CORRESPONDENCE
Relating to

THE WAR WITH SPAIN

INCLUDING THE
INSURRECTION IN THE PHILIPPINE ISLANDS
AND THE
CHINA RELIEF EXPEDITION

April 15, 1898, to July 30, 1902

Volume 2

Center of Military History
United States Army
Washington, D.C., 1993

CORRESPONDENCE

RELATING TO

THE WAR WITH SPAIN

AND CONDITIONS GROWING OUT OF THE SAME,

INCLUDING THE

INSURRECTION IN THE PHILIPPINE ISLANDS

AND THE

CHINA RELIEF EXPEDITION,

BETWEEN THE

ADJUTANT-GENERAL OF THE ARMY AND MILITARY COMMANDERS
IN THE UNITED STATES, CUBA, PORTO RICO, CHINA,
AND THE PHILIPPINE ISLANDS,

FROM

April 15, 1898, to July 30, 1902.

WITH AN APPENDIX

GIVING THE ORGANIZATION OF ARMY CORPS AND A BRIEF HISTORY
OF THE VOLUNTEER ORGANIZATIONS IN THE SERVICE OF THE
UNITED STATES DURING THE WAR WITH SPAIN.

IN TWO VOLUMES
VOLUME 2.

WASHINGTON:
GOVERNMENT PRINTING OFFICE
1902

CONTENTS.

Volume 1.

	Page.
Mobilization and concentration of troops in campaign, April 15 to June 22, 1898	7
Santiago campaign, June 22 to August 25, 1898	50
Porto Rico campaign, May 26 to August 30, 1898	259
China relief expedition, May 30, 1900, to June 1, 1901	407
Organization of army corps, war with Spain	507
Volunteer organizations in United States service in war with Spain	581

Volume 2.

Manila campaign, May 3 to August 13, 1898	635
Affairs in the Philippine Islands, August 13, 1898, to February 4, 1899	751
Philippine insurrection, February 4, 1899, to July 30, 1902	893

CORRESPONDENCE

RELATING TO

PHILIPPINE ISLANDS,

MAY 5, 1898, TO JULY 30, 1902.

CORRESPONDENCE RELATING TO THE PHILIPPINE ISLANDS, MAY 3, 1898, TO JULY 30, 1902.

HEADQUARTERS OF THE ARMY,
Washington, D. C., May 3, 1898.

The Honorable, the SECRETARY OF WAR.

SIR: I have the honor to recommend that Gen. Thomas M. Anderson be sent to occupy the Philippine Islands, in command of the following troops: Two battalions Fourteenth Infantry; two troops Fourth Cavalry; one regiment of infantry, California Volunteers; two batteries heavy artillery, California Volunteers; one regiment of infantry, Oregon Volunteers; one regiment of infantry, Washington Volunteers; the troops to go with all the necessary appliances, supplies, and equipment.

Very respectfully,

NELSON A. MILES,
Major-General Commanding U. S. Army.

EXECUTIVE MANSION, *Washington, May 4, 1898.*

The troops designated by General Miles, if approved by the Secretary of War, should be assembled at San Francisco, Cal., for such service as may be ordered hereafter.

W. McK.

The above is only carrying out verbal instructions heretofore given.

To the SECRETARY OF WAR.

VANCOUVER BARRACKS, WASH., *May 7, 1898.*
(Received 2.50 p. m.)

ADJUTANT-GENERAL, U. S. ARMY, *Washington, D. C.:*

Band, Companies C, D, E, and F, Fourteenth Infantry. Major Robe commanding, leave to-night for San Francisco. Oregon and Washington Volunteers will be forwarded there by battalions as fast as mustered.

MERRIAM, *Brigadier-General.*

WAR DEPARTMENT, PAYMASTER-GENERAL'S OFFICE.
Washington, May 10, 1898.

The ADJUTANT-GENERAL OF THE ARMY.

SIR: I have the honor to request that Maj. C. H. Whipple and Maj. C. E. Kilbourne, paymasters, be relieved by telegraph from their station at Portland, Oreg., and ordered to proceed to San Francisco and thence to the Philippine

Islands with the expedition now being organized; also that Maj. J. S. Witcher, paymaster, be relieved by telegraph from duty at San Francisco and ordered to Portland, Oreg., for duty as chief paymaster.

Very respectfully,

T. H. STANTON,
Paymaster-General U. S. Army.

ADJUTANT-GENERAL'S OFFICE,
Washington, May 10, 1898.

Maj. C. H. WHIPPLE, *Paymaster:*

(Through Headquarters Department Columbia, Vancouver, Wash.)

You are relieved from duty at Portland, Oreg., by the Secretary of War, who directs, as necessary for public service, that you proceed to San Francisco, Cal., and report in person for duty to the commanding officer of the expedition now being organized to proceed to the Philippine Islands, and that you accompany that expedition.

By command of Major-General Miles:

SCHWAN, *Assistant Adjutant-General.*

(Same as above to Maj. C. E. Kilbourne.)

ADJUTANT-GENERAL'S OFFICE,
Washington, May 10, 1898.

Maj. J. S. WITCHER, *Paymaster:*

(Through Headquarters Department California, San Francisco, Cal.)

You are relieved from duty at San Francisco by the Secretary of War, who directs, as necessary for the public service, that you proceed to Portland, Oreg., and report by letter to the commanding officer, Department Columbia, for duty as chief paymaster of that department.

By command of Major-General Miles:

SCHWAN, *Assistant Adjutant-General.*

ADJUTANT-GENERAL'S OFFICE,
Washington, May 11, 1898.

General OTIS, *Denver, Colo.:*

General Merritt has been assigned to the command of an expedition for the Philippine Islands. It will consist of two and possibly three divisions, which will be designated as the First Army Corps. The question of assignment of general officers is now under consideration, and the Secretary of War bids me say that if agreeable you will be sent second in command. Your pleasure in premises desired at earliest possible moment. Please acknowledge receipt.

H. C. CORBIN, *Adjutant-General.*

DENVER, COLO., *May 11, 1898.*
(Received 10.35 p.m.)

The ADJUTANT-GENERAL, U. S. ARMY. *Washington, D. C.:*

Am prepared to respond to any assignment which authorities may make. This in reply to telegram of this date concerning proposed expedition to Philippine Islands.

OTIS, *Major-General, U. S. Volunteers.*

WAR DEPARTMENT, ADJUTANT-GENERAL'S OFFICE,
Washington, May 12, 1898.

Maj. Gen. WESLEY MERRITT, U. S. Army,
    Commanding Department of the East,
        Governors Island, New York Harbor.

SIR: On being relieved from the command of the Department of the East, by direction of the President you are assigned to the command of the expedition being sent to the Philippine Islands. You will repair to San Francisco, Cal., and assume command of and organize troops assembling there. You will be accompanied by your authorized aids. General staff officers will be assigned you hereafter. The travel enjoined is necessary for the public service.

Very respectfully,

        H. C. CORBIN, *Adjutant-General.*

ADJUTANT-GENERAL'S OFFICE,
Washington, May 12, 1898.

General OTIS, *Denver, Colo.:*

Secretary War directs that you repair to San Francisco, and until General Merritt arrives there, that you assume command of all troops assembling at that place and to assist in their organization and equipment as rapidly as possible. It is uncertain as to time that General Merritt will arrive, but as you are near, it is suggested, agreeable to your telegram of last night, that you proceed at once. General Merritt is now here, and is gratified that you are willing to go with him.

        H. C. CORBIN, *Adjutant-General.*

NAVY DEPARTMENT,
Washington, May 12, 1898.

SIR: Referring to your letter of the 11th instant, concerning the steamship *City of Pekin* to be used for transporting troops and stores to the Philippine Islands, I have to transmit herewith the following copy of a telegram, dated the 11th instant, received in this Department from the commandant of the navy-yard, Mare Island, Cal.:

"Provision can be made for 1,200 men and 75 officers, including naval contingent, two officers in a room; allowance also made for camp equipage and rations for troops for six months. Weights will be as follows: Coal, 2,000 tons; officers, men, camp equipage, and six months' rations, 700 tons; leaving 1,300 tons for ammunition, stores, and other naval supplies. If troops are to be sent away, quartermaster should make immediate arrangement for same, as at least four days will be required to fit bunks.

        KIRKLAND."

This Department is desirous of expediting the departure of the *City of Pekin* as much as possible. She will be convoyed by the cruiser *Charleston*, and will probably be the first vessel to arrive at the Philippine Islands. I have the honor to request that you inform me, at the earliest possible date, how many men your Department desires to send by this vessel, and also what date they will be ready to embark, and I have also to request that the earliest practicable date be fixed for the embarkation of these men.

Very respectfully,

        JOHN D. LONG, *Secretary.*

The Honorable, the SECRETARY OF WAR.

ADJUTANT-GENERAL'S OFFICE,
Washington, May 12, 1898.

COMMANDING GENERAL, DEPARTMENT COLUMBIA,
Vancouver Barracks, Wash.:

The steamer *City of Pekin* has been chartered for use in carrying troops and freight to the Philippine Islands. She will sail from either Portland or Seattle direct for the Philippines, and has accommodations for 1,200 men and 75 officers. Could either the Washington or the Oregon regiment be put in readiness to take advantage of this transportation, say, within six or ten days; or, in brief, how soon could they go? Acknowledge receipt.

H. C. CORBIN, *Adjutant-General.*

WAR DEPARTMENT,
Washington, May 12, 1898.

MR. SECRETARY:

Referring to my request, as approved by the President and yourself in conversation this morning, I desire to have organized one battery of six Hotchkiss mountain guns, manned by the selection of 100 noncommissioned officers and men from the Eighth United States Cavalry, now stationed at Forts Meade, Robinson, and Washakie, who have had experience in handling and packing this peculiar weapon, with First Lieutenant Farrand Sayre, Eighth United States Cavalry, to command.

With great respect, your obedient servant,

W. MERRITT, *Major-General.*

The Honorable, the SECRETARY OF WAR.
(Through the Adjutant-General.)

PHILADELPHIA, PA., *May 12, 1898.*
(Received 7.42 p. m.)

The ADJUTANT-GENERAL, U. S. ARMY, *Washington, D. C.:*

Please telegraph me the present address of General Otis.

MERRITT, *Major-General.*

ADJUTANT-GENERAL'S OFFICE,
Washington, May 12, 1898.

General MERRITT, *Governors Island, New York Harbor:*

General Otis is at Denver, Colo.

H. C. CORBIN, *Adjutant-General.*

GOVERNORS ISLAND, N. Y., *May 13, 1898.*
(Received 11 a. m.)

ADJUTANT-GENERAL ARMY, *Washington, D. C.:*

Please hold the order relieving me here till I have a chance to communicate with the Secretary of War, for the present.

W. MERRITT,
Major-General Commanding.

ADJUTANT-GENERAL'S OFFICE,
Washington, May 13, 1898.

Maj. Gen. JOHN R. BROOKE,
Chickamauga Park, Battlefield Station, Ga.:

With approval Secretary War Major-General Commanding directs that you cause to be shipped six Hotchkiss mountain guns, with everything complete, including sufficient amount of ammunition for each gun, to the depot quartermaster, San Francisco, for use of General Merritt's command,

H. C. CORBIN, Adjutant-General.

ADJUTANT-GENERAL'S OFFICE,
Washington, May 13, 1898.

General MERRIAM,
Commanding Department Columbia, Vancouver Barracks, Wash.:

Secretary War is anxious to have reply to my telegram last night concerning troops for the *City of Pekin.* Yesterday the President assigned General Merritt to the command of expedition to the Philippines. Major-General Otis will go second in command. It is desired that you lend every assistance possible to the commanding generals of the two departments, and the authority given you heretofore in connection with organization of volunteers, to hasten the outfit of this expedition. It is now thought that it will probably consist of about 12,000 men, or one army corps. The Quartermaster's, Ordnance, and Subsistence departments have been directed to assemble in San Francisco sufficient stores to meet the demands of volunteers, who are not expected to arrive in anything like complete working order. The Thirteenth Minnesota left last night. Barring want of some articles of clothing, they are in fairly good condition. The General Commanding the Army would like for you to repair to San Francisco soon as possible and give the organization of these troops your personal attention. any way until the arrival of Generals Merritt and Otis, and then cooperate with them as heretofore stated. Acknowledge receipt.

H. C. CORBIN, Adjutant-General.

OFFICE OF CHIEF OF ORDNANCE,
Washington, May 13, 1898.

COMMANDING GENERAL, DEPARTMENT OF THE COLUMBIA,
Vancouver Barracks, Wash:

There are sufficient supplies at Benicia Arsenal, Benicia, Cal., for completing the equipment of the Washington or Oregon regiment for passage on steamer *City of Pekin,* mentioned in Adjutant-General's telegram of yesterday. As the use of these stores would affect supply collected for another purpose, request that if requisition is made it be sent to this office, that the order to Benicia may be telegraphed from here.

FLAGLER, Chief of Ordnance.

ADJUTANT-GENERAL'S OFFICE,
Washington, May 14, 1898. (Received 4.45 p. m.)

Major-General OTIS, Headquarters, Denver, Colo.:

The Secretary of War directs, if possible, that you reach San Francisco by Monday night, in order to sail on the *City of Pekin,* which will carry the First Regiment California Volunteers and four companies of Fourteenth United States

Infantry, amounting in all to 1,200 men. On arrival at the Philippines you will confer with Admiral Dewey with view to occupying such part of the islands as you may be able to do with this force until the arrival of other troops, which will be put under way in very near future. Acknowledge receipt.

By command Major-General Miles:

H. C. CORBIN, *Adjutant-General.*

(Same to Major-General Otis, on board train en route from Denver to San Francisco. Major-General Otis, San Francisco, Cal.)

ADJUTANT-GENERAL'S OFFICE,
Washington, May 14, 1898.

Col. JAMES A. SMITH,
First California Volunteers, San Francisco, Cal.:

The Major-General Commanding, with approval of the Secretary of War, has designated your regiment to sail for the Philippines on the *City of Pekin* Monday night, under command of Major-General Otis, who is expected to arrive in San Francisco during Monday. In the meantime you are enjoined to make every effort to thoroughly equip your command. The commanding officer of Benicia Arsenal has been directed to furnish you necessary arms, and you will see that you have necessary supply of tentage and not less than 400 rounds of ammunition per man. Acknowledge receipt, and give general report of the condition of your regiment.

H. C. CORBIN, *Adjutant-General.*

ADJUTANT-GENERAL'S OFFICE,
Washington, May 14, 1898.

COMMANDING OFFICER, BATTALION FOURTEENTH U. S. INFANTRY,
Presidio of San Francisco, Cal.:

The Major-General Commanding, with approval of the Secretary of War, has designated your battalion to sail for the Philippines on the *City of Pekin* Monday night, under command of Major-General Otis, who is expected to arrive in San Francisco during Monday. In the meantime you are enjoined to make every effort to thoroughly equip your command. You will see that you have necessary supply of tentage and not less than 400 rounds of ammunition per man. Acknowledge receipt, and give general report of the condition of your battalion.

H. C. CORBIN, *Adjutant-General.*

ADJUTANT-GENERAL'S OFFICE,
Washington, May 14, 1898.

Captain LONG,
Depot Quartermaster, San Francisco, Cal.:

The Major-General Commanding, with approval of the Secretary of War, has given orders for the First California Volunteers and the four companies of the Fourteenth Infantry in camp at the Presidio to sail from San Francisco, on the *City of Pekin,* to the Philippine Islands, Monday night. You are enjoined to make every effort to see that these troops are as thoroughly equipped as possible before sailing. Acknowledge receipt, and report the general condition in which these troops will be able to leave on Monday evening.

H. C. CORBIN, *Adjutant-General.*

ADJUTANT-GENERAL'S OFFICE,
Washington, May 14, 1898.

COMMANDING GENERAL, DEPARTMENT CALIFORNIA,
San Francisco, Cal.:

Secretary War directs that General Otis embark on steamer *City of Pekin,* sailing from port of San Francisco on Monday evening, carrying the First California Volunteer Regiment and the four companies of the Fourteenth Infantry now supposed to be in camp at the Presidio. Every effort will be made to thoroughly equip these troops by the time named for them to sail. Acknowledge receipt.

By command General Miles:

H. C. CORBIN, *Adjutant-General.*

ADJUTANT-GENERAL'S OFFICE,
Washington, May 14, 1898.

Major-General OTIS, *Headquarters, Denver, Colo.:*

Having reference to telegram sent you at 4.45, Secretary War authorizes you to take with you such staff officers and clerical assistance as you may desire. It is of first importance for you to reach San Francisco in time named in my previous dispatch, namely, Monday evening.

By command General Miles:

H. C. CORBIN, *Adjutant-General.*

(Same to General Otis on board train en route from Denver to San Francisco. Same to General Otis, San Francisco, Cal.)

ADJUTANT-GENERAL'S OFFICE,
Washington, May 14, 1898.

COMMANDING GENERAL, DEPARTMENT OF COLORADO, *Denver, Colo.:*

It is not known that General Otis has left, but in the event that he has, every effort will be made to reach him with the telegram sent at 4.45 this afternoon directing him to reach San Francisco by Monday night. Acknowledge receipt.

By command General Miles:

H. C. CORBIN, *Adjutant-General.*

ADJUTANT-GENERAL'S OFFICE,
Washington, May 14, 1898.

COMMANDING OFFICER, BATTALION FOURTEENTH U. S. INFANTRY,
Presidio, San Francisco:

Take 400 rounds ammunition per man. If not on hand, make requisition on commanding officer Benicia Arsenal by telegraph.

By order Secretary of War:

H. C. CORBIN, *Adjutant-General.*

ADJUTANT-GENERAL'S OFFICE,
Washington, May 14, 1898.

Col. L. S. BABBITT, *Benicia Arsenal, Benicia:*

Furnish First California Volunteer Infantry, Colonel Smith, 400 rounds ammunition per man and such arms as necessary to fully arm them; also, 400 rounds per man to Battalion Fourteenth United States Infantry, under orders to sail Monday night.

By order Secretary of War:

H. C. CORBIN, *Adjutant-General.*

ADJUTANT-GENERAL'S OFFICE,
Washington, May 14, 1898.

Col. JAMES A. SMITH,
First California U. S. Volunteers, The Presidio, San Francisco, Cal.:

Make requisition by telegraph on commanding officer Benicia Arsenal for 400 rounds ammunition per man; also, such arms as may be necessary to fully arm your regiment.

By order Secretary of War:

H. C. CORBIN, *Adjutant-General.*

DENVER, COLO., *May 14, 1898.*
(Received 9.20 p. m.)

ADJUTANT-GENERAL, U. S. ARMY,
Washington, D. C.:

Telegram just received. Can not catch evening train. Telegram later.

OTIS, *Major-General, U. S. Volunteers.*

DENVER, COLO., *May 14, 1898.*
(Received 9.33 p. m.)

ADJUTANT-GENERAL, U. S. ARMY,
Washington, D. C.:

Your telegram not received until too late to catch evening train. Staff officers and clerical force are fully prepared to start early to-morrow morning. Baggage has been shipped by express. Horses and all transportation left Denver early this morning by fast freight. We leave early to-morrow morning by special car and reach San Francisco Tuesday evening. All arrangements have been perfected. Officials and clerks are now beyond reach with orders to report promptly to-morrow morning.

OTIS, *Major-General, U. S. Volunteers.*

ADJUTANT-GENERAL'S OFFICE,
Washington, May 14, 1898.

General MERRIAM,
Headquarters, Vancouver Barracks, Wash.:

By direction of the Secretary War, following instructions have been given to the commanding officer Fourteenth Infantry, Presidio of San Francisco: "The Major-General Commanding, with approval of the Secretary of War, has designated your battalion to sail for the Philippines on the *City of Pekin* Monday night under command of Major-General Otis, who is expected to arrive in San Francisco during Monday. In the meantime you are enjoined to make every effort to thoroughly equip your command. You will see that you have necessary supply of tentage and not less than 400 rounds of ammunition per man. Acknowledge receipt and give general report of the condition of your battalion." This has been sent direct by reason of want of time to communicate through your headquarters. The same instructions have been given to the commanding officer of the First Regiment of California Volunteers, San Francisco, Cal. Benicia Arsenal will furnish arms for the volunteers. Acknowledge receipt.

H. C. CORBIN, *Adjutant-General.*

SAN FRANCISCO, CAL., *May 14, 1898.*
(Received 11.18 p. m.)

ADJUTANT-GENERAL, U. S. ARMY,
   Washington, D. C.:

Telegram this day relative to embarkation of troops on *City of Pekin* just received. Bearing on this subject following telegram has just been sent to General Merriam at Portland. Captain Ruhlen, who in company with Captain Long and Commander Gibson, of the Navy, and general manager Pacific Mail Steamship Company, inspected *City of Pekin, City of Sydney,* and *Australia* to-day, reports that vessels can not possibly be ready to sail before Friday, May 20, but may be able to leave Saturday. Captain Ruhlen says to facilitate matters and prevent further delay it is necessary to know designation of commands and number of men to go on each vessel, also if artillery or cavalry horses are to go. Number of animals must be known, because thus far no arrangements have been made on any vessels for live stock. Space for stock on three vessels named very limited, and must necessarily take up nearly all deck room now allotted to me for exercise.

FIELD,
Acting Assistant Adjutant-General,
In absence of Department Commander.

EXECUTIVE MANSION,
Washington, May 14, 1898.

MY DEAR SIR: The President has just received the inclosed letter from General Merritt, and directs me to say that he would be glad to have you read it and that he wishes to talk with you about it.

Very truly, yours,

JOHN ADDISON PORTER,
Secretary to the President.

Hon. R. A. ALGER,
   Secretary of War.

[Inclosure.]

HEADQUARTERS DEPARTMENT OF THE EAST,
Governors Island, New York City, May 13, 1898.

To His Excellency WILLIAM MCKINLEY,
   President of the United States.

MR. PRESIDENT: As I promised yesterday in my interview with you. I have the honor to furnish the following as my estimate of troops necessary to constitute an expedition to the Philippines with a fair chance of success after arriving there.

In this connection I desire to point in very emphatic terms to the fact that the volunteers from the Northwest are not as well drilled or disciplined as those from any State in the East or interior. For that reason I urgently request the number of regular troops I have asked for. I feel that I would be doing the country, the force in Manila Harbor, and myself a great injustice to attempt to carry out your wishes with a smaller force or one differently constituted. I make this representation because I feel sure, Mr. President, that you will consider it in all its bearings, after which I am thoroughly willing to leave the matter in your hands and to cheerfully obey your instructions.

In the above connection I desire to call your attention to the fact that an immense volunteer reserve can be advanced to perfection as soldiers day by day here, and are within supporting distance of any force operating against Cuba or Porto Rico, should it be necessary, while the command that goes to the Philippines must depend on itself in the face of casualties from sickness or other causes and can not be readily reenforced. If I neglected to represent this matter to you fully and freely, I would feel that I had failed in an important duty.

It is my purpose later to ask for the general and staff officers necessary for the command.

With great respect, your obedient servant,

WESLEY MERRITT, *Major-General.*

Estimate of composition of a field force of 12,000 effectives for the Philippine expedition.

Regulars:
Four regiments infantry	4,800
Two squadrons cavalry	800
Two field batteries	350
One mountain battery	100
	6,050

Volunteers:
Six regiments infantry	7,200
One squadron cavalry	400
Two field batteries	350
One mountain battery	100
	8,050

Two companies of engineers (regulars) 300

All appliances, including mines and instruments to work them.
Necessary men of Hospital Corps and Signal Corps.
Total, 14,400 men, supposing every organization full.

This would give about 12,000 effectives on landing and taking the field. It is agreed that these must go in two detachments, about one-half at a time.

W. MERRITT, *Major-General.*

ASHLAND, OREG., *May 15, 1898.*
(Received 3.35 p. m.)

Adjutant-General CORBIN, *Washington, D. C.:*

Chief quartermaster reports *Pekin, Sydney,* and *Australia* will require a week to prepare for sea transport. I do not know who has been charged with preparation of transports, but have ordered quartermaster to rush whatever is required.

MERRIAM, *Major-General, Commanding.*

SAN FRANCISCO, CAL., *May 15, 1898.*
(Received 5.45 p. m.)

ADJUTANT-GENERAL, U. S. ARMY, *Washington, D. C.:*

The First Regiment California Volunteers and four companies of Fourteenth Infantry can and will be immediately and thoroughly equipped with clothing and equipage from this depot. Have seen quartermasters of organization. They will submit requisitions to complete equipment, which will be filled early Monday. Regarding sailing of *Pekin,* please see telegrams to Quartermaster-General of yesterday afternoon and to-day.

LONG,
Quartermaster in Charge.

SURGEON-GENERAL'S OFFICE,
Washington, May 15, 1898.

The ADJUTANT-GENERAL OF THE ARMY.

SIR: I have the honor to request that the commanding general, Department of California, be directed to send five hospital stewards or acting hospital stewards from posts in the Department of California and of the Columbia with the expedition for the Philippine Islands, and that these instructions be communicated by telegraph.

Very respectfully,
GEORGE M. STERNBERG,
Surgeon-General U. S. Army.

HEADQUARTERS DEPARTMENT OF THE EAST,
Governors Island, New York City, May 15, 1898.
(Received May 16, 1898.)

The ADJUTANT-GENERAL, U. S. ARMY, *Washington, D. C.*

SIR: I inclose copy of letter written to the President on May 13, which explains itself. This letter was written for the reason that, on the President's invitation, I was to put before him what was wanted, in my opinion, for the expedition to the Philippines.

Since posting the letter it has occurred to me that your office should have a copy of it, and I accordingly inclose a copy.

Very respectfully, your obedient servant,
W. MERRITT,
Major-General, Commanding.

(Inclosure is found on pp. 643 and 644.)

HEADQUARTERS DEPARTMENT OF THE EAST,
Governors Island, New York City, May 15, 1898.
(Received May 16, 1898.)

His Excellency WILLIAM MCKINLEY,
President of the United States.

SIR: Since my letter to you of May 13, I have been studying the problem before me with all the assistance I can get from my staff and from men who have lived in the Philippine Islands.

To the list submitted on the 13th of necessities for the expedition, I desire to add: One siege battery, fully manned and equipped; an ordnance detachment of 2 officers and 25 men, with necessary tools.

The question of trains must necessarily be postponed until more definite information can be had, but present information indicates that it will be imperative to carry with the expedition an advance guard pontoon train and all the draft animals for artillery and trains. The most suitable horses and mules can be purchased on the Pacific coast.

I need hardly urge the importance of my learning at the earliest possible moment what Admiral Dewey reports of the military situation, and if cable communication can not be had with him at an early date it seems to me that a dispatch should be got to him from Hongkong in order to obtain answers to the following inquiries:

First. What is the total strength of the Spanish forces in the island?
Second. How much of this force is in or about Manila?
Third. What proportion of the troops is Spanish and what native?
Fourth. What amount and caliber of field artillery have they?

Fifth. Can we operate field artillery, or will mountain artillery alone be practicable?

Sixth. What number of horses can be had in or near Manila? What work are they equal to?

Seventh. What food supplies is it imperative to bring?

Eighth. Will bridge trains be needed, and how much?

I have been in consultation with an intelligent physician who has passed much time in the eastern country, including the Philippines, and I am convinced that the expedition must be fitted out very carefully with reference to the conditions to be met there. These conditions are not the same as those obtaining in Cuba. If the Quartermaster's Department has no reliable man to furnish this information, I can send such a man to Washington.

There is urgent necessity that the chiefs of the staff departments be appointed at once to assist in organizing and equipping their specialties. They will need time to get information of the conditions and to study their respective problems. We are going too far from our base to permit of any guesswork.

The following list of staff officers is given as being those that I would select, but any capable men, chosen by their respective chiefs, would be agreeable to me:

Adjutant-general, Col. J. B. Babcock.
Inspector-general, Col. R. P. Hughes.
Judge-advocate, Col. John W. Claus, or Capt. Francis J. Kernan.
Chief quartermaster, Col. J. G. C. Lee, or Col. J. W. Pope.
Chief engineer, Col. G. W. Goethals, or Col. H. M. Chittenden.
Chief surgeon, Col. J. Van R. Hoff, or Maj. C. E. Woodruff.
Chief commissary, Col. David R. Brainard.
Chief signal officer, Maj. R. E. Thompson.
Chief paymaster, Col. F. M. Coxe, or Maj. G. R. Smith, or Maj. J. L. Bullis.
Ordnance officer. Capt. W. A. Simpson, Seventh Artillery, and Lieut. L. M. Fuller, Ordnance Department.

Personal staff as now constituted, with Lieut. C. S. Babcock as additional aid.

I do not yet know whether it is your desire to subdue and hold all of the Spanish territory in the islands, or merely to seize and hold the capital.

It seems more than probable that we will have the so-called insurgents to fight as well as the Spaniards, and upon the work to be accomplished will depend the ultimate strength and composition of the force.

With great respect, your obedient servant,

W. MERRITT, *Major-General, U. S. Army,*

ADJUTANT-GENERAL'S OFFICE,
Washington, May 16, 1898.

COMMANDING GENERAL, DEPARTMENTS CALIFORNIA AND COLUMBIA,
San Francisco, Cal.:

Assistant Secretary War directs that five hospital stewards or acting hospital stewards from posts in Departments California and Columbia be sent with expedition for Philippines.

WARD, *Assistant Adjutant-General.*

WAR DEPARTMENT,
OFFICE OF THE ASSISTANT SECRETARY, *May 16, 1896.*

MEMORANDUM FOR THE ADJUTANT-GENERAL.

The Assistant Secretary has the honor to state that the War Department has been informed by Captain Long, quartermaster, U. S. Army, San Francisco, that

Commander Gibson, of the Navy, has positively stated that the *City of Pekin* will not be ready to sail before Friday, the 20th instant, and possibly not before the 21st instant.

Secretary of the Navy has wired for advices.

GOVERNORS ISLAND, N. Y., *May 16, 1898.*
(Received 4.43 p. m.)

The COMMISSARY-GENERAL, *Washington, D. C.:*

I think that Colonel Brainard should go to San Francisco and report to General Otis, now in charge there, in order to make every preparation for the subsistence of the command going to the Philippines.

MERRITT, *Major-General.*

ADJUTANT-GENERAL'S OFFICE,
Washington, May 16, 1898.

Major-General MERRIAM, *Vancouver Barracks, Wash.:*

Secretary of War directs that until further orders you establish your headquarters at San Francisco, Cal. You will continue to exercise command of both the Departments of the Columbia and of California.

You are authorized to retain possession, for yourself and authorized aids, of the quarters now occupied by you at Fort Vancouver. Acknowledge receipt.

SCHWAN, *Assistant Adjutant-General.*

SAN FRANCISCO, CAL., *May 16, 1898.*
(Received 10.41 p. m.)

SCHWAN, *Assistant Adjutant-General, Washington, D. C.:*

Telegram directing my headquarters San Francisco until further orders received.

MERRIAM,
Major-General, Comanding Departments California and Columbia.

HEADQUARTERS OF THE ARMY,
Washington, D. C., May 16, 1898.

The Honorable, the SECRETARY OF WAR.

SIR: I have the honor to submit the following: In order to make the United States force as strong and effective as possible, with a view to its maintaining our possession and our flag on the Philippine Islands, and at the same time relieve our navy as speedily as possible, I suggest that the command sent there consist of the Fourteenth and Fifteenth United States Infantry, two squadrons Fourth Cavalry, one battery of heavy artillery from the Seventh, and two batteries of light artillery from the Seventh, and in addition 12,975 volunteers from California, Colorado, Kansas, Montana, Nebraska, Oregon, Utah, Washington, North Dakota, South Dakota, Idaho, Wyoming, Minnesota, already designated. I also recommend that two 12-inch guns, two 10-inch guns, with disappearing carriages, and eight mortars, to be dismounted, also two 8-inch guns now at Benicia Barracks—all to be placed on board ships at San Francisco and sent to Manila, there to be mounted as speedily as possible for the defense of that harbor, and used together with any rapid-fire guns that can be spared from the fleet now at that place. When this is accomplished the fleet can be released for more important service. The guns and mortars referred to should be replaced as soon as possible by others sent to San Francisco from the gun foundries and arsenals on the Atlantic coast.

Very respectfully, yours,
NELSON A. MILES,
Major-General, Commanding.

ADJUTANT-GENERAL'S OFFICE,
Washington, May 16, 1898.

COMMANDING GENERAL, DEPARTMENT EAST,
Governors Island, New York:

Recommendations of Major-General Commanding Army concerning composition of expedition to Philippine Islands this day referred to you by Secretary War for remark.

SCHWAN, *Assistant Adjutant-General.*

[First indorsement.]

WAR DEPARTMENT, ADJUTANT-GENERAL'S OFFICE,
Washington, May 16, 1898.

Respectfully referred to Maj. Gen. W. Merritt, U. S. Army, Governors Island, N. Y., for an expression of his opinion on the subject contained herein, and for any suggestions he may desire to make.

By order of the Secretary of War:
H. C. CORBIN, *Adjutant-General.*

[Second indorsement.]

HEADQUARTERS DEPARTMENT OF THE EAST,
Governors Island, May 17, 1898.

Respectfully returned to the Adjutant-General of the Army.

I consider the composition of the force outlined by the Major-General Commanding the Army as unsuited to the ends to be accomplished, and insufficient in efficiency for the expedition to the Philippines.

Two regiments of regular infantry, two-thirds of a regiment of regular cavalry, and two light batteries is a very small proportion of the 42 regular regiments in the Army when the work to be done consists of conquering a territory 7,000 miles from our base, defended by a regularly trained and acclimated army of from 10,000 to 25,000 men, and inhabited by 14,000,000 of people, the majority of whom will regard us with the intense hatred born of race and religion.

Besides, if I am not greatly mistaken, the suggested command is only on paper, as the Fourteenth Infantry is only partially available. My letters of May 13 and 15 give the composition and minimum strength of the regular force I deem necessary.

W. MERRITT,
Major-General, Commanding.

[Third indorsement.]

HEADQUARTERS OF THE ARMY,
Washington, D. C., May 18, 1898.

Respectfully submitted to the Secretary of War.

The reference to the Spanish troops is believed to be very much exaggerated. No reports have been received thus far that there is anything like the number indicated in the above indorsement, while the population of that territory is probably nearer one-half the number stated. The number of troops already ordered to the Philippine Islands is three times as many as Admiral Dewey called for.

The force ordered at this time is not expected to carry on a war to conquer an extensive territory, and the chief object of the within letter was to suggest a means of quickly establishing a strong garrison to command the harbor of Manila, and to relieve the United States fleet under Admiral Dewey with the least possible delay. This, in my judgment, is of preeminent importance. The troops mentioned in the within letter as available to send to that department number 15,425. The Tenth Pennsylvania Volunteers, ordered to-day, will be approximately 1,000 more. These troops, in my judgment, are all that would be advisable to send to the Philippine Islands at this time. If it be deemed advisable to send additional regiments, they can be sent from New Orleans or Tampa, but the force now ordered to be sent is, as already indicated, 10 000 more than will be required for the purpose. It is, however, in my judgment, of the highest importance that orders should be sent to place the six high-power guns and eight 12-inch mortars, with at least 50 rounds of ammunition per gun and mortar, on vessels at San Francisco, and possibly Puget Sound, with the least possible delay, and sent to the harbor of Manila and mounted as speedily as possible. It may be advisable to send additional guns. These orders should be sent by telegraph, and the Engineer and Ordnance Departments should be directed to expedite the work by every possible means.

NELSON A. MILES,
Major-General, Commanding.

ADJUTANT-GENERAL'S OFFICE,
Washington, May 16, 1898.

Maj. Gen. WESLEY MERRITT, U. S. Army,
Governors Island, New York Harbor:

Order this day issued assigns you to command of Department of the Pacific.

The department is intended to include Philippine Islands only; but this fact is not mentioned in orders, and will be communicated to you in confidential letter of instructions.

Secretary War directs that you proceed without unnecessary delay, accompanied by your personal staff, to San Francisco, Cal.

The travel enjoined is necessary for the public service. Please acknowledge receipt.

SCHWAN, *Assistant Adjutant-General.*

GOVERNORS ISLAND, N. Y., *May 16, 1898.*
(Received 8.34 p. m.)

The ADJUTANT-GENERAL, *Washington, D. C.:*

Telegram containing assignment to the Department of the Pacific received. Who will succeed me in command here?

W. MERRITT, *Major-General.*

DEPARTMENT OF STATE,
Washington, May 17, 1898.

The Honorable, the SECRETARY OF WAR.

SIR: I have the honor to transmit herewith for your information copies of three dispatches from the consul at Manila, dated February 22, March 19, and March 27, 1898, respectively, relative to the political situation in the Philippine Islands.

Respectfully, yours,

THOS. W. CRIDLER,
Third Assistant Secretary.

[Inclosure No. 1.]

No. 9.]
CONSULATE OF THE UNITED STATES,
Manila, Philippine Islands, February 22, 1898.

Hon. THOS. W. CRIDLER,
Third Assistant Secretary of State, Washington, D. C.

SIR: Without specific instructions it seems my duty at this critical period to inform the Washington Government somewhat as to the political conditions here. But as I have been here less than a month vigilance has not overcome all difficulties, and the rigid censorship of the press in general and the suppression of such publications as uttered the truth have made news gathering onerous.

I have before me a lengthy dispatch giving dates of many warlike and political matters, with rumors, observations, and conclusions, but deem it wise to write more briefly to-day, to bide events and wait specific instructions from you.

Peace was proclaimed, and since my coming, festivities therefor were held, but there is no peace and has been none for about two years. Conditions here and in Cuba are practically alike. War exists, battles are of almost daily occurrence, ambulances bring in many wounded, and hospitals are full. Prisoners are brought here and shot without trial, and Manila is under martial law.

The Crown forces have not been able to dislodge a rebel army within 10 miles of Manila, and last Saturday, February 19, a battle was there fought and 5 dead left on the field. Much of such information is found in my longer dispatch referred to, and which is at your command.

The governor-general, who is amiable and popular, having resigned, wishes credit for pacification, and certain rebel leaders were given a cash bribe of $1,650,000 to consent to public deportation to China. This bribe and deportation only multiplied claimants and fanned the fires of discontent.

Insurgents demand fewer exactions from Church and State, a half of public offices, and fewer church holidays, which seriously retard public business.

A republic is organized here as in Cuba. Insurgents are being armed and drilled, are rapidly increasing in numbers and efficiency, and all agree that a general uprising will come as soon as the governor-general embarks for Spain, which is fixed for March.

While some combatant regiments have recently been returned to Spain, it was for appearance only, and all authorities now agree that unless the Crown largely reenforces its army here it will lose possession.

Command me for any desired information.

Your obedient servant,
OSCAR F. WILLIAMS, *Consul.*

[Inclosure No. 2.]

CONSULATE OF THE UNITED STATES,
Manila, Philippine Islands, March 19, 1898.

Hon. THOS. W. CRIDLER,
Third Assistant Secretary of State.

SIR: Matters are in a serious state here. I have daily communication by cable and letter with Commodore Dewey, but we pass letters by British and other shipmasters and by private parties, because cables and letters are tampered with.

Insurrection is rampant, many killed, wounded, and made prisoners on both sides. A battle ship, the *Don Juan de Austria*, sent this week to the northern part of Luzon to cooperate with a land force of 2,000 dispatched to succor local forces overwhelmed by rebels.

Last night special squads of mounted police were scattered at danger points to save Manila.

I caution Americans against bearing arms in violation of local law, although threats have been made by Spaniards that all Americans would soon have their throats cut. Certain ones are so frightened as to frequently come to my consulate and hotel, and spies watch all my movements.

Yesterday I examined stock of an American who had been threatened and abstracted his ledger. To-day his inventory and accounts were placed in my safe. To-day two others came to me to send their effects to some American ship lying in the bay, and I have so planned.

I have no instructions from you as to these delicate complications, but so far have gotten on well. I fly our flag all the time; give double hours to the consulate, and have notified Americans that they can find me all the time at the consulate, or at my hotel, or on the path between. We have many holidays, but I keep open consulate every day, including Sundays, so Americans may find me.

Rebellion never more threatening to Spain. Rebels getting arms, money, and friends, and they outnumber the Spaniards resident and soldiery probably an hundred to one.

Report says that holy week the insurgents plan to burn and capture Manila. But if so you will learn it by wire before you receive this dispatch.

My March quarterly reports may be delayed or captured. If no trouble thwarts my work, all reports from here will be sent by first mail after March 31, but my consular agents at Cebu and Iloilo are both absent, and hence I may not receive their reports for transmission as early as I send my own.

All news comes indirect from Washington. I hear nothing as to relations between United States and Spain, and depending upon unofficial reports I must act as if peace reigned. I can only assure you of vigilance and loyalty, await your instructions, and remain,

Your most obedient servant, OSCAR F. WILLIAMS,
Consul.

[Inclosure No. 3.]

Special.] CONSULATE OF THE UNITED STATES,
Manila, Philippine Islands, March 27, 1898.

Hon. THOS. W. CRIDLER,
Third Assistant Secretary of State, Washington, D. C.

SIR: Because of having given daily information to Commodore Dewey as to disturbances here I have assumed that he informed the Washington Government, and I have written little on war matters.

Cuban conditions exist here possibly in aggravated form. Spanish soldiers are killed and wounded daily, despite claimed pacification, and the hospitals are kept full.

The majority of casualties are reported from the ranks of the native insurgents and the cruelties and horrors of war are daily repeated.

Cavite is the naval port of Luzon, situated about 8 miles across the bay from Manila and about 20 miles distant by way of bay shore and public highway, and last Thursday, March 24, a Crown regiment of natives, the Seventy-fourth, stationed there, was ordered to advance against native insurgents near by. The regiment refused to obey orders, and eight corporals were called out and shot to death in presence of the regiment, which was again ordered to advance and threat made that a refusal would be death to all. All did refuse and were sent to barracks to await sentence. On the morning following, Friday, March 25, the entire regiment, with arms and equipments, marched out of the barracks and deserted in a body to the insurgents, saying they were willing to fight the foreign enemies of Spain but would not fight their friends.

Since beginning this dispatch I learn of the desertion to the insurgents of another entire regiment. These are said to be the severest setbacks received by Spain during the two years' insurrection here.

On Friday morning, March 25, a church holiday, a meeting of natives was being held near my consulate in Manila, the natives being unarmed. The building was surrounded by police and military, the meeting broke up, 12 natives wantonly shot to death, several wounded, and 62 taken prisoners. Saturday morning, March 26, the 62 prisoners were marched in a body to the cemetery and shot to death, although it was shown that several were chance passers-by or employees in ships adjoining—not being in attendance at the meeting.

It was cold comfort to the widows and orphans of innocent men to have Spanish officers present them the mangled corpses of husbands and fathers.

Such horrors, usually on a smaller scale, but at times attended by greater disregard for modern rules of war, occur almost daily; and the piteous cry goes up, "Will it ever stop?"

The Crown forces are now building a cordon of small forts on city's outskirts for defense against provincial natives, who are expected to soon attack Manila. In fact, two detectives and one messenger have come to me this evening with information that attack was to be made to-night, and everybody is anxious, as 8,000 native insurgents are encamped only 5 miles away.

The insurgents seem to lack arms and organization, but, so far as I can learn, outnumber the Spanish forces and inhabitants twenty to one. Arms are being obtained and organization slowly effected, and all classes fear the near future. It is said that the only reason why Manila has not been taken and burned is because a vast majority of its population is in perfect accord with the insurgents.

Because of anxiety among Americans and my wish to keep in reach of all demands I keep the consulate open double hours and on all holidays and Sundays, with biggest flag flying, so any needing a refuge may find it.

Barbarities are reported as daily practiced, such as placing prisoners and suspects in black hole dungeons in the walls of old Manila, so placed that with rise of tide prisoners are drowned. Several hundred reported to have so perished.

Cruelties too horrid for an official report are detailed to me every day, and it seems that the cry of outraged humanity would soon compel Spain to abolish Middle Age methods of warfare.

Christian nations are such only in name when such atrocities as daily blacken the calendar are known to be perpetrated here and no effort made to protect the weak.

There is to-day no Christian nation. Policy and mock diplomacy govern all, and the vilest cruelties of war are added to the mangling of old men, women, and children to make full the measure of iniquity.

The American Indians would not permit one of their tribes to practice such barbarities. Why should so-called Christian nations decline to call a halt upon Spanish outrages?

All information as to defenses of Manila has been sent to Commodore George Dewey, at Hongkong.

For fear of confiscation this dispatch and other mail goes by messenger to Hongkong, to be there mailed.

Cable is cut in three places. I keep copies of dispatches, etc., but at present for reasons they are not copied on the register at consulate.

I remain, sir, your most obedient servant,

OSCAR F. WILLIAMS,
United States Consul, Manila.

ADJUTANT-GENERAL'S OFFICE,
Washington, May 17, 1898.

COMMANDING GENERAL, UNITED STATES TROOPS, *Tampa, Fla.*:

Secretary War directs as necessary for public service that Lieutenant-Colonel Babcock, assistant adjutant-general, proceed to San Francisco, Cal., for duty as adjutant-general of the Department of the Pacific (General Merritt), to whom he will report by letter for instructions. Adjutant-General appreciates your action in waiving your prior claim to Colonel Babcock, and requests that you designate someone of the recently nominated lieutenant-colonels and assistant adjutants-general of volunteers as your adjutant-general.

H. C. CORBIN, *Adjutant-General.*

GOVERNORS ISLAND, N. Y., *May 17, 1898.*
(Received 1.07 p. m.)

ADJUTANT-GENERAL ARMY, *Washington, D. C.:*

In the event of my having command of the expedition to the Philippine Islands I would request that Capt. Putman Bradlee Strong, assistant adjutant-general, U. S. Volunteers, be ordered to report to me for duty with the expedition.

W. MERRITT,
Major-General, Commanding.

GOVERNORS ISLAND, N. Y., *May 17, 1898.*
(Received 3.03 p. m.)

The ADJUTANT-GENERAL, *Washington, D. C.:*

Telegram in which Secretary orders me report in Washington before leaving for San Francisco received. I expect to hear from General Otis, reporting situation, to-day or to-morrow. As soon as this information comes I will start for Washington.

W. MERRITT, *Major-General.*

SAN FRANCISCO, CAL., *May 17, 1898.*
(Received 7.50 p. m.)

The COMMISSARY-GENERAL, U. S. ARMY,
Washington, D. C.:

Army and Navy officers going on *Pekin* report that the charter does not provide messing or room attendance for officers. The general manager Pacific Mail says he will not subsist officers or furnish room attendance unless all expenses first guaranteed. I report this as a matter of information to be laid before the Secretary. Pacific Mail willing to do all above if guaranteed by Government and officers are willing to pay cost. Can not such arrangement be made?

CLOMAN, *Acting Commissary.*

SAN FRANCISCO, CAL., *May 17, 1898.*
(Received 8.23 p. m.)

QUARTERMASTER-GENERAL, *Washington, D. C.:*

City of Sydney is equipped and will be coaled ready to load Saturday. Everything possible has been quickly done to make her comfortable. Steamship authorities heartily cooperating. Recommend steamship company should cook and serve rations for troops and furnish bill of actual expenses to Government; Government to supply rations. The company insists upon this, and that Government should guarantee payment of board of officers, either through commissary or otherwise. Is it intended that *City of Sydney* should stop at Honolulu? Provisions of charter not known.

LONG, *Quartermaster in Charge.*

SAN FRANCISCO. CAL., *May 17, 1898.*
(Received 8.50 p. m.)

QUARTERMASTER-GENERAL, *Washington, D. C.:*

Australia will be equipped and coaled ready to load Saturday. Everything possible has been done to make her comfortable for long journey. Extra ventilation, lighting, lavatories, berths, galleys, life-preservers, and tanks for water have been placed. Ship carries 1,200 tons coal, which includes 500 tons in ballast. She should stop at Honolulu for coal and water. Is it intended by charter that the company should furnish and cook rations for troops at 60 cents per day, or shall troops furnish, cook, and serve their own rations? This is important. Requirement of charter not known here.

LONG, *Quartermaster in Charge.*

WAR DEPARTMENT, *Washington, May 17, 1898.*

MEMORANDUM FOR THE SECRETARY OF WAR TO TAKE TO THE CABINET MEETING.

Herewith contains all the information it is possible to furnish from the office of the Adjutant-General upon the questions submitted by General Merritt—from 1 to 9. The Secretary of the Navy has cabled Commodore Dewey to get this information, but it will require a week or ten days.

MAY 25, 1898.

ADJUTANT-GENERAL:

Let this be referred to General Merritt for his information.

R. A. ALGER, *Secretary of War.*

SPANISH TROOPS IN THE PHILIPPINE ISLANDS.

According to the latest authentic sources of information the Spanish troops in the Philippine Islands are the following:

	Officers.	Men.		Horses.
		White.	Native.	
7 regiments of infantry	372		11,368	
15 "expeditionary" battalions	461	20,149		
1 cavalry regiment	31		453	249
1 expeditionary squadron	11	161		126
2 artillery regiments	61	2,196		104
1 ordnance detachment	4	72		
1 regiment of engineers	31		1,266	
3 tercie of guardia civil (gendarmery)	155		3,530	26
Carabineros (custom guards)	14		415	
Train			15	88
Sanitary detachment	4	245		
Total	1,144	22,823	17,047	593

Grand total, 41,014 officers and men.

The "expeditionary" battalions are those which were organized in Spain and sent to the islands to assist in the suppression of the insurrection.

In estimating the present strength of these troops it is well to take account of a statement contained in the Spanish press during the month of March. This statement announced the return of a battalion of marine infantry from the Philippine Islands, with a total strength of 322 officers and men out of an original 800. It is of course not improbable that some troops suffered more than others, but there can be little doubt that the Spanish contingent of the army in the Philippines, as given above, may be safely cut down 50 per cent or more, and these troops probably do not number more than 10,000 men to-day.

No data are available regarding the native troops. It is known that some of them joined in the insurrection, but it is not known how far their defection spread. These natives probably never were very loyal to Spain and are no doubt a questionable element of strength of the Spanish army at this time.

The organizations that make up the above force are the following:

(1) Regimiento de Legazpi, No. 68, Colonel ———; headquarters at Jolo; in the field in Luzon and Mindanao, and detachments in Carolina and Paragua Island.

(2) Regimiento de Iberia, No. 69, Colonel Real; headquarters at Zamboanga; in the field in Mindanao and Manila.

(3) Regimiento de Magallanes, No. 70, Colonel Camiña; headquarters at Manila; in the field in Luzon.

(4) Regimiento de Mindanao, No. 71, Colonel Lasala; headquarters at Iligan; at Manila, and in the field in Mindanao.

(5) Regimiento de Visayas, No. 72, Colonel Seijas; headquarters at Manila; at Manila, and in the field in Mindanao.

(6) Regimiento de Jolo, No. 73, Colonel ———; headquarters at Manila; in the field in Luzon and Mindanao.

(7) Regimiento de Manila, No. 74, Colonel Pazos; headquarters at Manila; in the field in Luzon and Mindanao.

The expeditionary battalions are called " Battalones cazadores expedicionarios," expeditionary rifle battalions; there are 15 in all. In addition to this infantry there were three battalions of marine infantry, all of which have returned to Spain since January 1, 1898, in a most deplorable condition.

The cavalry regiment is called " Regimiento caballeria de Filipinas," and has its headquarters at Manila, where the squadron above enumerated as "expeditionary" is also located. This last-named squadron is called the " Escadron de Lanceros Expedicionario," No. 1. Whether it actually is a lancer squadron, as the name would imply, is not known.

Of the two artillery regiments one is a fortress artillery regiment, stationed at Manila, and probably badly cut up by the fire of the United States squadron in the naval battle of Manila. The other regiment is a mountain artillery regiment, organized by royal order of July 1, 1896, and its organization is unknown, but, judging from the small number of guns of a caliber suitable for the field, it contains but few batteries; it is not unlikely that in view of the subsidence of the insurrection the organization was never completed.

The artillery material sent to the Philippine Islands up to May 1, 1897, in connection with the insurrection is as follows (according to official Spanish statements): 6 guns, compressed bronze, caliber 9 cm.; 6 guns, steel, long, caliber 8 cm.; 6 guns, steel, short, caliber 8 cm.; 2 guns, compressed bronze, caliber 12 cm.; 4 guns, field, caliber 57 mm.; 2 howitzers, compressed bronze, caliber 15 cm.; 2 mortars, compressed bronze, caliber 15 cm.; 4 mortars, compressed bronze, caliber 9 cm., and approximately 10,000 rounds of artillery ammunition.

Small arms: 24,521 Mausers, caliber 7 mm.; 478 Mauser carbines, caliber 7 mm.; 18,000 converted Remingtons, model 1871–89; 100 carbines, model 1871, Remington; 2,302 machetes, model 1881; 980 cavalry sabers, model 1895; 300 sabers for foot troops, model 1879; 120 lances.

Ammunition: 15,486,750 rounds Mauser, caliber 7 mm.; 33,500,000 rounds Remington, model 1871–89; 66,000 rounds revolver ammunition, Lefaucheux (rim-fire pattern); 200,000 rounds revolver ammunition, Smith; 20,000 pounds of powder and supply of reloading materials.

Question 2. It is impossible to tell how many of the Spanish troops are now near Manila. It is safe to say none can get there now that were not there before the destruction of the Spanish fleet. Probably Admiral Dewey could get a definite answer from the insurgents, with whom he is, no doubt, in communication.

Question 3. The proportion of white troops to natives is given in answer to Question I. If the natives have all remained loyal to Spain they outnumber the white troops at this time probably 2 to 1.

Question 4. The answer to this question is contained in the answer to the first question.

Question 5. It is difficult to answer this question, on account of lack of definite information of a topographical character. All maps and charts are extremely defective, except for coasts. However, the whole surface of the Philippine Islands is essentially mountainous, the only plains being alluvial districts at the rivers' mouths and in the spaces made by the intersection of the ranges. The highest mountain is estimated at from 8,800 to 11,000 feet. Only natural roads exist, rough, stony, and in very bad condition, except in Luzon and Cebu, where there are some highways. During the rainy season the inundations of the rivers make traveling in the interior almost impossible. Roads are neglected on account of the great number of water ways in the archipelago. On the whole, it would seem as though mountain artillery would be better than field artillery. The Spaniards, however, have some field artillery, as mentioned elsewhere.

Question 6. No specific information on this subject exists in this office. Many horses are raised in the two northernmost islands, 30 miles from Luzon, and, according to one of the authorities, horses are found in all of the islands. In the island of Panay there is a celebrated breed of horses. In time of peace draft horses are more or less plentiful in Manila, but are now probably an article of food.

Question 7. Rice is the staple food, though frequently the supply is not equal to the demand. Potatoes, pease, and even wheat are raised in the higher localities. Buffalo are found everywhere in number, both wild and domesticated. As communication with the interior will be more or less difficult, it would be best to take along a full supply of the United States Government ration as now fixed for service in Cuba.

Question 8. While the mountain torrents could probably not be bridged by ordinary pontoon bridges, there is plenty of wood on the banks with which to bridge these streams, with men familiar with this work. During the rainy season, however, large tracts of low-lying regions are known to be covered with water, and in this case a large bridge train would be very useful. Then there is also to be considered that the city of Manila is divided into two parts by the river Pasig, and occasions might arise when a pontoon bridge train would be necessary to establish communication between the two cities.

The above contains all the information this office can give on the questions submitted to the President by General Merritt.

H. C. CORBIN, *Adjutant-General.*

PORTLAND, OREG., *May 12, 1898.* (Received May 18, 1898.)
The PAYMASTER-GENERAL OF THE ARMY, *Washington, D. C.*

SIR: I have the honor to report that I will this day proceed to San Francisco, Cal., for the purpose of reporting to the commanding officer of the expedition now forming to proceed to the Philippine Islands, in compliance with the telegraphic instructions from the office of the Adjutant-General of the Army, dated May 10, 1898.

Very respectfully, your obedient servant,

CHAS. H. WHIPPLE,
Major and Paymaster, U. S. Army.

PORTLAND, OREG., *May 12, 1898.* (Received May 18, 1898.)

The ADJUTANT-GENERAL OF THE ARMY.

(Through the Paymaster-General, U. S. Army.)

SIR: I have the honor to inform you that I will this day proceed to San Francisco, Cal., for the purpose of reporting to the commanding officer of the expedition now forming to proceed to the Philippine Islands, in compliance with telegraphic instructions from the Adjutant-General's Office, dated May 10, 1898.

Very respectfully,

CHAS. E. KILBOURNE,
Major and Paymaster, U. S. Army.

SURGEON-GENERAL'S OFFICE,
Washington, May 18, 1898.

The ADJUTANT-GENERAL OF THE ARMY.

SIR: I have the honor to recommend that the following-named medical officers be ordered to report to Maj. Gen. Wesley Merritt for duty with the expedition to the Philippines:

Lieut. Col. Henry Lippincott, deputy surgeon-general, U. S. Army, now on duty at Fort Sheridan, Ill.

Maj. Robert H. White, surgeon, U. S. Army, now on duty at the Presidio of San Francisco, Cal.

Maj. William H. Corbusier, surgeon, U. S. Army, now on duty at Angel Island, California.

Capt. William O. Owen, assistant surgeon, U. S. Army, now on duty at Fort Bayard, N. Mex.

Capt. Edward R. Morris, assistant surgeon, U. S. Army, now on duty at Fort Spokane, Wash.

Capt. Harlan E. McVay, assistant surgeon, U. S. Army, now on duty at Alcatraz Island, California.

First Lieut. Henry Page, assistant surgeon, U. S. Army, now on duty at the Presidio of San Francisco, Cal.

It is requested that this order be communicated by telegraph.

Very respectfully,

GEO. M. STERNBERG,
Surgeon-General U. S. Army.

ADJUTANT-GENERAL'S OFFICE,
Washington, May 18, 1898.

Lieut. Col. HENRY LIPPINCOTT, *Deputy Surgeon-General:*

(Through Commanding Officer, Fort Sheridan, Ill.)

Order made to-day directs you report to Maj. Gen. Wesley Merritt, San Francisco. Cal., for duty with the expedition to the Philippines.

SCHWAN, *Assistant Adjutant-General.*

ADJUTANT-GENERAL'S OFFICE,
Washington, May 18, 1898.

Capt. WILLIAM O. OWEN, *Assistant Surgeon:*

(Through Commanding Officer, Fort Bayard, N. Mex.)

Order made to-day directs you report to Maj. Gen. Wesley Merritt, San Francisco, Cal., for duty with the expedition to the Philippines.

SCHWAN, *Assistant Adjutant-General.*

ADJUTANT-GENERAL'S OFFICE,
Washington, May 18, 1898.

Capt. EDWARD R. MORRIS, *Assistant Surgeon:*
(Through Commanding Officer, Fort Spokane, Wash.)
Order made to-day directs you report to Maj. Gen. Wesley Merritt, San Francisco, Cal., for duty with the expedition to the Philippines.

SCHWAN, *Assistant Adjutant-General.*

ADJUTANT-GENERAL'S OFFICE,
Washington, May 18, 1898.

Lieut. HENRY PAGE, *Assistant Surgeon:*
(Through Commanding Officer, Presidio of San Francisco, Cal.)
Order made to-day directs you report to Maj. Gen. Wesley Merritt, San Francisco, Cal., for duty with the expedition to the Philippines.

SCHWAN, *Assistant Adjutant-General.*

SAN FRANCISCO, CAL., *May 18, 1898.*
ADJUTANT-GENERAL, U. S. ARMY, *Washington, D. C.:*
Recommended that commanding general Philippine expedition be authorized to transfer enlisted men from organizations to Hospital Corps equitably as service may require.

MERRIAM, *Major-General, Commanding.*

HOUSE OF REPRESENTATIVES, UNITED STATES,
Washington, D. C., May 17, 1898. (Received May 18, 1898.)
General ALGER, *Secretary of War.*

DEAR GENERAL: Should you decide to send any Eastern troops to Manila, I would respectfully request that the Tenth Pennsylvania Volunteers be taken. They are anxious to go.
Sincerely, yours,   J. B. SHOWALTER.

ADJUTANT-GENERAL'S OFFICE,
Washington, May 18, 1898.

Col. A. S. HAWKINS,
Tenth Regiment Pennsylvania Volunteer Infantry, Mount Gretna, Pa.:
The destination of Tenth Pennsylvania has been changed to San Francisco, where it will form part of expedition to the Philippines.
By order Secretary War:

H. C. CORBIN, *Adjutant-General.*

(Same to governor of Pennsylvania, Harrisburg, Pa.; adjutant-general Pennsylvania, Mount Gretna, Pa.; commanding officer, Mount Gretna, Pa.)

ADJUTANT-GENERAL'S OFFICE,
Washington, May 18, 1898—11.30 a. m.

Col. A. S. HAWKINS,
Tenth Regiment Pennsylvania Volunteer Infantry, Mount Gretna, Pa.:
Referring to my telegram this morning, Tenth Regiment will be placed immediately en route for San Francisco.
By order Secretary War:

H. C. CORBIN, *Adjutant-General.*

(Same to governor of Pennsylvania, Harrisburg, Pa.; adjutant-general Pennsylvania, Mount Gretna, Pa.; commanding officer, Mount Gretna, Pa.)

MOUNT GRETNA, PA., VIA LEBANON, *May 18, 1898.*
(Received 2.08 p. m.)

ADJUTANT-GENERAL, U. S. ARMY, *Washington, D. C.*:

Orders to report my command to San Francisco received; 175 men without uniforms or equipment; 160 men unarmed. Would like to be armed and equipped here.

HAWKINS, *Colonel.*

ADJUTANT-GENERAL'S OFFICE, *Washington, May 18, 1898.*
Colonel HAWKINS, *Mount Gretna, Pa.*:

To delay your command at Mount Gretna for the arms and uniforms would bring you to San Francisco after the time appointed for sailing. Hope to have these things ready for you when you reach San Francisco.

H. C. CORBIN, *Adjutant-General.*

MEMORANDUM FOR THE QUARTERMASTER-GENERAL.

It is requested that the Quartermaster-General take the necessary steps to provide the uniforms and all other things needed for this command when it reaches San Francisco.

H. C. CORBIN, *Adjutant-General.*

MEMORANDUM FOR THE CHIEF OF ORDNANCE.

ADJUTANT-GENERAL'S OFFICE, *Washington, May 18, 1898.*
Copy of dispatch to Colonel Hawkins from the Adjutant-General, referred to the Chief of Ordnance, who is requested to see that this regiment is provided with the necessary arms and equipments upon reaching San Francisco.

H. C. CORBIN, *Adjutant-General.*

HARRISBURG, PA., *May 18, 1898.*
Gen. H. C. CORBIN, *Adjutant-General, Washington, D. C.*:

I have your telegram this date announcing the Tenth Regiment will be placed immediately en route for San Francisco.

HASTINGS, *Governor of Pennsylvania.*

SAN FRANCISCO, CAL., *May 18, 1898.*
(Received May 19—1.32 a. m.)

ADJUTANT-GENERAL, U. S. ARMY, *Washington, D. C.*:

Arrived last evening. Have spent entire day in investigations and inspections and will telegraph result at length.

OTIS, *Major-General of Volunteers.*

SAN FRANCISCO, CAL., *May 18, 1898.*
(Received May 19, 1898—6.45 a. m.)

ADJUTANT-GENERAL, U. S. ARMY, *Washington, D. C.*:

Have to-day examined conditions and made careful inquiry into work of supply departments in fitting out expedition. Have inspected the three vessels already chartered and casually the troops which have arrived. The vessels secured are the *City of Pekin*, *City of Sydney*, and the *Australia*. The two first are in about the same stage of preparation; should be ready to load on Saturday. Galleys and bunks should be complete on Friday. The *Australia* should be ready for troops on Monday. These vessels can not carry any quartermaster's transportation (animals and wagons). Will have these vessels inspected to ascertain if seaworthy and in good sanitary condition. Their carrying capacity when crowded will not be over 175 officers and 2,500 men, independent of Navy contingent which goes on *Pekin*. Plans of all decks of these vessels will be furnished me as soon as carrying arrangements completed. No other vessels suitable for the transportation of troops can be secured by Government at present. Those sailing from this port are the *Ohio*, the *Senator*, the *China*, the *Colon*, the *St. Paul*, the *Columbia*, and *State of California*. The *Ohio* is en route for Seattle, and advertised to leave that port for Alaska June 15. The *Senator, St. Paul, Columbia*, and *State of California* can not be chartered; available only by seizure. The *China*, from Hongkong, will reach this port about June 2 and the *Colon*, from Panama, about May 24; the *Conemaugh*, not suited for troops but adapted for animals and freight, now en route to Seattle. Any of these vessels if secured must be put in condition for troop transportation, and it is doubtful if troops could be sent in them from this port in less time than four weeks, present absence of vessels considered. The *Pekin* is to take on eighty odd officers and men of Navy and a large tonnage of naval stores, etc., and doubtful if more than single full regiment of troops of army can be safely transported. Vessel has made no provision for messing officers and will not unless high rate stipulated for and money guaranty. Troops present and intended for embarkation are band and four companies Fourteenth Infantry (9 officers and 276 men), two regiments and two battalions of California infantry (thirty-four companies in all), two companies of California heavy artillery, giving for California nearly 3,000 officers and men. First Oregon Regiment, twelve companies, arrived this afternoon. A regiment from Minnesota, Nebraska, Kansas, Colorado, each, and the Wyoming battalion will arrive on or before the 20th instant. None of the troops are properly equipped, but a few can be made available for service in distant country with means at hand. Articles of ordnance, tentage, and light clothing especially needed. Some of the California troops have old .50-caliber Springfield muskets. I have not assumed command here of incoming troops in obedience to my orders of the 12th instant, and I am at a loss to understand that it is the intention of the authorities that I, with staff and not to exceed an infantry regiment of untrained troops, proceed to the Philippines and occupy such parts of the islands as I may be able until other troops are sent to that distant point. I might be of service in putting the troops here in condition. I request immediate instructions.

OTIS, *Major-General of Volunteers.*

SAN FRANCISCO, CAL., *May 18, 1898.*
(Received May 19, 1898—7.33 a. m.)

ADJUTANT-GENERAL, U. S. ARMY, *Washington, D. C.:*

Brigadier-General Anderson with two companies Fourteenth Infantry reached Seattle from Alaska to-day. Will arrive Vancouver Barracks to-morrow.

MERRIAM, *Major-General Commanding.*

SURGEON-GENERAL'S OFFICE,
Washington, May 19, 1898.

The ADJUTANT-GENERAL, U. S. ARMY, *Washington, D. C.*

SIR: I have the honor to recommend that the commanding general Department of the Colorado be directed to send without delay three hospital stewards or acting hospital stewards (preferably stewards), to San Francisco, Cal., and that they be ordered to report for duty to the general commanding the Philippine expedition.

It is requested that all the necessary orders in the case be communicated by telegraph.

Very respectfully,
GEO. M. STERNBERG,
Surgeon-General U. S. Army.

ADJUTANT-GENERAL'S OFFICE,
Washington, May 19, 1898.

COMMANDING OFFICER, DEPARTMENT COLORADO, *Denver, Colo.:*

Assistant Secretary War directs three hospital stewards, or acting hospital stewards (preferably former), sent at once to San Francisco to report for duty to general commanding Philippine expedition.

WARD, *Assistant Adjutant-General.*

GOVERNORS ISLAND, N. Y., *May 19, 1898.*
(Received 10.16 a. m.)

ADJUTANT-GENERAL, *War Department, Washington, D. C.:*

I hear from General Otis that he has asked if he should proceed to the Philippines on the *Pekin* or remain in San Francisco temporarily. By all means he should remain in San Francisco. I can't see that there is any reason for a general officer going with these first troops.

W. MERRITT, *Major-General.*

ADJUTANT-GENERAL'S OFFICE,
Washington, May 19, 1898.

Gen. E. S. OTIS, U. S. Army, *San Francisco, Cal.:*

Your telegram of last evening has been submitted to the Secretary War and by him to the President. After full consideration of situation it has been decided that it is not necessary for you to embark with the troops first going to the Philippines, but that Brig. Gen. T. M. Anderson go in your stead. The Secretary War further directs you assume command of all troops assembling in San Francisco for Philippine expedition. This of course will not mean that you are to assume command of either military departments. The ships *Australia*, 2,755 tons, the *City of Sydney*, 3,000 tons, and the *Centennial*, 2,100 tons, have been chartered for the expedition for the Philippines. The *Zealandia*, 2,500 tons, will arrive in San Francisco May 27. Mr. Huntington offers the *China*, 5,000 tons, to arrive May 27, and the *Colon*, 2,600 tons, to arrive in San Francisco May 23. All the above steamers have been chartered except *China* and *Colon*. Secretary War desires report from you as to largest number troops that can be accommodated on these ships, after which it may be deemed advisable, even necessary, to press into service the ships named in your telegram. Arrangements for the messing of officers will be made in best way to meet interests of all concerned. It is desirable that you confer with Mr. Huntington to ascertain from him whether it is not possible to get charter of other ships. Also desirable that you make frequent reports upon situation and progress until General Merritt's arrival. Acknowledge receipt.

By command General Miles:

H. C. CORBIN, *Adjutant-General.*

ADJUTANT-GENERAL'S OFFICE,
Washington, May 19, 1898.

General MERRIAM, U. S. Army,
Vancouver Barracks, Wash.:

Following has been sent General Otis, and is transmitted to you for your information and guidance:

(Here is repeated telegram to General Otis, as above.)

Secretary War directs that General Anderson repair to San Francisco, to go in command of first troops leaving for the Philippines. He will be guided by instructions heretofore telegraphed General Otis. Acknowledge receipt.

By command Major-General Miles:

H. C. CORBIN, *Adjutant-General.*

DENVER, COLO., *May 19, 1898.*
(Received 3.10 p. m.)

ADJUTANT-GENERAL, U. S. ARMY, *Washington, D. C.:*

In obedience to your telegram 19th, Acting Hospital Steward Thomas D. Hare, Whipple Barracks, and Acting Hospital Steward Shelby G. Cox, Fort Bayard, have been ordered by telegraph to San Francisco to report to general commanding Philippine expedition. Chief surgeon department recommends that Hospital Steward Land, on furlough until September 6th (last address Oroville, Cal.,) have his furlough revoked by Adjutant-General Army, by telegraph, and be ordered to report in like manner at San Francisco.

In absence department commander—

VOLKMAR, *Assistant Adjutant-General.*

ADJUTANT-GENERAL'S OFFICE,
Washington, May 19, 1898—11.45 p. m.

Major-General MERRITT, *Governors Island, New York Harbor:*

Agreeable to your request of this date, General Otis has been directed to remain in San Francisco, and not go with first expedition leaving in few days. General Anderson, brigadier-general volunteers, will go in charge.

H. C. CORBIN, *Adjutant-General.*

ADJUTANT-GENERAL'S OFFICE,
Washington, May 19, 1898.

General MERRITT, *Governors Island, New York:*

The Major-General Commanding directs that you be notified that the Eighteenth and Twenty-third Infantry have been ordered from New Orleans to San Francisco, to report on arrival to General Otis.

By order Major-General Miles:

H. C. CORBIN, *Adjutant-General.*

ADJUTANT-GENERAL'S OFFICE,
Washington, May 19, 1898—11.45 p. m.

General MERRITT,
Commanding General, Department East, Governors Island, New York.

Having reference to previous telegrams concerning expedition to Philippines, Secretary War bids me inform you that to the regular force the Eighteenth and Twenty-third Regiments Infantry have been ordered from New Orleans this evening.

H. C. CORBIN, *Adjutant-General.*

AFFAIRS IN THE PHILIPPINE ISLANDS. 663

SAN FRANCISCO, CAL., *May 19, 1898.*
(Received May 20, 1898—2.05 a. m.)

ADJUTANT-GENERAL, U. S. ARMY, *Washington, D. C.:*

Preparations on steamer *City of Pekin* progressing as rapidly as possible. Promised that she will be ready for troops on Saturday. Bunks and galleys to be completed to-morrow. Sanitary board of medical officers called this morning to determine number of troops that can be safely transported under existing necessities. Reports at length, fixing number at 1,000 in steerage; number could be increased 200 if upper deck used, which is not practicable. The Navy contingent and First California number 59 officers and 1,041 enlisted men, all that can with any prudence be transported by *Pekin.* Can not obtain plans of decks until to-morrow afternoon, after completion of bunks, but doubt if that number can be provided with bunks. Vessel's tonnage, 4,000 tons dead weight, and with coal and naval stores already taken and to be taken on after leaving dock only about 6,000 tons can be loaded for Army; may be necessary to reduce subsistence stores. Both vessels, *City of Sydney* and the *Australia*, will be ready to load on Saturday; both now as far advanced as *Pekin.* Have deck plans of *Sydney;* can not take more than 800 men, and them closely packed. The *Australia* may be able to transport 600 men. Will make further examination to-morrow and will endeavor to have sanitary inspection of both *Sydney* and *Australia* made. Those two vessels would transport the battalion of Fourteenth Infantry and the regiment of Oregon volunteers now here and in fair shape. Will make further suggestions when more definite information obtainable. I still await further instructions.

OTIS, *Major-General of Volunteers.*

HOUSE OF REPRESENTATIVES, U. S.,
Washington, D. C., May 19, 1898. (Received May 20, 1898.)

General ALGER, *Secretary of War.*

DEAR GENERAL: The officers and men of the Fifteenth Pennsylvania Volunteers desire to be ordered to the Philippines. They are a splendid regiment, as well drilled as regulars. I would be gratified to learn, should you determine to send any more volunteers from the East to the Philippines, that the Fifteenth had been selected.

Respectfully, J. B. SHOWALTER.

VANCOUVER BARRACKS, WASH., *May 20, 1898.*
(Received 2.16 p. m.)

ADJUTANT-GENERAL, U. S. ARMY, *Washington, D. C.:*

Telegram 19th instant to General Merriam, transmitting for his information and guidance instructions sent to General Otis, received and forwarded to General Merriam at San Francisco, Cal.

DAVIS, *Acting Assistant Adjutant-General.*

SAN FRANCISCO, CAL., *May 20, 1898.*
(Received 4.40 p. m.)

ADJUTANT-GENERAL, U. S. ARMY, *Washington, D. C.:*

Telegram directing that I remain here temporarily, received. Will send First California Volunteers by steamer *City of Pekin*, which, with Navy contingent, will require all vessel's space. It is well outfitted, and will have six months' supply from all supply departments. This freight, together with personal baggage of troops, will fully meet carrying capacity of vessel. The three vessels, *City of Pekin*, *City of Sydney*, and the *Australia*, should sail together, as reported in my dispatch of last night. All equally prepared, and together will transport 2,500 men, with their officers, although crowded. Can send out, besides First California, the battalion of Fourteenth Infantry, and another regiment of volunteers, increased by necessary detachments. Suggested in telegram of last night that First Oregon be sent, but several cases of measles developed and isolated camp ordered. First Colorado, of full regimental strength, well equipped, well officered, and having superior medical officers. will arrive in morning, and I suggest that it be placed on vessel as soon as practicable. Will not delay *Pekin* materially. If plan approved, will use some discretion in matters. Have telegraphed General Anderson to be here Sunday morning.

OTIS, *Major-General of Volunteers.*

ADJUTANT-GENERAL'S OFFICE,
Washington, May 20, 1898.

Major-General OTIS, *San Francisco, Cal.:*

Your telegram this date has been submitted to Secretary War and Major-General Commanding, who approve of plan therein set forth.

H. C. CORBIN, *Adjutant-General.*

SAN FRANCISCO, CAL., *May 20, 1898—4.58 p. m.*

General CORBIN, *Adjutant-General, Washington, D. C.*

Your telegram directing General Otis to take command of expeditionary troops here and General Anderson to report to him, received and action taken. This will relieve pressure here.

MERRIAM,
Major-General, Commanding Department.

SAN FRANCISCO, CAL., *May 20, 1898.*
(Received May 21, 1898—2.11 a. m.)

ADJUTANT-GENERAL, U. S. ARMY, *Washington, D. C.:*

Telegram this date approving suggestions received. *City of Pekin*, with naval contingent, First California Volunteers, hospital detachment, with six months' supplies and baggage of troops, will be loaded to full capacity. Vessel will take troops on board, proceed to Mare Island, take on 400 tons navy ammunition, and can then clear. She should be ready to go to Mare Island early Monday morning. In meantime First Oregon Volunteers and battalion of Fourteenth Infantry, nearly 1,400 enlisted men, and possibly increased by detachments, will take *City of Sydney* and the *Australia* and join *Pekin* Tuesday morning, 24th instant, when all vessels depart. All organizations properly equipped and supplied for six months. Navy finished loading *Pekin* this evening, except Mare Island freight and army freight, about 600 tons, loaded to-morrow, and troops follow next day. Commander Gibson, who goes in charge of *Pekin*, has instructions to proceed to Honolulu, and from there proceed to Philippines under orders of commanding officer of cruiser *Charleston*, still here being repaired. *Charleston* will not make more than 9 knots an hour from Honolulu, while *Sydney* and *Australia* can make about 14. This will greatly delay progress of troops. If convoy by *Charleston* not necessary, the three vessels should be permitted to proceed together to Philippines at usual rate of speed. They are coaled for full distance. Can not naval authorities modify Commander Gibson's instructions in this respect?

Have assumed command of troops. Mr. Huntington left city Wednesday for the East. Will confer with his representative to-morrow about steamers *China* and *Colon*. Will report number of troops that can be transported by vessels, as directed in telegram of yesterday.

OTIS, *Major-General of Volunteers.*

ADJUTANT-GENERAL'S OFFICE,
Washington, May 21, 1898.

GENERAL OTIS, *San Francisco, Cal.:*

Referring to your telegram of last evening, instructions to Commander Gibson have been modified, and ships will follow movements of *Pekin*, and conform to the instructions of the navy commander of the *Pekin*.

By command Major-General Miles:

H. C. CORBIN, *Adjutant-General.*

ADJUTANT-GENERAL'S OFFICE,
Washington, May 21, 1898.

Brig. Gen. THOMAS M. ANDERSON,
Vancouver Barracks, Wash.:

Order issues to-day directing you report in person to commanding general, Department Pacific, San Francisco, for duty with expedition to Philippine Islands. Similar telegram sent you yesterday. Please acknowledge receipt.

SCHWAN,
Assistant Adjutant-General.

ADJUTANT-GENERAL'S OFFICE,
Washington, May 21, 1898.

COMMANDING GENERAL, UNITED STATES TROOPS,
San Francisco, Cal.:

Assistant Secretary War authorizes commanding general Philippine expedition to transfer enlisted men from organizations to hospital corps equitably, as service may require.

WARD, *Assistant Adjutant-General.*

DEPARTMENT OF STATE,
Washington, May 21, 1898.

The Honorable, the SECRETARY OF WAR.

SIR: By direction of the Secretary of State I have the honor to inform you that a telegram has been received from the consul at Hongkong, China, dated May 19, 1898, in the following words:

"This answers Long's cable to Dewey. From best information obtainable Dewey can not reply under a week. Twenty-one thousand Spanish troops, of which 4,000 natives, 2,000 volunteers. All but 1,000 at Manila. They have 10 mountain guns, no large field artillery, proven last rebellion not practicable. Plenty good ponies 12 hands high. No food Philippines but rice. Large supply rifles should be taken for insurgent allies."

Respectfully yours,

ALVEY A. ADEE,
Second Assistant Secretary.

Official copy respectfully referred to Major-General W. Merritt, U. S. Army, commanding Department of the Pacific, San Francisco, Cal., for his information.

By command of Major-General Miles:

WM. H. CARTER,
Assistant Adjutant-General.

ADJUTANT-GENERAL'S OFFICE, *May 26, 1898.*

ADJUTANT-GENERAL'S OFFICE,
Washington, May 21, 1898.

General BROOKE, *Chickamauga Park, Ga.*

Please state whether the Hotchkiss guns sent to San Francisco for the Philippine expedition were mountain guns with pack saddles.

H. C. CORBIN, *Adjutant-General.*

WASHINGTON, *May 21, 1898.*

ADJUTANT-GENERAL, U. S. ARMY.

SIR: I desire to call your attention to the fact that, as the Fifteenth Infantry is not to accompany me on the Philippine expedition, one regular regiment to replace the same be ordered to San Francisco for the expedition. Either the Fourth or the Twentieth would be satisfactory to me, or any other regiment that can better be spared. No orders as yet have been received with reference to the Third Artillery, now at San Francisco, which, I understand, is to accompany my expedition. It should be recruited to war strength. In this request is only considered the batteries that will probably accompany me, as the two at San Diego and Fort Canby will probably not be sent.

In the matter of the Fourth Cavalry, there are four troops at the Presidio and four troops in Washington and Idaho.

I take it for granted, from conversation already had, that these will accompany the expedition, and it is with a view to this that I ask that Major Kellogg, who is a ranking major, be sent with the command.

The matter of machine guns has been called to my attention as being most important on the mission that I am to undertake. Of the Gatling guns, model 1883, there are, as I learn from the Ordnance Department, 6 at Springfield Armory, and corresponding carriages for these 6 guns at Rock Island Arsenal. I should like to have these batteries sent. Of Gatling guns, model 1881, there are 7 guns at Springfield Armory, 4 carriages at Rock Island Arsenal, and 3 carriages at Allegheny Arsenal. I should be glad to have these also sent. There are 2 guns and carriages at the Presidio of San Francisco of the Gatling type, with long barrels; 1 gun and carriage at Angel Island, San Francisco Harbor. This makes a total of 16 guns and carriages, which would be eminently useful to me with my command. It is understood that 6 Hotchkiss guns, 1.65-inch caliber, with carriages and pack outfits complete, have been ordered from Chickamauga to San Francisco for the use of this expedition. If this has not been done I hope it will be attended to. I desire especially to call attention to the necessity for the additional infantry regiment for which I have asked. If this is sent the regular troops at my disposal will be less than those originally promised, namely, 5,000.

Very respectfully,

W. MERRITT, *Major-General.*

WASHINGTON, D. C., *May 21, 1898.*

The ADJUTANT-GENERAL, U. S. ARMY, *Washington, D. C.*

SIR: In addition to the troops applied for this morning I should like two companies of engineers to report for duty to me at San Francisco. A consultation with the Chief of Engineers results in his statement that he has at least 60 men at

Willets Point, and Lieutenant Echols, well instructed, who could be sent to me. If I can not do better I should be glad to have these. I fear it is futile to apply for Griffin's entire organization of engineers, but if it is possible to get them in shape before the last expedition leaves I should be glad to have them.

In conversation with the President yesterday he was very much impressed with the advantage that would result from having mines, submarine, and appliances on hand at Manila. If these can be furnished I request that it may be done. An ordnance detachment of mechanics is, in my opinion, especially necessary. It is also important that a siege battery should be sent with the command, and this I consider rather more important than the two regular light batteries applied for in my first estimate, which I am willing should not be sent at present.

Very respectfully,
W. MERRITT, *Major-General, U. S. Army.*

WASHINGTON, D. C., *May 21, 1898.*

The ADJUTANT-GENERAL, UNITED STATES, *Washington, D. C.*

SIR: I find, in my letter of this date, that I omitted to mention the general officers who are, in my opinion, necessary to the success of my expedition. Otis and Anderson are already in San Francisco and have received the necessary orders. I should like, in addition, to have four other general officers, and I request them in the following order: Brig. Gen. George W. Davis, Brig. Gen. A. R. Chaffee, and if Col. Edwin V. Sumner, Seventh Cavalry, is appointed to a brigadier-generalcy, as I recommend, I would also like to have him.

If the President appoints general officers from civil life I should be particularly glad to have Col. F. V. Greene, of the Seventy-first New York, and Colonel Garretson, of Ohio, to report to me. These officers, as I understand it, have expressed a willingness to go.

If the officers above named, in addition to Otis and Anderson, can not join me I request that at least four others be sent with me, and leave the selection to yourself.

Very respectfully,
W. MERRITT, *Major-General, U. S. Army.*

WASHINGTON, *May 21, 1898.*

ADJUTANT-GENERAL, U. S. ARMY.

SIR: The following officers for service on my staff, who have not yet been ordered and whose services I consider essential, are reported, as you requested, in order that you may give the necessary orders in the case: Judge-advocates, Crowder and Kernan; attending surgeon, Woodruff; ordnance officers, Simpson and Sturgis; engineers, Bement and Potter, of the engineers.

I also desire that Dr. Bourns be appointed a division or brigade surgeon and accompany my command. He is a citizen from Georgia.

It would be greatly in my favor if Major Kellogg could be ordered with the battalions of the Fourth Cavalry that are going. I should like also to have young Babcock, who has just graduated from the Academy, and whose father is assistant adjutant-general of the expedition, be appointed as an additional aid.

Very respectfully,
W. MERRITT, *Major-General.*

SAN FRANCISCO, CAL., *May 21, 1898—11.20 p. m.*

ADJUTANT-GENERAL, U. S. ARMY, *Washington, D. C.:*

Have seen vice-president of Pacific Mail Steamship Company, from which *City of Pekin* and *Sydney* chartered, about charter of steamers *China* and *Colon*, and he informs me that he has received proposition from Assistant Secretary of War, which he has answered. The three vessels, *Pekin*, *Sydney*, and *Australia*, will be prepared to depart on Tuesday, transporting the navy contingent, the First California and the First Oregon regiments of volunteers, an officer and 50 men detached from the battalion of heavy artillery California Volunteers, which includes all members who have any knowledge of the service of artillery, and the battalion of the Fourteenth Infantry; in all, 125 officers and nearly 2,400 men. These are all that can be safely transported. Delay may be caused by failure to receive the contracts of charter of *City of Sydney* and *Australia*. Copies must be furnished the captains of vessels before sailing, and they have not been received. If not received I would suggest that I may be authorized to direct new charter parties to be made here in accordance with the charter party of *Pekin*, which would be satisfactory except as to *Sydney*, wherein owners would require that deck stores be furnished by Army, which would not amount to $500. I would further suggest that on each vessel, *Sydney* and *Australia*, an officer of the Navy, chosen from those taking passage on *Pekin*, be detailed to direct those transports, sailing on same, and to represent the Army in same way as Commander Gibson represents the Navy. This I thought might be arranged through conference of Navy and War Department authorities, and would be of great benefit should emergency arise.

OTIS, *Major-General of Volunteers.*

SAN FRANCISCO, CAL., *May 21, 1898.*
(Received May 22, 1898—6 a. m.)

ADJUTANT-GENERAL, U. S. ARMY, *Washington, D. C.*:

The speed of vessels *Pekin*, *Sydney*, and *Australia* reported by me last evening as about 14 knots is the best speed of vessels and can not be maintained without great consumption of coal, leaving little in bunkers upon arrival at Manila. Careful consideration of the subject by Commander Gibson and captain of *Pekin* has resulted in following conclusion, viz: That an average run of 12 knots would cover the distance in twenty-five days, and with 11 knots in a little more than twenty-six days. That it would be prudent and in the interests of good seamanship to call at Honolulu with all three ships and take on coal, which would not require more than two days: this to meet any unexpected emergency from the enemy or the elements. Coal in two of the vessels constitute the ballast, and good supply must be kept on hand. Will leave this subject to the discretion of navy officers.

OTIS, *Major-General Volunteers.*

PORTLAND, OREG., *May 17, 1898.* (Received May 23, 1898.)
PAYMASTER-GENERAL, U. S. ARMY, *Washington, D. C.*

SIR: I have the honor to report that I arrived at Portland, Oreg., this morning, and have complied with the telegraphic instructions of the Adjutant-General of the Army, dated 10th instant.

Very respectfully,

JOHN S. WITCHER,
Major and Paymaster, U. S. Army.

ADJUTANT-GENERAL'S OFFICE,
Washington, May 23, 1898.

Gen. E. S. OTIS, *San Francisco, Cal.*:

The Secretary of War directs that General Anderson, or the senior officer of the troops sailing on the *Pekin*, *Australia*, and *Sydney* for the Philippines, on arrival will confer fully with Admiral Dewey as to whole situation and dispose of the troops so as to have them under the protection of the guns of the Admiral's fleet until the arrival of the main force of the army under General Merritt and General Otis. Importance of the speedy return of transports going with these troops should be kept in view. This instruction is not intended to deprive General Anderson of the fullest discretion after consultation with Admiral Dewey. Hearty cooperation with the senior officer of the Navy is enjoined. He must, however, be governed by events and circumstances of which we can have no knowledge. The President and Secretary of War rely upon the sound judgment of the officer in command. Acknowledge receipt.

By command Major-General Miles:

H. C. CORBIN, *Adjutant-General.*

ADJUTANT-GENERAL'S OFFICE,
Washington, May 23, 1898.

Gen. E. S. OTIS, *San Francisco, Cal.:*

Having reference to telegram of this date giving instructions of the President and Secretary of War to General Anderson, the President and Secretary War remark that in event of General Anderson not joining, or not being able to go, that it will be expected that General Otis himself will assume immediate command and proceed to join Admiral Dewey. Acknowledge receipt.

By command Major-General Miles:

H. C. CORBIN, *Adjutant-General.*

SAN FRANCISCO, CAL., *May 23, 1898—12 m.*
ADJUTANT-GENERAL, U. S. ARMY, *Washington, D. C.:*

City of Pekin with troops on board, consisting of 11 officers and 76 enlisted men of the Navy, 50 officers and 970 men of the First California, is about to leave dock to anchor in bay and take on 400 tons of ordnance and ordnance stores. It will require at least twenty-four hours to load these stores. The *City of Sydney* and the *Australia* are nearly loaded. They will take on to-morrow the Second Oregon (50 officers and 965 men), the band and five companies of the Fourteenth Infantry (9 officers and 340 men), and detatchment of California Heavy Artillery (1 officer and 50 enlisted men). General Anderson is here and will embark on *Australia* with staff. *City of Sydney* and *Australia* will then join *City of Pekin* in bay, when all vessels will sail together under modified instructions received by Commander Gibson, of the Navy. The entire force, Navy and Army combined, will exceed 2,500; accurate numerical strength later. Vessels should leave port to-morrow evening or early Wednesday morning. Nothing yet heard of charter parties for steamers *City of Sydney* and *Australia*. Will telegraph more accurate details later, and will report strength of forces now encamped here, independent of departing troops. Will furnish General Anderson written instructions to govern him en route and after arrival at destination.

OTIS, *Major-General of Volunteers.*

NEW YORK, *May 23, 1898.*
(Received 3 p. m.)
Gen. H. C. CORBIN, *Adjutant-General U. S. Army, Washington, D. C.:*

No papers received. Have arranged to start for San Francisco Tuesday afternoon at 5. Will I receive papers in time?

PUTNAM BRADLEE STRONG,
12 West Fifty-seventh Street.

CORRESPONDENCE.

ADJUTANT-GENERAL'S OFFICE,
Washington, May 23, 1898.

BRADLEE STRONG,
12 West Fifty-Seventh Street, New York City.:
Papers will reach you in due time. Do not delay your departure for San Francisco on their account.

H. C. CORBIN, *Adjutant-General.*

SAN FRANCISCO, CAL., *May 23, 1898.*
(Received 9.35 p. m.)
ADJUTANT-GENERAL, U. S. ARMY, *Washington, D. C.*:
Telegram of this date received. General Anderson arrived yesterday morning. Has completed all arrangements and takes quarters on steamer *Australia*. I telegraphed fully several hours ago. *City of Pekin* left dock at 1 o'clock and is now loading in bay. *City of Sydney* and *Australia* will be loaded and join *Pekin* as soon as or before she is loaded. The three vessels should sail to-morrow evening fully equipped and supplied for six months.

OTIS, *Major-General of Volunteers.*

ADJUTANT-GENERAL'S OFFICE,
Washington, May 23, 1898—10 p. m.
Gen. E. S. OTIS, *San Francisco, Cal.*:
Immediate report desired as to number of troops armed and equipped sufficiently efficient to take steamer on Saturday or even Monday next.
By command Major-General Miles:

H. C. CORBIN, *Adjutant-General.*

SAN FRANCISCO, CAL., *May 23, 1898*,
(Received May 24, 1898—4 a. m.)
ADJUTANT-GENERAL, U. S. ARMY, *Washington, D. C.*:
The Pacific Mail Steamship Company will not consent to let *City of Sydney* sail without knowledge of stipulations of charter party, which probably will not reach this point before 26th instant, as Quartermaster-General telegraphs it was not mailed until 20th. Company believes from information received that that contract now en route will prove unsatisfactory and not in accordance with its propositions. The vessel will leave forcibly or otherwise, although I may direct quartermaster here to enter into contract with stipulations similar to those contained in navy charter party for *City of Pekin*, omitting all mention of deck stores.

OTIS, *Major-General of Volunteers.*

ADJUTANT-GENERAL'S OFFICE,
Washington, May 24, 1898.
General OTIS, *San Francisco Cal.*:
Secretary of War desires me inform you that the Secretary Navy has given instructions that the *Charleston* convoy the *Pekin* and other ships from Honolulu to the Philippines. See that this information reaches General Anderson, if possible, before steamer sails.
By command Major-General Miles:

H. C. CORBIN, *Adjutant-General.*

AFFAIRS IN THE PHILIPPINE ISLANDS.

ADJUTANT-GENERAL'S OFFICE,
Washington May 24, 1898.

Capt. CHARLES E. WOODRUFF,
Assistant Surgeon, Jackson Barracks, New Orleans, La.:
Order issues to-day directing you proceed at once to San Francisco and report to General Merritt. commanding Department Pacific, for duty in that Department.
SCHWAN, *Assistant Adjutant-General.*

ADJUTANT-GENERAL'S OFFICE,
Washington, May 24, 1898.

Lieut. FRANCIS J. KERNAN,
7 Myrtle Avenue, Brooklyn, N. Y.:
Order issues to-day directing you proceed at once to San Francisco and report to General Merritt, commanding Department Pacific, for duty in that department.
SCHWAN, *Assistant Adjutant-General.*

SAN FRANCISCO, CAL., *May 24, 1898.*
(Received 5.24 p. m.)

ADJUTANT-GENERAL, U. S. ARMY, *Washington, D. C.:*
The troops now in camp and intended for expedition, First California, Second Oregon, Fourteenth United States Infantry, and detachment of California Heavy Artillery. Already shipped are Seventh California, First Colorado, Thirteenth Minnesota, First Nebraska, Twentieth Kansas regiments, averaging 47 officers and 968 enlisted men, having a total of 236 officers and 4,842 enlisted men. Also here in camp a battalion of California Heavy Artillery, two battalions Idaho, one battalion Wyoming, and the Utah Artillery, numbering 63 officers, 1,464 men; total, all told, 299 officers, 6,306 enlisted men. Tenth Pennsylvania Regiment will arrive to-day. Of these troops the Colorado, Minnesota, and Nebraska regiments are in fair condition; need to be outfitted with certain necessary stores not yet received, but arrive in two or three days. These regiments are being inspected to ascertain what ordnance necessary. They can be placed in condition to sail early next week. All other infantry organizations can not be put in condition in less than two weeks. Carefully inspected yesterday by an officer of my staff. The Utah Battery, if it had horses and harness, could leave at any time. The great obstacle to moving is vessel transportation. Only one small vessel chartered; full capacity, 800 men; and she can not discharge freight upon arrival and be put in condition to transport troops before the 31st instant. Have reported on this subject. Quartermaster making every effort here and not meeting with much success. Think seizure only possible solution.
OTIS, *Major-General of Volunteers.*

SAN FRANCISCO, CAL., *May 24, 1898.*
(Received 8.35 p. m.)

ADJUTANT-GENERAL, U. S. ARMY, *Washington, D. C.:*
Steamer *City of Sydney*, with troops on board and prepared to sail, anchored in bay beside *City of Pekin*. *Australia* loaded and ordered to leave dock at 4 o'clock this afternoon and anchor in bay. Am not sufficiently informed when *Pekin* will complete loading naval stores, but understand that it will be this evening. The hour of departure of the three vessels depends upon Navy authorities. Strength of

General Anderson's command, 117 officers and 2,382 enlisted men. Navy contingent, 11 officers and 76 enlisted men. Total for vessels, 128 officers, 2,458 enlisted men. Request made on owners of *Sydney* to let *Sydney* go. If not acceded to, then impressment ordered. Request has been complied with. Report on this subject by mail.

OTIS, *Major-General of Volunteers.*

NEW YORK, *May 24, 1898.*
(Received 7.42 p. m.)

Gen. H. C. CORBIN, *Washington, D. C.:*
I leave for San Francisco to-night.

PUTNAM BRADLEE STRONG.

SAN FRANCISCO, *May 24, 1898.*
(Received May 25, 1898—1 a. m.)

Gen. G. M. STERNBERG, *1016 Sixteenth street NW., Washington:*
As Lippincott is chief, pray retire me thirty-years. Substitute Parkhill here. Recent bereavement overwhelming. Written General Moore.

WHITE.

FORT SPOKANE, WASH., *May 25, 1898.*
(Received 2.38 p. m.)

ADJUTANT-GENERAL, U. S. ARMY, *Washington, D. C.:*
Received telegram Wednesday that order had been issued sending me to San Francisco. Order not yet received. Shall I proceed at once?

MORRIS, *Assistant Surgeon.*

ADJUTANT-GENERAL'S OFFICE,
Washington, May 25, 1898.

Capt. EDWARD R. MORRIS, *Fort Spokane, Davenport, Wash.:*
Telegram to you 18th instant from this office was sent to notify you of necessity for your departure for San Francisco.

SCHWAN, *Assistant Adjutant-General.*

TACOMA, WASH., *May 25, 1898.*
(Received 4.26 p. m.)

G. D. MEIKLEJOHN,
Assistant Secretary of War, Washington, D. C.:
Referring to telegrams passed between Secretary Alger and myself about two weeks ago relative chartering *Pakshan* to Government, Senator Cockrell wires me to-day that you express some doubt of steamer's safety for ocean voyage. *Pakshan* has always been engaged in ocean trade; made trip from Hongkong here last January, which is stormiest month. Lloyd classes her A1. Captain Robinson, quartermaster, Seattle, has examined her; report filed in General Ludington's office. There is no safer or more suitable steamer on this coast than *Pakshan* for transporting Manila troops. This is easily demonstrable.

HUGH C. WALLACE.

ADJUTANT-GENERAL'S OFFICE,
Washington, May 25, 1898.

Gen. WESLEY MERRITT, *San Francisco, Cal.:*

Secretary of War desires report of the number of troops of the different arms necessary for the defense of Pacific coast.

By command Major-General Miles:

H. C. CORBIN, *Adjutant-General.*

ADJUTANT-GENERAL'S OFFICE,
Washington, May 25, 1898.

COMMANDING-GENERAL, DEPARTMENT PACIFIC,
San Francisco, Cal.:

Order made relieving Maj. R. H. White, surgeon, from duty with Philippine expedition. Please notify him at once.

SCHWAN, *Assistant Adjutant-General.*

SAN FRANCISCO, CAL., *May 25, 1898.*
(Received 10.10 p. m.)

ASSISTANT SECRETARY OF WAR, *Washington, D. C.:*

Your two dispatches received at 5 p. m., and understood. Endeavored to communicate with General Anderson, but too late, as vessels with troops were moving and *City of Pekin* had crossed the bar.

OTIS, *Major-General of Volunteers.*

ADJUTANT-GENERAL'S OFFICE,
Washington, May 26, 1898.

General MERRIAM, *San Francisco, Cal.:*

Secretary of War is anxious to have you report the number of troops and the several arms thereof, in your opinion, necessary to garrison the posts on the Pacific coast.

By command of Major-General Miles:

H. C. CORBIN, *Adjutant-General.*

SAN FRANCISCO, CAL., *May 26, 1898.*

ADJUTANT-GENERAL, U. S. ARMY, *Washington, D. C.:*

Will report number and kind of troops for coast defenses in a day or two. The greatest need is competent staff officers to replace those ordered east and west from both departments and who were familiar with local conditions. Clerks and messengers also taken away, and still we have our full share of war preparations.

MERRIAM, *Major-General, Commanding.*

ADJUTANT-GENERAL'S OFFICE,
Washington, May 27, 1898.

Major-General MERRIAM, *San Francisco, Cal.:*

Your statement that the number of your staff officers and clerks is insufficient is fully appreciated here. Steps will be taken to remedy this as soon as possible. It is the same everywhere. The staff for an army of 25,000 does not fill the needs of an army of 250,000.

H. C. CORBIN, *Adjutant-General.*

NAVY DEPARTMENT, *Washington, May 27, 1898.*

SIR: I have the honor to transmit herewith, for your information, the following copy of an extract from a dispatch, dated the 24th instant, received in this Department from Rear-Admiral Dewey, U. S. Navy, commanding the United States naval forces on the Asiatic Station:

"Organizing forces near Cavite, and may render assistance that will be valuable. I do not consider submarine mines practicable here on account of great depth and width of bay and entrance. If attacked by superior force, the squadron will endeavor to give good account of itself."

Very respectfully,

JOHN D. LONG,
Secretary.

The SECRETARY OF WAR.

SAN FRANCISCO, CAL., *May 27, 1898—4 p. m.*
ADJUTANT-GENERAL, U. S. ARMY, *Washington, D. C.:*

I am badly in need of general officers to take charge of camp to organize command. Have any of the officers asked for in my communication of the 21st been ordered to report to me? If yes, please state who; if no, please have two or three ordered at once. This I consider an imperative necessity.

W. MERRITT, *Major-General.*

ADJUTANT-GENERAL'S OFFICE,
Washington, May 27, 1898.
Col. F. V. GREENE,
Seventy-First New York Volunteers, Tampa, Fla.:

You have been nominated brigadier-general of volunteers to-day, and will be ordered to duty with expedition to Philippine Islands. Please telegraph Maj. Gen. Wesley Merritt, San Francisco, probable date of your arrival there. Acknowledge receipt.

H. C. CORBIN, *Adjutant-General.*

(Telegraph same to Colonel Garretson, Cleveland, Ohio.)

ADJUTANT-GENERAL'S OFFICE,
Washington, May 27, 1898.
Maj. Gen. WESLEY MERRITT, *San Francisco, Cal.:*

Col. F. V. Greene, of New York, Colonel Garretson, of Ohio, and Col. Marcus P. Miller, Third Artillery, this day nominated brigadier-generals, and will be ordered to report to you for duty with Philippine expedition. Secretary War desires to know what other general officers, if any, you wish to join that expedition. The above is reply to your telegram this date.

H. C. CORBIN, *Adjutant-General.*

SAN FRANCISCO, CAL., *May 27, 1898.*
(Received 10.15 p. m.)
ADJUTANT-GENERAL, U. S. ARMY, *Washington, D. C.:*

Minimum force needed to garrison Pacific coast defenses 2,600 well-trained heavy artillery, 2,000 infantry, 500 cavalry. This provides barely for two reliefs at the guns mounted, and small supports and patrols, also leaving Puget Sound to depend upon naval protection.

MERRIAM, *Major-General.*

CLEVELAND, OHIO, *May 27, 1898.*
(Received 8.47 p. m.)

H. C. CORBIN, *Adjutant-General, Washington, D. C.:*
Your telegram received. I will report to General Merritt by telegraph at once.

G. A. GARRETSON.

ADJUTANT-GENERAL'S OFFICE,
Washington, May 27, 1898—12 midnight.

Major-General OTIS, *San Francisco, Cal.:*
Your telegram for interpreter and stenographer received. I will submit it to Secretary War to-morrow, and, if possible, get approval. The Secretary War remarked to-day that he expected you would accompany the second expedition sailing for the Philippines. Acknowledge receipt.

By command Major-General Miles:

H. C. CORBIN, *Adjutant-General.*

ADJUTANT-GENERAL'S OFFICE,
Washington, May 28, 1898.

COMMANDING GENERAL, DEPARTMENT OF CALIFORNIA,
San Francisco, Cal.:
Having reference to your telegram of last night, giving number of men necessary for protection of your coast, you mention 2,600 well-trained heavy artillery. Could not two regiments infantry be utilized for this purpose, as there is no heavy artillery, as such, available in the service? Early reply desired.

By command Major-General Miles:

H. C. CORBIN, *Adjutant-General.*

NAVY DEPARTMENT,
Washington, May 28, 1898.

SIR: I have the honor to transmit herewith a translation of a cipher dispatch, dated the 25th instant, at Cavite, received in this Department from Rear-Admiral George Dewey, U. S. Navy, commanding the United States naval force on the Asiatic Station, containing certain information obtained at the request of the War Department.

Very respectfully,

JOHN D. LONG, *Secretary.*

The Honorable, the SECRETARY OF WAR.

[Inclosure.]

HONGKONG, *May 27, 1898.*

SECRETARY OF NAVY, *Washington:*

CAVITE, May 25.—The following is information required for General Merritt:

FIRST. Between 35,000 and 40,000 Spanish troops of all kinds in Philippine Islands.
SECOND. Fifteen thousand at Manila.
THIRD. About 60 per cent Spanish.
FOURTH. Seven 8-centimeter and two 12-centimeter field guns at Manila; can not ascertain number outside.
FIFTH. Light field guns best.
SIXTH. Nearly impossible to get horses near Manila.
SEVENTH. All supplies must be brought.
EIGHTH. Bridge train not necessary.

Cavite now in my possession. Would be excellent base. Plenty forage and water to be had. Very difficult to obtain coal of any kind. Rainy season will shortly begin. Climate extremely hot. The discipline and efficiency of the Spanish troops is very low.

DEWEY.

WAR DEPARTMENT,
Washington, May 28, 1898.

GENERAL: I transmit herewith, for your information, copy of a dispatch from Rear-Admiral Dewey, dated Cavite, May 25th, instant.

Very respectfully,

R. A. ALGER, *Secretary of War.*

Maj-Gen. WESLEY MERRITT,
Commanding Army of Occupation to the Philippines,
Palace Hotel, San Francisco, Cal.

Inclosure (copy of foregoing dispatch).

WAR DEPARTMENT,
Washington, May 28, 1898.

Maj. Gen. WESLEY MERRITT, U. S. Army,
Commanding Army of Occupation to the Philippines,
Washington, D. C.

GENERAL: The following instructions of the President are communicated to you for your information and guidance:

EXECUTIVE MANSION,
Washington, May 19, 1898.

To the SECRETARY OF WAR.

SIR: The destruction of the Spanish fleet at Manila, followed by the taking of the naval station at Cavite, the paroling of the garrisons, and acquisition of the control of the bay, have rendered it necessary, in the further prosecution of the measures adopted by this Government for the purpose of bringing about an honorable and durable peace with Spain, to send an army of occupation to the Philippines for the twofold purpose of completing the reduction of the Spanish power in that quarter and of giving order and security to the islands while in the possession of the United States. For the command of this expedition I have designated Maj. Gen. Wesley Merritt, and it now becomes my duty to give instructions as to the manner in which the movement shall be conducted.

The first effect of the military occupation of the enemy's territory is the severance of the former political relations of the inhabitants and the establishment of a new political power. Under this changed condition of things the inhabitants, so long as they perform their duties, are entitled to security in their persons and property and in all their private rights and relations. It is my desire that the people of the Philippines should be acquainted with the purpose of the United States to discharge to the fullest extent its obligations in this regard. It will therefore be the duty of the commander of the expedition, immediately upon his arrival in the islands, to publish a proclamation declaring that we come, not to make war upon the people of the Philippines nor upon any party or faction among them, but to protect them in their homes, in their employments, and in their personal and religious rights. All persons who, either by active aid or by honest submission, cooperate with the United States in its efforts to give effect to this beneficent purpose will receive the reward of its support and protection. Our occupation should be as free from severity as possible.

Though the powers of the military occupant are absolute and supreme and immediately operate upon the political condition of the inhabitants, the municipal laws of the conquered territory, such as affect private rights of persons and property and provide for the punishment of crime, are considered as continuing in force, so far as they are compatible with the new order of things, until they are suspended or superseded by the occupying belligerent; and in practice they are not usually abrogated, but are allowed to remain in force and to be administered by the ordinary tribunals substantially as they were before the occupation. This enlightened practice is, so far as possible, to be adhered to on the present occasion. The judges and the other officials connected with the administration of justice may, if they accept the authority of the United States, continue to administer the ordinary law of the land as between man and man, under the supervision of the American commander in chief. The native constabulary will, as far as may be practicable, be preserved. The freedom of the people to pursue their accustomed occupations will be abridged only when it may be necessary to do so.

While the rule of conduct of the American commander in chief will be such as has just been defined, it will be his duty to adopt measures of a different kind if, unfortunately, the course of the people should render such measures indispensable to the maintenance of law and order. He will then possess the power to replace or expel the native officials in part or altogether, to substitute new courts of his own constitution for those that now exist, or to create such or supplementary tribunals as may be necessary. In the exercise of these high powers the commander must be guided by his judgment and his experience and a high sense of justice.

One of the most important and most practical problems with which the commander of the expedition will have to deal is that of the treatment of property and the collection and administration of the revenues. It is conceded that all public funds and securities belonging to the government of the country in its own right, and all arms and supplies and other movable property of such government, may be seized by the military occupant and converted to the use of this Government. The real property of the state he may hold and administer, at the same time enjoying the revenues thereof, but he is not to destroy it save in the case of military necessity. All public means of transportation such as telegraph lines, cables, railways, and boats belonging to the state, may be appropriated to his use, but unless in the case of military necessity they are not to be destroyed. All churches and buildings devoted to religious worship and to the arts and sciences, all schoolhouses, are, so far as possible, to be protected, and all destruction or intentional defacement of such places, of historical monuments or archives, or of works of science or art, is prohibited, save when required by urgent military necessity.

Private property, whether belonging to individuals or corporations, is to be respected, and can be confiscated only as hereafter indicated. Means of transportation, such as telegraph lines and cables, railways, and boats, may, although they belong to private individuals or corporations, be seized by the military occupant, but unless destroyed under military necessity are not to be retained.

While it is held to be the right of a conqueror to levy contributions upon the enemy in their seaports, towns, or provinces which may be in his military possession by conquest, and to apply the proceeds to defray the expenses of the war, this right is to be exercised within such limitations that it may not savor of confiscation. As the result of military occupation the taxes and duties payable by the inhabitants to the former government become payable to the military occupant, unless he sees fit to substitute for them other rates or modes of contribution to the expenses of the government. The moneys so collected are to be used for the purpose of paying the expenses of government under the military occupation, such as the salaries of the judges and the police, and for the payment of the expenses of the army.

Private property taken for the use of the army is to be paid for, when possible, in cash at a fair valuation, and when payment in cash is not possible receipts are to be given.

In order that there may be no conflict of authority between the Army and the Navy in the administration of affairs in the Philippines, you are instructed to confer with the Secretary of the Navy, so far as necessary, for the purpose of devising measures to secure the harmonious action of these two branches of the public service.

I will give instructions to the Secretary of the Treasury to make a report to me upon the subject of the revenues of the Philippines, with a view to the formulation of such revenue measures as may seem expedient. All ports and places in the Philippines which may be in the actual possession of our land and naval forces will be opened, while our military occupation may continue, to the commerce of all neutral nations, as well as our own, in articles not contraband of war, and upon payment of the prescribed rates of duty which may be in force at the time of the importation.

WILLIAM MCKINLEY.

Very respectfully,

R. A. ALGER. *Secretary of War.*

SAN FRANCISCO, CAL., *May 28, 1898.*
(Received 6.33 p. m.)

ADJUTANT-GENERAL, U. S. ARMY, *Washington, D. C.*:

I have not yet received President's instructions for the conduct of affairs in the Philippines. Unsigned copy was shown me at White House, and I was told official copy would be furnished. Also, when order was issued directing me to assume command of the Department of the Pacific I was informed that special confidential instructions would be sent me. These have not been received.

MERRITT, *Major-General.*

ADJUTANT-GENERAL'S OFFICE,
Washington, May 28, 1898.

Major-General MERRITT, *San Francisco, Cal.*:

Your telegram received; your instructions for the conduct of affairs in Philippines, I think, was mailed yesterday. Secretary War remarked they would be. Will see him early in morning, and if they have not been sent they will reach you by following mail.

H. C. CORBIN, *Adjutant-General.*

SAN FRANCISCO, CAL., *May 28, 1898—1.04 p. m.*

ADJUTANT-GENERAL, U. S. ARMY, *Washington, D. C.*:

Telegram yesterday regarding interpreter and my expected movements received.

OTIS, *Major-General of Volunteers.*

ADJUTANT-GENERAL'S OFFICE,
Washington, May 28, 1898.

Major-General MERRITT, *San Francisco, Cal.*:

After further consideration Secretary War does not wish General Garretson to go to the Philippines. Brig. Gens. Charles W. King, Francis V. Greene, and Harrison Gray Otis, of the new generals, have been ordered to report. Would you like the services of Gen. Marcus P. Miller or any other general not already assigned?

H. C. CORBIN, *Adjutant-General.*

LAKELAND, FLA., *May 28 1898—4.36 p. m.*
ADJUTANT-GENERAL, *Washington, D. C.:*
  Order from Shafter to proceed to San Francisco immediately. Will leave to-night unless otherwise instructed. Telegraph will reach me St. Charles Hotel, New Orleans. Sunday evening.
  F. V. GREENE, *Brigadier-General.*

ADJUTANT-GENERAL'S OFFICE,
Washington, May 28, 1898.
Gen. F. V. GREENE, *St. Charles Hotel, New Orleans, La.:*
  Secretary War is very glad of your prompt compliance with orders to report to General Merritt. I hope the assignment pleases you. This order was made on the earnest solicitation of the General himself. I take more satisfaction in your promotion than that of any other, and, as I told the President, am sure you will give fully as good account of yourself as any of the distinguished men nominated in same list. With world of good wishes.
  H. C. CORBIN, *Adjutant-General.*

ADJUTANT-GENERAL'S OFFICE,
Washington, May 28, 1898.
Gen. HARRISON GRAY OTIS, *Los Angeles, Cal.:*
  The President bids me say to you, in anticipation of your confirmation as brigadier-general, you will be assigned to duty with General Merritt for duty with expedition going to Philippines. Acknowledge receipt and let me know if this will be agreeable. If you go with General Merritt, it will be necessary for you to report soon as possible.
  H. C. CORBIN, *Adjutant-General.*

ADJUTANT-GENERAL'S OFFICE,
Washington, May 29, 1898.
Major-General MERRITT, *San Francisco, Cal.:*
  Secretary War just informed me your instructions for government and guidance after your arrival in Philippines were mailed you yesterday.
  H. C. CORBIN, *Adjutant-General.*

CLEVELAND, OHIO, *May 28, 1898.* (Received May 29, 1898.)
Gen. H. C. CORBIN, *Washington.*
  MY DEAR GENERAL: Since I talked to you to-day I have learned to my very great chagrin that an officious friend of mine had telephoned Senator Hanna that I did not want to go to the Philippines with General Merritt, and asked the Senator to use his influence to have the order changed. I do not know whether this caused the Secretary to change the order or not, but if it did I am extremely mortified, and want him and you to know that it was done entirely unknown to me and unwarranted by me. It causes me extreme annoyance to be apparently guilty of such an unsoldier-like proceeding. I do not care particularly for the detail, to be sure, but I would have gone to the end of the earth before I would have asked, directly or indirectly, for the change of an order.

Will you kindly show this letter to the Secretary of War, so that he may understand my feelings in the matter?

With many thanks for your kind messages of congratulation, I am,

Yours, sincerely,

G. A. GARRETSON.

ADJUTANT-GENERAL'S OFFICE,
Washington, May 29, 1898.

Major-General MERRITT, *San Francisco, Cal.:*

The Secretary War directs me to inform you that the force going to the Philippines will be increased so as to make the effective force 20,000. I would be glad if you will intimate the States from which you would like to have the additional force sent.

H. C. CORBIN, *Adjutant-General.*

ADJUTANT-GENERAL'S OFFICE,
Washington, May 29. 1898.

MEMORANDUM FOR THE QUARTERMASTER-GENERAL.

The Secretary of War directs that clothing and equipments of all kinds be prepared for 20,000 men for the expedition to the Philippines.

H. C. CORBIN, *Adjutant-General.*

ADJUTANT-GENERAL'S OFFICE,
Washington, May 29, 1898.

MEMORANDUM OF THE COMMISSARY-GENERAL.

The Secretary of War directs that rations be prepared for 20,000 men for the expedition for the Philippines for three months.

H. C. CORBIN. *Adjutant-General.*

SAN FRANCISCO, CAL., *May 29, 1898.*
(Received 6.15 p. m.)

The ADJUTANT-GENERAL, *War Department, Washington, D. C.:*

In reply to your dispatch of to-day, the additional force should be sent from States having their troops in best order for immediate shipment. The greatest difficulty to contend with here is want of organization. The addition of the Twentieth and Fifteenth regiments of infantry would be of greatest value. Some of the unorganized volunteers would have a better chance to become efficient in posts now occupied by the Fifteenth Infantry than they would have if shipped immediately on a long voyage. This request for an increase to the regular force for the expedition is in keeping with the promise made to me by the President and Secretary of War when the organization of the Philippine expedition was put under discussion.

WESLEY MERRITT. *Major-General.*

ADJUTANT-GENERAL'S OFFICE,
Washington, May 29, 1898.

Major-General MERRITT, *San Francisco, Cal.:*

Secretary War desires to know number of animals in your opinion should be taken with the several expeditions of your command going to Philippines.

By command Major-General Miles:

H. C. CORBIN, *Adjutant-General.*

AFFAIRS IN THE PHILIPPINE ISLANDS.

ADJUTANT-GENERAL'S OFFICE,
Washington, May 29, 1898.

Major-General MERRITT, United States Army,
San Francisco, Cal.:

Secretary War directs that you call upon all commanders of troops in San Francisco to forward to this office a trimonthly field return on the 31st instant, also that a similar return showing strength and names of all officers on date of sailing of any expedition for the Philippines.

H. C. CORBIN. *Adjutant-General.*

ADJUTANT-GENERAL'S OFFICE,
Washington, May 29, 1898.

COMMANDING OFFICER, U. S. FORCES FIRST ARRIVING AT PHILIPPINES,
Care Admiral Dewey, via Hongkong, China:

Report required by cable as to desirability of transporting animals to meet requirements of troops operating in Philippines.

By order Secretary War:

H. C. CORBIN, *Adjutant-General.*

SAN FRANCISCO, CAL., *May 30, 1898.*
(Received 3.40 p. m.)

ADJUTANT-GENERAL, WAR DEPARTMENT,
Washington, D. C.:

I find a constant and growing necessity for a sum of money which shall be available for use in carrying out my plans, and I request that a contingent fund of at least $10,000 be placed to my credit for such use as I find the interests of the service demand.

WESLEY MERRITT, *Major-General.*

SAN FRANCISCO, CAL., *May 30, 1898.*
(Received 4.48 p. m.)

The ADJUTANT-GENERAL, *Washington, D. C.:*

When in Washington I was informed that eight batteries of Third Artillery and two squadrons of Fourth Cavalry were to constitute part of Philippine expedition. Am I to take these troops without further orders from your office. They must have ample notice to make preparations.

MERRITT, *Major-General.*

MEMORANDUM MADE BY COLONEL CARTER.

Major-General Miles stated to Colonel Carter, May 30, afternoon, that he did not think it advisable to send any of the Third Artillery on the Philippine expedition. That it could not be spared from Pacific coast. Two squadrons of the Fourth Cavalry to accompany expedition, but should not take their horses, because there is nothing for them to eat there and would probably die on the way over. Two light batteries of the Seventh Artillery detailed for the expedition in accordance with the General's wishes. Did not think the Fourth and Twentieth or any other regular infantry regiment should be moved to go with that expedition. He has no suggestion to make as to what volunteer regiments should go in place of the Fourth and Twentieth, if any were sent.

Secretary of War directs that on Tuesday morning the composition of General Merritt's forces, as far as determined, including the general officers detailed thereto, be reported to him, showing exactly what expedition now consists of and what is necessary to complete it up to 20,000 men.

SAN FRANCISCO, CAL., *May 30, 1898.*
(Received 5.55 p. m.)

ADJUTANT-GENERAL, UNITED STATES ARMY,
   War Department, Washington, D. C.:

Replying to inquiry of Secretary of War, I hesitate to take with command all the animals that will probably be needed, as well-informed persons tell me they probably will not stand the climate and other changed conditions. The cavalry horses of the squadrons of Fourth Cavalry which accompany the expedition, two animals to each gun and caisson taken, and not to exceed 50 wagons and teams in the quartermaster's department, and say 25 horses to be purchased here to provide for contingencies, should, in my opinion, be taken.

                MERRITT, *Major-General.*

SAN FRANCISCO, CAL., *May 30, 1898.*
(Received 9.46 p. m.)

The ADJUTANT-GENERAL, *Washington, D. C.:*

In my letter of May 15 I requested that certain information be obtained by cable from Admiral Dewey. Has this information been received? If not can I hope to obtain it soon?

                W. MERRITT, *Major-General.*

ADJUTANT-GENERAL'S OFFICE,
Washington, May 30, 1898—Midnight.

Major-General MERRITT, *San Francisco, Cal.:*

Having reference to your expressed wish that all regular troops possible be sent with your expedition to Philippines, Secretary of War desires to know if, in your opinion, there is a regiment of volunteers now on Pacific coast that you think would be willing to take post of Fifteenth Infantry in Arizona and New Mexico. Secretary of War desires, far as possible, to ascertain whether this is practicable and report accordingly.

                H. C. CORBIN, *Adjutant-General.*

ADJUTANT-GENERAL'S OFFICE,
Washington, May 31, 1898—12.30 a. m.

Major-General MERRITT, *San Francisco, Cal.:*

Admiral Dewey was requested, under date May 15, to give information asked for in your letter of that date. As yet no reply has been received. The moment it is it will be sent you.

                H. C. CORBIN, *Adjutant-General*

ADJUTANT-GENERAL'S OFFICE,
Washington, May 31, 1898.

Major-General MERRITT, *San Francisco, Cal.:*

The Secretary of War has just approved requisition upon Treasury Department for $10,000, to be placed to your credit with assistant treasurer in San Francisco, as per your telegram on this subject.

                H. C. CORBIN, *Adjutant-General.*

ADJUTANT-GENERAL'S OFFICE,
Washintgon, May 31, 1898.

Major-General MERRITT, San Francisco, Cal.:

The Secretary of War directs me to inform you that the charter for the *China* and the *Colon* has been perfected. These ships will be ready to sail from San Francisco for the Philippines within three or four days. The Secretary of War desires to know the number of men you will have ready to embark on these two ships. Will telegraph you later in day the organizations that will be ordered to fill your expedition.

H. C. CORBIN, *Adjutant-General.*

NAVY DEPARTMENT, *Washington, May 31, 1898.*

SIR: The Department is to-day in receipt, by your reference, of an official copy of the instructions of the President to Maj. Gen. Wesley Merritt, United States Army, commanding the army of occupation to the Philippines.

Very respectfully,

JOHN D. LONG, *Secretary.*

Hon. R. A. ALGER,
Secretary of War, Washington, D. C.

SAN FRANCISCO, CAL., *May 31, 1898.*
(Received 4.20 p. m.)

ADJUTANT-GENERAL, *War Department, Washington, D. C.:*

In reply to your telegram, General Miller has received orders to report to me, which is very satisfactory. For additional brigadier-generals I would like Hall, Gilmore, and MacArthur.

W. MERRITT, *Major-General, Commanding.*

ADJUTANT-GENERAL'S OFFICE,
Washington, May 31, 1898—12 midnight.

Major-General MERRITT, San Francisco, Cal.:

After careful consideration Secretary War directs but one battalion of four companies of Third Artillery be detailed for expedition to Philippines. Thinks that four troops of Fourth Cavalry, dismounted, are all that can be spared. If, however, after conferring with General Merriam, he feels he can spare eight troops, you will be instructed to order them to report to you. It is not thought any horses should be taken for cavalry. The artillery and cavalry organizations going with you will be filled to maximum before leaving—cavalry to 100 per troop and artillery to 200 men. Are you able to report that any volunteer regiment in your command can be sent to relieve the Fifteenth Infantry? In meantime we are making efforts on this side of continent to secure services of volunteer regiments in order that Fifteenth may come to you, which will be recruited to maximum before sailing. General MacArthur will be ordered to report to you. General Gilmore will remain on duty with General Miles, and Secretary War, for reasons that will occur to you, does not care to order General Hall before first ascertaining that these services will be agreeable to him.

H. C. CORBIN, *Adjutant-General.*

ADJUTANT-GENERAL'S OFFICE,
Washington, June 1, 1898—12.15 a. m.

General MERRIAM, San Francisco, Cal.:

Secretary War directs me inform you that four batteries Third Artillery, recruited to maximum, and four troops Fourth Cavalry will be ordered to report to General Merritt to form part of expedition for the Philippines. I shall be able to telegraph you in a day or two the volunteer regiments that will be ordered to report for duty in your command for the two departments. Secretary War desires to know if remaining batteries of Third Artillery are recruited to maximum. With assistance of infantry proposed ordered, they will be able to man guns on Pacific coast.

H. C. CORBIN, *Adjutant-General.*

ADJUTANT-GENERAL'S OFFICE,
Washington, June 1, 1898.

Major-General MERRITT, *San Francisco, Cal.:*
General MacArthur has been ordered to report to you.

H. C. CORBIN, *Adjutant-General.*

WAR DEPARTMENT, *June 1, 1898.*

GOVERNOR OF IOWA, *Des Moines, Iowa:*
I desire to know if it will be agreeable for a regiment from your State now awaiting assignment to be ordered to report to General Merritt, San Francisco, for duty with expedition to the Philippines. Consider this confidential, and it should not be known to troops for obvious reasons.

R. A. ALGER, *Secretary of War.*

(Same to governor of Tennessee, Nashville, Tenn.; governor of Kentucky, Frankfort, Ky.; governor of Virginia, Richmond, Va.)

SAN FRANCISCO, CAL., *June 1, 1898.*
(Received 5.46 p. m.)

ADJUTANT-GENERAL, *War Department, Washington, D. C.:*
Your telegram received. Every effort has been made to discover a volunteer regiment willing to relieve the Fifteenth Infantry, as directed in your telegram. No regiment will accept this duty voluntarily. I still think it important that one should be ordered for this service.

W. MERRITT, *Major-General.*

DENVER. COLO., *June 1, 1898.*
(Received 7.26 p. m.)

Senator TELLER, *Washington, D. C.:*
The Colorado boys in Torrey's cavalry are anxious to go to Philippines instead of Cuba.

ALVA ADAMS, *Governor.*

SAN FRANCISCO, CAL., *June 1, 1898.*
(Received 9.26 p. m.)

ADJUTANT-GENERAL, *War Department, Washington D. C.:*
Referring to your telegram relating to the Fourth Cavalry and Third Artillery, General Merriam tells me he could spare the eight troops probably, certainly six troops, of the Fourth Cavalry. In regard to taking this cavalry dismounted, I am of the opinion that it would be feasible and very desirable to take the serviceable horses now with the cavalry command—say forty or fifty horses to the troops.

MERRITT, *Major-General, Commanding.*

AFFAIRS IN THE PHILIPPINE ISLANDS. 685

ADJUTANT-GENERAL'S OFFICE,
Washington, June 2, 1898.

General MERRIAM, *San Francisco, Cal.:*

Secretary War directs you confer with General Merritt as to number of troops of Fourth Cavalry you can spare for his expedition, and to order the number you and he agree upon.

By command of Major-General Miles:

H. C. CORBIN, *Adjutant-General.*

ADJUTANT-GENERAL'S OFFICE,
Washington, June 2, 1898.

Major-General MERRITT, *San Francisco, Cal.:*

Secretary War directs that you exercise your own judgment as to taking horses with the six or eight troops of the Fourth Cavalry as General Merriam may determine he can spare for this duty. Secretary War thinks it would be well to make an experiment, with a view, if successful, to have others follow in a later expedition.

H. C. CORBIN, *Adjutant-General.*

ADJUTANT-GENERAL'S OFFICE,
Washington, June 2, 1898.

Major-General MERRITT, *San Francisco, Cal.:*

Referring to your telegram of May 30 concerning eight batteries of Third Artillery and two squadrons of Fourth Cavalry, Secretary War directs you confer with General Merriam on this subject. In previous telegram to-day you were informed that either six or eight troops of the Fourth Cavalry would be taken. He does not think that more than four batteries of Third Artillery should go at this time, but these should be filled to the maximum.

H. C. CORBIN, *Adjutant-General.*

SAN FRANCISCO, CAL., *June 2, 1898.*
(Received 4.56 p. m.)

ADJUTANT-GENERAL, *Washington, D. C.:*

Under your telegram yesterday four batteries Third Artillery, Major Hess commanding, ordered to report to General Merritt. These batteries not yet filled to maximum, but recruiting rapidly. To make up cavalry squadron have ordered one troop from Vancouver and three from Presidio, Major Kellogg to command. This leaves two troops at Walla Walla with Major Rucker, one at Boise, one old and two new troops with band at Presidio, Lieutenant-Colonel Morris commanding, and two troops in National Park. If more of this cavalry is to join Merritt's force, Morris desires to go with it, but I doubt his fitness for field service.

MERRIAM, *Major-General.*

SAN FRANCISCO, CAL., *June 2, 1898.*
(Received 6.15 p. m.)

ADJUTANT-GENERAL, *War Department, Washington, D. C.:*

Replying to your dispatch of 31st ultimo, there are more men ready to embark than the ships *China* and *Colon*, which you mention, will accommodate. The *Zealandia* it is understood here is also to sail at the same time, and there are more than sufficient men armed and equipped ready to load her also. The total capacity of the three ships is reported by the board of survey as 205 officers and 2,313 men, and the ships are reported staunch and in good sanitary condition. They will not be ready to sail under a week. It is important of course that additional transports be chartered at once.

W. MERRITT,
Major-General, Commanding.

SAN FRANCISCO, CAL., *June 2, 1898.*
(Received 8.20 p. m.)

ADJUTANT-GENERAL, U. S. ARMY, *Washington, D. C.:*

Adjutant-General Cowles, Raleigh, N. C., has some competent men for Signal Corps. Request they be enlisted at Raleigh and ordered here to report to Major Thompson for Volunteer Signal Corps.

W. MERRITT,
Major-General, Commanding.

SAN FRANCISCO, CAL., *June 2, 1898.*
(Received 8.40 p. m.)

ADJUTANT-GENERAL, *War Department, Washington, D. C.:*

Request authority to transfer operators from volunteer and regular regiments to Volunteer Signal Corps in cases meeting approval of regimental commanders.

MERRITT,
Major-General, Commanding.

MILWAUKEE, WIS., *June 2, 1898.*
(Received 3.25 p. m.)

Gen. H. C. CORBIN, *War Department, Washington, D. C.:*

Chicago papers report General Greene on way to Pacific yesterday. Am eagerly awaiting orders here.

CHARLES KING.

ADJUTANT-GENERAL'S OFFICE,
Washington, June 2, 1898.

Maj. Gen. WESLEY MERRITT,
San Francisco, Cal.:

Commissions of Major Hale, assistant adjutant-general, Major Strother, chief engineer, and Captain Mott, assistant adjutant-general, mailed to them at San Francisco. They can accept and execute oaths at once.

CARTER, *Assistant Adjutant-General.*

ADJUTANT-GENERAL'S OFFICE,
Washington, June 3, 1898.

Major-General MERRITT, *San Francisco, Cal.:*
Major-General MERRIAM, *San Francisco, Cal.:*

With exceptions noted below, orders issued to-day provide for the detail from each battalion of a regiment and from each independent battalion, by the commanding officer thereof, of one recruiting party, to consist of one officer and four enlisted men, one of whom should be qualified to perform clerical work; and in a like manner from each troop or battery not otherwise provided for above, a recruiting party of one officer and one enlisted man, and in addition from each regiment or organization consisting of two battalions, one medical officer for service with recruiting parties therefrom. Each party to proceed to locality where organization was raised for the purpose of enlisting recruits to fill such organization already in service to the maximum published in General Orders, 29, current series, from these headquarters. The names of the officers, their respective organizations, and the points to which sent to be reported as early as possible to the Adjutant-General of the Army. You will give the necessary orders for transportation and subsistence, the travel enjoined being necessary for the public service. Instructions for recruiting officers and blank forms will be sent on or about the 7th instant to adjutant-general of the state, to whom officers in charge of recruiting parties should apply for the same. Complete returns not having been received here, each recruiting officer, before proceeding to comply with these instructions, will inform himself, by conference with his commanding officer and inspection of returns, of the number of enlisted men required under this plan by the organization for which he is to recruit, which detailed information you will please compile and report to the Adjutant-General of the Army. Each recruiting officer thus detailed will also be an acting quartermaster.

Organizations from the following States, whose apportionment under the first call exceeded their quota under both calls, will not be considered in this order, namely: Delaware, Idaho, Montana, Wyoming, Arizona, Nevada, North Dakota, South Dakota, Vermont, District of Columbia, New Mexico, Oklahoma, Indian Territory.

The organization of additional companies except cavalry necessary for the completion of regiments to twelve-company basis, battalions to four-company basis, will be taken up in the near future under the same rules that governed the organizations and muster in of the troops raised under the President's first call, but it is not intended that this latter work shall interfere with the above, and it is therefore not begun at this time.

Each commander detailing a recruiting officer under these instructions will promptly mail to the chief commissary and chief quartermaster, respectively, of the department into which the recruiting officer is sent a copy of the order of detail, with the signature of the recruiting officer inscribed upon the same. Acknowledge receipt.

H. C. CORBIN, *Adjutant-General.*

ADJUTANT-GENERAL'S OFFICE,
Washington, June 3, 1898.

Major-General MERRITT, *San Francisco, Cal.:*

Your telegram concerning effort to get volunteer regiment to relieve the Fifteenth is received. Every effort is being made on this side of continent, but without results.

H. C. CORBIN, *Adjutant-General.*

NEW YORK, N. Y., *June 3, 1898.*
(Received 11.46 a. m.)

QUARTERMASTER-GENERAL, U. S. ARMY, *Washington, D. C.:*

Have bought for delivery in St. Louis, June 10, 25 horses and 100 mules for Astor Battery; also harness and saddles, all subject to Government acceptance. Please instruct depot quartermaster at St. Louis to accept and care for everything until battery can take charge on its way to Philippines.

J. J. ASTOR.

ADJUTANT-GENERAL'S OFFICE,
Washington, June 3, 1898.

General WESLEY MERRITT, *San Francisco, Cal.:*

Should batteries and cavalry intended for your expedition be provided with horses and mules and transported to San Francisco, or should they be sent there without them?

H. C. CORBIN, *Adjutant-General.*

SAN FRANCISCO, CAL., *June 3, 1898.*
(Received 3.22 p. m.)

ADJUTANT-GENERAL, *War Department, Washington, D. C.:*

You informed me under date of May 29 that special instructions for my government of the Philippines had been mailed me. The paper has not yet been received. Will you see if it was mailed the date indicated?

MERRITT, *Major-General, Commanding.*

WAR DEPARTMENT, *June 3, 1898.*

Major-General MERRITT, *San Francisco, Cal.:*

Special letter of instructions for government of the Philippines mailed to you by me on morning of May 31 by special delivery; also at same time another letter inclosing copy of dispatch from Admiral Dewey.

JOHN TWEEDALE, *Chief Clerk.*

SAN FRANCISCO, CAL., *June 3, 1898.*
(Received 3.41 p. m.)

ADJUTANT-GENERAL, *War Department, Washington, D. C.:*

After careful consideration of the subject in consultation with General Merriam, I have decided to take but six troops of the Fourth Cavalry. The suggestion of the Secretary of War in regard to shipping a portion of the horses first will be complied with.

MERRITT, *Major-General, Commanding.*

SAN FRANCISCO, CAL., *June 3, 1898.*
(Received 7.26 p. m.)

ADJUTANT-GENERAL, *War Department, Washington, D. C.:*

On May 12 I was informed by Secretary of War that I could have 100 men of Eighth Cavalry to man Hotchkiss mountain guns. In letter of same day I asked that these men, with Lieutenant Sayer commanding them, be ordered to San Francisco at once. Has this been done?

W. MERRITT, *Major-General, Commanding.*

ADJUTANT-GENERAL'S OFFICE,
Washington, June 3, 1898.

Major-General MERRITT, *San Francisco, Cal.:*

Major Bement has just been ordered to report to you.

H. C. CORBIN, *Adjutant-General.*

AFFAIRS IN THE PHILIPPINE ISLANDS. 689

ADJUTANT-GENERAL'S OFFICE,
Washington, June 4, 1898.

General MERRITT, *San Francisco, Cal.:*

Secretary of War directs that you be informed that owing to the reported serious condition of the frontier bordering the Sioux Indian reservations and the trouble between the Apaches and reservation Indians in Indian Territory, it is regarded as absolutely necessary to keep the Eighth Cavalry at their present stations. You are authorized, however, to select from the Fourth Cavalry men to man the Hotchkiss guns shipped to you, but none of these should be taken from the two troops now in the Yellowstone Park.

CARTER, *Assistant Adjutant-General.*

SAN FRANCISCO, CAL., *June 4, 1898.*
(Received 4.19 p. m.

ADJUTANT-GENERAL, *War Department, Washington, D. C.:*

Referring to your dispatch of June 3, it is my intention to take the horses of the regular cavalry that are now here, but not the horses for Utah batteries now here. If additional batteries and cavalry are intended for the expedition, it will probably be necessary to take them without horses or mules. Please inform me what other batteries and cavalry it is the intention to assign to this command.

MERRITT, *Major-General, Commanding.*

ADJUTANT-GENERAL'S OFFICE,
Washington, June 4, 1898.

Major-General MERRITT, *San Francisco, Cal.:*

Should you desire General Hughes to command a brigade, you are, of course, at liberty to assign him; General Babcock also. All such assignments are left to your discretion.

By command Major-General Miles:

H. C. CORBIN, *Adjutant-General.*

ADJUTANT-GENERAL'S OFFICE,
Washington, June 5, 1898.

General MERRITT, *San Francisco, Cal.:*

Following telegram, June 4, from commanding officer, Fort McPherson, is repeated for your information:

"Troops for Eighteenth and Twenty-third Infantry left this evening; first section at 7.40; last section at 9.15; Eighteenth Infantry, 472; Twenty-third Infantry, 423; arrive at San Francisco Thursday."

H. C. CORBIN, *Adjutant-General.*

BOSTON, MASS., *June 4, 1898.* (Received June 5, 1898.)

Gen. H. C. CORBIN,
Adjutant-General's Office, War Department, Washington, D. C.

DEAR SIR: In accordance with the request of the honorable Secretary of War, which came to us from you, we have written to General Merritt in regard to the Philippines, and inclose copy for your reading.

We remain, very truly, yours, HENRY W. PEABODY & CO.

BOSTON, MASS., *June 4, 1898.*

Maj. Gen. WESLEY MERRITT, U. S. Army, *San Francisco, Cal.*

SIR: In accordance with our overtures and the official indorsements which we inclose, we are pleased to respond to the request of the honorable Secretary of War in submitting to you some information regarding the Philippines. Our close business relations there the past eight years, and especially the residence at Manila nearly four years of Mr. Charles L. Smith, now connected with our Boston office, enable us, perhaps, to have some information that may be useful, at least in confirming what you find from other sources.

His description of the recent conditions at Manila, received by private advices, we believe to be equally reliable to the facts which he states from his earlier observations, viz:

Climate.—The southeast monsoon sets in during April, and rains are frequent in the afternoon during May and become heavier in June, while July is generally the rainiest month of the year, there being a downpour of rain for ten to twelve days at a time, so that the country is practically under water. During August the rains become more spasmodic, though there are usually many heavy storms. September is the last of the southeast monsoon, and with October we have the northeast monsoon, with almost uniform clear, dry weather until April again. The rainy season in Manila is generally considered as healthy a season as any, as, coming after the long hot, dry period, it washes the country and air clear of all impurities, and practically the only danger from this season is the exposure to the weather, with consequent chills and colds.

Location.—Manila is built entirely on the low, swampy land at the mouth of the river Pasig, and the country back of the city, extending to the foothills, some 20 to 25 miles away, is of the same swampy character, and is given up chiefly to the cultivation of rice. Consequently, during the wet season the country inland from Manila is practically impassable, especially for troops of any kind. There are very few roads, and these narrow and poorly made. In fact, it would be very difficult at this season for troops to maneuver to any extent in the rear of the city. The city is built on both banks of the Pasig, and is intersected in every direction by a network of creeks and canals. Most of these are only 10 to 20 feet wide and easily spanned by portable bridges, but very difficult to cross by fording, as they all have a soft mud bottom. The river Pasig has two bridges and one or two smaller ones.

Natives.—My own experience with the natives, and especially with the native troops, is that they have no particular love for the Spaniards, and, while they will fight under the Spanish rule with the utmost valor so long as they think the Spanish are invincible, yet when they once become convinced that the Spanish are to be defeated they will immediately turn against their commanders and join the opposing forces. This has happened several times in the recent insurgent engagements, and, in my opinion, would be sure to be the case if they were attacked by American forces. It may be interesting for you to know that, in all the recent troubles with the natives in Manila, not one Englishman or English-speaking man in the islands has been interfered with by the natives. On the contrary, they have been doing everything possible to win the sympathy of the English-speaking people, and it seems reasonable to suppose that they would help the American troops, and that, with the Spaniards once conquered, we should have no trouble in bringing the natives into submission.

Spanish troops.—There have been apparently about 50,000 troops sent to the Philippines from Spain, but of these apparently only about one-half are now fit for service, the balance having died or been invalided home. Of these 25,000 now in the islands apparently nearly one-half are south of Manila, distributed in small detachments at the various ports throughout the archipelago. A month and a half ago it was supposed that there were some 7,000 to 8,000 Spanish troops in Manila and about 3,000 to 4,000 native troops, making a total fighting force of not exceeding 12,000, which might be added to by volunteers. It is obviously impossible for the troops in the southern islands to return to Manila, as there is no possible communication except by water. The Spanish troops that were distributed throughout the island of Luzon to curb the recent insurgent uprising will find it extremely difficult to return to Manila, as there are no thoroughfares by land even on that island.

Defenses.—You are undoubtedly fully advised in regard to the principal fortifications in Manila. Since the recent troubles with the insurgents the Spanish have arranged a system of three-story blockhouses at the back of the city, forming a chain covering 6 to 8 miles in extent, there being about fifteen of these houses, occupied by 50 to 100 troops each. My recollection of the fortifications and defenses of the city leads me to believe that the best approach to take the city with troops would be to land on the beach just above Malate, which is about a mile and a half to the south of the old walled city and on the same side of the river. There are no fortifications to speak of at this point, and there is good ground for the formation of troops to advance on the city. All the fortifications that protect the city are on this side of the river, and the advance could be made without having to count on crossing the bridges.

Health.—The chief danger to our troops at this season of the year would be constant exposure to the weather. The Spanish troops endeavor to avoid camping on the ground as much as possible. In Manila the troops live in barracks, and when out of the city they always make a great effort to spend the night in some village where they can be quarted in the houses. Of course, at times this is impossible, and they then wrap themselves in heavy blankets and sleep on the ground. Their uniform consists of a light gauze suit of underclothes and blue and white stripe cotton drill. Yellow fever and cholera are unknown. While there is more or less smallpox, it is not epidemic. The great danger arises from dysentery, which is very easily contracted if one is allowed to get chilled. My own experience proved that the greatest protection from illness during the rainy season was wearing a woolen band around the abdomen, commonly known as a "cholera belt." This proved very effective in preventing the dangerous chills to the stomach. To be thoroughly wet during the rainy season and then sleeping without proper protection or warmth is almost sure to bring on a chill, and dysentery follows quickly. This constant exposure to the weather during the rainy season would be the chief danger to our troops, but with Manila once ours there would be ample accommodations for troops in the Spanish barracks or in the large warehouses erected for the storing of hemp and sugar, which must be more or less vacant while the blockade of Manila continues.

We have the honor to be, sir, very respectfully, yours,

HENRY W. PEABODY & CO.

SAN FRANCISCO, CAL., *June 6, 1898.*
(Received 6.30 p.m.)

ADJUTANT-GENERAL, *War Department, Washington, D. C*:

I consider it important that the authorities in Washington should know how matters are dragging with the Philippine expedition. Owing to changes necessary to be made in the chartered transports, the next detachment can not sail before about the 15th. This includes the *China, Colon,* and *Zealandia.* They will carry, all told, about 2,500 men and officers. This, including the detachment already sailed, will be, in round numbers, about 5,000, only about one-fourth the entire expeditionary force contemplated. There are plenty of men as fit to go as these already ordered. The need being transports, as already reported (see dispatch of 2d instant), can they not be hurried? I am not complaining, but report the facts, as they do not seem to be understood in Washington. In the meantime we are doing all that is practicable in instructing the commands in camp here.

MERRITT, *Major-General Commanding.*

ADJUTANT-GENERAL'S OFFICE,
Washington, June 6, 1898.

General MERRITT, *San Francisco, Cal.:*

The Secretary of War directs that you be informed that Light Batteries B and G, which have been ordered to report to you, can not be supplied with ammunition for several weeks. It is expected ammunition will arrive in San Francisco not later than the 30th, and will be hurried before that time if possible. The batteries come without horses. In order that more men may be selected for one of these batteries it is desired to know about what date you would expect them to leave San Francisco for the Philippines, and also that they may have as much time as possible to complete fitting out here.

CARTER, *Assistant Adjutant-General.*

ADJUTANT-GENERAL'S OFFICE,
Washington, June 7, 1898.

Major-General MERRITT, *San Francisco, Cal.:*

Your telegram last evening concerning the lack of transports has been submitted to the Secretary of War and to the President, and every effort is being put forth to secure transportation needed. Any action on your part looking to speedy supply of transportation will be approved. The same, however, should be reported at once to this office. The President as well as the Secretary of War give you the widest latitude in this matter.

H. C. CORBIN, *Adjutant-General.*

SAN FRANCISCO, CAL., *June 7, 1898.*
(Received 5.50 p. m.)

ADJUTANT-GENERAL, *War Department, Washington, D. C.:*

The question of the necessity of taking with us machines of sufficient capacity to distill water for drinking purposes has been strongly brought to my attention by the chief surgeon of the expedition. Inquiries directed by me ascertain the facts that distiller's pumps, boilers, and tanks of sufficient capacity for drinking water for the command can be obtained in a reasonable time here at a cost not to exceed $12,000. I desire authority to proceed in this matter. I also find that at a cost not to exceed $7,500 we could procure three or four good portable steam boilers and engines and the necessary pump and about 2 miles of wrought-iron pipe and fittings for the purpose of taking water from a tower to a higher level and providing large camps with water from one or more sources of supply. I consider this also as a necessary matter, and request authority to carry it out.

MERRITT, *Major-General, Commanding.*

SAN FRANCISCO, CAL., *June 7, 1898.*
(Received 5.55 p.m.)

ADJUTANT-GENERAL, *War Department, Washington, D. C.:*

In reference to the fleet of transports to sail next week, I assume that the question of a naval convoy has been considered by the authorities in Washington, this in view of the information given me that it was contemplated to request Admiral Dewey to meet the fleets en route.

MERRITT. *Major-General, Commanding.*

SAN FRANCISCO, CAL., *June 7, 1898.*
(Received 6.27 p.m.)

ADJUTANT-GENERAL, *War Department, Washington, D. C.:*

Archbishops Ireland and Riordan recommend as the priests who would be of special service to us the appointment of Father Francis Brooks Doherty as chaplain, U. S. Army. I approve and earnestly recommend this appointment.

MERRITT, *Major-General, Commanding.*

HEADQUARTERS DEPARTMENT OF THE PACIFIC,
OFFICE OF THE CHIEF PAYMASTER,
San Francisco, Cal., May 30, 1898. (Received June 8, 1898.)

The PAYMASTER-GENERAL OF THE ARMY, *Washington, D. C.*

SIR: I have the honor to request that authority be given the pay department of the army in the Philippines to issue checks on New York and San Francisco to officers and soldiers for money which they may wish to send to their families.

In order to do this the existing Treasury regulations should be rescinded which forbids a disbursing officer to issue a check for less than $100 "for money to pay troops."

After pay day the men can make application to the paymaster for checks for money for mailing, and it will keep the money so received in the pay department and lessen the amount to be sent from the United States. Moreover, it would be a great accommodation to both the officers and men paid on headquarters and company rolls.

Very respectfully, your obedient servant,

CHAS. MCCLURE,
Major and Paymaster, U. S. Army, Chief Paymaster.

[First indorsement.]

WAR DEPARTMENT, PAYMASTER-GENERAL'S OFFICE,
Washington, June 8, 1898.

Respectfully referred to the Honorable the Secretary of the Treasury, through the Secretary of War, inviting attention to the within suggestions of the chief paymaster, Department of the Pacific, that officers and enlisted men may receive from the paymaster checks in exchange for money.

Reference is made to sections 3620 and 5488, Revised Statutes, and rules of the Treasury Department made in accordance therewith, as published in inclosed Treasury Department circular, No. 125, 1897.

Paymasters are authorized by Army Regulations (1349) to issue to enlisted men checks for amount of pay due them on the pay roll, but the suggestion of Major McClure relates to any sum which a soldier may desire to remit by mail.

It is hoped that the views of the Honorable Secretary of the Treasury may be received before the departure of paymasters ordered for duty with the Philippine expedition.

T. H. STANTON,
Paymaster-General U. S. Army.

[Second indorsement.]

WAR DEPARTMENT, *June 8, 1898.*

Respectfully submitted to the Honorable the Secretary of the Treasury.

G. D. MEIKLEJOHN,
Assistant Secretary of War.

Third indorsement.]

TREASURY DEPARTMENT, *June 10, 1898.*

Respectfully returned to the Honorable the Secretary of War, with the information that checks drawn for the purpose herein mentioned would not be a violation of the regulations of this Department, and the convenience to the paymaster in obtaining ready money in this manner, as well as the accommodation to both officers and men at that far-away place, would seem to warrant the War Department in modifying Article 1349, Army Regulations, herein referred to, so far as it relates to disbursements at the Philippine Islands. If a check is drawn for a portion of pay due, it should be drawn in favor of the soldier, and the object or purpose should be stated as "part pay for month of ———." If for any sum which the soldier may desire in exchange for money after he has been paid, the check should be drawn by the paymaster in favor of himself and indorsed by him, payable to the order of the soldier, and the object or purpose should be stated as "to obtain cash to make payments at a distance from a depositary."

L. J. GAGE, *Secretary.*

[Fourth indorsement.]

WAR DEPARTMENT, PAYMASTER-GENERAL'S OFFICE,
Washington, June 11, 1898.

Respectfully referred to the Adjutant-General U. S. Army, recommending modification of Army Regulations 1349 in accordance with foregoing decision of the Secretary of the Treasury.

T. H. STANTON,
Paymaster-General U. S. Army.

[Fifth indorsement.]

The Secretary of War approved the recommendation of the Paymaster-General.

H. C. CORBIN, *Adjutant-General.*

ADJUTANT-GENERAL'S OFFICE, *June 14, 1898.*

(General Orders, No. 70, June 16, 1898, issued accordingly.)

ADJUTANT-GENERAL'S OFFICE,
Washington, June 8, 1898.

Major-General MERRITT, U. S. Army,
Commanding Department Pacific, San Francisco, Cal.:

The following dispatch, dated 24th ultimo, received by Navy Department from Rear-Admiral Dewey, is repeated for your information:

"Organizing forces near Cavite, and may render assistance that will be valuable. I do not consider submarine mines practicable here on account of great depth and width of bay and entrance. If attacked by superior force, the squadron will endeavor to give good account of itself."

By command of Major-General Miles:

CORBIN. *Adjutant-General.*

SAN FRANCISCO, CAL., *June 8, 1898.*
(Received 5.10 p. m.)

ADJUTANT-GENERAL, U. S. ARMY,
    Washington, D. C.:

The prospects as to transports is improving; hope to have five sail about the 15th, carrying 4,000 men and officers. The *Indiana, Ohio, Belgic,* and *City of Puebla* should be ready to sail about June 25. Capacity not yet determined. I again call attention to the consideration of the Government at Washington of the question of convoys for these transport ships, which must of necessity be helpless in a fight.

    MERRITT, *Major-General Commanding.*

WAR DEPARTMENT,
Washington, June 8, 1898.

The SECRETARY OF THE NAVY.

SIR: I have the honor to transmit herewith a telegram just received from General Merritt, commanding the expedition to the Philippines. I desire to know what reply shall be made.

Very respectfully,

    R. A. ALGER, *Secretary of War.*

ADJUTANT-GENERAL'S OFFICE,
Washington, June 9, 1898.

Major-General MERRITT, *San Francisco, Cal.:*

Instructions have been given Commissary-General about loading ships, but this must not delay departure of troops.

By order Secretary of War:

    H. C. CORBIN. *Adjutant-General.*

ADJUTANT-GENERAL'S OFFICE,
Washington, June 9, 1898.

Major-General MERRITT, *San Francisco, Cal.:*

Secretary War regrets there is no fund available for the hire of trained cooks for enlisted men on transports. The men will have to be instructed to do their own cooking. There seems to be universal complaint throughout the service, and the sooner the men understand that they are to do the work themselves, and the officers so instructed, the better it will be for the service. For a hundred years the soldiers of the Army have cooked for themselves, and it is not understood why at this late day change should be made. This, however, is immaterial, as there is no fund available.

By order Secretary War:

    H. C. CORBIN, *Adjutant-General.*

WAR DEPARTMENT, *Washington, June 9, 1898.*

MEMORANDUM.

Hon. W. S. Shallenberger, Assistant Postmaster-General, telephones War Department that urgency of the case makes it necessary to wire to San Francisco to-day so as to get the Railway Mail Service in touch with the Philippine expedition.

The Postmaster-General has designated one railway mail superintendent and one clerk from San Francisco to accompany the expedition, and desires to obtain rations and quarters for them. They will be on ship and on land, serving the troops. How can this be done? Wants an early reply to-day.

WAR DEPARTMENT, *June 9, 1898.*

Maj. Gen. WESLEY MERRITT, *San Francisco, Cal.:*

Postmaster-General has designated F. W. Vaille, assistant superintendent Railway Mail Service, and one clerk, to be selected by postal authorities at San Francisco, to proceed to Philippine Islands to establish and facilitate postal connections and mail service with American forces at Manila. You are directed to transport them to Manila, and requested to extend such aid and facilities in prosecution of their work as you consistently can.

G. D. MEIKLEJOHN,
Assistant Secretary of War.

WAR DEPARTMENT, *Washington, June 9, 1898.*

DEAR SIR: Referring to your telephonic message of this date regarding the establishment of postal relations with American forces in Asiatic waters, I beg to invite your attention to the inclosed copy of a telegram which has just been transmitted to General Merritt, commanding the Philippine expedition, which it is hoped will subserve the ends in view.

Very respectfully, G. D. MEIKLEJOHN,
Assistant Secretary of War.

Hon. W. S. SHALLENBERGER,
Second Assistant Postmaster-General.

Inclosure (see preceding telegram).

ADJUTANT-GENERAL'S OFFICE,
Washington June 9, 1898.

Maj. Gen. WESLEY MERRITT, U. S. Army,
San Francisco, Cal.:

For use of expedition Secretary of War approves expenditure not exceeding $12,000 for purchases of machines for distilling drinking water. Secretary also approves expenditure not exceeding $7,500 to purchase portable steam boilers, engines, pump, wrought-iron pipe, and fittings for purpose set forth in your telegram of 7th instant.

H. C. CORBIN, *Adjutant-General.*

SAN FRANCISCO, CAL., *June 9, 1898.*
(Received 6 p. m.)

ADJUTANT-GENERAL, *War Department, Washington, D. C.:*

I have been asked to make requisition for Battery A, Light Artillery, Second Brigade, Massachusetts Volunteer Militia. This battery, without guns, could be useful if they could be given me in addition to the troops originally contemplated, as I now have 21 Gatling guns and could assign a portion of them to these men.

MERRITT, *Major-General, Commanding.*

ADJUTANT-GENERAL'S OFFICE,
Washington, June 9, 1898.

Maj. Gen. WESLEY MERRITT, *San Francisco, Cal.:*

Capt. F. M. Linscott's First Troop Nevada Cavalry, U. S. Volunteers, unequipped and without tentage, mustered in and now at Cheyenne, Wyo., has this day been ordered to San Francisco without horses.

H. C. CORBIN, *Adjutant-General.*

ADJUTANT-GENERAL'S OFFICE,
Washington, June 10, 1898.

Major-General MERRITT, *San Francisco, Cal.:*

Replying to your telegram of June 9, Light Battery A, Second Brigade, Massachusetts Volunteer Militia, will not be taken into the service under the second call.

H. C. CORBIN, *Adjutant-General.*

NAVY DEPARTMENT, *Washington, June 10, 1898.*

The Honorable, the SECRETARY OF WAR.

SIR: The Department finds that it has no available man-of-war fast enough and with sufficient steaming radius to convoy the army transports mentioned in General Merritt's telegram to the Adjutant-General of the 8th instant, as preparing to start for Manila about the 15th instant. It is considered that no danger of capture would be incurred by the transports in crossing the Pacific at present, but as a precaution Admiral Dewey will be requested to send, if practicable, one of his cruisers to Guam, there to meet the army transports and convoy them to Manila.

Very respectfully,

CHAS. H. ALLEN, *Acting Secretary.*

NAVY DEPARTMENT, *Washington, June 10, 1898.*

The SECRETARY OF WAR.

SIR: Referring to my letter of the 10th instant concerning the departure, about the 15th instant, of a division of the army for Manila, you are requested to communicate to this Department the sailing day of the division above mentioned, when finally settled, as also the places at which it will touch, and its estimated sea speed, in order that Admiral Dewey may be requested to have a cruiser at Guam in time to convoy the division thence to Manila.

Very respectfully,

CHAS. H. ALLEN, *Acting Secretary.*

SAN FRANCISCO, CAL., *June 10, 1898.*
(Received 4.53 p. m.)

ADJUTANT-GENERAL, U. S. ARMY, *Washington, D. C.:*

Request that three Webster's Unabridged Dictionaries and three English-Spanish dictionaries be furnished for use of these headquarters, and that proportionate share of funds for contingent expenses for Adjutant-General's Office, Military Department, for next fiscal year be allotted this department.

MERRITT, *Major-General, Commanding.*

ADJUTANT-GENERAL'S OFFICE,
Washington, June 11, 1898.

Major-General MERRITT, *San Francisco, Cal.:*

One hundred thousand dollars, appropriation for contingencies of the Army for Philippine expedition, is available for your use. To whose credit shall this sum be placed, and at what place, so as to be available for your purposes?

H. C. CORBIN, *Adjutant-General.*

ADJUTANT-GENERAL'S OFFICE,
Washington, June 11, 1898.

Major-General MERRITT, *San Francisco, Cal.:*

The President regrets his inability to appoint the Catholic priest mentioned in your telegram to chaplaincy in Army, but he bids me say you can have the services of any one or all the Catholic priests in the service.

H. C. CORBIN, *Adjutant-General.*

ADJUTANT-GENERAL'S OFFICE,
Washington, June 11, 1898.

COMMANDING OFFICER, ASTOR BATTERY, *Westchester, N. Y.:*

Secretary War directs you put your battery in readiness to proceed to San Francisco, to report to Maj. Gen. Wesley Merritt, as part of expedition to Philippines. The question of horses is one that Mr. Astor will have to determine for himself. No horses will be taken with any artillery troops going to Philippines; so the question of their transportation need not delay your departure. Quartermaster-General remarks that unless too much money has been paid for these horses that he can take them and pay cost price. Mr. Astor's agent had better correspond with Quartermaster-General on subject. All other appointments of battery, such as harness, had better go; also any ammunition, and everything belonging to battery, except horses. They will have to be supplied from native stock after arrival of troops. This will be authority for Quartermaster's Department to furnish transportation. Colonel Kimball, Army building, New York City, is the officer to whom you should apply; also chief commissary, in same building, with view to your securing travel rations. Acknowledge receipt, and report action taken.

H. C. CORBIN, *Adjutant-General.*

WAR DEPARTMENT, *June 13, 1898.*

Maj. Gen. WESLEY MERRITT, *San Francisco, Cal.:*

The following has been received from the Navy Department, and is sent to you for your information:

"The Department finds that it has no available man-of-war fast enough, and with sufficient steaming radius, to convoy the army transports mentioned in General Merritt's telegram to the Adjutant-General of the 8th instant, as preparing to start for Manila about the 15th instant. It is considered that no danger of capture would be incurred by the transports in crossing the Pacific at present, but as a precaution Admiral Dewey will be requested to send, if practicable, one of his cruisers to Guam, there to meet the army transports and convoy them to Manila."

H. C. CORBIN, *Adjutant-General.*

AFFAIRS IN THE PHILIPPINE ISLANDS. 699

ADJUTANT-GENERAL'S OFFICE,
Washington, June 13, 1898.

Gen. WESLEY MERRITT, *San Francisco, Cal.:*

The Astor Battery leaves Jersey City this afternoon at 5 p. m., via Pennsylvania Railroad for San Francisco, to report to you for duty, with full equipment in every respect, including ammunition, but without horses or mules. Acknowledge receipt.

H. C. CORBIN, *Adjutant-General.*

SAN FRANCISCO, CAL., *June 13, 1898.*
(Received 4.18 p. m.)

ADJUTANT-GENERAL, *War Department, Washington, D. C:*

The ships *Zealandia, Colon, China,* and *Senator* will be ready to sail on Wednesday, carrying about 3,300 troops. Are there any special orders in regard to route to be followed, and in regard to naval convoy for these vessels?

MERRITT, *Major-General Commanding.*

SAN FRANCISCO, CAL., *June 13, 1898.*
(Received 6.15 p. m.)

ADJUTANT-GENERAL, *War Department, Washington, D. C:*

Please request Navy Department to place its coal at Honolulu at the disposal of the army transports, four in number, to sail on the 15th en route to Manila.

MERRITT *Major-General Commanding.*

(MEMORANDUM, A. G. O., JUNE 13, 1898.)

Colonel Carter presented the above dispatch to Captain Bradford, Chief of the Bureau of Equipment, who agrees to telegraph to consul at Honolulu, through General Merritt, authorizing the fleet sailing from San Francisco on June 15, consisting of four steamers, to use the naval coal at Honolulu, the cost of the same to be repaid by the Quartermaster's Department, provided the Quartermaster's Department has no coal of its own at that point.

SAN FRANCISCO, CAL., *June 13, 1898.*
(Received 9.45 p. m.)

ADJUTANT-GENERAL, *War Department, Washington, D. C.:*

The troops now present, those en route to the Philippine Islands, and the Tennessee Infantry and Nevada cavalry, and batteries which I have been informed will be sent me, will constitute in all about 17,000 men. I request that the 20,000 troops promised me may be filled by the assignment of the First Maine, now at Chickamauga, and the Ninth New York, now at Chickamauga.

MERRITT, *Major-General, Commanding.*

ADJUTANT-GENERAL'S OFFICE,
Washington, June 13, 1898.

Major-General MERRITT, *San Francisco, Cal.:*

The Secretary of War directs that you communicate to the War Department the sailing day of the next detachment of the Army for Manila, which it is reported will sail about the 15th instant, and also the places at which it will touch and its estimated sea speed, in order that Admiral Dewey may be requested to have a cruiser at Guam in time to convoy the detachment thence to Manila.

H. C. CORBIN, *Adjutant-General.*

SAN FRANCISCO, CAL., *June 13, 1898.*
(Received 10.04 p.m.)

ADJUTANT-GENERAL, *War Department, Washington, D. C.:*

In reply to your telegram in relation to convoy, the *China, Zealandia, Colon,* and *Senator* will sail on the 15th and keep an estimated sea speed of 10 knots. They will touch at Honolulu, and probably remain there not longer than two days.

MERRITT, *Major-General, Commanding.*

SAN FRANCISCO, CAL., *June 13, 1898.*
(Received 10.05 p.m.)

ADJUTANT-GENERAL, *War Department, Washington, D. C.:*

In reply to your telegram in relation to appropriation of $100,000 for contingencies, I suggest that this sum may be placed to my credit as follows: Fifty thousand in the subtreasury of New York City and fifty thousand in the subtreasury of San Francisco.

MERRITT, *Major-General, Commanding.*

ADJUTANT-GENERAL'S OFFICE,
Washington, June 14, 1898—12.15 a. m.

Major-General MERRITT, *San Francisco, Cal.:*

Your request for additional troops to be assigned to expedition for Philippines is received. Our returns show that your command, present and having sailed, amounts to 15,700. To fill these regiments will require 3,300 recruits, which you should receive within few days. This will make your force quite 20,000. The President remarks, however, after reading your telegram, as fast as transportation is provided you should have the full 20,000, or even more if required. This request will be kept in mind and additional troops, if need be, furnished you as fast as transportation can be provided. We have information that Shafter's expedition is sailing at this hour.

H. C. CORBIN, *Adjutant-General.*

SAN FRANCISCO, CAL., *June 14, 1898.*
(Received 3.48 p.m.)

ADJUTANT-GENERAL, *Washington, D. C.:*

I recommend, as important to facilitate the objects of this command, that the troops of the Philippine expedition be constituted an army corps, and I further recommend the following-named officers, now practically serving as corps staff officers, should be promoted to fill vacancies made by the creation of an additional army corps, as follows: Maj. Thomas H. Barry, assistant adjutant-general U. S. Army, as lieutenant-colonel and assistant adjutant-general U. S. Volunteers; Maj. E. H. Crowder, judge-advocate U. S. Army, as lieutenant-colonel and judge-advocate U. S. Volunteers; First Lieut. Charles L. Potter, Corps of Engineers, U. S. Army, as lieutenant-colonel and chief engineer U. S. Volunteers; Capt. Charles W. Whipple, Ordnance Department, U. S. Army, as lieutenant-colonel and inspector-general U. S. Volunteers. Letter in detail on this subject mailed you yesterday.

MERRITT, *Major-General, Commanding.*

AFFAIRS IN THE PHILIPPINE ISLANDS. 701

ADJUTANT-GENERAL'S OFFICE,
Washington, June 14, 1898—11.40 p. m.

Major-General MERRITT, *San Francisco, Cal.:*

Secretary War desires to know what general officers you have designated to command outgoing expedition about leaving San Francisco for Philippines.

H. C. CORBIN, *Adjutant-General.*

ADJUTANT-GENERAL'S OFFICE,
Washington, June 15, 1898.

General MERRITT, *San Francisco, Cal.:*

The Chief of Bureau of Equipment of the Navy will telegraph his agent to your care authorizing use of naval coal at Honolulu. Quartermaster here will pay for amount used. In case Quartermaster's Department should have coal on hand at that point of course you will make use of it.

By order Secretary War:

H. C. CORBIN, *Adjutant-General.*

NAVY DEPARTMENT,
Washington, D. C., June 15, 1898.

CONSUL-GENERAL OF THE UNITED STATES, *Honolulu, Hawaiian Islands:*

(Care Maj. Gen. Wesley Merritt, U. S. Army, San Francisco, Cal.)

If army need coal for four transports sailing from San Francisco about June 16 please provide it. Use navy coal if necessary.

BRADFORD.

ADJUTANT-GENERAL'S OFFICE,
Washington, June 15, 1898.

Major-General MERRITT, *San Francisco, Cal.:*

Secretary War is inclined to approve your request to organize an army corps for expedition to the Philippines. In that event, would you expect to be assigned or have General Otis assigned and you command the Department expedition. It would seem, for many reasons that will occur to you, that it would be better to have General Otis announced as corps commander. Of this, however, your views are requested.

H. C. CORBIN, *Adjutant-General.*

SAN FRANCISCO, CAL., *June 15, 1898.*
(Received 3.07 p. m.)

ADJUTANT-GENERAL, U. S. ARMY, *Washington, D. C.:*

Replying to your telegram, Brig. Gen. Francis V. Greene, U. S. Volunteers, will command the expedition about leaving for Philippines.

MERRITT, *Major-General, Commanding.*

SAN FRANCISCO, CAL., *June 15, 1898.*
(Received 8 p. m.)

ADJUTANT-GENERAL, *War Department, Washington, D. C.:*

The transports *Zealandia, China, Colon,* and *Senator* sailed at 1.45 p. m. to-day, under command of Gen. F. V. Greene. Troops embarked: Tenth Pennsylvania, First Colorado, First Nebraska, one battalion Eighteenth United States

Infantry, one battalion Twenty-third United States Infantry, Batteries A and B, Utah Artillery, detachment United States Engineer Corps, with general and staff officers, surgeons, Hospital Corps men, post-office employees. The total embarked is 3,540. Special return of troops embarked will be submitted as soon as possible.

MERRITT, *Major-General, Commanding.*

Official copy respectfully furnished the Honorable the Secretary of the Navy. By order of the Secretary of War:

H. C. CORBIN, *Adjutant-General.*
ADJUTANT-GENERAL'S OFFICE, *June 18, 1898.*

WAR DEPARTMENT, *June 15, 1898.*
Maj. Gen. WESLEY MERRITT, *San Francisco, Cal.:*
I have informed the Post-Office Department that the transports going to Manila will carry such mail as may be turned over to them to the Hawaiian Islands.

R. A. ALGER, *Secretary of War.*

WASHINGTON, D. C., *June 14, 1898.* (Received June 15, 1898.)
Gen. H. C. CORBIN.

MY DEAR SIR: I have received the following very satisfactory dispatch from General Merritt:

"SAN FRANCISCO, CAL., *June 14, 1898—1.59 p. m.*
"MURAT HALSTEAD, *Washington, D. C.:*
"Will be very glad to have you go with the expedition in the capacity you mention, and you may say so to the President.

"WESLEY MERRITT,
"*Major-General, U. S. Army.*"

That settles it very agreeably. I sent a copy of the General's dispatch to the President. I would be glad to know—indeed it's of importance to me to have the earliest information—as to when General Merritt will start. I have pretty nearly two thousand things to do. If there happens to be any reason for secrecy as to the movements of the General, I will take a hint and make the trip absolutely confidential; but do not suppose that there will be any hesitation in announcing his departure.

Yours, truly, with old-fashioned regards, MURAT HALSTEAD.

ADJUTANT-GENERAL'S OFFICE,
Washington, June 15, 1898.
Major-General MERRITT, *San Francisco, Cal.:*
The President is anxious that Murat Halstead accompany you to the Philippines. Will you kindly telegraph me for Mr. Halstead's information the probable date of your departure, as he has many matters of importance on hand, and does not desire to tarry any considerable time in San Francisco.

H. C. CORBIN, *Adjutant-General.*

SAN FRANCISCO, CAL., *June 16, 1898.*
(Received 8.47 p. m.)
SECRETARY OF WAR, *Washington, D. C.:*
In reply to your dispatch relative to the establishment of a cable from Manila to Hongkong, it has been suggested to me by an officer of high rank in the West-

ern Union Company that it would be unnecessary to land the cable. He thinks cable could be worked from a hulk or war vessel anchored outside of marine league.

MERRITT, *Major-General, Commanding.*

SAN FRANCISCO, CAL., *June 16, 1898.*
(Received 9.30 p. m.)

ADJUTANT-GENERAL, *War Department, Washington, D. C.:*

Referring to your telegram 15th instant in relation to the organization of an army corps for the expedition to the Philippines, which was addressed to General Merriam, but no doubt intended for me, and in which you ask my views as to the officer to be announced assigned as corps commander, I request consideration of my letter 11th instant, in which my views are fully expressed, and which should reach you by to-morrow. I deem it of great importance that I should be orignally assigned to the command with discretionary power to transfer the corps to General Otis after the assembling of all the troops at the Philippines, retaining myself command of the Department.

MERRITT, *Major-General, Commanding.*

SAN FRANCISCO, CAL., *June 17, 1898.*
(Received 3.02 p. m.)

ADJUTANT-GENERAL, *Washington, D. C.:*

Replying to your dispatch of 15th instant, I can not tell definitely when I will start for Philippines. Certainly not for ten days, when the next expedition starts, and may not then. I will keep Mr. Halstead informed, through you, of the exact date of my departure.

W. MERRITT, *Major-General, Commanding.*

SAN FRANCISCO, CAL., *June 17, 1898.*
(Received 4.41 p. m.)

ADJUTANT-GENERAL, *War Department, Washington, D. C:*

Little or no information can be obtained here in regard to coal supply now available at Manila for return of transports. If nothing definite is known at War Department, should not this information be asked of the naval commander at Manila? In view of his statement in telegram furnished from the War Department that it is difficult to obtain coal, it is possible that colliers should be taken from here. Very desirable to know privately at once in regard to this matter.

MERRITT, *Major-General, Commanding.*

SAN FRANCISCO, CAL., *June 17, 1898.*
(Received 9.50 p. m.)

ADJUTANT-GENERAL, *Washington, D. C.:*

I intend, if everything is propitious, to sail with the next detachment to Manila. In view of this and the growing necessity for a convoy, I request that the *Philadelphia*, now at the navy-yard here, may be placed at my disposal for transportation, and to act as a convoy to the transports. She can return to this port at once after the performance of the duty, or remain at the Philippines under such orders as may be given. I ask that this request may be laid before the President.

MERRITT, *Major-General, Commanding.*

SAN FRANCISCO, CAL., *June 17, 1898.*
(Received 11.03 p. m.)

ADJUTANT-GENERAL, *War Department, Washington, D. C.:*

The transports *Morgan City, Ohio, Indiana, Valencia,* and *City of Para* are now being fitted out with the total capacity for about 4,000 men. It is expected these ships will be ready to sail in about ten days.

MERRITT, *Major-General, Commanding.*

NAVY DEPARTMENT, *Washington, June 18, 1898.*

SIR: This Department requests to be informed whether the commanding officer of the military expedition that sailed from San Francisco to Manila on the 15th instant was instructed to touch off Guam to meet a convoy from Admiral Dewey, in case one is there. This course was recommended in a letter from this Department to the War Department, dated the 10th instant.

Very respectfully,

JOHN D. LONG, *Secretary.*

The SECRETARY OF WAR.

CAMP MERRITT, CAL., *June 12, 1898.*
(Received June 18, 1898.)

DEAR GENERAL CORBIN: General Merritt was good enough to assign me on arrival here to command the next detachment sailing to the Philippines, consisting of First Battalion, Eighteenth Infantry; First Battalion, Twenty-third Infantry; detachment Company A, Engineer Battalion, United States; First Colorado Infantry; First Nebraska Infantry; Tenth Pennsylvania Infantry; two batteries Utah Artillery; in all, something over 4,000 men. The troops are thoroughly equipped, well drilled, and in every way a splendid body of men. I have spent nearly all this week inspecting and drilling them. We have four ships, *China,* the finest vessel on the Pacific, *Colon, Zealandia,* and *Senator.* The bunks, galleys, sinks, and other arrangements for the men are as far superior to those of the transports I was on in New York Harbor as can possibly be imagined. We expect to sail on Wednesday, June 15. I belive it is General Merritt's intention to sail in person with the next detachment, about ten days later, but I have no positive knowledge.

I do not know whether we shall have much or little fighting to do at Manila, or what the nature of our work will be there. But I feel that the President, Secretary of War, and yourself, as well as General Merritt, have done everything that could possibly be done for me personally, and if I fail to do my part in justifying their confidence in me, I assure you it will not be for lack of trying.

I inclose a photograph taken just before I left New York, and hope you will find a place for it in your collection.

I trust the country will appreciate the tremendous amount of hard and successful work you have done during the last sixty days, and with best wishes I remain,

Very sincerely, yours,

F. V. GREENE.

Gen. H. C. CORBIN, *Washington.*

ADJUTANT-GENERAL'S OFFICE,
Washington, June 18, 1898.

Major-General MERRITT, *San Francisco, Cal.:*

In reply to your telegram of yesterday, Secretary War has been unable to see Secretary Navy about the *Philadelphia.* Either he or I will see him this evening and send his reply to-morrow morning. Agreeable to your request, I laid your telegram before the President, who remarked that he was glad you intended going with next detachment to Manila.

H. C. CORBIN, *Adjutant-General.*

BROOKLYN, N. Y., *June 18, 1898—12 m.*

HENRY C. CORBIN,
 Adjutant-General, War Department, Washington, D. C.:
 If the change announced hurries Merritt's sailing, please telegraph me, Hotel Margaret, Brooklyn; otherwise, nothing to say.

MURAT HALSTEAD.

ADJUTANT-GENERAL'S OFFICE,
Washington, June 18, 1898.

Hon. MURAT HALSTEAD,
 Hotel Margaret, Brooklyn, N. Y.:
 General Merritt says he will not sail for at least ten days and probably not that soon, but will advise me later so that I may keep you informed.

H. C. CORBIN, *Adjutant-General.*

SAN FRANCISCO, CAL., *June 18, 1898—5.57 p. m.*

ADJUTANT-GENERAL, *War Department, Washington, D. C.:*
 I request that the special attention of the President and the Secretary of War may be invited to the necessity of placing transports at my command after arrival of expedition at Philippines. The flag must be carried to outlying islands, and it is obvious that I must have ships. Suggest permanent assignment of sufficient vessels to carry 2,500 men at a trip.

MERRITT, *Major-General, Commanding.*

LISBON, *June 18, 1898.*

ADJUTANT-GENERAL, *Milago, Washington:*
 Spanish reserve fleet sailed 16th instant. Five auxiliary cruisers accompany it with 4,000 troops. Every newspaper rumor believes for China Sea.

LIEUTENANT SLOCUM.

HEADQUARTERS UNITED STATES EXPEDITIONARY FORCES
AND DEPARTMENT OF PACIFIC,
San Francisco, Cal., June 11, 1898. (Received June 19, 1898.)

The ADJUTANT-GENERAL, *Washington, D. C.*

SIR: I have the honor to state that, in my opinion, it will greatly facilitate future operations of the Philippine expedition under my command if the troops comprising the expeditionary forces (20,000 in number) should be constituted an army corps, and that I be given discretionary power to assign in the future the next in command under me, after the occupation of the islands, to the command of the corps, should I see fit in the public interest to do so. By making the command an army corps many matters of military administration would be better served so far as the interests of the troops are concerned, and I would be left free, if I find it desirable to transfer the command of the corps, to devote my attention to the important matters of the government of the vast territory and the general military operations.

In the event that this is approved and the eighth corps created, I very earnestly ask that the officers heretofore selected by me, and now in reality performing the duties of corps staff officers, may be appointed to, and assigned with, the volunteer rank to which they would be entitled under section 10 of the act of Congress approved April 22, 1898, as follows: Maj. Thomas H. Barry, assistant adjutant-general, U. S. Army, as lieutenant-colonel and assistant adjutant-general, U. S. Volunteers; Maj. E. H. Crowder, judge-advocate, U. S. Army, as lieutenant-colonel and judge-advocate, U. S. Volunteers; First Lieut. Charles L. Potter, Corps of Engineers, U. S. Army, as lieutenant-colonel and chief engineer, U. S. Volunteers; Capt. Charles W. Whipple, Ordnance Department, U. S. Army, as lieutenant-colonel and inspector-general, U. S. Volunteers. This last nomination with a view to giving Captain Whipple, as ordnance officer, the rank to which his important services entitle him, and for which no provision is made in the law.

Very respectfully, W. MERRITT,
Major-General, U. S. Army.

ADJUTANT-GENERAL'S OFFICE,
Washington, June 19, 1898.

Maj. Gen. WESLEY MERRITT, *San Francisco, Cal.:*

In case the recruits and regiments now with you do not reach 20,000, as agreed upon for your army corps, would you still prefer the First New York, Colonel Barber, over all others? It looks now as though one additional regiment would have to be ordered to report to you. Would like to know your preference as to regiments. It is understood First New York is very desirous of going with you. It is now on garrison duty at Governors Island and other posts in that vicinity, and is becoming efficient and well equipped, so that it would leave and sail the day after it reached San Francisco if it was agreed upon.

H. C. CORBIN, *Adjutant-General.*

PAYMASTER-GENERAL'S OFFICE,
Washington, June 19, 1898.

The SECRETARY OF WAR.

SIR: I desire to submit the following matter for your consideration:

After the occupation of the Philippine Islands it will be quite difficult for disabled officers ordered to their homes to obtain transportation (as transportation by transports will be very irregular) unless mileage can be advanced to them.

I would therefore recommend that the President be requested to authorize the payment of mileage in advance to disabled officers ordered to their homes from that point.

Very respectfully, T. H. STANTON,
Paymaster-General U. S. Army.

OAKLAND PIER, CAL., *June 20, 1898.*
(Received 10.45 a. m.)

ADJUTANT-GENERAL U. S. ARMY, *Washington, D. C.*

Astor Battery arrived Oakland 10 p. m. June 19.

MARCH.

ADJUTANT-GENERAL'S OFFICE,
Washington, June 20, 1898.

Capt. P. C. MARCh,
    Astor Battery, Presidio, San Francisco, Cal.

Muster-in rolls of your battery not received. What has become of them?

HEISTAND, Assistant Adjutant-General.

ADJUTANT-GENERAL'S OFFICE,
Washington, June 20, 1898.

Capt. GRANVILLE K. PALMER, Cheyenne, Wyo.,
    Commanding Light Battery A, Wyoming U. S. Volunteer Artillery:

By direction of the Secretary of War you will proceed at once, without horses, taking such guns, carriages, harness, ammunition, and ordnance supplies as you now have, with your battery to San Francisco, Cal., and report to Major-General Merritt. Upon receipt of this order you will at once communicate with chief quartermaster, Denver, Colo., for the necessary transportation, and with the chief commissary, Denver, Colo., for ten days' field rations, the necessary travel rations, and coffee money. The Quartermaster-General and Commissary-General have instructed the chief quartermaster and chief commissary, Denver, to provide the transportation, rations, and coffee money.

Send direct to Quartermaster-General and Chief of Ordnance, respectively, separate telegraphic lists of the exact state of your equipment, including tentage and ammunition. Also to General Merritt, reporting to him at the same time and to this office the date of your departure. Acknowledge receipt.

H. C. CORBIN, Adjutant-General.

SAN FRANCISCO, CAL., June 20, 1898.

The ADJUTANT-GENERAL, Washington, D. C.:

In reply to your telegram, would still prefer Colonel Barber and the First New York. The Kansas regiment and the Tennessee troops now with me are, in my opinion, unlikely to be fit for some time to become a part in this expedition, and in that view it would be well to assign me at once two good regiments, including Colonel Barber's. The Kansas regiment has been here some time, and has made itself prominent by its want of capacity, so far as officers are concerned. The recent arrival of the colonel may improve these conditions, but as it now stands the regiment is unfit to embark. The Tennessee regiment, which just arrived, is completely destitute of equipment in any direction, and of instruction and drill to a great extent. Colonel Smith, of the Tennessee regiment, impresses me as a very excellent soldier, and he tells me he has good officers in his command, but the prospects are that it will be some time before the regiment can be put in shape for duty in the field. For the above reasons I am anxious that other regiments be assigned my command.

MERRITT, Major-General.

HEADQUARTERS OF THE ARMY,
ADJUTANT-GENERAL'S OFFICE,
Washington, June 21, 1898.

GENERAL ORDERS.

The following order has been received from the War Department:

WAR DEPARTMENT, Washington, June 21, 1898.

By direction of the President the forces comprising the Philippine expedition under command of Maj. Gen. Wesley Merritt, U. S. Army, are hereby constituted an army corps, to be known as the Eighth. Major-General Merritt is assigned to the command of the Eighth Corps, with authority to transfer the command of the corps to Major-General Otis or the next officer in rank at such time as he may deem it expedient as a matter of military administration.

R. A. ALGER, *Secretary of War.*

By command of Major-General Miles:

H. C. CORBIN, *Adjutant-General.*

WAR DEPARTMENT,
Washington, June 21, 1898.

General MERRITT, *San Francisco, Cal.:*

By direction of the President the forces comprising the Philippine expedition under command of Maj. Gen. Wesley Merritt, U. S. Army, are hereby constituted an army corps, to be known as the Eighth. Major-General Merritt is assigned to the command of the Eighth Corps, with authority to transfer the command of the corps to Major-General Otis or the next officer in rank at such time as he may deem it expedient as a matter of military administration.

R. A. ALGER, *Secretary of War.*

SAN FRANCISCO, CAL., *June 21, 1898.*
(Received 2.44 p. m.)

ADJUTANT-GENERAL, *Washington, D. C.:*

Since my arrival here the duties performed by myself and staff have required our being stationed in this city, where there are no public quarters. Commutation of quarters denied under decision, it is understood, of the War Department. Request authority of Secretary of War for commutation for myself and staff for one month.

W. MERRITT, *Major-General.*

SAN FRANCISCO, CAL., *June 21, 1898.*
(Received 7.50 p. m.)

ADJUTANT-GENERAL, *War Department, Washington, D. C.:*

Dispatch from General Greene received by carrier pigeon which left the ship 40 miles at sea gives his opinion that the sea speed of 11 knots instead of 10 knots can be maintained by that fleet. Possibly Admiral Dewey should be notified accordingly.

MERRITT, *Major-General, Commanding.*

ADJUTANT-GENERAL'S OFFICE,
Washington, June 21, 1898—12 midnight.

Maj. Gen. WESLEY MERRITT, *San Francisco, Cal.:*

Secretary of War decides you and your staff are entitled to commutation of quarters while in the city of San Francisco.

H. C. CORBIN, *Adjutant-General.*

ADJUTANT-GENERAL'S OFFICE,
Washington, June 21, 1898—12 midnight.

Major-General MERRITT, *San Francisco, Cal.:*

Having reference to your telegram June 18, Secretary War directs that such of the transports as may be needed to the carrying capacity of 2,500 men will be provided from the transports carrying the last of your command to Philippines. The hire or purchase of these steamers will be arranged, and you will be notified.

H. C. CORBIN, *Adjutant-General.*

ADJUTANT-GENERAL'S OFFICE,
Washington, June 22, 1898.

Major-General MERRITT, *San Francisco, Cal.:*

Careful inquiry has been made of naval commander at Manila to ascertain coal supply available there for return of transports. More definite plans can be entered into when we have report of the expedition that went under command of Brigadier-General Anderson. Secretary War desires that you obtain all possible information concerning supply of coal on which to base your recommendation as to the advisability of colliers going with you.

H. C. CORBIN, *Adjutant-General.*

SAN FRANCISCO, CAL., *June 22, 1898.*
(Received 5.30 p. m.)

ADJUTANT-GENERAL, *Washington, D. C.:*

Authority requested to purchase here such surgical instruments as are needed for Philippine expedition, bills to be paid by medical purveyor in city. The instruments needed are for treatment of eye, ear, and throat troubles. The necessity is urgent.

W. MERRITT, *Major-General.*

[First indorsement.]

WAR DEPARTMENT, SURGEON-GENERAL'S OFFICE,
June 23, 1898.

Respectfully returned to the Adjutant-General of the Army.

I do not agree with General Merritt that the instruments referred to are urgently needed. Captain Woodruff, assistant surgeon, United States Army, now on duty with General Merritt, and recently appointed brigade surgeon, asked to have a lot of instruments for the treatment of eye, ear, and throat troubles, and which had been purchased for his use, sent to him by express from Jackson Barracks, La. This request has been complied with. He has since telegraphed for authority to buy additional instruments, and I declined to authorize the purchase because I consider it an unnecessary expenditure. This telegram from General Merritt indicates an attempt on his part to get what he wants in spite of my disapproval. I have been extremely liberal in authorizing purchases for the Manila expedition, but I am unwilling to give Dr. Woodruff carte blanche for the purchase of special instruments not on the supply table of the Army. He has already been greatly favored in this way and, as stated, the instruments selected by himself have been sent to him by express.

GEO. M. STERNBERG,
Surgeon-General U. S. Army.

ADJUTANT-GENERAL'S OFFICE,
Washington, June 22, 1898.

Major-General MERRITT, *San Francisco, Cal.:*

The commission of Maj. Carroll H. Potter will be mailed to him to-morrow. He will be assigned to the Fourteenth Infantry.

CARTER, *Assistant Adjutant-General.*

SAN FRANCISCO, CAL., *June 22, 1898.*
(Received 8.31 p. m.)

ADJUTANT-GENERAL, *Washington, D. C.:*

Five transports, with about 4,000 troops, will sail on the 27th. The ship *Newport* will start in time to overtake advance fleet, with from 500 to 600 men and officers. Before my own departure I request definite information on following points: Can I have the *Philadelphia* by July 1? The prestige and importance of my mission would be more clearly indicated in the islands by the arrival of a Government vessel with my headquarters. Also referring to my telegram on the subject, is it necessary to take colliers from here for the return supply of coal for the transports? If no Government vessel accompanies this fleet, I ask that arrangements be made for convoy in dangerous zone. This precaution seems more important as time for the enemy to prepare to intervene transpires. Also, in view of possibility of foreign interference with my troops landing at the Philippines, I desire instructions to how far, in the opinion of the Government, force should be used to enforce our rights.

MERRITT, *Major-General.*

ADJUTANT-GENERAL'S OFFICE,
Washington, June 22, 1898.

To General MERRITT, *San Francisco, Cal.:*

Please inform this office whether the third Philippines expedition has been ordered to stop at any place, where and at about what date. In case a stop at the Caroline Islands or in that vicinity is made it is the intention to send a war ship from Manila to meet the expedition.

H. C. CORBIN.

SAN FRANCISCO, CAL., *June 22, 1898.*
(Received 10.05 p. m.)

ADJUTANT-GENERAL, *Washington, D. C.:*

Cipher telegram of this date just received. Third expedition to the Philippines has not been ordered to stop at any place except Honolulu, where it coals, nor is it the intention to stop at the Caroline Islands or elsewhere. I sent a cipher dispatch this morning to you on the subject of a convoy, and presume that this is not the answer to that dispatch.

W. MERRITT, *Major-General.*

ADJUTANT-GENERAL'S OFFICE,
Washington, June 23, 1898.

Major-General MERRITT, *San Francisco, Cal.:*

The Secretary War desires to know whether the commanding officer of the military expedition that sailed from San Francisco to Manila on 15th instant was instructed to touch off Guam to meet convoy from Admiral Dewey in case one is there.

H. C. CORBIN, *Adjutant-General.*

SAN FRANCISCO, CAL., *June 23, 1898.*
(Received 4.11 p. m.)

ADJUTANT-GENERAL, *Washington, D. C.:*

The commanding officer of the military expedition that sailed from San Francisco for Manila on the 15th instant was duly instructed to touch off Guam to meet convoy furnished by fleet to Manila. It was with a view to this that the carrier-pigeon message from General Greene was transmitted to Washington, as he is making faster time than was at first supposed he would.

MERRITT, *Major-General.*

SAN FRANCISCO, CAL., *June 23, 1898.*
(Received 5.15 p. m.)

ADJUTANT-GENERAL, U. S. ARMY, *Washington, D. C.:*

No information direct from Manila in regard to the available coal supply there. Appears to be obtainable in this city so far as my chief quartermaster has been able to ascertain. It was learned that arrangements for 5,500 tons from Australia for navy at Manila had been made; but whether this supply has actually been received or how much remains can not be ascertained. If anything is heard from General Anderson or Admiral Dewey on this subject, please let me know at once.

MERRITT, *Major-General.*

ADJUTANT-GENERAL'S OFFICE,
Washington, June 23, 1898—11.30 p. m.

Major-General MERRITT, *San Francisco, Cal.:*

Your request to purchase surgical instruments such as are needed for Philippine expedition, and that bills be paid by medical purveyor in city, is received, and referred to Surgeon-General, who, among other things, remarks that "a very liberal supply of all instruments and medical supplies has been furnished for Manila expedition," and declines to authorize further purchase, because he considers it unnecessary expenditure. He says he has been extremely liberal in authorizing purchases for your expedition and is unwilling that further purchases shall be made, in which Secretary of War concurs.

By command Major-General Miles:

H. C. CORBIN, *Adjutant-General.*

SAN FRANCISCO, CAL., *June 24, 1898.*
(Received 2.30 p. m.)

ADJUTANT-GENERAL, *Washington, D. C.:*

Referring to my telegram concerning Father Doherty, I have been informed that the War Department states his going to Manila rests with me. If so, I would like to have him go.

W. MERRITT, *Major-General.*

ADJUTANT-GENERAL'S OFFICE,
Washington, June 24, 1898.

Maj. Gen. WESLEY MERRITT, *San Francisco, Cal.:*

The Department would be glad for Father Doherty to accompany you to Manila, but there is no way in which he can be given rank or pay, as there is no vacancy for chaplain. Of course, if he desires to accompany you at his own expense, or that of his church, it will be viewed with favor.

H. C. CORBIN, *Adjutant-General.*

SAN FRANCISCO, CAL., *June 24, 1898.*
(Received 2.35 p. m.)

ADJUTANT-GENERAL, *Washington, D. C.:*

If it is intended to assign the California regiment now being mustered under second call for volunteers to my command for duty in Philippines I would be glad to have it.

W. MERRITT, *Major-General.*

ADJUTANT-GENERAL'S OFFICE,
Washington, June 24, 1898.

Maj. Gen. WESLEY MERRITT, *San Francisco, Cal.:*

The disposition of the new regiment of California Volunteers has not been determined.

H. C. CORBIN, *Adjutant-General.*

SAN FRANCISCO, CAL., *June 24, 1898.*
(Received 8.32 p. m.)

ADJUTANT-GENERAL, *War Department, Washington, D. C.:*

My chief quartermaster has now concluded a contract for supply of coal at Manila, varying from 3,000 to 6,000 tons, deliveries of which are to begin on or about July 31. It should, however, be considered in reference to subject of sending collier from here that no company will guarantee the time of delivery, the "on or about" being construed liberally. Therefore the Government can not depend upon having a supply of coal delivered as a result of contracts made here before some time in August. I have now definite information that the coal for the Navy Department, referred to in my telegram of the 23d instant, about 5,400 tons started for Manila on the steamer *Nyanza* from Newcastle, Australia, Thursday, the 23d instant.

MERRITT, *Major-General, Commanding.*

NAVY DEPARTMENT, *Washington, June 24, 1898.*

The Honorable, the SECRETARY OF WAR.

SIR: Referring to the telegram of General Merritt, of date the 22d instant, regarding the expedition to Manila in which he proposes to embark, I have to remark as follows:

The cruiser *Philadelphia* can not be ready for sea until several weeks after July 1.

The question of whether it will be necessary to take the colliers from San Francisco in order to coal the transports at Manila for the return voyage from the Philippines can best be settled by ascertaining on board the transports what their expenditure of coal will be in making the voyage out and back. It seems probable that some coal must be taken on board at Manila for the return voyage, though there is no information in this Department on that subject. It is not apparent that any man-of-war will be ready, of appropriate speed and endurance, in time to convoy the transports that leave on the 27th instant, and in view of the present movements of Admiral Camara it is uncertain whether Admiral Dewey will find it possible to detach any vessels from his fleet to convoy the transports when they approach the Philippines. However, Admiral Dewey will be communicated with on this subject.

The Navy has no reserve of coal at the Philippines, and it would seem that the transports will have to make some provisions for coal for the return voyage.

Respectfully,

CHAS. H. ALLEN, *Acting Secretary.*

ADJUTANT-GENERAL'S OFFICE,
Washington, June 24, 1898.

Major-General MERRITT, *San Francisco, Cal.:*

In reply to your cipher telegram of 22d, which has been read by both the President and Secretary War, I am instructed to inform you that the Navy Department reports that the *Philadelphia* will not be ready for any service in less period than thirty days. This would seem to take her out of list of availabilities for your service. The question of coal will be definitely determined within a day or two. It is thought, however, that sufficient coal can be furnished the transports to Manila, Commodore Dewey having considerable store accumulated. Definite information will, if possible, be obtained by cable. Transports should take with them all that is possible for them to carry. Arrangements will be made for convoy in the dangerous zone. The Secretary War bids me say that the last paragraph of your telegram is not understood. It reads: "Also in view of foreign interference with my troops landing at Philippines, I desire instructions as to how far, in opinion of Government, force should be used to enforce our rights."

By order Secretary War:

H. C. CORBIN, *Adjutant-General.*

SAN FRANCISCO, CAL., *June 24, 1898.*
(Received June 25, 1898—9.10 a. m.)

ADJUTANT-GENERAL, U. S. ARMY,
    War Department, Washington, D. C.:

My telegram in cipher, from which you quote, read: "Also, in view of possibility of foreign interference with my troops landing at the Philippines, I desire instructions as to how far, in the opinion of the Government, force should be used to enforce our rights." This inquiry was made in view of the many reports Germany was negotiating for control of Philippines. It perhaps is not important.

W. MERRITT, *Major-General.*

SAN FRANCISCO, CAL., *June 25, 1898.*

ADJUTANT-GENERAL,
    War Department, Washington, D. C.:

Five steamers will sail on the 27th, with about 4,000 men. I sail on the 29th on steamer *Newport*, with 500 men. Will overtake the first fleet at Honolulu. The fleet will maintain an estimated sea speed of 10 knots; possibly slightly less. Will require three days for coaling at Honolulu. I request that arrangements for convoy may be made, and invite attention to persistent reports that Spanish squadron is now on the way to western Pacific.

MERRITT, *Major-General Commanding.*

ADJUTANT-GENERAL'S OFFICE,
Washington, June 25, 1898.

Major-General MERRITT, *San Francisco, Cal.:*

Can you obtain collier? If so, you are authorized by Secretary of War.

H. C. CORBIN, *Adjutant-General.*

ADJUTANT-GENERAL'S OFFICE,
Washington, June 25, 1898.

General MERRITT, *San Francisco, Cal.:*

General Shafter's report just received confirms dispatches of Associated Press as regards engagement yesterday at Santiago.

H. C. CORBIN, *Adjutant-General.*

NAVY DEPARTMENT, *Washington, June 26, 1898.*

The Honorable, the SECRETARY OF WAR.

SIR: The appended telegram expresses the opinions of this Department in regard to the best course to be pursued by General Merritt in conducting his expedition, when he reaches the neighborhood of the Philippine Islands. It will probably be impracticable for Admiral Dewey to send the convoy any distance from Manila to meet the General, but if it so happens that the convoy could be dispatched, the best way to enable it to meet the military transports would be for the latter to run as described in this telegram. It is therefore suggested that, if it meets with your approval, the substance of the appended telegram be sent General Merritt.

Very respectfully,

J. D. LONG, *Secretary.*

[Appended telegram.]

General MERRITT,
Commanding Military Expedition to Manila:

Navy Department can not furnish a convoy for your expedition of June 27, and thinks the probability of meeting Spaniards very small, but recommends you to run at greatest safe speed on as direct a course as practicable for a point 600 miles east true from Cape Engano, at north end of Luzon, and thence to run west true until reaching that cape. Possibly Admiral Dewey may be able to send a convoying ship to look out for you upon this 600-mile line, but whether he can is uncertain, for if Admiral Camara's fleet goes on eastward, it will arrive Manila between July 30 and August 15, according to its rate of speed, and Dewey will need all his ships to meet Camara. Precious time will be saved by not touching anywhere unless necessary.

ADJUTANT-GENERAL'S OFFICE,
Washington, June 26, 1898—11.45 a. m.

Maj. Gen. WESLEY MERRITT, *San Francisco, Cal.:*

The Secretary of War directs me to inform you that the Navy Department can not furnish a convoy for your expedition of June 27, and thinks the probability of meeting Spaniards very small, but recommends you to run at greatest safe speed on as direct a course as practicable for a point 600 miles east true from Cape Engano, at north end of Luzon, and thence to run west true until reaching that cape. Possibly Admiral Dewey may be able to send a convoying ship to look out for you upon this 600-mile line, but whether he can is uncertain, for if Admiral Camara's fleet goes on eastward, it will arrive Manila between July 30 and August 15, according to its rate of speed, and Dewey will need all his ships to meet Camara. Precious time will be saved by not touching anywhere unless absolutely necessary.

In view of this statement and importance of your reaching Admiral Dewey, Secretary War directs you put forth every effort to leave at earliest possible moment. Acknowledge receipt and report action taken.

By order Secretary War:

H. C. CORBIN, *Adjutant-General.*

SAN FRANCISCO, CAL., *June 26, 1898.*
(Received 3.01 p. m.)

ADJUTANT-GENERAL, *Washington, D. C.:*

Telegram of this date just received. Will make preparations to sail as soon as possible. Five transports will load and sail to-morrow. My own vessel will sail next day. Will report further to-day.

MERRITT, *Major-General.*

AFFAIRS IN THE PHILIPPINE ISLANDS.

SAN FRANCISCO, CAL., *June 26, 1898.*
(Received 6.35 p. m.)

The ADJUTANT-GENERAL, U. S. ARMY, *Washington, D. C.:*

Referring to dispatch received this morning, I find by inquiry that it will be necessary to stop at Honolulu for from twenty-four to thirty-six hours to coal the vessels of the transport fleet. I purpose sending four of them ahead with a view to their coaling before the arrival of the other two. Four will start to-morrow at greatest safe speed, the *Valencia* on Tuesday, and the *Newport,* on which I sail, on Wednesday. These last two are faster than the other boats and will not delay them at Honolulu. They are both unavoidably detained until the days mentiond on account of necessary work.

MERRITT, *Major-General.*

ADJUTANT-GENERAL'S OFFICE,
Washington, June 27, 1898.

Major-General MERRITT, *San Francisco, Cal.:*

Orders issued to-day directing Colonel Barber's regiment New York Volunteers to report to you for duty in the Philippines.

H. C. CORBIN, *Adjutant-General.*

SAN FRANCISCO, CAL., *June 27, 1898.*

SECRETARY OF WAR, *Washington, D. C.:*

Your favor of June 22 just received, and I hasten to assure you that there was no speech made of the kind you indicate on the occasion in question. The dinner was a private affair given to me and a few friends by the mayor, and not a club dinner, as represented, and which I have uniformly refused, though several have been offered. There were no newspaper reporters present and nothing of the character indicated was said. I have not seen the reports of the speech mentioned, but the mayor applied to me and offered to contradict the whole thing if I considered it important. I did not suppose that my friends would think I was capable of such gratuitous folly as was indicated in the speech. Please assure the President that I have said and done nothing which would compromise the policy he has laid out in his treatment of the questions in the East. I am making every exertion to get the command off. Four vessels sail to-day, one to-morrow, and my own early Wednesday morning. Expect to overtake the concentrated fleet at Honolulu, and I will make no delay there that is not absolutely necessary. You may be assured of this.

W. MERRITT, *Major-General.*

SAN FRANCISCO, CAL., *June 27, 1898.*
(Received 8.50 p. m.)

ADJUTANT-GENERAL, *War Department, Washington, D. C.:*

The ships *Indiana, City of Para, Morgan City,* and *Ohio* sailed at 2 p. m. to-day, General MacArthur in command. *Valencia* sails to-morrow morning and the *Newport* Wednesday morning.

MERRITT, *Major-General, Commanding.*

ADJUTANT-GENERAL'S OFFICE,
Washington, June 28, 1898.
COMMANDING GENERAL, DEPARTMENT OF THE EAST,
Governors Island, N. Y.:

With approval Secretary War, Major-General Commanding Army directs you to give immediate instructions for the First New York Volunteer Infanty to proceed to San Francisco, Cal., and report to the commanding general, Eighth Army Corps, to accompany the Philippine expedition. Acknowledge.

HEISTAND, *Adjutant-General.*

GOVERNORS ISLAND, N. Y., *June 28, 1898.*
(Received 1.33 p. m.)
ADJUTANT-GENERAL, U. S. ARMY, *Washington, D. C.:*

Telegram directing First New York Volunteer Infantry to proceed to San Francisco received and orders issued accordingly.

ROYAL T. FRANK, *Brigadier-General.*

ADJUTANT-GENERAL'S OFFICE,
Washington, June 29, 1898.
Major-General OTIS, U. S. Army,
San Francisco, Cal.:

It is desired that return be made by telegraph of organizations that have left for Manila, giving names of commanding officers and strength of the several commands, commissioned and enlisted.

By command Major-General Miles:

H. C. CORBIN, *Adjutant-General.*

CAMP MERRITT,
San Francisco, Cal., June 29, 1898.
(Received 12.15 p. m.)
ADJUTANT-GENERAL OF THE ARMY, *Washington, D. C.:*

Three expeditions have embarked for Philippines. Strength of first, 115 officers and 2,386 enlisted men, General Anderson commanding. Of second expedition, 158 officers and 3,428 enlisted men, General Greene commanding. Field returns of these troops forwarded. Last expedition, General MacArthur commanding, General Merritt accompanying; strength, 197 officers, 4,650 enlisted men, and 35 civilians, made up of following organizations: Detachment of 6 enlisted men of First Regiment Nebraska Infantry, U. S. Volunteers. Headquarters, band, and Companies B, C, G, and L, Twenty-third United States Infantry, with recruits for First Battalion, Twenty-third United States Infantry, 11 officers and 481 enlisted men, Col. Samuel Ovenshine commanding. Headquarters, band, and Companies C, D, F, and H, Eighteenth Infantry, with recruits for First Battalion, Eighteenth Infantry, 9 officers and 519 enlisted men, Col. D. D. Van Valzah commanding. Batteries G, H, K, and L, Third United States Artillery, 9 officers, 722 enlisted men, Capts. W. E. Birkhimer and James O'Hara, Third United States Artillery, commanding. Company A, Engineer Battalion, 2 officers and 100 enlisted men, First Lieut. C. P. Echols, Engineer Corps, commanding. Thirteenth Regiment Minnesota Infantry, U. S. Volunteers, 44 officers and 963 enlisted men, Col. C. McReeve commanding. First and Second Battalions, First Regiment Idaho

Infantry, U. S. Volunteers, 32 officers and 657 enlisted men, Lieut. Col. J. W. Jones commanding. First and Second Battalions, First Regiment North Dakota Infantry, U. S. Volunteers, 30 officers and 642 enlisted men, Lieut. Col. W. C. Treumann commanding. First Battalion, First Regiment Wyoming Infantry, U. S. Volunteers, 14 officers and 322 enlisted men, Maj. F. M. Foote commanding. Company A, Signal Corps, U. S. Volunteers, 5 officers and 55 enlisted men, Capt. E. A. McKenna commanding. Artillery detachment Astor Battery, 3 officers and 99 enlisted men, First Lieut. P. C. March, Fifth United States Artillery, commanding. Thirty-six staff officers, 65 enlisted men of Hospital Corps, U. S. Army; 19 enlisted men attached to General Merritt's headquarters; 30 civilian clerks; 2 civilian messengers, and 8 newspaper correspondents; total, 197 officers, 4,650 enlisted men, 35 civilians.

E. S. OTIS, *Major-General.*

SAN FRANCISCO, CAL., *June 29, 1898.*
(Received 4.28 p. m.)

ADJUTANT-GENERAL, U. S. ARMY, *Washington, D. C.:*

General Merritt, with staff, sailed this morning on steamer *Newport*. Will overtake other five vessels of flotilla at Honolulu. Forty-five hundred officers and enlisted men constitute this expedition. Return of same by mail.

OTIS, *Major-General.*

ADJUTANT-GENERAL'S OFFICE,
Washington, June 29, 1898.

Col. T. H. BARBER,
First New York Volunteers, Governors Island, N. Y. H.:

Your telegram even date received. Uniforms should be obtained for recruits before leaving. Supply of uniforms for the Tropics will be furnished on reaching San Francisco, as will the additional arms and small parts thereof. This would seem to be better than to await these stores at this end of the line. It is not desired, however, that your regiment leave until the recruits are all comfortably clothed.

By command Major-General Miles:

H. C. CORBIN, *Adjutant-General.*

HONGKONG, *July 3, 1898.*
(Received 1.41 a. m.)

ADJUTANT-GENERAL, U. S. ARMY, *Washington:*

Cavalry, artillery, and riding horses desirable. Can get limited number of draft animals here.

ANDERSON.

OFFICE MAJOR-GENERAL COMMANDING PHILIPPINE EXPEDITION,
San Francisco, Cal., June 28, 1898. (Received July 4, 1898.)

SIR: As already reported, I sail on the *Newport* to-morrow about 10 o'clock, and expect to overtake the other vessels of the fleet at Honolulu.

I am sorry that more of the command can not accompany me, but it is out of the question, and I purpose doing the best I can with the means at hand. It may be possible to effect the capture of Manila with the troops that will be there when

I arrive. I will consult with Admiral Dewey, and do everything that is possible to carry out the wishes of the War Department and the President.

I can not leave the country without expressing my extreme satisfaction at the excellent work that has been done by the officers of my staff, both personal and general, in getting the commands in shape for service. My personal aids, as well as General Hughes, Major Simpson, Colonel Whipple, and in fact all of the staff, have done great work in teaching the new men their duties as soldiers, and we have succeeded in giving them all, so far as they have sailed, a short course of target practice. The material that I have sent is very fine, so far as I can judge. The men are enthusiastic and willing to learn, and most of the officers are quite satisfactory. Of course they have to contend with the want of experience in military matters, but I am satisfied they will give a good account of themselves if we have an opportunity to engage them at Manila.

I take it for granted that the possibility of the Spanish fleet arriving at Manila before our troops get there is not great, and I will strain every nerve to anticipate the Spaniards in arriving at Manila.

Thanking you, the President, and the Secretary of War, for the kindnesses extended to me, I am,

Very respectfully,
WESLEY MERRITT,
Major-General.

The ADJUTANT-GENERAL U. S. ARMY,
War Department, Washington, D. C.

DEPARTMENT OF STATE,
Washington, July 6, 1898.

The Honorable, the SECRETARY OF WAR.

SIR: I have the honor to transmit herewith for your information a copy of an unnumbered dispatch of May 12 last, from the consul at Manila, relative to the political situation in the Philippine Islands.

Respectfully, yours,
WILLIAM R. DAY.

[Inclosure.]

No. —, of May 12, 1898, from Manila, Philippine Islands.

CONSULATE OF THE UNITED STATES, MANILA, PHILIPPINE ISLANDS,
Special Cruiser Baltimore, Manila Bay, opposite Cavite, May 12, 1898.

Honorable Judge DAY,
Secretary of State, Washington, D. C.

SIR: To aid you, if possible, permit me to give assurance of the friendliness of the Philippine natives to our country and to me as its representative.

During the period of my residence in Manila every week was a history of barbarities by Spaniards and of efforts, often futile, of the natives to obtain rights and protect their homes.

Scores of times I have heard hopes expressed that either the United States or Great Britain would acquire these islands. In all this, foreign residents other than Spanish concurred, and all such classes are most friendly to me.

In the struggle between Spain and the insurgents the deaths have been many greater among the natives, first, because the Spaniards have been much better armed; second, because the Spaniards killed many noncombatants—old men, women, and children—while the natives refrained from such barbarities.

From concensus of opinions of many reliable people I estimate Spanish forces here about as follows:

First. Naval force, in ships, annihilated in the notable battle of Manila Bay, in which ten Spanish war ships were burned and sunk, two auxiliary gunboats ditto, and about thirty steamers, schooners, tugs, etc., captured.

Second. About 4,000 Spanish infantry, nearly a half of whom are in hospitals.

Third. About 6,000 native troops under Spanish officers: but if such officers were deported their soldiers would eagerly follow our flag.

An insurgent leader, Major Gonzales, reported to me last week on the *Olympia* that they had 37,000 troops under arms, good and bad, surrounding Manila, endeavoring to cooperate with us. In the main they are very poorly armed, but have about 6,600 rifles taken from the Spaniards. They have captured the entire railroad line and the River Pasig, thus cutting off supply lines, while we, by cutting off supply by bay and sea, can soon starve Manila into surrender.

These natives are eager to be organized and led by United States officers, and the members of their cabinet visited me and gave assurance that all would swear allegiance to and cheerfully follow our flag. They are brave, submissive, and cheaply provided for.

To show their friendliness for me as our nation's only representative in this part of the world, I last week went on shore at Cavite with British consul in his launch to show the destruction wrought by our fleet. As soon as natives found me out they crowded around me, hats off, shouting, "Viva los Americanos," thronged about me by hundreds to shake either hand, even several at a time—men, women, and children—striving to get even a finger to shake, so I moved a half mile shaking continuously with both hands. The British consul, a smiling spectator, said he never before saw such an evidence of friendship. Two thousand escorted me to the launch, amid hurrahs of good feeling for our nation. Hence I must conclude:

First. Our squadron can force surrender in a day—Spaniards are all cooped up in Manila.

Second. Spanish officers of native regiments away. These 6,000, together with selections from the 37,000 insurgents, can give us ample land force, and can be well armed with rifles of Spanish soldiers and from barracks and arsenals.

Third. Few United States troops will be needed for conquest and fewer still for occupancy. Expulsion of Spaniards, naval, civil, military, and cleric, will remove all discord and danger, and civil government, crude in the beginning, but better than the present, will be easy and be well received, while native priests, of which there are many, can fully and with perfect acceptability meet all religious requirements so far as present established religion is concerned.

All natives, all foreigners other than Spanish, and certain Spaniards in mercantile and retired life, will aid us to every extent. The people crave a change of flag.

Hence I believe ample assurances are at hand that civil government by us will be easy of organization and gratefully received by the people.

My communications to your Department are, these war days, supra-consular, but on other lines I endeavor to serve our fleet and thus serve our nation.

All rejoice over the merited promotion of our Commodore to the rank of rear-admiral, but every man of the fleet proved a hero, and it seems as if the shield of Providence warded off the enemy's shot, leaving our men unharmed, our ships and guns intact, and gave us the most important and unique victory of history.

The student of the next century will read with pride that the right arm of Spain was broken at the battle of Manila Bay, and from this must come the acquisition of these islands, many times more extensive, more populous, and more valuable than Cuba, or else their capture will force Spain to conditions of peace on basis of honor, so much sought by our nation.

I have the honor to be, sir, your most obedient servant,

OSCAR F. WILLIAMS,
United States Consul.

SAN FRANCISCO, CAL., *July 6, 1898.*
(Received 4.49 p. m.)

Adjutant-General HEISTAND, *Washington, D. C.:*

Your telegram of yesterday received. I am not expecting to send any troops abroad on transports. Your telegram furnished Major-General Otis, in charge of Philippine expedition in this city.

MERRIAM, *Major-General.*

MEMORANDUM FOR THE WAR DEPARTMENT.

NAVY DEPARTMENT, *Washington, July 7, 1898.*

A cablegram from Rear Admiral Dewey, dated Cavite, July 4—Hongkong, July 7—states: "The United States troops have landed, and have been comfortably housed at Cavite, Luzon Island. Insurgents still active. Aguinaldo proclaimed himself president of the revolutionary republic on July 1."

A. S. CROWNINSHIELD, *Secretary.*

WAR DEPARTMENT, *July 7, 1898.*

Gen. E. S. OTIS, *San Francisco, Cal.:*

The Secretary of War directs you to take the *Titania, Rio Janeiro, Peru, Pennsylvania,* and *City of Puebla,* and so many of your command as these ships will accommodate, and proceed to join General Merritt. This will be the last expedition going from the Pacific until the return of the transports now gone in advance. It is desired Brig. Gen. H. G. Otis go with you.

H. C. CORBIN, *Adjutant-General.*

ADJUTANT-GENERAL'S OFFICE,
Washington, July 7, 1898.

Major-General OTIS, *San Francisco, Cal.:*

First New York Volunteer Infantry, Col. T. H. Barber, should leave New York to-day. This regiment is reported to be a very fine one, in excellent state of equipment and discipline. It may be that you will wish it to go with the expedition mentioned in telegram sent you few minutes ago.

H. C. CORBIN, *Adjutant-General.*

ADJUTANT-GENERAL'S OFFICE.
Washington, July 7, 1898.

COMMANDING-GENERAL, DEPARTMENT CALIFORNIA,
San Francisco, Cal.:

Your telegram 6th instant, saying you are not expecting to send any troops abroad on transports and that Adjutant-General's telegram of 5th instant furnished Major-General Otis, in charge of Philippine expedition, is not understood.

HEISTAND, *Assistant Adjutant-General.*

NEW YORK, *July 7, 1898.*
(Received 5.12 p. m.)

ADJUTANT-GENERAL, U. S. ARMY, *Washington, D. C.:*

The First Regiment Infantry New York Volunteers, Colonel Barber, has left Jersey City for San Francisco; first section at 4 o'clock, and the fourth and last section at about 4.30.

GILLESPIE, *Brigadier-General Volunteers.*

UNITED STATES GEOLOGICAL SURVEY,
Washington, July 8, 1898.

Hon. G. D. MEIKLEJOHN,
Assistant Secretary of War, Washington, D. C.

DEAR SIR: I have the honor to acknowledge yours of July 7, in the matter of sending a geologist to the Philippine Islands.

I wish to personally thank you for the interest you have shown in sending Dr. Becker, and I trust that the results will fully justify the action taken. Dr. Becker has received a letter from the Secretary of the Navy to Admiral Dewey, and starts out under the most auspicious conditions.

Truly, yours, CHAS. D. WALCOTT.

ADJUTANT-GENERAL'S OFFICE,
Washington, July 8, 1898.

Major-General OTIS, *San Francisco, Cal.:*

The Secretary is desirous of having a regiment go to Honolulu for station; have you one available? He would also like you to go in advance, if possible, of your expedition, and remain at Honolulu until the forces overtake you.

H. C. CORBIN, *Adjutant-General.*

ADJUTANT-GENERAL'S OFFICE,
Washington, July 8, 1898.

General OTIS, *San Francisco, Cal.:*

Having reference to previous telegram concerning a garrison for Honolulu, you are informed that the First New York, under Colonel Barber, is now en route and will probably be more available than anything you have under command. This only by way of suggestion.

H. C. CORBIN, *Adjutant-General.*

SAN FRANCISCO, CAL., *July 8, 1898.*
(Received 7.10 p. m.)

ADJUTANT-GENERAL, U. S. ARMY,
Washington, D. C.:

The situation is as follows: Steamers *Pueblo* and *Peru* now loading with freight of troops designated to embark thereon. Troops are remainder of Fourteenth Infantry and remaining recruits for the two battalions of the Eighteenth and Twenty-third Infantry which have already gone to Manila, detachment of battalion Third Artillery also gone, squadron of Fourth Cavalry, two light batteries of Sixth Artillery, and the remaining enlisted men of battalions of volunteer organizations which have gone; all numbering 1,800, equal to full capacities of vessels. The vessels can sail early next week and assignments can not now be changed without making confusion. Steamer *Titania* not to be chartered for reasons telegraphed yesterday to Assistant Secretary of War, hence instructions in your telegram of yesterday can not be strictly carried out. The *St. Paul* can, I think, be secured, and is expected in port on or before Tuesday next. This, with *Rio de Janeiro* and *Pennsylvania*, now discharging cargo, can transport 3,000 men or more; vessels can be in condition about the same time, probably in twelve days. Have directed charter of *St. Paul* on same terms as former charters contained. I would recommend that I take the *Puebla* and *Peru* on to Honolulu as soon as prepared to sail, and there wait the remaining vessels of the flotilla; that a vessel be secured to transport a regiment to Honolulu for station, to sail with them.

This I think I can do. I would recommend that the Eighth California Volunteers be designated for the Honolulu station. The colonel is an excellent national guard officer of long standing and a good lawyer; the lieutenant-colonel (Carrington) is an army officer of experience, as is known. The remaining field officers and a majority of the enlisted men have a long national guard experience. If suggestions are approved, will put the Eighth California in condition to embark. Will telegraph more fully later, as soon as I can learn conditions in regard to transports.

OTIS,
Major-General, U. S. Volunteers, Commanding.

SAN FRANCISCO, CAL., *July 8, 1898.*
(Received 10.41 p. m.)

ADJUTANT-GENERAL, U. S. ARMY,
Washington, D. C.:

Have directed the charter of steamer *St. Paul*, expected here 10th instant or at latest by 12th. Excellent vessel and terms moderate. Also directed charter of sailing vessel *Tacoma*, at $200 per day, to transport stock and forage. She will leave about 18th instant. Can, I think, secure vessels to transport regiment to Honolulu—men per capita, freight per pound—at moderate rates. First mail steamer for Honolulu leaves on 13th instant.

OTIS,
Major-General, U. S. Volunteers, Commanding.

ADJUTANT-GENERAL'S OFFICE,
Washington, July 8, 1898.

Major-General OTIS, U. S. Volunteers,
San Francisco, Cal.:

Your telegram received. Would it be possible to send any considerable number, say a battalion, on mail ship? Will reply to remainder of questions after conferring with Secretary of War to-morrow morning.

H. C. CORBIN, *Adjutant-General.*

SAN FRANCISCO, CAL., *July 9, 1898.*

QUARTERMASTER-GENERAL, *Washington, D. C.:*

In accordance with telegraphic instructions this date, chartered steamship *City of Rio Janeiro*, also steamship *Pennsylvania*. Arrangements have been made to fit these vessels as rapidly as possible for transport service. Every endeavor will be used to promptly complete them. Under direction of General Otis have also chartered sailing ship *Tacoma*, which will be fitted as rapidly as possible for animals, and will also take a large quantity of coal in ballast; should transport about 225 animals. Will report further on this ship. This morning I notified General Otis that I could secure the steamship *St. Paul*, which is a sister ship of the *Senator*. Reference to telegram of 11th regarding *Senator*. *St. Paul* will carry about 1,000 men, and is a new ship, most complete in every particular, with every modern improvement, and can be rapidly fitted after arrival, and is expected Sunday or Monday next. Can arrange to charter for $1,000 per day, perhaps less, depending upon price fixed upon *Senator*. General Otis ordered me to charter her, which I will do upon arrival. General Otis has concluded not to take the *Titania*.

LONG, *Quartermaster in Charge.*

SAN FRANCISCO, CAL., *July 9, 1898.*

QUARTERMASTER-GENERAL, *Washington, D. C.:*

Reference to your telegram 7th instant, report regular line of steamers leave monthly for Honolulu on Oceanic Steamship Company, which now has only the *Alameda, Mariposa,* and the *Moata,* the latter being under the British flag; capacity, about 250 passengers each. Company reports no vessels available at present for carrying troops. *Alameda* and *Mariposa* about same capacity as transports *Zealandia* and *Australia.* Pacific Mail steamers have been run to Honolulu, but do not now on account of having chartered majority to the Government as transports. The Occidental and Oriental Line are British steamers and can not be utilized. There is no regular line of ships reported as carrying sugar, of which about 50,000 tons is brought here annually in small sailing ships. There are two methods available for transport of troops to Honolulu: First, by means of small steamships which have been used in Alaska trade, and with which I think arrangements can be made to transport at so much a head and so much freight per ton. These ships would carry, approximately, 250 passengers each, and on the return trip could load with sugar and other freight at Honolulu. The second is, if possible, to make arrangements with the Oregon Railway and Navigation Company for two or three of their steamships now used in trade for passengers and freight between here and Portland, which possibly could be utilized for this service as transports between this port and Honolulu if secured. Will see the manager in the early morning regarding the latter suggestion and report further.

LONG, *Quartermaster in Charge.*

SAN FRANCISCO, CAL., *July 9, 1898.*
(Received 4.40 p. m.)

ADJUTANT-GENERAL, U. S. ARMY, *Washington, D. C.:*

Ascertained that Honolulu mail steamer, which leaves this port on 13th or 14th instant, can transport 150 men in steerage and a few in after cabin. Price, $21 per head, steerage; cabin passage, $75. Vessel can not take any freight. No other mail steamer departing until latter part of the month.

OTIS,
Major-General, U. S. Volunteers, Commanding.

SAN FRANCISCO, CAL., *July 9, 1898.*
(Received 5.41 p. m.)

ADJUTANT-GENERAL, U. S. ARMY, *Washington, D. C.:*

With reference to troops for station at Honolulu, find that by 18th instant can secure four coast vessels, with capacity to transport 1,200 men and officers to Honolulu, at $35 per capita and $10 per ton for freight. Freight capacity sufficient for all purposes. If speedy action taken vessels promised by 15th instant.

OTIS,
Major-General, U. S. Volunteers, Commanding.

ADJUTANT-GENERAL'S OFFICE,
Washington, July 9, 1898.

Major-General OTIS, *San Francisco, Cal.:*

In making up the final expedition going with you to the Philippines the Secretary War would like, if possible, that you take the South Dakota regiment, and he would like to know if this is possible.

H. C. CORBIN, *Adjutant-General.*

SAN FRANCISCO, CAL., *July 9, 1898.*
(Received 7.56 p. m.)

ADJUTANT-GENERAL, U. S. ARMY, *Washington, D. C.:*
The South Dakota regiment can be taken, as you suggest.

OTIS,
Major-General, U. S. Volunteers, Commanding.

NAVY DEPARTMENT, *Washington, July 9, 1898.*

SIR: The Department has ten engineer officers which it is desired shall be transferred, as early as practicable, from the navy-yard, Mare Island, Cal., to the fleet in Asiatic waters, under the command of Rear-Admiral George Dewey, U. S. N., now stationed at Manila, Philippine Islands.

It is requested that these officers be allowed to take passage in an army transport, and that the necessary instructions be issued in order that they may take passage on the first convenient transport sailing for Manila. It is further requested that this Department be informed of the date upon which the steamer selected will sail.

I have the honor to be, very respectfully, your obedient servant,

JOHN D. LONG, *Secretary of the Navy.*

The SECRETARY OF WAR,
War Department, Washington, D. C.

ADJUTANT-GENERAL'S OFFICE,
Washington, July 9, 1898.

Major-General OTIS, *San Francisco, Cal.:*

Secretary War directs that you furnish transportation to ten engineer officers now at Mare Island, Cal., on one of the army transports to sail for the Philippine Islands, in order that they may join the Asiatic fleet. Telegraph date on which steamer will sail.

CARTER, *Assistant Adjutant-General.*

SAN FRANCISCO, CAL., *July 9, 1898.*
(Received 11.04 p. m.)

ADJUTANT-GENERAL, U. S. ARMY, *Washington, D. C.:*

Two transports will be prepared to sail by the 13th or 14th instant, and transportation can be furnished engineers enumerated in your telegram. The actual time of sailing will depend upon instructions now awaited from your office.

OTIS,
Major-General, U. S. Volunteers, Commanding.

ADJUTANT-GENERAL'S OFFICE,
Washington, July 10, 1898.

Major-General OTIS, *San Francisco, Cal.:*

Your telegram recommending that you take the *Puebla* and *Peru* and go in advance to Honolulu is approved. Have you fully determined on the regiment you will assign to garrison duty there? There is no objection to the Eighth California other than it is thought that as California has one regiment on the way to the Philippines the other States feel that details for service should be given to all the states alike. Two regiments from any one state are for these reasons objectionable. You have no idea the anxiety for service, and how any sign of favoritism is resented.

By order Secretary of War:

H. C. CORBIN, *Adjutant-General.*

ADJUTANT-GENERAL'S OFFICE,
Washington, July 10, 1898.

MEMORANDUM FOR THE HEADQUARTERS OF THE ARMY.

Agreeable to the instructions of the President, the Secretary of War has ordered the island of Honolulu to be garrisoned by one regiment of infantry. Provisions will be made accordingly. It has not been determined that the permanent garrison will be of this size, but will be for the present. It is probable this island will be attached to the Department of California, but this has not been fully determined.

By order of the Secretary of War:

H. C. CORBIN, *Adjutant-General.*

ADJUTANT-GENERAL'S OFFICE,
Washington, July 10, 1898.

Major-General OTIS, *San Francisco, Cal.:*

Under instructions of Assistant Secretary of War, it is understood that you are to make all arrangements necessary for the charter of steamers for transportation of troops to Honolulu. Have you determined what regiment you will send? All things being equal, by reason of well-known ability and education, etc., of Colonel Barber, of the First New York, it is thought it would be well to send his regiment, if agreeable to him and in accordance with your own views. With this suggestion the Secretary War leaves selection to you, but desires to know what regiment you select before orders are issued.

H. C. CORBIN, *Adjutant-General.*

ADJUTANT-GENERAL'S OFFICE,
Washington, July 10, 1898—9.10 p. m.

Major-General OTIS, *San Francisco, Cal.:*

Secretary War directs that on the embarkation of the expedition now being formed to go under your immediate charge that the remaining troops heretofore destined for the Philippines will, until return transportation or other orders issued, report to the commanding general Department of California for his orders.

By order Secretary War:

H. C. CORBIN, *Adjutant-General.*

ADJUTANT-GENERAL'S OFFICE,
Washington, July 10, 1898—9.15 p. m.

COMMANDING GENERAL, DEPARTMENT OF CALIFORNIA, *San Francisco·*

The following instructions have been sent General Otis:

"Secretary War directs that on the embarkation of the expedition now being formed to go under your immediate charge that the remaining troops heretofore destined for the Philippines will, until return transportation or other orders issued, report to the commanding general Department of California for his orders."

By order Secretary War:

H. C. CORBIN, *Adjutant-General.*

ADJUTANT-GENERAL'S OFFICE,
Washington, July 10, 1898—midnight.

Major-General OTIS, *San Francisco, Cal.:*

At a conference to-night the President and Secretary War agreed that the First New York Volunteers should be diverted from the force going immediately to the Philippines and assigned to duty for the time being at Honolulu. It was further agreed that the Hawaiian Islands should become a part of the geographical limits of the Department of California. Under this new order of things the troops going to Honolulu will report to the commanding general of that department, but you will stop en route, as heretofore directed.

By order Secretary War:

H. C. CORBIN, *Adjutant-General.*

ADJUTANT-GENERAL'S OFFICE,
Washington, July 10, 1898—midnight.

COMMANDING GENERAL, DEPARTMENT CALIFORNIA, *San Francisco, Cal.:*

Orders to-morrow will issue attaching the Hawaiian Islands to the Department of California. The First New York Volunteers, Colonel Barber commanding, will be assigned for the time being as the garrison at Honolulu. It is thought you will find Colonel Barber, by reason of his ability and training, an officer peculiarly fitted to the delicate duties devolving upon the first commanding officer of troops on these islands.

By order Secretary War:

H. C. CORBIN, *Adjutant-General.*

SAN FRANCISCO, CAL., *July 10, 1898.*
(Received July 11, 1898—3 a. m.)

ADJUTANT-GENERAL, U. S. ARMY, *Washington, D. C.:*

I understand that on application of Colonel Barber, First New York, to go to Philippines, General Merritt applied for regiment. It should reach Ogden to-morrow morning and I telegraphed Barber to know his desire and if regiment fully uniformed and equipped. Chicago papers report men without uniforms. Captain Murray informs me that he has completed muster of Eighth California, 1,287 strong, and reports that about 60 per cent are national guard men, well drilled; that officers and men are very superior and that colonel an excellent soldier and strong man. Unfortunately, it is not fully armed and many arms in possession captain has condemned. Benicia Arsenal has no .45-caliber rifles on hand, but expects them daily, as they were shipped on 1st instant. Will telegraph to-morrow, when I have more information as to actual conditions. Your three telegrams of to-day received.

OTIS,
Major-General, U. S. Volunteers, Commanding.

ADJUTANT-GENERAL'S OFFICE,
Washington, July 11, 1898—4.35 p. m.

Major-General OTIS, *San Francisco, Cal.:*

If you should find that the First New York is not suitable for service in Honolulu and Colonel Barber would prefer to go to the Philippines, the Secretary of War says that you can then select the California regiment. It was desired to send the First New York for the reason that Colonel Barber was an educated soldier and a man of such character and ability as commended him for this delicate and important duty. It is desired you confer with him before making final selection.

By order Secretary War:

H. C. CORBIN, *Adjutant-General.*

SAN FRANCISCO, CAL., *July 11, 1898.*
(Received 7.35 p. m.)

ADJUTANT-GENERAL, U. S. ARMY, *Washington, D. C.:*

The telegram of last night directing First New York to proceed to Honolulu received. Telegram from Colonel Barber says regiment uniformed and equipped and only needs light clothing, some tentage, and band instruments. Regiment will arrive Thursday. Am promised sufficient excellent coast transportation to send entire regiment on by 23d instant about or shortly after last steamer of next expedition will sail. Terms, $35 per capita, officers and men, which is cheaper than vessels can be chartered even if it were possible to charter any. Will direct contract on these terms as soon as parties notify me that they can execute it without fail.

OTIS,
Major-General, U. S. Volunteers.

WAR DEPARTMENT, *Washington, July 11, 1898.*

SIR: I have the honor to acknowledge the receipt of your letter of 21st ultimo, inclosing copy of a letter from Messrs. Merryweather & Sons, of London, England, asking that the carrying out of their contract with the fire authorities of Manila, Philippine Islands, for furnishing fire apparatus, be not interfered with by the United States officials when they occupy that city.

Replying thereto, I beg to inform you that the request of Messrs. Merryweather & Sons has been favorably considered by the Department, and the papers in the case will be transmitted to Major-General Merritt, commanding Department of the Pacific, for his information and guidance.

Very respectfully,

R. A. ALGER, *Secretary of War.*

The SECRETARY OF STATE.

SAN FRANCISCO, CAL., *July 12, 1898.*
(Received 3.20 p. m.)

Adjutant-General CORBIN, *Washington, D. C.:*

I recommend a board of engineer, artillery, quartermaster, and medical officers be sent at once to Honolulu to select sites for military stations and defensive works covering that harbor; necessary reservations should be secured at once.

MERRIAM, *Major-General.*

SAN FRANCISCO, CAL., *July 12, 1898.*
(Received 7.35 p. m.)

Hon. R. A. ALGER, *Secretary of War, Washington, D. C.:*

Public sentiment favors California regiment going Honolulu. Eighth California Infantry has most efficient field and good line officers. Men greatly superior to average enlistments, representing all professions and skilled labor. It would fulfill reasonable expectations in discipline and general soldier conduct.

W. L. BARNES.

LOS ANGELES, CAL., *July 13, 1898.*
(Received 2.20 p. m.)

Hon. R. A. ALGER, *Washington, D. C.:*

It is the earnest wish of our whole people, myself as well, that heavy batteries A and D, U. S. Volunteers, California, be sent to Manila next expedition. The boys are anxious to be in it.

GEO. H. BONEBRAKE.

SAN FRANCISCO, CAL., *July 13, 1898.*
(Received 2.40 p. m.)

Maj. H. O. S. HEISTAND, *War Department, Washington, D. C.:*

Please use strong influence to have First Battalion California Heavy Artillery assigned to Manila. My brother lieutenant Battery A, part of which already gone first expedition, rest sidetracked for unknown reasons. Wire prospects and oblige.

GEORGE E. MORSE.

ADJUTANT-GENERAL'S OFFICE,
Washington, July 13, 1898.

GEORGE E. MORSE, *San Francisco, Cal.:*

Prospects not good for First Battalion California Heavy Artillery to be assigned to Manila.

H. O. S. HEISTAND,
Assistant Adjutant-General.

SAN FRANCISCO, CAL., *July 13, 1898.*
(Received 4.15 p. m.)

Secretary ALGER, *Washington, D. C.:*

I respectfully suggest that California troops be sent to Hawaii, on account of our geographical, commercial, and social relations, and particularly recommend for this service the Eighth California Regiment, Colonel Henshaw commanding.

JAMES D. PHELAN,
Mayor of San Francisco.

SAN FRANCISCO, CAL, *July 13, 1898.*
(Received 4.45 p. m.)

ADJUTANT-GENERAL, U. S. ARMY, *Washington, D. C.:*

Great difficulty experienced in securing vessels for transportation of Honolulu troops, as promises heretofore made can not be fulfilled. No ships in port can have one-half of regiment shipped within fifteen days and rest before August 10. Vessels *Peru* and *Puebla* loaded, and troops can be placed on board to-morrow morning. Vessels *Rio* and *Pennsylvania* ready for troops by 23d instant. *St. Paul* not yet arrived; probably will be ready for troops by same date. Admiral Miller can not start for Honolulu until after 20th instant—probably 23d or 24th. Shall I embark troops on steamers *Puebla* and *Peru* to-morrow and go on with ships to Honolulu and there await rest of fleet, or let vessels remain here two or three days to complete all necessary arrangements for entire flotilla? Please instruct me as to my duties in Honolulu. Colonel Barber arrived with a portion of the First New York. Entire regiment should be here to-morrow. Will consult him as soon as possible and telegraph result. Request reply at once.

OTIS,
Major-General, U. S. Volunteers, Commanding.

SAN FRANCISCO, CAL., *July 13. 1898*.
(Received 9.49 p. m.)

ADJUTANT-GENERAL, U. S. ARMY, *Washington, D. C.*:

Colonel Barber's regiment fully equipped except in the matter of light clothing, which can be obtained here. He desires to go to Honolulu, provided it does not prejudice his chances of going to Philippines ultimately. Have contracted for transportation, and one-half of regiment can be embarked this month; remaining early in August. Shall this regiment be sent?

OTIS,
Major-General, U. S. Volunteers, Commanding.

ADJUTANT-GENERAL'S OFFICE,
Washington, July 14, 1898—12.45 a. m.

Major-General OTIS, *San Francisco, Cal.*:

Your telegram of this date, asking if the First New York shall be sent to Honolulu, received, and the answer is in the affirmative. Your action in contracting for transportation, and one-half of regiment embarked this month, remaining early in August, is also approved. It is further remarked that Colonel Barber's station at Honolulu will not prejudice his chances in going to the Phillippines later on. May have to remain some three or four months, however.

By order Secretary War:

H. C. CORBIN, *Adjutant-General.*

ADJUTANT-GENERAL'S OFFICE,
Washington, July 14, 1898—1 a. m.

Major-General MERRIAM, *San Francisco, Cal.*:

Your recommendation that a board of engineer, artillery, quartermaster, and medical officers be sent to Honolulu is received. After due consideration, the Secretary of War is of the opinion that the number of officers available will not admit of this action, but he directs as necessary for the public service that you designate one officer in whom you have confidence to select sites for military stations, etc., as indicated in your telegrams.

H. C. CORBIN, *Adjutant-General.*

CONSULATE-GENERAL OF THE UNITED STATES OF AMERICA,
Honolulu, H. I., June 28, 1898. (Received July 14, 1898.)

Gen H. C. CORBIN,
Adjutant-General, U. S. Army, War Department, Washington, D. C.

SIR: I am in receipt of a communication from General Merritt at San Francisco, advising me that the Navy authorizes the use of naval coal at this place for the army transports. I am also in receipt of a letter from the chief quartermaster at San Francisco to the effect that he has contracted for 9,000 tons of coal to be delivered here for the use of future transports which are expected shortly. It hardly seems possible that this coal can arrive in time to coal the vessels of the third expedition. Should these vessels, however, arrive before the army coal does, I will coal them with navy coal, as I have done heretofore. I assure you that while the transports are in Honolulu every other duty which I have to perform will be laid aside so that the vessels may get away as quickly as possible.

I am, very respectfully, yours,

WM. HAYWOOD, *Consul-General.*

DEPARTMENT OF STATE,
Washington, July 14, 1898.

The Honorable, the SECRETARY OF WAR.

SIR: I have the honor to inclose herewith for your information an extract from a dispatch from our minister at Honolulu giving an account of the arrival at and departure from that place of the second American expeditionary force sent to the Philippines.

Respectfully, yours, WILLIAM R. DAY.

[Inclosure from minister to Hawaii, No. 175, June 27, 1898.—Extract.]

Copy No. 175.]
LEGATION OF THE UNITED STATES,
Honolulu, Hawaiian Islands, June 27, 1898.

Hon. W. R. DAY,
Secretary of State, Washington, D. C.

SIR: I have the honor to report that there arrived here on the evening of the 23d instant the United States transports *China*, *Zealandia*, *Colon*, and *Senator*, conveying the second expedition to the Philippines, Brig. Gen. F. V. Greene commanding. These troops received the same generous treatment accorded those of the first expedition, reported in detail in my No. 167 of June 8. There was nothing left undone for the entertainment and comfort of the officers and men which warm American sympathy and traditional Hawaiian hospitality could provide. Good order and general good feeling prevailed. The impression made upon the natives was very favorable, and it is noticed that they adopt a cordial attitude toward our men, and speak in a friendly way of impending annexation. On the morning of the 25th instant, having taken on board 1,667 tons of coal, the fleet left the harbor.

* * * * * * *

I have the honor to be, sir, your obedient servant,

HAROLD M. SEWALL.

DEPARTMENT OF STATE,
Washington, July 14, 1898.

The Honorable, the SECRETARY OF WAR.

SIR: I have the honor to inclose herewith for your consideration, and for such action as you may be pleased to take in the matter, a copy of a dispatch from our minister at Honolulu, calling attention to the urgent necessity of providing for officers and men of the expeditionary forces sent to the Philippines who have been or may be left behind at Honolulu.

Respectfully, WILLIAM R. DAY.

[Inclosure from minister to Hawaii, No. 176, June 28, 1898.]

[Copy, No. 176.]

LEGATION OF THE UNITED STATES,
Honolulu, Hawaiian Islands, June 28, 1898.

Hon. W. R. DAY,
Secretary of State, Washington, D. C.

SIR: I have the honor to call your attention to the urgent need for some provision on the part of our Government to meet the emergency created by officers and men left here for various reasons from our expeditionary forces en route to the Philippines.

From the second expedition these numbered 17, as will appear from inclosed memorandum; of these, 9 were cared for by the Red Cross Society of Hawaii; 1, Private H. C. Fisk, Company D, Nebraska Volunteers, died at the Red Cross Hospital, and was buried under the direction of the society (newspaper reports of the funeral inclosed); 1 is now at the Queen's Hospital in a very sick condition. The transportation of the convalescents home has been provided for by an order on the quartermaster at San Francisco, but little money was given them for their maintenance here.

Lieutenant Ritchie, of the Tenth Pennsylvania Volunteers, with a Red Cross surgeon of the same regiment, was left behind. Through the generosity of W. G. Irwin, esq., of Honolulu, they were enabled to take the *Belgic*, leaving the 26th instant for Hongkong, whence they hope to reach Manila.

A hospital steward of the Regular Army and a surgeon of the Volunteers are also here. I have requested Captain Leutze, of the *Monterey*, to take them on board the collier *Brutus*.

Four coal bearers from the *Colon* have been assisted at the consulate as distressed American seamen.

The Red Cross Society will accommodate all it can at its hospital, and carry on its work to the limit of its resources, but it is feared that coming expeditions may exhaust these, and there are some cases that can not be taken to its hospital for treatment.

As for the men who are well and left here by mistake, they must depend upon outside assistance, both for maintenance and transportation.

In my No. 166, of June 8, I suggested that it might be necessary for our Government to establish a military camp or sanitarium here. The need of the latter is already apparent. Already the town is exposed to an epidemic of measles, a disease that is very fatal to the natives, brought by the troops, and against which there is established here on passenger steamers a strict quarantine. If the necessity for isolation and Government medical supervision of our troops here exist now, it will certainly be greater when they begin to be sent back from Manila, and are landed here, as many will have to be, because unable to continue the journey.

It will be plain, I think, on the above statement that the emergency created, which will become more serious at each succeeding expedition, and which neither the consulate nor this legation are able to meet, ought to be brought to the attention of the War Department, to which I respectfully suggest a copy of this dispatch with inclosure be submitted.

I have the honor, etc., HAROLD M. SEWALL.

[Inclosure in No. 176.]

Memorandum of officers and men left at Honolulu from the second expeditionary force, United States troops, to the Philippines.

Private W. J. Malone, Company L, will be sent to San Francisco per *Rio Janeiro*.

Corporal C. A. Shuler, Company L, will be sent to San Francisco per *Rio Janeiro*.

Private Charles Butler, Company C, First Nebraska Volunteers, will be sent to San Francisco per *Rio Janeiro*.

Sergeant Leonard Stafford, Company E, First Nebraska Volunteers, will be sent to San Francisco per *Rio Janeiro*.

Private Charles Craig, Company F, sick at Red Cross Hospital.

Private H. C. Fisk, Company D, died at Red Cross Hospital.

Paul Miller, Company D, Twenty-third Infantry, Regular, now at Queen's Hospital, but will be sent to San Francisco per *Rio Janeiro*.

Moneton Dene, hospital steward, U. S. Army, Plattsburg, by *Brutus*.

Dr. McAllister, surgeon, Tenth Pennsylvania Volunteers.

Herbert Stanon, Hospital Corps, First Regiment Colorado.

Herbert Howard, private, Company H, First Regiment Colorado, have ticket to San Francisco by *Rio*.

Lieutenant Ritchie, Tenth Pennsylvania, W. F. Warrick, Tenth Pennsylvania, went by *Belgic*.

Four firemen to go by *Rio* to San Francisco.

WASHINGTON, D. C., *July 14, 1898.*

Hon. RUSSELL A. ALGER,
    Secretary of War, Washington.

SIR: I would respectfully urge that the First California Heavy Artillery be ordered to Manila, if such course is consistent.

Very respectfully,

E. F. LOUD.

ADJUTANT-GENERAL'S OFFICE,
Washington, July 14, 1898.

Maj. Gen. E. S. OTIS, *San Francisco, Cal.:*

It is reported here that Colonel Barber objects to going to Honolulu. If this is true, you will designate another regiment. It is the desire of this Department to meet Colonel Barber's wishes as far as consistent with the interests of the service.

H. C. CORBIN, *Adjutant-General.*

ADJUTANT-GENERAL'S OFFICE,
Washington, July 14, 1898—3.30 p. m.

Major-General OTIS, *San Francisco, Cal.:*

Having reference to telegram that you should stop at Honolulu, the Secretary of War now directs that you need not give the matter any further consideration than to confer with General Merriam and have the regiment to take station there to report to him. This to enable you to give your entire attention to the embarkation and departure of your command for the Philippines. It is feared any delay on your part at Honolulu might interfere with the expedition.

By order Secretary of War:

H. C. CORBIN, *Adjutant-General.*

ADJUTANT-GENERAL'S OFFICE,
Washington, July 14, 1898—3.45 p. m.

Major-General MERRIAM, *San Francisco, Cal.:*

General Otis will order a regiment to report to you to occupy the Hawaiian Islands. You will cause arrangements to be made on the lines understood by General Otis, which we will explain to you. Should you deem it best to go in person, with one aid, to examine sites, etc., you are authorized to do so.

By order Secretary War:

H. C. CORBIN, *Adjutant-General.*

SAN FRANCISCO, CAL., *July 14, 1898.*
(Received 3 55 p. m.)

ADJUTANT-GENERAL, U. S. ARMY, *Washington, D. C.:*

Troops placed on board steamers *City of Puebla* and *Peru* to-day, and I await answer to my request for instructions in telegram of yesterday.

OTIS,
Major-General, U. S. Volunteers, Commanding.

SAN FRANCISCO, CAL., *July 14, 1898.*
(Received 4.02 p. m.)

ADJUTANT-GENERAL, U. S. ARMY, *Washington, D. C.:*

Colonel Barber is a good soldier and says he can not object to any service which Government assigns. He is preparing his regiment for Honolulu and will doubtless sail with a portion of it in a very few days.

OTIS,
Major-General, U. S. Volunteers, Commanding.

SAN FRANCISCO, CAL., *July 14, 1898.*
(Received 8.01 p. m.)

ADJUTANT-GENERAL, U. S. ARMY, *Washington, D. C.:*

Your telegram of to-day just received and not understood. Former expeditions have had sailing orders how to proceed, where convoys are to be met, and ultimate destination. The steamers *Peru* and *Puebla* are loaded and ready to start under orders given men to go with them and stop at Honolulu and there await for remainder of expedition, to leave 23d instant, and disposition of officers, property, and freight has been made accordingly. All orders were issued yesterday and to-day for the loading of remaining vessels, and if steamer *St. Paul* arrives within next two days the last vessel can leave here by 21st unless ordered to the contrary. I will sail on *Peru* to-morrow or Saturday and await at Honolulu for the remaining transports, as intended, but request definite sailing orders.

OTIS, *Major-General.*

ADJUTANT-GENERAL'S OFFICE,
Washington, July 14, 1898—9.30 p. m.

Major-General OTIS, *San Francisco, Cal.:*

The Secretary War is glad you are going to be able to stop at Honolulu, and approves your going to-morrow. The impression obtained that possibly this would delay the expedition. To avoid this the telegram this afternoon was sent you, and was not in any way intended to interfere with your plans already made. Get away accordingly, and may good fortune go with you.

By order Secretary War:

H. C. CORBIN, *Adjutant-General.*

BUTTE, MONT., *July 16, 1898.*
(Received 4.30 p. m.)

Hon. R. A. ALGER, *Secretary War, Washington, D. C.:*

First Regiment Montana Volunteer Infantry is ordered to sail for Manila on 23d instant. Please permit no change to be made in these orders which will leave our regiment behind. Answer.

LEE MANTLE.

SAN FRANCISCO, CAL., *July 16, 1898.*
(Received 6.21 p. m.

SECRETARY OF WAR, *Washington, D. C.:*

I request permission to join my regiment at Manila.

JAMES E. BARNETT,
Lieutenant-Colonel Tenth Pennsylvania Infantry, U. S. Volunteers.

ADJUTANT-GENERAL'S OFFICE,
Washington, July 17, 1898—12.35 p. m.

Hon. LEE MANTLE, *Butte, Mont.:*

Your telegram 16th to Secretary War. No change contemplated here.

H. C. CORBIN, *Adjutant-General.*

CAMP MERRITT, CAL., *July 17, 1898.*
(Received July 18, 1898—1.50 a. m.)

ADJUTANT-GENERAL OF THE ARMY, *Washington, D. C.*

SIR: I am appealed to by the officers and men of the Seventh California Infantry, and by a multitude of the regiment's friends, to urge the selection of that regiment for early dispatch to Manila. I do not mean to interfere with the orders of my superiors, who have already chosen the troops for the fourth expedition, but, without exceeding my authority I will earnestly request the President, through the Secretary of War, to order the early advance of this faithful, efficient, well-disciplined, and excellent regiment, and I earnestly recommend the charter of the necessary vessels for that purpose.

HARRISON GRAY OTIS,
Brigadier-General, U. S. Volunteers,
Commanding Third Brigade.

WAR DEPARTMENT,
Washington, July 18, 1898.

SIR: I have the honor to acknowledge the receipt of your letter of the 6th instant, inclosing copy of a dispatch dated May 12, from our consul at Manila, relative to the political situation in the Philippine Islands.

Very respectfully,

R. A. ALGER, *Secretary of War.*

The SECRETARY OF STATE.

ADJUTANT-GENERAL'S OFFICE,
Washington, July 18, 1898.

Major-General MERRIAM,
Commanding Department California, San Francisco, Cal.:

Secretary War directs that any portion of troops originally assigned to the Philippine expedition remaining in San Francisco report to you for purposes of further equipment, drill, and discipline. Secretary War further directs that Camp Merritt be abandoned and these troops be placed in camp on the Presidio Reservation. This will be authority for the commanding officer of these troops to report as herein directed. Acknowledge receipt.

H. C. CORBIN, *Adjutant-General.*

WASHINGTON, D. C., *July 18, 1898.*
(Received 1.35 p. m.)

Hon. GEORGE D. MEIKLEJOHN,
Assistant Secretary of War, Washington, D. C.:

I shall feel personally obliged if you will direct that the recruits for the Tenth Regiment, Pennsylvania Volunteers, now in San Francisco, be immediately equipped for service, and that Lieut. Col. James E. Barnett, of the same regiment, be ordered to immediately proceed to Manila with the recruits as soon as transportation can be provided. I make this as a personal request. Kindly reply by wire.

BOIES PENROSE.

SAN FRANCISCO, CAL., *July 18, 1898.*
(Received 8.32 p. m.)

ADJUTANT-GENERAL, U. S. ARMY, *Washington, D. C.:*

Complying telegram directing report to be rendered regarding transports: *Pennsylvania* sails 19th, 54 officers, 1,294 enlisted men, 1,280 rifles, caliber .45, and 200 rounds ammunition per man.

MERRIAM, *Major-General, Commanding.*

SAN FRANCISCO, CAL., *July 18, 1898.*
(Received 9.27 p. m.)

Hon. R. A. ALGER, *Secretary of War, Washington, D. C.:*

Seventh California Infantry has been in camp in San Francisco since May 7. It is splendidly equipped, drilled, and disciplined. It was once ordered aboard ship to go to the Philippines and orders subsequently revoked. Officers and men greatly disappointed being withheld from active service. I earnestly hope you can consistently order them to Philippines by next transport. Your many California friends will greatly appreciate your interest in their behalf. Please answer.

GEORGE C. PERKINS.

SAN FRANCISCO, CAL., *July 18, 1898.*
(Received 9.30 p. m.)

Adjutant-General CORBIN, *U. S. Army, Washington, D. C.:*

Your many friends in California earnestly hope you can comply with request Seventh Regiment California Infantry wired Secretary War to-day.

GEORGE C. PERKINS.

SAN FRANCISCO, CAL., *July 18, 1898.*
(Received 9.51 p. m.)

ADJUTANT-GENERAL, U. S. ARMY, *Washington, D. C.:*

Telegram reference new Washington battalion and abandonment of Camp Merritt as assignment to me expeditionary forces received.

MERRIAM, *Major-General, Commanding.*

SAN FRANCISCO, CAL., *July 18, 1898.*
(Received 11.28 p.m.)

Hon. R. A. ALGER, *Washington, D. C.:*

Will it not be possible to have Seventh California Regiment ordered West Indies or Manila? They are equipped and personnel equal to any in service. Were among first mustered in. Very anxious to go to the front.

U. S. GRANT, Jr.

ADJUTANT-GENERAL'S OFFICE,
Washington, July 19, 1898.

General MERRIAM, *San Francisco, Cal.:*

What troops—give letters of companies—sailed with General Otis 15th instant?

H. C. CORBIN, *Adjutant-General.*

ADJUTANT-GENERAL'S OFFICE,
Washington, July 20, 1898—12.30 a. m.

COMMANDING GENERAL, DEPARTMENT OF CALIFORNIA,
San Francisco, Cal.:

Report by telegraph the number and strength of each regiment now in your command originally intended for the Philippine expedition.

By order Secretary War:

H. C. CORBIN, *Adjutant-General.*

SAN FRANCISCO, CAL., *July 20, 1898.*
(Received 3.45 p.m.)

ADJUTANT-GENERAL CORBIN, *Washington, D. C.:*

Complete Philippine organizations still here as follows: United States Volunteer Engineer battalion, ten officers, 347 men; battalion California Heavy Artillery, 13 officers, 453 men; Twentieth Kansas, 46 officers, 1,243 men; First Tennessee, 46 officers, 1,257 men; Seventh California, 40 officers, 1,232 men; Fifty-first Iowa, 50 officers, 1,336 men; First South Dakota, 45 officers, 998 men. Total, 250 officers and 6,868 men. Besides these, the First Washington and Eighth California, both good full regiments, will be available here for field service shortly.

MERRIAM, *Major-General.*

SAN FRANCISCO, CAL., *July 20, 1898.*
(Received 7.10 p.m.)

ADJUTANT-GENERAL, U. S. ARMY, *Washington, D. C.:*

Following organizations sailed with General Otis, 15th instant: C, E, G, I, K, and L, Fourth Cavalry; D and G, Sixth Artillery; G, I, K, L, and M, Fourteenth Infantry. Balance were detachment Signal Corps, recruits, etc.

MERRIAM, *Major-General.*

NAGASAKI, *received July 21, 1898—8.50 a. m.*

ADJUTANT-GENERAL, *Washington:*

Cavite, July 21.—Steamer *City Sydney* sails San Francisco to-day.

ANDERSON, *Commanding.*

HEADQUARTERS DEPARTMENT OF THE PACIFIC,
Honolulu, Hawaiian Islands, July 6, 1898. (Received July 21, 1898.)
The ADJUTANT-GENERAL, U. S. ARMY, *Washington, D. C.*

SIR: I have the honor to suggest the steamer *Newport*, in which I am now proceeding to the Phillippine Islands, as a vessel admirably adapted in every way for one of the permanent fleet of transports which, I have been officially informed, it is the intention of the War Department to furnish for the use of this expedition.

This vessel has recently had her boilers and engines thoroughly overhauled and replaced, and will probably not require repairs in that direction for some time come.

The inclosed tables show the more than ordinary facilities for ventilation possessed by this vessel and the economical expenditure of coal at a speed of 10 knots. The ship is capable of making 14 knots, and she is undoubtedly a very excellent sea boat, as indicated by her behavior in a severe blow which we encountered soon after leaving San Francisco.

I desire to call the attention of the War Department particularly to this last quality of the ship, as this is now the season of typhoons in the Philippines, and it would be unwise to navigate in those waters with transports loaded with troops, unless the ships were in every way fit to ride out a storm of great severity. For a short run this ship could carry almost a full regiment.

For the reasons above stated I particularly recommend the purchase or hire of this ship for the permanent use of the expedition in carrying troops to and from the outlying islands, and that authority may be given me (by cable) to retain her on arrival at Cavite, if I consider it desirable to do so.

Very respectfully,
W. MERRITT,
Major-General Commanding.

FACILITIES FOR VENTILATION, STEAMSHIP NEWPORT.

Forward of midships, in the steerage deck, there are three hatches; one is a hatch 14 feet square. There are two companion ways 5 by 4, and one about 4 feet square. Besides, there are two 14-inch iron ventilators—all forward. The side hatches on the quarters are so situated that they can be left open in any kind of weather. Then she has, on the deck below, capacity in the shape of cargo ports for throwing the whole side open. There are also ventilators in the aft part of the ship—one of 24 inches, and 2 of about 14 inches. She is well supplied with windsails—two 3 feet in diameter, and one of 2 feet. There are no bulkheads in the cargo space on the steerage deck, and therefore there is free passage for currents of air. There are on this deck deadhead lights of about 10 inches, which can be opened in fair weather. The cargo ports above referred to may be opened when the vessel is lying in port, and give perfect ventilation in the steerage deck, and the upper portion can be opened at sea in smooth weather.

Table showing economy in the consumption of coal, steamship Newport.

Knots.	Tons per day.
10.2	28.8
10.96	30
10.27	32
11.33	27
10.10	28
10.3	20
63.16	165.8
10.52	27.6

Average: Knots, 10.52; consumption, 27.3.

U. S. S. MOHICAN (3D RATE),
Honolulu, Hawaiian Islands, July 6, 1898. (Received July 21, 1898.)

SIR: Two army stragglers from the second expedition to Manila received on board this vessel for rations have this day been transferred to the troopship *Indiana.*

Very respectfully,
G. M. BOOK,
Commander, U. S. Navy, Commanding.

The SECRETARY OF THE NAVY,
Navy Department, Washington, D. C.

DEPARTMENT OF STATE, *Washington, July 21, 1898.*

The SECRETARY OF WAR.

SIR: I have the honor to apprise you of the receipt of a telegram from Mr. Rounsevelle Wildman, consul-general of the United States at Hongkong, China, reading as follows:

"CONSULATE-GENERAL OF THE UNITED STATES,
"*Hongkong, July 21, 1898.* (Received 6.23 a. m.)
"DAY, *Washington:*
"Second expedition arrived Manila Sunday. *Monterey* not arrived.
"WILDMAN."

A copy of this telegram has been given to the Secretary of the Navy.

Respectfully, yours,
WILLIAM R. DAY.

NAVY DEPARTMENT, *Washington, July 21, 1898.*

MEMORANDUM FOR THE WAR DEPARTMENT.

The following telegram received to-day from Admiral Dewey:

"CAVITE, *July 17.*

"Situation unchanged. Second army detachment arrived to-day. All well on board. The health of the squadron continues good. No sickness whatever. In view of information received, shall retain *City of Pekin* and *China* as auxiliaries. Shall return other transports to the United States as soon as possible."

JOHN D. LONG, *Secretary.*

ADJUTANT-GENERAL'S OFFICE, *Washington, July 21, 1898.*

Maj. Gen. HENRY C. MERRIAM,
Commanding Department of California, San Francisco, Cal.

SIR: I have the honor to inform you that I have forwarded by to-day's mail, in two mail bags, 1,200 copies of Customs Tariff and Regulations for the Philippine Islands, addressed to Maj. Gen. Wesley Merritt, commanding Department of the Pacific, Manila, Philippine Islands, in your care, which please cause to be safely forwarded to General Merritt at the earliest practicable date, and inform this office of the date of shipment.

Very respectfully,
H. C. CORBIN, *Adjutant-General.*

P. S.—The publication referred to is a confidential one.

BURLINGTON, IOWA, *July 21, 1898.*
(Received 3.47 p. m.)

Honorable SECRETARY OF WAR, *Washington, D. C.:*

Not one Iowa regiment mentioned in any expedition against Spaniards. Special demands in this State for assignment of Fifty-first Iowa to next expedition to Manila. Such orders would give great satisfaction in State.

JOHN GEAR.

CAMP MERRITT, *San Francisco, Cal., July, 16, 1898.*
(Received July 22, 1898.)

Hon. R. A. ALGER, *Secretary of War, Washington, D. C.*

SIR: As per telegram this day sent, I hereby make application for permission to rejoin my regiment, the Tenth Pennsylvania Infantry, U. S. Volunteers, at Manila.

I have here 248 recruits which I have organized into a provisional battalion under command of Lieut. C. C. Crowell. Their equipment and drill will proceed as satisfactorily as if I were present, and consequently I feel that my duty lies with my regiment.

I have the honor to be, your most obedient servant,

JAMES E. BARNETT,
Lieutenant Colonel Tenth Pennsylvania U. S. Volunteers.

TOPEKA, KANS., *July 22, 1898,*
(Received 12.16 p. m.)

Honorable SECRETARY OF WAR, *Washington, D. C.:*

Twentieth Kansas disappointed at not being sent to Manila. Say California and Iowa assigned ahead of them. They are as well drilled and as efficient as other regiments. The people of Kansas would be pleased to have you look into this matter and send the Kansas regiment in its turn.

CHARLES CURTIS.

DEPARTMENT OF STATE,
Washington, July 22, 1898.

The Honorable, the SECRETARY OF WAR.

SIR: Referring to my letter of the 14th instant, inclosing a copy of a dispatch from our minister to Hawaii, in which he called attention to the urgent necessity of providing for officers and men of the expeditionary forces sent to the Philippines, who have been or may be left behind at Honolulu, I have the honor to inclose herewith, for your information, a copy of a dispatch from the minister reporting the action taken by Major-General Merritt to meet the emergencies set forth in the minister's earlier dispatch.

Respectfully, yours, WILLIAM R. DAY.

[Inclosure: From Mr. Sewall, No. 180, July 8, 1898.]

No. 180.] LEGATION OF THE UNITED STATES,
Honolulu, July 8, 1898.

Hon. W. R. DAY, *Secretary of State, Washington, D. C.*

SIR: Referring to my dispatch No. 176, of June 28, I have the honor to report that having called the attention of Major-General Merritt to the needs it presents, he at once took steps to provide for them. Funds will be furnished for the care of the sick left here, and arrangements have been effected for the establishment of a Government hospital here, which will be in operation so soon as a building which has been leased can receive necessary alterations, and the equipment of supplies and medical staff can be brought here.

The Red Cross Society will continue its work to the extent of its powers.

I have the honor to be, sir, your obedient servant,

HAROLD M. SEWALL.

DEPARTMENT OF STATE,
Washington, July 22, 1898.

The Honorable, the SECRETARY OF WAR.

SIR: I have the honor to inclose herewith for your information copies of dispatches from our minister at Honolulu, reporting the arrival at that place on the 5th–7th instant of the third expeditionary force of American troops sent to the Philippines.

Respectfully, yours,

WILLIAM R. DAY.

[Inclosures: From minister to Hawaii, Nos. 181 and 182, of July 8, 1898.]

No. 181.]
LEGATION OF THE UNITED STATES,
Honolulu, Hawaiian Islands, July 8, 1898.

Hon. W. R. DAY, *Secretary of State, Washington, D. C.*

SIR: I have the honor to report that the United States troop ships *Ohio* and the *City of Para*, of the third expedition to the Philippines, arrived here on the 5th instant, the *Morgan City* and the *Indiana* the 6th, and the *Newport* and *Valencia* the 7th instant.

The troops of this expedition have been received with the same hospitality that has been so generously extended to the previous expeditions.

After taking on 1,812¼ tons of coal, the ships left the harbor at noon. To-night they have returned, two of them within the harbor, the *Indiana* being in tow.

I have the honor to be, sir, your obedient servant,

HAROLD M. SEWALL.

No. 182.]
LEGATION OF THE UNITED STATES,
Honolulu, Hawaiian Islands, July 8, 1898.

Hon. W. R. DAY, *Secretary of State.*

SIR: Referring to my dispatch No. 181, of to-day's date, I have the the honor to report that the United States steamer transport *Newport* did not return with the other transports, but has continued on her course.

General Merritt informed me yesterday that it was his intention to proceed with the *Newport* at good speed and overtake the *Monterey;* and this is, I believe, what he has done.

I have the honor to be, sir, your obedient servant,

HAROLD M. SEWALL.

SAN FRANCISCO, CAL., *July 25, 1898.*
(Received 10.18 p. m.)

General CORBIN, *Adjutant-General U. S. Army, Washington, D. C.:*

Secretary of War has intimated Seventh Regiment California Volunteers, that have been in camp since first of May, can be sent in next expedition to Manila. May I venture to urge you to kindly expedite the detail, and thereby favor a splendid regiment of soldiers.

GEO. C. PERKINS.

Los Angeles, Cal., *July 26, 1898.*
(Received 8.16 p. m.)

Adjt. Gen. H. C. Corbin, *Washington, D. C.:*

Much feeling with reference to Seventh Regiment, now at San Francisco; criticisms extend outside military circles. If possible, kindly aid in procuring permission to sail.

Stephen M. White.

Adjutant-General's Office,
Washington, July 26, 1898—11.15 p. m.

General Merriam, *San Francisco, Cal.:*

There is great pressure being brought to bear upon the Department for the shipment of the Seventh California to the Philippines. Secretary of War would be glad, if you can do so with due regard to the rights of others and plans already made, to hasten the departure of this regiment.

H. C. Corbin, *Adjutant-General.*

Quartermaster-General's Office,
Washington, July 27, 1898.

Brig. Gen. H. C. Corbin.

Sir: Referring to attached communication from General Merritt respecting the steamer *Newport*, I have the honor to state that steps have been taken to ascertain the price at which this ship can be purchased; that such price is so much in excess of her intrinsic value that it would not be advantageous for the Government to purchase her. She is now chartered at a price of $1,000 per day and General Merritt can retain her as long as may be absolutely necessary, but it is hoped that two ships recently purchased by the Government, the *Scandia* and *Arizona*, will give General Merritt adequate transportation facilities for the permanent use of the expedition in carrying troops to and from the outlying islands.

Yours, respectfully,

Frank J. Hecker,
Colonel and Quartermaster Volunteers, Chief of Transportation.

San Francisco, Cal., *July 27, 1898.*
(Received 3.08 p. m.)

Adjutant-General Corbin, *Washington, D. C.:*

Referring to your telegram regarding Seventh California, I found expeditionary camp here filled with odd detachments of recruits and battalions of broken regiments. My selections for embarkation are made with a view of restoring organization as a matter of first importance. As shipments continue the Seventh California can take precedence if desired.

Merriam, *Major-General.*

Adjutant-General's Office,
Washington, July 27, 1898—3.30 p. m.

General Merriam, *San Francisco, Cal.:*

As shipments continue, Secretary War desires that the Seventh California be given precedence as far as can be done without interfering with arrangements you have already made,

H. C. Corbin, *Adjutant-General.*

ADJUTANT-GENERAL'S OFFICE,
Washington, July 27, 1898.

General MERRIAM, *San Francisco, Cal.:*

Secretary of War desires to report as to whether Lieut. Col. James E. Barnett, Tenth Regiment, Pennsylvania Volunteers, at Camp Merritt, in charge of recruits for his regiment, has been sent to join his regiment.

H. C. CORBIN, *Adjutant-General.*

SAN FRANCISCO, CAL., *July 27, 1898.*
(Received 7.31 p. m.)

Adjutant-General CORBIN, *Washington, D. C.:*

Replying to your telegram this date, Lieut. Col. James E. Barnett, Tenth Pennsylvania, is still on duty at Camp Merritt.

MERRIAM, *General.*

ADJUTANT-GENERAL'S OFFICE,
Washington, July 29, 1898.

The COMMANDING GENERAL, EIGHTH ARMY CORPS
AND DEPARTMENT OF THE PACIFIC.
(Via San Francisco, Cal.)

SIR: Referring to your communication of the 6th instant, suggesting the steamer *Newport* as a vessel admirably adapted for one of the permanent fleet of transports, the Secretary of War desires me to inform you that steps have been taken to ascertain the price at which this ship can be purchased; that such price is so much in excess of her intrinsic value that it would not be advantageous for the Government to purchase her; and that she is now chartered at a price of $1,000 per day, and you can retain her as long as may be absolutely necessary, but it is hoped that two ships recently purchased by the Government, the *Scandia* and *Arizona*, will give you adequate transportation facilities for the permanent use of the expedition in carrying troops to and from the outlying islands.

Very respectfully,

H. C. CORBIN, *Adjutant-General.*

SAN FRANCISCO, CAL., *July 29, 1898.*
(Received 4.38 p. m.)

ADJUTANT-GENERAL, U. S. ARMY, *Washington, D. C.:*

Steamer *St. Paul* sails to-day for Philippine Islands with companies C, H, I, and K, First South Dakota Volunteers, Lieutenant-Colonel Stover commanding; 310 recruits, Thirteenth Minnesota Volunteers; 155 recruits, First Colorado Volunteers; detachment Medical Department, etc. Total, 25 officers, 814 enlisted men, 3 civilians, 794 rifles, caliber .45, and 279 rounds ammunition per man. One million rounds ammunition shipped on *Rio de Janeiro* 22d instant and not reported heretofore.

MERRIAM, *Major-General.*

HONGKONG, *received July 30, 1898—1.03 a. m.*

ADJUTANT-GENERAL, U. S. ARMY, *Washington:*

Cavite, July 25. Arrived to-day about 12. Health of commands good. Remainder fleet four days in rear. All troops assigned me will probably be needed.

MERRITT, *Major-General, Commanding.*

ROME, *July 31, 1898.* (Via France.)

Monsignor MARTINELLI, *Apostolic Delegate, Washington*:

The vicar apostolic of Hongkong telegraphs that the monks prisoners of the rebels are in danger of death. The Holy Father wishes that you take steps at once to have the Government of the United States prevent this evil.

M. CARDINAL RAMPOLLA.

ROME, *July 31, 1898.* (Via France.)

Monsignor MARTINELLI, *Apostolic Delegate, Washington*:

Those monks are in Cavite, Philippines.

M. CARDINAL RAMPOLLA.

HONGKONG, *received August 1, 1898—4.05 a. m.*

ADJUTANT GENERAL, *Washington:*

Situation difficult. Insurgents have announced independent government; some are unfriendly, fearing they will not be permitted to enter Manila with my troops. Will join Dewey in note demanding surrender, with assurance of protection from insurgents.

It may be important have my whole force before attacking if necessary to hold insurgents while we fight Spanish.

MERRITT.

ADJUTANT-GENERAL'S OFFICE,
Washington, August 1, 1898.

General MERRITT, *Manila, Philippines:*

Information has been received that monks and other prisoners in hands of the insurgents at Cavite are in danger of being put to death. This should not be permitted if you are in position to prevent it.

H. C. CORBIN, *Adjutant-General.*

SAN FRANCISCO, CAL., *August 1, 1898.*
(Received 5.56 p. m.)

Hon. R. A. ALGER, *Secretary of War, Washington, D. C.:*

The Eighth California Volunteers, being thoroughly organized, equipped, and drilled, are anxious to be ordered into active service at earliest possible moment. Can not this be done? Please answer.

W. S. LEAKE, *Manager Call.*

SAN FRANCISCO, CAL., *August 1, 1898.*
(Received 11.23 p. m.)

Hon. R. A. ALGER, *Secretary of War, Washington, D. C.:*

The Eighth California Volunteers are anxious to be ordered into active service as soon as possible. This regiment is well drilled and equipped and in perfect health. Can you not expedite the matter?

JOHN D. SPRECKELS.

ADJUTANT-GENERAL'S OFFICE,
Washington, August 2, 1898—12.15 a. m.

General MERRIAM,
Commanding Department of California, San Francisco, Cal.:

The President directs that if any of the military force of the island of Hawaii desires to become a part of your volunteer army, that you are authorized to organize, not to exceed a battalion of infantry, nominating the officers, and causing the officers and men to be mustered into the service, and have them to report to Colonel Benham for duty.

By order of the Secretary of War:

H. C. CORBIN, *Adjutant-General.*

SAN FRANCISCO, CAL., *August 2, 1898.*
(Received 1.40 p. m.)

Gen. R. A. ALGER, *Secretary of War, Washington, D. C.:*

I have a brigade of infantry which would be ready for Manila in three weeks if accepted.

MATTHEW SCHLAUDEIKER.

SANTA ROSA, CAL., *August 2, 1898.*
(Received 4.12 p. m.)

Hon. R. A. ALGER, *Secretary of War, Washington, D. C.:*

Strong California influences desire Eighth Regiment California U. S. Volunteers, now unattached, be given opportunity for service at front. Regiment well drilled, equipped, and of exceptionally high personnel, and anxious for active service. Can you not do something for them?

J. A. BARHAM, *M. C.*

SAN FRANCISCO, *August 2, 1898.*
(Received 4.20 p. m.)

Hon. R. A. ALGER, *Secretary of War, Washington, D. C.:*

The California State Red Cross Society feels the urgent need of more nurses at Philippines, and asks for transportation for ten trained male nurses on *Arizona* or *Scandia*, and 12 feet square space for supplies to establish and maintain hospital at Manila.

Mrs. W. B. HARRINGTON, *President.*
Mrs. O. F. LONG,
M. H. HECHT,
CHARLES SONTAG,
Committee.

CARSON, NEV., *August 2, 1898.*
(Received 8.03 p. m.)

ASSISTANT SECRETARY MEIKLEJOHN, *Washington, D. C.:*

First Battalion Nevada Infantry Volunteers, 415 strong, in fine condition, and anxious for service; telegraph if you can send them to Manila or elsewhere and when.

WM. M. STEWART.

DEPARTMENT OF STATE,
Washington, August 3, 1898.

The Honorable, the SECRETARY OF WAR.

SIR: Referring to my confidential letter of the 28th ultimo, inclosing a copy of a dispatch from our minister to Hawaii reporting a delay in the departure of the U. S. S. *Monadnock* from Honolulu, and which was accompanied also by a copy of a memorandum on the Ladrone and Caroline Islands, prepared by the minister, I have the honor to inclose herewith a copy of a revised memorandum on the same subject, which he desires to have substituted for the former one.

Respectfully, yours,

WILLIAM R. DAY.

[Inclosure: From Mr. Sewall, No. 185, July 19, 1898, with accompanying memorandum.]

No. 185.]
LEGATION OF THE UNITED STATES,
Honolulu, Hawaiian Islands, July 19, 1898.

Hon. WILLIAM R. DAY, *Secretary of State,*
Washington, D. C.

SIR: Referring to my confidential dispatch of July 8, 1898, I have the honor to inclose a revised memorandum on the Caroline and Ladrone groups of islands, which I respectfully ask may replace that on the files of the Department.

I have the honor to be, sir, your obedient servant,

HAROLD M. SEWALL.

MEMORANDUM ON THE CAROLINE AND LADRONE GROUPS.

The only Spanish colony at Ponape is located on a point in the harbor sloping gradually toward the water, the site of an American mission, destroyed by the Spanish at the time of a native uprising. A wall of adobe and coral surrounds the inland portion of the colony from water to water. There are no defenses on the front or water portion of the colony. Outside this wall there was a moat in progress, with a few watchtowers and sentries, and within this a small fort, evidently built for storage of ammunition and place of refuge in case of attack by natives. There are no mounted guns on the wall nor on the water front or landing side of the colony. On the inner fort there are some small guns, evidently old-fashioned. No access is allowed here. The residences of the governor-general and all the Spanish colony are on the point of land within this large inclosure. There are 200 Spanish officers and men, a captain being the ranking officer.

In the harbor there are what are known as the inner and outer anchorage. Beacons are on all the numerous shoals in the harbor. The inner anchorage is the nearest to the colony; outside of this a larger and deeper anchorage, and within a mile, anchorage for a whole fleet. To land at the colony in a boat a straight course must be made from the inner anchorage until the rear portion of the colony bears right abeam; then steer direct for the landing, otherwise a boat is likely to ground in shoal water unless at the highest tides. The Spanish had begun a boat passage from the colony to the inner anchorage, but that is no sign that it will ever be finished.

In this inner anchorage is usually anchored the Spanish gunboat *Quiros*, somewhat similar to the *Callao* recently captured by Admiral Dewey at Manila. The *Quiros* is a wooden vessel of not over 400 tons, officered by a captain and two lieutenants. She carries 1 rifled gun on each side and 1 on her stern, and on her bow a larger gun. The officers for the most part of the time are on shore.

All the natives of Ponape are well armed with knives, Winchester rifles, and ammunition, and are violently hostile to the Spanish.

The Island of Hogoleu, Rouk, or Turk has probably the finest harbor of all, with good passage, with short intervals, around the entire reef, which is 80 miles in circumference. There are few coral patches in this lagoon and the water is deep, say from 20 to 40 fathoms, and still deeper in places. The ships of the world could anchor there at one time. The surrounding reef is low and dangerous, with a few trees or shrubbery on it in places. The islands in the lagoon, on board a vessel approaching from any direction, can be seen a long time before the surrounding reef, as some of them are eight and ten hundred feet high.

The Island of Yap, northeast of the Pelews, has an excellent harbor and an inner and outer anchorage. The inner anchorage has water deep enough for any craft, but is very contracted. There are no Spanish fortifications here of any sort. A Spanish governor is here, with a body guard of native police.

The same description applies to the Guam of the Ladrones, but here is a large town of 4,000 people. A large ship can not anchor very near to the island proper or the boat landing. There is a boat landing on the outside of reef, near town. A bold headland marks the right side of the entrance, and has on it what appears to have been a fort.

The *Saturnus*, a Spanish unarmed merchant steamer of about 1,000 tons, runs regularly between Manila, Yap, Guam, and Ponape, taking about six weeks for the round trip. When the American missionary vessel *Morning Star* was at Ponape, the 28th of February last, the *Saturnus* was then daily expected and several days overdue.

The weather about the groups is not variable, the trades blowing quite regularly from the east the year around; November, December, and January are the months of wet and squally weather.

In regard to coal, it is to be had at Jaluit, in the Marshall Group, of the German firm, and at Butaritari, of the Gilbert Group, of a Chinese firm, which keeps on hand a good quality, and the price charged is about $12.50 a ton.

OAKLAND, CAL., *August 3, 1898.*
(Received 2.25 p. m.)

Hon. R. A. ALGER, *Secretary of War, Washington, D. C.:*

The Eighth Regiment California Volunteer Infantry, unassigned, anxious for active service at front. It is well drilled, equipped, of excellent personnel, both officers and men, and in good health; also backed by strong California influences. Can you not help them?

S. G. HILBORN.

SAN FRANCISCO, CAL., *August 4, 1898.*
(Received 5.42 p. m.)

ADJUTANT-GENERAL, *Washington, D. C.:*

Light Battery C, Utah Volunteer Artillery, has reported at these headquarters. What disposition is intended for these troops?

MERRIAM, *Major-General Volunteers.*

ADJUTANT-GENERAL'S OFFICE,
Washington, D. C., August 4, 1898.

COMMANDING GENERAL, DEPARTMEMT OF CALIFORNIA,
San Francisco, Cal.:

Make any use you can of Light Battery C, Utah Volunteers. If you have transportation, and battery is in serviceable condition, you may send it to the Philippines; otherwise, dispose of it the best you can.

By order Secretary War:

H. C. CORBIN, *Adjutant-General.*

DEPARTMENT OF STATE,
Washington, August 5, 1898.

Hon. RUSSELL A. ALGER, *Secretary of War.*

MY DEAR SIR: The Secretary of the Chinese legation called this morning to say that Mr. Chin has been appointed by the Chinese Government as its consul at Manila, and to request that Mr. Chin be allowed freely to pass into that city. I assured him that I had no doubt that Mr. Chin would be permitted to go to his post without hindrance. If this view is in accordance with your own, may I ask you to communicate it in such manner as you deem proper to the military authorities at Manila.

Very truly, yours,
WILLIAM R. DAY.

ADJUTANT-GENERAL'S OFFICE,
Washington, August 6, 1898.

Mrs. W. B. HARRINGTON,
President California State Red Cross Society, San Francisco, Cal.:

Secretary of War has referred your telegram of August 2 to commanding general Department California.

H. C. CORBIN, *Adjutant-General.*

COLD SPRING, PUTNAM COUNTY, N. Y., *August 6, 1898.*

Major-General CORBIN, *Washington, D. C.:*

Will be very gratified if my old regiment, Twelfth New York, can be ordered to Merritt. Please do it if possible.

D. BUTTERFIELD.

ADJUTANT-GENERAL'S OFFICE,
Washington, August 6, 1898—8.50 p. m.

Gen. DANIEL BUTTERFIELD,
Cold Spring, Putnam County, N. Y.:

It is not probable any more troops will be ordered to Merritt. If so, the Twelfth will have consideration.

H. C. CORBIN, *Adjutant-General.*

ADJUTANT-GENERAL'S OFFICE,
Washington, August 7, 1898.

General MERRITT, *Manila, via Hongkong:*

At the request of the Secretary of State, you will allow Mr. Chin, the Chinese consul, to pass in and out of Manila as freely as the circumstances will admit, and extend to him the courtesies shown the most favored of diplomatic agents.

By order Secretary War:

H. C. CORBIN, *Adjutant-General.*

WAR DEPARTMENT,
Washington, August 7, 1898.

Hon. WILLIAM R. DAY, *Secretary of State.*

SIR: In reply to your letter of August 5, I beg to inform you that the following cable has this day been sent, via Hongkong, to Major-General Merritt:

"At the request of the Secretary of State, you will allow Mr. Chin, the Chinese consul, to pass in and out of Manila as freely as the circumstances will admit, and extend to him the courtesies shown the most favored of diplomatic agents."

R. A. ALGER, *Secretary of War.*

HONGKONG, *received Washington, August 9, 1898—7.28 a. m.*
ADJUTANT-GENERAL, *Washington:*

MacArthur's troops arrived 31st. No epidemic sickness; five deaths. Lieutenant Kerr, Engineers, died spinal meningitis. Landing at camp delayed account high surf. Artillery outposts behaved well. Held position. Unnecessary to call out brigade. To gain approach to city Greene's outposts were advanced to continue line from the Camino Real to beach on Sunday night. Spanish attacked sharply. Spanish loss rumored heavy. Our loss, killed, Tenth Pennsylvania Infantry, John Brady, jr., Walter E. Brown, William E. Brinton, Jacob Hull, jr., Jesse Noss, William H. Stillwagon; First California, Maurice Justh; Third Artillery, Ell Dawson; First Colorado, Fred E. Springstead. Seriously wounded, Tenth Pennsylvania, Sergt. Alva M. Walters, Privates Lee Snyder, Victor H. Holmes, C. S. Carter, Arthur J. Johnson; First California, Capt. R. Richter, Private C. J. Edwards; Third Artillery, Privates Charles Winfield, J. A. McIlroth. Thirty-eight slightly wounded.

MERRITT.

SAN FRANCISCO, *August 9, 1898.*
(Received 4.50 p. m.)
ADJUTANT-GENERAL, *Washington, D. C.:*

Government transports *Scandia* and *Arizona* will sail about Saturday with Seventh California Regiment, remainder of Eighteenth and Twenty-third Infantry, and all recruit detachments. This will leave expeditionary troops still here as follows: Twentieth Kansas, First Tennessee, Fifty-first Iowa, Eighth California, battalion California Heavy Artillery, Light Battery C, Utah volunteers; aggregate, about 6,000 men. So far as I am informed, Quartermaster's Department is making no provision for transportation of these troops. What action is desired.

MERRIAM, *Major-General.*

SAN FRANCISCO, CAL., *August 9, 1898.*
(Received 8.31 p. m.)
ADJUTANT-GENERAL, *Washington, D. C.:*

Company E and 44 men, Company D, First New York, Captain Pickard commanding, sail for Honolulu on steamer *Mariposa* Wednesday night. Total, 4 officers, 150 men; 147 rifles, caliber .45; 40 rounds ammunition per man. Supply of 200 per man will go on next steamer.

MERRIAM, *Major-General.*

SAN FRANCISCO, CAL., *August 9, 1898.*
(Received 9.28 p. m.)
ADJUTANT-GENERAL, *Washington, D. C.:*

Report Companies C, I, K, L, M, First New York Volunteers, Major Chase commanding, 1 officer and 38 men; Company K, Second Volunteer Engineers; total, 589 officers and men, sailed on steamer *Charles Nelson*. Companies I, L, M, and remainder of K, Captain Rickon commanding, total, 239 officers and men, sailed on steamer *Lakme* for Honolulu August 6. Total rifles, 889, caliber .45; 40 rounds ammunition per man. Previous report has not been made.

MERRIAM, *Major-General.*

ADJUTANT-GENERAL'S OFFICE,
Washington, August 9, 1898—11.55 p. m.

General MERRIAM, *San Francisco, Cal.:*

The Secretary of War instructs me to inform you that it is desirable that all the expeditionary force remaining at San Francisco be put under way for the Philippines at the earliest possible day. A report of what can be done is desired.

H. C. CORBIN, *Adjutant-General.*

SAN FRANCISCO, CAL., *August 10, 1898.*
(Received 9.30 p. m.)

Adjutant-General CORBIN, *Washington, D. C.:*

Regarding shipping of remainder Philippine troops, I believe returning transports promise quickest results. *Australia* and *Sydney*, due here about 14th, could sail about 17th, taking 1,500; the *Pekin*, expected about 23d, could sail about 26th, taking about 1,300; other returning transports not yet reported, but may be expected at corresponding dates. No other desirable ships for charter known, possibly some may be available later.

MERRIAM, *Major-General.*

ADJUTANT-GENERAL'S OFFICE,
Washington, August 10, 1898.

General MERRITT, *Manila, via Hongkong:*

Six thousand troops at San Francisco. Can charter no more transports. What ships have left Manila returning and on what dates? When ought first returning ships reach San Francisco?

H. C. CORBIN, *Adjutant-General.*

DEPARTMENT OF STATE,
Washington, August 11, 1898.

The Honorable, the SECRETARY OF WAR.

SIR: I have the honor to apprise you of the receipt of a telegram from Mr. Rounsevelle Wildman, Consul of the United States at Hongkong, China, reading as follows:

CONSULATE OF THE UNITED STATES,
Hongkong, August 11, 1898. (Received 7.46 a. m.)

MOORE, *Washington:*

Information General Corbin, Steamship *Sydney* left Nagasaki 27th; *Australia*, 29th; *Pekin*, 6th. All direct Frisco without stop.

WILDMAN.

Respectfully yours,

WILLIAM R. DAY.

BURLINGTON, IOWA, *August 12, 1898.*
(Received 4.07 p. m.)

Honorable SECRETARY OF WAR, *Washington, D. C.:*

All Iowa interested in movement of troops. Great disappointment if Fifty-first Iowa doesn't sail on *Arizona*. Is such an order possible? Meeting being held. Please answer.

THOMAS STIVERS, *Editor Gazette.*

ADJUTANT-GENERAL'S OFFICE,
Washington, August 12, 1898—4.23 p. m.

Major-General MERRITT, *Manila:*

The President directs all military operations against the enemy be suspended. Peace negotiations are nearing completion, a protocol having just been signed by representatives of the two countries. You will inform the commander of the Spanish forces in the Philippines of these instructions. Further orders will follow. Acknowledge receipt.

By order Secretary of War:

H. C. CORBIN, *Adjutant-General.*

ADJUTANT-GENERAL'S OFFICE,
Washington, August 12, 1898—5 p. m.

General MILES, *Ponce, Porto Rico:*
General MERRITT, *Manila:*
General SHAFTER, *Santiago:*

The Secretary of War directs that the following proclamation of the President be sent you for your information and guidance:

"BY THE PRESIDENT OF THE UNITED STATES OF AMERICA.

"A PROCLAMATION.

"Whereas by a protocol concluded and signed August twelfth, eighteen hundred and ninety-eight, by William R. Day, Secretary of State of the United States, and His Excellency Jules Cambon, Ambassador Extraordinary and Plenipotentiary of the Republic of France at Washington, respectively representing for this purpose the Government of the United States and the Government of Spain, the United States and Spain have formally agreed upon the terms on which negotiations for the establishment of peace between the two countries shall be undertaken; and

"Whereas it is in said protocol agreed that upon its conclusion and signature hostilities between the two countries shall be suspended, and that notice to that effect shall be given as soon as possible by each Government to the commanders of its military and naval forces:

"Now, therefore, I, William McKinley, President of the United States, do, in accordance with the stipulations of the protocol, declare and proclaim on the part of the United States a suspension of hostilities, and do hereby command that orders be immediately given through the proper channels to the commanders of the military and naval forces of the United States to abstain from all acts inconsistent with this proclamation.

"In witness whereof I have hereunto set my hand and caused the seal of the United States to be affixed.

"Done at the city of Washington, this twelfth day of August, in the year of our Lord one thousand eight hundred and ninety-eight, and of the Independence of the United States the one hundred and twenty-third.

(Signed) "WILLIAM McKINLEY.

"By the President:
"WILLIAM R. DAY, *Secretary of State.*"

Acknowledge receipt.

By order Secretary War:

H. C. CORBIN, *Adjutant-General.*

THE PROTOCOL PROVIDES

1. That Spain will relinquish all claim of sovereignty over and title to Cuba.
2. That Porto Rico and other Spanish islands in the West Indies, and an island in the Ladrones, to be selected by the United States, shall be ceded to the latter.
3. That the United States will occupy and hold the city, bay, and harbor of Manila, pending the conclusion of a treaty of peace which shall determine the control, disposition, and government of the Philippines.
4. That Cuba, Porto Rico, and other Spanish islands in the West Indies shall be immediately evacuated, and that commissioners, to be appointed within ten days, shall, within thirty days from the signing of the protocol, meet at Havana and San Juan, respectively, to arrange and execute the details of the evacuation.
5. That the United States and Spain will each appoint not more than five commissioners to negotiate and conclude a treaty of peace. The commissioners are to meet at Paris not later than the 1st of October.
6. On the signing of the protocol hostilities will be suspended, and notice to that effect will be given as soon as possible by each Government to the commanders of its military and naval forces.

SAN FRANCISCO, CAL., *August 12, 1898.*
(Received 6.51 p. m.)

ADJUTANT-GENERAL, *Washington, D. C.:*

Suspension of hostilities carries suspension of shipment of troops to Manila unless otherwise instructed. In that case shall transports carry supplies for troops now at Manila?

MERRIAM, *Major-General.*

ADJUTANT-GENERAL'S OFFICE,
Washington, August 13, 1898—12.15 a. m.

General MERRITT, *Manila:*

Under the changed conditions, set forth in telegram of yesterday, Secretary of War desires your views as to necessity of sending you that part of your command waiting transportation in San Francisco.

H. C. CORBIN, *Adjutant-General.*

SAN FRANCISCO, CAL., *August 13, 1898.*
(Received 9.31 p. m.)

Adjutant-General CORBIN, *Washington, D. C.:*

Can you hurry answer on question of further shipment of troops to Manila? *Arizona* ready to sail, and troops under General King waiting to go aboard.

MERRIAM, *Major-General.*

ADJUTANT-GENERAL'S OFFICE,
Washington, August 13, 1898—midnight.

Major-General MERRIAM,
Commanding Department of California, San Francisco, Cal.:

The Secretary of War has caused inquiry to be made of General Merritt as to his needs for further force. You will hold the *Arizona* and General King's troops in readiness to sail at once should it be so ordered. Will advise you soon as possible.

By order Secretary War:

H. C. CORBIN, *Adjutant-General.*

SAN FRANCISCO, *August 14, 1898.*
(Received 8.85 p. m.)

Hon. R. A. ALGER,
 Secretary of War, Washington, D. C.:

I request permission individually to rejoin Tenth Pennsylvania by steamer *Arizona;* colonel sick.

           BARNETT, *Lieutenant-Colonel.*

WASHINGTON, D. C., *August 15, 1898.*
(Received 6.55 p. m.)

Gen. H. C. CORBIN,
 Adjutant-General, U. S. Army, Washington, D. C.:

I shall feel obliged if you will direct Lieutenant-Colonel Barnett, Tenth Pennsylvania Volunteers, now at San Francisco, to join his regiment without delay at Manila. Please wire by reply to United States Senate Annex.

           BOIES PENROSE.

ADJUTANT-GENERAL'S OFFICE,
Washington, August 15, 1898.

COMMANDING GENERAL, *San Francisco, Cal.:*

The Secretary of War directs that one of the transports belonging to the Government now at San Francisco be immediately fitted up for a hospital ship for Manila. Which do you recommend? Can not the work be largely done en route, putting a large force upon it, to be completed by the time it arrives, and shipping the workmen by returning transports? Your views and recommendations desired.

           H. C. CORBIN, *Adjutant-General.*

SAN FRANCISCO, CAL., *August 15, 1898.*
(Received 10.30 p. m.)

Adjutant-General CORBIN, *Washington, D. C.:*

Chief Surgeon and Majors Ruhlen and Long all recommend the *Scandia* for hospital ship. She will be ready to sail about Saturday. Requires no considerable changes beyond those planned already, but work can not be well done at sea. She can take a large amount of supplies needed at Manila, now loading, and also balance of garrison for Honolulu. *Arizona* is ready for sea, including also large amount of supplies for troops already at Manila. Troops assigned for this ship under General King consist entirely of detachments of organizations now at Manila and incomplete.

           MERRIAM, *Major-General.*

HONGKONG, *August 15, 1898.* (Received 11.50 p. m.)

DAY, *Washington:*

Augustin says Dewey bombarded Manila Saturday. City surrendered unconditionally. Augustin was taken by Germans in launch to *Kaiserin Augusta* and brought to Hongkong. I credit the report.

           WILDMAN.

STATE OF WASHINGTON, EXECUTIVE DEPARTMENT,
Olympia, August 8, 1898. (Received August 16.)

Hon. RUSSELL A. ALGER,
 Secretary of War, Washington, D. C.

MY DEAR SIR: I have the word of General Merriam, department commander at San Francisco, that the First Washington Volunteers is one of the very best infantry regiments in the United States service. The men of this regiment are desirous of service abroad. I sincerely hope that you will give them the opportunity of serving their country in the Philippines.

Yours, very truly, J R. ROGERS, *Governor.*

WAR DEPARTMENT, *Washington, D. C., August 16, 1898.*
Hon. J. R. ROGERS,
    Governor of Washington, Olympia, Wash.

MY DEAR SIR: In reply to your letter of August 8, I beg to inform you that if there are any more troops ordered to the Philippines the First Regiment of Washington Volunteers will doubtless go. We have had this in mind all the time.

Very truly, yours,

R. A. ALGER, *Secretary of War.*

WASHINGTON, D. C., *August 16, 1898.*
(Received 11.42 a. m.)
Gen. H. C. CORBIN,
    Adjutant-General, U. S. Army, Washington, D. C.:

It is quite important, which I can explain when I next see you, that Lieutenant-Colonel Barnett, of the Tenth Pennsylvania Volunteers, be ordered to rejoin his regiment at Manila by first steamer. I trust that you will advise me that my request has been complied with. Answer by wire to United States Senate Annex.

BOIES PENROSE.

ADJUTANT-GENERAL'S OFFICE,
Washington, August 16, 1898.
General MERRIAM, *San Francisco, Cal.:*

Secretary War directs Lieutenant-Colonel Barnett, Tenth Pennsylvania Volunteers, be ordered to join his regiment at Manila by first steamer, turning over command to next senior officer.

CARTER, *Assistant Adjutant-General.*

ADJUTANT-GENERAL'S OFFICE,
Washington, August 16, 1898.
Senator BOIES PENROSE, *Senate Annex:*

Lieutenant-Colonel Barnett, Tenth Pennsylvania Volunteers, ordered to join regiment at Manila by first steamer.

CARTER, *Assistant Adjutant-General.*

ADJUTANT-GENERAL'S OFFICE,
Washington, August 16, 1898—11.30 p. m.
COMMANDING GENERAL, DEPARTMENT OF CALIFORNIA,
    San Francisco, Cal.:

Your recommendation that the *Scandia* be used for hospital ship is approved. The necessary changes to this end will be made under your direction. In loading her with supplies the Secretary of War directs that plenty of hospital and medical stores be included. Note is made that the *Arizona* will carry the troops assigned, consisting of detachments for regiments now in Manila under command of General King, and is approved.

By order Secretary War:

H. C. CORBIN, *Adjutant-General.*

ADJUTANT-GENERAL'S OFFICE,
CAVITE, *August 13, 1898*. (Received August 17, 1898.)

Send the following telegram to the Adjutant-General:

"Since occupation of the town and suburbs the insurgents on outside are pressing demand for joint occupation of the city. Situation difficult. Inform me at once how far I shall proceed in forcing obedience in this matter and others that may arise. Is Government willing to use all means to make the natives submit to the authority of the United States?

"MERRITT.
"DEWEY."

ADJUTANT-GENERAL'S OFFICE,
Washington, August 17, 1898.

Major-General MERRITT, *Manila, Philippines:*

The President directs that there must be no joint occupation with the insurgents. The United States in the possession of Manila City, Manila Bay, and harbor must preserve the peace and protect persons and property within the territory occupied by their military and naval forces. The insurgents and all others must recognize the military occupation and authority of the United States and the cessation of hostilities proclaimed by the President. Use whatever means in your judgment are necessary to this end. All law-abiding people must be treated alike.

By order Secretary War:

H. C. CORBIN, *Adjutant-General.*

MANILA, *August 13, 1898*. (Via Hongkong.)
(Washington, August 18, 1898—9.40 a. m.)

ADJUTANT-GENERAL, *Washington:*

On 7th instant Admiral Dewey joined me in forty-eight hours' notification to Spanish commander to remove noncombatants from city. Same date reply received expressing thanks for humane sentiments, and stating Spanish without places of refuge for noncombatants now within walled town. On 9th instant sent joint note inviting attention to suffering in store for sick and noncombatants in case it became our duty to reduce the defenses; also setting forth hopeless conditions of Spanish forces, surrounded on all sides, fleet in front, no prospect of reenforcement, and demanded surrender as due every consideration of humanity. Same date received reply admitting their situation, but stating council of defense declares request for surrender can not be granted, but offered to consult Government if time was granted necessary for communication via Hongkong. Joint note in reply declining on the 13th. Joined with navy in attack with following result: After about half hour's accurate shelling of Spanish lines, MacArthur's brigade on right and Greene's on left, under Anderson, made vigorous attack and carried Spanish works. Loss not accurately known, about fifty in all. Behavior of troops excellent. Cooperation of the navy most valuable. Troops advanced rapidly on walled city, upon which white flag shown, and town capitulated. Troops occupy Malate, Binondo, walled city San Miguel. All important centers protected. Insurgents kept out; no disorder or pillage.

MERRITT.

SAN FRANCISCO, CAL., *August 18, 1898.*
(Received 1.29 p.m.)

Hon. G. D. MEIKLEJOHN,
Assistant Secretary of War, Washington, D. C.:

Confidentially, may I suggest that State and national politics are being complicated here, seemingly by whims of Regular Army officers, who appear to be gratifying personal ends. Seventh California been repeatedly promised, and each time new excuses intervene. The Seventh had detail guarding Indians, which took other troops. Was slated for the *Arizona*, and at General King's request recruits put on her. Now guarding *Scandia*, and that ship to be taken for hospital purposes. Southern California feels this a conspicuous discrimination against her regiment, which, first ready, roused local conditions; makes it wisdom to send Seventh instead of recruits. States having regiments in Manila do not care whether recruits are sent or not, but southern California wishes a representation in Philippines.

MARTIN FRANK PIERCE.

SAN FRANCISCO, CAL., *August 18, 1898*.
(Received 9.45 p. m.)

ADJUTANT-GENERAL, *Washington D. C.*:

Companies F, G, H, First New York Volunteers, Surgeon Davis and Chaplain Schwartz, sail on steamer *Alliance* to-day for Honolulu. Total, 11 officers and 313 men, 312 rifles, caliber .45, and 200 rounds per man.

MERRIAM, *Major-General*.

SACRAMENTO, CAL., *August 19, 1898*.
(Received 12.03 p. m.)

The PRESIDENT, *Washington:*

The people here are anxious to have Seventh California regiment to go to Manila. We hope nothing will interfere with arrangements to send them on *Scandia* or *Arizona*.

STEPHEN M. WHITE, *Senator*.
JAMES G. MAGUIRE, *M. C.*

WAR DEPARTMENT, *August 19, 1898—3.30 p. m.*
Hon. MARTIN FRANK PIERCE, *San Francisco, Cal.*:

There has been no intention on the part of this Department to discriminate against California or any other State. It is not deemed expedient to send any regiment to the Philippines at this time, as it is held, under conditions of the protocol, that the troops and detachments belonging to the organizations now there could only be sent; also supplies; but it is doubtful whether new or independent organizations could be added to General Merritt's force. Should this be decided in the affirmative, I would take great pleasure in instructing General Merriam to send a California regiment among first going to Philippines.

R. A. ALGER, *Secretary of War*.

SAN FRANCISCO, CAL., *August 19, 1898*.
(Received 10.51 p. m.)

The PRESIDENT, *Washington:*

I beg to urge the forwarding of the Seventh California to Manila. I speak as the friend and associate of Gen. E. G. Otis, whose earnest wish it was that this command should be given a place in the field.

L. E. MOSHER, *Editor Los Angeles Times*.

RUSH.] EXECUTIVE MANSION, *Washington, August 20, 1898.*
COMMANDING GENERAL, *U. S. Army, San Francisco, Cal.:*

Have detachment under General King await order at Honolulu. If the *Arizona* has sailed, and she can be overtaken with this message, send fast boat to do so.

By order Secretary of War:

H. C. CORBIN, *Adjutant-General.*

ADJUTANT-GENERAL'S OFFICE,
Washington, August 20, 1898—noon.
COMMANDING GENERAL, DEPARTMENT CALIFORNIA,
San Francisco, Cal.:

The Secretary of War directs that the troops of General Merritt's department remaining in San Francisco be sent to Honolulu, as transportation is available, there to await further orders. At least four months' subsistence and abundant medical stores and medicines should be provided. All the medical officers should go with this command. Where there is not the full complement, you are authorized to employ acting assistant surgeons. The transports going to Honolulu should remain in the harbor there until further orders. Acknowledge receipt and report action taken.

By order Secretary War:

H. C. CORBIN, *Adjutant-General.*

HONGKONG, *received August 20, 1898—2.25 p. m.*
ADJUTANT-GENERAL, *Washington:*

Reply your cablegram 13th regard sending forward troops now San Francisco, my opinion no necessity for sending troops. Difficulty landing supplies here much greater than anticipated. Shall transports now here, which brought second and third expeditions, and are not yet unloaded, be held to return as many troops to Un ted States as exigencies of terms upon which hostilities were suspended, and which are not known to me, will justify?

MERRITT.

ADJUTANT-GENERAL'S OFFICE,
Washington, August 20, 1898.
General MERRITT, *Manila:*

The President is glad to know you have ample force. Keep only such ships as you may require for transportation purposes. Will you want a hospital ship, or can you provide for all necessary hospitals at Manila? Every provision will be made by you for the health of your command and comfort of your sick. One of your ships may be found useful for hospital purposes; if so, you are authorized to make any change necessary. In this connection, the Navy Department reports the Government owns a hospital at Yokohama, with capacity for 600, and that there is also hospital at Hongkong which you can use. A report of the health of the troops of your command desired.

By order of the Secretary of War:

H. C. CORBIN, *Adjutant-General.*

HONGKONG, *received August 20, 1898—2.40 p. m.*
ADJUTANT-GENERAL, *Washington:*

Cablegram 12th, directing military operations be suspended, received afternoon 16th. Spanish commander notified. Acknowledge receipt of cablegram same date containing proclamation of President.

MERRITT.

HONGKONG, *received August 20, 1898—5 p. m.*
ADJUTANT-GENERAL, *Washington:*

The following are the terms of the capitulation:

The undersigned having been appointed a commission to determine the details of the capitulation of the city and defenses of Manila and its suburbs, and the Spanish forces stationed therein, in accordance with agreement entered into the previous day by Maj. Gen. Wesley Merritt, U. S. Army, American commander in chief in the Philippines, and his excellency Don Fermín Jardenes, acting general in chief of the Spanish army in the Philippines, have agreed upon the following:

1. Spanish troops, European and native, capitulate with the city and defenses with all honors of war, depositing their arms in the places designated by the authorities of the United States, and remaining in quarters designated and under the orders of their officers and subject to control of the aforesaid United States authorities until the conclusion of a treaty of peace between the two belligerent nations. All persons included in the capitulation remain at liberty, the officers remaining in their respective homes, which shall be respected as long as they observe the regulations prescribed for their government and the laws in force.

2. Officers shall retain their side arms, horses, and private property; all public horses and public property of all kinds shall be turned over to staff officers designated by the United States.

3. Complete returns in duplicate of men by organizations, and full lists of public property and stores shall be rendered to the United States within ten days from this date.

4. All questions relating to the repatriation of officers and men of the Spanish forces and of their families, and of the expenses which said repatriation may occasion, shall be referred to the Government of the United States at Washington. Spanish families may leave Manila at any time convenient to them; the return of arms surrendered by the Spanish forces shall take place when they evacuate the city or when the American army evacuates.

5. Officers and men included in the capitulation shall be supplied by the United States, according to their rank, with rations and necessary aid as though they were prisoners of war, until the conclusion of a treaty of peace between the United States and Spain. All the funds in the Spanish treasury and all other public funds shall be turned over to the authorities of the United States.

6. This city, its inhabitants, its churches and religious worship, its educational establishments and its private property of all descriptions, are placed under the special safeguard of the faith and honor of the American army.

F. V. GREENE,
Brigadier-General of Volunteers, U. S. Army.
B. L. LAMBERTON,
Captain, U. S. Navy.
CHAS. A. WHITTIER,
Lieutenant-Colonel and Inspector-General.
E. H. CROWDER,
Lieutenant-Colonel and Judge-Advocate.
NICHOLAS DE LA PEÑA,
Auditor-General Excts.
CARLOS REYES,
Colonel de Ingenieros.
JOSÉ MARIA OLAQUEN FELIA,
Coronel de Estado Major.

MERRITT.

SAN FRANCISCO, CAL., *August 20, 1898.*
(Received 10.15 p. m.).

Adjutant-General CORBIN, *Washington, D. C.:*

Referring to your telegram just received, *Australia* and *Sydney*, now coaling, will sail in about three days with troops and supplies for Honolulu, and can repeat trip twice a month. *Pekin* expected hourly; can do same. Colonel Barber reports great difficulty in finding ground for regimental camp at Honolulu. Larger camp still more difficult. *Arizona* sails to-night with supplies for General Merritt and detachments under General King. I am also aboard to carry out order of August 9 at Honolulu, and will also look into locations for camps there. General Miller will supervise my office here in my absence. *Scandia*, converted for hospital service under your order of 16th August, is loaded with hospital supplies and detachments for Manila, including money for pay of troops, and will sail in three days.

MERRIAM, *Major-General.*

SAN FRANCISCO, CAL., *August 20, 1898.*
(Received 10.50 p. m.).

ADJUTANT-GENERAL, U. S. ARMY, *Washington, D. C.:*

Transport *Arizona* sails to-day for Philippine Islands, with Brig. Gen. Charles King, Third Battalion, Twenty-third Infantry, recruits for Tenth Pennsylvania, First Nebraska, and First Colorado Volunteer Infantry. Total, 26 officers, 1,171 enlisted men, 9 civilians, 476 rifles, caliber .30; 690 rifles, caliber .45, and 196 rounds of ammunition per man. In addition to small-arms ammunition in hands of troops, 1,000,000 rounds in bulk, caliber .30. Maj. Gen. H. C. Merriam, one aid, one mustering officer, and Lieut. Col. George Ruhlen, quartermaster, with three clerks, also sailed *Arizona* for Honolulu.

MERRIAM, *Major-General.*

MANILA, *received Washington August 20, 1898—11.12 p. m.*
ADJUTANT-GENERAL, *Washington:*

Cable is now working to this point.

MERRITT.

HONGKONG, *received August 20, 1898.*
ADJUTANT-GENERAL, *Washington:*

In assault on Manila, August 13, General Anderson commanded division; General MacArthur, First Brigade; General Greene, Second. Losses were as follows: Killed—First Sergeant Holmes, Astor Battery; Sergeant Crimins, Astor Battery; Bugler Patterson, Thirteenth Minnesota; Private Thollen, Twenty-third Infantry; Private Dinsmore, First California. Wounded—Captain Seabeck, Thirteenth Minnesota, serious; Captain Bjornstad, same regiment, badly; Lieutenant Bunker, same regiment, slightly, and 40 enlisted men.

MERRITT.

MANILA, *received August 21, 1898—4.43 a. m.*
ADJUTANT-GENERAL, *Washington:*

Major-General Otis, with steamers *Peru* and *City of Puebla*, has arrived: all well; no casualties.

MERRITT.

WASHINGTON, D. C., *August 21.*
Major-General MERRITT, *U. S. Army, Manila, via Hongkong:*
In my own behalf and for the nation I extend to you and the officers and men of your command sincere thanks and congratulations for the conspicuously gallant conduct displayed in your campaign.
WILLIAM MCKINLEY.

ST. PAUL, MINN., *August 21, 1898.*
(Received 12.37 p. m.)
SECRETARY OF WAR, *Washington, D. C.:*
Please have Merritt wire names of enlisted men killed or wounded at Manila. He reports 40 enlisted men without naming them, but names officers. People here notice this and want names of enlisted men, especially from Minnesota.
C. K. DAVIS.

ADJUTANT-GENERAL'S OFFICE,
Washington, August 21, 1898—1.30 p. m.
General MERRITT, *Manila, Philippines:*
The Secretary of War desires names enlisted men wounded and killed; also names of those died in hospital since arrival troops at Manila.
H. C. CORBIN, *Adjutant-General.*

ADJUTANT-GENERAL'S OFFICE,
Washington, August 22, 1898—1 a. m.
COMMANDING GENERAL, DEPARTMENT OF CALIFORNIA,
San Francisco, Cal.:
Did the telegram to General Merriam of last night, instructing him to hold General King's command at Honolulu, reach him before sailing?
H. C. CORBIN, *Adjutant-General.*

SAN FRANCISCO, CAL., *August 22, 1898.*
(Received 2 p. m.)
ADJUTANT-GENERAL, U. S. ARMY, *Washington, D. C.:*
Dispatch to hold General King's command at Honolulu reached General Merriam before sailing, and he will act accordingly.
FIELD,
Major, Second Artillery, Acting Assistant Adjutant-General.

ADJUTANT-GENERAL'S OFFICE,
Washington, August 22, 1898—4.15 p. m.
General MERRITT, *Manila, Philippines:*
Troops of your entire command should be put in camp or quarters as you decide. The question of returning any can only be decided after the ratification of the report of the Peace Commission, which may not be for some weeks, even months. *Arizona* left yesterday and will be retained by you so long as needed. She is the property of the Government. Also the *Scandic,* which has been furnished as a hospital ship. All other transports not needed for immediate use of your command you will order sail for San Francisco as soon as possible.
By order Secretary War:
H. C. CORBIN, *Adjutant-General.*

ADJUTANT-GENERAL'S OFFICE,
Washington, August 23, 1898—1 a. m.

General MERRITT, *Manila, Philippines:*

The President will be pleased to receive any recommendations you may desire to make of officers serving in your command.

By order Secretary War:

H. C. CORBIN, *Adjutant-General.*

MANILA, *received August 23, 1898—4.40 a. m.*

ADJUTANT-GENERAL, *Washington:*

President's direction in cipher dispatch have been anticipated. Feared at first force would be necessary with insurgents; they rendered little assistance on the 13th, but some managed to enter unimportant suburbs which they have now agreed to vacate. Conditions seem favorable. Health and spirits of troops excellent.

J. B. BABCOCK, *Adjutant-General.*

ST. PAUL, MINN., *August 23, 1898.*
(Received 1.20 p. m.)

Hon. RUSSELL A. ALGER, *Secretary of War, Washington, D. C.:*

Can't Merritt's second report, giving names and condition sick and wounded at Manila, be hastened? People here in great distress.

THIRTEENTH MINNESOTA AUXILIARY ASSOCIATION.

MANILA, *received August 30, 1898—1.28 p. m.*

ADJUTANT-GENERAL, *Washington:*

Following is list killed, wounded, and deaths of enlisted men in this command since August 1:

August 2.—Killed: Lears, William P., private, E, First Nebraska. Wounded severely: Duncan, John F., private, E, First Nebraska; Connor, Lawrence P., private, E, First Nebraska; Hansen, George, private, A, First Nebraska; Wickham, Henry A., private, A, First Nebraska. Wounded slightly: Oviatt, Joseph S., private, A, First Nebraska; Peltzer, Charles E., private, E, First Nebraska; McCauley, John P., private, A, First Nebraska.

August 5.—Killed: McCann, Robert, private, C, Fourteenth Infantry; Howell, Samuel F., private, D, Fourteenth Infantry; Lauer, Clemens, private, F, Twenty-third Infantry. Wounded severely: Head, Claud F., musician, A, First Nebraska; Lambert, Clinton, private, C, Fourteenth Infantry; Snow, Lucius, private, D, Fourteenth Infantry. Wounded slightly: Ballard, Henry W., private, F, Twenty-third Infantry; O'Connor, Daniel J., private, D, Fourteenth Infantry; Sterling, William W., private, K, First Colorado; Englehorn, George, private, K, First Nebraska.

August 13.—Wounded severely: Newman, Fenton F., private, C, Twenty-third Infantry; Smith, Joseph, private, Twenty-third Infantry; Turk, Richard L., private, C, Twenty-third Infantry; Hayden, Thomas, private, Astor Battery; Carleton, Mervin, sergeant, E, Thirteenth Minnesota; Williams, Henry E., corporal, E, Thirteenth Minnesota; Crowl, Frank M., private, G, Thirteenth Minnesota; Little, Charles, private, F, Thirteenth Minnesota. Slightly wounded: McCann, Robert E., private, C, Twenty-third Infantry; Morgan, Charles A., private, C, Twenty-third Infantry; Parker, Robert R., private, C, Twenty-third Infantry;

Perg, Peter, private, H, Twenty-third Infantry; Booker, Harry, private, C, Twenty-third; Van Pelts, Charles E., private, Astor Battery; Sillman, Robert H., sergeant, Astor Battery; Hakel, George E., private, Astor Battery; Van Horn, Hallard, corporal, Astor Battery; Seumore, William, Astor Battery; Baker, William B., Astor Battery; Smith, Frank, private, F, First Colorado; Brady, Edward F., private, K, First Colorado; Hammerson, Alfred T., private, First Colorado; Jones, William A., private, G, Thirteenth Minnesota; Wallace, Lewis H., private, H, Thirteenth Minnesota; Thorsen, Guiman, artificer, H, Thirteenth Minnesota; Rice, Clarence T., private, E, Thirteenth Minnesota; Barrowman, Henry E., private, E, Thirteenth Minnesota; Twenty, George T., private, E, Thirteenth Minnesota; Ulmer, Louis, private, L, Thirteenth Minnesota; Kahl, George, private, L, Thirteenth Minnesota; Moore, William S., private, L, Thirteenth Minnesota; Rider, Ernest L., private, L, Thirteenth Minnesota; Fitzloff, Henry, private, C, Thirteenth Minnesota; Trenham, Milton A., private, D, Thirteenth Minnesota; McDonald, Robert, private, K, First Colorado; Hansen, Albert S., private, F, Thirteenth Minnesota; Ahlere, Charles J., private, G, Thirteenth Minnesota; Wood, Charles P., private, E, Thirteenth Minnesota.

Died as result of wounds received in action:

Winfield, Charles, private, H, Third Artillery. August 2.
Snyder, Lee, private, E, Tenth Pennsylvania. August 3.
McIlrath, John A., Battery H, Third Artillery. August 3.
Dunstore, John G., private, First California. August 14.
Dunn, Charles, private, Astor Battery. August 15.
Burnston, Charles, sergeant, G, Thirteenth Minnesota. August 16.
Phineas, Charles, private, I, First Colorado. August 18.

Died in hospital as result of disease:

Evans, William J., sergeant, C, First Nebraska. July 24.
Nicholas, Daniel J., private, H, First California. July 26.
Johnson, Edgar J., private, D, Second Oregon. July 28.
Berdine, Walter, private, E, Twenty-third Infantry. July 31.
Robeson, William B., Hospital Corps. August 2.
Paden, Leslie B., private, E, Thirteenth Minnesota. August 6.
Perkins, George H., private, B, First California. August 7.
Holbrook, Rufus R., private, C, Second Oregon. August 10.
Young, Edward C., private, A, Second Oregon. August 11.
Firn, Philip, musician, G, Eighteenth Infantry; Howard Neill, private, Hospital Corps, August 14.
Minnich, Leroy S., private, C, First Wyoming. August 15.
Dickson, Henry, private, Thirteenth Minnesota. August 16.
Sergeant, Thomas H., private, Hospital Corps. August 17.
Sanders, William; August 17.
Pratt, Sidney, private, Thirteenth Minnesota, August 18.
Jobbling, Arthur, private, H, Eighteenth Infantry. August 19.

MERRITT.

ADJUTANT-GENERAL'S OFFICE,
Washington, August 23, 1898—11.50 p. m.

COMMANDING GENERAL, DEPARTMENT CALIFORNIA, *San Francisco, Cal.:*

Scandia should leave with supplies as soon as possible and not take any troops. She will be used as hospital ship if needed after reaching Manila. Inform Colonel Long.

By order of the Secretary of War:

H. C. CORBIN, *Adjutant-General.*

ADJUTANT-GENERAL'S OFFICE,
Washington, August 24, 1898.

Hon. C. K. DAVIS, *St. Paul, Minn.:*

General Merritt's list killed, wounded, and deaths enlisted men in his command since August 1, just received, shows following names of enlisted men from Minnesota: Killed, none. Wounded severely: Mervin Carleton, sergeant, Company E; Henry E. Williams, corporal, E; Frank M. Crowl, private, Company G; Charles Little, private, Company F. Slightly wounded: William A. Jones, private, Company G; Lewis H. Wallace, private, Company H; Guiman Thorson, artificer, H; Clarence T. Rice, private, Company E; Henry E. Barrowman, private, Company E; George T. Twenty, private, Company E; Louis Ulmer, private, Company L; George Kahl, private, Company L; William S. Moore, private, Company L; Ernest L. Rider, private, Company L; Henry Fitzloff, private, Company C; Milton A. Trenham, private, Company D; Albert S. Hansen, private, Company F; Charles L. Ahlere, private, Company G; Charles P. Wood, private, Company E. Died as result of wounds received in action: August 16, Charles Burnston, sergeant, G. Died in hospital as result of disease: August 6, Leslie B. Paden, private, E.; August 16, Henry Dickson, private; August 18, Sidney Pratt, private—all of the Thirteenth Minnesota.

H. C. CORBIN, *Adjutant-General.*

ADJUTANT-GENERAL'S OFFICE,
Washington, August 24, 1898.

THIRTEENTH MINNESOTA AUXILIARY ASSOCIATION,
St. Paul, Minn.:

Hon. C. K. Davis, St. Paul, Minn., has been furnished with General Merritt's list Minnesota troops killed, wounded, and deaths enlisted men in his command since August 1.

HEISTAND, *Assistant Adjutant-General.*

SAN FRANCISCO, CAL., *August 24, 1898.*
(Received 8.40 p. m.)

ADJUTANT-GENERAL OF THE ARMY, *Washington, D. C.:*

A very large sum of money is now on board *Scandia* by authority Secretary of War. Guard is necessary. Can detachment First New York, about 275 men, under Lieutenant-Colonel Stackpole, be sent as guard and to complete Colonel Barbar's regiment as garrison of Honolulu. As guard from Honolulu to Manila, 1 commissioned officer and 25 men, California Heavy Artillery, are available. Fifty men of same organization have preceded them by two months. The sending of these men will not interfere with the carrying of medical and other stores.

MILLER, *Brigadier-General Volunteers.*

SAN FRANCISCO, CAL., *August 24, 1898.*
(Received 8.41 p. m.

SURGEON-GENERAL, U. S. ARMY, *Washington, D. C.:*

General Miller says ordered to send no more men to Manila. One hundred and fifty Hospital Corps men here belonging there. Can not they go on the *Scandia?*

MIDDLETON, *Chief Surgeon.*

SAN FRANCISCO, CAL., *August 24, 1898.*
(Received 10.40 p. m.)

ADJUTANT-GENERAL, U. S. ARMY, *Washington, D. C.:*

Colonel Babbitt asks for information as to disposition of ordnance stores sent for use at Manila. Request telegraphic authority to ship 200 steel shells, 1,600 cartridges for 5-inch siege guns, and 4 azimuth telescopes to Manila, and retain two 7-inch breech-loading howitzers, two carriages for same, 400 shells, and 912 cartridges at the arsenal.

MILLER, *Brigadier-General.*

SAN FRANCISCO, CAL., *August 24, 1898.*
(Received 11 p. m.)

Adjutant-General CORBIN, *Washington:*

Am here with two majors, band, and two and one-half companies of First New York Volunteers; total, 300 men. Please send us on *Scandia* to join balance regiment at Honolulu. Colonel Barber desires his full regiment with him.

STACKPOLE, *Lieutenant-Colonel.*

ADJUTANT-GENERAL'S OFFICE,
Washington, August 24, 1898—midnight.

COMMANDING GENERAL, DEPARTMENT CALIFORNIA,
San Francisco, Cal.:

Your telegram concerning *Scandia* is received. The detachment of First New York can be sent as guard as far as Honolulu, and from Honolulu a commissioned officer and 25 men from California heavy artillery should be sent, as recommended in your telegram of this date. This, of course, will not interfere with carrying medical stores and should not delay departure of ship.

By order of the Secretary of War:

H. C. CORBIN, *Adjutant-General.*

ADJUTANT-GENERAL'S OFFICE,
Washington, August 24, 1898—midnight.

Brigadier-General MILLER, *San Francisco, Cal.:*

The Secretary of War approves of your telegram of this date to ship 200 steel shells, 1,600 cartridges for 5-inch siege guns, and 4 azimuth telescopes to Manila, and retain two 7-inch breech-loading howitzers, 2 carriages for same, 400 shell and 912 cartridges at the arsenal.

H. C. CORBIN, *Adjutant-General.*

MANILA, *received August 25, 1898—8.35 a. m.*

ADJUTANT-GENERAL, *Washington, D. C.:*

Rio de Janeiro and *Pennsylvania* arrived 24th; all well; no casualties, excepting Private Wenks, First South Dakota, who died between San Francisco and Honolulu.

MERRITT.

SAN FRANCISCO, CAL., *August 25, 1898.*
(Received 4.22 p. m.)

Hon. WILLIAM MCKINLEY:

Detail of 50 men from California heavy artillery by orders from Washington to leave on transport *Scandia* in command of a lieutenant. Please have my brother, Second Lieut. J. B. Morse, now in command of Battery A, First Battalion, detailed to take command, and greatly oblige.

GEORGE E. MORSE.

ADJUTANT-GENERAL'S OFFICE,
Washington, August 25, 1898—5.10 p. m.
General MERRITT, *Manila, Philippines:*

Whatever information you have which will be of value to the President and the Peace Commission should be sent in cipher, and cable fully.

By order Secretary of War:

H. C. CORBIN, *Adjutant-General.*

ADJUTANT-GENERAL'S OFFICE,
Washington, August 25, 1898—11 p. m.
COMMANDING GENERAL, DEPARTMENT CALIFORNIA,
San Francisco, Cal.:

Referring to Chief Surgeon Middleton's telegram of yesterday to the Surgeon-General, the Secretary of War directs that the 150 Hospital Corps men be put on the *Scandia,* if that number does not overcrowd the boat.

H. C. CORBIN, *Adjutant-General.*

MANILA, PHILIPPINES, *received August 26, 1898—12.27 a. m.*
ADJUTANT-GENERAL, *Washington:*

Request order to return home via Paris commission, leaving command here to Otis. If not via Paris, request order to return direct, to be accompanied by such member of my staff as can be spared.

MERRITT.

CAMP MERRIAM,
San Francisco, Cal., August 25, 1898.
(Received August 26, 1898, 1.04 a. m.
ADJUTANT-GENERAL, U. S. ARMY, *Washington, D. C.:*

Shall 150 Hospital Corps be sent to Manila on *Scandia,* in accordance with recommendation of medical director, who urges their departure and claims they are not troops as contemplated in telegram of 23d? Their going will cause no delay; preparations already made.

MILLER, *Brigadier-General Volunteers.*

ADJUTANT-GENERAL'S OFFICE,
Washington, August 26, 1898.
COMMANDING GENERAL, DEPARTMENT OF CALIFORNIA,
San Francisco, Cal.:

Secretary of War directs that you send orders by the *Scandia* for the *Arizona,* which is at Honolulu, to go at once to Manila with the stores for both army and navy which she has aboard. Both of these ships, the *Scandia* and the *Arizona,* are loaded with supplies for the commands at Manila, and should proceed at once to that point. Acknowledge receipt and report your action.

H. C. CORBIN, *Adjutant-General.*

SAN FRANCISCO, CAL., *August 26, 1898.*
(Received 2.09 p. m.)
ADJUTANT-GENERAL, U. S. ARMY, *Washington, D. C.:*

Telegram regarding *Arizona* just received, and your instructions will be carried to General Merriam, at Honolulu, by *Scandia,* which leaves to-morrow morning at 9 a. m.

MILLER, *Brigadier-General Volunteers.*

ADJUTANT-GENERAL'S OFFICE,
Washington, August 26, 1898—5 p. m.

General MERRITT, *Manila, Philippines:*

The President directs that you transfer your command, with all your instructions and general staff officers now on duty with you, to Major-General Otis, U. S. Volunteers, and proceed without delay to the city of Paris, France, for conference with the Peace Commission. You will be accompanied by your three regular aides. The commission will meet in Paris October 1. You should consult fully with Admiral Dewey, so you can present his views as well as your own to the commission.

By order Secretary of War:

H. C. CORBIN, *Adjutant-General.*

MANILA, PHILIPPINES, *received August 27, 1898—12.43 a. m.*
ADJUTANT-GENERAL, *Washington:*

In the event of no army representation appearing with the commission at Paris, I withdraw my application of yesterday.

MERRITT.

MANILA, PHILIPPINES, *received August 27, 1898.*
ADJUTANT-GENERAL, *Washington:*

Situation here as follows: About 10,000 armed Filipinos near Manila City and suburb in this Parochial. Filipinos and their chief anxious to be friendly. Little confidence is to be placed in their professions. They are superior as a people than is generally represented; their leaders are mostly men of education and ability.

Spanish prisoners now in city, 13,300; Spanish arms, 22,000; with large supply of ammunition; also seacoast batteries and several batteries of field pieces. These figures are close approximation only. Exact amount of Spanish public funds in this Parochial, $882,451.39. Custom-house occupied since 15th instant. Receipts up to the 26th, $51,283.58.

MERRITT.

ADJUTANT-GENERAL'S OFFICE,
Washington, August 27, 1898—Midnight.

The PRESIDENT UNITED STATES, *Somerset, Pa.:*

Following just received in cipher from General Merritt, Manila:

"Situation here as follows: About 10,000 armed Filipinos near Manila City and suburb in this Parochial. Filipinos and their chief anxious to be friendly. Little confidence is to be placed in their professions. They are superior as a people than is generally represented; their leaders are mostly men of education and ability.

"Spanish prisoners now in city, 13,300; Spanish arms, 22,000, with large supply of ammunition; also seacoast batteries and several batteries of field pieces. These figures are close approximation only. Exact amount of Spanish public funds in this Parochial, $882,451.39. Custom-house occupied since 15th instant. Receipts up to the 26th, $51,283.58."

H. C. CORBIN, *Adjutant-General.*

ADJUTANT-GENERAL'S OFFICE,
Washington, August 27, 1898—Midnight.

COMMANDING GENERAL, U. S. FORCES, *Manila, Philippines:*

Secretary War directs that Maj. F. V. Greene, U. S. Volunteers, be relieved from further duty with your command and report to Adjutant-General Army for orders. He should come on first returning ship.

H. C. CORBIN, *Adjutant-General.*

MANILA, PHILIPPINES, *received August 28, 1898—5.55 a. m.*
ADJUTANT-GENERAL, *Washington:*

Regard coming of *Scandia* fitted up as hospital ship as most desirable. Will not be necessary in that case to use any ships now here for that purpose. Such of sick and wounded capable of making journey in transports about to leave will be sent home. Will not be necessary to use the hospitals at Yokohama and Hongkong for the present at least. Wounded are doing well. There are 180 patients of all kinds in hospital Manila and 69 in hospital Cavite, chiefly made up cases that are likely to return duty soon. Total number deaths from disease since first landing is 17: typhoid fever 9, cerebro-spinal meningitis 1, septicæmia 1, paralysis 1, pneumonia 3, dysentery 2. If Major Corbusier, medical purveyor, is not on way out recommend funds in his possession intended for purchase medical supplies be transferred by wire to Captain McVay, assistant surgeon. Also recommend Chief Surgeon Lippincott be furnished $1,000 for hospital-fund purposes.

MERRITT.

MANILA, PHILIPPINES, *received August 28, 1898—7 a. m.*
ADJUTANT-GENERAL, *Washington:*

Thank the President and you for highly satisfactory order. I now earnestly request authority to order chief staff, General Babcock, to United States direct. Otis has General Hughes chief of staff and Barry adjutant. General Babcock not needed. His services campaign entitle him to this consideration. Also ask authority to take Major Scriven with me on account of his fluency in French. His position here is military secretary.

MERRITT.

SAN FRANCISCO, CAL., *August 28, 1898.*
(Received 4.22 p. m.).
ADJUTANT-GENERAL OF THE ARMY, *Washington, D. C.:*

Steamer *Scandia* sailed yesterday with remainder First New York Volunteers, 10 officers, 293 men, 293 rifles, caliber .45, and 235 rounds ammunition per man, for Honolulu. One officer, 25 men, 3 paymasters, 5 medical officers, 139 Hospital Corps men, etc., for Manila.

FIELD,
*Acting Assistant Adjutant-General,
in the absence of the Department Commander.*

MANILA, PHILIPPINES, *received August 29, 1898.*
ADJUTANT-GENERAL, *Washington:*

Paymasters have had no increased rank. McClure, Kilbourne, and Whipple, with me, have been efficient. Recommend McClure brevet brigadier-general volunteers, Whipple and Kilbourne colonels volunteers, brevet.

MERRITT.

ADJUTANT-GENERAL'S OFFICE,
Washington, August 29, 1898—11.30 p. m.
COMMANDING GENERAL, U. S. FORCES, *Manila, Philippines:*

The President will not entertain recommendation for promotion by brevet other than for services rendered in battle. This will govern in all cases.

By order Secretary War:

H. C. CORBIN, *Adjutant-General.*

ADJUTANT-GENERAL'S OFFICE,
Washington, August 29, 1898—11.30 p. m.

COMMANDING GENERAL, *Manila, Philippines:*

Major Simpson will return to the United States and report to the Adjutant-General of the Army. Simpson and Babcock should return on our own transports direct to San Francisco.

H. C. CORBIN, *Adjutant-General.*

ADJUTANT-GENERAL'S OFFICE,
Washington, August 29, 1898—11.45. p. m.

COMMANDING GENERAL, UNITED STATES FORCES, *Manila, Philippines:*

Order General Babcock to return to the United States direct, reporting to this office by telegraph upon arrival at San Francisco. You are also authorized to order Major Scriven to accompany you to Paris.

By order Secretary War:

H. C. CORBIN, *Adjutant-General.*

HDQRS. FIRST BRIGADE, U. S. EXPEDITIONARY FORCES,
Cavite Arsenal, Philippine Islands, July 11, 1898.
(Received August 29, 1898.)

ADJUTANT-GENERAL, U. S. ARMY.

GENERAL: I have the honor to transmit the required reports of the voyage of the transports of this expedition.

I need only summarize a few suggestions: When possible, it would seem expedient to let the commandant of an expedition have some control before his transports start. Copies of the charters should be given the quartermaster on each vessel. The promises of the agents to make changes and improvements should not be taken for granted as fulfilled.

On our transports the cooking facilities were inadequate. The temperature of the sea water being over 82° F., raised the temperature of the cold-storage rooms so that there was great loss of beef.

In the *Australia* only 800 gallons of water could be distilled per diem, and the water supply was inadequate.

Convoys should be able to run more than 9 knots an hour. A thirty-six days' voyage in the Tropics is very trying when the vessels are crowded and not intended for transports.

Men should not be allowed to take their bedticks on deck, even if allowed to sleep there.

Very respectfully, THOMAS M. ANDERSON,
Brigadier-General, U. S. Volunteers, Commanding.

Nine inclosures.

[Inclosure 1.]

ON BOARD S. S. CITY OF PEKIN, *June 1, 1898.*
(Received August 29, 1898.)

ASSISTANT ADJUTANT-GENERAL,
First Brigade, United States Expeditionary Forces.

SIR: I have the honor to submit the following report as to the sanitary condition of the S. S. *City of Pekin* and of the troops on board from May 25, 1898, to June 1, 1898.

After leaving the port of San Francisco, May 25, 1898, I discovered a case of measles (private, Company G), and at once used precautionary measures to avoid contagion. On May 28 one more case developed from Company G, and on May 31 one suspected case from the same company was placed in quarantine; on May 28 a severe case of tonsillitis was placed in the hospital, otherwise the health of the command is good, excepting ordinary seasickness.

Dating from May 27 I have issued orders placing each battalion, sanitary condition of quarters, and health of men under the special charge of an assistant surgeon, from whom I receive daily a written report.

A detail of the sanitary corps on duty with the battalion surgeons make hourly inspection of the quarters of enlisted men, and report to the surgeon in charge. As per special orders from this department, blankets, mattresses, and pillows are brought on deck and thoroughly aired for two hours or more daily. Bunks and woodwork are scoured with mercuric chloride solution.

Surgeons in charge of battalions each morning make a personal examination of the men under their charge.

During the past four days, weather permitting, the men of this command have received daily a hose bath under charge of a noncommissioned officer. Also special days assigned for the washing and cleaning of clothes. Sinks for officers and men under the special care of the sanitary corps. Average temperature of sleeping quarters of men from date of leaving San Francisco, 70 degrees in fore and aft parts of ship. The amidships very uncomfortable on account of heat generated from fire room and boilers.

I have ordered men from that part of the ship to sleep on deck. Proper supervision and care is taken to see that food is properly cooked and cleanly served. A carcass of diseased beef was reported by this department and condemned by a board of survey as unfit for food on May 27. I have made my informal inspections during the day, also one inspection daily with the captain of the ship, representing the Pacific Mail Steamship Company, and one inspection daily with Col. James F. Smith, commanding this regiment. After consultation with the naval officers and surgeons I learned that it would be unsafe to fumigate vessel on voyage on account of explosives on board, therefore used the method of cleaning quarters of men with mercuric chloride. The only method we had for fumigating was formaldehyde, which is liable to generate gases that would be dangerous if in contact with explosives.

May 29 every man was vaccinated and his name checked by his company commander (976 men). I have made special investigation as to facility for supplying fresh water. The condensers have a capacity of 2,500 gallons per day. Fresh water is used only for cooking purposes, for drinking, and in officers' quarters. For bathing and washing salt water only is used.

Very respectfully,

WM. D. MCCARTHY,
Major and Surgeon, U. S. Volunteers.

[Inclosure 2.]

CITY OF SYDNEY, *June 1, 1898.* (Received August 29, 1898.)
ADJUTANT-GENERAL UNITED STATES EXPEDITIONARY FORCES,
S. S. Australia.

SIR: I have the honor to submit the following report concerning the commissary department on board *City of Sydney:*

The means for cooking are so limited that it is not practicable to serve more than two meals each day and have the food well prepared. To serve two meals each day the galley is used day and night.

Fresh bread has been served but three times, and then the quality was such that hard bread was preferable.

Articles for sales to officers and enlisted men are almost exhausted, with the exception of cigars and tobacco. This is due to the fact that I could not secure the articles I asked the purchasing commissary for on such short notice.

I have on hand 8,400 pounds of fresh beef. The supply of rations provided for in Special Orders, No. 4, paragraph 1, is properly segregated and can be issued when required.

Very respectfully,

WM. A. BURNSIDE,
Second Lieutenant, Fourteenth Infantry, Commissary, City of Sydney.

[Inclosure 3.]

UNITED STATES EXPEDITIONARY FORCES, S. S. CITY OF SYDNEY,
En route to Philippine Islands, June 2, 1898.
(Received August 29, 1898.)

ADJUTANT, SECOND REGIMENT OREGON VOLUNTEERS,
S. S. Australia.

SIR: I have the honor to herewith make the following report as regards the detachment of the Third Battalion, under my command, on board this vessel:

The detachment reported at the Pacific Mail dock at 11 o'clock a. m. on June 24, and were immediately assigned to quarters, taking them in a very orderly manner, without undue confusion.

On board I found a detachment of five companies of the Fourteenth Infantry, U. S. Army, Capt. John Murphy, commanding, and a detachment of 50 men from the California Heavy Artillery, Capt. D. Geary, commanding. Being the ranking officer on the vessel, I assumed command. Captain McVea, U. S. Army, reported to me as surgeon; Lieutenant Burnside, U. S. Army, reported as commissary officer of the vessel.

As soon as practicable the command was divided into two divisions, the first division consisting of the Fourteenth Infantry, numbering 387 soldiers; the second division consisting of a detachment of the Third Battalion, Second Oregon, numbering 231 soldiers, and a detachment of the California Heavy Artillery, consisting of 50 soldiers, making a total of 281 soldiers.

On the morning of the 25th of June Chief Engineer Chalker, U. S. Navy, reported on board with 20 sailors, with an order from Brigadier-General Otis to furnish them transportation and subsistence until the arrival at the destination of the vessel. These sailors were put in the second division.

As regards the commissary department, I beg to say that upon examination of the ship's galley I found it inadequate to supply the demands made upon it. Have therefore adapted myself to circumstances, and instructed the commissary officer of the vessel to issue full rations to every man and to have the same served in two meals, breakfast beginning at 8 o'clock a. m. and dinner at 4 o'clock p. m., daily, the first and second divisions alternating daily as to which goes first. The subdivisions of the divisions alternate the same as the divisions. At first there was some confusion in serving the soldiers, and the meals were not what they should be. However, after several days of unceasing effort upon the part of myself and officers on board, we finally systematized affairs, so that the meals are now served in a very orderly manner, and the men have plenty of good food, well cooked, and are adapting themselves to the cramped quarters and circumstances.

On the main deck I have had shower baths arranged so that the soldiers can take baths. However, at the present time they are inadequate to supply the demands made upon them, and I am endeavoring to perfect arrangements so that the men can bathe every other day. Owing to the cramped quarters, it is very difficult to manage affairs as they should be, but I am endeavoring to adapt myself to circumstances and make the best of the facilities at hand.

As regards the medical department, I will say that we have been particularly fortunate in the matter of serious illness. We have had, however, a number of cases in the hospital, among them two cases of measles, which are at present improving very rapidly. The bedding is brought on deck twice a week for airing, and the sanitary condition of the vessel is very fair, particular attention being paid to the ventilation of the berth deck and to the cleanliness of the water-closets. Each commanding officer of the companies is held personally responsible for the cleanliness of the quarters occupied by his command. Besides this, I have appointed a provost-sergeant, who is responsible for the general policing of the ship. The officer of the day is required to make three inspections daily of the entire ship. The commanding officers of subdivisions are required to make frequent inspections of their quarters. I make two inspectious daily, one at 11 o'clock a. m. and one immediately after taps.

In general, I may say that the discipline of the troops on board this vessel, and the general health of the same, are very good; and I am pleased to report that no infractions, worthy of note, of any of the rules and regulations, as laid down for the government of the troops, has occurred.

Very respectfully,

P. G. EASTWICK, Jr.,
Major, Second Oregon Volunteers,
Commanding troops on board S. S. City of Sydney.

[Inclosure 4.]

UNITED STATES EXPEDITIONARY FORCES, S. S. CITY OF SYDNEY,
En route to Philippine Islands, June 2, 1898.
(Received August 29, 1898.)

ASSISTANT ADJUTANT-GENERAL,
First Expedition to Philippine Islands,
S. S. City of Pekin.

SIR: In compliance with the regulations, I have the honor herewith to make the following report as regards the troops under my command on board the *City of Sydney.*

The troops on board this vessel are a detachment of the Fourteenth Infantry, U. S. Army, 387 soldiers and 10 officers, Capt. John Murphy commanding; 20 sailors of the Navy, Chief Engineer Chalker in charge; a detachment of California Heavy Artillery, 50 soldiers, Capt. D. Geary commanding; and a detachment of the Third Battalion, Second Oregon Volunteers, Maj. P. G. Eastwick, jr., commanding.

All of the above-mentioned troops were embarked at San Francisco by 1 o'clock p. m., May 24, 1898, and the vessel immediately swung into the stream and anchored.

As soon as possible after embarkation I divided the troops into two divisions and assigned them to sections of the deck, in accordance with a letter of instruction dated May 24, 1898, signed by Major-General Otis.

The first division consists of the Fourteenth Infantry, numbering 387 soldiers. The second division consists of the sailors of the Navy, numbering 20 men; the detachment of California Heavy Artillery, numbering 50 men; and a detachment of the Third Battalion, Second Oregon Volunteers, numbering 231 soldiers.

The quarters on the berth deck, assigned to the troops for sleeping purposes, have been made as comfortable as possible; and I have paid especial attention to the cleanliness of the quarters and the ventilation of the same, which, under the circumstances, I consider very good.

In regard to facilities for baths for the soldiers, arrangements have been made on the main deck whereby baths can be had daily, if necessary, the second division using the baths in the forenoon and the first division using them in the afternoon. However, the bathing facilities are not yet perfected, and it is hoped that better arrangements can be made at an early date.

In regard to the commissary department, I will say that it was found impracticable to serve three meals a day, owing to the small galley which was at our disposal. We therefore serve full rations in two meals, breakfast beginning at 8 a. m., and dinner beginning at 3.30 p. m. To serve these two meals the galley is used day and night. The troops have plenty of good wholesome food, the first and second divisions alternating daily as to the service of meals.

The medical department, under the charge of the surgeon, is in a very satisfactory condition, and his report is filed herewith.

In general, I will say that the troops are being cared for in the best manner possible, under the existing circumstances.

Very respectfully,
P. G. EASTWICK, Jr.,
Major Second Oregon Volunteers,
Commanding troops on board City of Sydney.

[Inclosure 5.]

UNITED STATES EXPEDITIONARY FORCES, S. S. CITY OF SYDNEY,
At Sea, June 30, 1898. (Received August 29, 1898.)
ADJUTANT, SECOND REGIMENT OREGON U. S. VOLUNTEERS,
S. S. Australia.

SIR: I have the honor to make the following report regarding the troops of my battalion, consisting of Companies F, I, and M, under my immediate command, and on board the *S. S. City of Sydney.*

The detachment embarked on May 24, 1898, comprising 12 officers, 1 hospital steward, and 231 enlisted men. At Honolulu, where we stopped, 2 men reported to M Company, in compliance with regimental order No. 34.

I desire to say that the discipline of the troops during the trip has been excellent. No serious breach of discipline has been reported, and all the volunteer forces seem to be endeavoring to profit by their surroundings to learn all that is possible and that a soldier should know. Officers' schools have been held daily, Saturday and Sunday excepted, and instructions given in drill regulations, guard manual, troops in campaign, and Army Regulations.

Noncommissioned officers' schools have also been held on the same days, and I would respectfully recommend that a first sergeants' and company clerks' school be organized for all of the first sergeants and company clerks in the regiment for instruction in their respective duties, thus insuring a uniform observance in the manner and custom of making out papers.

In general, I would state that, barring one unfortunate event, which was the death of Private Elias Hutchinson, Company M, who was operated on for appendicitis on June 16, and died on June 20, and was buried at sea with due military honors on the same date, the voyage has been very successful.

Owing to the cramped quarters in the galley, we were unable to give but two meals a day, but this has proven to be sufficient.

Very respectfully,
P. G. EASTWICK, Jr.,
Major Second Regiment Oregon U. S. Volunteers,
Commanding U. S. Troops on board City of Sydney.

[Inclosure 6.]

UNITED STATES EXPEDITIONARY FORCES, S. S. CITY OF SYDNEY,
At Sea, June 30, 1898. (Received August 29, 1898.)

ACTING ASSISTANT ADJUTANT-GENERAL,
First Brigade, First Expeditionary Forces, S. S. Australia.

SIR: In accordance with regulations, I have the honor to herewith submit my report as regards the troops under my command on board the S. S. *City of Sydney* as follows:

DATE OF EMBARKATION AND TROOPS EMBARKED.

On the 24th day of May, 1898, the following troops embarked on this vessel: Five companies of the Fourteenth Infantry, under command of Capt. John Murphy, 387 enlisted men and 8 officers; a detachment of California heavy artillery, Capt. Dennis Geary commanding, 50 enlisted men and 1 officer; 20 sailors of the U. S. Navy, in charge of Chief Engineer J. H. Chalker; three companies of the Third Battalion, Second Oregon Volunteers, Maj. P. G. Eastwick, jr., commanding, 231 enlisted men and 12 officers. Capt. H. E. McVay, surgeon, U. S. Army, and Second Lieut. W. A. Burnside, commissary, reported, making a total of 668 enlisted men and 24 officers; Lieut. Commander T. S. Phelps, jr., U. S. Navy, being the naval officer on board.

ASSIGNMENT OF QUARTERS.

Immediately upon coming on board and assuming command, I assigned quarters to the troops in accordance with instructions received from Major-General Otis, under date of May 24, 1898.

For some twenty-four hours after embarkation affairs on board were in a confused state, owing to cramped quarters, but after that time rapidly improved, and finally order was resumed.

SANITARY CONDITIONS.

In this connection I would respectfully state that under the existing circumstances and the cramped quarters the sanitary conditions on board were very fair. Frequent inspections of the ship were made by myself and the officer of the day each day. Bedding of the men has been brought on deck for airing Wednesdays and Saturdays, weather permitting. The water-closet facilities are sufficient; but I would respectfully recommend in this connection that should this vessel be again used to transport troops a stronger stream of water be kept constantly running through the closets; and I would also recommend that a temporary structure be built on the after part of the hurricane deck, to be used as an hospital to isolate contagious diseases. During the voyage 22 cases of measles were reported by the surgeons. However, all have become convalescent, and 18 cases have been discharged.

SLEEPING ACCOMMODATIONS.

Sleeping accommodations for the enlisted men number 801 berths, and are distributed as follows: One hundred and forty-one berths in the forward steerage, 318 berths in the main steerage, and 342 berths in the aftersteerage. As regards the ventilation of the forward and main steerage, I will state that it is very good, but in the aftersteerage very poor, the temperature reaching as high as 86°. As regards the circulation of air, I will say in connection with the aftersteerage that the wind sail does not seem sufficient to supply the requisite amount of air; and I would respectfully recommend that, if practicable, an artificial current of air be arranged to perfect the ventilation on this steerage.

During the voyage as many as could be accommodated have been allowed to sleep on the hurricane deck during the hottest portion of the trip.

COOKING FACILITIES.

In this connection, I would report that the galley facilities for the accommodation of the number of men on board is entirely too small, and we were forced to serve only two meals—breakfast at 8 o'clock a. m. and dinner at 4 o'clock p. m.—the galley being used day and night, the facilities being much cramped, and practically impossible to make as good bread as required.

As regards the galleys, I would most respectfully recommend that the two rooms immediately aft of the galley on the starboard side be arranged for cooking purposes, as an additional galley; and I believe that by so doing three meals a day may be served, or at least two meals and coffee.

COMMISSARY DEPARTMENT.

The commissary department has been managed as satisfactorily as could be expected under the circumstances. However, I would recommend that, if consistent, prunes should be issued to the soldiers.

BATHING FACILITIES.

No provisions having been made for the bathing of the soldiers, I arranged with the officer of the vessel to have a shower bath made forward on the starboard side for the use of the men. However, this we found insufficient, and I would respectfully recommend that at least four or five shower baths be erected at or near the place at present occupied by the one bath being used.

WATER.

The capacity of the condenser on this vessel is practically about 1,500 gallons per day. The consumption, including wastage, averages in the neighborhood of 2,000 gallons during the hottest days. In order not to run short, it was deemed advisable, after having cautioned the men regarding the willful waste of water, to lock the pumps at night and distribute barrels full of water for drinking purposes on the deck. This we found to do away with most of the waste.

EXERCISE.

Twenty minutes daily, Saturday and Sunday excepted, has been devoted by each company to the setting-up exercises; also squad drill for recruits, as many as could be accommodated on deck, has been had for forty-five minutes daily, excepting Saturday and Sunday. Once a week fire and boat drill has been practiced in connection with the ship's officers and crew.

During the voyage "call to arms" was sounded, and the following disposition made of the troops to act in case of emergency. Three companies were placed on the hurricane deck, lying down and concealed from view as effectually as possible; also two companies were placed on the main deck, one company on the port side and one on the starboard side, practically hidden from sight. The balance of the troops on board were held in their quarters as a reserve.

SCHOOLS.

In compliance with General Orders, No. 2, headquarters First Brigade, United States Expeditionary Forces, officers and noncommissioned officers' schools were organized and held.

OFFICERS OF TRANSPORTS.

In this connection, I will say that the officers of the transport have been courteous and obliging in all respects, and have by their efforts aided materially in the comfort of the troops on board.

However, I would respectfully recommend that the commanding officer of the troops, before sailing, be furnished with a copy of the charter, and also written instructions as regards the authority of the ship's officers in regard to the troops under his immediate command, by this means obviating any misunderstanding that might arise.

On the 16th day of June, Private Elias Hutchinson, Company M, Second Regiment Oregon Volunteers, was operated on for appendicitis, but after lingering for several days died at 6.20 a. m. June 20, and was buried at sea off the Island of Guam, Ladrone group, 2° northwest of Point Orote, on the same day, with due military honors.

Very respectfully,
P. G. EASTWICK, Jr.,
Major, Second Regiment Oregon Volunteers,
Commanding U. S. Troops on board S. S. City of Sydney.

[Inclosure 7.]

ON BOARD S. S. CITY OF PEKIN,
July 1, 1898. (Received August 29, 1898.)

ASSISTANT ADJUTANT-GENERAL,
First Brigade, United States Expeditionary Forces.

SIR: I have the honor to submit the following report as to the sanitary condition of the transport *City of Pekin* and the health of troops on board from June 1 to July 1 1898:

I have taken every precaution to keep the men clean and free from vermin; having them bathe daily, wash their clothes at least thrice a week; the surgeons in charge of battalions examine bodies and clothing of men weekly. The quarters of the men have been washed well with bichloride solution and the berth deck and walls sprayed with a solution of phenol and acid carbol. The result has been most gratifying; a careful individual inspection of every man, his clothing, bedding, and quarters show that the entire command is free from vermin, a condition I think unique on a troopship. The sick report shows that the methods adopted by this department to have pure air have been most successful. The officers and enlisted men have all shown a ready willingness to carry out all orders and suggestions from the medical department. The Hospital Corps have had litter drill daily, the limited space on board ship preventing any marching exercises. They have also been instructed daily in calisthenic exercises.

I and my assistant surgeons have delivered several lectures to the officers and noncommissioned officers on sanitation, hygeine, and how best to preserve health in this climate, the use and abuse of fruits and vegetables indigenous to this country.

The condition of the ship's drainage and plumbing is not good, having on several occasions broken through and flooded the sleeping quarters of men.

The hourly inspection by members of the sanitary corps and several inspections daily by the surgeons have been continued as before; each surgeon giving a written report every evening.

As was stated in last report to you, the men were all vaccinated on May 29. I find that about 80 per cent were successful.

I have in use "social hall" for a hospital, which is fairly large, very airy, and comfortable, giving facilities for doing even more work than has been necessary. We have had only two serious cases this month—one a case of acute mania, developing upon the evening of the 28th, and a concussion of the spine, owing to a fall on June 30. This accident was apparently due to carelessness on the part of the "ship crew," a bunker hatch being left open without the officer of the day being informed of the fact, therefore the danger was unknown, no sentry being posted, and the man on his way to his quarters dropped through. The other cases in the hospital consisted mostly of influenza and minor surgery.

The battalion surgeons have each been giving daily lectures to their sections of the sanitary corps and the company bearers every afternoon in "first-aid" work.

Very respectfully,

WM. D. MCCARTHY,
Major and Surgeon.

[Inclosure 8.]

HDQRS. FIRST REGIMENT CALIFORNIA U. S. VOLUNTEER INFANTRY,
Cavite Arsenal, P. I., July 7, 1898. (Received August 29, 1898.)
ACTING ASSISTANT ADJUTANT-GENERAL,
First Brigade, United States Expeditionary Forces.

SIR: In compliance with directions from brigade headquarters, I have the honor to report that the First Regiment California U. S. Volunteer Infantry, at 10.40 o'clock on the morning of May 23, 1898, bound for Cavite, Philippine Islands, boarded the transport *City of Pekin*, chartered by the Navy Department, for which port it sailed at 4.50 p. m. on the 25th of May.

On the 30th of May, 1898, the command participated in the memorial exercises held on Decoration Day, at sea, arriving at Honolulu, Hawaiian Islands, at 6.50 p. m. June 1.

On the morning of June 4, at 10 a. m., the transport began its voyage to the island of Guam, convoyed by the United States cruiser *Charleston*, and sighted the island at 4 o'clock in the morning, June 20, casting anchor in San Luis D'Apra Harbor at 1.50 p. m. of the same day.

On June 22, at 4.05 o'clock p. m., the transport resumed its voyage for Cavite, on the island of Luzon, Philippine Islands, where it arrived on June 30 at 5 o'clock p. m.

The entire distance run was 7,246 miles. The voyage was without event, there being no storms of any kind until the evening of June 29, one day out from Cavite.

The enlisted men, 980 in number, were quartered in the steerage deck, in a space 10 feet high, 425 feet long and 60 feet wide, exclusive of the space located in the bow. Some of the berth-deck space was occupied by commissary supplies.

The bunks were well constructed and arranged in tiers three high, and, in some places, four high. The tiers were from three to seven bunks deep, and I think they were not sufficiently cut up by passages. Had there been a passageway, however narrow, between every two bunks in the same tier, the ventilation would have been somewhat improved and some of the inconveniences resulting from seasickness avoided.

The full strength of the regiment on board the transport was 57 officers and 980 enlisted men. In addition she carried 123 naval officers and about 50 or 60 of a crew—in all over 1,200 persons. While such a number of persons might be readily transported in the Temperate Zone in a vessel of the size and tonnage of the *Pekin* without any discomfort whatever, still I am of the opinion that the number should be considerably lessened for a voyage in the Tropics, in view of the fact that during storms the troops would all be compelled to remain below, under battened hatches and without the advantage of windsails. However that may be, I must say that during the trip the health of the command might be said to be excellent, not more than 8 or 9 men being confined to hospital at any one time. I am inclined to believe that this small sick list was due largely to daily salt-water bathing, morning and evening, sleeping in the open air on deck, calisthenic and other exercises, and sanitary precautions taken by medical officers.

The rations furnished were ample, but I am of the opinion that some alteration of the prescribed ration should be made to meet the changed condition of a life in the Tropics.

I would, however, respectfully recommend that, for the purpose of cooking the rations, a separate and distinct galley, adequate for the preparation of meals, be set apart for the exclusive use of troops, and that over that galley neither the captain of the vessel nor his crew be permitted to exercise any control whatever.

During the voyage in the warm belt practically but two meals a day were allowed to the men. After reveille coffee and a piece of bread was given to each man. At about 11 o'clock a regular meal was had, and at 5 o'clock dinner was served.

Each morning the arms were inspected, and once a week a general inspection was had. The quarters were inspected several times a day.

Officers and noncommissioned officers had instruction every day, except Saturday and Sunday and the two days during which the transport was at Guam.

Drill in the manual and calisthenic and other exercises, prescribed by the brigade commander, took place each morning, Saturdays and Sundays excepted.

The discipline of the regiment was satisfactory.

I have the honor to be, very respectfully,

JAMES F. SMITH,
Colonel First Regiment California U. S. Volunteer Infantry.

[Inclosure 9.]

HEADQUARTERS SECOND REGIMENT OREGON U. S. VOLUNTEERS,
Cavite, P. I., July 8, 1898. (Received August 29, 1898.)
ASSISTANT ADJUTANT-GENERAL,
First Brigade, U. S. Expeditionary Forces, Cavite Arsenal, P. I.

SIR: In compliance with Army Regulations, I have the honor to make my report in regard to transportation of troops of my command from San Francisco to this point.

On May 24, 1898, we embarked at San Francisco on board the S. S. *Australia* with part of my command, consisting of my headquarters and Companies A, B, C, D, E, G, H, K, and L, and proceeded out into the bay and there dropped anchor, awaiting final departure. About 3 p. m. May 25 we steamed out of the harbor, heading for these islands, and arrived at Honolulu on the 1st day of June. We left Honolulu on June 3 and arrived at Guam, Ladrone Islands, on the 20th about 7 a. m. After a stoppage of about two days we left Guam at 2 p. m. June 22 and sailed for these islands, and arrived in the harbor off Cavite at 5 p. m. June 30.

Outside of the ordinary complaints usual to a sea voyage of this kind the health of the command during the trip was very satisfactory, considering the general arrangements made for the comfort and the condition of the men while in transit.

A daily system of rations was arranged, after a few days out, in adapting ourselves to the different departments and the handling and custody of matters of this kind.

A general system of work was organized for the trip, so far as it related to the health and comfort of the command. We established a system of two meals a day, with a luncheon of coffee and hard bread in the morning.

A system of drill was kept up, so far as practicable, aboard ship. Setting-up exercises and the drill of the manual of arms was adhered to every day (Saturday and Sunday excepted) and strictly complied with.

The bathing of the men was watched very closely, they being compelled to bathe by companies twice a week, commencing by three companies each day on the first three days of each week, to be followed up in like manner on the latter three days of the week.

A general inspection of the quarters of the ship was followed out each day, Major Jones, of the brigade staff, acting as inspecting officer, accompanied by the commanding officer of this regiment.

Officers' schools were kept up each day during the trip as follows: From 10.30 to 11.30 a school was given for the benefit of commissioned officers under the auspices of one of the brigade officers, where a system was given out in regard to the construction of a quartermaster department, commissary department, and the adjutant-general's department, according to regulations. General Anderson himself kindly assisted in giving valuable information in regard to field maneuvers at these schools. In the afternoons a school for noncommissioned officers was given under the auspices of each battalion commander, the First Battalion having a school from 2 to 3 p. m., and the Second Battalion from 3.30 to 4.30 p. m. In the evening a school was held from 8 to 9 for commissioned officers on general tactics and field maneuvers under the auspices of the commanding officer of the regiment.

Church services were held every Sunday, and, so far as practicable, a general military discipline was conducted all through the voyage.

The distance traveled by this command was as follows: San Francisco to Honolulu, 2,102 miles; from Honolulu to Guam, 3,339 miles; from Guam to Cavite, 1,756 miles; making a total of 7,197 miles.

I would respectfully state that the accommodations aboard ship were entirely inadequate, so far as sleeping accommodations and a general healthful condition was concerned. We were quite fortunate in having a very pleasant and satisfactory voyage all through, the time consumed in the trip being thirty-six days. Also, I regret that conditions were such that compelled my command to come into the field for service only partially equipped, so far as actual necessities, such as clothing, shoes, and equipment, required for field service, owing to the limited provisions made for these matters in the quartermaster department at San Francisco. We are very short on these things that would be absolutely necessary for a successful field campaign.

Accompanying this report you will find reports as made by Maj. P. G. Eastwick, jr., who was placed in command of Companies F, I, and M, of my regiment, which sailed on board the S. S. *City of Sydney* on the same date.

Very respectfully,

O. SUMMERS,
Colonel Second Regiment Oregon U. S. Volunteers.

HDQRS. FIRST BRIGADE, U. S. EXPEDITIONARY FORCES,
Cavite Arsenal, Philippine Islands, July 9, 1898.
(Received August 29, 1898.)

ADJUTANT-GENERAL, U. S. ARMY, *Washington, D. C.*

GENERAL: As the major-general assigned to the command of this expedition has not reached here, and his time of coming is uncertain, I submit to you a statement of the present condition of the expedition and of the character of our surroundings.

The town of Cavite entirely covers the point of a narrow peninsula, 7 miles from Manila by water; 27 by land. About one-third of this point of the peninsula is occupied by the buildings of a navy-yard and arsenal; the rest by the town. But on the sea side of the town there is a line of stone forts and casemated sea wall so extensive that 2,000 Spanish prisoners are confined therein, with room for more.

There is also in the town an infantry barrack, formerly used by the Seventh Spanish Infantry and now by the Second Oregon Infantry.

Between the town and the navy-yard there is a small inclosed stone fort, in which we hold confined the 60 Spanish prisoners taken at Guam, kept as a matter of comity for navy, the admiral commanding promising to reimburse the War Department for the value of their rations.

Here I would state that as I had no orders or instructions in relation to the capture of any of the Ladrone Islands, I allowed the navy to take the entire responsibility, giving them a reinforcement of two companies; rationing and guarding their prisoners—6 officers, 54 soldiers—on the way over.

The buildings of the navy-yard and arsenal are large and commodious, of stone and brick. The houses of the town are built of stone and pesa, and resemble closely the houses to be seen in Mexican cities. The villages of the natives on the upper part of the peninsula are bamboo structures.

This command was landed within two days after our arrival, with five days' rations and from 100 to 200 rounds of ammunition per man.

Apprehending that a strong Spanish squadron might arrive before our monitors, Admiral Dewey strongly advised that we should not land anything more than absolutely necessary subsistence and impedimenta. I acted upon this advice, although it involved, of course, retaining the transports much longer than I would otherwise have kept them.

As soon as it became probable that the monitors and the second land expedition would soon arrive, I took the responsibility of landing our stores. This was advisable, as the canvas clothing was damp and in many cases wet, and needed to be opened and aired as soon as possible.

This has been a slow process, as the transports were anchored far from the shore and all the impedimenta had to be carried by hand.

The ponies here are too small for transportation work, and loads of any weight have to be hauled in carts drawn by the water buffalo, and they can only be obtained by sending out some distance in the country for them. Very little in the way of transportation, fuel, or forage can be obtained in this vicinity.

The district of Cavite—all the part south of the island from Manila—has been for many years the head center of insurrections and the scene of warfare, and consequently ordinary supplies can only be found here in small quantities. As it is now the scene of insurgent warfare, the opposing forces have killed off nearly all the cattle, and appropriate all the subsistence supplies they can seize.

General Aguinaldo tells me he has about 15,000 fighting men, but only 11,000 armed with guns. Most of these he has taken from the Spaniards. He claims to have in all, 4,000 prisoners.

When we first landed he seemed very suspicious and not at all friendly, but I have now come to a better understanding with him, and he is much more friendly and seems willing to cooperate; but he has declared himself dictator and president and is trying to take Manila without our assistance. This is not probable, but if he can effect his purpose he will, I apprehend, antagonize any attempt on our part to establish a provisional government.

Manila is strongly fortified, and is difficult of approach from the land side on account of dense bamboo thickets and swamp land in rainy season.

My information is that there are from 4,000 to 8,000 effective soldiers—regulars—in Manila, and an uncertain number of half-breed volunteers, who are not likely to give much trouble.

As a result of experience, I would respectfully submit a statement as to supplies. I was only in San Francisco two days before sailing, and never saw the command or had any control of it until I saw one regiment of it on board the steamer on which I took passage myself. I had no opportunity to inspect it—to ascertain its wants.

I was assured, however, that it was fully equipped and supplied with subsistence for six months. I found at Honolulu that a large part of the command had no change of underclothing and were beginning to be infested with graybacks. I ordered a purchase to meet the emergency.

All quartermaster supplies have been invoiced to the regimental quartermasters and all the subsistence to the regimental commissaries.

The estimates of the quartermasters for clothing had been cut down to a very inadequate amount, upon a representation that they should only require for what was absolutely essential, and that a full supply would be sent them hereafter.

Being entirely inexperienced, the regimental quartermasters made no protest, and accepted what was given them. The result is that a number of men have not a single garment of underclothing, the steaming process resorted to on the steamers to kill the vermin having destroyed the clothing.

The men of the Second Oregon Volunteer Infantry have only one pair of shoes each, mostly badly worn, and nearly all of them shoes of their own, which they were wearing when mustered in. Very few of them have Government shoes, as a small lot sent them were nearly all too large. While thus cut down on essentials the Second Oregon Volunteer Infantry was directed to take with them their State tents, about 500 in number, which were useless to them, as we have no transportation for tents and the weather is too hot to use them if we had.

I do not wish to reflect on the administrative organization. The conditions here could not well be anticipated in San Francisco.

We have succeeded in buying a reasonable amount of fresh meat from steamers bringing supplies in on speculation.

The health of the command is good, excepting the Second Oregon Volunteer Infantry, which has 145 men on the sick report.

A refugee from Manila, just in, tells me that the people there have eaten up nearly all their horses.

With great respect, your obedient servant,

THOMAS M. ANDERSON,
Brigadier-General Volunteers, U. S. Army, Commanding.

HDQRS. FIRST BRIGADE, U. S. EXPEDITIONARY FORCES,
Cavite Arsenal, Philippine Islands, July 14, 1898.
(Received August 29, 1898.)

ADJUTANT-GENERAL, U. S. ARMY,
Washington, D. C., U. S. A.

GENERAL: As I have an unexpected and very short notice of a sailing of a merchant steamer to Hongkong, I will endeavor to give a concise statement of this situation.

All the military stores of the expedition have been landed and stored in the buildings of the navy-yard and arsenal. The soldiers are being drilled, instructed, and disciplined. They have been sent out on practice marches, reconnoissances, and target practice.

We are now beginning to collect water buffalo and carts for transportation, and also to make scaling ladders of bamboo, etc.

One battalion of the First California Volunteer Infantry is under orders to cross the bay and go into camp between Parañaque and Manila, to secure a good camp and to guard transportation to be collected there. A number of discreet officers have made personal reconnoissances. Lieutenants McCain and Clark, of the brigade staff, and Captain Case and Lieutenant Bryan, of the Second Oregon Volunteer Infantry, have obtained valuable information as to the defenses of Manila, landings on the bay, roads, trails, and camping places.

We have succeeded in getting out of Manila a gentleman who has heretofore given very valuable information to Admiral Dewey. I have also obtained valuable, and, I believe, trustworthy information, as it has been tested with varied reports from other quarters. A small reconnoitering party has started from here to-day to make, if possible, the circuit of the city.

The insurgents have the Spanish forces in Manila closely besieged by a bushwhacking force of brave and adventurous men, but of very loose organization. A moderate amount of supplies go through their lines into the city, either by connivance or negligence. Provisions are scarce, but under present conditions the city will not be starved out.

Telegraphic intelligence is said to go to the city by way of a telegraph line to Borneo; and they receive their mails quite regularly through the foreign men-of-war in the harbor.

As you are aware, we have no artillery or cavalry. As Admiral Dewey gave all the captured guns and ammunition to the insurgents, the 50 heavy artillerymen have no guns to use and are only acting as infantry, and are at present guarding prisoners.

I have no intelligence except newspaper reports from Hongkong as to what reinforcements are coming and whether there will be light batteries or cavalry in the expected command. Nor is it known, certainly, whether it will venture to come on from Guam without convoy. I have no orders about the two transports *Australia* and *City of Sydney*, but have kept them at Admiral Dewey's advice. He stated to me, as I before advised you, that if the Spanish fleet arrived before the monitors, he would not fight them, and that I should keep the transports to get to a place of safety, as this place, Cavite, would be indefensible. He subsequently told me that he thought he would make his fight in Subig Bay, and suggests that I should move my forces there; that if defeated in a naval action my command would be safe there; and, if successful, I could march to the termination of a railroad, and move on Manila from the north. Upon this I stated that I would, if in command, move my forces to the north side of the bay directly from here by water. My reason for expressing this preference was that from Subig to reach the railway I would have had to march over an almost impassable mountain trail to the railroad, 131 miles from Manila, with inadequate transportation. Whereas by going directly beyond Manila by water, and a short march, the move can be made in a few hours; and by taking that position we would be able to intercept any Spanish force attempting to reinforce Manila from the north.

But Admiral Dewey has just informed me this morning that he has resolved to make his fight here in this bay. In the event that the Spanish fleet comes on by way of the Red Sea, he proposes to attack Manila as soon as the monitors arrive.

I only fear that, in an attack on formidable land batteries, his fleet may be so seriously injured as to lessen its chance of victory over the Spanish squadron.

Very respectfully,

THOMAS M. ANDERSON,
Brigadier-General, U. S. Volunteers, Commanding.

NOTE.—News from Borneo reaches Manila via Iloilo.

HDQRS. FIRST BRIGADE, U. S. EXPEDITIONARY FORCES,
Cavite Arsenal, Philippine Islands, July 18, 1898.
(Received August 29, 1898.)

ADJUTANT-GENERAL, U. S. ARMY,
Washington, D. C.

GENERAL: Since reading the President's instructions to General Merritt, I think I should state to you that the establishment of a provisional government on our part will probably bring us in conflict with the insurgents, now in active hostility to Spain.

The insurgent chief, Aguinaldo, has declared himself dictator and self-appointed president. He has declared martial law and promulgated a minute method of rule and administration under it

We have observed all official military courtesies, and he and his followers express great admiration and gratitude to the great American republic of the North; yet in many ways they obstruct our purposes, and are using every effort to take Manila without us.

I suspect also that Aguinaldo is secretly negotiating with the Spanish authorities, as his confidential aid is in Manila.

The city is strongly fortified and hard to approach in the rainy season. If a bombardment fails, we should have the best engineering ability here.

Very respectfully,

THOMAS M. ANDERSON,
Brigadier-General, U. S. Volunteers, Commanding.

HEADQUARTERS DEPARTMENT OF THE PACIFIC,
Manila Bay, Philippine Islands, July 25, 1898.
(Received August 29, 1898.)

ADJUTANT-GENERAL, *Washington, D. C.*

SIR: As cabled to-day, I arrived here at noon, and found the condition of things as follows:

The insurgents seem to have surrounded the town of Manila and are lying off at a distance, but making no attempt for its capture. I have conferred with Admiral Dewey, and he is very anxious that nothing should be done until the two monitors arrive. However, much will depend upon when the monitors reach here and what I may discover in the meantime, that I will not attack at once after the remainder of the fleet arrives. Before this reaches you it may be that I will have cabled news which will make this unimportant, and for that reason I will not enter into particulars.

As you have probably been informed, though I have not as yet seen General Greene, there were four fatal cases of sickness in his fleet, one an officer—Lieutenant Lazelle. I have not heard the names of the men, but they probably have been communicated by General Greene. The *Newport*, on which I sailed, has arrived in this port with but one case of typhoid fever, which has been sent to the hospital on shore. There were other cases of sickness confined to two or three of the passengers, but they have all recovered.

The difficulties in the way of a preparation for attack, outside the absence of the monitors, are very great, though not insurmountable. The landing of supplies and troops and the stores generally on vessels is very slow business. It all has to be done by lighters having very little capacity, and there are very few under the control of the Army. Beyond Cavite and south of Manila the troops already landed occupy very good camps, and everything is being done to insure the health of the men, which at present is good; but I fear very much that a long delay will result in considerable sickness, and for that reason I am anxious to make a demand for the surrender of Manila, and an attack, if need be, at as early date as possible. In view of the critical condition of affairs, Admiral Dewey, however, hesitates to expose his unarmored boats to the fire of the forts, in which, it is said, some powerful modern guns are mounted, but as soon as the monitors arrive he assures me that he will be able to make an attack which undoubtedly will prove successful.

The approaches from the camp to Manila are narrow and inclosed by rice fields and swamps which are practically impassable. There is one good main road about 30 feet wide, but in places not wide enough for more than two vehicles to pass each other. This is the best road that the vehicles can take, though approach is also practicable by the beach. I am very much in hopes that the *Monterey* will be here by the 1st of August and the other monitor only a few days later.

I visited the camp yesterday and made a reconnoissance of the approaches to the city, so that I speak by personal knowledge of the above facts.

Very respectfully,

W. MERRITT,
Major-General, U. S. Army.

MANILA, PHILIPPINES, *received August 30, 1898—6.40 a. m.*
ADJUTANT-GENERAL, *Washington:*

On eve of departure to-day, and having received no reply to my cablegram on subject, have ordered General Babcock to proceed on first transport with official report. This I believe will get approval of War Department. In view of custom in such cases have also ordered Major Sturgis, acting aid, to accompany General Babcock.

MERRITT.

ADJUTANT-GENERAL'S OFFICE,
Washington, August 30, 1898.
DEWEY, *Manila:*

The President directs use your discretion in regard to transportation of priests and Spanish civil authorities that desire to leave Hongkong, determining, first, attitude of English authorities there. The Secretary of War agrees to use of transports.

(Signed) ALLEN, *Acting Secretary.*

ADJUTANT-GENERAL'S OFFICE, *August 30, 1898.*
COMMANDING GENERAL, DEPARTMENT OF CALIFORNIA,
San Francisco, Cal.

SIR: General Babcock and Major Sturgis, now en route from the Philippines, should, on arrival at San Francisco, report by telegraph to the Adjutant-General of the Army and await orders at San Francisco.

Very respectfully,

H. C. CORBIN, *Adjutant-General.*

ADJUTANT-GENERAL'S OFFICE, *Washington, August 30, 1898.*
COMMANDING GENERAL, *Manila:*

Confer with Admiral Dewey as to use of transports in connection with cable to him from Secretary Navy this date.

H. C. CORBIN, *Adjutant-General.*

NEW YORK, *August 30, 1898.*
Hon. R. A. ALGER, *Secretary of War, Washington, D. C.*:
Major Wadsworth telegraphs from Manila wishing to be ordered home. Hope it can be done.
T. C. PLATT.

LOS ANGELES, CAL., *August 30, 1898.*
(Received 10.05 p. m.)
Gen. H. C. CORBIN, *War Department, Washington, D. C.*:
Condition Seventh Regiment something awful. Sickness arising from grossly inadequate arrangements is fast accomplishing what enemy's bullets can not do. Company H, from Ventura, especially suffering. In humanity's name urge these unfortunates, citizens and soldiers, be mustered out or relieved from present unspeakable distress, for which someone other than themselves must be responsible.
STEPHEN M. WHITE.

ADJUTANT-GENERAL'S OFFICE,
Washington, August 30, 1898—11.45 p. m.
COMMANDING GENERAL, DEPARTMENT OF CALIFORNIA,
San Francisco, Cal.:
The following received from Stephen M. White, Los Angeles, Cal.:
"Condition Seventh Regiment something awful. Sickness arising from grossly inadequate arrangements is fast accomplishing what enemy's bullets can not do. Company H, from Ventura, especially suffering. In humanity's name urge these unfortunates, citizens and soldiers, be mustered out or relieved from present unspeakable distress, for which someone other than themselves must be responsible."
The Secretary War desires immediate report on condition of this regiment, and every remedy within your command applied.
H. C. CORBIN, *Adjutant-General.*

MANILA, *received Washington August 31, 1898—2 a. m.*
ADJUTANT-GENERAL, *Washington*:
No casualties in August among regular officers.
OTIS.

PALACE, MANILA, PHILIPPINES, *received August 31, 1898—2.38 a. m.*
ADJUTANT-GENERAL, U. S. ARMY, *Washington*:
General Merritt left for Hongkong yesterday noon, General Babcock accompanying. Your instructions to General Babcock sent to Hongkong. Major Scriven here ordered to Hongkong to join General Merritt at once. Major Simpson here will return to San Francisco first opportunity. Telegraphic instructions of 13th instant concerning Admiral Dewey received.
OTIS,
Major-General, U. S. Volunteers.

NAHANT, MASS., *August 31, 1898.*
(Received 9.28 a. m.)
Maj. Gen. H. C. CORBIN, *War Department, Washington, D. C.*:
Should be greatly obliged if Major Wadsworth, General Merritt's staff, Manila, could be ordered home. Senator Platt makes same request. Wadsworth personal friend.
H. C. LODGE.

ST. PAUL, MINN., *August 31, 1898.*
(Received 1.41 p. m.)

Adjutant-General CORBIN, *Washington, D. C.:*

Please cable Manila and advise me as to truth of report of death of Lieutenant Morley, Company G, Thirteenth Minnesota.

C. K. DAVIS.

ADJUTANT-GENERAL'S OFFICE, *Washington, August 31, 1898.*

Hon. C. K. DAVIS, *St. Paul, Minn.:*

We have received complete reports from General Merritt, giving names of officers and men who have died, and the name of Lieutenant Morley of the Thirteenth Minnesota does not appear.

H. C. CORBIN, *Adjutant-General.*

ADJUTANT-GENERAL'S OFFICE, *Washington, August 31, 1898.*

COMMANDING GENERAL, UNITED STATES TROOPS,
Manila, Philippines.

SIR: The Secretary of War directs me to inclose copy of a communication received from a reliable source, together with newspaper clipping concerning the subject-matter of the said communication, with request that you give the matter a thorough investigation and report the result of same to this office.

Very respectfully,

H. O. S. HEISTAND,
Assistant Adjutant-General.

MANILA, *September 1, 1898—3.20 a. m.*

ADJUTANT-GENERAL, U. S. ARMY, *Washington:*

Steamer *St. Paul,* last of the five transports conveying fourth expedition from San Francisco, arrived yesterday; troops in good health. Have steamers *Arizona* and *Scandia* sailed, or will they sail from San Francisco for this point, and, if so, what troops will they transport?

OTIS,
Major-General, U. S. Volunteers, Commanding.

ADJUTANT-GENERAL'S OFFICE,
Washington, September 1, 1898—9.45 a. m.

COMMANDING GENERAL, UNITED STATES FORCES, *Manila:*

Arizona and *Scandia* have sailed for Manila. They bring no troops beyond Honolulu.

H. C. CORBIN, *Adjutant-General.*

DEPARTMENT OF STATE,
Washington, September 1, 1898.

The SECRETARY OF WAR.

SIR: In compliance with the request of the Chinese minister, I have the honor to ask that instructions may be telegraphed to the commander in chief of the United States military forces at Manila to recognize Chen Chien Shan, a Chinese merchant at Manila, as consular agent at that port till the arrival of the Chinese consular representative, Chen Chung.

Very respectfully, yours,

J. B. MOORE, *Acting Secretary.*

ADJUTANT-GENERAL'S OFFICE,
Washington, September 1, 1898—4.30 p. m.

COMMANDING GENERAL, UNITED STATES FORCES, *Manila:*

The President directs that Chen Chien Shan, a Chinese merchant at Manila, be recognized as consular agent at Manila, pending arrival of Chinese consular representative, Chen Chung.

By order of Secretary of War:

H. C. CORBIN, *Adjutant-General.*

ADJUTANT-GENERAL'S OFFICE,
Washington, September 1, 1898.

COMMANDING GENERAL, *Manila:*

Order Major Wadsworth, quartermaster, home.

H. C. CORBIN, *Adjutant-General.*
W. H. C.

SAN FRANCISCO CAL.,
September 2, 1898—10.38 p. m.

ADJUTANT-GENERAL, U. S. ARMY, *Washington, D. C.:*

Following is summary of General Miller's report upon telegram of August 30–31, about sickness in Seventh California. Condition September 1: Typhoid, 19; recovering from measles, 12; malarial, 5; bronchial, 16; surgical cases, 5; pneumonia, 6; sick in quarters, 10. Enlisted strength of regiment, 1,260; total sick, 73; per cent of sickness, 6; per cent of typhoid, 1½. Deaths during the month of August, 6. Remedies: clean camps, liberal disinfectants, removal of garbage, kitchens placed further from latrines. Medical board making exhaustive inquiry into origin and spread of disease. Chief surgeon holds percentage not excessive, no deaths occurring at present.

FIELD, *Major Second Artillery,*
Acting Assistant Adjutant-General, in the absence of the Department Commander.

HONGKONG, *September 2, 1898—11.05 p. m.*

ADJUTANT-GENERAL, *Washington:*

I recommend Chance, of Signal Corps, be commissioned.

MERRITT.

HELENA, MONT., *September 2, 1898—11.08 p. m.*

Hon. RUSSELL A. ALGER,
Secretary of War, Washington, D. C.:

Please do not take action on discharging any Montana volunteers at Manila until you hear from me.

THOS. H. CARTER.

MANILA, *September 3, 1898—8.35 a. m.*

ADJUTANT-GENERAL, *Washington:*

May 26 Stanton telegraphed if Manila is occupied by our forces the Quartermaster's Department will hire quarters necessary for public service. Will necessary quarters be hired for officers?

OTIS, *Major-General.*

ADJUTANT-GENERAL'S OFFICE,
Washington, September 3, 1898.

Hon. T. H. CARTER, *Helena, Mont.:*

No action will be taken on discharging Montana volunteers at Manila for the present.

H. C. CORBIN, *Adjutant-General.*

MANILA, *September 3, 1898—5.25 p. m.*

ADJUTANT-GENERAL, *Washington:*

Some insurgent forces entered suburb of city behind United States troops day of occupation and number since augmented. General Merritt insisted on withdrawing, but Aguinaldo has thus far postponed action by correspondence and has failed to comply. He insists upon occupation of suburb, withdrawing of American troops therefrom, and other concessions. They fear resumption of Spanish authority, and Spanish residents increase fear insurgents pardoning of native inhabitants; aspire to and determine to fight even United States for Philippines. Large number of remaining natives prefer prolonged American protection. Insurgent army, large part of which resentful and desire hostilities against American troops. Principal men, including Aguinaldo, desire peaceful relations, I think. Am preparing communication withdrawing of insurgents from suburb within certain time. May be necessary to forcibly eject them, in which event war may result. Any indication by United States Government looking to removal Spanish prisoners, or to insurgents that Manila will not soon be remanded to Spain, will greatly relieve situation.

OTIS.

ST. PAUL, MINN., *September 3, 1898—12.53 p. m.*

Maj. Gen. H. C. CORBIN,
Adjutant-General U. S. Army, Washington, D. C.:

Please wire Manila and inform me as to truth of report of death of Harry G. Watson, Company C, Thirteenth Minnesota Infantry.

C. K. DAVIS.

ADJUTANT-GENERAL'S OFFICE,
Washington, September 3, 1898.

Hon. C. K. DAVIS, *St. Paul, Minn.:*

We have received complete reports of all deaths of soldiers in Manila, and the name of Harry G. Watson, Company C, Thirteenth Minnesota Volunteers, does not appear thereon.

H. C. CORBIN, *Adjutant-General.*

ADJUTANT-GENERAL'S OFFICE,
Washington, September 4, 1898.

Major-General OTIS, *Commanding, Manila*:

The Secretary of War directs that you telegraph immediately what there is of the report that a ship with 700 insurgents has left Manila to attack Spaniards in the Philippines. Are any similar insurgent expeditions fitting out? Telegraph generally the present state of insurgent operations against the Spaniards.

H. C. CORBIN, *Adjutant-General.*

MANILA, *September 5, 1898—2.40 a. m.*

ADJUTANT-GENERAL, *Washington:*

June 23, Aguinaldo declared revolution. Last week he proclaimed independence of Philippines; is reported that is about to seek recognition of foreign powers. Yesterday officers traversed entire railroad line between Manila and Dagupan, 120 miles. They report activity among insurgents, who claim capture of Spanish port Vigan, western coast Luzon. Officers report conference between principal men of interior and upper provinces of Luzon with Aguinaldo, and apparent settlement former difficulties. Chiefs of priest party and Aguinaldo have conferred and claim to be in accord. Insurgents constructing defenses on railroad line and elsewhere; no insurgent vessel having troops has left Manila nor Manila Bay, recently. Rumor reports the insurgents have three or four small vessels, two of which carry guns; that about August 10, two vessels with from 100 to 200 troops left the bay, destination unknown. Rumor reports insurgents meditate attack from Iloilo, Panay, where 4,000 disaffected residents are prepared to assist. All rumors lack confirmation. The largest insurgent vessel will not carry more than 250 men. Our relations friendly but require delicate manipulation.

OTIS, *Major-General.*

ADJUTANT-GENERAL'S OFFICE,
Washington, September 5, 1898.

Major-General OTIS, *Manila, P. I.:*

When troops are in quarters, if none are available for officers without renting, hire regulation allowance.

H. C. CORBIN, *Adjutant-General.*

SALEM, OREGON, *September 5, 1898—7.50 p. m.*

Adjutant-General CORBIN, *Washington, D. C.:*

I earnestly request that the 330 recruits to fill the Second Oregon Regiment to maximum be either mustered out and sent to homes in Oregon, or that they be promptly forwarded to their regiment at Manila. These men were recruited three months ago, and in the latter part of June the mustering officer, under order of the War Department, sent them in details, without uniforms or equipments, from their various stations, as fast as mustered, in charge of one of their number, to San Francisco, where they now are, as reported to me, in disorganized and demoralized condition, many of them suffering from physical and moral illness for want of proper care, discipline, sanitation, and camp regulations. I beseech your active interference.

WM. P. LORD, *Governor.*

ADJUTANT-GENERAL'S OFFICE,
Washington, September 5, 1898.

COMMANDING GENERAL, DEPARTMENT OF CALIFORNIA:

Following received from Governor of Oregon:

"I earnestly request that the 330 recruits to fill the Second Oregon Regiment to maximum be either mustered out and sent to homes in Oregon, or that they be promptly forwarded to their regiment at Manila. These men were recruited three months ago, and in the latter part of June the mustering officer, under order of the War Department, sent them in details, without uniforms or equipments, from their various stations, as fast as mustered, in charge of one of their number, to San Francisco, where they now are, as reported to me, in disorganized and demoralized condition, many of them suffering from physical and moral illness for want of proper care, discipline, sanitation, and camp regulations. I beseech your active interference."

Report of condition of these troops desired. If not sufficient officers with this detachment, officers should be detached from other regiments to see to their comfort, drill, and discipline.

By order Secretary of War:

H. C. CORBIN, *Adjutant-General.*

DEPARTMENT OF STATE,
Washington, September 6, 1898.

The Honorable, the SECRETARY OF WAR.

SIR: By direction of the President, I have the honor to request that a telegram may be sent to the commander of the United States military forces in the Philippines instructing him " to exert his influence during the suspension of hostilities between the United States and Spain to restrain insurgent hostilities against Spaniards, and, while maintaining a position of rightful supremacy as to the insurgents, to pursue, as far as possible, a conciliatory course toward all."

Very respectfully,

J. B. MOORE, *Acting Secretary.*

ADJUTANT-GENERAL'S OFFICE,
Washington, September 7, 1898—10.35 a. m.

Major-General OTIS,
Commanding United States Forces, Manila:

Secretary War directs you to exert your influence during the suspension of hostilities between the United States and Spain to restrain insurgent hostilities against Spaniards, and, while maintaining a position of rightful supremacy as to the insurgents, to pursue, as far as possible, a conciliatory course toward all.

H. C. CORBIN, *Adjutant-General.*

MANILA, *September 7, 1898—11.25 a. m.*

ADJUTANT-GENERAL, *Washington:*

Insurgents have captured all Spanish garrisons in island and control affairs outside of Cavite and this city. Number in city and outskirts under arms large and increasing. Admiral Dewey and myself consider affairs critical. Will send to Aguinaldo to-morrow long communication in reply to his demands on General Merritt in which conditions and our international obligations under the terms of capitulation are fully discussed, and which concludes as follows:

"It only remains for me to respectfully notify you that I am compelled by my instructions to demand that your armed forces evacuate the entire city of Manila, including its suburbs, and that I shall be obliged to take action with that end in view within a very short period of time should you decide not to comply with my Government's demands, and I hereby serve notice upon you that unless your troops are withdrawn beyond the lines of the city's suburbs before Thursday, the 15th instant, I shall be obliged to resort to forcible action, and that my Government will hold you responsible for any unfortunate consequences that may ensue. Permit me to believe my confidence in the sound judgment and patriotism of yourself and associates is not misplaced. In conclusion, I beg to inform you that I have conferred freely with Admiral Dewey upon the contents of this communication, and am delegated by him to state that he fully approves of the same in all respects; that the commands of our

Government compel us to act as therein indicated, and that between our respective forces there will be unanimity and complete concert of action.

"I am, with great respect, your obedient servant,

"E. S. OTIS,
"*U. S. Military Governor in the Philippines.*"

Copy of all correspondence by mail. I respectfully ask instructions if the course indicated above is not approved. Sentiment divided as to whether insurgents will comply with our demands.

OTIS, *Military Governor.*

ADJUTANT-GENERAL'S OFFICE,
Washington, September 7, 1898.

Major-General OTIS, *Manila:*

Your cablegram of this date has been submitted to the President and the Secretary of War, and your action, as therein outlined, is approved.

H. C. CORBIN, *Adjutant-General.*

SAN FRANCISCO, CAL., *September 9, 1898—5.54 p. m.*

H. C. CORBIN, *Adjutant-General U. S. Army, Washington, D. C.:*

If further troops are needed for Manila, I would consider it a special favor that the Sixth, Seventh, and Eighth California Volunteer Regiments be given an opportunity for active duty.

JAMES H. BUDD, *Governor of California.*

SAN FRANCISCO, CAL., *September 9, 1898—6.47 p. m.*

Honorable SECRETARY OF WAR, *Washington, D. C.:*

If troops be needed for Manila immediately, I would consider it a special favor if the Sixth, Seventh, and Eighth California Volunteer Regiments were ordered to the front for active duty. They are willing and anxious for a chance.

JAMES H. BUDD, *Governor.*

ADJUTANT-GENERAL'S OFFICE,
Washington, September 9, 1898—9.30 p. m.

Governor BUDD, *San Francisco, Cal.:*

It is not thought probable any considerable number of troops, more than are now in Manila, will be required there.

H. C. CORBIN, *Adjutant-General.*

DEPARTMENT OF STATE,
Washington, September 10, 1898.

The Honorable, the SECRETARY OF WAR.

SIR: I have the honor to state that by reason of an error in the transmission to it of the name of the consular representative of China who is to go to Manila, this department in its letter to you of August 5 last incorrectly described such representative as Mr. Chin, and in its letter of the 1st instant as Chen Chung. I am now informed by the Chinese minister at this capital that the correct name of the official is Chen Kang.

I have the honor therefore to request that the commanding officer of our military forces at Manila be advised by telegraph that the name of the Chinese consul-general who is to be sent to the city is Chen Kang, and not Chin or Chen Chung.

Respectfully, yours,

J. B. MOORE, *Acting Secretary.*

ADJUTANT-GENERAL'S OFFICE,
Washington, September 11, 1898—1 p. m.

COMMANDING GENERAL, UNITED STATES FORCES, *Manila:*

Correct name of consular representative China to go to Manila is Chen Kang.

H. C. CORBIN, *Adjutant-General.*

ADJUTANT-GENERAL'S OFFICE,
Washington, September 14, 1898—10.45 p. m.

COMMANDING GENERAL, *Manila:*

Report of situation desired.

H. C. CORBIN, *Adjutant-General.*

MANILA, *September 15, 1898—10.19 a. m.*

ADJUTANT-GENERAL, *Washington:*

Affairs much more satisfactory. Demands for withdrawal insurgent forces complied with and all withdrawn or withdrawing to-day except small forces in outlying districts which are not obeying insurgent leader. Aguinaldo requests few days in which withdraw them by detachments and punish their commanding officers. Over 2,000 already withdrawn. No concessions granted insurgents, but strict compliance with demands of 8th instant required. General good feeling prevailing. Manila quiet and business progressing favorably. No difficulty anticipated. Have been compelled to confine Spanish prisoners temporarily within limits of walled city.

OTIS, *Commanding.*

ADJUTANT-GENERAL'S OFFICE,
Washington, September 15, 1898—3 p. m.

COMMANDING GENERAL, *Manila:*

Acting Secretary War directs you cable names of chartered transports at Manila, stating names of those which will be required in service, and those which can be ordered to San Francisco for cancellation of charters.

H. C. CORBIN, *Adjutant-General.*

ADJUTANT-GENERAL'S OFFICE,
Washington, September 15, 1898—10.50 p. m.

COMMANDING GENERAL, *Manila:*

In your opinion, will any further force be required for service with you?

H. C. CORBIN, *Adjutant-General.*

DEPARTMENT OF STATE,
Washington, September 16, 1898.

The Honorable, the SECRETARY OF WAR.

SIR: I have the honor to communicate to you, for such action as may be available or expedient, within the actual sphere of control of the United States forces at Manila, the translated text of a telegram addressed by Cardinal Rampolla, the secretary of the Vatican, to the Apostolic Delegate in Washington, a copy of which has been informally left at the Executive Mansion by the secretary of the apostolic delegation with a request for such action as may seem proper:

"ROME, *September 13, 1898.*

"Monsignor MARTINELLI,

"*Apostolic Delegate, Washington, D. C.:*

"News comes from Manila that the bishop of New Segovia and some priests have been captured by the insurgents and are being treated in a brutal manner by them.

The Holy Father wishes that you should present the matter to the Government of the United States and try to move it to take some opportune step regarding it.

"M. CARD. RAMPOLLA."

Respectfully, yours,

WILLIAM R. DAY.

MANILA, *September 16, 1898—3.55 a. m.*
ADJUTANT-GENERAL ARMY, *Washington, D. C.:*
Twelve transports have been returned to San Francisco, six remaining in Manila Harbor, namely, *City of Para, City of Puebla, Morgan City, Peru, St. Paul,* and *Rio Janeiro;* last named leaves for San Francisco 22d instant with sick soldiers. With the present, desire to retain the *Peru* and *City of Para* for possible movement of troops in harbor; remaining vessels will depart in course week; every effort to unload and coal; facilities primitive.

OTIS, *Commanding.*

MANILA, *September 16, 1898—7.35 a. m.*
ADJUTANT-GENERAL ARMY, *Washington:*
In my opinion, based upon present indications, no further force required; insurgent leaders in politics and army in excitable frame of mind, but better portion amenable to reason, and desire to make approved reputation before civilized world.

OTIS, *Commanding.*

MANILA, *September 16, 1898—11.45 a. m.*
ADJUTANT-GENERAL ARMY, *Washington, D. C.:*
Telegraphed situation briefly yesterday. Insurgents have acceded demand and evacuated entire city of Manila, except small force in one outlying district. No difficulty anticipated and no concessions made to them. They express strong desire to maintain friendly intercourse with the United States Government in all particulars. They organized congress Thursday at Malolos, 20 miles north of city, to frame plan of government. May injure commerce by exacting tariffs at ports in their possession. They can place under arms at short notice, possibly 30,000 men. Manila very quiet, military government being perfected gradually, and large force policing and cleansing city. Health of command fairly satisfactory. Trade and commerce active. Treasury receipts since August 14, $540,000, Mexican current money. Philippines monthly expenses will aggregate at least $350,000, nearly one-half required to subsist 13,000 Spanish prisoners; believe that receipts will largely exceed expenditures; tariffs and duties imposed as directed by President on July 12, but received in currency of country as on gold basis would almost double former Spanish duties. United States laws applied for admission of Chinese and opium, sales of licenses for lotteries and other pastimes opposed by public morals discontinued; private claims against Spanish Government received in large numbers, aggregating large amounts, are being investigated, but it is not intended that any claims shall be paid which originated prior to our occupation.

OTIS, *Commanding.*

MANILA. (Received Washington, September 17, 1898—2.32 a. m.)
ADJUTANT-GENERAL ARMY, *Washington:*
Paymasters Whipple, treasurer of public funds; Kilbourne, auditor of public accounts in military government; duties complex and onerous; service very impor-

tant for proper administration of public affairs. Paymaster Keleher, disbursing officer provost marshal, and fully occupied by department proper, limited, and withdrawal of paymaster would embarrass situation; request reconsideration of telegraphic order.

OTIS, *Commanding.*

ADJUTANT-GENERAL'S OFFICE,
Washington, September 17, 1898—11.45 a. m.
COMMANDING GENERAL, *Manila:*
Order of Paymaster-General revoked. You are authorized to retain paymasters.
H. C. CORBIN, *Adjutant-General.*

MANILA. (Received Washington, September 18, 1898—3.13 a. m.)
ASSISTANT SECRETARY OF WAR, *Washington:*
Senator and *China* left port August 24 and 30; *Indiana,* September 1; *Ohio* and *Valencia,* September 3; *Pennsylvania,* September 9; *Newport,* September 13; *Zealandia,* August 24—in dry dock Nagasaki repairing; *Pekin* under contract of Navy; date of departure unknown; part of vessels proceeded by way of Nagasaki and part Honolulu.

OTIS, *Commanding.*

SAN FRANCISCO, CAL., *September 19, 1898—3.50 p. m.*
ADJUTANT-GENERAL, *Washington, D. C.:*
Recommend that battalion of California Heavy Artillery, consisting of commanding officer and adjutant and portions of Batteries A and D, which have all along belonged to the expeditionary forces, be included in the forces to go to Manila. Two officers and 76 men of these two batteries are now in Manila or en route there.

M. P. MILLER,
Brigadier-General, U. S. Volunteers.

ADJUTANT-GENERAL'S OFFICE,
Washington, September 19, 1898.
Brig. Gen. M. P. MILLER,
U. S. Volunteers, San Francisco, Cal.:
Your recommendation that California Heavy Artillery, consisting of commanding officer, adjutant, and portion of Batteries A and D, go to Manila is approved by Acting Secretary of War. They will proceed to that point with other troops ordered, reporting upon arrival to the commanding general for duty. Acknowledge receipt.
By command Major-General Miles:

H. C. CORBIN, *Adjutant-General.*

SAN FRANCISCO, CAL., *September 20, 1898—2.32 p. m.*
ADJUTANT-GENERAL, U. S. ARMY, *Washington, D. C.*
Referring to telegram of yesterday, regarding recruits and detachments for Manila, I recommend that the *Arizona,* now nearing Manila, be returned at once to Honolulu to take General King and his detachments to Manila. We can meet the *Arizona* at Honolulu with supplies to complete her cargo for Manila. These detachments are disappointed at delay in Honolulu and should go forward to regiments or be promptly mustered out.

MERRIAM, *Major-General.*

AFFAIRS IN THE PHILIPPINE ISLANDS. 793

CAMP MERRIAM, SAN FRANCISCO, CAL.,
September 20, 1898—2.09 p. m.

ADJUTANT-GENERAL, U. S. ARMY,
  Washington, D. C.:

Your telegram approving my recommendation that the California Heavy Artillery go to Manila is received.

           MILLER, *Commanding.*

SAN FRANCISCO, CAL., *September 20, 1898—2.10 p. m.*

ADJUTANT-GENERAL, U. S. ARMY,
  Washington, D. C.:

Arrived this morning from Honolulu.

           MERRIAM, *Major-General.*

ADJUTANT-GENERAL'S OFFICE,
Washington, September 20, 1898.

General OTIS, *Manila:*

Secretary Vatican advises bishop and priests New Segovia captured by insurgents and brutally treated. If under control, your forces protect from inhuman treatment.

By order Acting Secretary of War:

           H. C. CORBIN, *Adjutant-General.*

WAR DEPARTMENT,
Washington, September 21, 1898.

The Honorable, the SECRETARY OF STATE.

SIR: Replying to your letter of the 16th instant, communicating the translated text of a telegram addressed by Cardinal Rampolla, the secretary of the Vatican, under date of September 13, 1898, to the apostolic delegate in Washington, advising that the bishop of New Segovia and some priests have been captured by insurgents, Philippine Islands, and are being treated in a brutal manner by them, I have the honor to inclose herewith for your information copy of a cablegram of this Department, dated September 20, 1898, to General Otis at Manila on the subject.

Very respectfully,

           G. D. MIEKLEJOHN,
           Acting Secretary of War.

MANILA. (Received, Washington, September 21, 1898—12.53 a. m.)

ADJUTANT-GENERAL, *Washington:*

Has Reeve been promoted brigadier?

           OTIS.

ADJUTANT-GENERAL'S OFFICE,
Washington, September 21, 1898.

General OTIS, *Manila:*

Reeve promoted brigadier September 5.

           CORBIN, *Adjutant-General.*
W. H. C.

ADJUTANT-GENERAL'S OFFICE,
Washington, September 21, 1898.

COMMANDING GENERAL, Manila:

Do you think any change in the rations for troops serving in the Philippines called for? Your views and recommendations desired by Acting Secretary of War. The question of suitable clothing should be considered and reported on.

H. C. CORBIN, Adjutant-General.

SAN FRANCISCO, CAL., September 21, 1898—7.40 p. m.

ADJUTANT-GENERAL, U. S. ARMY,
Washington, D. C.:

General Miller has received no orders relative to Manila; is very anxious to go as brigade or division commander; has spent much time and labor in equipping and instructing troops. On account of his services and ability I recommend that authority be given by telegraph for General Miller to accompany last contingent of the expedition.

MERRIAM,
Major-General, Commanding.

MANILA. (Received Washington, September 22, 1898—6.41 a. m.)

ADJUTANT-GENERAL, Washington:

Transport *Rio de Janeiro* left to-day for San Francisco with 7 officers, 116 men sick, 2 men insane. Acting Surgeon Daywalt in charge. Notify Surgeon-General.

OTIS, Major-General.

ADJUTANT-GENERAL'S OFFICE,
Washington, September 22, 1898.

COMMANDING GENERAL, DEPARTMENT CALIFORNIA,
San Francisco, Cal.:

Your telegram concerning recruits and detachments now at Honolulu, under General King, is received, and the Acting Secretary of War directs that the recommendations contained in your telegram to meet the *Arizona* at Honolulu with supplies to complete her cargo for Manila, and the shipment of detachments to destination, be carried into effect. Acknowledge receipt.

By command Major-General Miles:

H. C. CORBIN, Adjutant-General.

ADJUTANT-GENERAL'S OFFICE,
Washington, September 22, 1898.

COMMANDING GENERAL DEPARTMENT,
San Francisco, Cal.:

Your telegram concerning General Miller received. Acting Secretary of War directs you give necessary orders for General Miller to go with contingent of expeditionary force now at San Francisco. Are any other officers required? Acknowledge receipt.

By command Major-General Miles:

H. C. CORBIN, Adjutant-General.

AFFAIRS IN THE PHILIPPINE ISLANDS. 795

SAN FRANCISCO, CAL., *September 23, 1898.*
ADJUTANT-GENERAL, *Washington:*
Orders should be cabled to Manila to unload the *Arizona* and return her at once to Honolulu for use of General King's command and supplies from that port. *Arizona* due at Manila to-morrow.
MERRIAM, *Major-General.*

ADJUTANT-GENERAL'S OFFICE,
Washington, September 23, 1898—11 p. m.
COMMANDING GENERAL, *Manila.*
Acting Secretary War directs that the *Arizona* be unloaded and returned at once to Honolulu for use General King's command and supplies from that port.
H. C. CORBIN, *Adjutant-General.*

ADJUTANT-GENERAL'S OFFICE,
Washington, September 23, 1898—11 p. m.
Major-General MERRIAM, *San Francisco, Cal.:*
Orders have been cabled to Manila to unload the *Arizona* and return her at once to Honolulu, as referred to in your telegram this date.
H. C. CORBIN, *Adjutant-General.*

SAN FRANCISCO, CAL., *September 23, 1898—3.05 p. m.*
ADJUTANT-GENERAL, *Washington, D. C.:*
Telegram of yesterday directing General Miller be sent to Manila with expeditionary troops received. No other officers required.
MERRIAM, *Major-General.*

MANILA. (Received Washington, September 25, 1898—5.06 a. m.)
ADJUTANT-GENERAL, *Washington:*
Arizona will be sent Honolulu upon arrival and discharge of freight.
OTIS.

ADJUTANT-GENERAL'S OFFICE,
Washington, September 25, 1898—12.30 p. m.
Major-General MERRIAM, *San Francisco, Cal.:*
Following received from General Otis, Manila, and sent you for your information and guidance:
"*Arizona* will be sent Honolulu upon arrival and discharge of freight."
H. C. CORBIN, *Adjutant-General.*

MANILA. (Received Washington, September 26, 1898—6.14 a. m.)
ADJUTANT-GENERAL, *Washington:*
Understand reporters sent exaggerated account sickness; total in hospital to-day, highest of any day, 529; typhoid fever patients, 95; all doing well and mostly convalescent; about 1,200 excused from duty, mostly slight ailments, showing condition fair for this latitude; 19 deaths from disease this month, 23 in August.
OTIS, *Commanding.*

St. Paul, Minn., *September 26, 1898—1.19 p. m.*

Hon. R. A. Alger,
 Secretary of War, Washington, D. C.:

Please report names and physical condition of Minnesota men on transport *Rio Janeiro* from Manila to San Francisco.

L. Fletcher.
F. C. Stevens.

Adjutant-General's Office,
Washington, September 27, 1898.

Commanding General, Department California,
 San Francisco, Cal.:

Please report names and physical condition of Minnesota volunteers arrived on transport *Rio Janeiro.*

H. C. Corbin, *Adjutant-General.*

San Francisco, Cal., *September 27, 1898—8.24 p. m.*

Adjutant-General, *Washington, D. C.:*

Referring to your telegram of this date, I have no knowledge of date of sailing of transport *Rio Janeiro* for this port. If she is coming with sick and wounded, full situation should be reported in order to make arrangements for their care and comfort here.

Merriam, *Major-General.*

St. Paul, Minn., *September 29, 1898—1.56 p. m.*

Hon. H. C. Corbin,
 Adjutant-General, Washington, D. C.:

Can you inform me about when hospital ship that left Manila recently with sick soldiers will arrive at San Francisco?

D. M. Clough, *Governor.*

Adjutant-General's Office,
Washington, September 29, 1898.

Governor Clough, *St. Paul, Minn.:*

The *Rio Janeiro* left Manila September 14 with 140 sick soldiers, and should arrive in San Francisco about October 7.

H. C. Corbin, *Adjutant-General.*

Manila, *September 29, 1898—11.07 p. m.*

Adjutant-General, *Washington:*

Simpson left for Washington by steamer *Newport* September 13; has important papers showing conditions and action taken here.

Otis, *Commanding.*

Adjutant-General's Office,
Washington, September 30, 1898—9.15 a. m.

Commanding General, Department California,
 San Francisco, Cal.:

Referring to your telegram 27th, *City of Rio Janeiro* sailed from Manila for San Francisco September 16 with 7 officers and 116 sick and 2 insane soldiers. Acting Surgeon Daywalt in charge.

H. C. Corbin, *Adjutant-General.*

ADJUTANT-GENERAL'S OFFICE,
Washington, September 30, 1898.

Hon. L. FLETCHER, *St. Paul, Minn.:*

Referring to your telegram 26th, *Rio Janeiro* sailed from Manila for San Francisco September 16, and it will be a week or ten days before she arrives. As soon as she does will furnish you information called for.

H. C. CORBIN, *Adjutant-General.*

ADJUTANT-GENERAL'S OFFICE,
Washington, September 30, 1898.

General MERRIAM,
Department California, San Francisco, Cal.:

Secretary of War desires to know what transports, if any, have returned from Manila and are available for the waiting troops for the Philippines.

H. C. CORBIN, *Adjutant-General.*

[Personal.]

MADISON, WIS., *September 30, 1898—4.54 p. m.*

Gen. H. C. CORBIN, *Adjutant-General, Washington, D. C.:*

I sincerely hope that General King may be permitted to go to Manila. What is the prospect? Would like to know confidentially if there has been any personal reason for holding him back. Please advise me.

JOHN C. SPOONER.

ADJUTANT-GENERAL'S OFFICE,
Washington, September 30, 1898.

Hon. JOHN C. SPOONER, *Madison, Wis.:*

General King, with his command, has been ordered from Honolulu to Manila.

H. C. CORBIN, *Adjutant-General.*

MANILA. (Received Washington, September 30, 1898.)

ADJUTANT-GENERAL, *Washington:*

Replying telegram 21st, state necessity modifications made in rations by telegraphic authority Commissary-General September 19; carefully considered clothing and just ascertained amounts here and to arrive; light quality manufactured here and Hong-kong obtained at cheap rates. Will soon be abundantly supplied with clothing suitable to climate. Nothing needed.

OTIS.

MANILA. (Received Washington, October 2, 1898—1.15 a. m.)

ADJUTANT-GENERAL, *Washington:*

Arizona leaves port for Honolulu to-morrow per instructions 24th ultimo.

OTIS, *Commanding.*

MANILA. (Received Washington, October 3, 1898—2.20 a. m.)

ADJUTANT-GENERAL, *Washington:*

Deaths among troops in Philippines July, August, and September: July, 4 officers, 83 enlisted men; August, 2 officers, 50 enlisted men, of whom 1 officer and 16 enlisted men killed in action; 7 died of wounds; deaths for September, 25 enlisted men.

Total deaths: Seventeen killed in action, 7 died of wounds, 14 typhoid fever; cause of remaining deaths accident and miscellaneous diseases.

OTIS.

MANILA. (Received Washington, October 3, 1898—6.56 a. m.)
ADJUTANT-GENERAL, *Washington:*
Steamer *Scandia* arrived to-day without accident. Private Jacobs, Hospital Corps, died at sea, typhoid fever; remains brought here.

OTIS, *Commanding.*

MANILA, *October 3, 1898.*
ADJUTANT-GENERAL, *Washington:*
Meditate extending present trade facilities to permit free transit foreign merchandise between Manila, Iloilo, and Cebu, Philippine ports of entry, when duties paid at port original importation and properly certified; when duties greater in one port than other, excess to be paid in port levying excess. This in interests of trade and to be tentative in character. Recommend appointments as United States vice-consuls W. S. Duncan, Iloilo, and J. Sidebotham, Cebu; new British vice-consul those ports.

OTIS.

Above telegram referred to the Secretary of Treasury with following indorsement, by Assistant Secretary of War:

"Referred to Secretary of Treasury with request for recommendation regarding that portion of cablegram relating to Philippine tariff.
"October 7, 1898."

WAR DEPARTMENT,
Washington, October 3, 1898.
The Honorable, the SECRETARY OF STATE.
SIR: I have the honor herewith to submit copy of cablegram received this date from Major-General Otis, commanding the Department of the Pacific, for such action as you may judge to be in the interest of the public service.
Very respectfully,

R. A. ALGER, *Secretary of War.*

(Inclosure: Cable from General Otis dated October 3.)

MANILA, *October 4, 1898—2.58 a. m.*
ADJUTANT-GENERAL, *Washington:*
Informed mule and wagon transportation shipped from San Francisco, and of greatest necessity here detained for use Honolulu; vessel returned because vessel's condenser unsatisfactory; repaired Honolulu about to continue voyage when turned back; same authority retained my quartermaster—only one having knowledge of shipment of stores—causing confusion here and overthrow my orders for transportation of troops to accompany me when I proceeded to Honolulu; anomalous position in which Government placed me last May one of incessant labor and annoyance, but believe spirit of War Department instructions can be successfully consummated if interference ceases; request that none but duly authorized persons be sent to this port by Government transports.

OTIS.

AFFAIRS IN THE PHILIPPINE ISLANDS. 799

ADJUTANT-GENERAL'S OFFICE,
Washington, October 4, 1898—10.30 a. m.

COMMANDING GENERAL, DEPARTMENT OF CALIFORNIA,
San Francisco, Cal.:

Following telegram, received this day from General Otis, is sent you for your information:

Informed mule and wagon transportation shipped from San Francisco, and of greatest necessity here detained for use Honolulu; vessel returned because vessel's condenser unsatisfactory; repaired Honolulu about to continue voyage when turned back; same authority retained my quartermaster—only one having knowledge of shipment of stores—causing confusion here and overthrow my orders for transportation of troops to accompany me when I proceeded to Honolulu; anomalous position in which Government placed me last May one of incessant labor and annoyance, but believe spirit of War Department instructions can be successfully consummated if interference ceases; request that none but duly authorized persons be sent to this port by Government transports.'

The Secretary of War directs that the request of General Otis receive immediate attention. This transportation should reach him at very earliest opportunity. Acknowledge receipt.

H. C. CORBIN, *Adjutant-General.*

ADJUTANT-GENERAL'S OFFICE,
Washington, October 4, 1898—10.30 a. m.

General OTIS, *Manila:*

Your cablegram received and commanding general, San Francisco, directed to give your request immediate attention; transportation will reach you at first opportunity.

H. C. CORBIN, *Adjutant-General.*

SAN FRANCISCO, CAL., *October 4, 1898—8.10 p. m.*

ADJUTANT-GENERAL, *Washington, D. C.:*

Telegram quoting General Otis received. Please inform him by what authority troops and transports and Quartermaster Ruhlen designated for Manila were retained here and at Honolulu, and Red Cross nurses sent on the *Arizona* and *Scandia;* animals and wagons now at Honolulu will be shipped to Manila as soon as *Tacoma* can be fitted with proper condenser.

MERRIAM, *Major-General.*

SAN FRANCISCO, CAL., *October, 4, 1898—9.37 p. m.*

ADJUTANT-GENERAL, *Washington, D. C.:*

Transport *Senator*, arrived this date from Manila, is being put in condition for return voyage.

MERRIAM, *Major-General.*

MANILA. (Received Washington, October 7, 1898—1.40 a. m.)

ADJUTANT-GENERAL, *Washington:*

Former Captain-General Jaudenes reports summons to Spain to answer for action here; announces intention to depart soon. Admiral Montojo permitted to go few days since. Admiral Dewey having no objection, shall General Jaudenes be permitted to leave or shall I hold him as prisoner of war under articles of capitulation?

OTIS, *Commanding.*

SAN FRANCISCO, CAL., *October 6, 1898—2.36 a. m.*
VAN ANTWERP, *Washington, D. C.:*
We receive dozens inquiries every day from mothers and fathers of Philippine troopers. They are almost crazed by the uncertainty. Can you not induce War Department to get by cable list of dead to date and have daily list cabled hereafter the same as from Cuba? That would be a small favor for the Government to render the families of its volunteer soldiers.

F. W. LAWRENCE.

ADJUTANT-GENERAL'S OFFICE,
Washington, October 6, 1898.
General OTIS, *Manila:*
Animals and wagons at Honolulu. Will be forwarded on *Tacoma* soon as fitted with condenser.

H. C. CORBIN, *Adjutant-General.*

MANILA. (Received Washington, October 7, 1898—6.31 a. m.)
ADJUTANT-GENERAL, *Washington:*
Request permission to allow sick Spanish officers prisoners of war to depart for Spain; Spanish general commanding urgently requests.

OTIS, *Commanding.*

ADJUTANT-GENERAL'S OFFICE,
Washington, October 7, 1898—2 p. m.
General OTIS, *Manlia:*
With the approval of the President, the Secretary of War directs that General Jaudenes be permitted to return to Spain, as referred to in your cable this date.

H. C. CORBIN, *Adjutant-General.*

ADJUTANT-GENERAL'S OFFICE,
Washington, October 7, 1898—2 p. m.
General OTIS, *Manila:*
Secretary War approves your request to allow sick Spanish officers, prisoners of war, to depart for Spain.

H. C. CORBIN, *Adjutant-General.*

MANILA. (Received Washington, October 7, 1898—11.57 p. m.)
ADJUTANT-GENERAL, *Washington:*
Transport *Peru*, here since August 21, leaves for San Francisco to-day. *City Para* and *Scandia* only transports remaining in harbor.

OTIS, *Commanding.*

ADJUTANT-GENERAL'S OFFICE,
Washington, October 8, 1898.
COMMANDING GENERAL, DEPARTMENT CALIFORNIA,
San Francisco, Cal.:
General Otis reports *Peru* leaving for San Francisco to-day.

H. C. CORBIN, *Adjutant-General.*

ADJUTANT-GENERAL'S OFFICE,
Washington, October 8, 1898.

General OTIS, *Manila:*

Secretary War directs names and regiments be furnished by cable of the dead of your command, from leaving San Francisco to date. Hereafter weekly list will be cabled.

H. C. CORBIN, *Adjutant-General.*

ADJUTANT-GENERAL'S OFFICE,
Washington, October 8, 1898.

COMMANDING GENERAL, DEPARTMENT CALIFORNIA,
San Francisco, Cal.:

Have you report of the arrival of the *Ohio* and *Valencia?* When will they return to Manila? The Secretary of War desires to know troops that will go and in the order of their going.

By command Major-General Miles:

H. C. CORBIN, *Adjutant-General.*

SAN FRANCISCO, CAL., *October 8, 1898—4.15 p. m.*

ADJUTANT-GENERAL, *Washington, D. C.:*

Transports *Ohio* and *Valencia* arrived this port from Manila last night.

MERRIAM, *Major-General.*

MANILA. (Received Washington, October 9, 1898—5.52 a. m.)

SECRETARY WAR, *Washington:*

Private Paul M. Crosby, Company E, Thirteenth Minnesota, died October 4; tuberculosis.

OTIS.

ADJUTANT-GENERAL'S OFFICE,
Washington, October 9, 1898.

Major-General OTIS, *Manila:*

Are the services of any more quartermasters needed with your command? This in connection with considering the reenforcements by General Miller's command in San Francisco, which will be sent you as soon as transportation is available. Also report any surplus staff officers of other departments, or the needs of any further staff officers in your department.

By order Secretary War:

H. C. CORBIN, *Adjutant-General.*

ADJUTANT-GENERAL'S OFFICE,
Washington, October 9, '1898—11 a. m.

COMMANDING GENERAL, DEPARTMENT CALIFORNIA,
San Francisco, Cal.:

Constant inquiries are being made as to disposition of First New York Volunteers, it being generally reported throughout the country that you have relieved them from Honolulu and ordered them to Philippines. It is necessary, to quiet anxiety, to have an official denial from you.

H. C. CORBIN, *Adjutant-General.*

SAN FRANCISCO, CAL., *October 9, 1898—2.45 p. m.*
ADJUTANT-GENERAL, *Washington, D. C.:*
Entire First New York Regiment and Major Langfitt's battalion, Volunteer Engineers, remain at Honolulu doing garrison duty.

MERRIAM, *Major-General.*

SAN FRANCISCO, CAL., *October 9, 1898.* (Received 2.48 p. m.)
ADJUTANT-GENERAL, *Washington, D. C.:*
Senator expected to sail about Thursday with battalion Twenty-third Infantry and detachments of recruits. *Ohio* and *Valencia* will take Washington regiment; sail in about one week.

MERRIAM, *Major-General.*

MANILA. (Received Washington, October 10, 1898—11.44 a. m.)
ADJUTANT-GENERAL, *Washington:*
Need 4 additional quartermasters of experience; 1 should have rank of major. Subsistence department requires 3 additional officers and 2 commissary-sergeants. Commissary Lee Linn ordered report to you; left Saturday; mail sent then explains. Chief surgeon needs 6 additional medical officers. Sickness increasing, not in anywise alarming; 13 cases of smallpox in two weeks, 8 of which fatal; disease epidemic here; in hospital to-day, 720; typhoid fever, 119. Weather still hot. Hospitals good, and supplies abundant for present. Two assistant adjutants-general and two experienced inspectors would prove very useful. No surplus staff officer present.

OTIS.

SAN FRANCISCO, CAL., *October 10, 1898—9 p. m.*
ADJUTANT-GENERAL, *Washington, D. C.:*
Transport *Indiana* and sailing vessel *Tacoma* arrived in port to-day.

MERRIAM, *Major-General.*

ADJUTANT-GENERAL'S OFFICE,
Washington, October 11, 1898.
COMMANDING GENERAL, DEPARTMENT CALIFORNIA,
San Francisco, Cal.:
Secretary of War directs careful inspection be made of First Tennessee Volunteers, with view to eliminating, by discharge, such of the men who, for good and sufficient reasons, should be discharged. For instance, boys who are not fully developed and not calculated to stand service in Manila, and married men who have families dependent upon them, and those who have failed in developing aptitude for service. Report number that in your opinion should be mustered out before regiment sails.
By command Major-General Miles:

H. C. CORBIN, *Adjutant-General.*

MANILA. (Received Washington, October 11, 1898—4.30 p. m.)
ADJUTANT-GENERAL, *Washington, D. C.:*
Following have died since leaving San Francisco: Fourth Cavalry, Private Albert J. McCane; Third Artillery, Privates Isaac Strickland, Charles Winfield, John A. McIlrath, Eli Dawson, Albert D. Fairfax, George Edgell, Thomas Roache; Sixth Artillery, Privates Ray Horton, Harry A. Suether, William P. Griffin; Astor Battery, First Sergt. Marcus Holmes, Sergt. Dennis Crimmens, Private Charles Dunn; Utah

Light Artillery, Private George H. Hudson; Fourteenth Infantry, Privates Robert McCann, Samuel F. Howell, E. W. Gildersleve, Philip Hicks, William A. Hill, Harry S. Culver; Eighteenth Infantry, Privates Elmer B. Madder, William S. Sanders, Arthur Jobbling, Charles Crowley, Frank Berry, William A. Flosser, Musicians Philip Fisk, Marian Hurley, Lieut. Jacob H. Lazelle; Twenty-third Infantry, Privates Steve R. Roddy, Walter Berdine, Clemens Lauer, Augustus Thallen, Elmer E. Vaughn; Company A, Engineers, Lieut. Robert D. Kerr, Private James F. Cardoza; Signal Corps, Privates Ralph R. Bowers, Leonard Garsuch; Hospital Corps, Privates William B. Robberson, Neil Howard, Thomas Sargent, Francis Dickelman, William Fields, Frederick G. Jacobs; First California Infantry, Capt. Reimbold Richter, Privates Daniel J. Nicholls, George H. Perkins, John V. Dunmore, Maurice Justh, Peter S. H. Fisher, Joseph Tomer, Edward Braham, H. M. Bowers; First Colorado Infantry, Sergt. Neil C. Sullivan, Privates Walter Wise, Charles Phenix, F. E. Springstead, John A. Scroggs, Herbert Sarazon; First Idaho Infantry, Private Bird L. Adams; Thirteenth Minnesota Infantry, Bandmaster C. H. Watson, Lieut. Frank A. Morley, Musicians Fred Duckland, Archie Patterson, Privates Leslie B. Paden, Harry Nickson, Charles Burnson, Sidney Pratt, John S. Wood, Henry G. Watson, Charles Schwartz, Albert Dennis, William Sullivan, Payseon C. E. Caldwell, Harry L. Currier, F. S. Wanrick, George H. Cooty, Joseph O. Daily, Paul Crosby, William O. Marlinson; First Nebraska Infantry, Sergt. William J. Vans, Privates C. H. Nieke, William P. Lewis, Roy C. Maher, Walter M. Hayne, Horace G. Falkner, John Black, Theodore Larson; First Montana Infantry, Privates John C. Adams, William C. O'Leary, Cary Taylor; First North Dakota Infantry, Private John Buckley; Second Oregon Infantry, Privates Elias P. Huckinson, Edgar W. Johnson, Rufus R. Holbrooke, Edwin C. Young, Richard E. Perry, Charles Miner, Frank Rufino, George Stormer, James J. Reid, Harry M. Wheeler; Tenth Pennsylvania Infantry, Corpl. Walter E. Brown, Privates Be. Snyder, John Brady, jr., Jesse Noss, William Stillwagon, Jacob Hull, jr., William E. Bunton, William H. Crable, Robert L. Fox, William Braden; First South Dakota Infantry, Privates Newell Jenks, Joseph Whitmore, Martin Martinson; First Wyoming Infantry, Privates Ernest S. Bowker, Leroy S. Mimick.

OTIS.

SAN FRANCISCO, CAL., *October 11, 1898—9.18 p. m.*
ADJUTANT-GENERAL, *Washington, D. C.:*
Transport *Newport* arrived this port from Manila to-day.

MERRIAM, *Major-General.*

SAN FRANCISCO, CAL., *October 12, 1898—4.45 p. m.*
ADJUTANT-GENERAL, *Washington, D. C.:*
Soldier cooks can not be relied on at sea. Transports usually but one system of galleys. I recommend ship's cook be increased at expense of quartermaster's department to meet this demand Immediate action on this matter required, as transports are now loading.

MERRIAM, *Major-General.*

ADJUTANT-GENERAL'S OFFICE,
Washington, October 14, 1898.
COMMANDING GENERAL, *Manila:*
Secretary War directs, upon arrival Battery A, California Artillery, Lieutenant Hayne collect information regarding agriculture in Philippines for Secretary Agriculture.

CARTER.

ADJUTANT-GENERAL'S OFFICE,
Washington, October 14, 1898—2.30 p. m.

COMMANDING GENERAL, *Santiago:*

Replying to cablegram from commissaries and quartermasters, Secretary War desires to know if there are not capable and deserving young officers, preferable from regular regiments, in your command, who are competent to perform this duty with increased volunteer rank. If so, send names.

H. C. CORBIN, *Adjutant-General.*

(Same to General Otis, Manila.)

MANILA. (Received Washington, October 14, 1898—10.57 p. m.)

ADJUTANT-GENERAL, *Washington:*

Lieutenant Hayne assigned October 11 as directed in your telegram 14th instant. Orders by mail.

OTIS.

MANILA. (Received Washington, October 15, 1898—9.30 a. m.)

ADJUTANT-GENERAL, *Washington:*

Following deaths since last report: October 10, Privates Charles A. Howe, Second Oregon, dysentery; Ernest M. Forster, Fourteenth Infantry, malarial cerebritis. October 11, Private Fred Greenilet, First South Dakota, typhoid fever. October 12, Privates A. H. Bird, First Nebraska, typhoid fever; Daniel Paryibel, Astor Battery, tuberculosis.

OTIS.

MANILA. (Received Washington, October 16, 1898—10 a. m.)

SECRETARY WAR, *Washington:*

No existing codification of Spanish tariffs; schedules will be prepared and mailed in three days.

OTIS.

ADJUTANT-GENERAL'S OFFICE,
Washington, October 18, 1898.

General OTIS, *Manila:*

Considerable anxiety felt about cruel treatment of religious orders by insurgents. You will use your good offices discreetly for their protection.

By order Secretary War:

H. C. CORBIN, *Adjutant-General.*

HEADQUARTERS DEPARTMENT OF THE PACIFIC AND EIGHTH ARMY CORPS,
Manila, P. I., September 12, 1898. (Received Washington, October 19, 1898.)

The ADJUTANT-GENERAL, U. S. ARMY,
Washington, D. C.

SIR: I have the honor to inclose herewith copies of all correspondence by and between the United States military authorities and General Aguinaldo, commanding the insurgent forces of the Philippines, which are of record. I am of the impression that certain notes have passed between the parties of which no record was made, and I conclude thus from expressions in the letters of Aguinaldo, copies of which are inclosed. To my long communication, in which I make demands upon the insurgents to evacuate the city of Manila and its defenses by the 15th instant, I have not yet received any response. I am informed that Aguinaldo's advisers are quite evenly divided in sentiment—the one strongly advocating a compliance with the demands, the other urging refusal. I can not as yet reach any decided opinion as to which party will prevail. Should I promise them that in case of the return of the city to Spain upon United States evacuation their forces would be placed by us in positions which they now occupy, I thoroughly believe that they would evacuate at once. But of course under the international obligations resting upon us by reason of the articles of capitulation no such promise can be given.

The insurgents are very strong, estimated by some to number 30,000 troops. They have been receiving a good many arms and much ammunition within the last few weeks, and I am informed have contracted with the Japanese Government for a considerable supply. I shall not yield to any of their requests or make any concessions which affect in any way our international obligations to Spain. Should war result, more troops would be required, for which I shall make request by telegraph. Admiral Dewey approves thoroughly of my action and heartily unites in the course which I am pursuing. I continue in the hope that hostilities can be avoided. It is reported to me that the best legal talent which the insurgents possess (and they have among them some able men) state that the arguments used in my communication are unanswerable, but the difficulties lie in their inability to control their irresponsible military organizations. They want the arguments coupled with requests and not demands, so that Aguinaldo can make proclamation in his paper which will appeal to their sense.

I send these papers in care of Maj. W. A. Simpson, assistant adjutant-general, U. S. Army, who has been directed to proceed to Washington by War Department orders.

Very respectfully,

E. A. OTIS,
Major-General, U. S. Volunteers, Commanding.

HEADQUARTERS FIRST BRIGADE, U. S. EXPEDITIONARY FORCES,
Cavite Arsenal, Philippine Islands, July 4, 1898.

Señor Don EMILIO AGUINALDO Y FAMY,
Commanding Philippine Forces, Cavite, Luzon.

GENERAL: I have the honor to inform you that the United States of America, whose land forces I have the honor to command in this vicinity, being at war with the Kingdom of Spain, has entire sympathy and most friendly sentiments for the native people of the Philippine Islands.

For these reasons I desire to have the most amicable relations with you, and to have you and your people cooperate with us in military operations against the Spanish forces.

In our operations it has become necessary for us to occupy the town of Cavite as a base of operations. In doing this I do not wish to interfere with your residence here and the exercise by yourself and other native citizens of all functions and privileges not inconsistent with military rule.

I will be pleased to be informed at once of any misconduct of soldiers under my command, as it is the intention of my Government to maintain order, and to treat all citizens with justice, courtesy, and kindness.

I have, therefore, the honor to ask your excellency to instruct your officials not to interfere with my officers in the performance of their duties, and not to assume that they can not visit Cavite without permission.

Assuring you again of my most friendly sentiment and distinguished consideration, I remain, with all respect,

THOMAS M. ANDERSON,
Brigadier-General, U. S. Volunteers, Commanding.

Received July 5, 1898. From Aguinaldo, Emilio. No date or place. Brief: Expresses an interpretation of sentiments of natives of the Philippine Islands toward the great North American nation, and announces his agreeable relations with the United States military authorities, etc. Action: Forwarded to General Merritt, July 27, as an inclosure to L. S. 45.

HEADQUARTERS FIRST BRIGADE, U. S. EXPEDITIONARY FORCES,
Cavite Arsenal, Philippine Islands, July 6, 1898.

Señor Don EMILIO AGUINALDO Y FAMY,
Commanding Philippine Forces.

GENERAL: I am encouraged by the friendly sentiment expressed by your excellency in your welcome letter received on the 5th instant to endeavor to come to a definite understanding which I hope will be advantageous to both.

Very soon we expect a large addition to our forces, and it must be apparent to you as a military officer that we will require much more room to camp our soldiers, and also storeroom for our supplies. For this I would like to have your excellency's advice and cooperation, as you are the best acquainted with the resources of this country.

It must be apparent to you that we do not intend to remain here inactive, but to move promptly against our common enemy. But for a short time we must organize and land supplies and also retain a place for storing them near our fleet and transports.

I am solicitous to avoid any conflict of authority which may result in having two sets of military officers exercising command in the same place.

I am also anxious to avoid sickness, by taking sanitary precautions. Your own medical officers have been making voluntary inspections with mine and fear epidemic disease if the vicinity is not made clean.

Would it not be well to have prisoners work to this end under the advice of the surgeons?

I again renew my assurances of distinguished consideration.

I am, with great respect,

THOMAS M. ANDERSON,
Brigadier-General, U. S. Volunteers, Commanding.

[Extract of letter from Headquarters First Brigade, U. S. Expeditionary Forces.]

"CAVITE ARSENAL, P. I., *July 9, 1898.*

"The ADJUTANT-GENERAL, U. S. ARMY,
"*Washington, D. C.*

"General Aguinaldo tells me he has about 15,000 fighting men, but only 11,000 armed with guns, which mostly were taken from the Spaniards. He claims to have in all 4,000 prisoners.

"When we first landed he seemed very suspicious and not at all friendly, but I have now come to a better understanding with him, and he is much more friendly, and seems willing to cooperate.

"But he has declared himself dictator and president, and is trying to take Manila without our assistance This is not probable, but if he can effect his purpose he will, I apprehend, antagonize any attempt on our part to establish a provincial government."

The letter from which the above extract was taken was signed,

"THOMAS M. ANDERSON,
"*Brigadier-General, U. S. Volunteers, Commanding.*"

HEADQUARTERS FIRST BRIGADE,
U. S. EXPEDITIONARY FORCES,
Cavite Arsenal, P. I., July 14, 1898.

Señor Don EMILIO AGUINALDO,
Commanding Philippine Forces.

GENERAL: Wishing to get complete information of the approaches to Manila from every direction, I therefore have the honor to request that you give my officers all possible assistance in making reconnoissance to the lines and approaches, and that you favor them with your advice.

Officers coming from me will have a note to that effect.

With great respect,

THOMAS M. ANDERSON,
Brigadier-General, U. S. Volunteers, Commanding.

L. R. No. 122. Received July 20, 1898. From Aguinaldo, Emilio, general Philippine forces. Dated at Bacoor, P. I., July 15, 1898. Brief: States that his government has seen necessity of adopting form and organization more adequately popular. Expresses friendly and harmonious relations with "the Great North American Nation."

HEADQUARTERS EXPEDITIONARY FORCES TO THE PHILIPPINE ISLANDS,
CHIEF QUARTERMASTER'S OFFICE,
Cavite, P. I., July 17, 1898.

Gen. EMILIO AGUINALDO,
Addressed.

SIR: General Anderson wishes me to say that the second expedition having arrived he expects to encamp in the vicinity of Parañaque from 5,000 to 7,000 men. To do this, supply this army, and shelter will require certain assistance from the Filipinos in this neighborhood. We will want horses, buffaloes, carts, etc., for transportation, bamboo for shelter, wood to cook with, etc. For all this we are willing to pay a fair price, but no more. We find so far that the native population are not willing to give us this assistance as promptly as required. But we must have it, and if it becomes necessary we will be compelled to send out parties to seize what we may need. We would regret very much to do this, as we are here to befriend the Filipinos. Our nation has spent millions of money to send forces here to expel the Spaniards, and to give a good government to the whole people, and the return we are asking is comparatively slight.

General Anderson wishes you to inform your people that we are here for their good, and that they must supply us with labor and material at the current market prices. We are prepared to purchase 500 horses at a fair price, but can not undertake to bargain for horses with each individual owner.

I regret very much that I am unable to see you personally, as it is of the utmost importance that these arrangements should be made as soon as possible.

I will await your reply.

Very respectfully,

S. R. JONES,
Major and Quartermaster, U. S. Volunteers, Chief Quartermaster.

[Indorsement.]

FIRST BRIGADE HEADQUARTERS, *July 17, 1898.*

The request herein made by Major Jones, chief quartermaster, was made by my direction.

THOMAS M. ANDERSON,
Brigadier-General, U. S. Volunteers, Commanding.

The within communication was delivered to me personally by a staff officer of General Aguinaldo, who stated that General A. requested to know whether it was sent by my authority. The above indorsement was placed on the paper, which was then returned to the staff officer.

THOMAS M. ANDERSON,
Brigadier-General, Volunteers, Commanding.

L. R. No. 137. Received July 22, 1898. From Jones, Sam R., chief quartermaster first brigade. Dated at Cavite, P. I., July 20, 1898. Brief: States that it is impossible to secure transportation except upon Señor Aguinaldo's order, in this section, who has an inventory of everything. The natives have removed their wheels and hid them.

HEADQUARTERS FIRST BRIGADE, U. S. EXPEDITIONARY FORCES,
Cavite Arsenal, P. I., July 18, 1898.

The ADJUTANT-GENERAL UNITED STATES ARMY.

GENERAL: Since reading the President's instructions to General Merritt I think I should state to you that the establishment of a provincial government on our part will probably bring us in conflict with insurgents, now in active hostility to Spain.

The insurgent chief, Aguinaldo, has declared himself dictator and self-appointed president. He has declared martial law and promulgated a minute method of rule and administration under it. We have observed all official military courtesies, and he and his followers express great admiration and gratitude to the great American Republic of the North, yet in many ways they obstruct our purposes and are using every effort to take Manila without us.

I suspect also that Aguinaldo is secretly negotiating with the Spanish authorities, as his confidential aid is in Manila.

The city is strongly fortified and hard to approach in the rainy season. If a bombardment fails we should have the best engineering ability here.

Very respectfully, your obedient servant,

THOMAS M. ANDERSON,
Brigadier-General, U. S. Volunteers, Commanding.

HEADQUARTERS FIRST BRIGADE, U. S. EXPEDITIONARY FORCES,
Cavite Arsenal, P. I., July 19, 1898.

Señor Don EMILIO AGUINALDO,
Philippine Forces.

GENERAL: The bearer, Maj. J. F. Bell, U. S. Army, was sent by Maj. Gen. Wesley Merritt, U. S. Army, to collect for him, by the time of his personal arrival, certain information concerning the strength and position of the enemy and concerning the topography of the country surrounding Manila.

I would be obliged if you would permit him to see your maps and place at his disposal any information you may have on the above subjects and to facilitate his passage along the lines upon a reconnoissance around Manila on which I propose to send him.

I remain, with great respect, your obedient servant,

THOMAS M. ANDERSON,
Brigadier-General, U. S. Volunteers, Commanding.

L. R. No. 47 (new series). Received August 8, 1898. From Aguinaldo, Emilio. Dated at Bacoor, P. I., near Manila, July 18, 1898. Brief: Relative to the assistance of his people to us in furnishing supplies and transportation. Retains his great admiration for the great North American nation. No action recorded.

HEADQUARTERS FIRST BRIGADE, U. S. EXPEDITIONARY FORCES,
Cavite Arsenal, P. I., July 19, 1898.

Señor Don EMILIO AGUINALDO,
Commanding Philippine Forces.

GENERAL: I have the honor to acknowledge the receipt of your letter of the 18th instant. Your offer of assistance is appreciated and your assurances of good will are most gratifying. The difficulty of collecting supplies, referred to by you, is apprehended and will be considered in fixing compensation.

As a medium of communication with your people, we will be pleased to have you assure them that there will be no confiscation of their property, that our requisition will be reasonable, and that a fair compensation will always be given.

I remain, General, with all respect, your obedient servant,

THOMAS M. ANDERSON,
Brigadier-General, Commanding.

[Extract of letter from Headquarters First Brigade, United States Expeditionary Forces.]

"CAVITE ARSENAL, P. I., *July 21, 1898.*

"ADJUTANT-GENERAL, U. S. ARMY,
" *Washington, D. C.:*

"Since I wrote last Aguinaldo has put in operation an elaborate system of military government under his assumed authority as dictator, and had prohibited any supplies being given us except by his order. As to this last, I have written him that our requisitions on the country for horses, ox-carts, fuel, and bamboo (to make scaling ladders) must be filled, and that he must aid in having them filled. His assumption of civil authority I have ignored, and let him know verbally that I could and would not recognize it, while I did recognize him as a military leader.

"It may seem strange that I have made no formal protest against his proclamation as dictator, his declaration of martial law, and publication and execution of a despotic form of government. I wrote such a protest, but did not publish it, at Admiral Dewey's request and also for fear of wounding the susceptibilities of Major-General Merritt, but I have let it be known in every other way that we do not recognize the dictatorship.

"These people only respect force and firmness. I submit, with all deference, that we have heretofore underrated the native. They are not ignorant, savage tribes, but have a civilization of their own; and though insignificant in appearance are fierce fighters, and for a tropical people they are industrious. A small detail of natives will do more work in a given time than a regiment of volunteers."

The letter from which the above extract was taken was signed,

"THOMAS M. ANDERSON,
Brigadier-General, U. S. Volunteers, Commanding."

HEADQUARTERS FIRST BRIGADE, U. S. EXPEDITIONARY FORCES,
Cavite Arsenal, P. I., July 21, 1898.

Señor Don EMILIO AGUINALDO,
Commanding General Philippine Forces.

GENERAL: I have the honor to request that passes and such other assistance as practicable be given to the bearer, Lieut. E. J. Bryan, and party, who are making reconnoissance of the surrounding country.

Thanking you for the assistance given on previous occasions, I remain, with great respect, your obedient servant,

THOMAS M. ANDERSON,
Brigadier-General, U. S. Volunteers, Commanding.

L. R. No. 138. Received July 22, 1898. From Aguinaldo, Emilio, commanding general Philippine forces. No date or place. Brief: Objects to United States troops occupying warehouse No. 1, Calle Colon, as it is property of a Filipino named Don Antonio Osorio, and is under insurgents' protection. Requests the removal of same. Action: Forwarded to General Merritt, July 27, as an inclosure to L. S. No. 45.

L. R. No. 166. Received July 25, 1898. From Aguinaldo, Emilio, general Philippine forces. Dated at Bacoor, P. I., July 24, 1898. Brief: Makes a statement as to the house of Osorio in Cavite, and also makes a full statement of his connection with the revolution and the United States forces. Action: Forwarded to General Merritt July 27, as an inclosure to L. S. No. 45.

HEADQUARTERS FIRST BRIGADE, U. S. EXPEDITIONARY FORCES,
Cavite Arsenal, P. I., July 22, 1898.

Señor Don EMILIO AGUINALDO,
Commanding Philippine Forces.

GENERAL: Replying to your excellency's letter in relation to the property of Don Antonio Osorio, I have the honor to state that if he transferred the property to you personally before the capture of Cavite by our forces, it will give me great pleasure to transfer the property to you, in question. If, however, the property was not transferred to your excellency until after the capture of Cavite, the property would appear to have been public Spanish property, or contraband of war, and subject to capture.

This property will be held subject to investigation, but Don Osorio must make his claim and offer his proof to the commanding officer of the American army.

I observe that your excellency has announced yourself as a dictator and proclaimed martial law. As I am here simply in a military capacity, I have no authority to recognize this assumption. I have no orders from my Government on the subject, and, so far as I can ascertain, your independent status has not been recognized by any foreign power. Your fine intellect must perceive that, happy as I am to see you fighting so bravely and successfully against a common enemy, I can not, without orders, recognize your civil authority.

I remain, with great respect,

THOMAS M. ANDERSON,
Brigadier-General, U. S. Volunteers, Commanding.

HEADQUARTERS FIRST BRIGADE, U. S. EXPEDITIONARY FORCES,
Cavite Arsenal, P.I., July 23, 1898.

Señor Don EMILIO AGUINALDO,
Commandiny Philippine Forces.

GENERAL: When I came here three weeks ago I requested your excellency to give what assistance you could to procure means of transportation for the American army, as it was to fight in the cause of your people.

AFFAIRS IN THE PHILIPPINE ISLANDS. 811

So far we have received no response.

As you represent your people, I now have the honor to make requisition on you for 500 horses and 50 oxen and ox-carts.

If you can not secure these, I will have to pass you and make requisition directly on the people.

I beg leave to request an answer at your earliest convenience.

I remain, with great respect,

——— ———,
Brigadier-General, U. S. Volunteers, Commanding.

L. R. No. 167. Received July 25, 1898. From Aguinaldo, Emilio, general Philippine forces. Dated at Bacoor, P. I , July 24, 1898. Brief: States that he misunderstood the desires of the United States forces before, but now he will assist in supplying all requisitions for transportation if given reasonable notice and time.

HEADQUARTERS FIRST BRIGADE, U. S. EXPEDITIONARY FORCES,
Cavite Arsenal, P. I., July 24, 1898.

Señor DON EMILIO AGUINALDO,
Commanding Philippine Forces.

GENERAL: Your favor of the 26th ultimo, [?] in relation to requisitions for cattle, horses, etc., is satisfactory. I regret that there should have been any misunderstanding about it. The people to whom we applied, even for the hiring of carromatos, etc., told our people that they had orders to supply nothing, except by your orders. I am pleased to think that this was a misapprehension on their part.

We are not so unreasonable as to suppose that all we want can be supplied at once or from one place. We may even have to send to other islands. Our quartermaster will establish a depot near the American camp, where he will receive and pay for supplies, and from which he will send out parties to whatever places your excellency will indicate, to transact business with your people.

With great respect, your obedient servant,

THOMAS M. ANDERSON,
Brigadier-General, U. S. Volunteers, Commanding.

HEADQUARTERS FIRST BRIGADE, U. S. EXPEDITIONARY FORCES,
Cavite Arsenal, P. I., July 27, 1898.

ADJUTANT-GENERAL, U. S. EXPEDITIONARY FORCES,
Manila Bay.

SIR: I have the honor to transmit the last letter I received from the insurgent chief, Aguinaldo, dated Bacoor, July 24, 1898. This letter has not been answered by me.

My whole correspondence with him is also inclosed.

Very respectfully,

THOMAS M. ANDERSON,
Brigadier-General, U. S. Volunteers, Commanding.

HEADQUARTERS FIRST BRIGADE, U. S. EXPEDITIONARY FORCES,
Cavite, P. I., July 30, 1898.

ADJUTANT-GENERAL, DEPARTMENT OF PACIFIC AND EIGHTH ARMY CORPS,
S. S. Newport, Manila Bay, P. I.

SIR: Referring to verbal instructions in relation to an issue of rations to Spanish prisoners, I have the honor to state that I have just received a verbal message from

General Aguinaldo, conveyed by Capt. Marti Burges, aid-de-camp, to this effect: That he (Aguinaldo) appreciates the kindness that prompts the offer, but fears that if this should become known in Manila, the Spaniards would regard it as an indication that resources were exhausted and would consequently take heart and make renewed resistance.

He will therefore endeavor to increase their rations, but reminds us that prisoners always complain. I made answer verbally that if prisoners were kept here they would have to be well fed, but that he could of course remove them if he saw fit to do so.

Very respectfully, THOMAS M. ANDERSON,
Brigadier-General, U. S. Volunteers, Commanding.

HEADQUARTERS SECOND DIVISION, EIGHTH ARMY CORPS,
Cavite Arsenal, P. I., August 5, 1898.

ADJUTANT-GENERAL, DEPARTMENT OF THE PACIFIC.

SIR: I have the honor to inform you that General Aguinaldo, through a staff officer, complains that the Signal Corps, United States Army, in putting up wires, has interrupted his communications; that he was promised that this interruption would not last more than one day, but that it has now been out of working order for three days; that he is very glad to have the army use his telegraph poles, but it is so important to keep his communication that he earnestly requests prompt action in the matter.

Very respectfully, THOMAS M. ANDERSON,
Brigadier-General, U. S. Volunteers, Commanding.

AUGUST 10, 1898.

INSTRUCTIONS FROM GENERAL MERRITT BROUGHT BY GENERAL BABCOCK.

1. No rupture with insurgents. This is imperative. Can ask insurgent generals or Aguinaldo for permission to occupy their trenches, but if refused not to use force.

2. No extension of lines as proposed in memorandum of August 9, which will bring partial engagement resulting in loss prior to general assault.

3. One gun can be placed within two hours after receiving the order in the insurgent emplacement on the road facing No. 14; not as good a position as farther to the front and right. Three more guns can be placed in trenches near the beach without precipitating an engagement. Embrasures can be cut through trenches to-night.

4. Troops can occupy trenches on two hours' notice, but are not prepared to make a determined assault without carrying out memorandum of August 9, requiring three days. We can hold trenches against any possible attack and bring eight field guns into action in front of enemy's lines.

CAMP DEWEY (NEAR MANILA),
August 10, 1898.

Gen. EMILIO AGUINALDO,
Commanding Philippine Forces, Bacoor:

Will your excellency consent to my occupation of the intrenchment facing blockhouse No. 14, on the road from Pasay to Singalon? Our object is to place artillery to destroy the blockhouse. If you consent, please issue necessary orders to-night. I shall highly appreciate a prompt reply.

THOMAS M. ANDERSON,
Brigadier-General, Commanding Division.

BACOOR, *August 10, 1898.*

Brig. Gen. THOMAS M. ANDERSON, *U. S. Volunteers, Camp Dewey.*

SIR: Replying to your note of this date, in which you ask me the occupation by your troops of the intrenchments facing blockhouse No. 14, on the road from Pasay to Singalon, I have the pleasure to tell you that I [am] giving the necessary orders so that your troops may occupy the mentioned intrenchments, and my troops will pass to the immediate intrenchments or to any other place where they think convenient to intrench themselves.

E. AGUINALDO.

MANILA, P. I., *August 13, 1898.*

General AGUINALDO, *General in Chief, Filipino Forces:*

Serious trouble threatening between our forces. Try and prevent it. Your forces should not force themselves in the city until we have received the full surrender. Then we will negotiate with you.

ANDERSON.

[Most urgent.]

PIÑEDA (Received from Bacoor, 10.50 a. m., 13).

General Aguinaldo, president of revolutionary government, Ermita, to General Anderson, Ermita.

I received a telegram. My interpreter is in Cavite; in consequence of this I have not answered till now. My troops are forced by yours by means of threats of violence to retire from positions taken. It is necessary to avoid conflict, which I should lament, that you order your troops that they avoid difficulty with mine, as until now they have conducted themselves as brothers to take Manila. I have given strict orders to my chiefs that they preserve strict respect to American forces and to aid them in case they are attacked by a common enemy.

I do not doubt that the good relations and friendship which unite us will be continued if your soldiers correspond to the conduct imposed upon mine.

E. AGUINALDO.

[Memorandum without date. In General Anderson's handwriting.]

If you apparently have been treated harshly, it is from military necessity and not for want of confidence.

We had to take Manila to effect the purpose of our war.

While we may admit the justice of your insurrection, to prevent all possible complications still it is thought judicious and necessary to have only one army in Manila at once.

[In General Merritt's handwriting.]

The Government of the United States, you may be assured, which as its agent I can make no promises, will deal fairly with the Filipinos, but we must now insist for the good of all there shall be no joint occupation of Manila.

NOTE.—This note is apparently the draft of a telegram sent in reply to General Aguinaldo's message dated 10.50 a. m., August 13, and marked "Most urgent."

BACOOR, *August 14, 1898.*

General ANDERSON:

My troops who have been for so long besieging Manila have always been promised that they could appear in it, as you know and can not deny, and for this reason and on account of the many sacrifices made of money and lives, I do not consider it prudent to issue orders to the contrary, as they might be disobeyed against my authority. Besides, I hope that you will allow the troops to enter because we have given proofs, many times, of our friendship, ceding our positions at Parañaque, Pasay, Singalon, and Matubig. Nevertheless, if it seems best to you, and in order to enter into a frank and friendly understanding and avoid any disagreeable conflict before the eyes of the Spaniards, I will commission Don Felipe Buencamino and others, who will to-day go out from our lines to hold a conference with you, and that they will be safe during the conference.

E. AGUINALDO.

BACOOR, *August 14, 1898.*

General ANDERSON, *Manila.*

DEAR GENERAL: Not being able to leave government, have conferred special powers to —— Buencamino, Araneta, and others, who left here for you at 8 o'clock this morning.

E. AGUINALDO.

[From Aguinaldo, Emilio, dated Bacoor, P. I., August 15, 1898.]

Brief: Mis comisionados me dicen que V. ha promitiss enviarme antes el plans del radio que quiiren ustedes solos occupar; sin embargo iran alli mañana mismo mis comisionados para hacer arreglos despues de los enales vere si conviene la retirado de mis tropas desersco siempo de conservar la mistad y un a burao intelligencio.

NOTE.—This document was received in the War Department in the form in which it is here given, and in which it was printed in the report of the Major-General Commanding the Army, 1899, volume 2, page 343. It is found not to have been correctly rendered in Spanish and it is evident that it should have read as follows:

[From Aguinaldo, Emilio, dated Bacoor, P. I., August 15, 1898.]

Mis comisionados me dicen que V. ha prometido enviarme cuanto antes el plan del radio que quieren Vds. ocupar; sin embargo irán allí mañana mis comisionados para hacer arreglos, después de los cuales veré si conviene la retirada de mis tropas. Deseo siempre conservar la amistad y una buena inteligencia.

A translation of it reads:

[From Aguinaldo, Emilio, dated at Bacoor, P. I., August 15, 1898.]

My commissioners tell me that you have promised to send me as soon as possible the map of the zone that you wish to occupy; without doubt my commissioners will come to-morrow to make the arrangements, after which I shall see if it is possible to withdraw my troops. I desire always to maintain friendship and a good understanding.

[Memorandum.]

General Merritt remarks in relation to the telegrams you sent us that it would be well to inform General Aguinaldo as follows:

We can not permit joint occupation of the city. The city surrendered to the United States forces, and all the headway that you have been able to make was due entirely to the assistance furnished you by the United States. We now hold the city, which includes all the outlying districts of the city properly within the city limits. We most earnestly and sincerely hope and trust that there may be no conflict between us, but we are prepared to enforce our orders in this matter, and expect from time to time large additions to our strength. We desire most sincerely to remain friendly with the Filipinos, and have nothing but their best interests at heart in all our dealings with them.

We have given orders to our troops as well as to General Aguinaldo that there shall be no violence whatever.

(NOTE.—Apparently a memorandum prepared for General Anderson by General Babcock.)

HEADQUARTERS DEPARTMENT OF THE PACIFIC
AND EIGHTH ARMY CORPS,
Manila, P. I., August 15, 1898.

Brig. Gen. T. M. ANDERSON,
U. S. Volunteers, Commanding Second Division, Eighth Army Corps.

SIR: The commanding general directs that in any arrangement made with the insurgents in regard to retiring from the vicinity of the city, care will be taken to make them understand that they must not hold a line encircling the city. The commanding general will not tolerate a line of troops or works which would give the appearance that our troops were hemmed in by a besieging force. The insurgents may billet their commands in villages in the vicinity, but under no circumstances will they be allowed to hold a line as above indicated.

Very respectfully,

J. B. BABCOCK, *Adjutant-General.*

NOTES TO GENERAL ANDERSON.

First. We concede the military disposition of the town of Manila, always that there be understood by said town, the jurisdiction of the old municipal limits or walled city and its suburbs, Binondo, Tondo, Santa Cruz, Quiapo, Sampaloc, San Miguel, Concepcion, Ermita, Malate, and Paco or San Fernando de Dilao.

Second. We concede the source of potable water always that [on condition that] the ayuntamiento of Manila bear the cost of repairing the machinery and piping, and current expenses of the machinery, such as coal, and the pay of the working force. We will be responsible for order and security at that place.

Third. We ask free navigation for the *Patria*, with entrance and exit to the port and river Pasig, and that our products be admitted free of duty, and free entrance to and departure from the city to all the Filipinos, the arms of our chiefs and officers being respected.

Fourth. The sacrifices that we have made in contribution to the siege and capture of Manila being notorious, it is just that we should have a part of the booty of war.

Fifth. We ask for our use the palace at Malacanan and the convents at Malate, Ermita, and Paco or San Fernando de Dilao.

Sixth. We ask that the civil offices of Manila be filled by North Americans and never by Spaniards. But if General Merritt should have need of Filipinos, we would be pleased that he concede to our president, General Don Emilio Aguinaldo, the right of nominating those Filipinos who would be most energetic and apt. The jurisdiction of the authorities of Manila will not be recognized outside of the municipal radius [limits].

Seventh. The American forces can not [will not be permitted to] approach nor pass through our military positions without permission of the respective commanders, and all positions outside of the municipal limits shall be evacuated. Spaniards who pass through our lines without permission of the commander will be considered as spies.

Eighth. We ask the return of the arms of the 150 military [men] who were disarmed by the American officers.

Ninth. All arrangements [negotiations] must be made in writing and afterwards ratified by both generals in chief.

Tenth. We are pleased, lastly, to be certain [to affirm] that our own commissions and positions do not signify acknowledgment on our part of North American sovereignty in these islands any more [or longer] than the necessity of actual war [demands].

NOTE.—This is presumably a memorandum drawn up and submitted to General Anderson by the commissioners (of Aguinaldo) mentioned in the preceding telegram. Both the pumping station (at Santolan) and the reservoir (at San Juan del Monte) had been taken from the Spaniards by and were in the possession of the insurgents prior to our entry into Manila.

HEADQUARTERS DEPARTMENT OF THE PACIFIC
AND EIGHTH ARMY CORPS,
Manila, P. I., August 20, 1898.

The COMMANDING GENERAL OF THE PHILIPPINE FORCES.

SIR: The commanding general of the American forces has received a memorandum addressed to General Anderson, which purports to contain a statement of certain desires on the part of the Filipinos.

As most of them seem to be reasonable, it gives him much pleasure to say that he agrees to the following:

The forces of the Filipinos are to withdraw entirely beyond the jurisdiction of the old municipal limits or walled city and its suburbs, Binondo, Tondo, Santa Cruz, Quiapo, Sampaloc, San Miguel, Concepcion, Ermita, and Paco, or San Fernando de Dilao. The Filipinos will repair at once whatever may be needed in order that the water may be turned on to the city, and the expenses of the repairs and current expenses of the works will be paid by the city. The commander of the Filipinos agrees to be responsible for order and security at the pumping station.

Permission for the free navigation of the *Patria* to entrance and exit of the port and river passage, and that country products for sale be admitted free of duty, is granted.

Free entrance and departure from the city of all Filipinos without arms is granted. Chiefs and officers of the Filipino army may, as a matter of courtesy, wear their side arms, though this is deprecated as possibly leading to disturbance of quiet of city.

No pistols should be carried. The major-general having taken for his own use the palace at Malacanan, the request that it be turned over to the Filipinos can not be granted, and the convents at Malate, Ermita, and Paco can not be turned over and must be evacuated. The civil offices at Manila are being filled as rapidly as possible by Americans, and the commanding general will be glad to receive recommendations for appointments to office of such Filipinos as may be considered fitted for the duties of subordinate officers.

American soldiers without arms are to be allowed to pass through the Filipino's position outside the city, just as the Filipinos without arms are permitted to enter the city.

The return of the arms of the 150 men will be granted by the general in immediate command.

The opening of the waterworks at once, and the retirement of your soldiers from the positions now occupied within the municipal jurisdiction, will be sufficient notice on your part that everything is satisfactorily arranged on the terms of this letter. With the sincere hope that it may be speedily accomplished, I am

Very respectfully,

W. MERRITT,
Major-General Commanding.

NOTE.—I delivered this letter the day it was written, and was to verbally convey the contents of the memorandum which follows the answer thereto at the same time; but Aguinaldo was absent from his headquarters at the time the letter was delivered and I did not mention the contents of the memorandum, except that portion relating to opening the waterworks immediately. His associates claimed that General A. had already ordered this done (and I feel certain that he had). They promised that it should be done at once, and sent a message to again order it done at once while I was there. I made an engagement to see General Aguinaldo at 11 a. m. the next day.

J. F. BELL.

BACOOR, *August 21, 1898.*

The COMMANDING GENERAL OF THE AMERICAN FORCES IN THE PACIFIC.

SIR: The commanding general of the Philippine forces has been favored by your excellency with a letter of the 28th instant, containing the conditions that you will accept from the Filipinos provided the latter abandon the posts that they now occupy within the suburbs of Manila. The aforesaid letter speaks of permission for the free navigation of the *Patria,* and as the Filipinos have no boat of that name the undersigned takes the liberty of clearing up that point, as he considers it understood that the Filipinos desire the protection of the American squadron for the free navigation of all their boats, and free entrance and exit in the ports that are in charge of the same.

Moreover, in substitution for the conditions proposed (in a previous communication), which the aforesaid letter does not mention, the Filipinos desire to go on occupying that part of the suburbs of San Fernando de Dilao or Paco, adjacent to the east side of the bridge and creek of the same name, the undersigned answering for the foreign interests which exist in that district. They also desire that if in consequence of the treaty of peace which may be concluded between the United States of America and Spain the Philippines should continue under the domination of the latter, the American forces should give up all the suburbs to the Filipinos in consideration of the cooperation lent by the latter in the capture of Manila.

With these conditions and others which you have already accepted in the aforementioned letter the undersigned promises in the name of the Filipinos to evacuate the positions they now hold in the suburbs; and the acceptance of the same on the part of your excellency will be one more proof that you have in consideration the innumerable lives sacrificed in the siege of Manila, and that you are able to appreciate the unqualified friendship which he, the undersigned, will try to preserve at all costs.

Very respectfully, EMILIO AGUINALDO.

NOTE.—This answer was already prepared and was handed me on my arrival at 11 a. m. Therefore it was prepared before the contents of the memorandum which follows were made known to Aguinaldo and his associates.

[Memorandum for Major Bell.]

1. In case you find Aguinaldo inclined to be generous in his arrangements with us you may communicate to him the following:

(1) [a] That if a meeting between himself and the commanding general here could be arranged I would be very glad to meet him and have a talk with him upon the general situation.

(2) That it is of the utmost importance to us that the water supply of the city be at once turned on, as the rainy season having suspended it is important that the sewers be flushed and the city gotten in fair sanitary condition.

(3) That I have every disposition to represent liberally the Government at Washington, which I know is inclined to deal fairly with him and his people; but not knowing what the policy of that Government will be I am not prepared to make any promises except that in the event of the United States withdrawing from these islands care will be taken to leave him *in as good condition as he was found by the forces of the Government.* [b]

(4) That I agree with Mr. Williams, the consul, in thinking that it would be well for him and some of his leaders to visit Washington and represent the case to the American authorities. I feel sure that good would result from this course. However, it is not considered necessary.

(5) It is my intention to depose the Spanish officials from all important positions hitherto held by them, and this already has been done to a considerable extent. I will be very glad to receive recommendations from him for Filipinos who are especially trustworthy, though I can not agree to make any appointments in the immediate future. The American officers and men will be employed as far as is practicable in conducting the affairs of the municipality.

(6) I expect daily a considerable accession to the forces which I now have here, and it is my design to lodge them in Cavite provided room can be found. In conclusion I sincerely trust that there will be no friction in the future between our commands, and that the good feeling that we have made every attempt to foster will be encouraged by Aguinaldo and his chiefs. For myself and the officers and men under my command I can say that we have conceived a high respect for the ability and qualities of the Filipinos, and if called upon by the Government to express an opinion it will be to that effect.

WESLEY MERRITT, *Major-General.*

---

[a] Aguinaldo told me to thank General Merritt for his kind offer and to say that just as soon as his health would permit of such a thing (he had been sick) he would send a staff officer to General Merritt to ascertain when it would be convenient to meet him. He had not sent the staff officer, as far as I know, when General Merritt left. Soon after General Merritt's arrival he sent a staff officer on board the *Newport* to arrange for an interview with him, but the General sent back word that he was exceedingly pressed by business just then, but as soon as he could he would send him word when he could see him.

[b] I was pressed to explain further just what meaning General Merritt meant to convey by the underscored portion of this remark, but I replied that I had repeated the language General Merritt had used to me and I preferred they should seek any further explanation from him, lest I might unwittingly fall into error if I undertook to explain the meaning myself. Their lack of definiteness and my unwillingness to comment upon the language seemed to arouse their apprehensions and suspicions. They have been trying ever since to obtain in writing some definite promise on this subject.

BACOOR, *April (August) 21, 1898.*

Without losing a moment, you will proceed to open [start] the machinery of the water works, being sorry that up to the present my orders have not been completed [fulfilled], for said object, and I expect that the present will be immediately completed [fulfilled].

I inform you that this order will be carried to you by Majors Bemont (engineer) and Bell, accompanied by an assistant, Mr. Infante, with the object of examining said machinery.

E. AGUINALDO.

NOTE.—Aguinaldo and his associates seemed much gratified when I made known to them the contents of the preceding memorandum. I asked for a written order to the officer in charge of the forces holding the reservoir and pumping station, to be delivered by myself. The above was prepared and handed me. Captain Infante, one of Aguinaldo's adjutants, was also sent with me to make sure that his object (the immediate opening of the works), was accomplished. On arriving at the pumping station next day, I found that the delay had been due not to official obstruction, but to the inability of these mañana people to overcome the inertia incident to starting up machinery which had lain idle for some months.

OFFICE OF THE MILITARY GOVERNOR AND
HEADQUARTERS DEPARTMENT OF THE PACIFIC,
Manila, August 24, 1898.

Gen. EMILIO AGUINALDO,
Bacoor, Philippine Islands.

SIR: The commanding general of the American land forces has the honor to acknowledge the receipt of your communication of August 21, and in reply to inform you as follows:

The error which you speak of which needs clearing up as to the navigation of the Patria, seems to have arisen from a request on your part that the Filipinos of the country should be permitted to trade freely, and navigate without obstruction the streams and bays surrounding Manila. So far as the products of the country are concerned this has been acceded to, and there will be no obstruction placed by the American land forces in the way of a free trade in the products of the country between the residents of this island and the city of Manila.

The protection which you ask from the American squadron rests with Rear-Admiral Dewey and it is for him to determine whether it can be granted or not.

A commission of your appointment, which had an interview with the undersigned about the 15th instant, agreed that if a line were designated by a proper commission on my part that the armed Filipinos should retire beyond it. While this had been done in some instances it has been neglected in others, and it is now desired to call your attention to the fact that the occupation of the suburbs of Manila or any part of them can not be acceded to by the undersigned. It has already been pointed out to you that dual occupation of Manila was impossible in the interests of either party; and as the troops of the United States are in possession of Manila, I must insist upon the carrying out of the original agreement between your commissioners and myself. I am the more insistent in this particular because recent instructions from my home Government contemplate this course.

So far as any promises as to what should be done in the event of a conclusion of a treaty between the United States and Spain is concerned, it is utterly impossible for me as the military representative only of the United States to make any promises such as you request. As you have already been informed, you may depend upon the good will of the Americans out here, and the Government of which you already know the beneficence, to determine these matters in the future.

This answer to your communication has been delayed by a press of business which could not very well be neglected.

I thank you in the name of my country for the good will expressed toward it, and feel assured that nothing will occur to mar the friendly feeling that now exists. It is for the interests of all that the good feeling that now exists between us should be carefully fostered and maintained.

Very respectfully,   WESLEY MERRITT, *Major-General.*

[Telegram received from Aguinaldo, 5.13 a. m., August 25, 1898. To General Merritt: Concerning trouble between Filipino and American forces at Cavite.]

I have received notice of the death of one American soldier and three wounded. It is said that this happened by their being drunk. They fired in the air in the beginning but afterwards fought among themselves. General Anderson says death has been occasioned by my people on account of which I have ordered investigations to ascertain the truth and demonstrate that the Filipinos try to be in harmony with the Americans. If I shall find any one of my people guilty I shall order severe punishment.

Yours, respectfully,   AGUINALDO.

[Reply to telegram received from Aguinaldo, 5.13 a. m., August 25, 1898.]

MALACANAN, *August 25, 1898—3.05 a. m.*

General AGUINALDO,
Commanding Philippine Forces, Bacoor:

Thanks for your telegram. I am glad to learn of your intention to investigate fully. I am desirous with you that harmony should prevail, and request you always in event of trouble to communicate directly with me, as you have so wisely done this time.

MERRITT.

REVOLUTIONARY GOVERNMENT OF THE PHILIPPINES,
Bacoor, August 27, 1898.

Gen. WESLEY MERRITT, *Manila.*

MY DEAR SIR: Knowing the contents of your letter of the 24th instant, I can not do less than manifest my surprise at knowing that you have formed the idea that my commissioners compromised themselves in the conference of the 15th, to retire my troops outside of the line that you would designate.

I understood, and still understand, as well as the commissioners, that the evacuation of my troops of the posts that they occupy to-day on the outskirts of the city would take place when the proposed conditions were accepted by you, among which figured the condition that the agreement [treaty] should be in writing to be valid; for which reason, not having yet accepted some of the propositions made at the time, nor those that were substituted in my previous communication, I do not think that up to now I have contracted said obligation.

If I have permitted the use of the water before the formalization of the treaty, it was more to demonstrate that I am disposed to sacrifice to friendship everything that does not prejudice too much the rights of the Philippines. I comprehend as well as yourself the inconvenience of a double occupation of the city and its suburbs, given the conditions stipulated in the capitulation with the Spaniards; but you ought to understand without the long siege sustained by my forces you might have obtained possession of the ruins of the city, but never the rendition of the Spanish forces, who could have retired to the interior towns.

I do not complain of the disowning of our help in the mentioned capitulation, although justice resents it greatly, and I have to bear the well-founded blame of my people. I do not insist upon the retention of all the positions conquered by my forces within the city limits at the cost of much blood, of indescribable fatigues, and much money. I promise to retire, then, to the following lines:

In Malate, the continuation of the Calzada of Singalon to the bridge that joins the road; from this bridge in straight line to that of Paco; from this last bridge, following the creek Paco and leaving outside the suburb of Tanque, to the river Pasig; following this river and entering by the creek that goes to the bridge of Aviles; from this bridge following the road (Calzada) of the same name and that of Santa Mesa, that are the dividing lines between Sampaloc and the village of Pandacan, to the jurisdictional limit of the suburbs of Sampaloc, Trozo, and Tondo.

But before I retire to this line I pray you to reclaim from Admiral Dewey the protection of our ships for free navigation, and permit me to insist, if you wish, upon the restitution of the position that we are now going to leave if, in the treaty of peace to be celebrated between Spain and the United States, they acknowledge the domination of Spain in the Philippines. I expect as well that you order the American forces outside of the above line to retire within the city, as already agreed to. I do not believe that the acceptation of the conditions proposed will prejudice the smallest right of your people, as it signifies nothing more than the acknowledgment of a part of the rights of a friendly people.

I am now compelled to insist upon the said conditions to quiet the complaints of my chiefs and soldiers, who have exposed their lives and abandoned their interests during the siege of Manila. I hope that this time you will manifest the spirit of justice that pertains to such a free and admirably constituted Government as that of the United States of America.

Very respectfully,   EMILIO AGUINALDO.

NOTE.—No position whatever, with a possible exception of Paco (San Fernando de Dilao), were conquered within the city limits by Aguinaldo's forces. Definite information can be procured of General MacArthur as to whether the insurgents or our forces forced the Spanish to retire from that place.

The Calzada á Aviles merges at the crossroads, [where] there is really a round open space with a fountain in the center and called the "Plaza de Rotondo," into the road to Santa Mesa, marked on the map "A" Mariquina, to which place it also goes. The First Colorado Regiment has a picket post on this road a half mile beyond the limit mentioned by Aguinaldo.

I gather from the statement of many naval officers that Aguinaldo was invited here and given much assistance and encouragement by Admiral Dewey, who of course did not anticipate any complication, and probably never supposed Aguinaldo would at once assume an independence of American control. He has been much concerned and displeased by Aguinaldo's course of conduct, and told me several days ago that he had ceased to recognize him in any way, and had refused any longer to receive his representatives. This prayer to you to "reclaim" Admiral Dewey's protection is doubtless due to this change of attitude on the Admiral's part, who, if permitted to follow his own inclinations, will not only grant Aguinaldo no protection, but will seize boats and launches at the first overt act.

Attention is invited to General Merritt's promise (page 11, paragraph 3), made known to Aguinaldo by me verbally, namely, that in the event of the United States withdrawing from these islands care would be taken to leave Aguinaldo in as good condition as he was found by the forces of the Government. From a remark the

General made to me I inferred he intended to interpret the expression "forces of the Government" to mean the naval forces should future contingencies necessitate such an interpretation. At the time of the entry of the American forces into Manila, which was accomplished without assistance from the insurgents being either needed, requested, received, or desired, the insurgents held the following lines: Joining onto the American trenches facing Mytubig (the Indian name for the locality at the south end of Malate, in the vicinity of the old fort and bridge), their trenches extended in a large circle around and outside of the Spanish line of blockhouses. The Spanish held Santa Ana, Concordia, Paco, Singalon, and Malate; then the line dropped back to blockhouse No. 8, to McLeod's house in Santa Mesa, and continued on around to the bay at Bancu Say, including within it all the suburbs on the northern side of Manila. The lines are indicated in map accompanying my report of July 27. Parañaque, Pasay, San Pedro Macati, Mandaloian, Pasig, Guadalupe, Partero, Santolan (where is situated the pumping station), San Juan del Monte (where the reservoir is located), Cabiao, Santol, San Francisco del Monte, Caloocan, and Malabon are the villages, towns, and places (immediately in rear of the insurgent trenches and positions) where the insurgent forces were generally located. After our entry into the city they all advanced their positions and encroached upon our outposts without anyone's authority or permission save their own, and in the face of repeated objections on the part of General Merritt. They can lay no just claim to having conquered from the Spanish the positions now held, except those at the pumping station and reservoir. Prior to the 13th of August they had for weeks been straining every resource in an effort to capture Manila without the assistance of Americans and before they got ready, without making the slightest progress. Of course, they could never have made the progress they did in investing the city had it not been for the destruction of the Spanish fleet by Admiral Dewey, but they did do much hard fighting and did drive the Spanish from positions in the provinces immediately surrounding Manila into the confines of the city itself. This credit they are entitled to.

OFFICE OF THE MILITARY GOVERNOR
AND HEADQUARTERS DEPARTMENT OF THE PACIFIC,
Manila, August 30, 1898.

Colonel BARRY,
 Adjutant-General Eighth Army Corps.

DEAR COLONEL: Inclosed you will find a letter from General Aguinaldo and a blue print of Manila. The letter was brought by his aid two days ago, and he was informed that a reply would be sent within four days. The matter should have immediate attention as General Merritt has not been able to take it up, owing to his hurried departure. The letters referred to by Aguinaldo from General Merritt will be found in the press copy book at the department headquarters and here.

The demand now made by Aguinaldo is to retain his people just outside of the interior black pencil mark on the map. The outside pencil marks indicate the positions that General Merritt desired to have the insurgents withdraw to. I inferred from what the aid said that what Aguinaldo particularly desires is, that in case his requests are are not granted, that reasons are to be given which he can use to satisfy his people. The trouble seems to be that he does not think it prudent to give positive orders for his people to withdraw from the city.

Very respectfully,

—— ——, *Chief of Staff.*

AFFAIRS IN THE PHILIPPINE ISLANDS. 823

[Telegram.]

OFFICE OF THE GOVERNOR-GENERAL,
Manila, P. I., August 31, 1898.

General AGUINALDO, *Bacoor, P. I.:*

Referring to promise made by General Merritt to reply to your letter of August 27 within four days, I desire to state that General Merrett was unexpectedly ordered away and had not opportunity to reply. Being unacquainted with the situation I must take time to inform myself before replying, which I will do at the earliest opportunity.

OTIS, *Commanding.*

OFFICE OF THE U. S. MILITARY GOVERNOR IN THE PHILIPPINE ISLANDS,
Manila, P. I., September 8, 1898.

The COMMANDING GENERAL OF THE PHILIPPINE FORCES.

SIR: I have the honor to acknowledge the receipt of your communication of the 27th ultimo, addressed to General Merritt, my predecessor, and by him transferred to me on the eve of his departure from Manila. By telegram of the 31st ultimo, I informed you of General Merritt's hurried departure in obedience to orders from my Government; that his necessarily hurried preparations did not permit him to make reply to the communication and that such duty devolved upon me, which I would perform at the earliest opportunity and as soon as I could acquaint myself with the condition of affairs of which (as I had but recently arrived) I had but slight knowledge. To my telegrams you made a most courteous response. Having now carefully considered the situation, I have the honor to make reply as follows:

First. In your note of the 27th ultimo you are pleased to manifest surprise that the United States military governor should have reached an erroneous conclusion as to the result of a conference with your commissioners on August 15, as apparently manifested by his letter to you of August 24. I do not know the extent of any conversation which may have been indulged in at that conference and the nature of the impression which may have been conveyed. Referring to a written memorandum in my possession, which purports to contain the substance of propositions discussed at the time, I find that certain concessions were made by the commissioners in expected return for specific privileges to be conferred, and as there has not been a mutual agreement concerning these matters between the interested parties I do not understand that any obligations have arisen by reason of that conference.

Second. I note with pleasure your allusion to your very friendly disposition toward my Government, as manifested by your prompt attendance to our request for a supply of water; also your expression as to the inconvenience of a dual occupation of the city of Manila, and I do not forget that the revolutionary forces under your command have made many sacrifices in the interest of civil liberty and for the welfare of your people, and to this I will be pleased to allude hereafter.

Third. In connection with your remark as to the injustice of the United States in not properly appreciating your assistance in the capture of Manila, I beg a full consideration on your part of the mandatory conditions which accompany the occupation, which I am sure you fully appreciate, but to which I will respectfully invite your attention in a subsequent portion of this reply.

Fourth. You designate certain lines within the suburbs of the city of Manila to which you promise to retire your troops, and name as conditions precedent—first, protection to your shipping by the United States Navy and the free navigation of your vessels within the waters of United States occupation; second, restitution to your forces of all positions which are now occupied by your troops in the event that treaty stipulations between the United States and Spain surrender to the last-named Government the territory occupied by the former; and, thirdly that United States troops now occupying positions beyond the lines which you name shall retire within the same.

A discussion of your proposition to hold jointly with the United States Government the city of Manila involves consideration of some of the other concessions you desire to be made, and to that I will at once refer. I wish to present the matter, in the first instance, in its legal aspect, although from remarks contained in former correspondence I am of the opinion that you are fully aware how untenable the proposition is. The United States and Spain were and are belligerent parties to a war, and were so recognized by the civilized world. In the course of events the entire city of Manila, then in full possession of the Spanish forces, was surrendered to the first-named belligerent power. The articles of agreement and capitulation gave to the United States Government full occupancy of the city and defenses of Manila, and that Government obligated itself to insure the safety of the lives and property of the inhabitants of the city to the best of its ability. By all the laws of war and all international precedents United States authority over Manila and its defenses is full and supreme, and they can not escape the obligations which they have assumed.

By the able representatives who have charge of the interests of the Philippine revolutionary forces this conclusion will be admitted to be incontrovertible and argument on the point unnecessary. Can they who seek civil and religious liberty and invite the approval and assistance of the civilized world afford to enter upon a course of action which the law of nations must condemn?

But conceding, as you do, the strictly legal right of my Government to hold and administer the affairs of the city of Manila and all of its suburbs (I thus conclude from expressions contained in former correspondence and from my appreciation of your intellectual attainments) you base your proposal of joint occupation upon supposed equitable grounds, referring to the sacrifices your troops have made and the assistance they have rendered the American forces in the capture of Manila. It is well known that they have made personal sacrifices, enduring great hardships and have rendered aid. But is it forgotten that my Government has swept the Spanish navy from the seas of both hemispheres, sent back to Spain the Spanish army and navy forces recently embarked for your destruction and for the secure holding of its Philippine possessions; that since May 1 last its navy has held the city of Manila at its mercy, but out of consideration of humanity refused to bombard it, preferring to send troops to demand surrender and thereby preserve the lives and property of its inhabitants? Is it forgotten that the destruction of the Spanish navy and the retention of Spanish armed men in its European possessions has opened up to you the ports of the island of Luzon and held Spain helpless to meet its refractory subjects?

As between my Government and the revolutionary forces of the Philippines, I fail to discover on what principle of common justice a joint occupation of Manila can be maintained. Equity, in the legal acceptance of the term, would most assuredly condemn it. A sense of justice should, in my opinion, have prompted the revolutionary forces to aid those of my country in every way possible in return for the great assistance they have received. You remark in substance, that had you not prevented the Spanish forces from retreating from the city, the United States would have received naught but its ruined streets and buildings. Possibly; but had all Spanish subjects, elsewhere and here, been the contented subjects of Spain, war between it and my Government would not have been waged. It was undertaken by the United States for humanity's sake, and not for their aggrandizement, or for any National profit they expected to receive, and they have expended millions of treasure and hundreds of the lives of their citizens in the interests of the Spanish suffering colonists.

Apart from all legal and equitable considerations, and those having their origin in personally-conceived ideas of justice, I wish respectfully to call your attention to the impracticability of maintaining a joint occupation of Manila and its suburbs; and in this I know that I shall have the approval of your excellent judgment. It would be extremely difficult to prevent friction between our respective forces, which might result in unfortunate consequences, labor as we may for continued harmonious relations. Located in close proximity, irresponsible members of our organizations, by careless or impertinent action, might be the means of inciting grave disturbances; and in this connection I cite the recent shooting affair at Cavite, which still requires investigation. There might also arise conflicts of authority between our respective officers. Even now, within precincts in entire actual possession of our troops, I find that permits are given to citizens, who are styled local presidents, to make arrests, to carry arms, etc., in violation of our instructions and authority, and that several cases of kidnaping have taken place. In pursuance of our obligations to maintain, in so far as we can, domestic tranquillity, our officers have arrested suspected parties, and they have asserted (with what element of truth I know not) that the insurgent forces are the offenders. I have declined to accept their statements, as I prefer to believe the contrary, although it would appear that officers connected with these forces have issued the permits to which I allude. Such interference with our administration of civil affairs must eventually result in conflict.

Again (reverting to a legal aspect of the subject) the affairs of the entire city corporation must be administered from a common center. The trust accepted by the Government from those who surrendered actual possession confers a discretionary power which can neither be shared nor delegated. The validity of this conclusion will be readily understood by yourself and associates as a well-established legal proposition, and does not require argument. And here permit me to remark upon a view of the subject you have advocated in support of the plea for dual occupation of the city's suburbs. Your forces, you say in substance, should have a share in the booty resulting from the conquest of the city, on account of hardships endured and assistance rendered. The facts on which you base your conclusion granted, the conclusion under the laws of war, which are binding on my Government, does not follow. It has never recognized the existence of spoils of war, denominated booty, as have many European Governments. No enemy's property of any kind, public or private, can be seized, claimed, or awarded to any of its officers and men; and should they attempt to appropriate any of it for their individual benefit, they would be very severely punished through military tribunals, on which have been conferred by law very sweeping jurisdiction. The enemy's money and property (all that is not necessary to be expended in administering local affairs in the enemy's surrendered territory) must be preserved for final arbitrament or settlement by and between the supreme authorities of the nations concerned. My troops can not acquire booty nor any individual benefits by reason of capture of an enemy's territory. I make this comment believing you hold erroneous opinions in respect to individual advantages which occupation bestows.

I request your indulgence while I briefly consider the concessions you ask us to make as conditions precedent to the retirement of your forces to the line indicated by your note of the 27th ultimo. The first is protection to your shipping and free navigation to your vessels. Neither the extent of protection nor the limit of free navigation you request is understood. Certainly you could not mean protection on the high seas or in ports not in the rightful possession of the United States. That, as you are fully aware, could only be effected by a treaty of guaranty following international recognition of the belligerent rights of a Philippine revolutionary government. While the existing armistice continues the United States are in rightful possession, in so far as the navigable waters of the Philippine Islands are concerned, only of the Bay of Manila and its navigable tributaries. Within the same all vessels of trade and commerce and the war vessels of recognized national powers sail freely as long as the sovereignty of my Government is not assailed nor the peace of the locality threatened. In this respect whatever concessions are extended by way of relaxation of trade restrictions incident to war to citizens of these islands will be extended to all alike; no discrimination in this regard is intended or will be permitted. Admiral Dewey exercises supervisory jurisdiction over all navy matters, and they are in no way related to the duties conferred upon me by law. Nor would it avail should I seek his consent for greater latitude of action, for even if disposed to grant special concessions he could not do so, and I doubt if the supreme authority of my Government could now, under the prevailing truce with Spain, invest him with the requisite powers to do so and at the same time preserve its international obligations.

The second concession named by you is restitution of positions in the city of Manila to your forces, in case a treaty of peace remands to Spain the territory surrendered by her in the late capitulation articles; and the third and last is a promise to retire our troops within the lines indicated by you as the lines which you desire your troops to remain permanently. These propositions having a kindred nature may be considered together, and indeed have already been impliedly answered. From previous statements of facts and logical conclusions made and stated in this communication, concerning the nature of the obligations resting upon the United States with regard to the territory to which they have the legal right of possession under contracting articles with Spain, it is evident that neither in law nor morals can the concessions be made. I would be powerless to grant them in any aspect of the case, being nothing more than an agent to carry out the instructions of the executive head of my Government, and not being vested with discretionary powers to determine matters of such moment. In the present instance I am not only powerless to accede to your request but have been strictly enjoined by my Government, mindful of its international promises and national honor, which it has never broken or sacrificed, not to concede joint occupation of the city and suburbs of Manila, and am directed specially to preserve the peace and protect persons and property within the territory surrendered under the terms of the Spanish capitulation. These mandates I must obey.

Thus have I endeavored with all candor and sincerity, holding nothing in reserve, to place before you the situation as understood by me, and I doubt not by the Republic which I represent. I have not been instructed as to what policy it intends to pursue with regard to its legitimate holdings here, and hence I am unable to give you any information on the subject. That it will have a care, and labor conscientiously for the welfare of your people I sincerely believe. It remains for you, beneficiaries of its sacrifices, to adopt a course of action which will manifest your good intentions and show to the world the principles which actuate your motives.

You and your associates could not regret more than I any conflict between our forces which would tend to excite the citizens of my country, who are always a unit in action when its sovereignty is attacked or when its rights to fulfill its international obligations are called into question. Then they never count cost; and, as you are fully aware, resources are abundant. Rather than see the ships of the Navy of the United States controlling the navigable waters of these islands and its armies devastating their territory, I would greatly prefer to advise my Government that there is no longer need to send more of its troops to this section of country, and that those whom it holds waiting on its Pacific slope can be remanded to their homes or employed elsewhere, as it may determine.

It only remains for me to respectfully notify you that I am compelled by my instructions to demand that your armed forces evacuate the entire city of Manila, including its suburbs and defenses, and that I shall be obliged to take action with that end in view within a very short period of time should you decline to comply with my Government's demands; and I hereby serve notice upon you that unless your troops are withdrawn beyond the lines of the city's defenses before Thursday, the 15th instant, I shall be obliged to resort to forcible action, and that my Government will hold you responsible for any unfortunate consequences that may ensue.

Permit me to believe that my confidence in the sound judgment and patriotism of yourself and associates is not misplaced.

You will please pardon me for my apparent unnecessary delay in replying to your communication of the 27th ultimo, but the press of duties connected with the administration of the affairs of the city is my excuse.

In conclusion, I beg to inform you that I have conferred freely with Admiral Dewey upon the contents of this communication, and am delegated by him to state that he fully approves of the same in all respects; that the commands of our Government compel us to act therein indicated; and that between our respective forces there will be unanimity and complete concert of action.

I am, with great respect, your obedient servant,

E. S. OTIS,
Major-General, U. S. Army, and U. S. Military Governor in the Philippines.

[End of inclosures to letter of General Otis dated September 12, 1898.]

SAN FRANCISCO, CAL., *October 19, 1898—3.35 p.m.*
ADJUTANT-GENERAL, *Washington, D. C.:*

Transport *Valencia* sails to-day for Philippines with Companies F, G, I, and L, First Washington Volunteers and part of Battalion California Heavy Artillery; total, 16 officers, 488 enlisted men, 515 rifles (caliber .45), and 240 rounds ammunition per man. Senior officer, Lieutenant-Colonel Fife, First Washington.

MERRIAM, *Major-General.*

MANILA. (Received, Washington, October 19, 1898—4.13 p. m.)
ADJUTANT-GENERAL, *Washington:*

Situation Luzon somewhat improved. Influence of Filipinos of education and property, not desiring independent government, but hostile to Spain, gaining ascendency in revolutionary councils. Believe Spanish residents constantly plotting to inaugurate hostilities between our forces and insurgents; freedom press permitted but greatly abused, many articles published entirely devoid truth; have no effect here. Insurgent authority crude, information and application acknowledged by inhabitants in two-thirds Luzon, North. Aguinaldo moderately recognized. Will make endeavors to gain possession of Spanish priests; now treated better than formerly. Do not anticipate trouble with insurgents; promise nothing but enforcement of law, and no encouragement given for American assistance or protection in southern islands; Spanish authority precarious, confined mostly to stations of troops. Insurgents there not allied to those in Luzon; appear determined to resist Spanish rule; would welcome that of United States. These complications seriously affect interisland commerce and diminish revenue receipts half million Mexican monthly. Affairs progressing favorable, though sick report increasing, owing mostly to carelessness enlisted men; health of officers good; condition of city and facilities for quartering troops improving; fevers decreasing; intestinal troubles about same; many slight ailments; smallpox apparently arrested. During month 28 deaths, 8 smallpox, 8 typhoid fever, 5 malarial and intestinal complaints, 3 accidental.

OTIS.

WAR DEPARTMENT,
Washington, October 19, 1898.

The SECRETARY OF STATE.

SIR: I have the honor to hand you herewith copy of cablegram received this date from Major-General Otis, Manila, relating to the situation in the Philippines.

Very respectfully,

R. A. ALGER, *Secretary of War.*

ADJUTANT-GENERAL'S OFFICE,
Washington, October 19, 1898.

Major-General OTIS, *Manila:*

Secretary War directs that General Whittier, accompanied by private secretary, return to United States via Hongkong and Yokohama, and that before starting he be given facility for investigating trade conditions.

H. C. CORBIN, *Adjutant-General.*

ADJUTANT-GENERAL'S OFFICE,
Washington, October 20, 1898.

Major-General OTIS, *Manila:*

Secretary directs Whittier return United States via Paris, reporting to Peace Commission there.

CORBIN.

MANILA, *October 20, 1898—9.33 a. m.*

ADJUTANT-GENERAL, *Washington:*

Names mentioned in cablegram 19th should read: Clemens Sauer, Twenty-third Infantry; H. M. Powers, First California; Henry Dickson, Thirteenth Minnesota; C. H. Fiske and Walter Hogue, First Nebraska.

OTIS.

MANILA, *October 20, 1898—10.46 a. m.*

ADJUTANT-GENERAL, *Washington:*

Captain-General Philippines, Iloilo, requests 27 Spanish officers, prisoners of war, mostly surgeons and administrative staff officers of late Captain-General Jaudenes, be permitted to join him on word of honor not to commit hostilities against the United States. Shall they be permitted to go? I do not perceive objection.

OTIS.

ADJUTANT-GENERAL'S OFFICE,
Washington, October 20, 1898.

General OTIS, *Manila:*

Secretary of War approves allowing Spanish officers to join their general on parole, as named in your cable of to-day.

H. C. CORBIN, *Adjutant-General.*

[Cable-received cipher which could not be deciphered.]

MANILA, *October 20, 1898.*

ADJUTANT-GENERAL, *Washington, D. C.:*

Cable regarding General Whittier received. He made application to visit southern Philippines on the 7th instant, and was refused. His services not considered necessary there. Are here. Request that his investigations do not extend to trade conditions in these islands, and that he be ordered direct to the United States; have had request in contemplation some days, but awaited developments.

OTIS.

ADJUTANT-GENERAL'S OFFICE,
Washington, October 20, 1898—10.30 p. m.

General OTIS, *Manila:*

Can not decipher one word of your message this date. Please repeat in War Department code.

H. C. CORBIN, *Adjutant-General.*

ADJUTANT-GENERAL'S OFFICE,
Washington, October 21, 1898.

Hon. R. A. ALGER, *Secretary of War,*
   49 Broadway, New York City:

Following is General Otis's telegram, received in cipher last night, which we could not make out; has since been deciphered:

"Cable regarding General Whittier received. He made application to visit southern Philippine Islands on 7th instant, and was refused. His services not considered necessary there. Are here. Request that his investigations do not extend to trade conditions in these islands, and that he be ordered direct to the United States; have had request in contemplation some days but awaited developments."

   H. C. CORBIN, *Adjutant-General.*

ADJUTANT-GENERAL'S OFFICE,
Washington, October 21, 1898.

General OTIS, *Manila:*

Cipher message of yesterday has been deciphered. Secretary War directs General Whittier proceed to United States first opportunity via Paris.

   H. C. CORBIN, *Adjutant-General.*

MANILA. (Received Washington, October 22, 1898—7 a. m.)
ADJUTANT-GENERAL, *Washington:*

Ernest M. Foster, Fourteenth Infantry. Correct name; see muster rolls C, Fourteenth Infantry.

   OTIS.

SAN FRANCISCO, CAL., *October 22, 1898—4.10 p. m.*
ADJUTANT-GENERAL, *Washington, D. C.:*

Rio Janeiro arrived from Manila; brings 6 officers and 110 enlisted men. Names of officers: Lieutenant-Colonel Bailey, Eighteenth U. S. Infantry; Major Wadsworth, Quartermaster's Department; Captain Murphy, First Idaho; Captain McCain, Fourteenth Infantry; Lieutenant Moore, Second Oregon; Lieutenant Bunker, Thirteenth Minnesota. Wounded 8 enlisted men died on the voyage. Their names will be wired as soon as possible.

   MERRIAM, *Major-General.*

SAN FRANCISCO, CAL., *October 22, 1898—7.05 p. m.*
ADJUTANT-GENERAL, *Washington, D. C.:*

Rio Janeiro brought 6 officers and 111 enlisted men, all convalescent and improving rapidly except Private W. S. Johnson, D, First Colorado, typhoid. Deaths en route: Private Elliot T. Ordway, Second Oregon; Private Edward S. Fiske, Hospital Corps; Private Henry S. Stube, F, First California; Sergt. John A. Glover, A, First Nebraska; Private Frank W. Tucker, C, Twenty-third; Private Lewis D. Passmore, I, First Nebraska; Private Henry D. Shuter, Astor Battery. All buried at sea except Ordway, Fiske, and Shuter.

   MERRIAM, *Major-General.*

MANILA. (Received Washington, October 23, 1898—9.33 a. m.)
ADJUTANT-GENERAL, *Washington:*

Following deaths since last report: October 15, Q. M. Sergt. William D. Gillespie, First Idaho, gunshot wound. October 16, Corpl. Christopher Rockefeller, Twenty-third Infantry, drowned; Private Jonas B. Adams, Band, Eighteenth Infantry, alcoholism. October 17, Private George F. Hansen, First Nebraska, typhoid fever. October 20, Privates Ira Griffin, First Nebraska, typhoid fever; Charles H. Ruhl, Second Oregon, meningitis. October 21, Corpl. William H. Jones, First Idaho, dysentery; Musician Thomas F. Fitzgerald, Twenty-third Infantry, diarrhea; Private Sage F. Freestrom, First California, pneumonia. October 22, Private Daniel McElliot, First Montana, dysentery; date unknown, Sergt. John A. Glover, First Nebraska, pneumonia; Privates Henry A. Stube, First California, dysentery; Frank W. Tucker, Twenty-third Infantry, typhoid fever; Edward S. Fiske, Hospital Corps, dysentery; last four died between Manila and Nagasaki on transport *Rio Janeiro*.

OTIS.

MANILA. (Received Washington, October 24, 1898—11.58 p. m.)
ADJUTANT-GENERAL, *Washington:*
Spanish transport ship expected to arrive to-morrow from Barcelona wishes to transport Spain 800 of the 1,100 sick Spanish prisoners of war now here; this would relieve situation; shall permission be given?

OTIS.

WAR DEPARTMENT, ADJUTANT-GENERAL'S OFFICE,
Washington, October 25, 1898.
Governor WILLIAM F. FORD,
Salem, Oreg.
SIR: I am directed by the Secretary of War to acknowledge the receipt of your letter of October 4, in reference to the danger of our troops in Manila contracting disease from the afflicted Spanish prisoners, and to inform you that your letter has been referred to the commanding general at Manila with instructions to take action immediately.
Very respectfully,

WM. H. CARTER,
Assistant Adjutant-General.

ADJUTANT-GENERAL'S OFFICE,
Washington, October 25, 1898.
General OTIS, *Manila:*
Secretary War approves sending sick Spanish prisoners to Spain. Let them go when convenient opportunity offers.

H. C. CORBIN, *Adjutant-General.*

MANILA. (Received Washington, October 26, 1898—3.24 p. m.)
ADJUTANT-GENERAL, *Washington:*
Transport *City of Para* leaves to-day for San Francisco via Nagasaki; large mail; Major Whipple, pay, Lieutenant Williams, ordnance, on board; transports *Scandia* and *Candor* still in port; *Scandia* probably leaves within ten days for San Francisco; can be utilized freight purposes. Quiet here and conditions believed to be improving.

OTIS.

SAN FRANCISCO, CAL., *October 26, 1898.*
(Received Washington, 8.10 p. m.)
ADJUTANT-GENERAL, *Washington, D. C.:*
Customs officers here refuse permit to land surplus stores, public and Red Cross, from the *Rio Janeiro*, recently arrived with sick and wounded from Manila. Please have proper permit wired from Washington.

MERRIAM, *Major-General.*

AFFAIRS IN THE PHILIPPINE ISLANDS. 831

WAR DEPARTMENT, *Washington, October 28, 1898.*
OTIS, *Manila:*
Cardinal Gibbons has received information from Cardinal Rampolla, secretary of state to the Pope, that bishop of New Segovia and 130 priests and nuns are being barbarously treated in captivity by insurgents. Investigate fully, and use every possible means to secure their release and care for them. Answer.
R. A. ALGER, *Secretary of War.*

MANILA. (Received Washington, October 30, 1898—9.56 a. m.)
ADJUTANT-GENERAL, *Washington:*
Following deaths since last report: October 21, Sergt. Maj. Roy W. Hover, First South Dakota, malarial fever. October 22, Privates Henry H. Weaver, K, Tenth Pennsylvania, chronic dysentery; Alfred J. Erisman, G, First Nebraska, typhoid fever; Thomas W. P. Harney, E, Fourteenth Infantry, malarial fever. October 23, Corpl. Arthur C. Sims, F, First Nebraska, acute diarrhea; Private Frank H. Heely, Hospital Corps, typhoid fever. October 25, Private B. Lee, Twenty-third Infantry, smallpox. October 26, Privates Charles J. Jorgenson, F, Eighteenth Infantry, typhoid fever; John Morgan, H, First North Dakota, acute dysentery; Corpl. Royal H. Smith, E, First South Dakota, smallpox. October 27, Private Earl W. Osterhout, E, First Nebraska, typhoid fever. October 28, Private Walter J. McLean, L, First Montana, typhoid fever. September 8, Private Edward Manches, M, First South Dakota, typhoid fever, not reported at time.
OTIS.

SAN FRANCISCO, CAL., *October 30, 1898.*
(Received Washington, 2.40 p. m.)
ADJUTANT-GENERAL, *Washington, D. C.:*
Transport *Zealandia* sails to-day for Manila with headquarters and Companies A, B, C, E, F, L, and M, First Tennessee Volunteers, and 5 privates, Hospital Corps; total 24 officers, 543 enlisted men; 538 rifles, caliber .45, and 539 rounds ammunition per man. Senior Officer Col. William C. Smith, First Tennessee.
MERRIAM, *Major-General.*

MANILA. (Received Washington, October 30, 1898—6.55 p. m.)
SECRETARY OF WAR, *Washington:*
Have endeavored to secure better treatment for priests, with some success. Relations with insurgents strained on demand made on 14th instant for their removal from city's defenses, with which they complied. Our relations now apparently friendly. Will endeavor to secure release, though Segovia does not recognize to any extent Aguinaldo's authority.
OTIS.

SAN FRANCISCO, CAL., *October 31, 1898—3.40 p. m.*
ADJUTANT-GENERAL, *Washington, D. C.:*
Transports now loading for Manila. Can take remainder of expeditionary troops, including Utah Battery and Nevada Troop of Cavalry. These organizations are in excellent condition, fully equipped, including harness and horse equipments, but no horses. I recommend they go forward as originally assigned.
MERRIAM, *Major-General.*

ADJUTANT-GENERAL'S OFFICE,
Washington, October 31, 1898.

COMMANDING GENERAL, DEPARTMENT CALIFORNIA,
San Francisco, Cal.:

Secretary of War approves your request to send remainder of expeditionary troops, including Utah Battery and Nevada Troop of Cavalry, on transport now loading for Manila.

By command Major-General Miles:

H. C. CORBIN, *Adjutant-General.*

ADJUTANT-GENERAL'S OFFICE,
Washington, November 1, 1898—10.50 p. m.

COMMANDING GENERAL, DEPARTMENT CALIFORNIA,
San Francisco, Cal.:

When will the last of the expeditionary forces to the Philippines sail? According to our reckoning, you have only the Fifty-first [Iowa] and the Second Oregon.

H. C. CORBIN, *Adjutant-General.*

SAN FRANCISCO, CAL., *November 1, 1898.*
(Received 7.35 p. m.)

ADJUTANT-GENERAL, *Washington, D. C.:*

Error in telegram of yesterday relative to troops for Manila. Should have read Wyoming Battery instead of Utah Battery.

MERRIAM, *Major-General.*

SAN FRANCISCO, CAL., *November 2, 1898.*
(Received 3.15 p. m.)

ADJUTANT-GENERAL, *Washington, D. C.:*

Fifty-first Iowa now embarking on *Pennsylvania*; one battalion Kansas regiment, one battalion Tennessee regiment, Wyoming Battery, Nevada Cavalry, and detachments under General Miller will go on *Puebla* and *Newport*, to sail probably next Tuesday. This completed expedition except the *Tacoma*, with horses and mules, to sail in about fifteen days.

MERRIAM, *Major-General.*

ADJUTANT-GENERAL'S OFFICE,
Washington, November 4, 1898.

General MERRIAM, *San Francisco, Cal.:*

Has General King and detachment First Nebraska left Honolulu for Manila? What troops now at Honolulu?

CORBIN, *Adjutant-General.*

SAN FRANCISCO, CAL., *November 4, 1898.*
(Received 8 p. m.)

ADJUTANT-GENERAL, *Washington, D. C.:*

Latest official from Honolulu, October 12, Nebraska recruits are among General King's detachments, ordered to sail for Manila on the *Arizona*. Press news via British Columbia, indicate *Arizona* not reached Honolulu, October 27. After King sails only New York regiment and engineer battalion will remain at Honolulu.

MERRIAM, *Major-General.*

AFFAIRS IN THE PHILIPPINE ISLANDS. 833

MANILA. (Received Washington, November 7, 1898—3.39 a. m.)
ADJUTANT-GENERAL, *Washington:*
Following deaths since last report: October 28, Walter J. McLean, private, L, First Montana, typhoid fever. October 29, William S. Sullivan, private, F, Fourteenth Infantry, typhoid fever. November 1, James D. Jones, private, C, First Idaho, dysentery. November 2, Charles P. Oliver, private, H, Second Oregon, typhoid fever; Roy P. Anderson, private, K, First South Dakota, smallpox; John H. Leppman, private, K, Fourth Cavalry, typhoid fever; Charles Connelly, sergeant, C, Fourteenth Infantry, abscess of liver; William S. McMurray, private, C, First Colorado, drowned, accident. November 3, Frank Dwent, sergeant A, First Idaho, smallpox; Asked O. Eidsness, private, D, First South Dakota, typhoid fever; Sidney T. Garrett, private, F, Thirteenth Minnesota, pemphigus. November 4, James G. Monroe, private, H, Tenth Pennsylvania, dysentery; William Cook, private, F, First California, typhoid fever.
OTIS.

MANILA. (Received Washington, November 7, 1898—7.12 a. m.)
ADJUTANT-GENERAL, *Washington:*
German war ship *Ancona,* which entered port several days ago, failed to salute flag, but subsequently gave admiral's salute. German war vessel *Irene,* which entered yesterday, has failed to give salute of any character.
OTIS.

MANILA. (Received Washington, November 7, 1898—8.55 a. m.)
ADJUTANT-GENERAL, *Washington:*
Spanish transport leaves Manila to-day taking about 900 prisoners, officers and enlisted men; touches at Iloilo for mail and sick; United States officer to that point to return from there. Admiral Dewey has war vessel in southern waters on Panay coast.
OTIS.

MANILA. (Received Washington, November 7, 1898—9.08 a. m.)
ADJUTANT-GENERAL, *Washington:*
Information from southern Philippine Islands indicates insurgents very active; that Spanish forces at certain points will be obliged to concentrate soon at Iloilo, Panay. Possibly Iloilo will soon be only port under Spanish control.
OTIS.

MANILA. (Received Washington, November 7, 1898—9.17 a. m.)
ADJUTANT-GENERAL, *Washington:*
October 31, $12\frac{1}{5}$ per cent of command report sick; one-half cases slight ailments; typhoid malarial fevers predominate in severe cases. Forty-five deaths October, three-tenths of 1 per cent of command. Eleven deaths this month. Conditions are now improving and sick list decreasing.
OTIS.

SAN FRANCISCO, CAL., *November 7, 1898.*
(Received 9.10 p. m.)
ADJUTANT-GENERAL, *Washington, D. C.:*
Transport *Newport* will sail under General Miller to-morrow at 3 p. m., taking the last of the Philippine expedition, except horses and mules, to go on the sailing transport *Tacoma,* which will sail in about two weeks.
MERRIAM, *Major-General.*

SAN FRANCISCO, CAL., *November 8, 1898.*
(Received 3.04 p. m.)

ADJUTANT-GENERAL, *Washington, D. C.:*

Transport *Newport* sails to-day for Manila with Brig. Gen. M. P. Miller, United States Volunteers, and his headquarters; Companies A, B, F, and L, Twentieth Kansas, and Light Battery A, Wyoming Artillery. Total, 20 officers, 457 men. Four 3.2 B. L. rifles with 1,200 pounds powder, 900 shrapnel, and 304 shell, 382 rifles, caliber, .45, and 229 rounds ammunition per man.

MERRIAM, *Major-General.*

ADJUTANT-GENERAL'S OFFICE,
Washington, November 8, 1898.

General OTIS, *Manila:*

The last of the Philippine expedition sails to-day under General Miller. Horses and mules will sail in two weeks. The several expeditions sailed as follows: October 19, 27, 20, 30, and November 6.

H. C. CORBIN, *Adjutant-General.*

DENVER, COLO., *November 11, 1898.*
(Received 3.04 a. m.)

Hon. RUSSELL A. ALGER, *Washington, D. C.:*

Intense anxiety prevails among relatives and friends thousand Colorado men at Manila. Statements signed by dozens of credible men of regiment allege bad and insufficient food, poor hospitals, wretched sanitary arrangements, and much disease. One statement signed by forty-five men says: "Since we landed on Luzon we have not eaten a decent meal unless we paid for it with our own cash. Weak with hunger and growing weaker, hollow eyed and with sunken cheeks, we are expected to do our duty, to fight and win our country's victories in the name of someone else, to sleep in the mud and rain, to walk our posts and stay awake on an empty stomach, and, hardest of all, we are expected to live and resist the ravages of a strange climate upon our weak and undermined constitutions. On August 13 First Colorado charged upon the Spanish intrenchments when we were so weak from constant hunger that we could hardly carry our ammunition. Had the Spanish forces remained in their intrenchments they would have experienced little trouble in dispatching us, for we were utterly exhausted and for a few minutes almost helpless, the excitement alone sustaining us." Can you not furnish authoritative statement of facts and give suggestion what may be done here to better condition at Manila? Friends of soldiers ready to do anything possible. Please wire reply.

ROCKY MOUNTAIN NEWS.

ADJUTANT-GENERAL'S OFFICE,
Washington, November 12, 1898.

ROCKY MOUNTAIN NEWS, *Denver, Colo.:*

Your telegram of 11th received. Have asked General Greene, Savannah, Ga., who was at the battle of Manila, for information as to condition of troops.

R. A. ALGER, *Secretary of War.*

ADJUTANT-GENERAL'S OFFICE,
Washington, November 12, 1898.

Major-General GREENE, *Savannah, Ga.:*

Following telegram has been received:
(Telegram from Rocky Mountain News, as copied above.)
What was the condition of the troops on the day of the battle of Manila?

H. C. CORBIN, *Adjutant-General.*

SAVANNAH, GA., *November 12, 1898.*
(Received 8.17 p. m.)

ADJUTANT-GENERAL, *Washington, D. C.:*

Telegram received. Colorado regiment, in common with all others under my command at Manila, suffered great hardship in trenches due to incessant rains, deep mud, and difficulty of landing provisions through high surf, but the essential components of ration were obtained every day by one in twenty-four.

There was practically no sickness; the men were in fine health and spirits, appreciated the fact that the difficulties arising from bad weather were what was to be expected in war, and made no complaints.

The Colorado regiment, in particular, was extremely anxious to go to Manila, was always eager for duty, and performed enthusiastically whatever was required of them. They led in the assault of August 13, and were justly proud of being the first to enter the Spanish works.

I inspected the regiment August 28, two days before leaving Manila. They were then quite comfortably quartered in San Sebastian Convent and adjacent buildings, and were in good health and spirits.

I can not believe that these complaints fairly represent the regiment, which contains splendid material, sturdy, courageous men and well-instructed officers. I suggest you cable Brigadier-General Irving, Hale, or McCoy for the facts concerning present situation.

F. V. GREENE, *Major-General.*

ADJUTANT-GENERAL'S OFFICE,
Washington, November 12, 1898.

Major-General OTIS, *Manila:*

Reports give great distress and lack of food in First Colorado. What are the facts? How is your supply of provisions?

H. C. CORBIN, *Adjutant-General.*

ADJUTANT-GENERAL'S OFFICE,
November 12, 1898.

General OTIS, *Manila, P. I.:*

On arrival Miller's command would you recommend the return of any of the troops now with you?

H. C. CORBIN, *Adjutant-General.*

MANILA. (Received Washington, November 13, 1898—9.43 a. m.)

ADJUTANT-GENERAL, *Washington:*

First Colorado supplied with full rations and addition 30 cents per day from public fund for each man sick. Reported to have cleared $700 last week from regimental exercise. The regiment has food, clothing, and money in abundance. Enlisted men desire to return home and telegraphed governors. Official papers in mail explain. Are now recovering from demoralization caused largely by State action. Abundant supply of provisions here of all kinds, including stores for sale; except there are periodical shortages in fresh vegetables which will not keep in climate. Regular regiments materially increasing company funds.

OTIS.

ADJUTANT-GENERAL'S OFFICE,
Washington, November 13, 1898.

ROCKY MOUNTAIN NEWS, *Denver, Colo.:*

Substance of your telegram of November 12 was cabled General Otis, commanding at Manila, and also General Greene, at Savannah, who commanded the brigade in which the First Colorado served in the campaign resulting in the surrender of Manila.

The replies are as follows:

[Reply from General Otis as copied on page 835.]

[Reply from General Greene as copied on page 835.]

R. A. ALGER,
Secretary of War.

MANILA. (Received Washington, November 13, 1898—9.40 a. m.)
ADJUTANT-GENERAL, *Washington:*

Prudence dictates that all troops here and soon to arrive be retained. Situation as follows: Revolutionary government Luzon progressing; cabinet divided on questions of policy; better element declare people are not capable of self-government and favor United States control; Aguinaldo ambitious, acting with unscrupulous members of cabinet and advisers, cries independence, secretly assert Americans must be driven out; his authority in northern provinces of islands outwardly acknowledged, not secured to any extent; asserted that Japanese Government has promised protection, favored by some, as Japanese kindred race. Arms and ammunition for insurgents received at northern ports of island; Aguinaldo accepted draft of $100,000 about to be sent to Hongkong for arms to be landed in upper ports if possible. In southern islands condition as follows: Insurgents in full possession Negros, Cebu, Panay, all but city Iloilo and adjacent islands Spanish forces concentrated and surrounded in Iloilo, and doubts expressed of ability to hold out. Glass, Navy, two vessels Admiral Dewey's fleet there now, also probably Bell, Army, who left here on Spanish vessel *Buenos Ayres* 7th instant. Southern insurgents acting to limited extent with those of Luzon. Aguinaldo's name in southern islands powerful incentive, but authority not recognized. Many important problems constantly arising here but no serious difficulty anticipated. Necessary to maintain adequate force to meet possible emergencies.

OTIS.

(Copy sent Secretary of State November 13, 1898.)

MANILA. (Received Washington, November 13, 1898—9.50 a. m.)
ADJUTANT-GENERAL, *Washington:*

Sylvester in Hongkong has completed contract to furnish arms, and $100,000 have been advanced. Arms will be shipped from Hongkong to Shanghai in vessel bearing German flag to clear for Aparri, Luzon, or insurgent port in Gulf of Lingayen. He will commence operations within very few days; possibly vessel may leave Hongkong for upper Chinese port and there clear for Manila, taking in insurgent ports on voyage.

OTIS.

(Copies sent Secretary of State and Secretary of Navy November 13, 1898.)

MANILA. (Received Washington, November 13, 1898—10 a. m.)
ADJUTANT-GENERAL, *Washington:*

Following deaths since last report: November 6, Morley L. Hassard, private, A, First Wyoming, cerebro-spinal meningitis. November 8, Lewis E. Miller, private,

A, Second Oregon, cerebro-spinal meningitis; David G. Willing, private, band, Eighteenth Infantry, typhoid fever. November 9, Charles B. Lemon, sergeant, B, First California, dysentery. November 10, John H. Fenton, private, B, Second Oregon, pupura hæmorrhagica. November 11, Albert S. Snowden, private, L, Fourth Cavalry, smallpox.

OTIS.

ADJUTANT-GENERAL'S OFFICE,
Washington, November 14, 1898.

General OTIS, *Manila, P. I.:*

Cable saying no troops can be spared received. Should any more be required they will be sent you promptly. Six regular regiments will be held in readiness for this purpose.

H. C. CORBIN, Adjutant-General.

WAR DEPARTMENT, *November 14, 1898.*

General OTIS, *Manila:*

Great pressure to send female nurses. President asks if you could use them. They have been of great benefit in hospitals here.

ALGER, Secretary.

SACRAMENTO, CAL., *November 14, 1898.*
(Received 3.32 p. m.)

Gen. H. C. CORBIN, *Adjutant-General, Washington, D. C.:*

I understand the First New York is ordered returned from Honolulu. Can you arrange to send the Eighth California in their place? Shall consider it personal favor anything you can do.

A. W. BARRETT, Adjutant-General.

ADJUTANT-GENERAL'S OFFICE,
Washington, November 15, 1898.

General OTIS, *Manila:*

Do you desire volunteers to be armed with heavy Jorgensen rifles, or will smokeless powder cartridges answer?

CORBIN.

ADJUTANT-GENERAL'S OFFICE,
Washington, November 15, 1898.

General BARRETT, *Sacramento, Cal.:*

There will be no troops sent to Honolulu to relieve the First New York Volunteers. The battalion of engineers and the native troops now there meet the requirements of the public service.

H. C. CORBIN, Adjutant-General.

WAR DEPARTMENT, ADJUTANT-GENERAL'S OFFICE,
Washington, November 15, 1898.

SIR: In compliance with instructions from the Secretary of War, the Major-General Commanding the Army directs that you take immediate steps to fill your regiment to its maximum strength with selected recruits and apply for the return to it of all officers now absent; and make thorough preparation in all matters of equipment, supplies, and instruction, and hold your command in readiness for a protracted period of tropical field service beyond the limits of the United States.

Very respectfully, your obedient servant,

H. C. CORBIN, *Adjutant-General.*

The above letter forwarded by mail this date to:

Through Commanding General, Department of Lakes: Fourth United States Infantry, Fort Sheridan, Ill.; Sixth United States Infantry, Fort Thomas, Ky.; Seventeenth United States Infantry, Columbus, Ohio.

Through Commanding General, Department of Missouri: Twelfth United States Infantry, Jefferson Barracks, Mo.; Twentieth United States Infantry, Fort Leavenworth, Kans.; Twenty-second United States Infantry, Fort Crook, Nebr.

Through Commanding General, Department of Dakota: Third United States Infantry.

Through Commanding General, Department of Colorado: Twenty-fourth United States Infantry.

MANILA. (Received Washington, November 16, 1898—6.30 a. m.)
ADJUTANT-GENERAL, *Washington, D. C.:*

Should like 8,000 Krag-Jorgensen rifles and 5,000,000 rounds of ammunition for same; also 100,000 smokeless powder cartridges for Springfield rifles, caliber .45, for experiment.

OTIS.

MANILA. (Received Washington, November 17, 1898—6.34 a. m.)
ADJUTANT-GENERAL, *Washington:*

Spanish authorities in these islands request permission to send to Spain volunteer recruits whose term of service expired in June last. I see no objection.

OTIS.

ADJUTANT-GENERAL'S OFFICE,
Washington, November 17, 1898.

General OTIS, *Manila:*

Your request for arms and ammunition will be met.

CORBIN.

SAN FRANCISCO, CAL., *November 17, 1898.*
(Received 9.08 p. m.)

ADJUTANT-GENERAL, *Washington, D. C.:*

Reports from Honolulu to November 9: General King's detachments boarded *Arizona* November 7, leaving 150 sick in hospital. *Arizona* was still anchored outside the harbor for observation of men with reference to typhoid. General King himself ill, but disease not reported. Surgeon reports 292 cases in hospital, 65 being typhoid and 40 malarial fever; remainder convalescent or other causes. Following deaths reported in First New York Regiment: Private Clarence H. Porter, Company H, malaria; Private Charles H. Thompson, Company H, tuberculosis; Private Webster McCarthy, Company A, typhoid; Private Charles F. Carter, Company G, typhoid; Sergt. William Goodrich, Company C, typhoid; Private George Van Beuren, Company M, typhoid; Private Thomas F. Lemon, Company A, typhoid; Corpl. Oscar R. Wheeler, Company E, typhoid; Dates of deaths not given and no lists of other regiments given.

MERRIAM, *Major-General.*

ADJUTANT-GENERAL'S OFFICE,
Washington, November 18, 1898.

General OTIS, Manila:
There is no objection to Spanish authorities returning volunteer recruits to Spain.
CORBIN, Adjutant-General.

SAN FRANCISCO, CAL., November 18, 1898.
(Received 5.08 p. m.)

ADJUTANT-GENERAL, Washington, D. C.:
Steamer *St. Paul* sails to-day with Lieutenant Dismukes, First Tennessee, and 48 enlisted men, consisting of recruits for Eighteenth Infantry and casuals rejoining regiment; Asst. Surg. R. M. Kirby-Smith, First Tennessee, and 2 hospital corps privates; Anthony M. Timke, employee subsistence department; Henry D. Walfe, interpreter, and 17 female nurses for Manila; two acting assistant surgeons and 17 female nurses for Honolulu.
MERRIAM, Major-General.

MANILA. (Received Washington, November 19, 1898—7.04 a. m.)
ADJUTANT-GENERAL, Washington:
Following deaths since last report: November 14, Jay A. Smith, private, G, First South Dakota, apoplexy following malarial fever.
OTIS.

MANILA. (Received Washington, November 21, 1898—11.52 p. m.)
ADJUTANT-GENERAL, Washington:
Transports *Senator* and *Valencia* arrived this morning. No deaths, little sickness.
OTIS.

ADJUTANT-GENERAL'S OFFICE,
Washington, November 21, 1898.

General MERRIAM, San Francisco, Cal.:
Secretary of War desires to know the probability of the retention of the present site of Camp Otis at Honolulu for military purposes.
H. C. CORBIN, Adjutant-General.

SAN FRANCISCO, CAL., November 22, 1898.
(Received 7.39 p. m.)

ADJUTANT-GENERAL, Washington, D. C.:
Camp Otis entirely abandoned when *Arizona* sailed, and will not be reoccupied. Camp McKinley troops also removed to new ground and every sanitary precaution taken.
MERRIAM, Major-General.

ADJUTANT-GENERAL'S OFFICE,
Washington, November 25, 1898.

General OTIS, Manila:
In the event of our retaining the entire Philippines, the Secretary of War desires to know what number of troops will be required for permanent garrison. Give number of cavalry, artillery, and infantry.
CORBIN, Adjutant-General.

MANILA. (Received Washington, November 26, 1898—3.17 a. m.)
ADJUTANT-GENERAL, *Washington:*
Arizona, from Honolulu, arrived yesterday. *Ohio*, from San Francisco this morning. Little sickness, no deaths.

OTIS.

MANILA. (Received Washington, November 27, 1898—11.35 a. m.)
ADJUTANT-GENERAL, *Washington:*
Following deaths since last report: November 21, Frank M. Harden, private, K, First North Dakota, dysentery; Ole T. Lakken, private, K, First North Dakota, typhoid fever. November 22, Clyde Perkins, private, K, Second Oregon, smallpox; Walter Downing, private, L, First Colorado, dysentery. November 23, Charles McKinnon, private, F, Second Oregon, smallpox. November 25, Robert Davidson, private, G, Fourteenth U. S. Infantry, malarial fever; James M. Clark, private, K, First South Dakota, dysentery,

OTIS.

MANILA. (Received Washington, November 27, 1898—7 p. m.)
ADJUTANT-GENERAL, *Washington:*
Event retention entire Philippines, at least seven posts, with several detached garrisons, must be maintained for a time; strength of posts to depend on action of inhabitants on question of absolute independence. Should United States assume Philippine debt, interest wealthy inhabitants with United States. Aguinaldo's cabinet divided; some discord. He assumes dictatorship, disregards opinion of congress and cabinet, not in his interest. Will endeavor to retain power. On question of independence he can unite disaffected influential men and lower class. Delegation from different parts of Luzon at Malolos to-day and question of loan discussed. Aguinaldo trying to establish bank with large capital, and urging subscriptions; $350,000 subscribed, but result doubtful. Bank to be established at Manila, where I advise location for purpose of control. Aguinaldo wishes to borrow $1,500,000 to expend purchase of arms. Reported that he has made arrangements for purchase with Hongkong and Shanghai house. Thus far he has sent $100,000, but no arms. Recently received report that delegation sent to Japan to ask protectorate. Three men composing delegation left yesterday for Hongkong. No one can determine result of United States action should she take island. Think that disaffection among inhabitants can at least be produced. Policy now to preserve quiet and to act vigorous when time for action arrives. Should Aguinaldo succeed in arousing decided opposition to United States authority generally, 25,000 men will be required here, as campaign must be made; although in southern island, do not now apprehend serious difficulty. There would be required 1,000 mounted cavalry, 15 light batteries, 22,000 infantry. The six regular regiments infantry should be sent from San Francisco as soon as practicable to meet possible emergency, as little dependence placed on some volunteer organizations now here. Hope to report more favorable indications soon, and may succeed in destroying much of Aguinaldo's authority. This dispatch should be kept secret, as publication in the United States quickly followed by publication here.

OTIS.

MANILA. (Received Washington, November 29, 1898—10.20 a. m.)
ADJUTANT-GENERAL, *Washington:*
Transport *Zealandia*, with headquarters and seven companies First Tennessee, arrived this morning. No casualties.

OTIS.

WAR DEPARTMENT, *November 30, 1898.*

GENERAL OTIS, *Manila:*

By direction of the President you will permit no arms or munitions of war to be landed in the Philippines, except by joint consent of yourself and the Admiral.

ALGER, *Secretary.*

MANILA. (Received Washington, December 1, 1898—7.04 a. m.)

ADJUTANT-GENERAL, *Washington:*

Transport *Indiana*, headquarters, two battalions Kansas Volunteers, arrived this morning. No deaths, little sickness.

OTIS.

HEADQUARTERS OF THE ARMY,
Washington, D. C., December 1, 1898.

The Honorable, the SECRETARY OF WAR.

SIR: I have the honor to invite attention to the following:

Upon a recent visit to Fort Crook, near Omaha, Nebr., I ascertained the condition of the Twenty-second Infantry at that time to be as follows:

Left Tampa June 14 for Cuba, 39 officers, 481 men; returned to Fort Crook, 5 officers, 176 men; killed, 1 officer, 10 men (3 men died from wounds); wounded, 6 officers, 31 men; present for duty at that time, October 15, 12 officers, 198 men; absent sick, whereabouts known, 31 men; absent sick, whereabouts unknown, 147 men; present sick, 83 men.

Attention is invited to the large number of men belonging to this regiment that are absent, whereabouts unknown. These men, I learn, have been sent to hospitals and retained there or furloughed, and the latter are wandering about the country. Similar reports were made to me, but not so serious, concerning regiments at Fort Snelling, Fort Sheridan, and other places, showing a large number of men absent from their commands.

The latest report concerning the regiments that have been directed to be ready for service in the Philippine Islands shows that out of 7,411 men 1,819 are sick or absent from their commands.

As artillery will be needed in the Philippine Islands, and the artillery regiments are armed with rifles and can do infantry duty if required, I recommend that the Seventh U. S. Artillery, now numbering 2,319 men, be prepared for service in those islands in place of the Fourth, Twentieth, and Twenty-third Infantry.

As Manila will undoubtedly be held for an indefinite time by the United States, I recommend that high-power guns, mortars, carriages, etc., and ample ammunition, with all other necessary appliances, be sent to that place, for the purpose of fortifying the harbor and rendering it untenable for any foreign fleet or battle ship; also that torpedoes and submarine mines be stored there where they can be instantly placed in position to protect the harbor against any foe.

The necessity of having officers in command of departments who are actively interested in all the requirements of the service I regard as highly important. General Merriam is commanding two departments, Gen. E. V. Sumner two, and General Bacon two. It it impossible for them to be at the headquarters of more than one department at a time, and I therefore suggest that General Chaffee be assigned to the command of the Department of the Missouri, General Bates to the Department of the Lakes, and Gen. S. S. Sumner to the Department of the Columbia.

Very respectfully,

NELSON A. MILES,
Major-General Commanding.

MANILA. (Received Washington, December, 2, 1898—11.26 a. m.)
ADJUTANT-GENERAL, *Washington:*
Per cent of sick of command, November 30, 10¼ as against 12¼ October 31. November deaths 26, as against 45 for October. Sick rate in command about same as among troops of other governments serving in tropical countries. One-half of present sick suffering from typhoid and malarial fevers, one-sixth intestinal troubles, remaining half of ailments slight in character.

OTIS.

ADJUTANT-GENERAL'S OFFICE,
Washington, December 2, 1898— 10.30 p. m.

COMMANDING OFFICER, FOURTH U. S. INFANTRY, *Fort Sheridan, Ill.*
COMMANDING OFFICER, TWENTIETH INFANTRY, *Fort Leavenworth, Kans.*
COMMANDING OFFICER, TWENTY-SECOND INFANTRY, *Fort Crook, Nebr.:*

Report by telegraph for information Secretary War, the number of officers and enlisted men present for duty; also the total strength of regiment.

H. C. CORBIN, *Adjutant-General.*

HEADQUARTERS, TWENTIETH INFANTRY,
Fort Leavenworth, Kans., December 3, 1898.

The ADJUTANT-GENERAL, U. S. ARMY,
Washington, D. C.

SIR: I have the honor to report that the Twentieth Infantry is being instructed and outfitted for service contemplated in confidential letter from your office.

Requisitions have been forwarded, stores not yet arrived; six special recruiting parties are now established, and the prospects are that the regiment will be filled to the maximum during month of December. These parties, as well as officers on court-martial duty at Fort Riley and those on short leaves, can be recalled within twenty-four hours.

A list of officers absent, not including above, is inclosed. Of these Captain Moon is not in good physical condition, and Lieutenant Sehon is absent sick at Columbus, Mo., awaiting retirement.

I would recommend the following:

(1) That authority be granted to discharge or transfer all married men of this regiment upon application made by them; the vacancies thus created can easily be filled by desirable men.

(2) That early information as to destination of this regiment be furnished, in order that officers can make provision for the future for their families. If the regiment is to be stationed in the Philippines, different arrangements would be necessary than would be the case if Cuba or Porto Rico is to be the station.

(3) That officers' families be permitted to occupy quarters at this post, not required by the regular garrison, until other arrangements can be made.

(4) That information be given whether it is intended that transportation for officers, allowance of baggage in changing station be furnished.

Very respectfully,

WM. S. MCCASKEY,
Lieutenant-Colonel Second Infantry, Commanding.

FORT LEAVENWORTH, KANS., *December 4, 1898.*
(Received 3.30 p. m.)

ADJUTANT-GENERAL, *Washington, D. C.:*

Twentieth Infantry present for duty 16 officers, 857 men. Total strength, 42 officers and 1,038 men.

MCCASKEY, *Lieutenant-Colonel Commanding.*

FORT SHERIDAN, ILL., *December 3, 1898.*
(Received 11.55 a. m.)
ADJUTANT-GENERAL, U. S. ARMY, *Washington, D. C.:*

There are present for duty in Fourth Infantry, 19 officers and 788 men; present sick, 2 officers and 63 men; there are absent, 18 officers, 63 men. Total strength of regiment, 953.

BAKER, *Commanding.*

FORT CROOK, NEBR., *December 3, 1898.*
(Received 1.30 p. m.)
ADJUTANT-GENERAL U. S. ARMY, *Washington, D. C.:*

Present for duty, 22 officers and 800 enlisted men; present and absent, 40 officers and 939 enlisted men.

PARKER, *Commanding.*

MANILA. (Received Washington, December 3, 1898.)
ADJUTANT-GENERAL, *Washington:*

Manila receipts from customs and taxes since occupation to November 30, 1,577,978 pesos; expended and in hands of disbursing office is 1,125,778 pesos; November receipts, 428,000 pesos; interisland commerce affected by action of insurgents; tariff regulations imposed November 10 working smoothly.

OTIS.

OFFICE OF THE U. S. MILITARY GOVERNOR IN THE PHILIPPINE ISLANDS,
Manila, P. I., October 25, 1898.
(Received December 3, 1898.)
The ADJUTANT-GENERAL, U. S. ARMY,
Washington, D. C.

SIR: I have the honor to inclose copy of correspondence, with explanatory notes, between these headquarters and those of the insurgent forces. The accompanying blue prints are explanatory of my letter of the 14th instant, and show the lines to which the insurgent forces are now retiring.

The friction between the United States military authorities and the insurgent troops is decreasing daily, and the latter are gradually ceasing their open interference in city affairs.

Aguinaldo, his cabinet and congress, remain in the city of Malolos. I understand that dissensions among them are frequent. The inhabitants of the north of Luzon Island (a different race of people from the Tagalos of the south) refuse to be subject to Aguinaldo's authority, although he could probably manage to use them by uniting against some common enemy.

The fear of the return of Spanish authority excites all classes, and persons acting in the interests of Spain are continually agitating them. This is one of the difficulties which has confronted us ever since our occupation of the city, and still stoutly confronts us.

Very respectfully,
E. S. OTIS,
Major-General, U. S. Volunteers.

[Note of explanation to accompany communication of September 13, 1898.]

MANILA, P. I., *October 20, 1898.*

In lengthy letter of September 8, a copy of which has been forwarded to the Adjutant-General of the Army, a final demand was made upon General Aguinaldo to withdraw his forces from the city of Manila, its suburbs and defenses, by the 15th of that month or stand responsible for consequences. On September 13 I was waited on by a number of representatives of Aguinaldo, who verbally requested that I make certain concessions, which I peremptorily declined to do, and called for full compliance with demands. Finally these gentlemen asked that I write a short note to Aguinaldo in the form of a request for the withdrawal of the insurgent troops, as Aguinaldo could not make known the contents of my letter of September 8 to his general officers and successfully control their movements, as they would not listen to reason; that if I would write a short note couched in friendly terms, which he could publish to his people, he would be able to withdraw the forces without bringing on any conflict. I declined the proposition, replying that the letter of September 8 would stand in every particular. The gentlemen replied that they fully understood that such would be the case, but they merely wished a short friendly expressed note containing a request which they could show to their people who were unable to understand conditions, as they fully believed that they had rendered more service in the capture of Manila than the United States troops and had, unaided, taken positions from which we sought to remove them; that they had been virtually promised a share of the victory, as they expressed it. I finally consented to draw up the following communication and delivered it, warning them at the time that if the demands of September 8 were not obeyed the United States forces would act as therein expressed. This short communication of September 13 Aguinaldo used successfully and withdrew his forces beyond the Manila suburbs as understood by him, with the exception of Paco, which he promised, as reported to me by his representatives, to relieve by detachments, as his general officer stationed there was refractory and needed discipline. This, I replied, would be satisfactory.

E. S. OTIS, Major-General Volunteers.

"OFFICE OF THE U. S. MILITARY GOVERNOR IN THE PHILIPPINE ISLANDS,
"*Manila, P. I., September 13, 1898.*
"The COMMANDING GENERAL OF THE PHILIPPINE FORCES.

"SIR: Referring to my communication of September 8, I have the honor to inform you that I have had a most agreeable conversation with certain gentlemen who are in the interest of your revolutionary government upon the matters therein contained. We have discussed at length the complications now existing, which will exist, and will doubtless increase while our troops continue to occupy jointly certain districts of the city of Manila. I have urged upon them the necessity of the withdrawal of your troops, in order that the friendly relations which have always been maintained by and between them and the forces of the United States Government may be perpetuated. I am sure that the gentlemen fully appreciate my sentiments and will clearly report them to you. May I ask you to patiently listen to their report of our conversation?

"It is my desire that our friendly intercourse and mutual amicable relations be continued; that they be not jeopardized, if we can by consistent action avoid it, and such, I am certain, is the desire of yourself and associates.

"May I ask, therefore, that you withdraw your troops from Manila?

"Permit me to add, in conclusion, that I have that confidence in your ability and patriotism which will lead you to accede to this request.

"I am, with great respect, your most obedient servant,

"E. S. OTIS,
"*Major-General, U. S. Volunteers, U. S. Military Governor in the Philippines.*"

[Note.]

MANILA, P. I., *October 20, 1898.*

The following is a translation from the Spanish of letter of September 16, received from Aguinaldo. I am informed that he denied emphatically that he had ever received my communication of September 8, and that I ever made any demands upon him for the withdrawal of troops. This letter of September 16 is confirmatory of that report.

E. S. OTIS, *Major-General Volunteers.*

"MALOLOS, BULACAN, *September 16, 1898.*
"The COMMANDING GENERAL OF THE AMERICAN FORCES.

"MY DEAR SIR: Referring to your esteemed communication dated the 13th instant, I have the honor to inform you that I have given appropriate orders that my troops should abandon their most advanced positions within some of the suburbs, and that they should retire to points where contact with yours [your troops] would be more difficult, in order to avoid all occasion for conflict.

"I hope that by the present [i. e. this letter] you will be fully convinced of my constant desire to preserve amicable relations with the American forces, even at the risk of sacrificing a part of the confidence placed in my government by the Phillippine people.

"A consideration of my many occupations [or duties] will serve to excuse me for not having answered with the promptness desired.

"Your very respectful servant, EMILIO AGUINALDO."

[Note.]

MANILA, P. I., *October 20, 1898.*

I am creditably informed that Aguinaldo made endeavors to withdraw his refractory general from Paco district, and part of the forces were withdrawn, but affairs there remained unsatisfactory. It became evident that in order to avoid all future misunderstanding a line around the city of Manila must be described and Aguinaldo informed to retire beyond it. To secure such a line directions were given Lieutenant-Colonel Potter, chief engineer officer, to search the records of Manila for the true limits of the city and to lay the same out on a city map, which would include the suburbs and defenses. In his endeavors he met with great difficulty. It was ascertained that the city limits had not been fixed by any decree; that they were indefinite. While pursuing this labor affairs at Paco became more unsatisfactory, and as soon as the inclosed blue print could be secured, the letter of October 14, which follows, was forwarded to Aguinaldo on the 14th instant, and is explanatory.

E. S. OTIS, *Major-General Volunteers.*

"OFFICE OF THE U. S. MILITARY GOVERNOR,
"*Manila, P. I., October 14, 1898.*
"Gen. EMILIO AGUINALDO,
"*Commanding Philippine Revolutionary Forces, Malolos, P. I.*

"GENERAL: I have the honor to acknowledge the receipt of your favor of the 16th ultimo, and beg to apologize for the late official recognition of the same, presenting as a reason for my delay the necessity of obtaining certain information in order to arrive at conclusions in matters materially affecting the substance of our late correspondence—the securing of which has been attended with considerable difficulty.

"I fully appreciate the friendly spirit manifested toward my Government in your expressions of regard which your action in retiring your troops has confirmed; but I believe that there has existed and still exists some misunderstanding as to the limits of territory which that Government is compelled to occupy and administer under its international obligations with Spain, the responsibilty for which it can not escape.

"The articles of capitulation transferred the city of Manila with suburbs and all defenses, as I had the honor to inform you in my letter of September 8. It was found impossible to determine definitely on any existing map either the limits of the city or the lines of its defenses. The latter had been variously placed, at some points retired and at others thrust out beyond conceded city limits. I therefore directed my chief engineer, by a careful search of the municipal records and an actual survey, to ascertain the lines within which occupation by United States troops was obligatory by reason of the terms of the surrender. He has finally concluded these directed labors, and has presented a map, of which the inclosed blue print is a copy, on which is traced in white the lines determined upon. By reference to this print and a comparison of the same with all former existing maps of the city and suburbs, it will be perceived that the latter vary materially from it, especially as to the trend of the Pasig River and the location of the Spanish defenses. The lines of circumvallation on the print begin at the Bocana de Vitas; from thence they follow Maypajo Creek until they reach the line of the Lico road produced; thence proceed along said line and road to Lico; thence to the junction of the two roads in front of the Chinese hospital; thence along the road in front of said hospital to the north corner of the hospital wall; thence to blockhouse No. 4; thence by blockhouses Nos. 5, 6, and 7 to San Juan del Monte Creek at the Aqueduct Bridge; thence down said creek and up the Rio Pasig to the mouth of Concordia Creek; thence by Concordia and Tripa de Gallinas creeks to a point opposite the place where the road from Singalon to Piñeda (Pasai) turns sharply to the right; thence by road to Matubig, and thence to the mouth of Malate Creek.

"This map is believed to be correct, as the surveying and platting were executed with the greatest care and with a desire for accuracy. The lines do not include all of the territory which the late Spanish chief engineer of the city has described as lying within its suburbs, and a larger proportion of them are drawn within the lines of the city's defenses, but they are practical, and include all portions of the suburbs which my Government, under its promises to Spain, could be expected to hold possession of under any demands which Spain might present.

"In your withdrawal of troops I note that to the north they retired to the line described on the map furnished by my predecessor, General Merritt, while to the east and south his request was not observed. As far as Paco is concerned it was understood that the troops in that section would be withdrawn within a short period of time, and I have now the honor to represent that the retention of that mutually conceded suburb has been a source of great annoyance to the American authorities, and, as I fully believe, to yourself, while the revolutionary forces along the Singalon and connecting roads have been the cause of complaint from the inhabitants in that section.

"I am therefore compelled, by reason of my instructions which direct me to execute faithfully the articles of the Spanish capitulation, because of the interests of my Government, and, as I sincerely believe, the welfare of your own forces, to ask that you withdraw all your troops beyond the lines marked in the accompanying blue print, which are above described, and I must request such withdrawal on or before the 20th instant, else I shall be forced into some action looking to that end.

"Permit me in conclusion, General, to bring to your attention facts of which you are doubtless ignorant, and which all connected with the American authorities, especially that vast majority who have entertained a decided and pronounced friendly interest in the Philippine people, have viewed with more or less indignation.

"In a number of instances kidnaping and robbery have been committed recently within this city by parties who claim to be connected with your forces, some of whom stated that they were acting under your instructions. This I can not believe, but the high-handed offenses committed by these persons show how important it is for the interests of all concerned to withdraw your troops as herein requested.

"In numerous instances my officers have submitted complaints to me that they have been arrested and been compelled to turn back to the city, though journeying as unarmed and peaceful citizens merely with the intent to seek health and recreation; and on Sunday last, a funeral party of the British war ship *Powerful*, now lying within this harbor, was so delayed by the insurgent forces at Paco, when proceeding to its English cemetery, that it was obliged to return to its vessel and repeat the journey on the following day. I fail to see how such proceedings can be justified before enlightened public opinion, and it is a matter of profound surprise to me that a people seeking relief from control of a government, by which in the pronounced judgment of a large portion of the civilized world it has been oppressed for centuries, should permit its armed authorities to so conduct themselves as to arouse the indignation of friendly and assistant nations. The indignities which my Government has suffered from the revolutionary forces, still illegally maintained at Paco (few of them are cited herein), can not be tolerated in future. Resistance to the high-handed proceedings there committed is not merely considered a duty from which there is no escape, but would be esteemed a virtue by any civilized government cognizant of the facts. I do not for a moment permit myself to entertain the impression that either you, or the able advisers by whom you are surrounded, have authorized these insults to my Government, but I must bring them to the notice of the authorities which maintain these troops and upon which rests the legal responsibility for their conduct.

"There is another matter which I beg respectfully to present for your distinguished consideration. There is a great number of United States troops within this city, and a large accession, primarily intended and equipped by my Government for use against the armed forces of Spain, is en route for this port. The continued unhealthfulness of the city, notwithstanding the strenuous efforts we are making for a thorough police of the same, may make it necessary to temporarily encamp such troops as are suffering from diseases contracted here on some point of land near promising favorable sanitary conditions for restoration to health. Should the emergency become imminent the dictates of humanity and the overwhelming demands of my Government would oblige me to establish a convalescent camp in this locality to which troops could be sent for recuperation and to relieve the congested situation which must attend the presence of so large a body of armed men within a thickly populated city. I have in mind for this possible camp the grounds on the shore of the bay formally occupied by the United States troops and designated "Camp Dewey," or the high ground to the east of the city. It is my great desire to place it in a locality which would not inconvenience any organizations connected with your forces or the surrounding inhabitants, and to the emergency of this anticipated proceeding I respectfully invite your consideration and ask your assistance should execution become necessary. Should action of this character be decided upon I beg of you to rest firmly in my unqualified assurance that it will be undertaken in a spirit of the greatest friendliness and with the sincere desire to neither compromise nor affect in the slightest degree your interests and those of the people whom you represent, but, on the contrary, to enhance them.

"Permit me to subscribe myself, General, with highest respect,
"Your most obedient servant,
"E. S. OTIS,
Major-General, U. S. Volunteers, U. S. Military Governor in the Philippines."

[Note.]

MANILA, P. I., *October 20, 1898.*

On the 18th instant General Aguinaldo's representatives called in person and delivered a letter, of which the following is a translation:

E. S. OTIS, *Major-General Volunteers.*
"MANILA, *October 18, 1898.*

"His Excellency Major-General OTIS,
"*Military Governor of the United States Forces in the Philippines.*

"GENERAL: I have the honor to place in your hands this note, which I bring personally, in which I make known the object of the mission confided to me by President Aguinaldo, and which I will reiterate verbally.

"The letter dated the 15th (14th) of this month, which you directed to General Aguinaldo, reached his hands, and, desirous of complying with your desires, he called in council all of his generals and made known to them the desires which you expressed in your letter. Highly appreciating the spirit of friendship and good feeling which is continually noted in your honorable letters, and which reflects the sentiments of Americans and of their policy toward us, the generals of Mr. Aguinaldo cheerfully accede to that which you ask.

"But the idea of the possibility that Spain may return to this territory and occupy Manila as the result of the decision of the Americo-Spanish conference now in session in Paris has caused said generals to try and obtain a modification of the demands which you make in your letter of the 15th (14th).

"Having verbally explained for your consideration the reasons which influence the manner of thought of the Philippine generals, I shall make also the following propositions, made by President Aguinaldo:

"First. The Filipinos will retire beyond the line of demarcation indicated in the blue map, as you desire.

"Second. The Filipinos will retain Pandacan under their jurisdiction.

"Third. The Filipinos consider it of the greatest importance to occupy blockhouses with their forces of the line with view of the possible return of the Spanish, promising not to pass [never] with arms.

"Fourth. General Aguinaldo asks of you an extension of the time indicated for evacuation by his troops.

"I repeat, sir, with the greatest consideration and respect,

"T. H. PARDO DE TARVERA."

All concessions were refused, and finally a request was made to extend the time for the withdrawal of the troops until the 25th instant, which was granted, and promises were given that the troops would be withdrawn as indicated in my communication. I have every confidence that the desired results will follow. The officer at Paco who has made himself disagreeable has been removed, I am informed. His subordinate officers, who attempted kidnaping in the city, were arrested and are now serving sentences of confinement in the city prison, which were imposed by our provost court. Matters very quiet throughout the city and the condition of affairs is constantly improving.

E. S. OTIS, *Major-General Volunteers.*

[Note.]

OCTOBER 25, 1898.

The question of removal of insurgent troops from the outer defenses of the city appears to have agitated Aguinaldo, his advisers, and officials of his government more than was anticipated here. Excited discussions among them seem to have caused a division of party, one announcing the United States' demands unjust and advising noncompliance, the other counseling acquiescence. On or about the 20th instant a concentration of insurgent troops was partially effected to the north of the city, but under instructions to cease the concentration, most of the forces were removed. On the 23d instant I received a communication, of which the following is a copy:

[Translation.]

"REVOLUTIONARY GOVERNMENT OF PHILIPPINE PRESIDENCY,
"*Malolos, October 22, 1898.*

"Gen. E. S. OTIS,
"*Commander in Chief of the American Forces, Manila, P.I.*

"GENERAL: In view of your favor of the 14th instant, I consulted the opinion of my generals and advisory counsel, and I have appointed Dr. Pardo de Tarvera in order that he might place before you the wishes of all, as he did it on the 18th. Said commissioner, upon giving me an account of your wishes, told me that you had consented to postpone the ultimatum for the withdrawal of our troops until the 25th, and the retention by our forces of the blockhouses situated on the line shown on the blue map, which you sent me with said letter, but had not acceded to the desire of the Philippine people that my forces continue to occupy Pandacan. Relative to the latter point, I take the liberty of telling you that your predecessor, General Merritt, understood that the American forces only ought to occupy, according to the terms of capitulation of Manila, the city and its environs, i. e., Binondo, Tondo, Santa Cruz, Quiapo, Sampaloc, San Miguel, Concepcion, Ermita, Malate, and Paco or San Fernando de Dilao; and thus he clearly puts it in his letter of the 20th of August last. The town of Pandacan has always been considered outside of the old municipal limits of Manila, which the General himself mentions in said letter, and I hope your high sense of judgment will see it thus.

"Nevertheless, I understand that your forces are already occupying the Uli-uli, Nactahan, and Santa Mesa districts, which, although belonging to the jurisdiction of Pandacan, they can continue to do so, in order to prevent the continual encounters with mine, which cause disagreeable incidents.

"I take pleasure in manifesting to you that it is not lack of confidence, and much less animosity, that prompts me to write in this manner. To-day, more than ever, the Filipinos desire to live in peace and perfect harmony with the Americans, because they will take care that the Philippines do not return under the odious Spanish dominion.

"When it is possible for a formal convention to pacify and harmonize the interests of the two peoples, then the suspicions of my people, which I can not completely quiet with my prestige and authority, no matter what good desires move me, will disappear.

"I beg of you not to consider as an insult to your flag, a bad interpretation of my orders, which I will severely punish according to the gravity of the offense. You, with your keen perception, will understand that a people agitated by a revolution return gradually, not suddenly, to their normal life, no matter how educated they are supposed to be. It becomes necessary for me to act with much tact in order to give no cause for internal dissensions.

"And this consideration is what obliges me to ask you about the form and conditions with which you wish to establish a sanitarium within my lines, because I wish at all cost to prevent the possibility of your complaints being renewed concerning acts emanating from the continual contact of our forces. I understand that you have considered it necessary to demand the withdrawal of our forces, notwithstanding the friendship that binds us, in order to prevent friction. On this account, although I highly appreciate the humane sentiments that prompt you, I do not dare allow it without previous explanations, for the very reason that I wish to preserve the friendship that constitutes the welfare of both peoples.

"I hope you will pardon me, as the necessity of consulting various advisers has obliged me to delay my answer.

"I am, General, with the greatest consideration,
  "Your most obedient servant,

'EMILIO AGUINALDO."

To this I briefly replied orally to Aguinaldo's representative that the subject had been discussed sufficiently, and the insurgent troops must retire on the specified day or suffer the consequences. Last evening I was authoritatively informed that all those troops would be retired to-day. The force to the east of the city has already been removed. I do not, therefore, anticipate any difficulty. The transport *City of Para* doubtless leaves to-morrow, and should any difficulty ensue a statement will be included in this report.

E. S. OTIS, *Major-General, Volunteers.*

MANILA. (Received December 4, 1898, 6.39 a. m.)

ADJUTANT-GENERAL, *Washington:*

Following deaths since last report: November 29, Otis W. Drew, private, B, Second Oregon, smallpox. November 30, Irving J. Willett, musician, F, First South Dakota, dysentery. December 1, James E. Link, private, I, First South Dakota, dysentery; John J. Mahoney, private, K, First South Dakota, typhoid fever; Clyde D. Pitts, private, L, Third Artillery, acute melancholia; Charles F. O'Donnell, musician, F, First Idaho, dysentery; Frank Temple, private, I, First California, smallpox.

OTIS.

ADJUTANT-GENERAL'S OFFICE,
Washington, December 4, 1898.

General OTIS, *Manila, P. I.:*

By direction of the Secretary of War, following from the President is sent you for your early consideration.

CORBIN.

"The President desires that Admiral Dewey and General Otis shall have an early conference and advise him what force and equipment will be necessary in the Philippine Islands; whether high-power guns, mortars, carriages, etc., will be required for the purpose of fortifying the harbor or harbors; also whether torpedoes or submarine mines are desired to protect the harbors, or harbors which we may hereafter occupy. The President would be glad to have suggestions from these commanders as to the government of the islands, which of necessity must be by the Army and the Navy for some time to come. When these islands shall be ceded to us, it is his desire that peace and tranquillity shall be restored and as kind and beneficent a government as possible given to the people, that they may be encouraged in their industries, and made secure in life and property. The fullest suggestions are invited.

"WILLIAM MCKINLEY."

MANILA. (Received Washington, December 5, 1898—1.21 p. m.)

ADJUTANT-GENERAL, *Washington:*

Dispatch dated 4th, containing directions Secretary War received. The most important preliminary action is the shipment of 10,000 Spanish prisoners of war from Manila to Spain; they have given trouble and anxiety. Will confer with Admiral Dewey and submit suggestions. Situation as given in my cablegram November 27, continues, though insurgent government quite pronounced in asserting unqualified independence. Has my request for regulars been favorably considered.

OTIS.

ADJUTANT-GENERAL'S OFFICE,
Washington, December 5, 1898.

General OTIS, *Manila:*

Send all messages of importance in cipher.

CORBIN

MANILA. (Received December 6, 1898—8.41 a. m.)

ADJUTANT-GENERAL, *Washington:*

Transport *Pueblo* arrived. No deaths; little sickness.

OTIS.

SAN FRANCISCO, CAL., *December 3, 1898.*
(Received 3.05 p. m.)

ADJUTANT-GENERAL, *Washington, D. C.:*

Headquarters band and Companies A, B, D, I, and L, First New York Regiment, arrived from Honolulu this morning on steamship *Australia.* Colonel Barber commanding, 21 officers and 470 enlisted men; sick list to-day, 4 enlisted men.

MERRIAM, *Major-General.*

MANILA. (Received Washington, December 7, 1898—8.57 a. m.)
ADJUTANT-GENERAL, *Washington:*

Transports *Newport* and *Pennsylvania* arrived to-day; no casualties; little sickness.

OTIS.

ADJUTANT-GENERAL'S OFFICE,
Washington, December 7, 1898.

COMMANDING GENERAL, DEPARTMENT CALIFORNIA,
San Francisco, Cal:

When the First New York Volunteer Infantry arrives and the regiment is assembled, order it to New York, where it will be given thirty days' furlough, pending question of further service. The regiment should be routed to New York City; thence the companies will be sent to their home stations.

By command Major-General Miles:

H. C. CORBIN, *Adjutant-General.*

ADJUTANT-GENERAL'S OFFICE,
Washington, December 7, 1898.

General OTIS, *Manila:*

Secretary of War directs you to send Astor Battery home on first returning transport. If you can spare volunteers to take returning ships, send them in the order of their arrival. Six regular regiments are in course of preparation to report to you. It is probable that part of them will sail direct from this coast via canal. This to get you good transports available for service from San Francisco.

CORBIN.

MANILA. (Received at Washington, December 8, 1898—6.14 p. m.)
SECRETARY WAR, *Washington:*

Condition improving and signs of revolutionary disintegration. Have conferred with number members of revolutionary government and think that majority will favor peaceful submission to United States authority. Aguinaldo holding out strenuously and is endeavoring to levy war contributions. Has excited public with cry for independence, but his influence waning. Bank project abandoned, and doubtful if he can obtain possession of arms for which he has contracted and sent nearly one-half million to Hongkong. Conference this evening of a number of leading men of revolutionary government who favor United States authority or annexation. I expect favorable report. Have conference with Admiral Dewey. He will cable fully regarding coast and harbor requirement. Army needs are as expressed in my dispatch of November 27. We think very necessary to occupy Iloilo and Cebu as soon as possible. Report of very active hostilities at Iloilo. Vessels and troops available and can be dispatched as soon as ordered. Later, Aparri, Vigan and Dagupan, in Luzon and Iligan, Mindanao, should be occupied; also other ports of islands, with quick occupancy in south; no serious difficulty apprehended there. Provincial governments should be established in Luzon under immediate charge of intelligent citizens and general supervision army and navy; they can be supervised from Manila; judicial system can be restored; courts to exercise both civil and criminal jurisdiction, with court of last resort at Manila. Can appoint as chief justice a distinguished Philippine lawyer of culture and integrity, universally respected by all classes. He has been of great aid to me in controlling insurgents. Competent lawyers can be found to fill other judicial positions. Composition of courts here simple and method of procedure not difficult. Believe establishment of judicial system imperative for peace and restoration of business; local civil government of primitive character in all outlying districts essential. They can be established in short space of time, under supervision of military government, and will answer every purpose while that government exists. Am now obtaining names of prominent and most trusted men for use, should it become necessary. These governments would be crude at first, but could be developed. The military governments which have always prevailed in the southern islands could, for temporary purpose, be restored. The natives there, except in Mindanao, are easily controlled, and by kind treatment some system of civil government could be worked out. I do not make any suggestions looking to permanence, but only in aid of efficient military government.

OTIS.

HEADQUARTERS OF THE ARMY,
Washington, D. C., December 10, 1898.

The SECRETARY OF WAR.

SIR: In my judgment, of the eight regiments of infantry recommended by your instructions of November 15, 1898, to hold themselves in readiness for a protracted period of tropical field service beyond the limits of the United States, the first six should be sent in the following order: Twentieth Infantry, Third Infantry, Twelfth Infantry, Seventeenth Infantry, Fourth Infantry and Twenty-second Infantry. This is based on the percentage, in reverse ratio, of the losses sustained by each regiment in the campaign in Cuba.

Very respectfully,

NELSON A. MILES,
Major-General, Commanding.

Approved by the Secretary of War:

H. C. CORBIN, *Adjutant-General.*

December 12, 1898.

ADJUTANT-GENERAL'S OFFICE,
Washington, December 10, 1898—3.10 p. m.

COMMANDING GENERAL, DEPARTMENT CALIFORNIA,
San Francisco, Cal.:

As soon as transport *Scandia* arrives, the Secretary of War desires a report as to her suitability for carrying a regiment of regular infantry to the Philippines. About how soon, in your judgment, should a regiment reach San Francisco in order to make close connection for the time of her sailing?

H. C. CORBIN, *Adjutant-General.*

MANILA. (Received Washington, December 11, 1898—9.27 a. m.)

ADJUTANT-GENERAL, *Washington:*

Following deaths since last report: December 3, Amasa J. Hawkins, private, I, Thirteenth Minnesota, smallpox. December 4, Harry A. McDonwell, private, M, First

Colorado, suicide by cutting throat. December 5, Frank S. Glover, private, A, First Nebraska, typhoid fever. December 7, William P. Vancel, private, I, Twentieth Kansas, typhoid fever, on board transport *Indiana* in Manila Harbor. December 8, Fred J. Norton, private, F, Second Oregon, dysentery; Frank M. Hobbs, private, A, Second Oregon, dysentery, heart failure. December 9, Harry G. Hibbard, corporal, K, Second Oregon, typhoid fever.

OTIS.

MANILA. (Received Washington, December 14, 1898—9 a. m.)
ADJUTANT-GENERAL, *Washington:*

Bankers and merchants, Manila, with business houses at Iloilo, petition American protection at Iloilo. Spanish authority there still holding out, but would receive United States troops. Insurgents reported favorable to American annexation. Can send troops. Shall any action be taken?

OTIS.

ADJUTANT-GENERAL'S OFFICE,
Washington, December 14, 1898—5.10 p. m.

Hon. R. A. ALGER, *Secretary War, Atlanta, Ga.:*

What reply shall be made to General Otis's query of this morning?

H. C. CORBIN, *Adjutant-General.*

ADJUTANT-GENERAL'S OFFICE,
Washington, December 14, 1898—5 p. m.

COMMANDING GENERAL, DEPARTMENT OF CALIFORNIA,
San Francisco:

Secretary War directs by telegraph to-day that the Twentieth United States Infantry be relieved from Department of Missouri, and proceed by rail to San Francisco in time to embark on transport *Scandia*, for the Philippines on next trip, reporting upon arrival at Manila to the commanding general, Department of Pacific.

Officers and enlisted men permitted to take full amount baggage allowed on change of station.

Families of officers and noncommissioned staff officers to go on transport.

Mounted officers may take their horses.

Commanding general Department Missouri, directed to communicate with you to arrange details of movement so that regiment will not be in San Francisco longer than is necessary to load and embark.

Every provision should be made by way of clothing, food, and equipment to insure comfort of troops en route.

By command of Major-General Miles:

H. C. CORBIN, *Adjutant-General.*

ADJUTANT-GENERAL'S OFFICE,
Washington, December 14, 1898.

COMMANDING GENERAL, DEPARTMENT OF MISSOURI,
Omaha, Nebr.:

Referring to letter from this office of November 15, Secretary War directs that the Twentieth United States Infantry be relieved from duty in the Department of Missouri and proceed by rail to San Francisco in time to embark on transport *Scandia*, for the Philippine Islands, on her next trip; reporting upon arrival at Manila to the commanding general, Department of Pacific, for duty.

Report will be made of the name, rank, and length of service of men, who, in the surgeon's opinion, are too ill to make the journey, and of all married enlisted men, and other enlisted men who have less than three months to serve and who do not intend to reenlist, with a view to their transfer or discharge.

Officers and enlisted men will be permitted to take the full amount of baggage allowed on change of station.

Officers and noncommissioned staff officers will be permitted to take their families on transports. Mounted officers may take their horses.

Communicate with commanding general, Department of California, to arrange details of movement. Regiment will arrive in San Francisco so as not to be there longer than is absolutely necessary for loading on baggage and embarkation.

Every provision should be made in the way of clothing, food, and equipment to insure the comfort of the troops en route and after arrival.

It is impossible to state the duration of the tour of service of this character at the present time, but preparations should be made with a view to at least two or three years' service before returning to the United States.

Quartermaster's Department will furnish the necessary transportation, the Subsistence Department suitable travel rations, and the Medical Department ample provision for medical attendance and stores en route.

By command Major-General Miles:

H. C. CORBIN, *Adjutant-General.*

ADJUTANT-GENERAL'S OFFICE,
Washington, December 15, 1898.

COMMANDING GENERAL, DEPARTMENT OF THE MISSOURI.

(By direction of the Secretary of War.)

Twelfth Infantry has been selected for service in the Philippine Islands. The date of embarkation and the port of sailing have not yet been decided, and depend upon transportation facilities which may be available.

Report will be made of the name, rank, and length of service of men who, in the surgeon's opinion, are too ill to make the journey, and of all married enlisted men, and other enlisted men who have less than three months to serve and who do not intend to reenlist, with a view to their transfer or discharge.

Officers and enlisted men will be permitted to take the full amount of baggage allowed on change of station.

Officers and noncommissioned staff officers will be permitted to take their families on transports, but will be required to pay for meals. Mounted officers may take their horses.

It is impossible to state the duration of the tour of service of this character at the present time, but preparations should be made with a view to at least two or three years' service before returning to the United States.

It is not the intention to send additional wagon transportation to Philippines.

By command of Major-General Miles:

H. C. CORBIN, *Adjutant-General.*

(Same to commanding general, Department of Colorado, for Twenty-fourth Infantry; commanding general, Department of Dakota, for Third Infantry; commanding general, Department Lakes, for Fourth and Seventeenth Infantry.)

OMAHA, NEBR., *December 15, 1898.*
(Received 2.53 p. m.)

ADJUTANT-GENERAL, U. S. ARMY,
Washington, D. C.:

Is it contemplated that Twentieth United States Infantry take any wagon transportation or ambulances to Philippines?

HUTCHESON,
Assistant Adjutant-General in absence of Department Commander.

ADJUTANT-GENERAL'S OFFICE,
Washington, December 15, 1898.

COMMANDING GENERAL, DEPARTMENT OF MISSOURI,
Omaha, Nebr.:

Reference your telegram even date, it is not the intention to send additional wagon transportation to Philippines, as regiments going there can use transportation left by regiments embarking for the United States.

By command of Major-General Miles:

H. C. CORBIN, *Adjutant-General.*

ADJUTANT-GENERAL'S OFFICE,
Washington, December 15, 1898.

General MERRIAM, *San Francisco, Cal.:*

It is the intention of this Department to send the Twentieth Infantry to Manila on the *Scandia*. Please report her capacity for officers and men, and the regiment will take only the number she can carry with comfort. The Secretary of War directs that the ship be thoroughly cleaned before sailing. The regiment will leave its station only in time to make close connection in San Francisco.

H. C. CORBIN, *Adjutant-General.*

SAN FRANCISCO, CAL., *December 15, 1898—6.49 p. m.*

Adjutant-General CORBIN,
Washington, D. C.:

Your telegram regarding regiment to go on the *Scandia* received. Vessel expected in port about Sunday. We will have her thoroughly cleaned and disinfected, and will report her capacity and date for sailing. Question of shipment of officers' horses may cause delay and some expense for preparation.

MERRIAM, *Major-General.*

ADJUTANT-GENERAL'S OFFICE,
Washington, December 15, 1898.

COMMANDING GENERAL, DEPARTMENT OF MISSOURI,
Omaha, Nebr.:

Scandia will not sail from San Francisco until about January 5.

CORBIN, *Adjutant-General.*

MANILA. (Received Washington, D. C., December 16, 1898.)

ADJUTANT-GENERAL, *Washington·*

Transport *Senator* left to-day for San Francisco via Nagasaki with Astor Battery, sick and furloughed officers and men.

OTIS.

ADJUTANT-GENERAL'S OFFICE,
Washington, December 16, 1898.

COMMANDING GENERAL, DEPARTMENT OF MISSOURI,
Omaha, Nebr.:

Referring to telegram of yesterday, concerning movement of Twelfth Infantry to Philippines, the Twenty-second Infantry is also to be designated for the same service, and the same telegraphic instructions apply.

By command Major-General Miles:

H. C. CORBIN, *Adjutant-General.*

ADJUTANT-GENERAL'S OFFICE,
Washington, December 16, 1898.

COMMANDING GENERAL, DEPARTMENT OF COLORADO,
Denver, Colo.:

Telegram yesterday (December 15), concerning Twenty-fourth Infantry for duty in the Philippines, was intended for the Twenty-second Infantry, in the Department of Missouri, and was by error sent to your department, and the same is therefore recalled.

By command Major-General Miles:

H. C. CORBIN, *Adjutant-General.*

ADJUTANT-GENERAL'S OFFICE,
Washington, December 16, 1898.

General OTIS, *Manila:*

The Third, Fourth, Twelfth, Seventeenth, Twentieth, and Twenty-second Infantry are under orders to report to you. Hope to get them all under way early next month.

CORBIN.

MANILA. (Received Washington, December 17, 1898—8.46 a. m.)

ADJUTANT-GENERAL, *Washington:*

Following deaths since last report, December 10: George O. Larson, corporal, A, Utah Artillery, typhoid fever; James Healy, private, I, Eighteenth Infantry, cerebral hemorrhage, result of fall, accident.

OTIS.

ADJUTANT-GENERAL'S OFFICE,
Washington, December 18, 1898—12.10 p. m.

General OTIS, *Manila:*

President and Secretary War absent from city. Cablegram of 14th asking for certain movements was forwarded. They instructed me to say for you to wait until their return, which will be Wednesday.

CORBIN.

FORT LEAVENWORTH, KANS., *December 18, 1898.*
(Received 5 p. m.)

ADJUTANT-GENERAL, U. S. ARMY,
Washington, D. C.:

Would respectfully ask that Twentieth Infantry be not ordered to move from this station before January 2, by which time it will be thoroughly equipped and filled to maximum.

MCCASKEY, *Commanding.*

ADJUTANT-GENERAL'S OFFICE, *December 19, 1898.*

MCCASKEY,
Commanding, Fort Leavenworth, Kans.:

Referring to your message 18th instant, Secretary War directs movement Twentieth Infantry be timed so as not to delay sailing *Scandia* from San Francisco, which, from present information, will be about January 5. Measures should be taken to have the regiment fully equipped with that date in view.

By command Major-General Miles:

H. C. CORBIN, *Adjutant-General.*

SAN FRANCISCO, CAL., *December 19, 1898.*
(Received 11.41 p. m.)

ADJUTANT-GENERAL, *Washington, D. C.:*

Scandia arrived. Capacity as arranged for troopship was 56 officers and 1,500 men. Can easily carry full regiment. But little space suitable for families. Will require some repairs. Time for sailing being estimated by depot quartermaster, to be reported later. Strongly advise against shipment of officers' horses; reported suitable horses can be purchased in Hongkong at about $30, and subsist on native forage.

MERRIAM, *Major-General.*

(Foregoing telegram repeated to commanding officer Twentieth Infantry, Fort Leavenworth, Kans., December 21, 1898.)

ADJUTANT-GENERAL'S OFFICE,
Washington, December 21, 1898—4 p. m.

General OTIS, *Manila:*

Complaints of disorderly conduct of our troops in Manila reach here. Secretary of War desires report of facts.

CORBIN.

ADJUTANT-GENERAL'S OFFICE,
Washington, December 21, 1898.

General OTIS, *Manila:*

Answering your message of December 14, the President directs that you send necessary troops to Iloilo to preserve the peace and protect life and property. It is most important that there should be no conflict with the insurgents. Be conciliatory but firm.

By order of the Secretary War:

CORBIN.

ADJUTANT-GENERAL'S OFFICE,
Washington, December 21, 1898.

COMMANDING GENERAL, DEPARTMENT LAKES,
Chicago, Ill.:

The Fourth and Seventeenth Infantry will embark for the Philippine Islands from New York City not later than January 15.

By command Major-General Miles:

H. C. CORBIN, *Adjutant-General.*

ADJUTANT-GENERAL'S OFFICE,
Washington, December 21, 1898.

COMMANDING GENERAL, DEPARTMENT MISSOURI,
Omaha, Nebr.:

The Twelfth Infantry will embark for the Philippine Islands from New York City not later than January 15.

By command Major-General Miles:

H. C. CORBIN, *Adjutant-General.*

ADJUTANT-GENERAL'S OFFICE,
Washington, December 21, 1898.

COMMANDING GENERAL, DEPARTMENT CALIFORNIA,
San Francisco, Cal.:

Major-General Commanding approves your recommendation against shipment of officers' horses. Regiments will be notified.

H. C. CORBIN, *Adjutant-General.*

ADJUTANT-GENERAL'S OFFICE,
Washington, December 21, 1898.

COMMANDING GENERAL, DEPARTMENT COLORADO,
Denver, Colo.:

The Twenty-fourth Infantry is not one of the regiments selected for immediate movement, and need make no preparations beyond that specified in letter from this office of November 15.

H. C. CORBIN, *Adjutant-General.*

ADJUTANT-GENERAL'S OFFICE,
Washington, December 21, 1898.

Maj. Gen. E. S. OTIS,
United States Volunteers, Commanding Department of the Pacific,
and Military Governor of the Philippine Islands, Manila.

SIR: By direction of the Secretary of War, I have the honor to transmit herewith instructions of the President relative to the administration of affairs in the Philippine Islands·

EXECUTIVE MANSION, *Washington, December 21, 1898.*

"The SECRETARY OF WAR.

"SIR: The destruction of the Spanish fleet in the harbor of Manila by the United States naval squadron commanded by Rear-Admiral Dewey, followed by the reduction of the city and the surrender of the Spanish forces, practically effected the conquest of the Philippine Islands and the suspension of Spanish sovereignty therein.

"With the signature of the treaty of peace between the United States and Spain by their respective plenipotentiaries at Paris, on the 10th instant, and as the result of the victories of American arms, the future control, disposition, and government of the Philippine Islands are ceded to the United States. In the fulfillment of the rights of sovereignty thus acquired, and the responsible obligations of government thus assumed, the actual occupation and administration of the entire group of the Philippine Islands becomes immediately necessary, and the military government heretofore maintained by the United States in the city, harbor, and bay of Manila is to be extended with all possible dispatch to the whole of the ceded territory.

"In performing this duty the military commander of the United States is enjoined to make known to the inhabitants of the Philippine Islands that, in succeeding to the sovereignty of Spain, in severing the former political relations of the inhabitants, and in establishing a new political power, the authority of the United States is to be exerted for the security of the persons and property of the people of the islands, and for the confirmation of all their private rights and relations. It will be the duty of the commander of the forces of occupation to announce and proclaim in the most public manner that we come, not as invaders or conquerors, but as friends, to protect the natives in their homes, in their employments, and in their personal and religious rights. All persons who, either by active aid or by honest submission, cooperate with the government of the United States to give effect to these beneficent purposes, will receive the reward of its support and protection. All others will be brought within the lawful rule we have assumed, with firmness if need be, but without severity so far as may be possible.

"Within the absolute domain of military authority, which necessarily is and must remain supreme in the ceded territory until the legislation of the United States shall otherwise provide, the municipal laws of the territory in respect to private rights and property and the repression of crime are to be considered as continuing in force and to be administered by the ordinary tribunals so far as practicable. The operations of civil and municipal government are to be performed by such officers as may accept the supremacy of the United States by taking the oath of allegiance, or by officers chosen as far as may be practicable from the inhabitants of the islands.

"While the control of all the public property and the revenues of the State passes with the cession, and while the use and management of all public means of transportation are necessarily reserved to the authority of the United States, private property, whether belonging to individuals or corporations, is to be respected except for cause duly established. The taxes and duties heretofore payable by the inhabitants to the late Government become payable to the authorities of the United States, unless it be seen fit to substitute for them other reasonable rates or modes of contribution to the expenses of government, whether general or local. If private property be taken for military use it shall be paid for when possible in cash, at a fair valuation, and when payment in cash it not practicable receipts are to be given.

"All ports and places in the Philippine Islands in the actual possession of the land and naval forces of the United States will be opened to the commerce of all friendly nations. All goods and wares, not prohibited for military reasons by due announcement of the military authority, will be admitted upon payment of such duties and other charges as shall be in force at the time of their importation.

"Finally, it should be the earnest and paramount aim of the military administration to win the confidence, respect, and affection of the inhabitants of the Philippines by assuring them in every possible way that full measure of individual rights and liberties which is the heritage of free peoples, and by proving to them that the mission of the United States is one of benevolent assimilation, substituting the mild sway of justice and right for arbitrary rule. In the fulfillment of this high mission, supporting the temperate administration of affairs for the greatest good of the governed, there must be sedulously maintained the strong arm of authority to repress disturbance, and to overcome all obstacles to the bestowal of the blessings of good and stable government upon the people of the Philippine Islands under the free flag of the United States.

"WILLIAM McKINLEY."

Very respectfully,

H. C. CORBIN, *Adjutant-General*.

[This letter was sent to General Otis, Manila, by cable, in cipher, December 27, 1898, 9 p. m.]

ADJUTANT-GENERAL'S OFFICE,
Washington, December 21, 1898.

COMMANDING OFFICER, THIRD U. S. INFANTRY,
Fort Snelling, Minn.:

(Official copy through Commanding General, Department Dakota.)

Upon further consideration Secretary War directs that horses will not be transported to the Philippines. Quartermaster-General reports that it has been impossible to transport animals over so long a voyage, and reports suitable horses can be purchased in Hongkong at $30 per head.

By command Major-General Miles:

H. C. CORBIN, *Adjutant-General*.

[Same telegram to Fourth U. S. Infantry, Fort Sheridan, Ill.; Seventeenth U. S. Infantry, Columbus Barracks, Ohio; Twenty-second Infantry, Omaha, Nebr.; Twelfth

Infantry, Jefferson Barracks, Mo. Official copies by mail sent all commanders above.—W. H. A.]

ADJUTANT-GENERAL'S OFFICE,
Washington, December 21, 1898.

COMMANDING GENERAL, DEPARTMENT CALIFORNIA,
San Francisco, Cal.:

Secretary War has decided to ship the Fourth, Twelfth, and Seventeenth Infantry to the Philippines via New York. They will embark about January 15, 1899.

H. C. CORBIN, *Adjutant-General.*

MANILA, *December 22, 1898.*
(Received 7.11 a. m.)

ADJUTANT-GENERAL, *Washington:*

Believe city never more quiet. Order prevails. Native population greatly augmented in three months. Volume of business increasing. Criminal class large. Representatives of that class from United States and Asiatic shores seek entrance and are closely watched. Conduct of troops good; most favorably commented on by citizens. Discipline improving. Disorders promptly punished, as business of courts show. Newspaper articles published in United States, Hongkong, and Singapore without element of truth. Military rule firm, as demanded by circumstances. Outbreaks likely to occur. Request to be furnished with names of complainants and I will furnish animus. Most of the trouble experienced comes from Spanish authorities and Spanish prisoners.

OTIS.

ADJUTANT-GENERAL'S OFFICE,
Washington, December 22, 1898—5 p. m.

General OTIS, *Manila:*

The President, no less than Secretary War, is very much gratified by reports contained in your cable to-day.

CORBIN.

SAN FRANCISCO, CAL., *December 22, 1898.*
(Received 8.20 p. m.)

ADJUTANT-GENERAL, *Washington, D. C.:*

For the benefit of the regiment designated to embark on *Scandia*, I report, in absence of definite information as to the exact time required for repairs, that depot quartermaster is of the opinion that the ship can not be ready to sail before 15th proximo, but that that date will probably find the ship ready for embarkation of the regiment.

MERRIAM, *Major-General.*

Foregoing telegram repeated to commanding officer, Twentieth Infantry, December 23, 1898.

FORT LEAVENWORTH, KANS., *December 22, 1898.*
(Received 7.04 p. m.)

ADJUTANT-GENERAL, U. S. ARMY, *Washington, D. C.:*

Strength of regiment, 1,396, including those to arrive 1,473. Have closed all regimental recruiting offices and wired Major Craigie to forward no more recruits until wish of Department concerning general orders 40 men and others recommend to be discharged or transferred is known. Recommend that if these men can not be discharged now that they be transferred to general service, in order that we can utilize long term men available. Reference to telegram of 20th December.

McCASKEY, *Commanding.*

ADJUTANT-GENERAL'S OFFICE,
Washington, December 23, 1898.

COMMANDING GENERAL, *Manila:*

By direction of the Secretary of War the following order of the President is furnished for your information:

Until otherwise ordered, no grants or concessions of public or corporate rights or franchises for the construction of public or quasi-public works, such as railroads, tramways, telegraph and telephone lines, waterworks, gas works, electric-light lines, etc., shall be made by any municipal or other local governmental authority or body in the Philippine Islands, except upon the approval of the major-general commanding the military forces of the United States in the Philippine Islands, who shall, before approving any such grant or concession, be so especially authorized by the Secretary of War.

H. C. CORBIN, *Adjutant-General.*

ADJUTANT-GENERAL'S OFFICE,
Washington, December 24, 1898—11 a. m.

COMMANDING GENERAL, DEPARTMENT LAKES,
Chicago, Ill.:

Referring telegram relative to movement of Seventeenth and Fourth United States Infantry to Philippines, Secretary War directs me to say Department desires to be liberal in matter of transportation of worthy families of enlisted men who are married at the time order for movement issues, and will offer no objection to the transportation of such families as the regimental and company commanders may believe worthy, leaving such determination to their judgment. Members of families of officers and enlisted men will be required to pay for their meals en route. The contents of this message, so far as it relates to married soldiers, is confidential and intended to serve as a basis for individual action and selection, and not to be a subject of general information. Acknowledge receipt.

By command Major-General Miles:

H. C. CORBIN, *Adjutant-General.*

(Same to commanding general Department of Missouri, for the Twelfth Infantry.)

MANILA, *December 26, 1898.*
(Received Washington, 7.40 a. m.)

ADJUTANT-GENERAL, *Washington:*

Following deaths since last report: December 15, Frank M. Knouse, private, C, First Nebraska, drowned in Pasig River, accident. December 18, Marwin M. Carleton, sergeant, E, Thirteenth Minnesota, gunshot wound, accident. December 19, Fred Taylor, private, L, First Nebraska, typhoid fever. December 20, Frank C. Hayden, private, D, Fourteenth Infantry, ulcer of stomach; Joe D. Wilson, private, L, Twenty-third Infantry, smallpox; David I. Saunders, private, I, First Colorado, smallpox. November 29, Ole G. Hagberg, sergeant, D, First Idaho, exhaustion following typhoid fever, not previously reported.

OTIS.

MANILA, *December 26, 1898.*
(Received Washington, 9.05 a. m.)

ADJUTANT-GENERAL, *Washington*:

General Miller, with Battery G, Sixth Artillery, Eighteenth Infantry, Fifty-first Iowa Volunteers, three transports, escorted by cruiser *Baltimore*, leave this evening for Iloilo. Further particulars to-morrow.

OTIS.

MANILA, *December 27, 1898.*
(Received Washington, 1.04 a. m.)

ADJUTANT-GENERAL, *Washington:*

Sent Colonel Potter on fast vessel to Iloilo on 24th, to communicate with Spanish General Rios. Latter evacuated evening of 24th, and Potter thirty-nine hours late. Insurgents took possession of city on 26th and Potter found Aguinaldo's flag flying. Had expedition started three days earlier would have been no difficulty in taking peaceable possession. Can not now report probable results; will not hear from there for four days, as no cable communications. Spanish forces have evacuated all stations in southern islands except Zamboanga, Mindanao, by orders, as they say, from Madrid. Several calls here for troops from southern ports.

OTIS.

MANILA, *December 27, 1898.*
(Received Washington, 8.17 a. m.)

ADJUTANT-GENERAL, *Washington:*

Iloilo expedition left last night. Reported that Spanish forces evacuated 24th instant. Report not confirmed. General Miller fully instructed as to action whether Spanish forces there or not, action to accord fully with the President's directions. Will cable result as soon as possible. Expedition should reach Iloilo to-morrow morning.

OTIS.

ADJUTANT-GENERAL'S OFFICE,
Washington, December 27, 1898.

COMMANDING GENERAL, DEPARTMENT CALIFORNIA,
San Francisco, Cal.:

It is desirable that the Twentieth Infantry make close connection at San Francisco. The Secretary of War directs that you report the day the regiment should reach San Francisco.

By command Major-General Miles:

H. C. CORBIN, *Adjutant-General.*

ADJUTANT-GENERAL'S OFFICE,
Washington, December 27, 1898.

COMMANDING OFFICER, TWENTIETH INFANTRY,
Fort Leavenworth, Kans.:

The date of departure of your regiment has not been definitely determined, but will be early in the month. Exact date will depend upon the complete furnishing and refitting of transport *Scandia* that is to take you to Manila, report of which is expected hourly.

H. C. CORBIN, *Adjutant-General.*

AFFAIRS IN THE PHILIPPINE ISLANDS. 863

SAN FRANCISCO, CAL., *December 27, 1898.*
(Received 4.12 p. m.)

ADJUTANT-GENERAL, *Washington, D. C.:*

Referring to your telegram of this date, information of number of officers, women, and children, and approximate amount of baggage to be provided for, was asked from commanding general, Department Missouri, by wire December 15th. Is required before we can determine amount of modification to be made and time required to fit the *Scandia* for sea.

MEERIAM, *Major-General.*

ADJUTANT-GENERAL'S OFFICE,
Washington, December 27, 1898.

COMMANDING GENERAL, DEPARTMENT MISSOURI,
Omaha, Nebr.:

Secretary War directs that you furnish by wire commanding general, Department California, approximate information as to number of officers, women, and children, and amount of baggage to be provided for Twentieth Infantry on *Scandia*. This information needed at once, in order to determine amount of modification to be made and time required to fit *Scandia* for sea.

By command Major-General Miles:

H. C. CORBIN, *Adjutant-General.*

MANILA, *December 29, 1898.*
(Received Washington, 8.10 a. m.)

ADJUTANT-GENERAL, *Washington.*

Instructions of President relative to administration of affairs received.

OTIS.

MANILA, *December 29, 1898.*
(Received Washington, 8.35 a. m.)

ADJUTANT-GENERAL, *Washington:*

When will Regular troops, to be sent here via San Francisco, leave that city?

OTIS.

WAR DEPARTMENT, *December 29, 1898.*

Major-General OTIS, *Manila:*

At suggestion of Professor Worcester it is thought best for you to occupy all strategic points in the island possible before the insurgents get possession of them. Dr. Burns of your staff can give you full information about these places. Answer.

ALGER, *Secretary.*

ADJUTANT-GENERAL'S OFFICE,
Washington, December 29, 1898—4.30 p. m.

General OTIS, *Manila:*

Twentieth Infantry will sail from San Francisco on *Scandia* about 7th or 8th January, and others will follow rapidly as transportation can be had. Fourth, Twelfth, and Seventeenth will sail from New York by way of canal on new transports about 10th to 15th January.

CORBIN.

FORT LEAVENWORTH, KANS., *December 29, 1898.*
(Received 1 p. m.)

ADJUTANT-GENERAL, U. S. Army,
Washington, D. C.:

The following received from a medical officer, U. S. Army, just arrived *Scandia*, furnished for information of Secretary of War:

Scandia is a freighter fitted up with bunks for troops, built for cold climates. It is insufferably hot. Though 1,500 soldiers can be crowded in, it is unsafe to take more than 700, and they will be frightfully uncomfortable. Request that the comfort of this regiment on this long journey be given full consideration, and that the crowding and discomfort experienced on the Cuban campaign be avoided. An additional ship should be chartered.

MCCASKEY, *Commanding.*

MANILA, *December 30, 1898.*
(Received Washington, 12.30 p. m.)

SECRETARY WAR, *Washington:*

Have perfect knowledge of all strategic points in Philippine Islands. All military stations, outside Luzon, with exception of Zamboanga, turned over by Spaniards to inhabitants, who may be denominated insurgents, with more or less hostility to United States. Some points we can take without friction, and could have taken nearly all outside Luzon peaceably before 23d and 24th of month, when Spain withdrew her forces without our knowledge. Am waiting to hear results from Iloilo, and am meditating action in islands of Samar, Leyte, and Cebu, in all of which Luzon insurgents have been at work for several months.

Conditions here at Manila and character of invigorating secretly not understood in United States. Large numbers of insurgent troops still in the field, scattered throughout Luzon Province, and about 6,000 outside this city, which contains large numbers of sympathizers who have threatened uprising. Former insurgent cabinet disrupted, one formed consisting mostly of irresponsible men, who demand complete independence or war with United States. Situation requires delicate manipulation, and our troops here can not be widely scattered at present. Great majority of men of property desire annexation. Those without property seek personal advancement and plunder, promises of which hold insurgents together; but already much dissatisfaction in ranks and conflicts with inhabitants in middle provinces. Will report further in few days. Am in consultation with Admiral Dewey, now engaged in efforts to stop shipment of insurgent arms from China and Japan, through meditated seizure. We will probably send another force south within a short time.

OTIS.

EXECUTIVE MANSION,
Washington, December 30, 1898—11 p. m.

OTIS, *Manila:*

Message received. It is not expected that you will prosecute the occupation too rapidly, but proceed with great prudence, avoiding conflict if possible, and only resort to force as the last extremity. Be kind and tactful, taking time if necessary to accomplish results desired by peaceful means.

ALGER, *Secretary of War.*

ADJUTANT-GENERAL'S OFFICE,
Washington, December 30, 1898—4 p. m.

General OTIS, *Manila:*

Cable received. President and Secretary War are pleased that you are in consultation with Admiral Dewey, and desire you to do so in all important matters affecting government in the Philippines. Also to avail yourself of the personal knowledge Dr. Burns, of your staff, is possessed of.

CORBIN.

ADJUTANT-GENERAL'S OFFICE,
Washington, December 30, 1898.

COMMANDING OFFICER, TWENTIETH INFANTRY,
Fort Leavenworth, Kans.:

Paragraph 1019, Army Regulations, amended in General Orders to-day by addition of following sentence:

"For officers when embarking under orders for extended service over the sea for duty, the allowance of baggage to be transported by the Quartermaster's Department from initial point to port of embarkation, and from port of destination to garrison station, will be three times the allowance prescribed above for change of station."

SCHWAN, *Assistant Adjutant-General.*

(Same telegram, signed by Adjutant-General, December 30, 1898, sent to commanding officer, Third Infantry, commanding officer, Fourth Infantry, commanding officer, Twelfth Infantry, commanding officer, Seventeenth Infantry, commanding officer, Twenty-second Infantry.)

SAN FRANCISCO, CAL., *December 30, 1898.*

QUARTERMASTER-GENERAL, *Washington, D. C.:*

Reference your telegram 28th instant, regarding complaint from McCaskey, commanding Twentieth Infantry, will make detailed report to-morrow. Despite his complaint about insufficiency of accommodations, am satisfied *Scandia* will carry full regiment with officers comfortably, but has no accommodations for ladies of regiment. The comfort of regiment will be given full consideration. *Scandia* is now being thoroughly fitted; she has been dry docked, cleaned, and painted, and will be at wharf in this city to-morrow afternoon. Thorough inspection will be made and information furnished as requested on arrival here.

LONG, *Depot Quartermaster.*

ADJUTANT-GENERAL'S OFFICE,
Washington, December 31, 1898.

COMMANDING GENERAL, DEPARTMENT CALIFORNIA,
San Francisco, Cal.:

Colonel Long wires Quartermaster-General that the *Scandia* has no cabins for officers' families. As the regiment going on this transport is to stay an indefinite period, the Department is anxious to allow the officers to take their families. What do you suggest to meet situation?

H. C. CORBIN, *Adjutant-General.*

MANILA. (Received Washington, January 1, 1899—9.55 a. m.)
ADJUTANT-GENERAL, *Washington:*

General Miller reports from Iloilo, city and environs in possession insurgents, 2,500 armed with rifles, 10,000 with [bolos?]. Recognized Aguinaldo and can not surrender without his orders. Miller can take city with force at hand, but not without great loss of life among inhabitants and destruction of property. Merchants who petitioned for troops now ask Miller to avoid conflict. His troops in harbor close to city and he awaiting instructions. His first instructions were to occupy city in case insurgents in possession through peaceful means, followed later by orders to seize city if he could do so without great loss of life and destruction of property. Excited condition of affairs in and surrounding Manila. Insurgents active. Can not weaken force here very much. Am prepared to send 1,100 men south. Cable of yesterday just received. Will act with caution.

OTIS.

ADJUTANT-GENERAL'S OFFICE,
Washington, January 1, 1899—4.30 p. m.

General OTIS, *Manila:*

The President considers it of first importance that a conflict brought on by you be avoided at this time if possible. Can not Miller get into communication with insurgents, giving them President's proclamation and informing them of the purposes of the Government, assuring them that while it will assert its sovereignty, that its purpose is to give them a good government and security in their personal rights.

It is most desirable that Miller should hold his ground, and as health of soldiers may not permit of their remaining on transports, could not a landing at some healthful place be effected without a conflict?

Your report of excited condition in Manila makes it incumbent upon you not to weaken your forces at that point.

By order Secretary War:

CORBIN.

ADJUTANT-GENERAL'S OFFICE,
Washington, January 1, 1899—5.30 p. m.

General OTIS, *Manila:*

Twentieth Infantry will sail from San Francisco not later than January 7. Fourth, Twelfth, and Seventeenth Infantry, full equipment of officers and men, on new transports, from New York, via Canal, not later than 12th, Major-General Lawton in command, and will be for duty with you after his arrival. As far as possible, all officers will come with regiments. The Third and Twenty-second will follow rapidly as we can arrange water transportation from San Francisco.

CORBIN.

MANILA. (Received Washington, January 2, 1899—2.59 a. m.)
ADJUTANT-GENERAL, *Washington:*

Following deaths since last report: December 24, Lewis W. Ferguson, private, B, Twentieth Kansas, purpura hæmorrhagica; Ira L. Kelly, private, K, Fourth Cavalry, drowned in Pasig, accidental. December 27, Noah Davis, private, K, Third Artillery, typhoid fever. December 28, Emmet W. Manley, private, D, Twenty-third Infantry, smallpox. December 30, Thomas C. North, private, G, First Nebraska, smallpox.

OTIS.

MANILA. (Received Washington, January 2, 1899—4.27 p. m.)
ADJUTANT-GENERAL, *Washington:*

General Miller's instructions in conformity to cable just received. He holds Iloilo in his grasp, but will not attempt landing until instructed. Conditions in Manila improving. Insurgent government becoming weak and unable to hold representative men. Aguinaldo's troops driven out from province of Tarlac and his officials murdered. Has called congress for to-morrow, but there will be but small representation. General Miller has President's proclamation. Not issued here yet, as time not opportune. Will be in two or three days. Sent one regiment south Wednesday morning, which will reach General Miller and be sent to Cebu. No further movement contemplated at present. Believe that it is possible to avoid conflict.

OTIS.

SAN FRANCISCO, CAL., *January 2, 1899.* (Received 3.55 p. m.)
ADJUTANT-GENERAL, *Washington, D. C.:*

Long's report on *Scandia* cabins correct. She was a freight steamer and converted for troops, including officers only. See my telegram dated December 19. I suggest that families be sent on other transports or via Hongkong, unless the new army transport service can meet the emergency.

MERRIAM, *Major-General.*

WASHINGTON, *January 3, 1899.*
COMMANDING GENERAL, DEPARTMENT OF THE PACIFIC,
Manila, P. I.

GENERAL: The Secretary of War is desirous that you direct all commanders of stations, posts, or substations under your command to render a monthly post return of their respective commands promptly to this office, care being taken to give in all cases, under the heading "Record of events," the dates of occupation of towns, establishment of posts or stations.

Division, district, and brigade commanders should be directed to show each separate command, post, or station on their respective returns.

Attention should also be invited to paragraph 795, Army Regulations, requiring special field returns.

Very respectfully, H. C. CORBIN, *Adjutant-General.*

SAN FRANCISCO, CAL., *January 3, 1899.* (Received 9.10 p. m.)
ADJUTANT-GENERAL, *Washington, D. C.:*

Depot quartermaster says can not yet state exact date when *Scandia* will be ready to sail. Is pushing repairs and will be able to notify regimental commander exact date for sailing in season for regiment to be there for embarkation. Can not sail before 15th, and may be a few days later. Baggage and property not required for use on voyage should come forward at once.

MERRIAM, *Major-General.*

WAR DEPARTMENT, *Washington, January 4, 1899.*
The Honorable, the SECRETARY OF STATE.

SIR: Replying to your communication of December 28, quoting telegram received from the consul at Osaka and Hiogo, Japan, as follows: 'People here arranging ship arms Aguinaldo; authority asked to employ detective to watch them," I have the honor to request that favorable action be taken upon the recommendation of Mr. Lyon and that authority to employ the detective be given.

Very respectfully, R. A. ALGER, *Secretary of War.*

MANILA. (Received Washington January 4, 1899.)
ADJUTANT-GENERAL, *Washington:*

Under date December 31, Miller reports situation at Iloilo unchanged; awaiting orders. Insurgents defiant. Instructions sent Miller to retain position and not commence hostilities. Considerable excitement here; many rumors afloat; uprising of Filipino organizations in city threatened to accompany attack of insurgents from without; the troops here can manage situation. Friendly Filipinos, men of influence, in consultation with Aguinaldo insurgents at Malolos. Have furnished them proclamation to be issued to-day. Expect good results. If Aguinaldo and advisers have not fully determined on war, friendly Filipinos think prospect very favorable. Have regiment on transports in bay for southern waters, but held awaiting developments.

OTIS.

OMAHA, NEBR., *January 4, 1899.* (Received 5.50 p. m.)
ADJUTANT-GENERAL, U. S. ARMY,
    War Department, Washington, D. C.:

Have received notice that *Scandia* will be ready to sail the 15th instant. Have ordered the Twentieth Infantry to leave post on 11th instant. All heavy baggage has been forwarded.

SUMNER, *Brigadier-General, Commanding.*

ADJUTANT-GENERAL'S OFFICE,
Washington, January 4, 1899.
COMMANDING OFFICER, TWENTIETH INFANTRY,
    Fort Leavenworth, Kans.:

Government contemplates chartering steamer *Morgan City* to carry families and portion of troops of your regiment. Quartermaster San Francisco says of her following quote: Upper deck, 15 staterooms, accommodating 30 people; saloon deck, 58 staterooms, accommodating 234 people. In addition, will carry 2,500 tons of freight.

H. C. CORBIN, *Adjutant-General.*

ADJUTANT-GENERAL'S OFFICE,
Washington, January 4, 1899.
The COMMANDING GENERAL, DEPARTMENT OF CALIFORNIA,
    San Francisco, Cal.:

The following has been given the Quartermaster-General: "The Secretary of War authorizes you to charter the *Morgan City* under the best terms obtainable, and, in addition to the freight which she is to take to Manila, she will be put in order to carry such officers and their families and men of the Twentieth Infantry as will equal her accommodation, and will sail on the same day as the *Scandia*, carrying Twentieth Infantry, from San Francisco to Manila. The quartermaster at Manila will be informed in advance that this ship is under charter and instructed to have her discharged as rapidly as possible and returned to San Francisco for revocation of charter. You will also use her for the return of such troops and freight as General Otis may have to send to San Francisco."

H. C. CORBIN, *Adjutant-General.*

ADJUTANT-GENERAL'S OFFICE,
Washington, January 4, 1899.
COMMANDING OFFICER, TWENTIETH INFANTRY,
    Fort Leavenworth, Kans.:

Secretary of War authorizes charter of *Morgan City*, referred to in telegram even date. Communicate with commanding general Department California in regard to her.

H. C. CORBIN, *Adjutant-General.*

ADJUTANT-GENERAL'S OFFICE,
Washington, January 5, 1899.

COMMANDING GENERAL, DEPARTMENT LAKES,
Chicago, Ill.:

Referring to previous orders concerning movement of troops to Philippines via New York, the Secretary War directs that the Fourth Infantry and six companies of the Seventeenth Infantry proceed by rail to New York City in time to embark, with General Lawton and his staff on transport *Mohawk* on 15th instant.

Communicate with commanding general, Department East, concerning details of movement and arrival of troops and baggage in such way as to prevent delay as far as possible by the troops after arrival.

The Twelfth Infantry, the headquarters, and remaining companies of the Seventeenth Infantry will move as directed later.

Direct commanding officers to report as soon as possible exact number of officers and men, and number of families to occupy cabins.

Quartermaster's Department will furnish the necessary transportation, the Subsistence Department suitable travel rations and coffee money, and the Medical Department proper medical attendance and stores. Acknowledge receipt.

By command Major-General Miles:

H. C. CORBIN, *Adjutant-General.*

ADJUTANT-GENERAL'S OFFICE,
Washington, January 5, 1899.

COMMANDING GENERAL, DEPARTMENT EAST,
New York Harbor:

The Fourth Infantry and six companies Seventeenth Infantry have been ordered to embark with General Lawton and staff on transport *Mohawk* from New York City for the Philippines the 15th instant. Commanding general, Department Lakes, has been directed by the Secretary War to communicate with you to arrange the details of movements and have the arrival of troops and baggage so timed as to make the least possible delay of troops after arrival in New York. Acknowledge receipt.

By command Major-General Miles:

CORBIN, *Adjutant-General.*

ADJUTANT-GENERAL'S OFFICE,
Washington, January 5, 1899.

COMMANDING GENERAL, DEPARTMENT CALIFORNIA,
San Francisco, Cal.:

Secretary of War directs you exercise your best judgment in giving comfort to the officers and their families and men of the Twentieth Infantry sailing on the *Scandia* and *Morgan City*, which have been chartered for this purpose. The Secretary desires you to make careful inspection of these two ships and your recommendation as to best disposition that can be made to take officers and their families and men. It may be possible that one or more companies of the regiment should go on the *Morgan City*. Anyway, it is desirable that some officers go aboard this ship, along with such of the families as can embark thereon.

By command Major-General Miles:

H. C. CORBIN, *Adjutant-General.*

ADJUTANT-GENERAL'S OFFICE,
Washington, January 5, 1899.

General OTIS, *Manila:*

Shall regular troops bring mattresses?

CORBIN.

MANILA, *January 5, 1899.*
(Received 10 p. m.)

ADJUTANT-GENERAL, *Washington:*

Mattresses not used in this country.

OTIS.

CHICAGO, ILL., *January 6, 1899.*

ADJUTANT-GENERAL, U. S. ARMY, *Washington, D. C.:*

Telegram touching movement Fourth Infantry and six companies Seventeenth Infantry received. Instructions issued in accordance therewith.

M. V. SHERIDAN,
Brigadier-General, U. S. Volunteers, Commanding.

GOVERNORS ISLAND, N. Y., *January 6, 1899.*
(Received 1.17 p. m.)

ADJUTANT-GENERAL, U. S. ARMY, *Washington, D. C.:*

Telegram received directing arrangements be made with commanding general, Department Lakes, to have arrival of Fourth Infantry and six companies Seventeenth Infantry so timed as to make least possible delay of troops after arrival in New York. In this connection depot quartermaster, New York, emphasizes request that these troops should not leave home stations until notified by him that transports are entirely ready for their reception. The transport service is not under the order or control of the commanding general, Department of the East.

SHAFTER,
Major-General, Commanding.

ADJUTANT-GENERAL'S OFFICE,
Washington, January 7, 1899.

COMMANDING OFFICER, TWELFTH INFANTRY,
Jefferson Barracks, Mo.:

General Otis telegraphs mattresses are not used in the Philippines.

H. C. CORBIN, *Adjutant-General.*

Same to commanding officer, Third Infantry, Fort Snelling, Minn.; commanding officer, Fourth Infantry, Fort Sheridan, Ill.; commanding officer, Seventeenth Infantry, Columbus Barracks, Ohio; commanding officer, Twentieth Infantry, Fort Leavenworth, Kans.; commanding officer, Twenty-second Infantry, Fort Crook, Nebr.

ADJUTANT-GENERAL'S OFFICE,
Washington, January 7, 1899.

COMMANDING GENERAL, DEPARTMENT LAKES,
Chicago, Ill.:

Secretary War has decided to send three transports from New York carrying four regiments of infantry to the Philippines. The Fourth and Twelfth and Seventeenth have already been designated, and in addition thereto the Third Infantry, now stationed at Snelling, will go by that route. Each transport will carry one regiment and one battalion of another regiment.

The telegraphic order of January 5 directing that six companies of the Seventeenth Infantry accompany the Fourth Infantry, to sail January 15, is modified to read one battalion of four companies of the Seventeenth; the remaining eight companies to sail later. Acknowledge.

By command Major-General Miles:

H. C. CORBIN, *Adjutant-General.*

CHICAGO, ILL., *January 7, 1899.*
(Received 5.05 p. m.)

ADJUTANT-GENERAL, U. S. ARMY, *Washington, D. C.:*

Telegram making modification in number of companies to go from Seventeenth Infantry received, and instructions issued accordingly.

M. V. SHERIDAN,
Brigadier-General, U. S. Volunteers, Commanding.

SAN FRANCISCO, CAL., *January 7, 1899.*
(Received 5 p. m.)

ADJUTANT-GENERAL, *Washington, D. C.:*

Personal inspection made *Scandia* and *Morgan City;* can not be ready for sea till January 25; work is progressing night and day; have so wired commanding general, Omaha, with reference to the Twentieth Infantry.

MERRIAM, *Major-General.*

OMAHA, NEBR., *January 7, 1899.*
(Received 7.42 p. m.)

ADJUTANT-GENERAL, U. S. ARMY, *Washington, D. C.:*

Telegram just received from commanding general, Department California, announcing transports *Scandia* and *Morgan City* will not sail until January 25. Orders for movement of Twentieth Infantry altered accordingly. That regiment now ordered to leave Fort Leavenworth January 21.

HUTCHESON,
Assistant Adjutant-General, in absence of Department Commander.

[Memorandum for Quartermaster-General, Surgeon-General, Commissary-General Subsistence, Chief of Ordnance.]

The Secretary of War directs that before the sailing of transports from New York with troops for the Philippines special attention be given all matters pertaining to the equipments, supplies, medical attendance, food, etc., and provision for the health, comfort, and welfare of the commands during the journey be thoroughly provided for.

H. C. CORBIN, *Adjutant-General.*

ADJUTANT-GENERAL'S OFFICE,
Washington, January 7, 1899.

General OTIS, *Manila:*

What transports are on the way back to San Francisco?

CORBIN.

ADJUTANT-GENERAL'S OFFICE,
Washington, January 7, 1899.

BROOKE, *Habana:*

It is of great importance that *Mobile* be discharged and returned New York soon as possible, as she is greatly needed to transport troops Philippines.

CORBIN.

MANILA. (Received Washington, January 8, 1899—12 noon.)
ADJUTANT-GENERAL, *Washington:*

Situation unchanged. On 4th instant issued conservative proclamation stating declared intention of President to insure individual rights. Quoted last sentence President's proclamation. Declared it my belief that was intention of United States while directing affairs generally, to appoint representative men of Philippines to civil positions of trust and responsibility; to draw from people as much of necessary military force as consistent with constituted authority, and to establish most liberal form of government, in which people shall have full representation as conditions permit. Aguinaldo met this by counter proclamation, declaring the Philippines independent; had been allies until Manila taken; that Philippine flag had been recognized, and that Filipinos had conquered the Philippines. Our proclamation received favorably by all foreigners except Spanish, who say it is temporizing preparatory to force, and that American rule would be harsher than that of Spain. Spanish circulate inflammatory reports constantly, and number of Spanish soldiers now in insurgent ranks. Filipinos received our proclamation favorably, but ignorant masses under Aguinaldo's influence radical; insurgent leaders now in charge fear this has gone too far, and can not control army and masses. They sought conference; declined to recognize them as representing insurgent government, but conferred with them individually. They desire protection of United States and independence. Have no clear idea of meaning of these words, but think definite arrangements can be made which United States will hold supervisory control and they conduct government, United States to assist when necessary. Conference still in progress, but have told them that they must await action of Congress. This they fail to understand. Miller's conditions at Iloilo same. He begs to be permitted to take city, which would doubtless result in great destruction of property and lives of many natives. He issued President's proclamation, and in this I think made mistake. Has received no response. Reported that natives as early as December 21 advised by Spanish to resist all foreign nations, especially United States, most cruel of all, and natives believe they recognize and execute orders of Luzon insurgent congress. Spanish turned over to Aguinaldo's men military station in south, and Spanish priests and claims. Sedulously advise resistance to United States. Conflict at Iloilo or any southern port means war in all the islands. The leading insurgents here fear and beg that we temporize at Iloilo. Regiment on transports still in Manila Harbor. The abler Filipinos who wish annexation have withdrawn from Aguinaldo despondent. Many of them fear assassination. I believe that the more radical and intelligent insurgent leaders also fear for individual safety, as they can not control army and masses. That Aguinaldo too has apprehensive fear for personal safety; dominates masses, and they obey army and secret clubs which terrorize them. Peace maintained here and business active, though the underlying elements of society excited. Secret clubs endeavor to foment discord. Spanish prisoners of war and Spanish citizens are able to prejudice constantly capability of United States.

OTIS.

ADJUTANT-GENERAL'S OFFICE,
Washington, January 8, 1899—7.15 p. m.

General OTIS, *Manilla:*

I am directed to transmit the following. To save toll but one message is sent, so that you will at once furnish copy to Admiral Dewey. Please acknowledge receipt, and also request Admiral Dewey to acknowledge receipt to Secretary Navy.

CORBIN.

OTIS and DEWEY, *Manilla:*
We transmit to you the following message from the President.

ALGER.
LONG.

"Am most desirous that conflict be avoided. Your statement that a conflict 'at Iloilo or other southern port means war in all the islands' increases that desire. Such conflict most unfortunate, considering the present, and might have results unfavorable affecting the future. Glad you did not permit Miller to bring on a conflict. Time given the insurgents can not hurt us and must weaken and discourage them. They will come to see our benevolent purpose and recognize that before we can give their people good government our sovereignty must be complete and unquestioned. Tact and kindness most essential just now. Am sure you both having full knowledge of situation can be trusted to accomplish purposes of this Government with the least discord and friction. We accepted the Philippines from high duty in the interest of their inhabitants and for humanity and civilization. Our sacrifices were with this high motive. We want to improve the condition of the inhabitants, securing them peace, liberty, and the pursuit of their highest good. Glad you are conferring with them in their unofficial capacity. Will send commissioners if you think desirable, to cooperate with you both in your delicate task. They can not leave here for two weeks or reach Manila for two months. Will send them as above on hearing from you.

"If possible to hasten repatriation of Spanish soldiers before treaty ratified it will be done. You are masters of the situation there and must not relax your power or vigilance. Hope good counsels will prevail among the inhabitants and that you will find means to save bloodshed and restore tranquillity to that unhappy island.

"How is the health of Miller's command?

"WILLIAM MCKINLEY."

MANILA. (Received Washington, January 8, 1899—3.41 a. m.)
ADJUTANT-GENERAL, *Washington:*
Transports *Senator* and *Ohio* left for San Francisco, December 16 and 18. Five transports here, one to return this week. Three at Iloilo.   OTIS.

CHICAGO, ILL, *January 8, 1899.*
(Received 12.38 p. m.)
ADJUTANT-GENERAL ARMY, *Washington, D. C.:*
Thirty-eight officers and 26 members of their families, 1,291 enlisted men and eight members of their families, go with Fourth Infantry. Companies B, G, I, and M, Seventeenth Infantry, designated for first movement, have 8 officers, 416 enlisted men, 3 wives of enlisted men, 1 medical officer and wife, and 5 enlisted Hospital Corps.

SHERIDAN, *Brigadier-General, Commanding.*

HABANA, *January 8, 1899.* (Received 9.28 p. m.)
Adjutant-General CORBIN, *Washington, D. C.:*
Mobile arrived afternoon January 5, 90 officers, 2,082 men, animals, baggage, subsistence and quartermaster stores. Sailed for New York 5.30 p. m., January 7, with orders to make the voyage in the least time practicable.

HUMPHREY.

MANILA. (Received Washington, January 9, 1899—6.20 a. m.)
ADJUTANT-GENERAL, *Washington:*

Require 15 additional medical officers, regulars in part; 72 now present with command, 4 to be discharged, and some sick. If contracts made, should be for one year, unless sooner discharged by Government.

OTIS.

ADJUTANT-GENERAL'S OFFICE,
Washington, January 9, 1899.

COMMANDING GENERAL, DEPARTMENT LAKES,
Chicago, Ill.:

Transport to carry Fourth Infantry and one battalion Seventeenth will not be able to leave New York before 17th instant. Secretary War directs that movement of troops be directed accordingly, and that communication be opened with Colonel Kimball, depot quartermaster New York City, so as to time their arrival to best suit the conditions for quick loading and comfort and welfare of troops. Heavy baggage should arrive in New York two days in advance of troops.

By command Major-General Miles:

H. C. CORBIN, *Adjutant-General.*

ADJUTANT-GENERAL'S OFFICE,
Washington, January 9, 1899.

COMMANDING OFFICER, FOURTH INFANTRY,
Fort Sheridan, Ill.:

Major-General Commanding Army directs you notify Quartermaster-General by wire number and kind of tents required for service abroad, which will be delivered to regiment at place of embarkation. It is not intended that tentage now in hands of companies shall be taken with them.

WM. H. CARTER, *Assistant Adjutant-General.*

FORT RILEY, KANS., *January 9, 1899.*
(Received 6.07 p. m.)

The ADJUTANT-GENERAL, U. S. ARMY,
Washington, D. C., War Department:

Arrived here to-day; will reach Jefferson Barracks to-morrow evening. Of the Twelfth Infantry battalions here, 70 per cent of the men are recruits undrilled and untried. Little can be known their character or stamina.

LAWTON, *Major-General.*

PAYMASTER-GENERAL'S OFFICE,
Washington, January 9, 1899.

The SECRETARY OF WAR.
(Through the Office of the Adjutant-General of the Army.)

SIR: I have the honor to state that application for payment for month of January has been made by an officer of the Third Infantry, whose regiment is about to depart for the Philippine Islands.

I would respectfully recommend that, under the act of May 26, 1898, in General Orders, No. 56, Adjutant-General's Office, authority be granted to pay all of the troops designated to sail this month for the Philippine Islands, for the month of January before they start.

Respectfully,

G. W. BAIRD,
Major, Pay Department, U. S. Army,
Acting Paymaster-General, U. S. Army.

VEDADO, HABANA, *January 9, 1899.*
(Received 8 p. m.)

ADJUTANT-GENERAL, *Washington:*
Mobile sailed for New York seventh.

JOHN R. BROOKE, *Commanding.*

ADJUTANT-GENERAL'S OFFICE,
Washington, January 9, 1899.

Major-General LAWTON, *Fort Riley, Kans.:*
Quartermaster reports transport *Grant*, upon which you and your headquarters are to sail, will not leave before the 17th instant.

HEISTAND, *Assistant Adjutant-General.*

GENERAL ORDERS,
No. 3.

HEADQUARTERS OF THE ARMY,
ADJUTANT-GENERAL'S OFFICE,
Washington, January 9, 1899.

I. The following order has been received from the War Department:

"WAR DEPARTMENT, *Washington, January 7, 1899.*

"The three transports now being prepared for the Philippines will be named as follows:

"The *Mohawk* shall hereafter be known as *Grant*, in honor of the late Gen. U. S. Grant.

"The *Mobile* shall hereafter be known as *Sherman*, in honor of the late Gen. William T. Sherman.

"The *Massachusetts* shall hereafter be known as *Sheridan*, in honor of the late Gen. P. H. Sheridan.

"R. A. ALGER, *Secretary of War.*"

MANILA. (Received Washington, January 10, 1899—2.10 a. m.)
ADJUTANT-GENERAL, *Washington:*
President's instructions of yesterday received. Have cabled fully.

OTIS.

MANILA. (Received Washington, January 10, 1899—7.45 a. m.)
ADJUTANT-GENERAL, *Washington:*
General Rios, late Spanish captain-general, with staff, has arrived from Mindanao, where he left southern Spanish troops. Desires to commence settlement of Spanish civil affairs. Requests that papers connected therewith be handed over to him. Informed that Washington instructions necessary. Think such action should be deferred. Cable instructions.

OTIS.

MANILA. (Received Washington, January 10, 1899—8.30 a. m.)
ADJUTANT-GENERAL, *Washington:*
January 1, Arthur Saunders, private, C, Eighteenth Infantry, diphtheria. January 3, Bert Cornett, private, E, Twentieth Kansas, smallpox. January 4, Harlan E. McVay, captain, medical department, typhoid fever. January 5, Harry Archbold private, M, First Montana, typhoid fever; Gilbert C. Perrine, private, D, Thirteenth Minnesota, smallpox; William H. Bash, private, F, Twentieth Kansas, smallpox; Lee K. Morse, sergeant, L, Second Oregon, gunshot wound, accidental. January 6, Charles Beiser, sergeant, K, Fourth Cavalry, dysentery.

OTIS.

MANILA. (Received Washington, January 10, 1899—9.10 a. m.)
ADJUTANT-GENERAL, *Washington:*
Have conferred with Admiral Dewey. We think commissioners of tact and discretion could do excellect work here. Great difficulty is leaders can not control less intelligent elements. Health of Miller's command good.
OTIS.

CHICAGO, ILL., *January 10, 1899.* (Received 12.40 p. m.)
ADJUTANT-GENERAL, U. S. ARMY, *Washington, D. C.:*
Telegram indicating delay in sailing of transport until 17th received and necessary instructions given.
M. V. SHERIDAN,
Brigadier-General, U. S. Volunteers, Commanding.

MANILA. (Received January 10, 1899—2.15 p. m.)
ADJUTANT-GENERAL, *Washington:*
Revolutionary government anxious for conference and action on my part, to enable them to allay excitement which they appear powerless to control. Believe revolutionary proclamation more result of fear for personal safety than determined hostility to American Government. City very quiet. Great suppressed excitement. Families leaving. Business progressing briskly. Insurgents increasing their force about city, and say that native population will rise if hostilities commence. Our troops well in hand and confident we can meet emergencies. Long conference last night and concessions asked, but insurgents have no definite idea of what they want. Further conference to be held. If peace kept for few days, immediate danger will have passed.
OTIS.

ADJUTANT-GENERAL'S OFFICE,
Washington, January 10, 1899—3 p. m.
COMMANDING OFFICER, FOURTH INFANTRY,
Fort Sheridan, Ill.:
Secretary War has approved recommendation of Paymaster-General, that officers and men about to start for the Philippines be paid for the month of January under provision of act of Congress published in General Orders, No. 56, current series.
HEISTAND, *Assistant Adjutant-General.*

(Same to commanding officer, Seventeenth Infantry, Columbus Barracks, Ohio; commanding officer, Twentieth Infantry, Fort Leavenworth, Kans.; commanding officer, Twelfth Infantry, Jefferson Barracks, Mo.)

ADJUTANT-GENERAL'S OFFICE,
Washington, January 10, 1899—4.30 p. m.
COMMANDING OFFICER, THIRD INFANTRY,
Fort Snelling, Minn.:
Secretary War has directed that troops sailing for the Philippines in the month of January be paid for the month before starting.
HEISTAND, *Assistant Adjutant-General.*

Fort Snelling, Minn., *January 10, 1899.*
Adjutant-General, U. S. Army, *Washington, D. C.:*
Recommend that authority be granted allowing wives and families of worthy married enlisted men of regiment, not exceeding fifteen, to accompany command on transport to Philippines.

Page, *Commanding.* [*Third Infantry.*]

Manila. (Received Washington, January 11, 1899—6.34 a. m.)
Adjutant-General, *Washington:*
Cable company recommends writing words period, colon, comma, instead using stops, which confuse transmission of messages.

Otis.

Adjutant-General's Office,
Washington, January 11, 1899—11.30 a. m.
Commanding Officer, Third Infantry,
Fort Snelling, Minn.:
Reference your telegram January 10, Secretary War directs me to say Department desires to be liberal in matter of transportation of worthy families of enlisted men who are married at the time order for movement to Philippines issued, and will offer no objection to the transportation of such families as the regimental and company commanders may believe worthy; leaving such determination to their judgment. Members of families of officers and enlisted men will be required to pay for their meals en route. The contents of this message, so far as it relates to married soldiers, is confidential, and intended to serve as a basis for individual action and selection, and not to be subject of general information.

By command Major-General Miles:

H. C. Corbin, *Adjutant-General.*

Manila. (Received Washington, January 11, 1899—3.15 p. m.)
Adjutant-General, *Washington:*
Condition unchanged. Sent communication to General Aguinaldo yesterday, expressing desire that peace would be maintained. Informed him that instructions of President would not permit us to bring on conflict. His trusted adviser informed bearer of letter that they desired peace, but could not control people beyond certain limit. Expect that conference will be continued. If excitement can be suppressed for few days, believe that affairs will greatly improve. Insurgent forces have increased in number, still threaten attack, and rising. Citizens believe we can meet any emergency. Thirty thousand citizens left city within the last week. Still going out.

Otis.

War Department, *January 11, 1899—5.35 p. m.*
Otis, *Manila:*
If you think it advisable on account of conditions at Manila, you might recall General Miller's command.

Alger, *Secretary.*

MANILA. (Received January 12, 1899—7.20 a. m.)

ADJUTANT-GENERAL, *Washington:*

Conditions apparently improving. Citizens feel more secure. Many natives returning. City quiet and business active. Constant watchfulness required.

OTIS.

MANILA. (Received January 13, 1899—8.45 a. m.)

ADJUTANT-GENERAL, *Washington:*

Transport *Valencia* left this afternoon for San Francisco by way of Nagasaki; 61 officers and enlisted men, 9 civilians.

OTIS.

ADJUTANT-GENERAL'S OFFICE,
Washington, January 13, 1899.

General OTIS, *Manila:*

Secretary War directs you cause press dispatches to be censored at your end of the line.

CORBIN.

SAN FRANCISCO, CAL., *January 13, 1899.*
(Received 10.15 p. m.)

ADJUTANT-GENERAL, U. S. ARMY,
Washington, D. C.:

Astor Battery arrived here to-day. No casualties on trip. Guns and ammunition turned over in Manila by order of Otis. To whom should I report in New York on arrival there. Leave Sunday night.

MARCH.

MANILA. (Received January 14, 1899—6.50 a. m.)

ADJUTANT-GENERAL, *Washington:*

Learn Spanish officers have cabled Madrid that our conditions most critical. Spaniards still inciting insurgents, misrepresenting intention of United States in order to defeat ratification of treaty. Conditions improving. Insurgent government seeking further conference. Troops can meet any emergency. Incendiarism and mob violence in city all that is feared. Police force strong and efficient. Our troops can readily handle all insurgent troops, should attempt conflict. Murders and robbery outside of city frequent, showing inefficiency of insurgent government to restrain people. More intelligent members of that government admit their dependence on United States assistance.

OTIS.

CHICAGO, ILL., *January 14, 1899.*
(Received 3.31 p. m.)

ADJUTANT-GENERAL ARMY, *Washington, D. C.:*

The Fourth Regiment will leave Fort Sheridan for New York early to-morrow forenoon as soon as loaded. The battalion of the Seventeenth will leave Columbus barracks in the afternoon. Both commands due in New York early Tuesday morning the 17th.

SHERIDAN, *Brigadier-General, Commanding.*

No telegram received reporting the sailing of the Fourth Infantry and one battalion of the Seventeenth Infantry. Returns show that the *Grant* sailed from New York January 19, 1899, with Fourteenth Infantry and one battalion of the Seventeenth Infantry, General Lawton in command.

MANILA. (Received Washington, January 16, 1899—6.49 a. m.)
ADJUTANT-GENERAL, *Washington:*
Following deaths since last report: January 8, Edward A. Rothemeyer, private A, Twentieth Kansas, smallpox. January 9, Powhatan T. Hackett, private F, Twentieth Kansas, smallpox; Eugene Merwin, corporal M, First California, cirrhosis of liver; Lewis R. Badger, private F, Twentieth Kansas, smallpox. January 11, A. Brent McClain, private G, First Tennessee, smallpox; Wilman H. Bell, private C, First California, smallpox; Eteyl P. Blair, private A, Twentieth Kansas, smallpox.
OTIS.

MANILA. (Received January 16, 1899—10.52 a. m.)
ADJUTANT-GENERAL, *Washington:*
General Miller reports 13th instant quiet and good health. His officers visit city and insurgents visit vessels. Insurgent authorities say can not surrender city without instructions from Aguinaldo. Seem desirous to do so. Foreign vessels destined for neutral ports loading in harbor; receiving cargo from city by lighters. Insurgents reported as collecting duties. Am I authorized to enforce payment of duties to United States?
OTIS.

FORT SNELLING, MINN., *January 16, 1899.*
(Received 11.34 a. m.)
ADJUTANT-GENERAL, U. S. ARMY, *Washington, D. C.:*
Is it necessary for men to take full-dress uniform to Philippines?
PAGE, *Commanding.* [*Third Infantry.*]

ADJUTANT-GENERAL'S OFFICE,
Washington, January 16, 1899.
COMMANDING GENERAL, DEPARTMENT EAST,
Governors Island, N. Y.:
Ascertain from Colonel Kimball hour of sailing of the *Grant* Wednesday morning, in order that a major-general's salute may be given as the transport passes Governors Island, and by all other posts in the harbor that she passes.
By command Major-General Miles:
H. C. CORBIN, *Adjutant-Genera*

MANILA. (Received January 16, 1899—4.06 p. m.)
ADJUTANT-GENERAL, *Washington:*
Conditions improving. Confidence. Citizens returning. Business active. Conference held Saturday. Insurgent commissioners presented following statement and asked that it be cabled:
"Undersigned commissioners of commander in chief, revolutionary army of these islands, state to Commissioners General Otis that aspiration of Filipino people is

independence, with restrictions resulting from conditions which its government may agree with American when latter agrees to officially recognize the former." Insurgent commissioners unable to maintain in conference position declared in statement. No conclusion reached. Another conference to-morrow evening. I understand insurgents wish qualified independence under United States protection.

OTIS.

SYRACUSE, N. Y., *January 16, 1899.*
(Received 4.22 p. m.)

ADJUTANT-GENERAL, *Washington, D. C.:*

Left Columbus Barracks at 7 last night, with 8 officers and 411 men Seventeenth Infantry, for New York. Expect to reach Weehawken about 11 to-night, en route to Philippines.

ROGERS, *Commanding.*

ADJUTANT-GENERAL'S OFFICE,
Washington, January 16, 1899.

COMMANDING GENERAL, DEPARTMENT CALIFORNIA,
San Francisco, Cal.:

On the arrival of the *Senator* and *Ohio*, the Secretary of War directs that you make a thorough inspection of these ships and report the number of officers and men each can carry, having in mind the health and comfort of troops to be carried, and at the same time utilize the full capacity of the ships. Also give the earliest date these ships can be put in order and made ready to sail for Manila.

By command General Miles:

H. C. CORBIN, *Adjutant-General.*

WEEHAWKEN, N. J., *January 17, 1899.*
(Received 6.35 a. m.)

ADJUTANT-GENERAL, U. S. ARMY,
Washington, D. C.:

Arrived at this point at 2.46 this morning with battalion Seventeenth Infantry. Have instructions from department commander to report to and await instructions from you. Have two mild cases of measles developed en route. Medical officer's opinion is there will be more cases and advises an isolation ward made ready on transport and these cases sent ahead or left on Governors Island. Battalion held at this point awaiting instructions from you.

ROGERS, *Commanding.*

ADJUTANT-GENERAL'S OFFICE,
Washington, January 17, 1899.

General LAWTON, *Army Building, New York City:*

Leave cases of measles and suspected cases. Remainder of battalion should go.

By order Secretary War:

H. C. CORBIN, *Adjutant-General.*

ADJUTANT-GENERAL'S OFFICE,
Washington, January 17, 1899—2.15 p. m.

COMMANDING GENERAL, DEPARTMENT EAST,
Governors Island, New York Harbor:

Secretary War directs that owing to the very limited number of blank cartridges for use with the guns placed on the *Mohawk*, you notify commanding officer troops on board the vessel that the salutes to be fired in honor of Major-General Lawton by the forts at New York will be returned by lowering of the flag and not by firing guns.

By command Major-General Miles:

CARTER, *Assistant Adjutant-General.*

ADJUTANT-GENERAL'S OFFICE,
Washington, January 17, 1899—4 p. m.

COMMANDING OFFICER, THIRD INFANTRY,
Fort Snelling, Minn.:

Secretary War decides that it is not necessary for men to take full-dress uniforms to the Philippines.

By command Major-General Miles:

H. C. CORBIN, *Adjutant-General.*

SAN FRANCISCO, CAL., *January 17, 1899.*
(Received 5.34 p. m.)

ADJUTANT-GENERAL, *Washington, D. C.:*

Have inspected transports *Senator* and *Ohio*. Each can carry 40 officers and 760 enlisted men. This gives staterooms to some noncommissioned officers, so that more first class and less second class can be provided for. If required, they can be ready for troops January 26.

MERRIAM, *Major-General.*

MANILA. (Received January 17, 1899—11 p. m.)

ADJUTANT-GENERAL, *Washington:*

No discrimination by press censor. Numerous baseless rumors circulated here, tending to excite outside world, stricken from proposed press cablegrams. Correspondents permitted to cable established facts.

OTIS.

ADJUTANT-GENERAL'S OFFICE,
Washington, January 18, 1899.

COMMANDING GENERAL, DEPARTMENT OF DAKOTA,
St. Paul, Minn.:

Referring to previous orders, Secretary War directs that the Third United States Infantry proceed to New York City and embark on transport to be provided for Philippine Islands, reporting upon arrival at destination to commanding general, Department Pacific.

Communicate with Colonel Kimball, depot quartermaster, New York City, to time arrival of baggage and troops in such manner as to facilitate loading and cause the least possible delay and inconvenience.

The headquarters and four companies of the Seventeenth Infantry from the Department of the Lakes will go on same transport with the Third Infantry. Acknowledge receipt and report hour of departure of regiment from present station.

By command Major-General Miles:

H. C. CORBIN, *Adjutant-General.*

ADJUTANT-GENERAL'S OFFICE,
Washington, January 18, 1899.

COMMANDING GENERAL, DEPARTMENT LAKES,
Chicago, Ill.:

Referring to previous orders, Secretary War directs that the headquarters and one battalion of four companies of the Seventeenth Infantry proceed to New York City and embark on transport to be provided for Philippine Islands, reporting upon arrival at destination to commanding general, Department Pacific.

Communicate with Colonel Kimball, depot quartermaster, New York City, to time arrival of baggage and troops in such manner as to facilitate loading and cause the least possible delay and inconvenience.

The Third Infantry from the Department of Dakota will go on same transport. Acknowledge receipt and report hour of departure of command from present station.

By command Major-General Miles:

H. C. CORBIN, *Adjutant-General.*

ADJUTANT-GENERAL'S OFFICE,
Washington, January 18, 1899.

COMMANDING GENERAL, DEPARTMENT MISSOURI,
Omaha, Nebr.:

Referring to previous orders, Secretary War directs that the Twenty-second Infantry proceed to San Francisco, Cal., there to embark on transports *Senator* and *Ohio* for Philippine Islands, reporting upon arrival to the commanding general, Department of the Pacific, for duty. Each vessel has capacity for 40 officers and 760 enlisted men.

Communicate with commanding general, Department California, with view to arranging details of movement and to so time arrival of troops and baggage as to offer greatest facility for loading and to cause least delay and inconvenience to troops after arrival at San Francisco. Instructions concerning movement of families of officers and enlisted men, issued in connection with the movement of the Twelfth Infantry, are applicable alike to this regiment. Acknowledge receipt and direct commanding officer to report strength of command and time of departure from present station and port embarkation.

By command Major-General Miles:

H. C. CORBIN, *Adjutant-General.*

ST. PAUL, MINN., *January 19, 1899.*
(Received 11.45 a. m.)

ADJUTANT-GENERAL, U. S. ARMY, *Washington:*

Your telegram directing the movement Third Infantry to New York en route to Philippine Islands received. Will report hour of departure of regiment after arrangements have been completed with Colonel Kimball. Baggage now being loaded.

BACON, *Brigadier-General Commanding.*

CHICAGO, ILL., *January 19, 1899—12.42 p. m.*

ADJUTANT-GENERAL, U. S. ARMY,
Washington, D. C.:

Telegram directing that headquarters and one battalion of Seventeenth Infantry proceed to New York City and embark for Philippines received, and instructions will be given accordingly.

M. V. SHERIDAN,
Brigadier-General, U. S. Volunteers, Commanding.

OMAHA, NEBR., *January 19, 1899.*
(Received 1.12 p. m.)
ADJUTANT-GENERAL, U. S. ARMY,
Washington, D. C.:
Telegram directing Twenty-second Infantry be sent to San Francisco for embarkation received, and all matters of detail will be attended to. Regiment is practically ready.
HUTCHESON,
Assistant Adjutant-General, in absence of Department Commander.

ADJUTANT-GENERAL'S OFFICE,
Washington, January 19, 1899.
COMMANDING GENERAL, DEPARTMENT OF CALIFORNIA,
San Francisco:
Twenty-second Infantry has been ordered to embark on transports *Senator* and *Ohio*. Commanding general, Department Missouri, directed to communicate with you for arrangement of detail of movements.
H. C. CORBIN, *Adjutant-General.*

ADJUTANT-GENERAL'S OFFICE,
Washington, January 19, 1899.
General OTIS, *Manila:*
What amount of funds from customs collections have you on hand?
CORBIN.

ADJUTANT-GENERAL'S OFFICE,
Washington, January 19, 1899.
General OTIS, *Manila:*
Following received from President. One telegram sent to save expense. Deliver copy to Admiral Dewey.
"OTIS and DEWEY:
Schurman, president of Cornell University, Worcester of Ann Arbor, who spent four years in the islands, and Denby, twelve years our minister to China, will leave here in a few days, going via Vancouver for Manila. These gentlemen, with Otis and Dewey, will constitute a commission. Instructions will accompany them.
"WILLIAM MCKINLEY."
By order Secretary War:
CORBIN.

ADJUTANT-GENERAL'S OFFICE,
Washington, January 19, 1899—4.10 p. m.
General OTIS, *Manila:*
The President desires no forcible measures be used for the present in collecting custom duties at Iloilo.
CORBIN.

SURGEON-GENERAL'S OFFICE,
Washington, January 19, 1899.

The ADJUTANT-GENERAL OF THE ARMY.

SIR: In view of the increasing amount of sickness at Manila, I have the honor to recommend that the hospital ship *Relief*, now in New York Harbor, be sent to Manila by way of the Suez Canal, to serve as a hospital ship for the troops at Manila, or for conveying convalescents to any more northern point that may be selected as a location for a convalescent hospital. General Otis has recently called for more medical officers, and these could be sent upon the *Relief*, together with some additional hospital stewards and female nurses, also a liberal supply of medicines.

Very respectfully,

GEO. M. STERNBERG,
Surgeon-General, U. S. Army.

Approved.

The Quartermaster-General will immediately make all arrangements necessary to carry this plan into effect.

R. A. ALGER, *Secretary of War.*

January 19, 1899.

MANILA. (Received January 20, 1899—4.20 a. m.)

ADJUTANT-GENERAL, *Washington:*

Public funds on hand, 1,869,546 pesos, exclusive of amount turned over by Spanish Government August 14 and not touched; 979,401 pesos received from customs since August 14; 2,270,811 pesos from all sources; 3,239,165 pesos accounts current of expenditures to December 31 transmitted.

OTIS.

MANILA. (Received January 20, 1899—8.25 a. m.)

ADJUTANT-GENERAL, *Washington:*

Admiral Dewey asks me to cable if Edward W. Harden acceptable as secretary of commission. Have no official information regarding commission. Harden not acceptable here in any capacity. See his abusive article published in San Francisco Chronicle, November 11.

OTIS.

ST. PAUL, MINN., *January 20, 1899.*
(Received 1.04 p. m.)

ADJUTANT-GENERAL, *Washington, D. C.:*

Colonel Kimball wires me that ship for Third Infantry will not be ready to sail much before February 1. Will have baggage and troops at destination in New York when he is ready for them.

BACON, *Brigadier-General.*

CHICAGO, ILL., *January 20, 1899.*
(Received 2.18 p. m.)

ADJUTANT-GENERAL ARMY, *Washington, D. C.:*

Companies D, H, K, and L, Seventeenth Infantry, have been designated to proceed to New York City with headquarters and hospital detachment of Seventeenth. Commanding officer, Columbus Barracks, reports 15 officers and 450 men to go, also 5 officers' wives and 7 wives and 3 children of enlisted men; that Captain Shanks and Lieutenant Sheldon are expected to join in New York, but does not know if they have families. Colonel Kimball, quartermaster, New York City, reports that ship will not be ready to receive troops before about February 1 next. Baggage will be sent some days in advance.

SHERIDAN,
Brigadier-General, U. S. Volunteers, Commanding.

MANILA. (Received January 21, 1899—6.44 a. m.)
ADJUTANT-GENERAL, *Washington:*
Construction hospital Nagasaki unnecessary. Health command good. Diseases successfully treated here, except chronic bowel difficulty and rheumatism. Send number such cases Monday by transport *Zealandia* to San Francisco for treatment. If peace prevailed, might establish hospital in mountains, where recuperation rapid. Convalescent hospital Corregidor successful.

OTIS.

EXECUTIVE MANSION,
Washington, January 21, 1899.
Major-General OTIS, *Manila:*
The President directs me to say: In accordance with your recommendation, defer action on the matter referred to in your cable of the 10th.

CORBIN, *Adjutant-General.*

WAR DEPARTMENT, *January 21, 1899.*
OTIS, *Manila:*
Spanish Government is most urgent for release of prisoners in hands of Tagals. The President is also very desirous that you should make another strenuous effort immediately to that end. Answer.

ALGER, *Secretary.*

ADJUTANT-GENERAL'S OFFICE,
Washington, January 21, 1899.
COMMANDING GENERAL, DEPARTMENT LAKES,
Chicago, Ill.:
Referring to movement Third Infantry and battalion Seventeenth, Secretary War directs that only four companies Seventeenth Infantry accompany Third Infantry, and that headquarters Seventeenth Infantry remain behind and accompany the Third Battalion, which will sail with Twelfth Infantry.
By command Major-General Miles:

H. C. CORBIN, *Adjutant-General.*

CHICAGO, ILL., *January 21, 1899.* (Received 5.05 p. m.)
ADJUTANT-GENERAL ARMY, *Washington, D.C.:*
Telegram directing that headquarters Seventeenth Infantry remain behind received, and instructions will be given accordingly.

SHERIDAN, *Brigadier-General Commanding.*

MANILA. (Received January 22, 1899—7.20 a. m.)
SECRETARY WAR, *Washington:*
No vessel trans-Atlantic steamship company now here. *Uruguay* should report soon. *Reina Cristina* due 28th instant. No vessels available on which to ship prisoners of war. Copies of all dispatches relating to joint operations have been furnished admiral.

OTIS.

MANILA. (Received January 22, 1899—12.48 p. m.)
ADJUTANT-GENERAL, *Washington:*
Informed by prominent insurgents last month that Spanish prisoners would be released; that such the desire of majority of Malolos insurgent congress. Do not think that Malolos government will release, believing detention will involve Spain and United States. Efforts to secure release of priests gives basis for charge that I am in sympathy with priests, and priests confirm rumor. Do not think I can effect anything at present, as can not recognize in correspondence insurgent government. Insurgent radical element comfortable, full possession and with aid of Spaniards and circulation of falsehoods are intensifying sentiment against Americans. Conservative educated Filipinos fear for personal safety should they resume prominence in affairs. Situation remains critical, but quiet prevails.

OTIS.

MANILA. (Received January 23, 1899—8.50 a. m.)
ADJUTANT-GENERAL, *Washington, D. C.:*
Am informed insurgent congress has adopted constitution which was proclaimed to-day, and Aguinaldo proclaimed president Philippine republic. Informed decree passed liberating Spanish civil prisoners and invalid military prisoners. Excitement at Malolos, and threats to drive invader from soil.

OTIS.

MANILA. (Received January 23, 1899—11.54 a. m.)
ADJUTANT-GENERAL, *Washington:*
Following deaths since last report: January 14, Benjamin W. Squires, private, L, Twentieth Kansas. 15, John D. Young, private, A, Twentieth Kansas; Frank Brain, private, C, Tenth Pennsylvania. 18, Norman E. Hand, private, L, Twentieth Kansas. 19, Harry C. Falkenburg, principal musician First Colorado; David L. Campbell, private, E, Twentieth Kansas. 20, Arthur W. Tilden, private, K, Fourteenth Infantry; all smallpox. 16, Allen E. Carlyle, private, I, First Washington, typhoid fever; Wister Hawthorne, private, C, Second Oregon, diphtheria.

OTIS.

ADJUTANT-GENERAL'S OFFICE,
Washington, January 23, 1899.
Major-General SHAFTER,
Department California, San Francisco, Cal.:
The Secretary of War is anxious that you have every preparation made for the transfer of the Twentieth Infantry, now en route to San Francisco, to the *Scandia* and *Morgan City*, and he suggests that you make personal inspection of the vessels to-day or to-morrow and of its arrangements, to ascertain whether everything possible has been done for the health and comfort of this command.

AFFAIRS IN THE PHILIPPINE ISLANDS. 887

The Twenty-second Infantry will reach San Francisco by the 28th and go on the *Ohio* and *Senator*, and the Secretary War desires the same care and precautionary measures taken for this regiment as herein directed for the Twentieth Infantry.

H. C. CORBIN, *Adjutant-General.*

CHICAGO, ILL., *January 23, 1899.*
(Received 2.35 p. m.)

ADJUTANT-GENERAL ARMY, *Washington, D. C.:*

In view of telegram received 21st instant, directing that Headquarters Seventeenth Infantry remain behind, commanding officer Columbus Barracks makes following report as to number of officers, men, and families to go on transport with Third Infantry: Officers, 10; enlisted men, 422; members officers' families, 5; enlisted men's families, 1; 100,000 pounds baggage.

SHERIDAN,
Brigadier-General Commanding.

OMAHA, NEBR., *January 23, 1899.*
(Received 6.34 p. m.)

ADJUTANT-GENERAL, U. S. ARMY,
War Department, Washington, D. C.:

Twenty-second Infantry will leave Fort Crook for San Francisco on the 27th, to arrive on 31st.

SUMNER, *Brigadier-General Commanding.*

ADJUTANT-GENERAL'S OFFICE,
Washington, January 25, 1899.

COMMANDING GENERAL, DEPARTMENT MISSOURI,
Omaha, Nebr.:

Secretary War directs that you detail from the Twenty-second Infantry an officer to act as commissary and one sergeant to act as commissary sergeant, and three enlisted men to act as clerks; to proceed immediately to San Francisco to receive stores to be placed aboard the transports *Ohio* and *Senator*. The officer, upon arrival, will confer with Lieutenant-Colonel Baldwin, depot commissary, San Francisco.

By command Major-General Miles:

H. C. CORBIN, *Adjutant-General.*

OMAHA, NEBR., *January 25, 1899.*
(Received 5 56 p. m.)

ADJUTANT-GENERAL, U. S. ARMY,
Washington, D. C.:

Referring to your telegram this date, Lieutenant Stanley left here yesterday for San Francisco to take charge of baggage and supplies of his regiment. Will it be necessary to send another officer with the enlisted men mentioned? Will be sent to-day.

SUMNER, *Brigadier-General Commanding.*

MANILA. (Received January 26, 1899—8.30 a. m.)

ADJUTANT-GENERAL, *Washington:*

Transport *Zealandia* left yesterday for San Francisco, 124 officers and enlisted men.

OTIS.

WAR DEPARTMENT, *January 26, 1899.*

OTIS, *Manila:*

You can load *Cristina* 1,200 enlisted men and as many officers as she can carry. Also *Uruguay* 800 men; same conditions for officers. See ships provisioned and in good condition. Terms to be accepted bid. Bids open February 1.

ALGER, *Secretary.*

ADJUTANT-GENERAL'S OFFICE,
Washington, January 26, 1899.

COMMANDING GENERAL, DEPARTMENT MISSOURI,
Omaha, Nebr.:

Referring telegram 25th, directing detail an officer Twenty-second Infantry to act as commissary, Secretary War directs a detail in addition to Lieutenant Stanley be made. By command Major-General Miles:

H. C. CORBIN, *Adjutant-General.*

MANILA. (Received January 27, 1899—2 ⁓. m.)

ADJUTANT-GENERAL, *Washington:*

Conditions apparently improving. Less excitement prevailing. Conferences with insurgent representatives still held. More moderation in demands. The following received:

"PHILIPPINE NATIONAL GOVERNMENT,
"OFFICE OF SECRETARY OF FOREIGN AFFAIRS.

"Maj. Gen. E. S. OTIS,

"*Commander in chief of the American forces of occupation in Manila:*

"My government has promulgated the political constitution of the Philippine republic, which is to-day enthusiastically proclaimed by the people because of its conviction that its duty is to interpret faithfully the aspirations of that people, a people making superhuman efforts to revindicate their sovereignty and their nationality before the civilized powers. To this end, of the governments to-day recognized and observed among cultured nations, they have adopted the form of government most compatible with their aspirations, endeavoring to adjust their actions to the dictates of reason and of right, in order to demonstrate their aptitude for civil life; and taking the liberty to notify your excellency, I confidently hope that, doing justice to the Philippine people, you will be pleased to inform the Government of your nation that the desire of mine, upon being accorded official recognition, is to contribute to the best of its scanty ability to the establishment of a general peace.

"May God keep your excellency many years.

"Malolos, January 23, 1899.

"EMILIO AGUINALDO.

[Seal of the revolutionary government of the Philippines.]

"A. MABINI."

OTIS.

SAN FRANCISCO, CAL., *January 27, 1899.*
(Received 6.30 p. m.)

ADJUTANT-GENERAL, *Washington, D. C.:*

Referring to telegram your office, 6th January last, report that *Scandia* sailed 6 and *Morgan City* 6.45 yesterday afternoon, with Twentieth Infantry, as follows: Thirty-two officers, 4 officers attached, 1,253 men, 1 surgeon, 3 acting assistant surgeons, 4 hospital stewards, 11 privates Hospital Corps. Five hundred thousand rounds small-arms ammunition, caliber .30. Two officers and 17 men were left ashore when the ships sailed, and will be sent by next transports. Both ships in excellent condition.

SHAFTER, *Major-General.*

OMAHA, NEBR., *January 27, 1899.*
(Received 6.20 p. m.)

ADJUTANT-GENERAL, U. S. ARMY, *Washington, D. C.:*

Twenty-second Infantry, 35 officers, 1,220 enlisted men, left Fort Crook to-day for San Francisco.

SUMNER, *Brigadier-General, Commanding.*

MANILA. (Received January 30, 1899—8.45 a. m.)

ADJUTANT-GENERAL, *Washington:*

Following deaths since last report: January 26, John A. Moyers, private, H, First Tennessee, smallpox; 26, Earl A. Jeans, private, I, First Washington, typhoid fever. 27, Otto J. Berg, private, F, First South Dakota, diphtheria.

OTIS.

MANILA. (Received January 30, 1899.)

ADJUTANT-GENERAL, *Washington:*

On what date did Twentieth Infantry leave San Francisco, and on what dates did other troop vessels leave United States?

OTIS.

ADJUTANT-GENERAL'S OFFICE,
Washington, January 30, 1899.

General OTIS, *Manila:*

Fourth Infantry and four companies Seventeenth Infantry, 1,728 officers and men, under General Lawton, sailed from New York January 19.

Twentieth Infantry, 37 officers and 1,268 men, under General Wheaton, sailed from San Francisco January 27.

Twenty-second Infantry sails January 31, from San Francisco, on *Ohio* and *Senator.*

Third Infantry and four companies Seventeenth Infantry sails from New York February 2.

Twelfth Infantry and four companies and headquarters Seventeenth Infantry sails from New York February 9.

CORBIN.

ST. PAUL, MINN., *January 30, 1899*.
(Received 2.15 p. m.)

ADJUTANT-GENERAL, U. S. ARMY, *Washington, D. C.:*

The Third Infantry left Fort Snelling and this city at 11.45 this morning for New York City en route to Manila, P. I. Strength 24 officers and 1,269 men, also 1 chaplain, 3 acting assistant surgeons, 15 men of Hospital Corps, and 1 of Signal Corps.

BACON, *Brigadier-General, Commanding.*

CHICAGO, ILL., *January 30, 1899*.
(Received 5.19 p. m.)

ADJUTANT-GENERAL ARMY, *Washington, D. C.:*

Companies D, H, K, and L, Seventeenth Infantry, leave Columbus Barracks 5 p. m. to-day, 9 officers, 426 enlisted men.

SHERIDAN,
Brigadier-General, U. S. Volunteers, Commanding.

No telegram received reporting the sailing of the Third Infantry and Second Battalion of the Seventeenth Infantry. Returns show that the *Sherman* sailed from New York February 3, 1899, with Third Infantry and Second Battalion of the Seventeenth Infantry, Colonel Page, Third Infantry, in command.

VICTORIA, B. C., *January 31, 1899*. (Received 9.20 a. m.)

Hon. JOHN HAY,
    Secretary of State, Washington, D. C.:

Already sailing; all well; due Yokohama 13th, Hongkong 21st.

J. G. SCHURMAN.

ADTUTANT-GENERAL'S OFFICE,
Washington, January 31, 1899.

General OTIS, *Manila:*

Discretionary authority granted reliable firms cabling business code messages, code book and unciphered messages being filed with censor.

CORBIN.

WAR DEPARTMENT, *January 31, 1899.*

OTIS, *Manila:*

Senate asks number and cause of death by sickness among troops since landing, number of deaths per week now, condition and health of command. When does so-called sickly season begin?

ALGER, *Secretary of War.*

ADJUTANT-GENERAL'S OFFICE,
Washington, January 31, 1899.

General LAWTON,
    U. S. transport Grant, Gibraltar:

Report at each station, where there is cable communication, arrival and condition of troops.

CORBIN.

ADJUTANT-GENERAL'S OFFICE,
Washington, January 31, 1899.

COMMANDING GENERAL, DEPARTMENT LAKES,
Chicago, Ill.:

Referring to previous telegrams concerning movement Seventeenth Infantry to Philippines, Secretary of War directs that the headquarters and remaining companies of that regiment sail from New York on transport *Sheridan* about February 9, and that the arrival of troops and baggage in New York may, by communication with depot quartermaster, New York City, be so timed as to facilitate loading and prevent, as far as possible, delay and inconvenience to troops. Twelfth Infantry goes on same transport. Acknowledge receipt and direct commanding officer to report departure of regiment from present station and strength of command.

By command Major-General Miles:

H. C. CORBIN, *Adjutant-General.*

CHICAGO, ILL., *January 31, 1899.*
(Received 1 10 p. m.)

ADJUTANT-GENERAL, U. S. ARMY,
Washington, D. C.:

Telegram touching movement of headquarters and remaining companies of Seventeenth Infantry received and necessary instructions issued.

M. V. SHERIDAN,
Brigadier-General, U. S. Volunteers, Commanding.

ADJUTANT-GENERAL'S OFFICE,
Washington, January 31, 1899.

COMMANDING GENERAL, DEPARTMENT MISSOURI, *Omaha, Nebr.:*

Referring to previous telegrams concerning movement of Twelfth Infantry to Philippines, Secretary War directs that the regiment sail from New York on transport *Sheridan* about February 9, and that the arrival of troops and baggage in New York may, by communication with depot quartermaster, New York City, be so timed as to facilitate loading and prevent, as far as possible, delay and inconvenience to troops. Headquarters and one battalion, Seventeenth Infantry, go on same transport. Acknowledge receipt and direct commanding officer to report departure of regiment from present station, and strength command.

By command Major-General Miles:

H. C. CORBIN, *Adjutant-General.*

OMAHA, NEBR., *January 31, 1899.*
(Received 3.04 p. m.)

ADJUTANT-GENERAL, U. S. ARMY,
Washington, D. C.:

Telegram regarding movement of Twelfth Infantry received.

HUTCHESON,
Assistant Adjutant-General, in absence of Department Commander.

MANILA. (Received February 1, 1899—6.45 a. m.)

ADJUTANT-GENERAL, *Washington:*

Receipts, taxes and duties, January, $745,000. Future receipts less if present conditions continue. City quiet. No material change. Insurgents threaten; make no active demonstration in force.

OTIS.

ADJUTANT-GENERAL'S OFFICE,
Washington, February 1, 1899.

General OTIS, *Manila:*

Civilian members Philippine Commission sailed Vancouver yesterday, due Hongkong 21st.

CORBIN.

CHICAGO, ILL., *February 1, 1899.*
(Received 1.37 p. m.)

ADJUTANT-GENERAL, U. S. ARMY,
Washington, D. C.:

Commanding officer Columbus Barracks reports that with headquarters, noncommissioned staff and band, and Companies A, C, E, and F, Seventeenth Infantry, there will be 16 officers and 448 enlisted men, 5 wives of officers, and 2 children under five years, 5 wives of enlisted men, 2 children over five and 2 under five, 125,000 pounds advance baggage.

M. V. SHERIDAN,
Brigadier-General, U. S. Volunteers, Commanding.

GIBRALTAR, *February 1, 1899.*
(Received 5.15 p. m.)

CORBIN, *Washington:*

Placed under strict quarantine. Allowed to coal only.

LAWTON.

GIBRALTAR, *February 1, 1899.*

SECRETARY STATE, *Washington:*

Grant permitted coal under quarantine restrictions. Officers and passengers may land, but not crew nor soldiers. Weather stormy.

SPRAGUE, *United States Consul.*

GIBRALTAR, *February 1, 1899.*
(Received 5.28 p. m.)

CORBIN, *Washington:*

Voyage uneventful. Health fairly good. Three cases measles, 2 mumps, 4 pneumonia, 3 meningitis, developed on trip. All improving. Private Prettyman, Company M, Seventeenth Infantry, died January 21, meningitis, seriously ill before sailing. Body hermetically sealed; casket brought into port. Coal here. Remain at least forty-eight hours.

EDWARDS, *Major.*

SAN FRANCISCO, CAL., *February 1, 1899.*
(Received 5.19 p. m.)

ADJUTANT-GENERAL, *Washington, D. C.:*

Total enlisted strength Twenty-second Infantry to sail for Manila, 1,182; on hand 100 rounds per man small ammunition, caliber .30; sail to-day at noon on steamers *Senator* and *Ohio*.

SHAFTER, *Major-General.*

MANILA. (Received February 2, 1899—3.45 a. m.)
SECRETARY WAR, *Washington:*
Deaths among troops in Philippines since arrival to February 1, seven months, 220, of which 40 due to wounds and accidents. Of remaining 179, 65 died of typhoid, 43 smallpox, 22 dysentery, 8 malarial fever. Remaining deaths due to many various diseases. Smallpox causes apprehension. Entire command vaccinated several times. Twelve physicians engaged several weeks vaccinating natives. More sickly season during hot months, March, April, May, when fevers, smallpox, and dysentery more prevalent. Nine per cent of command now reported sick; great majority cases slight ailments. Average death rate January, $6\frac{3}{4}$; from all causes other than smallpox, $2\frac{1}{2}$.

OTIS.

WAR DEPARTMENT, *February 3, 1899.*
OTIS, *Manila:*
How many Spanish officers and soldiers were taken prisoners on capture of Manila? How many of those have been returned to Spain? How many remain at Manila to be returned?

ALGER, *Secretary of War.*

ADJUTANT-GENERAL'S OFFICE,
Washington, February 4, 1899—2 p. m.
COMMANDING GENERAL, DEPARTMENT MISSOURI,
Omaha, Nebr.:
Quartermaster's Department reports transport *Sheridan* will not be ready before February 14. Notify troops to sail on her accordingly, and keep in communication with superintendent transport service in New York City.
By command Major-General Miles:
(Same to commanding general, Department Lakes, Chicago, Ill.)

H. C. CORBIN, *Adjutant-General.*

MANILA. (Received February 5, 1899—8.05 a. m.)
SECRETARY OF THE NAVY, *Washington:*
Insurgents have inaugurated general engagement yesterday night which is continued to-day. The American army and navy is generally successful. Insurgents have been driven back and our line advanced. No casualties to Navy. In view of this and possible future expenditure, request ammunition requisition doubled.

DEWEY.

ADJUTANT-GENERAL'S OFFICE,
Washington, February 5, 1899—1 p. m.
General OTIS, *Manila:*
Grant, with Lawton's command, coaled Gibraltar Thursday and Friday. *Sherman* with Third Infantry and four companies Seventeenth Infantry, sailed from New York early Friday morning, with Colonel Page commanding.

CORBIN.

ADJUTANT-GENERAL'S OFFICE,
Washington, February 5, 1899—4.20 p. m.
General OTIS, *Manila:*
We have cable from Dewey through Navy Department of engagement at Manila. Secretary War desires report from you soon as can be made, giving casualties. Company and regiment of each.

CORBIN.

MANILA. (Received February 5, 1899.)

SIGNAL:

February 5. Action continues since early morning. Losses quite heavy. Lines badly cut at first. Communication now satisfactory. Everything favorable to our arms.

R. E. THOMPSON,
Lieutenant-Colonel, Signal Corps.

MANILA, *February 5, 1899.*
(Received 10.52 p. m.)

ADJUTANT-GENERAL, *Washington:*

February 5. Insurgents in large force opened attack on our outer lines at 8.45 last evening. Renewed attack several times during night. At 4 o'clock this morning entire line engaged. All attacks repulsed. At daybreak advanced against insurgents and have driven them beyond the lines they formerly occupied, capturing several villages and their defense works. Insurgent loss in dead and wounded large. Our own casualties thus far intimated at 175, very few fatal. We are still driving enemy and think we shall punish him severely. Troops enthusiastic and acting fearlessly. Navy did splendid execution on flanks of enemy. City held in check and absolute quiet prevails. Believe that insurgent army attacked contrary wishes of their government. Insurgents have secured good many Mauser rifles, a few field pieces and quick firing guns, with ammunition, during last month.

OTIS.

MANILA. (Received February 5, 1899—10.55 p. m.)

ADJUTANT-GENERAL, *Washington:*

February 5. Have established our permanent lines well out, and have driven off and punished the insurgents severely. The troops have conducted themselves with great heroism. The country about Manila is peaceful and the city perfectly quiet. List of casualties to-morrow.

OTIS.

MANILA. (Received February 6, 1899—1.12 a. m.)

ADJUTANT-GENERAL, *Washington:*

Situation most satisfactory; no apprehension need be felt; perfect quiet prevails in city and vicinity. List of casualties being prepared and will be forwarded soon as possible. Troops in excellent health and spirits.

OTIS.

MANILA. (Received February 6, 1899—1.40 a. m.)

ADJUTANT-GENERAL, *Washington:*

Following deaths since last report: January 28, Royal E. Fletcher, private, B, First Washington, typhoid fever. January 29, Albert W. Alson, private, B, Thirteenth Minnesota, variola; Walter Dugard, private, G, First Idaho, typhoid fever. January 30, Isaac Cooper, private, B, Twentieth Kansas, variola. February 1, Burgher R. Jones, private, F, Twenty-third Infantry, variola; Charles Snodgrass, private, B, Twentieth Kansas, variola; Fred. Maxwell, private, K, Twentieth Kansas, variola. February 3, James Owen, private, L, Third Artillery, variola; Miles E. Kyger, corporal, I, First Washington, typhoid fever; Chester W. Hubbard, private, K, Third Artillery, variola; Olavus T. Felland, private, M, First South Dakota, variola. February 4, Pearl Doty, private, B, Second Oregon, variola.

OTIS.

AFFAIRS IN THE PHILIPPINE ISLANDS. 895

MANILA. (Received February 6, 1899—12.21 p. m.)
ADJUTANT-GENERAL, *Washington:*

Following casualties in First Brigade, First Division: Tenth Pennsylvania, Maj. E. Brierer, flesh wound, arm, slight; Lieut. Albert J. Buttermore, flesh wound, slight; Company H, Sergt. Joseph Sheldon, slight flesh wound, thigh; Private Hiram Conger, abdomen penetrated, serious; D, Private Edward Caldwell, lung penetrated, serious; C, Private Debalt, flesh wound, back, slight. First Montana, H, Private Reynolds, slight wound in ear; Private Charles Rummels, flesh wound in leg, slight; Corporal Hayes, missing, probably killed; L, Private John Serenson, head wounded, probably dead; I, Private Mayersick, lungs penetrated, serious; Corpl. I. Skinner, slight thigh wound. First Colorado, B, Private Orton Twever, wounded, left thigh; Private Charles S. Morrison, wounded, left hand; Private Maurice Parkhurst, wounded in pubes; D, Private C. D. White, missing, supposedly drowned; I, Private Elmer F. Doran, killed, shot in chest; Corpl. William H. Earle, wounded in left cheek and arm; L, Private Charles Carlson, killed, shot in head; Private Charles B. Boyce, flesh wound in left knee; First Lieut. Charles Haughwount, flesh wound in left knee. First South Dakota, H, Private Horace J. McCrancken, killed; I, Private Fred. E. Green, killed; Private Wm. Z. Lewis, killed; Private Benj. Phelps, wounded, right thigh; K, Corpl. Eugene E. Stevens, wounded in right thigh; G, Private Frank G. McLain, wounded in right hip; I, Private Hiram Fay, wounded in right knee; F, Corpl. Carl H. Osgood, sprained knee; I, Private A. Haskell, slight wound in neck. Third Artillery, L, Sergt. Bernard Sharp, flesh wound leg, slight; Private Orian Ryan, shot in head, serious; Private Edward Lundstrom, shot through hand, slight; Private James Gleason, flesh wound, thigh, slight.

Further reports will follow.

OTIS.

MANILA. (Received February 6, 1899—12.53 p. m.)
ADJUTANT-GENERAL, *Washington:*

Additional casualties: Killed in action—Fourteenth Infantry, Corpls. Guy B. Soden, E, and Henry F. Thompson, M; Privates Jesse A. Hale, A; Maurice L. Seeman, A; Louis V. Dietz, D; James Harvey Knight, Charles W. Douglass, Frank H. Issinghausen, Charles A. Seitz and Alphonso Bonner, M; Peter M. Storment, I. Sixth Artillery, Private W. A. Goodman, D. First Idaho, Maj. Ed. McConville, Corpl. Frank R. Calwerel, B; Private James Frazer, C. First California, Privates J. J. Dewar, K; Tom Bryan, H; Joseph Maher, M. First Washington, Corpl. George W. McGowan, A; Privates Ralph W. Simonds, A; George B. Reichart, Frank Smith, and Matthias H. Cherry, E; Sherman Harding and Edward H. Perry, I; Walter N. Hanson, L; Arno H. Maickel, H. Wounded in action—Fourteenth Infantry, Sergt. Samuel E. Boakler, I; Corpl. James Neary, M; Musician Joseph W. Osberger, M; Privates Dixon A. Everett, A; Michael Kennedy and Augustin Berry, F; Benjamin A. Harbour, Hugh P. McClellan, Herman Steinhagen and O. B. Wright, I; William Sloat, K; Arthur L. Osleurn, Richard Hughes, and Albert E. Barth, M. Died of wounds—Lieut. James Mitchell, Fourteenth Infantry, at 12 p. m. February 6; Private George W. Hall, G, First Idaho. Col. Wm. C. Smith, First Tennessee, died apoplexy at head of his command on firing line February 5.

OTIS.

ADJUTANT-GENERAL'S OFFICE,
Washington, February 6, 1899.

General OTIS, *Manila:*

What number of Spanish prisoners in your hands will have to be provided for transportation under treaty?

CORBIN.

MANILA. (Received February 7, 1899—2.48 a. m.)
ADJUTANT-GENERAL, *Washington:*
Preparing to capture Iloilo. Conditions and business interests demand it. Unless ordered to contrary, will proceed.

OTIS.

MANILA. (Received February 7, 1899—4 20 a. m.)
ADJUTANT-GENERAL, *Washington:*
Positive insurgent attack not ordered by insurgent government, which has shown inability to control army concentrated around Manila from Luzon provinces, numbering over 20,000, possessing several quick-firing and Krupp field guns; good portion of enemy armed with Mausers, latest pattern. Two Krupp and great many rifles captured. Insurgents fired great quantity ammunition. Quite a number of Spanish soldiers in insurgent service who served artillery. Insurgents constructed strong intrenchments near our lines, mostly in bamboo thickets; these our men charged, killed or capturing many of the enemy. Our casualties probably aggregate 250. Full reports to-day. Casualties of insurgents very heavy. Have buried some 500 of their dead and hold 500 prisoners. Their loss, killed, wounded, and prisoners, probably 4,000. Took waterworks, pumping station, yesterday, 6 miles out. Considerable skirmishing with enemy, which made no stand. Pumps damaged; will be working in week. Have number of condensers set up in city, which furnish good water. Troops in excellent spirits. Quiet prevails.

OTIS.

MANILA. (Received February 7, 1899—5.40 a. m.)
ADJUTANT-GENERAL, *Washington:*
Spanish prisoners war surrendered August 13 to United States, 5,600 officers and enlisted men; still present, 3,801. To Spain will send 180 officers and 1,800 enlisted men on 11th instant. Ignorant terms of treaty and class prisoners United States stipulates to deport.

OTIS.

WAR DEPARTMENT, *Washington, February 7, 1899.*
OTIS, *Manila:*
The President is satisfied to leave occupation of Iloilo to the judgment of yourself and Dewey.

ALGER, *Secretary of War.*

MANILA. (Received February 7, 1899—2.38 p. m.)
ADJUTANT-GENERAL, *Washington:*
Additional casualties: Utah Light Artillery—killed, Battery A, Sergt. Harry A. Young, Corpl. John G. Young, Private Wilhelm I. Goodman; slightly wounded, B, Corpl. George B. Wardlaw, Private Peter Anderson. First Washington—wounded slightly, Capt. Albert H. Otis, First Lieut. Edward K. Irwin, Second Lieut. Joe Smith, Q. M. Sergts. Rufus B. Clark and Oliver Clancy; Company A, Corpls. Kendall Fellowes, Charles F. Deloga, John F. Mitchell, Fred W. Schander, James A. Timewell; I, Corpl. Miles M. McDougall; seriously wounded, A, Privates Joseph E. Dougherty, James F. Greik, John C. Kline, Richard H. McLean, Oscar Sowards; D, William C. Hopwood, Nicholas C. Polly; E, Walter P. Fox; G, George M. Duncan,

William J. Hays; I, Ernest H. A. Fischer; L, John Pruitt; M, Jesse M. Morgan, Civilian J. B. Weatherby, cook; slightly wounded, A, Privates William E. Everett, William R. Fait, Otto H. Hoppe, Albert W. Owen, Frank Rivers; B, Lawrin L. Lawson, Albert F. Pray; C, Augustus Zeloder; E, Herbert E. Osborn; I, Mira Cusker, Rolla Proudfoot; M, Joseph P. Bernier, Wesley Walton; G, George McNeil, William J. Hayes; M, Daniel Camgobell; killed, E, Private Ralph E. Shearer. First Idaho—wounded, Company C, Musician Frederick W. Beck, Privates Fred. H. Streeter, Howard Hallor, Thomas P. Burke; B, John Switzens; G, Will C. Payne; B, Frank A. McCall; H, James Hansen; F, Lewis B. Beach; G, Harry Rutherford, Fred Shell; B, William M. Keller; Q. M. Sergt. Ernest Scott; C, Privates James Payne, Piley Walton; B, Robert Jones; F, Enoch Koth; G, Sidney Bailey. Twentienth Kansas—wounded, Company F, Chas. A. Hammond, Privates Daniel Conway, William Nelson; M, George M. Battersly. First California—wounded, Company A, Corpl. John Murphy, Privates John Slade; G, A. F. Sherer; M, Sergt. William L. Wall; I, Privates David A. Cutting; F, William Hogue; H, Oscar H. Heimroth, William A. Rogers, Richard Jentzen, First Lieut. Charles J. Hogan. First Wyoming—killed, C, Sergt. George Rogers; wounded, C, Sergt. Rogers, Private Ray Wiedeer. First Nebraska—wounded, C, First Sergt. Orren F. Curtis, Corpl. Henry Epp, Musician James Pierce; A, Corpl. Harry L. Hull; B, Privates John L. Bronson; F, Harry Brown; I, William Madox; K, Condrad Egan, Simon J. Simonson; L, James P. McKinney; M, Hugh Kenoyer, Howard L. Kerr; killed, L, Charles Ballanger; I, Privates Lewis Pegler; F, Egger. Sixth Artillery—wounded, Battery D, Private Jesse G. Lowerberg; Hospital Corps—wounded, Acting Hospital Steward Frank L. Hemstead. Third Artillery—killed, Battery G, Corporal Dean, K, Sergeant Whittaker; wounded, G, Privates Albert J. Corbert; E, Neimeyer E. Clampitt, Sergt. William McQuade, Privates Roscoe L. Mitchell; K, Andrew Johnson; M, George S. Schulemrie, David Krider, Holmer E. Hawkins, Christ E. Ploeger, John A. Gray, Second Lieut. Robert S. Abernethy. Discharged soldiers still with regiments—wounded, Isaac Russel, Battery A, Utah Artillery; George L. Clother, Company B, First Nebraska; Douglas L. Bridges, Company F, First Nebraska; Emmett H. A. Fisher, unknown. Tenth Pennsylvania—killed, C, Corpl. Jacob Landis; C, Private Allen B. Rockwell; wounded, D, James Kessler.

OTIS.

EXECUTIVE MANSION,
Washington, February 7, 1899—12.36 p. m.

OTIS and DEWEY, *Manila:*

Congratulations to you and your brave officers and men on your decisive victory. You have won an added title to the confidence and gratitude of your country.

WILLIAM MCKINLEY.

WAR DEPARTMENT, *February 7, 1899.*

Major-General OTIS, *Manila:*

Accept my best congratulations upon your magnificent victory of Sunday, all the more creditable because you were not the aggressor.

ALGER, *Secwar.*

EXECUTIVE MANSION,
Washington, February 7, 1899—12.40 p. m.

OTIS, *Manila:*

Have you or Dewey copy of treaty?

ALGER, *Secretary War.*

ADJUTANT-GENERAL'S OFFICE,
Washington, February 7, 1899—4 p. m.

General OTIS, *Manila:*

Following is contained in the text of the treaty ratified yesterday. Full text and appendices by mail.

CORBIN.

[Here follows part of treaty.]

MANILA. (Received February 7, 1899—11.41 p. m.)

SECRETARY WAR, *Washington:*

Sincere thanks for congratulations. All credit due to hearty response of troops to orders of officers.

OTIS.

MANILA. (Received February 8, 1899—1.58 a. m.)

ADJUTANT-GENERAL, *Washington:*

Situation rapidly improving. Reconnoissance yesterday, to south several miles, to east to Laguna de Bay, to northeast 8 miles, driving straggling insurgent troops in various directions, encountering no decided opposition. Army disintegrated and natives returning to village displaying white flag. Near Caloocan, 6 miles north, enemy made stand behind intrenchments, charged by Kansas troops, led by Colonel Funston, close encounter resulting in rout of enemy with very heavy loss. Loss to Kansas, Lieutenant Alford, killed; 6 men wounded. Night of 4th, Aguinaldo issued flying proclamation charging Americans with initiative and declared war. Sunday issued another, calling all to resist foreign invasion. His influence throughout this section destroyed. Now applies for cessation of hostilities and conference. Have declined to answer. Insurgent expectation of rising in city on night of 4th unrealized. Provost marshal-general with admirable disposition of troops defeated every attempt. City quiet. Business resumed. Natives respectful and cheerful. The fighting qualities of American troops a revelation to all inhabitants.

OTIS.

MANILA. (Received February 8, 1899—10.22 p. m.)

ADJUTANT-GENERAL, *Washington:*

Additional casualties: Twentieth Kansas—killed, First Lieut. Alfred C. Alford; Company M, Private Charles E. Pratt; wounded, B, Artificer Charles A. Kelson, Privates Dan Hewitt, John Gillilan; D, Raymond Clark; I, Sergt. Jay Sheldon, Privates Wm. A. McGraw, Ernest Fritz; M, Edward Ziebel. Fourteenth Infantry—killed, M, Privates Ransom Clase, Newton Henry; wounded, A, Privates Frank A. Goodon; B, Hans Jensen; D, Elmer D. Hough; C, Nicholas N. Foulks; D, Corpl. Manford Bennington, Privates John Brady; I, William S. Kennedy, Charles A. Clanton; G, Corpls. Spencer K. Lipscomb, Howard Middleton, Privates, John Carey, Patrick Horgan, Charles Read, Fred Goezenback; K, John Powers, William Howard, James Kane, Jerry A. Heckathorn; M, James Miller. First Idaho—killed, G, Private Orian L. Darras; wounded, D, Sergt. William Teller, Privates John N. Lutjens; C, James Ryan; B, Richard B. Jones. First California—wounded, Company E, Privates David J. Sinclair; G, Frank Aust; K, Henry M. Kalkins. First Washington—wounded, Private (M) John J. Carlile, Corpl. Charles C. Augstein; missing, Private Oval F. Gibson. First Montana—wounded, H, Private George W.

Rowland. Third Artillery—killed, Battery G, Private Braney Haag; wounded, L, Sergt. D. C. Sissenouth; G, Privates Herman Hansen, A. D. Philo; K, John Stadleman; wounded, Battery D, Private Robert B. Pstrom[?]. First Wyoming—wounded, Company F, Private Harry E. Crumrine.

OTIS.

ADJUTANT-GENERAL'S OFFICE,
Washington, D. C., February 8, 1899.

General OTIS, Manila:

Complaints are made that New York Herald correspondent is discriminated against; of course all should be treated alike.

CORBIN.

MANILA. (Received February 9, 1899—7 a. m.)

ADJUTANT-GENERAL, Washington:

Should our operations extend to southern islands, another signal company greatly needed.

OTIS.

ADJUTANT-GENERAL'S OFFICE,
Washington, February 9, 1899.

General OTIS, Manila:

Secretary War orders transfer 60 suitable volunteers to Signal Corps. Have Thompson organize Nineteenth Signal Company, selecting noncommissioned officers largely from First and Eighteenth companies.

CORBIN.

MANILA. (Received February 9, 1899—8 a. m.)

ADJUTANT-GENERAL, Washington:

Instructions to Miller last night to occupy Iloilo. First Tennessee sent. Shall learn results 14th instant. San Roque, adjoining Cavite, occupied to-day. Insurgents endeavoring to collect force few miles north of Manila. Aguinaldo there in person. Affairs in city quiet. Inhabitants in surrounding villages ask American protection.

OTIS.

MANILA. (Received February 9, 1899—11.07 a. m.)

ADJUTANT-GENERAL, Washington:

Additional casualties: Thirteenth Minnesota—wounded, Company M, Private Alexander F. Burns. First Montana—wounded, C, Private Lester Pierestoff. First Nebraska—killed, B, Artificer Gustave E. Edlund; F, Privates William Philpot; M, H. G. Livingston; wounded, A, Privates Charles Keckley; B, George L. Clother; Robert E. Childers; C, Fred Kuhn; E, Oral F. Gibson; F, Douglas T Bridges; H, Harry Seabrooke; K, Grant Boyd; L, Francis Hanson; M, Moro C. Shiperd, Daniel Campbell. Third Artillery—wounded, Battery K, Privates James J. Grateg; L, James T. Leahy. First Colorado—wounded, Company A, Private Clyde E. McVay. Fourteenth Infantry—wounded, Private William Bush. Total casualties resulting from all engagements since evening of February 4, aggregate 268, as follows: Killed, 3 officers, 56 enlisted men; wounded, 8 officers, 199 enlisted men; missing, 2 enlisted men.

OTIS.

MANILA. (Received February 9, 1899—11.56 p. m.)

ADJUTANT-GENERAL, *Washington:*

Cass White, D, First Colorado, body recovered from river; shot in head.

OTIS.

MANILA. (Received February 10, 1899—10.15 p. m.)

ADJUTANT-GENERAL, *Washington:*

February 10, insurgents collected considerable force between Manila and Caloocan, where Aguinaldo reported to be, and threatened attack and uprising in city. This afternoon swung left of MacArthur's division, which is north of Pasig River, into Caloocan, driving enemy easy. Our left now at Caloocan. Our loss slight. That of insurgents considerable. Particulars in morning. Attack preceded by one-half hour's firing from two of Admiral Dewey's vessels.

OTIS.

PORT SAID, EGYPT, *February 11, 1899.*
(Received 9.47 a. m.)

CORBIN, *Washington:*

Arrived noon. Voyage safe; pleasant. No serious illness. Fourteen cases mumps, ten measles, developed since Gibraltar. Sick doing well. Coal here. Leave to-night. Inform Quartermaster-General. Wire us news Suez.

LAWTON.

ADJUTANT-GENERAL'S OFFICE,
Washington, February 11, 1899.

General LAWTON, *Suez:*

Treaty ratified. Insurgents in the Philippines attacked General Otis, resulting in general engagement; enemy routed. Our loss some 300 killed and wounded. The enemy's loss many times more than ours. MacArthur's division had a very successful engagement yesterday. Give honorable discharge to Thomas Hardy, Company C, Seventeenth Infantry; requested by British Government.

H. C. CORBIN.

MANILA. (Received February 11, 1899—9.40 a. m.)

ADJUTANT-GENERAL, *Washington:*

MacArthur's division is north of Pasig River. Yesterday his left wing, Otis's brigade, which had been refused, made partial wheel to right, resting left of brigade on Caloocan. Insurgents in considerable force were sharply driven, leaving good many dead. Our casualties as follows: Killed, Private John A. Gibbons, Hospital Corps; Private Alonzo Rickets, Company I, Twentieth Kansas Volunteer Infantry; Private Fred Hall, Company I, First Montana Volunteer Infantry. Wounded, First Montana Volunteer Infantry, Lieut. Col. R. B. Wallace; Privates Thomas Maloy, Company K; Zeth H. Dibble, Company D; Everett Metcalf, Company B; Joseph Crafer, Company F; William J. Borthwick, Company G; Clarence Briggs, Company H; Capt. W. L. Hill; Privates Henry G. Reynolds, Company D; John C. Bullan, Company A; James W. Kennedy, Company G; Delos D. Babcock, Company G;

Carl J. Peterson, Company G; John W. Campbell, Company M. Third Artillery, Private Oscar Portwich, Battery G; Jeremy R. Cleveland, Battery H; Leo Heisler, Battery H; Bert M. Dorton, Battery K; Corpl. David C. McKelvey, Battery K; Privates Jerry Kramer, Battery H; James Leonard, Battery K; Rufus B. Blume, Battery K. Twentieth Kansas Volunteer Infantry, Corpl. Edward D. Willing, Company B; Private Harry S. Harris, Company B; James S. Mills, Company E; David M. Horkman, Company H; Privates I. J. Howard, Company B; Elmer E. Unie, Company B; William C. Barber, Company E; Bert Sanson, Company K. First Idaho Volunteer Infantry, Private James R. Willard, Company D. Thirteenth Minnesota Volunteer Infantry, Private Ben Ohtan, Company L. Troops in excellent condition; supplied with all necessities; hospitals, notwithstanding wounded, have fewer patients than before engagements of 4th and 5th instant. In yesterday's engagement most successful. Belief of old residents that Aguinaldo will be unable to gather in future any considerable force.

OTIS.

MANILA. (Received February 11, 1899—11.59 a. m.)

ADJUTANT-GENERAL, *Washington:*

Additional casualties: First South Dakota—wounded, Sergt. William H. Lock, Company G. Third Artillery—wounded, Private B. L. Patzker, Battery K. Utah Artillery—wounded, Corpl. Andrew Peterson, Battery B. First Montana—wounded, Second Lieut. William Gardenhire, Company F; Privates William Kennedy, Company G; Harry Slack, B; Percy G. Bullard, C; G. W. Boardman, A; J. M. Box, D; David Burns, M; Frank Gotti, I. Twentieth Kansas—wounded, Privates John O. Morse, Company K; Sydney Morrison, M. First Idaho—killed, Private Harry McClure, Company H; wounded, Capt. T. R. Hamer; Corpl. Howard Barkley, Company E.

OTIS.

ADJUTANT-GENERAL'S OFFICE,
Washington, February 11, 1899.

OTIS, *Manila:*

Can khaki suits, Jones's estimate, be procured advantageously Manila, or be sent from States? Will all forage have to be shipped from States, or can you arrange for supply cheaper from Australia? Are the 50 two-horse wagons your telegram required, in addition to 36 delivery wagons, Jones's estimate? Ninety-five thousand pounds oats shipped on *Tacoma.*

CORBIN.

ADJUTANT-GENERAL'S OFFICE,
Washington, February 11, 1899.

General OTIS, *Manila:*

Chinese Government anxious as to safety of Chinese in Philippines. Please extend them all practicable protection.

CORBIN.

MANILA. (Received February 12, 1899—2.55 a. m.)

ADJUTANT-GENERAL, *Washington:*

Am protecting Chinese where possible; most danger in Manila and Jolo islands, which can not be reached at present. Had regular troops left United States on dates stated in your dispatch of December 29, we ought soon turn in that direction.

OTIS.

MANILA. (Received February 12, 1899—3 a. m.)
ADJUTANT-GENERAL, *Washington:*
Have contracts with Shanghai and Hongkong houses for 50,000 khaki uniforms, 20,000 to be delivered in March, rest within four months; have 10,000 white uniform suits delivered. No khaki or white uniforms required from United States, only 50 two-horse wagons required. Inquiries concerning Australian forage unsatisfactory. Baled hay should be shipped from United States, cheaper than forage to be gathered here, which only suits native ponies. Large amount originally shipped on *Tacoma* should not have been taken off. Have oats here now to last few months.
OTIS.

MANILA. (Received February 12, 1899—8.04 a. m.)
ADJUTANT-GENERAL, *Washington:*
Additional casualties: Fourteenth Infantry—wounded, Privates Bernhart C. Hensel, William P. H. Ransom, Company F. First Idaho—wounded, Private M. W. Koskela, Company F. Utah Artillery—wounded, Private Charles B. Hill, Battery B. Third Artillery—killed, Private Fred. Good, Battery K. Thirteenth Minnesota—wounded, Privates James Hartley, William C. Fitch, Company D. First Montana—wounded, Private Thomas Malloy, Company K. First California—killed, Privates Anton B. Nilson, Guy V. Packer, Company C. Fourth Cavalry—wounded, Private James Thorsen, Troop E. Twentieth Kansas—wounded, Private Alexander M. Mitchell, Company B. Private Frank Gaut, Company I, First Montana, reported missing yesterday, has reported to his company commander.
OTIS.

MANILA. (Received February 12, 1899—10.27 a. m.)
ADJUTANT-GENERAL, *Washington:*
Reported that insurgent representative at Washington telegraphed Aguinaldo to drive out Americans before arrival reenforcements. The dispatch received Hongkong and mailed Malolos, which decided on attack to be made about 7th instant. Eagerness of insurgent troops to engage precipitated battle. Very quiet to-day on lines from Caloocan on north to Panay on south. Yesterday small reconnoitering party 12 miles south city fired on two men, slightly wounded. Two insurgents, with arms, captured. Affair of 10th, MacArthur's Division, very successful. Enemy's loss considerable; have collected 70 dead bodies; more not yet discovered. Insurgents reported to be gathering force 12 miles north on railway, but evidently perplexed. If regular troops en route were here could probably end war or all determined active opposition in twenty days.
OTIS.

SUEZ, EGYPT. (Received February 12, 1899—5.25 p. m.)
CORBIN, *Washington:*
Wait here until to-morrow morning for several men left at Port Said.
LAWTON.

MANILA. (Received February 13, 1899—1 a. m.)
ADJUTANT-GENERAL, *Washington:*
Surgeon reports Colonel Wallace out of danger; temperature, pulse, respiration normal. Thank you and Schwan for congratulations. Everything quiet this morning; business in city resuming former activity.
OTIS.

AFFAIRS IN THE PHILIPPINE ISLANDS.

MANILA. (Received February 13, 1899—3.10 a.m.)

ADJUTANT-GENERAL, *Washington:*

Following deaths since last report, not including those killed in action: February 4, Victor E. Schofield, private, I, First South Dakota, variola. February 6, Michael P. Crowley, private, D, Second Oregon, dysentery; John C. Marrior, private, K, Third Artillery, suppurative tonsilitis; James A. Garvey, private, A, First Tennessee, variola. February 8, Daniel T. Kyger, private, I, First Washington, typhoid fever. February 10, Charles Lillie, private, I, First Colorado, acute diarrhea. From gunshot wounds in action: February 8, Jay Sheldon, sergeant, I, Twentieth Kansas; Wm. C. Hopwood, private, D, First Washington. February 11, I. J. Howard, private, B, Twentieth Kansas.

OTIS.

MANILA. (Received February 13, 1899—2.17 p.m.)

ADJUTANT-GENERAL, *Washington:*

Additional casualties, engagement at Caloocan, February 10: Twentieth Kansas—wounded, Capt. Charles M. Christy, Company E; Corpl. James W. Kershner, A; Private Charles Bennett, M. First Montana, wounded, Sergt. George E. Lowman, Company D; Private Adolph T. Charette, A. Following casualties in trenches at Malolos, night 12th and morning 13th: First Montana—wounded, Private Steve Stevens, Company G; Charles Brinton, B; Joseph Callahan, M. Utah Artillery—wounded, Second Lieut. George A. Seaman, Battery B. Twentieth Kansas—wounded, Private Ira M. Payne, Company A. First California—wounded, February 6, Private Edward J. O'Neil, Company E. Morseberg, Twentieth Kansas, reported February 11, should read Morse. All foregoing slightly wounded.

OTIS.

NEW YORK, *February 13, 1899.* (Received 4.15 p.m.)

Adjutant-General CORBIN, *Washington:*

Storm here almost unprecedented. Hopkins just from *Sheridan*. She is nearly ready, but would be too cold for troops while storm lasts. Kimball just here. He says ship ought not to leave port for twenty-four hours after storm abates, on account of heavy sea; neither can men go aboard safely until storm abates. I suggest troops leave Columbus early to-morrow and take the chances.

R. A. ALGER, *Secretary of War.*

CUMBERLAND, MD., *February 13, 1899.*
(Received 5.14 p.m.)

ADJUTANT-GENERAL OF THE ARMY, *Washington, D. C.:*

Twelfth Infantry delayed by storm. Men well provided for. Inform Commissary-General have rations for Tuesday and Wednesday.

SMITH, *Lieutenant-Colonel, Commanding.*

MANILA. (Received February 13, 1899—11.50 p.m.)

ADJUTANT-GENERAL, *Washington:*

General Miller reports from Iloilo that town taken 11th instant and held by troops. Insurgents given until evening of 11th to surrender, but their hostile action brought on engagement during morning. Insurgents fired native portion of town, but little loss to property of foreign inhabitants. No casualties among United States troops reported.

OTIS.

MANILA. (Received February 14, 1899—4.22 a. m.)
ADJUTANT-GENERAL, *Washington:*
One hundred eighty officers, 1,800 men, Spanish prisoners war, left port, 12th and 13th instant, by steamers *Reina Cristina* and *Uruguay* en route to Spain. Can awards on Didi, opened Washington, 4th instant, be communicated?

OTIS.

CUMBERLAND, MD., *February 14, 1899.*
(Received 1.05 p. m.)
ADJUTANT-GENERAL OF ARMY, *Washington, D. C.:*
Twelfth Infantry still blocked here. Third section will arrive from West this afternoon, and all may get off to-morrow. One case of measles. Am providing hot meals for men. Very comfortable here.

SMITH, *Lieutenant-Colonel, Commanding.*

ADJUTANT-GENERAL'S OFFICE,
Washington, D. C., February 14, 1899.
COMMANDING OFFICER, SEVENTEENTH INFANTRY,
Columbus Barracks, Ohio:
Following telegram received from Secretary of War, dated New York, February 13: "*Sheridan* is nearly ready. Ship ought not to leave port for twenty-four hours after storm abates on account of heavy sea; neither can men go aboard safely until storm abates. I suggest troops leave Columbus early 14th." Twelfth Infantry, in three sections, is about twelve hours from New York. Confer with railroad officials and take train for New York as soon as possible, wiring this office and Colonel Jones, New York City, hour of departure and number men, officers, and families.

H. C. CORBIN, *Adjutant-General.*

COLUMBUS, OHIO, *February 14, 1899.*
(Received 5.58 p. m.)
ADJUTANT-GENERAL, U. S. ARMY, *Washington, D. C.:*
Headquarters, noncommissioned staff, band, Companies A, C, E, and F, Seventeenth Infantry, and detachment Hospital Corps, 15 officers and 479 enlisted men, leave at 9 p. m. for New York. Officers' families—4 wives, two children under 5; enlisted men's families—5 wives, two children under 5, and two over 5.

O'BRIEN, *Commanding.*

MANILA. (Received February 15, 1899—3.20 a. m.)
ADJUTANT-GENERAL, *Washington:*
Cablegram 6th should read Chester W. Hubbard, K, Second Oregon,

OTIS.

MANILA. (Received February 15, 1899—9.35 a. m.)
ADJUTANT-GENERAL, *Washington:*
Twentieth Kansas, wounded, 12th instant, engagement Caloocan: Sergt. Ira Keithley, Company D, slight. First California, wounded by desultory firing yesterday: Privates Allan Brant, severe; Albert Eggerm, slight; Ray L. Hursh, Company C, slight; William C. Walsh, severe; Sergt. William F. Dunne, severe; Corpl. Henry Ritter, H, slight. Lieut. Edwin A. Harting, First South Dakota, drowned last night while attempting to land a Hotchkiss at Pasig.

OTIS.

DEPARTMENT OF STATE, *Washington, February 15, 1899.*
The Honorable, the SECRETARY OF WAR.

SIR: I have the honor to apprise you of the receipt of a telegram from the consul of the United States at Gibraltar, dated February 15, 1899, reading as follows: "*Sherman* arrived."

I have the honor to be, sir, your obedient servant,

JOHN HAY.

ADJUTANT-GENERAL'S OFFICE,
Washington, February 15, 1899—2.30 p. m.

General OTIS, *Manila:*

Sherman reached Gibraltar to-day. *Sheridan* leaves New York to-morrow.

CORBIN.

CHICAGO, ILL., *February 15, 1899.*
(Received 12.20 p. m.)

ADJUTANT-GENERAL, U. S. ARMY, *Washington, D. C.:*

Headquarters, band, noncommissioned staff, Companies A, C, E, and F, Seventeenth Infantry, and detachment Hospital Corps, 15 officers, 479 enlisted men, left Columbus for New York last night.

M. V. SHERIDAN,
Brigadier-General, U. S. Volunteers, Commanding.

ADJUTANT-GENERAL'S OFFICE,
Washington, February 16, 1899.

General OTIS, *Manila:*

Instruct all commanders to forward casualty returns also by mail.

H. C. CORBIN.

MANILA. (Received February 17, 1899—9.40 a. m.)

ADJUTANT-GENERAL, *Washington:*

First California, wounded, in skirmish at Pateros, 14th: Private Harry W. Fawke, C, cheek, slight; Corpl. Oscar C. Nelson, C, chest, slight; Private W. A. Cornish, H, thigh, slight. Wounded from desultory firing, 15th and 16th: Private Howard H. Holland, Company D, First Washington, shoulder, slight; Ralph Wintler, Troop K, Fourth Cavalry, armpit, slight; Joseph J. Engberg, Battery H, Third Artillery, leg, slight, accidental. Wounded in engagement at Jaro, near Iloilo, Island of Panay, February 12: Second Lieut. Frank C. Bolles, Eighteenth Infantry, leg, severe; Corpl. Hugh Sparks, Company A, Eighteenth Infantry, shoulder and lung, serious; Private Fred Smith, Company A, Eighteenth Infantry, leg, slight.

OTIS.

PERIM, ARABIA, *February 17, 1899.*
(Received February 17, 1899—1.24 p. m.)

CORBIN, *Washington:*

Arrived this evening. Stop for coal only, leave before morning. Ideal voyage. Sick improving; 8 measles, 3 mumps, 2 meningitis; latter very light. Since last report, except meningitis, no serious illness. Will reach Colombo about 23d. Wire us.

LAWTON.

MANILA. (Received February 17, 1899—2.45 a. m.)
ADJUTANT-GENERAL, *Washington:*
Dispatches 7th, 8th, 13th, and 16th give full information casualties Washington regiment; all missing soldiers found. Insurgents have not made single capture.

OTIS.

ADJUTANT-GENERAL'S OFFICE,
Washington, February 17, 1899.

Colonel SMITH,
Commanding Twelfth Infantry, Care Army Building (Colonel Jones), New York City:
The Secretary of War desires the moment your troops are on board that you put to sea, as the importance of your early arrival at Manila is very great. Confer with Colonel Jones, of the Quartermaster Department, as to the necessities for the comfort of your voyage, and get away at earliest possible moment, reporting the hour of your departure.

H. C. CORBIN, *Adjutant-General.*

MANILA. (Received February 18, 1899—7.43 a. m.)
ADJUTANT-GENERAL, *Washington:*
Conditions follow: Troops occupy line well advanced in all directions from city with heavy interior police force; insurgents active, collecting force from different provinces; reported 5,000 on a line 5 miles south of city; much larger force 8 or 10 miles north and east; yesterday portion First Nebraska, Stotsenburg, encountered force north pumping station, 8 miles out, which it drove back 2 miles, killing 1 officer, 8 men, and capturing prisoners; Stotsenburg's casualties, 2 officers, 6 men wounded. Most barbarous order given inhabitants of city by insurgent government to rise en masse on night of 15th; the scheme defeated by activity provost-marshal, who has city well in hand; can hold ground, but not extend operations very much with present force.

OTIS.

MANILA. (Received February 18, 1899—10.35 a. m.)
ADJUTANT-GENERAL, *Washington:*
Casualties in skirmish on Mariquina road, north of pumping station, yesterday: First Nebraska—wounded, Company A, Privates Geo. M. Andrews, chest, forearm, and knee, died last night; Edward D. Day, head, severe; F, Charles E. Parks, right thigh, slight; G, John Williams, left elbow, severe; Sergt. Wilber E. Camp, left thigh, slight; F, First Sergt. H. Cook, neck, severe; C, Capt. Albert H. Hollingworth, wrist and thigh, severe; Second Lieut. Bert D. Whedon, right thigh, severe; Private Frank A. Huling, Company K, Twentieth Kansas, shot through knee yesterday, accidental, serious. Cable 11th, First Montana, wounded, James W. Kennedy and William Kennedy, G, identical, latter name error, shot right thigh, severe; Lieutenant Gardenhire, First Montana, wounded, is William Gardenhire, formerly private, G.

OTIS.

MANILA. (Received February 19, 1899—9.39 a. m.)
ADJUTANT-GENERAL, *Washington:*
Additional casualties: First Washington—wounded, 17th, Sergts. Reno D. Hoppe, slight; Leroy L. Childs, Company L, moderate; Corpl. Edward D. Smith, Private Edward L. Dwyer, wagoner; Henry Mullen, Company C, injured slightly, explo-

sion Springfield rifle on 17th instant. First Nebraska—wounded, 15th, Musician William H. Disbrow, Company H, severe, right thigh. Lieut. Bert D. Whedon, First Nebraska, doing well, "for Meiklejohn."

OTIS.

MANILA. (Received February 19, 1899—9.46 a. m.)
ADJUTANT-GENERAL, *Washington:*
Following deaths since last weekly report: February 5, Private Daniel E. White, C, Eighteenth Infantry, Iloilo, malarial fever and pneumonia; 11, Damian Grossman, C, First Washington, chronic diarrhea; 14, Com. Sergt. Arthur J. Smith, U. S. Army, retired, heart failure; 15, Corpl. Wilson M. Osborn, F, First South Dakota, variola; 17, Private Jacob Stassen, H, Twenty-third Infantry, heart failure under chloroform. Died of wounds received in action: 12, Privates Clarence G. Briggs, band, First Montana; Bruno L. Putzker, K, Third Artillery; 13, William B. Myersick, I, First Montana; 16, John J. Campbell, M, First Montana.

OTIS.

ADJUTANT-GENERAL'S OFFICE,
Washington, February 19, 1899—2 p. m.

General OTIS, *Manila:*
Acknowledging your cable of yesterday, Secretary War, with approval of the President, suggests that you continue to hold your forces well in hand and not extend your lines of occupation, except as they may be made necessary by local conditions, of which you must be the judge. What ports and places should, in your judgment, be early occupied by our forces? We should not occupy any faster than is necessary to our safety and control. Health of men is also a most important element to be considered. The six infantry regiments heretofore mentioned are all under way, *Sheridan* having left New York to-day. Recruits to fill regular regiments with you leave San Francisco this week. What more do you suggest in way of reenforcements, and what about return of volunteers on *Grant*, *Sherman*, and *Sheridan*, the transports bringing regulars?

CORBIN.

BROOKLYN, N. Y., *February 19, 1899.* (Received 4.25 p. m.)
ADJUTANT-GENERAL, U. S. Army,
Washington, D. C.:
Transport *Sheridan* sailed at 3 p. m. to-day, 1,792 enlisted men, 57 officers, and 56 wives and children, all well and send farewell.

J. H. SMITH,
Lieutenant-Colonel, Commanding Twelfth Infantry.

MANILA. (Received February 20, 1899—7 a. m.)
ADJUTANT-GENERAL, *Washington:*
Chaplain John R. Thompson, First Washington Infantry, died in hospital this city at 5.10 p. m., February 19, yesterday, of acute enterocolitis.

OTIS.

MANILA. (Received February 20, 1899—4.30 p. m.)

ADJUTANT-GENERAL, *Washington:*

Insurgents acknowledge Manila and outlying districts lost to them unless they dislodge our forces before arrival of reenforcements; therefore, making utmost effort to concentrate and attack, relying for assistance on simultaneous rising of inhabitants of city. Twentieth Infantry expected latter part of week; Twenty-second on 2d of March; transport *Grant*, March 4.

Our lines thin; no more extended than safety of entire city and waterworks system demand. Hold four regiments in city to suppress attempted interior violence. My long dispatch to Washington of November 27 last, in cipher, calling for regular troops, gives number of troops required to hold islands as 25,000; to conquer them 30,000 at least necessary, with continued assistance from Navy. Spanish abandonment of southern islands has rendered conditions there difficult. In Luzon, Manila, Dagupan, Aparri, and Legaspi should be occupied, and in the south, Iloilo, Cebu, Zamboanga, and Jolo as soon as practicable, with small garrisons at six other points. Volunteers can not be spared until conditions greatly changed. When United States able to furnish full protection, men of property and education will give adherence; now fear the assassin.

OTIS.

HEADQUARTERS DEPARTMENT OF THE PACIFIC AND EIGHTH ARMY CORPS,
Manila, P. I., January 12, 1899.
(Received February 20, 1899.)

The ADJUTANT-GENERAL, U. S. ARMY,
Washington, D. C.

SIR: Some time since I forwarded by cable information that the conservative men of the revolutionary government of the Filipinos had withdrawn from its councils, stating that they were unable to exert any further beneficial influence. I am of the impression that they were also influenced by apprehensions of personal danger.

The cabinet of President Aguinaldo resigned in a body, as it was not able to come to an agreement upon the terms of the proposed constitution. Aguinaldo's chief adviser, a man of very radical views, undertook to form a new cabinet, but found it impossible to secure the services of representative men. He finally succeeded in forming a provisional cabinet, composed of men of limited importance, and Aguinaldo called his congress, to which call the conservative members failed to respond, and therefore it was controlled by its radical element. Although many of the members who put in an appearance greatly desire to avoid any difficulty with the United States, and so declare themselves in private conversation, they fear to give public expression to their views. There were, however, a number who were unremitting in their secret endeavors to maintain peace. They approached me asking that I assist them to secure a conference with the United States authorities in order that they might work upon their congress in the interests of harmony. I replied through a civilian (an American citizen) that I would gladly meet any of the representative men of the Filipinos, and Aguinaldo himself, in their individual capacities, but was powerless to recognize the "de facto" government of which they boasted, or to receive any of its members in an official capacity. I further informed them that I would appoint a committee to meet a similar committee appointed by General Aguinaldo, commanding the revolutionary army, if such was their desire. They appealed to me to make some concession which they could use with their people in the interests of peace. Conditions were very fully explained to them, and while I discovered that they had a very fair understanding of affairs, they urged the difficulty of making their ignorant people understand them. The people had gone wild on the words "protection" and "independence," whereas the words "sovereignty," "annexation," and "United States control" served to excite them greatly. These gentlemen worked faithfully with the Malolos people, and finally I received a letter from Aguinaldo, of which the inclosed marked "Exhibit 1," is a translation, and to which I made reply, a copy of which is inclosed, marked "Exhibit 2." I appointed General Hughes, Colonel Smith, of the First California, and Lieutenant-Colonel Crowder, of the Judge-Advocate's Department, as members of the commission, and General Aguinaldo appointed two officers and a civilian of considerable judicial ability. A long conference ensued, in which the Filipino gentlemen failed to establish a single proposition for which they contended. The most amiable exchange of views was had and the result of the conference was beneficial. These Filipino gentlemen are still laboring for desired results and I think that another conference will be called. In the meantime affairs here are much strained. The insurgent army and city mobs view the quiet conduct of United States troops as a sign of weakness or fear and are very boastful of their prowess. In this lies the danger of the situation; and, should these insurgents, defying the orders of the Malolos government, bring on a conflict, a slaughter of their people will result. The troops are on the alert and well in hand.

I am of the opinion that some of our worst foes are those of our own household. I inclose an article cut from the Singapore Free Press of December 12 (Exhibit 3), which the insurgents declare was written by United States Consul Pratt, now on duty in that city. The better class of the insurgents have complained of this article, as it has had quite an exciting effect upon their people. The active intermeddling of other United States consuls has also given us considerable trouble. I inclose also copies of two proclamations issued by Aguinaldo. One was prepared and withdrawn by advice, I understand, and the second sent out—both of same date. A few copies of the one first prepared got into circulation after the second one was posted. I think that Aguinaldo was as pacific as he had the courage to be under the circumstances in which he found himself placed. He does not desire war, but finds it difficult to stem the dangerous current of excitement which he and his advisers have in motion.

Very respectfully, your obedient servant,

E. S. OTIS,
Major-General, U. S. Volunteers, Commanding.

EXHIBIT 1.

MALOLOS, *January 9, 1899.*

Maj. Gen. E. S. OTIS,
General of the American Forces of Occupation in Manila.

SIR: I have been informed, after the interview between the commissioners of my government and Mr. Carman, that there will be no inconvenience on your part in naming, as commanding general, representatives that will confer with those whom I will name for the same object.

Although it not being explained to me the reason why you could not treat with the commissioners of my government, I have the faculty for doing the same with those of the commanding general "who can not be recognized." Nevertheless, for the sake of peace, I have considered it advisable to name as "commanding general" a commission composed of the following gentlemen: Mr. Florentino Flores, Eufrasio Flores, and Manuel Arguelles, that they may together represent me and arrive at an accord with those whom you will name, with the object of using such methods as will normalize the actual situation created by the attitude of your Government and troops.

If you will deign to attend to said commissioners, and through these methods come to some understanding, "if only temporary," that will insure the peace and harmony amongst ourselves, the Filipino public would reach a grateful glory.

I am, yours, General, with the highest consideration.

Your most respected servant, EMILIO AGUINALDO.

EXHIBIT 2.

HEADQUARTERS DEPARTMENT OF THE PACIFIC AND EIGHTH ARMY CORPS,
Manila, P. I., January 9, 1899.

Gen. EMILIO AGUINALDO,
Commanding Revolutionary Force, Malolos, P. I.

GENERAL: I have the honor to acknowledge the receipt of your communication of to-day, and am much pleased at the action you have taken. I greatly regret that you have not a clear understanding of my position and motives, and trust that my explanation, assisted by the conference I have invited, will make them clear to you.

In my official capacity I am merely the agent of the United States Government to conduct its affairs under the limits which its Constitution, laws, precedents, and specific instructions prescribe. I have not the authority to recognize any national or civil power not already formally recognized by my Government, unless especially authorized so to do by the instructions of the Executive of the United States. For this reason I was unable to receive officially the representatives of the revolutionary government, and endeavored to make that inability clear to the distinguished gentlemen with whom I had the pleasure to converse a few evenings since. You will bear witness that my course throughout my entire official connection with affairs here has been consistent, and it has pained me that I have not been able to receive and answer communications of the cabinet officers of the government at Malolos, fearing that I might be erroneously charged with lack of courtesy. Permit me now briefly, General, to speak of the serious misunderstanding which exists between the Philippine people and the representatives of the United States Government, and which I hope that our commissioners, by thorough discussion, may be able to dispel. I sincerely believe that all desire peace and harmony, and yet by the machinations of evil-disposed persons we have been influenced to think that we occupy the position of adversaries. The Filipinos appear to be of the opinion that we meditate attack, while I am under the strict orders of the President of the United States to avoid conflict in every way possible. My troops, witnessing the earnestness, the comparatively disturbed and unfriendly attitude of the revolutionary troops and many of the citizens of Manila, conclude that active hostilities have been determined upon, although it must be clearly within the comprehension of unprejudiced and reflecting minds that the welfare and happiness of the Philippine people depend upon the friendly protection of the United States. The hand of Spain was forced, and she has acknowledged before the world that all her claimed rights in this country have departed by due process of law. This treaty acknowledgment, with the conditions which accompany it, awaits ratification of the Senate of the United States, and the action of its Congress must also be secured before the Executive of that Government can proclaim a definite policy. That policy must conform to the will of the people of the United States, expressed through its representatives in Congress. For that action the Philippine people should wait, at least before severing the existing friendly relations. I am governed by a desire to further the interests of the Philippine people and shall continue to labor with that end in view. There shall be no conflict of forces if I am able to avoid it, and still I shall endeavor to maintain a position to meet all emergencies that may arise.

Permit me to subscribe myself, General, with highest respect,
  Your most obedient servant,
                    E. S. OTIS,
       Major-General, U. S. Volunteers, Commanding.

The government of the Philippines has considered it its duty to set forth to the civilized powers the facts determining the rupture of its amicable relations with the Army of the United States of America in these islands to the end that they may thereby reach the conviction that I, for my part, have done everything possible to avoid it, although at the cost of many rights uselessly sacrificed.

After the naval combat which occurred on May 1 of last year, between the Spanish squadron and that of America, the commander of the latter consented to my return from Hongkong to this beloved soil, and he distributed among the Filipinos some rifles found in the arsenal at Cavite, doubtless with the intention of reestablishing the revolution, somewhat quieted by the convention of Biacnabato, in order to have the Filipinos on his side.

The people, influenced by the declaration of war between the United States and Spain, understood the necessity of fighting for its liberty, feeling sure that Spain would be destroyed and rendered incapable of leading it along the road to prosperity and progress. The Filipinos hailed my advent with joy, and I had the honor of being proclaimed leader on account of the services which I had rendered in the former revolution. Then all the Filipinos, without distinction of classes, took arms, and every province hastened to expel from its frontiers the Spanish forces. This is the explanation of the fact that after the lapse of so short a period of time my government rules the whole of Luzon, the Visaya Islands, and a part of Mindanao.

Although the North Americans took no part in these military operations, which cost no little blood and gold, my government does not disavow the fact that the destruction of the Spanish squadron and the gift of some rifles from the arsenal to my people influenced the progress of our arms to some extent. It was also taken for granted that the American forces would necessarily sympathize with the revolution which they had managed to encourage, and which had saved them much blood and great hardships; and above all we entertained absolute confidence in the history and traditions of a people which fought for its independence and for the abolition of slavery, which posed as the champion liberator of oppressed peoples. We felt ourselves under the safeguard of the faith of a free people.

The Americans, seeing the friendly disposition of the Filipino people, disembarked forces at the town of Parañaque and took up positions all along the line occupied by my troops as far as Matubig, taking possession of many trenches constructed by my people by the employment of astuteness, not unaccompanied by violence. They forced a capitulation on the garrison of Manila which, inasmuch as it was invested by my troops, was compelled to surrender at the first attack. In this I took a very active part, although I was not notified, my forces reaching as far as the suburbs of Malate, Ermita, Paco, Sampaloc, and Tondo.

Notwithstanding these services, and although the Spaniards would not have surrendered but for the fact that my troops had closed every avenue of escape to the towns of the interior, the American generals not only ignored me entirely in the stipulations for capitulation but also requested that my forces should retire from the port of Cavite and the suburbs of Manila.

I represented to the American generals the injustice done me and requested in friendly terms that they should at least expressly recognize my cooperation, but they utterly declined to do so. Nevertheless, being always desirous of showing friendliness and good feeling toward those who called themselves liberators of the Philippine people, I ordered my troops to evacuate the port of Cavite and the suburbs of Ermita, Malate, Sampaloc, and Tondo, retaining only a portion of the suburb of Paco.

In spite of these concessions, not many days passed before Admiral Dewey, without any reason whatever, arrested our steam launches which had been plying in the bay of Manila with his express consent. Almost at the same time I received a letter from General Otis, commander of the American army of occupation, demanding that I should withdraw my forces beyond the lines marked on a map which he also sent me, and which showed within the lines the town of Pandacan and the hamlet of Singalon, which never have belonged to the municipal area of Manila and its suburbs.

In view of this unjustifiable attitude of both American leaders I summoned a council of my generals and asked the advice of my cabinet, and in conformity with the opinion of both bodies, I named commissioners who placed themselves in communication with these Americans. Although Admiral Dewey received in a most insolent manner and with aggressive phrases my commissioners, whom he did not permit to speak, I yielded to the friendly suggestions of General Otis, withdrawing my forces to the desired line for the purpose of avoiding contact with his troops. This gave rise to many misunderstandings, but I hoped that once the Paris conference was at an end my people would obtain the independence promised them by the consul-general in Singapore, Mr. Pratt, and that the friendship formerly assured and proclaimed in manifestos and speeches would be established by the American generals who have reached these shores.

But it did not turn out thus; the said generals accepted my concessions in favor of peace and friendship as indications of weakness. Thus it is that, with rising ambition, they ordered forces to Iloilo on December 26, with the purpose of acquiring for themselves the title of conquerors of that portion of the Philippine Islands occupied by my government.

Such procedure, so foreign to the dictates of culture and the usages observed by civilized nations, give me the right to act without observing the usual rules of intercourse; nevertheless, in order to be correct to the end, I sent to General Otis commissioners charged to solicit him to desist from his rash enterprise, but they were not listened to.

My government can not remain indifferent in view of such a violent and aggressive seizure of a portion of its territory by a nation which has arrogated to itself the title, "champion of oppressed nations;" thus it is that my government is disposed to open hostilities, if the American troops attempt to take forcible possession of the Visaya Islands. I denounce these acts before the world, in order that the conscience of mankind may pronounce its infallible verdict as to who are the true oppressors of nations and the tormentors of human kind.

Upon their heads be all the blood which may be shed.

EMILIO AGUINALDO.

MALOLOS, *January 5, 1899.*

SUPPLEMENT TO THE HERALD OF THE REVOLUTION.

[Official.]

Proclamation from the president of the revolutionary government to my brothers, the Filipinos, all the honorable consuls, and other foreigners:

Maj. Gen. E. S. Otis's proclamation, published yesterday in the Manila papers, obliges me to circulate the present one in order that all who read and understand it may know of my most solemn protest against said proclamation, for I am moved by duty and my conscience before God, by my political obligations with my beloved people, by my official and private relations to the North American nations.

In the above-mentioned proclamation General Otis calls himself "Military governor in the Philippines," and I protest one and a thousand times with all the energy in my soul against such an authority.

I solemnly proclaim that I have never had, either at Singapore, or at Hongkong, or here in the Philippines, any verbal or written contract for the recognition of American sovereignty over this cherished soil.

On the contrary, I say that I returned to these islands, conveyed by an American man-of-war, on the 19th day of May of last year, with the firm and clear purpose of fighting the Spaniards in order to reconquer our liberty and independence, and so I expressed myself in the declaration made on the 24th of said month of May. Thus

I published it in a proclamation directed to the Philippine people on the 12th of last June, when in my natal town, Kawit, I for the first time unfurled our sacred national flag as a holy emblem of that sublime aspiration; and, lastly, the American general, Merritt, predecessor of Mr. E. S. Otis, has confirmed that same thing in a proclamation addressed to the Philippine people days before the surrender of the town of Manila was proposed to General Jaudenes, which proclamation clearly and decisively stated that the land and naval forces of the United States came to give us our freedom and to displace the bad Spanish Government.

In a word, our countrymen and foreigners are witnesses that the land and naval forces of the United States existing here have recognized by act the belligerency of the Filipinos, not only respecting but also doing public honor to the Philippine banner, which triumphantly traversed our seas in view of foreign nations, represented here by their respective consuls.

As in his proclamation General Otis alludes to some instructions issued by His Excellency, the President of the United States, relative to the administration of affairs in the Philippines, I solemnly protest, in the name of God, root and source of all justice and all right, who has visibly acceded me the power to direct my dear brethren in the difficult task of our regeneration, against this intrusion of the United States Government in the administration of these islands.

In the same manner, I protest in the name of the Filipino people against the referred-to intrusion; for when they gave me their votes in confidence, electing me, although unworthy to be so, president of the nation, they imposed upon me the duty of sustaining until death its liberty and independence.

And in conclusion, I protest against such an unexpected act which treats of American sovereignty in these islands in the face of all the antecedents that I have in my possession referring to my relations with the American authorities, which are unequivocal testimony that the United States did not take me out of Hongkong to make war against Spain for their own benefit, but for the benefit of our liberty and independence to which end said authorities verbally promised me their active support and efficacious cooperation.

So that you all may understand it, my beloved brothers, it is the principle of liberty and absolute independence that has been our noble ambition for the purpose of obtaining the desired object, with a force given by the conviction, now very widespread, not to retrace the path of glory that we have passed over.

EMILIO AGUINALDO.

MALOLOS, *January 5, 1899.*

MANILA. (Received February 21, 1899—3.35 p. m.)
ADJUTANT-GENERAL, *Washington:*
Following issued by an important officer of insurgent government at Malolos, February 15, 1899, for execution during that evening and night in this city.

OTIS.

"First. You will so dispose that at 8 o'clock at night the individuals of the territorial militia at your order will be found united in all of the streets of San Pedro, armed with their bolos and revolvers, or guns and ammunition, if convenient.

"Second. Philippine families only will be respected; they should not be molested; but all other individuals, of what race they may be, will be exterminated without apprisement [or] compassion after the extermination of the army of occupation.

"Third. The defender of the Philippines in your command will attack the guard at Bilibid and liberate the prisoners and 'presidiarios,' and this accomplished they will be armed, saying to them: 'Brothers, we must avenge ourselves on the Americans and exterminate them, that we may take our revenge for the infamy and treachery which they have committed upon us; have no compassion upon them; attack with vigor; all Filipinos en masse will second you.' 'Long live Filipino independencia.'.

"Fifth. The order which will be followed in the attack will be as follows: The sharpshooters of Tondo and Santa Ana will be the attack from without, and these shots will be the signal for the militia of Trozo, Binondo, Quiapo, and Sampaloc to go out into the street and do their duty. Those of Paco, Ermita and Malate, Santa Cruz, and San Miguel will not start out until 12 o'clock, unless they see that their companions need assistance.

"Sixth. The militia of Tondo will start out at 3 o'clock in the morning. If all do their duty our revenge will be complete. Brothers, Europe contemplates us. We know how to die as men shedding our blood in defense of the liberty of our country. Death to the tyrants! War without quarter to the false Americans who have deceived us! Either independence or death!"

MANILA. (Received February 21, 1899—5 a. m.)
ADJUTANT-GENERAL, *Washington:*

General Miller reports, 19th instant, insurgent forces few miles out from Iloilo; believed to be disintegrating. Can maintain his position with present force. Business in city being resumed. He has sent up four representative men—officials from capital of island Negros—where American flag raised and American protection requested against small insurgent force in island. Affairs there and in Cebu very encouraging. Had regular troops arrived would have little difficulty in most important Visaya Islands. Shall endeavor to maintain and improve present promising conditions. Affairs here quiet; small insurgent force east of city driven away yesterday with considerable loss to enemy.

OTIS.

MANILA. (Received February 21, 1899—9.47 a. m.)
ADJUTANT-GENERAL, *Washington:*

Additional casualties: First Washington—wounded, February 19, Company L, Private Carson E. Ellis, elbow, accidental; killed, February 20: K, Privates Alton A. Rinehart; M, John F. Adams. First California—wounded, February 20: L, Privates Arthur Buhl, thumb; John W. Parnow, arm; Max R. Kruse, arm; Thomas C. Haly, thigh. Casualties near Iloilo, Panay Island, February 14: Eighteenth Infantry—killed—A, Corpl. Robert L. Grigsby; wounded, A, Sergt. Robert Jennings, thigh; K, Corpl. James F. Saunders, nipple. All wounds above slight.

OTIS.

MANILA. (Received February 22, 1899—a. m.)
ADJUTANT-GENERAL, *Washington:*

Following casualties in intrenchments yesterday caused by men exposing themselves to enemy: First California—Company K, Sergt. Frank N. Turton, wounded forehead, slight; Private James P. Cassidy, killed. Following during reconnoissance this morning, vicinity San Pedro Macati, First Washington—wounded slightly, Company E, Privates Amos H. Waddington, Christian O. Horn, H. D. Hazzard; wounded seriously, H, Corpl. W. B. Tucker; killed, Private Ed. W. Hampton, H, Second Oregon. Following in skirmish near Waterworks this morning: First Nebraska—wounded, Company D, Privates John S. Alley, neck, very severe; F, Alonzo M. Fike, elbow, slight; K, Charles Govryck, knee, slight.

OTIS.

MANILA. (Received February 23, 1899—3.35 a. m.)
ADJUTANT-GENERAL, *Washington:*
Determined endeavors to burn city last night. Buildings fired in three different sections of city; fires controlled by troops after severe labor a considerable number of incendiaries shot and few soldiers wounded; early this morning a large body of insurgents made demonstration off MacArthur's front, near Caloocan, and were repulsed. Loss of property by fire last night probably half million dollars.

OTIS.

MANILA. (Received February 23, 1899—8.30 a. m.)
ADJUTANT-GENERAL, *Washington:*
Casualties caused by insurgent sharpshooters yesterday and to-day in districts of Tondo and Binondo Mabla: Thirteenth Minnesota—wounded, Company C, Capt. Noyes C. Robinson, lip, moderately severe; Sergt. George K. Sheppard, leg, moderate; Privates Thomas F. Galvin, shoulder, severe; George S. Wooding, thigh, severe; D, Merton G. Grinnell, armpit, severe; Private Enoch Davis, H, First Nebraska, shot in hand, self-inflicted, accidental, severe; Private Clyde A. McVay, A, South Dakota, doing well, fourth toe, right, amputated.

OTIS.

MANILA. (Received February 24, 1899—1.48 a. m.)
ADJUTANT-GENERAL, *Washington:*
Scandia arrived last night. On nights 21st and 22d and yesterday morning insurgent troops gained access to outskirts of city behind our lines, many in hiding, and about 1,000 intrenched themselves; completely routed yesterday, with loss of killed and wounded about 500 and 200 prisoners. Our loss very slight. City quiet. Confidence restored. Business progressing.

OTIS.

PORT SAID, EGYPT. (Received February 24, 1899—2.50 a. m.)
ADJUTANT-GENERAL, *Washington:*
Arrived last night; sail to-day; all well.

READ, *Quartermaster (Sherman).*

MANILA. (Received February 25, 1899—12.42 p. m.)
ADJUTANT-GENERAL, *Washington:*
Additional casualties, February 22, during reconnoissance near San Pedro Macati: First Washington—killed, Company H, Private Albert J. Ruppert. Following in engagement near Caloocan, February 22–23: First South Dakota—killed, C, Private Oscar Felker; M, Sergt. William B. Smith, died of wounds; wounded, B, Privates Fred. Tobin, neck and lungs, moderate; M, Martin Eide, arm, slight; Musician Charles Hultberg, neck, severe. Third Artillery—wounded, Battery G, Sergts. Jasper A. Lewis, wrist, slight; H, Charles W. Wheeler, head, slight. Twentieth Kansas—killed, Company F, Private George H. Monroe; wounded, L, Lieut. William A. Callahan, thigh, slight; I, Privates John M. Webber, hand, slight; C, James E. Riley, scalp, slight; F, Corpls. Herbert Sands, leg, severe; K, Oscar Mallicoat, head, serious; L, Private William Wolf, thigh, severe; Musician Tolando Blesh, thigh, severe. First Montana—killed, Company L, Second Lieut. Eugene S. French; wounded, K, Second Lieut. Philip Greenan, side, slight; F, Privates Fred Chaxel, elbow, slight; B, Martin Hyman, leg, severe; William A. Stedman, thigh, severe; D, William F. Kra-

mer, scalp, slight; I, William A. Bonham, shoulder, slight; C, Glen W. Hurd, foot, slight; G, Theodore E. Manchester, thighs and hand, severe; L, Thomas D. Dunn, head, serious; C, John F. Dunn, thigh and wrist, slight; A, Otto Nelson, shoulder, slight. Casualties in Tondo District, Manila, February 23: Thirteenth Minnesota—wounded, D, Privates Herman H. Hillman, chest, slight; M, Egidius J. Fehr, arm, thigh, and across chest, severe; Oscar Frykman, buttock, slight; G, George W. Baker, neck, severe. Twenty-third Infantry—killed, F, Private Edward Reaver; wounded, M, Private John L. Barker, thigh and forehead, severe. Private William Bush, A, Fourteenth Infantry, cabled wounded 9th, is error.

OTIS.

ADJUTANT-GENERAL'S OFFICE,
Washington, February 24, 1899.

General LAWTON, *Colombo:*

Situation in Manila critical. Engagements of greater or less importance every day. Your early arrival great importance.

CORBIN.

DEPARTMENT OF STATE,
Washington, February 24, 1899.

The Honorable, the SECRETARY OF WAR.

SIR: I have the honor, by direction of the Secretary of State, to append for your information a copy of a telegram from the consul-general of the United States at Singapore, S. S., in regard to the evacuation of Sulu by the Spaniards, and stating that civil war is imminent there.

A copy has also been sent to the Secretary of the Navy.

I have the honor to be, sir, your obedient servant,

ALVEY A. ADEE,
Second Assistant Secretary.

MANILA. (Received February 25, 1899—6.20 a. m.)

ADJUTANT-GENERAL, *Washington:*

Seventy-five officers, 991 men, prisoners of war, sailed for Spain on *Rio Negros* yesterday.

OTIS.

MANILA. (Received February 25, 1899—1.11 p. m.)

ADJUTANT-GENERAL, *Washington:*

Condition of affairs quiet, progressing favorably. Anxiety need not be felt in regard to the situation. Will send small body of troops to Cebu, where Navy took quiet possession. Will return Negros commissioners with battalion of troops for their protection against Luzon insurgents, upon commissioners' request.

OTIS.

COLOMBO, CEYLON. (Received February 25, 1899—6.17 p. m.)

CORBIN, *Washington:*

Situation unchanged last cable. No serious illness; sick improving. Sail to-night; Singapore 5th.

LAWTON.

COLOMBO, CEYLON. (Received February 25, 1899—7.14 p. m.)

CORBIN, *Washington:*

Situation anticipated; utmost effort for expedition; hope to sail by noon to-day.

LAWTON.

MANILA. (Received February 26, 1899.)

ADJUTANT-GENERAL, *Washington:*

Additional wounded, February 24-25, in trenches near Caloocan, Second Oregon—Company G, Corpl. William W. Ponath, chest, slight. Third Artillery—Battery H, Privates John W. Corder, thigh, slight; K, Michael J. Crowley, leg, slight. First Idaho—Company F, Charles S. Lamb, thigh, severe. Twentieth Kansas—D, Privates Larry Jones, head, serious; Campbell Scott, arm, severe. First Montana—A, Privates Francis G. Auspach, arm, severe; Albert S. Hicks, lung, severe. Private John Anderson, F, First Idaho, injured, fractured ankle. Answering inquiries, Private Harry R. Crumrine, in First Wyoming Infantry, dorsum of foot, returned to quarters. Private Ralph W. Kells, L, First Nebraska, killed in action February 4. Private Peter M. Storment, I, Fourteenth Infantry, killed in action February 5.

OTIS.

ADJUTANT-GENERAL'S OFFICE,
Washington, February 26, 1899.

OTIS, *Manila:*

In order to reduce expenses, hereafter it will be necessary to use as far as possible Western Union telegraphic code.

CORBIN.

SAN FRANCISCO, CAL., *February 26, 1899.*
(Received 3 p. m.)

ADJUTANT-GENERAL, *Washington, D. C.:*

Lieutenant Brambila, Twenty-third Infantry, with 17 recruits Fourteenth, 10 casuals Twentieth, and 2 casuals and 57 recruits Twenty-third Infantry sailed this day on transport *Roanoke* for Manila; also 1 acting assistant surgeon, 1 hospital steward, and 3 privates, hospital corps.

SHAFTER, *Major-General.*

MANILA. (Received February 27, 1899—9.45 a. m.)

ADJUTANT-GENERAL, *Washington:*

Following deaths since last weekly report: February 18, Private James J. Morros, M, First Tennessee, variola. 19, Chaplain John R. Thompson, First Washington, acute enterocolitis; Privates William F. Stanley, F, First Montana, malarial fever. 20, Arthur Ransey, F, First Colorado, spinal meningitis; Robert L. Van Eman, I, Thirteenth Minnesota, variola; Henry K. Saunders, F, Fourteenth Infantry, dysentery. 21, Corpl. Harry R. S. Strand, L, First Washington, dysentery; Private James Ganong, D, First Idaho, variola. 22, Jacob Huth, K, Fourteenth Infantry, variola. 23, Andrew O. Cole, D, Fourteenth Infantry, variola; Adolph Agidius, F, First Idaho, dysentery. 24, Albert Haviland, F, First Colorado, variola. Died of wounds received in action: 18, First Sergt. W. H. Cook, F, First Nebraska. 19, Privates Eli E. Clampitt, G, Third Artillery. 20, John Sorenson, L, First Montana. 21, Edward Day, A, First Nebraska. 24, John Alley, D, First Nebraska.

OTIS.

ADJUTANT-GENERAL'S OFFICE,
Washington, February 27, 1899.

General OTIS, *Manila:*

In filling your requisition for regular troops could you make use of the Twenty-Fourth Infantry; it is available and in good condition.

CORBIN.

WAR DEPARTMENT, *February 27, 1899.*

OTIS, *Manila:*

President authorizes Eastern Company to extend cable from Capiz to Iloilo under conditions now existing, so that all rights of United States shall be preserved.

ALGER, *Secwar.*

WAR DEPARTMENT, *February 27, 1899.*

OTIS, *Manila:*

Pratt, consul-general Singapore, cables Spaniards about evacuate Sulu. Sultan anxious Americans come at once, as unable to withstand army opposition. Advise immediately action to prevent civil war. This for your information.

ALGER, *Secwar.*

WAR DEPARTMENT, *February 27, 1899.*

SIR: Referring to the letter of the 24th instant from your Department, quoting dispatch from Consul Pratt at Singapore, dated February 24, I have the honor to inform you that the following dispatch has this day been sent to General Otis:

"WASHINGTON, D. C., *February 27, 1899.*

"OTIS, *Manila:*

"Pratt, consul-general Singapore, cables Spaniards about evacuate Sulu. Sultan anxious Americans come at once, as unable to withstand armed opposition. Advise immediately action to prevent civil war. This for your information.

"ALGER, *Secwar.*"

I am, very truly, yours,

R. A. ALGER, *Secretary of War.*

The Honorable, the SECRETARY OF STATE.

MANILA. (Received February 28, 1899—7.53 a. m.)

ADJUTANT-GENERAL, *Washington:*

Not considered wise to send Twenty-fourth Infantry here at present.

OTIS.

MANILA. (Received February 28, 1899—7.55 a. m.)

ADJUTANT-GENERAL, *Washington:*

Battalion Twenty-third Infantry sailed Cebu 26th instant. Battalion California Volunteers sails Negros to-morrow. Everything quiet here past three days.

OTIS.

MANILA. (Received February 28, 1899—10.32 a. m.)

ADJUTANT-GENERAL, *Washington:*

Additional wounded, February 26, in trenches, before Caloocan: Twentieth Kansas—Company F, Private Howard Olds, abdomen, severe. Thirteenth Minnesota—H, Private Andrew J. Meidle, arm, severe. First Montana—G, Private Edward S. Moore, abdomen, severe. Tenth Pennsylvania—C, Private Gilbert Cuize, elbow, severe; John A. Hennessey, foot, severe, accidental. Additional in Tondo and Binondo districts, Manila, February 22–23, Thirteenth Minnesota—Company C, Private Ira B. Smith, sternum, slight; D, John Hartfield, side, slight. Second Oregon—E, Private Martin Hildebrant, finger, slight. Additional near San Pedro Macati, February 18 and 27, respectively, First Idaho—Company D, Private William H. Lillie, foot, slight. First California—B, Private Charles F. Bussman, shoulder, severe.

OTIS.

DEPARTMENT OF STATE,
Washington, February 28, 1899.

The Honorable, the SECRETARY OF WAR.

SIR: The President requests that you will wire General Otis, in the absence of a German naval force at Manila, to undertake the protection of German subjects and of those under German protection in the Philippines.

I have the honor to be, sir, your obedient servant,

JOHN HAY.

WAR DEPARTMENT, *February 28, 1899.*

OTIS, *Manila:*

The President directs, in the absence of a German naval force at Manila, that you give protection to German subjects and those under German protection in the Philippines, to the utmost of your ability.

ALGER, *Secwar.*

WAR DEPARTMENT,
Washington, February 28, 1899.

SIR: I beg to acknowledge receipt of your letter of the 23th instant relative to the protection of German subjects in Manila. The following dispatch in cipher has this day been sent to General Otis:

"The President directs, in the absence of a German naval force at Manila, that you give protection to German subjects and those under German protection in the Philippines to the utmost of your ability."

I have the honor to be, your obedient servant,

R. A. ALGER, *Secretary of War.*

The Honorable, the SECRETARY OF STATE.

PERIM. (Received March 1, 1899—3 a. m.)

ADJUTANT GENERAL, *Washington:*

Arrived this morning; depart this afternoon; all well.

READ,
Quartermaster, Transport Sherman.

MANILA, *March 1, 1899.*

SECRETARY WAR, *Washington:*

Informed Spanish authorities several days ago that proposition to vacate Jolo premature. Spain responsible until final confirmation of treaty. No troops to send to that distant island at present. Mindanao and Paragua likewise in dangerous turbulent condition. Have furnished Admiral Dewey copy your message.

OTIS.

920   CORRESPONDENCE.

MANILA. (Received March 2, 1899—2.18 a. m.)
ADJUTANT-GENERAL, *Washington*:

Morgan City arrived this morning; passengers good health; no deaths. *Tacoma* arrived yesterday; animals excellent condition, no loss; only one month's long forage brought.

OTIS.

MANILA. (Received March 2, 1899, 10.07 a. m.)
ADJUTANT-GENERAL, *Washington:*

Casualties near Caloocan, First South Dakota, February 27: Company B, Private Herman Bellman, knee, severe; L, Sergt. Robert B. Ross, scalp, slight. Twentieth Kansas, February 28: G, Capt. David S. Elliott, killed. First Montana, February 28: A, Privates Alvin F. Plottner, shoulder, slight; K, Howard L. Tanner, thigh, moderate; M, William J. Cheastey, hand, slight. Near San Pedro Macati, First California, February 28: F, Privates Arthur M. Smith, neck, severe; K, Harold E. Parks, arm, slight. First Washington, March 1: C, Corpl. Alfred B. Reichelt, shoulder, moderate; Private Herbert L. Osborne, chest, severe. Chaplain Lewis L. Leland, First Tennessee, died at Iloilo, February 26, smallpox. Answering inquiries, Capt. Thomas R. Hamer, slight flesh wound, convalescent, able sit up; for Meiklejohn. Private Hiram C. Conger, H, Tenth Pennsylvania, shot through right lobe of liver, improving rapidly; for Meiklejohn. Private George Church, A, Thirteenth Minnesota, doing full duty with company.

OTIS.

ADJUTANT-GENERAL'S OFFICE,
Washington, March 2, 1899.
GENERAL OTIS, *Manila:*

Further reinforcement of regulars and relief of volunteers will be hastened by the speedy return to San Francisco of transports now at Manila and to arrive.

CORBIN.

WAR DEPARTMENT, *March 2, 1899.*
OTIS, *Manila*:

The treaty of peace was signed December 10. By its terms the Government was to ship to Spain all prisoners taken at Manila. Of course, that would not include any shipped by Spanish authorities before December 10. How many have been shipped? How many have you ready to ship under those terms, and are there any other prisoners on hand under article 6 of the treaty? Why are ships kept waiting at Manila for prisoners? Answer immediately.

ALGER, *Secwar.*

WAR DEPARTMENT, *March 2, 1899.*
OTIS, *Manila:*

Agreeably to the request of the Secretary of State, and in accordance with the wishes of the Spanish Government, as communicated through the French charge d'affaires, that the interests of the Spanish subjects in the Philippines be confided to the French consul at Manila for the purpose, you will see that this request is complied with to the extent of your ability.

ALGER, *Secretary of War.*

AFFAIRS IN THE PHILIPPINE ISLANDS. 921

ADJUTANT-GENERAL'S OFFICE,
Washington, March 2, 1899.

General OTIS, *Manila:*

With wagons for Manila 300 mules go. Do you require civilian teamsters? Shipment steamer *Conamaugh* in few days.

CORBIN.

WAR DEPARTMENT, *March 2, 1899.*

OTIS, *Manila:*

Reports are insurgents have 600 of your people prisoners. What are facts?

ALGER, *Secretary of War.*

GIBRALTAR. (Received March 3, 1899—6.54 a. m.)

CORBIN, *Washington:*

One death, Private Timothy Donalm, Company H, Twelfth Infantry; 28 sick, only 3 serious.

SMITH (*Transport Sheridan*).

GIBRALTAR. (Received March 3, 1899—5.23 p. m.)

ADJUTANT-GENERAL, *War Department, Washington:*

Surgeons report no smallpox on *Sheridan*.

SMITH (*Transport Sheridan*).

MANILA. (Received March 3, 1899.)

SECRETARY WAR, *Washington.*

Spanish prisoners of war shipped before December 10, 364 officers, 803 enlisted men; these reported sick. From December 13 to January 16, 2,700 enlisted men shipped. Since shipped by United States, 254 officers, 2,787 enlisted men. Remaining on hand this date, 264 officers, 2,339 enlisted men. To be shipped 6th instant, 120 officers, 963 enlisted men. All remaining soldiers, prisoners of war, to be shipped on 11th instant. No ships have been kept waiting by United States authorities; in all instances departure urged and hastened. Nearly all civilian officials captured by insurgents still in their hands.

OTIS.

MANILA. (Received March 3, 1899—4.30 a. m.)

SECRETARY WAR, *Washington:*

Insurgents have not taken nor do they hold single prisoner of war; they have 3 soldiers in Mololos picked up in January, who, without permission, went among them near Cavite and Caloocan; am looking after them, providing money. Have captured over 1,500 insurgent soldiers since February 4; hold majority as prisoners of war. Detrimental reports which reached United States manufactured mostly in Hongkong. Troops here in splendid condition and eager for active employment, which they will soon have.

OTIS.

MANILA. (Received March 3, 1899—2.22 a. m.)

ADJUTANT-GENERAL, *Washington:*

Thirty civilian teamsters should be sent with mules; remaining teamsters from natives hired here.

OTIS.

MANILA. (Received March 3, 1899—5.20 a. m.)

ADJUTANT-GENERAL, *Washington:*

Following transports in Philippines: *Arizona, Morgan City, Scandia, Newport,* Manila; *St. Paul* and *Indiana,* Iloilo and Negros; *Pennsylvania,* Cebu. *Newport* temporarily disabled. *Arizona* just arrived from Iloilo. *Scandia* and *Morgan City* being unloaded and coaled. *Arizona, Newport, Scandia,* and *Morgan City* sail for San Francisco different days, all by 12th instant.

OTIS.

WAR DEPARTMENT, *March 3, 1899.*

OTIS, *Manila:*

As rapidly as possible volunteers should be returned upon ships that bring regulars to you. Will it be safe to send back at once as many as the *Scandia* and *Morgan City* took to you?

ALGER, *Secretary of War.*

MANILA. (Received March 4, 1899—7.20 a. m.)

ADJUTANT-GENERAL, *Washington:*

Transport *Senator* just arrived; troops in good health; one casualty, accidental drowning.

OTIS.

MANILA. (Received March 4, 1899—7.56 a. m.)

SECRETARY WAR, *Washington:*

Can not dispense with volunteers now; do not think they wish to return at present; have expressed desire to remain until better conditions prevail.

OTIS.

MANILA. (Received March 4, 1899—9.35 a. m.)

ADJUTANT-GENERAL, *Washington:*

Casualties near Caloocan, First Montana, March 2: Band, Private Alfred Cashmore, thigh, slight. Near San Pedro, Macati, Third Artillery, March 1: Battery G, Sergt. Dennis Shea, hand, severe. Just reported as missing, Private Grant Cullams, C, Tenth Pennsylvania, sent outside lines for information January 27, not seen since. Answering inquiries, Maj. Fred A. Williams, First Nebraska, suffering from lumbago and muscular rheumatism, not improving, probably never fit for duty here. Remains Major McConville, Idaho Infantry, not yet sent home; will go first transport. Private Christ B. Ploeger, K, Third Artillery, good physical condition, doing full duty. Lieutenant Seaman, Utah Artillery, flesh wound, right leg, doing well; for Meiklejohn. Corpl. Andrew Peterson, B, Utah Artillery, wounded right thigh, doing well; for Meiklejohn. James Thorson, E, Fourth Cavalry, well and doing duty; for Meiklejohn.

OTIS.

SINGAPORE. (Received March 4, 1899—1.05 p. m.)

CORBIN, *Washington:*

Arrived to-night. Stop six hours for coal. No serious illness; favorable conditions still continue. Probably reach Manila early morning 10th. Inform Ludington. Have so informed Otis.

LAWTON.

ADJUTANT-GENERAL'S OFFICE,
Washington, March 4, 1899.

Otis, Manila:

Secretary War desires to know if you have made appointment of superintendent of schools at Manila. If so, who?

CORBIN.

ADJUTANT-GENERAL'S OFFICE,
Washington, March 4, 1899.

General Otis, Manila:

Do you desire any of the 300 mules equipped for pack purposes? If so, how many?

CORBIN.

GIBRALTAR. (Received March 4, 1899—11.10 p. m.)

SECRETARY STATE, Washington:

Sheridan coaled; just left Port Said.

SPRAGUE.

MANILA. (Received March 5, 1899—5.38 a. m.)

ADJUTANT-GENERAL, Washington:

Chaplain McKinnon successfully performing duties of superintendent of schools under verbal instructions; no formal orders of appointment issued.

OTIS.

MANILA. (Received March 5, 1899—5.40 a. m.)

ADJUTANT-GENERAL, Washington:

Desire 150 aparejos. Can then use for pack purposes any mules sent. Of the 30 civilian teamsters applied for 10 should be packers.

OTIS.

MANILA. (Received March 5, 1899—6.17 a. m.)

ADJUTANT-GENERAL, Washington:

Transport Ohio arrived this afternoon; troops in good condition; one casualty. Private Clarence W. Overton, G, Twenty-second Infantry, died 2d instant; spinal meningitis.

OTIS.

MANILA. (Received March 5, 1899—9.30 a. m.)

ADJUTANT-GENERAL, Washington:

Following deaths since last weekly report—February 25, Privates Richard M. Bryant, K, First Colorado, variola; Verne A. Barker, I, Thirteenth Minnesota, variola. 26th, Harry L. Plowman, H, First Idaho, variola; William Donohue, F, First Colorado, variola. 27th, Sim Barber, L, Twentieth Kansas, variola. March 1, John A. Ewing, G, First North Dakota, typhoid; Frank Upham, C, First North Dakota, dysentery; Joseph Marx, C, First Montana, variola; George L. Doran, F, Eighteenth Infantry, diarrhea and pneumonia. Died of wounds received in action—February 27, Privates Richard H. McLean, A, First Washington; Howard A. Olds, F, Twentieth Kansas. 28th, Edward S. Moore, G, First Montana.

OTIS.

MANILA. (Received March 6, 1899—7 a. m.)

ADJUTANT-GENERAL, *Washington:*

Following from Iloilo, 4th instant:

"*Government, congress, inhabitants of Negros to General Miller, Iloilo:*

"We affectionately salute you and congratulate ourselves for the happy arrival of Colonel Smith and troops under his orders, and beg you to send this salute and congratulations to General Otis, Manila, as representative of the Government of the United States in the Philippines.

"LACSON."

OTIS.

MANILA. (Received March 6, 1899—9.55 a. m.)

ADJUTANT-GENERAL, *Washington:*

Additional casualties March 4, near San Pedro Macati, Luzon: Killed—Third Artillery, Battery G, Private John Toiza. Wounded—First California, Company G, Privates Louis H. Barieau, abdomen, severe; L, Wilban H. Wheeler, thigh, moderate. Twenty-third Infantry, E, First Sergt. Henry S. McFadden, chest, slight. Injured—First California, G, Sergt. Frank S. McNally, sprained ankle in action. First Nebraska, K, Private James E. Weldon, ruptured in action, February 22. At Jaro, Panay, March 1 and 2, respectively: Killed—Eighteenth Infantry, C, Privates Joseph W. Everington; A, William F. Briggs. Answering inquiries, no such man as Nute Wilson in First Nebraska; for Meiklejohn. Private Dickson A. Everitt, A, Fourteenth, doing well; wound nearly healed.

OTIS.

ADJUTANT-GENERAL'S OFFICE,
Washington, March 6, 1899.

OTIS, *Manila:*

Section 15 of the army bill reads in part as follows:

"That the President is authorized to enlist temporarily in service for absolutely necessary purposes in the Philippine Islands volunteers, officers and men, individually or by organization, now in those islands and about to be discharged, provided their retention shall not extend beyond the time necessary to replace them by troops authorized to be maintained under the provisions of this act and not beyond a period of six months."

The President inquires as follows:

"If we are not able to get you sufficient force to replace volunteers under your command before exchange of ratification of treaty, will you be able to enlist your present volunteer force under this section?"

By order Secretary of War:

CORBIN.

MANILA. (Received March 7, 1899—2.58 a. m.)

ADJUTANT-GENERAL, *Washington:*

Articles of clothing asked by Pope, not procurable here, approved by me, intended to meet emergencies and for reserve supply; canvas clothing and light kersey trousers might be cut one-half.

OTIS.

ADJUTANT-GENERAL'S OFFICE,
Washington, March 7, 1899.

OTIS, *Manila:*

No answer Pope cable February 24 regarding site refrigerator. Do you recommend such plant?

CORBIN.

MANILA. (Received March 8, 1899—7.38 a. m.)

ADJUTANT-GENERAL, *Washington:*

Corpl. George A. Abbott, D, Twenty-second Infantry, fell overboard from transport *Senator* during storm morning February 1; efforts recover body successful.

OTIS.

MANILA. (Received March 8, 1899—7.50 a. m.)

ADJUTANT-GENERAL, *Washington:*

Citizens contemplate construction large refrigerator plant here, which will accommodate army. Do not recommend that Government construct one at present.

OTIS.

MANILA. (Received March 8, 1899—8.41 a. m.)

ADJUTANT-GENERAL, *Washington:*

Wish to withdraw cable refrigerator plant. Definite dispatch to-morrow.

OTIS.

MANILA. (Received March 8, 1899—9 55 a. m.)

ADJUTANT-GENERAL, *Washington:*

Casualties March 4, near San Pedro Macati: Wounded—First Washington, Company C, Corpl. Frank A. Johnson, breast, slight. March 6: Wounded—Sixth Artillery, Battery D, Blacksmith Louis Heibeck, leg, slight. First Washington, Company K, Privates Frank L. Rose, chest, slight; H, Solomon Russell, thigh, moderate. Injured, First Washington, M, Private Fred C. Shorey, foot crushed on Mariquina road. Wounded—First Nebraska, F, Corpl. Walter J. Hunting, chest, severe; I, Privates Charles A. Lewis, hip, severe; John Trimble, thigh, severe. Second Oregon, G, Privates Harold L. Stanton, leg, moderate; Albert A. Eide, abdomen, severe. Hospital Corps, Private Cornelius Monahan, leg, severe. March 7, near San Pedro Macati: First Washington, C, killed, Private Frank A. Lovejoy.

OTIS.

ADJUTANT-GENERAL'S OFFICE,
Washington, March 8, 1899.

The COMMANDING OFFICER, SIXTH ARTILLERY, *Fort McHenry, Md.*
(Through commanding general, Department of the East.)

SIR: Referring to General Orders, No. 35, dated Adjutant-General's Office, March 3, 1899, which directs that your regiment be put in readiness for service in the Philippine Islands, the Secretary of War directs me to say that the families of officers and noncommissioned staff officers will be permitted to accompany the troops on the transports.

The Department also desires to be liberal in the matter of transportation of worthy families of other enlisted men who are married at the time order for movement issues, and will offer no objection to the transportation of such families as regimental and company commanders may believe worthy.

Members of families of officers and enlisted men will be required to pay for meals en route at the rate of $1 per capita per day for adults and children over 10 years of age; 50 cents per day for children between the ages of 5 and 10 years, and children under 5 years free.

Owing to the difficulty of transporting animals, officers' horses will not be taken. It is reported that suitable horses can be purchased in Hongkong at about $30 per head.

Mattresses are not used in the Philippines, and will not be taken.

The regiments designated will leave the United States in the following order: Ninth Infantry, Sixth Artillery, Twenty-first Infantry, Thirteenth Infantry, Sixth Infantry, Sixteenth Infantry. Specific orders for the movement will be communicated later, and preparation should be made with the view to sending the heavy baggage, under charge of an officer and detachment, to the port of embarkation in advance of the troops.

Very respectfully, H. C. CORBIN, *Adjutant-General.*

[Same to commanding officer, Sixth Infantry, Fort Sam Houston, Tex.; and on March 9, 1899, same order to commanding officer, Ninth U. S. Infantry, Madison Barracks, N. Y.; commanding officer, Twenty-first Infantry, Plattsburg Barracks, N. Y.; commanding officer, Thirteenth U. S. Infantry, Fort Porter, N. Y.; commanding officer, Sixteenth U. S. Infantry, Fort Crook, Nebr.]

COLOMBO, ISLAND CEYLON. (Received March 9, 1899—5.30 a. m.)
ADJUTANT-GENERAL, *Washington:*

Arrived this morning; depart to-morrow morning. All well.

READ,
Quartermaster, Transport Sherman.

MANILA. (Received March 9, 1899—8.38 a. m.)
ADJUTANT-GENERAL, *Washington:*

Cold-storage plant proposed by citizens not sufficient capacity; 5 acres public land in city, well located for plant, desired; available; quartermaster will cable details asked for by Quartermaster-General.

OTIS.

MANILA. (Received March 9, 1899—9.10 a. m.)
ADJUTANT-GENERAL, *Washington:*

Casualties March 7, near pumping station: Killed—First Nebraska, Company B, Privates Roscoe Young; G, Guy C. Walker. Wounded—First Nebraska, B, Capt. Claude H. Ough, thigh, moderate; Private Herbert Hedges, neck, moderate. Twentieth Infantry, M, Privates Frank Young, second arm, moderate; H, John Curran, chest, lung, severe. First Wyoming, F, Capt. John D. O'Brien, forearm, moderate; C, Private Joseph Spaeth, penis, severe. Engineers, Maj. J. F. Bell, side, slight. Near San Pedro Macati: Wounded—First Wyoming, G, Musician George E. Small, knee, moderate. First Washington, H, Private Sidney O. Dickinson, breast, slight.

Answering inquiries, Privates Albert S. Hicks, William Stedman, First Montana, doing well. Corporal Willing, Twentieth Kansas, doing well. (For Alger.)

OTIS.

ADJUTANT-GENERAL'S OFFICE,
Washington, March 9, 1899.

General OTIS, *Manila:*

In sending sick and wounded soldiers home it is particularly desirable that they have descriptive lists, as it is not intention to return them to service, but to discharge them on arrival at San Francisco.

CORBIN.

HEADQUARTERS DEPARTMENT OF THE PACIFIC AND EIGHTH ARMY CORPS,
Manila, P. I., January 23, 1899. (Received March 9, 1899.)
The ADJUTANT-GENERAL, U. S. ARMY,
Washington, D. C.

SIR: I have the honor to inclose a pamphlet which has been circulated in the Philippines, prepared by Mr. Howard W. Bray, an American citizen, and issued last month. I respectfully call attention to the dedicatory page; also to pages 34, 35, and 36. The paragraph on page 35 sets out the false position which the insurgent government assumes. I am of the opinion that nearly all of our difficulties have arisen from the intermeddling of American citizens of the type of this Mr. Bray, some of whom have been holding places under the Government.

With regard to the occupation of Iloilo and Cebu, those ports might have been occupied easily on December 14, when I cabled for permission to send troops there. Had that been done promptly, the influence of Aguinaldo in those islands would have been met and destroyed. So firmly was I impressed with the necessity for quick action that I had determined to send troops there without waiting instructions, and requested the protection and assistance of the Navy, contending that the petition of the citizens for our interference and the invitation of General Rios to send down troops were sufficient to authorize immediate action. As I had cabled for authority, Admiral Dewey thought it best to await it and not take the responsibility, believing that the Spaniards would hold out a little longer, and in this belief I also shared. The reply to my cabled request was not received till eight days had passed. Had the movement taken place three days sooner, it would have given us a firm foothold in the southern islands without conflict. We may still be successful in peaceably securing it, but I am unable to give assurance in the matter.

At this moment and since writing the above I have received a report from Iloilo, of which the inclosed is a copy. It is self-explanatory. Major Mallory, the writer, was sent there by me to assist General Miller in his delicate duties.

Very respectfully, your obedient servant,

E. S. OTIS,
Major-General, U. S. Volunteers, Commanding.

[Inclosure No. L.]

U. S. TRANSPORT NEWPORT,
Iloilo Bay, Panay, January 20, 1899—12 m.

GENERAL: I arrived here Wednesday, the 18th, and reported to General Miller immediately, turning over to him your two letters of instructions and copies of my orders, and explaining why I was sent here. I also acquainted him fully with the situation at Manila, and the necessity of avoiding a conflict with the insurgents and of correcting any false impressions the insurgents may have received as to the policy our Government proposes to pursue toward the people of these islands. He fully understands the situation now and will act in accordance with your instructions, based upon the expressed wishes of the President.

From all accounts, no harm was done by the publication here of the President's letter of instructions to you, as the insurgent authorities, General Miller informs me, have remarked to him that they found no material difference between the President's letter and your proclamation, which latter he furnished them as soon as it was received.

The situation here is highly satisfactory. The insurgents understand that we do not propose to attack them, but desire to win their confidence and to maintain the friendly relations now existing.

General Miller and Captain Dyer, of the *Baltimore*, were invited a few days ago by the "President of the Biscayan Republic" to visit Iloilo and the neighboring towns of Jaro and Molo as his guests, and the invitation was accepted unofficially, and General Miller has invited me to accompany him. We are to go this afternoon, and this visit should serve to confirm the expressions of friendly feeling already communicated to them.

There was a general exodus of Europeans and natives from Iloilo shortly after the arrival of our troops, most of them taking refuge on the opposite island of Guimaras, where they hired native huts at a high rate or else remained in sailing boats near the shore. Now that confidence has been restored, these refugees have returned to Iloilo, reestablished themselves in their homes, opened their shops and gone about their usual avocations. Most of the Europeans have also returned, and at least one bank is open and business generally has been resumed.

According to all accounts, only a small insurgent force, probably several hundred, is now under arms at Iloilo, and the hill men (bolo men), who had come down to loot the town, if not to resist the threatened attack, have returned to their hills. It is said that in their disappointment they burned two large villages in the vicinity of Iloilo before they left. The Iloilo paper of the 17th says the bolo men deposited their weapons here before leaving, and express satisfaction at this and at their departure.

I will remark here that General Miller had established friendly relations with the insurgents before I arrived, and had assured them that should it ever become necessary to attack the town he would give them three days' notice.

In my opinion there is less danger of a conflict here as long as our troops do not attempt a landing than there is at Manila, where the opposing lines confront each other, and the friction in the city itself is almost constant.

General Miller appears to be showing all due forbearance, patience, and judgment, and I think you need feel no special uneasiness about the situation in this quarter.

General Miller has probably informed you that a new man, a lawyer named Malisa, has been in the last few days elected "President of the Biscayan Republic," the former president, Lopez, becoming general of the army. This Malisa is the Mabini of the Biscayas, I understand—a smart, tricky fellow, who furnishes the brains and who detests Americans. This is the account I hear of him. I do not know the truth of it.

I write in haste, as the *Rattler*, carrying the mail, leaves presently.

Very respectfully,

JOHN S. MALLORY,
Major and Inspector-General.

Gen. E. S. OTIS,
Military Governor.

MANILA. (Received March 10, 1899—2 a. m.)
ADJUTANT-GENERAL, *Washington:*

Transport *Grant* arrived; troops in good condition. *Arizona*, *Newport* leave to-day for San Francisco; *Arizona* via Hongkong, *Newport* via Nagasaki.

OTIS.

ADJUTANT-GENERAL'S OFFICE,
Washington, March 10, 1899.

COMMANDING GENERAL, DEPARTMENT OF EAST,
Governors Island, New York:

Transport *City of Puebla*, with capacity for 800 men, will be ready to load troops at San Francisco 16th instant. Transport *Zealandia*, with capacity for 600 men, will be ready to load at same port 24th instant.

Ninth Infantry will embark on these vessels and should leave present stations, if possible, not later than March 17. The arrival of troops and baggage to be timed by communication with depot quartermaster, San Francisco, so as to facilitate loading and prevent, as much as possible, delay after arrival. Acknowledge receipt.

By command Major-General Miles:

H. C. CORBIN, *Adjutant-General.*

ADJUTANT-GENERAL'S OFFICE,
Washington, March 10, 1899.

General OTIS, *Manila:*

Do you favor officers' families going with regiments to Manila?

CORBIN.

ADJUTANT-GENERAL'S OFFICE,
Washington, March 10, 1899.

General OTIS, *Manila:*

As transports are ready, regiments will come to you in following order: Ninth Infantry, Sixth Artillery, Twenty-first Infantry, Thirteenth Infantry, Sixth Infantry, Sixteenth Infantry.

CORBIN.

ADJUTANT-GENERAL'S OFFICE,
Washington, March 10, 1899.

COMMANDING GENERAL, DEPARTMENT EAST,
Governors Island, New York:

Transports *Arizona* and *Senator* will be available for Sixth Artillery to embark not later than April 15. Transports *Scandia* and *Morgan City* for the Twenty-first Infantry not later than April 18.

CORBIN, *Adjutant-General.*

ADJUTANT-GENERAL'S OFFICE,
Washington, March 11, 1899.

OTIS, *Manila:*

For information Secretary War statement desired as to sufficiency or otherwise of all character of supplies. This in order that any deficiency may be at once supplied.

CORBIN.

MANILA. (Received March 11, 1899—11.41 p. m.)

ADJUTANT-GENERAL, *Washington:*

How many light battery organizations will Sixth Artillery bring?

OTIS.

MALTA. (Received March 11, 1899—11.45 a. m.)

AGWAR, *Washington:*

Arrived 8th, depart 12th, after repairing machinery; troops landed for exercise; health troops good, except two pneumonia. Four children of soldiers died pneumonia. Authorities most courteous.

SMITH.

MANILA. (Received March 11, 1899—1.10 a. m.)

ADJUTANT-GENERAL, *Washington:*

Manila not safe place for officers' families; great difficulty experienced in caring for those now here, and their safety one of the chief causes of anxiety. Officers' families should remain in the United States.

OTIS.

[Telegram sent to all department commanders in the United States.]

ADJUTANT-GENERAL'S OFFICE,
Washington, March 11, 1899.

COMMANDING GENERAL, DEPARTMENT OF THE EAST,
Governors Island, New York:

Following cablegram received from General Otis:

(Here follows as copied immediately above.)

Under such conditions Secretary War regrets that no more families of officers or enlisted men will be permitted to accompany troops. Families of officers and all noncommissioned officers for which quarters are legally provided will be permitted to retain their quarters at the posts from which troops depart according to the provisions of memorandum circular dated Adjutant-General's Office, January 19, 1899

By command Major-General Miles:

H. C. CORBIN,
Adjutant-General.

ADJUTANT-GENERAL'S OFFICE,
Washington, March 11, 1899.

The COMMANDING GENERAL, DEPARTMENT OF THE EAST,
Governors Island, New York.

SIR: I have the honor to inform you that one battalion of the Sixth Artillery will be assigned to garrison Honolulu, and that the Secretary of War directs that you select three of the old batteries and one of the new batteries, to be organized at Fort McHenry, to constitute this battalion, to be commanded by Maj. S. M. Mills, Sixth Artillery. Instructions as to the organization of these new batteries and the recruitment of the regiment have this day been mailed to the commanding officer of the Sixth Artillery through your office.

It is expected that the regiment will be ready to sail by April 15, 1899.

By command of Major-General Miles.

Very respectfully, your obedient servant,

WM. H. CARTER,
Assistant Adjutant-General.

MANILA. (Received March 12, 1899—12.01 p. m.)

ADJUTANT-GENERAL, *Washington:*

Transport *Scandia* left Nagasaki for San Francisco yesterday. *Morgan City* leaves this evening same route. Will transport *Grant* be sent to San Francisco? Can leave in ten days.

OTIS.

SAN FRANCISCO, CAL., *March 11, 1899.*
(Received March 12, 1899—4.40 a. m.)

ADJUTANT-GENERAL, *Washington:*

Transport *Conemaugh* sailed to-day for Manila with cargo of 295 mules; Captain Butner, quartermaster volunteers, 30 civilian employees in charge of animals, and three Hospital Corps privates took passage on ship.

SHAFTER, *Major-General.*

ADJUTANT-GENERAL'S OFFICE,
Washington, March 12, 1899.

Otis, Manila:

Conemaugh sailed from San Francisco yesterday, 295 mules.

CORBIN.

MANILA. (Received March 12, 1899—7.15 a. m.)

Adjutant-General, *Washington:*

Following deaths since last weekly report: March 8, Privates Alexander R. Chapline, M, Fourteenth Infantry, accidentally shot. 9th, Henry O. O'Flaherty, L, Second Oregon; Edward J. Sutton, I, Thirteenth Minnesota, variola. 10th, Albert J. Hartrigsen, E, Fourth Cavalry, accidentally shot. 11th, Louis E. Westphal, jr., D, First California, dysentery. Died of wounds received in action, 9th, Private Joseph M. Spaeth, C, First Wyoming.

OTIS.

WAR DEPARTMENT, *March 13, 1899.*

Otis, Manila:

Under new law but two major-generals except regulars can be retained, Shafter and you. Of brigadier-generals besides regulars you will have three, including Lawton, who is to be retained. Whom do you recommend for the remaining two? However, none of your officers will be mustered out in near future unless you so recommend.

ALGER, *Secwar.*

MANILA. (Received March 13, 1899—10.31 a. m.)

Adjutant-General, *Washington:*

Casualties near San Pedro Macati: Wounded—March 7, Company M, Private Warner Marshall, First Washington, thumb, slight. March 10, D, Capt. Edward Smith, First Idaho, leg, slight. March 11, C, Private A. W. Seigenthaler, Twenty-second Infantry, severe. Near San Felipe: March 7, C, Private John A. McConnell, First Wyoming, ankle, slight. Near Caloocan: March 11, Twentieth Kansas, killed, F, Oscar G. Thorne; wounded, I, Corpl. William M. Rumbley, hand, moderate. March 12, wounded, Twentieth Kansas, C, Private Arthur C. Howe, shoulder, severe.

OTIS.

MANILA. (Received March 14, 1899—9.56 a. m.)

Adjutant-General, *Washington:*

Until yesterday field operations here since capturing Caloocan of minor nature, consisting of driving back small bands insurgents with considerable loss to latter. Yesterday General Wheaton with Twentieth, Twenty-second Infantry, the Oregon and Washington troops, section Sixth Artillery and squadron Fourth Cavalry, attacked large force of enemy, drove them back and took line of Pasig River, which he now holds. Two improvised gunboats in lake have captured considerable property. Insurgent loss heavy; our own killed and wounded slight, aggregating 35, mostly slightly wounded. Insurgents made no determined stand.

OTIS.

WAR DEPARTMENT, *Washington, March 14, 1899.*

OTIS, *Manila:*
In no case give men discharges that will entitle them to travel pay. It is not just to those who remain.

ALGER, *Secwar.*

ADJUTANT-GENERAL'S OFFICE,
Washington, March 14, 1899.

OTIS, *Manila:*
Do you need more light batteries? Mountain guns also available.

CORBIN.

DEPARTMENT OF STATE,
Washington, March 14, 1899.

The Honorable, the SECRETARY OF WAR.

SIR: I have the honor by direction of the Secretary of State to inform you that the following telegram has to-day been received from the consul at Malta:

"Six *Sheridan* soldiers and seamen left behind. Wire authority to act."

I should be glad to be advised as early as possible as to what reply shall be telegraphed to the consul.

I have the honor to be, sir, your obedient servant,

THOS. W. CRIDLER,
Third Assistant Secretary.

WAR DEPARTMENT,
Washington, March 14, 1899.

SIR: I have the honor to inform you that the following dispatch has this day been sent to the consul at Malta:

"Have men put aboard United States-hospital ship *Relief*, soon due. If she does not stop there, can not you send them at once to Suez, where *Relief* would be sure to pick them up?"

Very respectfully, your obedient servant,

R. A. ALGER, *Secretary of War.*

The Honorable, the SECRETARY OF STATE.

WAR DEPARTMENT, *March 14, 1899.*

CAPTAIN, U. S. S. RELIEF,
Gibraltar:

Six men from *Sheridan* left at Malta. Stop and get them, or if forwarded to Suez pick them up there.

ALGER, *Secwar.*

(Service cablegram says *Relief* left Gibraltar before cable was received, and that it was recabled to Malta.)

MALTA, *March 14, 1899.* (Received 10.08 p. m.)

ALGER, *Secretary of War, Washington:*

Better order *Relief* here from Gibraltar, for men can't catch *Relief* if she passes. Might send them to Port Said and be too late. Wire authority to support them Government account.

GROUT, *United States Consul, Malta.*

WAR DEPARTMENT, *March 14, 1899.*
UNITED STATES CONSUL, *Malta:*
Have men put aboard United States hospital ship *Relief,* soon due. If she does not stop there can not you send them at once to Suez, where *Relief* would be sure to pick them up?

ALGER, *Secwar.*

GENERAL ORDERS, } HEADQUARTERS OF THE ARMY,
No. 56. } ADJUTANT-GENERAL'S OFFICE,
Washington, March 27, 1899.

By direction of the Secretary of War the following batteries will be relieved from duty at their present stations and put in readiness to proceed to the Philippine Islands via San Francisco:

Light Batteries E, First; F, Fourth, and F, Fifth Artillery.

Each battery will take twenty-four selected horses. The remainder will be turned over to the Quartermaster's Department for such disposition as may hereafter be determined upon.

The Quartermaster's Department will arrange for transportation; the Subsistence Department for the necessary subsistence, and the Medical Department for medical attendance and supplies for these batteries.

Departure from present stations will be arranged by department commanders so that the batteries will arrive in San Francisco in time to take the steamer to be hereafter designated to convey them to Manila.

Maj. John L. Tiernon, First Artillery, is assigned to command the Light Artillery Battalion, and will proceed to Jefferson Barracks, St. Louis, Mo., in time to move with Light Battery E, First Artillery, to San Francisco.

By command of Major-General Miles:

H. C. CORBIN, *Adjutant-General.*

MANILA. (Received March 15, 1899—12.50 a. m.)
ADJUTANT-GENERAL, *Washington:*
Need 3 additional light batteries and 6 additional Hotchkiss mountain guns, with equipments and supply of ammunition; at least 500 rounds per gun.

OTIS.

MANILA. (Received March 15, 1899—7.32 a. m.)
ADJUTANT-GENERAL, *Washington:*
Transports *Ohio* and *Senator* leave 20th instant; *Grant* on 25th. Removal freight and recoaling necessary. Asked on 12th instant if *Grant* should be sent to San Francisco; no reply.

OTIS.

ADJUTANT-GENERAL'S OFFICE,
Washington, March 15, 1899.
General OTIS, *Manila:*
If *Grant* can sail before 25th, have her do so. *Sherman* and *Sheridan* to follow as soon as possible. Regular regiments all ready, but must wait for these transports. No officers' families will come until you say they may.

CORBIN.

ADJUTANT-GENERAL'S OFFICE,
Washington, March 15, 1899.

General OTIS, *Manila:*

Having reference to cable of to-day, *Grant* and all returning transports should go to San Francisco.

CORBIN.

MANILA. (Received March 15, 1899—9 a. m.)

ADJUTANT-GENERAL, *Washington:*

Three thousand insurgents moved down last night to towns of Pasig and Pateros, on shore Laguna de Bay, confronting Wheaton's troops on Pasig River line. By heavy fighting Wheaton has dislodged and driven them back, taking 400 prisoners and inflicting heavy loss in killed and wounded; he reports his loss as very moderate. He now occupies those towns with sufficient force to hold them.

OTIS.

MANILA. (Received March 15, 1899—10.35 a. m.)

ADJUTANT-GENERAL, *Washington:*

Casualties March 13, near Caloocan: Killed—Twentieth Kansas, Company L, Private James W. Kline. Near Guadalupe: Killed—Twenty-second Infantry, B, Privates George E. Stewart; K, Wynne P. Munson; D, Wesley J. Henessy. Wounded—Twenty-second Infantry, M, Privates William Reinhard, leg, moderate; D, Willett M. Harman, scalp, slight; William S. O'Brien, head, severe; John Mulvahill, scalp, slight; A, Theodore A. Misner, finger, severe; Daniel W. Carroll, forearm, slight; E, Joseph Hoffman, thigh, severe; Joseph B. Cox, thumb, severe; I, John Blazek, chest, severe; David Mulholland, arm, moderate. Twentieth Infantry, K, Corpl. Christ Thompson, side, severe; B, Privates Charles Simon, back, moderate; K, Thomas Miller, hand, severe; D, Frank Nash, knee, severe; M, Richard J. Piper, thigh, slight; G, Lester M. Folger, neck, slight; H, Charles F. Sharpless, thigh, slight; Charles A. Davis, neck, severe. Second Oregon, B, Private Walter Erwin, foot, moderate. Accidentally injured: Twenty-second Infantry, B, Corpl. Charles I. Easly, contusion, side. Twentieth Infantry, E, Privates William Sempson, sprain, ankle; M, Adolph G. Koehler, sprain, ankle; B, Peter J. Thelen, hand, moderate; F, Corpl. John E. Hoffman, sprain, ankle. March 14, near Guadalupe: Killed—First Washington, E, Private Ralph E. Van Buskirk. Wounded—Second Oregon, D, Privates Alfred O. Carden, chest, severe; F. D. B. Dodson, ankle, slight; E, Charles Olson, foot, severe. Answering inquiry Private Charles S. Lamb, F, First Idaho, severe flesh wound thigh; doing well.

OTIS.

DEPARTMENT OF STATE,
Washington, March 15, 1899.

Hon. R. A. ALGER, *Secretary of War, War Department.*

DEAR SIR: By direction of the Secretary of State, I have the honor to transmit to you a copy of a telegram just received from our consul at Gibraltar.

Very respectfully, yours,

WM. H. MICHAEL, *Chief Clerk.*

GIBRALTAR, *March 15, 1899.*
(Received 1.53 p. m.)

SECRETARY STATE, *Washington:*

Inform Alger, Secretary of War, have rewired his cable to Malta. *Relief* left yesterday; uncertain whether calling Malta.

SPRAGUE.

ADJUTANT-GENERAL'S OFFICE,
Washington, March 15, 1899.

General OTIS, *Manila:*

All volunteer soldiers returning to San Francisco should be provided with descriptive lists that they may be discharged on arrival, as none will be returned. Some have reached there unprovided.

CORBIN.

GOVERNORS ISLAND, N. Y., *March 15, 1899.*

ADJUTANT-GENERAL, U. S. Army,
Washington, D. C.:

Referring to your telegraphic instructions March 11, commanding officer, Sixth Artillery, has designated Batteries I and K of his regiment at Fort Monroe, one from St. Francis Barracks, and one new battery to be organized at Fort McHenry, letter not yet known, for garrison of Honolulu. Is this satisfactory?

W. MERRITT,
Major-General Commanding, U. S. Army.

MANILA. (Received March 16, 1899—12.08 a. m.)

ADJUTANT-GENERAL, *Washington:*

Reports from Iloilo indicate improvement; less activity on the part of insurgents of island. Reports from Negros most encouraging. Inhabitants enthusiastic for American supremacy. Quiet prevails throughout island, and Colonel Smith directing affairs in framing internal government. Cebu quiet. Business progressing under United States protection. Reports from Samar and Leyte indicate desires of inhabitants for United States troops. These islands occupied. Insurgents' control confined to Luzon, and the occupation of the Pasig River line, with control of Laguna de Bay, has cut the country occupied by the Tagals in nearly two equal parts.

OTIS.

SINGAPORE. (Received March 16, 1899—2.38 a. m.)

ADJUTANT-GENERAL, *Washington:*

Depart for Manila daybreak to-morrow; all well.

READ, *Quartermaster, Transport Sherman.*

MANILA. (Received March 16, 1899—6.15 a. m.)

ADJUTANT-GENERAL, *Washington:*

Believed after inquiry majority volunteer organizations willing to reenlist for six months from ratification of treaty, provided that upon original discharge are paid traveling allowances to places of muster in, and that after expiration of second enlistment they are transported to those places by United States.

OTIS.

ADJUTANT-GENERAL'S OFFICE,
Washington, March 16, 1899.

General OTIS, *Manila:*

It was hoped that volunteers, as now organized, would be willing to remain at least until sufficient regulars can reach you to relieve them. Of course this must continue until treaty of peace is formally declared. In the meantime you are given full authority to send individual men, or organizations, to San Francisco for discharge as you may think best.

CORBIN.

CORRESPONDENCE.

PORT SAID. (Received March 16, 1899—9.35 a. m.)

AGWAR, *Washington:*
Depart 5; all well.

SMITH,
Colonel Twelfth Infantry, Transport Sheridan.

MANILA. (Received March 16, 1899—8.20 a. m.)

ADJUTANT-GENERAL, *Washington:*

Casualties March 13, near Guadalupe: Wounded—Twentieth Infantry, Company M, Sergt. William Barkley, shoulder, slight. Near San Pedro Macati: Sixth Artillery—Battery D, Private Fred J. Kelly, shoulder, slight. March 14, near Guadalupe: Killed—Fourth Cavalry, Troop E, Saddler Samuel Jones. Accidentally wounded—Fourth Cavalry, E, Capt. Fred Wheeler, hand, slight; Privates Michael Good, leg, severe; Horace H. Smith, thighs, severe; George B. Parks, chest, severe; Ernest Wilcox, arm, moderate. Twenty-second Infantry, C, Private Alfred Behm, ribs, severe; Marshal E. Coombs, palm, slight. Near Pateros: Wounded—Second Oregon, E, Private Walter Doran, eyebrow, slight. Injured, First Washington—C, Private Rodney S. Church, powder burn, slight. March 15, near Pateros: Wounded—Second Oregon, E, Private Edward D. Oesch, hip, slight.

OTIS.

ADJUTANT-GENERAL'S OFFICE,
Washington, March 16, 1899.

General OTIS, *Manila:*

Shall horses be sent with light batteries? Mountain guns will be sent. Ninth Infantry sailing the 24th of this month.

CORBIN.

SAN FRANCISCO, CAL., *March 16, 1899.*
(Received 5.58 p. m.)

ADJUTANT-GENERAL, U. S. ARMY. *Washington, D. C.:*

Arrangements for immediate transportation of the Ninth Infantry completed. About April 10 the steamers *Hancock, Warren, Morgan City, Newport,* and *Senator* will be available. These steamers can transport three regiments and part of a fourth.

SHAFTER, *Major-General.*

ADJUTANT-GENERAL'S OFFICE,
Washington, March 16, 1899.

COMMANDING GENERAL, DEPARTMENT OF THE EAST,
Governors Island, N. Y.

As recommended by you, following will constitute Honolulu Battalion: Batteries A, I, K, and N, Sixth Artillery.

By command Major-General Miles:

CARTER, *Assistant Adjutant-General.*

MANILA. (Received March 17, 1899—3.50 a. m.)

AGWAR, *Washington:*

Believe patriotism of volunteers will induce them to remain if actual necessity exists, and that important results will be accomplished within three weeks.

OTIS.

AFFAIRS IN THE PHILIPPINE ISLANDS. 937

MANILA. (Received March 17, 1899—4.12 a. m.)

AGWAR, *Washington:*

Seventy-two horses should be sent with three light batteries. Can supply other battery transportation necessities with mules.

OTIS.

MANILA. (Received March 17, 1899—9.55 a. m.)

AGWAR, *Washington:*

Casualties March 15, at Caloocan: Killed—First Montana, Company A, Private Henry C. Beecher. At Pasig: Killed—Twentieth Infantry, L, Private Charles Farnoff. Wounded—Twentieth Infantry, F, Privates Ralph E. Truman, chest, moderate: L, Thomas H. Rogers, side, severe. March 16, action at Cainta: Killed—Twentieth Infantry, C, Corpl. Ole Johnson; L, Private John McAvoy. Wounded—Twentieth Infantry, C, Corpl. James C. Tinkler, forearm, severe; Privates Oscar C. Kinniey, forearm, severe; Mike Kelly, leg, slight; Edward M. Brady, arm, moderate; F, William A. Ealy, shoulder, moderate; Thomas Filley, shoulder, slight; G, Thomas Varley, shoulder, slight; L, Virgil H. Mahan, shoulder, severe; John J. Griffiths, forehead, moderate; George McFarlane, chest, severe; William A. Lafeyth, hip, severe; Sergt. William D. Cheek, foot, moderate. Injured—Twentieth Infantry, F, Corpl. S. S. Householder, bruise, forehead. Near Mariquina: Wounded—First Colorado, Maj. Charles H. Anderson, ankle, slight; L, Corpl. Charles W. Haskell, thigh, moderate; K, Private Edward R. Pyncheon, back, moderate.

OTIS.

SACKETTS HARBOR, N. Y., *March 17, 1899.*
(Received 5.25 p. m.)

ADJUTANT-GENERAL, U. S. ARMY, *Washington, D. C.:*

Ninth Infantry with 30 officers and about 1,200 men left Madison Barracks and Fort Ontario to-day, the last of sixth section leaving Sacketts Harbor at 4 p. m.

POWELL, *Commanding.*

ADJUTANT-GENERAL'S OFFICE,
Washington, March 18, 1899.

OTIS, *Manila:*

Can Australian horses be purchased light batteries? Transportation difficult.

CORBIN.

DEPARTMENT OF STATE,
Washington, March 18, 1899.

The Honorable, the SECRETARY OF WAR.

SIR: Referring to this Department's letter of the 17th instant, concerning the seamen and soldiers left by the transport *Sheridan* at Malta, I now have the honor by direction of the Secretary of State to inform you that the following telegram has just been received from the consul at Malta:

"Instructions wanted disposition *Sheridan* deserters, also regarding money their support. No opportunity send Port Said. *Relief* passed. Can [?] catch her."

I should be glad to receive as early as possible a reply from you in regard to the matter in order that the consul may be promptly instructed.

I have the honor to be, sir, your obedient servant,

THOS. W. CRIDLER,
Third Assistant Secretary.

WAR DEPARTMENT,
Washington, March 18, 1899.

The Honorable, the SECRETARY OF STATE.

SIR: I have the honor to acknowledge receipt of your communication of this date, relating to the seamen and soldiers left behind by the steamer *Sheridan* at Malta, and to inform you in reply that the following cablegram was sent to the consul at Malta this date:

"Send account support *Sheridan* men to War Department. Did they join *Relief?* Any commercial line by which could sail for Manila?

I have the honor to be, sir, very respectfully, your obedient servant,

G. D. MEIKLEJOHN,
Acting Secretary of War.

ADJUTANT-GENERAL'S OFFICE,
Washington, March 18, 1899.

Consul GROUT, *Malta:*

Send account support *Sheridan* men to War Department. Did they join *Relief?* Any commercial line by which could sail for Manila?

CORBIN.

MALTA, *March 18, 1899.* (Received 4.21 p. m.)

CORBIN, *Care Secwar, Washington:*

Men here. No commercial line. Suggest await *Vixen.* Total weekly subsistence, $15.

GROUT.

MANILA. (Received March 19, 1899—1.40 a. m.)

AGWAR, *Washington:*

Negotiations Australian horses unsatisfactory; bidders ask £40 Melbourne; £47 delivered without right of rejection. About sending cavalry officer there to examine field.

OTIS.

MANILA. (Received March 19, 1899—7.50 a. m.)

AGWAR, *Washington:*

Our improvised gunboat under Captain Grant, Utah Artillery, has full possession of Laguna de Bay. Troops, inhabitants, and property on shore of lake at our mercy. Wheaton's Brigade on Pasig River line drove enemy northeast into province Morong last evening. Enemy attacked portion of his force south of Pasig, killing 2 men and wounding 20 of the Twenty-second Infantry. This morning Wheaton moved against this insurgent force, driving it to the south 15 miles, experiencing very slight loss; enemy left 200 dead on field.

OTIS.

MANILA. (Received March 19, 1899—9.52 a. m.)

ADJUTANT-GENERAL, *Washington:*

Have purchased all gunboats in Philippines of Spain, 13 in number, now at Zamboanga. Half are in serviceable condition. Payment in cash from public funds upon delivery at Manila. They will be sent for this week.

OTIS.

AFFAIRS IN THE PHILIPPINE ISLANDS. 939

MALTA, *March 19, 1899.* (Received 10.31 a. m.)

SECWAR, *Washington:*

If two hundred deposited with Secstate and I cabled draw expenses and use own judgment will settle affair. My plan get seamen employment, other vessels; send two soldiers New York.

GROUT, *Consul.*

MANILA. (Received March 20, 1899—7.53 a. m.)

AGWAR, *Washington:*

Following deaths since last weekly report: March 11, Privates Timothy Enright, B, Thirteenth Minnesota, electric shock. 14th, George J. Smith, H, First Nebraska, typhoid; John Spierings, H, Second Oregon, dysentery; Corpl. John T. Kennedy, A, Utah Artillery, dysentery. 18th, Private Andrew Mickelson, A, Nevada Cavalry, typhoid. Died of wounds received in action, March 15, Private Charles A. Davis, H, Twentieth Infantry.

OTIS.

ADJUTANT-GENERAL'S OFFICE,
Washington, March 20, 1899.

General OTIS, *Manila:*

Secretary War is anxious that volunteers be sent home the moment you feel any can be spared, utilizing the returning transports. Of course, your judgment must determine. It is going to take a long time at best, and as you have matter so well in hand, can you not safely load the troop ships as they arrive, including *Grant?*

CORBIN.

DEPARTMENT OF STATE,
Washington, March 20, 1899.

The Honorable, the SECRETARY OF WAR.

SIR: I have the honor to invite your early consideration of the following telegram just received from the United States ambassador at London:

"HAY, *Secretary, Washington:*

"Governor at Malta telegraphs London War Office 13 British deserters from British army have secreted themselves at that port on board American transport *Sheridan* proceeding to Philippines via Colombo. War Office informally requests instructions be given commander of *Sheridan* to put deserters ashore at Colombo. Please reply.

"CHOATE."

Awaiting your reply, in order that I may inform the ambassador by cable of the action taken, I have the honor to be, sir,

Your obedient servant,

JOHN HAY.

WAR DEPARTMENT,
Washington, March 20, 1899.

The Honorable, the SECRETARY OF STATE.

SIR: Having reference to your favor of even date, I have the honor to hand you herewith copy of instructions cabled the commanding officer of the transport *Sheridan.*

Very respectfully,

R. A. ALGER, *Secretary of War.*

ADJUTANT-GENERAL'S OFFICE,
Washington, March 20, 1899.

COMMANDING OFFICER, TRANSPORT SHERIDAN, *Colombo*:

Reported that 13 deserters from British army have secreted themselves on your transport. Secretary of War directs that you cause them to be put ashore at Colombo.

CORBIN.

WAR DEPARTMENT,
Washington, March 21, 1899.

The Honorable, the SECRETARY OF STATE.

SIR: Having reference to previous correspondence relative to 13 deserters from the British army secreting themselves on the transport *Sheridan*, I have the honor to inclose herewith copy of instructions cabled to the commanding officer of the *Sheridan* at Perim.

Very respectfully, R. A. ALGER, *Secretary of War.*

ADJUTANT-GENERAL'S OFFICE,
Washington, March 21, 1899.

COMMANDING OFFICER, TRANSPORT SHERIDAN, *Perim:*

Reported that 13 deserters from British army have secreted themselves on your transport. Secretary War directs that you cause them to be put ashore at Perim. Acknowledge.

CORBIN.

(Service cablegram from Perim says: "Commanding officer, transport *Sheridan*, undelivered; did not call.")

MANILA. (Received March 21, 1899—6.45 a. m.)

AGWAR, *Washington:*

Transports *Ohio* and *Senator* left 20th; *Grant* delayed for necessary repairs; starts 25th; carries all sick and wounded necessary to ship; *Sherman* expected to-night; can not commence shipment volunteers at present; hope to do so soon. Ship additional battalion California to Negros this afternoon.

OTIS.

ADJUTANT-GENERAL'S OFFICE,
Washington, March 21, 1899.

COMMANDING GENERAL, DEPARTMENT CALIFORNIA:

The following is repeated for your information:
(Preceding cable from General Otis.)

H. C. CORBIN, *Adjutant-General.*

MANILA. (Received March 21, 1899.)

AGWAR, *Washington:*

Casualties March 17, near Blockhouse No. 4: Wounded—Tenth Pennsylvania, Company E, Second Lieut. John G. Thompson, thigh, moderate; Private John A. McVay, shoulder, moderate; C, Sergt. Alexander McCouch, forearm, moderate. March 18, near Taguig: Killed—Twenty-second Infantry; E, Privates John Schmidt,

Charles W. Fredericks; K. Henry W. Johnson. Wounded—E, Capt. Frank B. Jones, thigh, moderate; Privates Robert Rice, abdomen, severe; Charles E. Parmer, back, severe; Raleigh T. White, hip, severe; William Ellis, thigh, severe; Leander Mingee, thumb, severe; Carl Crumpholz, forearm, slight; Merritt Porter, toe, severe; D, Nels Arvidson, thigh, severe Frank Yount, chest, moderate; Berry H. Young, leg, severe; G, Charles E. Haley, foot, slight; Frank Ruefer, chin, slight; K, Earl Edwards, foot, severe; M, Corpls. James Comerford, thigh, moderate; Edward F. Wilson, finger, severe. Injured—E, Privates George Schneider, clubbed by enemy, severe. March 19: Wounded—K, August Schmidt, arm, slight. Near Pasig: Killed—Second Oregon, D, Private James Page. Wounded—M, Corpl. Fred W. Bowne, thigh, slight. Near Taguig: First Washington—K, Corpl. Robert E. Bucklin, thigh, severe; D, Hugh Waters, lung, severe; Privates Henry O. Ness, arm and side, severe; Edward R. Bartlett, lung, severe.

OTIS.

WAR DEPARTMENT, *March 21, 1899.*

OTIS, *Manila:*

If it would not interfere with your military operations, I see no objection to your allowing Spanish agents to pass your lines to arrange with the insurgents for release of prisoners. I do not think the money consideration should deter or influence your action. This Government is pledged to aid in this release.

ALGER, *Secwar.*

ADJUTANT-GENERAL'S OFFICE,
Washington, March 21, 1899.

General OTIS, *Manila:*

Secretary War desires to know whereabouts and condition of First Tennessee Volunteers.

CORBIN.

MANILA. (Received March 21, 1899—10.20 p. m.)

AGWAR, *Washington:*

First Tennessee in Iloilo; good condition; performing excellent work.

OTIS.

MANILA. (Received March 21, 1899—11.30 p. m.)

AGWAR, *Washington:*

In taking possession of islands, 100 mules in addition to 295 en route could be advantageously used; desire them sent.

OTIS.

MANILA. (Received March 22, 1899—7 a. m.)

AGWAR, *Washington:*

Sherman just arrived; troops good condition.

OTIS.

MANILA. (Received March 22, 1899—7.08 a. m.)

AGWAR, *Washington:*

Under construction treaty, article 5, believe that all public movable property not belonging to Spanish land and naval forces belongs to the United States. Spanish authorities here hold that such property remains the property of Spain. Which construction is correct?

OTIS.

942   CORRESPONDENCE.

[Indorsement.]

MARCH 22, 1899.

I should say property belongs to the United States. What says the Attorney-General?

R. A. ALGER, *Secretary War.*

OFFICE OF THE ATTORNEY-GENERAL,
Washington, D. C., March 22, 1899.

Gen. H. C. CORBIN, *Adjutant-General.*

SIR: Referring to the annexed dispatch to the Secretary of War from General Otis, I recommend that an answer in the form which I have prepared and inclose be sent by the War Department.

Very respectfully,

JOHN W. GRIGGS, *Attorney-General.*

WAR DEPARTMENT, *March 22, 1899.*

OTIS, *Manila:*

Attorney-General advises that public movable property belonging to Spanish central Government remains to Spain. Fixtures intended for permanent use in connection with immovable property regarded as immovable. Archives and legal and judicial records useful for government of islands or security of private titles belong to United States. If important doubtful property in question, telegraph character.

R. A. ALGER, *Secretary of War.*

ADJUTANT-GENERAL'S OFFICE,
Washington, March 22, 1899.

General OTIS, *Manila:*

Are pack or draft mules required?

CORBIN, *Adjutant-General.*

MANILA. (Received March 22, 1899—11.48 p. m.)

AGWAR, *Washington:*

Immaterial whether mules draft or pack; can use for either purpose as necessities demand.

OTIS.

DEPARTMENT OF STATE,
Washington, March 22, 1899.

The Honorable, the SECRETARY OF WAR.

SIR: Referring to a telegram from the consul of the United States at Malta of March 19, 1899, which was left personally at the Department yesterday and which read as follows:

"SECRETARY WAR, *Washington:*

"If two hundred deposited with Secretary State and I cabled draw expenses and use own judgment will settle affair. My plan get seamen employment other vessels; send two soldiers New York.

"GROUT."

I have now the honor to quote for your information a copy of a telegram which was addressed to the consul of the United States at Malta, reading as follows:

"Referring to your cable Secretary War, send soldiers New York. Draw expenses on Secretary of State."

When the draft of Mr. Grout is received covering the expenses of sending these two soldiers to New York it will be presented to your Department for payment.

I have the honor to be, sir, your obedient servant,

THOS. W. CRIDLER,
Third Assistant Secretary.

MANILA. (Received March 23, 1899—9.04 a. m.)

AGWAR, *Washington:*

Casualties, March 16, near San Pedro Macati: Wounded—First Idaho, H, C. A. Benedict, forearm. March 21, near Mariquina: Wounded—First Colorado, E, Artificer Archie A. Aldrich, armpit, moderate. March 16, at Jaro, Panay: Killed—Eighteenth Infantry, B, Private Louis Biehl. Wounded—Eighteenth Infantry, B, Joseph Daly, thigh; Theodore Burr, chest; Preston Savage, forearm; William Bruschke, chest; L, Max Horne, forearm; C, Joseph R. McCreary, hand; William Lohman, thigh; John E. Rodgers, thigh; William Bixman, leg; H, Riley G. Callaghan, scalp; William R. Rodenberger, hand; K, William Markwood, leg; E, William Buster, leg; I, Corpl. Charles E. Bates, foot. First California L, Private T. A. Marlow, shoulder.

OTIS.

MANILA. (Received March 24, 1899—11.20 p. m.)

SIGNALS, *Washington:*

MacArthur's division swinging northward; Otis directing disposition and operations from central telegraph station.

THOMPSON.

MANILA. (Received March 24, 1899—11.41 p. m.)

ADJUTANT-GENERAL, *Washington:*

City quiet; business progressing; no indications of excitement. Fighting far beyond city limits, and firing can not be heard. Old battle lines surrounding city maintained, as city can not be safely uncovered.

OTIS.

SAN FRANCISCO, CAL., *March 24, 1899.*
(Received 9.40 p. m.)

ADJUTANT-GENERAL, *Washington:*

Transport *City of Puebla* sailed at 4.30 p. m. this date, with headquarters, band, two medical officers, and Companies A, F, G, I, L, and M, Ninth Infantry. Fifteen officers, 623 men with caliber .30 arms, 100 rounds ammunition per man. In addition to above, ship carried 70 recruits for Ninth Infantry, assigned from Presidio; also Lieutenant Stewart, Fourth Cavalry, quartermaster and commissary of ship; Lieutenant Vitale, military attaché Italian embassy; Captain Beall, Third Infantry; Lieutenant Bunker, Thirteenth Minnesota; Lieutenant Mitchell, Fifty-first Iowa; Lieutenant Stickle, United States Engineers; Mr. Samuel Steele, Mr. Daily, and Commissary-Sergeant Wikander. Captain Regan, Ninth Infantry, in command.

SHAFTER, *Commanding.*

MANILA. (Received March 25, 1899—2.35 a. m.)

ADJUTANT-GENERAL, *Washington:*

MacArthur, with two brigades, commenced advance on Novaliches, northeast Caloocan, and center of insurgent line at daylight this morning; advancing rapidly and successfully, suffering little. From Novaliches MacArthur will swing to left and strike north of Polo. Wheaton's brigade fronting Caloocan will press forward proper time. Hall's brigade on old line north of Pasig demonstrating west of pumping station. Enemy 12,000 strong on line. Am endeavoring to take large fraction in reverse.

OTIS.

ADJUTANT-GENERAL'S OFFICE,
Washington, March 25, 1899.

General OTIS, *Manila:*

All gratified by your account of splendid work being done. Greatest interest all over the country. Would be grand if work could be pushed to immediate completion. Am instructed to suggest that you make such use of the *Sherman* and *Sheridan* for hospital and other purposes as your judgment may deem best.

CORBIN.

MANILA. (Received March 25, 1899—7.05 a. m.)

AGWAR, *Washington:*

Transport *Grant* leaves for Nagasaki, San Francisco, this afternoon.

OTIS.

MANILA. (Received March 26, 1899—12.08 a. m.)

AGWAR, *Washington:*

Projected northern movement not yet completed; Otis's and Hale's brigades, with mounted troops Fourth Cavalry, the turning column met heavy resistance over difficult country, and are camped to-night 6 miles east of Polo and 6 miles north of line from which advance was taken up. Wheaton's brigade, Caloocan, drove enemy 1½ miles north across river. Hall on extreme right encountered considerable force and routed it. Fighting heavy near Caloocan. Movement continues in morning. Our casualties about 160, 25 killed; enemy lost in killed alone 200.

OTIS.

MANILA. (Received March 26, 1899—5.25 a. m.)

AGWAR, *Washington:*

Attacks on Hall and pumping station last night easily repulsed. MacArthur, with moving column, has driven enemy but can not gain point north of Polo on account of roughness of country; must strike railway south that point. This will enable most of Aguinaldo's troops to escape north; still he may oppose as best of his army, consisting of released prisoners of war, former native Spanish troops, concentrated there. This northern army will be pressed south of city. Three thousand insurgent troops from southern Luzon provinces have concentrated. Lawton will take care of them. Affair satisfactory.

OTIS.

AFFAIRS IN THE PHILIPPINE ISLANDS. 945

MANILA. (Received March 26, 1899—8.22 p. m.)

AGWAR, *Washington:*

Entire casualties yesterday—1 officer, 25 enlisted men killed; 8 officers, 142 men wounded. Officer killed, Captain Stewart, First Colorado. List cabled immediately. To-day's fighting south and around Polo determined; MacArthur, with three brigades united, having artillery and cavalry, engaging enemy. Colonel Egbert, Twenty-second Infantry, killed. Our loss thus far, moderate; enemy's heavy. Army gunboats on coast and in esturaries west and north of Polo very efficient. Troops in excellent condition and spirits.

OTIS.

MANILA. (Received March 26, 1899—8.26 a. m.)

AGWAR, *Washington:*

Time, 4.30 p. m. MacArthur has driven enemy, strongly intrenched in large force north of Polo; will continue to press him. Insurgents have strong intrenchments from Caloocan to Malolos, which have taken them months to construct.

OTIS.

MANILA. (Received March 26, 1899—10.25 p. m.)

AGWAR, *Washington:*

MacArthur has advanced beyond Meycauayan, 2 miles beyond Polo, 9 miles from Manila and 15 miles from Malolos; railroad will be repaired to advance point to-morrow and troops supplied by cars. MacArthur will press on to-morrow; is now in open country; insurgents stoutly resisting behind succeeding lines of intrenchments, from which troops continually drive them. City perfectly quiet and native inhabitants appear to be relieved of anxiety and fear of insurgents. Captain Krayenbuhl, commissary, lieutenant, Third Artillery, mortally wounded.

OTIS.

MANILA, *March 26, 1899.* (Received 5.15 p. m.)

AGWAR, *Washington:*

Casualties, March 24, 25, 26: Killed—Twentieth Kansas, E, Privates H. L. Plummer; Curran C. Craig; G, A. S. Anibal. Third Artillery—Battery H, Privates William Patten, James A. O'Neil, Sergt. William Fogarty; G, Private Herbert Rass; K, Thomas Thompson, Clarence V. Watts. Second Oregon, Company B, Privates H. P. Adams; D, William M. Cook; L, Charles Hubart, Guy Millard. First Montana: Company F, Privates Joseph Beckman, G, Percy R. Lockhart, Steve Stevens; M, William Mietschke. Third Infantry, Company M, Private William J. Merrill, Corporal Cummings. Tenth Pennsylvania, Company E, Private Alex. Newell. First Nebraska, Company A, Sergt. Walter Poor. First Colorado, Company A, Capt. John S. Stewart. Twenty-second Infantry, Col. H. C. Egbert.

Wounded—Tenth Pennsylvania, Company C, Privates Charles O. Walker, back, severe; D, Eugene R. Morgan, foot, slight; K, Vernon Kelly, hand, severe. First Montana, Company D, Privates Thomas Rickard, thigh, severe; E, James McCreary, chest, slight; James Enright, chest, slight; John Calanary, neck, slight; Edward McWrarer, forearm, slight; Corpl. George T. Banks, arm, slight; G, Privates Robert Brown, chest, severe; Joseph P. Meyer, coccyx, severe; Gomer Williams, arm, slight; William H. McCarty, thigh, severe; Hays Axtell, thighs, slight; H, Louis Pallat, leg, slight; I, Edward J. Lynn, groin, severe. Third Infantry: Company

E, Private Martin O'Malley, forearm, moderate; G, Corpl. William H. Heaperling, chest, severe; M, William E. Fitzgerald, arm, slight; Charles Tenton, leg, slight; William G. Schenk, thigh and leg, severe; George S. Owens, knee, severe. Seventeenth Infantry, Company M, Capt. Charles D. Clay, neck, slight. Hospital Corps: Privates Gordon A. Peel, chest and head, severe; Peter F. West, jaw, severe; Eugene J. Owen, chest and shoulder, severe. Fourth Infantry, Company G, Privates Jas. O'Neil, knee, severe; Herman Bleeker, thigh, slight. Twenty-second Infantry, Company C, First Lieut. Harold L. Jackson, thigh, severe; E, Privates Fred. W. Arndt, leg, severe; D, George C. Richards, thigh and hand, severe; E, Edward B. Miller, knee, slight; William Howard, chest, severe; F, William Meyers, face, severe; G, Bert E. Clough, leg, severe; H, Albert E. Axt, forearm, moderate; L, Merton Hunricker, chest, severe; M, Edward H. Lammers, forearm, severe; Lewis T. Skillman, arm, slight; Nicholas Gearin, thigh, slight; Sergt. La Vergne Gregg, hand, slight. First South Dakota, Company G, Private Walter E. Brown, forearm. Twentieth Kansas, Company A, Privates Frank Steward, scalp, slight; C, Thaddeus J. A. Wiegant, thigh, severe; D, George C. Nichols, thorax, severe; E, George H. Cravens, thigh, severe; Joseph H. Heflin, leg, severe; Andrew W. Evans, neck, moderate; Corpl. James H. Bryant, elbow, slight; G, Private Orville E. Parker, shoulder and arm, severe; H, Capt. Adna G. Clarke, shoulder: severe; Privates Edward R. Hook, shoulder and neck, slight; I, William Tull, tibia, severe. First Nebraska, Company A, Privates Harry A. Shuman, jaws, severe; C, Roscoe C. Ozman, forearm, moderate; G, Ward G. Roberts, head, slight; C. E. Young, hand, severe; Capt. Lee Forby, abdomen, severe; K, Privates Ottis V. Fent, elbow, silght; L, William J. Koopman, elbow, moderate; David O. Barnell, thigh, moderate; Edward A. Pegan, forearm, moderate; Clarence A. Fay, forearm and thigh, severe; Ward C. Crawford, hip, severe; Robert E. Fritscher, hand, slight; Capt. Wallace C. Taylor, forearm, moderate; M, Private John E. Robinson, hand, slight. Second Oregon: D, Sergt. A. Lee Morelock, foot, severe; D, Corpl. A. L. Roberts, sprain, ankle; Company B, Privates William J. Armitage, arm, severe; C, Elmer O. Roberts, chest, severe; B. B. Chandler, jaw, severe; James E. Snodgrass, thigh, moderate; Elwin Crawford, scalp, moderate; Earl Mount, shoulder, slight; D, First Sergt. James West, knee and hand, severe; Corpl. William E. Searcy, buttock, severe; E, Privates John E. Davis, shoulder, severe; George C. Snyder, chest, severe; Jacob N. Smith, forehead, slight; First Lieut. A. J. Brazee, forearm, severe; F, Privates Charles W. Ruedy, forehead, severe; G, George Spicer, jaw, severe; Albert J. Jordan, leg, severe; George Eichhammer, chest, severe; Edgar Samson, arm, moderate Corpl. C. A. Marcy, back, severe; H, Private Frank H. Thompson, face, severe; I, Corpl. Rudolph Gantenbein, leg, moderate; K, Privates Ray L. Antrim, thigh, slight; John Janzen, eye, severe; Emmet L. Jones, back, slight; William F. Schwartz, knee, slight; L, John A. Bailey, hand and arm, severe; William T. Allen, thigh, severe; Carleton E. Sanders, thigh, slight; Guy N. Sanders, neck and arm, severe; B. F. Dunseth, foot, slight; M, Corpl. B. F. Burnett, shoulder, severe; Leon G. Holland, chest, severe; Privates E. D. Cosper, foot, severe; John H. Blosser, head and side, severe; Albert J. Califf, forearm, severe; A, William B. Ungerman, thigh and scrotum, severe; D. J. C. Headlee, arm, severe. Third U. S. Artillery: G, Second Lieut. Winfield S. Overton, thigh, moderate; Privates W. L. Duplisser, shoulder, slight; A. W. Lintner, chest, severe; Thomas F. Lynch, arm, severe; H, Corpl. Timothy Fitzpatrick, thigh, slight; Privates Chauncey Tesh, thigh, severe; Julius C. Buhlert, leg, slight; William Patten, abdomen, severe; K, David J. Sullivan, thumb, severe; Maurice Reynolds, thigh, moderate; Patrick Cooney, stomach, slight; Alfred Harlow, arm, moderate; Jules Kuester, leg, slight; Sergt. Earl Fisher, thigh, severe; Fred. Clark, head, severe; Private Joseph J. Motz, armpit, moderate; L, E. A. Stockton, shoulder, slight; Herman E. Warner, thigh and thumb, severe; Ollie Miller, stomach, slight; Herbert W. Ogilvie, foot, slight; Oscar Gustafson, foot moderate; James Barrett, tibia, severe; Sergts. Frank A. Ernsberger, thigh, severe; Herbert A. McKenzie, finger, severe; Corpl. Thomas A. Galvin. Fourth United States Cavalry, Troop E, First Sergt. Alexander H. Davidson, side, severe; Sergt. Charles Hiatt, jaw, severe; Privates Leroy Grundhand, thigh, severe; Harry Howe, chest, severe; William E. Tufts, head, severe; Charles Rie, face, serious; Samuel H. Evans, leg, slight; I, Farrier Rankins Nebinger, leg, severe; K, Private John Cotter, neck, slight. First Washington Infantry, Company B, Capt. George H. Fortson, mortal; Q. M. Sergt. William D. Covington, thigh, severe; Privates Reginald S. Patterson, thigh, slight; William C. Courtney, probably mortal; Frank Pinny, arm and chest, severe; Oliver D. Ward, thumb, slight; K, William Hinchcliffe, hand, slight. Utah Light Artillery, B, Corpl. Henry L. Southers, thigh, moderate; Private Parker J. Hall, thigh, severe. First Colorado, Company A, Privates Edwin E. Pitts, breast, severe; M, Malcolm H. Maccoe, abdomen, severe; Charles Brill, thigh, severe; E, Merton W. Esshom, thigh, slight. Thirteenth Minnesota, Company A, Privates Andrew Martenson, foot and ankle, severe; Arnold Arneson, head, slight; C, Bert W. Parsons, hand severe; I, Fred Ekman, thigh, severe; Lennard Porter, groin, severe; Sergt. Edward McInness, hand slight; K, Privates John T. Whelan; abdomen, severe; James C. McGee, thumb, slight; Corpls. John Connelly, jr., thigh, severe; L, Harry M. Glazier, abdomen, severe; Privates Avery Grimes, jaw, severe; M, Paulinus Huhn, chest, severe.

OTIS.

MANILA. (Received March 27, 1899—4.48 a. m.)
AGWAR, *Washington:*
Following deaths have occurred since last report: March 17—William J. Tracey, private C, First Idaho, drowned, accidental; Joseph L. Walker, private B, First Tennessee, variola. 18, Hugh B. McClellan, private I, Fourteenth Infantry, appendicitis; Bernard J. Smith, musician, Band, First Colorado, variola. 19 William J. Harms, private L, Fourth Infantry, typhoid. 20, William Wallace, private L, First Tennessee, variola; Edward R. Pyncheon, private K, First Colorado, from wound in action; Benjamin Hubbard, private G, Fourteenth Infantry, jaundice; Henry Leimbacher, private G, First Washington, drowned, accidental. 22, Milton S. Melse, private D, First Washington, from wound in action. 23, Horace G. McCordic, private F, First South Dakota, variola. 24, William H. Bush, private I, First Colorado dysentery.

OTIS.

MANILA. (Received March 27, 1899—7.45 a. m.)
AGWAR, *Washington:*
Hugh B. McClellam, I, Fourteenth Infantry, wounded February 5, recurring appendicitis March 15, died 18th. See weekly list deaths cabled to-day.

MANILA. (Received March 27, 1899—8.55 a. m.)
AGWAR, *Washington:*
MacArthur holds Marilao; severe fighting to-day and our casualties about 40. The insurgents had destroyed bridges, which impeded progress of train and artillery. Our troops met the concentrated insurgent forces on northern line to-day, commanded by Aguinaldo in person, and drove them with considerable slaughter. They left nearly 100 dead on field, and many prisoners and small arms were captured. The column will press on in the morning.

OTIS.

ADJUTANT-GENERAL'S OFFICE,
Washington, March 27, 1899.

OTIS, Manila:

J. W. Pope, February 2, sends estimate for bunks, mattresses, pillows, barrack chairs. Shall we send?

CORBIN.

MANILA. (Received March 27, 1899—12.30 p. m.)

AGWAR, Washington:

Additional casualties, March 23, 24, 25, 26: Killed—Third Artillery, First Lieut. M. G. Krayenbuhl, Captain and Commissary, U. S. Volunteers. Twentieth Kansas, Company B, Sergt. Morris J. Cohen; D, Private Tray E. Fairchild. Twenty-second Infantry, L, Sergt. Charles F. Brooks. Second Oregon, L, Privates Liew Strawderman, Hayes B. Taylor. Wounded—Twentieth Kansas, E, Private John C. Muhr, lung, fatal; D, Artificer James E. Hested, neck, moderate; B, Samuel F. Barton, leg, moderate. Twentieth Infantry, Ira Wright, foot, severe. Twenty-second Infantry, A, Privates Harry J. Scanlan, shoulder, slight; William Geyer, forearm, slight; B, First Sergts Patrick J. Byrne, leg, slight; F, Ole Walve, shoulder, slight; Artificer William Hagebaum, back; I, Private John Miller, head; K, Musician Spurgeon Cain, toe, slight; L, Private William J. Dunlap, hand, severe. First Montana, Maj. F. J. Adams, surgeon, thigh, slight; Company B, Private Edward Morrissey, arm, slight; Third Artillery, Battery K, Private Robert H. Vorfeld, leg, severe; Patrick O'Brien, forearm, severe; L, Mason Calloway, side, severe. First South Dakota, Company C, Private George D. Benson, leg, slight; I, Byron F. Hasting, knee; Sergt. Hiram A. Pratt, thigh, slight; Private Fred. Barber, chest, severe; K, Artificer Arne Haugse, thigh, moderate; L, Privates Allison Myers, hand and arm, moderate; Fred C. Lorenzen, chest, severe. Thirteenth Minnesota, E, Privates Jack Hamilton, thigh and knee, slight; G, Robert L. C. Geib, thigh, moderate. Second Oregon, A, Privates Leo D. Grace, neck, moderate; D, Daniel C. Bowman, hand, severe; F, Richard E. Brickdale, leg, moderate; G, Charles E. Cockrane, sprained ankle; M, Corpl. Frank E. Edwards, thigh, severe. Tenth Pennsylvania, C, Private William D. Collins, shoulder, severe; Musician Elmer E. Barnes, elbow, slight; H, Privates Ralph M. Hodgens, elbow, moderate; I, William H. Stauffer, chest, severe; K, Sergt. Charles T. Wallace, neck, slight. First Idaho, A, Private Claude Hill, chest, severe. First Nebraska, C, First Lieut. Joseph A. Storch, arm, slight; A, Private Weldon R. Robbins, thigh, moderate; D, Fred R. Wagner, chest, severe; Harry E. Fitchie, hand, moderate; E, Walker L. Smedley, thigh, moderate; I, William J. Finke, thigh, severe; M, Mate Sumers, neck, severe. First North Dakota, H, Private Harry W. Donovan, forearm, moderate. March 25, wounded, not heretofore reported: Sixth Artillery, Battery D, Private Frederick J. Kelly, shoulder, slight, 13th. First Washington, C, Private E. Morin, hand, slight, 18th.

OTIS.

MANILA. (Received March 28, 1899—2.37 a. m.)

ADJUTANT-GENERAL, Washington:

MacArthur had severe fighting yesterday afternoon beyond Marilao; brilliant charge by South Dakota led by Frost, against famed troops of Aguinaldo brought from Malolos; repulsed enemy with slaughter; Adjutant Lien and Lieutenants Adams and Morrison and four enlisted men, that regiment, killed; Lieutenant McClelland and 22 enlisted men wounded; loss yesterday mostly confined to this regiment. Partial destruction of railroad, which is being rapidly repaired, impedes MacArthur's progress; supply railway trains have now reached Marilao and MacArthur is pushing

AFFAIRS IN THE PHILIPPINE ISLANDS. 949

on. Our small gunboats are in Bulacan River, where great execution done yesterday; they will relieve pressure on MacArthur's front materially. Troops in excellent condition and spirits. Proclamation signed, Luna, general in chief insurgent forces, directs that all towns abandoned be burned. In consequence thereof much country north in flames.

OTIS.

MANILA. (Received March 28, 1899—3.28 a. m.)
ADJUTANT-GENERAL, *Washington:*

Prince Loewenstein, with Wheaton's command morning 26th, took refreshments to officers, Second Oregon, on firing line; was cautioned as to danger, but advanced with line when it charged insurgent intrenchments. He was killed by enemy and a friend with him wounded. His remains delivered to friends in city.

OTIS.

MANILA. (Received March 28, 1899—7.08 a. m.)
ADJUTANT-GENERAL, *Washington:*

Following from Iloilo: "All quiet here. Smith's additional troops received at Enrique with great show of gladness.

"VAN VALZAH."

The additional troops, Second Battalion, California, sent to Colonel Smith to protect inhabitants from raids of hill robbers. Negros developing internal government under Smith's supervision; reports very encouraging.

OTIS.

ADJUTANT-GENERAL'S OFFICE,
Washington, March 28, 1899.

General OTIS, *Manila:*

Brief cable desired stating how far supplies of all kinds meet requirements of your army, particularly subsistence present and past.

CORBIN.

MANILA. (Received March 28, 1899—12.05 p. m.)
ADJUTANT-GENERAL, *Washington:*

Casualties, March 27: Killed—First South Dakota, First Lieut. and Adjt. Jonas H. Lien; Company H, First Lieut. Frank H. Adams; E, Second Lieut. Sidney E. Morrison; D, Privates James W. Nelson, Matthew N. Ryan; E, Harry R. Keogh, Lewis Chase, Peter Ryan, Frank A. Shroeder. Twentieth Kansas, G, Corpl. John Scherrer D, Private William Carroll; I, Wiliam Keene. Tenth Pennsylvania. H, Private J. O. Cline. Wounded—First South Dakota, I, First Lieut. Paul D. McClelland, arm; C, Sergt. Sidney J. Cornell, ankle, severe; Privates George A. Moore, thigh, severe; D, Ray L. Washburn, shoulder, severe; Isaac Johnson, arm, severe; First Sergt. Ernest Madden, thigh and hand, severe; E, Sergt. Arthur A. Northrop, thigh, severe; Corpl. Frank E. Wheeler, testicle, slight; Privates John Stauke, lung, chest, severe; William F. Pankey, arm, moderate; I, Warren E. Crosiar, shoulder, slight; F, Benjamin Strobel, neck, severe; Peter J. Tierney, ankle, slight; Guy P. Squire, leg, severe; G, Corpls. Alexander W. Hardy, hip, moderate; I, William R. Amos, arm, slight; Privates Jacob H. Stockmyer, knee, severe; Will May, abdomen, severe; K, Ray S. Nichols, shoulder; L, Allison Myers, arm; Fred. C. Brunger, arm, moderate; M, Matt Schueler, leg, slight; Charles H. Jackson, head, severe. First Sergt. Charles B. Preacher, chest, severe; Musician David Elmes, leg, moderate. Tenth

Pennsylvania, I, Privates Morrison Barclay, side, severe; J. C. Mickey, leg, moderate. First Nebraska, F, Capt. C. W. Jens, elbow, slight; A, Privates Joe Scott, knee, slight; B, W. T. Rymer, arm, severe; D. W. Scriven, knee, severe; F, Frank A. Peterson, knee, severe; George Newhoff, leg, severe; H, H. E. Wright, foot, severe; I, Isa Holbrook, shoulder, severe; Herman Bensel, knee; Musician Albert C. Taylor, scalp; L, Privates M. E. Sayles, chest, serious; R. E. Riley, thigh, severe; M, George L. Sears, hip, severe; Pearley M. Busic, forearm, severe; D, John Gretzer, jr., scalp, severe. Twentieth Kansas, A, Corpl. Fred A. Recob, thigh, severe; H, Privates Joseph A. Wahl, neck, severe; L, Leslie G. Setzer, arm, severe. First Montana, A, Private Harry R. Athey, thigh, severe; B, J. O. Bolkey, neck, severe; F, Joseph Lorenz, back, severe; G, William H. Yost, hip, severe; H, Frank A. Gibson, leg, severe; I, Seymour Addison, chest, severe; A. K. Lunskeenan, chest, severe; John Tierney, thigh, severe. First Colorado, H, Private Harry B. Kerr, chest, severe. Twenty-second Infantry, I, Private John A. Hogebom, shoulder, slight. Third Artillery, Battery H, Sergt. Benjamin H. Hiett, abdomen, severe; Musician Henry J. Rath, forearm, severe; Privates John McCandless, leg, severe; K, Frank B. Catron, thigh, severe; Oren A. McKay, leg, severe; A. A. Boeckling, knee, severe; John D. Gillilan, foot, slight; L, Tom Culbeson, ilium, severe; Clarence E. Chappell, thigh, severe; Alexander C. Pike, hip, severe; Capt. J. C. Read, commissary subsistence, U. S. Volunteers, finger, trifling, spectator.

OTIS.

MANILA, *March 28, 1899.*
(Received 2.27 a. m.)

AGWAR, *Washington:*

Neither bunks, mattresses, pillows, nor barrack chairs needed here.

OTIS.

[Copy of foregoing sent to commanding generals, Department of the Lakes, Chicago Department of the Gulf, Atlanta; Department of Missouri, Omaha; Department of California, San Francisco.]

MANILA. (Received March 28, 1899—12.50 a. m.)

AGWAR, *Washington:*

Battalion Twenty-third Infantry withdrawn to city; replaced by entire Third Infantry.

OTIS.

MANILA. (Received March 29, 1899—3.22 a. m.)

ADJUTANT-GENERAL, *Washington:*

MacArthur's advance yesterday only to outskirts of Marilao; took until late afternoon to repair road and railway bridges and send cars through with supplies. Commenced march 6 this morning. Marched rapidly on Bocaue and will continue to Bigaa, 7 miles from Malolos. Enemy had destroyed railway and telegraph line. Construction train following our forces. Enemy's resistance not so vigorous to-day. Our loss thus far slight. Towns in front of our advance being destroyed by fire. Troops in excellent spirits.

OTIS.

MANILA. (Received March 29, 1899—8.48 a. m.)

ADJUTANT-GENERAL, *Washington:*

Casualties March 28: Killed—Third Artillery, Battery G, Sergt. I. J. Whitney; Private Charles Johnson. Wounded—Tenth Pennsylvania, Company E, Private Christer Sibert, hand, severe, accidental. Third Artillery, Battery G, First Sergt. John C. O'Connor, eye, slight. Injured—Twentieth Kansas, Company B, Private Louis J. Rouse, foot, slight.

OTIS.

MANILA. (Received March 29, 1899—6.20 a. m.)

ADJUTANT-GENERAL, *Washington:*

Supplies of all kinds sufficient for immediate wants and will continue to be ample if cables and estimates which have been made are promptly filled.

OTIS.

ADJUTANT-GENERAL'S OFFICE,
Washington, March 29, 1899.

OTIS, *Manila:*

Cablegram in reference to supplies received. Comments on character supplies specially desired.

CORBIN.

SAN FRANCISCO, CAL., *March 29, 1899.*
(Received 2.45 p. m.)

ADJUTANT-GENERAL, *Washington:*

Zealandia sailed yesterday evening with companies B, C, D, E, H, and K, Ninth Infantry; 11 officers and 2 medical officers, 8 Hospital Corps. Total enlisted, 599, including 29 recruits. Total equipped, 537; caliber arms, .30; 100 rounds ammunition per man. Ship carried, additional, Captain Bickham, quartermaster Volunteers, quartermaster and commissary of ship; Lieutenant Clinton, Twenty-second Infantry; and Chaplain Wells, First Tennessee. Captain Rockefeller, Ninth Infantry, in command.

SHAFTER, *Major-General.*

MANILA. (Received March 30, 1899—12.02 a. m.)

ADJUTANT-GENERAL, *Washington:*

MacArthur advanced at 6 yesterday morning from Marilao; passed rapidly to Bocaue; at 11.45 took up advance for Bigaa, and at 3.15 afternoon for Guiguinto, 3½ miles from Malolos, reaching that point at 5.05. Casualties for the day about 70. Fierce fighting in the afternoon. Troops made crossing of river at Guiguinto by working artillery over railroad bridge by hand and swimming mules against fierce resistance. Column will pass on railroad to extreme front, nearly repaired, and will resupply troops to-day.

OTIS.

MANILA. (Received March 30, 1899—1.30 a. m.)

ADJUTANT-GENERAL, *Washington:*

Subsistence supplies excellent and abundant. Meats deteriorating in this hot climate are sold at public auction at high figure. Considerable hard bread spoiled; will be some loss. Supplies in all other departments good. Medical supplies abundant. Light clothing short. Shanghai and Hongkong contractors do not deliver as rapidly as expected. Little inconvenience suffered thereby.

OTIS.

MANILA. (Received March 30, 1899—10.50 p. m.)

ADJUTANT-GENERAL, *Washington:*

MacArthur made disposition yesterday for attack on Malolos to-day; engagement opened at 7 o'clock this morning and is now progressing. Casualties yesterday, 4 killed and 23 wounded; all brought to Manila last night. Hall moved out from pumping station at daylight this morning with three battalions, northeast; attacked, and has taken Mariquina and is pursuing enemy. Ordered to return this afternoon.

OTIS.

MANILA. (Received March 30, 1899—8 a. m.)

ADJUTANT-GENERAL, *Washington:*

Answering inquiries, Gordon A. Peel, Hospital Corps, out of danger; doing well. Andrew Bank, I, Tenth Pennsylvania, discharged March 3; probably left on *Grant*, 25th.

Deaths on transport *Sherman*—Private George Devlin, M, Third Infantry, fever, February 15; buried Gibraltar, 16th. Chief Musician Edward M. Matter, Third Infantry, malarial fever, March 11; buried at sea, 11th. Private Frederick Kuhn, L, Seventeenth Infantry, drowned at sea February 22.

OTIS.

MANILA, *March 30, 1899.*
(Received 1.05 p. m.)

AGWAR, *Washington:*

Additional casualties, March 25: Killed—Second Oregon: Company A, Private Birt I Clark. Wounded—L, Capt. H. L. Wells, stomach, spent ball, slight; Sergt. W. W. Wilson, hand, slight; Privates Charles R. Rubart, leg, slight; Frank E. Adams, side, severe; F, Benjamin F. Smith, jr., legs, severe. Injured—K, Q. M. Sergt. E. R. Colgan, leg, slight; M, Private Edward Jaques, hand, slight.

Twenty-sixth: Wounded—Second Oregon, C, Privates Frank Woodruff, heel, moderate; G, E. C. Thornton, hand, moderate.

Twenty-ninth: Killed—First Nebraska, D, Private John J. Boyle. Wounded, First Nebraska: B, First Sergt. Charles B. Robbins, scalp, moderate; C, Privates Bruce E. Macy, shoulder, severe; D, Charles Knapp, thigh, severe; E, Gustave Meyer, knee, severe; G, Lewis E. Reed, chest, severe; H, Emory W. Grossman, arm, moderate; Charles H. Youngs, thigh, severe; I, James A. Carroll, thigh, severe; L, Joseph A. Wither, leg, moderate; M, Corpl. Monroe W. Spence, foot, slight. Twentieth Kansas, Maj. Wilder S. Metcalf, foot, severe; F, Privates Henry Ratcliff, thigh, severe; Walter Kemp, abdomen, moderate; William A. Ebert, hip, severe; Thadeus G. Alderman, thigh, slight; I, John E. Ballou, elbow, slight; L, Walter A. Wyatt, forearm, slight; K, Sergt. Joseph DeWald, wrist, severe; Private Adrian Hatfield, wounded March 27, dead. First Montana, A, Corporals William H. Tolbert, wrist, severe; H, Soren H. Smith, arm, moderate; Privates Fred Wheaton, back, severe;

D, William G. Marshall, head, severe; F, Edward B. Bowen, eye, slight. Tenth Pennsylvania: D, Corpl. Thomas B. Critchfield, groin, severe; Privates Patrick Cummings, head, moderate; C, Ralph W. E. Downs, thigh, severe; E, William H. West, leg, slight; H, Alexander B. Young, arm, slight; I, Archibald W. Powell, elbow, severe. Second Oregon, K, Private Thomas C. Townsend, foot, slight. Injured—Tenth Pennsylvania, A, Private Alex Coulter, groin, slight.

OTIS.

FORT MCHENRY,
Baltimore, Md., March 30, 1899. (Received 3.05 p. m.)
ADJUTANT-GENERAL, *Washington, D. C.:*
New battery, Sixth Artillery, will be ready to accompany others to Honolulu.

VOSE, *Commanding Post.*

ADJUTANT-GENERAL'S OFFICE,
Washington, March 30, 1899.
COMMANDING GENERAL, DEPARTMENT OF THE EAST,
Governors Island, N. Y.:
The three batteries, Sixth Artillery, from Fort McHenry and Fort Monroe, should arrive in San Francisco in time to take the steamer sailing April 12, on which passage has been engaged for them.

By command of Major-General Miles:

CARTER, *Assistant Adjutant-General.*

ADJUTANT-GENERAL'S OFFICE,
Washington, March 30, 1899.
OTIS, *Manila:*
Ninth Infantry sailed 24th and 28th, *Puebla* and *Zealandia.* Three light and 8 heavy batteries sail about April 20 Twenty-first and Thirteenth Infantry, marines, recruits, about April 13, followed by Sixteenth and Sixth Infantry. Are 72 light-battery horses for draught or saddle?

CORBIN.

MANILA. (Received March 31, 1899—1.25 a. m.)
ADJUTANT-GENERAL, *Washington:*
MacArthur captured Malolos at 10.15 this morning. Enemy retired after slight resistance and firing city. Particulars later. Hall had quite severe engagement beyond Mariquina. Casualties, 20. Enemy driven.

OTIS.

MANILA. (Received March 31, 1899—6 a. m.)
ADJUTANT-GENERAL, *Washington:*
Troops resting at Malolos. Considerable portion of city destroyed by fire. Our casualties, 1 killed, 15 wounded. Hall has returned with his troops to former position north of Manila.

OTIS.

ADJUTANT-GENERAL'S OFFICE,
Washington, March 31, 1899.
OTIS, *Manila:*
All reports of operations by mail desired soon as convenient.

CORBIN.

CORRESPONDENCE.

GOVERNORS ISLAND, N. Y., *March 31, 1899.*
(Received 11.28 a. m.)
ADJUTANT-GENERAL, U. S. ARMY, *Washington, D. C.:*

Does your telegram of 30th, referring to movement of batteries Sixth Artillery from Fort McHenry and Monroe, refer to Honolulu battalion or the batteries for the Philippines? Please specify the batteries intended to sail from San Francisco not later than April 12.

W. MERRITT,
Major-General, U. S. Army, Commanding.

ADJUTANT-GENERAL'S OFFICE,
Washington, March 31, 1899.
COMMANDING GENERAL, DEPARTMENT OF THE EAST,
Governors Island, N. Y.:

Batteries A, I, K, and N, Sixth Artillery, are the ones designated to sail from San Francisco to Honolulu April 12.

By command of Major-General Miles:

CARTER,
Assistant Adjutant-General.

MANILA. (Received March 31, 1899—2.21 p. m.)
ADJUTANT-GENERAL, *Washington:*

Additional casualties, March 29: Killed—Twentieth Kansas, Band, Privates Orlin L. Birlew; Company G, Alva L. Dix; M, Samuel M. Wilson. Tenth Pennsylvania, I, Privates Daniel W. Stevens; C, Frederick M. Jennewine; I, Bert F. Armburst. First South Dakota, M, Private Oscar Fallen. March 30: First Nebraska, A, Privates Milton F. Linde; William S. Orr; L, James H. Whitemore. March 31: Fourth Infantry, First Lieut. John C. Gregg. Wounded—March 25: First Montana, K, Second Lieut. Myles Kelley, wrist, slight; C, Privates Theodore Volkey, neck and shoulder, severe; E, John Cavanaugh, neck, slight; Musician John H. McQuary, sternum, slight; I, Privates Edward M. Weaver, forearm, slight; G, Charles E. Young, hand, slight; M, John E. Robinson, forearm, slight. March 29: E, Privates Axel Petersen, forearm, slight; James P. Lenox, knee, severe; F, William Borkowski, shoulder, severe; H, Alfred Smith, cheek, moderate; Charles F. Myers, groin, severe. Twentieth Kansas—E, Capt. William J. Watson, chest, severe; Privates Albert Shaughnessy, knee, severe; Fred Carter, forearm, severe; A, Charles A. Waters, head, slight; B, Charles M. Pease, thigh, slight; Wilson B. Smith, hand, severe; Corpl. Claude Sperlock, breast, slight; K, George B. Daily, side, slight; L, Harris E. Kuhns, shoulder, slight; Sergt. Joseph W. Murray, leg, slight; Privates Michael H. Garritty, knee, severe; C, Henry L. Johnson, forearm, slight; D, Edward Crane, forearm, moderate; James F. Rice, knee, moderate; G, Fred Atchison, knee, moderate; Corpl. James C. Hammerberg, chest, severe; H, Ernest Criss, shoulder, severe; Band, Private Courtland Fleming, abdomen, severe. First South Dakota, C, Private Lewis F. Barber, thigh, severe; John H. Benedict, lung, severe; D, Emanuel Rickman, thigh, severe; Homer A. Baker, leg, slight; Frank E. Furguson, scapula, severe; L, John W. Ortman, thigh, severe; Knut K. Peterson, hip and thigh, severe; M, John Donnelly, leg, moderate; H, Corpl. Oscar E. Johnson, flesh, slight. Tenth Pennsylvania, I, First Sergt. Augustus C. Remaley, thigh, severe; C, Sergt. Charles W. Ashcraft, leg, slight; Privates William D. Lewis, thigh, severe; D, James Novrcki, forearm, moderate; E, Richard G. Baer, hip, slight; H, George A. Taylor, abdomen, severe; K, Solomon F. Rush, pelvis, severe. First Nebraska, F, First Sergt. Arthur H. Vickers, groin, severe; C, Privates Roy G.

Campbell, leg, moderate; G, Henry M. Heckman, thigh, severe; H, William Otto Kastenborder, shoulder, slight; M, Jack L. Beach, forearm, slight. March 30: First Nebraska, D, Sergts. Hugh E. Clapp, thigh, severe; H, Robert B. McConnell, breast, slight; A, Privates Herbert P. Barber, wrist, thigh, and buttock, severe; C, William Logsdon, chest, severe; George R. Boomer, forearm, slight; Charles F. Durhem, chest, severe; Bert W. Watts, thigh, slight; B, Herbert Hedges, leg, slight; D, Erich Newfeldt, thigh and shoulder, severe; G, Jonathan Dowis, hand, slight; Claude M. Chenoweth, thigh, slight; H, Lloyd Spottenstein, hand, severe; Edward S. Downing, thigh, slight; John C. Marshall, leg, slight; Walter A. Elifritz, arm, severe; Roy Dunken, leg, slight. First Colorado, Second Lieut. Fred L. Perry, chest, slight; E, Private C. S. Carty, dorsal region, severe. Tenth Pennsylvania, E, Privates Roy J. D. Knox, foot, severe. First South Dakota, C, Sergt. Frank B. Stevens, heel, moderate. Twentieth Kansas, F, Private Todd L. Wagoner, leg, severe. First North Dakota, E, Private Harry W. Donovan, elbow, slight. Putnam Bradlee Strong, major, assistant adjutant-general volunteers, shoulder, slight; Henry T. Hoyt, major, chief surgeon volunteers, thigh, slight. Injured March 29: First South Dakota, Company M, Private Charles D. A. Theiss, powder burn, abdomen. March 13: Tenth Pennsylvania, C, Private William M. Engleheart, back and foot.

OTIS.

MANILA, *April 1, 1899.* (Received 4.25 a. m.)

AGWAR, *Washington:*

Impossible to embalm and ship bodies now. Experiment failure; weather warm, decomposition rapid. Process of embalming immediately after death unsuccessful. Of twelve bodies already sent to United States doubtful if some reach port. The work was stopped because of danger to health of inhabitants and uncertainty of preservation of remains during voyage. The dead can probably be shipped after six months' period.

OTIS.

ADJUTANT-GENERAL'S OFFICE,
Washington, April 1, 1899—10 a. m.

General OTIS, *Manila:*

Acting Secretary War directs, in view of your cable, no further effort be made to bring home the dead at this time. Not only the graves but the boxes containing the dead will be marked with care.

CORBIN.

MANILA, *April 1, 1899.* (Received 6.43 a. m.)

AGWAR, *Washington:*

Quiet prevails. Have directed troops at Malolos and on railroad on reconnoitering duty. Find insurgents only in small forces in surrounding country, who retire on the approach of our troops. Few of our troops moving to new positions. Preparing for continued active campaign. Army in excellent spirits.

OTIS.

COLOMBO. (Received April 1, 1899—5.20 a. m.)

AGWAR, *Washington:*

Depart 1st. Private Philip F. McGuire, F, Twelfth, drowned, bathing here. Health troops improving.

SMITH.

CORRESPONDENCE.

MANILA, *April 1, 1899.* (Received 1.10 p. m.)

AGWAR, *Washington:*

Additional casualties, March 30: First Nebraska: Wounded—Company L, Private Gaylord S. Blakeley, hand and thigh, slight. March 31: Killed—First Nebraska, E, Private R. M. Lawton. Wounded—Twenty-third Infantry, C, Musician High R. Ashby, forearm, moderate; Privates Peter O. Olesen, forearm, moderate; Harry W. Stephenson, thighs, severe; Corporals Frank G. Armstrong, abdomen, severe; L, Wiley Barnes, thigh, severe; Privates William G. Alvey, chest, severe; E, Oliver B. Cason, back, severe; Charles H. Anderson, thigh, severe; Band, William E. House, abdomen, severe. Fourth Infantry, Company H, Corpl. Richard F. Schmidt, forearm, moderate. Third Infantry, H, Corpl. Ernest A. Kuver, leg, moderate; A, Privates Emil Krohn, abdomen, severe; D, Robert C. Kistler, forearm, moderate; M, Charles C. Dehart, forehead, moderate. First Nebraska, D, First Lieut. P. James Cosgrave, abdomen, slight; Privates John Webtever, shoulder, severe; D, William L. Whitcomb, forearm, moderate; E, Albert S. Hisey, neck, severe; F, Walter P. Stockton, shoulder, severe; K, John M. Everson, thigh, severe; Pertinax Donaldson, leg, severe; L, Emil Saal, chest, severe. First South Dakota, C, Wagoner Joseph D. Waugh, thigh, severe; F, Corpl. L. S. Richmond, knee, moderate; E, Privates William Grundy, knee, severe; K, Herman F. Kruger, arm, severe. First Colorado, C, Privates Charles L. Hutchinson, thigh, severe; D, John Dennis, neck, severe; G, Henry E. Redmond, cheek, severe; Corpls. John T. McCorkle, thigh, severe;L. E. Philippi, head, severe.

Answering inquiries, Colonel Egbert, Twenty-second Infantry, killed at Malinta, 12.20 p. m., March 26. Lieutenant Krayenbuhl, Third Artillery, shot near Meycanayan, 4.30 p. m., March 26; died 5.15 same afternoon. Charles O. Ballenger, D, First Nebraska, killed February 5. Harry R. Athey, A, First Montana, doing well. Dalzell well (for Meiklejohn).

OTIS.

MANILA, *April 2, 1899.* (Received 3.25 a. m.)

AGWAR, *Washington:*

First Lieut. John C. Gregg, Fourth Infantry, aid Brigadier-General Hall, killed in battle with insurgents 11 a. m., March 31, near Mariquina, Luzon.

OTIS.

MANILA, *April 2, 1899.* (Received 10.07 a. m.)

AGWAR, *Washington:*

Deaths since last report. March 25: Thomas F. Whiteside, private, M, First Colorado, dysentery.

March 28: Adolph Koplen, private, A, First North Dakota, drowned, accidental. Smallpox, March 25: Edward Pratt, private, L, Thirteenth Minnesota; Wallace A. Bolin, quartermaster sergeant, Fifty-first Iowa.

March 26: Frank M. Martin, private, I, Twenty-third Infantry.

March 27: Nelson B. McKellar, private, F, First South Dakota.

March 28: James O. Stovall, private, D, Sixth Artillery.

From wounds in action, March 29: David Campbell, private, M, First Washington.

March 26: Robert Brown, private, G, First Montana; John Miller, private, I, Twenty-second Infantry; William C. Courtney, private, B, First Washington; George H. Fortson, captain, B, First Washington.

March 28: Mat Sumers, private, M, First Nebraska; Lee Forby, captain, G, First Nebraska.

March 31: Charles Preachers, first sergeant, M, First South Dakota; Will May, private, I, First South Dakota; William H. Heasperling, corporal, G, Third Infantry; Fred H. Wheaton, private, H, First Montana; Joseph Wahl, private H, Twentieth Kansas.

April 1: George A. Taylor, private, H, Tenth Pennsylvania.

OTIS.

MANILA, *April 3, 1899.* (Received 7.53 a. m.)

AGWAR, *Washington:*

Casualties not heretofore reported. March 25, Twenty-second Infantry: Wounded—Company H, Private Fritz Herter, wrist, moderate. April 1, First North Dakota, H, Second Lieut. Dorman Baldwin, jr., leg, severe; D, Corpl. John C. Byron, forearm, moderate; Private Elijah Morgan, eyebrow, slight. Third Infantry, Second Lieut. Chauncey B. Humphrey, forearm, slight. First Nebraska, D, Capt. Martin Herpolsheimer, forearm, moderate, accidental. Cable February 7, reporting Egger, First Nebraska, killed, is error; no such man.

OTIS.

MANILA, *April 3, 1899.* (Received 12.43 a. m.)

AGWAR, *Washington:*

Present indications denote insurgent government in perilous condition. Its army defeated, discouraged, and shattered; insurgents returning to their homes in cities and villages between here and points north of Malolos, which our reconnoitering parties have reached, and desire protection of Americans. Movements to the south and east now in contemplation will have beneficial results. News from Visayan Islands more encouraging every day.

OTIS.

ADJUTANT-GENERAL'S OFFICE,
Washington, April 4, 1899.

OTIS, *Manila:*

Will ship with 72 artillery horses 170 mules, steamer *Leelanaw*, about 15th. Shall any packers and teamsters be sent? If sent, how many? Have plenty mules. Shall any additional be shipped later?

CORBIN.

HEADQUARTERS OF THE ARMY,
Washington, April 4, 1899.

Memorandum for the Adjutant-General: In view of the cablegram from General Otis of the 3d instant reporting "present indications denote insurgent government in perilous condition, its army defeated, etc.," the Major-General Commanding recommends that a cablegram be sent to General Otis asking whether the services of three light batteries ordered to Manila will be necessary.

J. C. GILMORE, *Brigadier-General.*

MANILA. (Received April 5, 1899—2.40 a. m.)

AGWAR, *Washington:*

Transport *Sherman* left 3d instant, Nagasaki, San Francisco; 6 officers; 67 enlisted men, mostly sick and wounded; 7 civilians.

OTIS.

ADJUTANT-GENERAL'S OFFICE,
Washington, April 5, 1899.

COMMANDING GENERAL, DEPARTMENT OF CALIFORNIA,
San Francisco, Cal.:

Following received from General Otis and sent you for your information and guidance:

"Transport *Sherman* left 3d instant, Nagasaki, San Francisco; 6 officers; 67 enlisted men, mostly sick and wounded; 7 civilians."

H. C. CORBIN, *Adjutant-General.*

ADJUTANT-GENERAL'S OFFICE,
Washington, April 5, 1899.

COMMANDING GENERAL, DEPARTMENT OF CALIFORNIA,
San Francisco, Cal.:

General Otis cabled March 25 that transport *Grant* left that day for Nagasaki, San Francisco. This for your information.

H. C. CORBIN, *Adjutant-General.*

MANILA. (Received April 5, 1899—7.13 a. m.)

AGWAR, *Washington:*

One hundred nineteen mules received; 295 en route steamer *Conemaugh;* 170 to come by *Leelanaw;* no more required. Cabled March 5 for 150 aparejos, 30 civilian teamsters, of which 10 should be packers. Would like in addition 20 teamsters and 20 packers.

OTIS.

MILLBRAE, CAL., *April 6, 1899.* (Received 1.35 p. m.)

Gen. H. C. CORBIN,
War Department, Washington, D. C.:

Delayed answer to consult General Babcock about Government nurses. Still think desirable to send 6 offered by Mrs. Reid's society. Need great nurses there; ask for them. These cost Government nothing, serve on transports going over and under surgeons there.

WHITELAW REID.

MANILA. (Received April 6, 1899—8.46 a. m.)

AGWAR, *Washington:*

Huber, Hospital Corps, insurgent prisoner, passed beyond lines without permission seven days before hostilities commenced, having camera and revolver; was arrested near Malolos because armed and taking photographs; was in civilian clothes; claimed to be British seaman; was in fair health February 10, when money furnished him with promise of more to follow; he and 3 other prisoners arrested before hostilities commenced were at Malolos ten days before capture of city; believe that all are alive.

OTIS.

MANILA. (Received April 7, 1899—7.45 a. m.)

AGWAR, *Washington:*

Transport *Valencia* arrived this morning; successful passage.

OTIS.

MANILA. (Received April 7, 1899—8.40 a. m.)

AGWAR, *Washington:*

Casualties not heretofore reported: Killed—Third Artillery, March 25, K, Sergt. Edwin W. Wall. Wounded—H, Privates Richard King, scalp, slight; L, William B. French, forearm, slight; Fred J. A. John, hand, slight.

March 27: L, Second Lieut. Lloyd England, finger, slight; Sergt. John Montgomery, hand, slight.

First Washington—March 28: B, Private William Pyncheon, hand, slight.

Tenth Pennsylvania—March 30: D, Private George B. Gemas, foot, slight.

First Colorado—March 31: C, Private George P. Dickerman, shoulder, slight. Twenty-third Infantry, L, Corpl. John A. Jones, hand, moderate.

First Montana—Killed, April 4: L, Corpl. Owen H. Rowlands. Wounded—Band, Sergt. George W. Crowell, ankle, slight; G, Privates William J. Boast, knee, severe; M, Frank Landermann, chest, severe.

Answering inquiry, Albert W. Hartrigsen, E, Fourth Cavalry, accidently shot in barracks March 10 with revolver in hands Private Stolkman, same troop. Hartrigsen died following morning. Investigation board of officers mailed.

OTIS.

MANILA. (Received April 7, 1899—11.11 a. m.)

ADJUTANT-GENERAL, *Washington:*

MacArthur's division still at Malolos and vicinity. Enemy apparently concentrating to north and east, with advance 13 miles south of San Isidro in Tagalic Province, Nueva Ecija, to which point insurgent government moved. Lawton moves to-morrow on shore cities surrounding Laguna de Bay and insurgents in southern province. Many Negros seeking entrance to Manila. City very quiet. Business active. Confidence restored.

OTIS.

ADJUTANT-GENERAL'S OFFICE,
Washington, April 8, 1899.

Hon. WHITELAW REID, *Millbrae, Cal.:*

Replying to your telegram of the 6th instant, the commanding general, Department California, San Francisco, has been ordered to send the 6 nurses. Please communicate with the commanding general, San Francisco.

H. C. CORBIN, *Adjutant-General.*

ADJUTANT-GENERAL'S OFFICE,
Washington, April 8, 1899.

COMMANDING GENERAL, DEPARTMENT OF CALIFORNIA,
San Francisco, Cal.:

At the request of Hon. Whitelaw Reid, the Acting Secretary of War directs that 6 nurses, to be furnished by Mrs. Reid's society, be furnished transportation on Government transport from San Francisco to Manila.

H. C. CORBIN, *Adjutant-General.*

ADJUTANT-GENERAL'S OFFICE,
Washington, April 8, 1899.

General OTIS, *Manila:*

The Twenty-first Infantry is en route to San Francisco and will sail on the *Hancock*, the light batteries on the *Newport*. It is assumed, in absence of other recommendation, that these troops are required.

CORBIN.

SAN FRANCISCO, CAL., *April 8, 1899.*
ADJUTANT-GENERAL, U. S. ARMY,
  Washington, D. C.:
  Transport *Newport* arrived to-day. Passengers: Capt. Charles McClure, Eighteenth Infantry, acting judge-advocate; First Lieut. Harry H. Seckler, Twentieth Kansas; 7 ladies, wives of officers Army and Navy; 1 seaman, 1 quartermaster's clerk, no enlisted men of volunteers or regulars.

                                            BABCOCK,
                    In absence of Department Commander.

SINGAPORE. (Received April 8, 1899—9.06 a. m.)
ADJUTANT-GENERAL, *Washington:*
  Sail to-morrow 7. All well.

                                            SMITH.

MANILA. (Received April 9, 1899—3 p. m.)
ADJUTANT-GENERAL, *Washington:*
  Transport *Sheridan* expected 14th instant; Twenty-first Infantry, April 25 and 9. You say Twenty-first Infantry en route to San Francisco to sail on *Hancock*, light batteries on *Newport*. These troops are required, also all others mentioned in your dispatch of March 10. The large island of Mindanao and Jolo Archipelago will require 2,500 men for a time at least, the Visayan Islands 5,000, and in Luzon the more employed the sooner peace established. Insurgent northern troops, though demoralized, holding together fairly well. Will be attacked again soon. Extreme heat our greatest difficulty. About 6,000 armed insurgents in Luzon northern provinces. Two thousand have returned near to and south of Manila. Lawton now opposite Laguna de Bay with 1,500 men and improvised navy; will visit cities. Refugees returning; no hostile demonstration threatened. Insurgents consider Commissioners' proclamation sign of United States' weakness; has produced good effect among better classes pacifically inclined. Condition of troops excellent. Sickness light.

                                            OTIS.

ADJUTANT-GENERAL'S OFFICE,
Washington, April 9, 1899—7 p. m.
General OTIS, *Manila:*
  The President is most anxious that every provision shall be made for the health and comfort of your troops during the rainy season. He does not doubt that you are giving the matter your earnest attention, but wants you to know that no expense should be spared for their welfare and protection.

                                            CORBIN.

MANILA. (Received April 9, 1899—10.35 a. m.)
AGWAR, *Washington:*
  Following deaths since last report: March 31, Jacob Hamberger, private, H, Eighteenth Infantry, gunshot wound, accidental. April 4, George B. Fargo, private, F, First Washington, dysentery.
  From wounds in action: April 1, Frank G. Armstrong, assumed name, real name Frank O'Keefe, corporal, C, Twenty-third Infantry; Leonard E. Phillippi, corporal,

AFFAIRS IN THE PHILIPPINE ISLANDS. 961

G, First Colorado. 2d, William Marshall, private, D, First Montana. 4th, Arthur H. Vickers, first sergeant, F, First Nebraska. 6th, Joseph J. Motz, private, K, Third Artillery; William E. House, private, band, Twenty-third Infantry; William Tufts, private, E, Fourth Cavalry.

OTIS.

MANILA. (Received April 9, 1899—1.10 p. m.)

AGWAR, *Washington:*

Casualties not heretofore reported: March 25: Killed—Third Infantry, G, Privates John Ingham Nelson; M, Thomas P. Morris. Wounded—California Artillery, D, Private Lionel Sturman, arm, slight. Third Infantry, E, Privates Jack Hamilton, leg, slight; M, Joseph Slack, arm slight; John McCullough, arm slight; John W. Parrot, foot slight; Joseph D. Sweet, heel, severe. Twentieth Kansas, G, Privates Wesley D. Mathews, above eye, slight; K, George Meyer, abdomen, slight. 27th, H, Q. M. Sergt. Larrance Page, foot, slight. 29th, Band, Cortland Fleming, abdomen, severe. First Montana: 25th, G, Private John T. McLaughlin, hand, slight. First Washington: 26th, K, Private Thomas L. Munroe, scalp and hand, slight. Tenth Pennsylvania: 28th, K, Sergt. Frank Sharp, abdomen, severe. 29th, D, Private Charles Rosenecker, leg, slight. First South Dakota: 28th, C, Private Guy P. Davis, hand, slight. 29th, L, Private John F. Rogers back, semisevere. Utah Artillery: 31st, B, Private John A. Pender, thigh, severe; H, Private Alfred J. Borderwine, Fifty-first Iowa, missing.

OTIS.

MANILA. (Received April 10, 1899—2.32 a. m.)

AGWAR, *Washington:*

Transport *Portland* arrived no casualties.

OTIS.

MANILA. (Received April 10, 1899—8.47 a. m.)

AGWAR, *Washington:*

Spanish authorities seek permission to send to Caroline Islands, to be used as garrison, 270 of their former native soldiers held at Manila by United States as prisoners of war and released when discharged from Spanish army. These natives are Macabebes, hostile to Tagalos, and are afraid to return to their native province north of Manila and are still in walled city. They desire to accept military service from Spain and go to Carolines with their families. Are there objections?

OTIS.

ADJUTANT-GENERAL'S OFFICE,
Washington, April 10, 1899.

OTIS, *Manila:*

The President sees no objection to the transfer of any proportion of the Spanish forces to Carolines.

CORBIN.

MANILA. (Received April 10, 1899—10.20 a. m.)

AGWAR, *Washington:*

Lawton's command captured Santa Cruz, chief city of Laguna de Bay, this morning; casualties, 6 wounded. Insurgent troops driven, leaving 68 dead on field and larger number wounded; a considerable number captured. Lawton will pursue westward.

OTIS.

ADJUTANT-GENERAL'S OFFICE,
Washington, April 10, 1899.

OTIS, *Manila:*
Should recruits be armed and equipped before leaving here?

CORBIN.

MANILA. (Received April 11, 1899—12.11 a. m.)

AGWAR, *Washington:*
Recruits should bring equipments, not arms. Three thousand additional Krag-Jörgensen now en route. Three thousand in use by volunteers here.

OTIS.

MANILA. (Received April 11, 1899—7 a. m.)

AGWAR, *Washington:*
Lawton's success at Santa Cruz more complete than reported yesterday. Enemy left 93 uniformed dead on field and number seriously wounded. Lawton captured city without destruction property. His loss 10 wounded, slight, except 2; 1 since died. Lieutenant Eltinge only officer wounded, slight in hand. Enemy retired eastward; Lawton in pursuit early this morning. Expects to capture all insurgents' craft and gunboats formerly in lake.

OTIS.

MANILA. (Received April 11, 1899—8.30 a. m.)

AGWAR, *Washington:*
Insurgents attacked MacArthur's line of railway communication last night in considerable force. Repulsed by Wheaton with heavy loss; Wheaton's casualties 3 killed, 20 wounded. Shall have water base at Malolos in few days; railway communication immaterial; with new base secured farther advance into interior of island practicable. Railway and telegraph communication with Malolos intact.

OTIS.

ADJUTANT-GENERAL'S OFFICE,
Washington, April 11, 1899.

General OTIS, *Manila:*
Treaty signed and exchanged 3 p. m. to-day.

CORBIN.

ADJUTANT-GENERAL'S OFFICE,
Washington, April 11, 1899.

OTIS, *Manila:*
Twenty-first Infantry left Plattsburg yesterday. Regiment with 1 battery leaves 17th, *Hancock.*

Warren, 8 batteries Sixth Artillery and recruits; *Newport,* 260 marines and 2 batteries; *Morgan City,* recruits. These sail between 15th and 20th. *Ohio* and *Senator* expected April 20; take Thirteenth Infantry and recruits; should leave before end month. *Grant* expected April 25; will take Sixth Infantry and recruits. *Sherman* expected May 3; will take Sixteenth Infantry and recruits.

For reasons heretofore stated, *Sheridan* and other transports should be hurried back.

CORBIN.

MANILA. (Received April 12, 1899—2.15 a. m.)

AGWAR, *Washington:*
Relief arrived; all well. Notify Surgwar.

OTIS.

MANILA. (Received April 12, 1899—12.57 p. m.)

AGWAR, *Washington:*
Casualties not heretofore reported: Killed, Fourteenth Infantry, April 10: G, Private John W. Pitts. Second Oregon, 11th: M, Privates Henry Payne, Edward Hoffman, Joseph L. Berry. Thirteenth Minnesota, 10th: L, Private Jesse J. Cole. 11th: C, Private Maurice P. Beaty. Wounded, Hospital Corps, 9th: Acting Hospital Steward Benno Altmann, forearm, moderate. Thirteenth Minnesota, 10th: B, Private Henry Foss, leg, moderate. 11th: F, First Lieut. Charles N. Clark, scalp, slight; A, First Sergt. Eugene Hanscom, thumb, moderate; Corpls. Holden P. Guilbert, hand, slight; I, Walfred A. Ryberg, arm, slight; B, Private William J. Oberle, ear, slight; Eugene A. Harvey, thumb, slight; Charlie J. Meggison, back, slight; Charles F. Brackett, hands, slight; C, John J. Young, jaw, severe; Bjorn B. Gislason, scalp, slight; Harry C. Anderson, ear, slight; L, Richard H. Kelly, forehead, severe; Adam Hotchkiss, thigh, severe. Fourteenth Infantry, 10th: D, Private William Somers, arm, severe. Fourth Cavalry, 11th: C, Private Joe Grabowsky, head, severe. First North Dakota: H, Corpl. Herman P. Wolf, foot, moderate. First Idaho: A, Private Arthur Pearson, forearm, severe. Second Oregon: M, Privates Everett Millard, abdomen, severe; Arthur Pullen, arm, slight.

OTIS.

MANILA. (Received April 12, 1899—9.45 a. m.)

AGWAR, *Washington:*
Yesterday, in the lake region, Lawton pursued insurgents eastward from Santa Cruz, dispersing them; captured all the larger vessel used in the lake trade and Spanish gunboat. He is now endeavoring to pass them from river, where concealed, into lake. He moves to-night by water to another point where considerable insurgent force has assembled. This morning Wheaton drove enemy 10 miles to eastward of railway line of communication with Malolos; Lawton's and Wheaton's casualties few and light, as enemy made no stand. Notified by Spain that she will evacuate Mindoro and Polo soon. Two thousand troops required in those waters; will send them as soon as possible.

OTIS.

MANILA. (Received April 14, 1899—8.38 a. m.)

AGWAR, *Washington:*
Spanish liquidation commission asks delivery of all movable property in public buildings formerly occupied by Spanish officials, Colonial Island and city; in all public school, civil court, library, art buildings, etc.; the delivery of all records, constitution, archives of patronage which Spain exercised over church; of all records relating to right of Spain, and useful in collection of credits, taxes, rents, etc., accruing prior to August 13; delivery of all records which concern Philippine loan; of all Spanish deposits made by private individuals in treasury; of all Spanish bonds, and, finally, of all funds in Spanish treasury of Manila at time of capitulation. Nothing yet delivered, but property of military character and records and property in which United States no interest. How far shall Spanish request be complied with?

OTIS.

WAR DEPARTMENT, *April 14, 1899.*

The Honorable, the ATTORNEY-GENERAL.

SIR: I have the honor herewith to hand you copy of cablegram received from Maj. Gen. E. S. Otis, Manila, in reference to delivery of certain property to Spain, and to ask the views of your Department thereon.

Very respectfully, G. D. MEIKLEJOHN,
Acting Secretary of War.

ADJUTANT-GENERAL'S OFFICE,
Washington, April 14, 1899.

OTIS, *Manila:*

We are getting inquiries from State authorities as to muster out of the Nebraska, Washington, and Minnesota regiments in your command. Have understood from your dispatches that it is their desire to remain as long as they are needed, which under the law can not exceed six months. The President is solicitous that there shall be no misunderstanding among the volunteers, and that their preference shall be regarded.

If it is their wish to be mustered out, that should be done at the very earliest time practicable. If you need them, their retention must be voluntary. These volunteers have done noble service, which the President appreciates. He wants them to choose whether they will come home or remain temporarily in case the exigencies of public service require it.

CORBIN.

NEW YORK, N. Y. (Received April 14, 1899.)

Hon. GEORGE D. MEIKLEJOHN,
Acting Secretary of War, Washington, D. C.

SIR: On March 4, 1899, the honorable Secretary of War entered into a contract for the transportation of the Spanish prisoners from Manila to Spain. The contractors, Messrs. J. M. Ceballos & Co., agreed to provide a sufficient number of steamships in the harbor of Manila to perform the entire service as stipulated in said contract, so that the embarkation of the last Spanish prisoners of war and other persons should be made not later than May 1, 1899. The ships to be used for that purpose are also named and described in the detailed list which was annexed to the contract.

The contractors have called my attention on several occasions to the fact that they are holding two steamships in the harbor of Manila to comply with the terms of the agreement, and they are desirous of knowing if the Government would permit them to use these steamers in the regular course of business, in which event the contract should be so modified that, should the Government be ready to transport more prisoners of war before May 1, sufficient time should be allowed them to send their steamers to Manila. Their demands are, of course, perfectly just, and if there are no more prisoners to be shipped, or the Spanish prisoners in the hands of the Philippine insurgents are not likely to be surrendered before May 1, it would seem wise and proper to allow them to use their ships, for if you ask them to hold their ships then the question of demurrage will arise, and this is one of the questions that I have been most anxious to avoid, and so far no demurrage that I know of has been incurred.

The only solution that I can suggest is for you to indicate to me or assure me that, in the event of their using the steamers which they now have in Manila for their regular business between Manila and Spain for the transshipment of passengers and freight, due notice will be given to the contractors when the Government is ready for any additional transportation of Spanish prisoners under the terms of the contract and that time will be allowed to send the steamers from Spain to Manila, calculating, say thirty days, for the transmission of orders and for the passage of the steamers from Spain to Manila. With this assurance from you, I will advise them to dispatch their steamers back to Spain with passengers who are now anxious to return and such of the Spanish officers—prisoners of war—who, I am informed, are awaiting transportation, but who were, on account of the smallness of their number and by arrangement with General Otis, held back awaiting a full load.

Your usual prompt consideration of this matter will be greatly appreciated by me, in order that I may be able to advise the contractors as to the proper course to pursue.

Very respectfully, yours,

R. A. C. SMITH.

WAR DEPARTMENT, *Washington, April 14, 1899.*

MY DEAR SIR: I have the honor to acknowledge the receipt of your letter of the 8th instant, asking on behalf of Messrs. J. M. Ceballos & Co., contractors for the transportation of Spanish prisoners from the Philippines to Spain, that the Government permit them to use their vessels in their regular business, and that their contract be modified so that, should the Government require prisoners to be transported before May 1 proximo, sufficient time be allowed them to send their ships to Manila, say thirty days' notice.

Replying thereto, I beg to inform you that I have this day, with a view to meeting your request, directed that General Otis be cabled for report as to whether there are any more Spanish prisoners ready to send to Spain, and if not that he be instructed to release the ships of Messrs. Ceballos & Co., now at Manila, in order that they may resume their regular business.

Very respectfully, G. D. MEIKLEJOHN,
Acting Secretary of War.

R. A. C. SMITH, Esq., *100 Broadway, New York, N. Y.*

MANILA. (Received April 14, 1899—7.55 a. m.)

AGWAR, *Washington:*

Eastern Extension Australia and China Telegraph Company requests United States recognition of concessions made by Spain, which include exclusive cable privileges between Manila and Hongkong until 1940. Also same for twenty years with respect to its Visayan lines, with annual subsidy of about $20,000 gold; see Spain royal decrees, April 10, 1897, March 28, 1898; also pages 241 and 262, Senate Document No. 53, containing argument of commission on recent Paris treaty. Shall the above and other related concessions be recognized?

OTIS.

WAR DEPARTMENT, *Washington, April 14, 1899.*

The Honorable, the SECRETARY OF STATE.

SIR: I have the honor herewith to hand you copy of cablegram received from Maj. Gen. E. S. Otis, in reference to the request of the Eastern Extension Australia and China Telegraph Company that the United States recognize certain concessions made by Spain, and to ask the views of your Department thereon.

Very respectfully, G. D. MEIKLEJOHN,
Acting Secretary of War.

MANILA. (Received April 14, 1899—12.11 a. m.)

AGWAR, *Washington:*

Sheridan arrived. Casualties: Lieutenant Meyer, 3 enlisted men, died; 4 deserted; 6 children of enlisted men died en route. Health of troops now very good.

OTIS.

MANILA. (Received April 15, 1899—8 a. m.)

AGWAR, *Washington:*

Cable company will place cable between Iloilo and Cebu, giving Manila direct communication with latter city if desired. Consider this extension important for military purposes. This to be considered in connection with my dispatch of yesterday regarding recognition.

OTIS.

[Telephone from Attorney-General.]

ADJUTANT-GENERAL:

The Attorney-General wishes to get from the War Department a copy of a cablegram which he drew up about three weeks or a month ago to General Otis, concerning the disposition of property in the Philippine Islands. Please send it to the office of the chief clerk to the Attorney-General.

APRIL 15, 1899.

ADJUTANT-GENERAL'S OFFICE,
Washington, April 15, 1899.

The Honorable, the ATTORNEY-GENERAL.

SIR: In compliance with telephonic request from your Department this morning, I have the honor to hand you herewith the copy of the cablegram you drew up March 22, concerning the disposition of property in the Philippine Islands.

Very respectfully,

H. C. CORBIN, *Adjutant-General.*

DEPARTMENT OF JUSTICE,
Washington, April 15, 1899.

The SECRETARY OF WAR.

SIR: Referring to your note of yesterday, I recommend an answer as per inclosure to the cablegram of to-day from Maj. Gen. E. S. Otis, Manila.

Respectfully,

JOHN W. GRIGGS, *Attorney-General.*

(See cipher cable sent April 25, 1899.)

MANILA. (Received April 16, 1899—12.55 a. m.)

AGWAR, *Washington:*

Casualties not heretofore reported: Killed—Third Artillery, April 13, H, Sergt. John L. Lang; L, Private Ernest Seifert. Wounded—First Washington, April 9, D, Corpl. Calvin Welbon, hip, slight. Twenty-second Infantry, K, Private Robert H. Haley, forearm, moderate. Thirteenth Minnesota, April 11, C, Privates Charles Still, knee, slight; D, Charles C. Conley, clavicle, slight. April 12, E, Corpl. Robert J. Kelliher, leg, severe. First Montana, April 13, B, Private Joseph Wright, thigh, severe. Third Artillery, K, Second Lieut. Conrad H. Lanza, leg, moderate; Privates Ralph Golden, cheek, severe; L, Henry V. Tjarnel, thigh, severe; George C. Wampler, cheek, slight; Robert Moles, hand, slight.

OTIS.

MANILA. (Received April 16, 1899—10.10 a. m.)

AGWAR, *Washington:*

Casualties not heretofore reported: Wounded—First Nebraska, March 26, H, Private Nels G. Forsberg, abdomen, slight. March 28, F, Private Ora Ross, side, slight. March 29, C, Privates Jesse P. Baird, hand, slight; E. Edward Matthews, wrist, slight; K, William L. Gilbert, side, slight. March 31, L, Sergt. William L. Baehr, shoulder, slight; B, Privates Herbert Rasmussen, thigh, severe; E, Frank A. Graham, leg, slight. First Washington, April 13, H, First Lieut. Edward E. Southern, forearm, severe; First Sergt. John J. Harlton, leg, slight. Fourteenth Infantry, A, Privates Moses P. Pritchard, thigh, severe; K, Alonzo R. Johnson, hip, severe. Second Oregon, April 15, A, Second Lieut. Jonathan A. Young, foot, serious. First North Dakota, I, Private Herbert L. Files, axilla, severe. Killed—Corpl. Isadore Driscoll, Wagoner J. Peter W. Tompkins, Privates Alfred C. Almen, William G. Lamb; I, Musician George J. Schneller.

OTIS.

MANILA. (Received April 16, 1899—10.15 a. m.)

AGWAR, *Washington:*

Deaths since last report: Smallpox—April 5, Don L. Noble, recruit, Eighteenth Infantry. April 9, Nathaniel F. Prickett, private, G, Twenty-third Infantry. April 11, Julius Hohlfeld, corporal, M, Fourth Infantry. April 13, Algernon A. Gardner, private, G, Fourth Infantry; John Turner, private, H, Fifty-first Iowa. Typhoid fever—April 8, Charles A. Kaiser, private, K, First Montana. General collapse—April 9, Walter M. Riley, corporal, F, First Nebraska. Fever, undetermined—April 13, Charles Eschels, private, B, First South Dakota. Dysentery—April 13, Alfred H. Whitaker, sergeant, A, First North Dakota. Suicide—April 12, George Briggs, private, G, First Wyoming Infantry, real name Harry D. Wicks.

OTIS.

ADJUTANT-GENERAL'S OFFICE,
Washington, April 17, 1899.

OTIS, *Manila:*

Telegraph whether British deserters from Malta on *Sheridan* were left at Colombo.

CORBIN.

ADJUTANT-GENERAL'S OFFICE,
Washington, April 18, 1899.

OTIS, *Manila:*

If there are no more Spanish prisoners ready to send Spain, release ships of Ceballos & Co., now at Manila to resume their regular business.

CORBIN.

SAN FRANCISCO, CAL., *April 18, 1899.*
(Received 3.39 p. m.)

ADJUTANT-GENERAL, *Washington, D. C.:*

Hancock sailed 5.20 a. m. to-day with headquarters, band, and 12 companies Twenty-first Infantry, 32 officers, 1,326 enlisted men; Light Battery E, First Artillery, 3 officers, 99 enlisted men; 4 medical officers, and 21 Hospital Corps men, attached; 3 men Fourth Artillery and 2 men Ninth Infantry. Ammunition, small arms per man, Twenty-First Infantry, 205; calibre, .30.

BABCOCK,
In Absence Department Commander.

MANILA. (Received April 18, 1899—2.50 a. m.)

AGWAR, *Washington:*

One British deserter turned over at Port Said, one at Colombo; others probably left *Sheridan* at ports en route as they could not be found.

OTIS.

ADJUTANT-GENERAL'S OFFICE,
Washington, April 18, 1899.

OTIS, *Manila:*

Regiment infantry recalled from Porto Rico. This makes it available for you, if so desired.

CORBIN.

MANILA. (Received April 19, 1899—2.15 a. m.)

AGWAR, *Washington:*

Transport *Portland* left for San Francisco, via Nagasaki, 16th; 23 passengers, mostly discharged and sick soldiers. *Valencia* 18th; 41 passengers, of whom 34 discharged soldiers. *Sheridan* will leave 25th. All cargo discharged to-day, but undergoing necessary repairs to machinery.

OTIS.

MANILA. (Received April 19, 1899—4.10 a. m.)

AGWAR, *Washington:*

All prisoners war, except few Spanish authorities wish to retain, have been shipped. No vessel of Spanish trans-Atlantic Company retained here at any time; none to release. Future shipments confined to prisoners held by insurgent government. Few in Manila escape from insurgents.

OTIS.

MANILA. (Received April 19, 1899—8.54 a. m.)

AGWAR, *Washington:*

Deaths on *Sheridan:* Second Lieut. Ralph E. Meyer disappeared at sea about April 11, accident or suicide; Private Timothy Donohue, H, of pneumonia March 1, buried at sea March 2; Corpl. June M. Brackette, C, of pneumonia March 23, buried at sea same date; Private Philip F. McGuire, F, accidentally drowned March 29, bathing harbor, Colombo, Ceylon, buried same date, general cemetery, Colombo, Ceylon. All members Twelfth Infantry.

OTIS.

MANILA. (Received April 19, 1899—11.40 a. m.)

ADJUTANT-GENERAL, *Washington:*

Lawton returned from Lake country 17th instant, bringing captured vessels. Movement to north projected, employing 7,000 troops. Insurgents much scattered; retreat before our force; await opportunity to attack detachments. Better class of people tired of war, desire peace. Enemy build hopes on return Volunteers. Its army much demoralized, and losses by desertion and death large. Will probably prosecute guerrilla warfare, looting and burning country which it occupies. Excessive heat and lack of roads and transportation makes campaigning difficult. Health and spirits of troops good. Volunteers will not reenlist; return will commence about May 5. Will render willing service until return transports available. Embarkation will continue through June and July, when, if expected conditions continue, the force here will be too weak to meet demands. Reports from Visayan Islands continue very encouraging. Interisland commerce heavy; customs receipts increasing. Can not formulate decided opinion on results; from present war outlook am encouraged to hope for great improvement.

OTIS.

ADJUTANT GENERAL'S OFFICE,
Washington, April 19, 1899—12.30 p. m.

OTIS, *Manila:*

Total regular troops with you, under orders and en route, 22,260. What additional troops will you require after return of volunteers as per your cable to-day?

CORBIN.

ADJUTANT GENERAL'S OFFICE,
Washington, April 19, 1899.

OTIS, *Manila:*

Twenty-first Infantry and one Light Battery sailed *Hancock*, April 18.

H. C. CORBIN,
Adjutant-General.

MANILA. (Received April 19, 1899—4 a. m.)

AGWAR, *Washington:*

Regiment recalled from Porto Rico needed here.

OTIS.

ADJUTANT-GENERAL'S OFFICE,
Washington, April 20, 1899.

OTIS, *Manila:*

Is there anything the Department can do to help you in matter transportation or any other assistance needed?

CORBIN.

MANILA. (Received April 20, 1899—9.31 a. m.)

AGWAR, *Washington:*

Prudence will not permit reduction November estimate of 30,000. Anticipate difficulty in Luzon and extreme southern islands. Can now capture any place on coast or in interior, but permanent occupancy in many instances necessary, as withdrawal of troops always followed by reappearance of enemy who terrorize inhabitants whatever their desires. Majority people, better classes, wish peace and stable government, but armed insurgents, drawn from lower classes, prefer to riot rather by looting than honest labor. Hope to report greatly improved conditions within month, but dislike to anticipate facts by submitting present opinion. In Negros at present native organizations, paid by quartermaster, efficient police, and most of troops can be withdrawn soon. Believe this policy can be employed in all Visayan Islands, and ultimately to limited extent in Luzon and southern islands. Can pay these organizations from civil funds, now materially increasing. Am reestablishing civil courts in Manila and will endeavor to reconstruct soon civil government Manila Province.

OTIS.

ADJUTANT-GENERAL'S OFFICE,
Washington, April 20, 1899.

General OTIS, *Manila:*

Would it be possible for you to organize a regiment or more from the volunteers to serve until 1901, under act approved March 2, you to nominate officers from those with you?

CORBIN.

SAN FRANCISCO, CAL., *April 20, 1899.*
(Received 9.33 p. m.)

ADJUTANT-GENERAL, *Washington, D. C.:*

Transport *Newport* sailed this day at 3.30 p. m. with Major Tiernon, First Artillery; Light Batteries F, Fourth and Fifth Artilleries; 8 officers, and 222 enlisted men, 2 acting assistant surgeons, 6 Red Cross nurses, 6 nurses employed by medical department, Commissary-Sergeant Favier, Mr. Umstetter, agent Greater American Exposition, and wife; 15 officers and 260 enlisted men of battalion marines. Colonel Pope, marines, senior officer on ship.

BABCOCK,
In absence Department Commander.

MANILA. (Received April 21, 1899—1.03 a. m.)

AGWAR, *Washington:*

Conemaugh arrived yesterday. Lost 10 mules before reaching Honolulu; two since. Two hundred eighty-three remaining not in as good condition as those by *Tacoma*.

OTIS.

MANILA. (Received April 21, 1899—1.05 a. m.)

AGWAR, *Washington:*

May be possible to organize regiment or more under conditions indicated in your dispatch yesterday. Will make endeavor.

OTIS.

MANILA. (Received April 21, 1899—2.35 a. m.)

AGWAR, *Washington:*

General King sick; ordered San Francisco 18th instant, under your instructions January 24. Leaves soon. Not able to perform service here. This in view your dispatch yesterday naming general officers. Colonel Smith, First California, should be advanced.

OTIS.

MANILA. (Received April 21, 1899—5.25 a. m.)

AGWAR, *Washington:*

No assistance needed except what already called for and will be called for from time to time. Troops abundantly supplied and sickness—wounded included—only seven and fraction per cent of command. Newspapers and state cablegrams received advising no reenlistments, and action United States citizens here and on Asiatic coast only demoralizing influences at work among soldiers.

OTIS.

AFFAIRS IN THE PHILIPPINE ISLANDS. 971

MANILA. (Received April 21, 1899—8.59 a. m.)

AGWAR, *Washington:*

Additional casualties: Wounded—Second Oregon, April 17, A, Private William O. Walker, foot, moderate. Thirteenth Minnesota, 20th, A, Private Nicholas Hansen, thigh, severe. First Washington, D, Privates Albert R. Straub, face, severe; William Winder, chest, severe; H, Corpl. George M. Burlingham, side, slight.

OTIS.

SAN FRANCISCO, CAL., *April 21, 1899.*
(Received 4.40 p. m.)

ADJUTANT-GENERAL, *Washington, D. C.:*

Warren sailed 3.40 p. m. yesterday with headquarters, band, 8 batteries Sixth Artillery, 20 officers and 936 men; 6 hospital corps men attached to regiment; Major Edie, surgeon; 2 assistant surgeons, 3 acting assistant surgeons; also Lieutenants Marsh, Fifth Artillery; Leonard, Fourteenth Infantry, with following detachments: Hospital corps, 50. Cavalry, 41 casual, 56 recruits. Artillery, heavy, Third, 1 casual, 45 recruits. Infantry, Third, 2 recruits; Ninth, 8 casuals, 4 recruits; Twelfth, 3 casuals; Fourteenth, 1 casual, 10 recruits; Seventeenth, 27 casuals, 12 recruits; Eighteenth, 2 recruits; Twentieth, 4 casuals, 11 recruits; Twenty-second, 3 recruits. Brigadier-General Williston, commanding.

BABCOCK,
In absence Department Commander.

ADJUTANT-GENERAL'S OFFICE,
Washington, April 21, 1899.

OTIS, *Manila:*

Any objection to families coming, provided go to China or Japan, if restrictions in force on arrival?

CORBIN.

MANILA. (Received April 22, 1899—1.36 a. m.)

ADJUTANT-GENERAL, *Washington:*

General Lawton's column of 2,500 left vicinity Caloocan this morning for Novaliches, San José, Norzagaray, and Biacnabato. Column 1,200, under colonel Second Oregon, leaves Bocaue on railway to-morrow, proceed northeast, and join Lawton at Norzagaray. On 24th, MacArthur, with column of 4,000, moves on Calumpit; thence northeasterly to San Miguel, where he joins Lawton. Latter encountered enemy 6 miles out this morning. Enemy and heat impeding progress. March to San Miguel will require at least ten days. Subsequent movements depend on developments.

OTIS.

MANILA. (Received April 22, 1899—11.41 p. m.)

SECWAR, *Washington:*

City of Puebla arrived this morning. No casualties. Troops in good condition.

OTIS.

ADJUTANT-GENERAL'S OFFICE,
Washington, April 22, 1899.

OTIS, *Manila:*

Warren sailed April 20, eight batteries Sixth Artillery and recruits.

CORBIN.

MANILA. (Received April 22, 1899—6.30 a. m.)

AGWAR, *Washington:*
Families can not be provided for in islands now. Can visit China and Japan and await there more permanent conditions if desired.

OTIS.

ADJUTANT-GENERAL'S OFFICE,
Washington, April 22, 1899.

OTIS, *Manila:*
Can any or all the dispatches discouraging enlistments be confidentially transmitted here? Important.

CORBIN.

MANILA. (Received April 23, 1899—9.34 a. m.)

AGWAR, *Washington:*
Following deaths since last weekly report: From wounds in action—April 15, Joseph Grabowsky, private, C, Fourth Cavalry. 18th, Archie A. Aldrich, private, E, First Colorado. 20th, Bruce E. Macy, private, C, First Nebraska. Drowned, accidental—21st, John Montgomery, sergeant, K, Third Artillery. 22d, Jacob Boyd, sergeant, K, Fourth Infantry. Variola—6th, Samuel J. February, private, I, Eighteenth Infantry. 21st, Thomas O. Cauble, private, D, Third Infantry. Diarrhea—15th, Joseph Gompman, private, G, Eighteenth Infantry. Malarial fever—5th, Bert B. Chandler, private, C, Second Oregon. Erysipelas—20th, Charles Parsons, private, A, First Washington. Tuberculosis—20th, Jay Taylor, B, Second Oregon. Peritonitis—21st, Michael Ryan, sergeant, A, Fourteenth Infantry.

OTIS.

MANILA. (Received April 23, 1899—10.17 a. m.)

AGWAR, *Washington:*
A reconnoissance on Quingua, place 6 miles northeast of Malolos, made by Major Bell and troop of cavalry this morning, resulted in contact and battle, in which 4 battalions of infantry and 4 pieces of artillery became engaged. Enemy driven from strong intrenchments at Quingua with considerable loss; our casualties quite severe. Colonel Stotsenburg and Lieutenant Sisson, First Nebraska, killed; also several enlisted; a considerable number wounded not yet reported. MacArthur will advance his force to-night or very early in morning. Lawton's column proceeding north from Novaliches; little resistance. Advance slow on account of rough roads and thick brush. Is some 20 miles from Manila. Bocaue column marched 5.30 this morning; no opposition reported.

OTIS.

MANILA. (Received April 23, 1899—10.50 p. m.)

AGWAR, *Washington:*
Casualties at Quingua today: First Nebraska, 2 officers and 2 enlisted killed; 2 officers and 26 enlisted wounded. Fourth Cavalry, 2 enlisted men killed, 5 wounded. Fifty-first Iowa, 7 enlisted men wounded. Utah Light Artillery, 1 officer and 2 enlisted men wounded; total, 49. Names in morning.

OTIS.

AFFAIRS IN THE PHILIPPINE ISLANDS. 973

MANILA. (Received April 23, 1899—9.45 a. m.)

ADJUTANT-GENERAL, *Washington:*

Attention called to following dispatches, dated April 13, 14, 19, first anonymous:

"OMAHA.

"To OMAHA, *Manila:*
"Boys, don't reenlist. Insist immediate discharge.

"———."

"GREENBURG, PA.

"HAWKINS, *Manila:*
"People demand that Tenth return.

"ROBBINS."
"DAYTON.

"COMPANY I, DAYTONITES, WASHINGTON VOLUNTEERS, *Manila:*
"Don't reenlist.

"CITIZENS."
OTIS.

ADJUTANT-GENERAL'S OFFICE,
Washington, April 24, 1899.

OTIS, *Manila:*

Propose to send remaining six troops Fourth Cavalry. Should they bring horses?

CORBIN.

MANILA. (Received April 24, 1899—11.30 p. m.)

AGWAR, *Washington:*

Horses Fourth Cavalry should be sent; sailing vessel *Tacoma* leaves to-day for San Francisco well equipped for this business; can bring 200 head.

OTIS.

WAR DEPARTMENT, *April 25, 1899.*

OTIS, *Manila:*

Edward Atkinson is sending out pamphlets entitled, "The Cost of a National Crime, The Hell of War with Its Penalties, Criminal Aggression, by Whom Committed." You will have all such pamphlets, if any are sent, taken from the mails and destroyed. Complaints are made against the present censor, Thompson, and it is asked would not Judge-Advocate Crowder be a more moderate and considerate man? This, however, is left to your own discretion.

ALGER, *Secwar.*

MANILA. (Received April 25, 1899—4.50 a. m.)

AGWAR, *Washington:*

Hale's brigade, MacArthur's division, moved down right bank Quinqua River yesterday to vicinity Calumpit; now joined by Wheaton's brigade on left bank. Hale encountered fierce opposition, driving enemy with heavy loss, taking his intrenchments in flank. Hale's casualties, 6 killed, 12 wounded. The division has now invested Calumpit, which will be taken to-day. Lawton, with part of his command, reaches Norzagary this evening, where he will be joined by center column from Bocaue. Extreme heat, rain, high streams, bad roads made march very difficult. He has not met opposition since leaving Novaliches; enemy retreating in his front. South of and near Manila enemy has force 4,000, making demonstrations daily; can easily be taken care of; it can not communicate with north. List of casualties of day before yesterday cabled to-day.

OTIS.

MANILA. (Received April 25, 1899—11.22 a. m.)

AGWAR, *Washington:*

Additional casualties: Killed—First Nebraska, April 23, Col. John M. Stotsenburg; K, Second Lieut. Lester E. Sisson; B, Q. M. Sergt. James F. Storch; H, Sergt. Charles Mellick. Fourth Cavalry, I, Privates William B. Jackson, William K. Skinner. Wounded—K, Musician Charles Power, ankle, severe; Privates Ralph Wintler, buttock, severe; Edward Quinn, shoulder, severe; John B. Carey, thigh, slight; Patrick O'Connor, head, severe. First Nebraska, H, First Lieut. William K. Moore, leg, moderate; B, Second Lieut. Andrew S. Wardsworth, leg, severe; Privates William C. Richards, arm, severe; D, Lee H. Stoner, jaw, severe; Edwin O. Peterson, cheek, severe; James Richard, jaw, severe; Charles M. Swartz, iliac region, severe; F, John W. White, leg, moderate; Musician Walter G. Tingley, neck, severe; H, Privates Walter Aloy Elifritz, shoulder, severe; Guy E. Minor, leg, severe; I, Edwin F. Gregg, forearm, severe; James T. Keenan, buttock, severe; David H. Wilkins, chest, severe; Sergt. Clyde Vosburgh, iliac region, severe; Corpls. Dallas Henderson, leg, moderate; K, Harry Brookover, arm, severe; Frank J. Fouke, leg, severe; Privates Robert L. Smith, side, severe; William H. LaRue, hand, severe; Frederick Gibbs, back, slight; Otto Hembd, leg, slight; Eli I. Sisson, thigh, slight; James R. Allen, knee, severe; M, Orson E. Humphrey, shoulder, severe; Sergt. Horace F. Kennedy, chest, severe; Corpl. Arden R. Chapman, forearm, moderate. Fifty-first Iowa, E, Corpls. George E. Mariner, forearm, severe; Louis L. Hunter, hand, severe; L, Privates Carl M. Gardner, thigh, severe; Walter C. Larson, thigh, moderate; Robert L. Daily, dorsal region, severe; M, Adrian L. Hackett, jr., leg, severe; Bert Thomas, thigh, severe. Utah Artillery, A, Privates David J. Davis, leg, severe; B, John Alpbanalp, head, severe. First California, Corpl. Charles N. Davis, foot, slight.

Answering inquiries: Charles H. Hultberg, First South Dakota, doing well. William M. Winders, First Washington, doing well; for Meiklejohn. William K. Warren, A, Fourteenth, will recover; for Alger.

OTIS.

WAR DEPARTMENT,
Washington, April 25, 1899.

OTIS, *Manila:*

Attorney-General advises furniture, hanging pictures, and like property belonging to Spanish Peninsular government, for example, in captain-general's palace, deliverable to owners. Property in public buildings, used by colonial, island, city governments, in public schools, courts, libraries, art buildings, remain for same or like use. Archives and records useful for government and history of Philippines remain, including church patronage archives. Deposits in treasury belonging private individuals remain for them. Explain question about Spanish bonds, how owned. Records relating to credits, taxes, rents, remain for use. Deliver records, exclusively concerning Philippine loan, including bonds never issued. Spain probably entitled some moneys in treasury and uncollected. Cause expert or legal examination concerning moneys collected and collectible, how, when, and for what objects and periods, and report fully; also how said objects accomplished during period for which uncollected tax levied, also whether there are unpaid salaries of local officials to come out of such moneys,

ALGER, *Secwar.*

MANILA. (Received April 26, 1899—11.33 p. m.)

AGWAR, *Washington:*

Lawton at Norzagaray and Angat. His two columns united, have driven enemy to north and west; slight casualties, names not reported. Only means of communication couriers. MacArthur has taken portion of Calumpit south of river. Movement attended with difficulties on account of jungle heat and strong intrenchments. His casualties yesterday, 3 killed, 11 wounded. Developments thus far satisfactory.

OTIS.

MANILA. (Received April 26, 1899—11.55 p. m.)

AGWAR, *Washington:*

Sheridan for San Francisco to-day, via Nagasaki. Just completed necessary repairs.

OTIS.

MANILA. (Received April 26, 1899—1.38 p. m.)

AGWAR, *Washington:*

Casualties not heretofore reported: Killed—Hospital Corps, April 24, Private Holland I. Laidler. First South Dakota, Wagoner Mortimer C. Bowen; Company H, Corpl. Oscar E. Johnson, Private Charles Stulz. 25th, B, Corpl. Harvey M. Breed; H, Privates Charles W. Peterson, Guy Jones; K, James A. Lizer; L, Harlowe DeJean. First Nebraska: I, Private Harry O. McCart. Utah Artillery, B, Private Max Madison. Hospital Corps, Private Paul Gompertz.

Wounded—First Idaho, 9th, C, Private George B. Manning, foot, slight. Fourteenth Infantry, 10th, A, First Sergt. George Wall, hand, slight; E, Privates Bertie A. Lowe, arm, slight; Allen M. Shelledy, cheek, slight. Thirteenth Minnesota, F, Private Ira S. Towle, arm, severe. First South Dakota, 22d, B, Private Fred Hanche, chest, severe. 24th, B, Sergt. Charles L. Butler, ankle, slight; G, Privates Paul Weiss, forehead, slight; L, David C. Dean, neck, severe; Axel S. Sjoblom, hand, severe. 25th, B, Sergts. Arthur W. Swenson, hip, slight; I, Oliver C. Lapp, leg, severe; L, Q. M. Sergt. Antone Jurich, jr., elbow, slight; E, Corpls. Christ L. Myhre, shoulder, slight; F, William W. Reaman, leg, slight; B, Privates Frank H. Goebel, knee, slight; James Gibb, shoulder, slight; D, John Murphy, face, severe; E, Thomas H. Coleman, head, slight; I, Charles P. Wagner, head, slight; Herbert A. Putnam, knee, slight; K, Don J. Rancus, knee, slight; Guy E. Skinner, knee, slight; L, James H. Davis, foot, slight; E, Robert W. Hawkins, back, slight. First Nebraska, 24th, C, Second Lieut. W. G. Lungan, eye, severe; Artificer John S. Roller, arm, moderate; F, Privates Charles I. Cadwell, thigh, severe; L, Martin O. Legg, abdomen, severe; George A. Wageck, neck, severe. 25th, Maj. Frank D. Eager, foot, severe; C, Corpl. Charles S. Brewster, foot, moderate; E, Privates David E. Gillispie, shoulder, slight; I, Lucius W. Pangborn, knee, severe; L, William V. Carter, forearm, slight; Francis E. Hansen, neck, severe; Harvey W. Majors, shoulder, severe. Fifty-first Iowa: 24th, Maj. William J. Duggan, arm, slight; C, Corpl. Louis E. Wyland, thigh, moderate; M, Private John Behm, leg, moderate. 25th, B, Privates John Kernen, back, slight; D, Nathan A. Hodges, leg, severe; Elmer F. Narver, shoulder, severe; H, Patrick H. Dwyer, leg, slight. Utah Artillery, B, Corpl. Mourits C. Jensen, abdomen, severe; Privates Frederick A. Burniller, abdomen, severe; John Braman, knee, slight. Hospital Corps, Private Charles H. Slater, foot, severe. Twentieth Kansas, K, Sergt. Arthur C. Snow, forearm, severe; Private Walter A. Hubbard, foot, slight. First Montana, H, Musician William A. Patton, neck, slight; Private Joseph E. Jette, forehead, severe. Sixth Artillery, D, Private Nels A. Tornquest, hand, slight.

OTIS.

MANILA. (Received April 27, 1899—11.36 a. m.)

SECWAR, *Washington:*

To guard against circular pamphlets mentioned in dispatch of yesterday through mails, instructions should be given San Francisco, where army mail put up and sent direct to organizations. Only mixed mail distributed here. Manila postmaster instructed.

OTIS.

SAN FRANCISCO, CAL., *April 27, 1899—6.45 p. m.*

ADJUTANT-GENERAL, *Washington, D. C.:*

The Thirteenth Infantry has arrived and is on board transports *Ohio* and *Senator*. Expected to sail 6 this p. m.

SHAFTER, *Major-General.*

MANILA. (Received April 27, 1899—11.18 a. m.)

AGWAR, *Washington:*

Casualties not heretofore reported: Killed—First Montana, April 26: B, Sergt. Thomas Anderson; K, Private James A. Callahan. Twentieth Kansas, A, Private Resiel Manahan. Wounded—Fourth Cavalry, 10th: G, Second Lieut. Leroy Eltinge, hand, slight. First Montana, 26th: F, Privates Frank E. Tate, nose, slight; Adolph M. Clay, jaw, severe; I, Edward B. Harvey, neck, severe. Twentieth Kansas, E, Second Lieut. Collin H. Ball, jaw, severe; A, Privates James W. Kershner, axilla, severe; I, Joseph Scott, side, moderate; Lyle L. Knox, shoulder, slight; K, Edward E. Harris, thigh, severe. Utah Artillery, A, Private Emil F. Selmer, back, severe. Sixth Artillery, D, Private Moses S. Simmons, knee, moderate. First Nebraska, D, Privates Harold K. Blake, thigh, moderate; E, Noah B. Land, chest, slight.

OTIS.

MANILA. (Received April 27, 1899—7.53 a. m.)

SECWAR, *Washington:*

Question about Spanish bonds refers to provisional bonds issued to subscribers of Spanish loan, subsequently taken up by Spain when regular bonds issued and deposited in treasury. They have been delivered to Spanish Government.

OTIS.

ADJUTANT-GENERAL'S OFFICE,
Washington, April 27, 1899.

OTIS, *Manila:*

Do you recommend that horses Fourth Cavalry be shipped by sailing vessels only? If so, horses can not reach you for about two months after men. Believed horses can be shipped by steamer with as little casualty as by sail and will arrive much sooner.

CORBIN.

MANILA. (Received April 28, 1899—7.05 a. m.)

AGWAR, *Washington:*

Messrs. Ceballos & Co. have fulfilled their contract to transport prisoners of war to Spain, in so far as United States permits their vessels in harbor to take remaining few, but held by United States authority for specific necessary purposes. Two of the vessels will not depart before May 10; will take United States troops to Zamboanga and Jolo and there take on Spanish troops, not prisoners of war, for Spain.

OTIS.

AFFAIRS IN THE PHILIPPINE ISLANDS. 977

MANILA. (Received April 28, 1899—8.35 a. m.)

AGWAR, *Washington:*

After taking Calumpit MacArthur's Division crossed Ric Grande River in face of great obstacles, driving the concentrated forces of enemy back on railroad two miles. MacArthur reports that passage of river remarkable military achievement, the success of which due to daring skill and determination of Colonel Funston, under discriminating control of General Wheaton. Casualties slight; number not yet ascertained. This morning chief of staff of commanding general of insurgent forces entered our lines to express admiration of the wonderful feat of the American Army in forcing passage of river, which was thought impossible. Staff officer reports that insurgent commanding general has received from insurgent government directions to suspend hostilities, pending negotiations for the termination of the war. The staff officer, with party, is now en route to Manila and will arrive soon. Lawton's forces well in hand in vicinity of Angat, east of Calumpit, where he is awaiting supplies to be sent to-morrow. Yesterday morning force of 1,500 insurgents attacked troops at Taguig; driven back by Washington regiment with considerable slaughter. Our loss 2 killed, 12 wounded.

OTIS.

ADJUTANT-GENERAL'S OFFICE,
Washington, April 28, 1899.

OTIS, *Manila:*

Thirteenth Infantry sailed yesterday from San Francisco on *Ohio* and *Senator*.

CORBIN.

SAN FRANCISCO, CAL., *April 28, 1899.*
(Received 8.07 p. m.)

ADJUTANT-GENERAL, *Washington, D. C.:*

Detachment of 10 signal corps men, reported to have sailed on *Senator*, were transferred to *Ohio* for better accommodation, and sailed on that ship.

SHAFTER, *Major-General, Commanding.*

MANILA. (Received April 28, 1899—1.55 p. m.)

AGWAR, *Washington:*

Additional casualties: Killed—First Washington, April 27: F, Corpl. Edward W. Strain; H, Private Joseph Eno. First Montana, M, Private Charles S. Murphy. Wounded—First Washington, F, First Lieut. Charles A. Booker, scalp, slight; Privates Harvey R. Smith, face, moderate; D, William J. Marshall, neck, slight; H, Clyde Z. Woods, abdomen, severe; Robert Hovey, leg, severe; Sidney O. Dickinson, chest, severe; Abel Nilsson, cheek, severe; William E. Howard, thigh, severe; Sherman T. Shepard, chest, severe; Edward M. Curley, thumb, slight; Arthur H. Ellis, loin, slight; Corpl. George W. Hovey, abdomen, severe; L, Private Edward R. Ennis, chest, slight. Twentieth Kansas, M, Capt. William H. Bishop, hip, moderate; A, Sergt. Charles A. Woolworth, groin, moderate; K, Corpl. Ernest R. Kincaid, arm, slight; Privates Lossen B. Whiteker (Company A) side, severe; L, Albert H. Terry, abdomen, severe; M, Henry H. Morrison, chest, severe. First South Dakota, B, Sergt. Charles L. Butler, leg, slight; Corp. Hammon H. Buck, arm, slight. First Montana, Maj. John R. Miller, shoulder, severe; E, Capt. Andrew Jensen, forearm, severe; B, Privates James Tierney, thigh, severe; I, John T. Schultz, scalp, slight; K, John Kirley, shoulder, moderate.

OTIS.

SAN FRANCISCO, CAL., *April 28, 1899.*
(Received 4 p. m.)

ADJUTANT-GENERAL, *Washington, D. C.:*

Transports *Senator* and *Ohio* sailed at 5.30 a. m. to-day. On *Senator*, headquarters, 16 officers and 682 men Thirteenth Infantry; Lieutenant Frazier, Ninth Infantry, 1 surgeon, 2 acting assistant surgeons, 1 commissary sergeant, 10 Signal Corps men, and 6 Hospital Corps men. On *Ohio* 13 officers and 643 men Thirteenth Infantry; 2 acting assistant surgeons, 2 commissary sergeants, 33 Hospital Corps men, and 75 recruits assigned to infantry as follows: Thirteenth, 1; Fourteenth, 3; Eighteenth, 34; Twenty-third, 37; 100 rounds ammunition, caliber .30, per man, Thirteenth Infantry.

SHAFTER, *Major-General, Commanding.*

MANILA. (Received April 28, 1899—7 a. m.)

AGWAR, *Washington:*

Recommend horses Fourth Cavalry be sent expeditiously as possible. Sailing vessel to be utilized to bring additional stock upon arrival San Francisco.

OTIS.

MANILA. (Received April 29, 1899—4 a. m.)

AGWAR, *Washington:*

Conference with insurgent representatives terminated this morning. Their request, cessation of hostilities three weeks to enable them to call their congress to decide whether to continue prosecution of war or propose terms of peace. Proposition declined and full amnesty promised on surrender. Believe insurgents weary of war, but seek to secure terms of peace through what they denominate their representative congress.

OTIS.

MANILA. (Received April 29, 1899—4.05 a. m.)

AGWAR, *Washington:*

The congratulations of His Excellency the President, for which all grateful, will be conveyed as directed.

OTIS.

ADJUTANT-GENERAL'S OFFICE,
Washington, April 29, 1899.

General OTIS, *Manila:*

Report scheme for return of volunteers when matured. Secretary of War desires organizations to return in the order of their going to Manila—first to go, first to return.

CORBIN.

ADJUTANT-GENERAL'S OFFICE,
Washington, April 29, 1899.

OTIS, *Manila:*

Referring to your cablegram April 28, what number additional stock do you need, and kind?

CORBIN.

AFFAIRS IN THE PHILIPPINE ISLANDS. 979

MANILA. (Received April 30, 1899—11 a. m.)
AGWAR, *Washington:*

Following deaths since last weekly report: From wounds in action—April 24, William Kastenberger, private, H, First Nebraska; Charles M. Swartz, private, D, First Nebraska. 25th, David C. Dean, private, L, First South Dakota. 26th, Mourits C. Jensen, corporal, B, Utah Artillery; Frederick A. Bumiller, private, B, Utah Artillery; Martin O. Legg, private, L, First Nebraska; George Lichamer, private, G, Second Oregon. 28th, Francis E. Hanson, corporal, L, First Nebraska; Henry H. Morrison, private, M, Twentieth Kansas; Clyde Z. Woods, private, H, First Washington; George W. Hovey, corporal, H, First Washington; Albert H. Terry, private, L, Twentieth Kansas. Drowned, accidental—23d, Patrick Manning, private, L, Seventeenth Infantry. 24th, Frederick Lundin, private, D, First California. 25th, James Kennedy, private, K, First Montana. 28th, M. Wilson, private, E, Twelfth Infantry. Typhoid fever—25th, Maynard E. Sayles, private, L, First Nebraska. 27th, Oliver W. Davis, private, D, First South Dakota. 29th, Richard Carroll, private, B, Third Infantry. Smallpox—23d, John Sheehan (probably Otto Seaholm), private, L, Seventeenth Infantry. 26th, Robert Carter, private, F, Third Infantry. Dysentery—17th, Herbert A. Hopkins, private, F, First California. 24th, William Burgess, private, E, First Idaho. Ptomaine poisoning—15th, William Clark, private, E, Eighteenth Infantry.

OTIS.

MANILA. (Received April 30, 1899—4.12 a. m.)
AGWAR, *Washington:*

With mules sent and complement of horses for Fourth Cavalry forwarded believe shall have sufficient stock if waste in horses can be supplied here; if not, will require additional ones from United States. Before *Tacoma* arrives San Francisco intelligent opinion can be reached.

OTIS.

MANILA. (Received May 1, 1899—1.15 a. m.)
AGWAR, *Washington:*

Under authority recent appropriation act request clerks Donnelly, Porter, Cardwells, Burton, be rated at $1,400 Request emergency clerk O'Loghlen be permanently assigned at $1,200. Desire instructions number clerks authorized this department and authority to secure same. Particulars by mail.

OTIS.

ADJUTANT-GENERAL'S OFFICE,
Washington, May 1, 1899.

OTIS, *Manila:*

Reference sending horses Fourth Cavalry, Colonel Long reports only vessels in sight for carrying animals are one large steamer due May 5 and two sailing vessels now there which would require six weeks to properly fit for comfortable and safe transportation of animals. *Tacoma* on way back by which would take about four months to deliver animals Manila, and *Conemaugh* could be returned at once and deliver about seventy days. *Leelanaw* leaves May 2; could return Manila one hundred days. These three ships already fitted for water and ventilation and could carry all horses necessary to mount six troops now under orders for Manila. What do you recommend? Shall foregoing vessels be utilized or animals sent by earliest steam vessels obtainable?

CORBIN.

MANILA. (Received May 2, 1899—11.35 p. m.)

AGWAR, *Washington:*

General Lawton's column passing westward from Norzagaray. Captured Baliuag and villages in vicinity yesterday, scattering and pursuing 1,600 insurgent troops. His only casualties, 2 wounded. Insurgents' loss several killed, large number wounded and captured; numbers not stated. Have opened communication with Lawton via Malolos by means of Hale's troops and detachments from city.

OTIS.

ADJUTANT-GENERAL'S OFFICE,
Washington, May 2, 1899.

OTIS, *Manila:*

Grant and *Sherman* have arrived. General Shafter reports it will require twenty days to put them in order for the return trip. Twenty-second of month has been fixed as date of their sailing to bring you the Sixth and Sixteenth Infantry and about 800 or 1,000 recruits for infantry regiments. Nineteenth Infantry will go to you on *Sheridan.*

CORBIN.

MANILA. (Received May 2, 1899—2.01 p. m.)

AGWAR, *Washington:*

In purchasing from private parties all Spanish gunboats in Philippine waters held at southern station advertised for sale at public auction, some of which insurgents were endeavoring to secure, I agreed to take them at fair figure, private parties to deliver all property in Manila Bay and navy to furnish protection en route. By some mistake navy did not protect boats; seized by insurgents near Zamboanga and greater portion of armament and ammunition taken by them. Think Spanish authorities, if not conniving, knew insurgent intention to capture. Spanish troops on most friendly terms with insurgents south, and desire to evacuate Zamboanga and Jolo before United States troops arrive, that may not be caught by hostilities, which will follow. Fearing another Iloilo experience at southern port, I have engaged two of the transports which return Spanish troops to Spain to take our troops south, thus holding Spanish garrisons until we arrive and secure peaceable possession of point to be garrisoned. Am paying demurrage on vessels until troops ready to embark, which will be about fifteen days.

OTIS.

ADJUTANT-GENERAL'S OFFICE,
Washington, May 2, 1899.

General OTIS, *Manila:*

Acting Secwar approves your action in engaging the two transports referred to in cipher to-day.

CORBIN.

MANILA. (Received May 3, 1899—12.05 a. m.)

AGWAR, *Washington:*

List prisoners in hands insurgents, just received, shows Lieutenant Gillmore and 7 enlisted men navy lost from *Yorktown,* and 6 enlisted men army, 3 of the 6 wrongfully arrested in January, before hostilities commenced. All reported to be doing well. Besides the above, 2 men in hands insurgents, south, and Captain Rockefeller still unaccounted for.

OTIS.

AFFAIRS IN THE PHILIPPINE ISLANDS.

MANILA. (Received May 3, 1899—12.45 p. m.)

AGWAR, *Washington:*

Casualties not heretofore reported. Wounded—March 26, Brig. Gen. Irving Hale, leg, slight. First South Dakota, H, Capt. Charles H. Englesby, shoulder, slight; G, Sergt. Oscar W. Coursey, leg, slight. Tenth Pennsylvania, Col. Alexander L. Hawkins, arm, slight; H, First Lieut. Blaine Aiken, arm, slight; Sergt. John H. Thompson, face, slight. Fifty-first Iowa, M, Private Fred E. Strong, scalp, slight. April 25, M, Private Samuel J. Tilden, shoulder, slight. 27th, H, Private Bertram H. Grace, foot, slight, accidental. First North Dakota, 12th, K, Private August W. Hensil, leg, slight. 30th, I, Private Emil J. Pepke, chest, severe. First South Dakota, 24th, G, Corpl. Charles P. Green, ear, slight. 25th, G, Second Lieut. Walter S. Doolittle, foot, slight; I, Privates William H. Harrison, shoulder, slight; K, Roy E. Ranous, leg, slight. First Montana, 27th, C, Private Gottlieb Molcan, arm, slight; H, Capt. Frank E. Green, hand, slight; I, Privates G. Muhlson, arm, slight; K, Robert Murphy, shoulder, slight. 28th, B, Privates Andrew Davis, cheek, slight; Charles Thompson, leg, slight; F, Martin G. Hall, ear, slight; M, Corpl. James O'Leary, shoulder, slight. Fourth Cavalry, 24th, I, Private William Heer, hand, severe. Twentieth Kansas, 25th, K, Sergt. Joseph Dewald, neck, slight. 27th, K, Private Oscar Nesbitt, wrist, slight. Third Infantry, D, Second Lieut. Charles C. Todd, thigh severe; F, Private Oscar Bevan, shoulder, severe. Thirteenth Minnesota. 28th, K, Sergt. William B. Burlingham, knee. First Colorado, May 1, K, First Sergt. Clifford H. Bowser, arm, severe. Third Infantry, 2d, G, Corpl. Jacob Fisher, abdomen, severe; M, Private Frederick Miller, thigh, severe. Killed—Thirteenth Minnesota, 1st, F, Private Frank Lewis.

OTIS.

MANILA. (Received May 3, 1899—3.50 a. m.)

AGWAR, *Washington:*

Commissioners from insurgent government reported yesterday, asking of United States Commission three months' suspension hostilities and general armistice entire archipelago, to consult opinion of people and appoint special commission to confer with United States. They requested that I use my influence with United States Commission, and state if attempt at forcible domination continue will prolong war indefinitely. Do not know action United States Commission; no truce will be accorded nor insurgent government recognized.

OTIS.

MANILA. (Received May 3, 1899—7.30 a. m.)

AGWAR, *Washington:*

Transports *Conemaugh*, *Leelanaw*, and *Tacoma* can bring 700 cavalry horses from San Francisco to this port by August 20. Advise they be so sent. Meantime will depend upon island ponies, which are cheap.

OTIS.

MANILA. (Received May 4, 1899—2.30 a. m.)

AGWAR, *Washington:*

Situation as follows: Lawton holds Baliuag, captured 2d instant, after rapid movement from Angat, where supplied with wagon train, pack animals, and rations. He scattered the strongly intrenched enemy to the north and northwestward, capturing large amounts food supplies, and has his detachments to north and eastward. His successful movement attended with great difficulty, because of character of country, rain, and heat. He now covers our railroad communication and will be supplied from Malolos. MacArthur's column, concentrated, took up advance on San Fernando at 6.30 this morning. Do not apprehend stout resistance on part of enemy, who will probably leave railroad and retire in northeasterly direction to north of Lawton. Destruction of railroad near Calumpit necessitates dependence on wagon transportation. Enemy to south and east of Manila about 9,000, opposed by sufficient force under Ovenshine and Hall; his demonstrations thus far promptly met by these officers with slight losses. Many requests received from outlying cities for protection against insurgent troops.

OTIS.

MANILA. (Received May 4, 1899—6.10 a. m.)

AGWAR, *Washington:*

Difficulties occasionally arise at Guam. Complaints and explanations sent here. Who exercises supervision of the island?

OTIS.

ADJUTANT-GENERAL'S OFFICE,
Washington, May 4, 1899.

General OTIS, *Manila:*

The President directs that for the present the navy under Admiral Dewey will exercise supervision over island of Guam.

CORBIN.

MANILA. (Received May 4, 1899—11.29 a. m.)

AGWAR, *Washington:*

Colonel Summers with six battalions Oregon, Minnesota, Third Infantry and Utah piece Light Artillery, of Lawton's Division, proceeded north this morning to Maasin; crossed river, charged enemy in strong intrenchments, driving him northward and inflicting considerable loss. His casualties, 2 wounded. Both Wheaton and Hale, of MacArthur's Division, found enemy in force strongly intrenched and commanded by Commander in Chief Luna about 4 miles south San Fernando. Hale on right dislodged enemy, and Wheaton on left, leading in person, made brilliant charge, scattering his forces, inflicting great punishment. Several officers and enlisted men seriously wounded. MacArthur proceeds to San Fernando in morning. Delayed by partial destruction of bridge across river. Not believed enemy will make another determined stand until he effects retreat to Mount Arayat, short distance from San Isidro.

OTIS.

MANILA. (Received May 4, 1899—9.28 a. m.)

AGWAR, *Washington:*

Casualties not heretofore reported: Killed—Fourth Cavalry, April 23: K, Corpl. John Golambeski. Wounded—K, Privates James F. McGreevy, hand, slight. First Nebraska, 1st, C, Private Paul Ossowski, hand, severe, accidental; 4th, F, Private John D. Keeney, hand, severe, accidental; 23d, I, Privates Charles E. Schaffer, leg, slight; K, William L. Gilbert, thigh, slight; Leo W. Hunter, hip, slight.

OTIS.

AFFAIRS IN THE PHILIPPINE ISLANDS. 983

MANILA. (Received May 5, 1899—3.35 a. m.)

AGWAR, *Washington:*

Following casualties at Santo Tomas yesterday: One officer, Lieutenant McTaggart, Twentieth Kansas, and 4 enlisted men killed; three officers, 22 enlisted men wounded. Among wounded General Funston, hand, slight. Lawton reports capture over 150,000 bushels rice, 265 tons sugar at Baliuag. Values of subsistence captured at Malolos, $1,500,000. Large captures rice and corn belonging to enemy at other points. Insurgents destroyed by fire yesterday town of Santo Tomas, and last evening fired city of San Fernando.

OTIS.

MANILA. (Received May 6, 1899—6.35 a. m.)

AGWAR, *Washington:*

Additional casualties. Killed—Twentieth Kansas, May 4: Company G, Second Lieut. William A. McTaggart; H, Private Merton A. Wilcox. First Nebraska, G, Privates James H. Spivey; L, William O. Belden. First Montana, K, Private Thomas Scallon. Wounded—Twentieth Kansas, Col. Frederick Funston, hand, moderate; C, Capt. William S. Albright, thigh, moderate; Sergt. Maj. Cassius E. Warner, hand, moderate; D, Sergt. Joseph A. Robinson, leg, slight; K, Corpls. Elvie Allison, foot, slight; H, Benjamin F. Oliver, thigh, slight; C, Frank I. Sample, head, severe; Privates William Landenschlager, knee, severe; F, William McDougall, shoulder, severe; H, Thomas J. Davidson, leg, severe; I, Chris W. Clapp, jr., chest, severe; Band, Benjamin Conchman, lung, severe. Engineer Corps, C, Private Frederick H. Buttner, head, severe. First Nebraska, E, Privates Benjamin F. Dunning, thigh, severe; K, William I. Johnson, knee moderate; Grant Chinn, leg, severe; L, Willard B. Mason, hip, slight. First Montana, K, Capt. Thomas S. Dillon, chest, severe; Privates Bruce F. Belknap, breast, slight; C, Fred W. Smith, ear, moderate. First South Dakota, K, Musician Robert Van Hook, leg, severe. Fifty-first Iowa, C, Corpl. John H. Cushing, scalp, slight; E, Privates Everett Brunson, abdomen, slight; H, Charles L. Bander, heel, slight. Second Oregon, 1st, A, Private John T. Reeves, knee, moderate; K, Corpl. Edgar J. Chamberlain, thigh, moderate.

OTIS.

ADJUTANT-GENERAL'S OFFICE,
Washington, May 6, 1899.

Gen. W. R. SHAFTER,
Commanding Department California, San Francisco, Cal.:

Can not the crew and passengers of the *Grant* be put in quarantine somewhere on land to enable the repairs on the transport to be begun? If this is feasible Acting Secretary War desires it done.

H. C. CORBIN, *Adjutant-General.*

MANILA. (Received May 6, 1899—7.45 a. m.)

AGWAR, *Washington:*

Cable between Iloilo and Negros broken by United States transport. Cable company manifests willingness to repair line and extend cable to Cebu without prejudice to United States' interests, waiving all demands which could arise thereby for recognition by United States of Spanish concessions to company. On these conditions I have authorized execution of the work. Is this action approved? Cable communication to Cebu necessary for military and civil interests.

OTIS.

ADJUTANT-GENERAL'S OFFICE,
Washington, May 6, 1899.

OTIS, *Manila:*

Action in reference to repair cable between Iloilo and Negros and extending cable to Cebu, referred to in your cable this date, approved by Acting Secwar.

CORBIN.

ADJUTANT-GENERAL'S OFFICE,
Washington, May 6, 1899.

General OTIS, *Manila:*

By the President's direction you have, from time to time, been requested to make suggestions as to change of rations for your troops, which you have complied with, but to better enable the President to determine under provisions section 1146, Revised Statutes, what alterations, if any, in established ration would be conducive to the better health of troops serving in tropical climates, Acting Secretary War directs that you institute board of 3 officers, noted for their ability and experience, serving, respectively, in the line, medical, and subsistence departments, to fully examine into subject of any desired changes in the rations for the troops of your command, and that you submit substance of report of its investigation by cable and full report by mail, together with your recommendation. Refer to board previous correspondence and other available information relative to dietetics. Particularly should the experience of officers and enlisted men of long service in the Tropics receive full consideration.

CORBIN.

MANILA. (Received May 8, 1899—8.20 a. m.)

AGWAR, *Washington:*

Weekly report of deaths: Variola—May 3, Edward Vaughn, private, C, Fifty-first Iowa. May 4, John P. Smith, private, L, Fourteenth Infantry. Drowned—April 29, William L. Higgins, corporal, B, Ninth Infantry; Harris W. Mallory, private, B, Ninth Infantry. Septicæmia from phlegmon—April 30, Myron O. Stearns, sergeant, B, First Nebraska. Gunshot wound, accident—May 1, James S. Lynch, private, C, Ninth Infantry. Wounds in action—May 4, Guy Nebergall, private, I, Twentieth Kansas. Ulcerative colitis—John A. Moore, sergeant, K, Fourth Infantry.

OTIS.

MANILA. (Received May 8, 1899—10.09 a. m.)

AGWAR, *Washington:*

Casualties not heretofore reported: Killed—Thirteenth Minnesota, May 4, L, Private Fred W. Buckendorf. Wounded—H, Private James Barrett, shoulder, moderate. Second Oregon, A, Capt. Herbert L. Heath, leg, slight. Sixth Artillery, D, Private William Betzold, arm, slight. Fifty-first Iowa, 5th, C, Private George Shannon, hip, slight. Twentieth Kansas, H, Private Arthur K. Moore, hand, severe. First Washington, April 27, L, Corpl. William Schemerhorn, arm, slight.

OTIS.

MANILA. (Received May 8, 1899—10.21 a. m.)

AGWAR, *Washington:*

Situation as follows: Lawton at Maasin and Baliuag; scouting parties to north and east; MacArthur at San Fernando. Both columns awaiting necessary preparation for continued advance. Population of country between Manila and northern points, held by troops, returning to homes; appear cheerful and contented. Army gunboats, operating in rivers, have cleared country west of MacArthur of insurgents. Armed insurgents south of Manila—about 6,000—hold together; still threaten attack on city. Signs of insurgents' weakness more apparent daily.

OTIS.

SAN FRANCISCO, CAL., *May 8, 1899.*
(Received 8.45 p. m.)

ADJUTANT-GENERAL, *Washington, D. C.:*

Transport *Roanoke* arrived to-day with following military passengers: Capt. Amos W. Kimball, quartermaster; surgeon S. J. Frazer, and 7 enlisted men and 23 discharged soldiers. No deaths during voyage.

SHAFTER, *Major-General.*

MANILA. (Received May 9, 1899—7.06 a. m.)

AGWAR, *Washington:*

Transport *Puebla* left for San Francisco 7th. *Zealandia* to-day.

OTIS.

ADJUTANT GENERAL'S OFFICE,
Washington, May 9, 1899.

COMMANDING GENERAL, DEPARTMENT CALIFORNIA,
San Francisco, Cal.:

General Otis advises transport *Puebla* left for San Francisco 7th; *Zealandia* 8th.

H. C. CORBIN, *Adjutant-General.*

ADJUTANT-GENERAL'S OFFICE,
Washington, May 9, 1899.

OTIS, *Manila:*

Executive order provides for appointment officer regular army treasurer Philippine Islands. Declares Manila, Iloilo, Cebu ports of entry. Officers regular army are to be assigned to each as collectors. You authorized to fill positions reporting action. Change Manila collector when you deem advisable.

CORBIN.

MANILA. (Received May 10, 1899—8.57 a. m.)

AGWAR, *Washington:*

Transport *Pennsylvania* left for San Francisco to-day; *Nelson* leaves 11th; *Cleveland* 12th; *St. Paul* 13th instant.

OTIS.

[Copy sent General Shafter May 10, 1899.]

ADJUTANT-GENERAL'S OFFICE,
Washington, May 10, 1899—10.02 a. m.

OTIS, *Manila:*

Cablegrams reporting transports leaving Manila received. What do these ships bring?

CORBIN.

ADJUTANT-GENERAL'S OFFICE,
Washington, May 10, 1899—10.57 a. m.

OTIS, *Manila:*

Secwar anxious to know when volunteers will begin to leave for home. He feels that all returning transports should be utilized for this purpose.

CORBIN.

MANILA. (Received May 11, 1899—12.44 a. m.)

AGWAR, *Washington:*

Health conditions troops arrived on *Hancock* excellent. Two deaths en route—Privates Die E. Jones and Elmer H. Chevalier, Companies L and E, Twenty-first Infantry, April 24 and 26.

OTIS.

MANILA. (Received May 11, 1899—12.45 a. m.)

AGWAR, *Washington:*

Volunteer organizations first to return now at Negros and 45 miles from Manila at front. Expected that transports now arriving will take returning volunteers. Volunteers understand they will begin to leave for United States latter part of month; know importance of their presence here at this time and accept sacrifice which United States' interests make imperative. *Hancock* now entering harbor. Transports returning this week carry sick and wounded men; *Pennsylvania* and *St. Paul* not needed longer in southern waters where they have been retained, hence dispatched. Transports *Nelson* and *Cleveland* brought freight; return without cargo.

OTIS.

ADJUTANT-GENERAL'S OFFICE,
Washington, May 11, 1899.

OTIS, *Manila:*

Cable to-day concerning return of volunteers is approved by Secwar, who is very glad to receive this encouraging information. He is also gratified at excellent condition troops as reported arrived on *Hancock*.

CORBIN.

MANILA. (Received May 11, 1899—1.05 a. m.)

AGWAR, *Washington:*

Situation as follows: Succeeded in passing army gunboats to Calumpit for use in Rio Grande. Railway connection with that point secured this week. Passage of gunboats through Macabebe country hailed with joyful demonstrations by inhabitants. Active operations to north practicable in few days. In country passed over by troops temporarily civil administration inaugurated and protection to inhabitants against insurgent abuses given as far as possible. Signs of insurgent disintegration daily manifested. Obstacles, which natural features of country present, can be overcome.

OTIS.

MANILA. (Received May 12, 1899—7.25 a. m.)

AGWAR, *Washington:*

Casualties not heretofore reported: Wounded—First North Dakota, May 2, G, Private Charles Olstad, hand, moderate. Thirteenth Minnesota, 8th, Maj. Arthur M. Diggles, forehead, severe. Second Oregon, F, Corpl. John G. Miller, arm, slight. First Montana, 9th, K, First Sergt. Patrick McBride, chest, severe; M, Private Swift D. Hunter, forearm, severe. Frank Smith, F, Thirteenth Minnesota, reported killed May 1, should read Frank C. Lewis.

OTIS.

MANILA. (Received May 12, 1899—9.10 a. m.)

AGWAR, *Washington:*

Casualties not heretofore reported: Wounded—Thirteenth Minnesota, April 25, D, Privates Frank Wiplinger wrist, slight; G, Allan T. Williams, shoulder, slight. Third Infantry, 29th, K, Private Edward Rea, thigh, slight. May 11th, I, Private Benton W. Landrum, thumb, moderate. Fourth Cavalry, I, Private Charles H. Coe, thigh, moderate.

OTIS.

MANILA. (Received May 12, 1899—10.40 p. m.)

AGWAR, *Washington:*

Nebraska regiment suffered severely in casualties. Health fairly good; now resting at San Fernando. Am considering relief of that and South Dakota regiment from front.

OTIS.

[Telegram.]

WAR DEPARTMENT, *May 13, 1899.*

OTIS, *Manila:*

How many obsolete cannon have you that would be suitable to send to the States from which troops have served, and for monuments?

ALGER, *Secwar.*

WAR DEPARTMENT, QUARTERMASTER-GENERAL'S OFFICE,
Washington, May 13, 1899.

The ADJUTANT-GENERAL OF THE ARMY.

SIR: Messrs. J. M. Ceballos & Co., contractors for the transportation of Spanish prisoners from the Philippine Islands to Spain, have presented an account for the services rendered under their contract, amounting in the aggregate to $1,104,974.39.

The contract entered into between the Secretary of War and J. M. Ceballos & Co. provides for the payment of $215 for each commissioned officer and $73.75 for each enlisted man or other person designated by the Secretary of War for transportation from the Philippine Islands to Spain, an account of the number of officers, enlisted men, or other persons to be taken at the time of embarkation by a representative of the Government and a representative of J. M. Ceballos & Co., and pay to said company to be made upon the basis of the number of officers, enlisted men, and persons counted on each ship.

The bills of Messrs. Ceballos & Co. include charge for officers' wives and children at the same rate per capita as charged for officers, $215 each, charging one fare only for two minor children, and for wives and children of enlisted men at same rate as charged for enlisted men, $73.75, counting one fare for two minor children.

This office has no report of the number of prisoners counted on the ships, and it is repectfully requested that Major-General Otis be requested by cable to report the number of officers, enlisted men, and other persons counted upon each of the ships, giving names of the ships and dates of sailing.

The account presented shows that eleven vessels were employed in transporting the prisoners, and that two of them made a second trip.

Very respectfully,

JAMES M. MOORE,
Assistant Quartermaster-General, U. S. Army,
Acting Quartermaster-General.

ADJUTANT-GENERAL'S OFFICE,
Washington, May 13, 1899.

OTIS, *Manila:*

Referring transportation Spanish prisoners. Secwar desires know number officers, enlisted men, and other persons counted upon each ship, giving names ships and dates sailing. This to enable settlement of account.

CORBIN.

MANILA. (Received May 14, 1899—6.06 a. m.)

AGWAR, *Washington:*

Situation is as follows: Lawton, from Baliuag, has taken Ildefonso and San Miguel to north, with slight loss, and driving considerable force of enemy. Gunboats and cascoes accompany 1,500 men, under Kobbé, up Rio Grande River from Calumpit; start 16th. MacArthur remains at San Fernando covering country. Insurgents retain large force south of Manila. Yesterday messenger from Aguinaldo, expressing wish to send commission to Manila for conference with United States Commission, to arrange terms of peace; directions given to pass body representative insurgents to Manila, should it present itself.

OTIS.

ADJUTANT-GENERAL'S OFFICE,
Washington, May 14, 1899.

OTIS, *Manila:*

How many Spanish troops do you estimate are yet in Philippines, and where located?

CORBIN.

MANILA. (Received May 14, 1899—9.21 a. m.)

AGWAR, *Washington:*

Following deaths since last weekly report: Thermic fever and Bright's disease— May 9, Arthur S. Hunt, private, K, Third Infantry. Typhoid fever—10th, Albert M. Wooters, private, B, Twenty-third Infantry. Dysentery—12th, James Kelly, G, Second Oregon. Alcoholism—Richard H. McReynolds, wagoner, G, Fourth Cavalry. Gunshot wound, accidental—Peter Laporte, private, Hospital Corps.

OTIS.

MANILA. (Received May 14, 1899—12.20 p. m.)

AGWAR, *Washington:*

Reported that Zamboanga insurgents attacked Spanish troops 11th instant, using quick-firing guns and arms captured from Spanish gunboats. Spanish general, two other officers wounded; few casualties among troops. Spanish garrisons now besieged, water supply cut off, and troops calling for relief. This attack surprising, as I hold proof that Spanish and insurgent troops on most friendly terms, united in sentiment on necessity of opposing Americans. Can not now send sufficient troops to take and hold securely city and evironments, including water supply, because of extended field of campaign in Luzon. Can permit Spanish troops to withdraw and take town hereafter, though with probable destruction to considerable property. Meditate sending, present week, troops to Jolo to relieve Spanish garrison there.

OTIS.

WAR DEPARTMENT, *May 14, 1899.*

The PRESIDENT, *Hot Springs, Va.:*

Concerning Otis's dispatch of affairs at Zamboanga I suggest that a gunboat be ordered there, also transports to take off Spanish troops if upon arrival there it is thought advisable to do so, and that a company or battalion be sent with discreet officer to act as situation may demand. Secretary Long is absent from city.

R. A. ALGER, *Secretary of War.*

HOT SPRINGS, VA., *May 14, 1899.*
(Received 6.35 p. m.)

Lieut. Col. B. F. MONTGOMERY,
Executive Mansion, Washington, D. C.:

Please give to the Secretary of War the following from the President: "Immediate. I fear it would not be prudent at this great distance to give orders concerning affairs at Zamboanga. General Otis has such knowledge of the situation and of the strength at his disposal that the largest discretion in such matters should be left to him. It would be entirely prudent to inquire of General Otis whether the suggestion of your dispatch is practicable, and if he and Admiral Dewey concur. It could then be done."

WILLIAM MCKINLEY.

WAR DEPARTMENT, *May 14, 1899.*

OTIS, *Manila:*

Is it practicable to send gunboat to Zamboanga and a company or battalion with discreet officer to act as situation demands, also transport to take off Spanish troops, if thought advisable? This is the President's suggestion, and also that you confer with Admiral Dewey.

ALGER, *Secwar.*

MANILA. Received May 15, 1899—7.48 a. m.)

SECWAR, *Washington:*

All obsolete cannon in Philippines Spanish property under terms of treaty.

OTIS.

MANILA. (Received May 15, 1899—7.55 a. m.)

SECWAR, *Washington:*

About 1,900 Spanish troops still in Philippines; 500 at Jolo, 1,000 at Zamboanga, 50 at Baler, east coast of Luzon.

OTIS.

CORRESPONDENCE.

WAR DEPARTMENT, *May 15, 1899.*

OTIS, *Manila:*

Complaint is made that South Dakota and other volunteers are using black powder and Springfield rifles. Is this true? Have you not enough smokeless powder and Krag-Jörgensens for your command?

ALGER, *Secwar.*

MANILA. (Received May 16, 1899—7.55 a. m.)

SECWAR, *Washington:*

All volunteers supplied with Springfield rifle and black-powder ammunition when leaving San Francisco. Applied several months ago for 8,000 Krags and smokeless-powder cartridges for Springfields. Five thousand Krags received and issued pro rata. Smokeless-powder ammunition for Springfields issued and on hand; has caused casualties by bursting gun; five casualties in one regiment; men somewhat afraid of it. At medium range Springfield preferred to Krag; volunteers have done great execution with it. All volunteer expert shots have Krag; have not sufficient Krags for entire command. Do not want more; the volunteers return by the time they could be received. The complaint cabled extends back to August; do not consider it of merit.

OTIS.

ADJUTANT-GENERAL'S OFFICE,
Washington, May 16, 1899.

The STAR, *Kansas City, Mo.:*

The Secretary of War instructs me to inform you that if your staff correspondent will report to General Shafter in San Francisco, transportation will be furnished him to Manila on transport sailing the 22d of this month.

H. C. CORBIN, *Adjutant-General.*

ADJUTANT-GENERAL'S OFFICE,
Washington, May 16, 1899.

General SHAFTER, *San Francisco, Cal.:*

The following has been sent the Star, Kansas City, and is repeated for your information and guidance:

"The Secretary of War instructs me to inform you that if your staff correspondent will report to General Shafter in San Francisco, transportation will be furnished him to Manila on transport sailing the 22d of the month."

H. C. CORBIN, *Adjutant-General.*

MANILA. (Received May 17, 1899—3.25 a. m.)

AGWAR, *Washington:*

Situation as follows: Lawton, with tact and ability, has covered Bulacan Province with his column and driven insurgent troops northward into San Isidro, second insurgent capital, which he captured this morning. Is now driving enemy northward into mountains. He has constant fighting, inflicting heavy losses and suffering few casualties. Appearance of his troops on flanks of enemy, behind entrenchments thrown up at every strategic point and town, very demoralizing to insurgents, and has given them no opportunity to reconcentrate scattered troops. Kobbé's column, with gunboats, proceeding up Rio Grande. Will encounter strong resistance; enemy can not withstand. It will unite with Lawton's columns soon. MacArthur still at San Fernando and vicinity confronting Luna's forces, which we desire to keep in position now occupied for few days. No change south of Manila.

OTIS.

MANILA. (Received May 17, 1899—4.42 a. m.)

SECWAR, *Washington:*

Will send two battalions to Jolo to-morrow to relieve Spanish garrison there. Will endeavor to relieve Zamboanga in few days. Force 1,500, at least, required. Transport *Warren* expected to-morrow from San Francisco with 1,000 men. Admiral Dewey has sent war vessel to Zamboanga; will convoy Jolo troops, also Zamboanga relief, when sent. Spanish authorities send transport to Zamboanga this afternoon to take away Spanish garrison.

OTIS.

MANILA. (Received May 17, 1899—12.31 p. m.)

AGWAR, *Washington:*

Names vessels transporting Spanish prisoners: *Buenos Aires, Cashemire, Isla de Luzón, León XIII, Monserrat, Reina Cristina, Uruguay, Rio Negro, Satrustegui, Buenos Aires, Alicante, Isla de Luzón, Cadiz, Cataluña.* Dates of departure: November 8; December 13, 20; January 11, 16; February 12, 13, 25; March 6, 10, 13, 17; April 8; May 6. Number officers transported in vessels in order as above named, 97, 30, 74, 71, 46, 100, 79, 75, 140, 83, 72, 93, 159, 71; total, 1,190. All these vessels transported enlisted men except *Alicante*, and in numbers on each vessel in order above named, as follows: 814, 1,037, 660, 625, 479, 807, 989, 991, 1,094, 984, 35, 93, 30; total, 8,668. Transporting contractors claim additional on all vessels 103 officers, 291 enlisted men, and claim transported 417 wives and 905 children of officers and enlisted men; also 533 civilian employees with 198 wives and 293 children, or a total of 12,598 persons all descriptions.

OTIS.

MANILA. (Received May 17, 1899—10.52 a. m.)

AGWAR, *Washington:*

Additional casualties: Killed—Utah Artillery, May 14, A, Sergt. Ford Fisher. Second Oregon, 16th, G, Private James Harrington. Wounded—First North Dakota, 13th, C, Private William R. Trulock, thigh, severe; Civilian William H. Young, chief of scouts, died. 16th, Thirteenth Minnesota, H, Private Albert Erickson, chest, moderate. 15th, K, First Sergt. Harry M. Howard, wrist, slight. Missing, First California Infantry, K, Private Ralph C. Coates, since April 6.

OTIS.

ADJUTANT-GENERAL'S OFFICE,
Washington, May 17, 1899.

General OTIS, *Manila:*

Unless field ovens and cooking utensils in hand of volunteer organizations should, in your judgment, be retained for reissue they will be returned with troops. Tents should be retained in Philippines.

CORBIN.

MANILA. (Received May 18, 1899—8.24 a. m.)

AGWAR, *Washington:*

Representatives, insurgent cabinet, and Aguinaldo in mountains 12 miles north San Isidro, which abandoned 15th instant. Will send in commission to-morrow to seek terms of peace. Majority of force confronting MacArthur at San Fernando has retired to Tarlac, tearing up 2 miles railway; this force has decreased to about 2,500. Scouting parties and detachments moving to-day in various directions; Kobbé with column at Candaba on Rio Grande. Great majority inhabitants of provinces over which troops have moved anxious for peace; supported by members of insurgent congress. Aspect of affairs at present favorable.

OTIS.

SAN FRANCISCO, CAL., *May 18, 1899.* (Received 5.11 p. m.)
ADJUTANT-GENERAL, *Washington, D. C.:*
Transport *Portland* arrived last night with following military passengers: Acting Assistant Surgeon McCulloch and 1 private, Hospital Corps, on duty; 12 discharged soldiers; 3 soldiers to be discharged; 2 sick soldiers transferred to general hospital, Presidio. Sergt. Jeremiah Shea, Battery A, California Artillery, died April 19, of chronic dysentery and was buried at sea same date.

SHAFTER, *Major-General.*

WAR DEPARTMENT, *May 18, 1899.*
OTIS, *Manila:*
Three thousand Krag-Jörgensen guns have been in Benicia Arsenal subject to your orders since April and 10,000 more have been added.

ALGER, *Secwar.*

MANILA. (Received May 19, 1899—10.37 a. m.)
AGWAR, *Washington:*
Additional casualties: Killed—Twenty-second Infantry, May 18, L, Corpl. Henry Langford. Wounded—H, Sergt. Peter Cosgrove, arm, slight; Privates Carl A. Carlson, abdomen, moderate; L, Simon Shueller, abdomen, severe. Thirteenth Minnesota, 15th, F, Private Martin E. Tew, thigh, slight. Second Oregon, L, Frank M. Butts, thigh, slight.

OTIS.

OLYMPIA, WASH., *May 19, 1899.* (Received 2.09 p. m.)
Hon. R. A. ALGER,
Secretary of War, Washington, D. C.:
Friction among officers in First Washington Volunteers at Manila seems to have culminated. Colonel Wholly, when appointed, was first lieutenant Twenty-fourth Infantry, United States Army. Volunteer officers desire to have him recalled to his regiment. Have just received from Manila following telegram: "Wholly unjustifiably arrested Major Canton, Captain Otis, Captain Scudder, Lieutenant Hazzard. Nearly all officers will resign if Wholly is not recalled to his regiment. Signed, Lieutenant-Colonel Fife, Major Weisenberger." The whole matter is turned over to the War Department.

J. R. ROGERS,
Governor of Washington.

WAR DEPARTMENT, *May 19, 1899.*
OTIS, *Manila:*
Trouble reported in Washington Volunteer Regiment. Colonel Wholly causing much disturbance and officers demand his return to his own regiment. Investigate and act as you deem best.

ALGER, *Secwar.*

MANILA. (Received May 19, 1899—4 a. m.)
SECWAR, *Washington:*
Applied for 8,000 Krags November 16. Was informed December 25 that 8,000 Krags stopped at Benicia to be forwarded in lots as called for; December 29 called for 3,000, which have been received; April 8 called for 3,000, received these, issued

to volunteers. All regular troops have Krags, and as volunteers are soon to return not necessary to ship for their use; however, recruits arriving without arms additional, 3,000 should be sent to meet possible emergency.

OTIS.

WAR DEPARTMENT, *May 19, 1899.*

Maj. Gen. WILLIAM R. SHAFTER,
Commanding Department of California, San Francisco, Cal.:
Send 5,000 Krag-Jörgensen rifles with ammunition to General Otis at once by first ship. They are stored at Benicia Arsenal.

R. A. ALGER, *Secretary of War.*

WAR DEPARTMENT, *May 19, 1899.*

OTIS, *Manila:*
Have directed General Shafter to ship 5,000 Krag-Jörgensens with ammunition at once.

ALGER, *Secwar.*

MANILA. (Received May 20, 1899—10.48 a. m.)

AGWAR, *Washington:*
Commissioners of Aguinaldo arrived this morning. Wish to consult United States Commissioners, which they will do 22d instant. Their power limited and apparently armistice a condition precedent to negotiations. This unsafe to grant. Aguinaldo asks cessation hostilities to ascertain desires Filipino people and army, for peace or continue war.

OTIS.

MANILA. (Received May 21, 1899—10.15 p. m.)

AGWAR, *Washington:*
Transport *Warren* arrived 18th instant; no casualties.

OTIS.

MANILA. (Received May 21, 1899—11.15 p. m.)

AGWAR, *Washington:*
Following deaths since last weekly report: Dysentery—May 7, Stephen Burdell, private, M, First California. 13th, William Fahrenwald, private, C, First South Dakota. Typhoid fever—14th, John B. Elliott, private, B, Twelfth Infantry; John Corbett, private, G, Twenty-second Infantry. Diphtheria—16th, Herbert L. Keeler, private, C, Thirteenth Minnesota. Nephritis—William Hast, Corporal, H, Fourth Infantry. Suicide—17th, Christof Lov, private, G, Twentieth Infantry. Erysipelas—Frank Hassaurek, Second Lieutenant, K, Seventeenth Infantry, 9.45 p. m., 19th, at Manila.

OTIS.

MANILA. (Received May 22, 1899—7.10 a. m.)

AGWAR, *Washington:*
Conditions as follows: In Bulacan province troops maintained at Quingua, Baliuag, San Miguel; Lawton proceeding down Rio Grande River from San Isidro has driven enemy westward from San Antonio, Cabiao, and Arayat, where he was joined yes-

terday by Kobbe's column; will reach Santa Ana and Candaba to-day. MacArthur still at San Fernando and will occupy cities south and westward. Insurgent forces disintegrating daily; Luna's force at Tarlac much diminished; has destroyed several miles railway in his front. Number of officers of rank have deserted Luna and few have entered Manila for protection. In Pampanga and Bulacan inhabitants returning to homes. Only fear insurgent troops south of Manila. Insurgent disintegration progressing, though large force still maintained; conditions improving daily; send battalion troops and gunboat to Negros to-morrow to allay excitement in southern portion of island and west coast Cebu. Have denied request of Aguinaldo's commissioners for armistice.

OTIS.

SAN FRANCISCO, CAL., *May 23, 1899.* (Received 4.12 p. m.)
ADJUTANT-GENERAL, *Washington, D. C.:*

Transport *Sheridan* arrived last night with following military passengers: General Miller; Colonel Lippincott, deputy surgeon-general; Captains Clay, Seventeenth Infantry; Hill, First Montana; Ough, First Nebraska; Jensen, assistant surgeon, First Nebraska; First Lieutenants Jackson and Newell, Twenty-second Infantry; Coffin, assistant surgeon Tenth Pennsylvania; Bothwell, First Washington; Rud, Volunteer Signal Corps; Second Lieutenants Cavenaugh, Twentieth Infantry; Zolars, First Colorado. Twenty-two sick and convalescent soldiers; 44 discharged. List of casualties will be reported later.

SHAFTER, *Major-General.*

SAN FRANCISCO, CAL., *May 23, 1899.* (Received 6.15 p. m.)
ADJUTANT-GENERAL, *Washington, D. C.:*

Record of casualties on *Sheridan*: Private John W. Flynt, C, Thirteenth Minnesota, died at sea 14th instant, dysentery; body on board ship.

SHAFTER, *Major-General.*

MANILA. (Received May 23, 1899—7.25 a. m.)
AGWAR, *Washington:*

Second Lieut. Pierce C. Foster, Third Infantry, died at Manila, 12.25, May 22, typhoid fever.

OTIS.

MANILA. (Received May 24, 1899—12.08 a. m.)
AGWAR, *Washington:*

Newport arrived yesterday; no casualties.

OTIS.

MANILA. (Received May 24, 1899—10.36 a. m.)
AGWAR, *Washington:*

Additional casualties: Wounded—Twenty-first Infantry, May 14, E, Private Leonard J. Edling, nates, moderate. Twelfth Infantry, 22d, I, Private John G. Pender, skull, severe. Ninth Infantry, C, Private Charles H. Knepa, thumb, slight. Fourth Cavalry, K, Private Jow Costello, breast, severe; Thomas H. Turner, thumb, moderate; Hans C. Mathieson, thigh, severe. Twenty-second Infantry, K, Privates Robert V. Cassidy, knee, severe; L, Simon Schuller, nates, severe. Killed—First Idaho, G, Corpl. George Scott. First Colorado, 23d, C, Private Harry L. Doxsee.

OTIS.

SAN FRANCISCO, CAL., *May 24, 1899.* (Received 1.35 p. m.)
ADJUTANT-GENERAL, *Washington, D. C.:*
The *Sheridan* will be ready to receive troops on June 7.

SHAFTER, *Major-General.*

ADJUTANT-GENERAL'S OFFICE,
Washington, May 24, 1899.

OTIS, *Manila:*
Sherman sailed 22d, with Sixth Infantry, 28 officers, 1,371 men; also Generals Bates and Grant, and Colonels Liscum and Powell, and other staff and line officers. Also hospital, engineer, signal corps men, and recruits.

CORBIN.

MANILA. (Received May 25, 1899—10.10 a. m.)
AGWAR, *Washington:*
On 23d instant, Third Infantry, returning to Baliuag from San Miguel, were attacked morning, noon, and evening by a large force of enemy, suffering in casualties 2 men killed and 13 wounded; enemy repulsed, leaving on field 16 killed, large number wounded and prisoners. Yesterday enemy appeared in vicinity San Fernando; attacked by Kansas and Montana regiments, which suffered slight loss. Enemy driven through rice field, leaving 50 dead, 38 wounded, and 28 prisoners; 50 rifles and other property captured. Their retreat through swamp lands saved them from destruction. Lawton returning, leaving with MacArthur on the front regular troops to replace volunteers.

OTIS.

MANILA. (Received May 25, 1899—11.32 a. m.)
AGWAR, *Washington:*
Additional casualties. Killed—Third Infantry, May 23, M, Corpl. Ashel E. Pipes; Private Guy L. Whitlock. Twentieth Kansas, 24th, A, Private William Sullivan. Wounded—California Heavy Artillery, May 20, D, Private George Cathelin, leg, severe. Third Infantry, May 23, A, First Lieut. John C. McArthur, leg, moderate; Privates Anthony Brefka, foot, severe; Charles Deitrich, arm, moderate; C, Richard T. Frank, scalp, slight; F, Fred A. Baker, abdomen, moderate; Samuel Alpren, leg, slight; Musician William P. Lemay, leg, slight; H, Sergt. Joseph W. Miller, shoulder, severe; Privates Peter Higgins, foot, moderate; Benjamin E. Ledgerwood, foot, moderate; K, John E. Nelson, thigh, severe; David J. Parcell, thorax, severe; James W. Baker, thigh, moderate. First Montana, 24th, F, Privates Joseph Frantzen, cheek, slight; Corpl. Joseph C. Taylor, scalp, slight; G, George B. Raymond, arm, severe. Twentieth Kansas, H, Second Lieut. Robert S. Parker, thigh, slight; B, Privates Peter M. Sorenson, shoulder, severe; E, Elmer H. Ashcroft, neck, moderate; Arthur Hollingshead, abdomen, severe; L, Ernest Ryan, abdomen, severe; Sergt. Charles W. Tozier, head, slight; Corpl. Albert Dooley, thigh, moderate.

OTIS.

MANILA. (Received May 25, 1899—5.30 a. m.)
AGWAR, *Washington:*
Referring dispatch, 17th instant reporting Spanish prisoners war transported to Spain, transportation company reported all Spanish troops carried, whether prisoners of war or those drawn from Zamboanga and other southern Spanish stations; our

count only covers prisoners of war sent from this port. Company reported 1,123 wives and children of prisoners of war transported; also separately wives and children of troops not Spanish prisoners of war, and civilian employees, not knowing whether United States or Spain would pay transportation of families of prisoners of war. Discrepancies in our count of prisoners and those reported by company not very material.

OTIS.

ADJUTANT-GENERAL'S OFFICE,
Washington, May 26, 1899.

COMMANDING GENERAL, DEPARTMENT CALIFORNIA,
San Francisco, Cal.:

Nineteenth Infantry has not yet been able to get away from Porto Rico, so that the regiment will hardly be ready to sail on the *Sheridan*. The Secretary of War feels that the better way would be to send recruits to the capacity of the *Sheridan* as soon as she can leave, as it is desirable to have this transport at Manila for the return of volunteers. In this connection it is desired to know if there are any field officers going to Manila now in San Francisco. We will be able to get a number of young officers to go, but you can understand the importance of having a number of officers of experience and high rank. If you have not sufficient the Department will make an effort to get officers, now on leave, in time to sail on the *Sheridan*.

H. C. CORBIN, *Adjutant-General.*

ADJUTANT-GENERAL'S OFFICE,
Washington, May 26, 1899.

COMMANDING GENERAL, DEPARTMENT CALIFORNIA,
San Francisco, Cal.:

Having reference to my telegram of this date referring to recruits going on *Sheridan*, Secretary of War is of opinion that you should organize them into temporary companies for purposes of discipline and control while en route. Failing in getting sufficient and satisfactory officers to command that belong in Manila, Secretary of War directs that you detail field officers from captains in your department to conduct these recruits there.

H. C. CORBIN, *Adjutant-General.*

MANILA. (Received May 26, 1899—11.10 p. m.)

AGWAR, *Washington:*

Morgan City with recruits arrived this morning; no casualties.

OTIS.

WAR DEPARTMENT, *May 27, 1899.*

OTIS, *Manila:*

Reports not credited by the President are being circulated that you and commissioners disagree. What are the facts?

ALGER, *Secwar.*

MANILA. (Received May 27, 1899—6.24 a. m.)

AGWAR, *Washington:*

Additional casualties: Wounded—First Montana, May 24, M, Private Barney O'Neill, thigh, slight. First South Dakota, 25th, A, First Sergt. George E. Barker, hand, slight; C, Corpl. David Martindale, leg, slight; G, Privates Carl W. McConnell, foot, slight; Edwin W. Heald, foot, severe; G, Bert Kellett, arm, slight; James Black, abdomen, slight. Killed—G, Private Daniel E. Coleran.

OTIS.

AFFAIRS IN THE PHILIPPINE ISLANDS.

MANILA. (Received May 28, 1899—9.55 a. m.)

SIGNALS, *Washington:*

Captain Tilly, one of a party landed at Escalante, Negros, cable work, treacherously attacked by insurgents. Tilly missing. Worst feared.

THOMPSON.

MANILA. (Received May 28, 1899—9.38 a. m.)

AGWAR, *Washington:*

Two battalions Twenty-third Infantry, in quiet possession Jolo. Spanish troops withdrawn from Zamboanga after battle with insurgents, with severe loss to latter. Spanish loss 9 killed, 27 wounded, among whom Commanding General Montero, died from wounds, buried here yesterday. Insurgents used rifles, artillery, and ammunition captured from gunboats, expending major part of ammunition. Conference followed between General Rios, who went from Manila to withdraw troops, and insurgents. Latter stated to him would not oppose landing Americans, but would accept conditions in Luzon. Spanish troops withdrawn now here depart for Spain to-morrow. Feeble attack by insurgents on inhabitants southeast portion Negros necessitated sending battalion troops from Manila there. Will soon restore order. Insurgent falsehoods circulated in southern islands of overwhelming insurgent victories in Luzon keep up excitement in that section among more ignorant classes, although intelligent people know American arms have never met reverse and they call for United States protection. Have turned over to Navy for use on coast southern islands number of purchased Spanish gunboats, from which excellent results expected.

OTIS.

MANILA. (Received May 28, 1899—4.46 a. m.)

SECWAR, *Washington:*

Majority Oregon volunteers desire to be sent by vessel to Portland. Washingtons express wish to go to San Francisco.

OTIS.

MANILA. (Received May 29, 1899—2 a. m.)

AGWAR, *Washington:*

Transports *Ohio*, *Senator*, with Thirteenth Infantry, just arrived. Private David R. Johnson, I Company, drowned, and 5 desertions Honolulu. No other casualties.

OTIS.

MANILA. (Received May 29, 1899—10.13 a. m.)

ADJUTANT-GENERAL, *Washington:*

Following deaths since last weekly report: Typhoid malaria—May 10, Claude R. White, private, A, Twenty-third Infantry. Malaria—21st, Denny Hayes, private, E, Twenty-second Infantry; 26th, Edward Hylin, corporal, D, Sixth Artillery. Typhoid—22d, Joseph Salwitshka, private, E, Third Infantry; 23d, Vernon E. Taggart, private, F, Thirteenth Minnesota; 25th, Charles Milkowski, corporal, F, Twenty-second Infantry. From wounds in action—24th, John C. Byron, corporal, D, First North Dakota; 25th, Ernest Ryan, private, L, Twentieth Kansas; 26th, Arthur M. Diggles, major, Thirteenth Minnesota. Drowned in Pasig River on duty—privates, G, Twelfth Infantry, 23d, Nels Anderson, Jasper L. Whims, Joseph Nuneville, Corpl. Ernest Herrmann, Webber Harrison.

OTIS.

CORRESPONDENCE.

MANILA. (Received May 29, 1899—4.16 p. m.)

ALGER, *Secwar:*

Have attended only few meetings commission for lack of time. Recommendations to President and President's responsive instructions unknown to me until called upon to unite in proclamation publishing them. Declined, believing time not opportune. Know nothing of cable dispatches President Schurman has sent or is sending. Declined to be compromised or advised by commission in war measures and am not aware that disposition to interfere exists. Do not think that gentlemen, Worcester excepted, understand conditions or mental adroitness of inhabitants, though Denby rapidly grasping situation. Commission has been beneficial in gaining confidence of leading, well-disposed natives in beneficent intentions United States. Doubt if it has accomplished anything further. Leading Filipinos unite with me in asserting that continued applications of force followed by kind treatment and the establishment of a strong United States Government will alone bring about desired results. Shall be no friction between commission and myself if I can avoid it.

OTIS.

MANILA. (Received May 30, 1899—2.30 a. m.)

AGWAR, *Washington:*

Cable company's vessel, placing cable between Iloilo and Cebu, ran to Escalante, east coast Negros, to remove old cable connection. Captain Tilly, Signal Corps, accompanied, and with captain of vessel and three men visited town, natives making friendly demonstrations. While there ambushed. Vessel's captain and one man escaped to vessel in launch; Tilly and two men taking to water and not rescued. Vessel then reported at Iloilo. General Smith informed, who immediately took 75 men and proceeded to Escalante. He reports this morning that body Captain Tilly found floating in river; marks of violence on head; body sent to Iloilo. Smith remains at Escalante for the present.

OTIS.

SAN FRANCISCO, CAL., *May 30, 1899.* (Received 3.44 p. m.)

ADJUTANT-GENERAL, U. S. ARMY, *Washington, D. C.:*

Entire regiment consisting of 30 officers and 1,295 enlisted men, with 4 surgeons, 1 chaplain, and 15 enlisted men of Hospital Corps, left this point on transport *Grant* at 5 p. m. to-day en route to Philippines.

SPURGIN, *Commanding.*

SAN FRANCISCO, CAL., *May 30, 1899.* (Received 5.08 p. m.)

ADJUTANT-GENERAL, *Washington:*

Transport *Grant* will sail at 4.30 p. m. to-day with Sixteenth Infantry, 30 officers, 1,295 men, 250 rounds per man, caliber .30 ammunition, 1 surgeon, 3 acting assistant surgeons, 1 chaplain; and 15 Hospital Corps men. Attached passengers, Lieutenant-Colonel Friedrick, Thirteenth Minnesota; Lieutenants Dove, Twelfth; Wickham, Eighteenth; Walker, Third Infantry; Acting Assistant Surgeon Grandy; also 20 discharged volunteer engineers for Honolulu; Lieutenants Merritt, First Artillery, and Waldron, Ninth Infantry, on duty with casuals and recruits, and following enlisted men: Signal Corps, 5; Hospital Corps, 50; casuals Sixth Infantry, 8; recruits cavalry, Fourth, 1; artillery, Third, 5; infantry, Fourteenth, 157; Eighteenth, 7; Sixth, 6; Twenty-third, 137. Recruits all had previous service.

SHAFTER, *Major-General.*

AFFAIRS IN THE PHILIPPINE ISLANDS. 999

WAR DEPARTMENT, *May 31, 1899.*

OTIS, *Manila:*

The Adjutant-General reports you will have approximately 24,000 troops when those ordered to the Philippines have arrived and all volunteers have returned. In your judgment will you need more troops? If so, how many? They should be sent at once if required, that they may be in condition for service at the end of the rainy season.

ALGER, *Secwar.*

MANILA. (Received May 31, 1899—7.05 a. m.)

AGWAR, *Washington:*

Additional casualties: Wounded—Fourth Cavalry, May 2, E, Private James Thorson, leg, slight. Seventeenth Infantry, 17th, A, Private Homer A. Hall, eye, slight. Twenty-second Infantry, 18th, C, Private Charles L. Diedel, breast, slight. Fifty-first Iowa, 27th, M, Private James J. Markey, leg, moderate. Third Infantry, C, Privates Charles J. Gamble, head, severe; Stanley Anderson, thigh, severe. Fourth Infantry, 27th, A, Private Excelsion H. Wiedberg arm, slight.

OTIS.

MANILA. (Received June 1, 1899—7.15 a. m.)

AGWAR, *Washington:*

Smith reports from Negros has punished insurgents who murdered Captain Tilly. That eastern coast of island now under American flag and inhabitants ask protection against robber bands. Bands pursued into mountains by us and native troops and severely punished.

OTIS.

MANILA. (Received June 1, 1899—8.11 a. m.)

AGWAR, *Washington:*

Additional casualties: Missing—Ninth Infantry, April 28, B, Capt. Charles M. Rockefeller. Wounded—Third Infantry, May 23, K, Sergt. Jacob Hellriegel, chest, slight. Fourteenth Infantry, 29th, F, Private Alonzo B. Castner, foot, severe, accidental. Fifty-first Iowa, 31st, H, Privates Clifford P. Stevenson, thigh, moderate; I, Harley M. Stretch, chin, slight; Corpl. Walter R. Combs, forearm, slight.

OTIS.

MANILA. (Received June 1, 1899—11.17 a. m.)

SECWAR, *Washington:*

Still of opinion that 30,000 effective troops needed here and that it will require 25,000 to govern islands after all opposition by large armed body has ceased. Class of insurgent natives who indulge in robbery and murder, always large, now increased and having arms, will give great annoyance.

OTIS.

WAR DEPARTMENT, *June 1, 1899.*

OTIS, *Manila.*

Volunteers mustered out at San Francisco will receive travel pay approximately as follows: Men of companies, Colorado, $59 to $95; Idaho, $51 to $81; Iowa, $82 to $130; Kansas, $83 to $131; Montana, $53 to $84; Nebraska, $74 to $117; Nevada, $55 to $87; North Dakota, $86 to $136; Oregon, $32 to $51; Pennsylvania, $127 to $201; South

Dakota, $82 to $130; Tennessee, $107 to $169; Utah, $36 to $57; Washington, $39 to $62; Wyoming, $55 to $87; Minnesota $89 to $142. Of course the higher sums are graded among the noncommissioned officers. Railroad fares are, San Francisco to St. Louis and Fargo, $43; Chicago, $44; Washington and Philadelphia, $59; New York, $60; Salt Lake, $24; Lincoln and Topeka, $37; Des Moines, $40; Sioux Falls, $41; Cheyenne and Denver, $35; not including subsistence. Officers, of course, get larger sums. Submit these facts to each regiment and let them determine by vote whether they will be mustered out at San Francisco and take travel pay or in their own states, transported by Government. Cable vote of each regiment.

ALGER, *Secwar.*

MANILA. (Received June 2, 1899—5.43 a. m.)
AGWAR, *Washington:*
Under War Department directions, May 6, approved report board on proper components ration; recommends no change in field and travel ration, but modifies garrison ration as follows: Issue fresh beef eight and bacon two days; one day's salmon in lieu of beef, if desired. Reduction ration fresh beef and flour to 16 ounces; 2 ounces rice, 2 dried fruit, in lieu of beef; 2 ounces oatmeal in lieu of flour; no savings. Issue beans, rice, fresh vegetables, coffee, tea, continued in quantities as at present. Sugar ration increased to 20 pounds, with sirup in lieu, as now authorized; increased for use with oatmeal or dried fruit; no savings. Vinegar reduced one-half; pickles substituted. No other modifications. Full report mailed.

OTIS.

SAN FRANCISCO, CAL., *June 2, 1899.*
(Received 4.35 p. m.)
ADJUTANT-GENERAL, U. S. ARMY, *Washington, D. C.:*
The general superintendent of army transport service reports that serious defects have been discovered in the boilers of the *Sheridan*, which will delay the date of sailing of the ship from the 7th to the 22d.

SHAFTER, *Major-General.*

SAN FRANCISCO, CAL., *June 2, 1899.*
(Received 6 p. m.)
ADJUTANT-GENERAL, *Washington, D. C.:*
Transport *City of Puebla* arrived last evening with Brigadier-General King; Major Brinkerhoff, Third Infantry; Captains Chance, Signal Corps; Stockham, First Nebraska; Lieutenants Hutton, First California; Vannice, First Colorado; Fox, First South Dakota; Dorn, First Montana. Seventy-five sick and 46 discharged soldiers. No casualties.

SHAFTER, *Major-General.*

ADJUTANT-GENERAL'S OFFICE,
Washington, June 2, 1899.
OTIS, *Manila:*
Secwar desires to know how far, in your judgment, it would be advisable to call into service natives, organizing them into battalions, officers to be appointed on your recommendation.

With travel allowances given officers and men on discharge for reenlistment in volunteers, how many volunteers and discharged regulars will remain with you?

CORBIN.

MANILA. (Received June 3, 1899—11.30 p. m.)

AGWAR, *Washington:*

Spanish gunboats obtained, paid for from public civil funds, cost 330,000 pesos; now loaned to Navy, which is manning them. Claim for 81,000 pesos still pending for armament, large amount of which stolen by insurgents at Zamboanga, and which must probably be paid, as claimants allege promise to convoy, which was not fulfilled. Would be glad to turn boats over to Navy if there are no objections.

OTIS.

MANILA. (Received June 3, 1899—7.53 a. m.)

AGWAR, *Washington:*

Not advisable to call into service in Luzon native organizations of any character at present; could not be trusted in Negros. Have force 200 doing excellent work; carried as scouts, paid by Quartermaster's Department from public funds. Understand travel allowances not granted volunteers enlisting for six months; only for long term. They now express desire to go home and enjoy reception from friends; may undergo some change in desire from present indications; do not think two regiments could be obtained from all volunteers here.

OTIS.

MANILA. (Received June 4, 1899—4.23 a. m.)

AGWAR, *Washington:*

Lawton's troops maneuvering Morong, where Pilar, with 2,000 insurgents, has robbed and murdered inhabitants for several months; insurgents will at least be driven into mountains. Hope to capture many with property. Hall with column 2,500 strong moved on Antipolo yesterday; force of 600 threaten towns to the westward and to-day 1,100 men with gunboats move on city of Morong.

Oregon regiment will leave for United States this week. Shall it be sent to San Francisco or Portland? Character of transports used will depend on reply.

OTIS.

MANILA. (Received June 4, 1899—6.18 a. m.)

AGWAR, *Washington:*

Following deaths since last weekly report: Typhoid fever—May 27, William Donsley, private, C, First California. 28th, Fred Krueger, private, K, Third Infantry. Cerebro-spinal meningitis—28th, Charles Karger, private, M, Third Infantry. Strangulated hernia—James McCormick, private, B, Fourth Infantry. Alcoholism—27th, Patrick Byrnes, private, L, Twentieth Infantry. Suppurative typhlitis—28th, Edward Patterson, private, C, Third Infantry. Suppurative tonsilitis—29th, Lyman Kelsay, private, D, Second Oregon. Variola—Edward A. Campbell, private, F, Fourteenth Infantry. Suicide—31st, Thomas Rock, private, F, Twentieth Infantry. Dysentery—David L. Williams, private, F, First Montana. Drowned, accidental—June 1, Lawrence McCray, corporal, G, Twenty-second Infantry. Drowned on duty—April 12, Frederic Grabow, private, F, Fourteenth Infantry.

OTIS.

SAN FRANCISCO, CAL., *June 4, 1899.*
(Received 3.40 p. m.)

ADJUTANT-GENERAL, *Washington, D. C.:*

Transport *Zealandia* arrived yesterday evening. Lieutenant Hawkins, Tenth Pennsylvania, and 11 enlisted men. No casualties en route.

SHAFTER, *Major-General.*

MANILA. (Received June 4, 1899—9.05 a. m.)

SECRETARY OF WAR, *Washington:*

Informed that Mr. Schurman has cabled his policy for terminating war and establishing civil government. He stands alone, unsupported by a single member of Commission. Only know from report what his opinions are, and don't know where he obtained them. Negotiations and conference with insurgents cost soldiers' lives and prolong our difficulties. Advise no action on part of authorities. Policy apparently dictates that Commission quietly continue its labors until discontinued by natural and inherent reasons. Ostensibly it will be supported by War Department authorities here, and to outside world gentle peace shall prevail.

OTIS.

EXECUTIVE MANSION, *June 4, 1899.*

OTIS, *Manila:*

Yours of June 4 received. The President has sent an instruction to Mr. Schurman which he has asked him to communicate to all Commissioners.

The President is glad to have your assurance in regard to "outside world." It is of highest importance if any differences exist the knowledge should be confined to the Commission itself. He sends congratulations upon the success of your military operations.

CORBIN.

ADJUTANT-GENERAL'S OFFICE,
Washington, June 5, 1899.

OTIS, *Manila:*

Acting Secwar directs me say there are no objections to turning over to navy the Spanish gunboats mentioned cable June 3.

CORBIN.

ADJUTANT-GENERAL'S OFFICE,
Washington, June 5, 1899.

OTIS, *Manila:*

Accident boilers *Sheridan* delay sailing until 22d.

CORBIN.

ADJUTANT-GENERAL'S OFFICE,
Washington, June 5, 1899.

OTIS, *Manila:*

Acting Secwar directs Oregon regiment be sent direct to Portland, where it will be mustered out at Vancouver Barracks.

CORBIN.

ADJUTANT-GENERAL'S OFFICE,
Washington, June 5, 1899.

OTIS, *Manila:*

Secwar directs that on date of sailing total strength officers and men, each volunteer regiment, be reported and that where safe to do so bodies of dead be brought home with each regiment.

CORBIN.

ADJUTANT-GENERAL'S OFFICE,
Washington, June 5, 1899.

OTIS, *Manila:*

Has collector of customs for Manila been designated?

CORBIN.

AFFAIRS IN THE PHILIPPINE ISLANDS. 1003

MANILA. (Received June 5, 1899—11.05 p. m.)

AGWAR, *Washington:*

In orders May 25, Lieutenant-Colonel Miley and Captain Wortherspoon appointed collectors customs Manila, Iloilo. Entered upon duties 1st instant.

OTIS.

ADJUTANT-GENERAL'S OFFICE,
Washington, June 5, 1899.

OTIS, *Manila:*

Referring cable 3d, do you think one regiment of volunteers could be organized by you? The President and Acting Secwar are anxious to fix definitely the increase of the force that is to remain with you to full 30,000. One regiment would help. Would you view with favor raising of your infantry companies to one hundred forty or fifty, or would you prefer volunteer regiments be organized and sent you? Your views desired.

CORBIN.

ADJUTANT-GENERAL'S OFFICE,
Washington, June 5, 1899.

OTIS, *Manila:*

The Acting Secretary of War directs me to say that the congratulations of the President last evening had special reference and approval of the vigor with which you continue to push active operations.

CORBIN.

MANILA. (Received June 6, 1899—11.30 p. m.)

AGWAR, *Washington:*

Will volunteers reenlisting here for period to July 1, 1901, receive transportation to United States upon discharge?

OTIS.

MANILA. (Received June 6, 1899—7.23 a. m.)

AGWAR, *Washington:*

Additional casualties: Killed—Twelfth Infantry, June 3, G—Private David S. Goldsmith; 4th, G, Private Converse P. Warner. Second Oregon, H, Private William McElwain. Fourth Cavalry, C, Sergeants Seth Lovell; I, Benjamin Craig. Wounded, Second Oregon, April 25, Maj. Surg. Matthew H. Ellis, leg, slight; June 3, B—Privates Henry M. Wagner, iliac region, severe; H, Austin J. Salisbury, axillary region, severe; 4th, C, Privates Elmer L. Doolittle, arm, moderate; K, William E. Smith, arm, severe. Fourth Cavalry, 3d, G, Private Earl B. Miles, head, severe; 4th, C, Privates Patrick Branigan, leg, severe; G, Nelson E. Daily, chest, severe; I, Maurice Coffield, chest, moderate. First Colorado, 3d, A, Private Charles P. Hickman, foot, moderate. First Montana, C, Private Theodore Scheule, back, slight. Fourth Infantry, 4th, A, Private James McCarty, thigh, slight.

OTIS.

EXECUTIVE MANSION,
Washington, June 6, 1899.

OTIS, *Manila:*

The President is considering the necessity of enlisting regiments under volunteer act, March 2, 1899. He prefers not to do it if the military situation will permit. The following are the facts upon which he invites your judgment:

You have, and en route, 24,000 regulars, to which we can add 3,100 recruits, thus increasing the size of your companies. In addition, can send one regiment of regulars. If you can organize in the Philippines two or three skeleton regiments, to fill which we will send you volunteer recruits, it will give you more than 30,000. The President desires to know whether you can reenlist 1,000 or more of your volunteers to constitute the nucleus for three regiments, which we can readily fill to full quota by volunteer recruits from here. If this can be done he would want you to select from your best men, volunteers or regulars, as a reward for their gallantry and efficiency, the field officers and captains and as many lieutenants as the number of enlistments with you would entitle them to have. The remaining lieutenants to be sent from here with the recruits. A volunteer army of any size can be enlisted here for service in the Philippines, but it is the President's desire to keep the force within actual military needs.

By order Acting Secwar: CORBIN.

ADJUTANT-GENERAL'S OFFICE,
Washington, June 7, 1899.

OTIS, *Manila:*

Having reference to cable last night relating to organization skeleton volunteer regiments, Acting Secretary of War now directs that for enlistments in those regiments volunteers or men in Regular Army under Order 40, if any such there be still in service, you are authorized to discharge on final statements, with full travel pay to their homes, for both sea and land travel involved. This will not apply to commissioned officers. They will receive travel allowances under General Orders, No. 54.

CORBIN.

ADJUTANT-GENERAL'S OFFICE,
Washington, June 7, 1899.

OTIS, *Manila:*

You may also say to those enlisting in volunteer regiments with you that on discharge of said regiments the officers and men will be given actual transportation to their homes in the United States.

CORBIN.

ADJUTANT-GENERAL'S OFFICE,
Washington, June 7, 1899.

OTIS, *Manila:*

Proposed to send Nineteenth Infantry on first large steamer. When will one sail from Manila?

H. C. CORBIN.

ADJUTANT-GENERAL'S OFFICE,
Washington, June 7, 1899.

OTIS, *Manila:*

When in your best judgment making your command a division would promote military efficiency, recommendation will receive President's prompt attention. Necessary military departments could be created from time to time within the division.

CORBIN.

MANILA. (Received June 8, 1899—3.15 a. m.)

AGWAR, *Washington:*

Result movement Morong province was to drive insurgents into mountains, capturing Antipolo and other towns that section, with point of land projecting into

AFFAIRS IN THE PHILIPPINE ISLANDS. 1005

bay. They retreated and scattered before our advance, leaving 25 dead on field; our loss 4 killed, few wounded, mostly slight. City Morong, on only land route around bay, garrisoned; all other troops withdrawn. Inhabitants of provinces profess friendship; ask protection. Large numbers wish to enter Manila; refused, as city population increasing too rapidly. Leading natives throughout island, including active insurgent leaders, seek permission to send families to Manila; considered only place of personal security.

OTIS.

MANILA. (Received June 8, 1899—8.20 a. m.)

AGWAR, *Washington:*

Lieut. Fred Anderson Pearce, Sixth Artillery, died, Manila, 9.20 a. m., June 6, suicide.

OTIS.

ADJUTANT-GENERAL'S OFFICE,
Washington, June 8, 1899.

OTIS, *Manila:*

Arrangements completed with Navy to furnish Army fresh beef until refrigerator has been completed. Secretary of War authorizes purchase, for cash, subsistence supplies on the part of the Navy and Marine Corps, to be used by themselves, sailors, and marines. Notify all parties.

CORBIN.

MANILA. (Received June 8, 1899—2.15 a. m.)

AGWAR, *Washington:*

Nearly all volunteers inclined to go home; anxious to participate in State welcome. Believe good many will be equally anxious to return to Philippines in short time. Quite confident can form nucleus of three regiments as outlined in your dispatches; will know positively shortly. Oregons request to defer time of departure until 12th; will leave for Portland in transports *Ohio* and *Newport*. Sixth Infantry, upon arrival, will relieve Californians at Negros. *Hancock* sails in few days with Nebraska and other troops.

OTIS.

ADJUTANT-GENERAL'S OFFICE,
Washington, June 8, 1899.

General OTIS, *Manila:*

Your cable satisfactory. The Department waits with interest positive information that you can organize the skeleton regiments as indicated, when the lieutenants from here will be appointed and put to recruiting. Don't you think it would be well to appoint one major from here to take charge of the recruiting of each regiment? In sending volunteers home the Acting Secretary wants all the officers and men to come; the sick, so far as they are able to make the journey. Also anxious, in cases where it can be done with safety, that the dead of each regiment be sent on the same transport. General officers will come with their original commands, Smith with California regiment, Funston with Kansas, etc.

CORBIN.

ADJUTANT-GENERAL'S OFFICE,
Washington, June 9, 1899.

General OTIS, *Manila:*

Referring my cable May 17, will returning troops bring field ovens and mess utensils with them?

CORBIN.

MANILA. (Received June 9, 1899—11.45 p. m.)

AGWAR, *Washington:*

All volunteer tentage and field cooking outfits to remain here.

OTIS.

MANILA. (Received June 9, 1899—2.10 a. m.)

AGWAR, *Washington:*

Services General Smith in Negros very important; has that island under control and has confidence of all influential natives. Can he be retained a short time? Funston can return with regiment. Hughes now at Iloilo commanding Visayan military district.

OTIS.

ADJUTANT-GENERAL'S OFFICE,
Washington, June 9, 1899.

OTIS, *Manila:*

* * * You may retain General Smith. In all such matters exercise your best judgment. Under law we can retain for six months any volunteer officer with you, but at end of this time they must be discharged.

CORBIN.

ADJUTANT-GENERAL'S OFFICE,
Washington, June 10, 1899.

OTIS, *Manila:*

Secwar desires to know number men discharged in Philippines under General Orders, No. 40; number reenlisted; total enlisted strength each regular regiment; number in each still entitled to discharge under such orders who refuse to reenlist. Separate light and heavy artillery.

CORBIN.

MANILA. (Received June 10, 1899.—3.27 a. m.)

AGWAR, *Washington:*

Lawton with two provisional brigades, commanded by Wheaton and Ovenshine, 4,300 men, mostly regulars, proceeded south Manila early this morning, piercing center of insurgent line, with instructions, after passing beyond line, to swing right and left on flank and rear insurgents' stronghold. Fighting has been severe and insurgents driven. Particulars not yet reported; maneuvering in that section of the country may occupy several days.

OTIS.

AFFAIRS IN THE PHILIPPINE ISLANDS. 1007

MANILA. (Received June 10, 1899.—7.35 a. m.)

AGWAR, *Washington:*

At 3 this afternoon Lawton reported south of Parañaque; loss so far, 1 man killed, 2 officers, 21 men wounded; heat terrific. Have stopped to rest, will move over to Parañaque to-night; no good water all day, which accounts for much of suffering. Must stop at Parañaque for night. Wheaton soon cleared out Taguig contingent and was compelled to come over to right to help Ovenshine. Forty-seven days insurgents fell into our hands.

OTIS.

MANILA. (Received June 11, 1899—3.22 a. m.)

AGWAR, *Washington:*

Terrific heat yesterday did not permit troops to reach positions at hours designated. Enabled majority of insurgents to escape in scattered organizations south and westward, which they effected during the evening and night. Movement great success however; enemy disorganized and routed, suffering heavy loss. Troops resting to-day at Las Piñas and Parañaque. Navy did excellent execution along shore of bay, but many insurgent detachments retired in that direction, protected by presence of women and children who they drove along with them. Our loss, 4 killed and some 30 wounded. Report of casualties later. Conservative estimate of enemy's loss about 400.

OTIS.

MANILA. (Received June 11, 1899—8.07 a. m.)

AGWAR, *Washington:*

No discharges yet made under General Orders, No. 40; papers now being received; statistical information called for, cable to-day; furnished soon as practicable.

OTIS.

MANILA. (Received June 12, 1899—10.50 p. m.)

AGWAR, *Washington:*

Oregon regiment on transports *Ohio* and *Newport* ready to sail; too many for one vessel, not enough for two. Have therefore sent on *Newport* part battalion of Oregons, also officers and families Signal Company, and discharged men destined for San Francisco. Shall all these troops be unloaded and new combinations made, which will require several days? Larger vessel to carry entire Oregon regiment can not be sent up Columbia River safely; practically unanimous wish of Oregons to be sent to San Francisco.

OTIS.

EXECUTIVE MANSION,
Washington, June 12, 1899—11.18 p. m.

General OTIS, *Manila:*

Use your discretion as to transports. Let the Oregons sail for San Francisco.

CORBIN.

SAN FRANCISCO, CAL., *June 12, 1899.*

ADJUTANT-GENERAL, *Washington, D. C.:*

Transport *St. Paul* arrived to-day with following military passengers: Lieutenant Tompsett, First Nebraska; Acting Asst. Surg. Ira B. Ladd; and following soldiers: Twenty-six discharged, 2 sick, 1 insane, 1 guard, and 1 to be discharged. No casualties.

SHAFTER, *Major-General.*

CORRESPONDENCE.

MANILA. (Received June 12, 1899—10 a. m.)

AGWAR, *Washington:*

Following deaths since last weekly report: From wounds in action—May 20, Carl A. Carlson, private, H, Twenty-second Infantry; June 5, Melvin P. Daily, private, G, Fourth Cavalry; 8th, Patrick Branigan, private, C, Fourth Cavalry; 9th, Clifford H. Bowser, First Sergeant, K, First Colorado. Typhoid fever—3d, John A. Saxton, private, M, First Montana. Meningitis—George A. King (probably Geo. A. Kidd), private, L, Seventeenth Infantry. Cholera nostras, Frank L. Garrison, private, I, Seventeenth Infantry. Dysentery, Ralph A. Odell, private, A, Second Oregon. Ulcerative colitis, 4th, Oscar A. Fenniger, private, A, Utah Artillery. Drowned, J. J. Kehoe, private, G, Second Oregon.

OTIS.

MANILA. (Received June 12, 1899—2.08 p. m.)

AGWAR, *Washington:*

Additional casualties: Killed—First Washington, June 6, D, Private Carl M. Thygeson. First North Dakota, 9th, H, Private John H. Killian. Thirteenth Infantry, 10th, M, Private Thomas F. Healey. Wounded—Second Oregon, June 3, H, Privates Ezra A. Kirtz, wrist, slight; Charles E. Doughty, hand, slight; L, Clayton L. Ranson, head, slight. First Washington, 6th, G, Private Joseph Dobman, leg, slight. First Idaho, F, Private Hugh Hutchinson, buttock, severe. First Colorado, 10th, Lieut. Col. Cassius M. Moses, forearm, moderate; B, Sergt. George M. La Shell, elbow, moderate; Privates Bert E. Young, patella, moderate; Francis J. Henry, arm, severe; D, Asa P. Morrill, cheek, severe; E, William J. Currier, arm, slight; Harry H. Hegner, neck and chest, severe; Corpls. Robert F. Reed, chest, severe; Thomas Rylott, thigh, slight; Privates Frank Duvall, leg, severe; Harry Macklem, head, moderate. Thirteenth Infantry, D, Sergt. Boyle Christensen, ankle, moderate; E, Privates Charles Bess, leg, moderate; M. M. Henry, thigh, slight. Ninth Infantry, C, Privates Barney Gonyea, arm, slight; I, Arthur E. Prager, eye, severe; K, Joseph F. Beavers, hip, severe. Twenty-first Infantry, F, Privates Casper Cook, leg, moderate; Andrew McFarland, leg, slight. Fourteenth Infantry, D, Corpl. Conrad Hallaner, chest, severe; F, Private Walter Brogden, neck, slight. First Montana, D, Private Abraham Clem, thigh, severe; William Kramer, knee, slight. Twelfth Infantry, 11th, L, First Sergt. Henry Clark, leg, slight.

OTIS.

MANILA. (Received June 13, 1899—7.18 a. m.)

AGWAR, *Washington:*

Lawton's troops had severe engagement to-day with enemy in strong intrenchments at crossing Zapote River near Bacoor, Cavite province. Has driven enemy with heavy loss. Our casualties some 30. Insurgents in this southern section not molested until threatened attack in strong force on Manila. Now scattered and in retreat. Doubtful if they make further stand.

OTIS.

ADJUTANT-GENERAL'S OFFICE,
Washington, June 13, 1899.

OTIS, *Manila:*

Acting Secwar directs me say the President wishes you to extend all proper facilities to Spanish agencies who are endeavoring to effect release of prisoners.

CORBIN.

AFFAIRS IN THE PHILIPPINE ISLANDS. 1009

MANILA. (Received June 13, 1899—6.30 a. m.)
ADJUTANT-GENERAL, *Washington:*

It is believed that the killing of Lieutenant-General Luna on the 8th instant, near San Isidro, by Aguinaldo's guard, will be attended with important results not derogatory to United States' interests.

OTIS.

GENERAL ORDERS, } HEADQUARTERS OF THE ARMY,
                    ADJUTANT-GENERAL'S OFFICE,
No. 107.   }   *Washington, June 13, 1899.*

By direction of the Acting Secretary of War the following changes of station of troops are ordered:

The Twenty-fourth and Twenty-fifth Infantry, excepting 1 major and 4 companies of each regiment, will be assembled at San Francisco, Cal., and there put in readiness for duty in the Philippine Islands.

The following companies of each regiment will compose the battalion to be assembled at San Francisco, and those not already there will be put en route to that point without delay:

A, C, E, F, G, H, I, and K, Twenty-fourth Infantry; B, E, F, H, I, K, L, and M, Twenty-fifth Infantry.

The remaining companies of the Twenty-fourth Infantry will be distributed as follows:

B, Vancouver Barracks, Wash., with detachments at Fort Walla Walla, Wash., and Boise Barracks, Idaho.

D, at Fort Harrison, Mont., with detachments at Fort Missoula, Mont., and Fort Assinniboine, Mont.

L, Dyea, Alaska.

M, New Fort Spokane, Wash., with detachment at Fort Sherman, Idaho.

The major will be assigned to station by the commanding general, Department of the Columbia.

The remaining companies of the Twenty-fifth Infantry will retain their present stations, and the major will be assigned to station by the commanding officer, Department of Texas.

The commanding general, Department of the Colorado, will direct the following changes of troops in his department:

One troop of the Ninth Cavalry from Fort Huachuca, Ariz., to Fort Bayard, N. Mex.

A detachment of 1 officer and 25 men from Fort Duchesne, Utah, to Fort Douglas, Utah.

The commanding general, Department of the Missouri, will direct the following changes of station:

One troop of the First Cavalry from Fort Robinson, Nebr., to Fort Russell, Wyo.

One troop of the Sixth Cavalry from Fort Leavenworth, Kans., to Fort Logan, Colo.

One light battery of the Third Artillery from Fort Riley, Kans., to the Presidio, San Francisco.

The Quartermaster's Department will make the necessary arrangements for the transportation. The Subsistence Department will make the necessary arrangements for subsistence, and the Surgeon-General will make provision for medical supplies and attendance.

By command of Major-General Miles.

H. C. CORBIN, *Adjutant-General.*

MANILA. (Received June 14, 1899—5.20 a. m.)

AGWAR, *Washington:*

Additional casualities: Wounded—Thirteenth Infantry, June 9, M, Private Henry W. Marsfelder, thigh, slight. Fourth Cavalry, 10th, I, Private William F. Riordan, leg, moderate. Ninth Infantry, C, Privates August F. Porczeng, shoulder, slight; B, Deforest V. Hutchinson, head, severe. Twenty-first Infantry, C, Private Thomas Mullin, arm, slight. First Colorado, M, Private Joseph P. Kearns, leg, slight; 11th, H, Private Edgar T. Pate, knee, severe.

Cablegram 12th, Thomas Healy, private, M. Thirteenth Minnesota, should read Thirteenth Infantry.

OTIS.

MANILA. (Received June 14, 1899—5.30 a. m.)

AGWAR, *Washington:*

Lawton's troops under Wheaton and Ovenshine occupy country south to Bacoor; have scouted westward and some distance southward on line Zapote River and Bacoor road. Enemy appears to have retired on Imus, abandoning bay country. The fighting yesterday severe, our loss 10 killed and 40 wounded; majority at crossing Zapote River. Enemy driven from heavy and well-constructed intrenchments, to which they held tenaciously; their loss several hundred, of whom 50 buried this morning. Will not probably make any determined future stand in southern provinces.

OTIS.

MANILA. (Received June 14, 1899—4.33 a. m.)

AGWAR, *Washington:*

Transports *Ohio* and *Newport*, Oregons, First Signal Company, and discharged soldiers from different organizations, left for San Francisco this morning via Nagasaki. Oregons number 46 officers, 1,035 enlisted men; signal company, 4 officers, 32 enlisted men. Transport *Leelanaw* arrived yesterday.

OTIS.

ADJUTANT-GENERAL'S OFFICE, *Washington, June 14, 1899.*

OTIS, *Manila:*

Sheridan and *Pennsylvania* will leave in few days with fresh troops for Eighth Army Corps. Cable any requirements situation demands in way of arms, ammunition, medical, or other supplies, so they may be sent on these transports.

CORBIN.

ADJUTANT-GENERAL'S OFFICE,
Washington, June 14, 1899.

COMMANDING GENERAL, DEPARTMENT CALIFORNIA,
San Francisco, Cal.:

Quartermaster-General reports to-day charter having been made for *Valencia*. Capacity, 600. Acting Secretary War directs that you make arrangements to have her loaded promptly with all troops she can carry.

H. C. CORBIN, *Adjutant-General.*

SAN FRANCISCO, CAL., *June 14, 1899.*
(Received 3 p. m.)

ADJUTANT-GENERAL, *Washington, D. C.:*

Transport *Pennsylvania* arrived last night. No military passengers.

SHAFTER, *Major-General.*

AFFAIRS IN THE PHILIPPINE ISLANDS. 1011

MANILA. (Received June 14, 1899—9.05 a. m.)

ADJUTANT-GENERAL, *Washington*:

General Luna, killed 8th instant at Aguinaldo's headquarters, held supreme military command; was uncompromising for continuation of war; influenced lower and robber classes; demanded confinement or death of all who should advise peace, and greatly feared by natives in country occupied by his troops on account of cruelties practiced. He dominated Aguinaldo and all insurgent officers, civil and military. His death received with satisfaction by all influential Filipinos.

OTIS.

MANILA. (Received June 14, 1899—1.48 p. m.)

ADJUTANT-GENERAL, *Washington*:

Permission granted officer and two citizens of Spain to pass lines to negotiate for release Spanish prisoners. Citizens have doubtful reputation. Difficulties have been and are experienced on account Spanish intrigues with insurgents. Reported and believed Zamboanga February sales of arms to insurgents Samar, Leyte, and Lower Luzon aggregate $200,000. Their intrigues with Sultan archipelago defeated in part by unexpected arrival American troops at Jolo. Considerable number Spaniards in insurgent army, and disposition on part large class that population to make all trouble possible. Influential friendly Filipinos openly charge Spaniards with fomenting discord, and ask none be appointed to office. Insurgent attack on Zamboanga Spanish forces the result of Spanish officer permitting insurgents, if not conniving with them, to take arms and ammunition from gunboats purchased by us. Property landed near city without interference on insurgents' promise that they would use it wholly against Americans. Insurgents sought possession of city before United States troops could arrive; hence turned on Spaniards. Insurgents now ask that our forces occupy city. Say they will abide fate insurgent government in Luzon.

OTIS.

ADJUTANT-GENERAL'S OFFICE,
Washington, June 14, 1899.

OTIS, *Manila*:

Is organization skeleton volunteer regiments with you sufficiently advanced to warrant Department appointing recruiting lieutenants and putting them to work?

CORBIN.

MANILA. (Received June 15, 1899—4 a. m.)

AGWAR, *Washington*:

Prominent Filipino, friendly to Americans, assassinated at Cebu. Inhabitants that locality urgently requested American protection in stronger force. Have sent battalion Tennessee and two guns from Iloilo, which insures peace. Hughes now in charge of affairs in that section.

OTIS.

MANILA. (Received June 15, 1899—4.07 a. m.)

AGWAR, *Washington*:

Success Lawton's troops Cavite Province greater than reported yesterday. Enemy, numbering over 4,000, lost in killed, wounded, and captured more than one-third; remainder much scattered; have retreated south to Imus, their arsenal. Of 5 pieces of artillery, 3 captured. Navy aided greatly on shore of bay, landing forces occasionally. Inhabitants in that country rejoiced at deliverance, and welcome with enthusiastic demonstrations arrival of our troops.

OTIS.

MANILA. (Received June 15, 1899—7.10 a. m.)

AGWAR, *Washington:*

No supplies needed other than those estimated for, except as follows: Seven hundred sets horse equipments; 700 carbines, caliber .30; 6,000 shell mountain Hotchkiss, caliber 1.65; 5,000 shell point percussion Hotchkiss cannon, caliber 1.50; 3,000 brown canvas trousers.

OTIS.

ADJUTANT-GENERAL'S OFFICE,
Washington, June 15, 1899.

OTIS, *Manila:*

Supplies mentioned in cable to-day will be shipped at once, except the 5,000 shell point percussion Hotchkiss cannon, caliber 1.50, which will have to be procured, but will be shipped as soon as possible.

CORBIN.

ADJUTANT-GENERAL'S OFFICE,
Washington, June 15, 1899.

Gen. W. R. SHAFTER,
Commanding Department California, San Francisco, Cal.:

The Acting Secretary War desires you, as far as possible, to make your personal inspection of each transport before sailing for Manila; that you cause each to be loaded to its full capacity, but not a man more than can go with comfort and due regard to the health of officers and men. You will exercise your judgment as to the organizations to go on each ship; organizations, battalions, and companies might be well on each, and then fill up with recruits. Should you think it desirable, you can hasten the arrival of the Twenty-fourth and Twenty-fifth Infantry with a view to their early or immediate departure. In all this do by Otis as you would wish him to do by you under like conditions.

H. C. CORBIN, *Adjutant-General.*

SAN FRANCISCO, CAL., *June 15, 1899.*

ADJUTANT-GENERAL, *Washington, D. C.:*

The arrangements already contemplated in assignment of troops to four ships now available is precisely as indicated in your telegram to-day, viz: assigning organizations and completing complement with recruits. The present assignment depending upon the arrival of the troops in time will be as follows: *Zealandia* to sail 20th, second headquarters, four companies of Twenty-fourth or Twenty-fifth Infantry, and about 100 recruits; *Pennsylvania* to sail 24th, headquarters and eight companies Twenty-fourth or Twenty-fifth Infantry and about 75 recruits; *Sheridan* to sail 24th, two troops Fourth Cavalry, two companies Fourteenth Infantry, Signal Corps detachment, and 1,275 recruits; *Valencia* to sail 25th, four companies Twenty-fourth or Twenty-fifth Infantry and 100 recruits. Please inform me at once if this can stand, or is it intended to send the Nineteenth on the *Pennsylvania*. Have wired Merriam to hasten arrival companies Twenty-fourth and Twenty-fifth in his department, and request that commanding generals, Departments Gulf and Dakota, may also be ordered to expedite the arrival of companies from their departments and report probable date of arrival. Though not mentioned in telegram, I take it for granted that headquarters Twenty-fourth and Twenty-fifth are to go.

SHAFTER, *Major-General.*

ADJUTANT-GENERAL'S OFFICE,
Washington, June 15, 1899.

OTIS, *Manila:*

The President has ordered companies your command increased to 128 enlisted. Three thousand recruits awaiting transportation at San Francisco. Many have seen service in volunteer regiments. Shafter having them drilled daily, making target practice a feature.

CORBIN.

ADJUTANT-GENERAL'S OFFICE,
Washington, June 16, 1899.

COMMANDING GENERAL, DEPARTMENT CALIFORNIA,
San Francisco, Cal.:

Your disposition of troops for the *Zealandia, Pennsylvania, Sheridan,* and *Valencia* is approved by the Acting Secretary War.

H. C. CORBIN, *Adjutant-General.*

MANILA. (Received June 16, 1899—4.27 a. m.)

AGWAR, *Washington:*

Northern insurgents concentrated large force near San Fernando, and early this morning attacked MacArthur's troops; enemy quickly repulsed and driven, leaving over fifty dead on field and large number wounded. Enemy in retreat; our casualties 14 wounded, mostly very slight. Preparations for this attack in progress several days; believed to be under personal direction Aguinaldo.

OTIS.

ADJUTANT-GENERAL'S OFFICE,
Washington, June 16, 1899.

OTIS, *Manila:*

Bills contractors for transportation Spanish prisoners disagree with your report in following shipments:

Buenos Aires, November 8, bill 104 officers 850 soldiers; you report 97 and 814.
Cashemire, bill 32 and 1,102; you report 30 and 1,067.
Isla de Luzon, bill 72 officers; you report 74.
Leon XIII, bill 63 officers, 583 soldiers; you report 71 and 625.
Monserrat, bill 47 officers, 375 soldiers; you report 46 and 479.
Uruguay, bill 65 officers, 551 soldiers; you report 79 and 939.
Rio Negro, bill 74 officers, 1,011 men; you report 75 and 991.
Satrustegui, bill 117 officers, 1 103 soldiers; you report 140 and 1,094.
Buenos Aires, March 10, bill 123 soldiers; you report 984.
Alicante, bill 64 officers, 1 soldier; you report 72 officers.
Isla de Luzon, March 17, bill 70 officers, 59 soldiers; you report 93 and 35.
Ciudad de Cadiz, bill 158 officers, 110 soldiers; you report 159 and 93.
Can payment properly be made on bills as rendered?

CORBIN.

ADJUTANT-GENERAL'S OFFICE,
Washington, June 16, 1899.

OTIS, *Manila:*

Lippincott recommends two laundries for troops. Machinery each laundry capable washing 10,000 men, 500 officers, cost about $20,000; require building 100 by 150 feet. Do you recommend? Can it be paid from island funds? Is it advisable to ship material for buildings?

CORBIN.

MANILA. (Received June 16, 1899—6.55 a. m.)

AGWAR, *Washington:*

Only single volunteer regiment yet in progress of organization; somewhat doubtful if others can be skeletonized; regiments scattered; communication difficult; sentiment not fully ascertained; desire of men to return home increasing, whence many will ask to return; only six reenlistments from Oregons; recruiting lieutenants should not be appointed in States yet.

OTIS.

MANILA. (Received June 17, 1899—9.17 a. m.)

AGWAR, *Washington:*

Discrepancy between contractors'. figures and ours in number prisoners war transported, sete (due) doubtless to different classification deaths en route, or to prisoners counted who left transports after loading and before sailing, presenting themselves subsequently for transportation. Safe to pay on contractors' bills as rendered.

OTIS.

ADJUTANT-GENERAL'S OFFICE,
Washington, June 17, 1899.

COMMANDING GENERAL, DEPARTMENT CALIFORNIA,
San Francisco, Cal.:

Quartermaster-General reports charter of *City of Para*, with capacity of 1,025, to sail July 12. This should be taken into consideration in your plan for sending men now under orders for General Otis's army.

H. C. CORBIN, *Adjutant-General.*

SAN FRANCISCO, CAL., *June 17, 1899.* (Received 11.22 p. m.)

ADJUTANT-GENERAL, *Washington, D. C.:*

Referring to your telegram reporting charter *City of Para*, with capacity for 1,025, to sail July 12, it is expected that the *Sheridan, Pennsylvania, Zealandia,* and *Valencia* will all be off before that time, notwithstanding the delay mentioned in my telegram of this date which may attend the concentration of the Twenty-fifth here. This being so, the *Para*, to sail July 12, is the latest date now known, and I advise, referring to your wire of this date regarding Nineteenth Infantry, that that regiment arrive here on that date, and so much of it as can be accommodated on the *Para* be sent on that ship. Any later information that postpones the time when the *Para* will be ready will be sent you.

SHAFTER, *Major-General.*

ADJUTANT-GENERAL'S OFFICE,
Washington, June 17, 1899.

OTIS, *Manila:*

General Schwan completed inspection Nineteenth Infantry yesterday. Ranks full and regiment good condition. Leave at early date for service with you.

CORBIN.

MANILA. (Received June 18, 1899—3.43 a. m.)

AGWAR, *Washington:*

Do not recommend construction of laundry at present; not necessity. Contracts let for building nipa hospital and barracks at Corregidor, and barracks for two regiments at Caloocan and Pasay; cost 250,000 pesos. Revenue will decrease as insurgent ports blockaded and interisland trade, except with Negros and Cebu, interdicted.

OTIS.

MANILA. (Received June 18, 1899—8 32 a. m.)

AGWAR, *Washington:*

All volunteer organizations here desire muster-out at San Francisco.

OTIS.

MANILA. (Received June 18, 1899—12.30 p. m.)

AGWAR, *Washington:*

Additional casualties: Killed—Fourteenth Infantry, at Zapote, June 13, L, Sergt. Thomas J. Laws, Corpl. John H. Moore; A, Corpl. David E. Dague; I. Nelson T. Lamoree. Fifty-first Iowa, A, Walter Wagner. Wounded—First Washington, at Cainta and Morong, June 3, I, Corpl. Benit F. Goldman, hand, slight; 4th, L, Charles G. Anderson, thigh, slight; 5th, H, William H. Adkins, thigh, slight. First Montana, near Bacolor, 10th, D, James A. Casebeer, arm, slight. Fourteenth Infantry, at Zapote, 13th, A, Second Lieut. Howard S. Avery, thigh, moderate; John Brannen, head, severe; Senro J. Brendel, ear, slight; William Cooper, leg, moderate; Henry Hulbe, hand, moderate; Harvey J. Lowe, lower extremity, severe; Pomroy Harned, thigh, moderate; D, William Curry, arm, moderate; I, Thorn H. Ballard, shoulder, moderate; L, Arthur Franz, hand, slight; William Lapp, buttock, severe. Twelfth Infantry, Arthur Rosebrock, back, slight; L, Charles Stephan, hand, moderate; M, Corpl. Charles J. Adams, foot, moderate. First Artillery, E, William C. Clayton, thigh, slight; Norman E. Danner, wrist, moderate; Samuel S. Wentworth, ankle, moderate; Sergt. Avery E. Long, forearm, moderate. Sixth Artillery, near Las Piñas, D, Mark D. Mynott, thigh, severe. Ninth Infantry, at Zapote River, B, George Clampffer, eyelid, slight; George L. Deforest, shoulder, moderate; C, Brayton Bretch, hand, slight; I, Arthur S. Odin, arm, slight. Twelfth Infantry, L, Myles Doyle, neck and chest, severe; John W. McHenry, arm, slight; Patrick J. Mulvihill, chest, moderate; William J. McGillicuddy, eye, severe; Michael Uline, thigh, moderate; First Lieut. James P. Harbeson, thigh, slight; Sergts. Frank J. Boy, hand, moderate; M, George Tiernan, thigh, moderate; Corpls. George Marshall, chest, severe; Frank E. Shirk, thigh, severe; Musician William Silence, leg, moderate. Twenty-first Infantry, F, John Henchy, hand, slight; John J. Ward, wrist, moderate; James McCue, leg, moderate; First Lieut. Joseph L. Donovan, thigh, severe; Corpls. Charles Neuvians, forearm, slight; John C. Whalen, elbow, moderate; I, Dennis A. Collins, thigh, slight; Patrick Houlihan, wrist, slight; Michael J. Mikulhki, clavicle, slight; Thomas M. Rayne, forearm, moderate; G, First Lieut. Patrick A. Connolly, leg, severe. Twenty-third Infantry, L, Second Lieut. Monroe C. Kerth, arm, severe.

OTIS.

MANILA. (Received June 18, 1899—8.25 a. m.)

AGWAR, *Washington:*

Following deaths since last weekly report: From wounds in action—June 11, Charles J. Gamble, private, C, Third Infantry. 14th, George Marshall, corporal, M, Twelfth Infantry; Mark D. Mynott, private, D, Sixth Artillery; John Brannen, private, A, Fourteenth Infantry.

Typhoid fever—May 22d, George Schultz, private, A, Twenty-third Infantry. June 11th, Charles W. Edmonds, private, E, First Artillery. 12th, Charles K. Prouty, private, C, First South Dakota.

Endocarditis—Charles Calkins, private, E, Third Infantry.
Diphtheria—13th, Fred L. Maxfield, private, B, Twentieth Kansas.
Dysentery—15th, William B. Gray, private, H, Twentieth Infantry. 13th, Joseph J. Madden, private, L, Third Artillery.

OTIS.

MANILA. (Received June 19, 1899—7 a. m.)

AGWAR, *Washington:*

Sherman arrived this morning; casualty, Edwin L. Gavett, I, Sixth Infantry. Colonel Kellogg, 12 men, left Honolulu sick; 17 cases typhoid fever en route. Sixth Infantry leaves for Iloilo to relieve Californians Negros. Transport *Indiana*, 134 officers and soldiers discharged as sick, with civilians, left for San Francisco via Nagasaki yesterday. *Hancock, Sherman*, with Nebraska, Pennsylvania, and Utah, leave for United States as soon as troops can be placed in readiness. Californians will leave as soon as collected. Colorado to follow on first available transport.

OTIS.

MANILA. (Received June 20, 1899—3.20 a. m.)

AGWAR, *Washington:*

Wheaton at Imus, Cavite Province, with 4 guns, 4 battalions Fourth and Fourteenth Infantry, Nevada troop cavalry; sent battalion south on reconnoissance, direction of Dasmariñas, yesterday morning, where enemy reported concentrating scattered forces; battalion encountered enemy's force, 2,000, marching to attack Imus. Successful impeding its progress. Wheaton with 2 guns and 2 battalions hurried forward, repulsed enemy with heavy loss, enemy leaving over 100 dead on field; our loss 5 killed, 23 wounded. Wheaton reenforced last night by battalion Ninth Infantry. Is driving enemy beyond Dasmariñas, now in his possession. Casualties to-day not reported. Wheaton's qualities for bold and successful attack unsurpassed.

OTIS.

GENERAL ORDERS, }   HEADQUARTERS OF THE ARMY,
                              ADJUTANT-GENERAL'S OFFICE,
No. 113.   *Washington, June 20, 1899.*

I. By direction of the Acting Secretary of War, the Nineteenth U. S. Infantry will be relieved from duty at Camp Meade, Pennsylvania, and will proceed to San Francisco, Cal., so as to reach that point on July 10, 1899.

The Quartermaster's Department will make the necessary arrangements for transportation, the Subsistence Department for subsistence, and the Medical Department will make provision for medical supplies and attendance.

II. By direction of the Acting Secretary of War, in addition to the articles for general prisoners required to be supplied by the Subsistence Department under General Orders, No. 33, August 3, 1896, from this office, such quantities of toilet paper as may be necessary for use of post guardhouse will be issued by the commissary on requisitions approved by the post commander, and the receipt of the officer of the day will be the commissary's voucher for dropping this article from his return.

By command of Major-General Miles:

H. C. CORBIN, *Adjutant-General.*

MANILA. (Received June 21, 1899—2.23 p. m.)

AGWAR, *Washington:*

Additional casualties: Killed—Fourteenth Infantry, June 10, G, Thomas W. Andrews, near Las Piñas. 13th, D, William S. Somers; Eli Goodreau, at Zapote

AFFAIRS IN THE PHILIPPINE ISLANDS. 1017

River. Fourth Infantry, near Dasmariñas, 20th, B, Corpl. Pete Goorskey; William Coak; D, Daniel Donovan; K, Charles Hope. Wounded—Second Oregon, at Norzagaray, April 25, F, Q. M. Sergt. Charles R. Herrington, head, slight. Fourteenth Infantry, near Las Piñas and Zapote, June 10, 11, 13, L, First Lieut. H. G. Learnard, leg, slight; K, Charles S. Girton, face, slight; L, Harry C. Emery, leg, severe; L, Robert Cryan, leg, severe; Enoch Wallgreen, eye, slight. Twelfth Infantry, L, William J. Gilliardy, head and hand, moderate; John H. Long, shoulder, moderate. First Montana, San Fernandino, 16th, C, Warren J. Morris, shoulder, slight; E, Charles N. Robb, thigh, slight; M, David Silver, abdomen, severe; A, Sergt. George W. Boardman, lip, slight; D, James W. C. Dennis, buttock, slight. Twentieth Kansas, M, William Eickworth, shoulder, severe. Seventeenth Infantry, G, Edward Baudreau, elbow, slight; Charles Ford, foot, slight; C, Sergt. James H. Laughlin, arm, slight. Fifty-first Iowa, C, David Walling. forearm, moderate; D, Nathan D. Rockafellow, lung, severe; Charles E. Lucas, ear, slight; Lewis S. Woodruff, finger, slight; K, Corpl. Lou D. Sheets, thigh, severe. Fourth Infantry, near Dasmariñas, 19th, B, Paul Wagner, face, severe; Frank Huss, leg, moderate; Frank Lukes, thigh, moderate; Herbert Mifflin, abdomen, severe; D, William F. Donnally, face, severe; Thomas E. Charlton, thigh, severe; Clarence C. Martin, abdomen, moderate; William G. Henry, arm, moderate; Samuel K. Haynes, chest; Artificer George Dilts, abdomen, severe; K, Charles F. Kreeger, forearm, slight; Charles A. Layman, arm, moderate; Thomas Parker, thigh, moderate; Artificer Edgar Kiphart, thigh, severe; L, Arnold A. Mason, chest, severe; Frederick A. Davis, leg, moderate; Minott C. Denniston, heel, moderate; John McHugh, leg, moderate; William Prignitz, knee and leg, moderate; Corpl. William T. Lang, neck, severe

OTIS.

MANILA. (Received June 22, 1899—2.37 a. m.)
AGWAR, *Washington:*
Hospital ship *Relief* for San Francisco this morning; 250 sick.

OTIS.

ADJUTANT-GENERAL'S OFFICE,
Washington, June 23, 1899.
OTIS, *Manila:*
Acting Secwar is advised there are four cartridge factories in the islands. That agent in Hongkong is shipping arms and ammunition through ports in our possession marked "agricultural implements."

CORBIN.

MANILA. (Received June 23, 1899—11.21 p. m.)
AGWAR, *Washington:*
Major Drennan, First Montana, died at 1 this morning, Manila, Bright's disease; ill three months.

OTIS.

SAN FRANCISCO, CAL., *June 23, 1899.*
(Received 7.55 p. m.)
ADJUTANT-GENERAL, *Washington, D. C.:*
Referring to my dispatch of 15th, indicating proposed assignment of troops to sail on the *Zealandia, Pennsylvania, Sheridan,* and *Valencia,* the *Zealandia* has sailed with troops as indicated, except headquarters Twenty-fourth Infantry, which I retained

here, and the *Sheridan* will sail to-morrow with the troops indicated in my dispatch; but owing to increase in size of the companies to 128 and necessary changes in the *Valencia*, which reduced her capacity, the *Pennsylvania* and *Valencia* will not carry as many organizations as mentioned in my dispatch of 15th. I therefore intend to take the *City of Para*, to sail about July 12, which, in dispatch of 17th, I recommended for the Nineteenth Infantry, and fill her with the overflow from the two ships just mentioned; also the four troops Fourth Cavalry, two here and two to arrive from Yellowstone, and the headquarters Fourth Cavalry; also Engineer company at Willets Point, which it is understood is to go, if you will send it in time, filling the balance of the ship with recruits. This will clear up the Twenty-fourth and Twenty-fifth Infantry, raised to 128 each company, the whole of the Fourth Cavalry, and leave the Nineteenth Infantry for some later ship, which would be a better arrangement in any event, as only a portion of the Nineteenth could go on the *Para*.

SHAFTER, *Major-General.*

ADJUTANT-GENERAL'S OFFICE,
Washington, June 24, 1899.

Major-General SHAFTER, *San Francisco, Cal.:*

Referring to your telegram 23d, engineer company at Willets Point has been instructed to arrange to arrive at San Francisco in time take the *Para* on July 12.

CORBIN, *Adjutant-General.*

SAN FRANCISCO, CAL., *June 23, 1899.*
(Received 2.10 p. m.)

ADJUTANT-GENERAL, *Washington, D. C.:*

Transport *Zealandia* sailed 6 p. m. yesterday with Companies C, E, G, and I, Twenty-fourth Infantry; Major Thompson and 7 officers, 406 enlisted men; 386 rounds per man, caliber .30 ammunition; 2 acting assistant surgeons; 12 men Signal Corps; 5 Hospital Corps; casuals Sixth Artillery; light, 1; Sixth Infantry, 1; Thirteenth Infantry, 1; Sixteenth Infantry, 17. Recruits, artillery, Third, heavy, 93; First, light, 5; Sixth, light, 6; infantry, Fourth, 8; Sixth, 1; Ninth, 11; Twelfth, 2; Thirteenth, 1; Twenty-first, 1; also 3 recruits for Sixth Artillery, heavy, at Honolulu. The detachments of this battalion on duty at Sequoia Park did not return in time to take the *Zealandia;* will be sent on the *Sheridan*.

SHAFTER, *Major-General.*

ADJUTANT-GENERAL'S OFFICE,
Washington, June 24, 1899.

General OTIS, *Manila:*

Report of situation and conditions desired by Acting Secretary of War.

CORBIN.

SAN FRANCISCO, CAL., *June 25, 1899.* (Received 5.07 p. m.)

ADJUTANT-GENERAL, *Washington, D. C.:*

Transport *Sheridan* sailed 6 p. m. yesterday with General Young and aids; Colonel Dagget, Major Quinton and Companies B and H, Fourteenth Infantry, 2 company officers, 239 enlisted men, 1 acting assistant surgeon, 215 rounds (caliber .30) ammunition per man. Troops A and F, Fourth Cavalry, 7 officers, 173 enlisted men, 1 acting assistant surgeon, 232 carbine and 116 pistol cartridges per man. Lieutenant Moss and 25 men Twenty-fourth Infantry, 100 cartridges (caliber .30) per man; Major Rodman, Twentieth Infantry; Major Howard, quartermaster; Captain Dodds, Ninth Infantry; Lieutenants Schreiner, Clyde S. Ford, Joseph H. Ford, assistant surgeons; Royden, Twenty-third Infantry; Sarratt, Sixth Artillery; Grimes, Twentieth Infantry; Dockery and Stewart, Third Infantry; Smith, Ninth Infantry; Elliott, Thirteenth Infantry; McMillan, Fourteenth Infantry; Dougherty, Hobbs, and Waldo, Seventeenth Infantry; McCaskey and Brewer, Twenty-first Infantry; 8 Hospital Corps men; 41 Signal Corps. Casuals: Twenty-third Infantry, 2 recruits; artillery, Third, 3; cavalry, Fourth, 186. Infantry, Fourteenth, 251; Eighteenth, 405; Twentieth, 40; Twenty-second, 41; Twenty-third, 323.

SHAFTER, *Major-General.*

ADJUTANT-GENERAL'S OFFICE,
Washington, June 26, 1899.
COMMANDING GENERAL, DEPARTMENT CALIFORNIA,
San Francisco, Cal.:
Secretary War particularly anxious that *Pennsylvania* and *Valencia* be gotten off as soon as practicable.

H. C. CORBIN, *Adjutant-General.*

MANILA. (Received June 26, 1899—4.30 a. m.)
ADJUTANT-GENERAL, *Washington:*
Rainy season. Little island campaigning possible in Luzon. We occupy large portion Tagalog country, lines stretching from Imus south to San Fernando; north, nearly sixty miles, and to eastward into Laguna province. Insurgent armies have suffered great losses and are scattered; only large force held together about 4,000 in Tarlac province and northern Pampanga. Their scattered forces in bands of fifty to five hundred in other portions Luzon; in Cavite and Batangas provinces could assemble possibly 2,000, though demoralized from recent defeat; mass of people terrorized by insurgent soldiers, desire peace and American protection; no longer flee on approach our troops unless forced by insurgents, but gladly welcome them; no recent burning of towns; population within our lines becoming dense, taking up land cultivation extensively; kept out Manila much as possible, as city population becoming too great to be cared for. Natives southeast Luzon combining to drive out insurgents; only hope insurgent leaders is United States aid. They proclaim near overthrow present administration, to be followed by their independence and recognition by United States. This is the influence which enables them hold out; much contention prevails among them and no civil government remains; trade with ports not in our possession, former source insurgent revenue now interdicted; not certain of wisdom of this policy, as people in those ports are without supply of food and merchants suffering losses; meditate restoring trade privileges, although insurgents reap benefits. Courts here in successful operation under direction of able Filipinos. Affairs in other islands comparatively quiet, awaiting results in Luzon. All anxious for trade and repeated calls for American troops received. Am giving attention to Jolo Archipelago and Palauan Islands. Our troops have worked to limit of endurance. Volunteer organizations have been called in; replaced by regulars, who now occupy salient positions. Nebraska, Pennsylvania, and Utah now taking transports, and Sixth Infantry sent to Negros to relieve California. These troops leave in good physical condition; sickness among troops has increased lately, due mostly to arduous service and climatic influences. Nothing alarming. Of the 12 per cent of the command reported sick, nearly 6 in general hospitals, of whom 3 per cent have typhoid and 17 malarial fevers; 25 per cent have intestinal trouble; remaining 55 per cent have various ailments, 14 of which due to wound injuries. Many officers and men who served in Cuba break under recurrence Cuban fever, and regular regiments lately received are inadequately officered.

OTIS.

MANILA. (Received June 26, 1899—8.20 a. m.)

ADJUTANT-GENERAL, *Washington:*

Reported situation just cabled. Will probably raise nucleus two volunteer regiments. Volunteers suffering from nostalgia. Will be too weak for a time to make extensive offensive movement in force, and, indeed, wet weather forbids it, except on isolated (?) towns. The insurgent cause may collapse at any time, and the ablest Philippine citizens expect it soon. I am not sanguine. Troops should be sent until 30,000 are on hand effective for the field, not counting staff corps. This requires from 35,000 to 40,000 troops of the line. That number is sufficient and is based on calculations of last November.

OTIS.

ADJUTANT-GENERAL'S OFFICE,
Washington, June 26, 1899.

OTIS, *Manila:*

Cipher cable translated reads: "Make directed offensive movement." No such directions have been given from here, hence not understood. All movements are left to your judgment and discretion. Troops will be sent to full number of your request as rapidly as transportation can be furnished.

CORBIN.

MANILA. (Received June 26, 1899—8.25 a. m.)

AGWAR, *Washington:*

Following deaths since last weekly report: From wounds in action—June 17, David Silver, M, First Montana Infantry. June 18, Miles Doyle, corporal, L, Twelfth Infantry. 19th, Sherman T. Shepard, H, First Washington; De Forrest Hutchinson, B, Ninth Infantry; Leonard J. Edling, E, Twenty-first Infantry. 20th, Herbert Mifflin, B, Fourth Infantry. 21st, George Dalts, artificer, D, Fourth Infantry. Drowned—Honolulu, May 9, David R. Johnson, I, Thirteenth Infantry. Erysipelas—June 18, Richard F. Havens, H, Twenty-first Infantry. Heat exhaustion—19th, Max Neugass, E, Fourth Infantry. Phthisis—20th, Edward Florentine, K, Third Artillery. Dysentery—22d, Frank E. King, G, Ninth Infantry. 24th, William H. Pilgrim, M, Thirteenth Minnesota. Variola—22d, Earl R. Cotton, H, Ninth Infantry.

OTIS.

SAN FRANCISCO, CAL., *June 26, 1899.*
(Received June 27, 1899—5.47 a. m.)

ADJUTANT-GENERAL, U. S. ARMY,
Washington, D. C.:

The *Valencia* and *Pennsylvania* will be gotten off just as soon as possible. Both are awaiting arrival of troops. Two companies Twenty-fifth Infantry now here and two more expected to-night.

Valencia can certainly get off by 30th and possibly by 29th. On account of companies being increased by assignment of recruits to 128 a little delay here is unavoidable. The *Pennsylvania* will be delayed a few days longer waiting arrival of companies of Twenty-fourth, one company of which regiment left Assinniboine to-day.

General Merriam telegraphs to-day companies Twenty-fourth at Douglas and Russell have just arrived at posts from riot duty in Idaho. I believe the *Pennsylvania* can be gotten away by the 3d or 4th.

There will not be a minute's unnecessary delay after arrival of troops.

SHAFTER, *Major-General.*

MANILA. (Received June 27, 1899—5 a. m.)

AGWAR, *Washington:*
Word "directed" unfortunately used; word "extensive" conveys meaning intended.

OTIS.

MANILA. (Received June 27, 1899—6.20 a. m.)

AGWAR, *Washington:*
Transport *Grant* arrived this morning; no casualties.

OTIS.

SAN FRANCISCO, CAL., *June 27, 1899.*
(Received 9.20 p. m.)

Gen. H. C. CORBIN,
Adjutant-General, U. S. Army, Washington, D. C.:
After consultation with the Surgeon-General it is the opinion that the provisions already made here are sufficient to take care of all the sick that may reasonably be expected. This means the retention in use as hospital of the brick barracks at Presidio, used as hospital at present, with the old and new general hospitals, which have a capacity for 800 sick, and this may be increased in three days' time to capacity for 1,000 by use of hospital tents. A detention camp with capacity for 1,500 men will be established at Angel Island in addition, for use in case of necessity arising therefor by arrival of transports with cases of contagious diseases.

SHAFTER, *Major-General.*

MANILA. (Received June 27, 1899—2.41 p. m.)

AGWAR, *Washington:*
Additional casualties: Killed—Fourteenth Infantry, at Guadalupe Hill, June 10, D, Gerard Strumper. Ninth Infantry, at Zapote, 13th, I, Alfred A. Mahoney. Twenty-first Infantry, F, Corpl. John B. Gerstner; I, Joseph Crogan. Wounded— Ninth Infanfry, C, First Sergt. Romeo T. Perry, back, slight. Twenty-first Infantry, I, Charles Overton, shoulder, slight; James Curran, back, moderate. Fourth Infantry, near Imus, 20th, B, William A. Mulhey, abdomen, severe; E, John Noland, head, moderate; G, David H. Wadlington, face, slight. Seventeenth Infantry, near San Fernando, 22d, D, Albert R. Davis, leg, slight; E, Musician William O. Carrol, forehead, slight.

OTIS.

SAN FRANCISCO, CAL., *June 27, 1899.*
(Received 12.20 p. m.)

ADJUTANT-GENERAL, U. S. ARMY, *Washington, D. C.:*
By sending companies of the Twenty-fourth and Twenty-fifth Infantry and Fourth Cavalry, now here, without regard to regimental or battalion organizations, and completing loading with about 500 recruits, of which there are at Presidio to-day 2,700, the *Valencia* can go to-morrow and the *Pennsylvania* two days later. I do not think that the troops sent this way will be as efficient on arrival as if sent in battalion organizations, but the early departure of the transports appearing to be the important consideration, I will send them as I have stated, headquarters, band and 2 troops of Fourth Cavalry, and 2 companies of the Twenty-fifth Infantry on the *Valencia*, band and 1 company of the Twenty-fourth Infantry, 2 companies of the Twenty-fifth Infantry, and about 500 recruits on the *Pennsylvania*.

This will leave headquarters and 6 companies of the Twenty-fifth Infantry, and 3 companies of the Twenty-fourth Infantry, to go on next transport. Please advise if this is satisfactory.

SHAFTER, *Major-General.*

ADJUTANT-GENERAL'S OFFICE,
Washington, June 27, 1899.

COMMANDING GENERAL, DEPARTMENT CALIFORNIA,
San Francisco, Cal.:

The Secretary of War has read your telegram of even date, and agrees with you that it would be better for organizations to go as such, but under the pressing demand that we get all transportation to Manila as soon as possible that the volunteers there may be returned, he directs that the plan set forth by your telegram be carried out, viz, the *Valencia* to leave to-morrow, and *Pennsylvania* two days later, sooner if possible to be done with good order and comfort of the men.

H. C. CORBIN, *Adjutant-General.*

AN FRANCISCO, CAL., *June 28, 1899.*
(Received 6.35 p. m.)

ADJUTANT-GENERAL, *Washington, D. C.:*

Medical officers report that it is almost certain there will be infectious diseases on returning transports. In anticipation I have directed erection of camp for 1,500 men on Angel Island, in vicinity of quarantine. Every provision will be made to make camp comfortable, and though while in quarantine the men would be under quarantine authorities, it is necessary to provide for them ourselves, as the quarantine has no accommodation except for Asiatic passengers.

SHAFTER, *Major-General.*

SAN FRANCISCO, CAL., *June 28, 1899.*
(Received 9.21 p. m.)

ADJUTANT-GENERAL, *Washington, D. C.:*

Referring to the detention camp on Angel Island, mentioned in my dispatch this morning, I have directed that the tents be floored and suitable places made for the men to eat, but without going to unnecessary expense, such as laying pipes to lead water, the water wagon being sufficient for the purpose. About $200 will have to be put into repair of a small wharf, but this is unavoidable. I trust all this will meet with approval of the Secretary of War.

SHAFTER, *Major-General.*

ADJUTANT-GENERAL'S OFFICE,
Washington, June 29, 1899.

COMMANDING GENERAL, *San Francisco, Cal.:*

Your two telegrams relating to hospital accommodations at Angel Island received, and your course and expenditure recommended approved by the Secretary of War.

H. C. CORBIN, *Adjutant-General.*

MANILA. (Received June 29, 1899—1.10 a. m.)

AGWAR, *Washington:*

Number late Spanish civil officials, held as prisoners by insurgents, enabled to escape and return to Manila by advance of troops into interior. Spanish authorities claim United States obligated to transport them to Spain under article 6 of treaty. Request decision to get this class of cases.

OTIS.

WAR DEPARTMENT, *June 29, 1899.*

OTIS, *Manila:*
Without admitting any obligation, you are authorized to use your own judgment as to whom you will return to Spain under article 6, having in mind the best interests of the United States in getting them away from the islands.

ALGER, *Secretary of War.*

ADJUTANT-GENERAL'S OFFICE,
Washington, June 29, 1899.

OTIS, *Manila:*
Zealandia left 22d, battalion Twenty-fourth Infantry, 10 officers, 406 enlisted men; also 12 signal corps and 148 recruits.

Sheridan left 24th, Companies B and H, Fourteenth Infantry; Troops A and F, Fourth Cavalry; General Young and number officers; 8 Hospital Corps; 41 Signal Corps and 1,251 recruits. Total, 37 officers, 1,737 men.

Valencia left 28th, headquarters, band, B and M, Fourth Cavalry; E and H, Twenty-fifth Infantry. Total, 12 officers, 454 men.

Pennsylvania sails to-morrow with 1 company Twenty-fourth, 2 companies Twenty-fifth, and 500 recruits.

CORBIN.

SAN FRANCISCO, CAL., *June 29, 1899.*
(Received 3.06 p. m.)

ADJUTANT-GENERAL, *Washington, D. C.:*
Transport *Valencia* left yesterday evening with headquarters band, Troops B, M, Fourth Cavalry, 7 officers, 195 men, 200 rounds carbine, 120 pistol ammunition per man. Companies E, H, Twenty-fifth Infantry, 3 officers, 253 men, 200 rounds rifle ammunition per man, 1 assistant surgeon, 1 acting assistant surgeon, 6 men Hospital Corps.

SHAFTER, *Commanding.*

MANILA. (Received June 30, 1899—2.35 a. m.)
AGWAR, *Washington:*
Transport *Morgan City* sailed San Francisco June 24, 464 sick.

OTIS.

ADJUTANT-GENERAL'S OFFICE,
Washington, June 30, 1899.

OTIS, *Manila:*
Department is advised that King Sudley, formerly wool dealer Philadelphia, is in Hongkong, acting as agent for insurgents for importation of firearms.

CORBIN.

ADJUTANT-GENERAL'S OFFICE,
Washington, June 30, 1899.

OTIS, *Manila:*
The Associated Press of the United States, represented by Mr. Collins and others at Manila, complain that preference is given to other press representatives by your censor; that they are constantly discriminated against and that you are prejudiced against it, and allege that its representatives are in the pay of the Filipino Junta at Hongkong. The Department does not believe that you are prejudiced against

this association, or that you hold such views concerning it, but that the whole complaint must be the result of some misunderstanding. These complaints are reported to us by their head office here. There is no desire here to interfere with your censorship of matter sent from Manila, but it is necessary that all shall be treated alike.

CORBIN.

ADJUTANT-GENERAL'S OFFICE,
Washington, June 30, 1899.

COMMANDING GENERAL, DEPARTMENT CALIFORNIA,
San Francisco, Cal.:

After sailing of *Pennsylvania* what number of officers and men will you have awaiting transportation to Manila?

H. C. CORBIN, *Adjutant-General.*

SAN FRANCISCO, CAL., *June 30, 1899.*
(Received 11.08 p. m.)

ADJUTANT-GENERAL, *Washington, D. C.:*

In reply to your telegram this date, after sailing of *Pennsylvania* there will remain awaiting transportation to Manila, headquarters and four companies Twenty-fourth Infantry, 14 officers, 512 men; Troops D and H, Fourth Cavalry, 5 officers, 166 men, and at this date 2,891 recruits and casuals, with 32 officers on duty with them. Of the above the *City of Para* will take Twenty-fourth Infantry and Fourth Cavalry, in addition to Engineer company from New York; 1,000 of the 2,891 recruits now here are quite well prepared for service, and others should be kept for some time yet for drill and target practice and to weed out men unsuited for the service.

SHAFTER, *Major-General.*

MANILA. (Received July 1, 1899—7.25 a. m.)

AGWAR, *Washington:*

Chief surgeon reports demand for additional medical officers; soon to lose 7, and number on sick list; says 24 vacancies. Reasonable allowance considered; response not received to request of January 9 and recent one for 15 and 10 medical officers, respectively.

OTIS.

ADJUTANT-GENERAL'S OFFICE,
Washington, July 1, 1899.

OTIS, *Manila:*

On receipt cable January 9, 27 regular medical officers and 29 acting assistant surgeons were ordered. Those that have not already reported are now en route. On receipt cable May 22, 7 regular medical officers and 9 acting assistant surgeons were ordered. Number of others have been ordered to sail on *City of Para* July 12. All troops en route have more than full complement medical officers.

CORBIN.

MANILA. (Received July 1, 1899—9.21 a. m.)

AGWAR, *Washington:*

Khaki uniform United States condemned, defective material and workmanship, unfit for issue; should not be sent. Uniform of excellent quality procured here at very low price.

OTIS.

AFFAIRS IN THE PHILIPPINE ISLANDS. 1025

MANILA. (Received July 1, 1899—2.30 p. m.)
ADJUTANT-GENERAL, *Washington:*

Associated Press without cause for complaint. Collins now here says that if anything prejudicial to press done satisfied not intentional. Names two instances when he thinks was beaten by other reporters by not receiving immediate action of censor. Bray, of Hongkong Junta Associated Press correspondent, last fall used position to send dispatches in interests insurgents. I made complaint at time to press representative. Have no interest in nor prejudice against any particular newspaper. Great care exercised to treat all alike.

OTIS.

SAN FRANCISCO, CAL., *July 1, 1899.*
(Received 7.30 p. m.)
ADJUTANT-GENERAL, *Washington, D. C.:*

Transport *Pennsylvania* sails to-day with Colonel Burt, headquarters band, Companies B, F, I, K, L, and M, Twenty-fifth Infantry, 17 officers, 701 enlisted men, and 80 colored recruits assigned to regiment, 170 rounds ammunition, caliber .30, per man; 1 surgeon, 2 acting assistant surgeons, 8 Hospital Corps men; also Lieutenant-Colonel Coolidge, Ninth Infantry; Major James, Twenty-third Infantry; Captain Johnston, Sixteenth Infantry, with 130 white recruits, as follows: For Philippines—cavalry, Fourth, 23; artillery, heavy, Third, 9; Sixth, 3; light, Fourth, 1;. infantry, Third, 44; Fourth, 4; Sixth, 1; Ninth, 5; Twelfth, 1; Fourteenth, 6; Sixteenth, 1; Seventeenth, 2; Eighteenth, 12; Twentieth, 2; Twenty-first, 2; Twenty-second, 3; Twenty-third, 11; for Honolulu, 2 recruits for Sixth Artillery.

SHAFTER, *Major-General.*

EXECUTIVE MANSION,
Washington, July 1, 1899—4.10 p. m.
OTIS, *Manila:*

By direction of the Secretary of War, the following is transmitted:
"OTIS, *Manila:*

"The President desires to express in the most public manner his appreciation of the lofty patriotism shown by the volunteers and regulars of the Eighth Army Corps in performing willing service through severe campaigns and battles against the insurgents in Luzon, when under the terms of their enlistments they would have been entitled to discharge upon the ratification of the treaty of peace with Spain.

"This action on their part was noble and heroic. It will stand forth as an example of the self-sacrifice and public consecration which have ever characterized the American soldier.

"In recognition thereof I shall recomend to Congress that a special medal of honor be given to the officers and soldiers of the Eighth Army Corps, who performed this great duty voluntarily and enthusiastically for their country.

"WILLIAM McKINLEY."
CORBIN.

ADJUTANT-GENERAL'S OFFICE,
Washington, July 14, 1899.
Major-General SHAFTER, *San Francisco:*

The following was transmitted to Major-General Otis, Manila, under date of the 1st instant. Publish it to the Oregon volunteers.
(Copy of telegram immediately preceding.)

CORBIN.

MANILA. (Received July 2, 1899—9 a. m.)

AGWAR, *Washington:*

Transports *Hancock* and *Senator*, with Nebraska, Pennsylvania, Utah, left for San Francisco yesterday. Nebraska, 42 officers, 812 enlisted. Pennsylvania, 34 officers, 712 enlisted. Utah, 9 officers, 258 enlisted. Nebraska left in Manila 1 sick—Private Lauterman, Company M; 1 deserter; 30 discharged. Pennsylvania, 1 prisoner of insurgents, Private Colloms, Company C; 7 discharged. Utah, 29 discharged.

OTIS.

MANILA. (Received July 2, 1899—11.42 a. m.)

AGWAR, *Washington:*

Number recruits required to fill companies to 128 each regular regiment infantry: Third, 336; Fourth, 304; Sixth, 175; Ninth, 305; Twelfth, 300; Thirteenth, 253; Fourteenth, 739; Sixteenth, 270; Seventeenth, 294; Eighteenth, 828; Twentieth, 338; Twenty-first, 195; Twenty-second, 460; Twenty-third, 680. Artillery: First, 8; Third, 256; Fourth, 2; Fifth, 2; Sixth, 93. Cavalry: Fourth, 493. Engineers, 7. Volunteers yet to be returned: Infantry, California, 1,188; Colorado, 1,144; Idaho, 598; North Dakota, 623; Wyoming, 300; Minnesota, 1,165; South Dakota, 917; Montana, 906. California Artillery, 358. Washington, 1,068; Tennessee, 946; Kansas, 1,052. Nevada Cavalry, 88. Wyoming Artillery, 85. Iowa, 995. Signal Corps, 106. California and Colorado preparing to take transports *Sherman* and *Warren;* leave shortly.

OTIS.

ADJUTANT-GENERAL'S OFFICE,
Washington, July 2, 1899.

COMMANDING GENERAL, DEPARTMENT CALIFORNIA,
San Francisco, Cal.:

There will be 6 officers of the medical regular corps and 8 acting assistant surgeons for General Otis's army, and the Secretary of War desires that rooms be reserved for them on *City of Para*, as it is important that they should surely go.

H. C. CORBIN, *Adjutant-General.*

MANILA. (Received July 3, 1899—9.15 a. m.)

AGWAR, *Washington·*

Additional casualties: Killed—Fourth Cavalry, at Muntinlupa, June 26, C, William Nolan. Seventeenth Infantry, near San Fernando, 13th, E, John C. McHuner. Wounded—Twelfth Infantry, A, William H. Dingey, elbow, slight; F, Aaron C. Wise, wrist, slight. Fifty-first Iowa, C, Edward F. Brown, nates, moderate.

OTIS.

WAR DEPARTMENT, *July 3, 1899.*

OTIS, *Manila:*

The *Sherman* has berths for 1,800 men; the *Warren* a regiment comfortably. If possible, fill them to their capacity, as there is a great demand in the United States for the return of volunteers. Use every possible means to get volunteers away as quickly as possible, and fill the ships as full as they can be fairly comfortable.

ALGER, *Secwar.*

MANILA. (Received July 4, 1899—7.43 a. m.)

AGWAR, *Washington:*

California Infantry and Artillery, number 1,400, and discharged men take *Sherman* now loading at Negros. *Warren* takes Colorado, 1,100, now preparing preparatory papers. Difficult to lighter transports in typhoon now prevailing. *Grant*, unloaded in four days, will take on Idaho, North Dakota, and Wyoming, 65 officers, 1,500 men, with other discharged men.

OTIS.

MANILA. (Received July 4, 1899—1.08 p. m.)

ADJUTANT-GENERAL, *Washington:*

Negotiations in progress six weeks. Now approaching completion. Promise surrender populous province Cavite in few days. Consummation will break power Tagalo insurrection. Affairs south progressing favorably. Large portion Cebu occupied without meeting resistance. All Negros occupied. Control about to extend to Bohol Islands. Matters in Jolo improving. General Bates (J. C.) about to leave for Jolo with instructions to make agreement with Sultan, subject to approval of President. Copy instructions by mail. Ports northern and southeastern Luzon, those of Samar, Leyte, Bohol, Cebu, and Negros opened for trade.

OTIS.

ADJUTANT-GENERAL'S OFFICE,
Washington, July 4, 1899.

OTIS, *Manila:*

Having in mind probable, even possible, needs future campaigns, report desired what, if any, mules or horses will be required for either mounts, packs, or otherwise. Large number trained mules on hand for Cuban war. If needed, they can be sent before sale now contemplated.

CORBIN.

MANILA. (Received July 5, 1899—7.45 a. m.)

AGWAR, *Washington:*

Following deaths since last weekly report: Typhoid fever—June 26, Fred. C. Fritzon, E, Thirteenth Minnesota. 28th, Paul J. Rhode, K, Thirteenth Minnesota; Arthur Froggatt, H, Ninth Infantry; Herbert Streator, C, Thirteenth Infantry. 29th, Fred. Przykalla, corporal, H, Ninth Infantry. July 1, Paul B. Pugh, L, Fifty-first Iowa. From wounds in action—June 25, Harvey J. Lowe, A, Fourteenth Infantry. 29th, William Lapp, L, Twelfth Infantry. Drowned, accidental—22d, Alfred H. Koch, F, Twenty-first Infantry. 25th, James Armstrong, L, Ninth Infantry. Tuberculosis—14th, Thomas Connors, M, Twelfth Infantry. Dysentery—22d, John Holoman, H, Seventeenth Infantry. Pneumonia—30th, William H. Hussey, C, Seventeenth Infantry. Variola—James Allan, G, Third Artillery.

OTIS.

WAR DEPARTMENT, *July 5, 1899.*

OTIS, *Manila:*

Some newspapers report you are to be relieved. Pay no attention to such reports. There is no truth in them. The President and myself are absolutely satisfied with your conduct of affairs.

ALGER, *Secwar.*

MANILA. (Received July 5, 1899—1.52 a. m.)

AGWAR, *Washington:*
Transportation sent relieves native transportation hired. Desire 50 escort wagons, 300 mules, one-third pack. Horses requested, expected on 3 transports September sufficient.

OTIS.

ADJUTANT-GENERAL'S OFFICE,
Washington, July 6, 1899.

OTIS, *Manila:*
Quartermaster-General says lack strength khaki a result of effort to produce very light garments suggested by many officers as necessary in Tropics. That will be corrected hereafter. In the meantime Secretary of War authorizes you charge men equitable prices for defective khaki garments issued, establishing same under Army Regulations 713. Continue purchases to meet wants six months, by which time it is believed here satisfactory khaki clothing can be placed Manila from here. Is regulation pattern khaki coat sent with troops satisfactory? They now have reenforced cuffs and no facings, except on shoulder straps.

CORBIN.

ADJUTANT-GENERAL'S OFFICE,
Washington, July 6, 1899.

OTIS, *Manila:*
Refer to your telegram of 5th. It is understood that you want 50 escort wagons, 300 animals, one-third pack horses? Are we correct?

CORBIN.

MANILA. (Received July 7, 1899—7.50 a. m.)

AGWAR, *Washington:*
Fifty escort wagons, 300 mules, one-third to be pack mules

OTIS.

MANILA. (Received July 8, 1899—7.25 a. m.)

AGWAR, *Washington:*
Desires of all volunteers in Philippines ascertained. Two skeleton regiments fairly well assured. In two three days will cable names of officers nominated for regiments so that appointments of lieutenant to recruit in United States can be made.

OTIS.

MANILA. (Received July 8, 1899—10.02 a. m.)

AGWAR, *Washington:*
Second Oregon left behind at Manila, Privates J. E. Lawrence, C. W. Mills, R. G. McCoy, Company M, missing since May 2, supposed in hands insurgents. Privates Daniel Carroll, A; Frank Boyd, D; L. F. Neumann, G; H. W. Kerrigan, H; absent without leave, supposed deserters. Privates Frank Kenney, A; Stephen Murphy, M, missed transport, to go on *Centennial.*

OTIS.

MANILA. (Received July 8, 1899—3.08 p. m.)

SECWAR, *Washington:*

Greatly appreciate expressed confidence. Have no individual desires nor personal ambition other than to promote interest of Government. Every movement so far-reaching in consequence and the best Filipinos so unappreciative of republican institutions are having so little confidence in humanity that extreme caution must be combined with boldness and celerity of execution. Every stroke of the Army given to secure political effect. In Visayan Islands troops hold comparatively quiet, exercising general supervision and faction will war with each other and Tagalos will be driven out. In Manila the families of the most distinguished insurgent officers now living, others coming in. Still some hard fighting necessary in Luzon soon as conditions permit. Weather and exchange of one army for another would neutralize attempted efforts at present. Army, Navy, and remaining members of commission in hearty accord and best of feeling prevails. Know source of abuse, care nothing for it. Do not want popularity, only credit for attempted honest administration. Indisposition last two days has delayed this acknowledgment.

OTIS.

MANILA. (Received July 9, 1899—4.50 a. m.)

AGWAR, *Washington:*

Following deaths since last weekly report: Typhoid fever—July 2, Charles Wilseck, G, First Wyoming Infantry. 5th, Edward Weldon, K, Fourteenth Infantry. William Miller, K, Fourth Infantry. 6th, Elmer Stevens, G, Twelfth Infantry. Dysentery—4th, William H. Hill, Hospital Corps. 5th, Thomas W. Fetro, M, Fourth Infantry. Drowned—4th, Charles Hiatt, sergeant, E, Fourth Cavalry.

OTIS.

MANILA. (Received July 9, 1899—4.52 a. m.)

AGWAR, *Washington:*

Two veteran regiments assured, will enlist about 1,000; you can appoint 11 second lieutenants for First and 9 for Second Regiment to recruit in United States. All other officers filled. Regiments styled First and Second Philippine United States Veterans Volunteer Infantry.

OTIS.

ADJUTANT-GENERAL'S OFFICE,
Washington, July 10, 1899.

OTIS, *Manila:*

Steps to get recruits for your volunteer regiments inaugurated at once. Ten are being raised here, styled Twenty-sixth to Thirty-fifth regiments of Infantry, U. S. Volunteers. Yours are designated Thirty-sixth and Thirty-seventh regiments of Infantry, U. S. Volunteers.

CORBIN.

WAR DEPARTMENT, *July 10, 1899.*

OTIS, *Manila:*

Do you not think it would be wise to mount 5,000 men to be used as mounted infantry; if so, would it not be best to send mules, unless you can purchase ponies there? Answer quick.

ALGER, *Secwar.*

MANILA. (Received July 11, 1899—4.33 a. m.)

SECWAR, *Washington:*
Can purchase ponies when country opened; now purchasing, daily, small number; just mounted Nevada Cavalry; have 4 mounted troops; have contracted for small number from China; don't think mules necessary for purpose indicated.

OTIS.

WAR DEPARTMENT, *July 11, 1899.*

OTIS, *Manila:*
I can not think otherwise than that a strong cavalry force would be of great use to you, especially when you have long distances to travel with your troops. If you wish, we will send you mounts for 4,000 or 5,000 men, or you can purchase horses in the island, Australia, China, or elsewhere. Let us get a full ready for a fall campaign.

ALGER, *Secwar.*

MANILA. (Received July 12, 1899—5.15 a. m.)

AGWAR, *Washington:*
Bell should rank June 9; Wallace, June 28; dates upon which they were directed to organize regiments. Is it desired that the third regiment be organized here if found practicable? Desire of many volunteers to reenlist again apparent.

OTIS.

EXECUTIVE MANSION, *July 12, 1899.*

OTIS, *Manila:*
The President approves organizing the third regiment should you find it practicable.

CORBIN.

FORT MASON, CAL., *July 12, 1899.*
(Received July 13, 1899—1 a. m.)

Gen. H. C. CORBIN,
Adjutant-General, Washington, D. C.:
Ohio and *Newport* arrived at 5 p. m. to-day; all well.

SHAFTER, *Major-General.*

MANILA. (Received July 13, 1899—8.40 a. m.,

SECWAR, *Washington:*
Cavalry force 2,000 or 3,000 essential. With horses to come in September thought we could meet necessity by purchase. Just informed failure China contract. China stopped shipment contraband war. Horses received from Australia; three lots not satisfactory. Two lots ponies from Sulu worthless, not received. Expect to secure 500 good ponies Cavite and Batangas. If 2,000 horses in addition to those asked for could be shipped from United States, would fill requirements even if expected purchases here can not be secured.

OTIS.

SAN FRANCISCO, CAL., *July 13, 1899.*
(Received 6.20 p. m.)

ADJUTANT-GENERAL, *Washington, D. C.:*
Report arrival yesterday of transports *Newport* and *Ohio* with Second Oregon, California Signal Corps, and following additional military passengers: Major Sears, addi-

tional paymaster; Major Bates, Eighteenth Infantry; Captain Jeffrey, quartermaster Volunteers; Acting Assistant Surgeon Anderson; 1 sick and 8 discharged soldiers.

SHAFTER, *Major-General.*

MANILA. (Received July 14, 1899—4.18 a. m.)
AGWAR, *Washington:*
Additional casualties: Wounded—Seventeenth Infantry at San Fernando, June 30, C, Corpl. Christian Jenson, arm, slight. July 4, E, George W. King, thigh, severe. 11th, First Lieut. Ira L. Reeves, cheek, hand, and foot, moderate. Fourth Cavalry, 5th, C, Frank Bouchard, hand, slight, at Pililla. 11th, Edward Reeves, foot, moderate; G, Amon Nall, abdomen, severe, near Santa Cruz.

OTIS.

SAN FRANCISCO, CAL., *July 14, 1899.* (Received 8.50 p. m.)
ADJUTANT-GENERAL, *Washington, D. C.:*
Transport *City of Para* sailed yesterday evening with Major Augur and two troops Fourth Cavalry, 4 officers, 175 men; headquarters, band and four companies Twenty-fourth Infantry, 14 officers, 542 men; Company B, Engineers, 3 officers, 150 men; 180 rounds, caliber .30, ammunition per man. With troops, 6 assistant surgeons, 10 acting assistant surgeons, 19 Hospital Corps, 1 officer and 21 men Signal Corps, 66 assigned men Twenty-fourth and 7 Twenty-fifth Infantry. Passengers, General Schwan and aid, Colonels Carpenter, Eighteenth; Bisbee, Thirteenth; Major Lee, Ninth; Captain Batchelor, Twenty-fourth Infantry.

SHAFTER, *Major-General.*

ADJUTANT-GENERAL'S OFFICE,
Washington, July 14, 1899.
OTIS, *Manila:*
Eighteen medical officers sailed *City of Para* yesterday.

CORBIN.

MANILA. (Received July 15, 1899—3.38 a. m.)
AGWAR, *Washington:*
Twenty inches rain July attended by typhoons made loading transports impossible. At Negros impossible to unload Sixth Infantry until last day or two. Californians now loading. Colorados leave to-morrow on *Warren.* Idahos, North Dakotas, and Wyomings next week soon as transport *Grant* can be coaled.

OTIS.

ADJUTANT-GENERAL'S OFFICE,
Washington, July 15, 1899.
OTIS, *Manila:*
City of Para sailed yesterday, two troops Fourth Cavalry, 4 officers, 179 men; headquarters' band; four companies Twenty-fourth Infantry, 14 officers, 542 men; Company B, Engineers, 3 officers, 150 men; 16 medical officers, 19 men, Hospital Corps; 1 officer, 21 men, Signal Corps; General Schwan, Colonels Carpenter, Eighteenth, and Bisbee, Thirteenth.

CORBIN.

ADJUTANT-GENERAL'S OFFICE,
Washington, July 15, 1899.

COMMANDING GENERAL, DEPARTMENT CALIFORNIA,
San Francisco, Cal.:

A general field return by wire of the Oregon regiment desired, showing number of men enlisted, number killed, discharged, promoted, total waiting muster out.

H. C. CORBIN, Adjutant-General.

ADJUTANT-GENERAL'S OFFICE,
Washington, July 15, 1899.

OTIS, Manila:

What size horses should be sent? Would a range between fourteen-two and fifteen-two, weighing from 900 and 1,000 be suitable? What will you require in way of equipment for horses asked for in your cable to Secwar? Will you require any additional mules for wagon or pack.

CORBIN.

MANILA. (Received July 16, 1899—8.25 a. m.)

AGWAR, Washington:

Full-chested, large-barreled, short-backed horses, weighing from 900 to 1,000, desired, and full cavalry equipment for all horses sent. Captain Lockett, Fourth Cavalry, directed to raise third regiment here and for cavalry purposes if no objection; think he will succced; need for it 1,500 carbines; will cable concerning mules later.

OTIS.

MANILA. (Received July 16, 1899.)

AGWAR, Washington:

Following deaths have occurred since last report: Dysentery—July 8, James J. Higgins, corporal, Thirteenth Infantry, Company H; George W. Warrington, I, First Colorado; Ernest Weidoff, Third Infantry, Company I. July 13, Ludwig P. Mohlin, Twelfth Infantry, Company B. July 14, Harry J. Heisig, M, First Colorado. Drowned, accidental—June 24, Michael Sullivan, M, Ninth Infantry. July 4, George J. Wilson, Sixteenth Infantry, Company E. Deaths from typhoid fever—July 7, August Nolte, Fourth Infantry, Company A. Nephritis—John Quinlan, sergeant, Band, Eighteenth Infantry. Hemiplegia—July 13, William Hodge, Fourteenth Infantry, Company C. From wounds in action—June 28, Frank A. Duval, F, First Colorado; death occurred on *Relief*, Nagasaki.

OTIS.

MANILA. (Received July 16, 1899—11.12 a. m.)

AGWAR, Washington:

Have in command 530 good mules, 100 escort wagons, 150 packs; asked 5th instant for 300 more mules, one-third pack, and 50 escort wagons. Now obliged to use native transportation, which poor; dispensing with it could use profitably additional 500 mules, 100 broad-tire escort wagons, 100 more aparejos. Better teamsters secured here than in the United States; none should be sent except sufficient to care for stock en route.

OTIS.

MANILA. (Received July 16, 1899—1.37 p. m.)
ADJUTANT-GENERAL, *Washington:*
Referring to your dispatch inviting suggestions to organizing military departments, four can be advantageously organized, with headquarters at Manila, Dagupan, Iloilo, and Zamboanga. Must await occupation Dagupan and Zamboanga, which will quickly follow active operations to be commenced soon as weather and arrival of troops en route permit.

OTIS.

MIDDLETOWN, PA., *July 17, 1899.* (Received 10.35 a. m.)
ADJUTANT-GENERAL, U. S. ARMY, *Washington, D. C.:*
Left Camp Meade at 9.20 this morning, strength as follows: Field, staff and band, 6 officers and 32 men; B, 2 officers, 119 men; D, 2 officers, 112 men; F, 2 officers, 124 men; G, 3 officers, 120 men; H, 2 officers, 115 men; I, 3 officers, 112 men; K, 2 officers, 114 men; M, 3 officers, 110 men. Attached 4 officers and 13 men; medical department, 1 assistant surgeon, 3 acting assistant surgeons, and 9 men.

SNYDER, *Commanding.*

MANILA. (Received July 18, 1899—10.05 a. m.)
AGWAR, *Washington:*
Continued heavy rain. Cyclonic storms impede business in harbor. Colorados sailed transport *Warren* yesterday; privates Horn and Wilder, Company G, left sick. In addition, 131 discharged men, various organizations, took passage. Californians, on *Sherman,* arrived from Negros. Vessel must be coaled. Await subsidence of typhoon now prevailing.

OTIS.

ADJUTANT-GENERAL'S OFFICE,
Washington, July 18, 1899.
OTIS, *Manila:*
The President approves your organizing a cavalry regiment as recommended.

CORBIN.

SAN FRANCISCO, CAL., *July 18, 1899.*
(Received 2.40 p. m.)
ADJUTANT-GENERAL, *Washington, D. C.:*
Replying to your telegram 15th instant, general field return Second Oregon as follows: Commissioned officers, 50; promoted from ranks, 6; resigned and discharged, 9; remaining to be mustered out, 47. Enlisted men: Enlisted, 1,316; discharged, 208; killed and died of wounds, 16; died of disease, 33; deserted, 2; remaining to be mustered out, 1,057.

SHAFTER, *Major-General.*

ADJUTANT-GENERAL'S OFFICE,
Washington, July 18, 1899—4 p. m.
COMMANDING OFFICER, CAMP MEADE,
Middletown, Pa.:
Acting Secretary War directs that battalion Nineteenth Infantry now on duty at Camp Meade proceed by rail, with baggage and equipment, to San Francisco, Cal., in time to reach there July 25, to embark same day two companies each on the

transports *Newport* and *Ohio* for the Philippine Islands, to be reported upon arrival to the commanding general.

Quartermaster's Department will furnish necessary transportation, Subsistence Department ample and suitable travel rations, and Medical Department attendance and supplies for journey.

Acknowledge receipt. Direct commanding officer to report arrival in San Francisco.

By command Major-General Miles:

HEISTAND,
Assistant Adjutant-General.

MANILA. (Received July 20, 1899—7.20 a. m.)

AGWAR, *Washington:*

Storm still prevailing; barometer rising, indicating improved weather conditions. Average rainfall July several years $14\frac{1}{2}$ inches; for twenty days fully, now closed, 41 inches; country flooded. Troops on outpost have suffered and former lines of communication cut in some instances; not serious. No material increase in sickness reported. Telegraphic communication maintained, San Fernando, Bacoor, and nearly all other points. Unable yet to coal returning transports.

OTIS.

MANILA. (Received July 20, 1899—7.23 a. m.)

AGWAR, *Washington:*

Desire decision word "immediately," second paragraph, General Orders, No. 67. Men discharged Jolo other southern points present themselves for reenlistment here twenty or thirty days after discharge. Men discharged Manila desire reenlist few days after discharge; will they come within meaning word "immediately?"

OTIS.

ADJUTANT-GENERAL'S OFFICE,
Washington, July 20, 1899.

OTIS, *Manila:*

Exercise your judgment and construction "immediately" to meet justice and interests of service.

CORBIN.

ADJUTANT-GENERAL'S OFFICE,
Washington, July 20, 1899.

OTIS, *Manila:*

Do you wish it understood that the departments are to be organized now? If so, who to command each? Brig. Gen. Joseph Wheeler ordered report to you for duty; sails 22d.

CORBIN.

ADJUTANT-GENERAL'S OFFICE,
Washington, July 20, 1899.

OTIS, *Manila:*

Have you seen dispatch from Hongkong signed by newspaper correspondents at Manila? If so, do you desire to make any statements relating thereto?

CORBIN.

MANILA. (Received July 21, 1899—6.55 a. m.)

AGWAR, *Washington:*

Do not think departments can be successfully organized at once; will make recommendation in short period.

OTIS.

MANILA. (Received July 21, 1899—7.50 a. m.)

AGWAR, *Washington:*

Capt. B. A. Byrne, Sixth Infantry, with 70 men surprised united robber bands, Negros, numbering 450; killed 115, wounded many, captured few rifles and revolvers, many hand weapons, large quantities stock; fighting at close distance; Byrne's loss, 1 killed, 1 wounded, names not given; this action very beneficial for quiet of Negros.

OTIS.

MANILA. (Received July 21, 1899—10.48 a. m.)

ADJUTANT-GENERAL, *Washington:*

Cabled explanation Hongkong dispatch yesterday. Charge made by press untrue. Believe have support of all officers. Most harmonious relations exist between army and navy.

Following extract letter just received from influential Philippine at Tarlac, center of insurgent main army:

"For some days have been trying to leave this band of thieves. Watched so closely impossible to leave. A great many of the people here look for American troops to advance, for every one is desperate with so much savagery committed by our army."

Future will show my dispatches very conservative.

OTIS.

ADJUTANT-GENERAL'S OFFICE,
Washington, July 21, 1899.

OTIS, *Manila:*

Desired you cable end each month brief field returns, giving total enlisted and commissioned each regiment your command.

CORBIN.

ADJUTANT-GENERAL'S OFFICE,
Washington, July 22, 1899.

OTIS, *Manila:*

Should 500 mules, refer to your telegram 16th, be all team mules, or should 100 be pack mules? If latter, shall we send equipment of packers with them and the aparejos?

CORBIN.

ADJUTANT-GENERAL'S OFFICE,
Washington, July 22, 1899.

OTIS, *Manila:*

Must we ship grain and hay from States for all animals you now have and 3,500 to be sent, or can you obtain all or part from other sources cheaper? About what quantity hay and grain can you take care of?

CORBIN.

MANILA. (Received July 20, 1899—2.36 p. m.)
ADJUTANT-GENERAL, *Washington:*

Press correspondent demanded permission to cable that official reports sent misrepresented conditions. Declined. Then demanded privilege to cable freely facts found by them and their opinions. Grant if interests of Government permitted. Answer not satisfactory to correspondents, and dispatch presented probably sent by mail to Hongkong, there cabled to United States. Not conscious of sending misrepresentations; in fact, think my dispatches at times too conservative. Press affair appeared to be threat to take certain action if demands not granted, which, on denial, undoubtedly taken. To my request to be informed wherein my dispatches misleading or misrepresenting, press offered nothing tangible except my conclusions unwarranted. To my charge that they had defied military authority and were amenable to punishment, found they courted martyrdom, which unwise to give. Do not know what engages them now. Willing to remove censorship and let them cable anything.

OTIS.

ADJUTANT-GENERAL'S OFFICE,
Washington, July 20, 1899.

COMMANDING OFFICER, THIRD CAVALRY,
Fort Ethan Allen, Vt.:

It is contemplated sending headquarters and eight troops your regiment for duty in Philippine Islands. Secretary of War directs that you designate the troops, having in view those that had least service in the Spanish-American war.

H. C. CORBIN, *Adjutant-General.*

FORT ETHAN ALLEN, VT., *July 20, 1899.*
(Received 5.07 p. m.)

ADJUTANT-GENERAL, U. S. ARMY,
Washington, D. C.:

Troops A, C, D, E, F, K, L, and M, with Majors Swigert and Steever, are designated. The regiment is in fine shape.

WESSELS, *Lieutenant-Colonel, Commanding.*

GENERAL ORDERS, }   HEADQUARTERS OF THE ARMY,
                     ADJUTANT-GENERAL'S OFFICE,
No. 135.   }   *Washington, July 22, 1899.*

By direction of the Secretary of War, the following changes in stations of troops are hereby ordered:

The headquarters and troops A, C, D, E, F, K, L, and M, Third U. S. Cavalry, are relieved from duty at their present stations, and will proceed by rail, properly equipped for field service, with their horses, baggage, and equipment, to Seattle, Wash., for transportation to the Philippine Islands, to be reported upon arrival to the commanding general, Department of the Pacific.

The band of the regiment will remain on duty at Fort Myer, Va.

Troops B, G, and I are relieved from duty at their present stations, and will proceed with their equipment and such horses as may be left with them to the Department of the East, for assignment at Fort Myer, Va.

Department commanders where troops affected by this order are now stationed will, from the forces remaining at their disposal, arrange for such detachments as may be necessary to guard and protect the public property and buildings left vacant, and will, by concert of action, arrange with the commanding general, Department of California, for the details of the movement.

Those troops designated for service in the Philippine Islands will be filled to the maximum strength of 120 men by transfer of recruits from the San Francisco depot, and the Quartermaster's Department will provide by transfer and purchase sufficient horses to mount the command.

Commanding officers will report their departure from present stations, stating strength of commands and hour of arrival at destination by telegraph to the War Department.

The Quartermaster's Department will provide the necessary transportation and forage, the Subsistence Department suitable travel rations, and the Medical Department medicines and medical attendance en route.

By command of Major-General Miles:

H. C. CORBIN, *Adjutant-General*.

MANILA. (Received July 23, 1899—9.06 a. m.)

AGWAR, *Washington:*

Will use some of 500 mules as pack; can take them from teams; don't want packers sent out; those already sent unsatisfactory.

OTIS.

MANILA. (Received July 23, 1899—9.12 a. m.)

AGWAR, *Washington:*

Can store two months' long and short forage for 800 animals, and in forty days can double capacity. No forage in this country but grass and rice, which fed occasionally, but very expensive. Forage should be sent from San Francisco once or twice each month, thus avoiding having large quantities on hand at any one time.

OTIS.

MANILA. (Received July 23, 1899—6.15 a. m.)

AGWAR, *Washington:*

Campaign against mountain robber bands, Negros, more successful than reported. Byrne with his 70 men killed one-third of the 450 assembled, including their leader, a Spaniard or Spanish mestizo. Pursuit then made by Lieutenant Evans and detachment Sixth Infantry, who killed 3 and captured 1 of the robbers; captured 100 head stock, many spears and bolos, large quantity provisions and destroyed 100 huts. The two casualties in Byrne's fight are Privates David S. Anderson, killed; Albert C. Jerks, slightly wounded; both Company K.

OTIS.

SAN FRANCISCO, CAL., *July 23, 1899.*
(Received 5.52 a. m., July 24.)

ADJUTANT-GENERAL, U. S. Army, *Washington, D. C.:*

Headquarters First and Third Battalions Nineteenth Infantry arrived 6 this evening.

SNYDER, *Commanding.*

MANILA. (Received July 23, 1899—10.25 p. m.)

AGWAR, *Washington:*

Zealandia arrived yesterday; no casualties; health good, exception few cases measles.

OTIS.

ADJUTANT-GENERAL'S OFFICE,
Washington, July 24, 1899.

COMMANDING-GENERAL, DEPARTMENT CALIFORNIA,
San Francisco, Cal.:

Transport *Morgan City* sailed from Manila June 24 with 464 sick. Records do not show you were notified. This repeated to insure provision made for their arrival.

CORBIN, *Adjutant-General.*

MANILA. (Received July 24, 1899—8.02 a. m.)

AGWAR, *Washington:*

Additional casualties: Killed—First California Infantry, at Bulong, Negros, July 1, E, Walter T. Sweenie. Ninth Infantry, near San Luis, 18th, K, Edward B. Webster. Wounded—First California Infantry, at Bulong, Negros, 1st, E, Claude W. Hulf, arm, slight. Twenty-first Infantry, near Morong, 17th, C, Francis Glancey, knee, moderate. Ninth Infantry, near San Luis, 18th, K, Sergt. Herbert L. Hartwick, arm, slight.

OTIS.

MANILA. (Received July 24, 1899—8.07 a. m.)

AGWAR, *Washington:*

Transport *Sheridan* arrived to-day; no casualties.

OTIS.

MANILA. (Received July 24, 1899—9.33 a. m.)

AGWAR, *Washington:*

Following deaths since last report: Dysentery, July 15, Michael Corrigan, K, First Montana. Suicide, July 19, John L. Moore, first lieutenant, L, Fifty-first Iowa. Intestinal tuberculosis, July 20, William L. Murray, C, Twenty-first Infantry. Death from typhoid fever, July 21, Floyd Allen, K, Twenty-first Infantry.

OTIS.

SAN FRANCISCO, CAL., *July 24, 1899.*

ADJUTANT-GENERAL U. S. Army, *Washington, D. C.:*

Morgan City, with sick, just arrived inside heads.

SHAFTER, *Major-General.*

MANILA. (Received July 24, 1899—12.55 a. m.)

AGWAR, *Washington:*

Great desire on part volunteer officers here to raise strictly volunteer regiments; all officers and men to be taken from volunteers here; scheme has appearance of success; can it be tried?

OTIS.

ADJUTANT-GENERAL'S OFFICE,
Washington, July 24, 1899.

OTIS, *Manila:*

Chief Ordnance reports on hand dozen Simms-Dudley dynamite guns. Do you need any? How many?

CORBIN.

ADJUTANT-GENERAL'S OFFICE,
Washington, July 25, 1899.

Otis, Manila:

Has storm abated sufficiently to start volunteers homeward? President anxious this be done with least possible delay. Wives regular officers begging to join husbands with you. Is it advisable to allow any just yet?

CORBIN.

SAN FRANCISCO, CAL., July 25, 1899.
(Received 3.49 p. m.)

ADJUTANT-GENERAL, Washington:

Transport *Tartar* sailed at 12 o'clock last night with Col. Simon Snyder, headquarters, band, Companies B, D, F, G, H, I, K, and M, Nineteenth Infantry, 28 officers, 948 men, 200 rounds ammunition, caliber .30, per man. Attached to regiment 1 assistant surgeon, 3 acting assistants surgeons, 8 Hospital Corps. Chaplain J. H. Sutherland. Second Lieuts. Cassels, Seventh Artillery; Purviance, Fourth Cavalry; Young, Sixth Infantry, and Weeks, Sixteenth Infantry. Lieutenant Lenoir, with 11 men, Signal Corps. Recruits: Artillery, First, 134; Sixth, 3. Cavalry, Fourth, 24. Infantry, Fourth, 2; Sixth, 293; Thirteenth, 12; Fourteenth, 21; Sixteenth, 4; Seventeenth, 76; Eighteenth, 21; Nineteenth, 5; Twentieth, 1; Twenty-second, 2; Twenty-third, 9; Twenty-fourth, 3; Twenty-fifth, 3. Passengers: General Wheeler and aid, Col. C. P. Miller and Captain Horton, quartermasters; Captain Hutchins, commissary, and Major Downey, paymaster.

SHAFTER.

MANILA. (Received July 26, 1899—12.20 a. m.)

AGWAR, Washington:

No supplies imperatively needed by steamer *Indiana*. Want ammunition for Astor Battery if Ordnance Department has secured it.

OTIS.

MANILA. (Received July 26, 1899—1 a. m.)

AGWAR, Washington:

Don't know anything of dynamite field gun mentioned; might experiment with two in opening up ports of islands. Could use, in addition to guns on hand, 12 Gatlings, long barreled, .45 caliber; 12 Colts, Navy automatic, caliber 6 millimeters, with 1,000,000 cartridges for same; 12 Hotchkiss mountain guns, 1.65, with 5,000 shells for same. Use heavy field guns in campaigning swampy country impracticable; request above be sent.

OTIS.

MANILA. (Received July 26, 1899—2.30 a. m.)

AGWAR, Washington:

Reported that mail, First Montana, held San Francisco; regiment desires it sent to Nagasaki for delivery to it when it reaches that place. Same in regard to mail First South Dakota, if held.

OTIS.

MANILA. (Received July 26, 1899—7 a. m.)

AGWAR, Washington:

Following from Cebu to-day: Bandits in Cebu Mountains robbing and impressing people, coast towns. On Monday Lieutenant Moore, with detachment Twenty-third Infantry, while scouting in mountains, fired upon from strongly fortified position; 1 private killed, name not given. No other casualties. Enemy's loss, 5 bandits killed, 7 captured.

OTIS.

MANILA. (Received July 26, 1899—8.32 a. m.)

SECWAR, *Washington:*

Settlement regarding shipping Spanish civil prisoners subject of correspondence; Spanish officials here claim that under sixth article treaty, United States obligated to transport to Spain all prisoners who escaped through aid United States troops, but not Spanish prisoners of war nor civil prisoners whose release effected through Spain's negotiations with insurgents. Hence, all prisoners who have escaped and entered our lines, and all who shall escape, United States must repatriate. To this argument shall reply that article 6 obligates United States to release prisoners through friendly intercession with insurgents, but not to fight for them, as when treaty signed insurgents friendly to us; therefore obligations at an end when friendly intercession tried and failed, but that under discretion conferred will furnish transportation to all prisoners who have thus far escaped from insurgents because of our advance inland; this not because of legal obligation, but through spirit of comity. This action not to be precedent for future action. Shall this position be taken?

OTIS.

WAR DEPARTMENT, *July 26, 1899.*

OTIS, *Manila:*

Your position as to escaped prisoners approved.

MEIKLEJOHN.

MANILA. (Received July 26, 1899—2.35 a. m.)

AGWAR, *Washington:*

Storm has abated. *Sherman* coaled, leaves to-day with all troops of California; *Grant* being coaled, leaves in about four days with all troops North Dakota, Wyoming, and Idaho. Minnesotas preparing to leave on *Sheridan* soon as transport can be unloaded and coaled; other volunteer organizations leave soon as transports are available. Wives and families of officers should not come until later; can not be cared for and officers will be scattered throughout islands; many families which came have departed on account of sickness.

OTIS.

WAR DEPARTMENT, *July 26, 1899.*

OTIS, *Manila:*

President anxious to assist Spanish Government in every practicable way to effect release Spanish prisoners in hands of Filipino insurgents.

Suggest you allow Spanish agent in Philippines to communicate with insurgent chief in cipher, or otherwise, such dispatches as may have been previously communicated to you.

MEIKLEJOHN, *Acting Secwar.*

ADJUTANT-GENERAL'S OFFICE,
Washington, July 26, 1899.

OTIS, *Manila:*

All our enlistments of volunteers were made under act of March 2. Do not understand full significance your cable 24th.

CORBIN.

AFFAIRS IN THE PHILIPPINE ISLANDS. 1041

MANILA. (Received July 27, 1899—3.20 a. m.)
AGWAR, *Washington:*
Sherman sailed midnight, 1,287 officers and men, California; 256 discharged; total passengers, 1,567.

OTIS.

SAN FRANCISCO, CAL., *July 27, 1899.*
ADJUTANT-GENERAL, *Washington, D. C.:*
Transport *Newport* sailed last night with Companies A and E, Nineteenth Infantry, Capt. F. H. French commanding, 4 officers, 238 men; 256 rifles, caliber .30; 230 rounds ammunition per man. Attached, Lieutenant Hartmann and 14 men, absent from first and third battalions of regiment, and 2 men Hospital Corps; Captain Shillock, assistant surgeon; Captain Dapray, Twenty-third Infantry; Lieutenants Fuller, Ordnance Department; Gilbert, Sixth Artillery; Bradford, Seventeenth Infantry; and Hardenbergh, Fourth Infantry; recruits, Infantry, Third, 57; Fourth, 107; Seventeenth, 66; Nineteenth, 5; also 9 Red Cross nurses.

SHAFTER, *Major-General.*

SAN FRANCISCO, CAL., *July 27, 1899.*
(Received 8.12 p. m.)
ADJUTANT-GENERAL, *Washington, D. C.:*
Transport *Ohio* sailed last night with Companies C and L, Nineteenth Infantry, 4 officers, 249 men; 256 rifles, caliber .30; 200 rounds ammunition per man; Major Sweet, Twenty-third Infantry, commanding troops on transport. Captain Collins, Lieutenants Noyes and Kent, Twenty-third; Van Schaick, Fourth; Hagadorn, Sixteenth; and Lang, Ninth Infantry. One acting assistant surgeon, and 3 members Hospital Corps; 1 private, Ninth Infantry; 1 private, Sixth Artillery, and following infantry recruits: Third, 27; Fourth, 2; Ninth, 112; Twelfth, 157; Twentieth, 83; Twenty-first, 17; Twenty-second, 79; also 5 Red Cross nurses.

SHAFTER, *Major-General.*

ADJUTANT-GENERAL'S OFFICE,
Washington, July 27, 1899.
OTIS, *Manila:*
Cable concerning complaints correspondents submitted to the President, who directs this, as other matters, be left to your discretion and judgment. Suggested that all consideration within limits of good of the service be shown.

CORBIN.

ADJUTANT-GENERAL'S OFFICE,
Washington, July 27, 1899.
COMMANDING GENERAL, DEPARTMENT CALIFORNIA,
San Francisco, Cal.:
The transport *Senator* with Pennsylvania Volunteers is due August 1; *Hancock*, July 29 with Nebraska and Utah; *Warren*, August 15, First Colorado; *Sherman*, August 25 with California Volunteers.

The Acting Secretary of War directs that every arrangement be made for their comfort and speedy muster out. He suggests that care be exercised against overcrowding camps.

H. C. CORBIN, *Adjutant-General.*

SAN FRANCISCO, CAL., *July 27, 1899.*
(Received 8.25 p. m.)

ADJUTANT-GENERAL, *Washington, D. C.:*

Every arrangement for comfort of incoming troops has been made. There will be no crowding. Fully prepared to care for them in best possible manner. Troops are satisfied. Criticism of newspapers without foundation.

SHAFTER, *Major-General.*

SAN FRANCISCO, CAL., *July 27, 1899.*
(Received 4.11 p. m.)

ADJUTANT-GENERAL, *Washington, D. C.:*

Transport *Tacoma* left last night with Captain Cress and 39 enlisted men Fourth Cavalry, Acting Asst. Surg. T. A. McCulloch, Veterinary Williamson, 200 horses, 65 rounds caliber .30 ammunition per man.

SHAFTER, *Major-General.*

MANILA. (Received July 27, 1899—7.25 a. m.)

AGWAR, *Washington:*

Following explanatory of cable 24th: Bell's, Wallace's, and Lockett's volunteer regiments being three already organized, officers of the withdrawing volunteer regiments desire permission to raise a fourth by reenlistments of their men, all officers of same to be appointed from withdrawing volunteer regiments now here; say they can raise regiment here if permitted.

OTIS.

ADJUTANT-GENERAL'S OFFICE,
Washington, July 27, 1899.

OTIS, *Manila:*

If the withdrawing volunteers can offer you a regiment, the President authorizes you to accept the same. Should not be a skeleton regiment.

CORBIN.

MANILA. (Received July 28, 1899—1.55 a. m.)

AGWAR, *Washington:*

Hall, with 1,000 men, captured Calamba, important strategic position Laguna de Bay, yesterday, driving out 300 insurgents. Command composed portions Fourth Cavalry, Twenty-first Infantry, Washington Volunteers, transported in launches and cascoes, gunboat accompanying. Casualties: Privates Charles Gleesupp, Fourth, and McDuffy, H, Twenty-first, killed; Corpl. Thomas Totten, G, Fourth, mortally wounded; Privates Michael Sheridan, Herbert Tracey, Napoleon White, K, seriously wounded; Privates Hinds and Plummer, G, and Sanson, C, Fourth; Phillipps, H, Christie and Hollister, D, and Ashland, I, Twenty-first, slightly wounded. Insurgent casualties unknown. Forty Spanish prisoners released. Spanish gunboat in good condition, long sought for in bay, captured. This town the directed objective of Lawton when he captured Santa Cruz and launches in April, but unable to reach town by boats on account of shoal water.

OTIS.

MANILA. (Received July 28, 1899—7.24 a. m.)

AGWAR, *Washington:*

In possession and to be delivered on contract, 68,000 khaki uniforms; troops arriving ask to exchange for them suits brought from United States; not permitted, but satisfactory deduction will be made; suits without facings or reinforced cuffs give best satisfaction.

OTIS.

MANILA. (Received July 28, 1899—8.48 a. m.)

AGWAR, *Washington:*
Transport *Sherman*, with California infantry and heavy artillery, left for San Francisco 26th; infantry, 41 officers, 1,000 enlisted; artillery, 9 officers, 276 enlisted. Infantry left at La Carlota, Negros, Privates Claude W. Huff, Company E; W. J. Clark, G. W. Iverson, Company F; John M. Nooman, Jas. M. Dabney, James F. Brown, Wm. D. Stewart, Company G; H. G. Collins, Company L, sick; private Benj. F. Hurd, Company E, nurse; Private Ralph Coates, Company K, missing in action near Manila, April 6.

OTIS.

ADJUTANT-GENERAL'S OFFICE,
Washington, July 28, 1899.

OTIS, *Manila:*
Shall we send farriers to remain in Manila with the 500 mules and 2,000 extra horses. Each ship will be accompanied by veterinary surgeon. Will you require their services in Manila?

CORBIN.

ADJUTANT-GENERAL'S OFFICE,
Washington, July 28, 1899.

OTIS, *Manila:*
Newport and *Ohio* sailed 26th with four companies Nineteenth Infantry and recruits. Total, 23 officers, 1,228 enlisted; also 14 nurses.

CORBIN.

MANILA. (Received July 28, 1899—7.57 a. m.)

SECWAR, *Washington:*
Spanish authorities given full liberty to negotiate with insurgents for exchange prisoners. Results of negotiations not reported to me. My information, obtained from secret sources, is that insurgents first demanded 35,000 stands of arms with ammunition and $7,000,000, then $6,000,000 and recognition. This reported to Madrid, which has authorized payment of $3,000,000; nothing more. Informed that Spanish officials would soon apply for permision to send vessel north, ostensibly to take provisions to prisoners, but really to discuss with insurgents this Madrid offer.

OTIS.

MANILA. (Received July 29, 1899—2.52 a. m.)

AGWAR, *Washington:*
Should have 2 veterinarians and 25 farriers with horses and mules sent over; difficult to get and keep blacksmiths here.

OTIS.

ADJUTANT-GENERAL'S OFFICE,
Washington, July 29, 1899.

OTIS, *Manila:*
Application for veterinarians, farriers attended to.

CORBIN.

MANILA. (Received July 29, 1899—11.46 p.m.)

AGWAR, *Washington:*
Transport *Valencia* arrived this morning; no casualties.

OTIS.

MANILA. (Received July 30, 1899—6.53 a. m.)

AGWAR, *Washington:*
North Dakota, Wyoming, and Idahos on transport *Grant* ready to depart. Desire to delay until to-morrow to receive monthly pay. Permitted.

OTIS.

MANILA. (Received July 30, 1899.)

SECWAR, *Washington:*
All Filipinos allowed to depart to United States covered by War Department instructions, except in two instances, orphan boys taken by officers.

OTIS.

FORT MASON, SAN FRANCISCO, CAL.,
July 30, 1899. (Received 10.27 p. m.)

HENRY C. CORBIN, *Adjutant-General, Washington, D. C.:*
Hancock arrived this morning. All well.

SHAFTER, *Major-General.*

Hancock had on board First Nebraska Infantry and two batteries of Utah Artillery Volunteers.

MANILA. (Received July 31, 1899—6.20 a. m.)

AGWAR, *Washington:*
Insurgents in considerable force appeared vicinity Calamba yesterday; were punished and driven off by Hall. Our casualties, 1 killed, 7 wounded. Captain Simpson, Sixth Infantry, struck robber band Negros, 28th instant, killing 19; no casualties.

OTIS.

MANILA. (Received July 31, 1899—10.22 a. m.)

ADJUTANT-GENERAL, *Washington:*
Additional casualties, July 26, at Calamba. Killed—Twenty-first Infantry, Company I, Q. M. Sergt. Fred Suppinal. Wounded—Fourth Cavalry, G, James A. Reese, leg, severe. First Washington Infantry, H, Fred. L. Ballau, shoulder, slight. Twenty-first Infantry, D, Peter Christie, temple, severe; F, Charles Grottendick, abdomen, severe; I, Corpl. Godwin J. Lane, back, severe; H. William H. Phillips, hand, slight. July 27, at San Fernando, Third Artillery, L. J. Virger, ear, slight.

OTIS.

MANILA. (Received July 31, 1899—12.17 p. m.)

AGWAR, *Washington:*
Following deaths have occurred since last report: Gunshot wound, accidental—May 6, Henry Lehmay, Third Infantry. Baccabulos—June 15, at Carlota, Negros, Charles Gardinell, F, First California. Tubercular meningitis—June 23, Frank J.

Murray, A, First California. Diarrhea—July 11, Frank Bohner, M, Twenty-third Infantry. July 22, Wesley Lytle, Wyoming Infantry. Deaths from typhoid fever—Peter Manz, Third Infantry, Company F. July 25, John F. Walker, corporal, G, Fifty-first Iowa. Shot, accidental—July 22, James McGuire, quartermaster-sergeant, Sixteenth Infantry, Company B. Syncope—Christian Bosold, M, Seventeenth Infantry. Dysentery—John J. Boman, G, First California. July 24, Thomas Brathor, sergeant Ninth Infantry, Company B. Peritonitis—Wm. Beauchene, F, First Idaho. Anæmia—July 23, Wm. H. Nichols, Fourth Infantry, Company E. Stabbed by natives—July 26, John M. Gamble, Third Artillery, Battery K. Enteritis—July 27, George Greller, Twelfth Infanty, Company A.

OTIS.

MANILA. (Received July 31, 1899—10.21 p. m.)

AGWAR, *Washington:*

Consul, Nagasaki, reports death, in hospital, Private Richard H. Ralph, B, Utah Artillery. Will pay interment bill and give instructions as to disposition of effects.

OTIS.

MANILA. (Received August 1, 1899—12.35 a. m.)

AGWAR, *Washington:*

Transport *Grant* sailed yesterday, 78 officers, 8 citizens, 1,353 soldiers and discharged men, Wyoming, North Dakota, and Idaho organizations; left behind about 200 discharged men; good many have reenlisted; only sick soldier left, Corpl. Frank Gere, H, Wyoming. Minnesota regiment and discharged men next transport in very few days.

OTIS.

MANILA. (Received August 1, 1899—2.10 a. m.)

AGWAR, *Washington:*

Transport *Pennsylvania* arrived this morning; no casualties.

OTIS.

MANILA. (Received August 1, 1899—7.48 a. m.)

AGWAR, *Washington:*

Number available sites between Bacoor and Cavite well protected, permitting building of wharves to deep water—about 24 feet. Price depends upon vicinity to villages, and now fluctuating.

OTIS.

ADJUTANT-GENERAL'S OFFICE,
Washington, August 1, 1899.

OTIS, *Manila:*

Secwar suggests expedite in every way possible sailing of transports from Manila, or transportation will be short at San Francisco to get troops to you.

CORBIN.

MANILA. (Received August 2, 1899—3.18 a. m.)

SECWAR, *Washington:*

Referring dispatch 28th July concerning Spanish prisoners, officials have applied as therein inexpedient. Have granted pass same commissioners to take vessel to San Fernando, northwestern Luzon, with provisions and clothing for prisoners and if opportunity permits to further negotiate for their release. Permission given to return overland, if desired. Believe Madrid offer will be submitted. If accepted and money paid, will enable insurgents to float loan contemplated.

OTIS.

ADJUTANT-GENERAL'S OFFICE,
Washington, August 2, 1899.

OTIS, Manila:
Is it to be understood by your cable to Secwar that you oppose Spanish commissioners offering or paying any money to the insurgents?

CORBIN.

MANILA. (Received August 2, 1899—10.12 a. m.)

AGWAR, Washington:
Additional casualties: Killed—Twenty-first Infantry, near Calamba, July 26, H, William A. Renned. Thirteenth, C, William Murphy; K, Corpl. Charles Henderson. Wounded—Fourth Cavalry, 26th, C, Edward Oberhausen, forearm, slight; 30th, John McGregor, knee, severe. First Washington Infantry, C, Spawn Woodruff, neck, slight. Twenty-first Infantry, Second Lieut. James M. Love, elbow, severe; K, Charles W. Winters, thigh, moderate.

OTIS.

ADJUTANT-GENERAL'S OFFICE,
Washington, August 2, 1899.

OTIS, Manila:
Strength of total enlisted desired; regulars and volunteers separately.

CORBIN.

SAN FRANCISCO, CAL., August 2, 1899.
(Received 8.45 p. m.)

ADJUTANT-GENERAL, Washington, D. C.:
Relief arrived this morning.

SHAFTER, Major-General.

SAN FRANCISCO, CAL., August 2, 1899.
(Received 11.35 p. m.)

ADJUTANT-GENERAL, Washington, D. C.:
Transport *Senator* arrived yesterday carrying Tenth Pennsylvania, 33 officers, 708 enlisted men; Captain Jennings, Utah Artillery; Capt. A. B. Dyer, Sixth Artillery; Lieuts. H. M. Merriam, Third Artillery; Fleming, Sixth Artillery, and Weigle, First Washington Volunteers; 9 privates Hospital Corps; 1 discharged soldier.

SHAFTER, Major-General.

MANILA. (Received August 3, 1899—7.24 a. m.)

AGWAR, Washington:
Four transports in harbor; cargoes discharged. *Pennsylvania* nearly coaled; takes on recruits for organizations in southern waters; leaves 6th instant and returns all men discharged under General Orders, No. 40. *Sheridan* being coaled, leaves for San Francisco 8th instant with Minnesota and South Dakota troops. *Valencia* and *Zealandia* require 1,200 tons coal; time of sailing indefinite as approaching typhoon interferes.

OTIS.

MANILA. (Received August 3, 1899—7.50 a. m.)

ADJUTANT-GENERAL, Washington:
Payment of money for Spanish prisoners supplies insurgents with funds to prolong war, and thus far I have opposed. Condition of prisoners arouses humanitarian

sentiment of world and question is, Should United States accept additional burdens that release may be effected? Supreme authority should determine this. Have no official information that Spain intends to pay money, but believe such to be the fact.

OTIS.

MANILA. (Received August 3, 1899—12.17 p. m.)

AGWAR, *Washington:*

* * * Scheme to raise additional volunteer regiment abandoned, as considered impossible to secure full regiment here.

OTIS.

ADJUTANT-GENERAL'S OFFICE,
Washington, August 3, 1899.

OTIS, *Manila:*

Secwar directs me inform you six of the ten regiments volunteers here are organized; other four well under way. They are well officered and many of the men have had service. They are being drilled in target practice and outpost duty. They will at least be available at once for garrison duty, enabling you to hold towns taken and have regulars for active campaign work.

It is expected to begin sending them on return of *Grant, Sherman,* and *Sheridan.*

CORBIN.

MANILA. (Received August 4, 1899—8.48 a. m.)

AGWAR, *Washington:*

What troops en route on transport *Tartar;* reported sailed July 24?

OTIS.

ADJUTANT-GENERAL'S OFFICE,
Washington, August 4, 1899.

OTIS, *Manila:*

Tartar sailed 25th, headquarters, B, D, F, G, I, K, and M, Nineteenth Infantry, and recruits, 41 officers and 1,163 enlisted.

CORBIN.

MANILA. (Received August 4, 1899—8.50 p. m.)

AGWAR, *Washington:*

Total strength, enlisted, commissioned, regulars, volunteers: Cavalry, Fourth, commissioned 26, enlisted 1,056; Nevada, commissioned 3, enlisted 83. Artillery, First, commissioned 4, enlisted 116; Third, commissioned 14, enlisted 801; Fourth, commissioned 5, enlisted 118; Fifth, commissioned 4, enlisted 115; Sixth, commissioned 32, enlisted 1,193. Battalion Engineers, commissioned 3, enlisted 126. Infantry, Third, commissioned 47, enlisted 1,209; Fourth, commissioned 44, enlisted, 1,191; Sixth, commissioned 48, enlisted 1,353; Ninth, commissioned 43, enlisted 1,271; Twelfth, commissioned 46, enlisted 1,303; Thirteenth, commissioned 44, enlisted 1,304; Fourteenth, commissioned 42, enlisted 769; Sixteenth, commissioned, 46, enlisted, 1,332; Seventeenth, commissioned 47, enlisted 1,271; Eighteenth, commissioned 45, enlisted 1,338; Twentieth, commissioned 45, enlisted 1,250; Twenty first, commissioned 44, 1,330 enlisted; Twenty-second, commissioned 45, enlisted 1,245; Twenty-third, commissioned 45, enlisted 1,213; Twenty-fourth, commissioned 10, enlisted 429; Twenty-fifth, commissioned 21, enlisted 1,022; Thirty-sixth, commissioned 38, enlisted 490; Thirty-seventh, commissioned 26, enlisted 462; Fifty-first Iowa, commissioned 47, enlisted 913; Twentieth Kansas, commissioned 46, enlisted 908; Thirteenth Minnesota, commissioned 46, enlisted 991; First Tennessee, commissioned 32, enlisted 753; First Montana, 45 commissioned, 764 enlisted; First South Dakota, 46 commissioned, 820 enlisted; First Washington, 44 commissioned, 914 enlisted. Total strength, regulars, commissioned, 812; enlisted, 23,307. Total strength, volunteers, commissioned, 309; enlisted, 6,146.

OTIS.

MANILA. (Received August 6, 1899—7.40 a. m.)

AGWAR, *Washington:*

Request 5,000 sets infantry equipments complete, except blanket bags.

OTIS.

MANILA. (Received August 6, 1899—9.22 a. m.)

AGWAR, *Washington:*

Following deaths since last weekly report: Cause unknown—April 6, Ralph C, Coates, K, First California. Drowned—July 14, John Mullaney, corporal in Twenty-first Infantry; William H. Murray, K, Twenty-first Infantry. August 3, Albert Roos, D, Sixteenth Infantry. Typhoid fever—July 14, Richard H. Ralph, B, Utah Artillery, on *Hancock*, at Nagasaki. Dysentery—July 12, Christian R. Spressor, corporal, K, Eighteenth Infantry. July 29, William O. Rasmunson, corporal, F, Twelfth Infantry. July 29, Levi W. Mellingerm, corporal, F, Thirteenth Infantry. August 4, Edward L. Bedell, A, Twenty-first Infantry. Malarial fever—July 25, James M. Dabney, G, First California. July 20, John Garvey, L, Ninth Infantry. August 2, Thomas J. Burchill, G, Twenty-second Infantry. From wounds in action—July 14, Michael Walsh, H, Sixth Infantry. July 26, Thomas Totten, L, Fourth Cavalry. July 31, Herbert S. Tracy, K, Twenty-first Infantry. Meningitis—July 30, Arthur Morse, D, Eighteenth Infantry. Pulmonary tuberculosis—July 31, James McCarron, corporal, B, Twenty-first Infantry. Pneumonia—July 31, Thomas Conway, M, Twelfth Infantry. Volvulus ileocæeum—August 1, James McHugh, M, Twelfth Infantry. Suicide—August 2, Marvin R. McHenry, H, Fourteenth Infantry. Appendicitis—August 3, Clarence W. Mason, Band, Fifty-first Iowa.

OTIS.

ADJUTANT-GENERAL'S OFFICE,
Washington, August 7, 1899.

OTIS, *Manila:*

There will be sent from Seattle and Tacoma, about August 20, 8 troops Third Regiment of Cavalry, with 1,050 of the horses, 500 mules, 100 wagons and harness, 100 aparejos, 10 citizen farriers. Later, same ports, 400 of the 2,000 horses, in accordance with your request, which are being bought. There also will be sent in the same ship 800,000 feet of the 1,200,000 feet lumber, requests by Pope, and a proportionate quantity of corrugated iron roofing. Arrangements completed to load in the same vessel carrying animals sufficient forage feed en route and last them about three months after arrival Manila. About 580 paulins, large size, will be sent in the same ship, in order to assist protecting forage. Will this be sufficient for present requirements? Fifty wagons and harness, 200 team mules, 126 pack mules, with equipment of aparejos and packers, 15 citizen farriers, and remainder of 2,000 horses will be sent from San Francisco, from time to time, probably within next forty days, with two or three months' forage supply. We propose sending in the same vessel carrying these animals 500 additional paulins, in order to protect forage. The problem of forage supply for a large number of animals going over is of the utmost importance, and until other arrangements can be made considerable supply will be sent at one time on animal vessels in order to complete their loading. When they arrive will be 5,000 to feed. Will necessitate large storage capacity.

CORBIN.

ADJUTANT-GENERAL'S OFFICE,
Washington, August 7, 1899.

Otis, *Manila:*

Following transports sailing: *Morgan City*, August 8; *Sydney* and *Senator*, one 9th and other 18th; *St. Paul* from Seattle, 20th, with 400 marines and recruits. Infantry equipments asked for in cable yesterday ordered. Are any further stores or supplies specially required?

CORBIN.

MANILA. (Received August 8, 1899—3.55 a. m.)

Agwar, *Washington:*

Three days' typhoon, rendering work on bay impossible, passed 6th instant. Transport *Pennsylvania* leaves Iloilo, Cebu, Jolo, this evening. *Sheridan* with Minnesotas, South Dakotas, and discharged men for San Francisco 11th instant. *Valencia*, *Zealandia*, when coaled, requiring ten days' good weather, leave with Montanas and discharged men. Suggest portion of transports coal at Nagasaki, both coming and returning, expedite business here where facilities for loading and unloading vessels primitive.

OTIS.

ADJUTANT-GENERAL'S OFFICE,
Washington, August 8, 1899.

Otis, *Manila:*

Refer to your cable of 8th, C. P. Miller selected apparatus to load 600 tons coal per day to be used Manila. Now en route.

CORBIN.

WAR DEPARTMENT, *August 8, 1899—4.20 p. m.*

Otis, *Manila:*

We can not consent to payment to insurgents of $3,000,000, or any sum sufficient to give them material aid, and must prevent if possible. What information have you of number and location of Spanish prisoners held by insurgents? When would it be practicable to send expedition for their release? Following confidential telegram received from Minister Storer, Madrid: Have been informed by minister for foreign affairs, confidentially, what was the result attempted, cipher negotiations for Philippine Island prisoners. Captors demand 6,000,000 Spanish dollars, which has been refused once for all.

ROOT, *Secwar.*

MANILA. (Received August 9, 1899—4.17 a. m.)

Agwar, *Washington:*

MacArthur with 4,000 men attacked insurgent army, 6,000 strong, concentrated around San Fernando 5.15 this morning. At 10 o'clock a. m. had driven it 5 miles in direction of Angeles. Casualties few. Attack ordered for 7th instant, but rain did not permit movement; railway from Angeles north badly washed by unprecedented floods of last six weeks beyond ability of insurgents to repair.

OTIS.

ADJUTANT-GENERAL'S OFFICE,
Washington, August 9, 1899.

Otis, *Manila:*

Acting Secretary of War has given instructions for ships coming to you to coal at Nagasaki. You will give same from your end of line until better facilities obtain at Manila.

CORBIN.

ADJUTANT-GENERAL'S OFFICE,
Washington, August 9, 1899.

OTIS, *Manila:*
Five thousand sets infantry equipments sent you June 26. Five thousand more, except blanket bags, ordered to be sent you from Benicia 7th instant.

CORBIN.

MANILA. (Received August 10, 1899—1.35 a. m.)
AGWAR, *Washington:*
MacArthur's movement yesterday very successful; serves to clear country rear and left and right of insurgents; has advanced north to Calulet, 6 miles from San Fernando, whence he is now reconnoitering; his casualties, 5 killed, 29 wounded; officers wounded, Major Braden, Captain Abernethy, Thirty-sixth Volunteers, leg and arm, moderate; Lieutenant Williams, Fifty-first Iowa, thigh, moderate. These troops operated to left and rear toward Santa Rita. McArthur's advance under Wheaton Liscum consists Ninth, Twelfth, Seventeenth, part of Twenty-second regiments, and portion Fifty-first Iowa; movement very difficult on account of mud and surface water. MacArthur reports insurgent loss 100 killed some 300 wounded. They were rapidly driven northward and last evening apparently abandoned Porac line where they blew up power works. Success of contemplated movements in that direction will greatly improve conditions.

OTIS.

ADJUTANT-GENERAL'S OFFICE,
Washington, August 10, 1899.

OTIS, *Manila:*
Secretary of War desires timely requisition for emergency rations should occasion for use arise.

CORBIN

MANILA. (Received August 10, 1899—10.53 a. m.)
SECRETARY OF WAR, *Washington:*
Reported that insurgents hold 2,000 Spanish prisoners, Abra province, northern Luzon; about 2,000 others scattered over Luzon. Can send troops north to relieve, latter part September. Minister Storer's dispatch misleading as to Madrid action taken. Madrid instructs Commission here to secure permission to take vessel, Spanish flag, to northern Luzon and ransom prisoners individually, promising insurgents full, final compliance with their demands; thus propose to allay suspicion Americans, and, as said, throw them off track. Vessel flying other than American flag will not be permitted to enter other than open ports, and Spanish application, now before me, will be denied. Delay in negotiations between Spain and insurgents, inspired latter with belief that their recognition seriously considered in Europe and they have issued decree closing Philippine port to American vessels, inviting those of foreign nations. This gratifying as enable us to resist importunities of resident merchants, and Luzon ports will be closed at once. Good condition to do so, as large stock of hemp and tobacco recently brought in, and tobacco house, Manila, employing large native force, can continue business. Policy adopted by insurgents mounted to ——— interests and gives us advantage. They have destroyed one merchant vessel north and may destroy others, but nearly all vessels in. Movements of our troops north will interfere with their international speculations.

OTIS.

MANILA. (Received August 10, 1899—3.35 a. m.)

ADJUTANT-GENERAL, *Washington:*

Captured letters, high insurgent authority, exhorting inhabitants to hold out a little longer; that European recognition will be granted by August 31, and that present United States administration will be overthrown.

OTIS.

MANILA. (Received August 11, 1899—10.05 a. m.)

AGWAR, *Washington:*

City of Para arrived; Private Cosley Reed, A, Twenty-fourth, died at sea. *Sheridan* sails to-day.

OTIS.

MANILA. (Received August 11, 1899—10.09 a. m.)

AGWAR, *Washington:*

MacArthur has taken possession Santa Rita; reconnoitered Porac, Angeles, and other points. Insurgents driven north. One casualty yesterday; none to-day. Condition roads makes movement troops difficult, but considered necessary to open up this section of country, as it virtually gives control of province of Bataan and relieves inhabitants there.

OTIS.

ADJUTANT-GENERAL'S OFFICE,
Washington, August 12, 1899—5.40 p. m.

OTIS, *Manila:*

Secretary of War specially desires to know what, with all the light you now have, you consider an undoubtedly adequate force for complete suppression of insurrection during the coming dry season. In view of the impatience of the public, which may effect legislative provision for conduct of war, rapid and thorough action is important. The Secretary would rather err on the safe side in sending too many troops than too few. He desires to know what conclusion you reach after full consultation with your general officers as to forces required, especially of cavalry.

CORBIN.

MANILA. (Received August 12, 1899—10.45 p. m.)

ADJUTANT-GENERAL, *Washington:*

Emergency rations regarded not suitable to Tropics, owing to meat component being all bacon and liability pea meal to heat and sour. Ration adopted satisfactory; will order 100,000 emergency rations for trial.

OTIS.

MANILA. (Received August 13, 1899—12.37 a. m.)

AGWAR, *Washington:*

Additional casualties: Killed—August 9, Thirty-sixth Infantry, near San Fernando, Corpls. Louis L. Wagner; M, Andrew Wilson. Wounded—Seventeenth Infantry, D, Nicholas J. Nolan, chest, very severe; John J. Woods, forearm, moderate; Celestine Bottino, elbow, severe; G, John Hammel, arm, severe; H, Edward Woods, thigh, severe; John W. Raymond, thigh, slight. Twelfth Infantry, H, Corpl. Albert Beyrow, shoulder, slight. Fifty-first Iowa Infantry, C, Peter J. Harriff, chest, severe. Thirty-sixth Infantry, Maj. John Q. A. Braden, knee, slight; Capt. Robert F. Abernethy, forearm, slight; C, Matthew E. Hann, arm, severe; D, James F. Higgins, thigh, slight; M, Michael McCarthy, knee, slight; John Ray, knee, slight. Twenty-fourth Infantry, at Deposito, E, Corpl. Lewis H. Price, foot, moderate. 11th, Fourth Infantry, near Novaleta, B, Clem Woughtel, leg, slight.

OTIS.

MANILA. (Received August 13, 1899—10.22 a. m.)

AGWAR, *Washington:*

Following deaths since last report: Drowned—July 20, Patrick Duffy, Corpl. H, Twenty-first Infantry; William Stafford, H, Twenty-first Infantry; August 7, Albert Pernitzki, A, Twenty-first Infantry. Dysentery, 6th, Thomas Maloney, E, Seventeenth Infantry; 8th, Walter E. Hutchison, A, Fifty-first Iowa; Frederick S. Batey, B, Twelfth Infantry. Typhoid fever, 1st, William Kunzig, B, Sixth Infantry; 8th, Rodney Clark, B, Fifty-first Iowa; 11th, Frank J. Halfry, E, Twelfth Infantry. Arterial sclerosis, 6th, Joseph Walker; M, Fourth Cavalry. Anæmia, Alvin E. Alder, Corpl. G, Third Infantry. Erysipelas, Gilbert Smith, E, Twenty-fourth Infantry. Enteritis, 9th, Emil Jessien, K, Third Artillery. From wounds in action, 11th Nicholas J. Nolan, D, Seventeenth Infantry.

OTIS.

MANILA. (Received August 14, 1899—12.55 p. m.)

AGWAR, *Washington:*

Additional casualties: Killed—Sixth Infantry, at Bobon, Negros, July 19, K, David S. Anderson; 30th, K, Vincent Seger. Near San Isidro, Negros, John Heichener. Twenty-third Infantry, near Pardo, Cebu, 24th, K, Robert H. Moore. Seventeenth Infantry, near San Fernando, Luzon, August 9, D, Corpl. Samuel T. Bollinger; Ninth Infantry, D, Corpl. George S. Welles; H, Charles J. Lavier, jr. Fourth Infantry, near Novaleta, 11th, I, Frank Lampman. Twenty-second Infantry, near San Luis, 12th, D, Ira W. Cox. Twenty-first Infantry, near Mariquina, B, Walling Collins; G, John A. Brennan. Twenty-fourth Infantry, E, James Noid; Fourth Cavalry, B, Sergts. James Robertson; F, Nick Sebilus. Wounded—Twenty-first Infantry, at Calamba, July 30, C, Corpl. Alexander Foster, chest, severe. Fifty-first Iowa, near San Fernando, August 9, M, Harry P. Brenholts, leg, severe. Twenty-first Infantry, near Mariquina, August 12, L, Second Lieut. Marion Merle Weeks, abdomen, moderate; E, Corpl. Louis Blood, thigh, moderate; B, First Sergt. George T. Rollins, arm, severe; Charles Wallington, leg, severe; G, James J. Canaly, thigh, moderate; Frank D. Vondle, arm, slight; E, George W. Howard, thigh, severe; Twenty-fourth Infantry, E, Samuel Wabster, chest, severe; Clarence Rucker, forearm, moderate; G, John Cecil, thigh, slight; Corpl. Willis Howe, thigh, moderate; Fourth Cavalry, B, Charles Jabelmann, arm, moderate.

OTIS.

ADJUTANT-GENERAL'S OFFICE,
Washington, August 14, 1899.

OTIS, *Manila:*

Apparatus to load 600 tons daily Manila Harbor en route. In addition, do you need steam collier to send coal other points? Vessel offered can load 800 tons daily, reach Manila in about three months. If collier actually needed can you buy, Manila, and what will it cost you?

CORBIN.

MANILA. (Received August 14, 1899—8.10 p. m.)

ADJUTANT-GENERAL, *Washington:*

Estimating necessary force, question enter, which depends for solution upon success negotiations, being conducted by J. C. Bates, Jolo. Should natives of Jolo

Archipelago and Mindanao become actively hostile, 15,000 men would be required in extreme southern waters. Have reason to believe that negotiations will be successful. Have consulted general officers repeatedly on force required in Philippines; none place it higher than 50,000 effectives. I estimate force here and being organized at 40,000 effectives for the field, after deducting probable ratios of sick and disabled. The force fully adequate for Luzon, central islands, and light garrisons of extreme south. With present force could send column through Luzon successfully, but inhabitants, when cities taken, appeal for permanent protection against returning insurgents. This scatters troops over large extent territory. To meet possible contingencies and demands of people United States that larger force be sent here, request that fifteen volunteer regiments in addition to those now being organized, be raised and sent to Philippines for garrison purposes. We are now exchanging armies and shipping troops as fast as received; necessarily great labor, with facilities at hand and primitive condition of harbors. The Third, Fourth, and Lockett's regiment (cavalry), will give sufficient mounted troops, as when country opens can secure ponies and mount infantry when necessary. American horses require American forage. United States overestimates insurgents' armed strength and cohesion. When Tagalos overpowered organized armed opposition will cease. Length of war depends upon celerity with which troops sent here. Active operations will not await return dry season, as that three months in future.

OTIS.

MANILA. (Received August 15, 1899—6.45 a. m.)
ADJUTANT-GENERAL, *Washington:*

Declined, 10th instant, to permit Spanish vessel to overload northern Luzon. Request resubmitted 12th instant, based on dictates humanity, still withheld, and meantime Madrid cabled that Spanish authorities here must not attempt anything not approved by home Government. To which Commission replied that Government should state wishes, otherwise voyage north useless and insurgents will charge their proposition not responded to. Government should state if willing to offer three million and promise payment certain bonds; that if commissioner obliged to return to Manila for information will excite suspicion Americans. To which Madrid replied that Commission must not make final agreement, but present to Madrid desire of insurgents; that in this affair it wishes to act in accord with and with frankness toward American Government. Now believe that request to send out Spanish vessel will be withdrawn.

OTIS.

MANILA. (Received August 16, 1899—6.45 a. m.)
AGWAR, *Washington:*

Do not need steam collier; can contract for delivery of coal in other ports as well as Manila. Need 3 lighters, capacity 200 tons, 2 for Manila, 1 for Iloilo Will cost, delivered here within eight and ten months, $22,000 gold each. Have been considering terms of bid received.

OTIS.

MANILA. (Received August 16, 1899—10.23 a. m.)
AGWAR, *Washington:*

MacArthur's troops occupy country from Candaba to point near Angeles, thence toward Porac, taking within his line Santa Rita, Guagua, Bacolor. Colonel Smith, with ten companies Twefth Infantry and two guns First Artillery, attacked to-day enemy in intrenchments, outskirts Angeles, estimated at 2,500, driving them north and inflicting upon them reported loss of 200 killed and wounded; our loss 2 killed, 12 wounded. On 11th instant, General Young's troops, consisting detachments Fourth Cavalry, Twenty-first, Twenty-fourth, and Twenty-fifth Infantry, drove insurgents northeast of Manila, through Maraquina, San Mateo, into mountains, returning following day. Column of insurgents, 500 strong, descending road east of Baliuag for the purpose of taking railway, driven by our Baliuag and Quingua troops and routed yesterday. This force in full retreat northward, carrying number of their wounded officers. Angeles will be permanently occupied at once.

OTIS.

ADJUTANT-GENERAL'S OFFICE,
Washington, August 16, 1899.

OTIS, *Manila:*

How many of Thirteenth Minnesota sailed? How many reenlisted and how many left sick at Manila?

CORBIN.

ADJUTANT-GENERAL'S OFFICE,
Washington, August 16, 1899.

OTIS, *Manila:*

Two thousand horses purchased by Quartermaster-General. This in addition to Third Cavalry horses. What additional do you require in way of transportation animals? Eight hundred are being loaded now.

CORBIN.

ADJUTANT-GENERAL'S OFFICE,
Washington, August 16, 1899.

COMMANDING GENERAL, DEPARTMENT OF CALIFORNIA,
San Francisco, Cal.:

State Department is informed that the Japanese Government authorizes landing of animals at Kobe for rest as well as at Nagasaki. Give instructions to officers in charge of transports to this effect so they can show them to the officials at Kobe.

CORBIN.

MANILA. (Received August 17, 1899—2.50 a. m.)

AGWAR, *Washington:*

Forty-one officers, 946 men, Minnesotas, sailed on *Sheridan*. Remained, mostly with intention of reenlisting, 2 officers, 41 men. One enlisted man left sick in hospital. Private W. J. Worthington, H, disappeared, Marilao; Joseph Walsh, L, Malibon, June 7 and 9; supposed to be in hands insurgents.

OTIS.

MANILA. (Received August 17, 1899—2.52 a. m.)

AGWAR, *Washington:*

The horses purchased in addition to those enumerated in your dispatch sufficient; no more transportation animals than those heretofore requested needed.

OTIS.

SAN FRANCISCO, CAL., *August 17, 1899.*
(Received 7 27 p. m.)

ADJUTANT-GENERAL, *Washington:*
* * * *Warren* arrived last night. Full report of military passengers will be telegraphed later.

SHAFTER, *Major-General.*

SAN FRANCISCO, CAL., *August 17, 1899.*
(Received 9.08 p. m.)

ADJUTANT-GENERAL, *Washington, D. C.:*
Following military passengers arrived on transport *Warren:* First Colorado, 46 officers, 937 enlisted men. * * *

SHAFTER, *Major-General.*

ADJUTANT-GENERAL'S OFFICE,
Washington, August 17, 1899.

OTIS, *Manila:*
Reliable information has been received of insurgents taking measures to obtain rapid-fire guns in Europe. Take every precaution to prevent such reaching the hands of the insurgents.
By order Secwar:

CORBIN.

MANILA. (Received August 18, 1899—5.22 a. m.)

AGWAR, *Washington:*
Conemaugh, 261 horses, arrived this morning.

OTIS.

MANILA. (Received August 18, 1899—8.35 a. m.)

AGWAR, *Washington:*
Additional casualties: Killed—near San Fernando, Ninth Infantry, August 9, K, William N. Munson. Near Bustos, Third Infantry, 14th, F, Charles A. Brooks. Wounded—near San Fernando, Twelfth Infantry, 9th, F, Corpl. William Barnes, arm, slight; M, George Plummer, abdomen, severe; Fifty-first Iowa, E, Second Lieut. Lamont A Williams, leg, severe; Twenty-second Infantry, H, William Kneisler, leg, moderate; Seventeenth Infantry, H, Corpl. Samuel H. Lamb, thigh, severe; 10th, E, William Rupel, chest, moderate; 13th, G, George W. Sharp, forearm, moderate; Ninth Infantry, 9th, D, James Linton, nates, slight; G, George H. B. Strauch, neck, severe. At Angeles, C, Richard E. Keenan, leg, severe; 13th, I, Henry P. Shierloh, foot, moderate. At Santa Rita, 12th, E, James Brown, forearm, slight. Near San Mateo, Twenty-fourth Infantry, E, Louden Ware, head, slight. Near Quingua, Third Infantry, 13th, B, William Foster, leg, severe. At Angeles, First Artillery, E, William Gartz, leg, moderate.

OTIS.

ADJUTANT-GENERAL'S OFFICE,
Washington, August 18, 1899.

OTIS, *Manila:*
Fix the responsibility for grounding of *Hooker.*

CORBIN.

MANILA. (Received August 19, 1899—10.48 p. m.)

AGWAR, *Washington:*

First Lieut. Alfred W. Drew, Twelfth Infantry, instantly killed and First Lieut. Willis Uline, same regiment, severely wounded yesterday in attack on insurgents, vicinity Angeles, by two companies Twelfth Infantry; no other casualties; enemy routed.

OTIS.

GENERAL ORDERS, }   HEADQUARTERS OF THE ARMY,
No. 151.   ADJUTANT-GENERAL'S OFFICE,
                         Washington, August 19, 1899.

By direction of the Secretary of War, the following changes in station of troops are hereby announced:

The Twenty-sixth, Twenty-seventh, Thirty-first, and Thirty-fourth Regiments Infantry, U. S. Volunteers, are hereby relieved from duty at their present stations and will proceed by rail to San Francisco, Cal., for embarkation at that point for the Philippine Islands, to be reported upon arrival to the commanding general, Department of the Pacific. Mounted officers may take their horses. The regiments will be fully armed and equipped and supplied with 200 rounds of ammunition per man and proper tentage. Personal baggage will be limited to clothing actually necessary for immediate field service.

Department commanders where troops affected by this order are now stationed will by concert of action arrange with commanding general, Department of California, for details of movement, and report hour of departure and strength of commands by telegraph to the War Department.

The quartermaster's department will provide the necessary transportation, the subsistence department suitable travel rations, and the medical department proper medical attendance and supplies.

By command of Major-General Miles:

H. C. CORBIN, *Adjutant-General.*

MANILA. (Received August 20, 1899—7.01 a. m.)

AGWAR, *Washington:*

Following deaths since last report: Tetanus, August 5, Cosley Reed, A, Twenty-fourth Infantry. Phthisis, 14th, Allie W. Lord, E, Twelfth Infantry. Typhoid fever, 15th, Second Lieut. Joseph B. Morse, I, Ninth Infantry. Acute dysentery, 15th, John Smith, K, First Washington; 17th, William Harrison, K, Thirteenth Infantry; 18th, John H. Dunn, D, Fourth Infantry. Abscess of liver, 17th, Adolph M. Kreitzer, F, Sixth Artillery. General arterio-sclerosis, 17th, John A. Martin, H, Thirty-sixth Infantry. Nephritis, 17th, Francis C. Miller, I, Twenty-first Infantry.

OTIS.

MANILA. (Received August 20, 1899.)

AGWAR, *Washington:*

Lieutenant Cole, Sixth Infantry, 80 men, attacked and routed 100 of enemy, entrenched at Tibuan, Negros Mountains, having 3 men slightly wounded; enemy left in entrenchments 19 dead, 6 rifles, all reserve ammunition; supposed to be armed Tagalos who few days since crossed from Panay in small boats.

OTIS.

SAN FRANCISCO, CAL., *August 21, 1899.*
(Received 5.50 p. m.)

ADJUTANT-GENERAL, *Washington, D. C.:*

Transport *Garonne* left Seattle with horses Third Cavalry 9 p. m. last night, Lieutenants Suplee and Morrison, 1 medical officer, 1 hospital steward, 1 veterinary surgeon, 1 farrier, 75 enlisted men, 389 horses.

SHAFTER, *Major-General.*

MANILA. (Received August 22, 1899—12.30 a. m.)

AGWAR, *Washington:*

Tartar arrived yesterday; all well; no deaths.

OTIS.

MANILA. (Received August 22, 1899—2.21 a. m.)

AGWAR, *Washington:*

Sailing *Zealandia* and *Valencia* with Montana and discharged men on board, arrested by prevailing typhoon; leave to-day.

OTIS.

MANILA. (Received August 22, 1899—4.25 a. m.)

AGWAR, *Washington:*

Additional casualties: Killed near Angeles—Twelfth Infantry, August 16, C, Musician Edwin S. Boatwright, John P. Brooks; D, Edward E. Householder; 19th, I, First Lieut. Alfred W. Drew. Wounded, at San Fernando—Hospital Corps, 9th, George W. Greenwell, head, moderate; Thirty-sixth Infantry, K, John G. Tahl, foot, slight. Twenty-second Infantry, near San Luis, 12th, D, James H. O'Connell, leg, slight. Twelfth Infantry near Angeles, 16th, First Lieut. Wm. H. Williams, eye, severe; B, Charles E. Knighton, arm, slight; C, Corpl. Frank J. Raft, foot, slight; Henry Malchus, elbow, severe; Fred P. Steiger, leg, moderate; D, Carl Hannigs, hand, severe; Jordon Rogers, leg, slight; Ansel T. Ware, arm, moderate H, William I. Messenheimer, arm, moderate; L, Charles H. Hane, thigh, moderate; Julius Weber, knee, moderate; M, Albert Irvine, abdomen, severe; Louis R. Stroup, forearm, slight; 18th, D, Musician Milton M. Roeder, leg, slight; E, Stephen Braddish, forearm, slight; 19th, H, First Lieut. Willis Uline, neck, severe. At Bacolor, 16th, K, Q. M. Sergt. Fred. S. Beach, thigh, moderate. First Washington, near San Pedro Macati, 18th, K, Corpl. Otis L. Denno, chest, severe. Twenty-third Infantry, near Guadalupe, Cebu, 12th, I, Second Lieut. Alexander J. Macnab, jr., scalp, slight.

OTIS.

MANILA. (Received August 24, 1899.)

AGWAR, *Washington:*

Following men Company F, Twenty-fourth Infantry, drowned morning 21st near pumping station, by jumping in panic from boat while crossing the swollen San Mateo River: Sergt. Thomas W. Countee, Privates William Carter, John Dean, James G. Johnson, Edward Jones, Thomas Russell, Emmett McMillan, Hampton Kendall, George Moody. Following drowned in attempting to rescue others: Private John E. Poole, Company H, Twenty-fourth, and one private, Fourth Cavalry, name not yet learned but has been telegraphed for.

OTIS.

MANILA. (Received August 24, 1899—4.52.a. m.)

AGWAR, *Washington.*

General Bates returned; mission successful; agreement made with Sultan and dattos whereby sovereignty United States over entire Jolo Archipelago acknowledged; its flag to fly on land and sea; United States to occupy and control all points deemed necessary, introducing firearms prohibited; Sultan to assist in suppressing piracy; agrees to deliver criminals accused of crime not committed by Moros against Moros; relations between United States troops and all Moros very friendly; two other points in archipelago will be occupied by United States troops soon, when trade and commerce can be controlled; Moros western Mindanao friendly, ask permission to drive out insurgents; reports by mail.

OTIS.

MANILA. (Received August 24, 1899—6.26 a. m.)

AGWAR, *Washington:*

Newport arrived. Private Elmer Raymond, E, Nineteenth, died August 7, uræmia; no other casualties. Montana enlisted strength, 711, sailed yesterday morning; took all enlisted men.

OTIS.

ADJUTANT-GENERAL'S OFFICE,
Washington, August 24, 1899.

OTIS, *Manila:*

Telegraph hereafter name of vessel, strength of each command, officers and men, sailing for the United States.

CORBIN.

ADJUTANT-GENERAL'S OFFICE,
Washington, August 24, 1899.

OTIS, *Manila:*

Cable 12th reference emergency ration not understood. Desires know exactly what you desire.

CORBIN.

ADJUTANT-GENERAL'S OFFICE,
Washington, August 25, 1899.

OTIS, *Manila:*

Secwar specially anxious hospital arrangements shall be made in Manila to meet proposed increase of your army. What money do you need for hospital buildings or pavilions? How many beds do your present hospitals afford? How many beds now vacant?

CORBIN.

MANILA. (Received August 25, 1899—3.36 a. m.)

AGWAR, *Washington:*

Transport *Ohio* arrived this morning; no casualties; 5 sick left at Honolulu.

OTIS.

SAN FRANCISCO, CAL., *August 25, 1899.*
(Received 9.11 p. m.)

ADJUTANT-GENERAL, *Washington, D. C.:*

Transport *Sherman* brought First California, California Heavy Artillery, and 251 discharged soldiers. Casualties: Sergt. Ernest Koenig, A, California Artillery, July

28, typhoid; Private Luther H. Dinsmore, B, First California, 5th instant, typhoid. Bodies brought to port. Private John J. Boman, G, First California, July 22, acute dysentery; body transferred at Manila.

SHAFTER, *Major-General.*

MANILA. (Received August 25, 1899—5.32 a. m.)

AGWAR, *Washington:*

Brainard cabled Commissary-General 12th instant for 100,000 emergency rations, giving components of same desired. My cable that date stated emergency rations not suited to Tropics for reasons therein given, and that ration in use gave satisfaction. Action on Brainard's cable will supply us with all emergency rations needed.

OTIS.

SAN FRANCISCO, CAL., *August 25, 1899.*
(Received 9.33 p. m.)

ADJUTANT-GENERAL, *Washington, D. C.:*

Transport *Athenian* sailed from Seattle 10.30 p. m. 24th instant, 3 commissioned officers, 102 enlisted men, 372 public and 24 private horses; Capt. George F. Chase, Third Cavalry, commanding; Acting Assistant Surgeon Driver, 1 private Hospital Corps, with transport.

SHAFTER, *Major-General.*

SAN FRANCISCO, CAL., *August 25, 1899.*
(Received 10.35 p. m.)

ADJUTANT-GENERAL, *Washington, D. C.:*

Transport *St. Paul* left Seattle for Manila 3.15 p. m. to-day seven troops Third Cavalry, Colonel Wessells commanding.

SHAFTER, *Major-General.*

ADJUTANT-GENERAL'S OFFCE,
Washington, August 26, 1899.

OTIS, *Manila.*

Reported here that eight batteries German field artillery have been purchased by insurgents and en route to the Philippines. Secwar directs this be communicated to you in order that you may be on the lookout for the arrival of any such batteries.

CORBIN.

MANILA. (Received August 26, 1899—11.20 p. m.)

AGWAR, *Washington:*

Valencia sailed August 23, 13 officers, 324 enlisted men, Montana Infantry; 10 officers, 86 discharged men, 2 Hospital Corps men, 5 civilians. *Zealandia* sailed August 23, 24 officers, 339 enlisted men, Montana Infantry; 8 officers, 179 discharged men, 8 men, Hospital Corps; 20 enlisted men, sick; 9 civilians. Montana Infantry left in Manila 5 officers, 62 enlisted men reenlisted, 9 sick; 2 officers, 90 enlisted men, discharged.

OTIS.

MANILA. (Received August 27, 1899—3.21 a. m.)

AGWAR, *Washington:*

Hughes, Iloilo, reports 4 soldiers ambushed, killed, mutilated, few miles south of city of Cebu; names not given; that robber bands, Negros, scattered, and most members of same returning to work on sugar plantations; that armed Tagalos who had entered that island severely punished, and that conditions favorable for formation of civil government under military supervision as has been instructed. Llittle change in Panay and Cebu islands; withdrawal of volunteers and regulars discharged under Order 40, last year, has prevented active campaigns in those islands, which meditated reenforcements will cure.

OTIS.

MANILA. (Received August 27, 1899—11.07 a. m.)

AGWAR, *Washington:*

Following deaths since last report: Drowned—August 5, John J. Blake, H, Sixth Infantry, near La Castellana, Negros; 21st, Jno. E. Poole, H, Twenty-fourth Infantry; 22d, Theodore J. Martens, M, Twentieth Infantry. Following, Company F, Twenty-fourth Infantry, drowned August 21: Sergt. Thomas W. Countee, Privates William Carter, John Dean, James G. Johnson, Edward Jones, Thomas Russell, Emmett McMillan, George Moody, Hampton Kendall. Typhoid fever—20th, Dickson W. Weeden, C, First Montana; 22d, Elmer R. Rothbone, I, Twenty-first Infantry; 22d, Frederick McDonald, H, Nineteenth Infantry; 23d, Abraham Gottreux, H, Twelfth Infantry; 23d, Samuel Fehl, recruit, Fourteenth Infantry. Cirrhosis of liver—18th, John T. Rogers, C, Fourth Cavalry; 23d, John W. Evans, F, Twenty-first Infantry. Dysentery—22d, William Harting, corporal, L, Thirteenth Infantry; 25th, Henry Keen, jr., private, I, Twenty-first Infantry. Diarrhea—17th, Murnan, C, Third Infantry. Accidental fall—16th, William A. Vanza, C, Seventeenth Infantry. From wounds in action—21st, Albert Irvine, M, Twelfth Infantry. Appendicitis—24th, Fred Anderson, C, Third Infantry.

OTIS.

MANILA. (Received August 28, 1899—3.20 a. m.)

AGWAR, *Washington:*

Datto Mundi, Zamboanga, attacked and defeated insurgents there, killing 30, this date; under Spaniards he supervised Moros of entire southwestern peninsula, Mindanao Island; he visited General Bates at Jolo to give adhesion to United States; Bates returned him to small island near Zamboanga, when he requested permission to drive out insurgents, but told that troops would be sent to Zamboanga soon. Insurgents there offered several weeks ago to turn over the city on promise of surrender in case Aguinaldo successful in Luzon; proposition declined. Dato Mundi, able man; educated abroad; thoroughly loyal to American interests. Bates leaves 30th to place troops in Sulu Islands; will soon place troops Zamboanga and Isabela, the naval station in Basilan Islands.

OTIS.

MANILA. (Received August 28, 1899—10.11 a. m.)

AGWAR, *Washington:*

Casualties: Wounded near San Fernando—Sixteenth Infantry, August 9, E, Sergt. Louis Steere, elbow, severe, accidental; Twenty-second Infantry, C, Edward Newman, leg, slight; Seventeenth Infantry, D, Corpl. Francis B. Eastman, neck, slight; James B. McGillioray, nates, slight; Frank Stickel, scalp, slight; E, Sergt. William Schroeder, scalp, slight; Fifty-first Iowa, near Calulum; 11th, A, Amon M. Slatten, leg, slight; Band, James T. Stuart, shoulder, slight; D, Theodore P. Saltgaver, shoulder, slight.

OTIS.

ADJUTANT-GENERAL'S OFFICE,
Washington, August 30, 1899.

OTIS, *Manila:*

When will *Pennsylvania* and any other transport with you now sail? We are anxious to know in order to provide transportation for the ten volunteer regiments which are now in readiness as soon as transportation can be provided.

CORBIN.

SAN FRANCISCO, CAL., *August 30, 1899.*
(Received 1.48 p. m. August 31.)

ADJUTANT-GENERAL, *Washington, D. C.:*

Transport *Grant* arrived last night with First North Dakota, First Idaho, First Wyoming Volunteer Infantry, and Battery A, Wyoming Light Artillery. Further report will be made later.

SHAFTER, *Major-General.*

MANILA. (Received August 31, 1899—7.55 a. m.)

AGWAR, *Washington:*

Para sailed to-day, 14 officers, 41 enlisted and 924 discharged men, 3 civilians.

OTIS.

ADJUTANT-GENERAL'S OFFICE,
Washington, August 31, 1899.

OTIS, *Manila:*

Headquarters seven troops Third Cavalry from Seattle August 25, on *St. Paul.* Horses and D Troop August 25, on *Athenian* via Dutch Harbor, Nagasaki and Kobe.

CORBIN.

MANILA. (Received August 31, 1899—3.07 a. m.)

AGWAR, *Washington:*

Referring to your cablegram August 30, *Para* sails August 31; *Tartar,* September 3; *Pennsylvania,* 5; *Newport* and *Ohio,* September 7.

OTIS.

MANILA. (Received September 1, 1899—7.38 a. m.)

AGWAR, *Washington:*

Nine hundred and twenty-four discharged soldiers sailed *Para* yesterday; final statements in possession Lieutenant Gordan, signal officer, acting quartermaster of transport, who will identify men to paymasters San Francisco; advisable make full preparation prompt payment arrival *Para.*

OTIS.

ADJUTANT-GENERAL'S OFFICE,
Washington, September 1, 1899.

Maj. Gen. W. R. SHAFTER,
Commanding Department California, San Francisco, Cal.:

Following has been received from General Otis: "Nine hundred twenty-four discharged soldiers sailed *Para* yesterday. Final statements in possession Lieutenant Gordan, signal officer, acting quartermaster of transport, who will identify men to paymasters San Francisco. Advisable make full preparation prompt payment arrival *Para.*"

H. C. CORBIN, *Adjutant-General.*

MANILA. (Received September 2, 1899—10.07 a. m.)

AGWAR, *Washington:*

Hughes transmits following: Lieutenant-Colonel Byrne on August 31 destroyed Argogila, most important bandit stronghold, killing 21, wounding many, capturing large quantities supplies, complete outfit reloading shells, bolos, spears, etc.; feat remarkable as town accessible only by road, almost perpendicular slope; constantly under fire for 1,000 feet; one officer and two men struck by bowlders rolled down on them, but not seriously hurt; no casualties reported; bandit strength, 400.

OTIS.

MANILA. (Received September 2, 1899—2.52 p. m.)

ADJUTANT-GENERAL, *Washington:*

Railway to Angeles completed in four days. Insurgents north opened on place this morning with shrapnel, which failed to explode; no casualties. Two columns, Lawton and MacArthur, move north in few days, soon as preparations can be completed. Kansas and Washingtons being loaded on transports. Two battalions Nineteenth Infantry relieve Tennessees at Iloilo and Cebu. Latter with Iowas, only remaining volunteer regiments, sail soon.

OTIS.

SAN FRANCISCO, CAL., *September 2, 1899.*
(Received 3.26 p. m.)

ADJUTANT-GENERAL, *Washington, D. C.:*

Transport *Victoria* sailed from Tacoma yesterday with Lieutenants Johnston and Chitty, Third Cavalry, 1 acting assistant surgeon, 1 veterinary surgeon, 80 men Third Cavalry and 3 stock tenders; 413 horses Third Cavalry.

SHAFTER, *Major-General.*

MANILA. (Received September 3, 1899—8.57 a. m.)

AGWAR, *Washington:*

Graves deceased members Tenth Pennsylvania decorated September 1 with fitting ceremonies, conducted by Chaplain Pierce; Chaplain Sutherland, personal friend Colonel Hawkins, delivered address.

OTIS.

ADJUTANT-GENERAL'S OFFICE,
Washington, September 3, 1899.

OTIS, *Manila:*

Secwar is much pleased with your projected movement of Lawton and MacArthur.

CORBIN.

MANILA. (Received September 3, 1899—1.40 p. m.)

AGWAR, *Washington:*

Following deaths since last report: Chronic dysentery—August 26, Jacob Goebel, L, Twelfth Infantry; August 28, Thomas Quinne, E, Fourth Cavalry; August 31, Frederick Hutfils, quartermaster-sergeant, H, Twenty-first Infantry; August 30, Palmer Helsen, H, Third Infantry; September 2, George J. Dahl, D, Fourteenth Infantry. Acute dysentery—August 30, John Kane, K, Seventeenth Infantry; September 1, John W. Fugate, Hospital Corps; Robert M. Nazor, E, Ninth Infantry. Chronic gastro enteritis—August 27, William S. Houck, K, Twenty-second Infantry.

Intestinal obstruction—August 31, William P. Seward, G, Twenty-first Infantry. Typhoid fever—August 28, Edwin H. Weber, E, Third Infantry; August 31, George Guess, corporal, I, Ninth Infantry; September 1, Thomas S. Ralph, M, Twenty-second Infantry. Pneumonia, lobar, double—August 27, Charles Todd, sergeant, E, Nineteenth Infantry; Hugh E. Noble, G, Seventeenth Infantry. Nephritis—August 26, Robert A. Crystal, F, First Washington. Meningitis, cerebral—August 26, Frederick C. Sharland, corporal, B, Twentieth Kansas. Uræmia—August 7, Eler Raymond, E, Nineteenth Infantry. Apoplexy—August 30, Otto H. Boehnke, G, Fourth Cavalry. Aneurism rupture—September 1, Fred. C. Buhmann, K, First Washington.

OTIS.

NAGASAKI, JAPAN. (Received September 3, 1899—11.50 p. m.)
ADJUTANT-GENERAL, U. S. ARMY, *Washington, D. C.:*
Transport *Morgan City*, under guidance experienced pilot, struck reef in Inland Sea, 8 miles from Onomichi, 250 miles from Nagasaki, about 4 a. m. September 1; backed off at daylight, vessel filled very rapidly, was beached, and all saved; officers and crew did splendid work; have telegraphed to Kobe for food; am sending wrecking crew, vessel food from here; cargo almost all lost. Can you send me transport from Manila? American money good here only, hence delay.

CASTNER, *Quartermaster.*

MANILA. (Received September 4, 1899—4.15 a. m.)
AGWAR, *Washington:*
Tartar left yesterday, San Francisco, 48 officers, 13 civilians, 400 discharged men, 735 enlisted men Kansas, 7 Hospital Corps; total, 1,210.

OTIS.

ADJUTANT-GENERAL'S OFFICE,
Washington, September 4, 1899.
OTIS, *Manila:*
Warren sailed yesterday. Fourteen officers, 54 casuals, 327 recruits; volunteers, Thirty-sixth regiment, 303; Thirty-seventh, 297; Eleventh Cavalry, 52. Sixty Krag-Jörgensen rifles and 12,000 rounds ammunition.

CORBIN.

MANILA. (September 4, 1899—4.45 a. m.)
AGWAR, *Washington:*
Ohio, to transport soldiers *Morgan City*, will leave here when facts ascertained from Minister Buck, to whom cable sent.

OTIS.

NAGASAKI, JAPAN. (Received 4.20 p. m.)
ADJUTANT-GENERAL, U. S. ARMY, *Washington, D. C.:*
Morgan City in hands of owners and crew; authority from Japanese Government secured to land troops here; have secured quarters; sending steamer for them to-morrow. *City of Para* expected here to-morrow.

CASTNER.

MANILA. (Received September 5, 1899—9 a. m.)

AGWAR, *Washington:*

Total strength enlisted, commissioned: Cavalry, Fourth, commissioned 21, enlisted 1,156; Eleventh, commissioned 37, enlisted 252. Artillery, First, commissioned 4, enlisted 117; Third, commissioned 15, enlisted 385; Fourth, commissioned 5, enlisted 119; Fifth, commissioned 4, enlisted 116; Sixth, commissioned 31, enlisted 1,120. Infantry, Third, commissioned 45, enlisted 1,293; Fourth, commissioned 43, enlisted 1,253; Sixth, commissioned 45, enlisted 1,358; Ninth, commissioned 40, enlisted 1,250; Twelfth, commissioned 42, enlisted 1,419; Thirteenth, commissioned 41, enlisted 1,289; Fourteenth, commissioned 42, enlisted 1,137; Sixteenth, commissioned 43, enlisted 1,299; Seventeenth, commissioned 44, enlisted 1,250; Eighteenth, commissioned 43, enlisted 1,180; Nineteenth, commissioned 46, enlisted 1,494; Twentieth, commissioned 43, enlisted 1,304; Twenty-first, commissioned 46, enlisted 1,267; Twenty-second, commissioned 44, enlisted 1,243; Twenty-third, commissioned 42, enlisted 1,370; Twenty-fourth, commissioned 32, enlisted 1,048; Twenty-fifth, commissioned 32, enlisted 1,042; Thirty-sixth, commissioned 39, enlisted 585. Engineer Battalion, commissioned 6, enlisted 276. Signal Corps, commissioned 10, enlisted 187. Total strength, commissioned 926, enlisted 26,329.

OTIS.

MANILA. (Received September 5, 1899—3.30 a. m.)

AGWAR, *Washington:*

Transport *Ohio* sails for Nagasaki to-day to receive *Morgan City* troops; round trip requires thirteen days.

OTIS.

MANILA. (Received September 6, 1899—4.20 a. m.)

AGWAR, *Washington:*

Pennsylvania sailed September 5, with 42 officers, 776 enlisted men, Washington Infantry; 2 officers, 34 discharged, 3 men Hospital Corps, 7 civilians. Washington Infantry left in Manila 10 officers, 47 enlisted, reenlisted. Two officers, 41 enlisted men discharged; none sick.

OTIS.

MANILA. (Received September 6, 1899—7.53 a. m.)

AGWAR, *Washington:*

Don't need money for hospital accommodations Manila. Nipa buildings, which will accommodate 2,000 sick, being erected in good location suburbs city; will be finished within month. These buildings supplement present hospital facilities.

OTIS.

MANILA. (Received September 6, 1899—8.46 a. m.)

AGWAR, *Washington:*

Casualties: Killed—Thirty-sixth Infantry, near Santa Rio, September 3, A, John J. Doering. Wounded—Twenty-first Infantry, at Calamba, July 26, E, Sergt. James Connelly, ankle, severe. Sixth Infantry, at Bobon, Negros, 19th, K, Albert C. Jenks, throat and jaw, severe. Ninth Infantry, near San Fernando, August 9, D, Edward Gorman, groin, slight; Thirty-sixth Infantry, September 3, A, Frank Rathmaner, loin, nates, leg, foot, severe.

OTIS.

MANILA. (Received September 8, 1899—7.35 a. m.)
AGWAR, *Washington:*
Newport sailed yesterday, 9 officers, 66 enlisted and 463 discharged men, 10 civilians; total, 548; 40 of enlisted men belong to volunteer signal company; remainder sick.

OTIS.

MANILA. (Received September 8, 1899—7.42 a. m.)
AGWAR, *Washington:*
Ask that in addition to ordnance already requested, 12 Hotchkiss mountain 12-pounder guns, with 2,000 shrapnel, 1,000 shell, filled and fused, and 3,000 charges smokeless powder be sent.

OTIS.

ADJUTANT-GENERAL'S OFFICE,
Washington, September 8, 1899.
OTIS, *Manila:*
Twelve mountain guns, 12-pounders, with ammunition-packing outfit shipped from London via Hongkong October 1. Vickers-Maxim pattern instead of Hotchkiss.

CORBIN.

SAN FRANCISCO, CAL., *September 8, 1899.*
(Received 5 p. m.)
ADJUTANT-GENERAL, *Washington, D. C.:*
Transport Sheridan arrived 7 p. m. yesterday morning, Thirteenth Minnesota and First South Dakota Infantry. Full report will be sent later.

SHAFTER, *Major-General.*

ADJUTANT-GENERAL'S OFFICE,
Washington, September 9, 1899.
OTIS, *Manila:*
The Secretary of War directs that all orders, decrees, and proclamations providing for or having in view the establishment of a form of government in any of the islands ceded or relinquished by Spain by the Treaty of Paris will be submitted to this office for his approval before the promulgation thereof.

CORBIN.

ADJUTANT-GENERAL'S OFFICE,
Washington, September 9, 1899.
OTIS, *Manila*:
[Confidential.] In view of the public misconception here, created by the allegations of Manila correspondents that they are not allowed to send accounts of the situation as viewed by them, the Secretary of War inclines to advise most liberal treatment, even to the point of practically meeting your expressed willingness of July 20 that the censorship be entirely removed, only continuing the requirement that all matter be submitted in advance, that you may deal, as you may deem best, with any liable to affect military operations or offending against military discipline. For reasons that are obvious, this should be done as of your own motion and without making any general or formal order of announcement. Do it without announcing that you are going to do it. Acknowledge receipt.

CORBIN.

SAN FRANCISCO, CAL., *September 9, 1899.*
(Received 4.07 p. m.)

ADJUTANT-GENERAL, *Washington, D. C.:*

Transport *Columbia* left here at 6 p. m. yesterday with headquarters, staff, band, Companies E, F, G, H, and L, Thirty-fourth Infantry Volunteers, 17 officers and 557 enlisted men, 3 Hospital Corps men; Captain Brewster, Ninth Infantry; 200 rounds per man ammunition, caliber .30.

SHAFTER, *Major-General.*

MANILA. (Received September 10, 1899—6.30 a. m.)

AGWAR, *Washington:*

Cable 9th received; course therein outlined practically followed now.

OTIS.

MANILA. (Received September 10, 1899—8.50 a. m.)

AGWAR, *Washington:*

Following deaths since last report: Chronic dysentery—September 2, Henry O. Bulson, H, Ninth Infantry; William Creelman, B, First Tennessee. Acute dysentery—First Sergt. Joseph Hogan, M, Fourth Infantry. Gunshot wound (accidental)—August 24, Daniel R. Edwards, E, Eighteenth Infantry; September 6, Thomas P. Guinan, K, Twelfth Infantry; Sergt. Edward H. Kemano, L, Fourth Cavalry. Typhoid fever—July 10, Henry Uppendah, K, First South Dakota; September 6, John Healy, K, Third Artillery. Drowned, arm of Manila Bay—August 29, Raymond D. Louth, M, Sixth Artillery. Chronic diarrhea—September 3, Owen V. Dunn, E, Fourth Infantry; 6th, James Hogan, F, Twenty-first Infantry. General peritonitis—John M. McCall, B, Twenty-second Infantry. Pulmonary phthisis—Michael McGrath, M, Twelfth Infantry. Pneumonia, lobar—Richard W. Tobin, F, Twenty-first Infantry. Gastritis, chronic—Henry L. Noble, G, Fifty-first Iowa. Alcoholism, acute—7th, Capt. Charles L. Collins, I, Twenty-first Infantry, at Cebu Island, 6 p. m. Appendicitis, chronic—8th, William H. Kennedy, G, Ninth Infantry. Fever, remittent malaria—9th, Joshua W. Johnson, Hospital Corps.

OTIS.

MANILA. (Received September 10, 1899—11.52 p. m.)

AGWAR, *Washington:*

Spanish authorities request delivery guns and other war material at Cavite; Navy declines to deliver, contending Cavite naval station with all property captured during active war not affected by treaty. Decision requested.

OTIS.

MANILA. (Received September 11, 1899—1.55 a. m.)

AGWAR, *Washington:*

Two companies Nineteenth Infantry left last night for Iloilo, to be followed to-morrow by headquarters and balance two battalions to relieve Tennessee regiment at Iloilo and Cebu.

OTIS.

MANILA. (Received September 11, 1899—2.10 a. m.)

AGWAR, *Washington:*

Following minor affairs reported: Captain Butler, Third Infantry, with portion Baliuag troops, drove insurgents at San Rafael, capturing 7 with arms. Insurgent forces made demonstration against Santa Rita, on Porac road; loss, 2 officers, 6 privates, with arms, captured by Colonel Bell; no casualties among our troops.

OTIS.

ADJUTANT-GENERAL'S OFFICE,
Washington, September 11, 1899.

OTIS, *Manila:*

Columbia sailed 8th, headquarters, band, and five companies Thirty-fourth Volunteer Infantry, 17 officers, 557 men; 200 rounds ammunition per man.

CORBIN.

MANILA. (September 11, 1899—7.45 a. m.)

CORBIN, *Washington:*

[Confidential.] Lawton pronounces utterly foundationless newspaper reports of interview asserting that he commented on military situation or criticised conduct of operations here. Declares beforehand as false all future accounts of such interviews.

SCHWAN.

MANILA. (Received September 12, 1899—2.50 a. m.)

AGWAR, *Washington:*

Request 5,000,000 rounds caliber .30 ammunition.

OTIS.

MANILA. (Received September 12, 1899—8.20 a. m.)

AGWAR, *Washington:*

Casualties: Killed at Cebu—Twenty-third Infantry, August 25, M, Sergt. Samuel Darcey; Lance Corpl. George E. Burger; Joseph Cummings. Wounded, at Tabuan, Negros—Sixth Infantry, 17th M, Corpl. Ben. A. Morton, forehead, severe; 19th, Corpl. George Timmerman, arm, slight; B, Stanislaw Meksa, hip, slight; Terrence E. O'Donnell, cheek, slight.

OTIS.

ADJUTANT-GENERAL'S OFFICE,
Washington, September 12, 1899.

OTIS, *Manila:*

Press reports have it that *Tartar* is in Hongkong, badly overloaded; men suffering in consequence; undoubtedly exaggerated. Why do transports put in there?

CORBIN.

ADJUTANT-GENERAL'S OFFICE,
Washington, September 12, 1899.

SCHWAN, *Manila:*

Secwar did not credit interview, but is gratified to receive and publish Lawton's denial. He is confident of everyone's loyal and cheerful efforts for early completion of work in hand.

CORBIN.

MANILA. (Received September 13, 1899—8.33 a. m.)

AGWAR, *Washington:*

Tartar sent Hongkong to dock, as requested by Major Long; no dock large enough at Nagasaki. She has capacity for 1,145 men and 111 cabin passengers. She took back 1,142 men and 61 cabin passengers. On her trip from San Francisco she carried comfortably 1,145 men and 55 cabin passengers.

OTIS.

HONGKONG. (Received September 13, 1899—7.32 a. m.)

CORBIN, *Washington:*
British authorities refuse to clear *Tartar* because overcrowded; authorize 824.

METCALF.

ADJUTANT-GENERAL'S OFFICE,
Washington, September 13, 1899.

OTIS, *Manila:*
Were complaints of overcrowding *Tartar* made before she sailed? Did food supplies differ from food supplies of Colorado, Wyoming, and South Dakota troops?

H. C. CORBIN.

ADJUTANT-GENERAL'S OFFICE,
Washington, September 13, 1899.

METCALF, *Hongkong:*
Is *Tartar*, in your opinion, overcrowded? Is there just cause of complaint of sufficiency or quality of food? What suggestions have you to make?

H. C. CORBIN.

ADJUTANT-GENERAL'S OFFICE,
Washington, September 13, 1899.

SCHWAN, *Manila:*
Newspapers say Lawton's denial insufficient. His words reported are: "What we want is to stop this accursed war. It is time for diplomacy; time for mutual understanding."

CORBIN.

MANILA. (Received September 14, 1899—2 a. m.)

AGWAR, *Washington:*
No complaints received of overcrowding *Tartar* before sailing; troops and other on *Tartar* supplied with same kind of food as troops you mention; discharged soldiers, of whom *Tartar* carries 407, apt to be fault-finding.

OTIS.

HONGKONG. (Received September 14, 1899—5.40 a. m.)

CORBIN, *Washington:*
No more crowded than other transports have been; no cause for complaint about food; complaints made by discharged regulars.

METCALF.

HONGKONG. (Received September 14, 1899—9.11 a. m.)

CORBIN, *Washington:*
Clearance allowed; sail to-day.

METCALF.

MANILA. (Received September 15, 1899—8.51 a. m.)

AGWAR, *Washington:*
Enlisted strength Eleventh Cavalry, 285; Thirty-sixth Infantry, 516; Thirty-seventh Infantry, 599.

OTIS.

ADJUTANT-GENERAL'S OFFICE,
Washington, September 15, 1899.

OTIS, Manila:
Information desired as to number Spanish prisoners—officers and enlisted men—shipped to Spain on Cashemire, December 13; Cataluña, May 6; Leon XIII, May 13; Satrustegui, June 3; Isla de Luzon, July 1.

CORBIN.

MANILA. (Received September 15, 1899—7.33 a. m.)
AGWAR, Washington:
After earnest effort neither Lawton nor those about him recall uttering words mentioned in your cablegram or like language.

SCHWAN.

MANILA. (Received September 16, 1899—7.40 a. m.)
AGWAR, Washington:
Shipped to Spain on Cachemire, 30 officers, 1,067 enlisted men; Cataluña, 71 officers, 30 men; Leon XIII, 4 officers, 6 men; Satrustegui, 11 officers, 79 men; Isla de Luzon, 13 officers, 16 men.

OTIS.

ADJUTANT-GENERAL'S OFFICE,
Washington, September 16, 1899.

OTIS, Manila:
Referring to your cables February 20 and July 16, will you not soon be ready to occupy Dagupan and other west coast ports? Secwar does not wish to interfere, but considers important to cut off insurgent supplies. Occupy railroad and supplant Tagolog (Tagalos) domination over other tribes soon as possible. Can have every possible cooperation by Navy, including landing marines.

CORBIN.

MANILA. (Received September 17, 1899—6.45 a. m.)
AGWAR, Washington:
Navada Cavalry booked for transport Ohio, which detained, because sent for wrecked Morgan City troops; will probably leave Manila 24th instant. Iowas leave on Wednesday when Tennessees arrive from south, and sail as soon as papers completed. This will finish shipment of all volunteers and discharged men from regular establishment.

OTIS.

SAN FRANCISCO, CAL., September 17, 1899. (Received 4.27 p. m.)
ADJUTANT-GENERAL, Washington, D. C.:
Transport Belgian King sailed yesterday at 5 p. m. with two battalions Thirty-fourth Infantry Volunteers, Companies A, B, C, D, I, and M; Lieutenant-Colonel Howze, and 26 officers, 740 enlisted men, 9 Hospital Corps men, and following casuals and recruits. * * * Two hundred and forty rounds per man ammunition, caliber .30.

SHAFTER, Major-General.

MANILA. (Received September 17, 1899—10.37 a. m.)
ADJUTANT-GENERAL, Washington:
Will be ready to operate Northern Luzon as soon as troops arrive. Shipments for some time have exceeded receipts. Still think can occupy Northern Luzon latter part of month. Lawton now moving troops and supplies San Fernando and Calum-

pit preparatory to circular and rapid movement. No difficulty in defeating insurgent forces. Difficulty consists in protecting lives of citizens after troops have conquered and passed cities, in case they exhibit any American tendency.

OTIS.

ADJUTANT-GENERAL'S OFFICE,
Washington, September 18, 1899.

OTIS, *Manila:*
Some feeling here over alleged desecration of churches by our soldiers. Have any churches been occupied by us not previously occupied by insurgents? What is their practice? Enjoin on your officers special respect and protection for all church property.

CORBIN.

ADJUTANT-GENERAL'S OFFICE,
Washington, September 18, 1899.

OTIS, *Manila:*
Secwar desires you to give every facility to Spanish commissioners for the care of Spanish prisoners being released by Aguinaldo.

CORBIN.

ADJUTANT-GENERAL'S OFFICE,
Washington, September 18, 1899.

OTIS, *Manila:*
Except when absolutely necessary, Secwar directs returning ships do not touch at either Hongkong or Yokohama.

CORBIN.

MANILA. (Received September 18, 1899—1.10 p. m.)
AGWAR, *Washington:*
Following deaths since last report: Nephritis, acute—September 9, James M. Leach, A, Seventeenth Infantry; 13th, James J. Higgins, C, Twenty-first Infantry. Pneumonia—3d, William B. Goldthwaite, recruit Twenty-third Infantry; 8th, Henry Back, E, Nineteenth Infantry. Homicide—shot by comrade at Pasay, 10th, Charles F. Wilson, C, Fourth Cavalry. Fever, typhoid—12th, Corpl. Matthew Kelleher, L, Seventeenth Infantry; John W. Hayes, B, Ninth Infantry. Dysentery, chronic— Q. M. Sergt. James Harrington, A, Fourteenth Infantry; 13th, Sergt. Martin Muller, E, First Artillery; Conley A. Ingle, G, Sixteenth Infantry; 14th, William G. Henry, D, Fourth Infantry; 16th, cook, George Steiger, G, Twenty-second Infantry. Fever, remittent malarial—12th, Otto T. Johnson, F, Fourteenth Infantry; 13th, Henry J. McNally, K, Twentieth Infantry. Meningitis, cerebral—14th, Frank Seil, B, Fourteenth Infantry. Diarrhea, subacute—15th, Philip Morris, L, Fourth Infantry.

OTIS.

ADJUTANT-GENERAL'S OFFICE,
Washington, September 18, 1899.

OTIS, *Manila:*
The Secretary of War intends early organization of the Division of the Philippine Islands, to be under your command, with four departments, as indicated in your dispatch of July 16. He invites your suggestions as to the lines of military departments, general officers to command, and location of department headquarters. He wishes to make this action coincident with movement to occupy Dagupan. He

highly approves your purpose to garrison all towns, necessary for protection of country, as they are taken, and to proceed with this as speedily as it can be done, without interfering with movements in force against assembled rebel forces and strenuous pursuit of their fragments when broken.

CORBIN.

MANILA. (Received September 19, 1899—3.40 a. m.)
AGWAR, *Washington:*
Transport *Ohio*, with *Morgan City* recruits, and *City of Sydney* arrived this morning; no casualties, except 1 desertion, *City of Sydney*, Nagasaki. *Ohio* left 2 sick Nagasaki.

OTIS.

MANILA. (Received September 19, 1899—3.44 a. m.)
AGWAR, *Washington:*
Transport *Tartar* sent to Hongkong by Major Miller without my knowledge on request San Francisco quartermaster; previous difficulties had warned me not to permit transports to enter there; *Tartar* left Hongkong 15 men; my intention to send *Ohio* there to receive them and coal, then proceed by way of Guam and Honolulu to San Francisco. Navy wishes to communicate with Guam and *Ohio* to be sent there for its accommodation. Shall this intention be carried out?

OTIS.

ADJUTANT-GENERAL'S OFFICE,
Washington, September 19, 1899.
OTIS, *Manila:*
Your recommendation in reference to transport *Ohio* approved. Her movements should be expedited, as presence of this ship on this side very much needed.

CORBIN.

MANILA. (Received September 19, 1899—7.15 a. m.)
AGWAR, *Washington:*
MacArthur reports from Angeles visit of 2 insurgent officers, with request for permission to send into our lines American prisoners; and sent to Manila prominent insurgent general officer for conference. The requested interview granted and insurgent officer at Angeles; return north this morning with information.

OTIS.

ADJUTANT-GENERAL'S OFFICE,
Washington, September 19, 1899.
OTIS, *Manila:*
Transport *Belgian King* sailed 16th; Companies A, B, C, D, I, and M, Thirty-fourth Volunteers, 26 officers and 740 enlisted men, and 28 recruits. Transport *Aztec* sailed 16th, with 2 officers, 8 enlisted volunteers, 366 horses, and 27 civilian employees.

CORBIN.

MANILA. (Received September 19, 1899—1.35 a. m.)
AGWAR, *Washington:*
Lieut. Col. John D. Miley, inspector-general volunteers, first lieutenant Second Artillery, died 12.37 September 19, at Manila; cause, cerebral meningitis attendant on typhoid fever.

OTIS.

MANILA. (Received September 19, 1899—8.31 a. m.)

AGWAR, *Washington:*

Spanish officials here ask to send vessel flying Spanish flag to Dagupan and other Northern Luzon ports to obtain large number civilian and sick military prisoners held by insurgents, to be released in accordance with insurgent decree of January 24. Under recent insurgent announcement delivery will not be made to American vessel. Spanish officers solemnly assert that no money will be paid insurgents for these prisoners. Thus far I have declined permission of this request, fearing execution of injurious secret negotiations and being unwilling to countenance insurgent presumption. Many of these prisoners reported sick and should be brought to Manila. If American vessel applied at northern ports for them they would be taken into interior. Spanish vessel in harbor awaiting result of decision. Shall ship be permitted to go for prisoners?

OTIS.

MANILA. (Received September 20, 1899.)

AGWAR, *Washington:*

Typhoon prevailing; rainfall forty-eight hours 8.2 inches; last twenty-four hours 6.3; delays shipment of volunteers; Iowas probably sail to-morrow; Tennessees detained south by storm.

OTIS.

WAR DEPARTMENT, *September 20, 1899.*

OTIS, *Manila:*

Your position regarding Spanish prisoners approved. Offer one of our vessels to receive prisoners from insurgents, and transport to Manila with every assurance to insurgents against hostile 'action by such vessel. We can not countenance direct official relation between the Spanish Government and insurgents under Spanish flag.

ROOT, *Secwar.*

MANILA. (Received September 21, 1899—8.26 a. m.)

AGWAR, *Washington:*

Casualties, wounded near El Pardo, island Cebu, Twenty-third Infantry, August 23, M, Second Lieut. Harry S. Howland, arm, severe; 25th, Charles Fisher, forearm, severe.

OTIS.

MANILA. (Received September 21, 1899—9.31 a. m.)

AGWAR, *Washington:*

Referring to your cablegram of September 18, sixteen churches, different localities, occupied by United States troops; four only partially occupied, and religious services not interfered with; also three convents occupied; these three and ten of sixteen churches formerly occupied by insurgents; church property respected, protected, by our troops.

OTIS.

MANILA. (Received September 21, 1899—12.55 a. m.)

AGWAR, *Washington:*

The six or eight days' mail sent by *Morgan City* lost in wreck; with slight exception nothing important received.

OTIS.

AFFAIRS IN THE PHILIPPINE ISLANDS. 1073

SAN FRANCISCO, CAL., *September 21, 1899.*
(Received 2.30 p. m.)

ADJUTANT-GENERAL, *Washington, D. C.:*

Transport *Tacoma* sailed at 3 a. m. to-day with headquarters, field, staff, band, and seven companies Twenty-seventh Infantry Volunteers, 26 officers, 729 men, 228 rounds ammunition per man, 1 acting assistant surgeon, 6 Hospital Corps; Colonel Bell, commanding.

SHAFTER, *Major-General.*

SAN FRANCISCO, CAL., *September 21, 1899.*
(Received 2.32 p. m.)

ADJUTANT-GENERAL, *Washington, D. C.:*

Transport *George W. Elder* sailed at 8 a. m. to-day with field, staff and five companies Twenty-seventh Infantry Volunteers, 20 officers, 485 men, 200 rounds ammunition per man, 3 assistant surgeons, 6 Hospital Corps; Lieutenant-Colonel Cummins, commanding.

SHAFTER, *Major-General.*

ADJUTANT-GENERAL'S OFFICE, *Washington, September 22, 1899.*

OTIS, *Manila:*

Chinese minister requests that 700 Chinese on steamer *Esmerelda*, with certificates of Amoy Taotoy, viséed by American consul, be allowed to land as exception to rule of exclusion based on military authority. This would relieve somewhat strained diplomatic situation, at the same time commit Chinese Government to recognition of the rule. Secretary of State considers permission very desirable. Secretary of War directs give permission unless the exception would cause substantial injury.

CARTER, *Acting Agwar.*

MANILA. (Received September 23, 1899—1.45 a. m.)

AGWAR, *Washington:*

Senator left yesterday Iowa Volunteers, 49 officers, 765 men; left in Manila, 4 men, 1 in hands insurgents; 4 officers, 111 discharged men.

OTIS.

MANILA. (Received September 23, 1899—7.30 a. m.)

AGWAR, *Washington:*

Insurgents succeeded in derailing section of train yesterday short distance from Angeles, then made attack on railway guards; result, Captain Perry, quartermaster, slightly wounded in arm: Private Charles Ziemans, Hospital Corps, killed; Private Sam Steele, I, Seventeenth Infantry, severely wounded; Civilian Charles S. Price, slightly wounded, and unknown civilian killed; insurgents driven, leaving 6 dead in their track, and troops immediately sent in pursuit.

OTIS.

MANILA. (Received September 23, 1899—11.35 p. m.)

AGWAR, *Washington:*

Hughes, Iloilo, reports Ignacio Lopez and 64 armed men surrendered to Byrne at Castellano, Negros; election in that island October 2; sought conference; wished to know what chief insurgents, Panay, promise could be given them in case of formal submission; told no arrangement possible until surrendered and force disbanded.

OTIS.

SAN FRANCISCO, CAL., *September 23, 1899.*
(Received 5.34 p. m.)

ADJUTANT-GENERAL, *Washington, D. C.:*

Transport *Zealandia* arrived here yesterday with headquarters band and six companies First Montana, 21 officers, 340 enlisted men. * * *

SHAFTER.

MANILA. (Received September 24, 1899—5.48 a. m.)

AGWAR, *Washington:*

Over 1,600 Chinese arrived from Amoy on steamers *Esmerelda* and *Salvadora;* mysteriously passed by United States Consul Johnson; after careful investigation, about half, having previous residence, permitted to land; have now allowed remainder to land, on promise of Chinese consul-general here that no more Chinese will leave Chinese ports for Philippines unless qualified to land under existing War Department regulations.

OTIS.

MANILA. (Received September 24, 1899—6.38 a. m.)

AGWAR, *Washington:*

Following deaths since last report: Dysentery, acute—August 24, at Jolo, Henry Baumler, E, Twenty-third Infantry; September 17, Isaac E. Rambo, E, Fourth Infantry; 21st, John Leclaire, I, Thirteenth Infantry; 22d, Martin Johnson, D, Third Infantry; 23d, Benjamin A. Tollefson, B, Third Infantry. Colitis, chronic—8th, at Jolo, Frank E. Armstrong, H, Twenty-third Infantry. Drowned, accidentally, at Bacolod, Negros—12th, Sergt. Frederick Simon, band, Sixth Infantry. Pneumonia—16th, John Nolan, H, Nineteenth Infantry. Diarrhea, chronic—17th, Louis E. Corbett, D, Ninth Infantry. Fever, typhoid—William H. Casey, G, Fourth Infantry. Appendicitis—18th, Thomas Holliday, A, Twenty-fourth Infantry. Paralysis, ascending—20th, Shubbell A. Snow, G, Twenty-first Infantry.

OTIS.

MANILA. (Received September 24, 1899—7.05 a. m.)

AGWAR, *Washington:*

Fourteenth Infantry received 312 recruits from *Indiana,* 295 from *Morgan City* and *Sydney;* is 177 above authorized strength. Shall excess be assigned elsewhere?

OTIS.

MANILA. (Received September 24, 1899—7.15 a. m.)

AGWAR, *Washington:*

Navy vessel *Culgon* not wanted by Army; draws 21 feet, and can not be used for harbor purposes.

OTIS.

MANILA. (Received September 24, 1899—7.45 a. m.)

AGWAR, *Washington:*

Bates returned from Jolo 21st instant, having placed garrisons at Siassi and Bongao, Tawi Tawi group, one company each place; affairs in archipelago satisfactory. Bates saw chief insurgents, Zamboanga; still anxious to receive United States garrison on condition of withdrawal should Aguinaldo succeed in Luzon; proposition not entertained; Zamboanga having more trouble with dattos in vicinity who have raised United States flag; Datto Cagayan, Sulu Island, visited Jolo, gave adhesion, and desired to raise American instead of Spanish flag on island; Cagayan not within lines of Paris treaty cession, through error of description doubtless, but will be considered United States territory and American flag will be raised there; ready to give six months' notice in order to establish in archipelago customs regulations, under protocol between Spain, Germany, and Great Britain of 1885; Bates's report by mail.

OTIS.

SAN FRANCISCO, CAL., *September 24, 1899.*
(Received 8.30 p. m.)

ADJUTANT-GENERAL, *Washington, D. C.:*

Transport *Sherman* sailed at 4.30 p. m. yesterday with Thirtieth Infantry Volunteers, 48 officers, 1,289 men, 275 rounds ammunition (caliber .30) per man. * * *

SHAFTER, *Major-General.*

MANILA. (Received September 25, 1899—1.56 a. m.

AGWAR, *Washington:*

Referring to your cablegram September 15, Robert M. Lee, F, Twentieth Kansas, died September 6, dysentery, Hongkong.

OTIS.

SAN FRANCISCO, CAL., *September 25, 1899.*
(Received 4.43 p. m.)

ADJUTANT-GENERAL, *Washington, D. C.:*

Transport *Valencia* arrived here yesterday with six companies First Montana, 18 officers, 276 enlisted men. * * *

SHAFTER, *Major-General.*

SAN FRANCISCO, CAL., *September 25, 1899.*

ADJUTANT-GENERAL, U. S. ARMY, *Washington, D. C.:*

City of Para arrived this morning. Full report later.

SHAFTER, *Major-General.*

MANILA. (Received September 26, 1899—12.20 a. m.)

AGWAR, *Washington:*

Casualties: Drowned—Third Infantry, at Bagbag River, Baliuag, in advance on enemy, August 14, C, Max Jackson; G, Corpl. Peter Larsen. Killed—Sixteenth Infantry, at Meycauayan, September 20, D, William Hardy. Wounded—Twenty-first Infantry, near Las Piñas, 17th, H, Alexander Hochberg, foot, moderate; Thirty-seventh Infantry, near Angeles, 22d, B, Corpl. Charles H. Lawson, arm, severe.

OTIS.

MANILA. (Received September 26, 1899—10.27 a. m.)

AGWAR, *Washington:*

On September 22 and 23 Snyder attacked strong insurgent positions about 5 miles west of Cebu with 265 officers and men Tennessee regiment, and 517 officers and men Nineteenth, Sixth, and Twenty-third Infantry and Sixth Artillery, driving enemy from works, capturing 7 forts, including smoothbore cannons mounted therein, and 14 intrenched and fortified places. Our loss, Private William M. Hanley, A, Sixth Infantry, killed, and 4 wounded. Enemy's loss estimated 40. Insurgents retreated to new fortifications far southwest. Snyder returned to Cebu with Tennessee troops, who had debarked from transport *Indiana* to take part in action. Two companies Nineteenth Infantry hold important positions in mountains.

OTIS.

SAN FRANCISCO, CAL., *September 26, 1899.*
(Received 9.12 p. m.)

ADJUTANT-GENERAL, *Washington, D. C.:*

Transport *Grant* sailed at 4 p. m. yesterday with Twenty-sixth Infantry Volunteers, 49 officers, 1,244 men; 208 rounds ammunition (caliber .30) per man. * * *

SHAFTER, *Major-General.*

ADJUTANT-GENERAL'S OFFICE,
Washington, September 28, 1899.

OTIS, *Manila:*

Reply to cable of 18th asking your recommendations for department lines and commanders in division proposed by you desired by Secretary War.

CORBIN.

MANILA. (Received September 29, 1899—3.05 a. m.

AGWAR, *Washington:*

Lawton's troops at Calumpit and San Fernando, where concentration taking place, ordered to cover country, Mexico, Guagua, Bacolor, and Santa Rita. MacArthur ordered to take his troops and clear country west and in vicinity of Porac, which he did yesterday, advancing on Porac at an early hour with Ninth Infantry and Thirty-sixth Volunteers, capturing Porac and driving enemy north. Wheaton, at Angeles, kept enemy back on his north and moved force westward to interrupt Porac insurgents, but they retreated by mountain roads. Results, clearing the country preparatory to future operation. Our casualties at Porac, 5 wounded. Wheaton does not report any casualties. Captured 1 officer and several enlisted men; some 20 of enemy killed; number wounded unknown.

OTIS.

MANILA. (Received September 29, 1899—8.40 a. m.)

AGWAR, *Washington:*

General Lawton permitted to organize two companies Macabebe scouts, under Lieutenant Batson, Fourth Cavalry, assisted by competent officers of the Army; they are performing excellent work in rivers and swamps on north and east shore Laguna de Bay, arresting robbers and securing rifles; their boats the only transportation required; compensation one-half that of soldiers, paid from civil funds.

OTIS.

MANILA. (Received September 29, 1899—11.51 p. m.)

AGWAR, *Washington:*

Communication dated 12th instant, from General Garcia, commanding all insurgent troops in eastern Mindanao, expresses desire to turn country over to United States authorities and surrender all insurgents' arms.

OTIS.

WAR DEPARTMENT, *September 29, 1899.*

OTIS, *Manila:*

State, Navy, and War Departments concur in decision that Spanish guns and other war material at Cavite should, under treaty, be deemed property of Spain.

ROOT, *Secwar.*

MANILA. (Received September 29, 1899—8.33 a. m.)
AGWAR, *Washington:*
Referring to our cablegram September 24, subject your approval, have assigned 120 surplus recruits from Fourteenth Infantry to Twenty-second Infantry.

OTIS.

ADJUTANT-GENERAL'S OFFICE,
Washington, September 29, 1899.
OTIS, *Manila:*
Secretary War confirms transfer 120 recruits Fourteenth Infantry to Twenty-second Infantry, and directs transfer remaining surplus recruits Fourteenth Infantry in Philippine Islands, and those on sea on arrival to Fourth Infantry. Cable number transfers as made.

SIMPSON.

MANILA. (Received September 29, 1899.)
ADJUTANT-GENERAL, *Washington:*
Four departments can be organized having headquarters Dagupan, Manila, Iloilo, and Zamboanga. First and last named places must be taken, which can be accomplished when necessary troops arrive. Recommend department lines as follows:

For Department Northern Luzon, all portion of island north of province Bataan, Pampanga, Bulacan, and Infanta.

For Department Southern Luzon, balance of Luzon and southern islands north of twelfth parallel of latitude, including Masbate, and including island of Busuanga and small islands immediately north of same and south of west pass of Apo. Also island of Samar.

For Department of the Visayas, all Philippine Islands situated entirely north of ninth parallel of latitude and east of meridian of longitude 121° 50' east of Greenwich.

For the Department of Mindanao and Jolo, all remaining islands of the Philippines. The names of general officers to command these departments cabled later.

OTIS.

MANILA. (Received September 30, 1899—7.13 a. m.)
AGWAR, *Washington:*
Ohio, 3 officers, 49 men Nevada Cavalry, 215 discharged men, sailed yesterday via Hongkong and Guam; 2 men Nevada Cavalry hands insurgents.

OTIS.

MANILA. (Received October 1, 1899—7.04 a. m.)
AGWAR, *Washington:*
From Iloilo Hughes reports improvement in Cebu and Negros, and that election in the last-named island will probably proceed satisfactorily; that insurgent Tagalos and Visayans in Panay in dissension and hostilities between them threatened.

OTIS.

SAN FRANCISCO, CAL., *October 1, 1899.* (Received 4.51 p. m.)
ADJUTANT-GENERAL, *Washington:*
Transport *Sheridan* sailed 4 p. m. yesterday with Thirty-third Infantry Volunteers. * * * [Here follows names of military passengers and numbers of recruits and casuals.]

SHAFTER, *Major-General.*

CORRESPONDENCE.

MANILA. (Received October 1, 1899—7.30 a. m.)

AGWAR, *Washington:*

Following deaths since last report: Pulmonary tuberculosis—September 1, Clarence Anderson, E, Twenty-third Infantry. Dysentery, chronic—16th, Peter O. Olson, C, Twenty-third Infantry; 23d, Allyn B. Wilmot, A, Twelfth Infantry; John M. Preston, G, Twelfth Infantry. Cirrhosis of liver—22d, Joseph Hines, D, Nineteenth Infantry. Nephritis—Stanislaus Stvan, D, Fourth Infantry. Typhoid fever—23d, Corpl. Ulysses G. Copley, F, Sixth Artillery; Joseph P. O'Rourke, I, Fourth Infantry; 26th, Richard E. Baylis, L, Sixth Artillery; 27th, Robert Marshall, D, Thirteenth Infantry; Christ Schwartz, A, Third Infantry. Meningitis, cerebro-spinal—25th, Sidney Rysdyk, F, Thirteenth Infantry. Splenic leucæmia—Luther M. Ellett, A, Twenty-fourth Infantry. Atrophy of the liver—28th, Henry Moreau, F, Fifth Artillery. Bright's disease, chronic—Corpl. Edward Fitzgerald, B, Fourth Cavalry. Gunshot wound, accidental—26th, Saul Copes, C, Twenty-fourth Infantry. Diarrhea, chronic—29th, John Moran, E, First Artillery.

OTIS.

MANILA. (Received October 2, 1899—9.38 a. m.)

AGWAR, *Washington:*

Transport *Sydney* sailed September 27 via Nagasaki, 9 officers, 10 civilians, 52 discharged soldiers, 66 *Hooker* crew.

OTIS.

MANILA. (Received October 2, 1899—11.05 a. m.)

AGWAR, *Washington:*.

Three insurgent officers permitted to enter our lines at Angeles with 12 of our soldiers and 2 citizens, whom they wished to present as released prisoners yesterday; in conference endeavored to present communication from insurgent government, which was declined; then presented paper signed by ten of the soldiers, in which soldiers gave parole; this received and held in abeyance; insurgent officers then said that Aguinaldo desired to end war and send in civil commission for conference, and were informed that it would not be received. They will be sent beyond lines to-morrow; the whole affair believed to be a ruse to obtain some acknowledgment by United States authorities. All soldiers returned were stragglers from within our lines, captured by robbers; they say they were obliged to sign parole to secure release, though two refused to sign; the whole affair of no significance; viewed as attempt at masquerading.

OTIS.

SAN FRANCISCO, CAL., *Octobor 2, 1899.*
(Received 8.19 p. m.)

ADJUTANT-GENERAL, *Washington:*

Transport *Charles Nelson* sailed from here 4.30 p. m. yesterday, with field, staff, Second Battalion, and Companies C and D, Thirty-second Infantry. * * * [Names of military passengers.]

SHAFTER, *Major-General.*

SAN FRANCISCO, CAL., *October 2, 1899.*
(Received 9.03 p. m.)

ADJUTANT-GENERAL, *Washington:*

Transport *Glenogle* sailed 4.15 p. m. yesterday, with field, staff, band, and seven companies Thirty-second Infantry. * * * [Companies A, E, F, G, K, L, M.]

SHAFTER, *Major-General.*

AFFAIRS IN THE PHILIPPINE ISLANDS. 1079

MANILA. (Received October 3, 1899—8.02 a. m.)

AGWAR, *Washington:*

St. Paul with seven troops Third Cavalry arrived October 1; no casualties. *Garonne* arrived September 30.

OTIS.

MANILA. (Received October 4, 1899—12.18 a. m.)

AGWAR, *Washington:*

Athenian arrived yesterday with 4 officers, 105 soldiers, 393 horses. No casualties.

OTIS.

[Above relates to Third Cavalry.]

MANILA. (Received October 4, 1899—7.45 a. m.)

AGWAR, *Washington:*

Captain Poore, Sixth Infantry, attacked intrenched robber band, western Negros, 1st instant; Lieutenant Grubbs, Sixth Infantry, killed; Dr. Shillock, 3 enlisted men, slightly wounded; 20 of enemy killed, including 2 leading robbers; 12 rifles, large supply ammunition and stores captured; Poore's action highly commended. Insurgents west of Bacoor and Imus, Luzon, attacked line of communication; Captain Eldridge, Fourteenth Infantry, killed; Lieutenant Burgess, Fifth Artillery, wounded; number enlisted men killed and wounded, 10 or 12; full report not yet received; enemy driven west and south with a reported heavy loss. Yesterday enemy attacked Calamba; driven off some distance into country; our casualties, 2 enlisted men killed, 7 wounded; 60 insurgents killed; number wounded unknown. Fourth Cavalry reconnaissance yesterday from San Fernando in direction of Santa Ana and Arayat; 1 man killed; no other casualties; insurgents driven with considerable loss. Advanced picket post, 3 men, cut from San Antonio and Santa Rita, west San Fernando, killed yesterday by bolomen, result of carelessness or overconfidence in natives.

OTIS.

ADJUTANT-GENERAL'S OFFICE,
Washington, October 4, 1899.

OTIS, *Manila:*

Sailed on *Sheridan*, September 30, Thirty-third Infantry; on *Nelson*, October 1, 37 officers, 210 men.

CORBIN.

MANILA. (Received October 4, 1899—8.35 a. m.)

AGWAR, *Washington:*

Capt. Bogardus Eldridge, Fourteenth Infantry, mortally wounded in action near Bacoor, Luzon, October 2, died 5.25 p. m. that date. First Lieut. Haydon Y. Grubbs, Sixth Infantry, killed in action at Tabuan, island of Negros, October 1.

OTIS.

MANILA. (Received October 4, 1899—6.07 p. m.)

AGWAR, *Washington:*

Total commissioned, enlisted, strength September 30: Cavalry, Fourth, commissioned, 44; enlisted, 1,135. Eleventh, commissioned, 43; enlisted, 288. Artillery, First, commissioned, 4; enlisted, 112. Third, commissioned, 15; enlisted, 387. Fourth, commissioned, 5; enlisted, 117. Fifth, commissioned, 4; enlisted, 114. Sixth, commissioned, 43; enlisted, 1,160. Infantry, Third, commissioned, 45; enlisted, 1,373. Fourth, commissioned, 43; enlisted, 1,347. Sixth, commissioned,

45; enlisted, 1,450. Ninth, commissioned, 41; enlisted, 1,425. Twelfth, commissioned, 42; enlisted, 1,497. Thirteenth, commissioned, 43; enlisted, 1,448. Fourteenth, commissioned, 42; enlisted, 1,632. Sixteenth, commissioned, 42; enlisted, 1,437.' Seventeenth, commissioned, 43; enlisted, 1,370. Eighteenth, commissioned, 42; enlisted, 1,442. Nineteenth, commissioned, 46; enlisted, 1,489. Twentieth, commissioned, 43; enlisted, 1,456. Twenty-first, commissioned, 45; enlisted, 1,330. Twenty-second, commissioned, 42; enlisted, 1,550. Twenty-third, commissioned, 42; enlisted, 1,170. Twenty-fourth, commissioned, 33; enlisted, 996. Twenty-fifth, commissioned, 34; enlisted, 1,039. Thirty-sixth, commissioned, 42; enlisted, 512. Thirty-seventh, commissioned, 41; enlisted, 607. First Tennessee, commissioned, 46; enlisted, 726. Engineer Battalion, commissioned, 3; enlisted, 134. Signal Corps, commissioned, 13; enlisted, 207.

OTIS.

SAN FRANCISCO, CAL., *October 5, 1899.*
(Received 5.11 p. m.)

ADJUTANT-GENERAL, *Washington:*

Transport *Sikh* sailed from Portland yesterday at 2.15 p. m., with 21 officers, 628 enlisted men, Thirty-fifth Infantry. * * * [Companies A, B, D, E, I, L.]

Rio left 6 p. m. yesterday, with 24 officers, 659 enlisted men, Thirty-fifth Infantry. * * * [Companies C, F, G, H, K, M.]

SHAFTER, *Major-General.*

ADJUTANT-GENERAL'S OFFICE,
Washington, October 5, 1899.

OTIS, *Manila:*

Sailed October 1: *Glenogle,* 29 officers, 713 men, Thirty-second U. S. Volunteer Infantry; October 4, *Sikh,* 21 officers, 628 men, Thirty-fifth U. S. Volunteer Infantry.

CORBIN.

MANILA. (Received October 6, 1899—7.20 a. m.)

AGWAR, *Washington:*

Steamer *Siam,* which left San Francisco August 19 with 45 horses, 328 mules, encountered typhoon, 1st instant, Northern Luzon, in which all but 16 mules lost. Animals killed by pitching of vessel and lack of air from necessary closing of hatches; no casualties among passengers.

OTIS.

ADJUTANT-GENERAL'S OFFICE,
Washington, October 6, 1899.

OTIS, *Manila:*

At the instance of Admiral Dewey, the naval force at Manila has been increased as follows: "Several vessels, including *Brooklyn,* already ordered; others probably follow."

The Admiral gives excellent reports of the conduct of affairs in the Philippines, and these ships are sent at his instance in order to accentuate his appreciation of the situation there to-day.

CORBIN.

ADJUTANT-GENERAL'S OFFICE,
Washington, October 6, 1899.

OTIS, *Manila:*

Whereabouts and day of sailing of Tennessee regiment desired.

CORBIN.

ADJUTANT-GENERAL'S OFFICE,
Washington, October 6, 1899.

OTIS, *Manila:*
Rio sailed October 4 remainder Thirty-fifth Infantry.

CORBIN.

SAN FRANCISCO, CAL., *October 6, 1899.*
(Received 5.52 p. m.)

ADJUTANT-GENERAL, *Washington, D. C.:*
Transport *Zealandia* left yesterday at 5.15 p. m., carrying field, staff, and five companies Twenty-ninth Infantry Volunteers. * * * (Companies D, E, F, G, H.)

SHAFTER, *Major-General.*

SAN FRANCISCO, CAL., *October 5, 1899.*
(Received 6.30 p. m.)

ADJUTANT-GENERAL, *Washington, D. C.:*
Transport *City of Para* sailed 5.55 p. m. yesterday with headquarters, field, staff, band, Companies A, B, C, I, K, L, and M, Twenty-ninth Infantry. Colonel Hardin in command. * * *

SHAFTER, *Major-General.*

MANILA. (Received October 6, 1899—7.46 a. m.)

AGWAR, *Washington:*
Additional casualties: Killed—First Tennessee, at Iloilo, September 15, F, Corpl. James C. Bullington. Fourteenth Infantry, near Bacoor, October 2, H, Corpl. Barney Mullen. Twenty-first Infantry, at Calamba, October 3, K, Frank J. Earley; D, Thomas P. Brothers. Fourth Cavalry, near Mexico, A, Charlie A. Radcliffe. Ninth Infantry, at Guagua, L, Arthur N. Chambers; Joseph F. Campbell. Wounded—Fifth Artillery, near Bacoor, F, First Lieut. Louis R. Burgess, leg, severe. Signal Corps, E, Frank L. Beals, knee, slight; October 2, Corpl. Ole Gunderson, groin, mortal. Fourteenth Infantry, 5th, Richard C. Neumann, leg, moderate; Charles E. Bevans, arms, severe; E, Max Gehleff, leg, slight. Fourth Infantry, M, Corpl. William Pillaus, thigh, moderate; M, George H. Brouillet, arms, severe; H, Corpl. Ole S. Erickson, lumbar, severe. Fourth Cavalry, near San Fernando, September 28, M, Frank J. McGrath, hand, severe. Twenty-first Infantry, at Los Baños, A, Harold T. Hely, knee, slight; at Calamba, October 3, D, Frank Yax, chest, severe; John H. Westerhoff, chest, severe; L, Corpl. John E. Gillman, foot, slight. Thirty-sixth Infantry, at Porac, September 28, E, Sergt. Joseph Bassford, head, arm, severe; D, Corpl. Louis J. Ingeterson, ankle, moderate; Corpl. Charles A. Waters, hand, slight; Woll Cooper, arm, moderate; L, Benton Wilson, buttock, moderate. Ninth Infantry, I, Corpl. Henry Morray, back, slight; Thomas F. McCarthy, neck, lung, severe; D, William Horan, foot, slight.

OTIS.

MANILA. (Received October 7, 1899—2.53 a. m.)

AGWAR, *Washington:*
Indiana sent south early in September to collect Tennessee regiment Iloilo and Cebu, picked up portion Iloilo, proceeded to Cebu, where regiment volunteered services to assist to drive off insurgents from mountains near that city; services accepted by General Snyder; insurgents overwhelmingly defeated, Tennessee taking prominent part; reembarked at Cebu, reaching this harbor 1st instant, detained in harbor to complete necessary discharge papers and will sail in *Indiana* to-morrow.

OTIS.

MANILA. (Received October 7, 1899—7.30 a. m.)

AGWAR, *Washington:*
Insurgents south Manila attacked Grant's Imus-Bacoor line again yesterday. Driven with considerable loss. Our casualty three slightly wounded. Will throw column into their midst to-morrow, Schwan commanding. This has delayed Lawton's movement north as some troops intended for him sent south with Schwan. Loss of mules *Siam* unfortunate and cripples us; 400 additional should be sent at once.

OTIS.

MANILA. (Received October 7, 1899.)

AGWAR, *Washington:*
Puebla sailed yesterday, 105 sick, 100 discharged men; *Garonne* sails to-day.

OTIS.

ADJUTANT-GENERAL'S OFFICE,
Washington, October 7, 1899.

OTIS, *Manila:*
Sailed October 6, *Para* and *Zealandia*, Twenty-ninth Volunteer Infantry and casuals. *Valencia* 13 officers, 427 recruits.

CORBIN.

MANILA. (Received October 8, 1899—9.45 a. m.)

AGWAR, *Washington:*
Following deaths since last report: Uræmia, September 29, Corpl. Joseph M. Callis, H, Sixth Infantry. Measles, 30th, Bert Pope, C, Twenty-second Infantry. Tuberculosis, pulmonary, Morradey E. Jones, I, Fourteenth Infantry. Dysentery, chronic, October 1, Samuel H. Alexander, C, Twenty-second Infantry; 4th, Sergt. Maj. Charles J. Giudici, Thirty-sixth Infantry. Dysentery, acute, J. Lewis Hellreigle, F, Fourteenth Infantry; 2d, John Cunningham, F, Twelfth Infantry. Drowning, accidental, 1st, James Ruffin, Twenty-fourth Infantry; 3d, Garfield Thompson, G, Twenty-fourth Infantry. Diarrhea, chronic, William Dunaway, C, Third Infantry; 4th, Henry G. Booth, B, Seventeenth Infantry; Walter Scott, G, Fourth Infantry; 5th, William C. Timmons, G, Twelfth Infantry. Gunshot wound in action, 3d, Corpl. Ole Gunderson, Signal Corps. Neuritis, general, 4th, Henry H. Gayer, M, Fourteenth Infantry. Typhoid fever, 3d, First Sergt. Julius Labodie, L, Sixth Infantry; 5th, Ernest C. Knapp, G, Ninth Infantry. Malaria, 6th, Demarest H. Smith, E, Seventeenth Infantry. Gunshot wound, accidental, Corpl. Frank B. Johnson, A, Twenty-second Infantry.

OTIS.

MANILA. (Received October 9, 1899—1.55 a. m.)

AGWAR, *Washington:*
Schwan, with column 1,726 men, Thirteenth Infantry, battalion Fourteenth Infantry, with cavalry and artillery, left Bacoor yesterday morning and proceeded to Noveleta, encountering heavy opposition old Cavite and beyond, but drove enemy, capturing two guns and inflicting damage; his casualties, Captain Saffold, Thirteenth infantry, killed; Captain McGrath, Fourth Cavalry, seriously wounded; 10 enlisted men wounded; column entering Rosario this morning, meeting slight opposition. Navy vessels and marines at Cavite made demonstration on Noveleta yesterday, while Schwan advanced at same time. Troops at Imus attacked insurgents at San Nicolas, 2 miles east of the city, and drove them from the road intersection there; 4 men slightly wounded; enemy left 6 bodies on field.

OTIS.

MANILA. (Received October 9, 1899—2.45 a. m.)

AGWAR, *Washington:*
Indiana sailed yesterday, 43 officers, 619 men, Tennessee volunteers; 100 general prisoners transferred Department California. Tennessee regiment left no sick.

OTIS.

ADJUTANT-GENERAL'S OFFICE,
Washington, October 9, 1899.

OTIS, *Manila:*
Refer to your telegram of 7th requesting 400 mules, *Port Albert*, Kobe, 3d, is expected to arrive Manila 14th, 500 mules. Do you wish us to send 400 requested in preference to horses?

CORBIN.

MANILA. (Received October 10, 1899—12.20 a. m.)

AGWAR, *Washington:*
Annual reports and appendixes, very long; printer, with all force obtainable, hard at work; will finish in about ten days; will send copies as far as completed next steamer.

OTIS.

MANILA. (Received October 10, 1899—1.45 a. m.)

AGWAR, *Washington:*
General Schwan's column moved early this morning from Santa Cruz de Malabon; now believed to be in San Francisco de Malabon; not meeting very determined resistance. Matters quiet in Imus section. General Young, with column, start northward to-morrow morning from San Fernando. Colonel Bell cleared country yesterday west of Guagua, to and including Florida Blanca, making captures of officers, men, and property.

OTIS.

MANILA. (Received October 10, 1899—4.30 a. m.)

AGWAR, *Washington:*
Let shipment horses precede that of mules; former much needed here.

OTIS.

ADJUTANT-GENERAL'S OFFICE,
Washington, October 10, 1899.

OTIS, *Manila:*
Inform Department when, in your opinion, it is advisable to allow officers' families to leave here for Manila. Pressure from every direction very great.

CORBIN.

SAN FRANCISCO, CAL., *October 10, 1899.* (Received 5.54 p. m.)
ADJUTANT-GENERAL, *Washington:*
Transport *Pennsylvania* arrived October 9, 1899, with First Washington Infantry.
* * *

SHAFTER, *Major-General.*

SAN FRANCISCO, CAL., *October 10, 1899.*
(Received 9.55 p. m.)

ADJUTANT-GENERAL, *Washington:*

Following arrived on transport *Newport:* Eighteenth Company Volunteer Signal Corps. * * * Twenty sick soldiers, 4 sick discharged soldiers, 300 discharged soldiers. * * *

SHAFTER, *Major-General.*

MANILA. (Received October 10, 1899—1.40 p. m.)

AGWAR, *Washington:*

Casualties: Wounded—near Cavite Viejo, Fifth Cavalry, October 8, First Lieut. Charles W. Fenton, ear, slight. Fourth Cavalry, G, Corpl. John P. Martin, leg, moderate. Thirteenth Infantry, B, Marshall D. Bibber, head, severe; George F. Bliel, leg, severe. Fourteenth Infantry, E, George D. Snapp, groin, moderate; F, John P. Flood, arm, moderate; G, Corpl. John Dwyer, leg, slight; Frank Richard, knee, moderate; James Milwee, forearm, moderate. Twenty-first Infantry, at Calamba, October 3, D, Alva K. Oliver; chest, slight; K, Sergt. Peter Kelly, shoulder, moderate; John T. Bratchey, ear, slight; L, Allie D. Fields, thigh, slight. Sixth Infantry, near Cebu, island Cebu, September 22, A, James Conway, leg, moderate; John H. Norton, arm, moderate; C, George W. Arthur, legs, severe. Nineteenth Infantry, K, Sergt. James Covey, breast, severe.

OTIS.

MANILA. (Received October 11, 1899—12.40 a. m.)

AGWAR, *Washington:*

Transport *Victoria* arrived night 9th instant with 403 horses; 10 died en route, several with glanders shot yesterday. *Garonne* sailed on 7th, *Athenian* on 9th; both for Seattle.

OTIS.

MANILA. (Received October 11, 1899—3.12 a. m.)

AGWAR, *Washington:*

Population Manila much congested; provision for officers' families can not be made; those already arrived, together with families enlisted men, have caused much perplexity; would not permit my own family to come under existing circumstances; nearly all officers and men here absent from Manila on duty; families should await more peaceful conditions.

OTIS.

MANILA. (Received October 11, 1899—3.12 a. m.)

AGWAR, *Washington:*

Schwan successful yesterday in driving insurgents south, with loss, from San Francisco de Malabon; he reports their force disintegrated and retiring on divergent roads, which are impassable for artillery or wagons; no intention of occupying this country permanently or temporarily; transportation will return by way of Rosario and column will move direction Dasmariñas, probably retiring on Imus; country of no strategic importance.

OTIS.

ADJUTANT-GENERAL'S OFFICE,
Washington, October 11, 1899.

OTIS, *Manila:*

Speedy return of *Columbia* and *Warren* desired.

CORBIN.

SAN FRANCISCO, CAL., *October 11, 1899.*
(Received 2.09 p. m.)

ADJUTANT-GENERAL, *Washington:*

Transport *Tartar* arrived here last night with the Twentieth Kansas; details later.

SHAFTER, *Major-General.*

MANILA. (Received October 11, 1899—6 a. m.)

AGWAR, *Washington:*

Capt. Woodbridge Geary, Thirteenth Infantry, died 3 o'clock this morning at San Francisco de Malabon from gunshot wound received in reconnoissance toward Buena Vista yesterday.

OTIS.

MANILA. (Received October 12, 1899—12.56 a. m.)

AGWAR, *Washington:*

Transport *Columbia* arrived last evening; no casualties. *Warren* leaves 15th instant; *Columbia* as soon as possible.

OTIS.

MANILA. (Received October 12, 1899—9.24 a. m.)

AGWAR, *Washington:*

Schwan's column moving on Sabang and Dasmariñas to-day, where opposition expected; his artillery and wagon transportation returning to Bacoor by way of Rosario; column 500 men marching from Imus to support Schwan if necessary. Young at north occupied Arayat, and supplies being moved up Rio Grande by cascos to that point. Lawton will command column when full concentration effected. Young's loss to-day, 1 enlisted man wounded. Yesterday insurgents attacked Angeles line; quickly repulsed; 6 enlisted men slightly wounded.

OTIS.

MANILA. (Received October 13, 1899—12.30 p. m.)

AGWAR, *Washington:*

Casualties: Wounded—Fourth Infantry, at Imus, September 29, B, Frank Huss, thigh, severe; John W. Smith, foot, moderate; K, Frank Hickade, thigh, moderate; October 3, A, Sergt. William L. Born, ear, slight; at San Nicolas, October 8, E, James McGlinchey, back, moderate. Fifth Artillery at Imus September 29, F, Louis Liever, knee, severe; at San Francisco de Malabon, October 10, Louis Arnold, chest, moderate. Twenty-second Infantry, at Arayat, October 5, F, Archie Huchison, arm, slight. Twenty-fourth Infantry, near Santa Ana, October 7, F, Sergt. David Holden, chest, severe; James Smith, thigh, severe; Fourteenth Infantry, near Mariquina, October 8, L, William Briney, neck, severe; at San Nicolas, G, Frank Frager, forearm, severe; Owen B. Hill, leg, severe. Hospital Corps, Alvin H. Bailey, leg, moderate. Thirteenth Infantry, at San Francisco de Malabon, October 10, F, Norman Norton, knee, moderate; G, Peter Kankiwicz, arm, severe; H, Charles E. Smith, thigh, severe. Fourth Artillery, F, Charles Wilson, thigh, moderate. Engineer Battalion, A, John I. Van Ness, leg, severe.

OTIS.

MANILA. (Received October 14, 1899—2.15 a. m.)

AGWAR, *Washington:*

Transport *Belgian King* arrived this morning seven companies Thirty-fourth Infantry; no casualties.

OTIS.

CORRESPONDENCE.

MANILA. (Received October 14, 1899—3.35 a. m.)

AGWAR, *Washington:*

Tacoma (sailing vessel) arrived last evening, delayed two weeks by typhoon, 191 horses, Fourth Cavalry, good condition; 9 lost.

OTIS.

MANILA. (Received October 14, 1899—4.56 a. m.)

AGWAR, *Washington:*

Schwan's column swung into Imus from Dasmariñas yesterday morning; camped at Bacoor last night; has scattered insurgents, who probably retiring by detachments on Indang; condition of roads prevented further pursuit. One hundred twenty-five men, Thirty-seventh Volunteers, Major Cheatham, drove insurgents south and westward from lake town Muntinlupa yesterday pursuing several miles and retired to Bacoor last night by Zapote River road; loss 3 men killed, 2 wounded, 1 missing; Schwan's movement very successful, inflicted heavy loss on men and property of southern insurgent army; he reports their casualties 200 killed and 400 wounded; their stored supplies destroyed. Young, moving from Arayat north and westward yesterday scattered insurgents, who returned northwestward; his casualties 3 slightly wounded; considerable store of grain captured.

OTIS.

MANILA. (Received October 15, 1899—6.50 a. m.)

AGWAR, *Washington:*

Following deaths since last report: Dysentery, chronic—October 8, Sergt. William Humphris, D, Fourteenth Infantry; Corpl. Matthias L. Harris, I, Twenty-first Infantry; 11th, Daniel McCarthy, E, Signal Corps; Sergt. Murtha Hennessy, B, Thirteenth Infantry; 13th, Patrick Ryan, C, Twentieth Infantry. Diarrhea, chronic—9th, Frank N. Cook, I, Twenty-first Infantry. Typhoid fever—7th, William J. Flynn, F, Fifth Artillery; 9th, Robert Paige, Hospital Corps; 11th, Lawrence V. Harris, I, Twenty-first Infantry; Lewis E. Jones, L, Thirteenth Infantry; Harry N. Whritenor, I, Twenty-first Infantry. Dysentery, acute—9th, Charles A. LaRose, B, Fourth Cavalry. Suicide—Alfred E. Bernard, Hospital Corps. Heart disease—Trumpeter Edward Parnell, E, Twenty-fifth Infantry. Enteritis—Henry Moller, B, Eighteenth Infantry. Pneumonia—13th, George Clayton, C, Nineteenth Infantry.

OTIS.

MANILA. (Received October 17, 1899—3.43 a. m.)

AGWAR, *Washington:*

Spirited night attack by insurgents on MacArthur's front at Angeles early yesterday morning; enemy repulsed; our loss, 1 killed; 8 wounded, most slightly.

OTIS.

MANILA. (Received October 17, 1899—1.30 p. m.)

AGWAR, *Washington:*

Casualties: Killed—Thirty-seventh Infantry, near Muntinlupa, October 12, A, Leslie D. Berry, Joseph T. Morisette, Joseph F. Maher. Wounded—Fourth Infantry, at Imus, October 5, E, Frank O. Stevens, foot, slight; October 6, C, Corpl. Ralph C. Haxton, hand and leg, severe; A, Harry Faulkner, hand, slight; F, Frank B. Conklin, leg and knee, severe. Ninth Infantry, at Angeles, October 11, C, Corpl. John W. Lattimore, foot, slight; F, Christopher E. Whiteside, chest, slight; Axel Skogsberg, leg, moderate; L, Frank W. Schork, forearm, slight; John F. McGraw, arm, slight; October 13, Leslie E. Cleland, arm, severe. Seventeenth Infantry, October 11, D, Corpl. William C. Rosselit, arm, slight. Thirty-seventh Infantry, near Muntinlupa, October 12, B, Andrew S. Garrett, thigh, moderate. Hospital Corps, Joseph S. Shapiro, thigh, moderate. Sixth Infantry, at Tabuan, island Negros, October 1, A, Sergt. George Stevens, arm, severe; Elmer F. Affeldt, thigh, slight; B, Harry Campbell, thighs, moderate.

OTIS.

MANILA. (Received October 18, 1899—5.35 a. m.)

AGWAR, *Washington:*

Lawton, with carefully selected strong column, reached Cabiao, 10 miles south San Isidro, this morning; has thirty days' supplies and more at Calumpit to be forwarded. Third and Fourth Cavalry with him under Young. Bell, Thirty-sixth Infantry, scouting northwest Santa Rita, with part of regiment, struck insurgents, killing and wounding several, capturing 13 prisoners, 15 rifles.

OTIS.

MANILA. (Received November 19, 1899—10.55 a. m.)

AGWAR, *Washington:*

Casualties: Killed—Sixth Infantry, near Cebu, island Cebu, September 18, A, Charles N. Cotay, Daniel E. Adams. Seventeenth Infantry, at Angeles, October 16, L, William Parker. Thirty-sixth Infantry, at Porac, October 17, H, Willard Winters. Wounded—October 16, at Angeles, Acting Asst. Surg. H. Eugene Stafford, breast, slight. Sixth Infantry, near Cebu, island Cebu, September 18, A, William Stovall, abdomen, severe; C, Horace Hutchinson, nates, severe. Fourth Infantry, near San Nicolas, October 8, F, James A. O'Reilly, hand, slight. Ninth Infantry, at Angeles, October 16, D, George K. Webster, head, moderate; H, John Kelley, thigh, severe; I, Albert Durand, back, severe; Charles S. Wilson, head, severe. Seventeenth Infantry, A, Corpl. Henry Rosser, head, slight; B, William Crosby, thigh, slight; H, Joseph B. Thackara, larynx, severe; Thomas E. Scully, thigh, slight. Sixteenth Infantry, at Guiguinto, October 13, F, Thomas Lynch, side, severe; Leslie Shores, foot, severe. Fourth Cavalry, near Arayat, October 13, D, First Sergt. Gustave Will, arm, moderate; Mathew W. Killion, leg, moderate. Thirty-sixth Infantry, at Porac, October 17, M, Sam Williams, cheek, moderate.

OTIS.

MANILA. (Received October 20, 1899.)

AGWAR, *Washington:*

Lawton's advance, under Young, in San Isidro where garrison will be established; considerable resistance encountered yesterday. Casualties: One killed, 3 wounded, Twenty-second Infantry. Enemy suffered considerably; 1 Spaniard, 15 insurgent soldiers captured. Young reports inhabitants in section of country most friendly.

OTIS.

MANILA. (Received October 21, 1899—4.15 a. m.)

AGWAR, *Washington:*

Transport *Elder* just arrived; 19 officers, 448 enlisted men; no casualties.

OTIS.

MANILA. (Received October 21, 1899—7.35 a. m.)

AGWAR, *Washington:*

Transport *Sherman* just arrived; Thirtieth Volunteers and recruits; no casualties.

OTIS.

MANILA. (Received October 21, 1899—11.22 a. m.)

AGWAR, *Washington:*

Following deaths have occurred since last report: Malaria—October 14, Sergt. James McLeod, E, Nineteenth Infantry; 16th, Robert Haeffele, H, Twenty-second Infantry. Gastro enteritis—15th, Charles E. Hummer, A, Thirty-sixth Infantry. Gunshot wound—in action, 17th, Sergt. Joseph H. Bassford, E, Thirty-sixth Infantry; accidental, 16th, Richard Jefferson, E, Twenty-fifth Infantry; 18th, Corpl. Eugene Wise, M, Sixteenth Infantry. Drowning, accidental—15th, Ira Jones, E, Twenty-fourth Infantry. Intestinal obstruction—17th, Jerry Sullivan, C, Seventeeth Infantry. Tetanus, James R. Cameron, E, Third Infantry.

OTIS.

MANILA. (Received October 22, 1899—5.30 a. m.)

AGWAR, *Washington:*

October 20, message received at Angeles, under flag of truce, expressed desire of honorable president Aguinaldo to send commission to Manila to arrange difficulties connected with delivery of Spanish prisoners and to discuss matter of a particular character. Reply returned that commission accredited by any one other than General Aguinaldo, general in chief insurgent forces, could not be recognized or received; no later correspondence.

OTIS.

SAN FRANCISCO, CAL., *October 22, 1899.*
(Received 5.55 p. m.)

ADJUTANT-GENERAL, *Washington, D. C.:*

Transport *Senator* has just arrived. (Fifty-first Iowa Volunteers.)

SHAFTER, *Major-General.*

MANILA. (Received October 23, 1899.)

AGWAR, *Washington:*

Capt. Guy Howard, assistant quartermaster and quartermaster of volunteers, killed yesterday near Arayat while on launch Rio Grande River, by concealed insurgents; his clerk, a civilian employee and native, wounded. Scouting detachment Thirty-sixth Volunteers encountered insurgents yesterday southwest Santa Rita; scattered them, killing 6, capturing 8 and 10 rifles; no casualties. General Lawton operating at San Isidro. The forwarding of supplies to that point continues attended with some difficulties on account lack of transportation, which will be supplied soon. Insurgents, southern Luzon, attacked Calamba; these were driven off; no casualties.

OTIS.

MANILA. (Received October 23, 1899—4.50 a. m.)

AGWAR, *Washington:*

This morning Kline, commanding at Calamba, vigorously attacked insurgent force concentrating on his front, routed them from trenches, and pursued 3 miles; his casualties, 1 private killed, 1 corporal and 3 privates wounded; enemy's loss unknown.

OTIS.

MANILA. (Received October 24, 1899—8.48 a. m.)

AGWAR, *Washington:*

Hughes reports Panay insurgents driven out of Negros. Byrne struck one band, killed 10, captured 13. Native troops struck another, killed 6; no casualties.

OTIS.

AFFAIRS IN THE PHILIPPINE ISLANDS.

MANILA. (Received October 25, 1899.)

AGWAR, *Washington:*
Transport *Grant*, Twenty-sixth Volunteers and recruits, arrived yesterday; no casualties. *Aztec* with horses and civilian employees this morning; 7 horses lost; all others in good condition.

OTIS.

SAN FRANCISCO, CAL., *October 26, 1899.*
(Received 4.46 p. m.)

ADJUTANT-GENERAL, *Washington:*
Transport *Newport* sailed this morning with Major Porter and companies I, K, L, and M, Twenty-eighth Infantry, 15 officers, 388 men. * * *

SHAFTER, *Major-General.*

SAN FRANCISCO, CAL., *October 26, 1899.*
(Received 4.54 p. m.)

ADJUTANT-GENERAL, *Washington:*
Transport *Manauense* sailed this morning with field, staff, and four companies Thirty-first Infantry, 15 officers, 375 men. * * *

SHAFTER, *Major-General.*

SAN FRANCISCO, CAL., *October 26, 1899.*
(Received 4.55 p. m.)

ADJUTANT-GENERAL, *Washington, D. C.:*
Transport *Tartar* sailed this morning with First and Second Battalions, Twenty-eighth Infantry, 31 officers, 829 men. * * *

SHAFTER, *Major-General.*

SAN FRANCISCO, CAL., *October 26, 1899.*
(Received 7.31 p. m.)

ADJUTANT-GENERAL, *Washington, D.C.:*
Transport *City of Sydney* arrived at noon. [Sick and discharged soldiers aboard.]

SHAFTER, *Major-General.*

MANILA. (Received October 27, 1899—3.45 a. m.)

AGWAR, *Washington:*
Transport *Tacoma*, headquarters, 7 companies, Twenty-seventh Volunteers, arrived; casualties, Corporal Henderson, C Company, washed overboard; 2 men deserted and 7 left sick at Honolulu, of whom Corporal Hunter, G, dead; no other casualties; command in good health.

OTIS.

MANILA. (Received October 27, 1899—6.45 a m.)

AGWAR, *Washington:*
Lawton's advance, under Young, north San Isidro, near Cabanatuan, San Isidro; established permanent station, three months' supplies being forwarded by San Juan River route; Lawton meets little resistance. Twenty-sixth Volunteers and battalion Nineteenth Infantry sent to Iloilo.

OTIS.

MANILA. (Received October 27, 1899—6.50 a. m.)
AGWAR, *Washington:*
Insurgent government submitted application to send five commissioners to Manila to arrange difficulties attending release Spanish sick prisoners and discuss peace conditions; declined, no negotiations necessary, as we would gladly receive all Spanish prisoners at our lines, welcome them from their cruel captivity and labor for their welfare. Correspondence by mail.

OTIS.

MANILA. (Received October 27, 1899—6.52 a. m.)
AGWAR, *Washington:*
Transport *Sheridan*, Thirty-third Volunteers and recruits, arrived; good condition; 1 casualty, Private Hulgan, Company K, died en route.

OTIS.

MANILA. (Received October 28, 1899—9.57 a. m.)
AGWAR, *Washington:*
Young struck iusurgents Santa Rosa, north San Isidro, yesterday, driving them capturing some of their property; casualties, 2 killed; 1 wounded. Evans, Sixth Infantry, struck robber band, Negros, 27th instant; killed 10, wounding many, capturing 20 prisoners. Simons, Sixth Infantry, struck small band; dispersed them, killing 3; no casualties.

OTIS.

SAN FRANCISCO, CAL., *October 28, 1899.*
(Received 5.12 p. m.)
ADJUTANT-GENERAL, *Washington, D. C.:*
City of Pekin will sail to-day with the remainder of Thirty-first Infantry and 125 recruits.

SHAFTER, *Major-General.*

MANILA. (Received October 28, 1899—10.55 p. m.)
AGWAR, *Washington:*
Casualties: Killed—civilian on tug *Oceania*, river Chico Pampanga, October 22, John D. Dean, blacksmith. Twenty-first Infantry, at Calamba, October 23, I, George Mitchell. Wounded—civilian employee on tug *Oceania*, river Chico Pampanga, October 22, W. P. Chamberlain, severe. Twenty-first Infantry at Calamba, B, Corpl. Jesse Elliott, shoulder, moderate. October 23, D, Ernest Knowles, thigh, severe; George Smith, knee, severe.

OTIS.

MANILA. (Received October 29, 1899—12.15 a. m.)
AGWAR, *Washington:*
Following deaths since last report: Uræmia—October 1, William E. Fauber, K, Sixth Infantry. Epilepsy—6th, Edgar A. Kenny, E, Nineteenth Infantry. Drowning, accidental—16th, John L. Hand, M, Fourth Cavalry. Pneumonia—19th, James Hart, oiler, ship *Yorktown*. Gastro enteritis—Michael Barry, H, Twenty-first Infantry. Pulmonary tuberculosis—21st, Robert H. Smith, E, Twelfth Infantry. Anæmia—22d, Charles H. Slater, B, Twenty-first Infantry. Gunshot wound, accidental—23d, Frank Gravely, H, Twenty-seventh Infantry. Dysentery, acute—Corpl. Edward Harris, F, Twenty-first Infantry; 24th, Charles Skinner, H, Fourth Infantry. Dysentery, chronic—Alexander M. Culross, K, Fourth Infantry; 27th, Robert M. Richwine, E, Thirty-seventh Infantry. Diarrhea, chronic—26th, Edward S. Bruce, I, Twelfth Infantry.

OTIS.

AFFAIRS IN THE PHILIPPINE ISLANDS. 1091

MANILA. (Received October 30, 1899—2.35 a. m.)

AGWAR, *Washington:*

Transport *Glenogle*, 29 officers, 716 men, Thirty-second Volunteers, arrived in good condition; 1 casualty, private Edward R. McCandless, company K, died at sea 21st instant; cause, septic peritonitis.

OTIS.

MANILA. (Received October 30, 1899—2.35 a. m.)

AGWAR, *Washington:*

Detachment Bell's regiment, Thirty-sixth Volunteers, reconnoitering toward Florida Blanca, West Guagua, struck body insurgents in newly constructed trenches; attacked and drove enemy, who left in hands of detachment 4 insurgent officers and 8 enlisted men killed, 3 prisoners, and 9 rifles; casualties, Captain French and Lieutenant Ferguson, wounded, not dangerously; 1 enlisted man killed, 6 wounded.

OTIS.

ADJUTANT-GENERAL'S OFFICE,
Washington, October 30, 1899.

OTIS, *Manila:*

Sailed October 26, *Tartar* and *Newport*, Twenty-eighth U. S. Volunteer Infantry; *Manauense*, battalion Thirty-first U. S. Volunteer Infantry; October 29, *Pekin*, remainder Thirty-first U. S. Volunteer Infantry. *Centennial* with casuals.

CORBIN.

MANILA. (Received October 30, 1899—11.45 p. m.)

AGWAR, *Washington:*

Young's advance north and east Cabanatuan will occupy Talavera and probably Aliaga to-day; objective, San José and Carranglan. Wet season has rendered roads in that section impracticable for wagon transportation, and progress difficult. Advance of another column in a few days.

OTIS.

MANILA. (Received October 31, 1899—4.45 a. m.)

AGWAR, *Washington:*

Capt. Charles French, Thirty-sixth Infantry, died, Manila, 11 a. m. October 31; cause, shock consequent on amputation leg below knee because of gunshot wound received in battle near Florida Blanca, October 30.

OTIS.

MANILA. (Received November 1, 1899—7.55 a. m.)

ADJUTANT-GENERAL, *Washington:*

Lawton's advance on Aliaga and Talavera, from Cabanatuan, which place now occupied, successfully; enemy driven north and westward; two small cannon captured, with considerable ammunition and large quantities corn, rice, river and land transportation, also telegraph operator with entire equipment and important insurgent dispatches; no casualties. Insurgents advancing from Tarlac to meet Lawton's troops, but they have lost strategic positions. Hope to hold majority of them on line of railroad, preventing escape to their recently announced capital of Bayombong, in mountains. Hughes reports Negros in better state of lawful submission than for twenty years—planters no longer in danger; quiet election; over 5,000 votes cast; no frauds attempted. Inauguration of military-civil government 6th instant. Hughes commences active operations against Tagalos in Panay as soon as condition of roads and trails permit.

OTIS.

ADJUTANT-GENERAL'S OFFICE,
Washington, November 1, 1899.

OTIS, *Manila:*

Orders to-day relieve two batteries Sixth Artillery from Honolulu to report to you at Manila for assignment station.

CORBIN.

SAN FRANCISCO, CAL., *November 1, 1899.*
(Received 6.28 p. m.)

ADJUTANT-GENERAL, *Washington, D. C.:*

The transport *City of Puebla* has just arrived. Details later. (Sick and discharged soldiers on board.)

SHAFTER, *Major-General.*

MANILA. (Received November 1, 1899—10.55 a. m.)

ADJUTANT-GENERAL, *Washington:*

Casualties: Killed—Twenty-second Infantry, at San Isidro, October 19, K, Corpl. Ephraim S. Yoder. Thirty-sixth Infantry, at Lupao, October 29, G, Windsor R. Stanley. Wounded—Twenty-first Infantry, at Calamba, October 23, D, Edward G. Hellen, foot, slight. Fourteenth Infantry, at Imus, October 6, H, Corpl. Henry Overbay, foot, severe. Twenty-second Infantry, at San Isidro, October 19, F, Griffin Andrews, forearm, severe; I, Charles H. Pierce, thigh, severe; K, Handy B. Johnson, leg, severe. Thirty-sixth Infantry, at Lupao, October 29, C, Corpl. John F. Swank, arms, slight; James Pitt, back, slight; H, William G. McCarty, forearm, slight; Hardy L. Laurence, thigh, slight; Third Artillery, K, Thomas H. Dow, shoulder, slight; Hospital Corps, Jesse Rutledge, thigh, slight; at San Isidro, October 19, Claude B. Day, hand, slight.

OTIS.

MANILA. (Received November 2, 1899—3.05 a. m.)

ADJUTANT-GENERAL, *Washington:*

Transport *Zealandia*, five companies Twenty-ninth Infantry and recruits, arrived. No casualties.

OTIS.

ADJUTANT-GENERAL'S OFFICE,
Washington, November 2, 1899.

COMMANDING GENERAL, DEPARTMENT CALIFORNIA,
San Francisco, Cal.:

Orders to-day send two batteries, Sixth Artillery, to be designated by you, from Honolulu for duty at Manila, reporting upon arrival to the commanding general Department Pacific, for assignment to station.

JOHNSTON,
Assistant Adjutant-General.

MANILA. (Received November 3, 1899—4.25 a. m.)

ADJUTANT-GENERAL, *Washington:*

MacArthur will advance 5th instant. Wheaton, with over 2,000 men, leaves for Lingayen Gulf 6th instant. Property now being placed on transports. We will block all roads on west coast Luzon leading north.

OTIS.

AFFAIRS IN THE PHILIPPINE ISLANDS. 1093

MANILA. (Received November 3, 1899—5 a. m.)

ADJUTANT-GENERAL, *Washington:*

On 1st instant Lieutenant Slavens and 18 men, reconnoitering MacArthur's front, struck 40 or more intrenched insurgents; immediately attacked and dispersed them, killing 3 and wounding a number; no casualties. Yesterday Lawton's advance at Aliaga struck enemy both west and south of city. Batson's Macabebe scouts reconnoitering south struck insurgents in ambush; Lieutenant Boutelle killed; 1 scout wounded; Batson routed enemy, who left dead in thicket. Yesterday Bell, Thirty-sixth Volunteers, with regiment and troop Fourth Cavalry, cleared country of all armed insurgents from Florida Blanca to considerable distance beyond Porac; pursuing them into mountains, capturing 9 of their cavalry horses, several guns, considerable property; killing, wounding, and capturing number of enemy; insurgent cavalry of that country practically destroyed. Bell's casualties, 1 man killed and 2 wounded.

OTIS.

SAN FRANCISCO, CAL., *November 3, 1899.*
(Received 4 p. m.)

ADJUTANT-GENERAL, U. S. ARMY,
Washington, D. C.:

The *Pennsylvania* and *Olympia*, with the Thirty-ninth Infantry and battalion Forty-fifth Infantry, sailed from Portland early this morning; will keep together; detailed reports of troops later.

SHAFTER, *Major-General.*

SAN FRANCISCO, CAL., *November 3, 1899.*
(Received 6 p. m.)

Gen. H. C. CORBIN, *War Department, Washington, D. C.:*

The arrival at this port yesterday on the transport *Puebla* from Manila of 100 discharged soldiers, nearly all of them without money, leads me to invite your attention again to the recommendation hitherto made that in future all soldiers be sent to San Francisco to be discharged and no more discharged in Manila. I would suggest that all men whose term of service expires in December be started for San Francisco early in November, thus bringing them here about the time their service expires, and that this plan of shipment be carried out in future in cases of all discharged soldiers in Manila. The adoption of this plan will insure the men having at least money enough to carry them to their respective homes after reaching San Francisco. As it is now many discharged soldiers are only able to reach home by reason of the charitable assistance of the good women of the Red Cross Society of this State. These discharged men of course receive their pay at Manila, but the pitfalls of Manila, Nagasaki, and Yokohama are too much for them and they consequently reach San Francisco in a destitute condition.

SHAFTER, *Major-General Commanding.*

MANILA. (Received November 3, 1899—3.50 p. m.)

ADJUTANT-GENERAL, *Washington:*

Total strength October 31: Cavalry, Third, commissioned 30, enlisted 956; Fourth, commissioned 43, enlisted 1,263; Eleventh, commissioned 43, enlisted 660. Artillery, First, commissioned 4, enlisted 111; Third, commissioned 12, enlisted 399; Fourth, commissioned 5, enlisted 132; Fifth, commissioned 4, enlisted 129; Sixth, commissioned 43, enlisted 1,161. Infantry, Third, commissioned 44, enlisted 1,415; Fourth, commissioned 43, enlisted 1,425; Sixth, commissioned 43, enlisted 1,514; Ninth, commissioned 43, enlisted 1,427; Twelfth, commissioned 44, enlisted 1,480; Thirteenth, commissioned 41, enlisted 1,453; Fourteenth, commissioned 43, enlisted 1,587; Sixteenth, commissioned 44, enlisted 1,445; Seventeenth, commissioned 42, enlisted 1,448; Eighteenth, commissioned 43, enlisted 1,412; Nineteenth, commissioned 45, enlisted 1,486; Twentieth, commissioned 43, enlisted 1,478; Twenty-first, commissioned 46, enlisted 1,374; Twenty-second, commissioned 43, enlisted 1,548; Twenty-third, commissioned 45, enlisted 1,203; Twenty-fourth, commissioned 17, enlisted 1,038; Twenty-fifth, commissioned 36, enlisted 1,081; Twenty-sixth, commissioned 49, enlisted 1,243; Twenty-seventh, commissioned 51, enlisted 1,238; Thirtieth, commissioned 50, enlisted 1,299; Thirty-second, commissioned 39, enlisted 997; Thirty-third, commissioned 49, enlisted 1,298; Thirty-fourth, commissioned 49, enlisted 1,299; Thirty-sixth, commissioned 48, enlisted 1,042; Thirty-seventh, commissioned 46, enlisted 895. Engineers, commissioned 5, enlisted 283. Signal Corps, commissioned 14, enlisted 247.

OTIS.

MANILA. (Received November 4, 1899—8.54 a. m.)
ADJUTANT-GENERAL, *Washington:*
Transports *Nelson, Para* arrived yesterday; no casualties; *Sherman* sailed October 31; *Tacoma* November 2; *Aztec* November 3.

OTIS.

ADJUTANT-GENERAL'S OFFICE,
Washington, November 4, 1899.
OTIS, *Manila:*
Secwar directs that enlisted men whose terms expire in December be sent to San Francisco on next transports to be discharged there.

WARD.

ADJUTANT-GENERAL'S OFFICE,
Washington, November 4, 1899.
Maj. Gen. W. R. SHAFTER,
Commanding Department of California, San Francisco, Cal.
The following has been sent General Otis to-day: "Secwar directs that enlisted men whose term expire in December be sent to San Francisco on next transports to be discharged there."

THOS. WARD,
Acting Adjutant-General.

NOTE.—No telegram or letter received reporting sailing of transport *Thomas* from New York November 4, 1899, with Forty-seventh Infantry, U. S. Volunteers.

MANILA. (Received November 4, 1899—10.13 a. m.)
ADJUTANT-GENERAL, *Washington:*
Do not protocols 1877 and 1885 between Spain, Germany, and Great Britain, whereby Spanish sovereignty over Sulu Archipelago acknowledged and free trade in Archipelago promised by Spain, fall with cession of territory to United States?

OTIS.

SAN FRANCISCO, CAL., *November 5, 1899.*
(Received 6.45 p. m.)
ADJUTANT-GENERAL, *Washington, D. C.:*
Transport *Ohio* arrived; details later. [Nevada Cavalry Volunteers on board.]

SHAFTER, *Major-General.*

AFFAIRS IN THE PHILIPPINE ISLANDS. 1095

MANILA. (Received November 6, 1899—3.20 a. m.)
ADJUTANT-GENERAL, *Washington:*

Wheaton's expedition, 2,500 strong, transports *Sheridan* and *Aztec* and two coasting steamers, convoyed by three war vessels, left for Lingayen Gulf this morning. MacArthur's troops advanced to Magalang yesterday, clearing country between Angeles and Arayat, encountered about 1,000 of enemy at different points. O'Brien with battalion Seventeenth Infantry, two troops Fourth Cavalry, and Slaven's scouts, moving on roads from Calulut, east of Angeles, encountered and drove enemy direction of Magalang, who left 49 dead on field. O'Brien captured 28 prisoners, 14 rifles. Colonel Smith with other two battalions Seventeenth, Hamilton's battery First Artillery, and Engineers and Signal Detachments, moved on direct road from Angeles to Magalang, capturing latter place, inflicting loss on enemy in killed and wounded of about 100, capturing 50 prisoners, large amount insurgent transportation; our casualties reported at 12 wounded in part. Severe heavy rains last three days have rendered decisive movements by Lawton's troops impossible; he now has abundant supplies at San Isidro and farther north, and will operate to the north and westward when the country now submerged permits.

OTIS.

MANILA. (Received November 6, 1899—4.40 a. m.)
ADJUTANT-GENERAL, *Washington:*

Following deaths since last report: Arterial sclerosis—October 13, Thomas Nagle, E, Seventeenth Infantry. Typhoid fever—John W. Porter, C, Sixth Artillery; 31st, Erwin A. Stephenson, L, Seventeenth Infantry. Malarial disease—Clarence Wilson, corporal, M, 17th Infantry; November 3, Frank P. Secrist, B, Seventeenth Infantry. Homicide—October 20, Paul E. Moran, sergeant, E, Sixth Infantry. Suicide, insane—31st, Charles A. Zaisser, D, Sixth Infantry. Chronic dysentery—30th, George F. Cooney, F, Twelfth Infantry; November 1, John F. Fitzsimmons, B, Twenty-first Infantry; 2d, James H. Grennan, D, Twentieth Infantry. Acute dysentery—1st, Daniel E. Webster, L, Ninth Infantry; October 28, Jacob Cavalaskie, E, Twenty-first Infantry. Pulmonary congestion—11th, James C. Hulgan, K, Thirty-third Infantry. Chronic diarrhea—13th, Michael B. Gavan, H, Thirteenth Infantry. Gastro intestinal catarrh—28th, Charles Curley, H, Twenty-first Infantry. Parotid abscess—30th, William E. Whitecotton, I, Fourth Infantry. Gastro enteritis—November 2, David R. Osborne, I, Twenty-first Infantry; John Moore, H, Twelfth Infantry; 4th, William Gallagher, L, Fourteenth Infantry. Drowned—2d, Louis Jansen, corporal, Band, Thirty-fourth Infantry.

OTIS.

MANILA. (Received November 7, 1899—9.06 a. m.)
ADJUTANT-GENERAL, *Washington:*

Transports *Rio, Sikh, Valencia,* arrived to-day. Private Patrick Cleary, G, Thirty-fifth Volunteer Infantry, died October 26, ptomaine poisoning.

OTIS.

MANILA, *November 7, 1899—11.05 a. m.*
ADJUTANT-GENERAL, *Washington:*

The following received from Negros, dated to-day: "To the President of the United States: The civil governor, counsellors, judges, and secretaries, who constitute the new government of this island in taking possession of their offices this day, have the high honor of saluting your excellency, and trust that in the inauguration of this form of government, based upon the liberal and democratic institutions which have made that great Republic so grand and prosperous, that a new era will open up to this region which will enable it to reach the legitimate goal of its aspirations. Melecio Severino."

OTIS.

MANILA. (Received November 8, 1899—2.28 p. m.)

ADJUTANT-GENERAL, *Washington:*

Casualties not previously reported: Hospital Corps, near Angeles, November 5, George C. Douglas, right arm, very severe. Fourth Cavalry, K, William L. Brett, right ankle, moderate; John F. Jackson, left chest, moderate. Thirty-sixth Infantry, at Porac, 2d, L, Wilburn Perry, right thigh, slight; E, August F. Shinke, abdomen slight; I, Frank J. Goldsberry, killed in action, 3d; 3d, Lieut. Col. William R. Grove, Thirty-sixth Infantry, right thigh, moderate. 5th, Seventeenth Infantry, near Magalan, Company D, Roy B. Motsinger, right thigh, slight; H, Clay M. Rogers, right thigh, slight; Michael Haggarty, right forearm, slight; K, John Hippert, left foot, slight; George E. Burdick, left leg moderate; Oliver H. Jones, forearm, slight.

OTIS.

MANILA. (Received November 8, 1899—3.05 a. m.)

ADJUTANT-GENERAL, *Washington:*

Capt. Hugh J. McGrath, Fourth Cavalry, died Manila 5.15 p. m. November 7, exhaustion, consequent gunshot wound in action October 8; body shipped *Zealandia* November 10.

OTIS.

MANILA. (Received November 8, 1899—7.50 a. m.

ADJUTANT-GENERAL, *Washington:*

Grant sailed yesterday.

OTIS.

MANILA. (Received November 9, 1899—10.11 a. m.)

ADJUTANT-GENERAL, *Washington:*

General Wheaton successfully landed expedition at Lingayen, west of Dagupan, afternoon of the 7th, against considerable opposition; slight casualties; rough sea not permitting landing at San Fabian, north of Dagupan, as directed; he is moving eastward. MacArthur seized Mabalacat on railroad 7th instant, Colonel Bell taking same on directed reconnoissance; slight opposition. General Lawton at Cabanatuan. Troops beyond Talavera and Aliaga have met with slight opposition, enemy being driven back in all instances; country still submerged, but water falling. Troops will move rapidly as soon as conditions permit. Hughes moved against Panay insurgents to-day.

OTIS.

MANILA. (Received November 9, 1899—10 a. m.)

ADJUTANT-GENERAL, *Washington:*

Spanish commission sent to Tarlac to make arrangements for release Spanish prisoners; returned few days ago. Aguinaldo would not treat with them as Spain had not formally recognized insurgent government. General MacArthur telegraphs to-day that he has just received at Mabalacat, under flag truce, communication from insurgent secretary war, dated 5th instant, asking that if I am powerless to formally receive Spanish prisoners from insurgent government, I cable Washington for permission to do so, as this in interests of humanity. Letter states if insurgent application not granted, insurgent government will regard its humane offer withdrawn, and remarks that their national pride imposes duty of not delivering prisoners except to a nation; that Spain can not receive them because Otis opposes, and Otis does not desire to receive them. Communication concludes by stating that in view of difficulties this affair will have to be completely terminated to the prejudice of the unfortunate prisoners, much to the regret and without any responsibility on the part of the insurgent government. In response to former insurgent application I have informed Aguinaldo that we would be glad to receive and take care of all the prisoners if he would simply send them in. The insurgents never intended to give prisoners up unless they could force money payments and recognition in exchange. They have not brought them in from the mountains. Aguinaldo now reported to be in full retreat for Bayombong; his government believed to be much scattered.

OTIS.

ADJUTANT-GENERAL'S OFFICE,
Washington, November 9, 1899.

OTIS, *Manila.*

Secwar approves your course in refusing to treat with Aguinaldo on the terms set forth in the letter of the insurgent secwar, sent by flag of truce to General MacArthur. The American and Spanish prisoners should be recovered by force as soon as possible. In the mean time you will inform the insurgent leader of the approval by the Department of your course, giving him to understand that any harm that comes to any of these prisoners will be visited upon him and his immediate followers, as last as they fall into our hands.

CORBIN.

MANILA. (Received November 10, 1899—7.30 a. m.)

ADJUTANT-GENERAL, *Washington:*

Report received yesterday concerning Wheaton's movement erroneous; he did land at San Fabian as directed and drove bulk of enemy back in desired direction toward Dagupan; his operations completely successful in every particular.

OTIS.

MANILA. (Received November 10, 1899—7.35 a. m.)

ADJUTANT-GENERAL, *Washington:*

Zealandia, Nelson, Glenogle sailed to-day.

OTIS.

MANILA. (Received November 10, 1899—10.30 a. m.)

ADJUTANT-GENERAL, *Washington:*

General Lawton experiences some difficulties on account of continued unprecedented rains in that section of country; his advance at San José yesterday; at Carranglan to-day; strong force put through on Aliaga route. Young captured yesterday considerable additional Cabanatuan Arsenal property in transit north, among which 144 two-inch, and 22 boxes of 1.65 inch ammunition for Hotchkiss guns; 50 projectiles for 5 and 8 inch breech-loading rifle cannon; 2 boxes of grenades; considerable other ordnance property; 2 tons casting and arsenal machinery, in parts. He is meeting with opposition, but advance not much impeded thereby. MacArthur reconnoitering north of Mabalacat yesterday, Bell to left; Slavens's scouts directed to front, and Smith. Seventeenth Infantry, on Magalang and Concepcion road. Bell, Thirty-sixth, with 5 of his officers and 2 privates of his regiment, mounted, 1 officer and 10 men Fourth Cavalry, struck 100 insurgents in mountains west of Mabalacat, charged, killing and wounding 19, captured 6, and 30 Mauser rifles. Railroad from Angeles to Bamban destroyed. MacArthur will have 40,000 rations to front to-day, and will take up advance to Tarlac to-morrow. Wheaton reports 28 Spanish prisoners secured; 300 insurgent recruits escaped to mountains from enemy during battle San Fabian; these recruits were en route to Dagupan. Wheaton says everything favorable to carrying out successfully his instructions and that cooperation of navy complete.

OTIS.

WAR DEPARTMENT, *November 10, 1899.*

OTIS, *Manila:*

Your course regarding prisoners held by insurgents is approved. Their location should be definitely ascertained and adequate force sent to recover them soon as possible. Insurgent secwar's letter implies a threat. Unless you see strong reasons to the contrary notify Aguinaldo that he and his advisers will be held personally responsible for any injury done to Spanish or American prisoners in violation of the laws and usages of war among civilized nations.

CORBIN.

MANILA. (Received November 11, 1899—4.25 a. m.)

ADJUTANT-GENERAL, *Washington:*

Lawton pushing troops through on Lupao, Humingan, and San Quintin road, but country submerged; bridges and recently constructed rafts washed out, and wheeled transportation can not move; his reliance on cavalry, few infantry, and native scouts, living mostly on country. MacArthur commenced advance early this morning; yesterday two companies Seventeenth Infantry, under Chynoweth, making reconnoissance on Magalang and Concepcion road, struck battalion of the enemy, which left 29 dead on field; our casualties reported 3 wounded.

OTIS.

MANILA. (Received November 11, 1899—7.35 a. m.)

ADJUTANT-GENERAL, *Washington:*

Severe typhoons over Panay last two days impeded march General Hughes's troops; his column several miles north of west of Iloilo; insurgents have abandoned strong defenses in that section.

OTIS.

MANILA. (Received November 11, 1899—8 a. m.)

ADJUTANT-GENERAL, *Washington:*

A number of official insurgent dispatches captured yesterday by General Young's troops in the north and forwarded by Lawton last night; they indicate directed abandonment by enemy of country in vicinity of Cabanatuan and San José and hurried movements by way Tayug over mountains to Bayombong; thence on to Aparri. Among the dispatches the following appears:

"TARLAC, *November 5, 1899.*

"Otis did not accept proposition to-day; enemy attacked our outposts because Otis promised McKinley to take Tarlac to-day; think they can not break through; take care of prisoners, as therein lies our great hopes, especially our wives. There is no use miscruit either by the government or by Miong. Spanish commissioners tried to deceive us, dealing with us as insurgents; our government sent them away and they withdrew greatly displeased; quadruple alliance between Germany, France, Russia, and Spain is a fact; before December we will know our fate; throughout Europe there is sympathy for our cause; American Democrats clearly in our favor; they are sure of Bryan's triumph next election; pay no attention to your affairs and never mind the rest."

OTIS.

SAN FRANCISCO, CAL., *November 11, 1899.*
(Received 3.45 p. m.)

ADJUTANT-GENERAL, *Washington:*

Transport *Indiana* just arrived. Details later. [On board First Tennessee Volunteers.]

SHAFTER, *Major-General.*

MANILA. (Received November 11, 1899—9.47 a. m.)
ADJUTANT-GENERAL, *Washington:*

The following deaths not heretofore reported: Œdema of larynx—November 6, James Horan, cook, A, Ninth Infantry. Traumatic cerebral hemorrhage—Joseph Pierce, recruit, Twenty-third Infantry. Apoplexy—4th, Eliphalet Price, E, Sixth Artillery. Chronic dysentery—8th, Gottfried Elfgang, C, Fourth Infantry. Chronic diarrhea—James Hamilton, sergeant, B, Twenty-first Infantry. Nephritis—Michael Walsh, H, Twenty-first Infantry. Aortic aneurism—7th, Samuel M Littrell, E, Sixteenth Infantry. Acute dysentery—11th, Martin Heffron, I, Fourteenth Infantry.

OTIS.

SAN FRANCISCO, CAL., *November 11, 1899.* (Received 4 p. m.)
ADJUTANT-GENERAL, *Washington, D. C.:*

Pursuant to your telegraphic instructions, Batteries A and N, Sixth Artillery, designated to go from Honolulu to Manila, and room will be left for them on transport *Benmohr*, to sail from here on 14th.

SHAFTER, *Major-General.*

MANILA. (Received November 11, 1899—4.31 p. m.)
ADJUTANT-GENERAL, *Washington:*

Insurgent plotting and subject of trade in Sulu Archipelago causing trouble. Consul Moseley reports from Singapore that merchants desire to clear several vessels for archipelago; have replied continuously that war emergency will not permit. Meanwhile Sandakan vessels clearing for Jolo, which declared free port, from there seek other Philippine ports with merchandise. One merchant vessel seized, brought here and fined; another reported here with merchandise and made to discharge―――― as manifested; have permitted some Sulu trade by Manila merchants in vessels chartered by government, supplying Sulu military station, which is constantly kept under guard. If protocol 1877 and 1885 granting free trade in archipelago, fall under Paris treaty, affair greatly simplified. Have been obliged to create military district in south and send Bates there to control matters; all serious trouble arises from endeavors Philippine, Sandakan, and Singapore merchants to establish trade in that section.

OTIS.

ADJUTANT-GENERAL'S OFFICE,
Washington, November 11, 1899.

OTIS, *Manila:*

Replying to your cablegram November 4, asking if protocols of 1877 and 1885 between Spain and Germany did not fall with the cession of the territory to the United States, the Secwar is of opinion that the protocols of 1877 and 1885 lapsed with the passage of Spain's sovereignty over the Philippines, and can not be invoked by Germany or Great Britain against the United States as the successor to Spain's title, and that this Government is as free to treat the navigation and commerce of those islands as in case of any other ceded territory, irrespective of the treaty relations which Spain may have entered into with other powers in regard to her colonial trade and navigation. You will be governed accordingly.

CORBIN.

MANILA. (Received November 12, 1899—6.25 a. m.)
ADJUTANT-GENERAL, *Washington:*

No news received from Lawton's advance since yesterday. MacArthur took Bamban and Capas, 4 miles north of Bamban, both on railroad, and Concepcion, to east of railroad, yesterday. Insurgents reported 1,500 strong retiring rapidly north, making slight resistance. Our casualties: Second Lieutenant Davis, Thirty-sixth Volunteers, killed; 3 enlisted men reported wounded. Strong reconnoissance from Capas in direction of Tarlac to-day. Condition of roads and streams render general advance with wagon transportation impracticable. Enemy appear to be in demoralized condition, and show much disorganization, as indicated by captured telegraphic dispatches and deserters from their ranks.

OTIS.

MANILA. (Received November 13, 1899—5.30 a. m.)
ADJUTANT-GENERAL, *Washington:*

MacArthur's advance, Thirty-sixth Volunteers and cavalry troop under Bell, entered Tarlac 7.10 p. m. yesterday; enemy fled; by great labor MacArthur succeeded in getting forward to Capas yesterday all artillery and quartermaster's transportation, and will have command in Tarlac to-day; his advance pushing forward to save as much of railroad as possible, which enemy trying to destroy on retreat. Many deserters from enemy, who passed into MacArthur some 30 rifles yesterday. Insurgents in that section reported to be short of provisions. Lawton pushing forward with great energy; his advance obliged to leave behind all transportation and depend to great extent upon country for subsistence. Hayes, Fourth Cavalry, in vicinity of Carranglan, has captured large amount insurgents' property and nearly half battalion of 400 bolomen transporting Aguinaldo's property north over mountains, together with his private secretary and seven of his officers. Young, with Third Cavalry, and Batson's Macabebe scouts, followed by Ballance's battalion Twenty-second Infantry, leaving behind all transportation, pushed out on San Jose, Lupao, San Quintin, and Tayug road, and scattered enemy stationed at these points, most of whom driven southwestward. Wessels, with squadron Third Cavalry, hastened forward to Tayug, where insurgents' supply depot captured, securing several hundred thousand pounds of rice, 3,500 pounds flour, 7,500 pounds salt, other provisions, 1,300 uniform coats, new, many blankets and other articles of clothing, also number of insurgent officers, and 69 Spanish and 2 American prisoners. Detachment sent north to San Nicolas, and is believed that Young established communication with Wheaton's troops last evening. Indications are that insurgents will not escape to mountain capital at Bayombong without great difficulty and loss, if at all. Our troops at Tarlac, Aliaga, Talavera, San José, Lupao, Humingan, San Quintin, Tayug, San Nicolas, on through to Lingayen Gulf, with strong stations at Arayat, San Isidro, and Cabanatuan, should cause insurgents some annoyance. Our troops have suffered great hardships and have performed most severe service, but are reported in excellent condition and spirits; the enterprise and indomitable will displayed by officers never excelled.

OTIS.

MANILA. (Received November 14, 1899—2.25 a. m.)
ADJUTANT-GENERAL, *Washington:*

Sheridan and *Aztec* transported Wheaton's troops to Lingayen Gulf; first left for Nagasaki on 9th and second on 12th instant.

OTIS.

AFFAIRS IN THE PHILIPPINE ISLANDS. 1101

MANILA. (Received November 14, 1899—3.20 a. m.),
ADJUTANT-GENERAL, *Washington:*

Rain continues, typhoon prevailing, nearly 4 inches this month in Manila; more central Luzon General Lawton has passed beyond telegraphic communication; nothing from him since yesterday. Wheaton reports engagement 10th instant, short distance from San Fabian; battalion Thirty-third under March attacked and defeated 400 of enemy intrenched; had 2 men wounded; enemy left 14 dead on field and 41 rifles. Wheaton about to attack San Jacinto; result not learned. Hughes, Panay, operating west Iloilo. Cordova, Maasin, Cabatuan; enemy makes no stand.

OTIS.

MANILA. (Received November 14, 1899—7.55 a. m.)
ADJUTANT-GENERAL, *Washington:*

Valencia sailed yesterday; *Para* sails to-day; *Sikh* 16th.

OTIS.

MANILA. (Received November 14, 1899—10.25 a. m.)
ADJUTANT-GENERAL, *Washington:*

Wheaton reports, November 12, engagement near San Jacinto, Thirty-third Volunteers and 1,200 intrenched insurgents; our loss, Major Logan, while gallantly leading battalion, and 6 enlisted men killed; Captain Green and 11 men wounded, mostly very slight; enemy routed, leaving 81 dead in trenches; his loss believed to be 300. Lawton reports from San José that in vicinity of San Nicolas, north of Tayug, Wessels captured 13 carts with insurgent war department records, printing press, complete, of insurgent newspaper; large quantities of rice also captured. Cavalry still actively engaged, and infantry pressing on from San José and Aliaga; roads impracticable for any wheel transportation; horses foraged on rice and growing rice straw.

OTIS.

MANILA. (Received November 15, 1899—8.07 a. m.)
ADJUTANT-GENERAL, *Washington:*

Capt. Magnus O. Hollis, Fourth Infantry, died hospital, Manila, 9 o'clock this morning; acute dysentery.

OTIS.

MANILA. (Received November 15, 1899—9.36 a. m.)
ADJUTANT-GENERAL, *Washington:*

Casualties not previously reported: Wounded—In action at San Mateo, November 11, James G. Wright, K, Sixteenth Infantry, both thighs, severe. In action at Arayat, October 12, James Turner, I, Twenty-fourth Infantry, neck, severe. In action, San Fabian Expeditionary Brigade, November 10, Sergt. James O'Neil, H, Thirteenth Infantry, chest, severe; Tony Eberhardt, E, Thirty-third Infantry, abdomen, slight; John F. Coates, G, right arm, slight; George Puehl, left arm, slight. In action at Bamban, 11th, James F. Wyatt, M, Thirty-sixth Infantry, right knee, moderate. In action at Mabalacat, 10th, Ernest W. Rodes, C, Seventeenth Infantry, back, severe; Dell Cudney, C right thigh, severe. In action on road to San Jacinto, November 11, killed, Oscar H. Mercier, acting hospital steward, Thirty-third Infantry; Lovell E. Casteel, sergeant, H; John A. Robinson, corporal, H; Willie F. Boone, H; Smack Mitchell, L; Andrew Pettus, E. Wounded—Arthur D. Radzinski, sergeant-major, left thorax, severe; Herbert B. Harpold, sergeant, G, right thigh, slight; George R. Sims, corporal, I, right leg, slight; George A. Matlock, artificer, A, left forearm, slight; Lazaro Castillo, E, left thorax, severe; Edward A. Hurth, H, left thigh, slight; Duke H. Howell, M, left side, slight; John F. Reffitt, M, left side, slight; John W. Stokes, M, left shoulder, slight; Francis C. Tanner, E, right wrist, slight; Charles Ulary, E, right leg, slight; Charles T. Throckmorton, L, right thigh, slight; Charles E. Rowe, corporal, M, sprain of back, severe; James Boyton, E, submaxillary, slight.

OTIS.

GIBRALTAR. (Received November 15, 1899—10.18 a. m.)
ADJUTANT-GENERAL, *Washington:*
Transport arrived to-day; condition of troops is excellent; all are well.

HOWE,
Forty-seventh Volunteer Infantry, Commanding.

SAN FRANCISCO, CAL., *November 15, 1899.*
(Received 3.31 p. m.)
ADJUTANT-GENERAL, *Washington:*
Transport *Pathan* sailed 4.40 yesterday afternoon with companies G, H, I, K, L, and M, Forty-sixth Infantry, 21 officers, 609 men. * * *

SHAFTER, *Major-General.*

SAN FRANCISCO, CAL., *November 15, 1899.*
(Received 4.51 p. m.)
ADJUTANT-GENERAL, *Washington:*
Transport *City of Sydney* left yesterday 4.30 p. m., with headquarters, field, staff, band, and six companies, Forty-sixth Infantry; 25 officers, 647 men. * * *

SHAFTER, *Major-General.*

MANILA. (Received November 16, 1899—2.50 a. m.)
ADJUTANT-GENERAL, *Washington:*
During thirty-six hours 4½ inches rain; still raining north; Lawton's telegraph line not beyond San José; last dispatch evening 14th reported capture money, supplies, transportation, north and east of San Nicolas, and our troops moving from Humingan and Tayug west on Urdaneta, where insurgent force reported. Lawton has abundant supplies, subsistence, forage, and transportation, San Isidro and Cabanatuan, but unable to move it. MacArthur has railroad between Bamban and Tarlac in operation; 5 miles road south Bamban being reconstructed; removed rails found north of Tarlac; MacArthur sends four battalions, troop cavalry, forward to Gerona to-day; advance from Aliaga at Victoria, 5 miles north of east Tarlac.

OTIS.

ADJUTANT-GENERAL'S OFFICE,
Washington, November 16, 1899.
OTIS, *Manila:*
From Seattle, November 12, *Garonne*, 79 passengers, 386 mules. November 14, *Sydney* and *Pathan*, Forty-sixth Volunteer Infantry. From New York, November 15, *Meade*, Forty-third Volunteer Infantry.

CORBIN.

SAN FRANCISCO, CAL., *November 16, 1899.*
(Received 4.22 p. m.)
ADJUTANT-GENERAL, *Washington:*
Transport *Senator* sailed 10 a. m. to-day with headquarters, field, staff, band, and five companies, Forty-fifth Infantry Volunteers. * * *
SHAFTER, *Major-General.*

SAN FRANCISCO, CAL., *November 16, 1899.*
(Received 4.31 p. m.)
ADJUTANT-GENERAL, *Washington:*
Transport *Benmohr* sailed 10 a. m. to-day with field, staff, and five companies Forty-fifth Infantry Volunteers. * * *
SHAFTER, *Major-General.*

NOTE.—No telegram or letter received reporting sailing of transport *Meade* with Forty-third Infantry, U. S. Volunteers, November 16, 1899, from New York.

MANILA, (Received November 18, 1899—5.20 a. m.)
ADJUTANT-GENERAL, *Washington:*
General MacArthur entered Gerona yesterday, and pushed advance to Panique, few miles beyond. Inhabitants remained in houses, receiving troops hospitably, first instance during entire advance from San Fernando. Railroad intact from washout north Tarlac to Panique, but engines and cars practically destroyed by insurgents on retreating; sufficient rolling stock can be repaired to insure railroad service. Nothing from General Lawton, as telegraph line only working to San José, south of Carranglan, and 35 miles east Tayug; his cavalry reported yesterday at Bayambang, railroad station south Dagupan. Reenforcements and supplies leave here for San Fabian, Wheaton's headquarters, to-night. Indications are that insurgent troops widely scattered, some retreating into the western Luzon province of Zambales.
OTIS.

MANILA. (Received November 18, 1899—8.55 a. m.)
ADJUTANT-GENERAL, *Washington:*
Dispatch from General Lawton, dated on road between San Nicolas and San Manuel, 10.15, 18th instant, transmits dispatches from General Young and Major Ballance at Asingan and Rosales, of November 15 and 16; former moving on Pozorrubio, about 12 miles east San Fabian and 25 miles west San Nicolas, where Major Swigert finds enemy strongly intrenched. Young and Ballance have had several skirmishes with enemy, driving them northwestward, capturing prisoners, guns, large amounts property; troops have subsisted on country, cordially received by inhabitants. Would appear that insurgents driven northwestward, off road, to Bayombong, their mountain capital. Lawton reports drowning Lieutenant Luna, Thirty-fourth Infantry, his aid, and two men of his escort, in crossing Agno river. Also reports still missing, Lieutenant Thayer and 10 men sent to communicate with Wheaton. He says must again recur to fortitude, endurance, and cheerfulness of command. Hayes just telegraphs from San Isidro that he holds Aguinaldo's secretary of interior. Indications now of good weather.
OTIS.

MANILA. (Received November 19, 1899—9 a. m.)

ADJUTANT-GENERAL, *Washington:*

The following deaths have occurred since November 11 and not reported: Acute dysentery—November 12, Jacob Fessler, Hospital Corps. Chronic diarrhea—Carl E. Crandall, A, Ninth Infantry; 3d, Marvin A. Coffel, civilian, late G, Seventeenth Infantry. Chronic dysentery—11th, Charles A. Guenther, B, Thirty-fourth Infantry; 15th, Reginald H. Horner, M, Thirty-sixth Infantry; 18th, Ignacy Romanonicz, sergeant, D, Third Infantry. Gastro-enteritis—10th, John Draney, musician, E, Sixteenth Infantry. Gunshot wound while resisting arrest—12th, William L. Murphy, A, Twenty-seventh Infantry. Variola—7th, William M. Curry, H, Sixth Infantry. Gunshot wound, accidental—12th, Norman Louis, K, Fourteenth Infantry. Endocarditis—Thomas Roach, L, Twenty-first Infantry. Typhoid fever—13th, James Clauer, C, Twenty-first Infantry; John La Rowe, H, Fourth Infantry. Mitral insufficiency—11th, James Williams, C, Thirteenth Infantry. Appendicitis—9th, James H. F. Hill, C, Nineteenth Infantry. Tuberculosis, pulmonary—15th, Henry G. Binier, C, Twentieth Infantry. Drowned accidentally in river at Oton—9th, John H. Woodard, artificer, L, Eighteenth Infantry.

OTIS.

MANILA. (Received November 20, 1899—2.15 a. m.)

ADJUTANT-GENERAL, *Washington:*

MacArthur's advance within 5 miles of Dagupan, to which point railroad intact from Bamban, excepting Tarlac break, the northern 5 miles destroyed, but rails recovered; large quantity rolling stock destroyed along line; probably either Lawton's or Wheaton's men in Dagupan; no report from those officers since 17th; should hear to-day; roads becoming practicable for transportation and troops moving from San José to Lawton's front; Leonhauser, with three companies Twenty-fifth Infantry, by night, much surprised and captured, without casualties, insurgent force at O'Donnell, 7 miles west railroad station, Bamban or Capas, one insurgent killed; force consisted of 4 officers and 200 men; their rifles, many thousand rounds ammunition, transportation, 4 tons subsistence, official records, and considerable clothing secured. Insurgents south Manila somewhat restless again, driven back from Imus; 6 men slightly wounded.

OTIS.

MANILA. (Received November 20, 1899—7.22 a. m.)

ADJUTANT-GENERAL, *Washington:*

MacArthur's advance entered Dagupan to-day; ascertained that Wheaton's troops had been there yesterday, and were withdrawn last evening; is believed that many insurgent detachments are west of railroad in province of Zambales, meditating concentration and future demonstration. They will be looked after. Nothing yet received from either Lawton or Wheaton.

OTIS.

MANILA. (Received November 20, 1899—3.35 a. m.)

ADJUTANT-GENERAL, *Washington:*

Petroleum indispensable to marines, Cavite; request authority for its sale from army supplies.

OTIS.

ADJUTANT-GENERAL'S OFFICE,
Washington, November 20, 1899.

OTIS, *Manila:*

Secwar approves authority for sale of petroleum to marines. In all such matters he authorizes you to act without reference to this office.

CORBIN.

MANILA. (Received November 20, 1899—3.50 a. m.)
ADJUTANT-GENERAL, *Washington:*

One of the contending insurgent factions at Zamboanga secured the city and turned same over to Captain Very, of United States war vessel in harbor; other insurgent faction made demonstration against city and Very called on Jolo for troops; one company sent; the commanding officer asked permission to send three additional, leaving two there; two companies will be dispatched from Jolo. Both Jolo and Zamboanga must be reenforced as soon as practicable; it will require several days. It was not intended to take possession of Zamboanga until later; no provision made. Latter part September members insurgent government in Cotabato district, southern Mindanao, beheaded. New government formed, which calls for United States troops; cities Cotabato, Davao Surigao, northeast point Mindanao, of importance; troops will be sent to these points when available. Hughes moving in Panay with two columns; insurgents have retreated from southeastern portion of island.

OTIS.

BROOKLYN, N. Y., *November 20, 1899.* (Received 8.40 p. m.)
ADJUTANT-GENERAL, U. S. ARMY, *Washington, D. C.:*

Report of strength of regiment on board *Logan* at hour of sailing: Field, 3; medical, 3; line 43; enlisted present, 1,313; 76 enlisted men absent; 4 commissioned and 12 enlisted attached.

RICHMOND, *Colonel Forty-first Infantry.*

ADJUTANT-GENERAL'S OFFICE,
Washington, November 21, 1899.

OTIS, *Manila:*

If the situation at Zamboanga, set forth in your cable 20th, calls for greater force than you have at your disposal, the use of marines is suggested. Any orders to render them available will be issued on your request. The following transports are due Manila on 26th: *Tartar, Newport,* and *Manauense,* with Twenty-eighth Volunteers and four companies Thirty-first Volunteers. *City of Pekin* due 28th, with eight companies Thirty-first Volunteers and recruits. Grand total, 88 officers and 2,495 men.

CORBIN.

SAN FRANCISCO, CAL., *November 21, 1899.*
(Received 4.28 p. m.)

ADJUTANT-GENERAL, *Washington:*

Transport *Duke of Fife* left 8.10 a. m. to-day with field, staff and six companies Thirty-eighth Infantry Volunteers, 19 officers, 618 men. * * *

SHAFTER, *Major-General.*

CORRESPONDENCE.

SAN FRANCISCO, CAL., *November 21, 1899.*
(Received 5.03 p. m.)

ADJUTANT-GENERAL, *Washington:*

Transport *Hancock* left here for Manila at 6 p. m. yesterday with headquarters, band, and nine companies Forty-fourth Infantry, 33 officers, 964 enlisted men. * * *

SHAFTER, *Major-General.*

SAN FRANCISCO, CAL., *November 21, 1899.*
(Received 6.07 p. m.)

ADJUTANT-GENERAL, *Washington:*

Transport *St. Paul* sailed 8.10 a. m. to-day with headquarters, field, staff, band, and companies E, F, G, H, K, and L, Thirty-eighth Infantry, 27 officers, 614 men. * * *

SHAFTER, *Major-General.*

SAN FRANCISCO, CAL., *November 21, 1899.*
(Received 6.52 p. m.)

ADJUTANT-GENERAL, *Washington:*

Transport *City of Puebla* left 6 p. m. yesterday with field and staff, and three companies, Forty-fourth Infantry, 12 officers, 310 men; two companies Forty-third Infantry, 6 officers, 205 men. * * *

SHAFTER, *Major-General.*

MANILA. (Received November 22, 1899—3.45 a. m.)

ADJUTANT-GENERAL, *Washington:*

Naval officer, personally acquainted with conditions, thinks troops sent from Jolo to Zamboanga sufficient for present needs. Will soon reenforce both points, sending all Twenty-third south and all Nineteenth to Cebu.

OTIS.

MANILA. (Received November 22, 1899—7.40 a. m.)

ADJUTANT-GENERAL, *Washington:*

Dispatch 21st from Lawton at Tayug reports Young with cavalry and Macabebe scouts at Aringay, with advance north to Baoang, near San Fernando; about to move on trail east to Trinidad. Young reports considerable insurgent force moving in that direction; that Aguinaldo in charge seeking to cross over to Bayombong; portion of Lawton's troops now being pushed through to Tayug with rations; battalion Twenty-fourth will join Lawton to-morrow. Nothing from Wheaton for several days. Intend to direct him first opportunity to occupy San Fernando and Vigan. MacArthur operating west of railroad and north of Tarlac; wire from Tarlac north not working. Troops on entire railroad line rationed without difficulty. Iloilo reports seven companies, Sixth and Twenty-sixth Volunteers, under Dickman, struck insurgents northeast Jaro; casualties 6 wounded; enemy left on field 18 killed. Dickman captured 7 prisoners, 4 one-pound brass field pieces, several thousand rounds ammunition. Eighteenth Infantry yesterday drove insurgents north of Santa Barbara. Hughes with column north and west of Santa Barbara. Reports of results not yet received.

OTIS.

AFFAIRS IN THE PHILIPPINE ISLANDS. 1107

MANILA. (Received November 23, 1899—8.10 a. m.)
ADJUTANT-GENERAL, *Washington:*
Transports *Tartar* and *Newport* arrived. No casualties.

OTIS.

[Twenty-eighth Volunteer Infantry on board transports.]

MANILA. (Received November 24, 1899—8.20 a. m.)
ADJUTANT-GENERAL, *Washington:*
Claim to government by insurgents can be made no longer under any fiction; its treasurer, secretary interior, and president of congress in our hands; its president and remaining cabinet officers in hiding, evidently in different central Luzon provinces; its generals and troops in small bands scattered through these provinces, acting as banditti, or dispersed, playing the rôle of amigos with arms concealed; indications are that Aguinaldo did not escape through the lines of Lawton or Wheaton, but fled westward from Bayambang railroad station. Telegraphic communication to Dagupan established probably to San Fabian to-day. By relaying 9 miles of track with material at hand railway communication to that point reestablished. Labor of troops must attend maintenance. To the south and east of Manila 4,000 armed insurgents concentrated in three bodies; they will receive attention soon.

OTIS.

MANILA. (Received November 24, 1899—8.34 a. m.)
ADJUTANT-GENERAL, *Washington:*
Hughes, Iloilo, reports enemy driven back into mountains; insurgent capital, Cabatuan, captured; only serious action that of Carpenter at Pavia; total casualties, 5 killed or since dead of wounds; 27 wounded; captured 10 prisoners, 18 cannon, 6 rifles, quantities of ammunition; enemy's casualties not stated.

OTIS.

MANILA. (Received November 24, 1899—8.30 a. m.)
ADJUTANT-GENERAL, *Washington:*
In Panay, 21st instant, when Dickman drove enemy vicinity Jaro, Carpenter with two battalions, Eighteenth Infantry and Bridgeman's Battery, had severe engagement at Pavia, north Iloilo; his casualties, 5 killed, 20 wounded, now in Iloilo hospital; others slightly wounded with command. Enemy driven north with reported very heavy loss; particulars not received. Carpenter passed on to insurgent's stronghold, Santa Barbara, which he captured 22d instant without loss. Nothing received from column under immediate command Hughes, which is moving rapidly and operating north and west of Santa Barbara. Apparently Visayans friendly, not taking active part; enemy consists of 2,000 Tagalos.

OTIS.

MANILA. (Received November 24, 1899—9.22 a. m.)
ADJUTANT-GENERAL, *Washington:*
Casualties not previously reported: Killed—In advance on Pavia, P. I., November 21, Howard W. Lowe, sergeant, G, Sixth Artillery; William S. Addy, F, Eighteenth Infantry. In action near Barrio Tenabang, 11th, Thomas E. Gardner, L, Seventeenth Infantry. Wounded—Charles E. Hapner, I, Seventeenth Infantry, right thigh, moderate; 10th, John E. Miller, A, Seventeenth Infantry, right chest and

abdomen, severe. In action at Mandurriao, Panay, Joseph (?) Casey, B, Eighteenth Infantry, left thigh, slight. In action near Jaro, Panay, Richard P. Corbett, C, Twenty-sixth Infantry, neck, severe; 18th, James E. Rooney, head, severe. In action at Anabo, Luzon, Paul P. Phenuer, F, Eleventh Cavalry, left thigh, moderate; Edward Johnson, head, moderate; William W. Hinman, corporal, right leg, moderate.

OTIS.

SAN FRANCISCO, CAL., *November 24, 1899.*
(Received 3.50 p. m.)

ADJUTANT-GENERAL, *Washington:*

Transport *Ohio* sailed for Manila 6.30 a. m. to-day, with headquarters, field, staff, band, Companies A, B, C, D, L, and M, Fortieth Infantry, 22 officers, 645 men. * * *

SHAFTER, *Major-General.*

SAN FRANCISCO, CAL., *November 24, 1899.*
(Received 3.57 p. m.)

ADJUTANT-GENERAL, *Washington:*

Transport *Indiana* sailed 6.30 this morning, with field, staff, and 6 companies Fortieth Infantry Volunteers, 20 officers, 620 men. * * *

SHAFTER, *Major-General.*

MANILA. (Received November 25, 1899—9.42 a. m.)

ADJUTANT-GENERAL, *Washington:*

Insurgents made feint on Imus last night; 3 enlisted men wounded; their loss 2 killed, 1 captured; quickly withdrew. Additional troops sent from Manila to-day; insurgents will be driven south. Reports from Negros encouraging; chief insurgent leader north of island surrendered voluntarily; more planting being done; more sugar mills at work than at any time since revolution against Spain began. Officers report people apparently cheerful and hopeful; that form of government in operation well suited to conditions and working smoothly.

OTIS.

MANILA. (Received November 25, 1899—10.35 a. m.)

ADJUTANT-GENERAL, *Washington:*

Vessel from Lingayen Gulf, with dispatches from Wheaton to 23d instant, brought in Buencamino, insurgent secretary state, captured 21st instant; he was with Aguinaldo, and party left Tarlac night 13th, to be escorted north by 2,000 troops from Bayambang and Dagupan; these troops Wheaton struck at San Jacinto, and Young eastward. Aguinaldo, with part of family, escaped north with 200 men, passing between Young and Wheaton; Young still in pursuit last accounts, and has been rationed at San Fernando. Aguinaldo's mother and oldest child, with Buencamino, separated from rest of party; mother lost in woods, and child, 4 years old, with Wheaton's troops; $2,000 gold belonging to mother captured and now in Manila treasury. Heavy storm in Lingayen has prevented loading of troops there for the north. MacArthur has captured insurgent director of railroad, who endeavored destroy railroad to Dagupan; also Captain Lawrence, Englishman, who served Aguinaldo's artillery. Telegraph not working north of Tarlac to-day. Lawton believed to be on military road to Bayambang. Roads now practicable for wagons, and supplies for him being forwarded.

OTIS.

MANILA. (Received November 26, 1899—10.45 a. m.)

ADJUTANT-GENERAL, *Washington:*

The following deaths since last report: Variola—October 28, John Evans, K, Nineteenth Infantry; November 17, John Miller, Fourth Infantry. Malaria—16th, Jacob Abel, K, Twenty-second Infantry; 22d, Charles Britenstine, hospital steward, Thirty-second Infantry. Nephritis—18th, Bert G. Flanders, K, Fourth Infantry; Samuel L. Davis, G, Twenty-eighth Infantry. Tuberculosis—19th, Lawrence Dinneen, sergeant, B, Thirteenth Infantry. Stabbed by comrade—16th, Pres Walker, C, Nineteenth Infantry. Typhoid fever—17th, Joseph Hallecka, D, Eighteenth Infantry. Phthisis, 21st, Benjamin R. Fairchild, L, Twenty-sixth Infantry. Chronic dysentery—25th, Charles Stader, A, Thirty-sixth Infantry; William G. Kennedy, C, Twentieth Infantry. Acute dysentery—21st, Frederick Bale, A, Thirty-sixth Infantry; 24th, Clarence W. Beall, K, Fourth Infantry; 17th, Charles W. Lamb, K, Thirty-fourth Infantry; 19th, Thomas Bell, A, Twenty-fourth Infantry. Heart disease—21st, Fred Stroutman, corporal, M, Thirty-second Infantry. Charles M. Smith, second lieutenant, Eighteenth Infantry, 10.20 o'clock a. m., November 22, at Iloilo, Panay, gunshot in action. 22d, result gunshot in action, Ernest W. Rhodes, C, Seventeenth Infantry; David A. McAdoo, B, Eighteenth Infantry, William J. Wallace, F. Maximiliano Luna, second lieutenant, Thirty-fourth Infantry, 3 o'clock p. m., November 15, drowned Agno River, near San Nicolas. Insect bite right forearm, 22d, Corpl. Jacob Brown, I, Fourteenth Infantry.

OTIS.

MANILA. (Received November 27, 1899—7.45 a. m.)

ADJUTANT-GENERAL, *Washington:*

Steamer from San Fabian yesterday brought 115 Spanish prisoners, $75,000 insurgent government money, and other property, captured by Lawton's troops near Tayug on 25th. Wheaton's troops, Fowler's company, Thirty-third, drove enemy westward from Mangataren, few miles southwest Dagupan; captured 5 8-inch muzzle-loading guns, 12 rifles, 12,000 rounds Maxim cartridges, 1,000 shrapnel, 800 pounds powder, and other property; also 94 Spanish and 7 American prisoners. Bell, with Thirty-sixth Infantry, in pursuit and will march down western Luzon coast. Indications are two or three bodies insurgent troops, numbering probably 500 or more men each, in mountains west of railroad; can be readily handled by MacArthur. They have the bulk of the insurgent artillery, all of which will be captured unless buried. Young still in pursuit of Aguinaldo, who is heading for Bangued, few miles east Vigan. Young, with cavalry and scouts, is followed by battalion Thirty-third and by Ballance's battalion Twenty-second; two battalions Thirty-third en route for Vigan by military post road. Young's reception by inhabitants enthusiastic; they give all aid possible. Aguinaldo has collected more than 1,000 of his troops at the north; probably most will desert him. Number small detachments insurgent troops throughout country north of Manila have been captured and inhabitants manifest gratitude for deliverance. Indications are that insurgent force south of Manila disintegrating and troops going to their homes. Reports from southern islands favorable. Zamboanga insurgents surrendered to our troops and no trouble anticipated there.

OTIS.

MANILA. (Received November 27, 1899—7.50 a. m.)

ADJUTANT-GENERAL, *Washington:*

Casualties not previously reported: Killed—Maxwell Keyes, second lieutenant, Third Infantry, engagement at Ildefonso, November 24, 2 o'clock p. m. Wounded—in action at Anabo, November 13, Quince E. Furman, C, Fourth Infantry, scalp, slight; James Maher, C, leg, slight; Edward S. Durkin, C, both thighs, moderate; John Homfeld, M, arm, moderate. In action at Imus, November 20, John C. Wetherby, L, shoulder, severe; Jesse R. Soper, corporal, E, knee, moderate. In action near San Mateo, 22d, Oscar McCulloch, K, Sixteenth Infantry, back, moderate.

OTIS.

MANILA. (Received November 27, 1899—11.51 p. m.)
ADJUTANT-GENERAL, *Washington:*
Transports *Pekin* and *Manauense*, Thirty-first Infantry, arrived; no casualties Regiment will garrison ports of Mindanao.

OTIS.

MANILA. (Received November 27, 1899—12.56 p. m.)
ADJUTANT-GENERAL, *Washington:*
Oregon landed marines at Vigan yesterday. Young's column at Namagpacan, 20 miles north San Fernando, on 23d, from which point passed north into mountains; troops will relieve marines at Vigan 29th. Bulk Spanish and American prisoners reported at Bangued, 20 miles east Vigan. Wheaton, San Fabian, just reports capture of 73 more rifles, $1,100 in money; also that he has been obliged to take mother and son of Aguinaldo under guard at San Fabian to prevent their murder by natives; they will be sent here first opportunity and delivered to friends. Natives in vicinity Bayombong, Nueva Vizcaya, offering services to drive out insurgents, and request arms; report only 400 insurgents there. Report from Zamboanga says insurgents surrendered heavy artillery to Navy, and since have surrendered to Nichols, commanding battalion Twenty-third Infantry, 179 rifles, 1 Nordenfeldt, and 4 breech-loading cannon. Order restored in town and vicinity; about 80 Tagalos scattered in mountains.

MANILA. (Received November 28, 1899—6.38 a. m.)
ADJUTANT-GENERAL, *Washington:*
Hospital ship *Missouri* just arrived; no casualties.

OTIS.

GIBRALTAR. (Received November 28, 1899—6.46 a. m.)
ADJUTANT-GENERAL, *Washington:*
Arrived in good condition. Receipt of your telegram acknowledged. Will arrive Malta Friday.

MURRAY,
Colonel, Forty-third Volunteer Infantry, on board Meade.

MANILA. (Received November 29, 1899—1.50 a. m.)
ADJUTANT-GENERAL, *Washington:*
General MacArthur reports from Bayambang that Bell, with Thirty-sixth and company Thirty-third Infantry, struck enemy commanded by Generals San Miguel and Alejandrino, in mountains west of Mangataren, and by series of combats, through mountains, has so scattered their forces, concentration impossible; Bell has captured all their quick-firing and Krupp guns, ammunition, their powder factory and arsenal, with thousands of pounds of lead and sheet copper, all their transportation, engineering tools, clothing, and food supplies; property scattered over the mountains now being collected; 20 of the killed and wounded of the enemy left on field; Bell does not report casualties; particulars expected this evening.

OTIS.

MANILA. (Received November 29, 1899—6.30 a. m.)
ADJUTANT-GENERAL, *Washington:*
The following from the northwest Luzon coast: Young left San Fernando 23d instant, where March's battalion Thirty-third Infantry arrived 26th, on which day Young at Namagpacan, where supplied by Navy gunboat *Samar*, he marched out next day; battle ship *Oregon* landed 200 men at Vigan 24th instant; no opposition; sailors welcomed by inhabitants; believe the Spanish and American prisoners still in vicinity of Bangued, guarded by small insurgent force; reports from northeast indicate that 500 insurgent troops at Bayombong, Nueva Vizcaya Province, surrendered yesterday to Lawton's troops; he advanced by both the San Nicolas and Carranglan trails.

OTIS.

MANILA. (Received December 1, 1899—2.34 a. m.)
ADJUTANT-GENERAL, *Washington:*
Hughes reports from central Panay that Iloilo Province one-third island cleared of insurgents; by forced marches with two battalions from Lambunao, by way of Calinog, he obliged enemy to fight at Pavia on 26th instant, and drove him, with loss, to the mountains in detached bodies, capturing 10 fieldpieces, of which 2 breechloaders, also 9 rifles, and several thousand rounds small ammunition. Hughes' casualties, Captain Warwick, Eighteenth Infantry, and Private Daniel W. Humphreys, K, Eighteenth Infantry, killed; he reports his troops in excellent health; is now converting wheel into pack transportation for purpose of entering mountains; expected that he will pass on to Capiz, northern coast of island. Dispatches from Lawton indicate Bayombong captured, 28th instant; both trails over mountains impracticable for wheel transportation of any kind; troops have subsisted on rice, and scant supply of that. MacArthur's troops have had several minor engagements, capturing men and rifles. Bell's capture in mountains includes 14 modern guns, all in good condition. Over 50 pieces of artillery captured by troops of corps in last three weeks. *Oregon* brought in 106 Spanish prisoners from Vigan yesterday; 94 received by rail previous evening. Young, with three troops cavalry and March's battalion Thirty-third Infantry, should have reached Vigan yesterday.

OTIS.

MANILA. (Received December 1, 1899—7.55 a. m.)
ADJUTANT-GENERAL, *Washington:*
Conditions Zamboanga satisfactory; additional ordnance surrendered, consisting 4 fieldpieces, 17 rifles, quantity ammunition; natives adjoining towns visiting city, and native military bands serenading troops; Thirty-first Infantry leaves Manila this evening to garrison several stations Mindanao coast; no difficulties anticipated.

OTIS.

SAN FRANCISCO, CAL., *December 1, 1899.* (Received 3.15 p. m.)
ADJUTANT-GENERAL, *Washington:*
The *Dabney Vostock* sailed yesterday 3 p. m. with field, staff and 7 companies Forty-second Infantry Volunteers, 25 officers, 716 men. * * *

SHAFTER, *Major-General.*

SAN FRANCISCO, CAL., *December 1, 1899.* (Received 10.51 p. m.)
ADJUTANT-GENERAL, *Washington:*
Transport *Columbia* sailed 3 p. m. yesterday with field, staff, band, and Companies H, I, K, L, and M, Forty-second Infantry, 21 officers, 539 men. * * *

SHAFTER, *Major-General.*

MALTA. (Received December 1, 1899—12.01 p. m.)
ADJUTANT-GENERAL, *Washington:*
Arrived in good condition Friday, 8 a. m.; no casualty.

MURRAY,
Colonel, Forty-third Infantry, on Meade.

MANILA. (Received December 2, 1899—1.15 a. m.)
ADJUTANT-GENERAL, *Washington:*
Report received that Bayombong, with province Nueva Vizcaya, surrendered November 28, to Lieutenant Munro, Fourth Cavalry, who commanded advance scouts on Carranglan trail, consisting 50 men Fourth Cavalry and 3 native scouts. Insurgent General Canon surrendered entire force numbering 800 men, armed with Mausers, and number officers; 70 Spanish and few American prisoners secured, and probably considerable insurgent property.

OTIS.

GIBRALTAR. (Received December 2, 1899—10.43 a. m.)
ADJUTANT-GENERAL, *Washington:*
Arrived Saturday 9 a. m. All are well.

RICHMOND,
Colonel, Forty-first Infantry, on Logan.

SAN FRANCISCO, CAL., *December 2, 1899.*
(Received 8.17 p. m.)
ADJUTANT-GENERAL, *Washington, D. C.:*
Transport *Warren* left to-day at 2.45 p. m. with headquarters, field, staff, band, and eight companies Forty-ninth Infantry Volunteers, 35 officers, 852 men. * * *

SHAFTER, *Major-General.*

MANILA. (Received December 2, 1899—12.28 p. m.)
ADJUTANT-GENERAL, *Washington:*
Casualties not previously reported: Killed—Harry O. Lee, B, Ninth Infantry, November 25, near Capas; Henry W. Landfeohr, E, Thirty-fifth Infantry, engagement Toboatin Bridge, November 24. Wounded in action, near Leon, Panay, November 20, Harry Hiscock, sergeant, H, Twenty-sixth Infantry, abdomen, mortal. In action, Imus, November 25, John Finger, F, Fifth Artillery, leg, moderate; George M. Duncan, B, Fourth Infantry, forearm, moderate. In action, Iloilo, Panay, November 21, Twenty-sixth Infantry, A, Abraham Frappier, thigh, severe; D, Eugene E. Blowers, corporal, head, severe; Edmund Sweet, leg, severe. Sixth Artillery, G, Edward C. England, sergeant, chest, severe; James T. Murphy, shoulder, severe; L, Lawrence E. Grennan, corporal, hand, severe; Paul Rink,

thigh, severe. Eighteenth Infantry, B, Charles J. Ling, shoulder, severe; Simeon T. Barker, shoulder, severe; George Beckwith, thigh, severe; Carl Strohm, elbow, slight; C, James O'Connell, thigh, severe; Harry L. Dunton, corporal, chest, severe; Brice Leach, hand, severe; Christopher C. Coats, leg, severe; F, Bert J. Reed, corporal, leg, severe; Timothy J. Flynn, arm, severe; James Jones, corporal, hand, severe; Charles Weber, corporal, chest, severe. In action beyond Mabalacat, November 28, Matthew Batson, first lieutenant, Fourth Cavalry, foot, severe.

OTIS.

MANILA. (Received December 3, 1899—6.45 a. m.)
ADJUTANT-GENERAL, *Washington:*

Following deaths since last report: Drowned—Rio Grande, October 27, Clem Bonaparte, K, Twenty-fourth Infantry. Acute dysentery—November 26, Thomas Smith, K, Twenty-second Infantry; 27th, Thomas B. Wall, E, Twenty-seventh Infantry; 28th, Dewane Goodrich, artificer, Ninth Infantry; 29th, Louis W. Mohun, corporal, L, Ninth Infantry. Gunshot in action—27th, Richard F. Corbett, C, Twenty-sixth Infantry; 24th, Harry Hiscock, sergeant, H, Twenty-sixth Infantry; 25th, James E. Rooney, A, Twenty-sixth Infantry; 29th, John C. Wetherby, E, Fourth Infantry. Typhoid fever—29th, Roy Storrs, L, Third Infantry. Uræmia—30th, John H. Williams, F, Sixth Artillery. Chronic diarrhea—30th, James M. Hart, A, Ninth Infantry; December 1, Fay Foster, D, Ninth Infantry.

OTIS.

MANILA. (Received December 5, 1899—6.31 a. m.)
ADJUTANT-GENERAL, *Washington:*

Maj. Frank C. Armstrong, surgeon, Thirty-second Infantry, died here 5.40 p. m., December 4, lymphatic leucæmia.

OTIS.

MANILA. (Received December 5, 1899—8.10 a. m.)
ADJUTANT-GENERAL, *Washington:*

Casualties not previously reported: Killed in action—Iloilo, Panay, November 21, Mert Fletcher, F, Eighteenth Infantry. Wounded in action—Iloilo, November 14, George D. Doble, C, Nineteenth Infantry, abdomen, severe. Skirmish, road to San Nicolas, November 19, Third Cavalry, K, Joseph F. Mangold, leg, slight; John J. Falls, elbow, slight; Dennis H. Wood, back, slight; Rufus A. Jackson, leg, slight; Ira W. Horton, C, buttock, slight. Action, Imus, November 25, August Bert, F, Fifth Artillery, shoulder, slight. Action, vicinity Rosario, November 14, Thirteenth Infantry, K, Albert Caplick, corporal, leg, slight; Charles E. White, abdomen, severe; L, John G. Fritz, arms, severe; B, Ulysses H. Gray, leg, slight Action, San Pedro, Magalang, Buston Witt, sergeant, H, Seventeenth Infantry, thumb, slight, November 5; Claude M. Mansfield, K, Fourth Cavalry, foot, slight, November 6.

OTIS.

MANILA. (Received December 6, 1899—6.30 a. m.)
ADJUTANT-GENERAL, *Washington:*

General Young, with thirteen companies infantry and nine troops cavalry, not heard from since 29th ultimo. He was then about 20 miles south Vigan, and most of troops marching to his support, but then had with him three troops cavalry, battalion Thirty-third Infantry, and Macabebe scouts. One company Thirty-third

Infantry sent by boat to Vigan to reenforce navy there. Lieutenant-Colonel Parker, Forty-fifth, reports from Vigan 5th instant that he has not heard from Young for a week. Insurgents, 800 strong, made attack on his force, consisting B Company and 153 sick and foot-sore men Thirty-third Infantry 4 o'clock morning 4th, entering city in darkness; severe street fighting ensued; continued four hours; enemy driven out, leaving behind 40 dead, 32 prisoners, including many officers, and 84 rifles. Now on outskirts intrenching. Parker says can hold out indefinitely; plenty rations and ammunition; his loss, 8 enlisted men killed, 3 wounded; 160 men now being transported from San Fabian to his relief. Young must be in vicinity with large force.

OTIS.

MALTA. (Received December 6, 1899—9.07 a. m.)
ADJUTANT-GENERAL, *Washington:*
Arrived Wednesday 6 a. m. All are well.

RICHMOND,
Colonel, Forty-first Infantry, on Logan.

MANILA. (Received December 6, 1899—5.18 p. m.)
ADJUTANT-GENERAL, *Washington:*
Total strength December 1: Cavalry, Third, commissioned, 28; enlisted, 730; Fourth, 43, 1,092; Eleventh, 48, 1,026. Artillery, First, 4, 411; Third, 13, 391; Fourth, 5, 134; Fifth, 4, 126; Sixth, 43, 1,177. Infantry, Third, 44, 1,437; Fourth, 41, 1,396; Sixth, 44, 1,507; Ninth, 43, 1,407; Twelfth, 44, 1,420; Thirteenth, 42, 1,433; Fourteenth, 43, 1,437; Seventeenth, 42, 1,590; Sixteenth, 43, 1,435; Eighteenth, 43, 1,440; Nineteenth, 46, 1,423; Twentieth, 44, 1,461; Twenty-first, 45, 1,371; Twenty-second, 42, 1,414; Twenty-third, 43, 1,372; Twenty-fourth, 23, 1,075; Twenty-fifth, 35, 1,087; Twenty-sixth, 50, 1,339; Twenty-seventh, 48, 1,231; Twenty-eighth, 48, 1,261; Twenty-ninth, 49, 1,275; Thirtieth, 49, 1,299; Thirty-first, 50, 1,398; Thirty-second, 37, 1,042; Thirty-third, 49, 1,312; Thirty-fourth, 47, 1,325; Thirty-fifth, 50, 1,286; Thirty-sixth, 48, 944; Thirty-seventh, 49, 1,058. Engineers, 6, 282. Signal Corps, 18, 272. Total commissioned, 1,493; enlisted, 43,823.

OTIS.

ADJUTANT-GENERAL'S OFFICE,
Washington, December 6, 1899.
OTIS, *Manila:*
State Department reports from trustworthy source large order Mauser ammunition placed at Kynochs, England; supposed destination insurgents Philippines, intending shipment Hamburg via China.

CORBIN.

PORT SAID. (Received December 6, 1899—10.12 a.m.)
ADJUTANT-GENERAL, *Washington:*
Arrived in good condition. No casualty.

MURRAY.

AFFAIRS IN THE PHILIPPINE ISLANDS.

MANILA. (Received December 7, 1899—10.09 a. m.)

ADJUTANT-GENERAL, *Washington:*

General Young reports arrival Vigan evening 5th, having encountered force of enemy Narvacan, 12 miles south of city, whom he drove to eastward of same into San Quintin canyon; his troops now pressing them back; country extremely rough; strongly intrenched; about 600 prisoners escaped; reported that insurgents allowed all but American and prominent Spanish prisoners to escape from Bangued; latter driven back into mountains; send transportation with subsistence and medical supplies to Vigan to-morrow, to bring prisoners to Manila, and to supply Young's troops with necessary quartermaster's stores. Our casualties, 1 killed, 12 wounded, wounds mostly slight; enemy left in trenches 25 dead, few rifles, several thousand rounds small ammunition, 40 shrapnel. Young has sufficient troops to meet all difficulties.

OTIS.

MANILA. (Received December 7, 1899—11.22 a. m.)

ADJUTANT-GENERAL, *Washington:*

In central Luzon no insurgent force of importance except in Bulacan province, near mountains, where Pilar holds together 1,000 or more men, which will be attacked soon. General Grant has moved small column down east coast of Bataan province, encountering little opposition. Column moving westward from mountains expected to reach western coast Luzon 10th instant. Many small insurgent armed bands in country robbing, and in some instances murdering, inhabitants, which are being pursued by troops quite successfully. To the south of Manila insurgents still maintain positions; necessary force to scatter them will be sent there soon.

OTIS.

MANILA. (Received December 7, 1899.)

ADJUTANT-GENERAL, *Washington:*

Believed that Captain Batchelor, with three companies Twenty-fourth Infantry, has descended Magat River from Bayombong in direction of Aparri contrary to instructions to General Lawton, November 22; courier sent from Tayug five days ago to arrest Batchelor; not yet heard from; if he has descended river probability is that he will not be successful. Admiral Watson sends two of his war vessels and two gunboats with battalion of marines to enter river at Aparri and give succor possible.

OTIS.

SAN FRANCISCO, CAL., *December 7, 1899.*
(Received 4.07 p. m.)

ADJUTANT-GENERAL, *Washington:*

Transport *Sherman* left yesterday 3 p. m., with field, staff and four companies Forty-ninth Infantry Volunteers. * * *

SHAFTER, *Major-General.*

MANILA. (Received December 8, 1899—2 a. m.)

ADJUTANT-GENERAL, *Washington:*

Informed outbreak natives in district south Negros, result of reported recent great insurgent victories in Luzon and Panay, which natives believe; extent of outbreak not ascertained; First Lieut. Augustus C. Ledyard, Sixth Infantry, killed; 2 privates wounded. One of our chief difficulties arises from circulation of falsehoods among natives. Defamatory newspaper articles of United States and Europe promptly published in Spanish in San Francisco, Madrid, and Hongkong Junta and circulated in Philippines. Insurgents have based all hopes of success upon false rumors.

OTIS.

MANILA. (Received December 8, 1899—2.05 a. m.)

ADJUTANT-GENERAL, *Washington:*

Thirty-ninth Infantry, battalion Forty-fifth, and recruits arrived last evening; transports *Olympia, Pennsylvania;* no casualties.

OTIS.

MANILA. (Received December 8, 1899—6.30 a. m.)

ADJUTANT-GENERAL, *Washington:*

Hospital ship *Relief* just returned from Vigan bringing 272 sick soldiers, 232 Spanish prisoners; reports several hundred Spanish prisoners at Vigan, for which we send transport this evening. Colonel Hare, Thirty-third Infantry, took Bangued 5th instant, and now with portion of regiment and battalion Thirty-fourth Infantry in pursuit insurgents on road southeast to Lepanto, thence to Bontoc, on which Aguinaldo and 300 insurgents supposed to be retreating with American prisoners. Inhabitants of western Luzon coast friendly and give assistance.

OTIS.

MANILA. (Received December 9, 1899—7.10 a. m.)

ADJUTANT-GENERAL, *Washington:*

Dispatch from Young, Vigan, yesterday, says escaped Spanish prisoners report four hours' engagement, 3d instant, between his troops and Aguinaldo's guard near Cervantes, 50 miles southeast Vigan, with heavy loss to enemy, who is being pursued; our loss, 1 killed, 6 wounded; inhabitants of own accord join troops repairing trail and carrying subsistence; have pushed column to San José, south Bangued; Howze's column on rear trail; Batchelor's battalion—Twenty-fourth—out of reach, north of Bayombong, evidently descending river; natives report fighting occurred 20 miles north; navy reaches Aparri to-morrow. Column of MacArthur's troops—Twenty-fifth Infantry—reported near Iba, west coast Zambales; Grant's column near Subig Bay; Lawton in Bulacan province to-day, with sufficient troops to overcome opposition and scatter enemy.

OTIS.

MANILA. (Received December 9, 1899—8 a. m.)

ADJUTANT-GENERAL, *Washington:*

Information received that Negros revolt of minor importance; Byrne in rapid pursuit of disaffected party; Hughes in mountains Panay en route Capiz.

OTIS.

ADJUTANT-GENERAL'S OFFICE,
Washington, December 9, 1899.

OTIS, *Manila:*

My telegram 6th; ammunition for insurgents; State Department advised delivery 37,000 rifles and 10,000,000 cartridges in progress. Proposed shipment secretly packed from Hamburg via Shanghai or Hongkong.

CORBIN.

PORT SAID. (Received December 10, 1899—9.08 a. m.)
ADJUTANT-GENERAL, *Washington:*
Arrived 2 (after) noon, Sunday; all are well.

RICHMOND,
Colonel, Forty-first Infantry, on Logan.

MANILA. (Received December 10, 1899—9.31 a. m.)
ADJUTANT-GENERAL, *Washington:*
Casualties not previously reported: Wounded in action—At Maasin, Luzon, November 24, Third Infantry, L. Stone, A, thigh, moderate. At Novaliches, Luzon, November 21, Sixteenth Infantry, William W. Tinch, K, thigh, slight. At San Mateo, Luzon, November 22, Sixteenth Infantry, Lewis Wilkes, A, wrist, slight; John Rogers, C, back, severe. At Jaro, Panay, November 21, Twenty-sixth Infantry, John J. Quigley, A, thigh, severe. At Ilaya and Pavia, Panay, November 21, Eighteenth Infantry, Robert B. Calvert, second lieutenant, chest, slight; Robert E. Brookling, B, thigh, slight; John Eager, B, slight, leg; Edward E. Lockhart, C, scalp, slight; Henry Barrett, first sergeant, leg, slight. Killed in action near Baliuag, Luzon, December 4, Third Infantry, Patrick J. Sullivan, C.

OTIS.

OFFICE OF THE MILITARY GOVERNOR IN THE PHILIPPINES,
Manila, P. I., December 10, 1899.
The SECRETARY OF WAR,
Washington, D. C.
SIR: I have the honor to acknowledge the receipt of War Department communication of October 27, 1899, containing information of the conditional approval of the agreement of August 20 last between General Bates and the Sultan of Sulu by His Excellency the President of the United States, and to inclose instructions on the subject which have been given to General Bates, who is now present in command of that section of the Philippines.

Very respectfully,
E. S. OTIS,
Major-General, U. S. V.,
U. S. Military Governor in the Philippines.

OFFICE OF THE U. S. MILITARY GOVERNOR IN THE PHILIPPINES,
Manila, P. I., December 10, 1899.
Brig. Gen. J. C. BATES, U. S. V.,
Commanding District of Mindanao and Jolo,
Zamboanga, Mindanao.
SIR: I am directed to inclose for your information, action, and guidance a copy of a confidential War Department communication dated October 27 last, which contains notice of the approval of His Excellency the President of the United States of the agreement of August 20, 1899, between yourself, as agent of the Government, and the Sultan and several dattos of the Jolo Archipelago, subject, however, to the conditions stipulated in the last clause of Article XI of the late Paris treaty, and which reads as follows:

"The civil rights and political status of the native inhabitants of the territory hereby ceded to the United States shall be determined by Congress."

This conditional approval, it will be seen by reference to the War Department communication, is given with the distinct understanding that the existence of slavery or involuntary servitude in any portion of the Philippines is in no wise authorized, as under the thirteenth amendment of the United States Constitution the authorization or recognition of the continued slavery status by the Executive of the Government is impossible.

You will carefully note the instructions in the communication which directs that when the Sultan is informed of the President's conditional approval of the agreement, that inquiry be made as to the extent which slavery is practiced in the archipelago, the number of people held as slaves, and what practical course of action looking to their emancipation can be adopted.

By reference to notes of your interviews and conferences with the Sultan and his representatives, which accompanied the agreement when submitted to this office, and from information obtained from other sources, it is believed that the market price of slaves in the archipelago is insignificant, ranging from $30 to $90 Mexican, and that in some instances owners will be pleased to grant freedom to their slaves if they can escape the burden of supporting them.

It is understood, too, that the character of domestic slavery existing in the archipelago differs greatly from the former slavery institutions of the United States in this that the Moro slave, so called, becomes a member of the owner's family, enjoying certain privileges, and that he often voluntarily sells himself to better his condition and to secure some slight temporary individual benefit. Hence it is desired that you report upon the character of this Moro slavery, in order that the institution as existing may be fully appreciated. The number of slaves secured by the Moros through capture or by purchase from other bands, tribes, or races, and now held by them, and the number of them in use who have voluntarily or involuntarily entered the condition of slavery, might be approximately stated.

You will conduct your inquiries with a caution prescribed in the inclosed War Department communication, making full report of the results of the same to this office as soon as practicable. You will also extend your investigation, with a report thereon, to other Philippine islands inhabited by Moros and where they have planted their domestic institutions.

Very respectfully,
C. H. MURRAY,
Major and Inspector-General, U. S. V., Military Secretary.

[Inclosure.]

WAR DEPARTMENT, *Washington, October 27, 1899.*
Maj. Gen. E. S. OTIS,
Commanding United States Forces in the Philippines, Manila, P. I.

SIR: The President instructs me to advise you that the agreement signed August 20, 1899, between Brig. Gen. John C. Bates, representing the United States, of the one part, the Sultan of Jolo, the Datto Rajah Muda, the Datto Attik, the Datto Calbi, and the Datto Joakanain, of the other part, is confirmed and approved, subject to the action of Congress provided for in that clause of the treaty of peace between the United States and Spain which provides "the civil rights and the political status of the native inhabitants of the territory hereby ceded to the United States shall be determined by Congress," and with the understanding and reservation, which should be distinctly communicated to the Sultan of Jolo, that this agreement is not to be deemed in any way to authorize or give the consent of the United States to the existence of slavery in the Sulu Archipelago, a thing which is made impossible by the thirteenth amendment to the Constitution of the United States.

At the same time, when you communicate to the Sultan the above-mentioned understanding, the President desires that you should make inquiry as to the number of persons held in slavery in the archipelago, and what arrangement it may be practicable to make for their emancipation. It is assumed that the market price referred to in the agreement of August 20, 1899, is not very high at present, and it may be that a comparatively moderate sum, which Congress might be willing to appropriate for that purpose, would suffice to secure freedom for the whole number.

It is needless to suggest that the inquiry should be prosecuted in such a way as not to create the impression that we now have authority to make such an arrangement, and in such a manner as not to create extravagant expectations.

Very truly, yours,

ELIHU ROOT,
Secretary of War.

MANILA. (Received December 11, 1899—8.43 a. m.)
ADJUTANT-GENERAL, *Washington:*

About 1,200 released Spanish prisoners here; steamship company contends can transport only on account of United States, as no contract with Spain; think sixth article treaty does not obligate United States to transport these prisoners, but we can send out the 1,200 by 16th instant if desired, as Spanish mail steamer here. Ask instructions.

OTIS.

ADJUTANT-GENERAL'S OFFICE,
Washington, December 11, 1899.

OTIS, *Manila:*

Replying cable this date, President and Secretary State agree with Secwar Spanish prisoners mentioned therein be given transportation to Spain at cost of the United States. Secwar so directs.

CORBIN.

ADEN. (Received December 11, 1899—6.56 a. m.)
ADJUTANT-GENERAL, *Washington:*

Arrived in good condition. No casualty.

MURRAY,
Colonel, Forty-third Infantry, on Meade.

MANILA. (Received December 11, 1899—1.47 p. m.)
ADJUTANT-GENERAL, *Washington:*

Following deaths since last report: Tuberculosis—at Nagasaki, Japan, September 20, First North Dakota Infantry Leslie R. Waterman. Quartermaster's Department, December 7, George F. Davidson, civilian employee, drowned in Pasig River, body identified December 8; September 11, Fourth Infantry, James Pattie, G, accidentally, attempting board launch at San Isidro; November 12, Fourth Cavalry, James E. Thompson, sergeant, C, bathing Mariquina River at Pasig, Luzon; December 3, Thirty-seventh, Henry M. Neatherly, F. Variola—at Tarlac, November 26, Thirty-sixth Infantry, Ewen W. Smith, M; Cebu, October 9, Twenty-third Infantry, Robert E. Welsh, A. Acute dysentery—November 22, Sixth Infantry, Thomas A. Heide, D. Malaria—November 23, Fourth Cavalry, Michael Sullivan, farrier, A; November 24, Peter P. Griewatz, D; December 3, Burt Heneger, K; December 1, Third Cavalry, Charles Branagan, E. Gunshot wounds in action—November 30, Sixth Infantry, Paul Rink, L. Accidental by comrade—November 27, Sixth Infantry, James Steele, K. Suicide—December 2, Thirty-fifth Infantry, George Montag, C. Diarrhea—December 2, Fourteenth Infantry, Joseph F. Williams, K. Erysipelas—December 6, Twenty-seventh Infantry, Harold F. Griffiths, G. Colitis—December

1, Thirty-sixth Infantry, Raymond Groll, I. Tricuspid insufficiency—December 3. Twenty-third Infantry, Thomas J. Murray, sergeant, A. Dysentery—December 7, Twelfth Infantry, Harry E. Gleason, F; December 2, Sixth Infantry, William J. Sherrell, K. Typhoid—December 3, Twenty-sixth Infantry, James E. Arlington, H. Anæmia, December 2, Twenty-first Infantry, George Sanford, I. Nephritis—December 9, Twenty-second Infantry, Edward H. Bliler, H. Cause not reported—November 28, Twenty-second Infantry, Herbert G. Hoor, K; December 2, George W. Rogers, K.

OTIS.

MANILA. (Received December 12, 1899—6.45 a. m.)
ADJUTANT-GENERAL, *Washington*.

Cable stating rifles and cartridges in progress for delivery received. Unless paid for delivery will not be attempted, as no longer any insurgent goverment or authorities. If delivered, too late to effect practical result. When is shipment from Europe expected? Watch will be maintained.

OTIS.

MANILA. (Received December 12, 1899—9.35 a. m.)
ADJUTANT-GENERAL, *Washington*.

Bulacan Province insurgents scattered and driven east to mountains; our casualties that section last few days, 10; insurgent casualties in killed, wounded, and prisoners aggregate 100; considerable insurgent property with records, arms, and ammunition captured; troops now in mountains in pursuit. Insurgents driven from Subig Bay country and marines now occupy naval station there; our column moving west from Tarlac, now on west coast Luzon, where supplied; encountered little resistance; column now moving west and south from Dagupan along coast; no concentrated insurgent force of importance in Luzon north of Manila; southern Luzon will not offer very serious resistance; troops moving for operations in that section; organized rebellion no longer exists, and troops active pursuing robber bands. All important and threatened centers of population, north, occupied.

OTIS.

MANILA. (Received December 12, 1899—12.33 p. m.)
ADJUTANT-GENERAL, *Washington*.

Two thousand additional Spanish prisoners secured in northern Luzon, making over 3,000 released within month; 700 now en route from Vigan, and transports will be sent for remainder.

OTIS.

MANILA. (Received, December 13, 1899—5 a. m.)
ADJUTANT-GENERAL, *Washington:*

Fifty men Navy and 50 men army, transported by navy, took Laoag 10th instant; General Young with staff followed next day; he reports Howze with Penn's battalion, Thirty-fourth, followed by portion Thirty-third Infantry, passed north to Piddig, east Laoag. March's battalion, Thirty-third, at Cayan, province Lepanto, on 7th instant. Third Cavalry along coast and in mountains pursuing enemy. Young states his extreme northern force passed over mountains, driving insurgents under General Tinio, who was badly wounded, killing 50, wounding many, making large captures of rifles and property, with all insurgent transportation, and released all Spanish prisoners in section to the number of about 2,000; our casualties, 2 wounded; our troops still pursuing remnant of Tinio's command. March's Thirty-third battalion reports from Cayan, Lepanto Province, 7th instant, that he has destroyed Aguinaldo's bodyguard; killed Gen. Gregorio Pilar; received surrender General Concepcion and staff, killed and wounded 52 insurgents; released 575 Spanish prisoners, including 150 friars, and captured considerable property; his loss, 2 killed, 9 wounded. My information is that Aguinaldo, disguised, has individually abandoned his troops and is hiding in province Benguet.

OTIS.

MANILA. (Received, December 13, 1899—5.10 a. m.)
ADJUTANT-GENERAL, *Washington:*
Admiral Watson informs me that province Cagayan surrendered unconditionally to Captain McCalla, of the *Newark*, on 11th instant; all arms surrendered Batchelor 90 miles south of Aparri; command in good condition; navy will take supplies to Batchelor in launch at once; this surrender doubtless includes the province of Isabela.

OTIS.

MANILA. (Received, December 13, 1899—5.15 a. m.)
ADJUTANT-GENERAL, *Washington:*
Bates, Zamboanga, reports affairs satisfactory; nearly all rifles surrendered. MacArthur, Bayambang, that he holds as prisoner of war Mabini, ablest of insurgents, founder of late government.

OTIS.

MANILA. (Received December 14, 1899—12.14 p. m.)
ADJUTANT-GENERAL, *Washington:*
General Lawton reports Bulacan Province freed of insurgents; yesterday troops Fourth Cavalry captured strong mountain position Biacnabato with food, supplies, clothing, cartridge factory, and barracks. MacArthur's troops occupied Iba and town south on western coast Luzon; slight opposition and few light casualties. Eighth instant Bates reported from Zamboanga that he has garrisoned Basilan, and is sending troops to Cotabato and Davao; that condition affairs satisfactory. Eighteen hundred Spanish prisoners received in Manila; over 2,000 more en route; 1,300 shipped to Spain 16th instant; these prisoners much better physical condition than Spanish troops surrendered when Manila capitulated.

OTIS.

MANILA. (Received December 15, 1899—3.52 a. m.)
ADJUTANT-GENERAL, *Washington:*
Transports *City of Sydney* and *Pathan*, Forty-sixth Infantry, arrived this morning; no casualties.

OTIS.

MANILA. (Received December 15, 1899—12.23 p. m.)
ADJUTANT-GENERAL, *Washington:*
Batchelor, Twenty-fourth Infantry Battalion, reports, 7th instant, had engagement at junction Magat and Rio Grande rivers, Isabela Province, enemy leaving 4 dead and 5 mortally wounded in trenches; our loss 1 drowned, 4 wounded. Says in need

clothing, provisions, and money; will reach Tuguegarao, Cagayan Province, shortly; doubtless navy relieved him yesterday. Four hundred and seventy-five Spanish prisoners arrived this morning; among them the sick at Vigan, numbering 120. Young, at Bangui, northwestern Luzon, reports troops still pursuing remnant insurgents, who have 23 American prisoners in their possession; country exceedingly rough; our men without shoes; still persistently pursuing few Spanish prisoners now in hands insurgents; probably 1,000, mostly in south; expect to effect their release in few days. Negros reports Sergt. Alfred Roeder, Sixth Infantry, 20 soldiers and 18 native police, attacked 400 insurgents Madrigal, Negros, this morning; no casualties; enemy's loss 28 killed and many wounded.

OTIS.

MANILA. (Received December 15, 1899—11.42 p. m.)

ADJUTANT-GENERAL, *Washington:*

Eighth instant, General Smith, Negros, reports that early in December number inhabitants four coast towns entered mountains, believing statements of Panay and Luzon agents that Americans overwhelmingly defeated in those islands, Aguinaldo about to dictate terms of peace, and American Congress to confer independence when established; civil government of island would be overthrown; also told that all Negros about to rise and drive out Americans; no depredations committed; no consequences of importance apprehended.

OTIS.

ADEN. (Received December 16, 1899—10.45 a. m.)

ADJUTANT-GENERAL, *Washington:*

Arrived Saturday, 1 [after]noon. All are well.

RICHMOND,
Colonel, Forty-first Infantry, on Logan.

MANILA. (Received December 18, 1899—4.05 a. m.)

ADJUTANT-GENERAL, *Washington:*

Hughes reports from Romblon Island his arrival Capiz, northern Panay, 10th instant, driving out all Tagalos; Carpenter with six companies occupying northern Panay, two companies on Romblon Island; Hughes with battalion Nineteenth Infantry has gone to Cebu to police that island; Young, northern Luzon, reports several minor engagements with few casualties; Colonel Hare with small column still in pursuit of insurgents; column which has the American prisoners has passed through mountains and is marching on Pamplona, short distance west of Aparri; navy cooperating; these prisoners will be released in few days; 731 Spanish prisoners arrived last evening; 500 more expected to-day; 1,400 leave for Spain this afternoon.

OTIS.

COLOMBO. (Received December 18, 1899—10.19 a. m.)

ADJUTANT-GENERAL, *Washington:*

Arrived in good condition; no casualty.

MURRAY,
Colonel, Forty-third Infantry, on Meade.

AFFAIRS IN THE PHILIPPINE ISLANDS.

MANILA. (Received December 18, 1899—2.30 a. m.)

ADJUTANT-GENERAL, *Washington:*

Following deaths since last report: Drowned—Rio Grande, near Cabanatuan, November 7, Twenty-second Infantry, George J. Marks, F; at Tayug, December 7, Twenty-fourth Infantry, John J. Johnson, corporal, H. Dysentery—November 25, Thirty-fourth Infantry, Frank Wells, A; December 9, Eleventh Cavalry, John Delaney, sergeant, E; 13th, Fourth Infantry, Otto Unger, M; 14th, Twenty-first Infantry, David E. Buckingham, I. Typhoid—November 27, Twenty-second Infantry, Charles O. Rainwater, C; December 8, Twelfth Infantry, Merrill E. Shearer, E. Gunshot wounds—in action, December 10, Thirty-third Infantry, Gilbert L. Baron, corporal, C; 15th, Thirty-sixth Infantry, Hardy L. Laurence, H, by comrade; December 9, Third Cavalry, Charlie Rist, F. Suicide—December 15, Thirty-sixth Infantry, Mark A. Hillis, corporal, E. Meningitis—December 10, Thirty-seventh Infantry, Lewis L. Eastwood, C. Variola—December 10, Third Cavalry, William McFarland, K. Tuberculosis—December 5, Thirty-fifth Infantry, Homer W. Paup, A; 15th, Twenty-second Infantry, Arthur Hollenbach, E. Colitis—December 7, Eighteenth Infantry, Thomas Smith, K. Septicæmia—December 15, Ninth Infantry, Henry Wolper, sergeant, band

OTIS.

MANILA. (Received December 19, 1899—3.18 a. m.)

ADJUTANT-GENERAL, *Washington:*

Transports *Hancock* and *City of Puebla*, Forty-fourth and portion Forty-third Infantry, arrived this morning; no casualties.

OTIS.

MANILA. (Received December 19, 1899—3.35 a. m.)

ADJUTANT-GENERAL, *Washington:*

Information from Hongkong and Negros shows late Negros uprising work Hongkong junta; three junta agents visited Negros latter part November; took in 300 Tagalos from Panay and much junta literature which they circulated; they announced great victories in Luzon; that insurgent independence would be recognized soon by United States; warned Negros of punishment in store and directed uprising throughout island for December 2; result, gathering of few hundred of the ignorant masses and robbers and consequent fright of better element. General Smith has imposed on towns concerned a fine to be paid into general treasury; reports guilt of two priests and says American clergymen needed; that Negros easily controlled if left to itself, but fears Tagalos vengeance when Aguinaldo fully establishes himself by driving Americans out of Luzon; most improbable statements believed by ignorant natives.

OTIS.

MANILA. (Received December 19, 1899—9.26 p. m.)

ADJUTANT-GENERAL, *Washington:*

General Lawton engaged in driving insurgents from San Mateo, section of country northeast of Manila, killed instantly 9.30 yesterday morning; a great loss to us and his country.

OTIS.

MANILA. (Received December 21, 1899—1.50 a. m.)

ADJUTANT-GENERAL, *Washington:*

Transports *Senator* and *Bermohr*, with Forty-fifth Infantry, two batteries Sixth Artillery, arrived this morning; no casualties.

OTIS.

CORRESPONDENCE.

SAN FRANCISCO, CAL., *December 21, 1899.*
(Received 2.30 p. m.)

ADJUTANT-GENERAL, *Washington, D. C.:*
Transport *Grant* sailed at 9 a. m. to-day for Manila with Forty-eighth Infantry Volunteers, 47 officers, 1,289 men. * * *

SHAFTER, *Major-General.*

MANILA. (Received December 22, 1899—11.53 a. m.)
ADJUTANT-GENERAL, *Washington:*
Casualties not previously reported: Killed—In action at Tila Pass, Luzon, December 2, Thirty-third Infantry, Henry F. Hill, G; John W. Joyner, G. Wounded—In action near San Mateo, December 19, Seventh Infantry, Second Lieut. Ethelbert L. D. Breckinridge, chest, slight; Eleventh Cavalry, Walter V. Cotchett, first lieutenant, leg, slight; Joseph C. Kessinger, D, jaw, severe; Patrick Burke, I, shoulder, moderate; Frank J. Clark, C, thigh, severe; Twenty-seventh Infantry, John Peters, corporal, A, foot, severe; Charles A. Littlefield, C, hips, moderate; Twenty-ninth Infantry, Frank Clarke, H, hand, slight. At Tila Pass, Luzon, December 2, Thirty-third Infantry, G, Marvin P. Hughes, sergeant, foot, moderate; Henry J. Smith, sergeant, foot, moderate; Chester L. Killpatrick, abdomen, severe; Elmo Cranford, eye, severe; William B. Bethea, abdomen, severe; Richard B. Sibley, leg, moderate; Harry D. Brown, corporal, E, abomen, severe; James A. Lane, H, thighs, moderate. At Tangadan Mountain, Luzon, December 4, Thirty-fourth Infantry, Oscar E. Dollen, G, pelvis, mortal. At Cabaruan, December 17, Seventeenth Infantry, Second Lieut. Lewellyn N. Bushfield, arm, slight. Near Carmen, December 1, Thirty-fifth Infantry, F, Harry W. Beatty, quartermaster-sergeant, nose, slight; Robert S. Clark, cook, forearm, slight; Lorenzo D. Hubbard, hand, slight. On Northern Expedition in mountains, December 20, Third Cavalry, John Dillinger, A, breast, moderate. Near Dingras, December 10, Thirty-fourth Infantry, Ernest B. Ziegler, F, forearm, slight. Near Vigan, December 4, Thirty-fourth Infantry, Samuel Faust, G, hip, slight. At Ildefonso, December 4, Third Artillery, L, Edward Mileon, sergeant, leg, severe; William A. Meyer, leg, severe; Elwyn C. Hulbert, neck, slight.

OTIS.

MANILA. (Received December 22, 1899—9.55 p. m.)
ADJUTANT-GENERAL, *Washington:*
Transport *Thomas*, Forty-seventh Infantry, arrived last evening; no casualties.

OTIS.

MANILA. (Received December 23, 1899—6.40 a. m.)
ADJUTANT-GENERAL, *Washington:*
General Young reports, 21st instant, from Vigan, Colonels Hare and Howze, heard from December 17, still in pursuit, through mountains, of insurgent column having our prisoners, of whom 4 captured. Captain Gillmore, remaining prisoners, one day in advance; pursuit continued; these pursuing troops have encountered great hardships, but will probably strike Aparri. Two hundred and one Spanish prisoners from Appari received this morning; 200 more in that section, mostly friars, awaiting transportation to Manila. Entire Sixteenth Infantry leaves for Aparri to-morrow for stations from that point as far south as Bayombong; Batchelor's battalion Twenty-fourth now on lower Rio Grande in good condition; to return to San José country.

Forty-fourth Infantry are being sent to Hughes, Iloilo, who reports Panay, Negros, and adjacent islands quiet; arriving troops and supplies being unloaded through service at Manila and Dagupan Railway; two trains daily. All ports northern Luzon open January 1.

OTIS.

ADJUTANT-GENERAL'S OFFICE,
Washington, December 23, 1899.

OTIS, *Manila:*
Have you provided for civil marriages in Philippines? If not, I think it desirable to do so without delay for reasons in letter of to-day.

CORBIN.

MANILA. (Received December 24, 1899—6.17 a. m.)
ADJUTANT-GENERAL, *Washington:*
Following deaths since last report; Nepro lithiasis—November 7, Sixth Infantry, John Smith, C. Gunshot wounds—November 16, Thirty-third Infantry, Arthur D. Radzinski, sergeant-major; Thirteenth Infantry, Charles E. White, K; December 7, Thirty-fourth Infantry, Oscar E. Dollen, G; December 21, Eleventh Cavalry, Joseph C. Kessinger, D; December 10, Thirty-fifth Infantry, Raynard N. Anderson, A, accidental. Typhoid fever—December 16, Third Artillery, Raymond Carpenter, L; December 7, Fourth Cavalry, Harry Reno, sergeant, K; December 19, Twenty-seventh Infantry, Claude E. Christman, corporal, K; December 19, Twenty-first Infantry, Henry C. Merriam, G; December 17, Sixth Infantry, John H. Free, K; December 22, U. S. transport *Hooker*, James Conway, cableman; December 23, Fourteenth Infantry, William Schneebele, H. Peritonitis—December 20, Twenty-ninth Infantry, Paul Gaines, L. Malaria—December 15, Twelfth Infantry, George Burg, I; December 8, Twenty-second Infantry, Kenneth M. Rodenberger, A; December 20, Twenty-fifth Infantry, Isaac Watson, F; December 21, Thirteenth Infantry, Paul H. Klick, H; December 12, Twenty-fourth Infantry, James Booker, K; December 18, Twenty-fourth Infantry, Henry Cunningham, F. Dysentery—December 19, Twenty-first Infantry, Edward N. Swanson, M; December 5, Twenty-second Infantry, Dimitri C. Buck, A; December 4, Thirty-fourth Infantry, Fred Morfoed, K; December 22, Hospital Corps, Albert Dusling; December 22, Fourteenth Infantry, Oscar Proske, G. Drowned—December 14, near Narrvcan, Luzon, accidentally, Thirty-third Infantry, William A. Axtell, K. Intestinal intussusception—December 5, Twenty-second Infantry, George H. H. McLean, F. General debility—December 11, Twenty-fourth Infantry, George Motley, H. Diarrhea—December 22, Twenty-first Infantry, Warren Bloushier, I.

OTIS.

MANILA. (Received December 24, 1899—1.40 a. m.)
ADJUTANT-GENERAL, *Washington:*
Full orders controlling marriages issued 18th instant; they also declare validity of recent marriages if either contracting party had good intent and solemnized before person professing authority to act; orders by mail.

OTIS.

SINGAPORE. (Received December 25, 1899—10.15 a. m.)
ADJUTANT-GENERAL, *Washington:*
Arrived in good condition. Died suddenly, 18th, alcoholic poisoning, Anthony Kerrigan, corporal, B.

MURRAY,
Colonel, Forty-third Infantry, on Meade.

MANILA. (Received December 26, 1899—6.40 a. m.)
ADJUTANT-GENERAL, *Washington:*
Following recent minor engagements: Capture San Mateo, December 19, General Lawton killed; Captain Kenan, Twenty-ninth Infantry, Lieutenant Breckinridge, Seventh Infantry, slightly wounded; 4 enlisted men slightly wounded. Capture, same date, Montalban, Lieutenant Cotchett, Eleventh Cavalry, and 6 enlisted men wounded, mostly slight; enemy's casualties heavy. In northern Zambales, 21st instant, Bell struck 150 insurgents; killed, wounded, and captured 28 and 20 rifles; Lieutenant Read, Thirty-sixth Infantry, right thigh, moderate. Hughes, Iloilo, reports insurgent band attacked Brownell's company Twenty-sixth Infantry near Jaro; repulsed with heavy loss in men and 26 rifles; insurgents are in Romblon surrendering arms. Twenty-third instant, Captain Dame, Thirty-fourth Infantry, struck insurgent band near Aritao, province Nueva Vizcaya, killing and wounding 15, capturing 7 rifles. Lieutenant Meade, Twenty-first Infantry, attacked insurgent outpost near Calamba 24th instant, killing 5, capturing 5 rifles. In mountains southern portion Bataan Province, 24th instant, Captain Comfort, Thirty-second Infantry, struck insurgent band, wounding 4 and having 1 man wounded. Major Spence, same regiment, same locality, captured insurgent corral with 125 cattle and ponies. Captain Hayson, same date, attacked in mountains near Sulug; 1 man missing.

OTIS.

ADJUTANT-GENERAL'S OFFICE,
Washington, December 26, 1899.
OTIS, *Manila:*
State Department has following from Acting Consul, Hamburg: "German steamer *Emma Luyken* sailed Hamburg Hongkong December 16, 30,000 Mauser rifles, 10,000,000 rounds ammunition to be transferred to Shanghai, and 3,000 Vetterli rifles to be transferred to Macao. Hamburg-American Line steamer *Savoia* sailed Hamburg Hongkong 22d December, 170 canvas-covered boxes rifles to be transferred to Macao. Large quantity ammunition arrived Hamburg Antwerp for shipping Philippines. Commander Beehler investigating."

CORBIN.

MANILA. (Received December 27, 1899—12.45 a. m.)
ADJUTANT-GENERAL, *Washington:*
Thirty-eighth and Fortieth Regiments arrived last evening. No casualties.

OTIS.

MANILA. (Received December 27,1899—1.18 p. m.)
ADJUTANT-GENERAL, *Washington:*
Casualties not previously reported: Killed in action—Engagement near Banna, December 11, Third Cavalry, A, Harry Sweger, Charles W. Frazee. Action against Romblon, Panay, December 10, Eighteenth Infantry, C, Charles J. Feley. Wounded— William J. Sheeley, Hospital Corps, abdomen and head, slight; wounded and taken prisoner during attack on train near Angeles, September 22; escaped during engagement near Mangataren, November 28. Action near Alimodian, Panay, P. I., November 28, Twenty-sixth Infantry, F, Thomas Russell, foot, slight; H, John Nadeau, thigh, severe; Nineteenth Infantry, A, William Hicks, arm, severe. Action La Granja, Samar, December 7, Sixth Infantry, M, Payton M. Womack, buttock, slight; Reed M. Keeney, shoulder, slight. Attack on Ginigaran, Samar, December 8, Sixth Infantry, D, Raymond D. Burbee, thigh, slight; William Huggard, both

wrists, slight. Advance on Sibul, December 10, Fourth Cavalry, B, Lorenzo A. Declairment, corporal, chest, moderate; H, Winthrop Richardson, corporal, thigh, severe. Action, Iba, December 19, Twenty-fifth Infantry, E, Gish Wade, leg, slight. Action near Tarlac, December 10, Twenty-fifth Infantry, H, Burt McCoy, corporal, thigh, severe.

OTIS.

MANILA. (Received December 28, 1899.)

ADJUTANT-GENERAL, *Washington:*
First Lieut. Edward R. Taylor, Twelfth Infantry, run over by train, crossing Agno River, died 4.40 p. m., December 26, at Bautista.

SINGAPORE, *December 29, 1899—6.45 a. m.*

ADJUTANT-GENERAL, *Washington:*
Arrived Friday 12 noon. All are well.

RICHMOND,
Colonel, Forty-first Infantry, on Logan.

MANILA. (Received December 29, 1899—8.47 a. m.)

ADJUTANT-GENERAL, *Washington:*
Colonel Lockett, with regiment, two battalions Forty-sixth, one Forty-fifth, and company Twenty-seventh Infantry, 2 guns, Captain Van Deusen, attacked enemy 600 strong on mountain stronghold beyond Montalban, northeast San Mateo. Large number killed and wounded, 24 prisoners taken. Lockett captured 1 cannon, 40 rifles, 20,000 rounds ammunition, 500 pounds powder, arsenal fortifications, all food supplies and considerable other property. This captured point located on mountain trail and formerly supposed to be impregnable. Our casualties, Lieutenant Enslow, Eleventh Cavalry, and 5 enlisted men wounded, mostly slight; Private Mattson, L, Forty-fifth Infantry, drowned.

OTIS.

WAR DEPARTMENT, *December 29, 1899.*

Major-General OTIS, *Manila:*
At suggestion of Professor Worcester it is thought best for you to occupy all strategic points in the island possible, before the insurgents get possession of them. Dr. Burns, of your staff, can give you full information about these places. Answer.

ALGER, *Secretary.*

MANILA. (Received January 2, 1900—9.08 a. m.)

ADJUTANT-GENERAL, *Washington:*
Three months' supply subsistence, issue and sales, for entire command on hand, excepting canned tomatoes, of which 75,000 cans required; all pending estimates will be examined at once and supplies required during next six months, not covered by estimates, will be cabled for.

OTIS.

CORRESPONDENCE.

MANILA. (Received January 3, 1900—9.12 a. m.)
ADJUTANT-GENERAL, *Washington:*
Transports arrived: *Indiana, Ohio* (Fortieth Infantry), *Duke of Fife, St. Paul* (Thirty-eighth Infantry), December 27, no casualties. *Dabney, Vostock, Columbia* (Forty-second Infantry), December 31; Private Curt E. Hall, L, Forty-second Infantry, died en route, December 20, acute meningitis. *Meade* (Forty-third Infantry), December 31. *Sherman, Warren* (Forty-ninth Infantry), January 2, no casualties. Transports sailed: *Pekin, Sydney*, December 29. *Benmohr, Missouri*, December 31. *Senator*, January 2.

OTIS.

MANILA. (Received January 4, 1900—4.35 p. m.)
ADJUTANT-GENERAL, *Washington:*
Present and absent, total strength, December 31: Artillery, First, commissioned 4, enlisted 116; Third, 11, 389; Fourth, 4, 133; Fifth, 4, 124; Sixth, 48, 1,413. Cavalry, Third, 30, 950; Fourth, 42, 1,359; Eleventh, 49, 1,058. Infantry, Third, 45, 1,441; Fourth, 44, 1,376; Sixth, 42, 1,495; Ninth, 44, 1,394; Twelfth, 42, 1,394; Thirteenth, 45, 1,426; Fourteenth, 46, 1,575; Sixteenth, 43, 1,439; Seventeenth, 43, 1,460; Eighteenth, 43, 1,430; Nineteenth, 45, 1,453; Twentieth, 44, 1,453; Twenty-first, 45, 1,409; Twenty-second, 43, 1,454; Twenty-third, 42, 1,449; Twenty-fourth, 34, 1,073; Twenty-fifth, 36, 1,086; Twenty-sixth, 49, 1,239; Twenty-seventh, 47, 1,235; Twenty-eighth, 49, 1,263; Twenty-ninth, 49, 1,270; Thirtieth, 50, 1,015; Thirty-first, 49, 1,184; Thirty-second, 49, 1,252; Thirty-third, 49, 1,007; Thirty-fourth, 49, 1,004; Thirty-fifth, 49, 1,286; Thirty-sixth, 48, 988; Thirty-seventh, 48, 1,042; Thirty-eighth, 48, 1,259; Thirty-ninth, 50, 1,284; Fortieth, 48, 1,286; Forty-second, 50, 1,296; Forty-third, 48, 1,271; Forty-fourth, 48, 1,326; Forty-fifth, 50, 1,280; Forty-sixth, 49, 1,231; Forty-seventh, 51, 1,272. Engineers, 5, 278. Signal Corps, 20, 290. Total, commissioned, 969; enlisted, 55,206.

OTIS.

MANILA. (Received January 5, 1900—12.55 a. m.)
ADJUTANT-GENERAL, *Washington:*
Casualties: Killed—In action at Paniqui, December 31, Twelfth Infantry, L, John Q. A. Carter. Engagement near Santa Rosa, October 28, Thirty-seventh Infantry, H, George A. G. Lamkin; Twenty-second Infantry, K, Herman H. Stone. Wounded—Action at Montalban, December 27, Forty-sixth Infantry, I, William G. Patton, chest, mortal; Eleventh Cavalry, D, Sergt. Joseph L. Hordemon, foot, slight; L, Harry Ross, thigh, slight; M, Sergt. Fred Stanley, leg, slight. Action near San Mateo, December 19, Twenty-ninth Infantry, H, Peter Thompson, corporal, thigh, slight.

OTIS.

MANILA. (Received January 5, 1900—7.55 a. m.)
ADJUTANT-GENERAL, *Washington:*
Transport *Wyefield* arrived yesterday; *Logan* to-day. No casualties.

OTIS.

MANILA. (Received January 5, 1900—7.08 a. m.)
ADJUTANT-GENERAL, *Washington:*
Colonels Hare and Howze just arrived at Vigan, northwest Luzon, with all American prisoners; their successful pursuit a remarkable achievement. Generals Schwan and Wheaton now with separate columns in Cavite Province; expect important results. Affairs in Luzon, north of Manila, greatly improved.

OTIS.

ADJUTANT-GENERAL'S OFFICE,
Washington, January 5, 1900.

OTIS, *Manila:*
Names of prisoners released by Hare and Howze desired to determine anxious inquiries.

CORBIN.

MANILA. (Received January 6, 1900—3.45 a. m.)
ADJUTANT-GENERAL, *Washington:*
Prisoners now en route from Vigan arrive to-night; list telegraphed to-morrow; Captain Gillmore among number.

OTIS.

MANILA. (Received January 7, 1900—7.43 a. m.)
ADJUTANT-GENERAL, *Washington:*
Admiral Watson has cabled names of navy rescued prisoners: 1 officer, 11 men; remaining 14 as follows: Civilians, G. W. Langford, Manila; David Brown, St. Paul; J. W. O'Brien, London. Soldiers: George T. Sackett, H, Archie H. Gordon, K, Third Infantry; William Bruce, Elmer Honnyman, First Nevada Cavalry; Frank Stone, Leland S. Smith, Signal Corps; Albert O. Bishop, H, Third Artillery; Sergt. Frank McDonald, L, Twenty-first Infantry; Harry F. Huber, Hospital Corps; Martin Brennan, K, James P. Curran, B, Sixteenth Infantry.

OTIS.

MANILA. (Received January 8, 1900—5.20 a. m.)
ADJUTANT-GENERAL, *Washington:*
Spanish civil officials, prisoners, released from insurgents apply for transportation to Spain, at United States expense, under terms Paris treaty. Shall it be given them? And if so, shall they be shipped on existing contract as officers or soldiers?

OTIS.

MANILA. (Received January 8, 1900—8.15 a. m.)
ADJUTANT-GENERAL, *Washington:*
First Lieut. Ward Cheney, Fourth Infantry, died at Imus, 11.45 a. m., January 7, of wounds received in skirmish there.

OTIS.

MANILA. (Received January 8, 1900—3.51 p. m.)
ADJUTANT-GENERAL, *Washington:*
Bates pursuing enemy in south with vigor. Schwan's column moving along shore Laguna de Bay, struck 800 insurgents under General Moriel, at Biñang, 6th instant, and drove them westward on Silang; captured place, from which point cavalry pushed through to Indang; Schwan captured 3 of Noriel's 6 pieces artillery and will take remainder; also his transportation with records and large quantity of ammunition. Two battalions Twenty-eighth, part of Wheaton's column, struck enemy near Imus yesterday, killing and wounding 140. Birkhimer, with battalion Twenty-eighth, struck enemy intrenched west of Bacoor yesterday morning; enemy left on field 65 in dead, 40 wounded, and 32 rifles; our loss thus far Lieutenant Cheney, Fourth Infantry, 4 enlisted men killed; 24 enlisted men wounded. Expected that Schwan's troops will cut off retreat of enemy's Cavite army. Wheaton moving

to-day on Dasmariñas. Boyd, Thirty-seventh Infantry, moved east from Los Baños, surrounded troops of General Rizal at daylight, capturing Rizal and considerable property. It is expected that Cavite and Batangas provinces will be cleared up soon. In the north Leonhaeuser, with three companies Twenty-fifth, attacked robber bands in Arayat Mountain, dispersed them, destroying their barracks and subsistence; found there 5 of our prisoners, whom they had picked up on railroad; 3 killed, 2 seriously wounded. These northern robber bands will be actively pursued.

OTIS.

MANILA. (Received January 8, 1900—4.18 p. m.)
ADJUTANT-GENERAL, *Washington:*

Deaths: Drowned—Rio Agno, November 15, Newton W. Reese, Albert E. Holter, I, Fourth Cavalry; Rio Grande, November 7, Clarence W. Crites, D, Third Cavalry; Rio Pasig, accidentally, January 2, Anton M. Bong, I, Thirtieth Infantry; Rio Zapote, accidentally, January 1, Aly C. Larrimore, A, Thirty-eighth Infantry; Rio Camiling, accidentally, December 29, William C. Bryant, corporal, G, Twelfth Infantry. Typhoid—December 27, George Lehfeld, C, Twenty-second Infantry; 26th, August Gruettert, M, Nineteenth Infantry; January 3, George N. Dudley, F, Fourteenth Infantry; 6th, Edward J. Derry, E, Sixth Artillery; 2d, Charles Harrison, H, Twenty-sixth Infantry; 4th, Jefferson M. Stirewalt, E, Eighteenth Infantry; 3d, William Rundy, N, Twenty-sixth Infantry. Dysentery—December 26, Jack Whitney, corporal, E, Sixth Infantry; January 1, Arthur J. Edgerton, L, Thirty-second Infantry; 2d, James Kelly, G, Third Artillery; 5th, John J. McGee, corporal, G, Fourteenth Infantry. Pneumonia—January 1, Theodore Gehring, C, Fourth Infantry; Thomas J. Lyons, D, Third Cavalry; 14th, William Moloney, corporal, L, Nineteenth Infantry. Malaria—December 29, Reuben Weathers, L, Twenty-fifth Infantry; 30th, George Burtchell, B, Engineers; January 5, Patrick Fallon, H, Twelfth Infantry; 4th, William Snyder, E, Twenty-first Infantry. Pernicious malarial fever—November 25, Willie Dance, K, Twenty-fourth Infantry. Chronic diarrhea—January 3, Peter H. Kean, sergeant, H, Fourth Cavalry. Inflammation of bowels—January 1, William Brown, D, Thirty-second Infantry. Aortic stenosis of heart—January 3, Edmond Crabtree, musician, K, Sixth Infantry.

OTIS.

MANILA. (Received January 9, 1900—8.05 a. m.)
ADJUTANT-GENERAL, *Washington:*

Casualties: Killed in action—Engagement near Imus, January 7, Fourth Infantry, Second Lieut. Ward Cheney; Twenty-eighth Infantry, L, Robert Shuman, sergeant; Fourth Infantry, C, August Harsch, August M. Erikson. Near Bacoor, January 2, Twenty-eighth Infantry, C, Michael E. Kané. Wounded—Engagement near Imus, January 7, Fourth Infantry, C, Stanley Millard, leg, slight; Twenty-eighth Infantry, C, John Corbit, hand, moderate; A, John J. Barry, arm, moderate; Henry J. Flood, sergeant, arm, moderate; Eleventh Cavalry, C, Ridgway H. Griscom, neck, severe; Thirtieth Infantry, F, Charles Cawetzka, both thighs, severe; Fifth Artillery, F, Terrence J. Mooney, thigh, moderate; William Protz, chest, severe. Action Cabanatuan, November 5, Ernest B. Barjaron, civilian in Lowe's scouts, chest, severe.

OTIS.

ADJUTANT-GENERAL'S OFFICE,
Washington, January 9, 1900.
OTIS, *Manila:*

Urgent inquiries and anxiety here about hemp. Whenever you are in position to give definite information about opening ports it would be great relief to Department.

CORBIN.

AFFAIRS IN THE PHILIPPINE ISLANDS. 1131

MANILA. (Received January 10, 1900—6.05 a. m.)
ADJUTANT-GENERAL, *Washington:*
While temporarily deranged, First Lieut. Daniel T. Bowman, Thirty-seventh Infantry, committed suicide, 4.10 a. m., January 9, by shooting himself.

OTIS.

MANILA. (Received January 10, 1900—6.10 a. m.)
ADJUTANT-GENERAL, *Washington:*
Obliged to use all available coasting vessels supplying troops in various islands; unable to move other troops to hemp districts as soon as anticipated; am now collecting vessels here for that purpose; the United States transports too great draft; have opened Romblon and Capiz; some hemp coming in; will open main hemp district as soon as possible, some time this month. Bates has about cleared up province Cavite, making large captures.

OTIS.

MANILA. (Received January 12, 1900—10.19 a. m.)
ADJUTANT-GENERAL, *Washington:*
Continued operations Bates's command south Manila, Thirty-seventh and Thirty-ninth regiments; Calamba commanded by Bullard. On January 1, Bullard, with two battalions Thirty-ninth, attacked force insurgents in vicinity, driving enemy, capturing town of Cabuyao; following day captured Biñang; enemy's loss, 30 killed, large number wounded, 20 prisoners and rifles captured; casualties, 3 men slightly wounded. January 3, Boyd, three companies Thirty-seventh, captured General Rizal official papers and property, 3 miles east of Los Baños. January 4, Long, detachment Thirty-ninth, attacked insurgents at Carmona, 25 killed, no casualties. January 9, Bullard, with portions Thirty-seventh and Thirty-ninth regiments, attacked enemy south Calamba, whom he drove beyond Santo Tomas, killing 24, capturing artillery; casualties, 1 private killed; Captain Baker and Lieutenant Petite, Thirty-ninth, slightly wounded. January 11, Cheatham, Thirty-seventh, 106 men, supported by artillery, attacked insurgents 2 miles west Santo Tomas, driving them from that section; no casualties. Schwan's column, consisting squadron Fourth, one of Eleventh Cavalry, Thirtieth, Forty-sixth Infantry, and 6 Nordenfeldt guns, under Captain Van Deusen, seized Biñang, Silang Naic, scattering enemy, who were severely punished. Wheaton's column, three troops Eleventh Cavalry, Fourth, Twenty-eighth, Thirty-eighth, and Forty-fifth regiments, Astor and Kenley's batteries, has driven enemy from all important points north of Silang line; had heavy fighting, captured considerable public property, inflicting heavy loss upon and scattering enemy. Schwan's column now moving in northern Batangas, in southerly direction. All Cavite Province occupied by Wheaton's command. Heavy loss to enemy during week, in men, ordnance, and other property. All operations very successful.

OTIS.

MANILA. (Received January 15, 1900—9.35 a. m.)
ADJUTANT-GENERAL, *Washington:*
Casualties: Killed—Action near Naic, January 9, Eleventh Cavalry, I, Robert Napier. Action, Comansi, January 5, Twenty-fifth Infantry, B, Morgan G. Washington, corporal. Prisoners killed near Comansi upon approach American troops, January 5—Ninth Infantry, B, Charles C. Cook, Alonzo Brown. Wounded—B, Joseph P. Cook, chest, severe; Twelfth Infantry, Christian Peterson, commissary-sergeant, thigh, severe; B, Edward E. Norval, groin, severe. Wounded in action—Barrio de Lum-

baro, January 7, Twenty-eighth Infantry, H, Ennis N. Williams, throat, mortal; L, Fred. J. McWhood, first sergeant, thigh, severe; Robert Cunningham, back, severe; Alexander Riddet, shoulder, slight; James A. Goodrich, neck, severe; I, Harry B. Landolt, knee, slight. Barrio Putol, January 7, Twenty-eighth Infantry, A, Martin Wentink, hand, slight; Angus Edder, corporal, neck, slight; Patrick McDonnell, elbow, slight; B, James Wareham, wrist, slight. Comansi, January 5, Twenty-fifth Infantry, L, James T. Quarles, ankle, severe; K, John Harvey, forehead, slight.

OTIS.

MANILA. (Received January 15, 1900—10.32 a. m.)
ADJUTANT-GENERAL, *Washington:*

Bolo men and armed insurgent robbers from Zambales mountains attacked two companies, Twenty-fifth Infantry, O'Neil, commanding at Iba, January 6; driven and pursued with loss to them of 50 men; no casualties. Schwan's troops east and south Santo Tomas, Batangas. Yesterday Cheatham's battalion Thirty-seventh struck enemy east Santo Tomas on San Pablo road; enemy left 5 dead on field; cavalry soon appearing pursued force eastward; no report of result; Cheatham's casualties, 1 wounded. Anderson, Thirty-eighth, en route to Lipa yesterday struck insurgents few miles south Santo Tomas, drove them through Lipa to Rosario; enemy's loss 20 dead and wounded, 60 Spanish prisoners, $20,000. Schwan has liberated about 200 Spanish prisoners; now en route to Manila. Anderson's casualties yesterday 1 man killed, 2 wounded. Wheaton's force actively operating in western Cavite and Batangas provinces; all important towns held and constant patrolling; great many Filipinos returning to homes, believed to be insurgent deserters.

OTIS.

MANILA. (Received January 16, 1900—10.40 a. m.)
ADJUTANT-GENERAL, *Washington:*

Deaths: Drowned—January 3, Cotabato, Mindanao, Thomas J. Williams, sergeant, G, Thirty-first Infantry; January 7, Aparri, Luzon, John K. Stoltsz, B, Sixteenth Infantry; January 8, Montalbon, Wilbon L. Webber, K, Twenty-seventh Infantry; Manila, Willie L. Wrenn, A, Forty-first Infantry; Pandan, Panay, Lahue H. Roormon, A, Nineteenth Infantry. Typhoid—October 31, Joshua L. McKnight, E, Twenty-fourth Infantry; December 30, Winfield Marshall, C, Twenty-fourth Infantry; 6th, Edward G. Major, L, Seventeenth Infantry; 18th, Harry Thomas, G, Seventeenth Infantry; 5th, Henry C. Whorton, E, Seventeenth Infantry; January 9, Benjamin Haworth, C, Third Infantry; William M. Bretherton, A, Eleventh Cavalry; 7th, Patrick Mason, I, Twenty-fourth Infantry. Dysentery—December 10, John M. Healy, K, Seventeenth Infantry; 25th, Adam Diehl, I, Sevententh Infantry; January 5, John S. Larkin, C, Thirty-fourth Infantry; 7th, William F. Lindsay, G, Fourth Cavalry; 9th, Arthur Euston, E, Twenty-sixth Infantry; 12th, Benjamin Gardner, D, Fourth Cavalry; 13th, Benjamin V. Grace, K, Sixth Infantry; Charles E. Harter, H, Eighteenth Infantry. Pneumonia—December 11, Price Williams, H, Thirty-fourth Infantry. Malaria—December 5, Joseph A. Crane, F, Seventeenth Infantry; 25th, Peter T. Robinson, K, Thirty-fourth Infantry; January 7, Clarence Whitford, Band, Thirty-fourth Infantry. Cerebral hemorrhage—December 14, George Kitchen, K, Twenty-fourth Infantry. Cerebral congestion—27th, Charles F. Adams, cook, D, Twentieth Infantry. Malarial fever—26th, Warren F. Tucker, Band, Twelfth Infantry. Neuralgia of heart—21st, James Leary, I, Thirty-fourth Infantry. Variola—December 25, Charles F. Easley, Band, Thirty-fourth Infantry; January 5, Austin Griggs, C, Twenty-fourth Infantry. Diphtheria—2d, John L. Porter, musician, H, Twenty-fourth Infantry. Cardiac dilatation—7th, Andrew P. Zwiefel, D,

Twelfth Infantry. Tuberculosis—13th, Harold J. Reisinger, L, Sixteenth Infantry. Pulmonary apoplexy—10th, William G. Llewellyn, H, Sixth Infantry. Enteritis—12th, Campbell Oswald, sergeant, E, Eighteenth Infantry. Gunshot wound—November 17, William S. Pollock, L, Third Cavalry; January 8, Ennis N. Williams, H, Twenty-eighth Infantry; 12th, Joseph P. Cook, B, Ninth Infantry. Accidental, 4th, William L. Miller, D, Thirty-eighth Infantry. Suicide—6th, Prestwood B. Craddock, F, Fourth Cavalry; 11th, George W. Curtis, G, Eighteenth Infantry.

OTIS.

ADJUTANT-GENERAL'S OFFICE,
Washington, January 16, 1900.

OTIS, *Manila:*

The Secretary of War desires that all captured records of interest be forwarded by first mail, particularly any showing connection or correspondence with parties here. Are there any such?

CORBIN.

MANILA. (Received January 17, 1900—1.12 a. m.)

ADJUTANT-GENERAL, *Washington:*

Large mass captured records; officers and clerks engaged in assorting and translating; will send on those most important soon.

OTIS.

MANILA. (Received January 17, 1900—2.55 a. m.)

ADJUTANT-GENERAL, *Washington:*

Schwan's troops in possession of Batangas province, about to move eastward into provinces of Tayabas and Laguna; Wheaton moving on Lemery and Taal and has navy cooperation; casualties slight; insurgent loss considerable in men and property, as keep up constant opposition. Expedition under Kobbé leaves for hemp ports to-night.

OTIS.

MANILA. (Received January 17, 1900—3.25 a. m.)

ADJUTANT-GENERAL, *Washington:*

Alicante, 88 officers, 1,039 enlisted men, Spanish prisoners, sailed 13th instant; 1,500 more now here awaiting shipment; probably 700 all told will be released in south; request answer to cable asking if United States ships Spanish civil prisoners.

OTIS.

MANILA. (Received January 17, 1900—3.30 a. m.)

ADJUTANT-GENERAL, *Washington:*

General Hughes absent on western coast Panay policing; section band 86 Tagalos, which landed Negros coast December, struck by Byrne in Negros Mountains, who killed 19, captured 28 rifles, and ammunition; no casualties; troops in Northern Luzon busy pursuing robber bands, with good results.

OTIS.

ADJUTANT-GENERAL'S OFFICE,
Washington, January 17, 1900.

OTIS, *Manila:*

Refer to your telegram of 8th: civil officials, prisoners, wives, and children entitled passage to Spain; contract provides for shipment civil officials as officers, $215; wives and children of officers, soldiers and civil officials, $73.75.

CORBIN.

ADJUTANT-GENERAL'S OFFICE,
Washington, January 17, 1900.

OTIS, *Manila:*

To whom do you refer in reporting correspondence with Aguinaldo September 12, 1898, mentioning impression certain notes passing between the parties of which no record made? Secretary of War desires fullest possible record for Congress.

CORBIN.

ADJUTANT-GENERAL'S OFFICE,
Washington, January 17, 1900.

OTIS, *Manila:*

Department advised that 400 boxes Mauser rifles, marked "ALS G, Hongkong," letter "G" is underneath "ALS," and "Hongkong" underneath all, have been shipped on the *Savio*, which left Hamburg for Hongkong December 26. Another lot of 400 boxes, with same mark, on *Bayern* for Hongkong from Bremerhaven; that 240 boxes of rifles are lying at present on a quay in Hamburg bearing marks "LWC," Macao underneath, and will be shipped from Hamburg via Hongkong for Macao within next few days. The marks on these latter boxes are on the side, and not on the face of the box, as on those first mentioned. The 800 boxes for Hongkong came from Berlin; the 240 cases for Macao from Solingen, believed to have been bought by Mario Cresto & Company, Hamburg, from Weyersberg, Kirshberg, of Solingen. Also advised of another lot on the way to Bremen from Berlin.

CORBIN.

MANILA. (Received January 19, 1900—1.25 a. m.)

ADJUTANT-GENERAL, *Washington:*

See twenty-ninth line, page 6, annual report; correspondence referred to, presume taken by General Merritt for use in preparing annual report; originals in part subsequently found Anderson's headquarters, Cavite, consisting letters and telegrams, Anderson to Aguinaldo, July 4, 6, 14, 19, 19, 21, 22, 23, 24, 27, August 10; Aguinaldo to Anderson, August 10, 13, 14, 14; Merritt to Aguinaldo, August 20, 24, 25; Aguinaldo to Merritt, August 21, 25; presume Anderson, Merritt, or Babcock have this original correspondence with them in United States.

OTIS.

MANILA. (Received January 19, 1900—6.30 a. m.)

ADJUTANT-GENERAL, *Washington:*

Hughes reports from San José de Buena Vista, western coast Panay, that crossed mountains, northwesterly direction, from San Joaquin, southern Panay, 17th, struck enemy crossing Antique River, capturing rifles, cannon, and Nordenfeldt; pursued insurgents through Antique, Egaña, and Sibalon, their capital, and marched to San José; casualties, 1 wounded; enemy loss, considerable; entire population fled to mountains; heat oppressive.

OTIS.

AFFAIRS IN THE PHILIPPINE ISLANDS. 1135

MANILA. (Received January 19, 1900—7.35 a. m.)
ADJUTANT-GENERAL, *Washington:*

MacArthur reports 17th instant that 35 rifles surrendered at Florida Blanca; that at Banibaug, McRae, Third Infantry, captured 3 insurgent officers, wife of General Mascardo, considerable insurgent property, and liberated 3 Spanish prisoners; that at Calang, captured 10 insurgents, burned 7 tons of rice and insurgent barracks; that Sullivan, Thirty-fourth Infantry, near San José, surprised insurgent force, captured 6 rifles and considerable live stock; that Lieutenant Houle, Third Infantry, captured, near Malolos, 1 officer, 25 men, and six rifles; that Van Horn, Seventeenth Infantry, struck Ladrones at Santa Cruz, killed 17, wounded 5, captured 13 and 9 rifles; MacArthur reports, 18th instant, strong mountain position west Mabalacat, occupied by General Hizon and 50 men, captured yesterday by McRae, Third Infantry; enemy left lieutenant and 4 men dead in trenches; McRae captured captain, 1 man, 130 rifles, several thousand rounds of ammunition, destroyed arsenal, quantity of rice; casualties, 1 man wounded. Bates reports that Schwan's column cavalry refitting at Batangas to move eastward on 19th; infantry now moving that direction; enemy retiring, suffering loss in men and property; our casualties few, mostly slight wounds; that portion Wheaton's troops will enter Lemery and Taal to-morrow, now meeting opposition in mountains which impedes march. Six officers, 54 enlisted men, 4 civil employees, 11 friars, all Spanish prisoners, released by Schawn, arrived from Batangas last evening; nearly 200 received Manila day before via Calamba. Young at Vigan reports number successful skirmishes in mountains with remnants insurgents' organization and robber bands with slight casualties among his troops. Kobbé's expedition, Randolph's light battery, Forty-third and Forty-seventh Infantry, convoyed by navy vessels *Helena* and *Nashville*, sailed for Albay Province and Samar and Leyte islands yesterday.

OTIS.

MANILA. (Received January 20, 1900—10.47 a. m.)
ADJUTANT-GENERAL, *Washington:*

Pack train 20 ponies, transporting rations between Santo Tomas and San Pablo, Laguna Province, escorted by 50 men under Lieutenant Ralston, Thirtieth Infantry, ambushed yesterday; 2 men killed, 5 wounded, 9 missing, pack train lost. Lieutenant and 34 men returned to Santo Tomas with killed and wounded. Affair being investigated. Dorst, Forty-fifth Infantry, struck insurgents in Batangas Mountains, prepared in ambush to receive him; he killed 8, wounded 3, captured 17, 1 Spaniard, 6 rifles; his casualties, 2 men slightly wounded.

OTIS.

ADJUTANT-GENERAL'S OFFICE,
Washington, January 20, 1900.

OTIS, *Manila:*

Associated Press representative charges favoritism shown some newspapers Manila; claims account landing Loyd Wheaton force, San Fabian, delayed fifteen hours because substitute censor attending matinee, thereby missing afternoon editions; that at one time substitute left all received commercial telegrams, involving important matters, untouched; reason given, pressure more important business. Secretary of War desires your careful consideration, even to change of officer in charge of office if allegations true.

CORBIN.

MANILA. (Received January 21, 1900—7.12 a. m.)
ADJUTANT-GENERAL, *Washington:*
Representative Associated Press here reports censorship quite satisfactory and no complaint made; says he sent the "Wheaton cable" to explain delay, attaching no blame to censorship for it, although he thinks person acting temporarily as censor did not understand situation; all press correspondents here satisfied with present censors.

OTIS.

MANILA. (Received January 21, 1900—9.35 a. m.)
ADJUTANT-GENERAL, *Washington:*
Deaths: Variola—December 28, John W. Goodling, H, Thirteenth Infantry; 31st, Everet Barker, G; January 13, William B. Sisk, F, Thirty-first Infantry. Dysentery—12th, John C. Bottorff, D, Twenty-third Infantry; 11th, William Brady, H, Ninth Infantry; 16th, James Ross, E, Thirty-fifth Infantry; 17th, William McQuade, sergeant, G, Third Artillery. Chronic diarrhea—14th, Frank E. House, F, Fourth Infantry. Rupture of aortic aneurism—15th, George Gatewood,[a] K, Twenty-fifth Infantry. Wounds in action—12th, Peter Madden, B, Fourth Cavalry; 18th, Charles W. Singlemann, G, Eleventh Cavalry. Found in Rio Agno, Bautista, covered with incised wounds, 6th, Joseph Crispi, musician, A, Seventeenth Infantry. Tuberculosis—16th, Robert Mills, corporal, E, Eleventh Cavalry. Pneumonia—Bert Myers, G, Twenty-ninth Infantry. Broncho-pneumonia—17th, Walter W. Harris, E, Fortieth Infantry. Gunshot, accidental—12th, Clarence S. Barkla, corporal, M, Twenty-seventh Infantry.

OTIS.

MANILA. (Received January 21, 1900—10.56 a. m.)
ADJUTANT-GENERAL, *Washington:*
Major Johnston, commanding battalion Forty-sixth Infantry, Wheaton's brigade, reports from Lemery, 18th and 20th instant, drove enemy through Balayan, eastward morning 18th, capturing 17 rifles, 1 fieldpiece; few hours later, through Calaca, captured 4 prisoners, 4 horses and equipments, 6 rifles; killed 3 insurgents; advanced toward Lemery that afternoon, captured enemy's outpost, 3 men, 6 horses; advanced on Lemery 5 o'clock p. m., enemy strongly intrenched; sent by navy gunboat to Batangas for assistance, when three companies Muir's battalion, Thirty-eighth Infantry, sent to Taal, insurgent headquarters; Johnston drove enemy through Lemery on Taal, where he attacked southern portion of city, and Muir northern portion; enemy dispersed, retreating in many directions; Johnston's casualties, 1 man killed, 1 seriously and 2 slightly wounded; four fieldpieces and quantity rifles captured. This movement of Johnston's ably conducted and important in results. Enemy reported in large force and heavily intrenched at and near Santa Cruz, Laguna de Bay; Schwan swinging his troops on that point; his left at town of Bay, few miles east Calamba, his right, consisting of cavalry, at city of Tayabas.

OTIS.

ADJUTANT-GENERAL'S OFFICE,
Washington, January 22, 1900.
OTIS, *Manila:*
Secretary of War desires to know name important officer insurgents mentioned in your telegram February 21, 1899.

CORBIN.

---

[a] Gatewood name not found; said to be assumed. See cable, June 21, 1900; June 24, 1900.

AFFAIRS IN THE PHILIPPINE ISLANDS. 1137

MANILA. (Received January 23, 1900—6.20 a. m.)
ADJUTANT-GENERAL, *Washington:*
Refer to our telegram of 21st February—Teodoro Sandico; whereabouts unknown; see page 182, annual report.

OTIS.

ADJUTANT-GENERAL'S OFFICE,
Washington, January 23, 1900.
OTIS, *Manila:*
Secwar desires to know position held in so-called government by Sandico February 15, 1899.

CORBIN.

MANILA. (Received January 23, 1900—10.41 a. m.)
ADJUTANT-GENERAL, *Washington:*
Killed in action—Vigan, Luzon, December 4, Thirty-third Infantry, A, Arthur Wright; B, Lawrence L. Spencer, quartermaster-sergeant; Frederick J. Bell, sergeant; Alfred P. Wachs, corporal; D, Dale Puckett; E, James A. Bennett, William N. Brandon; L, Norman M. Fry, sergeant. Near Santa Nicolas, November 15, Third Cavalry, A, Irving H. Palmer. Near Lemery, Luzon, January 18, Forty-fifth[a] Infantry, F, Frank Carr. Wounded in action—Vigan, December 4, Thirty-third Infantry, B, James R. Montgomery, musician; E, Fred W. Loyeaa; K, William H. Bostwisk; M, John Patterson. Tangadan Mountain, 4th, Third Cavalry, D, Hubert Muggy; K, Frank J. Kayser. Near Biñang, January 7, Fourteenth Infantry, William C. Geiger, first lieutenant. Near Lemery, 18th, Forty-sixth Infantry, H, William Boese; 19th, G, Algert T. Nelson; H, John Lenehan. Near Santo Tomas, November 19, Third Cavalry, K, Charles W. Grace.

OTIS.

ADJUTANT-GENERAL'S OFFICE,
Washington, January 23, 1900.
OTIS, *Manila:*
Senate has applied to us for information regarding aid or encouragement received by Aguinaldo and followers from person United States. What pamphlets, speeches, or other documents from United States against its authority and policy were circulated among Filipinos or our soldiers. Telegraph briefly facts. Send full details by letter.

CORBIN.

MANILA. (Received January 24, 1900—7.32 a m.)
ADJUTANT-GENERAL, *Washington:*
Second Lieut. Eugene G. Wing, Thirty-sixth Infantry, died 11.05 a. m., January 24, variola hemorrhagic.

OTIS.

MANILA. (Received January 24, 1900—8.07 a m.)
ADJUTANT-GENERAL, *Washington:*
Lieutenant Stockley, Twenty-first Infantry, missing since 12th instant, on reconnoitering duty Talisay, near Santo Tomas, Batangas; evidently captured; search still prosecuted.

OTIS.

---

[a] Twenty-sixth—not Forty-fifth. Cablegram from Otis February 7, 1900.

MANILA. (Received January 24, 1900—12.47 p. m.)
ADJUTANT-GENERAL, *Washington:*
MacArthur, 20th to 23d, reports four minor engagements, in which 5 insurgents killed, several wounded and captured; also captured few rifles and other property; no casualties; that Major Bishop, Thirty-sixth Infantry, in north Zambales with detachment 60 men, attacked 2 insurgent companies, killed 9, wounded and captured 14; secured 22 rifles, several thousand rounds of ammunition, 2 horses with equipments; casualties, 3 men wounded, 1 seriously. General Young reports action of Steever, Third Cavalry, against General Tinio's force in north; inflicted very heavy loss on insurgents in which 28 killed; that Dodd's troop attacked insurgents near Santa Lucia, killed 6; no casualties; reported south, enemy evacuated Santa Cruz; supposed to be on eastern coast; that city in our possession last two days; Schwan believed to be in pursuit; no late reports from him. Coast Laguna de Bay and neighboring sections of country opened to unrestricted traffic 27th instant; western coast island Panay opened for trade.

OTIS.

MANILA. (Received January 25, 1900—12.15 a. m.)
ADJUTANT-GENERAL, *Washington:*
Transport *Grant*, Forty-eighth Infantry, arrived this morning; no casualties.

OTIS.

WAR DEPARTMENT,
Washington, January 25, 1900.

Maj. Gen. E. S. OTIS,
Military Governor, Philippine Islands, Manila, P. I.

SIR: I have the honor to acknowledge receipt of your letter of December 10, 1899, inclosing copy of your instructions of the same date to Brigadier-General Bates, U. S. V., commanding district of Mindañao and Jolo, and communicating to him copy of the War Department communication dated October 27 last.

The instructions to General Bates contained therein are approved.

Very respectfully,

ELIHU ROOT, *Secretary of War.*

MANILA. (Received January 25, 1900—2.22 a. m.)
ADJUTANT-GENERAL, *Washington:*
Sandico organized Manila militia, so called; then withdrew to Malolos; was insurgent secretary of interior from January to May; wore colonel's uniform; claimed to be member of Aguinaldo's military staff.

OTIS.

MANILA. (Received January 25, 1900—11.43 a. m.)
ADJUTANT-GENERAL, *Washington:*
Schwan concentrated Thirtieth, battalion Thirty-seventh, and Thirty-ninth Infantry at and near San Pablo, Laguna Province, afternoon, 20th; Hayes with cavalry striking for Tayabas by lower road; enemy had advanced from Santa Cruz to very strongly fortified positions, San Diego, Majayjay, and adjacent points; country very broken and mountainous. Schwan struck enemy at San Diego in engagement lasting two hours; killed 82, wounded large number; our casualties, 1 enlisted man killed,

14 wounded, including 3 native scouts; captured several rifles, ammunition, bolos, and stock of uniform clothing. On 22d Schwan pushed on through to Lilio, driving enemy back on Majayjay, where force, as reported by escaped Spanish prisoners, numbering between 1,500 and 3,000, well equipped and supplied, had concentrated, waiting approach of troops; this position impregnable via roads or trails; troops working round on either flank of enemy; retreated rapidly; Thirtieth Infantry and cavalry in pursuit; believed that insurgents widely dispersed; country now covered by troops, and force occupies Santa Cruz; few minor engagements at other points, resulting considerable loss to enemy. MacArthur telegraphs that McRae struck insurgent post in mountains, northwest Porac, capturing arsenal, barracks, 10 cartloads powder, and ammunition, 3 insurgents with rifles; barracks and arsenal destroyed.

OTIS.

MANILA. (Received January 26, 1900—8.30 a. m.)
ADJUTANT-GENERAL, *Washington:*
Released Spanish prisoners, 74 officers, 1,000 enlisted men, 22 civilian officials, 21 wives, 34 children; furnished transportation Spain yesterday.

OTIS.

MANILA. (Received January 26, 1900—7.54 a. m.)
ADJUTANT-GENERAL, *Washington:*
Hayes's cavalry reported at Santa Cruz; drove enemy out of Lucena, Tayabas, and adjacent towns; rescued 20 Spanish prisoners and 5 women; other Spanish prisoners moved back in small detachments into mountains; enemy dispersed and greater part believed to be seeking homes at Tayabas found record, dated 15th instant, saying 11 American prisoners leave to-morrow; know not to what place; Hayes's casualties, 1 killed, 3 mortally wounded, 2 slightly wounded.

OTIS.

MANILA. (Received January 26, 1900—1.06 p. m.)
ADJUTANT-GENERAL, *Washington:*
Kobbé's troops occupy the hemp ports of Sorsogon, Donsol, Bulan, Albay, and Legaspi, southeastern Luzon; Virac, island Catanduanes; will probably occupy the ports of Calbayog, Catbalogan, and Tacloban, of the islands of Samar and Leyte before to-morrow evening. No opposition except at Legaspi, where 800 insurgents strongly intrenched, under Chinese general Powah, made stubborn resistance; troops landed under protection of guns of *Nashville*, which fiercely bombarded fortifications close range; enemy's loss over 50 killed or mortally wounded; 28 killed at bridge head, at almost hand-to-hand encounter, refusing to surrender. Our casualties: Captain Bradly (transport) *Hancock*, quartermaster volunteers, aid to Kobbé, wounded in hand; 6 men, including 1 sailor on *Nashville*, slightly wounded. These ports contain great quantity hemp ready for shipment and will be open on 30th instant.

OTIS.

ADJUTANT-GENERAL'S OFFICE,
Washington, January 27, 1900.
OTIS, *Manila:*
Can you give us any other further information concerning Stockley?

CORBIN.

MANILA. (Received January 28, 1900—8.32 a. m.)
ADJUTANT-GENERAL, *Washington:*
No further information in case Stockley; reported many Spanish and some American prisoners in towns Lopez, Calauag, Tayabas Province; Stockley possibly there; troops now moving on Atimonan, and will operate eastward; expect to liberate these prisoners.

OTIS.

MANILA. (Received January 28, 1900—8.37 a. m.)
ADJUTANT-GENERAL, *Washington:*
Rescued Spanish major reported that he saw Major Rockefeller in northern Zambales December 12; another Spanish officer, Southern Luzon, states he saw him there short time ago. No satisfactory conclusion can be reached.

OTIS.

MANILA. (Received January 30, 1900—5.05 a. m.)
ADJUTANT-GENERAL, *Washington:*
Casualties: Killed—Cebu, September 23, Herman Fritch, K, Twenty-third Infantry. Near Lipa, Luzon, January 13, Walter C. Young, corporal, L, Thirty-eighth Infantry. Between Tanauan and Lipa, 20th, Frank W. Summerfield, musician, F, Thirty-sixth Infantry. At Mangataren, wounded December 9, James W. Dunn, I, Twenty-fifth Infantry, head; John Goodman, M, leg, slight, at Botolan.

OTIS.

MANILA. (Received January 30, 1900—5.08 a. m.)
ADJUTANT-GENERAL, *Washington:*
Deaths: Drowned—December 4, Frank S. Thiel, E, Thirteenth Infantry. Malaria—January 5, Matthew McNulty, B. Twenty-second Infantry; 22d, William H. Doty, F, Fortieth Infantry. Typhoid—25th, Garfield Commer, C, Twelfth Infantry; 17th, George E. Rehl, E, Thirty-ninth Infantry. Variola—25th, Second Lieut. Eugene G. Wing, B, Thirty-sixth Infantry; 12th, Spencer S. Koontz, F, Thirty-sixth Infantry; 14th, William A. Holt, F, Thirty-third Infantry. Dysentery—24th, Daniel F. Shank, K, Ninth Infantry; Fred. W. Mathias, sergeant, F, Twenty-seventh Infantry. Pneumonia—21st, Newton Hollenbaugh, L, Sixth Artillery. Wounded in action—25th, Rufus Ridner, A, Thirty-seventh Infantry. Suicide—23d, William Gregory, H, Eleventh Cavalry.

OTIS.

MANILA. (Received January 30, 1900—9.42 a. m.)
ADJUTANT-GENERAL, *Washington:*
Casualties: Killed—Luzon, January 13, John H. Kelly, B, Twenty-second Infantry, near Caigan; 27th, James E. Nowland, sergeant, E, Twenty-seventh Infantry, at Morong. Wounded—6th, Michael J. Grady, C, Fourth Infantry, thigh, moderate, near Bacoor; 25th, Second Lieut. Dennis P. Quinlan, Eleventh Cavalry, foot, slight, at Bulacan; 25th, Thomas O'Rourke, E, Twenty-seventh Infantry, pelvis, mortal, at Morong, Panay; 18th, Christian A. Jorgensen, C, Nineteenth Infantry, leg, slight, at Antique.

OTIS.

AFFAIRS IN THE PHILIPPINE ISLANDS. 1141

MANILA. (Received February 1, 1900—9.47 a. m.)

ADJUTANT-GENERAL, *Washington:*

Casualties: Killed—Twenty-fifth Infantry, January 29, near Subig, Luzon, First Lieut. William T. Schenck; K. Tevis Bronston; L, Hilliard Boone; William Shannon. Wounded—Thirty-eighth Infantry, 19th, at Taal, Batangas, D, Edward H. Chapin, thigh, severe; C, Elmer E. Leasor, face; Ben. D. Chinn, arm; Thomas Brown, chest; Edward Weaver, shoulder, moderate; Henry Buchanan, leg. Thirty-sixth Infantry, 22d, at Balincaguing, F, Ira Allen, chest, severe; G, Lewis L. Wyles, thigh, slight; Preston A. Loyd, foot, severe. Nineteenth Infantry, 8th, near Cebu, Cebu, B, Alfred Berry, corporal, neck and face, severe; K, Willard R. Bell, leg, severe; M, Charles W. Sisler, arm, slight; I, Henry W. Summers, corporal, thigh, moderate.

OTIS.

ADJUTANT-GENERAL'S OFFICE,
Washington, February 1, 1900.

OTIS, *Manila:*

Has administration San José College been assumed by civil authority?

CORBIN.

MANILA. (Received February 2, 1900—12.55 a. m.)

ADJUTANT-GENERAL, *Washington:*

San José College established by Jesuits 1601. Jesuits expelled 1768; since administered by Spanish Government aid religious orders; latterly through Dominicans; not yet supervising administration; contemplate doing so when conditions of the many supporting trusts fully determine.

OTIS.

MANILA. (Received February 3, 1900—7.52 a. m.)

ADJUTANT-GENERAL, *Washington:*

Kobbé reports from Cebu, occupation by troops of Calbayog, Catbalogan, in Samar, and Tacloban, Leyte; opposition these three points; insurgents endeavored to burn Calbayog and Catbalogan without success, except very slight destruction in last town, when first put out by our troops. From this point Kobbé drove insurgents under General Lucban into mountains, capturing large arsenal, powder house, Lucban's baggage and money, all his artillery. Tacloban insurgent loss in killed, 10. No casualties. Kobbe captured at all points 30 pieces artillery, good many rifles, stores, and ammunition, large quantities hemp; at points seized by Kobbé 30 merchant vessels engaged in transporting same to Cebu and Manila.

OTIS.

MANILA. (Received February 4, 1900—4.01 p. m.)

ADJUTANT-GENERAL, *Washington:*

Deaths: Cerebro-spinal meningitis—December 30, George T. Mann, K, Thirty-eighth Infantry. Acute diarrhea—7th, Shelby H. Taylor, C, Twenty-second Infantry. Valvular heart disease—25th, Joseph C. Wilson, sergeant, F, Twenty-third Infantry. Septicæmia—January 25, John H. Cogan, F, Third Infantry. Variola—28th, Arthur J. Ellis, H, Forty-fourth Infantry; 27th, H. Cleide Conner, I, Thirty-sixth Infantry. Malarial—28th, Virgil J. Ferguson, C, Twelfth Infantry; 22d, Ralph L. Richar, K, Thirty-fourth Infantry; 28th, Nathan Coffee, A, Twenty-fourth; 11th, John Pleasant,

F, Twenty-fifth Infantry. Tuberculosis—30th, Charles L. Haefner, L, Thirty-second Infantry. Appendicitis—31st, John McGonagle, musician, C, Twenty-eighth Infantry; February 2, Fred P. Collins, battalion sergeant-major, Fourteenth Infantry. Dysentery—1st, Peter W. Helvie, D, Forty-fifth Infantry; 2d, Lewis Olimb, sergeant, C, Eleventh Cavalry; 1st, Charles Moore, E, Twenty-second Infantry; January 15, Samuel D. Long, C, Twenty-second Infantry. Typhoid—24th, Thomas H. Bennett, G, Fourth Cavalry; February 1, Louis McPherson, A, Thifty-fifth Infantry; January 27, Harry Radebaugh, G, Twenty-seventh Infantry. Abscess of liver—24th, Edgar M. Stucker, M, Thirty-first Infantry. Pneumonia—28th, John Cunningham, corporal, L, Ninth Infantry. Wounds in action—27th, Thomas O'Rourke, E, Twenty-seventh Infantry. Accidental gunshot—25th, Emmet C. Adams, M, Twenty-ninth Infantry; 18th, Herman A. Larson, K, Forty-sixth Infantry.

OTIS.

MANILA. (Received February 6, 1900—6.55 a. m.)
ADJUTANT-GENERAL, *Washington:*

Total strength present and absent, January 31: Artillery, First, commissioned, 4, enlisted, 119; Third, 15, 447; Fourth, 4, 129; Fifth, 4, 123; Sixth, 44, 1,387. Cavalry, Third, 30, 947; Fourth, 43, 1,390; Eleventh, 49, 1,053. Infantry, Third, 45, 1,421; Fourth, 42, 1,342; Sixth, 44, 1,484; Ninth, 44, 1,383; Twelfth, 42, 1,362; Thirteenth, 46, 1,383; Fourteenth, 46, 1,549; Sixteenth, 45, 1,442; Seventeenth, 44, 1,452; Eighteenth, 43, 1,422; Nineteenth, 47, 1,456; Twentieth, 44, 1,430; Twenty-first, 46, 1,374; Twenty-second, 46, 1,479; Twenty-third, 43, 1,608; Twenty-fourth, 34, 1,070; Twenty-fifth, 36, 1,082; Twenty-sixth, 49, 1,237; Twenty-seventh, 47, 1,275; Twenty-eighth, 49, 1,263; Twenty-ninth, 49, 1,246; Thirtieth, 50, 1,011; Thirty-first, 48, 1,182; Thirty-second, 50, 1,228; Thirty-third, 49, 1,002; Thirty-fourth, 48, 1,276; Thirty-fifth, 51, 1,280; Thirty-sixth, 47, 983; Thirty-seventh, 49, 987; Thirty-eighth, 48, 1,256; Thirty-ninth, 50, 1,284; Fortieth, 48, 1,285; Forty-first, 49, 1,330; Forty-second, 50, 1,296; Forty-third, 48, 1,270; Forty-fourth, 48, 1,325; Forty-fifth, 50, 1,282; Forty-sixth, 49, 1,230; Forty-seventh, 50, 1,273; Forty-eighth, 49, 1,349; Forty-ninth, 50, 1,223. Engineers, 5, 276. Signal Corps, 21, 301. Contract surgeons, 158. Hospital Corps, 67, 1,783. Total commissioned, 2,367; enlisted, 61,067.

OTIS.

ADJUTANT-GENERAL'S OFFICE,
Washington, February 6, 1900.

OTIS, *Manila:*

Captain Smith, Nineteenth Infantry, reported wounded, condition desired.

CORBIN.

ADJUTANT-GENERAL'S OFFICE,
Washington, February 6, 1900.

OTIS, *Manila:*

Reply to cable January 23, relating to aid to Aguinaldo, etcetera, desired.

CORBIN.

MANILA. (Received February 7, 1900—1 a. m.)
ADJUTANT-GENERAL, *Washington:*

Colonel Barry leaves on *Grant* to-day with papers furnished under your cable January 23; search being still made in captured records.

OTIS.

MANILA. (Received February 7, 1900—9.08 a. m.)
ADJUTANT-GENERAL, *Washington:*
Captain Smith, Nineteenth, died at Sogod, 8.30, evening February 5, gunshot wound; body in sealed casket; will be shipped San Francisco.

OTIS.

MANILA. (Received February 7, 1900—9 09 a. m.)
ADJUTANT-GENERAL, *Washington:*
First Lieut. James P. Toncray, Thirty-sixth Regiment, U. S. Volunteer Infantry, died to-day, 6.30 a. m., hemorrhagic smallpox.

OTIS.

MANILA. (Received February 7, 1900—9 14 a. m.)
ADJUTANT-GENERAL, *Washington:*
Escaped Spanish prisoners report they saw Lieutenant Stockley a prisoner in hands insurgents January 28, near Atimonan, Southern Luzon.

OTIS.

ADJUTANT-GENERAL'S OFFICE,
Washington, February 7, 1900.
OTIS, *Manila:*
The Secretary of War desires to know the date in your opinion officers' wives can reasonably count on joining their husbands in the Philippine Islands, the conditions permitting.

CORBIN.

MANILA. (Received February 8, 1900—4.20 a. m.)
ADJUTANT-GENERAL, *Washington:*
Impossible to secure quarters for officers' families in Manila; majority officers with troops scattered and moving through provinces where wives would not be safe; these conditions will prevail for some time.

OTIS.

MANILA. (Received February 8, 1900—7.50 a. m.)
ADJUTANT-GENERAL, *Washington:*
Casualties: Killed—Luzon, F, Twenty-fifth Infantry, January 3, at Iba, Sherman Shepard; E, Third Cavalry, 14th, at Bimmauya, George J. Mitchell; G, Thirty-sixth Infantry, 22d, at Dasol, Zambales, George G. Knapp; L, Thirty-fourth Infantry, 14th, at Carranglan, Nueva Ecija, Thomas Griffin; B, Forty-first Infantry, February 2, at Mabalacat, August Costa; G, Thirty-second Infantry, 6th, near Dinalupijan, Bataan, Lee S. Murphy, Corpl. Leonard T. Brann, Bert R. Lane, Oliver H. Martin, Algernon S. Pressley, George Welsh; K, Eighteenth Infantry, Panay, January 11, at Panitan, John H. Denny; L, Forty-third Infantry, Samar, 27th, at Catbalogan, Edward Logan. Wounded—Patrick Duffy, I, corporal, leg, severe.

OTIS.

ADJUTANT-GENERAL'S OFFICE,
Washington, February 8, 1900.
OTIS, *Manila:*
Suggested that home battalion for the regular regiments longest in Philippines desirable, as giving rest for invalided officers and men, and men with six months or less to serve. Your views desired.

CORBIN.

1144 CORRESPONDENCE.

MANILA. (Received February 10, 1900—4.10 a. m.)
ADJUTANT-GENERAL, *Washington:*
Suggestion home battalion might influence many regimental officers to seek to join it; withdrawal entire regiment, after period Philippine service, to receive men of different organizations about to be discharged, believed preferable.

OTIS.

MANILA. (Received February 11, 1900—10.12 a. m.)
ADJUTANT-GENERAL, *Washington:*
Deaths: Drowned—February 4, Wesley Randall, A; 5th, Arlendon Tucker, E, Forty-eighth Infantry, Rio San Juan de Deposito, Luzon. Fever, malarial—December 6, William H. Erwin, A, Fourth Cavalry; January 18, George H. Walters, I, Thirty-eighth Infantry; February 4, John F. Sellman, corporal, C, Twenty-seventh Infantry. Dysentery—3d, First Lieut. Assist. Surg. Brainard S. Higley, jr., United States Army, 12.30 p. m.; January 31, John H. Coakley, K, Thirty-fourth Infantry; February 2, Zade E. Kitchen, M, Seventeenth Infantry. Variola—January 25, William H. Street, G, Thirty-sixth Infantry; February 2, Preston B. Brook, H, Thirty-sixth Infantry; 10th, Leander Hobby, M, Thirty-sixth Infantry. Concussion of brain—1st, Louis O. Nelson, G, Twelfth Infantry. Abscess liver—3d, James H. Sullivan, C, Nineteenth Infantry. Organic heart lesion—5th, Maurice Cain, A, Twenty-second Infantry. Nephritis—6th, William A. Ogden, M, Thirty-second Infantry. Peritonitis—7th, Percy Leadberter, corporal, Band, Thirteenth Infantry. Sarcoma of stomach—4th, James Moloney, H, Twenty-sixth Infantry. Gunshot, accidental—December 23, Christy Underhill, corporal, B, Thirty-second Infantry; January 31, Lewis Whalery, A, Forty-ninth Infantry.

OTIS.

MANILA. (Received February 15, 1900.—11 a. m.)
ADJUTANT-GENERAL, *Washington:*
Bates left to-day with two regiments and battery artillery on transports for San Miguel Bay, province Camarines Sur, to move on Nueva Caceras and towns in that section; road east from Atimonan through province Tayabas not practicable for troops; insurgents in Camarines show considerable activity, and made attack on our troops along southeastern coast Luzon Island; reported that they hold several hundred Spanish and few American prisoners, vicinity Nueva Caceras; Kobbé, with two regiments, occupies southeastern extremity Luzon from Tabaco on north to Donsol on south; also all important points of islands Catanduanes, Samar, Leyte. Conditions throughout Philippines gradually improving; all coasting vessels engaged in transporting merchandise and products. Ladrone element troublesome in all islands and keeps troops very actively engaged.

OTIS.

ADJUTANT-GENERAL'S OFFICE,
Washington, February 15, 1900.
OTIS, *Manila:*
Telegraph the condition of Denis L. Hayes, William Dugan, Michael Tracy, Company F, Twenty-Sixth Infantry.

CORBIN.

MANILA. (Received February 17, 1900—1.30 a. m.)
ADJUTANT-GENERAL, *Washington:*
With reference to your telegram of 16th, Hayes, Dugan, Tracy, Company F, Twenty-sixth Infantry, missing in campaign near Calinog, Panay, since November 27. Officer now investigating thinks he can prove their throats were cut by order padre of Calinog. Remains not found nor report submitted.

OTIS.

MANILA. (Received February 17, 1900—6.40 a. m.)
ADJUTANT-GENERAL, *Washington:*
Casualties: Killed—Thirty-ninth Infantry, January 13, Lipa, Luzon, B, James C. Ryan; February 3, Bagbag, province Batangas, Luzon, K, Albert Votrie. Sixth Infantry, February 4, Antique, Panay, L, George A. Schuchard. Wounded— Fourth Cavalry, February 7, Magdalena, Luzon, A, Ross G. Miller, left hand, severe; C, Horace N. Munro, thorax, severe. Thirty-eighth Infantry, January 21, Sariaya, Tayabas, Luzon, L, Reuben C. Hieronymus, right thigh, severe. Thirty-second Infantry, January 2, Dinalupijan, Luzon, D, Claude L. Pearson, right hand, moderate. Thirty-third Infantry, January 24, Doninglay, Luzon, Sergt. Maj. Robert E. Wilson, right gluteal region, slight.

OTIS.

ADJUTANT-GENERAL'S OFFICE,
Washington, February 17, 1900.
OTIS, *Manila:*
Secretary of War interested to know quite fully present condition of relations between religious orders native church Tagalog people and present military government.

CORBIN.

MANILA. (Received February 19, 1900—6.32 p. m.)
ADJUTANT-GENERAL, *Washington:*
Archbishop Chapelle desires religious orders reinstated; says only means pacification. This announcement created excitement which military authorities allayed, assuring people they should enjoy religious liberty; that friars would not be forced upon them. Chapelle responded that he would not send friars where not wanted. Archbishop claims that United States has no supervision over landed and other properties religious orders; that church patronage exercised by Spain was conferred by Vatican and lapsed when Spain withdrew from islands; that Paris treaty guarantees religious orders all vested or acquired rights. Military authority responds that although United States can not exercise supervision ecclesiastical nature, has acquired from Spain her formerly exercised jurisdiction of civil character, or that which naturally existed in Spanish sovereignty; and even independent of right derived through conquest, United States, from nature of institutions, must exercise some measure of civil control. Correspondence by mail. People will not receive members of four of the eight religious orders, or those long domiciled here and possessing large estates. Tagalos will kill them, and will not be safe in other islands. Northern Panay now petitions that they be not sent there. Archbishop states can not supply place; that return to their parishes necessary for preservation religion and pacification people. In my opinion attempt to reestablish friars would unite people in many islands in hostility against United States. Recently ascertained that friars have transferred 130,000 acres Luzon estates to English syndicate, which now demand to be placed in possession. This complicates matters. Friar question will give great annoyance.

OTIS.

MANILA. (Received February 19, 1900—9.05 a. m.)
ADJUTANT-GENERAL, *Washington:*
Deaths: Malarial fever—January 2, Arlington Mayse, H, Twenty-second Infantry; February 10, Willis C. McMartin, corporal, G, Forty-fifth Infantry; 12th, Azariah Herron, K, Thirty-eighth Infantry. Drowned—January 15, Albert L. Perry, A, Thirty-second Infantry, bathing Rio Grande, Florida Blanca; 14th, John Magnusen, Band, Thirty-fourth Infantry, bathing Rio Grande, Cabanatuan, Luzon; 15th, Joseph F. Carnes, F, Thirty-fourth Infantry, Rio Agno, near San Nicolas, accidental. February 9, Daniel P. Jenkins, M, Twenty-second Infantry, gunshot. January 29, William Crawford, corporal, K, Twenty-fifth Infantry, Angeles, Luzon, fell on dagger worn by him. Gunshot in action—January 27, Amos O. Neal, F, Thirty-ninth Infantry. Heat prostration—February 9, Frederick Hegwein, H, Twenty-seventh Infantry. Pneumonia—11th, John P. Hill, C, Twenty-ninth Infantry. Variola—5th, Porter McGuyer, D, Forty-fourth Infantry; 12th, Cyrus E. Brittain, A, Thirty-sixth Infantry. Dysentery—14th, Andrew Anderson, H, Thirty-fifth Infantry; Carl L. Nessel, C, Fourth Cavalry. Typhoid fever—16th, Clarence Van Berger, corporal, B, Thirty-seventh Infantry.

OTIS.

MANILA. (Received February 20, 1900—4.20 a. m.)
ADJUTANT-GENERAL, *Washington:*
Casualties: Killed—Luzon, Thirty-seventh Infantry, January 11, at Santo Tomas, A, Lincoln Miller; 21st, Santiago, B, Harry E. Hosier, corporal; February 14, at Santa Cruz, Forty-second Infantry, G, John T. Larkin; G, William Shultz. Wounded—Luzon, Thirty-seventh Infantry, January 21, at Santiago, A, William Bullis, arm, severe; C, Marion F. Schaffer, leg, slight; D, Frank Chapman, foot, severe; D, Charles Silver, head, slight; D, Harry T. Seymour, first sergeant, hand, slight; L, Edward M. Holt, hand, slight; M, Anthony L. Schneider, forehead, slight. Thirty-ninth Infantry, February 16, San Francisco, Batangas, I, Perrin L. Smith, first lieutenant, arm, moderate; I, Napoleon D. Burgoyne, corporal, forearm, moderate; January 9, at Calamba, Hiram C. Baker, captain, ear perforated; Albert M. Petite, first lieutenant, legs, moderate. Forty-second Infantry, February 5, at Paquil, Edmund Dubois, captain, shoulder, severe; H, Milton Lane, arm, slight; 4th, at Pagsanjan, G, John Seeberger, corporal, face. Nineteenth Infantry, Cebu, 5th, at Consolacion, K, John W. Felts, thigh, slight.

OTIS.

MANILA. (Received February 21, 1900—1.45 a. m.)
ADJUTANT-GENERAL, *Washington:*
Have purchased with civil funds Spanish armored transport and two large gunboats, with entire armament; those particularly needed by navy now; request authority to transfer property to navy.

OTIS.

MANILA. (Received February 22, 1900—1.25 a. m.)
ADJUTANT-GENERAL, *Washington:*
Capt. Samuel R. Langworthy, Thirty-fifth Infantry, died Baliuag, Bulacan, 2.45 afternoon February 21, pernicious remittent malarial fever.

OTIS.

AFFAIRS IN THE PHILIPPINE ISLANDS.

MANILA. (Received March 1, 1900—3 a. m.)

ADJUTANT-GENERAL, *Washington:*

Casualties: Killed—Luzon, Third Cavalry, January 12, Bangar, C, Michael Barry, Charles Benson. Thirty-ninth Infantry, 9th, Santo Tomas, Province Batangas, E, Walter H. Hoskinson. Forty-seventh Infantry, 25th, Legaspi, H, Timothy Heneghan. Thirtieth Infantry, 18th, San Francisco, Batangas Province, H, William Sallisbury; C, Joseph O. Byunes. Jolo, Twenty-third Infantry, 30th, Bangao, Tawi-Tawi group, H, Egbert V. De Wolfe, Sergeant Webster F. Gibbons. Wounded—Luzon, Thirty-fourth Infantry, December 4, Tangadan, G, Patrick J. Murphy, arm, slight; James Smith, thigh, slight; Fred Carr, arm, slight. Forty-seventh Infantry, January 25, Legaspi, G, Ross Barton, first sergeant, arm, moderate; F, Matthew Gallivan, head, severe. Thirtieth Infantry, 18th, San Francisco, Batangas Province, C, Frank Junker, radius, severe; Harry M. Waite, corporal, abdomen, severe; Victor McMillen, hand, slight; K, Chris H. Anderson, thigh, slight; Leslie N. Tracy, arm, slight; B, Horace G. Baine, trachea, slight. Thirty-eighth Infantry, 27th, San Luis, B, Jerry W. Stephens, chest, slight; Charles W. Switzer, arm, slight; Charles H. Muir, major, heel, moderate. Thirty-ninth Infantry, 1st, Calamba, G, William F. Buchholz, corporal, knee, slight; H, Reuben Nichols, thigh, slight; Frank E. Youell, arm, slight; Jay Blaisdell, knee, slight; G, Jack Noel, leg, slight. Jolo, Twenty-third Infantry, 30th, Bangao, H, William T. Carter, lumbar region, severe; John A. Greathouse, neck, severe. Panay, Forty-fourth Infantry, 30th, Madalag, H, Noah L. Short, thigh, moderate.

OTIS.

MANILA. (Received March 1, 1900—8.05 a. m.)

ADJUTANT-GENERAL, *Washington:*

Received Manila since recent opening island ports, 13,000 tons hemp, 70,000 bales tobacco; large shipments abroad soon.

OTIS.

MANILA. (Received March 1, 1900—8.07 a. m.)

ADJUTANT-GENERAL, *Washington:*

Arrived to-day by Government transport from east coast Tayabas Province, 8 American and 410 Spanish soldiers, recent prisoners in hands insurgents; also 2 American citizens and 17 Spanish friars.

OTIS.

ADJUTANT-GENERAL'S OFFICE,
Washington, March 1, 1900.

OTIS, *Manila:*

Home battalions will be designated by you from Fourteenth Regiment, U. S. Infantry, Eighteenth Regiment, U. S. Infantry Twenty-third Regiment, U. S. Infantry, to be sent United States. Attach invalid officers desiring to return and those in your opinion who should be sent United States; invalid enlisted men and men having less than six months to serve who do not intend reenlist will be transferred to home battalions. Men having year or more to serve will be transferred to battalions remaining. Arriving San Francisco, commanding officer each battalion will report to the commanding general, Department of California, for instructions. Advise about what date departure, and strength commands, and if other troops should be sent to replace returning battalions.

CORBIN.

MANILA. (Received March 4, 1900—12.21 p. m.)
ADJUTANT-GENERAL, *Washington:*
Eighteenth Infantry at several stations Panay; Twenty-third Cebu, and three stations Jolo; will designate home battalions, transfer and attach as directed, and more within month; strength reported later. All troops here needed to protect inhabitants and in some sections country too few to meet requests. Guerrilla and robber bands still quite active in various sections of islands and considerable element natives untrustworthy. Developments of ensuing six weeks will alone permit intelligent answer to question concerning additional troops. Pronounced insurgents think they can tire out United States by keeping people in active state of unrest. However, conditions improving. Bates's movements in Camarines not yet known. Hamburg shipments reported from Washington January 18th have reached Hongkong and Shanghai. Hongkong junta active; said to have directed continued guerrilla warfare, expecting to secure thereby better conditions for insurgent cause. Encouraged by recent reports of attitude of Congress, which insurgents believe. Trade in all islands increasing; Manila never more bustling; but Insurgent junta working in our midst, requiring continual watching.

OTIS.

MANILA. (Received March 5, 1900—12.35 p. m.)
ADJUTANT-GENERAL, *Washington:*
Bates, two battalions Fortieth, Forty-fifth Regiments, detachments of artillery, Engineers, Signal Corps, total 2,200 men, landed troops on southeast, northwest, and southern coast San Miguel Bay, Camarines Province, to move on Nueva Caceres in three columns. Only strong opposition encountered by Godwin and battalion of his regiment at Libmanan, northwest Neuva Caceres. Godwin's loss: Adjutant Galleher died of wounds; 3 enlisted men severely, 5 slightly wounded. Enemy left 64 dead on field; many wounded, cared for by our medical officers. Godwin captured number armed insurgents, 18 Spanish prisoners, 30 rifles, considerable ammunition and property. Particulars of minor engagements of other columns not reported. Nueva Caceres found practically deserted; inhabitants in mountains. Troops now covering important points provinces Camarines, Albay, Sorsogon. Navy rendered most valuable aid in landing troops and supplies.

OTIS.

MANILA. (Received March 5, 1900—2.27 p. m.)
ADJUTANT-GENERAL, *Washington:*
Killed—Luzon, H, Fortieth Infantry, Albay, February 14, William H. Martin; Eleventh Cavalry, A, Sariaya, January 19, William R. Blanchard; C, Indang, 7th, James Freeman. Third Cavalry, D, San Juan, February 26, Mark Burns. Ninth Infantry, Tinuba, March 4, First Lieut. Edgar F. Koehler, at 8 a. m. Thirty-third Infantry, A, Tangadan Mountain, December 7, James A. Whalen. Panay, Nineteenth Infantry, A, Patnongon, February 15, George W. Morris; 6th, C, Frederick F. Parker. Wounded—Luzon, Fortieth Infantry, G, Albay, 8th, George Donaldson, thorax, severe; 12th, H, James A. Underwood, thigh, slight; Camalig, 22d, E, Thomas A. Killough, thorax, slight. Eleventh Cavalry, C, Sariaya, January 19, William T. Wright, foot, severe; F, John W. Hatfield, sergeant, leg, moderate; Heber Elkins, head, severe; Naic, 9th, E, John W. Maxwell, leg, moderate; Silang, 7th, M, George A. McCarter, sergeant, arm, moderate. Thirty-seventh Infantry, Magdalena, February 17, B, Frank Leers, wrist, severe; 28th, A, Sam Van Leer, captain, forearm, very slight; Cavinti, March 2, E, Albert L. Domce, thigh, severe; February 28, M, Andrew Hagland, forehead, slight. Twenty-fourth Infantry, San Luis, Isabela, December 3, F, Mack C. Nance, pelvis, severe; Naguilian, 7th, F, Alonzo B. Kelly,

musician, thigh, slight; H, Charles Wilson, scalp, slight; James Bentley, scalp, slight. Thirty-ninth Infantry Sampaloc, Tayabas, January 29, E, Simon Hudson, thigh, slight; San Pablo, 21st, George E. Quinn, corporal, shoulder, severe; F, Otis H. Sidener, abdomen, slight; G, Lanier Schley, corporal, leg, moderate; Maurice F. Lindsey, hand, slight. Panay, Sixth Infantry, Macato, February 24, C, Frank C. Bolles, first lieutenant, hand, moderate.

OTIS.

[This cable was repeated.]

MANILA. (Received March 6, 1900—11.57 a. m.)
ADJUTANT-GENERAL, *Washington:*
Deaths: Appendicitis—March 2, Tilden A. Logan, B, Twenty-ninth Infantry. Diarrhea—March 1, Charles L. Slocum, artificer K, Thirty-seventh Infantry. Dysentery—December 8, Henry Alexander, F, Twenty-fourth Infantry; February 7, John McEachran, corporal, B, Thirty-seventh Infantry; 24th, James H. Washington, A, Twenty-fourth Infantry; 24th, Willis C. Fulton, C, Seventeenth Infantry; 27th, William Banks, B, Forty-ninth Infantry; 27th, Ed. Stroup, K, Thirty-eighth Infantry; 28th, James J. Pryor, K, Twenty-fourth Infantry. Drowned—24th, John Hendrickson, E, Thirty-seventh Infantry, Rio Pagsanjan at Lumbang. Enteritis—25th, Harvey L. Leeman, F, Eighteenth Infantry. Fever, typhoid—7th, Moss B. Rode, C, Nineteenth Infantry; 22d, William Walker, L, Ninth Infantry. Fever, malarial—25th, Petronilo Gurule, L, Thirty-fourth Infantry; 27th, Mikal D. Grane, B, Thirty-fifth Infantry; 27th, Henry Tilley, quartermaster-sergeant, G, Ninth Infantry. Wounds in action—January 20, Felix George Baudain, F, Eleventh Cavalry; 20th, Patrick M. Phelan, I, Eleventh Cavalry; February 23, William F. Kinsell, D, Thirty-seventh Infantry; 28th, Thomas Brown, corporal, C, Thirty-eighth Infantry. Variola—17th, Fred. S. Johnston, I, Thirty-third Infantry; 22d, Paul H. Phillips, E, Fourth Cavalry; 25th, Joseph F. Martin, Hospital Corps; 26th, Charles E. Ramsey, C, Thirty-third Infantry; March 3, James M. Woodland, M, Seventeenth Infantry. Pleurisy—February 23, Taylor Johnston, F, Twenty-second Infantry. Chloroform anæsthesia—17th, Robert M. Bartlett, H, Forty-second Infantry.

OTIS.

MANILA. (Received March 8, 1900—7.30 a. m.)
ADJUTANT-GENERAL, *Washington:*
Officer, 60 enlisted men, 2 civilian officials, captured Spanish prisoners, received to-day from Tayabas.

OTIS.

ADJUTANT-GENERAL'S OFFICE,
Washington, March 9, 1900.
OTIS, *Manila:*
Major-General Commanding Army desires to know if there is any objection now to officers' families proceeding on transports to Manila.

CORBIN.

MANILA. (Received March 12, 1900—3.02 a. m.)
ADJUTANT-GENERAL, *Washington:*
Many officers' families have arrived; number leaving for Japan and United States. Until Philippines better pacified, do not consider them desirable place for officers' families; must remain in large cities while husbands in field; can not meet applications for houses and accommodations for those now here.

OTIS.

MANILA. (Received March, 12, 1900—7.55 a. m.)
ADJUTANT-GENERAL, *Washington:*

Casualties: Killed—Luzon, Sixteenth Infantry, February 28, Camalaniugan, C, Patrick J. Enright, corporal; March 2, Linao, B, Fred. Daniel. Thirtieth Infantry, January 15, Lipa, I, David Goldman. Forty-fifth Infantry, February 20, Calabanga, G, Wilson Bellis. Forty-seventh Infantry, February 21, Donsol, A, John P. Morrison, musician. Panay, Twenty-sixth Infantry, February 23, Iloilo, F, William Dugan, Denis L. Hayes, Michael Tracy. Wounded—Luzon, March 6, Peñaranda, Acting Asst. Surg. Walter C. Chidester, wounded in back, serious. Thirtieth Infantry, January 6, Biñang, Anthony Westrate, scalp, slight, Company F; January 19, San Pablo, D, Ernest F. Trepto, corporal, cheek, moderate; Jacob Lucas, lung, severe; January 28, Tayabas, D, Lieut. Guy A. Boyle, leg, moderate; Charles A. Hackworth, wounded in arm, moderate; February 4, Sampaloc, E, James L. Jones, abdomen, severe; H, Fred. Cliff, wounded in thigh, moderate. Thirty-sixth Infantry, March 6, Dasal, A, Second Lieut. Frank T. McNarney, thigh, slight. Thirty-seventh Infantry, March 7, Santa Cruz, L, David V. Kennedy, hip, slight. Fortieth Infantry, February 20, Libmanan, First Lieut. Adjt. John B. Galleher, abdomen, severe; A, Albert A. Widick, corporal, chest, slight; John F. Sandidge, corporal, side, slight; B, Alois C. J. Sick, corporal, head, serious; Robert D. Stewart, finger, slight; C, Earl R. Hutchison, sergeant, thigh, serious; William E. Biggs, thigh, slight; Edgar H. Garrett, shoulder, slight; Guy M. Ingersoll, breast, slight.

OTIS.

MANILA. (Received March 12, 1900—1.45 p. m.)
ADJUTANT-GENERAL, *Washington:*

Suicide—February 27, Daniel H. Collins, F, Seventeenth Infantry; March 6, Williams Parsons, C, Twenty-second Infantry; March 9, Second Lieut. Louis P. Weber, E, Forty-second Infantry, Friday, 11 p. m., while mentally deranged. Died from wounds received in action—February 23, Friday, 2 a. m., First Lieut. Bat. Adjt., John B. Galleher, Fortieth Infantry; February 5, James L. Jones, E, Thirtieth Infantry; March 5, William Boese, H, Forty-sixth Infantry. Variola—March 1, Louis Lille, corporal, G, Forty-first Infantry; March 2, Thomas M. Brooke, H, Thirty-sixth Infantry; March 5, Walter H. Burlingame, F, Thirty-ninth Infantry. Chronic diarrhea—March 3, Pinkney Flinn, E, Thirty-seventh Infantry. Subacute diarrhea—March 4, Theodore Shaffer, D, Thirty-second Infantry. Multiple neuritis—March 4, William Wightman, sergeant, I, Third Infantry. Typhoid fever—March 4, Charles Lee, E, Twenty-sixth Infantry; Henry O. Green, G, Eighteenth Infantry; March 5, Frank O. Ocker, B, Sixth Infantry; March 8, Henry Fitzgerald, F, Ninth Infantry. Enteritis—March 1, Charles F. Herrick, Battery G, Sixth Artillery. Accidental—March 6, William J. Wood, L, Sixth Artillery, run over by truck; March 4, Earl C. Ward, corporal, A, Thirtieth Infantry, shot by sentry; March 8, Albert Knittle, O, Sixth Artillery, fell through hatchway. Malarial fever—March 4, Edgar J. Manning, A, Ninth Infantry. Dysentery—March 6, Leon W. Wiltshire, E, Ninth Infantry; March 9, David A. Ferguson, I, Fourth Cavalry. Measles—March 7, Milton L. Smart, D, Thirty-eighth Infantry. Appendicitis—March 10, James Thompson, D, Forty-eighth Infantry.

OTIS.

MANILA. (Received March 13, 1900.)
ASSISTANT SECRETARY OF WAR, *Washington:*

Number Manila licensed saloons and hotels, sale liquors generally, 82; wine and beer, 74; beer, 2; nationality proprietors, Spanish, 67; American, 27; Filipinos, 26;

AFFAIRS IN THE PHILIPPINE ISLANDS. 1151

Chinese and Japanese, 11; unknown, 27. Twenty per cent decrease since June. Patrons mostly Americans and European; few natives. Licensed houses for sale native wine, 778, of which 15 distilleries. These conducted by Chinese and Filipinos. Under Spanish rule over 3,000 of these licensed shops existed. Can not ascertain number of liquor saloons under Spanish administration; fewer than at present time. Extended report by mail.

OTIS.

MANILA. (Received March 14, 1900—3.25 p. m.)
ADJUTANT-GENERAL, *Washington:*

Total strength, present and absent, February 28, as accurate as can be ascertained; impossible to get returns from some regiments: Third Cavalry, commissioned 30, enlisted 948; Fourth Cavalry, 45, 1,410; Eleventh Cavalry, 49, 998. First Artillery, 4, 128; Third Artillery, 13, 388; Fourth Artillery, 4, 128; Fifth Artillery, 4, 116; Sixth Artillery, 45, 1,394. Third Infantry, 45, 1,402; Fourth Infantry, 42, 1,320; Sixth Infantry, 44, 1,461; Ninth Infantry, 43, 1,346; Twelfth Infantry, 43, 1,489; Thirteenth Infantry, 46, 1,340; Fourteenth Infantry, 46, 1,537; Sixteenth Infantry, 43, 1,408; Seventeenth Infantry, 44, 1,424; Eighteenth Infantry, 45, 1,400; Nineteenth Infantry, 49, 1,406; Twentieth Infantry, 43, 1,409; Twenty-first Infantry, 44, 1,355; Twenty-second Infantry, 46, 1,449; Twenty-third Infantry, 46, 1,454; Twenty-fourth Infantry, 23, 1,029; Twenty-fifth Infantry, 31, 1,099; Twenty-sixth Infantry, 50, 1,239; Twenty-seventh Infantry, 50, 1,213; Twenty-eighth Infantry, 50, 1,253; Twenty-ninth Infantry, 49, 1,256; Thirtieth Infantry, 50, 1,280; Thirty-first Infantry, 50, 1,242; Thirty-second Infantry, 50, 1,218; Thirty-third Infantry, 49, 1,276; Thirty-fourth Infantry, 50, 1,254; Thirty-fifth Infantry, 46, 1,275; Thirty-sixth Infantry, 45, 979; Thirty-seventh Infantry, 50, 1,042; Thirty-eighth Infantry, 50, 1,248; Thirty-ninth Infantry, 49, 1,260; Fortieth Infantry, 48, 1,272; Forty-first Infantry, 50, 1,323; Forty-second Infantry, 48, 1,281; Forty-third Infantry, 50, 1,283; Forty-fourth Infantry, 47, 1,291; Forty-fifth Infantry, 49, 1,269; Forty-sixth Infantry, 49, 1,271; Forty-seventh Infantry, 50, 1,260; Forty-eighth Infantry, 49, 1,304; Forty-ninth Infantry, 42, 1,150. Battalion Engineers, 3, 123. Signal Corps, 21, 302. Hospital Corps, 68, 1,785. Total, 2,169 commissioned; 60,765 enlisted.

OTIS.

MANILA. (Received March 15, 1900—7 27 a. m.)
ADJUTANT-GENERAL, *Washington:*

Shipped to-day Barcelona, 84 officers, 427 enlisted men, Spanish prisoners war held by iusurgents; also 8 wives, 14 children of officers. Total, 533.

OTIS.

MANILA. (Received March 19, 1900—9 22 a. m.)
ADJUTANT-GENERAL, *Washington:*

Deaths: Dysentery—July 31, last year, Henry Haze, A, First California, at Tayabas, while prisoner of war; March 7, Timothy O'Hare, I, Twenty-sixth Infantry; Earl R. Bates, L, Thirty-seventh Infantry; March 12, Edward Bauman, E, Third Infantry. Malaria—February 26, Willie Chestnut, A, Twenty-second Infantry; March 11, William Tappe, M, Twelfth Infantry; March 13, William G. Burns, L, Ninth Infantry; March 10, Hugh McIntyre, L, Fortieth Infantry; March 15, John Mordin, G, Forty-sixth Infantry. Fever, cause not known—February 3, Clifton J. Paxton, D, Thirteenth Infantry. Variola—February 23, Bayles T. Reed, F, Third Infantry; February 18, Edgar J. Hurbough, F, Thirty-third Infantry; March 8,

Simon Hudson, E, Thirty-ninth Infantry; John Austin, K, Twenty-fourth Infantry; Romeo Jackson, K, Twenty-fourth Infantry; March 11, Daniel Lyons, H, Twenty-fourth Infantry; March 14, John M. Moore, C, Thirty-second Infantry. Nephritis—March 12, Abram L. Mauk, L, Fourth Cavalry; March 10, Harry B. Stranahan, K, Third Cavalry. Diarrhea—March 7, George W. Day, corporal, E, Eighteenth Infantry; March 8, John Sklensky, musician, F, Eighteenth Infantry. Beriberi—March 13, John E. Deasy, D, Twenty-first Infantry. Tuberculosis—March 12, Walter G. Webb, E, Seventeenth Infantry. Typhoid fever—March 14, William Diwell, L, Thirty-fifth Infantry; Edward Barth, G, Twenty-first Infantry; March 10, Joseph O. Cameron, D, Thirty-ninth Infantry. Pneumothorax—March 16, Patrick Dowdall, sergeant, E, Sixth Artillery. Pneumonia—March 4, Thomas A. Taylor, corporal, D, Fortieth Infantry. Drowned—February 6, Jacob Brandt, K, Thirtieth Infantry; March 3, Frank B. Keen, H, Twenty-fifth Infantry; March 11, William M. Brown, E, Twenty-fifth Infantry; March 13, Edward W. Beattie, A, Battalion Engineers; March 15, James Duddy, corporal, D, Twenty-eighth Infantry.

OTIS.

MANILA. (Received March 19, 1900—9.25 a. m.)
ADJUTANT-GENERAL, *Washington:*

Casualties: Killed—Luzon, Hospital Corps, March 2, Linao, Thomas D. Hare, hospital steward; Third Cavalry, March 14, Bagnotan, D, Arthur Hardwick; Sixteenth Infantry, March 2, Linao, B, Thomas F. Brady; Thirty-third Infantry, January 22, Quiangan, E, Edward Herrfeldt; March 9, Bangued, D, Chester A. Cress. Wounded—Luzon, Third Cavalry, March 14, Bagnotan, D, Michael J. Cooney, chest, moderate; Sixteenth Infantry, March 2, Linao, Maj. Henry C. Ward, leg; Thirty-ninth Infantry, March 10, Los Baños, F, Elmer E. Carr, chest, serious; Herman H. Frisch, head, serious; G, Noah W. Bullard, thigh, serious; Forty-second Infantry, March 4, Paete, E, Louis H. Teibell, side, severe; Panay, Eighteenth Infantry, February 16, San Remedio, E, Harry L. Gaylord, knee, slight; Cavitan, M, William O. McNulty, knee, slight; Nineteenth Infantry, February 16, San Remedio, E, James C. Gallaher, foot, slight; Cavitan, E, George Ross, leg, severe; L, George Therrien, corporal, leg, severe; Thomas Hosty, arm, serious; William Wenzelburger, leg, severe.

OTIS.

MANILA. (Received March 22, 1900—6.50 a. m.)
ADJUTANT-GENERAL, *Washington:*

Killed—Luzon, Third Cavalry, February 22, Alilem, C, Lewis B. Palmer; March 3, San Francisco, C, John B. King, corporal; Samuel G. Davis. Sixteenth Infantry, March 2, Iligan, E, Eugene S. Anderson. Thirty-third Infantry, March 9, Badoc, L, John W. Linn. Wounded—Third Cavalry, March 3, San Francisco, C, Henry Myers, scalp, slight. Sixteenth Infantry, March 1, Camalaniugan, C, Robert Borchart, sergeant, chest, serious; William Ryan, thigh, serious; March 2, Linas, B, Victor W. Lundblom, corporal, head, serious; Stewart C. Foultz, leg, slight; Edward McCully, thigh, slight; John F. Cannon, leg, severe; Enoch M. Fallis, clavicle, slight; John D. Coates, thigh, serious. Twenty-ninth Infantry, February 22, Alilem, H, William B. Kysh, corporal, thigh, serious. Thirty-third Infantry, March 5, Cabugao, L, Paul Rains, arm, slight; March 7, Bangued, D, Christopher C. Callaway, corporal, thorax, severe; March 9, Badoc, L, Elzy J. Guinn, corporal, knee, slight. Thirty-seventh Infantry, March 14, Magdalena, A, Earl E. Roberts, corporal, arm, slight; Ralph Henry, elbow, severe.

OTIS.

AFFAIRS IN THE PHILIPPINE ISLANDS. 1153

MANILA. (Received March 23, 1900—6.50 a. m.)
ADJUTANT-GENERAL, *Washington:*
Exports from Iloilo: October, none; December, sugar, 12,571,127 pounds; manufactured copper, $521 worth; dye, $132 worth; total duty, $11,020.

OTIS.

MANILA. (Received March 26, 1900—7.25 a. m.)
ADJUTANT-GENERAL, *Washington:*
Killed—Luzon Island, Fortieth Infantry, March 6, Mt. Isarog, B, Edmund Bullock, artificer; Bennett Blakely; Company C, Charles V. Huey, sergeant. Panay Island, Twenty-sixth Infantry, February 26, Pototan; B, Philip H. Nolan. Leyte Island, Forty-third Infantry, March 8, La Paz, Company A, Michael E. Corley; March 11, Dagami, A, Mike Pogorzelsk, beheaded while prisoner of war. Wounded—Luzon Island, Thirty-eighth Infantry, March 15, Cuenca, I, William D. Hoover, thigh; Noah W. Wingate, buttock, moderate. Panay Island, Sixth Infantry, February 24, Tangalan, C, George Hemphill, corporal, leg, severe; Horace Hutchinson, back, serious; Magruder Andrews, knee, slight. Nineteenth Infantry, January 28, Cavitan, C, Winfield S. Preston, arm, serious. Samar Island, Forty-third Infantry, March 8, Matuguinao, H, Joseph W. Alport, corporal, wounded in abdomen, serious.

OTIS.

ADJUTANT-GENERAL'S OFFICE,
Washington, March 26, 1900.
OTIS, *Manila:*
Having reference to previous cables on the subject, the Secretary of War desires to know if in your opinion the time has not now arrived to make order for your military division and to announce lines of the departments and name department commanders.

CORBIN.

MANILA. (Received March 27, 1900—5.50 a. m.)
ADJUTANT-GENERAL, *Washington:*
Malarial fever—February 28, Samuel Grimes, G, Eighteenth Infantry; March 21, Johnson H. Ray, B, Thirty-seventh Infantry; Chester Q. Dunn, E, Thirty-fourth Infantry; March 23, Charles Schleicher, corporal, M, Twenty-first Infantry. Died from wounds received in action—March 18, Joseph W. Alport, corporal, H, Forty-third Infantry. Alcoholism—March 17, Alexander S. Bruce, B, Twenty-ninth Infantry. Drowned—March 17, John F. Lynch, E, Thirty-seventh Infantry. Typhoid fever—March 17, Frank Apson, C, Forty-first Infantry; March 16, William Knuckles, E, Forty-second Infantry; March 19, Henry A. Sandman, C, Forty-second Infantry; March 21, Daniel Knight, K Forty-ninth Infantry. Dysentery—March 17, Charles W. Sutton, F, Forty-second Infantry; March 18, Sylvester F. Rothwell, sergeant, F, Thirty-seventh Infantry; Hugh McCall, A, Eighteenth Infantry; March 19, George Gongo, B, Twenty-seventh Infantry; March 20, Edward G. Roddy, D, Thirteenth Infantry; Cornelius E. Carter, E, Twenty-fourth Infantry; March 3, Peter M. Fallon, D, Sixth Infantry; March 21, Hurley B. Kellogg, D, Fourth Cavalry. Peritonitis—March 15, Alfred L. Ross, I, Thirty-third Infantry. Secondary operation: After operation chancroidal bubo—March 19, Zeph Parker, musician, I, Forty-eighth Infantry. Variola—March 20, Clarence H. Thomas, corporal, F, Signal Corps; March 22, George W. Dyer, B, Twenty-fifth Infantry. Tuberculosis—March 20, Joseph Strickland, H, Forty-eighth Infantry. General arterio sclerosis—March 23, William Linehan, F, Thirty-seventh Infantry.

OTIS.

MANILA. (Received March 27, 1900—9.45 a. m.)
ADJUTANT-GENERAL, *Washington:*
Recommend four departments, as follows: Department Northern Luzon—that portion Luzon north of the provinces of Manila, Morong, and Infanta, and all islands, Philippine group, north of Manila Bay and the provinces above named; Major-General MacArthur to command. Department Southern Luzon—balance Luzon and all Philippine Islands which lie south of south line of Department Northern Luzon, including Polillo, and north of line passing southeastwardly through west pass of Apo to twelfth parallel latitude; thence east on said parallel to meridian 124° 10′ east of Greenwich; thence northerly through San Bernardino Straits, and including entire island Masbate; Major-General Bates to command. Department of the Visayas—all islands south of southern lines Department Southern Luzon, east of longitude 121° 45′ east of Greenwich and north of ninth parallel of latitude, excepting therefrom all Mindanao and all islands east of Straits of Surigao; Brigadier-General Hughes to command. Department Mindanao and Jolo—remaining islands of the Philippines; Brigadier-General Kobbé to command. Commanders named acquainted with affairs in departments for which recommended. Should name General Schwam, but health failing; thinks he must leave islands soon.
OTIS.

ADJUTANT-GENERAL'S OFFICE,
Washington, March 29, 1900.
OTIS, *Manila:*
Orders to-day assign you command Division Philippines. Departments and commanders in accordance with your recommendation. Assign necessary troops, general and staff officers to put new commands into immediate working order.
Order of the Secretary of War:
CORBIN.

GENERAL ORDERS, } HEADQUARTERS OF THE ARMY,
ADJUTANT-GENERAL'S OFFICE,
No. 38. *Washington, March 29, 1900.*

The following order has been received from the War Department, and is published to the Army for the information and guidance of all concerned:

"WAR DEPARTMENT, *Washington, March 27, 1900.*

"By direction of the President the Department of the Pacific is discontinued and a military division, to be known as the Division of the Philippines, comprising all the islands ceded to the United States by Spain by the treaty of Paris ratified April 11, 1899, is created, under command of Maj. Gen. Elwell S. Otis, U. S. Volunteers, with headquarters in the city of Manila, who, in addition to command of the troops in the division, will continue to exercise the authority of military governor of the Philippine Islands, the division to be composed of the following departments:

"Department of Northern Luzon, to include all that part of the island of Luzon north of the provinces of Manila, Morong, and Infanta, the same being the provinces of Abra, Bontoc, Benguet, Bataan, Bulacan, Cagayan, Ilocos Norte, Ilocos Sur, La Isabela de Luzon, Lepanto, La Union, Nueva Vizcaya, Nueva Ecija, Principe, Pangasinan, Pampanga, Tarlac, and Zambales, and all the islands in the Philippine Archipelago north of Manila Bay and the provinces above named.

"Maj. Gen. Arthur MacArthur, U. S. Volunteers, is assigned to the command of this department.

"Department of Southern Luzon, to include all the remaining part of the island of Luzon the same including the following provinces: Albay, Batangas, Camarines Norte, Camarines Sur, Cavite, Infanta, La Laguna, Manila, Morong, and Tayabas, and all islands of the Philippine Archipelago which lie south of the south line of the Department of Northern Luzon, as above described, including the island of Polillo, and north of a line passing southeastwardly through West Pass of Apo to the twelfth parallel of north latitude; thence easterly along said parallel to 124° 10′ east of Greenwich, but including the entire island of Masbate; thence northerly through San Bernardino Straits.

"Maj. Gen. John C. Bates, U. S. Volunteers, is assigned to the command of this department.

"Department of the Visayas, to include all islands south of the southern line of the Department of Southern Luzon and east of longitude 121° 45′ east of Greenwich and north of the ninth parallel of latitude, excepting the island of Mindanao and all islands east of the Straits of Surigao.

"Brig. Gen. Robert P. Hughes, U. S. Volunteers, is assigned to the command of this department.

"Department of Mindanao and Jolo, to include all the remaining islands of the Philippine Archipelago.

"Brig. Gen. William A. Kobbé, U. S. Volunteers, is assigned to the command of this department.

"The division commander will designate the places for the several department headquarters, and will also assign the necessary staff officers and make such distribution of troops as in his judgment will best meet the requirements of the service in the division.

"ELIHU ROOT, *Secretary of War.*"

By command of Major-General Miles:

H. C. CORBIN, *Adjutant-General.*

MANILA. (Received March 30, 1900—3.05 a. m.)

ADJUTANT-GENERAL, *Washington:*

Killed—Luzon, Forty-fifth Infantry, March 20, Camilig, M, James T. Hill. Samar, Forty-third Infantry, March 3, Matuguinao, H, Elbridge H. Webster; March 11, Lanang, I, Ferdinand W. Meyer. Panay, Eighteenth Infantry, March 22, Cabug-Cabug, L, Max Hohne, corporal. Wounded—Luzon, Twenty-second Infantry, March 24, Peñaranda, First Lieut. Orrin R. Wolfe, lung, severe. Thirty-fourth Infantry, C, James E. Murphy, elbow, severe. Thirty-seventh Infantry, March 20, Camilig, G, Lloyd Hummer, sergeant, foot, serious. Forty-fifth Infantry, March 16, Polangui, A, Odis Smith, corporal, thigh, slight. Forty-seventh Infantry, March 14, Guinobatan, I, Thomas J. Gould, shoulder, moderate; March 20, Camilig, George H. Momeny, corporal, abdomen, serious. Leyte, Forty-third Infantry, March 13, Hilongos, C, James F. Burns, chest, serious. Panay, Eighteenth Infantry, March 22, Cabug-Cabug, L, John G. Carl, sergeant, mortally.

OTIS.

MANILA. (Received March 31, 1900—7.35 a. m.)

ADJUTANT-GENERAL, *Washington:*

Home Battalion Fourteenth Infantry leaves for San Francisco to-morrow; 4 officers, 211 men.

OTIS.

MANILA. (Received April 2, 1900—7.20 a. m.)

ADJUTANT-GENERAL, *Washington:*

Died from wounds received in action—March 13, James F. Burns, C, Forty-third Infantry; March 28, James E. Murphy, C, Thirty-fourth Infantry; March 23, John

G. Carl, sergeant, L, Eighteenth Infantry. Variola—December 31, last year, Evert Barker, G, Thirty-third Infantry; March 2, Alonzo Bare, D, Thirty-second Infantry; February 2, Ned Martin, M, Twenty-fifth Infantry. Typhoid fever—March 22, Claus A. Burke; March 21, Jacob Fuesguss, H, Forty-second Infantry; March 16, Clarence G. Brooks, M, Thirtieth Infantry; March 27, Lewis J. Leadly, M, Thirty-seventh Infantry; March 25, John C. Russell, jr., corporal, F, Forty-second Infantry. Dysentery—March 25, John McLaughlin, corporal, M, Ninth Infantry; Edward J. Scott, E, Seventeenth Infantry; March 19, Miles D. Jones, D, Sixth Infantry; March 23, Allen Cook, L, Twenty-sixth Infantry. Suicide—March 26, August Schoenknecht, musician, L, Seventeenth Infantry. Septicæmia—March 24, Frank A. Patton, K, Third Infantry. Malarial fever—March 26, Thomas A. Ehrheart, K, Forty-second Infantry; March 27, Thomas Hoar, sergeant, D, Eleventh Cavalry. Nephritis—March 28, Patrick Condon, sergeant, B, Twelfth Infantry. Abcess liver—March 21, Michael Kynan, F, Eighteenth Infantry. Undetermined fever—March 13, John J. Dougherty, B, Thirty-fourth Infantry. Accidental—March 24, Walter A. McCoy, I, Thirty-ninth Infantry. Gunshot—March 28, William Foster, A, Third Infantry. Drowned, killed by insurgents—September 29, last year, William F. Henry, I, Sixteenth Infantry.

OTIS.

ADJUTANT-GENERAL'S OFFICE,
Washington, April 2, 1900.

OTIS, *Manila:*
Give companies and commanding officers Home Battalion, Fourteenth Infantry.

CORBIN.

ADJUTANT-GENERAL'S OFFICE,
Washington, April 2, 1900.

OTIS, *Manila:*
Following transport sailed from New York for Manila on Saturday: *Sumner*, with 46 officers, 695 men.

CORBIN.

MANILA. (Received April 3, 1900—2.08 a. m.)
ADJUTANT-GENERAL, *Washington:*
Home battalion, Fourteenth Infantry, Companies A to D, inclusive, commanded by Captains Lasseigne, Yeatman, Biddle, Lieutenant Field.

OTIS.

MANILA. (Received April 3, 1900—9.03 a. m.)
ADJUTANT-GENERAL, *Washington:*
Private interests require my return to States; absent from family and business, attention to which important, since November, 1897, except few days; wish to sail by May 1 if possible; believe matters here can be placed in quite satisfactory condition by that date, although large repressive military force must be maintained some time.

OTIS.

MANILA. (Received April 3, 1900—9.34 a. m.)
ADJUTANT-GENERAL, *Washington:*
Since January 1, 124 skirmishes in Philipines reported; mostly very slight affairs. Our casualties 3 officers, 78 enlisted men killed; 13 officers, 151 men wounded. Insur-

gent and ladrone loss in killed and left on field, 1,426; captured, mostly wounded, 1,453. Small arms secured, 3,051; pieces artillery, 165, large; captured other insurgent property. Number important insurgent officers surrendering and situation gradually becoming more pacific.

OTIS.

ADJUTANT-GENERAL'S OFFICE,
Washington, April 3, 1900.

OTIS, *Manila:*
How many prisoners on *Sherman?*

CORBIN.

MANILA. (Received April 4, 1900—3.55 a. m.)
ADJUTANT-GENERAL, *Washington:*
With reference to your telegram of 3d, 149 general prisoners on *Sherman.*

OTIS.

ADJUTANT-GENERAL'S OFFICE,
Washington, April 4, 1900.

OTIS, *Manila:*
Replying to your cable of April 3, the Secretary of War instructs me to say that the President regrets to have you leave the Philippines, but he feels that your distinguished and successful service in both military and civil administration for nearly two years entitles you to prompt compliance with whatever wish you choose to express regarding your assignment to duty, and the requisite order will be made for your return May 1, by such route and taking such time as may be agreeable to you, with understanding that General MacArthur will succeed you as military govenor. Secretary of War wishes recommendation for commander of Department of Northern Luzon

CORBIN.

MANILA. (Received April 6, 1900—7.20 a. m.)
ADJUTANT-GENERAL, *Washington:*
Will remain until certain important modifications civil administration determined. New code, judicial, criminal procedure approaching completion and other matter receiving consideration; think can leave about May 1. Will cable latter part of month date I desire to be relieved and recommend officer for department commander;· probably Wheaton. Wish to return by most expeditious route and await orders short time until private business receives attention. No request to make regarding future sphere of duty.

OTIS.

ADJUTANT-GENERAL'S OFFICE.
Washington, April 8, 1900.

OTIS, *Manila:*
In order that he may fully understand military situation, Secretary of War desires Arthur MacArthur occupy his time until May 1 visiting all important points Division Philippines, in order to satisfy himself with reference to numbers and character troops required to meet existing conditions in several departments, and as far as possible determine number that will be required in the near future.

CORBIN.

MANILA. (Received April 9, 1900—3.55 a. m.)

ADJUTANT-GENERAL, *Washington:*

General Bates just returned from south, after placing Fortieth Infantry at Surigao, Cagayan, Iligan, Misamis, Dapitan, northern Mindanao, and attending to special matters intrusted to him, Department Mindanao and Jolo; attended by two naval vessels and two gunboats; troops occupied points without resistance; 241 rifles, 97 pieces artillery surrendered; eleven places in Mindanao and three in Jolo Archipelago now occupied by troops without the firing of a shot; affairs in that section quite satisfactory.

OTIS.

WAR DEPARTMENT, *April 9, 1900.*

OTIS, *Manila:*

Associated Press report from Manila as follows: "General Young, commanding in north Luzon, has made several requests for reenforcements, representing that his force is inadequate; that the men are exhausted by the necessity of constant vigilance; that he is unable to garrison the towns in his jurisdiction; that the insurgents are returning to the district and killing the amigos, and that it is necessary for him to inflict punishment in several sections before the rainy season begins. Gen. James Bell, who is commanding in Southern Luzon, has made similar representations. He says his forces are inadequate and that he merely holds a few towns, without controlling the territory. The president of the town of Samal, province of Bataan, Luzon, and another prominent native have been assassinated because they were known to be friendly to the Americans. The president of another town has joined the insurgents because they had threatened to kill him if he did not." What truth is there in these statements?

ROOT, *Secwar.*

WAR DEPARTMENT, ADJUTANT-GENERAL'S OFFICE.
Washington, April 9, 1900.

The COMMANDING GENERAL, DIVISION OF THE PHILIPPINES,
Manila, P. I.

SIR: By direction of the Secretary of War, I have the honor to furnish you, for your information and guidance, a copy of the President's instructions to the Philippine Commission.[a]

It is not deemed necessary to give you any instructions further than to remark that it is expected that you will give your cordial support to the Commission in the work with which it has been charged.

You will cause the Commission to be received with all the honors shown the most favored of similar bodies, and on arrival to at once place yourself in touch with it.

The subject-matter of this note will be held in confidence by you until its publication may become necessary in the way of information to the people and your command. On this point you and the Commission will agree and act in concert.

Very respectfully,

H. C. CORBIN, *Adjutant-General.*

MANILA. (Received April 10, 1900—7.03 a. m.)

ADJUTANT-GENERAL, *Washington:*

Shipped for Spain to-day 13 officers, 258 men Spanish army, released from insurgents; 17 wives and children.

OTIS.

---

[a] Printed on page 72 of the report of the War Department for 1900, volume 1.

AFFAIRS IN THE PHILIPPINE ISLANDS. 1159

MANILA. (Received April 10, 1900—2.15 p. m.)

SECRETARY OF WAR, *Washington:*

Insurgent force retreated to northern Luzon in November; greater number returned, but probably 600 remaining, much scattered, and operating with ladrones and mountain tribes; Aguinaldo believed to be in that section; part of this force passed to Cagayan Valley and attacked town there; small detachments then went to western coast; both Young and Hood called for troops; each furnished 2 battalions, and Young's scouts increased to 250; another battalion will probably be sent to Aringay, western coast, soon; Bell has now 2,600 men in Camarines and Albay; he reported that he needed more to police towns; both Bates and Kobbé, who have been there, think he has sufficient. Number of most prominent insurgent officers have surrendered. Murray, in Leyte, called for more troops; General Hughes supplying them, and believed to be there in person. Robberies and murders are committed, and have always been committed, throughout these islands; now guerrillas and ladrones murder each other, and occasionally rob and murder peaceable citizens; all the more important and many smaller towns are protected between Manila and Dagupan; 116 stations are maintained; similar disposition of troops south; neither guerrillas nor ladrones attack our troops unless in brush country in very small detachments, and then most always worsted; unfortunately, about one-half of 35,000 rifles possessed by insurgents still in possession of guerrilla bands and ladrones, or hidden by insurgents who have returned to cities, but our troops securing them daily; inhabitants now giving information—which until recently they feared to do—and better classes much encouraged; ignorance and character greater mass of natives will render secure; governments in these islands matter of time. The military organizations here if kept full are sufficient to meet any anticipated emergencies; three additional regiments could be used at once in some of the smaller islands not yet occupied, but immediate occupancy not material; we no longer deal with organized insurrection, but brigandage; to render every town secure against latter would require quarter million men; the war has increased brigandage in Luzon, though it has always prevailed in mountain sections, and in some of the islands much more than it does to-day; the above remarks considered by officers here rather pessimistic.

OTIS.

MANILA. (Received April 10, 1900—5.12 p. m.)

ADJUTANT-GENERAL, *Washington:*

Total strength present and absent March 31, as far as can be ascertained (impossible to get returns from some regiments): Third Cavalry, officers 29, enlisted men 927; Fourth Cavalry, 45, 1,410; Eleventh Cavalry, 48, 1,048. Battery E, First Artillery, 4, 129; Third Artillery, 12, 393; Battery F, Fourth Artillery, 4, 127; Battery F, Fifth Artillery, 4, 109. Sixth Artillery, 45, 1,401. Third Infantry, 45, 1,363; Fourth Infantry, 42, 1,320; Sixth Infantry, 45, 1,453; Ninth Infantry, 43, 1,317; Twelfth Infantry, 42, 1,470; Thirteenth Infantry, 43, 1,337; Fourteenth Infantry, 45, 1,520; Sixteenth Infantry, 45, 1,407; Seventeenth Infantry, 45, 1,393; Eighteenth Infantry, 42, 1,417; Nineteenth Infantry, 47, 1,440; Twentieth Infantry, 44, 1,386, Twenty-first Infantry, 45, 1,333; Twenty-second Infantry, 45, 1,432; Twenty-third Infantry, 45, 1,671; Twenty-fourth Infantry, 36, 1,045; Twenty-fifth Infantry, 37, 1,093; Twenty-sixth Infantry, 50, 1,242; Twenty-seventh Infantry, 49, 1,219; Twenty-eighth Infantry, 50, 1,251; Twenty-ninth Infantry, 50, 1,245; Thirtieth Infantry, 50, 1,230; Thirty-first Infantry, 50, 1,237; Thirty-second Infantry, 50, 1,207; Thirty-third Infantry, 50, 1,214; Thirty-fourth Infantry, 48, 1,275; Thirty-fifth Infantry, 49, 1,265; Thirty-sixth Infantry, 50, 973; Thirty-seventh Infantry, 50, 1,030; Thirty-eighth Infantry, 50, 1,248; Thirty-ninth Infantry, 49, 1,260; Fortieth Infantry, 46, 1,268; Forty-first Infantry, 50, 1,301; Forty-second Infantry, 50, 1,288; Forty-third Infantry, 50, 1,273; Forty-fourth

Infantry, 48, 1,287; Forty-fifth Infantry, 49, 1,258; Forty-sixth Infantry, 50, 1,268; Forty-seventh Infantry, 50, 1,252; Forty-eighth Infantry, 50, 1,366; Forty-ninth Infantry, 50, 1,292. Battalion Engineers, U. S. A., 6, 259. Signal Corps, U. S. A., 21, 356. Hospital Corps, 69, 1,875. Total, 2,211, 61,230.

OTIS.

MANILA. (Received April 11, 1900—10.03 a. m.)
ADJUTANT-GENERAL, *Washington:*
Deaths: Variola—March 30, William Sullivan, April 3, William E. Sliter, I, Thirty-third Infantry; March 28, Charles W. Steen, corporal, E, Forty-first Infantry; March 9, Pompy Hymes, G, Forty-ninth Infantry. Dysentery—March 4, John C. Lundberg, I; March 29, Charles Segal, corporal, L, Thirtieth Infantry; March 21, Thomas R. Edwards; March 4, William J. Nolan, K, Sixteenth Infantry; March 3, Michael Reilly, sergeant, G, Seventeenth Infantry; March 18, Arthur P. Van Ornum, C, Thirty-first Infantry. Typhoid fever—March 27, Arthur A. Brandan, D; April 3, Charles T. Row, K, Thirtieth Infantry. Malarial fever—March 20, Charles H. Thompson; March 22, Howard E. Miller, K; March 17, Thomas Morgans; March 18, Peter J. Eckert, L, Sixteenth Infantry. Died from wounds received in action—February 28, Frank Wysor, sergeant, B; March 11, James E. Davis, L, Nineteenth Infantry; April 1, Herman H. Frisch, F, Thirty-ninth Infantry. Brights disease—March 5, James McKenna, K, Sixteenth Infantry. Uræmia—March 31, George Thomas, I, Thirty-second Infantry. Heart disease—April 5, James E. Cullen, L, Thirtieth Infantry.

OTIS.

MANILA. (Received April 11, 1900—2.58 p. m.)
ADJUTANT-GENERAL, *Washington:*
Killed—Luzon, Ninth Infantry, March 31, Mabalacat, K, Alonzo L. Johnson, sergeant. Twelfth Infantry, April 6, Gerona, A, August Schuetz, artificer. Twenty-ninth Infantry, February 17, Tagudin, H, John W. Walker. Thirty-eighth Infantry, March 25, Batangas, C, Alex. Cooper, decapitated by Filipino. Panay, Eighteeth Infantry, March 27, San José de Buenavista, E, Frederick M. Dimler. Wounded—Luzon, Seventeenth Infantry, April 7, Camiling, First Lieut. Frank J. Morrow, wounded in leg, serious. Nineteenth Infantry, March 10, Valderrama, L, James E. Davis, wounded in abdomen, serious. Twenty-fourth Infantry, February 28, Bongabon, G, Kirk Fowlis, wounded in head, slight; James H. Thomas, leg, slight. Twenty-fifth Infantry, February 18, Botolan, H, Tony Grant, thigh, slight; Willis J. Johnson, thigh, slight. Twenty-ninth Infantry, February 17, Tagudin, H, James L. Husketh, head, slight, captured. Fortieth Infantry, March 1, San José, B, Ben. H. Marshall, leg, slight; William Lafler, jr., shoulder, slight; C, Emmett L. Tomlenson, musician, arm, slight; D, Charles L. Brooks, corporal, thigh, serious; Charles H. Huss, abdomen, slight. Panay, Eighteenth Infantry, March 22, Cabug Cabug, L, James G. Corning, leg, slight; March 27, San José de Buenavista, H, Clarence L. Messler, both thighs, serious. Nineteenth Infantry, March 10, Valderrama, A, Timothy Shea, corporal, forehead, slight. Cebu, Nineteenth Infantry, February 27, Danao, B, Frank Wysor, sergeant, abdomen, serious. Samar, Forty-third Infantry, March 8, Matuguinao, First Lieut. Joseph T. Sweeney, wounded in thigh, slight; H, Joseph H. Clancy, hip, slight; Clinton E. Mear, wrist, serious.

OTIS.

AFFAIRS IN THE PHILIPPINE ISLANDS. 1161

MANILA. (Received April 16, 1900—6 a. m.)

ADJUTANT-GENERAL, *Washington:*

Has time given Spaniards to declare decision to preserve allegiance under article 9, Paris treaty, been extended?

OTIS.

ADJUTANT-GENERAL'S OFFICE,
Washington, April 16, 1900.

OTIS, *Manila:*

Treaty extending time to declare citizenship before Senate. Not yet approved, but undoubtedly will be. Permit registration to continue.

CORBIN, *Adjutant-General.*

MANILA. (Received April 17, 1900—11.51 a. m.)

ADJUTANT-GENERAL, *Washington:*

Deaths: Malarial fever—March 15, Clinton G. Pressen, H, Fortieth Infantry; April 7, Christ Monsen, sergeant, I, Fourth Cavalry; April 10, First Lieut. Grant A. White, Thirty-third Infantry, 6 a. m., Tuesday; April 11, James J. Hallinan, G, Twenty-seventh Infantry. Diarrhea—April 12, William H. Shewman, artificer, E, Thirty-fourth Infantry; April 13, George A. Faul, M, Thirteenth Infantry. Tubercular peritonitis—April 2, Frank Southwood, B, Thirty-first Infantry. Alcoholism—April 7, William M. South, B, Twentieth Infantry. Suicide—April 6, Frank W. Foster, E, Thirtieth Infantry. Measles—April 8, Abner Farthing, B, Thirty-ninth Infantry. Shot by sergeant guard, self-defense—April 4, William Smith, I, Twenty-fifth Infantry. Tuberculosis—April 3, Frank J. Stone, L, Twenty-sixth Infantry. Nephrolithiasis—April 7, William V. McCray, G, Eleventh Cavalry. Dysentery—March 19, Ralph B. Patterson, M, Thirty-eighth Infantry; April 10, Philip Gallagher, sergeant, B, Twenty-first Infantry; April 13, William Bowman, D, Thirty-ninth Infantry; Edward Hale, A, Twenty-first Infantry. Aortic incompetency—March 31, Wiley M. Tudor, A, Twenty-second Infantry. Variola—Wilford B. Marlan, A, Forty-fourth Infantry. Typhoid fever—March 21, Daniel Gillespie, K, Twenty-third Infantry.

OTIS.

MANILA. (Received April 18, 1900—7.05 a. m.)

ADJUTANT-GENERAL, *Washington:*

Troops scattered call for canned roast beef when fresh beef difficult to obtain; 239,000 pounds issued since January 1; no complaint received; 96,000 cans called for should be delivered; no further shipments made until further request preferred; believe cattle more abundant soon.

OTIS.

MANILA. (Received April 20, 1900—1.43 p. m.)

ADJUTANT-GENERAL:

Killed—Luzon, April 11, Orion, C, Thirty-second Infantry, Donald MacDonald, Harry A. Easter; April 16, Batac, G, Thirty-fourth Infantry, Oscar F. Johnson, quartermaster-sergeant; Hardus Linstad; April 17, Pulilan, M, Thirty-fifth Infantry, Robert G. McKinnish; April 18, San Miguel de Mayumo, B, Thirty-fifth Infantry, John Orth, artificer; April 8, Nueva Caceres, K, Forty-fifth Infantry, Richard Eisenach; February 6, Legaspi, F, Forty-seventh Infantry, George E. Mead; H, Forty-seventh Infantry, Frank Kutschinsky. Samar, March 26, Calbayog, H, Forty-third Infantry, Adam Unsinn. Leyte, March 16, Jaro, B, Forty-third Infantry, Edward A. Ebig, musician. Mindanao, April 7, Cagayan, L, Fortieth Infantry, Rollie B. Killough; K, Fortieth Infantry, Frederick Brendel, Charles E. Guyer. Wounded— Luzon, March 17, Cabiao, I, Twenty-second Infantry, Charles W. Ray, sergeant, head, serious; April 17, Pulilan, M, Thirty-fifth Infantry, Andrew P. De Doux, first sergeant, arm, serious; April 18, Orion, Thirty-fifth Infantry, Second Lieut. John P. Hasson, leg, moderate. Samar, March 31, San José, I, Forty-third Infantry, Charles Dolloff, chest, serious. Leyte, March 29, Malitbog, K, Forty-third Infantry, Edward Hill, arm, serious. Mindanao, April 7, Cagayan, L, Fortieth Infantry, Benjamin F. Welch, abdomen, serious; Phineas F. Hustead, hand, slight; George M. Eagan, leg, slight; Clarence V. Taylor, chest, slight; Alfred Coad, legs, moderate; M, Fortieth Infantry, Capt. William J. Watson, foot, moderate; Elmer E. Shaffer, thigh, serious; I, Fortieth Infantry, Claude A. Adams, corporal, thigh, serious; Frank E. Farrow, shoulder, moderate; Charles Marshall, sergeant, thigh, serious.

OTIS.

MANILA. (Received April 23, 1900—10.35 a. m.)
ADJUTANT-GENERAL, *Washington:*
Deaths: Malarial fever—April 16, Charles V. Stiles, H, Forty-fourth Infantry; April 15, James E. Littleton, I, Fourth Cavalry; April 19, Harry E. Nash, D, Nineteenth Infantry. Accidental—April 7, Harry H. Schultz, H, Forty-fourth Infantry, dived on rock. March 23, John S. Dibble, M, Nineteenth Infantry, killed by comrade. Enteritis—April 8, Thomas Gillespie, G, Eighteenth Infantry. Typhoid fever— April 15, Frank J. Valdez, corporal, K, Eighteenth Infantry; April 14, Dock R. Isenbarger, B, Thirty-fifth Infantry. Colitis—April 11, Charles J. Major, G, Eighteenth Infantry. Septicæmia—April 7, Charles Lightell, C, Nineteenth Infantry. Dysentery—April 7, Llewellyn H. Converse, corporal, E, Sixth Infantry; March 10, James P. O'Shea, G, Sixth Infantry; April 14, John Bruner, H, Fourth Infantry; April 15, Henry Weibner, cook, G, Forty-second Infantry; April 16, Charles Brown, M, Twenty-sixth Infantry; April 2, Garland B. Sutherland, M, Sixth Infantry. Variola—April 15, Arthur Gwinn, first sergeant, Richard B. Harber, D, Thirty-second Infantry. Pneumonia—April 10, James J. Curran, K, Fourth Infantry. Died from wounds received in action—April 9, Benjamin F. Welch, L, Fortieth Infantry.

OTIS.

MANILA. (Received April 24, 1900—2.05 a. m.)
ADJUTANT-GENERAL, *Washington:*
Early morning 7th, several hundred Tagalos and Visayans attacked battalion Fortieth Infantry at Cagayan, north coast Mindanao; our casualties, 2 killed, 11 wounded; enemy's loss, 53 killed, 18 wounded and captured in city, besides other losses suffered on retreat. Young reports from northwestern Luzon several hundred natives, influenced by Aguinaldo's bishop Aglipay, attacked his troops at several points and in turn had been attacked; their loss in attack on Batac, 15th instant, 106 killed and during entire fighting from 15th to 17th, 333 killed; our loss during period, 2 killed, 4 wounded. Young has plenty troops and will have little further opposition. Affairs at other Luzon points improving; local presidentes and inhabitants of towns giving information and rendering assistance. Troops now taking possession of interior small islands.

OTIS.

AFFAIRS IN THE PHILIPPINE ISLANDS. 1163

SAN FRANCISCO, CAL., *April 26, 1900.*
(Received 2.41 p. m.)

ADJUTANT-GENERAL, *Washington:*

Transport *Sherman* has just arrived. (Home battalion Fourteenth Infantry on board.)

SHAFTER, *Major-General.*

MANILA. (Received April 24, 1900.)

ADJUTANT-GENERAL, *Washington:*

Spanish authorities ask for number cannon, formerly Spanish property, captured by our troops, various points in islands; shall turn them over if no objection.

OTIS.

MANILA. (Received April 30, 1900—11.34 a. m.)

ADJUTANT-GENERAL, *Washington:*

Killed—Luzon Island, April 21, Batac, A, Third Cavalry, Charles A. Harris; April 15, Pasacao, H, Forty-fifth Infantry, William H. Stone. Wounded—Luzon Island, April 17, Batac, L, Third Cavalry, Archie Black, shoulder, slight; March 28, Atimonan, K, Thirtieth Infantry, William J. Degnan, thigh, serious; April 16, Batac, B, Thirty-fourth Infantry, Samuel C. Wells, neck, slight; Taysan, C, Thirty-eighth Infantry, John J. Miller, leg below knee, moderate. Panay Island, February 12, Iloilo, A, Eighteenth Infantry, Fred Smith, leg below knee, serious; Hugh Sparks, shoulder, serious; March 31, Colasi, A, Nineteenth Infantry, Thomas J. Tangney, hand, moderate. Samar Island, March 23, Calbayog, E, Forty-third Infantry, Oliver M. Pendergrass, abdomen, serious; March 26, Calbayog, G, Forty-third Infantry, Ridgley M. Laird, arm, serious. Leyte Island, March 29, Cabang, B, Forty-third Infantry, Willis Quint, chest, slight; March 31, Tanauan, C, Forty-third Infantry, George H. Otto, arm, serious.

OTIS.

ADJUTANT-GENERAL'S OFFICE,
Washington, April 30, 1900.

OTIS, *Manila:*

Cable whether General Torres came to you under flag of truce February 5, 1899, and stated Aguinaldo declared fighting had begun accidentally and not authorized by him; that Aguinaldo wished it stopped and to end hostilities proposed establishment of neutral zone between the two armies of width agreeable to you, so during peace negotiations there might be no further danger conflict; whether you replied, "Fighting having begun, must go on to grim end."

CORBIN.

MANILA, *May 1, 1900.*

ADJUTANT-GENERAL, *Washington:*

Judge Torres, citizen and resident of Manila, who had served as member insurgent commission, reported evening February 5, asking if something could not be done to stop the fighting, such as establishment of neutral zone. I replied, Aguinaldo had commenced the fighting and must apply for cessation; I had nothing to request from insurgent government; he asked permission to send Colonel Arguellez to Malolos, and Arguellez was passed through lines, near Caloocan; next morning he went direct to Malolos, told General Aguinald and Mabini that General Otis would permit suspension of hostilities upon their request; they replied declaration of war had been made, a copy of which they furnished him; they said they had no objection to suspension of hostilities; but beyond this general remark made no response, but directed him to return with that message; Arguellez reported that he conveyed my statement that they had commenced the war and it must go on, since they had chosen that course of action, but did not attempt to induce them to make any proposition, as he feared accusation of cowardice; the insurgent chief authorities made no proposition and did not intend to make any, nor did they attempt to do so until driven out of Malolos; my hasty dispatch of about that date misleading; took in writing statement of Arguellez several days ago in order to fully understand temper of insurgents at early period of war.

OTIS.

MANILA. (Received May 1, 1900—9.43 a. m.)
ADJUTANT-GENERAL, *Washington:*

Deaths: Malarial fever—April 22, Company D, Ninth U. S. Infantry, George K. Webster; March 14, Company I, Sixteenth Infantry, Thomas H. Collison; Company K, Sixteenth Infantry, Joseph Kreanert, sergeant; Henry E. Hansen; March 15, Company L, Sixteenth Infantry, Lincoln G. Gray; March 11, Benj. F. West; March 26, Elmer R. Carruthers; April 13, Company M, Sixteenth Infantry, William J. Cleveland. Pneumonia—February 22, Company K, Thirty-first Volunteer Infantry, Porter Beck; April 20, Company K, Thirty-ninth Volunteer Infantry, Frederick I. Gleason. Drowning—March 23, Company K, Forty-eighth Volunteer Infantry, Wesley Merritt. Dysentery—March 15, Company K, Sixteenth Infantry, Albert T. Baker; April 22, Company L, Thirty-fifth Volunteer Infantry, Corpl. Henry E. Cull. Syphilis—April 14, Company K, Nineteenth Infantry, John D. McCann. Variola—April 23, Company B, Twenty-second Infantry, Alvin G. Baker; April 6, Company K, Sixteenth Infantry, Michael T. Lahey. Typhoid—April 16, Company B, Eighteenth Infantry, Samuel E. Hansen. Alcoholism—April 23, Company F, Thirty-fourth Volunteer Infantry, Sergt. John O'Malley. Died from wounds received in action—April 21, Company I, Fortieth Volunteer Infantry, Sergt. Charles Marshall.

OTIS.

MANILA. (Received May 3, 1900—12.23 p. m.)
ADJUTANT-GENERAL, *Washington:*

Request to be relieved 5th instant and ordered home via San Francisco. General MacArthur has made tour of islands; conditions very satisfactory and improving, although some difficulty in Samar and Leyte, which have been satisfactorily met. Recommend Brigadier-General Wheaton assignment to command Department Northern Luzon.

OTIS.

ADJUTANT-GENERAL'S OFFICE,
Washington, May 4, 1900.

OTIS, *Manila:*

Orders of President grant your request to surrender command to-day. Make transfer to MacArthur.

CORBIN.

ADJUTANT-GENERAL'S OFFICE,
Washington, May 4, 1900.

General MACARTHUR, *Manila:*

Orders of President assign you to succeed Elwell S. Otis. Secretary of War desires his departure be attended with all military honors.

CORBIN.

AFFAIRS IN THE PHILIPPINE ISLANDS. 1165

ADJUTANT-GENERAL'S OFFICE,
Washington, May 4, 1900.

OTIS, *Manila:*
Recommendation Loyd Wheaton to succeed Arthur MacArthur command Department approved.

CORBIN.

MANILA. (Received May 4, 1900—6.55 a. m.)

AGWAR, *Washington:*
April captures from enemy: Thirty pieces artillery, 1,209 rifles, considerable ammunition, large stores property. During early portion month enemy active in extreme northern and southern Luzon and some Viscayan Islands. Our reported losses for month, 13 enlisted men killed; 3 officers, 24 enlisted men wounded. Rumored recent loss in Samar of 19 killed and number wounded, not yet reported. This due to small detachments scouting in mountains in interior island. Enemy's losses, officially reported, 1,721 killed, wounded, and captured. Leading Filipinos express confidence in early pacification of islands; say war has terminated; leading insurgents surrendering.

OTIS.

MANILA. (Received May 6, 1900—1.05 a. m.)

AGWAR, *Washington:*
Meade sailed yesterday; Elwell S. Otis on board.

MACARTHUR.

MANILA. (Received May 7, 1900—4.12 a. m.)

ADJUTANT-GENERAL, *Washington:*
Deaths: Pyæmia—April 2, Company C, Nineteenth Infantry, John C. Howard. Malarial fever—May 1, Company K, Ninth Infantry, George C. O. Wienecke; April 28, Company E, Thirtieth Volunteer Infantry, Burton C. Cottrill. Typhoid—April 28, Company D, Thirty-ninth Volunteer Infantry, Henry J. Adamson; April 29, Company F, Forty-second Volunteer Infantry, Clayton S. Weed. Insolation—May 3, Company F, Fourth Infantry, Victor J. Senechal; April 27, Company H, Forty-eighth Volunteer Infantry, Thomas Hill. Cholecystitis—April 25, Company E, Twenty-sixth Volunteer Infantry, Thomas J. Welch. Variola—May 4, Company C, Twelfth Infantry, Thomas Osborn. Bright's disease—May 4, Company D, Forty-second Volunteer Infantry, James Jackson. Meningitis—May 1, Company B, Thirty-fifth Volunteer Infantry, Corpl. James R. Tyson. Died from wounds received in action—April 13, Company H, Forty-seventh Volunteer Infantry, Sergt. Wiley J. Brickey. Perinephritic abscess—May 1, Company M, Forty-seventh Volunteer Infantry, Joseph E. Rhodes. Dysentery—May 3, Troop C, Eleventh Volunteer Cavalry, George W. Howe; April 23, Company E, Forty-second Volunteer Infantry, Semon H. Sexton. Tuberculosis—May 4, Company C, Forty-fourth Volunteer Infantry, Courtney Smith. Killed by unknown parties: Manila, knife wounds of thorax—April 28, Company F, Signal Corps, U. S. Army, Sergt. Alexander C. Blair.

MACARTHUR.

MANILA. (Received May 8, 1900—3 a. m.)

SECWAR, *Washington:*
Dagupan unsuitable department headquarters; crowded native population; profitably employed; extensive building and forcible seizure private buildings unavoidable;

pacification, reduction, military eventually make Luzon single department; recommend modification lines; make department Northern Luzon comprise everything north Pasig; headquarters, Manila; facilitates materially administration and contemplated military operations.

MACARTHUR.

ADJUTANT-GENERAL'S OFFICE,
Washington, May 8, 1900.

MACARTHUR, *Manila:*
Have received your message to Secretary of War concerning departmental lines. It is under consideration. Secretary of War desires correspondence, as heretofore, be through Adjutant-General of the Army.

CORBIN.
W. H. C.

ADJUTANT-GENERAL'S OFFICE,
Washington, May 8, 1900.

MACARTHUR, *Manila:*
With reference to your telegram of 8th, you are authorized by Secretary of War, approved by President, to change department lines and headquarters as indicated.

CORBIN.

ADJUTANT-GENERAL'S OFFICE,
Washington, May 9, 1900.

MACARTHUR, *Manila:*
Cable continuation dividing line between Luzon departments Pasig east, also headquarters Southern Luzon.

CORBIN.

MANILA. (Received May 9, 1900—5.10 p. m.)
ADJUTANT-GENERAL, *Washington:*

Killed—Luzon Island: May 6, San Manuel, Company H, Thirteenth Infantry, Thomas Quinn; April 29, San Miguel de Mayumo, Company I, Thirty-fifth Volunteer Infantry, Corpl. Philip E. La Rivee.

Mindanao Island: April 26, Cagayan, Company K, Fortieth Volunteer Infantry, Richard J. Grady.

Leyte Island: April 26, La Paz, Company I, Twenty-third Infantry, Sergt. George A. Law, Corpl. George B. Koehler.

Wounded—Luzon Island: May 4, Naic, Troop F, Eleventh Volunteer Cavalry, Sergt. John W. Hatfield, wounded in side, slight; April 8, San Manuel, Company H, Thirteenth Infantry, Thomas F. Karns, wounded in foot, slight; April 11, Laigo, Company H, Forty-seventh Volunteer Infantry, Corpl. Charles A. Chapman, wounded in groin, serious; April 20, Malabog, Company I, Forty-seventh Volunteer Infantry, George W. Hunter, wounded in knee, serious; Elisha Tweed, wounded in thigh, serious.

Panay Island: April 17, Agsarab, Company H, Twenty-sixth Volunteer Infantry, Isaiah Lesher, wounded in leg, below knee, serious; Company G, Twenty-sixth Volunteer Infantry, Alexander W. Grinsel, wounded in shoulder, serious; Jacob Miller, wounded in neck, slight; Michael Maguic, wounded in head, slight.

Leyte Island: April 27, Tacloban, Company A, Forty-third Volunteer Infantry, Corpl. Humphrey E. Connors, wounded in legs and arms, serious; April 26, Lampag,

Company D, Forty-fourth Volunteer Infantry, Charles George, wounded in abdomen, serious; William E. Call, wounded in buttocks, slight; Company C, Forty-third Volunteer Infantry, Corpl. James L. Noble, wounded in thigh, slight; April 30, Company K, Forty-third Volunteer Infantry, James Leary, wounded in head, serious; Company I, Twenty-third Infantry, Rutherford B. Butts, wounded in foot, slight; Elmer E. Rose, wounded in arm, slight; John M. McMahon, wounded in hip, slight; George A. Thompson, wounded in foot, serious; George A. Mangum, wounded in leg below knee, serious; Sergt. Guy A. Wyeth, wounded in thigh, serious; Company A, Forty-third Volunteer Infantry Lucamo, Julius E. Bolt, wounded in arm, slight.

MacArthur.

MANILA. (Received May 12, 1900—7.30 a. m.)
ADJUTANT-GENERAL'S OFFICE:
With reference to your telegram of 11th, no objection to Bonesteel, Twenty-first Infantry, individually, but great objection to any regular officers leaving this command at present. Every military resource strained to limit and all possible efforts are necessary to maintain force in highest state of efficiency, to which end one of the most effective agencies would be to keep all officers with their regiments and send as many more as can possibly be spared from duty in United States.

MacArthur.

MANILA. (Received May 14, 1900—4.30 a. m.)
AGWAR, *Washington:*
With reference to your telegram of 9th. East of Pasig, Department Northern Luzon, includes provinces Morong and Infanta; department headquarters, Northern Luzon, Manila (Luzon), north of Pasig; department headquarters, Southern Luzon, Manila (Luzon), south of Pasig. Garrison of city and all civil affairs Manila province (Luzon) in my hands.

MacArthur.

MANILA. (Received May 14, 1900—12.52 p. m.)
ADJUTANT-GENERAL, *Washington:*
Deaths: Drowned—May 7, Troop C, Third Cavalry, John E. Adams; May 6, Company C, Twenty-fourth Infantry, Elisha Forche.
Jaundice—May 9, Company F, Seventeenth Infantry, Sergt. Frederick G. Reade.
Pneumonia—May 9, Company M, Forty-sixth Volunteer Infantry, Jay W. Cohen.
Typhoid fever—April 14, Company I, Eighteenth Infantry, Israel Cork; May 6, Company H, Twenty-sixth Volunteer Infantry, Frank L. Bigos; May 5, Company E, Forty-second Volunteer Infantry, Frank Bauer; April 27, Company G, Forty-fifth Volunteer Infantry, Mathieu Mikkula; April 7, Company C, Forty-seventh Volunteer Infantry, James K. Helder.
Malarial fever—May 8, Company I, Seventeenth Infantry, Roy Sayers; May 9, Company L, Seventeenth Infantry, Thomas Sullivan; Company H, Forty-sixth Volunteer Infantry, Napoleon L. Beaudette; May 10, Company D, Twenty-first Infantry, Alfred Tolck.
Chronic diarrhea—May 10, Company A, Twenty-first Infantry, William Londrigan; May 6, Company F, Twenty-first Infantry, Michael J. Farrell.
Tuberculosis—May 4, Company K, Forty-ninth Volunteer Infantry, Willie Bowan.
Nephritis—May 9, Company C, Forty-eighth Volunteer Infantry, John Furman.

Variola—April 7, Company K, Sixteenth Infantry, Robert N. Hoofer; April 24, Company K, Sixteenth Infantry, Corpl. Abraham Cross; April 28, Company C, Forty-third Volunteer Infantry, John C. Hunt; April 30, Company G, Forty-fourth Volunteer Infantry, Ferd Nichols; May 3, Company G, Forty-eighth Volunteer Infantry, Ed. Greenlee; Company H, Forty-eighth Volunteer Infantry, Elijah Sears; May 4, Peter Hairston.

Dysentery—May 6, Company B, Battalion of Engineers, U. S. Army, Frank W. Lehman; May 7, Company E, Twenty-second Infantry, Sergt. Patrick Malone; May 5, Company L, Thirty-fifth Volunteer Infantry, Henry E. Hamberg.

Peritonitis—April 23, Company D, Forty-fifth Volunteer Infantry, Edward M. Baker.

Abscess of liver—April 26, Battery G, Sixth Artillery, Fred Wilhelm; April 30, Company E, Twenty-sixth Volunteer Infantry, Robert Ed Laird.

Pyæmia—May 4, Company K, Twenty-ninth Volunteer Infantry, Sergt. William H. Clayton.

Gastroenteritis—April 16, Company D, Eighteenth Infantry, Alonzo Henley.

Died from wounds received in action—May 2, Company I, Twenty-third Infantry, First Sergt. Guy A. Wyeth; April 21, Company I, Forty-third Infantry, Charles Dolloff; April 1, Company E, Forty-third Volunteer Infantry, Oliver M. Pendergrass; May 3, Company F, Forty-third Volunteer Infantry, Thomas O. Bates.

Accidental pistol shot by comrade—April 22, Robert Stickles, Company C, Forty-ninth Volunteer Infantry.

MacArthur.

Adjutant-General's Office,
Washington, May 14, 1900.

MacArthur, Manila:

Persistent reports engagements companies Forty-third Regiment U. S. Volunteer Infantry, north Samar. What are the facts and casualties?

Corbin.

Manila. (Received May 16, 1900—9.03 a. m.)

Agwar, Washington:

With reference to your telegram of 14th. The rumored engagement in Samar, reported cablegram of General Otis May 4, has been confirmed by reports recently received from Henry T. Allen, Forty-third Regiment U. S. Volunteer Infantry, commanding Samar Island. That detachment of 31 men stationed at Catubig were attacked April 15 by 600 men with 200 rifles and 1 cannon. Our men quartered in convent, which was fired next day by burning hemp thrown from adjoining church. Detachment attempted escape by river. Men getting into boat were killed; remaining men intrenched themselves near river and held out two days longer, facing most adverse circumstances until rescued by Lieutenant Sweeney and 10 men; over 200 of attacking party, many of them are reported having come from Luzon Island, reported killed and many wounded. Lieutenant Sweeney reports streets covered with dead insurgents.

Killed—Sergts. Dustin L. George, William J. Hall; Corpls. Herbert H. Edwards, John F. J. Hamilton; cook Burton E. Hess; musician Burtan R. Wagner; privates Trefflie Pomelow, Otto B. Loose, Stefano Apperti, Joseph Noeil, John E. Kuhn, Ralph H. Ziun, Edward Braman, Chester A. A. Conklin, Walter E. Collins, Joseph J. Kerins, Henry Dumas, Philip Saling, and George A. Slack, all Company H, Forty-third Regiment U. S. Volunteer Infantry.

Wounded—Privates Lester Rushworth, Harry C. Lee, Michael J. Faron, James H. Clancy, Company H, Forty-third Regiment U. S. Volunteer Infantry; Corpl.

AFFAIRS IN THE PHILIPPINE ISLANDS. 1169

(Peter F.) White, Company F, Forty-third Regiment U. S. Volunteer Infantry. Copy of Henry T. Allen's report forwarded by mail yesterday. Iloilo (Panay) cable is broken by earthquake. Difficult procure more definite information.

MacArthur.

MANILA. (Received May 16, 1900—4.25 a. m.)
ADJUTANT-GENERAL, *Washington:*
Total strength, present and absent, April 30, ascertained as near as possible; impossible to get returns from some regiments: Third Regiment U. S. Cavalry, officers, 31, enlisted men, 913; Fourth Regiment U. S. Cavalry, 43, 1,420; Eleventh Regiment U. S. Volunteer Cavalry, 49, 1,047. Battery E, First Regiment U. S. Artillery, 4, 129; Third Regiment U. S. Artillery, 11, 393; Battery F, Fourth Regiment U. S. Artillery, 4, 127; Battery F, Fifth Regiment U. S. Artillery, 4, 109; Sixth Regiment U. S. Artillery, 44, 1,396. Third Regiment U. S. Infantry, 45, 1,364; Fourth Regiment U. S. Infantry, 47, 1,560; Sixth Regiment U. S. Infantry, 46, 1,440; Ninth Regiment U. S. Infantry, 43, 1,328; Twelfth Regiment U. S. Infantry, 42, 1,451; Thirteenth Regiment U. S. Infantry, 43, 1,301; Fourteenth Regiment U. S. Infantry, 39, 1,221; Sixteenth Regiment U. S. Infantry, 45, 1,403; Seventeenth Regiment U. S. Infantry, 45, 1,381; Eighteenth Regiment U. S. Infantry, 43, 1,399; Nineteenth Regiment U. S. Infantry, 46, 1,420; Twentieth Regiment U. S. Infantry, 44, 1,374; Twenty-first Regiment U. S. Infantry, 44, 1,318; Twenty-second Regiment U S. Infantry, 45, 1,415; Twenty-third Regiment U. S. Infantry, 45, 1,651; Twenty-fourth Regiment U. S. Infantry, 37, 1,035; Twenty-fifth Regiment U. S. Infantry, 36, 1,087; Twenty-sixth Regiment U. S. Volunteer Infantry, 50, 1,237; Twenty-seventh Regiment U. S. Volunteer Infantry, 49, 1,215; Twenty-eighth Regiment U. S. Volunteer Infantry, 50, 1,234; Twenty-ninth Regiment U. S. Volunteer Infantry, 50, 1,233; Thirtieth Regiment U. S. Volunteer Infantry, 50, 1,269; Thirty-first Regiment U. S. Volunteer Infantry, 50, 1,230; Thirty-second Regiment U. S. Volunteer Infantry, 50, 1,202; Thirty-third Regiment U. S. Volunteer Infantry, 50, 1,233; Thirty-fourth Regiment U. S. Volunteer Infantry, 49, 1,255; Thirty-fifth Regiment U. S. Volunteer Infantry, 50, 1,205; Thirty-sixth Regiment U. S. Volunteer Infantry, 50, 974; Thirty-seventh Regiment U. S. Volunteer Infantry, 50, 1,037; Thirty-eighth Regiment U. S. Volunteer Infantry, 50, 1,234; Thirty-ninth Regiment U. S. Volunteer Infantry, 50, 1,255; Fortieth Regiment U. S. Volunteer Infantry, 48, 1,272; Forty-first Regiment U. S. Volunteer Infantry, 50, 1,296; Forty-second Regiment U. S. Volunteer Infantry, 50, 1,288; Forty-third Regiment U. S. Volunteer Infantry, 50, 1,283; Forty-fourth Regiment U. S. Volunteer Infantry, 50, 1,276; Forty-fifth Regiment U. S. Volunteer Infantry, 49, 1,209; Forty-sixth Regiment U. S. Volunteer Infantry, 50, 1,265; Forty-seventh Regiment U. S. Volunteer Infantry, 50, 1,260; Forty-eighth Regiment U. S. Volunteer Infantry, 50, 1,366; Forty-ninth Regiment U. S. Volunteer Infantry, 50, 1,292. Company A, Battalion of Engineers, U. S. Army, 2, 182; Company B, Battalion of Engineers, U. S. Army, 2, 136. Hospital Corps, 73, 2,262. Signal Corps, U. S. Army, 21, 364. Total, 2,218, 61,246; acting assistant surgeons, 210.

MacArthur.

ADJUTANT-GENERAL'S OFFICE,
Washington, May 18, 1900.

MacArthur, *Manila:*
Secretary of War directs you detail an officer of rank, tact, good judgment to gather military information in China. He should repair to Hongkong and report by letter our minister China, retaining station Hongkong. Precise object ascertain doings junta there, particularly as their furnishing aid and assistance insurgents in

Philippines, and suggest how it can be frustrated. Funds employment detectives, etc., being sent him through minister. Cable name officer. Give him instructions as will give best results. Officer should report frequently to you, sending mail copies here through minister.

CORBIN.

GENERAL ORDERS, } HEADQUARTERS OF THE ARMY,
No. 70. ADJUTANT-GENERAL'S OFFICE,
Washington, May 19, 1900.

The following order has been received from the War Department, and is published to the Army for the information and guidance of all concerned:

"WAR DEPARTMENT, *Washington, May 8, 1900.*

"By direction of the President, the provinces of Morong and Infanta, and all that portion of the province of Manila north of the Pasig River, all in the island of Luzon, and now a part of the Department of Southern Luzon, are transferred to the Department of Northern Luzon.

"ELIHU ROOT, *Secretary of War.*"

By command of Major-General Miles:

H. C. CORBIN, *Adjutant-General.*

MANILA. (Received May 21, 1900—9.31 a. m.)
ADJUTANT-GENERAL, *Washington:*

Deaths: Dysentery—May 6, Band, Thirty-fourth Regiment U. S. Volunteer Infantry, Ray C. Perkins; Company C, Thirty-seventh U. S. Volunteer Infantry, Howard M. McCall; May 8, Company F, Forty-sixth U. S. Volunteer Infantry, Corpl. Edward N. Flood; May 10, Company C, Thirty-seventh U. S. Volunteer Infantry, James T. Heskett; May 12, Company F, Fourth Regiment U. S. Infantry, Sergt. Thomas Ryan; May 14, Troop I, Fourth Regiment U. S. Cavalry, Hugh H. Thompson; Company A, Thirty-ninth Regiment U. S. Volunteer Infantry, Gustav A. Krueger; May 15, Company B, Thirty-ninth Regiment U. S. Volunteer Infantry, Artificer Isaac N. Wise, Company A, Thirty-seventh Regiment U. S. Volunteer Infantry, Eugene S. Farnham; May 16, Company H, Thirteenth U. S. Infantry, William W. Crowell; Company C, Thirty-ninth U. S. Volunteer Infantry, George Roddin.

Typhoid fever—April 29, Company I, Forty-seventh U. S. Volunteer Infantry, Howard Templin; May 12, Company G, Thirty-ninth U. S. Volunteer Infantry, Scott L. Larson.

Drowned, accidentally—May 15, Company M, Fourth U. S. Infantry, Friedrik W. Franz; Company K, Forty-eighth U. S. Volunteer Infantry, Harrison Dirks.

Suicide—May 15, Troop D, Third Regiment U. S. Cavalry, Farrier Edward Watson.

Appendicitis—May 13, Company H, Forty-eighth U. S. Volunteer Infantry, Isaac M. Hoskins.

Malarial fever—May 13, Company D, Forty-first U. S. Volunteer Infantry, Edward Bastian (cook).

Peritonitis—May 11, Company A, Thirteenth U. S. Infantry, Lee Shepherd.

Septicæmia—May 6, Company E, Twenty-ninth U. S. Volunteer Infantry, Robert W. Floyd.

Pneumonia—May 12, Company A, Twenty-sixth U. S. Volunteer Infantry, James W. Moran.

Accidentally shot—May 3, Company M, Fortieth U. S. Volunteer Infantry, Corpl. Erskin H. Dorman.

Tetanus—May 17, Battery E, Sixth U. S. Artillery, Corpl. Chasei Sweeney.

MACARTHUR.

MANILA. (Received May 21, 1900—11.15 a. m.)

ADJUTANT-GENERAL, *Washington:*

Col. Edward A. Godwin, Fortieth Regiment U. S. Volunteer Infantry, reports engagement May 14, 80 men Fortieth Regiment U. S. Volunteer Infantry under Captain Elliott at Agusan, near Cagayan, Cagayan Province (Mindanao); enemy 500 strong in good position, routed; 52 killed, 31 Remingtons and quantity ammunition captured; our loss in killed, Company I, Fortieth Regiment U. S. Volunteer Infantry, Corpl. James O'Neill, John W Shaw; our loss in wounded, Company I, Fortieth Regiment U. S. Volunteer Infantry, Corpl. Jack Cook, wounded in thigh, moderate; Artificer Edwin E. Dodds, wounded in thigh, slight; Company K, Fortieth Regiment U. S. Volunteer Infantry, Mack D. Smith, wounded in thigh, moderate.

MACARTHUR.

MANILA. (Received May 22, 1900—10.05 a. m.)

ADJUTANT-GENERAL, *Washington:*

Wheaton reports two companies insurgents, comprising the comandante, 1 captain, 2 first lieutenants, 4 second lieutenants, 163 men, with 168 guns in good condition, small quantity ammunition, surrendered at Tarlac at 2 a. m. May 22. This is first instance in islands of surrender of organizations complete and is regarded as significant and important.

MACARTHUR.

MANILA. (Received May 22, 1900—8.28 a. m.)

ADJUTANT-GENERAL, *Washington:*

Request that I be granted authority to send officers Hongkong, Japan, and points in Asia, when necessities service require.

MACARTHUR.

MANILA. (Received May 23, 1900—7.20 a. m.)

ADJUTANT-GENERAL, *Washington:*

Transport *Sumner* arrived to-day.

MACARTHUR.

MANILA. (Received May 23, 1900—7.25 a. m.)

ADJUTANT-GENERAL, *Washington:*

With reference to your telegram of 18th, Lieut. Col. John S. Mallory. Forty-First Regiment, U. S. Volunteer Infantry, is officer selected for Hongkong.

MACARTHUR.

ADJUTANT-GENERAL'S OFFICE,
Washington, May 24, 1900.

MACARTHUR. *Manila:*

[Translation.] Secretary of War approves selection John S. Mallory Hongkong. You are authorized to send officers China, Japan, and other Asiatic ports when it becomes necessary.

CORBIN.

ADJUTANT-GENERAL'S OFFICE,
Washington, May 26, 1900.

MACARTHUR, *Manila:*

When you approve discharge officers for sickness, wounds, for the best interests of the service or on resignation for sufficient cause send them San Francisco, telegraphing arrival Adjutant-General of the Army. When reasons resignation are insufficient disapprove, informing those concerned.

CORBIN,
W. H. C.

ADJUTANT-GENERAL'S OFFICE,
Washington, May 26, 1900.

MACARTHUR, *Manila:*
Telegraph the condition of movement for return battalions Eighteenth Infantry and Twenty-third Infantry.

CORBIN.

MANILA. (Received May 27, 1900—7.40 a. m.)

ADJUTANT-GENERAL, *Washington:*
With reference to your telegram of 26th, will try send battalion Eighteenth Infantry June 15; good progress is being made. Organization battalion Twenty-third Infantry progress slow on account poor communication facilities.

MACARTHUR.

MANILA. (Received May 28, 1900—11.07 a. m.)

ADJUTANT-GENERAL, *Washington:*
Deaths: Typhoid—April 23, Company C, Thirty-first Volunteer Infantry, Lem Gordon; May 19, Company A, Forty-first Volunteer Infantry, Joseph H. Holbrow; May 21, Company B, Thirty-ninth Volunteer Infantry, Frederick Klinke; Company C, Thirty-ninth Volunteer Infantry, Temple B. Morrison; May 25, Company A, Thirty-ninth Volunteer Infantry, Henry J. Miller.

Variola—April 13, Troop E, Eleventh Volunteer Cavalry, George Overturf; May 12, Company H, Forty-eighth Volunteer Infantry, Judson Brown; May 20, Company M, Forty-sixth Volunteer Infantry, Charles Morehouse; May 21, Company H, Forty-eighth Volunteer Infantry, Alvin B. Winters.

Dysentery—May 19, Company L, Thirty-second Volunteer Infantry, William H. Thomas.

Malarial fever—May 19, Company K, Thirty-seventh Volunteer Infantry, Edward Thomas; May 22, Company M, Forty-first Volunteer Infantry, James W. Wilkerson.

Alcoholism—May 5, Troop F, Third Cavalry, John F. Dawson.

Intestinal obstruction—May 19, Company E, Forty-sixth Volunteer Infantry, Philip R. Prescott.

Polyneuritis—May 22, Company D, Forty-sixth Volunteer Infantry, William S. Robinson.

Dropsy—May 25, Company D, Sixth Infantry, Musician Milton D. Hernandez.

Suicide—April 4, Troop M, Fourth Cavalry, Victor Adair.

Homicide—May 19, Company F, Twenty-fifth Infantry, First Sergt. John Williams.

MACARTHUR.

MANILA. (Received May 28, 1900—7.50 a. m.)

ADJUTANT-GENERAL, *Washington:*
Three officers, 56 men, with 40 rifles, surrendered unconditionally at Cuyapo yesterday. Three officers, 46 men, with 55 rifles, surrendered unconditionally to-day at Tarlac. These spontaneous surrenders are very encouraging.

MACARTHUR.

MANILA. (Received at War Department May 28, 1900—10.35 a. m.)

ADJUTANT-GENERAL, *Washington, D. C.:*
Rapid conquest Luzon last fall from widely scattered enemy, resulted in corresponding dissemination our troops, necessity still obtain and may continue some

time yet. This extensive distribution strains to limit entire force now in island. In order prepare gradual decrease force necessary concentrate at central stations, relying for protection outlying districts upon rapid movements to threatened points. Successful development this policy depends largely upon good roads and bridges, which means probable expenditure million dollars gold, possibly more, and presence, at least, ten more engineer officers to work out detailed plans, which can be accomplished during rains, construction commence immediately thereafter. Foregoing based upon idea holding archipelago after March 1 with 45,000 troops; large proportion thereof must be cavalry; before March 1 not possible return any present force looking to concentration American troops. Proposed commence immediately organization native constabulary in towns where such action prudent; this to encourage people to self-protection against robber criminals, roving bands insurgents, with which country abounds. Propose arm this force with inferior weapon; possibly shotguns; if so will call for about 2,000. If possible to furnish, please advise, some length, views Department; if scheme approved, first step necessary is send engineer officers earliest possible date.

MacArthur.

Manila. (Received May 29, 1900—12.55 a. m.)
Adjutant-General, *Washington*:
Transport *Warren* arrived yesterday.

MacArthur.

Manila. (Received May 31, 1900—8.28 a. m.)
Adjutant-General, *Washington*:
Small surrenders continue Department of Northern Luzon. Corino, fugitive governor, Benguet, rich, active friend Aguinaldo, captured yesterday near Kabayan (Cabayan). Important. While scouting near San Miguel de Mayumo (Luzon) May 29, Capt. Chas. D. Roberts, Privates John A. McIntyre, Lyel W. Akins were captured; Sergt. John Gallen, Privates Joseph H. McCourt, John A. Greer, killed; George Kinger, wounded, thigh. All Company I, Thirty-fifth Regiment U. S. Volunteers.

MacArthur.

San Francisco, Cal. (Received May 31, 1900—4.51 p. m.)
Adjutant-General, *Washington, D. C.*:
Following military passengers arrived on transport *Meade:* General Otis, * * * Captains Sladen, Eighth; * * * Lieutenants Stanley, * * * Twenty-second. * * *

Shafter, *Major-General.*

Note.—Capt. F. W. Sladen, now of the Fourteenth Infantry, and Lieut. D. S. Stanley, Twenty-second Infantry, are aids to General Otis.

Manila. (Received June 2, 1900—1.45 a. m.)
Adjutant-General, *Washington:*
Killed—April 28, Patnongor, Panay, Company E, Forty-fourth Volunteer Infantry, Corpl. Joseph H. Griffin; Company G, Forty-fourth Volunteer Infantry, Corpl. John Ryan; May 15, Amontoc, Luzon, Company E, Forty-eighth Volunteer Infantry, Corpl. Lewis Washington; May 24, Mariquina, Luzon, Company B, Twenty-seventh

Volunteer Infantry, Sergt. James F. Berry. Wounded—April 29, Layagon [near Tinagaya], Panay, Company H, Twenty-sixth Volunteer Infantry, John F. Broderick, wounded in leg below knee, serious; April 28, Patnongon, Panay, Company E, Forty-fourth Volunteer Infantry, Second Lieut. Gustav F. Schlachter, wounded in thigh, serious; Edward Kuck, wounded in arm, slight.

MACARTHUR.

MANILA. (Received June 3, 1900—5.15 a. m.)
ADJUTANT-GENERAL, *Washington:*
Transport *Sumner* sailed June 1. Transport *Hancock* arrived to-day with Philippine Commission.

MACARTHUR.

MANILA. (Received June 4, 1900—6.35 a. m.)
ADJUTANT-GENERAL, *Washington:*
During engagement near San Miguel de Mayumo (Luzon) June 3, at 7 a. m., our loss in killed, Capt. George J. Godfrey, Twenty-second Infantry, and Perry G. Etheridge, Company A, Twenty-second Infantry.

MACARTHUR.

MANILA. (Received June 4, 1900—12.45 a. m.)
SECRETARY WAR, *Washington:*
Arrived, all well.

TAFT.

MANILA. (Received June 5, 1900—6.45 a. m.)
ADJUTANT-GENERAL, *Washington:*
Deaths: Dysentery—May 25, Company B, Thirty-eighth Volunteer Infantry, Carl H. Peterson; Company A, Thirtieth Volunteer Infantry, Frank E. Spears; Company K, Eighteenth Infantry, Corpl. Frank Kessler; May 27, Company D, Twenty-sixth Volunteer Infantry, Sergt. Earl H. Peck; May 28, Hospital Corps, Joseph V. Sheahan; May 31, Battery C, Sixth Artillery, First Sergt. Adolph Tross.

Typhoid fever—May 26, Company G, Thirty-ninth Volunteer Infantry, Louie W. Gowing; May 27, Company A, Thirty-fifth Volunteer Infantry, Frank O'Donovan; May 29, Company B, Thirty-ninth Volunteer Infantry, Arthur W. James; May 30, Company D, Thirty-ninth Volunteer Infantry, Charles M. Netherton.

Malarial fever—May 26, Company E, Forty-sixth Volunteer Infantry, George St. Clair; May 27, Troop A, Third Cavalry, Joseph Harris; May 30, Company B, Thirty-seventh Volunteer Infantry, Basil Owen; May 31, Troop K, Eleventh Volunteer Cavalry, John Moore.

Colitis—May 18, Company K, Eighteenth Infantry, William Crispen; May 29, Company A, Thirtieth Volunteer Infantry, James G. Lynch.

Variola—May 26, Company M, Forty-sixth Volunteer Infantry, Elwin R. Marsh.

Drowned—May 13, Company M, Forty-third Volunteer Infantry, Sergt. Ora Vestal.

Meningitis—May 28, Company B, Twenty-seventh Volunteer Infantry, Stewart King.

Heat exhaustion—May 29, Company E, Thirty-fifth Volunteer Infantry, David Davis.

Died from wounds received in action—April 20, Company H, Forty-third Volunteer Infantry, Sergt. William J. Hall.

*a*Sprue—May 29, Company H, Eighteenth Infantry, Ota L. Dehaven.
Alcoholism—May 13, Troop K, Eleventh Cavalry, John Kelly.
Carbunculosis of face—June 2, First Lieutenant Assistant Surgeon, Thirty-fourth Volunteer Infantry, 4.45 morning, Raphael A. Edmonston.

MACARTHUR.

MANILA. (Received June 5, 1900—9.34 a. m.)

ADJUTANT-GENERAL, *Washington*:

Propose immediate issue of amnesty offering complete immunity for past and liberty for future to all who have not violated laws of war and who will renounce insurrection and accept sovereignty and authority of the United States, this action to include Aguinaldo, who may possibly take advantage thereof, and whose voluntary surrender would greatly expedite pacification; at expiration of ninety days supplementary notice to issue, if situation requires, declaring all insurgents outlaws who decline amnesty within sixty days of second notice; prefer first notice should not refer to outlawry; effect probably best without threat of any kind. Hope second notice unnecessary. Judge Taft concurs. Can I proceed?

MACARTHUR.

WAR DEPARTMENT, *June 6, 1900.*

MACARTHUR, *Manila:*

Your proposal of June 5 for immediate issue of amnesty proclamation is approved by the President, the Secretary of War directing you to draft such proclamation and cable it here in full for revision before issue. It should read by direction of the President and contain no limitation of time or reference to any future proclamation. Future action must be determined when occasion arises.

CORBIN,
Adjutant-General, Major-General.

MANILA. (Received June 6, 1900—8.03 a. m.)

ADJUTANT-GENERAL, *Washington:*

Total strength present and absent, May 31, ascertained as near as possible: Third Cavalry, officers 26, enlisted men 904; Fourth Cavalry, 48, 1,459; Eleventh Volunteer Cavalry, 48, 1,043. Battery E, First Artillery, 4, 150; Third Artillery, 11, 382; Battery F, Fourth Artillery, 4, 150. Battery F, Fifth Artillery, 4, 140; Sixth Artillery, 42, 1,412. Third Infantry, 44, 1,424; Fourth Infantry, 45, 1,412; Sixth Infantry, 45, 1,426; Ninth Infantry, 44, 1,380; Twelfth Infantry, 42, 1,443; Thirteenth Infantry, 45, 1,395; Fourteenth Infantry, 39, 1,219; Sixteenth Infantry, 45, 1,299; Seventeenth Infantry, 45, 1,406; Eighteenth Infantry, 46, 1,363; Nineteenth Infantry, 46, 1,420; Twentieth Infantry, 44, 1,440; Twenty-first Infantry, 46, 1,408; Twenty-second Infantry, 43, 1,398; Twenty-third Infantry, 46, 1,661; Twenty-fourth Infantry, 37, 1,033; Twenty-fifth Infantry, 36, 1,048; Twenty-sixth Infantry, 50, 1,232; Twenty-seventh Infantry, 49, 1,205; Twenty-eighth Infantry, 50, 1,266; Twenty-ninth Infantry, 50, 1,238; Thirtieth Infantry, 50, 1,260; Thirty-first Infantry, 50, 1,227; Thirty-second Infantry, 50, 1,199; Thirty-third Infantry, 49, 1,233; Thirty-fourth Infantry, 49, 1,245; Thirty-fifth Infantry, 50, 1,251; Thirty-sixth Infantry, 49, 971; Thirty-seventh Infantry, 50, 1,027; Thirty-eighth Infantry, 50, 1,229; Thirty-ninth Infantry, 49, 1,236; Fortieth Infantry, 49, 1,261; Forty-first Infantry, 50, 1,294; Forty-second Infantry, 49, 1,065; Forty-third Infantry, 50, 1,262; Forty-fourth

---

a Disease: A sort of thrush.

Infantry, 50, 1,276; Forty-fifth Infantry, 49, 1252; Forty-sixth Infantry, 50, 1,252; Forty-seventh Infantry, 50, 1,260; Forty-eighth Infantry, 49, 1,309; Forty-ninth Infantry, 47, 1,269. Companies A and B, Battalion Engineers, U. S. Army, 4, 250. Signal Corps, U. S. Army, 21, 409. Hospital Corps, 75, 2,275. Total, 2,203, 61,099. Acting assistant surgeons, 216.

MACARTHUR.

MANILA. (Received June 7, 1900—7.32 a. m.)
ADJUTANT-GENERAL, *Washington:*

Killed—May 11, Matuguinao, Samar, Company K, Forty-third Volunteer Infantry, Corpl. Joseph McClellan; Company A, Forty-third Volunteer Infantry, Edward Hoyt; May 30, Indang, Luzon, band, Forty-sixth Volunteer Infantry, Herbert A. Percival, Sergt. David Langevin, Drum Major Stephen H. Leonard; May 30, Siniloan, Luzon, Company F, Forty-second Volunteer Infantry, Corpl. Henry F. Hart; February 3, Naporo, Samar, Company E, Forty-third Volunteer Infantry, Asa L. Johnson; February 24, Tayabas Province, Luzon, Company D, Thirtieth (Volunteer) Infantry, Charles Brandt; June 4, Norzagaray, Luzon, Company E, Thirty-fifth Volunteer Infantry, Clarence Quillion.

Wounded—May 11, Matuguinao, Samar, Company I, Twenty-third Infantry, Ralph M. Dickinson, wounded in arm, serious; Ralph L. Clark, wounded in knee, serious; Company E, Forty-third Volunteer Infantry, William G. Ten Eyck, wounded in shoulder, serious; Company K, Forty-third Volunteer Infantry, Thomas Mixon, wounded in knee, serious; May 6, Alava, Luzon, Troop M, Third Cavalry, Lawrence Creekbaum, wounded in neck, slight; Company K, Forty-eighth Volunteer Infantry, Corpl. Horace Cannon, wounded in shoulder, slight; Ulysses G. Heath, wounded in thigh, slight; Nathaniel Pettis, wounded in head, slight; May 13, Palauig, Luzon, band, Twenty-fifth Infantry, Sergt. George S. Thompson, wounded in knee, slight; May 29, Santa Lucia, Luzon, Company F, Thirty-third Volunteer Infantry, Harry Lichtman, wounded in abdomen, serious; May 4, Bonanguran, Luzon, Company A, Forty-seventh Volunteer Infantry, Sergt. Joseph J. Harvey, wounded in thigh, serious; Henry Hammermanson, wounded in face, slight; Company D, Forty-seventh Volunteer Infantry, Musician Sidney Lane, wounded in arm, slight; May 16, Paranas, Samar, Company I, Forty-third Volunteer Infantry, John Kopp, wounded in hand, slight; May 6, Pambujan, Samar, Company F, Forty-third Volunteer Infantry, James E. Murdock, wounded in leg above knee, slight; May 8, Catubig, Samar, Company F, Forty-third Volunteer Infantry, Ambrose W. Thompson, wounded in hand, slight; June 4, Norgazaray, Luzon, Company E, Thirty-fifth Volunteer Infantry, Musician Lee Speaker, wounded in abdomen, serious; Charles H. Dean, wounded in lung, serious; Corpl. William J. Bartlett, wounded in groin, serious; Pete Thompson, wounded in knee, slight; Ernest Hite, wounded in arm, slight; Hospital Corps, Morris Aronovitch, wounded in thigh, slight; May 22, Calbiga, Samar, Company M, Forty-third Volunteer Infantry, Clements L. Frazer, wounded in knee, serious; Company L, Forty-third Volunteer Infantry, Charles H. Weden, wounded in neck, slight.

MACARTHUR.

ADJUTANT-GENERAL'S OFFICE,
Washington, June 8, 1900.

MACARTHUR, *Manila:*

Detail officers of the Corps of Engineers road work under consideration. If you think it advisable to assign officer rank and special fitness under your immediate direction, vacancy brigadier-general volunteers open. Have you officer can fill all requirements?

CORBIN.

MANILA. (Received June 9, 1900—1.36 a. m.)

ADJUTANT-GENERAL, *Washington:*

Native police Manila captured insurgent General Pio del Pilar this morning. He was found lurking in neighborhood of San Pedro Macati.

MACARTHUR.

MANILA. (Received June 9, 1900—7 a. m.)

ADJUTANT-GENERAL, *Washington:*

Amnesty notice separate. Word proclamation, from long Spanish use, contracted, misleading, meaning, therefore, eliminated. Ninety days' limit necessary to insure speedy action. Otherwise natives discuss, procrastinate, and never act. Supplementary action, if necessary, in light of actual events, can be had at expiration of time limit.

MACARTHUR.

MANILA. (Received June 9, 1900—3.08 p. m.).

ADJUTANT-GENERAL, *Washington:*

Referring to your message June 9 (8), would like Thomas H. Barry, brigadier-general, chief of staff, provided he can also be assigned as adjutant-general, vice Barber (M), to go home. Juniors to do all office work under Barry. To retain Barber (M), or assign separate adjutant-general, would mean unceasing discord, and make chief of staff undesirable. Barber (M) been sick, and chief surgeon thinks return home wise.

Shall commence organizing constabulary armed with shotguns as soon as scheme approved; probably more shotguns required than first estimate. Early cable action important.

MACARTHUR.

MANILA. (Received June 9, 1900—4.19 p. m.)

ADJUTANT-GENERAL, *Washington:*

Notice of amnesty. The immediate purpose of the United States in this archipelago is to establish stable civil institutions according to the beneficient scheme of republican government, which alone is possible under the auspices of the American union. As an important step to this end, the undersigned, by special direction of the President, announces amnesty with complete immunity for the past and absolute liberty of action for the future, to all persons who are now or at any time since February 4, 1899, have been in insurrection against the United States in either a military or a civil capacity, and who shall within a period of ninety days from the date hereof formally renounce all connection with such insurrection, and subscribe to a declaration acknowledging and accepting the sovereignty and authority of the United States in and over the Philippine Islands. The privilege herewith published is extended to all concerned without any reservation whatever, excepting that all persons who have violated the laws of war during the period of active hostilities are not embraced within the scope of this amnesty. All who desire to take advantage of the terms herewith set forth are requested to present themselves to the commanding officers of the American troops at the most convenient station, who will receive them with due consideration according to rank, make special provisions for their immediate wants, prepare the necessary records, and thereafter permit each individual to proceed to any part of the archipelago according to his own wishes, for which purpose the United States will furnish such transportation as may be available, either by railway, steamboat, or wagon. Prominent persons who may desire to confer with the military governor or with the board of American commissioners will be permitted to visit Manila, and will, as far as possible, be provided with transportation for that purpose. In order to mitigate, as much as possible, consequences which have resulted from the various disturbances which since 1896 have succeeded each other so rapidly, and to provide in some measure for destitute Philippine soldiers during the transitory period which must inevitably succeed a general peace, the military authorities of the United States will pay 30 pesos to each man who presents a rifle in good condition. Whatever individual views may obtain in regard to the foregoing, it must be obvious to all that general acceptance thereof would contribute to the lasting material benefit of these beautiful islands.

MACARTHUR.

MANILA. (Received June 11, 1900—12.49 p. m.)
ADJUTANT-GENERAL, *Washington:*

Deaths: Dysentery—June 8, Company I, Thirty-fifth Volunteer Infantry, Frank P. Cushing; Company A, Forty-first Volunteer Infantry, Musician Thomas Young; Company E, Thirty-seventh Volunteer Infantry, Hans E. Espenson; June 7, Company L, Twenty-second U. S. Infantry, Peter Ley; June 5, Company G, Forty-sixth Volunteer Infantry, Oscar C. Mahoney; Company A, Thirty-ninth Volunteer Infantry, Hiram G. Robine; June 6, Company H, Thirteenth U. S. Infantry, Edwin R. Riley; Company E, Thirtieth Volunteer Infantry, Fred M. Truitt. Typhoid fever—June 8, Company H, Twenty-ninth Volunteer Infantry, John F. Owens; May 27, Company A, Thirty-ninth Volunteer Infantry, Patrick Dwyer; May 11, Company D, Thirty-ninth Volunteer Infantry, Eden C. Neeves; May 22, Company I, Thirty-first Volunteer Infantry, James Donahue; June 7, Company G, Twenty-first Infantry, Charles H. Cook. Diarrhea—June 8, Company F, Forty-sixth Volunteer Infantry, Herbert R. Nelson; June 7, Company M, Thirty-fourth Volunteer Infantry, Ford Hopkins; May 31, Company I, Thirty-sixth Volunteer Infantry, Joseph Sands. Malarial fever—June 7, Company L, Third Infantry, Joseph C. Patterson; June 6, Company L, Seventeenth Infantry, Richard M. Patton. Meningitis—May 18, Company I, Thirty-first Volunteer Infantry, William Keefe. Tetanus—May 21, Company I, Forty-third Volunteer Infantry, Alfred Fountaine. Suicide—June 3, Company I, Third Infantry, Charles Sawyer. Nephritis—June 5, Company B, Seventeenth Infantry, Frederick Hires. Variola—June 3, Company H, Forty-eighth Volunteer Infantry, Frank Haley. Tuberculosis—June 5, Company B, Forty-eighth Volunteer Infantry, Walter Allison.

MACARTHUR.

SAN FRANCISCO, CAL., *June 11, 1900—4.28 p. m.*
ADJUTANT-GENERAL, *Washington, D. C.:*

Following military passengers arrived on transport *Grant:* General Graham, retired; Major Balch, surgeon; Captain Tyler; Lieutenants Graham and Valentine, Nineteenth Infantry; Captain Gillenwater, Thirty-first, and Lieutenant McMillan, Thirtieth, Infantry; Lieutenants McIntyre, Sixth, and Cassels, Seventh, Artillery; 5 acting assistant surgeons, 30 discharged soldiers, 26 men, M, Sixth Artillery; 8 soldiers as guards, 18 Hospital Corps men; 57 soldiers to be discharged for disability, 17 insane soldiers, 125 general prisoners, 198 sick soldiers. Casualties during voyage, Corpl. George P. Clay, M, Forty-third Infantry, died May 19 of phthisis; Musician Balious Schooler, M [A], Thirty-ninth Infantry, died 7th instant of chronic dysentery; Private Harry J. Jackson, B, Thirty-ninth Infantry, died 8th instant of chronic dysentery.

SHAFTER, *Major-General.*

MANILA. (Received June 12, 1900—2.38 a. m.)
ADJUTANT-GENERAL, *Washington:*
Report capture Generals Hizon, near Mexico, and Cavestany, at Alcala, both important; latter very prominent leader guerillas Pangasinan Province (Luzon).

MACARTHUR.

MANILA. (Received June 13, 1900—7.50 a. m.)
ADJUTANT-GENERAL, *Washington:*
First Lieut. Jonathan Cilley, Forty-third Infantry, U. S. Volunteers, died in hospital 4.35 morning June 13, typhoid fever.

MACARTHUR.

ADJUTANT-GENERAL'S OFFICE,
Washington, June 13, 1900.
MACARTHUR, *Manila:*
Telegraph full particulars of death of Edward S. Thornton, sergeant-major, Third Cavalry. Report has been made to Paymaster-General of the Army, died June 1.

CORBIN.

ADJUTANT-GENERAL'S OFFICE,
Washington, June 15, 1900.
MACARTHUR, *Manila:*
Proposed notice amnesty approved with following amendments: Strike out following: "The immediate purpose of the United States in this archipelago is to establish stable civil institutions, according to the beneficent scheme of republican government, which mission is possible under the auspices of the American Union. As an important step to this end the undersigned, by special direction of the President," and substitute the following: "By direction of the President of the United States, the undersigned."

In the clause "without any reservation whatever, excepting that all persons who have violated the laws of war," strike out the word "all."

In the clause "in order to mitigate as much as possible the consequences which have resulted from the various disturbances," etc., strike out the words "which have resulted," substituting the word "resulting."

Strike out the last sentence, beginning "Whatever individual views" and ending "beautiful islands."

Date of issuance of notice to be cabled here.

CORBIN.

ADJUTANT-GENERAL'S OFFICE,
Washington, June 15, 1900.
MACARTHUR, *Manila:*
Organization constabulary as proposed by you May 25 and June 9 is approved. Do you desire shotguns sent from here? * * *

CORBIN.

MANILA. (Received June 15, 1900—5.48 a. m.)
ADJUTANT-GENERAL, *Washington:*
Transport *Hancock* sailed to-day with returning battalion Eighteenth Infantry.

MACARTHUR.

MANILA. (Received June 15, 1900—9.03 a. m.)
ADJUTANT-GENERAL, *Washington:*
General Macabulos, with 8 officers, 124 men, 124 rifles, surrrendered to Col. Emerson H. Liscum, Ninth Infantry, at Tarlac this morning. Macabulos the most important and last insurgent leader in Tarlac and Pangasinan.

MACARTHUR.

MANILA. (Received June 16, 1900—9.21 a. m.)
ADJUTANT-GENERAL, *Washington:*
Send quick as possible 2,000 shotguns, pattern furnished prison guards, necessary spare parts, 100 rounds per gun buckshot, ammunition and necessary material for 200 rounds per gun, and appliances for loading to be done here by ordnance department.

Force in Philippines has been disseminated to limitation of safety, concentration slow to avoid evacuation of territory now occupied which would be extremely unfortunate. Have not cared to emphasize this feature of situation.

Loss of a regiment at this time would be a serious matter, but if critical emergency arises in China can send a regiment two days' notice.

MACARTHUR.

DJUTANT-GENERAL'S OFFICE,
Washington, June 16, 1900.
MACARTHUR, *Manila:*
Shotguns ordered and will leave on first transport.

CORBIN.

ADJUTANT-GENERAL'S OFFICE,
Washington, June 15, 1900.
MACARTHUR, *Manila:*
The Surgeon-General has submitted a requisition for supplies from chief surgeon that in some particulars, at least, is deemed excessive. The Secretary of War directs that you examine the retained requisition and advise by cable what proportion is actually needed, and that in future requisitions for all stores and supplies for all departments of your army shall have your consideration and approval.

CORBIN.

ADJUTANT-GENERAL'S OFFICE,
Washington, June 18, 1900.
MACARTHUR, *Manila:*
If notice amnesty now satisfactory to you, Secretary War considers desirable to publish it promptly before rumors about it leak out. Quick reply desired.

CORBIN.

MANILA. (Received June 18, 1900—10.15 a. m.)
ADJUTANT-GENERAL, *Washington:*
Deaths: Dysentery—May 12, Company D, Seventeenth U. S. Infantry, Jacob Givens; June 7, Company K, Thirty-ninth Volunteer Infantry, Joseph Lovell; June 13, Company E, Thirtieth Volunteer Infantry, Ernest Seeley; Company K, Thirty-ninth Volunteer Infantry, John S. Hall; June 14, Company M, Thirty-fourth Vol-

unteer Infantry, Hardy Williams; Company K, Sixth U. S. Infantry, William T. Bailey; June 4, Company D, Thirty-seventh Volunteer Infantry, Robert Green; May 27, Company E, Fortieth Volunteer Infantry, Charles P. Schafer; May 24, Troop H, Eleventh Volunteer Cavalry, Jarvis Drew. Typhoid fever—May 24, Company D, Twenty-second U. S. Infantry, William Williams. Variola—June 5, Company E, Ninth U. S. Infantry, John J. Dwyer. Malarial fever—June 12, Company F, Third U. S. Infantry, William J. Keller; June 9, Company G, Ninth U. S. Infantry, Maurice Fitzgerald; June 8, Company E, Thirteenth U. S. Infantry, Ernest L. Palmer; June 14, Company C, Ninth Infantry, Ewing Shelton. Nephritis—June 12, Company B, Thirty-ninth Volunteer Infantry, John K. Wise. Peritonitis—June 12, Company F, Thirtieth Volunteer Infantry, Charlie Swanson. Appendicitis—June 12, Company M, Thirty-ninth Volunteer Infantry, Corpl. Frank Gould. Diarrhea—May 15, Company B, Twenty-second U. S. Infantry, James McNerney. Hæmoglobinuria—June 13, Company G, Twenty-eighth Volunteer Infantry, Glen V. Parke.

MacArthur.

Manila. (Received June 19, 1900—1.20 a. m.)
Adjutant-General, *Washington:*
Making every effort to expedite amnesty and prevent leak; mechanical work considerable. Will issue 21st.

MacArthur.

Adjutant-General's Office,
Washington, June 19, 1900.
MacArthur, *Manila:*
Report publication amnesty, that it may be released here simultaneously.

Corbin.

Manila. (Received June 19, 1900—7.51 a. m.)
Adjutant-General, *Washington:*
Drowned, June 10, off coast Albay, Capt. Orison P. Lee, Forty-fifth U. S. Volunteer Infantry.

MacArthur.

Manila. (Received June 20, 1900—4.50 a. m.)
Adjutant-General, *Washington:*
Amnesty in hands of department commanders for distribution; will be published in all Manila papers 21st. May be released in United States at once. Will be complete surprise here and hope very beneficial.

MacArthur.

Manila. (Received June 20, 1900—3.35 a. m.)
Adjutant-General, *Washington:*
Referring to my message of June 9 touching Thomas H. Barry, would like arrangement suggested therein carried out quickly as possible. Merritt Barber in hospital; office much confusion, which puts additional strain on myself.

MacArthur.

MANILA, *June 20, 1900.*

ADJUTANT-GENERAL, *Washington, D. C.:*

Killed—May 28, Labo, Luzon, Company B, Forty-fifth U. S. Volunteer Infantry, Corpl. Norwin Johnson, First Sergt. Clarence E. Miller; June 14, Callios [Papaya], Luzon, Troop G, Fourth Cavalry, First Sergt. Maurice O'Brian; May 26, Candaba, Luzon, Company M, Twenty-second Infantry, Arlington D. Jackson.

Wounded—June 14, Callios [Papaya], Luzon, Company I, Thirty-fourth Infantry, Hugh M. Duff, wounded in hip, slight; June 4, Norzagaray, Luzon, Company D, Thirty-fifth Volunteer Infantry, First Lieut. Grover Flint, wounded in arm and forearm, serious; Corpl. Charles J. McGibb, wounded in chest, serious; Harry Carter, wounded in neck, slight; Henry Gamble, wounded in thigh, serious; Company C, Thirty-fifth Volunteer Infantry, Henry Norris, wounded in chest, serious; June 4, Lemery, Luzon, Company A, Twenty-eighth Volunteer Infantry, Frank Smith, wounded in hip, serious; June 3, Malunu, Luzon, Company H, Sixteenth Infantry, John Allen, wounded in foot, serious; Millet L. Whitney, wounded in arm, slight; May 21, Libmanan, Luzon, Company L, Forty-fifth Volunteer Infantry, Elton A. Taylor, wounded in head, serious, wounded in neck, serious; June 11, Santa Cruz, Laguna, Troop L, Eleventh Cavalry, Sergt. Patrick Burke, wounded in back, slight; Company B, Thirty-seventh Volunteer Infantry, James Beer, wounded in leg above knee, serious; Company E, Thirty-third Volunteer Infantry, Corpl. Walter Trahern, wounded in thigh, serious; June 1, Sibul, Luzon, Company C, Thirty-fifth Volunteer Infantry, Lewis W. Jones, wounded in chest, serious; June 2, Balanga, Luzon, Company I, Twelfth Infantry, Rubert S. Pedigo, wounded in leg above knee, moderate; June 11, Buhi, South Camarines, Forty-fifth Volunteer Infantry, First Lieut. Temple H. Owens, accidentally shot himself through leg, serious.

MACARTHUR.

MANILA. (Received June 20, 1900—4.22 a. m.)

ADJUTANT-GENERAL, *Washington:*

With reference to your telegram of 16th, have examined retained requisition; can not recommend reduction. Read letter chief surgeon to Surgeon-General of the Army transmitting requisition. This will explain necessity. I fully concur.

MACARTHUR.

MANILA. (Received June 21, 1900—3.10 p. m.)

ADJUTANT-GENERAL, *Washington:*

Killed—May 14, Loculan, Mindanao, Company C, Fortieth Volunteer Infantry, Corpl. Edward H. Larue; Corpl. George F. Edwards, Thomas E. Bennett, James S. Calhoun, Charles Hanson, John L. Litchford, Oliver G. Woodford; June 14, Dumangas, Panay, Company G, 18th Infantry, John H. Glover; June 7, Company D, Twenty-sixth Infantry, Corpl. Albert M. Dennehy; May 3, Santa Cruz, Egaña Panay, Company F, Forty-fourth Volunteer Infantry, George D. McClure; May 7, Pamplona, Luzon, Company M, Forty-fifth Volunteer Infantry, Corpl. Thomas G. Day; June 14, Orion, Luzon, Company A, Thirty-second Volunteer Infantry, Fred W. Jenkins; June 9, Echagüe, Luzon, Company M, Sixteenth Infantry, Joseph Stratman.

Wounded: June 7, Dumangas, Panay, Company C, Twenty-sixth Volunteer Infantry, Thomas Gavigan, wounded in arm, serious; June 16, Santa Cruz, Panay, Troop G, Eleventh Volunteer Cavalry, William J. Byrne, wounded in knee, slight; May 7, Pamplona, Luzon, Company M, Forty-fifth Volunteer Infantry, Samuel Gray, wounded in arm, serious; June 14, Orion, Luzon, Company D, Thirty-second Volunteer Infantry, Ellet Scribner, wounded in face, slight; May 20, Boljoon Mountains, Cebu, Company A, Twenty-third Infantry, Axel W. Westran, wounded in leg above knee, slight; June 3, Barotac, Panay, Company C, Twenty-sixth Volunteer Infantry, Peter Dutran, wounded in thorax, serious; Sergt. Charles K. Osgood, wounded in arm, serious; Corpl. John Norton, wounded in knee, slight; May 1, Catarman, Samar, Company F, Forty-third Volunteer Infantry, Fred Myers, wounded in thigh, serious; May 10, Calabanga, Luzon, Company I, Forty-fifth Volunteer Infantry, Frank A. Welch, wounded in buttock, slight; May 11, Matuguinao, Samar, Company I, Twenty-third Infantry, Musician Ralph M. Davidson, wounded in shoulder, serious.

MacArthur.

ADJUTANT-GENERAL'S OFFICE,
Washington, June 22, 1900.

Shafter, *San Francisco:*

Will arrive San Francisco in time to sail for Manila by transport leaving about the 15th proximo.

Barry.

ADJUTANT-GENERAL'S OFFICE,
Washington, June 22, 1900.

MacArthur, *Manila:*

Barry appointed, assigned chief staff. Will sail San Francisco with 5 engineer officers July 15.

Corbin.

New York, *June 22, 1900—11.38 p. m.*

Corbin, *Adjutant-General, Washington, D. C.:*

Cable MacArthur as follows: "Secwar assumes that you will not enter into any negotiations about terms or conditions with former insurgents or entertain any proposition from them except unqualified acceptance of amnesty as offered."

Elihu Root, *Secretary of War.*

Manila. (Received June 23, 1900—11.37 a. m.)

Adjutant-General, *Washington:*

Detachment 4 officers, 10 men, Fortieth Infantry, Captain Miller commanding, left Cagayan midnight June 13 on reconnoissance up Cagayan River; morning June 14, ambushed by insurgents in strong position. Fifty men sent to reenforce from Cagayan; could not take position, and troops withdrew to post. Our loss in killed: Company H, Fortieth Infantry, Robert R. Coles, Lonie Fidler, John H. Haywood, Fred Holloway, John P. Pelham, Frank Sailsbury. Company M, Fortieth Infantry, Corpl. Jesse G. Moody, Alvin Landreth, Michael J. McQuirk. Wounded: Company I, Fortieth Infantry, Capt. Walter B. Elliott, slight; Company H, Fortieth Infantry, Capt. Thomas Miller, wounded in thigh, slight; Jesse Esig, moderate; James E. Jeffries, slight; Roxie Wheaton, moderate; George Hollars, slight; Turley Philips, severe; John W. Smith, severe; Company M, Fortieth Infantry, Edwin E. Williams, severe; Company K, Fortieth Infantry, George W. Wells, severe; Musician Lex. M. Kanters, moderate. Missing: Company H, Fortieth Infantry, Sergt. William P. Northcross. Full detailed report not received.

MacArthur.

ADJUTANT-GENERAL'S OFFICE,
Washington, June 23, 1900.

MACARTHUR, *Manila:*

Secretary of War assumes that you will not enter into any negotiations about terms or conditions with former insurgents or entertain any proposition from them except unqualified acceptance of amnesty as offered.

CORBIN.

MANILA. (Received June 25, 1900—3.20 p. m.)

ADJUTANT-GENERAL, *Washington:*

Referring to message of June 23, touching negotiations with former insurgents, it is necessary to have some conference with leaders in order to secure decisive results from present favorable conditions. Commission approving, I have assured them that any government instituted would embody the personal rights enumerated in instructions to Commission; that participation in insurrection would not bar future employment in civil or military service; that upon cessation of hostilities, private property not destroyed would be returned, but no damages paid them; there would be no church established by law; no minister interfered with or forced upon any community; no public funds used for support of religious organizations or any member thereof. Foregoing self-evident propositions not rightly understood, even by leaders, were put in form adapted to insure intelligent consideration. As a matter of expediency in agreement with Commission, have informed leaders I would release all claims to money now in their hands, at Hongkong and elsewhere, provided it be deposited in our treasury here, in which event it would become a trust fund for benefit of disabled Filipino soldiers, widows, orphans, of such as died in war. In consideration of such deposits I agreed to turn over an amount equal to that turned in by insurgents, provided such sum should not exceed amount captured by us. There has been nothing in the nature of negotiation—simply advice and instruction in regard to matters in which Commission and myself are in perfect accord.

MACARTHUR.

MANILA. (Received June 25, 1900—10.51 p. m.)

ADJUTANT-GENERAL, *Washington:*

Killed, February 2, Tabaco, Albay, Frank Hughes, Company E, Forty-seventh Infantry. Wounded, June 15, Monte Maradudon, Luzon, Troop E, Third Cavalry, wounded in hand, slight, Howard G. Myers.

MACARTHUR.

MANILA. (Received June 25, 1900—8.41 p. m.)

SECRETARY OF WAR, *Washington:*

No organized army of insurgents anywhere. Small bands under partisans invading territory not now occupied by our forces, compelled contribution and secret support by violence. Army working strenuously to capture and destroy bands, but with force progress slow. Many partisans can probably be reached by captured general and cabinet officers willing to take oath, apparently anxious for peace and seeking from General MacArthur information as to our future course to aid them in inducing general submission. Fully concur in General MacArthur's action in making statement contained in his dispatch to-day, not as condition of surrender, but as information of our policy, in any event given to strengthen those working for peace and to weaken arguments of irreconcilables. Even if mistaken as to good faith or influence of peacemaker, statement made detracts nothing from our position. See no ground

AFFAIRS IN THE PHILIPPINE ISLANDS. 1185

for withholding knowledge of our authority and settled purpose when knowledge may secure submission. Insurgent leaders evidently discouraged, but favorable outcome would be hindered by further reducing army and relaxing military grasp.

COMMISSION.

MANILA. (Received June 26, 1900—8.35 a. m.)
ADJUTANT-GENERAL, *Washington:*

Deaths: Dysentery—May 30, Company D, Thirty-first Infantry, Q. M. Sergt. Paul E. Melville; June 6, K, Sixth Infantry, William L. Weidriech; June 18, B, Thirty-ninth Infantry, Corpl. Howard G. Buck; B, Forty-first Infantry, Corpl. David M. Williams; L, Ninth Infantry, Jacob Klein; E, Thirty-second Infantry, James B. McCurry; June 12, F, Nineteenth Infantry, Corpl. John G. Markle; June 20, B, Thirty-ninth Infantry, Cassius A. Miner; June 23, M, Twenty-first Infantry, Patrick Hayes; G, Forty-sixth Infantry, Corpl. Jeremiah H. Hurley; June 21, L, Thirtieth Infantry, Richard Engstron; June 22, F, Thirty-ninth Infantry, John G. Turpin. Peritonitis—June 15, B, Twenty-eighth Infantry, Corpl. Henry Murphy. Drowned—May 5, L, Forty-ninth Infantry, John Gaskins; June 5, D, Thirty-ninth Infantry, Charles Woods; June 17, E, Fourth Cavalry, Trumpeter Michael Good. Typhoid fever—June 12, C, Thirty-ninth Infantry, William E. Lea; June 15, B, Thirtieth Infantry, Emil Lentz. Alcoholism—May 27, G, Sixteenth Infantry, Rudolph F. Stampff; May 31, C, Twenty-eighth Infantry, Robert Frame. Died from wounds received in action—May 9, M, Forty-fifth Infantry, Samuel Gray; June 15, A, Twenty-eighth Infantry, Frank Smith. Mania—June 22, I, Thirty-ninth Infantry, Edward Eaton. Suicide, shot, head—June 19, C, Thirty-sixth Infantry, Thomas Wilson. Opium poisoning, smoking and chewing—June 18, G, Eleventh Cavalry, William Heilig. Pyæmia—June 15, Company I, Fourth Infantry, William J. MacAndrew. Heart disease—June 12, F, Eighteenth Infantry, Sergt. Alex. B. Vanburen. Cerebral softening—June 19, D, Thirty-seventh Infantry, Sherman Taylor. Meningitis—May 27, G, Nineteenth Infantry, Bartholomew W. Howley. Variola—May 17, L, Forty-fourth Infantry, Vinton Richardson. Diarrhea—May 20, F, Forty-seventh Infantry, Russell Washburn.

MACARTHUR.

MANILA. (Received June 28, 1900—4.45 a. m.)
ADJUTANT-GENERAL, *Washington:*

Amnesty privilege extended prisoners Manila; following generals released upon taking oath renouncing revolution, recognizing sovereignty of United States: Garcia, Concepcion, Pilar, and several others of minor importance. Probably more to-day.

MACARTHUR.

MANILA. (Received June 28, 1900—8 a. m.)
ADJUTANT-GENERAL, *Washington:*

Killed—June 21, Monte Puruyan, Luzon, Troop E, Third Cavalry, William Barnes. Wounded—May 14, Malabog Hill, Luzon, B, Eleventh Cavalry, Fred. Swink, wounded in testicles, serious. May 22, Lipa, Batangas, Luzon, Second Lieut. Fred Bury, wounded in elbow, moderate. May 17, Aliang, Luzon, F, Forty-seventh Infantry, Corpl. John J. Amsler, wounded in chest, serious; Sergt. Henry Gardner, wounded in shoulder, serious.

MACARTHUR.

MANILA. (Received June 29, 1900—6 a. m.)

ADJUTANT-GENERAL, *Washington:*

Lyel W. Akins, I, Thirty-fifth Infantry, wounded in arm, moderate, and captured May 30; was sent in by insurgents June 27; reports health Charles D. Roberts, captain Thirty-fifth Infantry, and Private McIntyre good.

MACARTHUR.

ADJUTANT-GENERAL'S OFFICE,
Washington, June 29, 1900.

MACARTHUR, *Manila:*

Secretary of War instructs me to say there is no objection to explanations and assurances of purpose of this Government based upon the written instruction to new Philippine Commission, and your action stated in dispatch of June 25 is approved.

CORBIN.

WAR DEPARTMENT, *June 29, 1900.*

TAFT, *President, Manila:*

General MacArthur's action described in your dispatch June 25 is approved.

ROOT, *Secwar.*

MANILA. (Received June 30, 1900—6.43 a. m.)

ADJUTANT-GENERAL, *Washington:*

With reference to your telegram of 23, hold two officers of the Corps of Engineers in United States to purchase and ship material for road construction. Requisition by transport *Warren.*

MACARTHUR.

MANILA. (Received July 1, 1900—12.40 a. m.)

ADJUTANT-GENERAL, *Washington:*

General Aquino, prominent commander of insurgent forces, surrendered unconditionally to First Lieut. John J. O'Connell, with Macabebe scouts, June 29, with 64 rifles and ammunition.

MACARTHUR.

MANILA. (Received July 2, 1900—12.46 a. m.)

ADJUTANT-GENERAL, *Washington:*

General Ricarte, leader of threatened uprisings Manila during this year, recently very active, captured July 1 by native police between Paco and Stana. Event important in relation to conditions in Manila.

MACARTHUR.

MANILA. (Received July 2, 1900—4.44 p. m.)

ADJUTANT-GENERAL, *Washington:*

Following deaths have occurred since last report: Dysentery—July 2, William C. Geiger, first lieutenant, Fourteenth Infantry; June 23, E, Fourteenth Infantry, William H. Williams; Company L, Thirty-fifth Infantry, Robert E. Clark; June 21, G, Ninth Infantry, Corpl. Ernest L. Becker; June 12, I, Thirty-first Infantry, William

A. Cole; June 26, B, Thirty-seventh Infantry, Artificer George Floyd; M, Thirty-seventh Infantry, William J. Zeller; June 28, E, Ninth Infantry, Jeremiah Murphy. Drowned—March 28, K, Forty-ninth Infantry, William Lee; June 23, D, Thirteenth Infantry, Clinton Van Veghton; June 17, F, Third Cavalry, Louis Niemis, Harry A. Jones; June 12, M, Eleventh Cavalry, Harry Oswald; June 27, M, Twelfth Infantry, Joseph Groh. Alcoholism—June 23, L, Sixteenth Infantry, Q. M. Sergt. Frank Schmidt. Variola—June 21, H, Forty-eighth Infantry, Leroy C. Jones; June 25, H, Forty-eighth Infantry, Elijah Holland. Cardiac failure—June 28, B, Thirty-seventh Infantry, Ceasor. Died from wounds received in action—June 20, I, Forty-fifth Infantry, Frank Welch. Eclampsia—June 15, Band, Sixteenth Infantry, William Litzinger. Malarial fever—June 17, M, Sixteenth Infantry, Duncan G. Crawford. Pyæmia—June 29, D, Fourth Infantry, John J. Richards. Septicæmia—June 25, K, Third Infantry, Corpl. John W. Wonn. Died from effects of fall—June 28, K, Forty-second Infantry, Ira A. Stevens.

MACARTHUR.

MANILA. (Received July 3, 1900—12.11 p. m.)
ADJUTANT-GENERAL, *Washington:*
Casualties: February 13, Tabaco, Luzon, G, Forty-seventh Infantry, Corpl. Joseph C. Kauffman, thigh, serious; February 1, Albay, Luzon, G, Forty-seventh Infantry, George W. Parker, hand, serious; February 6, G, Forty-seventh Infantry, Capt. George H. Bently, arm, serious; Musician Robert J. Blystone, foot, serious; F, Forty-seventh Infantry, Musician Arthur W. Miles, wounded in leg above knee, serious; Herbert C. Shufelt, thigh, serious; H, Forty-seventh Infantry, Corpl. John W. Walter, arm, slight; Edwin N. North, foot, slight; Homer Gardner, heel, slight; F, Forty-seventh Infantry, Second Lieut. William R. Harrison, both arms, serious; February 2, Legaspi, Luzon, E, Forty-seventh Infantry, Frank B. Sayer, leg above knee, serious; Edward L. Harpster, thigh, serious; Sergt. Charles Craig, head, slight; Sergt. Robert A. Dunn, wounded in shoulder, slight.

MACARTHUR.

MANILA. (Received July 5, 1900—2.05 p. m.)
ADJUTANT-GENERAL, *Washington:*
Killed—July 3, Tibaguin, Luzon, H, Third Infantry, Sergt. Alfred W. Merriam, William Cheatham, Charles Geddy; July 4, near Malolos, G, Third Infantry, Corpl. Albert Goeke, Charles L. Hippler, Patrick Mullen. Wounded—May 29, Polo, Leyte, A, Forty-third Infantry, First Sergt. William Ebbert, abdomen, serious; May 5, D, Forty-third Infantry, Capt. Lucius E. Polk, arm, slight; C, Forty-third Infantry, Musician George R. Shaner, arm, serious; John J. Francis, hand, slight; May 22, Tabaco, Luzon, G, Forty-seventh Infantry, Frank Carney, arm, slight.

MACARTHUR.

ADJUTANT-GENERAL'S OFFICE,
Washington, July 5, 1900.
MACARTHUR, *Manila:*
With reference to your telegram of 30th ultimo, officers of the Corps of Engineers will sail as already ordered. Chief of Engineers, U. S. Army, will arrange purchase supplies road construction.

CORBIN.

MANILA. (Received July 7, 1900—6.40 a. m.)

ADJUTANT-GENERAL, *Washington:*

Killed—July 4, Maniling, Luzon, Company C, Twenty-fourth Infantry, Will Webb; June 10, Atlao, Panay, D, Twenty-sixth Infantry, Frank J. Tague; July 1, Rosario, Cavite, M, Thirty-eighth Infantry, Clyde M. Davis. Wounded—July 4, Maniling, Luzon, C, Twenty-fourth Infantry, Second Lieut. Edward B. Mitchell, shoulder, slight; Thomas Brown, shoulder, moderate; Peñaranda, Luzon, I, Thirty-fourth Infantry, Sergt. Samuel Bardelson, thigh, slight; July 3, Damageo Bridge, Luzon, E, Thirtieth Infantry, First Sergt. Ernest L. Hamilton, arm, slight; Wm. D. Cook, mouth, slight; May 6, Hilongos, Leyte, I, Twenty-third Infantry, transferred H, Twenty-third Infantry, Owen McCaffrey, thigh, slight.

MACARTHUR.

MANILA. (Received July 7, 1900—10.25 a. m.)

ADJUTANT-GENERAL, *Washington:*

Total strength present and absent June 30, ascertained as near as possible: Third Cavalry, officers, 27; enlisted men, 891; Fourth Cavalry, 47, 1,439; Eleventh Cavalry, 48, 1,040. Battery E, First Artillery, 4, 157; Third Artillery, 11, 380; Battery F, Fourth Artillery, 4, 149; Battery F, Fifth Artillery, 4, 138; Sixth Artillery, 40, 1,404. Third Infantry, 43, 1,436; Fourth Infantry, 45, 1,410; Sixth Infantry, 45, 1,214; Ninth Infantry, 49, 1,439, Taku, China; Twelfth Infantry, 42, 1,420; Thirteenth Infantry, 45, 1,375; Fourteenth Infantry, 45, 1,493; Sixteenth Infantry, 45, 1,295; Seventeenth Infantry, 45, 1,407; Eighteenth Infantry, 46, 1,360; Nineteenth Infantry, 46, 1,418; Twentieth Infantry, 43, 1,424; Twenty-first Infantry, 46, 1,395; Twenty-second Infantry, 41, 1,381; Twenty-third Infantry, 46, 1,650; Twenty-fourth Infantry, 37, 1,030; Twenty-fifth Infantry, 36, 1,080; Twenty-sixth Infantry, 50, 1,230; Twenty-seventh Infantry, 49, 1,252; Twenty-eighth Infantry, 50, 1,266; Twenty-ninth Infantry, 50, 1,233; Thirtieth Infantry, 50, 1,260; Thirty-first Infantry, 50, 1,217; Thirty-second Infantry, 50, 1,186; Thirty-third Infantry, 50, 1,229; Thirty-fourth Infantry, 49, 1,231; Thirty-fifth Infantry, 50, 1,242; Thirty-sixth Infantry, 49, 969; Thirty-seventh Infantry, 49, 1,017; Thirty-eighth Infantry, 50, 1,228; Thirty-ninth Infantry, 49, 1,235; Fortieth Infantry, 48, 1,228; Forty-first Infantry, 50, 1,292; Forty-second Infantry, 49, 1,061; Forty-third Infantry, 50, 1,240; Forty-fourth Infantry, 50, 1,260; Forty-fifth Infantry, 49, 1,248; Forty-sixth Infantry, 50, 1,250; Forty-seventh Infantry, 50, 1,256; Forty-eighth Infantry, 49, 1,309; Forty-ninth Infantry, 48, 1,260. Company A, Battalion Engineers, Company B, Battalion Engineers, 4, 250. Signal Corps, 25, 410. Hospital Corps, 78, 2,364. Total, 2,225, 61,059. Acting assistant surgeons, 218.

MACARTHUR.

MANILA. (Received July 8, 1900—7.32 a. m.)

ADJUTANT-GENERAL, *Washington:*

With reference to your telegram of 24th ultimo, in relation to returning cannon, Spanish authorities solicitous for answer.

MACARTHUR.

ADJUTANT-GENERAL'S OFFICE,
Washington, July 9, 1900.

MACARTHUR, *Manila:*

Secretary of War decides Spain has no just claim for arms captured from insurgents. Return of cannon refused.

CORBIN.

AFFAIRS IN THE PHILIPPINE ISLANDS. 1189

MANILA. (Received July 9, 1900—2 p. m.)

ADJUTANT-GENERAL, *Washington:*

The following deaths have occurred since last report: Dysentery—June 18, C, Twenty-second Infantry, Daniel Lynch; June 11, A, Twenty-second Infantry, Herbert E. Ellis; June 2, B, Thirty-second Infantry, Samuel Dearmond; June 4, F, Thirty-sixth Infantry, Jesse E. Barlow; June 1, D, Sixteenth Infantry, Martin J. Conway; June 27, C, Nineteenth Infantry, William Rauch; Eighteenth Infantry, unassigned, Charles Grimm; June 25, L, Sixth Infantry, John J. Coyle; June 4, D, Thirty-ninth Infantry, James A. Keller; July 3, A, Ninth Infantry, Cook Adolph Hug; July 5, G, Seventeenth Infantry, Wm. J. Regar; July 3, H, Forty-sixth Infantry, Oscar Peterson; July 4, M, Thirty-eighth Infantry, Benjamin M. Kerr; July 2, I, Thirtieth Infantry, Frank O'Brien; July 1, A, Thirty-ninth Infantry, Julius Anderson; July 7, C, Thirty-fourth Infantry, Matt. Ekola. Typhoid fever—July 3, K, Thirty-third Infantry, Wm. H. Bostwick; June 18, C, Twenty-sixth Infantry, John E. Farrell; July 4, B, Thirty-fourth Infantry, Corpl. Charles W. Gilpin; July 6, B, Thirtieth Infantry, Henry G. Blaesing. Died from wounds received in action—June 26, C, Twenty-sixth Infantry, Peter Dutran; June 16, C, Twenty-sixth Infantry, Thomas Gavigan; January 15, M, Third Cavalry, Austin A. Withers. Malarial fever—June 27, C, Forty-ninth Infantry, Thomas E. Swann; June 17, L, Twenty-first Infantry, Sergt. Henry N. Hall; July 2, G, Forty-sixth Infantry, Corpl. Samuel E. Regnier. Tuberculosis—July 2, L, Forty-seventh Infantry, Samuel C. Jackman; June 30, C, Thirty-ninth Infantry, Everette Kerbey; June 4, M, Sixth Infantry, Charles E. Ordd. Variola—July 3, H, Third Artillery, George L. Cross; July 2, D, Forty-eighth Infantry, Noah Lenoir; June 27, D, Forty-eighth Infantry, Henry Ballenger. Drowned—April 4, K, Twenty-second Infantry, Paul Fox. Pneumonia—June 24, F, Nineteenth Infantry, Edward G. Lane. Scorbutus—June 29, M, Eighteenth Infantry, Thomas M. Gray. Diarrhea—June 10, B, Twenty-second Infantry, Charles G. Peters. Mercurial poisoning, accidental—July 1, Hospital Corps, Joe A. Jarvis. Carcinoma—June 24, C, Twenty-second Infantry, James F. Kelly. Enterocolitis—July 1, H, Thirteenth Infantry, Philip Bindnagel. Peritonitis—July 6, H, Fourteenth Infantry, Q. M. Sergt. Charles T. Stowe.

MACARTHUR.

MANILA. (Received July 12, 1900—2 a. m.)

ADJUTANT-GENERAL, *Washington:*

Killed—July 8, Cabanatuan, K, Thirty-fourth Infantry, Oatis Harrison; Lapo, Luzon, F, Thirty-third Infantry, John W. Spencer. Wounded—April 26, La Paz, Leyte, I, Twenty-third Infantry, William Murphy, wounded in hip, serious.

MACARTHUR.

MANILA. (Received July 14, 1900—3.55 a. m.)

ADJUTANT-GENERAL, *Washington:*

Killed—June 18, Dumargas, Panay, C, Twenty-sixth Infantry, Thomas Lee. Wounded—June 27, Dumargas, Panay, F, Twenty-sixth Infantry, Corpl. Chas. S. Salmon, wounded in hand, slight; July 6, Taal, Luzon, C, Twenty-eighth Infantry, Hugh Clemerts, groin, serious; B, Twenty-eighth Infantry, Elmer G. Marsh, thigh, serious; Los. H. Roberts, back, serious; Sergt. Philip S. Gardner, foot, serious; D, Twenty-eighth Infantry, William Lynn, knee, slight; Samuel Franklin, knee, slight; June 20, Naga, Cebu, M, Nineteenth Infantry, John W. Bowling, arm, serious; James R. Hezlep, arm, slight; June 23, Florida Blanca, I, Thirty-second Infantry;

Corp. Henry G. Manning, leg above knee, slight; July 8, Lapo, Luzon, F, Thirty-third Infantry, Corpl. Charles E. Reynolds, slightly wounded. Died, gunshot wound, accidental—Charles A. Camel, band, Twenty-fourth Infantry, July 10.

MACARTHUR.

SAN FRANCISCO, CAL., *July 14, 1900*.
ADJUTANT-GENERAL, *Washington, D. C.:*
Transport *Hancock* arrived last night with battalion Eighteenth Infantry, number sick and prisoners. Particulars later.

SHAFTER, *Major-General.*

MANILA. (Received July 17, 1900—9 a. m.)
ADJUTANT-GENERAL, *Washington:*
Killed—January 31, San Isidro, Luzon, B, Thirty-fourth Infantry, Fred L. Williamson. Wounded—June 22, Malabagun, Luzon, D, Eleventh Cavalry, Andrew Workosky, hand, slight; June 24, Ligao, Luzon, I, Forty-seventh Infantry, Musician Robert R. Lynch, arm, slight; June 18, Guinobatan, Luzon, B, Eleventh Cavalry, Alexander D. Wipf, face, serious; June 24, Dumangas, Panay, L, Twenty-sixth Infantry, Michael Morrissey, head, slight

MACARTHUR.

MANILA. (Received July 17, 1900—5.20 p. m.)
ADJUTANT-GENERAL, *Washington:*
Following deaths have occurred since last report: Dysentery—May 27, D, Twenty-sixth Infantry, Sergt. Earl H. Peck; May 30, H, Forty-fourth Infantry, Jerry Deaton; July 14, A, Thirty-third Infantry, Hugh B. Duncan; July 7, F, Thirty-third Infantry, James E. McIntosh; July 6, K, Twenty-fifth Infantry, Musician Thomas G. Wilburn; July 9, L, Thirteenth Infantry, Morris Gordon; D, Thirty-second Infantry, Joseph M. Judy; M, Thirty-fourth Infantry, Albert M. Seeholts; July 10, M, Fourth Cavalry, Farrier George Farrow; July 8, B, Thirty-fifth Infantry, William Burke; June 27, B, Forty-fifth Infantry, Harry W. Thomas; June 2, B, Twenty-second Infantry, Charles Miller; June 28, K, Sixth Infantry, Thomas Sellers; July 12, H, Fourteenth Infantry, Joseph B. Moller; July 13, A, Twenty-first Infantry, John F. Young. Myocarditis—July 10, K, Fourth Cavalry, Willis L. McFarland. Purpura hæmorrhagica—June 16, G, Thirty-ninth Infantry, Gustave D. Dobel. Typhoid fever—May 30, K, Fortieth Infantry, Joseph Smith; June 21, A, Forty-third Infantry, Frederick S. Suter; June 2, E, Signal Corps, U. S. Army, Frank B. Burbank; March 14, L, Thirty-fifth Infantry, William Dowel. Variola—July 7, K, Forty-eighth Infantry, Louis Mitchell; July 9, I, Forty-sixth Infantry, Edward Rose; May 28, H, Forty-eighth Infantry, Albert Carter; March 26, E, Thirty-fourth Infantry, Albert L. Brown; February 24, L, Thirty-third Infantry, Vollie Knight. Died from wounds received in action—July 5, I, Twenty-third Infantry, William Murphy; July 6, I, Forty-ninth Infantry, Samuel Hardy. Diarrhea—July 8, A, Forty-fifth Infantry, Julius Johannsen; July 6, E, Forty-sixth Infantry, Cook George E. Manson. Drowned—July 8, A, Third Cavalry, George W. Robinson; Corpl. Calvin H. Eoff. Tuberculosis—July 8, Thirteenth Infantry, Sergt. Maj. George Binns. Typhlitis—July 8, A, Forty-ninth Infantry, Josh Lane. Suicide—Shot, head, July 7, L, Thirteenth Infantry, Oliver E. Green. Injuries while fighting—June 16, H, Forty-fourth Infantry, Elijah Webb. Alcoholism—July 9, H, Thirty-seventh Infantry, Edward Costello. Phthisis—June 29, D, Sixth Infantry, Alfred B. Congar. Malarial fever—June 30, D, Ninth Infantry, James H. McNerney; June 22, F, Twenty-

second Infantry, Samuel C. Wilson. Enterocolitis—June 11, H, Sixteenth Infantry, George W. Frey. Cause unreported—May 17, E, Fortieth Infantry, James L. Williams; April 5, K, Forty-seventh Infantry, William Fitzgerald; June 5, C, Twenty-sixth Infantry, Ivan L. Mills; May 4, C, Forty-seventh Infantry, Corpl. Ellis L. Guss. Pericarditis—March 17, M, Sixteenth Infantry, James Patten.

MacArthur.

MANILA. (Received July 19, 1900—10 a. m.)
Adjutant-General, *Washington:*
Killed—July 2, Legaspi, Luzon, F, Forty-seventh Infantry, John Pierce; June 30, Guinobatan, Luzon, B, Eleventh Cavalry, Sergt. Guy A. Furr; June 14, Tagatay, Luzon, H, Forty-seventh Infantry, Sergt. Frank W. Burns; July 15, Cabangan, Luzon, K, Twenty-fifth Infantry, Sergt. James R. Lightfoot; F, Twenty-fifth Infantry, Corpl. James Ward; July 19, Calamba, Luzon, E, Signal Corps, Sergt. Albert H. Cockayne. Wounded—July 14, Llana Hermosa, H, Thirty-second Infantry, Artificer Joseph Mallonee, thigh, serious; E, Thirty-second Infantry, Corpl. Edd F. Feist, leg above knee, slight.

MacArthur.

MANILA. (Received July 20, 1900—8.02 a. m.)
Adjutant-General, *Washington:*
Killed—July 11, Manadaan, Panay, G, Twenty-sixth Infantry, John Cullinane. Wounded—July 3, Tibaguin, Luzon, H, Third Infantry, Herman F. Burdt; Charles Wade, arm, serious.

MacArthur.

Adjutant-General's Office,
Washington, July 19, 1900.
MacArthur, *Manila:*
Secretary War directs on arrival battalion Third Regiment U. S. Artillery from San Francisco, consolidate the battalions with you into one at maximum strength, long-term men. Return other San Francisco for recruitment.

Corbin.

MANILA. (Received July 23, 1900—11.55 a. m.)
Adjutant-General, *Washington:*
Following deaths have occurred since last report: Dysentery—July 18, G, Forty-sixth Infantry, Charles W. Wild G, Fourth Cavalry, Hugh McRobert; July 19, G, Thirty-ninth Infantry, Corpl. Lanier Schley; E, Ninth Infantry, Frank Jacobs; July 15, M, Thirty-ninth Infantry, Archibald Roberts; June 28, E, Fortieth Infantry, George Oliver; June 7, Corpl. Albert G. Hemphill; July 17, M, Twentieth Infantry, Louis Eckhardt; July 3, G, Nineteenth Infantry, Louis Derr; July 16, H, Forty-first Infantry, Felix G. Crane; July 9, M, Fortieth Infantry, Frederick G. Burto; July 14, C, Forty-first Infantry, Sergt. Samuel H. Bevan; July 17, F, Thirtieth Infantry, Emil S. Sorensen. Enterocolitis—July 18, A, Fourth Cavalry, Joseph H. Shibley. Typhoid fever—July 20, D, Forty-third Infantry, Patrick H. Harrington. Variola—July 17, K, Forty-eighth Infantry, Corpl. Fletcher Williams; July 16, Al Wallace; July 14, Sergt. Samuel Taylor; July 19, Thomas Tolbert. Bronchitis—July 11, F, Eighteenth Infantry, Sergt. James Jones. Pneumonia—July 19, L, Third Cavalry, Edward Shilling. Erysipelas—July 18, M, Thirty-fifth Infantry, John Finncan. Killed by comrade—July 7, K, Forty-fourth Infantry, Enick L.

Allen. Malarial fever—July 10, A, Twenty-sixth Infantry, Frank A. Smith. Anæmia—June 5, F, Fortieth Infantry, Frank Hankley. Heart disease—July 20, D, Nineteenth Infantry; First Sergt. Thomas Burke; July 17, Ord. Sergt. Frederick Miller.

MacArthur.

Manila. (Received July 24, 1900—2.05 p. m.)

Adjutant-General, *Washington:*

Killed—July 21, Badoc, Luzon, F, Signal Corps, Sergt. Warren Billman; May 28, Labo, Luzon, B, Forty-fifth Infantry, James M. Philips; June 4, Dumangas, Panay, C, Twenty-sixth Infantry, Adelbert F. Cole; June 24, Hilongos, Leyte, A, Forty-fourth Infantry, Walter C. Booth; Sergt. Percy Hampson. Wounded—July 15, Tiamo, Luzon, G, Thirty-ninth Infantry, Corpl. Mark E. Lashley, knee, slight; July 18, Magadalena, Luzon, E, Eleventh Cavalry, Clyde J. Schrader, hip, slight; K, Thirty-seventh Infantry, Sergt. Fred Bombacher, arm, slight.

MacArthur.

Manila. (Received July 25, 1900—3.22 a. m.)

Adjutant-General, *Washington:*

Following telegram from alcalde of recently formed municipal government, Vigan, Luzon, is transmitted: "President, Washington: Alcalde and municipal council Vigan, installed under General Young's supervision, salute you and tender firm allegiance. Rivero, Alcalde."

MacArthur.

Manila. (Received July 26, 1900—4.35 a. m.)

Adjutant-General, *Washington:*

One hundred and seventeen stations without medical officers; something over 10,000 men with inadequate medical attendance; a large number of which without attention at all. In this connection refer to letter June 7 and cable July 14, Charles R. Greenleaf, deputy surgeon-general. John C. Bates remarks to-day, with regard to his department, that conditions are intolerable, and that remedial action has become imperative, in which view I concur and urgently request comprehensive and generous consideration of subject, and immediate dispatch 100 medical officers and 300 Hospital Corps men.

MacArthur.

Manila. (Received July 27, 1900—10.07 a. m.)

Adjutant-General, *Washington:*

Killed—July 21, Tanauan, Batangas, L, Thirty-eighth Infantry, James E. Easterly; E, Thirty-eighth Infantry, James S. Skaggs; July 22, Mount Corona, Luzon, C, Thirty-fourth Infantry, Albert Fryberger, William Hunter. Wounded—Sibert P. Aaron, wounded in thigh, slight; Capt. George E. Gibson, wounded in shoulder, face, serious; Oscar Lake, thigh, moderate; Charles Wright, knee, serious; Edward P. Frank, abdomen, serious; F, Twenty-second Infantry, William Mosby, chest, moderate; Musician John Montgomery, arm, moderate; July 24, Batangas, Luzon, B, Thirty-eighth Infantry, Robert C. Whitson, thigh, moderate; July 22, Cabanatuan, Luzon, K, Thirty-fourth Infantry, William Stratton, hand, slight; July 23, Batangas, Luzon, D, Thirty-eighth Infantry, William E. Lane, thigh, moderate.

MacArthur.

NAGASAKI, JAPAN. (Received July 27, 1900—10.10 p. m.)
ADJUTANT-GENERAL, *Washington:*
 Relief, Nagasaki, June 26, Claude D. Leslie, I, Fourteenth Infantry died of disease contracted in line of duty, dysentery; remains will be shipped San Francisco. Civilian employee, Arthur Hennessy, drowned June 21, buried Nagasaki.
HARRY O. PERLEY.

ADJUTANT-GENERAL'S OFFICE,
Washington, July 27, 1900.
MACARTHUR, *Manila:*
 With reference to your telegram of 26th, Secretary of War directs that you be advised medical officers will be sent as soon as possible. In the meantime medical officers there will, of course, be distributed best advantage. Every request yourself and General Otis for medical officers to July 14, has been promptly filled. You are authorized to make transfers from the line of the Army to Hospital Corps. Cable semimonthly number sick in hospitals of division.
CORBIN.

SAN FRANCISCO, CAL., *July 27, 1900.*
(Received 7.08 p. m.)
ADJUTANT-GENERAL, *Washington, D. C.:*
 Transport *Warren* arrived this day from Manila; particulars will be telegraphed later. (Battalion Twenty-third Infantry on board.)
SHAFTER, *Major-General.*

MANILA. (Received July 29, 1900—12.18 a. m.)
ADJUTANT-GENERAL, *Washington:*
 Nothing discouraging regarding health army; on contrary, comparative little sickness, not in excess of 9 per cent at any time since January 1. The greatest difficulty is from a large number medical officers required to give adequate service at the numerous stations into which army is necessarily divided. If officers have been sent to include call Chief Surgeon of July 14, as stated in accordance with your message July 27, this difficulty will soon be removed.
MACARTHUR.

MANILA. (Received July 30, 1900—2.55 a. m.)
ADJUTANT-GENERAL, *Washington:*
 Wounded—July 21, Lipa, Luzon, G, Thirty-eighth Infantry, Ben. F. Lillard, wounded in thigh, serious, both; E, Thirty-eighth Infantry, Vernon A. Adams, leg above knee, moderate; July 26, Panguil, Luzon, L, Thirty-seventh Infantry, Sergt. Robert McHaffy, arm, slight; E, Thirty-seventh Infantry, Edward M. Baytel, knee, serious; Joseph Flewelling, thigh, moderate; July 11, Lambuanao, Panay, G, Twenty-sixth Infantry, Edward C. Stone, thigh, slight; May 14, Loculan, Mindanao, C, Fortieth Infantry, Walter Lawrence, back, slight; Joseph W. Eastman, arm, serious; Corpl. Ross L. Pillsbury, thigh, serious; First Sergt. Walter C. Winkler, arm, serious.
MACARTHUR.

MANILA. (Received July 30, 1900—1 p. m.)

ADJUTANT-GENERAL, *Washington:*

Following deaths have occurred since last report: Dysentery—July 23, M, Thirtieth Infantry, Harry Caldwell; K, Twenty-first Infantry, Corpl. William L. Pierce; July 14, D, Twenty-sixth Infantry, John Baker; I, Eighteenth Infantry, Dennis Condon; July 25, C, Twelfth Infantry, Jerry Claypool; M, Thirty-ninth Infantry, Wallace McIntosh; July 10, B, Nineteenth Infantry, Samuel H. Dillon; July 16, F, Fortieth Infantry, Corpl. Fred. C. Gleason; July 21, A, Twentieth Infantry, Harry Jacobs; July 24, L, Thirtieth Infantry, Joseph W. Martin; July 18, K, Eighteenth Infantry, William Picken; July 19, K, Twenty-sixth Infantry, John Quinn; July 6, G, Fortieth Infantry, Clarence E. Ward. Diarrhea—July 15, F, Forty-fifth Infantry, Guy W. Henderson. Variola—July 18, K, Twenty-fourth Infantry, Levie Williams; July 22, F, Thirtieth Infantry, Elza Kline; July 27, D, Twenty-first Infantry; Albert C. Mercer. Malarial fever—July 25, H, Thirty-fifth Infantry, First Sergt. Ernest Edelsten; D, Twelfth Infantry, Musician Milton M. Roeder. Abscess liver—July 24, M, Thirty-ninth Infantry, Charles H. Murray; D, Thirty-ninth Infantry, Fred Stephens. Gastroenteritis—June 5, I, Forty-fifth Infantry, Q. M. Sergt. Morton H. Cook. Peritonitis—July 25, I, Twenty-first Infantry, Corpl. Erasmus Belk. Colitis—July 16, A, Twenty-sixth Infantry, Claude Taber. Drowned—July 20, A, Seventeenth Infantry, Earl E. Guyton. Murdered by comrade—July 23, I, Twenty-fifth Infantry, Shannon Proffett. Sprue—July 21, B, Twentieth Infantry, James O. Driver. Pneumonia—July 24, H, Thirty-fifth Infantry, William H. McNamara.

MACARTHUR.

MANILA. (Received July 31, 1900—6 a. m.)

ADJUTANT-GENERAL, *Washington:*

Paterno, who accepted American sovereignty some time ago, requested permission to organize banquet and fiesta, to last Saturday and Sunday, and assured me the ceremonies would be confined exclusively to celebrating the amnesty and expressing thanks to the United States therefor. Every facility was afforded to insure success, but strong tendency to questionable mottoes on arches. Aguinaldo's portrait and extreme sentiment entertained by speakers assigned to toasts necessitated considerable interference with programme arranged by Filipino committee. No speeches were made, and organized demonstration was practically a failure. The people were allowed unrestricted liberty on the streets for forty-eight hours and enjoyed the opportunity to the fullest limit as a popular holiday. The fiesta may be regarded as a great success. Military precautions were very complete, but there was absolutely no disposition to violence of any kind, and everything passed off very smoothly.

MACARTHUR.

MANILA. (Received July 31, 1900—7.10 a. m.)

ADJUTANT-GENERAL, *Washington:*

Sick, hospitals, 3,755; quarters, 1,081; 8.04 per cent.

MACARTHUR.

MANILA. (Received July 31, 1900—6 a. m.)

ADJUTANT-GENERAL, *Washington:*

Request authority to disburse when necessary under page 11, General Orders, No. 76, during recovery enlisted men.

MACARTHUR.

AFFAIRS IN THE PHILIPPINE ISLANDS. 1195

ADJUTANT-GENERAL'S OFFICE,
Washington, August 2, 1900.
MacArthur, Manila:
In returning to the United States sick soldiers, Secretary of War desires, in view of approaching end term of service volunteers, necessity soon bringing them to San Francisco and probability little if any service will be rendered from those in hospital, you be especially liberal in returning sick volunteers, but without injustice to regulars in condition requiring return; descriptive list in each case to accompany soldier. As soon as ready to enlarge your native volunteer force, authority will be telegraphed.

CORBIN.

ADJUTANT-GENERAL'S OFFICE,
Washington, August 2, 1900.
MacArthur, Manila:
Two thousand shotguns with ammunition Grant.

CORBIN.

MANILA. (Received August 2, 1900—2.47 a. m.)
Adjutant-General, Washington:
Transport Thomas sailed August 1. Mrs. Emerson H. Liscum aboard. Acting Asst. Surg. F. W. Hulseberg killed by insurgents 8.30 morning, August 1, near Majayjay, Luzon.

MACARTHUR.

SAN FRANCISCO, CAL., August 2, 1900.
(Received 3.18 p. m.)
Adjutant-General, Washington, D. C.:
Transport Meade sailed at 5 yesterday afternoon with * * * Company E, Battalion Engineers, 4 officers, 145 men; field, staff, band, Troops B, G, H, and I, Third Cavalry, 10 officers, 369 men; field, staff, Companies I, K, L, and M, Fifteenth Infantry, 13 officers, 512 men. Rifle and carbine ammunition—430 rounds per man Engineer Company; 487 rounds per man Third Cavalry; 419 rounds per man Fifteenth Infantry. Revolver ammunition—750 rounds Engineer Company; 72,000 rounds Third Cavalry; 9,000 rounds Fifteenth Infantry. Lieutenant-Colonel Williams, Fifteenth Infantry, commanding troops on transport.

SHAFTER, Major-General.

MANILA. (Received August 4, 1900—2.15 a. m.)
Adjutant-General, Washington:
Killed—July 26, Sariaya, Luzon, F, Thirtieth Infantry, Ellis Kindred, Charles J. Kriger; July 12, Oroquieta, Mindanao, I, Fortieth Infantry, Sergt. Ira N. Stanley. Wounded—Sergt. Harry N. Emmert, chest, slight; April 26, La Paz, Leyte, I, Twenty-third Infantry, Sergt. Gottlieb D. Schlewing, head, slight; Frank J. Knoffke, head, slight; June 30, Pavia, Panay, K, Twenty-sixth Infantry, Otto M. Utz, elbow, slight; July 21, Badoc, Luzon, G, Twelfth Infantry, Corpl. Thomas Smith, leg above knee, slight; Frederick B. Conklin, hand, slight; Arthur Saiter, leg above knee, slight; March 26, Calbayog, Leyte, G, Forty-third Infantry, Charles E. Mesick, hand, slight.

MACARTHUR.

CORRESPONDENCE.

MANILA. (Received August 4, 1900—10.20 a. m.)
ADJUTANT-GENERAL, *Washington:*
First Lieutenant Altstaetter, Corps of Engineers, U. S. Army, with escort 15 men, attacked, August 1, road between San Miguel de Mayumo, Luzon, and San Isidro, Luzon, by armed band insurgents, reported 350 strong. Entire party killed, wounded, or captured. Killed—Troop H, Fourth Cavalry, Richard Tischler. Wounded—Charles M. Newman, arm, serious; Walter Brewer, arm, serious; Company A, Battalion Engineers, Edward Long, abdomen, serious. Captured: Lieutenant Altstaetter; Company A, Battalion of Engineers, Henry T. Crenshaw, Henry J. Walsh; Troop H, Fourth Cavalry, Arthur Bates, Charles J. Luchsinger, Edward J. Cromer, George Knaub, William J. Gerity, John Coughlan, Robert F. Taylor, Joseph F. Mealey. Wounded sent San Isidro with note from Lacuna Maraimo announcing prisoners would be well treated.

MACARTHUR.

MANILA. (Received August 5, 1900—6.47 a. m.)
ADJUTANT-GENERAL, *Washington:*
Seven men, Company I, Twenty-fourth Infantry, en route from Cabaṇtuan to San José, were ambushed near Talavera August 1 by about 20 insurgents. Killed—Sergt. Charles H. Smith, Elijah Bethel, Eddie Fields. Captured—George W. Jackson, Robert H. Brooks. Captured men released by Sandico Marasmo.

MACARTHUR.

MANILA. (Received August 6, 1900—3.25 p. m.)
ADJUTANT-GENERAL, *Washington:*
Following deaths have occurred since last report: Dysentery—July 25, D, Thirtieth Infantry, Francis L. Tate; Company L, Thirtieth Infantry, Miles Joiner; July 29, Hospital Corps, George Wetzel; Company C, Forty-sixth Infantry, John Ellery, August 2, I, Twenty-seventh Infantry, John B. Wright; July 18, K, Thirty-first Infantry, Cook John C. McDaniel; July 22, I, Eighteenth Infantry, William H. Baker; July 31, Company I, Twenty-first Infantry, Daniel J. Breslin; Company B, Thirty-ninth Infantry, Joseph Collins; Company K, Third Infantry, John Jordan; July 21, Company D, Eighteenth Infantry, John Cerveny; July 17, Company G, Fortieth Infantry, Sam M. Daum; July 24, Company A, Twenty-sixth Infantry, William L. Daly; July 23, Company G, Thirty-first Infantry, James J. Cunningham; June 25, Company I, Thirty-first Infantry, Charles Hestilow; July 26, Company M, Thirty-first Infantry, Corpl. John A. Henderly; July 30, Company M, Thirty-seventh Infantry, William T. Hedges; Company E, Forty-second Infantry, Sergt. Frank Lange; August 1, Company B, Thirtieth Infantry, Corpl. Gustave Fromberg; July 28, Company B, Third Infantry, Russell Knapp; July 27, Company B, Sixth Infantry, John Hines; August 3, Company A, Thirtieth Infantry, George J. Schuster; Company B, Forty-first Infantry, Claud Wynn. Malarial fever—August 2, Company I, Thirty-fifth Infantry, Frank E. Annis; July 29, Company B, Forty-first Infantry, Musician Abraham H. Brubaker; Company E, Thirtieth Infantry, Charles E. Larsen; July 26, Company L, Thirty-fourth Infantry, Otis D. Cole; July 27, Company C, Thirty-first Infantry, Corpl. William E. Harney; July 31, Troop M, Fourth Cavalry, John W. Malakie; August 3, Company B, Thirty-seventh Infantry, Jesse S. Alexander; July 14, Company H, Forty-seventh Infantry, Wort Skinner. Typhoid fever—July 31, Company M, Thirty-seventh Infantry, Leon D. Cooledge; July 30, Company L, Thirtieth Infantry, Sergt. Joel R. Linsley; August 2, Company E, Forty-second Infantry, George I. Risner; August 3, Company G, Twenty-seventh Infantry, Andrew Muller. Variola—August 2, Company K, Forty-eighth Infantry, William

H. Bothwell; July 24, Company M, Thirtieth Infantry, William Brown; July 29, Company K, Twenty-fourth Infantry, Clarence Byrd; July 26, Company G, Thirtieth Infantry, Sergt. George Conley; July 31, Company K, Forty-eighth Infantry, Ulysses G. Heath; Company E, Forty-eighth Infantry, Moses Thomas; July 28, Company C, Thirty-third Infantry, Tilden H. Hayes; July 25, Company A, Thirtieth Infantry, Charles Pearson. Diarrhea—August 1, Company A, Thirteenth Infantry, Jacob Heinz; Company G, Eleventh Cavalry, Victor E. Sigler; July 30, Troop B, Fourth Cavalry, James A. Greens. Drowned—July 21, Company C, Forty-ninth Infantry, John Evans; July 22, Company F, Forty-fourth Infantry, Jesse G. Jackson. Died from wounds received in action—July 25, Company K, Forty-third Infantry, Thomas Mixon; August 1, Company H, Third Infantry, James Gray. Heart disease—August 1, Company E, Thirty-eighth Infantry, Asa T. Johns. Pericarditis—July 31, Company E, Fourth Infantry, John Crook. Shot while resisting arrest, having deserted— July 27, July 29, Company B, Twenty-ninth Infantry, Musician Joe Corren, Walter J. Mickler. Pneumonia—July 27, Company M, Twenty-sixth Infantry, Fred. Richter. Apoplexy—July 30, Company B, Thirty-ninth Infantry, John Porter. Overdose morphine—July 29, Company G, Forty-sixth Infantry, Percy Schryver. Pyæmia— July 20, Company A, Thirty-Fourth Infantry, William R. Davis. Acute mania— August 2, Company A, Seventeenth Infantry, Charles H. Faber.

MACARTHUR.

MANILA. (Received August 7, 1900—8.06 a. m.)
ADJUTANT-GENERAL, *Washington:*
With reference to your telegram of 2d, can not recommend any enlargement native volunteer command; conditions not propitious, nor, generally speaking, can natives be trusted. At present have 450 Macabebes, Major Batson's squadron, and 1,200 men in detachments, Samar, Leyte, Panay, Cebu, Negros, Luzon; these have been selected because of supposed loyalty American interests. The arming of native police with shot guns, revolvers, will add at least 3,000 men to armed force available for semimilitary duty. This is all can stand at present and more than I would risk, were it not for necessary reduction American troops early date.

MACARTHUR.

ADJUTANT-GENERAL'S OFFICE,
Washington, August 7, 1900.
MACARTHUR, *Manila:*
With reference to your telegram of 31st ultimo, page 11, General Orders, No. 76, disbursement $180,000 now confined to disbursements by chief commissaries in United States for returning organizations, and companies convalescents San Francisco. Secretary of War directs this policy must not be changed and disapproves request.

CORBIN.

MANILA. (Received August 8, 1900—10.41 a. m.)
ADJUTANT-GENERAL, *Washington:*
Left Manila April 3 in canoe for Apalit, have heard nothing since, dropped from rolls June 15, as killed by ladrones—Company K, Infantry, Sergt. George Deaner, Q. M. Sergt. Cornelius Sheehan, Christ E. Hansen. Wounded—July 31, Boac, Marinduque, Company A, Twenty-ninth Infanty, First Sergt. James T. Ellis, arm, serious; Corpl. Jefferson A. Upshaw, chest, slight; July 25, Palistina, Luzon, Troop I, Eleventh Cavalry, Lewis Rickle, leg above knee, moderate; August 1, Santa

Cruz, Luzon, Company H, Thirty-seventh Infantry, John M. Payne, buttock, slight; July 21, Bangued, Luzon, Company C, Thirty-third Infantry, Thomas J. Mallory, neck, serious, back, serious; June 30, Anistac, Luzon, Company F, Forty-seventh Infantry, William E. Fitzpatrick, thorax, serious; July 26, Sariaya, Luzon, Company F, Thirtieth Infantry, Oliver F. Gardner, chest, serious; August 4, Cavinti, Luzon, Company K, Thirty-seventh Infantry, Walter Heck, thigh, moderate; July 26, Siniloan, Luzon, Acting Asst. Surg. John G. Byrne, arm, slight.

MacArthur.

SAN FRANCISCO, CAL., *August 8, 1900.*
(Received 3.45 p. m.)

ADJUTANT-GENERAL, *Washington, D. C.:*

Garonne sailed 5 p. m. yesterday from Seattle; carries 21 officers, First Cavalry; * * * 745 enlisted men, First Cavalry. *Pakling* sailed 5.35 p. m. yesterday, carrying two officers, First Cavalry; * * * 3 enlisted, First Cavalry; 889 horses, First Cavalry; 12 mules.

SHAFTER, *Major-General.*

MANILA. (Received August 9, 1900—9.17 a. m.)

ADJUTANT-GENERAL, *Washington:*

Letters Surgeon-General of the Army, June 19, June 23, apparently reduce by half medical supplies and hospital stores requisition for quarter (or part) ending December 31. Dr. Charles R. Greenleaf submits formal report declaring if thus reduced supplies insufficient properly care for sick and wounded. Understand as matter of course Department is eager to do everything essential for this army, but seems some misconception exists as to medical necessity. Dr. Greenleaf has studied situation carefully and intelligently. Am satisfied will not be safe to ignore his advice, therefore recommend filling requisition in full. Impossible to make mistake side of prudence.

MacArthur.

MANILA. (Received August 9, 1900—12.23 p. m.)

ADJUTANT-GENERAL, *Washington:*

Total strength present and absent July 31, ascertained as near as possible: Third Cavalry, officers 27, enlisted men 884; Fourth Cavalry, 46, 1,440; Eleventh Cavalry, 48, 1,035; Philippine cavalry, natives, 13, 452. Battery E, First Artillery, 4, 153; Third Artillery, 11, 374; Battery F, Fourth Artillery, 4, 146; Battery F, Fifth Artillery, 4, 133, Taku; Sixth Artillery, 39, 1,408. Third Infantry, 44, 1,436; Fourth Infantry, 45, 1,406; Sixth Infantry, 44, 1,419; Ninth Infantry, 49, 1,419, Taku; Twelfth Infantry, 42, 1,436; Thirteenth Infantry, 45, 1,354; Fourteenth Infantry, 45, 1,491, Taku; Sixteenth Infantry, 45, 1,441; Seventeenth Infantry, 44, 1,431; Eighteenth Infantry, 46, 1,354; Nineteenth Infantry, 46, 1,415; Twentieth Infantry, 42, 1,436; Twenty-first Infantry, 46, 1,390; Twenty-second Infantry, 41, 1,400; Twenty-third Infantry, 46, 1,651; Twenty-fourth Infantry, 39, 1,026; Twenty-fifth Infantry, 36, 1,073; Twenty-sixth Infantry, 50, 1,226; Twenty-seventh Infantry, 49, 1,248; Twenty-eighth Infantry, 50, 1,265; Twenty-ninth Infantry, 50, 1,230; Thirtieth Infantry, 50, 1,244; Thirty-first Infantry, 50, 1,212; Thirty-second Infantry, 50, 1,279; Thirty-third Infantry, 50, 1,232; Thirty-fourth Infantry, 49, 1,223; Thirty-fifth Infantry, 50, 1,237; Thirty-sixth Infantry, 50, 957; Thirty-seventh Infantry, 49, 1,015; Thirty-eighth Infantry, 40, 1,219; Thirty-ninth Infantry, 49, 1,230; Fortieth Infantry, 48, 1,226; Forty-first Infantry, 50, 1,279; Forty-second Infantry, 49, 1,057; Forty-third Infantry, 50, 1,235; Fourty-fourth Infantry, 50, 1,254 Forty-fifth Infantry, 49, 1,243; Forty-sixth Infantry, 50, 1,247; Forty-seventh Infantry, 50, 1,249; Forty-eighth Infantry, 50, 1,292; Forty-ninth Infantry, 49, 1,104. Company A, Battalion Engineers, Company B, Battalion Engineers, 4, 247. Signal Corps, U. S. Army, 25, 394. Hospital Corps, 153, 2,357. Total 2,313, 61,504. Acting assistant surgeons, 212.

MACARTHUR.

ADJUTANT-GENERAL'S OFFICE,
Washington, August 9, 1900.

MACARTHUR, Manila:

Secretary of War desires to know whether articles for road building per your indorsement June 30 are to be paid for from revenues of island and if you can spare $100,000. No funds otherwise available.

CORBIN.

MANILA. (Received August 10, 1900—8.48 a. m.)

ADJUTANT-GENERAL, Washington:

Killed—August 4, Candelaria, Luzon, Company E, Thirtieth Infantry, William B. English, George N. Simpson. Wounded—Corpl. William R. Sullivan, thigh, slight; Corpl. Eugene E. Betwee, hand slight; Otto Adams, arm, slight; Maurice Frye, thigh, slight. Cavinti, Luzon, Troop A, Eleventh Cavalry, Corpl. George H. Cravens, leg above knee, slight. July 15, Cabangan, Luzon, Company L, Twenty-fifth Infantry, John Fleming, knee, serious.

MACARTHUR.

MANILA. (Received August 11, 1900—9.43 a. m.

ADJUTANT-GENERAL, Washington:

With reference to your telegram of 11th, money can be spared from island revenues for road supplies. Before final action examine my cable May 27, which contemplates expenditure possibly $3,000,000 Mexican from island revenues, or army appropriations, as ordered by Department. Sufficient money now in insular treasury, but control thereof passes entirely from my hands September 1. My policy is very comprehensive and far reaching in remote consequences. If it is approved something specific to this effect should issue from Department before any expense has been incurred. Road supplies will be quite useless unless plan suggested can be carried out in entirety.

MACARTHUR.

MANILA. (Received August 12, 1900—5.30 a. m.)

ADJUTANT-GENERAL, Washington:

Have directed requisition for Gatling, Colt's automatic, guns to meet a possible emergency when force reduced. Request careful consideration. Considerable demand already for machine gun to strengthen small garrisons. Requisition entirely precautionary, not regarded as indicating emergency.

MACARTHUR.

MANILA. (Received August 12, 1900—11.35 a. m.)

ADJUTANT-GENERAL, Washington:

Colonel Grassa, August 12, in vicinity of Tayug, surrendered command to Colonel Freeman, Twenty-fourth Infantry, consisting of 1 major, 6 captains 6 lieutenants, 169 men, 101 rifles, and 50 bolos.

MACARTHUR.

1200   CORRESPONDENCE.

MANILA. (Received August 13, 1900—6.30 a. m.)
ADJUTANT-GENERAL, *Washington:*
Maj. Folliot A. Whitney,. Sixth Infantry, died 10.50 morning August 11, heart disease, at post hospital, Silay, Negros.
MACARTHUR.

MANILA. (Received August 13, 1900—10.43 a. m.)
ADJUTANT-GENERAL, *Washington:*
Following deaths have occurred since last report: Dysentery—August 11, Company E, Seventeenth Infantry, Andrew C. Roper; August 5, Company B, Thirty-second Infantry, George Oglesby; Troop L, Eleventh Cavalry, Lewis Kugler; Company A, Forty-first Infantry, William T. Barnes; August 4, Company F, Eighteenth Infantry, Charles D. Huntley; August 6, Company M, Twenty-eighth Infantry, John M. Hanrahan; August 1, Company G, Eighteenth Infantry, Martin Glynn; July 17, Company I, Thirtieth Infantry, William Dimmick; July 29, Band, Sixth Infantry, Cook Herman C. Dingler; August 2, Company L, Sixth Infantry, James Campbell; August 9, Company I, Twenty-fourth Infantry, Richard Booze; Company I, Twenty-fifth Infantry, Milton T. Bates. Variola—August 7, Company L, Thirtieth Infantry, George H. Campbell; August 4, Company C, Thirtieth Infantry, Manley F. Milligan. Sprue—Company A, Twenty-sixth Infantry, Joseph L. Wright. Typhoid fever—Company I, Forty-fifth Infantry, William Barclay; August 9, Company M, Twenty-first Infantry, Thomas E. Cooper; July 29, Company K, Thirty-eighth Infantry, John W. Cox; August 10, Company A, Twenty-seventh Infantry, Charles Rice. Malarial fever—August 8, Company C, Forty-sixth Infantry, Henry J. Kranz; August 7, Company M, Sixteenth Infantry, Edward A. Yeagley. Syncope—July 17, Company D, Twenty-third Infantry, Anton Melchor. Diarrhea—August 11, Company H, Forty-sixth Infantry, John W. Collins. Abscess liver—August 4, Company K, Ninth Infantry, William G. Wilson. Tuberculosis—August 9, Company M, Twenty-ninth Infantry, Thurston Weeks. Encephalitis—August 8, Company M, Twenty-eighth Infantry, Frederick Morris. Heart disease—July 13, Company C, Sixth Infantry, Adolph Huttuna. Drowned—August 3, Company E, Twenty-second Infantry, George I. Soper; August 9, Troop I, Eleventh Cavalry, Frederick Smith.
MACARTHUR.

MANILA. (Received August 14, 1900—8.17 a. m.)
ADJUTANT-GENERAL, *Washington:*
With reference to your telegram of 7th, in reply to mine July 31, authority requested to issue when it becomes necessary under circumstances mentioned; ration fixed by chief surgeon and commissary differing from ordinary ration at no greater cost than .25 per ration.
MACARTHUR.

ADJUTANT-GENERAL'S OFFICE,
Washington, August 14, 1900.
MACARTHUR, *Manila:*
Since August 10, upon requisition your chief ordnance officer, 12 Gatling (10 barrels, long), caliber .30 inch (Bruce feed) complete ordered to the Philippines. First 12 Colt's automatic, on contract for 50, go Taku. Balance when delivered will be sent Manila. Contract to be completed in November.
CORBIN.

MANILA. (Received August 15, 1900—6.35 a. m.)
ADJUTANT-GENERAL, *Washington:*
Sick hospitals, 3,868; quarters, 1,261; 8.47 per cent.
MACARTHUR.

ADJUTANT-GENERAL'S OFFICE,
Washington, August 15, 1900.
MACARTHUR, *Manila:*
With reference to your telegram of 14th, Secretary of War authorizes issue rations if done under direction chief commissary, and convalescents be temporarily organized into companies or partial companies as distinguished from convalescents here and there. In latter case ordinary ration thought sufficient. No savings on substitute rations allowed.
CORBIN.

MANILA. (Received August 15, 1900—3.25 a. m.)
ADJUTANT-GENERAL, *Washington:*
Killed near Tanauan, 10 p. m., Tuesday, William L. Murphy, first lieutenant, Twenty-fourth Infantry, and captain, Thirty-ninth Infantry, U. S. Volunteers.
MACARTHUR.

SAN FRANCISCO, CAL., *August 21, 1900.*
(Received 8.10 p. m.)
ADJUTANT-GENERAL, *Washington:*
Transport *Sherman* sailed at noon to-day with * * * Second Battalion, Second Infantry, 12 officers, 504 enlisted men, 400 rounds per man rifle ball cartridges; Third Battalion, Fifth Infantry, 10 officers, 508 enlisted men; 386 rounds per man rifle ball cartridges and 6,000 rounds revolver ball cartridges; Third Battalion, Eighth Infantry, 8 officers, 474 enlisted men; 400 rounds per man rifle ball cartridges; Major Borden, Fifth Infantry, commanding troops on board. * * *
SHAFTER, *Major-General.*

MANILA. (Received August 20, 1900—3.40 a. m.)
ADJUTANT-GENERAL, *Washington:*
Following deaths have occurred since last report: Dysentery—August 13, Company C, Twenty-seventh Infantry, William H. Fulmer; Company F, Seventeenth Infantry, George Middleton; Company A, Thirty-seventh Infantry, Oscar Riblet; August 12, Company M, Thirty-sixth Infantry, Walter S. Keith; August 11, Company I, Twenty-first Infantry, Q. M. Sergt. Edward Murphy; August 14, Company A, Thirty-ninth Infantry, James E. Curtis; August 17, Company K, Third Infantry, Henry G. E. Voget; Company C, Forty-first Infantry, Harry Barnhart. Diarrhea—August 11, Company L, Sixteenth Infantry, Fred. Gordon. Enterocolitis—August 16, Company K, Thirty-fifth Infantry, Corpl. Coleman S. Stacey. Hemiplega, side—August 15, Company D, Seventeenth Infantry, Frank Dixon. Pyæmia—Company A, Thirty-eighth Infantry, Harve Collins. Variola—Company M, Thirtieth Infantry, Rufus N. Finney; August 14, Company L, Thirtieth Infantry, Jeff Summers. Pneumonia—Troop A, Eleventh Cavalry, William Lundy; August 16, Company F, Thirty-sixth Infantry, Charles Peterson. Heart disease—August 5, Company A, Thirty-eighth Infantry, Elmer R. Ward. Syncope—August 15, Company B, Twenty-seventh Infantry, Joseph R. Saunders Tuberculosis—August 13, Company B, Thirty-seventh Infantry, Corpl. Levi C. Woolley. Killed fighting comrade—August 4, Company A, Thirty-sixth Infantry, Joseph Kelly. Drowned—Company B, Thirty-eighth Infantry, Boyd M. Young.
MACARTHUR.

MANILA. (Received August 22, 1900—2.50 a. m.)

ADJUTANT-GENERAL, *Washington:*

Killed—August 9, Cristina, Panay, Company A, Nineteenth Infantry, Edward Baker, Henry W. Ericson. Wounded—July 24, Santa Fe, Leyte, Company B, Forty-third Infantry, James R. Campbell, foot, slight; June 19, Calivo, Panay, Company A, Sixth Infantry, Corpl. Otto O. Hanson, abdomen, slight; May 31, Lambunao, Panay, Company L, Eighteenth Infantry, George L. Borden, abdomen, serious; Edward J. Stewart, thigh, serious.

MACARTHUR.

MANILA. (Received August 25, 1900—8.52 a. m.)

ADJUTANT-GENERAL, *Washington:*

Wounded—July 1, Legaspi, Luzon, Company I, Forty-seventh Infantry, Randall McClellan, back, moderate; July 4, Company H, Forty-seventh Infantry, William Russell, arm, serious; Grover C. Sweet, arm, slight; John R. Keeble, shoulder, serious; July 6, Ezra L. Van Orden, buttock, slight; June 30, Leon, Panay, Company I, Twenty-sixth Infantry, Charles L. Fish, arm, serious; Herbert V. Spencer, hip, slight.

MACARTHUR.

MANILA. (Received August 27, 1900—2.49 p. m.)

ADJUTANT-GENERAL, *Washington:*

Following deaths have occurred since last report: Dysentery—August 19, Company D, Thirty-second Infantry, James Talley; August 11, Company K, Thirteenth Infantry, Arthur J. Swick; August 18, Company E, Thirteenth Infantry, Adolph T. Reyer; Company C, Forty-sixth Infantry, Charles P. Linderbeck; Company L, Twenty-sixth Infantry, Michael Fallon; August 15, Company C, Twenty-second Infantry, Irwin S. Lowe; August 8, Company A, Twenty-sixth Infantry, Pomeo Le Page; August 21, Company K, Third Infantry, William S. Kent; Company E, Signal Corps, Sergt. Marshall S. Greene; August 20, Company D, Forty-second Infantry, Irving W. Hale; Company B, Thirty-seventh Infantry, William Ceasor; August 14, Company D, Sixth Infantry, Charles F. Ellis; August 17, Band, Forty-sixth Infantry, William E. Belding. Sprue—August 23, Company C, Thirty-second Infantry, Monticue Steelman. Drowned—August 20, Company B, Forty-first Infantry, Worthy Warner, Joseph P. Sinclair; August 23, Company C, Twenty-fourth Infantry, Q. M. Sergt. Henry Giles; August 17, Company L, Thirty-sixth Infantry, Frank E. Coleman. Variola—July 13, Company F, Forty-third Infantry, Corpl. John E. Whitehead. Typhoid fever—August 9, Company L, Nineteenth Infantry, Lewis E. Thompson; August 21, Company A, Forty-eighth Infantry, Ernest Rice; August 23, Company A, Forty-sixth Infantry, Corpl. Roy L. Osborn. Undertermined—August 18, Company M, Thirty-eighth Infantry, Charles A. Cowan. Syphilis—August 19, Company M, Forty-fifth Infantry, Walter Rice. Appendicitis—July 22, Company F, Nineteenth Infantry, Sergt. George McAlvey. Heart disease—July 29, Troop I, Eleventh Cavalry, Joseph Ghant. Abscess liver—July 30, Company G, Nineteenth Infantry, Andrew Newman. Uræmia—August 16, Troop A, Eleventh Cavalry, William Janes. Extensive skin burn—August 22, Troop C, Fourth Cavalry, Cook George W. Graft. Nephritis—August 12, contract nurse Helen D. Cochrane. Died from wounds received in action—July 3, Company A, Twenty-fourth Infantry, Corpl. William Preston. Tuberculosis—August 16, Company F, Signal Corps, Sergt. Joseph A. Dronin. Malarial fever—July 31, Company M, Nineteenth Infantry, William H. Walters.

MACARTHUR.

NAGASAKI, JAPAN. (Received August 28, 1900—1.45 p. m.)
ADJUTANT-GENERAL, *Washington*·
 Transport *Meade* arrived at this port on the 25th; battalion Fifteenth Infantry, squadron of Third Cavalry, Company E, Battalion of Engineers; no casualties occurred.

WILLIAMS, *Commanding*.

MANILA. (Received August 31, 1900—3.35 a. m.)
ADJUTANT-GENERAL, *Washington:*
 Sick in quarters, 981; sick in hospital, 4,362; 8.94 per cent.

MACARTHUR.

MANILA. (Received August 31, 1900—11.22 a. m.)
ADJUTANT-GENERAL, *Washington:*
 Killed—August 24, Panguil, Luzon, Company L, Thirty-seventh Infantry, Thomas Johnson, Corpl. Thomas A. O'Toole; San Mateo, Luzon, Company D, Twenty-seventh Infantry, Corpl. William D. Clintman; August 17, Salvacion, Luzon, Forty-fifth Infantry, Capt. William Brown. Wounded—August 24, Panguil, Luzon, Company I, Thirty-seventh Infantry, Corpl. Robert J. Webster, abdomen, serious; Company L, Thirty-seventh Infantry, William F. Martin, shoulder, moderate; August 17, Salvacion, Company C, Forty-fifth Infantry, Mark J. Chaffee, foot, slight; August 15, Villavieja, Company H, Thirty-third Infantry, Second Lieut. William M. True, leg above knee, slight; John Rayburn, leg above knee, slight; August 23, Sariaya, Company F, Thirtieth Infantry, Corpl. William M. Lash, leg above knee, serious; August 20, Pagsanjan, Luzon, Troop G, Eleventh Cavalry, Charles Asselstine, thigh, serious; Troop A, Eleventh Cavalry, Corpl. Joseph C. Hertwick, buttock, slight; Ira A. Easton, wounded in leg below knee, moderate.

MACARTHUR.

NAGASAKI, JAPAN, (Received August 31, 1900—7 a. m.)
ADJUTANT-GENERAL, *Washington:*
 Band, field, and staff, First Cavalry, two squadrons, have arrived, August 30; no casualties occurred; health of command excellent.

LEBO.

MANILA. (Received August 31, 1900—9.02 a. m.)
ADJUTANT-GENERAL, *Washington:*
 Killed near Villavieja, Luzon, August 28, Henry N. Way, second lieutenant, Fourth Infantry.

MACARTHUR.

MANILA. (Received August 31, 1900—3.56 p. m.)
ADJUTANT-GENERAL, *Washington:*
 Meager result of amnesty, which expires September 21, raises question regarding supplementary action. Captured papers contain convincing evidence that insurgent leaders are making strenuous efforts to hold together until after election; indications also strong that disappointing result will induce many surrenders. Sandico, in carefully prepared paper, declares country requires peace, even if liberty is sacrificed to attain it, and says he will surrender immediately if President McKinley is elected. Considering foregoing, recommend amnesty be permitted to expire without remark, thus leaving future policy in abeyance until after election. Week by week, situation

shows little improvement; month by month, progress slow, but quite apparent, Unless rapid improvement sets in after election, which fortunately now seems very probable, it will not be possible to materially reduce present force for a long time, unless territory now occupied is abandoned; constrained to modify accordingly estimate of troops necessary to hold archipelago set forth in cable May 27. Hope large force will not be required, but as a possible contingency, touching army reorganization, it is submitted for early consideration.

MACARTHUR.

ADJUTANT-GENERAL'S OFFICE,
Washington, September 1, 1900.

MACARTHUR, *Manila:*

Suggested you reduce sick in hospital by sending all invalided volunteers on returning transports with descriptive lists that they may be discharged on arrival San Francisco, carefully guarding against stampede to hospitals for the purpose of home coming.

CORBIN.

SAN FRANCISCO, CAL., *September 1, 1900.*
(Received 8.20 p. m.)

ADJUTANT-GENERAL, *Washington:*

Transport *Logan* sailed at 3.15 p. m. to-day with headquarters, band, First and Second Battalions, First Infantry, 26 officers, 1,056 men, 485 rounds per man rifle cartridges; headquarters, band, Third Battalion, Second Infantry, 12 officers, 542 men, 595 rounds per man rifle and 110 rounds per man revolver cartridges.

* * * * * * *

SHAFTER, *Major-General.*

MANILA. (Received September 3, 1900—3.22 a. m.)

ADJUTANT-GENERAL, *Washington:*

Second Lieut. Roy L. Fernald, Twenty-sixth Infantry, drowned Jalaur River, near Pototan, Panay, September 1. Have not recovered body.

MACARTHUR.

MANILA. (Received September 3, 1900—6.30 a. m.)

ADJUTANT-GENERAL, *Washington:*

Capt. George H. Bentley, Forty-seventh Infantry, died 9.55 morning August 26 from wounds received near Camalig, Luzon, August 21.

MACARTHUR.

MANILA. (Received September 3, 1900—9.20 a. m.)

ADJUTANT-GENERAL, *Washington:*

Brig. Gen. Robert P. Hughes reports outbreak in Bohol. First Lieutenant Levack, Forty-fourth Infantry, reports engagement near Carmen, Bohol; our loss in killed, 1; wounded, 6. Enemy's loss in killed, 120; have not received further details.

MACARTHUR.

NAGASAKI, JAPAN. (Received September 3, 1900—1.55 p. m.)
ADJUTANT-GENERAL, *Washington:*
Col. Henry Page reports First Lieut. Easton Burchard, assistant surgeon, Fortieth U. S. Volunteer Infantry, died of disease contracted in line of duty, dysentery, 12 noon, Sunday, September 2, transport *Grant*, Nagasaki.

HYDE.

MANILA. (Received September 3, 1900—4.11 p. m.)
ADJUTANT-GENERAL, *Washington:*
Following deaths have occurred since last report: Dysentery—August 21, Company I, Twenty-second Infantry, First Sergt. Henry S. Booream; August 20, Company A, Seventeenth Infantry, Sergt. Heinrich Groth; August 22, Company F, Thirty-second Infantry, John Anderson; July 22, Company E, Forty-seventh Infantry, Thomas Henderson; August 27, Company D, Twenty-second Infantry, James Cullen; August 29, Company C, Seventeenth Infantry, William R. Estes; Company A, Thirty-ninth Infantry, John Gertz; August 26, Company E, Twenty-fifth Infantry, Benjamin Franks; August 25, Company B, Thirty-seventh Infantry, James Manning; July 25, Company K, Eighteenth Infantry, Joseph C. Pauley; August 19, Company L, Sixth Infantry George C. Mautte; June 9, Company G, Fortieth Infantry, Ulysses G. McCloud. Diarrhea—July 10, G, Forty-seventh Infantry, Corpl. Frank C. Smith; August 24, L, Thirty-second Infantry, Sidney L. Coonce; August 25, F, Thirtieth Infantry, Eldo Dellinger; August 29, B, Forty-second Infantry, Addison E. Kniffen. Typhoid fever—August 28, M, Twenty-first Infantry, Corpl. John W. Gardner; July 5, C, Eleventh Cavalry, Edward Carter; June 22, A, Forty-fifth Infantry, John Olson. Malarial fever—August 26, C, Forty-sixth Infantry, Charles V. Wigley; August 22, A, Forty-ninth Infantry, Henry Button. Pneumonia—August 31, I, Forty-eighth Infantry, William Smith. Septicæmia—August 29, M, Twenty-second Infantry, Corpl. Victor Leroy. Nephritis—August 26, L, Seventeenth Infantry, William H. Kingery. Splenitis—August 25, B, Thirty-seventh Infantry, Edward A. Crowe. Tuberculosis—August 30, K, Thirty-third Infantry, Victor A. Pool. Bright's disease—Company D, Thirty-third Infantry, George W. Keath. Variola—August 29, Company H, Forty-eighth Infantry, Augustus Riles. Drowned—August 18, A, Forty-eighth Infantry, John Fuller; Company K, Forty-eighth Infantry, James Saunders. Killed by comrade—August 16, L, Forty-ninth Infantry, James H. Green. Killed by native prisoner—August 17, C, Twenty-sixth Infantry, James T. Burgey. Accidental fall—August 22, E, Thirty-fourth Infantry, Joseph M. Ryan. Homicide—August 27, Company I, Twenty-fifth Infantry, William A. Weakley. Suicide, hanging—August 23, M, Thirty-third Infantry, Joe Marek.

MACARTHUR.

SAN FRANCISCO, CAL., *September 4, 1900.*
(Received 3.07 p. m.)
ADJUTANT-GENERAL, *Washington:*
Transport *Federica* will sail this morning with detachments Light Batteries C and M, Seventh Artillery, 3 officers, 37 enlisted men, 10,000 rounds revolver ammunition, 12 field guns with 2,800 rounds ammunition, * * * 259 horses, 168 mules.

SHAFTER, *Major-General.*

SAN FRANCISCO, CAL., *September 4, 1900.*
(Received 10.43 p. m.)

ADJUTANT-GENERAL, *Washington:*

Transport *Rosecrans* sailed at 5 p. m. yesterday with Major Greenough and Light Batteries C and M, Seventh Artillery, 5 officers, 291 enlisted men, 55 rounds per man revolver ammunition. * * *

SHAFTER, *Major-General.*

MANILA. (Received September 5, 1900—9.22 a. m.)

ADJUTANT-GENERAL, *Washington:*

Details outbreak Bohol develop Pedro Samson, comandante police, left Tagbilaran ostensibly inspect police various towns; this he did until heard from in Carmen with followers threatening attack garrison at Ubay. Two detachments ordered Carmen, found town peaceful. No trace of insurrection. Detachment 27 men under First Lieutenant Levack, August 31, were attacked near Carmen by 120 bolomen; latter nearly annihilated; over 100 killed; our loss as previously reported. Movement on interior now in progress.

MACARTHUR.

ADJUTANT-GENERAL'S OFFICE,
Washington, September 5, 1900.

MACARTHUR, *Manila:*

With reference to your telegram of the 5th, Secretary of War remarks Pedro Samson appears to have followed policy suggested by Aguinaldo in his order January 9, 1899, of pretending submission and loyalty to United States of America in order to secure opportunity to kill our soldiers. Killing brought about by these means should be treated as murder, and persons who appear guilty of it, as does Pedro Samson, should be tried, and if found guilty, convicted and punished.

CORBIN.

ADJUTANT-GENERAL'S OFFICE,
Washington, September 5, 1900.

MACARTHUR, *Manila:*

Allotment $1,000,000 American currency from insular funds for road building confirmed. Commission will be advised accordingly. Commission may appropriate any further sums for that purpose which they deem advisable.

CORBIN.

MANILA. (Received September 6, 1900—8.05 a. m.)

ADJUTANT-GENERAL, *Washington:*

Killed—September 1, Paete, Luzon, Company I, Thirty-seventh Infantry, Charles A. Wilson; September 2, Carmona, Luzon, Signal Corps, U. S. Army, Sergt. Ludlow F. North; August 24, Agutag, Panay, Company C, Sixth Infantry, Corpl. Willard L. Ditman; September 1, Rio Grande, Luzon, B, Thirty-fourth Infantry, Eldridge Harris. Wounded—August 24, San Mateo, Luzon, Company D, Twenty-seventh Infantry, Charles H. Carter, chest, serious; June 14, Rio Cagayan de Misamis, Company L, Fortieth Infantry, Corporal Jesse G. Moody. This soldier previously reported killed now known wounded and prisoner hands insurgents.

MACARTHUR.

AFFAIRS IN THE PHILIPPINE ISLANDS.

Nagasaki, Japan. (Received September 6, 1900—8.58 p. m.)
Adjutant-General, *Washington:*
Transport *Warren* arrived Nagasaki on September 6. Health of command excellent. (Two battalions Ninth Cavalry on board.)
McGregor.

Manila. (Received September 8, 1900—4.22 p. m.)
Adjutant-General, *Washington:*
Total strength, present and absent, August 31, ascertained as near as possible: Third Cavalry, officers 27, enlisted men 891; Fourth Cavalry, 47, 1,422; Eleventh Cavalry, 48, 1,034; Philippine Cavalry, 13, 451. Battery E, First Artillery, 4, 153; Third Artillery, 11, 374; Battery F, Fourth Artillery, 4, 146; Battery F, Fifth Artillery, China, 4, 132; Sixth Artillery, 38, 1,388. Third Infantry, 45, 1,426; Fourth Infantry, 45, 1,407; Sixth Infantry, 44, 1,422; Ninth Infantry, China, 49, 1,419; Twelfth Infantry, 44, 1,416; Thirteenth Infantry, 47, 1,370; Fourteenth Infantry, China, 45, 1,491; Sixteenth Infantry, 45, 1,395; Seventeeth Infantry, 45, 1,414; Eighteenth Infantry, 46, 1,354; Nineteenth Infantry, 46, 1,415; Twentieth Infantry, 46, 1,416; Twenty-first Infantry, 43, 1,390; Twenty-second Infantry, 46, 1,384; Twenty-third Infantry, 46, 1,651; Twenty-fourth Infantry, 39, 1,026; Twenty-fifth Infantry, 36, 1,058; Twenty-sixth Infantry, 50, 1,226; Twenty-seventh Infantry, 49, 1,248; Twenty-eighth Infantry, 50, 1,265; Twenty-ninth Infantry, 50, 1,230; Thirtieth Infantry, 50, 1,232; Thirty-first Infantry, 50, 1,212; Thirty-second Infantry, 50, 1,171; Thirty-third Infantry, 50, 1,232; Thirty-fourth Infantry, 50, 1,213; Thirty-fifth Infantry, 46, 1,231; Thirty-sixth Infantry, 50, 946; Thirty-seventh Infantry, 50, 994; Thirty-eighth Infantry, 49, 1,206; Thirty-ninth Infantry, 49, 1,230; Fortieth Infantry, 48, 1,226; Forty-first Infantry, 50, 1,202; Forty-second Infantry, 49, 1,057; Forty-third Infantry, 50, 1,235; Forty-fourth Infantry, 50, 1,254; Forty-fifth Infantry, 46, 1,243; Forty-sixth Infantry, 50, 1,247; Forty-seventh Infantry, 50, 1,249; Forty-eighth Infantry, 50, 1,284; Forty-ninth Infantry, 49, 1,225. Company A, Battalion Engineers, U. S. A.; Company B, Battalion Engineers, U. S. A., 4, 247. Hospital Corps, 75, 2,336. Signal Corps, 27, 419. Total, 2,247, 31,379. Acting assistant surgeons, 212. Hospital Corps, China, 4, 19.
MacArthur.

Manila. (Received September 9, 1900—3.50 a. m.)
Adjutant-General, *Washington:*
Board of officers on tariff revision reported August 25; report passed to Commission August 29.
MacArthur.

Manila. (Received September 10, 1900—2.27 a. m.)
Adjutant-General, *Washington:*
Transport *Garonne* arrived September 7. (First Cavalry aboard.)
MacArthur.

Manila. (Received September 10, 1900—11.35 p. m.)
Adjutant-General, *Washington:*
Transport *Pakling* arrived yesterday. (First Cavalry aboard.)
MacArthur.

1208   CORRESPONDENCE.

MANILA. (Received September 11, 1900—5.35 a. m.)
ADJUTANT-GENERAL, *Washington:*
With reference to your telegram of 8th, Lieutenant Brewer, with Francis Gallagher, Company I, Twenty-seventh Infantry, mounted, left Novaliches for Manila, 9.30 morning July 13. Reached point 6 miles Novaliches, 11 miles Manila; here completely disappeared. No trace yet found. Natives vicinity heard few shots fired near point last; * * * whole country scouted many days; every effort obtain trace missing without success; still continue to search. Any information will be reported.

MACARTHUR.

MANILA. (Received September 11, 1900—3.15 p. m.)
ADJUTANT-GENERAL, *Washington:*
Following deaths have occurred since last report: Dysentery—June 20, H, Fortieth Infantry, James W. Sears; September 7, I, Thirty-seventh Infantry, Archie Elliott; September 2, B, Thirty-ninth Infantry, Winnie Johnson; September 4, D, Sixteenth Infantry, Q. M. Sergt. John Reiss; September 1, E, Thirtieth Infantry, Edward H. Hegel; August 22, D, Sixth Infantry, George W. Scott; L, Eighteenth Infantry, Edward A. Rodden; Troop D, Eleventh Cavalry, James F. Kauffman; August 8, F, Twenty-fourth Infantry, William Lysle; August 16, G, Forty-fifth Infantry, Theodore F. Garvin; August 1, B, Thirty-first Infantry, William F. Braedler; August 25, M, Sixth Infantry, Cook Edward E. Anderson; August 26, H, Forty-seventh Infantry, John W. Walter. Paralysis heart—August 30, Hospital Corps, Frederick Hyner. Diarrhea—September 5, L, Twenty-second Infantry, James W. Hargrave; August 5, D, Thirty-first Infantry, Corpl. Rudolph Walter; August 28, I, Forty-fifth Infantry, James Boland. Typhoid fever—September 3, Company H, Thirteenth Infantry, Thomas H. Breeding; September 7, G, Twenty-fourth Infantry, John Taylor; September 4, Hospital Corps, Harold Whitting; August 17, F, Thirty-first Infantry, Carl Ankrim. Died from wounds received in action—September 4, D, Thirty-ninth Infantry, Corpl. James T. Dowdy; September 1, F, Thirtieth Infantry, Corpl. William M. Lash. Malarial fever—September 7, B, Twelfth Infantry, Henry R. Brock; August 15, F, Twenty-third Infantry, John W. Arnold. Pneumonia—August 18, K, Thirtieth Infantry, Henry C. Shearer; July 26, G, Thirty-eighth Infantry, Fayette Ott. Variola—July 12, I, Forty-fourth Infantry, Corpl. Samuel J. Overton; August 31, C, Thirtieth Infantry, Corpl. Sam A. Hall. Ascaris lumbricoides—August 27, M, Thirty-eighth Infantry, John Walls. Pyæmia—August 23, M, Eighteenth Infantry, John M. Bowling. Intestinal obstruction—August 17, E, Twenty-third Infantry, Sergt. William Flemming. Drowned—August 22, G, Twenty-fourth Infantry, Ernest King. Killed by comrade—July 31, H, Twenty-second Infantry, Corpl. Joseph Fox. Nephritis—September 4, A, Twenty-first Infantry, John J. Quinn. Dengue—September 2, I, Forty-first Infantry, Corpl. Oscar C. Hopkins.

MACARTHUR.

NAGASAKI, JAPAN. (Received September 11, 1900—3.55 p. m.)
ADJUTANT-GENERAL, *Washington:*
Arrived in good condition. [*Sherman* with battalion Second, Fifth, and Eighth Infantry.]

BORDEN.

ADJUTANT-GENERAL'S OFFICE,
Washington, September 13, 1900.

MacArthur, *Manila:*

In addition to those in China, [there are] on sea and ready to be shipped 2,000 horses, 1,400 mules. If animal transports return promptly additional 1,000 horses and 800 mules can be delivered before February. Do you need more? Can you use this number to advantage? Rush answer.

CORBIN.

Manila. (Received September 13, 1900—1.04 p. m.)
Adjutant-General, *Washington:*

Killed—August 27, Jaro, Leyte, D, Forty-fourth Infantry, Edward M. Agee; August 26, D, Forty-third Infantry, Carl F. Carlson; July 1, San Blas, Panay, I, Twenty-sixth Infantry, Richard O'Hearn; September 9, Cabugao, Luzon, K, Third Cavalry, Sergt. Matthew Simila; August 24, Nueva Caceres, Luzon, C, Forty-fifth Infantry, Corpl. Otis C. Newby. Missing—September 9, Cabugao, Luzon, K, Third Cavalry, James G. Lyons, Otto Schott. Wounded—Ernest A. Mussler, lung, moderate; August 27, Jaro, Leyte, D, Forty-fourth Infantry, John T. Mills, Corpl. William B. Parker, Thomas G. Donall, moderate; August 28, Dumangas, Panay, C, Twenty-sixth Infantry, Albert V. Rhodes, arm, head, moderate; September 3, Calamba, Luzon, B, Thirty-ninth Infantry, Garrett Farmer, leg above knee, slight; July 24, Oroquieta, Mindanao, I, Fortieth Infantry, Edward C. Underwood, pelvis, serious; August 24, Nueva Caceres, Luzon, C, Forty-fifth Infantry, Charles Brocker, arm, serious; Benjamin W. Madill, shoulder, slight; September 4, Gapan, Luzon, A, Fourth Cavalry, Corpl. Lennie L. Ruppert, thigh, serious; Harry B. Walkup, thigh, moderate.

MACARTHUR.

Manila. (Received September 14, 1900—10.30 a. m.)
Adjutant-General, *Washington:*

With reference to your telegram of 14th, animals referred to can be used to advantage. It is understood that this means 3,000 horses, 2,200 mules will be supply for the present; possibly later more can be employed usefully. Abundant supply animals means everything present situation. Send full cavalry equipments for horses; 250 escort wagons, 1,000 aparejos, drivers, packers, in proportion.

MACARTHUR.

Manila. (Received September 16, 1900—12.13 a. m.)
Adjutant-General, *Washington:*

Sick in quarters, 1,037; sick in hospital, 3,722; 8 per cent.

MACARTHUR.

Manila. (Received September 16, 1900.)
Adjutant-General, *Washington:*

Charles McQuiston, captain, Fourth Infantry, died yesterday, post hospital, Bacoor, Cavite Province, 8.30 evening, resulting from gunshot wound caused by private soldier. Captain McQuiston fit temporary insanity, attacked men of company, shot one or more, was shot himself, self-defense. Send further particulars when received.

MACARTHUR.

CORRESPONDENCE.

        MANILA. (Received September 17, 1900—2.16 a. m.)
ADJUTANT-GENERAL, *Washington:*
 Transports *Warren, Sherman* arrived yesterday.
                     MACARTHUR.

       KOBE, JAPAN. (Received September 17, 1900—6.40 a. m.)
ADJUTANT-GENERAL, *Washington:*
 Arrived. Two officers and 77 men, Ninth Cavalry, with horses and mules, on the *Strathgyle.*
                       STODTER.

           ADJUTANT-GENERAL'S OFFICE,
            Washington, September 17, 1900.
MACARTHUR, *Manila:*
 With reference to your telegram of 14th, 2,600 horses, 1,300 mules, 1,000 horse equipments, 250 wagons, 600 aparejos will be sent you, with 900 mules, 4,000 sets horse equipments, 400 each horses and aparejos, already shipped, will make number you ask.
                       CORBIN.

        MANILA. (Received September 18, 1900—8.40 a. m.)
ADJUTANT-GENERAL, *Washington:*
 Following deaths have occurred since last report: Dysentery—August 15, C, Nineteenth Infantry, Charles Sharp; August 31, Hospital Corps, Edward Nichols; August 29, L, Eighteenth Infantry, Herman Nagele; September 13, M, Twenty-ninth Infantry, Corpl. Harold McLaughlin; September 8, L, Third Cavalry, Fred. Lacharite; L, Thirty-ninth Infantry, Lawrence Curley; September 7, G, Thirteenth Infantry, Henry C. Hillman; August 21, C, Forty-third Infantry, Foy F. Gearhart; September 14, G, Fortieth Infantry, James P. Gardner; July 13, A, Thirty-first Infantry, Laurel Brown; August 5, M, Sixth Infantry, John A. Sloan. Diarrhea—September 11, L, Thirty-ninth Infantry, Harry F. Foin; L, Thirtieth Infantry, George M. Sampsel; September 10, L, Thirty-ninth Infantry, John Stone. Typhoid fever—September 12, H, Twenty-fourth Infantry, James T. Watson; September 1, F, Forty-seventh Infantry, Musician Arthur Q. Miles; August 29, B, Forty-third Infantry, James R. Campbell. Malarial fever—August 26, I, Forty-seventh Infantry, John E. Bryan. Drowned—September 6, M, Thirty-fourth Infantry, Milton E. Anderson, Frank W. Johnson; August 4, K, Eighteenth Infantry, Albert C. Laigle; August 24, Troop M, Fourth Cavalry, James Dixon. Killed by comrade—September 12, C, Seventeenth Infantry, Sergt. Joseph McEntee. Uræmic poisoning—September 10, I, Thirty-seventh Infantry, Q. M. Sergt. Raymond Clark. Anæmia—September 2, C, Twenty-sixth Infantry, Edson B. Moore. Œdematus laryngitis—August 23, L, Sixth Infantry, Cook Henry J. Klockenkemper. Appendicitis—September 8, G, Eleventh Cavalry, Frederick Gibson; September 14, M, Twenty-second Infantry, Frank McAdams. Pneumonia—September 11, Troop E, Fourth Cavalry, George Manderville. Cardiac degeneration—L, Thirtieth Infantry, Herman W. Kramer.
                      MACARTHUR.

           ADJUTANT-GENERAL'S OFFICE,
            Washington, September 18, 1900.
WOOD, *Habana:*
 Pack trains with experienced packers needed in Philippines. How many trains, with full complement packers and aparejos, can you spare from Cuba? Wire reply.
                       CORBIN.

AFFAIRS IN THE PHILIPPINE ISLANDS. 1211

SAN FRANCISCO, CAL., *September 18, 1900.*
(Received 9.53 p. m.)

ADJUTANT-GENERAL, *Washington:*

Transport *Thomas* sailed at 12.40 p. m. to-day with headquarters, band, and First Battalion, Fifth Infantry, 15 officers, 527 enlisted men, and 2 officers and 11 enlisted men of that regiment attached. Headquarters, band, and Second Battalion, Eighth Infantry, 14 officers, 531 enlisted men, and 1 officer and 7 enlisted men that regiment attached. * * * Four hundred and thirty-three thousand two hundred rounds ammunition in excess of that carried by troops.

SHAFTER, *Major-General.*

MANILA. (Received September 19, 1900—3.23 p. m.)

ADJUTANT-GENERAL, *Washington:*

Considerable activity throughout Luzon. Fighting reported vicinity Carig and Estella, Isabela Province. Insurgents estimated 500, probably much exaggerated, but sufficient force to make disturbance in district heretofore quiet. In the Ilocan provinces Brig. Gen. Samuel B. M. Young reports numerous small affairs, and has called so emphatically for more force that Kingsbury's squadron, Third Cavalry, and Borden's battalion, Fifth Infantry, been sent him; other battalion Fifth, same destination upon arrival. Country north Pasig, including all of Bulacan, very much disturbed, and numerous contacts with small parties throughout that district. South of Pasig, including Tayabas Province, Luzon, same conditions obtain. This activity has been anticipated and reported upon in letters, August 25, 29, and cable August 31. September 17 Capt. David D. Mitchell, Fifteenth Infantry, 90 men, Company L, Fifteenth Infantry, from Siniloan, Laguna Province, attacked insurgent General Cailles, who had 800 men in position at Mavitac, same province. Desperate fight ensued, which was pushed from the front with great pertinacity by Mitchell across causeway and through water waist deep; cooperative attack under Capt. George F. Cooke, Fifteenth Infantry, with 40 men, Company K, Fifteenth Infantry, and 10 men, Company B, Thirty-seventh Infantry, U. S. Volunteers; could not reach enemy's position because of high water in arm of lake, which could not be crossed; entire country was afloat in consequence recent rains; this very much impeded offensive action. After hour twenty minutes' fighting command withdrew to Siniloan. Upon renewal operations 18th found that insurgents had escaped from Mavitac previous night, most of them no doubt going back into contiguous barrios to appear for time being, or until called into fight again, as peaceful amigos. Casualties, which all occurred Mitchell's command, consisting of 130 men, 4 officers, were: Company L, Fifteenth Infantry—Killed and died wounds: David D. Mitchell, captain, Fifteenth Infantry; George A. Cooper, second lieutenant, Fifteenth Infantry; First Sergt. William Fitzgerald, Sergt. Evremonde DeHart, Corpl. Lauritz Jensen, Privates Edward C. Coburn, George R. Horton, Thomas P. Kelley, Thomas Mulray, John P. Brink, William L. Banker, Arthur S. Mansfield. Thomas I. Pitcher, Scott L. Smith, Richard Taylor, Edward M. Neal, Fred Duggan, Emanuel Kaufman. Wounded: Corpls. Charles Oswald, William H. Polley, Privates Benjamin Owens, Michael Kelly, Otto F. H. Bathe, Everette Matlock, Francis P. Flanagan, Michael J. Hennessey, Anthony Kearney, Harry Perry, Charles R. Debaugh. Company L, Thirty-seventh Infantry—Killed and died wounds: First Sergt. Thomas P. A. Howe, Privates Edwin J. Godahl, George A. Haight, Edward Stallcup, Alfred J. Mueller, James C. West. Wounded: Capt. John E. Moran, Sergt. Robert Mahaffy, Corpl. Frank A. Story, Privates Frank T. Bell, William S. Bradley, Worley T. Crosswhite, David Day, Cornelius Gentry. Thirty-three per cent is profoundly impressive loss and indicates stubbornness of fight, fearless leadership of officers and splendid response of men. Insurgent loss, as far as known, 10 killed, 20 wounded; among former, Colonel Fidel.

MACARTHUR.

HABANA. (Received September 20, 1900—4.40 p. m.)
ADJUTANT-GENERAL, *Washington:*
Will send you detailed statement of pack-train transportation available for Philippines at the earliest possible moment.

WOOD, *Commanding.*

MANILA. (Received September 21, 1900—5.40 a. m.)
ADJUTANT-GENERAL, *Washington:*
Transport *Aztec* arrived yesterday. [Two officers and horses Third Cavalry.]

MACARTHUR.

HABANA. (Received September 22, 1900—12.35 p. m.)
ADJUTANT-GENERAL, *Washington:*
Replying telegram 18th, can send three complete trains with packers from Matanzas; this is all that can be spared, as wagon transportation is useless for rapid work.

WOOD, *Commanding.*

ADJUTANT-GENERAL'S OFFICE,
Washington, September 24, 1900.
MACARTHUR, *Manila:*
Commission reports Spurgin retires. With reference to tariff circular 65, detail most competent officer available for collector. Physical condition of Captain Steinhauser desired.

CORBIN.

MANILA. (Received September 24, 1900—12.50 p. m.)
ADJUTANT-GENERAL, *Washington:*
Killed—August 31, Carmen, Luzon, C, Forty-fourth Infantry, Alpha E. Marshall; September 14, Maniclin, Luzon, C, Thirty-fourth Infantry, Edmond C. Johnson; September 18, Novaliches, Luzon, I, Twenty-seventh Infantry, Isadore Hansen; September 14, Carig, Luzon, L, Sixteenth Infantry, Richard C. Cummings; September 4, Biñang, Luzon, M, Twenty-eighth Infantry, David Allen; September 13, Maniclin, Luzon, C, Twenty-fourth Infantry, Sergt. Walter L. Washington; August 26, San Miguel, Leyte, F, Forty-third Infantry, Corpl. Michael F. McGovern; September 21, Naic, Luzon, B, Fourth Cavalry, Corpl. Levi B. Eichholtz. Wounded—September 18, Novaliches, I, Twenty-seventh Infantry, Marbel McCutcheon, hand, moderate; August 1, Pagsanjan, Luzon, A, Eleventh Cavalry, Joseph W. Ford, neck, slight; August 31, Carmen, Luzon, C, Forty-fourth Infantry, William J. Coan, hand, serious; Mike Martonchik, hand, slight; Ernest L. Noel, arm, moderate; John H. Brown, back, slight; William C. Harris, back, serious; Corpl. Andrew McDonal, head, serious; August 12, Catbalogan, Samar, C, Twenty-ninth Infantry, Zeb Grant, abdomen, slight; David J. Hornsby, hand, slight; Corpl. Thomas D. Blackmon, buttock, slight; Sergt. James P. Hamby, abdomen, moderate; September 12, Sinait, Luzon, G, Twelfth Infantry, Sergt. John F. Sentman, foot, serious; September 16, Guiguinto, Luzon, G, Third Infantry, Isaac J. Lamon, Max G. C. Helmcke, hand, moderate; September 15, Ackle, Luzon, E, Thirty-fifth Infantry, Capt. William G. Schreiber, thorax, severe; September 1, Cabanatuan, Luzon, B, Thirty-fourth Infantry, Herbert Carpenter, shoulder, slight; September 20, Malolos, L, Third Infantry, Wilburn Patton; hand, serious. With reference to my telegram 19th, reporting Neal, Duggan, Kaufman, L, Fifteenth Infantry, killed, incorrect, wounded. Arm, moderate; thigh, serious; arm, moderate, respectively.

MACARTHUR.

AFFAIRS IN THE PHILIPPINE ISLANDS.

MANILA. (Received September 25, 1900—7.22 a. m.)

ADJUTANT-GENERAL, *Washington:*

Following deaths have occurred since last report: Dysentery—September 15, M, Thirty-eighth Infantry, William A. Bower; September 14, I, Twenty-first Infantry, Carmac Brennan; September 17, F, Thirtieth Infantry, Paul Brum; September 18, B, Thirty-ninth Infantry, William T. Graham; September 10, M, Twenty-fifth Infantry, James M. Thomas; September 20, E, Forty-eighth Infantry, Corpl. Monroe M. Thomas; September 3, G, Thirty-first Infantry, Fred. Wetter; August 17, B, Thirty-first Infantry, Anthony H. Starkey; August 28, D, Twenty-third Infantry, Charles J. Neipp. Typhoid fever—September 22, 8 p. m., Saturday, First Lieut. Francis K. Meade, Twenty-first Infantry; September 12, G, Fourth Cavalry, William Hart; September 14, Hospital Corps, Walter B. Price; September 2, F, Thirty-first Infantry, Thomas Williams; August 12, A, Thirty-first Infantry, William R. Thompson. Endocarditis—September 19 A, Twentieth Infantry, Albert B. Crabb. Malarial fever—September 18, K, Thirty-fourth Infantry, Artificer Charles O. Daniel; A, Forty-ninth Infantry, Cook Alexander Whitesides; September 10, F, Signal Corps, U. S. Army, William F. Stevens. Died from wounds received in action—September 18, L, Fifteenth Infantry, Charles R. Debaugh; August 19, I, Twenty-third Infantry, Ralph L. Clark. Drowned—September 9, C, Sixteenth Infantry, Charles P. Parsons; August 29, L, Twenty-fifth Infantry, Corpl. Perrent Foster; September 20, C, Third Infantry, William D. Kelch. Diarrhea—September 16, B, Forty-first Infantry, Corpl. Frank Burke; September 20, M, Thirty-seventh Infantry, William H. Reed. Enteritis—September 19, A, Thirtieth Infantry, Ward Soper; September 17, Hospital Corps, Faitz O. Hagen; August 4, G, Thirty-eighth Infantry, Mathew W. Brown. Hydrophobia—September 15, M, Forty-eighth Infantry, Oliver Williams. Nephritis—September 14, A, Forty-sixth Infantry, Corpl. John F. Hayes. Diabetes—September 18, D, Twenty-first Infantry, George Kling. Killed by Capt. Charles McQuiston, Fourth Infantry, while demented—September 15, M, Fourth Infantry, Sergt. Frank S. Dunn. Septicæmia—August 21, K, Forty-fifth Infantry, Alva W. Petro. Tuberculosis—September 15, G, Third Infantry, George W. White. Abscess liver—September 10, A, Nineteenth Infantry, Corpl. Alexander L. Cartner. Paraplegia—September 16, M, Thirty-third Infantry, John J. Burns.

MACARTHUR.

ADJUTANT-GENERAL'S OFFICE,
Washington, September 25, 1900.

MACARTHUR, *Manila:*

What is the exact date deaths David D. Mitchell, George A. Cooper?

CORBIN.

MANILA. (Received September 26, 1900—7.20 a. m.)

ADJUTANT-GENERAL, *Washington:*

Transport *Athenian* arrived September 24. [Horses of Ninth Cavalry.]

MACARTHUR.

MANILA. (Received September 27, 1900—7.05 a. m.)

ADJUTANT-GENERAL, *Washington:*

Died 10.50 September 27, accidental discharge his pistol, Second Lieut. James D. Danner, Twenty-eighth Infantry, U. S. Volunteers.

MACARTHUR.

CORRESPONDENCE.

MANILA. (Received September 28, 1900—8.09 a. m.)
ADJUTANT-GENERAL, *Washington:*

September 11, Captain Shields, 51 men, Company F, Twenty-ninth Infantry, U. S. Volunteers, 1 Hospital Corps man, left Santa Cruz, Marinduque, by gunboat *Villalobos*, for Torrijos, intending return overland Santa Cruz. Have heard nothing since from Shields. Scarcely doubt entire party captured, with many killed, wounded, Shields among latter. Information sent by letter from commanding officer, Boac, dated September 20, received September 24, consisted of rumors through natives. *Yorktown* and two gunboats, George S. Anderson, colonel Thirty-eighth Infantry, U. S. Volunteers, two companies Thirty-eighth Infantry, U. S. Volunteers, sent Marinduque immediately. Anderson confirms first report as to capture, but unable September 27 to give details, present whereabouts Shields and party, names killed, wounded. This information probably available soon. Anderson has orders commence operations immediately and move relentlessly until Shields and party rescued. All troops expected soon. *Logan* will be sent Marinduque if necessary clear up situation.

MACARTHUR.

MANILA. (Received September 29, 1900—11.05 a. m.)
ADJUTANT-GENERAL, *Washington:*

Killed—September 23, Tanauan, Luzon, K, Thirty-ninth Infantry, John Niles; September 22, Badoc, Luzon, E, Twelfth Infantry, John E. Dupree; September 23, Cabanatuan, M, Thirty-fourth Infantry, William S. Mercer; September 17, Mavitac, Luzon, L, Thirty-seventh Infantry, Joseph N. Wells. With reference to my telegram of 19th, wounded in thigh, serious, instead of killed, Alfred J. Mueller, L, Thirty-seventh Infantry. Wounded—September 23, Tanauan, K, Thirty-ninth Infantry, John Burket, abdomen, moderate; September 22, Badoc, Luzon, E, Twelfth Infantry, John Manduka, hand, serious; James A. Kennedy, shoulder, serious; September 23, Cabanatuan, Luzon, Thirty-fourth Infantry, Company G, Capt. Cushman A. Rice, arm, slight; August 23, Alang-Alang, Leyte, F, Forty-third Infantry, William E. Dennis, leg above knee, serious; Fred Myers, severely; September 14, Carig, Luzon, L, Sixteenth Infantry, Sergt. Henry F. Schroeder, thigh, serious; September 15, Catubig, Samar, G, Twenty-ninth Infantry, Sergt. Leonidas O. Hollis, elbow, severe; August 17, Sorsogan, Luzon, M, Forty-seventh Infantry, George Kennedy, neck, mortal; August 20, San Miguel, Leyte, H, Forty-third Infantry, Corpl. Thomas A. Kennedy, abdomen, serious.

MACARTHUR.

MANILA. (Received October 1, 1900—4.12 a. m.)
ADJUTANT-GENERAL, *Washington:*

With reference to your telegram of 25th ultimo, Capt. David D. Mitchell, Fifteenth Infantry, Second Lieut. George A. Cooper, Fifteenth Infantry, killed 6.30 morning September 17.

MACARTHUR.

MANILA. (Received October 1, 1900—6.30 a. m.)
ADJUTANT-GENERAL, *Washington:*

Sick in hospital, 3,732; sick in quarters, 1,365; in United States of America, 1,715; per cent, 11.23.

MACARTHUR.

AFFAIRS IN THE PHILIPPINE ISLANDS. 1215

MANILA. (Received October 1, 1900—7.12 a. m.)
ADJUTANT-GENERAL, *Washington:*
Transport *Logan* arrived to-day.

MACARTHUR.

SAN FRANCISCO, CAL., *October 1, 1900.*
(Received 9.33 p. m.)
ADJUTANT-GENERAL, *Washington:*
Transport *Hancock* sailed at 2.35 p. m. to-day with companies B, D, and M, Twenty-fourth Infantry, 5 officers and 375 men; Companies A, C, D, and G, Twenty-fifth Infantry, 5 officers and 434 men; 3 officers and 100 men, Marine Corps; * * * 400 rounds rifle ammunition, caliber .30, per man. * * *

SHAFTER, *Major-General.*

MANILA. (Received October 2, 1900—7.32 a. m.)
ADJUTANT-GENERAL, *Washington:*
Killed between Pavia and Santa Barbara, Panay, October 1, Second Lieut. Max Wagner, Company A, Twenty-sixth Infantry.

MACARTHUR.

MANILA. (Received October 2, 1900—8.54 a. m.)
ADJUTANT-GENERAL, *Washington:*
Following deaths have occurred since last report: Dysentery—September 27, Company G, Fourth Infantry, Bernard Smith; Company B, Battalion of Engineers, Michael P. Corcoran; Company G, Thirty-ninth Infantry, George A. Wallace; September 20, H, Twenty-fourth Infantry, Leno A. Siler; Company M, Thirtieth Infantry, William W. Huesman; September 25, D, Thirty-ninth Infantry, Charlie Quick; F, Thirtieth Infantry, Berton England; September 17, I, Forty-seventh Infantry, Milo Jackson; September 24, E, Thirtieth Infantry, Thomas V. Hamilton; M, Thirty-eighth Infantry, Joe H. Asbery; September 22, D, Fourth Cavalry, Thomas L. Daft; September 23, A, Thirty-ninth Infantry, Charles H. Beach. Suicide—September 25, K, Thirty-fifth Infantry, John Eastman. Killed by comrade—September 17, D, Eleventh Cavalry, Joseph T. Mead. Died from wounds received in action—August 18, M, Forty-seventh Infantry, George Kennedy. Typhoid fever—August 22, F, Forty-fifth Infantry, Charles E. Hankins; September 18, G, Twenty-sixth Infantry, George Lyons; September 22, F, Thirtieth Infantry, Sydney H. Ball. Enteritis—September 23, C, Thirty-ninth Infantry, Benjamin Schupp; September 21, A, Sixteenth Infantry, First Sergt. Joseph Farrell; August 29, F, Thirty-eighth Infantry, Corpl. William Bouzey; August 22, E, Thirty-eighth Infantry, Henry S. Folds. Malarial fever—August 27, D, Thirty-seventh Infantry, Charles B. Dye; September 21, L, Eleventh Cavalry, Sergt. Patrick Burke. Septicæmia—September 16, I, Eighth Infantry, Theodore B. Basford. Appendicitis—September 9, A, Nineteenth Infantry, Otto J. Peters. Tuberculosis—September 21, M, Sixteenth Infantry, George S. Phillips. Atrophy liver—September 24, F, Third Cavalry, James J. Walsh. Heart disease—September 20, L, Fourth Infantry, Harry B. Murvin. Drowned—September 21, I, Third Cavalry, William A. Clarke.

MACARTHUR.

ADJUTANT-GENERAL'S OFFICE,
Washington, October 2, 1900.

MACARTHUR, *Manila:*

Transport *Hancock* left San Francisco on October 1, with one battalion each Twenty-fourth and Twenty-fifth Infantry.

CORBIN.

MANILA, P. I. (Received October 4, 1900—9.18 a. m.)

ADJUTANT-GENERAL, *Washington:*

First Infantry to Marinduque, October 6, on *Sumner*. General Hare to command island, with orders to push operations until insurrection is stamped out absolutely. He will have 12 full companies of infantry for the purpose. Anderson's first operations developed nothing. No report since October 2.

MACARTHUR.

MANILA. (Received October 4, 1900—10 a. m.)

ADJUTANT-GENERAL, *Washington:*

Reported having died in mountains Laguna province, after escape from insurgents, date unknown: Hospital Corps, Andrew B. Medlock, Edward F. Sexton; Company K, Thirty-seventh Infantry, John Dolan; Company F, Signal Corps, Olof Sundwall; Company A, Thirtieth Infantry, John N. Kenny. Killed by comrade—September 14, Pansanjan, Luzon, G, Eleventh Cavalry, Q. M. Sergt. William A. Hogan. Wounded—September 18, Novaliches, Luzon, I, Twenty-seventh Infantry, Otto Thiede, leg above knee, slight; Second Lieut. Matthew T. E. Ward, side, slight; September 25, Castillejos, Luzon, K, Twenty-fifth Infantry, James I. Carrick, moderately; August 18, Hilongos, Leyte, A, Forty-fourth Infantry, First Sergt. Charles O. Fort, chest, serious; September 14, Dingley, Panay, K, Eighteenth Infantry, Frank A. Arade, knee, serious; I, Eighteenth Infantry, Frederick W. Bender, arm, serious.

MACARTHUR.

MANILA. (Received October 4, 1900—7.52 a. m.)

ADJUTANT-GENERAL, *Washington:*

Transport *Strathgyle* arrived to-day. (Ninth Cavalry on board.)

MACARTHUR.

MANILA. (Received October 8, 1900—2.20 a. m.)

ADJUTANT-GENERAL, *Washington:*

With reference to your telegram of 6th, Andrew B. Medlock, Hospital Corps, John Dolan, K, Thirty-seventh Infantry, correct. Missing since September 4, John P. Kreidler, H, Thirty-eighth Infantry.

MACARTHUR.

MANILA. (Received October 8, 1900—7.12 a. m.)

ADJUTANT-GENERAL, *Washington:*

Killed—Near San Quintin, Luzon, October 4, Paul Jenkins, A, Thirty-third Infantry. Wounded, Robert L. Harris, B, Thirty-third Infantry. Wounded and captured, Eugene Todd, A, Thirty-third Infantry.

MACARTHUR.

AFFAIRS IN THE PHILIPPINE ISLANDS. 1217

MANILA. (Received October 8, 1900—11.07 a. m.)
ADJUTANT-GENERAL, *Washington:*
Following deaths have occurred since last report: Dysentery—September 25, L, Thirty-eighth Infantry, George W. Brewer; C, Sixteenth Infantry, Corpl. James A. Bush; September 29, C, Twenty-second Infantry, Walter O. Cunningham; September 12, K, Eighteenth Infantry, William J. Gardner; September 26, A, Nineteenth Infantry, Charles Mayer; September 13, F, Twenty-ninth Infantry, Archie Rice; September 17, D, Nineteenth Infantry, Julius Seitz; September 24, L, Sixth Infantry, Eugene Shine; October 3, E, Battalion Engineers, William Hobbs; October 4, G, Seventeenth Infantry, Sergt. Martin A. Madden. Typhoid fever—September 29, A, Thirty-ninth Infantry, Walter Morgan; Acting Hosp. Steward John. A. C. Huennekens; September 16, D, Twenty-ninth Infantry, John McCarthy; September 25, G, Twenty-sixth Infantry, Sergt. Clinton S. Baker; October 4, I, Thirty-fifth Infantry, Dennis Murphy; I, Twelfth Infantry, John A. Schisler. Endocarditis—September 24, F, Thirty-fourth Infantry, Beaure Reberger. Drowned—A, Eleventh Cavalry, Fred. R. Lyons. Septicæmia—September 15, I, Eighteenth Infantry, Porter H. Voorhies. Enteritis—September 12, K, Forty-third Infantry James E. Clark. Peritonitis—September 23, L, Sixth Infantry, Cock Francis Gould. Killed attempting escape while prisoner—September 28, E, Thirty-fourth Infantry, John Buchanan. Suicide, shot head—September 22, C, Thirteenth Infantry, James F. McLaughlin. Syphilis—October 1, Hospital Corps, Nels Hansen. Variola—October 3, L, Thirtieth Infantry, Courtland McLean. Alcoholism—October 5, B, Third Infantry, William P. Schall. Cirrhosis liver—September 13, K, Thirty-second Infantry, Aaron P. Haverman. Nephritis—October 1, recruit, unassigned, Hugh Smith.

MACARTHUR.

MANILA. (Received October 8, 1900—11 p. m.)
ADJUTANT-GENERAL, *Washington:*
Transports *Argyll*, *Rosecrans*, arrived yesterday. (Light Batteries C and M, Seventh Artillery, on board *Rosecrans*.)

MACARTHUR.

MANILA. (Received October 10, 1900—8.05 a. m.)
ADJUTANT-GENERAL:
Total strength present and absent, September 30, ascertained as near as possible: Officers, enlisted men, First Cavalry, 20, 714; Third Cavalry, 43, 1,319; Fourth Cavalry, 47, 1,420; Ninth Cavalry, 27, 734; Eleventh Cavalry, 50, 1,011; Philippine Cavalry, 13, 448. Battery E, First Artillery, 4, 151; Third Artillery, 11, 872; Battery F, Fourth Artillery, 4, 143; Battery F, Fifth Artillery, China, 4, 130; Sixth Artillery, 36, 1,378. First Infantry, 26, 1,037; Second Infantry, 25, 1,051; Third Infantry, 46, 1,397; Fourth Infantry, 45, 1,403; Fifth Infantry, 10, 504; Sixth Infantry, 45, 1,401; Eighth Infantry, 8, 491; Ninth Infantry, China, 49, 1,416; Twelfth Infantry, 45, 1,388; Thirteenth Infantry, 46, 1,354; Fourteenth Infantry, China, 45, 1,485; Fifteenth Infantry, 13, 500; Sixteenth Infantry, 46, 1,410; Seventeenth Infantry, 45, 1,398; Eighteenth Infantry, 46, 1,352; Nineteenth Infantry, 46, 1,413; Twentieth Infantry, 47, 1,393; Twenty-first Infantry, 46, 1,387; Twenty-second Infantry, 45, 1,372; Twenty-third Infantry, 46, 1,649; Twenty-fourth Infantry, 25, 1,024; Twenty-fifth Infantry, 35, 1,046; Twenty-sixth Infantry, 50, 1,224; Twenty-seventh Infantry, 50, 1,185; Twenty-eighth Infantry, 50, 1,263; Twenty-ninth Infantry, 50, 1,230; Thirtieth Infantry, 50, 1,221; Thirty-first Infantry, 50, 1,211; Thirty-second Infantry, 50, 1,164; Thirty-third Infantry, 50, 1,213; Thirty-fourth Infantry, 50, 1,215; Thirty-fifth Infantry, 50, 1,228;

Thirty-sixth Infantry, 50, 940; Thirty-seventh Infantry, 50, 957; Thirty-eighth Infantry, 49, 1,203; Thirty-ninth Infantry, 49, 1,230; Fortieth Infantry, 48, 1,223; Forty-first Infantry, 51, 1,262; Forty-second Infantry, 49, 1,053; Forty-third Infantry, 50, 1,232; Forty-fourth Infantry, 50, 1,253; Forty-fifth Infantry, 46, 1,240; Forty-sixth Infantry, 50, 1,243; Forty-seventh Infantry, 50, 1,246; Forty-eighth Infantry, 50, 1,279; Forty-ninth Infantry, 50, 1,195. Engineers, 6, 235. Hospital Corps, 77, 2,386. Signal Corps, U. S. Army, 23, 407. Total, 2,387, 66,429. Acting assistant surgeons, 284.

MacArthur.

MANILA. (Received October 10, 1900—11.17 p. m.)
Adjutant-General, *Washington:*
Died 7.30 evening October 3, hepatitis, Second Lieut. Robert Blakeman, Forty-ninth Infantry.

MacArthur.

MANILA. (Received October 12, 1900—5.08 p. m.)
Adjutant-General, *Washington:*
Killed—September 28, Pili, Luzon, Company M, Forty-fifth Infantry, James J. Ryan, John S. Pearson; September 19, Mount Malindy, Panay, Company G, Forty-fourth Infantry, Albin F. Carter. Wounded—September 28, Pili, Luzon, Thirty-seventh Infantry, First Lieut. Jesse G. Lowenberg, shoulder, serious; Company M, Forty-fifth Infantry, Edward T. Hyland, head, mortal.

MacArthur.

MANILA. (Received October 13, 1900—7.22 a. m.)
Adjutant-General, *Washington:*
Appropriation $1,000,000 gold contemplated for harbor improvement; another captain engineers indispensable to supervise this work. If detailed make him member Guam board sailing *Solace.* * * * Biddle indispensable here; work on road and bridges require his constant supervision; his presence Guam would be highly prejudicial to scheme; 100 engineer recruits required before January 1. Send as soon as possible.

MacArthur.

MANILA. (Received October 15, 1900—4.15 a. m.)
Adjutant-General, *Washington:*
Information from Marinduque just received that Captain Shields, 48 men Company F, Twenty-ninth Infantry, 2 corporals Company A, Twenty-ninth Infantry, 1 civilian American negro, prisoners hands insurgents, have been turned over to Brig. Gen. Luther R. Hare. More particulars soon, giving names killed, wounded.

MacArthur.

MANILA. (Received October 15, 1900—8.05 a. m.)
Adjutant-General, *Washington:*
Killed—October 6, Orion, Luzon, D, Thirty-second Infantry, Charles P. Hoffman. Wounded—Frank G. Schmidt, leg above knee, slight; Frank Sommers, arm, slight; Corpl. Ernest W. McDaniel, hip, slight; Ernest L. Hoeft, breast, severe. Killed—September 12, Baybay, Leyte, Company E, Forty-third Infantry, Burt Field; Sep-

tember 29, Palanas, Masbate, B, Twenty-ninth Infantry, Ira N. Pence; October 3, Carmen, Bohol, Company C, Forty-fourth Infantry, William O. Hollingsworth. Wounded—October 6, Bangued, Luzon, B, Thirty-third Infantry, Corpl. Orville H. Mills, leg above knee, slight; date unknown, Panda, Panay, Forty-fourth Infantry, First Lieut. Clyde B. Parker, four slight wounds.

MacArthur.

Manila. (Received October 15, 1900—8.46 a. m.)
Adjutant-General, Washington:
Transport Siam sailed October 13, Athenian October 14. Transport Federica arrived to-day. [Detachment Light Batteries C and M, Seventh Artillery, on board Federica.]

MacArthur.

Manila. (Received October 16, 1900—6.32 a. m.)
Adjutant-General, Washington:
Sick in hospital, 3,232; sick in quarters, 1,192; in United States of America, 2,015; 10.52 per cent.

MacArthur.

Manila. (Received October 16, 1900—6.40 a. m.)
Adjutant-General, Washington:
The following casualties are reported covering all recent operations that island; men not mentioned, present, well; wounded are present: Killed—September 13, Torrijos, Marinduque, F, Twenty-ninth Infantry, William R. Andrews, Elmore E. Murray, Erwin Niles; September 14, Frank Weigand. Wounded—September 13, Capt. Devereux Shields, neck, mouth, and in shoulder, serious; Livicns S. Colvin, hip, slight; Robert D. Jackson, cheek, slight; Toliver G. Johnson, head, slight; arm, serious; Juan B. Poole, head slight; John Shew, head, wrist, slight; shoulder, serious.

MacArthur.

Manila. (Received October 16, 1900—12.40 p. m.)
Adjutant-General, Washington:
Following deaths have occurred since last report: Dysentery—September 29, K, Sixth Infantry, Francis B. Bowling; September 25, C, Eleventh Cavalry, John J. Curry; September 17, A, Nineteenth Infantry, James McShearer; October 10, D, Forty-fifth Infantry, Peter Sodergren; October 12, I, Thirty-third Infantry, Jules D. St. Alexander; A, Forty-fifth Infantry, Daniel E. Roob; G, Thirtieth Infantry, Homer W. Poland; October 11, G, Fourth Cavalry, John E. Herndon; K, Seventeenth Infantry, Walter W. Fessenden; October 7, F, Thirtieth Infantry, Daniel Currie. Ulceration of intestines—October 8, K, Thirteenth Infantry, James P. Sullivan; October 6, C, Twelfth Infantry, Joseph B. Haller. Enteritis: October 12, F, Third Cavalry, John Linton. Typhoid fever—October 9, E, Twenty-fourth Infantry, Ermine Cook; October 4, Hospital Corps, Edward C. Roth; August 27, L, Forty-fifth Infantry, Thomas B. Riley; September 29, H, Twenty-sixth Infantry, John J. Dolan. Malarial fever—October 7, Hospital Corps, Henry G. Patterson; October 5, A, Forty-ninth Infantry, Arthur Hunt. Drowned—October 4, M, Fourth Cavalry, Leroy W. Plants. Tuberculosis—October 2, L, Forty-ninth Infantry, Corpl. James Robinson. Cardiac dilatation—October 10, M, Twenty-fifth Infantry, Smith Berhanan. Pneumonia—October 6, B, Thirty-seventh Infantry, Edwin L. Summers. Dengue—August

29, L, Forty-fourth Infantry, James P. Allbriten. Died from wounds received in action—September 30, M, Forty-fifth Infantry, Edward T. Hyland. Accidental discharge pistol—July 30, Hospital Corps, William D. Harper. Killed by comrade—October 7, C, Thirty-second Infantry, William Kilpatrick.

MACARTHUR.

ADJUTANT-GENERAL'S OFFICE,
Washington, October 18, 1900.

MACARTHUR, *Manila:*

Secretary of War directs when officers and men of volunteers desire to leave service to enter business and cast their fortune with Philippine Islands, if you are satisfied with their honesty, purpose, give men discharge and cable names, officers, for acceptance resignation.

CORBIN.

[From Manila to Associated Press, New York.]

Find censorship last quarter be more unreasonable, stringent any time past year. Transmission incontrovertible military occurrences some time suppressed, notably Marinduque story, which suppressed after officially reported Washington. Transmission established facts often delayed forty-eight hours more. Political news frequently suppressed or am forced rewrite suit censor. Word ambush in cablegrams prohibited. Our messages Iloilo to Manila blue penciled at Iloilo. Foregoing carefully asserted from personal experiences, censorship MacArthur characterizing untrue misleading permits transmission.

MARTIN.

ADJUTANT-GENERAL'S OFFICE,
Washington, October 19, 1900.

MACARTHUR, *Manila:*

Renewed complaint made of censorship. Without assuming there is cause for complaint, Secretary of War directs attention to telegram to General Otis same subject, September 9, 1899.

CORBIN.

MANILA. (Received October 20, 1900—7.43 a. m.)

ADJUTANT-GENERAL, *Washington:*

Killed—October 14, Jean, Luzon, C, Twenty-fourth Infantry, James H. Benjamin. Wounded—October 13, San Miguel de Mayumo, Luzon, K, Thirty-fifth Infantry, Roy Gage, thigh, moderate; Santa Cruz, Luzon, C, Thirty-fourth Infantry, Leonard Robinson, side, moderate; October 7, Guinobatan, Luzon, B, Eleventh Cavalry, Frank M. Trackler, foot, serious.

MACARTHUR.

MANILA. (Received October 22, 1900—12.44 p. m.)

ADJUTANT-GENERAL, *Washington:*

Following deaths have occurred since last report: Dysentery—October 14, C, Thirty-fifth Infantry, David C. Whiting; October 17, H, Thirty-fourth Infantry, William G. Parham; G, Forty-sixth Infantry, Corpl. Glan H. Jackson; October 12, K, Third Infantry, John Gragert; October 7, M, Thirty-fourth Infantry, Willard Elwood; October 11, D, Ninth Cavalry, Thomas Davis; October 18, K, Seventeenth Infantry,

AFFAIRS IN THE PHILIPPINE ISLANDS. 1221

Marion O. Bennett; C, Third Infantry, Joseph Barker. Typhoid fever—October 15, Battery B, Sixth Artillery, Curtis J. Rush; September 12, Band, Fortieth Infantry, Ralph C. Dunlap; September 4, B, Forty-third Infantry, Albert O. Bernard. Drowned—October 14, H, Fourth Cavalry, Frank M. Lick; October 5, H, Eleventh Cavalry, Corpl. Edward J. Inderbitzen; October 6, F, Forty-ninth Infantry, Robert Banks. Malarial fever—October 13, G, Thirty-fourth Infantry, Corpl. James E. Tanzy; October 18, E, Third Infantry, Allen P. Adams. Killed by comrade—October 8, F, Forty-ninth Infantry Clarence T. Flemming. Suicide, shot, head—October 18th, G, Twentieth Infantry, John L. Forbis. Tuberculosis—October 14, E, Seventeenth Infantry, Corpl. James L. Hickey. Diarrhea—October 13, F, Thirty-ninth Infantry, Corpl. Schuyler Weimer. Variola—September 23, L, Forty-fourth Infantry, William C. Wood. Anæmia—September 26, C, Nineteenth, Infantry, Sergt. John Hubberd.

MACARTHUR.

MANILA. (Received October 21, 1900—8.10 a. m.)
ADJUTANT-GENERAL, *Washington:*
With reference to your telegram of 20th, no complaint known here except from man named Martin, Associated Press, who has repeatedly tried to send misleading report of military operations. My only purpose has been to prevent garbled information and enormous lists killed and wounded reaching United States of America before accurate information was obtained for purpose official report. Personally would be very glad to dispense with censorship if the Department so desires. Will make order immediately.

MACARTHUR.

MANILA. (Received October 25, 1900—3.20 a. m.)
ADJUTANT-GENERAL, *Washington:*
To insure expedition service, transferring large class patients from various posts to Manila, Medical Department desires smaller vessel than *Relief*. Commercial liners formerly utilized for these cases, poorly equipped and irregular in dates sailing. Suitable ship, light draft, 800 net tonnage, equipped for 116 first-class, 400 steerage, passengers, offered at $175,000 gold. Authority requested for purchase if on inspection found every way suitable. *Relief* when available too heavy draft services contemplated herein.

MACARTHUR.

MANILA. (Received October 25, 1900—11.50 p. m.)
ADJUTANT-GENERAL, *Washington:*
Transport *Thomas* arrived yesterday. (One battalion each First and Eighth Infantry.)

MACARTHUR.

MANILA. (Received October 26, 1900—9.34 a. m.)
ADJUTANT-GENERAL, *Washington:*
October 24, First Lieutenant Febiger, 40 men Company H, Thirty-third Infantry, Second Lieut. Grayson V. Heidt, 60 men Troop L, Third Cavalry, attacked insurgents 14 miles east of Narvacan, Ilocos Sur Province, Luzon; developed strong position occupied by about 400 riflemen and 1,000 bolomen, under command Juan Villamor, subordinate of Tinio. Desperate fight ensued, which was most creditable to force engaged, though under heavy pressure overwhelming numbers; our troops

compelled to return Narvacan, which was accomplished in tactical, orderly manner. Acting Assistant Surgeon Bath and civilian teamster, captured early in fight, were released by Villamor. According to their accounts insurgents much stronger than reported herein, and their loss, moderate estimate, over 150. Our loss: Killed— First Lieut. George L. Febiger, Charles A. Lindenberg, William F. Wilson, H, Thirty-third Infantry; Andrew T. Johnson, Farrier Guy E. McClintock, Troop L, Third Cavalry. Wounded—Company H, Thirty-third Infantry, Floyd W. McPherson, hip, slight; John W. Gray, face, slight; Floyd H. Heard, cheek, slight; Henry S. Johnson, knee, serious; L, Third Cavalry, Corpl. Adam R. Wachs, arm, slight; Alfred Downer, lip, head, serious; Charles W. Martin, thigh, slight; Oscar O. Bradford, foot, slight; William E. Hunter, leg below knee, slight. Missing—H, Thirty-third Infantry, John J. Boyd, Samuel P. Harris; L, Third Cavalry, Samuel Davis, Fred Schwed. Twenty-nine horses missing; some known killed.

MACARTHUR.

MANILA. (Received October 26, 1900—11.18 a. m.)
ADJUTANT-GENERAL, *Washington:*

First Regiment U. S. Infantry in Marinduque will probably soon settle difficulty that island. Thereafter shall send regiment intact to operate in Samar in conjunction with Twenty-ninth Infantry, all of which will be concentrated therein. Shall concentrate Thirty-sixth Infantry for field column in Young's district, where insurgents very active at present. Desire organize similar column Thirty-eighth Infantry operations Panay under Hughes. Another of Twenty-eighth Infantry operations northern Mindanao under Kobbé. With these movable columns, in addition to troops at present in districts mentioned, hope to accomplish much. Full development this scheme requires about four months' time and all troops now in islands. In this connection urgently recommend movement volunteers homeward to be deferred last moment possible; request information this subject as soon as possible so my plans may conform fixed policy Department.

MACARTHUR.

MANILA. (Received October 27, 1900—8.40 a. m.)
ADJUTANT-GENERAL, *Washington:*

Killed—October 21, Nasugbu, Luzon, F, Twenty-eighth Infantry, John McBride; H, Twenty-eighth Infantry, John O'Hara; October 25, Bayambang, Luzon, L, Seventeenth Infantry, Corpl. William F. Steiner, Otto Seaholm; October 24, San Isidro, Luzon, A, Seventeenth Infantry, Thomas M. Sweeney; October 7, Moalbual, Cebu, K, Forty-fourth Infantry, Charles Brandenberg; October 10, Talavera, Luzon, I, Twenty-fourth Infantry, William H. Jones. Wounded—October 21, Nasugbu, Luzon, Twenty-eighth Infantry, Capt. George W. Biegler, leg, above knee, slight; F, Twenty-eighth Infantry, Raymond Sweeney; G, Twenty-eighth Infantry, Frank E. Mehailik, Fred M. Hunter. October 25, Bayambang, Luzon, L, Seventeenth Infantry, Arthur V. Farrar, James Carr, William Haler; October 6, Sinait, Luzon, H, Third Cavalry, William J. McMahan, hip, severe; October 19, Calamba, Luzon, D, Thirty-ninth Infantry, James S. McGinnis, arm, slight; Alva Cundiff, arm, serious; October 10, Munoz, Luzon, I, Twenty-fourth Infantry, Edward Skinner, thigh, serious; George W. Jackson, arm, serious.

MACARTHUR.

AFFAIRS IN THE PHILIPPINE ISLANDS. 1223

ADJUTANT-GENERAL'S OFFICE,
Washington, October 27, 1900.

MACARTHUR, *Manila:*

With reference to your telegram of 26th, movement volunteers will be regulated so as not to interfere with plans proposed, which Secretary of War desires prosecuted with vigor.

CORBIN.

MANILA. (Received October 28, 1900—7.15 a. m.)

ADJUTANT-GENERAL, *Washington:*

With reference to your telegram of 27th, movement into Samar, and Gen. Samuel B. M. Young's district will commence at once. Into departments, Gen. Samuel B. M. Young [General Robert P. Hughes], and Gen. William A. Kobbé, when troops have returned from China. Will retain for operations necessary water transportation without interfering semimonthly service San Francisco, Cal. Expect to have everything full operation November 15, which favorable time for offensive operations. Shall push everything with great vigor.

MACARTHUR.

MANILA. (Received October 29, 1900—2.25 a. m.)

ADJUTANT-GENERAL, *Washington:*

Killed—October 26, near Bangued, Luzon, Company I, Thirty-third Infantry, Sergt. Vincent Burgstaller. Wounded—Thomas C. Tucker, shoulder, moderate; Thomas B. Davis, thigh, moderate.

MACARTHUR.

MANILA. (Received October 29, 1900—10.47 a. m.)

ADJUTANT-GENERAL, *Washington:*

Following deaths have occurred since last report: Dysentery—October 25, E, Seventeenth Infantry, Albert W. Frisby; October 24, M, Twenty-first Infantry, Patrick J. Martin; I, Thirteenth Infantry, Dennis Murphy; October 22, G, Thirty-eighth Infantry, George F. Thornton. Tuberculosis—October 24, K, Fourth Cavalry, Fred P. Sullivan; F, Thirty-ninth Infantry, Charles T. Stearns; October 23, C, Seventeenth Infantry, William Gross; October 7, G, Thirtieth Infantry, Logan B. Jackson. Malarial fever—October 22, A, Forty-ninth Infantry, Robert L. Baker; F, Signal Corps, John H. Taylor; August 9, B, Twenty-eighth Infantry, John Engelhardt. Typhoid fever—October 26, K, Twenty-seventh Infantry, Charles Lennox. Meningitis—October 4, H, Eighth Infantry, William B. Phelps; October 20, F, Forty-first Infantry, William J. Miller. Nephritis—October 21, L, Third Cavalry, Alton J. Rumery. Drowned—October 17, C, Forty-ninth Infantry, Douglas Alston. Hemoglobinuria—October 21, I, Thirty-seventh Infantry, John J. England. Accidently killed by comrade—September 24, C, Forty-fourth Infantry, Verni Stockstill. Bronchitis—October 10, L, Thirty-seventh Infantry, William Chatman.

MACARTHUR.

MANILA. (Received October 29, 1900—10.34 p. m.)

ADJUTANT-GENERAL, *Washington:*

Transport *Hancock* arrived yesterday; *Algoa, Arab* October 29.

MACARTHUR.

QUARTERMASTER-GENERAL'S OFFICE,
Washington, October 29, 1900.

The ADJUTANT-GENERAL OF THE ARMY.

SIR: I have the honor to inform you that the army transports *Buford* and *Kilpatrick* will sail from New York for Manila on the following dates: *Buford*, November 7, 1900; *Kilpatrick*, November 13, 1900.

Respectfully,

M. I. LUDINGTON,
Quartermaster-General U. S. Army.

ADJUTANT-GENERAL'S OFFICE,
Washington, October 30, 1900.

MACARTHUR, *Manila:*

With reference to my telegram of 8th ultimo, troops from China for your command may be used to meet your requirements. They will not be needed in China. With reference to your telegram of 13th, another engineer is not available Guam board. Suggest Capt. George A. Zinn, serve chief engineer during the absence Biddle, subject future change if absence prolonged. * * *

CORBIN.

ADJUTANT-GENERAL'S OFFICE,
Washington, October 31, 1900.

MACARTHUR, *Manila:*

With reference to your telegram September 14, mules and horses referred to have all been shipped except 500 horses. These horses with 500 additional and 600 mules, including three fully equipped pack trains, are available for shipment by November 30. Do you need more of each? If so, how many do you want?

CORBIN.

MANILA. (Received November 1, 1900—1.40 a. m.)

ADJUTANT-GENERAL, *Washington:*

Sick in quarters, 1,475; sick in hospital, 3,860; in United States of America, 2,086; 11.96 per cent.

MACARTHUR.

ADJUTANT-GENERAL'S OFFICE,
Washington, November 1, 1900.

MACARTHUR, *Manila:*

* * * With reference to your telegram 1st, omit in the future number sick in United States.

CORBIN.

MANILA. (Received November 1, 1900—2.12 a. m.)

ADJUTANT-GENERAL, *Washington:*

With reference to your telegram of 31st ultimo, ship additional horses, mules referred to therein; for time being no more animals required; may need more when size army occupation definitely fixed by reorganization; smaller the force more animals needed. With reference to your telegram of 7th July, will Eighth Regiment Cavalry be sent?

MACARTHUR.

AFFAIRS IN THE PHILIPPINE ISLANDS.

MANILA. (Received November 1, 1900—4.30 a. m.)
ADJUTANT-GENERAL, *Washington:*
John G. Davis, major and surgeon, U. S.' Volunteers, died 1.58 this morning; chronic Bright's disease.

MACARTHUR.

ADJUTANT-GENERAL'S OFFICE,
Washington, November 1, 1900.
MACARTHUR, *Manila:*
Mr. Emery, Associated Press representative, will arrive on transport *Grant*, when he takes charge, relieving Martin; all censorship will be removed; this of your own motion. * * *

CORBIN.

MANILA. (Received November 2, 1900—1.42 a. m.)
ADJUTANT-GENERAL, *Washington:*
Killed—October 12, Laguan, Samar, F, Fourth Artillery, Fred. L. Rietz; September 30, Tacloban, Leyte, D, Forty-third Infantry, William M. Sugg; C, Forty-third Infantry, Corpl. James L. Noble; B, Forty-third Infantry, Aleade Gingras; October 30, Maasin, Luzon, E, Thirty-fifth Infantry, John H. Brewer; October 24, Narvacan, Luzon, L, Third Cavalry, Samuel Davis, previously reported missing; October 25, San Quintin, Luzon, I, Thirty-third Infantry, Sergt. Vincent Burgstaller; September 22, Langbasa, Leyte, K, Forty-third Infantry, Harry Veyon; October 15, Tubangan, Panay, B, Twenty-sixth Infantry, Herbert H. Brown; October 28, Sariaya, Luzon, C, Thirty-eighth Infantry, John Lanter. Wounded—October 30, Maasin, E, Thirty-fifth Infantry, William A. Staffeldt, neck, serious; D, Thirty-fifth Infantry, Matthew Majayjay, knee, serious; October 25, San Quintin, I, Thirty-third Infantry, Thomas C. Tucker, shoulder, moderate; Thomas B. Davis, thigh, moderate; September 22, Langbasa, Leyte, K, Forty-third Infantry, Edward J. Hill, foot, slight; L, Forty-Third Infantry, John South, thigh, serious; October 20, Legaspi, Luzon, D, Eleventh Cavalry, John Brittles, thigh, serious; October 30, Camilig. Luzon, G, Seventeenth Infantry, Clarence Parker, wounded in arm, serious; October 25, Bayambang, Luzon, L, Seventeenth Infantry, William Haler, chest, slight; October 8, Orion, Luzon, D, Thirty-second Infantry, Frank G. Schmidt, leg above knee, slight; October 24, Vintar, Luzon, H, Thirty-fourth Infantry, Earl Hale, arm, slight; November 1, Camilig, Luzon, L, Fourth Cavalry, John H. Rogers, arm, serious.

MACARTHUR.

ADJUTANT-GENERAL'S OFFICE,
Washington, November 3, 1900.
MACARTHUR, *Manila:*
With reference to your telegram of 1st, Eighth Regiment U. S. Cavalry will not be sent.

CORBIN.

MANILA. (Received November 4, 1900—1.30 a. m.)
ADJUTANT-GENERAL, *Washington:*
With reference to your telegram of 19th July, unless otherwise ordered shall defer temporarily consolidation of battalions, Third Regiment U. S. Artillery, as both are needed for pending field operations.

MACARTHUR.

MANILA. (Received November 5, 1900—1.06 p. m.)
ADJUTANT-GENERAL, *Washington:*
Following deaths have occurred since last report: Dysentery—October 31, E, Thirty-eighth Infantry, William Boling; October 29, M, Forty-first Infantry, John B. Bowers; October 7, A, Sixth Infantry, Charles A. Carroll; October 30, A, Twenty-sixth Infantry, Thomas Kane; B, Twenty-first Infantry, Michael J. Sullivan. Tuberculosis—G, Thirty-fourth Infantry, Richard M. Burns; September 14, G, Forty-third Infantry, Corpl. Patrick Maloney; October 28, L, Third Cavalry, Joseph P. Murphy. Malarial fever—October 16, M, Sixth Infantry, Henry L. Allison; October 29, L, Twenty-eighth Infantry, Edmund I. Dare; October 27, K, Thirty-fourth Infantry, Charles Hobson; October 30, M, Forty-fifth Infantry, William Jacobs; October 21, H, Thirty-ninth Infantry, Andrew J. Taylor; October 19, H, Eleventh Cavalry, Fretzsk Thomas. Variola—October 22, I, Forty-ninth Infantry, Walter Warren. Typhoid fever—October 30, L, Thirty-fifth Infantry, Patrick J. O'Connell. Diabetes—October 28, F, Fourth Cavalry, Robert J. Lilley. Asthma—October 18, G, Forty-ninth Infantry, Willie Johnson. Nephritis—October 26, C, Seventeenth Infantry, Sergt. Samuel M. Horn. Abscess liver—October 23, A, Nineteenth Infantry, Edward Farrell. Meningitis—October 20, M, Nineteenth Infantry, Philip F. Dindinger. Colonitis—October 22, M, Sixth Infantry, Sergt. Frank Braunwart. Drowned—September 8, C, Ninth Cavalry, Willie Clay; October 30, E, Twenty-eighth Infantry, William H. Moseback. Colitis—H, Sixteenth Infantry, John L. Chambers. Heart disease—October 15, B, Sixth Infantry, Frederick Deck. Alcoholism—November 1, H, Thirtieth Infantry, Musician John Maloney.

MACARTHUR.

ADJUTANT-GENERAL'S OFFICE,
Washington, November 5, 1900.
MACARTHUR, *Manila:*
* * * With reference to your telegram of 4th, Secretary of War directs no instructions from here be allowed interfere or impede progress your military operations, which he expects you force to successful conclusion; after which carry into effect instructions relating Third Regiment U. S. Artillery and home battalions generally. Home battalion scheme regarded best solution recruitment for regiments Philippine Islands. * * *

CORBIN.

MANILA. (Received November 6, 1900—6.57 a. m.)
ADJUTANT-GENERAL, *Washington:*
Stanley M. Stuart, assistant surgeon, Eleventh Cavalry, died 8.35 this morning, Santa Cruz, Luzon, fractured skull, thrown from horse.

MACARTHUR.

MANILA. (Received November 6, 1900—7.15 a. m.)
ADJUTANT-GENERAL, *Washington:*
Killed—1 p. m., Monday, October 29, near Cuartero, William D. Pasco, second lieutenant, K, Eighteenth Infantry; Lem Meador; Addison L. Eneix.

MACARTHUR.

MANILA. (Received November 8, 1900—1.30 p. m.)
ADJUTANT-GENERAL, *Washington:*
Total strength, present and absent, October 31, ascertained as near as possible: First Cavalry, officers, 20; enlisted men, 714; Third Cavalry, 42, 1,362; Fourth Cav-

alry, 47, 1,389; Sixth Cavalry, 4, 99; Ninth Cavalry, 27, 784; Eleventh Cavalry, 50, 1,005; Philippine Cavalry, 11, 436. Battery E, First Artillery, 4, 150; Third Artillery, 11, 370; Battery F, Fourth Artillery, 4, 140; Battery F, Fifth Artillery, China, no returns; Sixth Artillery, 37, 1,351. First Infantry, 26, 1,037; Second Infantry, 25, 1,049; Third Infantry, 46, 1,373; Fourth Infantry, 45, 1,401; Fifth Infantry, 25, 1,040; Sixth Infantry, 46, 1,380; Eighth Infantry, 23, 1,006 Ninth Infantry, China, no returns; Twelfth Infantry, 45, 1,379; Thirteenth Infantry, 46, 1,399; Fourteenth Infantry, China, no returns; Fifteenth Infantry, 13, 500; Sixteenth Infantry, 46, 1,396; Seventh Infantry, 46, 1,339; Eighteenth Infantry, 36, 1,148; Nineteenth Infantry, 47, 1,456; Twentieth Infantry, 47, 1,399; Twenty-first Infantry, 46, 1,391; Twenty-second Infantry, 46, 1,385; Twenty-third Infantry, 46, 1,640; Twenty-fourth Infantry, 46, 1,392; Twenty-fifth Infantry, 43, 1,487; Twenty-sixth Infantry, 50, 1,178; Twenty-seventh Infantry, 50, 1,167; Twenty-eighth Infantry, 50, 1,260; Twenty-ninth Infantry, 50, 1,229; Thirtieth Infantry, 50, 1,213; Thirty-first Infantry, 50, 1,211; Thirty-second Infantry, 50, 1,153; Thirty-third Infantry, 49, 1,199; Thirty-fourth Infantry, 51, 1,200; Thirty-fifth Infantry, 50, 1,218; Thirty-sixth Infantry, 50, 934; Thirty-seventh Infantry, 50, 968; Thirty-eighth Infantry, 49, 1,200; Thirty-ninth Infantry, 49, 1,227; Fortieth Infantry, 48, 1,220; Forty-first Infantry, 50, 1,254; Forty-second Infantry, 50, 1,162; Forty-third Infantry, 50, 1,174; Forty-fourth Infantry, 50, 1,238; Forty-fifth Infantry, 46, 1,232; Forty-sixth Infantry, 50, 1,240; Forty-seventh Infantry, 50, 1,249; Forty-eighth Infantry, 50, 1,279; Forty-ninth Infantry, 49, 1,219. Engineers, 6, 234. Hospital Corps, 83, 2,382. Signal Corps, 26, 431. Total, 2,352, 65,008.

MACARTHUR.

ADJUTANT-GENERAL'S OFFICE,
Washington, November 9, 1900.
MACARTHUR, *Manila:*
* * * Transport *Buford* left New York on November 7; transport *Kilpatrick* will leave New York on November 13; about 23 officers, 945 men each

CORBIN.

MANILA. (Received November 10, 1900—11.35 a. m.)
ADJUTANT-GENERAL, *Washington:*
Killed—November 1, Baliuag, Luzon, H, Fourth Cavalry, Sergt. William H. Bremer; November 3, Cebu, G, Sixth Artillery, Sergt. Edward F. Cleer. Wounded—November 1, Baliuag, Luzon, H, Fourth Cavalry, John H. Rodgers, arm, serious; November 5, Pasuquin, Luzon, F, Thirty-fourth Infantry, Thomas A. Cline, buttock, slight; November 4, O'Donnell, Luzon, D, Twelfth Infantry, John Price, arm, moderate; Carl Hannigs, eye, severe; October 18, Bataan, Luzon, E, Eighteenth Infantry, Lawrence E. Kilkenny, shoulder, serious; October 7, Moalbual, Cebu, K, Forty-fourth Infantry, Doughton H. Kimble, leg above knee, slight; October 11, Balasan, Panay, D, Twenty-sixth Infantry, Joseph Watson, arm, slight; Thomas McGee, arm, serious; October 10, Mambusao, Panay, L, Eighteenth Infantry, Thomas Noonan, back, slight; September 11, Sibalon, Panay, A, Nineteenth Infantry, Corpl. Richard K. Moffett, head, slight.

MACARTHUR.

ADJUTANT-GENERAL'S OFFICE,
Washington, November 10, 1900.
MACARTHUR, *Manila:*
When you can spare transports *Pennsylvania, Indiana, Garonne,* Secretary of War desires them sent San Francisco with volunteers sick and convalescent in hospitals; retaining *Warren, Sumner, Rosecrans.*

CORBIN.

CORRESPONDENCE.

MANILA. (Received November 11, 1900—7.03 a. m.)
ADJUTANT-GENERAL, *Washington:*

With reference to your telegram of 10th, *Warren, Sumner, Rosecrans,* two animal transports, required two months or more connection with military operations. *Indiana, Pennsylvania,* indispensable distribution supplies. Available resources local water transportation companies not sufficient. Can spare *Garonne* early date, which, in connection with regular transports, will clean up all sick and convalescents. With reference to your telegram of 27th ultimo, understood movement volunteers would not commence for four months; have arranged accordingly and based important military movements thereon.

MACARTHUR.

MANILA. (Received November 12, 1900—11.20 a. m.)
ADJUTANT-GENERAL, *Washington:*

Following deaths have occurred since last report: Dysentery—November 7, M, Thirty-ninth Infantry, Everett S. Wiley; October 7, G, Fortieth Infantry, Andrew Scott; L, Nineteenth Infantry, Edward J. McCarthy; November 3, K, Fourth Cavalry, Guy A. Rea; A, Twenty-eighth Infantry, Corpl. Edward Fitzgerald; November 6, K, Twenty-first Infantry, Raphael Magnus; H, Seventeenth Infantry, Charles B. Lageman; November 2, D, Thirtieth Infantry, William Krueger; M, Thirtieth Infantry, Artificer Walter D. Green; October 5, C, Twenty-ninth Infantry, Charles Wilson; November 8, M, Twenty-fifth Infantry, Albert Harris; October 20, K, Forty-fifth Infantry, William Sites; October 15, L, Eighteenth Infantry, Leonard Frey; I, Forty-seventh Infantry, Conoway O. Bullman. Diarrhea—November 7, E, Eleventh Cavalry, William Hall. Pneumonia—November 4, I, Forty-second Infantry, Sergeant Ezra W. Williams; October 27, A, Forty-fifth Infantry, Ed. Hunter. Enterocolitis—November 5, A, Louis Talmadge, Thirtieth Infantry. Gastroenteritis—November 1, F, Fourth Artillery, James E. Leighton. Cirrhosis liver—November 4, C, Thirty-sixth Infantry, Corpl. Asa C. Hylton; November 2, Band, Thirteenth Infantry, Corpl. Felix Franz. Malarial fever—November 4, A, Forty-ninth Infantry, Amos Reed. Insolation—October 10, I, Twenty-fourth Infantry, Corpl. Charles Henry. Variola—September 25, I, Forty-ninth Infantry, Lewis Horton. Tuberculosis—November 3, K, Forty-fifth Infantry, William H. McIntyre. Peritonitis—November 8, K, Forty-second Infantry, Edward P. Miller. Drowned—November 6, E, Fourth Infantry, Edward E. Davis.

MACARTHUR.

MANILA. (Received November 15, 1900—8.55 a. m.)
ADJUTANT-GENERAL, *Washington:*

Sick in quarters, 1,450; sick in hospitals, 3,403; 7.8 per cent.

MACARTHUR.

MANILA. (Received November 15, 1900—9.16 a. m.)
ADJUTANT-GENERAL, *Washington:*

Killed—November 10, Subig, Luzon, L, Twenty-fifth Infantry, James McCormick. Wounded—Elmer A. Price, shoulder, serious; James S. Cox, shoulder, slight; Walker D. Reason, foot, slight; Henry Warfield, shoulder, serious; October 26, Camilig, Luzon, G, Ninth Cavalry, Job McKinzie, back, serious; October 25, Cosucos, Luzon, H, Thirty-third Infantry, Henry S. Johnson, thigh, serious; November 2, Bangued, Luzon, A, Thirty-third Infantry, Albium M. Andrews, eye, slight; Capt. Charles Van Way, chest, serious; Corpl. William M. Miller, leg above knee, slight; John B. Clark, neck, slight; Peter Schomers, thigh, serious; William Nickel, scalp, slight.

MACARTHUR.

MANILA. (Received November 16, 1900—3.52 a. m.)
ADJUTANT-GENERAL, *Washington:*
Palmer G. Wood, jr., second lieutenant, Twelfth Infantry, died malarial fever, San Juan de Guimba, Luzon, 9.10 morning, November 16.
MACARTHUR.

NEW YORK, *November 16, 1900.*
(Received 3.55 a. m.)
PIERSON:
The Eastern Extension Company announces censorship on messages to and from Manila has been removed, but copies of press messages sent and received must be sent to the military governor.
CENTRAL CABLE COMPANY.

ADJUTANT-GENERAL'S OFFICE,
Washington, November 16, 1900.
MACARTHUR, *Manila:*
With reference to your telegram of 1st, 350 mules, 500 horses additional to those referred to in our telegram October 31, will be sent before December 31. Is it probable more of either will be required within next four months?
CORBIN.

MANILA. (Received November 17, 1900—9.28 a. m.
ADJUTANT-GENERAL, *Washington:*
Killed—October 27, Catbalogan, Samar, D, Twenty-ninth Infantry, Corpl. Herbert H. Chase; October 30, Bugason, Panay, First Lieut. Howard M. Koontz, Forty-fourth Infantry; November 12 La Paz, Luzon, H, Twelfth Infantry, John Lumbert. Wounded—Charles McCollister, severely; November 2, Point Bano, Luzon, C, Twenty-eighth Infantry, Patrick W. Crann, arm, serious; Cook John Bogt, thigh, serious; Corpl. Henry Kunkel, head, slight.
MACARTHUR.

MANILA. (Received November 19, 1900—10.30 a. m.)
ADJUTANT-GENERAL, *Washington:*
Following deaths have occurred since last report: Dysentery—November 15, B, Eleventh Cavalry, Melvin M. Hauk; November 9, H, Forty-seventh Infantry, James J. Tochel; October 31, E, Eighteenth Infantry, William H. Silvers; October 29, K, Sixteenth Infantry, John V. Ackley. Variola—November 8, F, Forty-eighth Infantry, William Jackson; November 11, H, Forty-eighth Infantry, Thomas Williams; November 9, E, Forty-eighth Infantry, Louis Kline. Drowned—November 6, G, Twenty-eighth Infantry, Guy F. Wooten; November 12, F, Twenty-second Infantry, William P. Miller. Died from wounds received in action—October 27, G, Ninth Cavalry, Job McKinzie; November 2, H, Thirty-third Infantry, Henry S. Johnson. Suicide—October 27, E, Eighteenth Infantry, Sergt. William T. Smith. Killed by comrade—November 5, K, Forty-ninth Infantry, Andrew Hardy. Cirrhosis liver—November 11, M, Seventeenth Infantry, Patrick B. Rooney; October 25, F, Fourth Artillery, John P. Watkins. Typhoid fever—November 5, M, Forty-seventh Infantry, George F. Thomas. Diphtheria—November 12, G, Thirty-fourth Infantry, Augustus F. Waite. Insolation—November 10, A, Seventeenth Infantry, Musician Harry T. Raub. Tuberculosis—November 12, G, Forty-eighth Infantry, Frank

Hunter. Appendicitis—November 14, M, Twenty-seventh Infantry, Henry Kind. Peritonitis—November 3, D, Twenty-sixth Infantry, Frank H. Crosby. Inanition—November 13, L, Forty-sixth Infantry, John D. Carpenter.

MACARTHUR.

MANILA. (Received November 21, 1900—3.50 a. m.)
ADJUTANT-GENERAL, *Washington:*
Transport *Leelanaw* arrived yesterday. All animals lost typhoon.

MACARTHUR.

MANILA. (Received November 21, 1900—4.40 a. m.)
ADJUTANT-GENERAL, *Washington:*
With reference to your telegram of 16th, ship immediately in addition to all previous orders 750 mules, 125 escort wagons. No more animals required for four months; this covers transport *Leelanaw's* loss, 237.

MACARTHUR.

ADJUTANT-GENERAL'S OFFICE,
Washington, November 21, 1900.
MACARTHUR, *Manila:*
* * * With reference to your telegram of August 15, reporting Capt. William L. Murphy killed Tuesday, which was August 14, report has been received since giving August 13. Suggest reports deaths give specific dates.

CORBIN.

ADJUTANT-GENERAL'S OFFICE,
Washington, November 21, 1900.
MACARTHUR, *Manila:*
What is the present status of Sergeant Kitchen, Company F, Forty-fourth Infantry, U. S. Volunteers? With reference to your telegram of 21st, no objection distribute annual report.

CORBIN.

MANILA. (Received November 23, 1900—1.37 a. m.)
ADJUTANT-GENERAL, *Washington:*
With reference to your telegram of 22d, death Murphy, 13th. Frederick W. Altstaetter, first lieutenant, Corps of Engineers, released by insurgents, November 20, now en route to Manila. Transport *Wyefield* arrived yesterday.

MACARTHUR.

MANILA. (Received November 23, 1900—7.35 a. m.)
ADJUTANT-GENERAL, *Washington:*
With reference to your telegram of 21st, Kitchen killed in action, Bugason, Panay, October 30. Never reported here.

MACARTHUR.

ADJUTANT-GENERAL'S OFFICE. (Received November 23, 1900.)
MACARTHUR, Manila:
What is the present status of Corporal Burns, Company F, Forty-fourth Infantry, U. S. Volunteers?

CORBIN.

MANILA. (Received November 24, 1900—7.10 a. m.)
ADJUTANT-GENERAL, Washington:
With reference to your telegram of 23d, Burns killed in action, Bugason, Panay, October 30.

MACARTHUR.

MANILA. (Received November 24, 1900—1.41 p. m.)
ADJUTANT-GENERAL, Washington:
Killed—November 11, Bulusan, Panay, L, Forty-seventh Infantry, Thomas W. Hollingsworth; November 14, Amulug, Luzon, F, Signal Corps, Sergt. Robin J. Todd; November 22, Montalban, Luzon, K, Twenty-seventh Infantry, William H. Hart, jr.; A, Forty-second Infantry, Lawrence P. Kappner. Wounded—Fred E. Riley, hand, slight; B, Twenty-seventh Infantry, Sergt. Daniel Gump, loin, slight; Harry S. Gatto, hand, slight; Twenty-seventh Infantry, Batt. Sergt. Maj. Daniel W. de Cardenas, face, slight; Pantijan, Luzon, I, Forty-sixth Infantry, Charles T. Smith, arm, slight; William E. Turner, thigh, moderate; November 11, Bulusan, Panay, L, Forty-seventh Infantry, Augustus Nelson, arm, serious; October 21, Guadalupe, Cebu, M, Nineteenth Infantry, John D. Hofman, hip, severe; Cook Joseph M. Potter, thigh, slight; November 16, Abucay, Luzon, F, Thirty-second Infantry, John G. Loos, thigh, moderate; October 16, Payo, Catanduanes, C, Forty-seventh Infantry, Corpl. John W. Jackson, head, serious; November 10, Subig, Luzon, L, Twenty-fifth Infantry, Corpl. Arthur R. D. Smith, thigh, serious; November 13, Santa Cruz, Luzon, E, Fourth Cavalry, Musician Thomas Matuchewica, neck, serious; November 16, Norzagaray, Luzon, Philippine Cavalry, Second Lieut. Clarence M. Condon, chest, slight.

MACARTHUR.

MANILA. (Received November 26, 1900—7.40 p. m.)
ADJUTANT-GENERAL, Washington:
Following deaths have occurred since last report: Dysentery—November 18, E, Forty-third Infantry, John H. Weld; November 22, K, Third Infantry, Harry Rich; November 17, A, Thirteenth Infantry, Thomas H. Doyle; D, Twenty-eighth Infantry, Charley Hulme; November 12, M, Sixth Infantry, Conrad Gautier; October 27, K, Forty-fifth Infantry, Hiram Gilpin. Variola—November 17, E, Forty-eighth Infantry, John Commons; November 15, G, Forty-eighth Infantry, Corpl. Frank Taylor. Tuberculosis—November 23, K, Thirty-fifth Infantry, Corpl. Jesse C. Dodson. Malarial fever—November 22, B, Thirty-fourth Infantry, Gilbert B. Lafflin. Anæmia—November 19, D, Thirty-fifth Infantry, Charles A. Miles. Heart disease—November 15, A, Twenty-fourth Infantry, Corpl. Louis Morgan. Died from wounds received in action—November 18, L, Twenty-fifth Infantry, Corpl. Arthur R. D. Smith. Alcoholism—November 19, K, Forty-ninth Infantry, Williams Ammons. Pulmonary congestion—November 21, G, Twenty-seventh Infantry, Raymond Lisk; November 4, F, Fourth Artillery, Charles Welch.

Pneumonia—November 19, G, Thirty-third Infantry, John W. Low. Pleurisy—November 11, G, Third Artillery, John B. Condlin. Cerebral hemorrhage—November 18, E, Seventeenth Infantry, William M. Rupel. Nephritis—November 19, E, Twenty-fifth Infantry, John M. Jones.

MacArthur.

MANILA. (Received December 1, 1900—12.28 a m.)

ADJUTANT-GENERAL, *Washington:*

Sick in hospital, 3,286; sick in quarters, 1,471; 8.8 per cent.

MacArthur.

MANILA. (Received December 2, 1900—7.25 a. m.)

ADJUTANT-GENERAL, *Washington:*

Service John S. Mallory (captain Second Infantry), Hongkong, practically of very little value, as impossible to arrange cooperation with consul-general. Request that I be granted authority to recall him.

MacArthur.

MANILA. (Received December 3, 1900—12.15 a. m.)

ADJUTANT-GENERAL, *Washington:*

Two thousand one hundred and eighty Katipunan insurrectos whom Connisque enrolled, bolomen, came from mountains and surrendered to Gen. Samuel B. M. Young to-day at Santa Maria. [They] renounced insurrection and swore allegiance to the United States. The oath was administered by the padre at the church with impressive religious ceremonies. General Young attributes the surrender to President's reelection and vigorous prosecution of the war. Although no rifles surrendered, this is important as indicating a reaction among the people Ilocos Sur. Movable columns Samar, Panay, commenced operations. Twenty-eighth Regiment U. S. Volunteer Infantry goes to Mindanao. Everything is to be pushed as vigorously as possible for the next thirty days.

MacArthur.

MANILA. (Received December 3, 1900—6.30 a. m.)

ADJUTANT-GENERAL, *Washington:*

Killed—November 26, Umbao, Nueva Caceres, Luzon, D, Ninth Cavalry, Samuel Walker; November 24, Malolos, Luzon, F, Third Infantry, Joseph H. Winkler. Wounded—L, Third Infantry, Otto Kruger; Daniel O. Harkins, head, serious; November 12, Cabatuan, Panay, H, Twenty-sixth Infantry, Otis Manchester, chest, slight.

MacArthur.

MANILA. (Received December 3, 1900—12.43 p. m.)

ADJUTANT-GENERAL, *Washington:*

Following deaths have occurred since last report: Dysentery—November 27, K, Fourth Cavalry, James A. Innis; November 18, F, Eighteenth Infantry, Harvey Bimson; A, Nineteenth Infantry, Frank J. Smith; November 25, B, Thirtieth Infantry, Christopher C. Keogel; November 6, A, Nineteenth Infantry, Musician William H. Dorey; November 30, B, Thirty-fourth Infantry, Frank E. Glumm. Diarrhea—November 26, B, Thirty-fourth Infantry, Edward Hoover. Heart disease—November 30, G, Twenty-second Infantry, John Vanzandt; H, Twenty-fifth Infantry,

Henry Gage. Typhoid fever—November 26, E, Fourteenth Infantry, Edward Pierson; M, Twenty-fourth Infantry, James H. Wilson; November 27, Thirtieth Infantry, Willard C. Gifford; November 20, I, Thirty-ninth Infantry, Sergt. Albert R. Krueger. Drowned—November 28, Twenty-fourth Infantry, unassigned recruit, Charles G. Geiger; November 24, G, Fourth Infantry, Jacob Wisler; October 12, D, Thirtieth Infantry, Andrew J. Nelson. Tuberculosis—November 26, A, Thirtieth Infantry, John M. Ramdles; November 14, E, Third Cavalry, William M. Renner. Nephritis—November 18, A, Twenty-ninth Infantry, Joseph C. Morgan; September 10, E, Twenty-fifth Infantry, John Bell. Alcoholism—November 23, M, Twenty-first Infantry, John B. Sullivan; October 12, G, Thirty-eighth Infantry, Joseph L. Mowrey. Malarial fever—November 26, I, Forty-first Infantry, William S. Brown. Syphilis—October 18, F, Eleventh Cavalry, Sergt. Vernie J. Edwards. Tetanus—November 26, B, Forty-eighth Infantry, Isaac Reeves. Diphtheria—November 24, B, Third Cavalry, Farrier Herman J. A. Jordens. Uræmia—November 26, F, Thirty-eighth Infantry, Ray W. Mihart. Hemorrhage—November 4, L, Nineteenth Infantry, John J. Barry. Killed by comrade—November 24, L, Twelfth Infantry, Patrick O'Day; November 25, H, Third Cavalry, Samuel Byers. Killed by sentry—October 30, L, Twenty-fifth Infantry, William Burles. Suicide, shot head—November 26, Thirty-fifth Infantry, Principal Musician Lewis E. Gale. With reference to my telegram of 5th November, death Burns, October 29.

MACARTHUR.

MANILA. (Received December 4, 1900—9.03 a. m.)
ADJUTANT-GENERAL, *Washington:*
Killed—November 30, Pilar, Luzon, A, Thirty-sixth Infantry, Cornelius J. Leahy. Wounded—H, Thirty-sixth Infantry, Samuel A. Roberts, arm, serious; F, Thirty-sixth Infantry, Ulric Jusseaume, abdomen, serious; K, Thirty-sixth Infantry, Frank Hilliker, groin, moderate; L, Thirty-sixth Infantry, Courtney Morris, leg above knee, slight; G, Thirty-sixth Infantry, Charles Clark, foot, slight; H, Thirty-sixth Infantry, John G. Kertz, arm, serious; I, Thirty-sixth Infantry, Albert Padesky, leg above knee, slight. Killed—November 21, San Vicente, Luzon, L, Forty-fifth Infantry, George R. Whittier.

MACARTHUR.

MANILA. (Received December 6, 1900—3.55 p. m.)
ADJUTANT-GENERAL, *Washington:*
Total strength, present and absent, November 30, ascertained as near as possible: Officers, enlisted men, First Cavalry, 35, 843; Third Cavalry, 41, 1,336; Fourth Cavalry, 47, 1,355; Sixth Cavalry, 15, 354;. Ninth Cavalry, 35, 837; Eleventh Cavalry, 50, 1,003; Philippine Cavalry, 11, 435. Battery E, First Artillery, 4, 154; Third Artillery, 13, 396; Battery F, Fourth Artillery, 3, 148; Sixth Artillery, 42, 1,352. First Infantry, 34, 1,065; Second Infantry, 35, 1,058; Third Infantry, 46, 1,402; Fourth Infantry, 44, 1,402; Fifth Infantry, 25, 1,045; Sixth Infantry, 46, 1,395; Eighth Infantry, 24, 1,004; Twelfth Infantry, 46, 1,373; Thirteenth Infantry, 47, 1,428; Fourteenth Infantry, 40, 1,114; Fifteenth Infantry, 11, 496; Sixteenth Infantry, 46, 1,451; Seventeenth Infantry, 45, 1,408; Eighteenth Infantry, 37, 1,144; Nineteenth Infantry, 35, 1,372; Twentieth Infantry, 47, 1,392; Twenty-first Infantry, 46, 1,348; Twenty-second Infantry, 46, 1,378; Twenty-third Infantry, 36, 1,402; Twenty-fourth Infantry, 37, 1,004; Twenty-fifth Infantry, 48, 1,530; Twenty-sixth Infantry, 50, 1,172; Twenty-seventh Infantry, 50, 1,153; Twenty-eighth Infantry, 50, 1,213; Twenty-ninth Infantry, 49, 1,217; Thirtieth Infantry, 50, 1,174; Thirty-first Infantry, 49, 1,189; Thirty-second Infantry, 50, 1,122; Thirty-third Infantry, 49, 1,191; Thirty-fourth Infantry, 50, 1,189,

Thirty-fifth Infantry, 50, 1,209; Thirty-sixth Infantry, 49, 934; Thirty-seventh Infantry, 50, 936; Thirty-eighth Infantry, 49, 1,181; Thirty-ninth Infantry, 50, 1,179; Fortieth Infantry, 49, 1,195; Forty-first Infantry, 50, 1,249; Forty-second Infantry, 50, 1,133; Forty-third Infantry, 47, 1,195; Forty-fourth Infantry, 50, 1,230; Forty-fifth Infantry, 50, 1,202; Forty-sixth Infantry, 50, 1,200; Forty-seventh Infantry, 48, 1,230; Forty-eighth Infantry, 50, 1,270; Forty-ninth Infantry, 50, 1,200. Engineers, 6, 232. Hospital Corps, 84, 2,771. Signal Corps, 26, 454. Total, 2,420, 66,044. Acting assistant surgeons, 311.

MACARTHUR.

MANILA. (Received December 10, 1900—12.25 p. m.)
ADJUTANT-GENERAL, *Washington:*

Wounded—September 19, Novaliches, Luzon, I, Twenty-seventh Infantry, June E. Plemons, thigh, slight; September 18, K, Twenty-seventh Infantry, William J. Armour, scalp, slight; December 4, Cabiao, Luzon, L, Twenty-second Infantry; William Dold, abdomen, serious; December 3, Capas, Luzon, C, Twelfth Infantry, John P. Ritchey, * * *; December 6, Rio Chico, Luzon, A, Fourth Cavalry, Sergt. John Schwartz, face, severe; First Sergt. James Alexander, shoulder, moderate; November 20, San Roque, Luzon, B, Forty-seventh Infantry, Peter J. O'Brien, knee, moderate; November 22, Bulasan, Luzon, Acting Asst. Surg. Frederick J. Jackson, knee, moderate; August 5, San Ildefonso, Thirty-third Infantry, First Lieut. Thomas L. Sherbourne, hand, moderate; September 2, San Gregorio, Luzon, C, Thirty-third Infantry, Corpl. Richard Geiger, arm, serious.

MACARTHUR.

MANILA. (Received December 10, 1900—12.50 p. m.)
ADJUTANT-GENERAL, *Washington:*

Following deaths have occurred since last report: Dysentery—December 3, K, Eighth Infantry, Michael Welch; November 30, I, Second Infantry, Henry Waldschmidt; November 24, E, Thirty-third Infantry, Owen Reilly; August 1, M, Forty-seventh Infantry, Henry Carnahan. Suicide—December 5, K, Thirty-second Infantry, Leroy Taylor; December 6, F, Third Cavalry, Alfred Hartley; October 17, B, Nineteenth Infantry, Sergt. John Dudley. Died from wounds received in action—December 2, F, Thirty-sixth Infantry, Ulric Jusseaume; December 4, C, Twelfth Infantry, John P. Ritchey; December 6, L, Twenty-second Infantry, William Dold. Variola—December 4, G, Forty-eighth Infantry, William K. Harden; December 8, E, Forty-eighth Infantry, Grant Latimer. Killed by comrade—November 30, M, Forty-ninth Infantry, Sergt. George Givens. Killed by sentry by mistake—November 21, B, Forty-fifth Infantry, Shan Doyle. Drowned—December 1, D, First Cavalry, Vincent Zlatnicki. Uræmia—December 8, B, Thirty-fourth Infantry, Isaac Thomas. Chloroform narcosis—December 2, C, Seventeenth Infantry, Charles H. Stinnett. Tuberculosis—December 1, H, Forty-eighth Infantry, Samuel Hardy. With reference to my telegram of 4th October, death John Dolan, K, Thirty-seventh Infantry, mistake; Corpl. John A. Dolan, C, Thirty-seventh Infantry, correct.

MACARTHUR.

ADJUTANT-GENERAL'S OFFICE,
Washington, December 11, 1900.
MACARTHUR, *Manila:*

Send volunteer convalescents to capacity next transport returning and volunteer regiment by transport following. As you report 69,000 now, Secretary of War directs you start home volunteer regiments until force reduced to 60,000, number fixed before reenforcement regulars. Will send you regular regiments to further relieve volunteers.

CORBIN.

ADJUTANT-GENERAL'S OFFICE,
Washington, December 12, 1900.

MacArthur, *Manila:*

Under ice plant agreement, July 8, 1899, La Verne Company was entitled second payment $65,000 on erection plant. Obligation provide suitable building rested on us. Machinery delivered Manila February and March last. Building apparently will not be ready short of full year. They need money and ask second payment without delay. Secretary of War thinks claim just. Inspect their machinery, and if appears to be in accordance with contract and you can see no objection, Secretary will direct compliance demand.

CORBIN.

Manila. (Received December 13, 1900—8.56 a. m.)

Adjutant-General, *Washington:*

With reference to your telegram of 11th, Thirty-seventh Infantry, transport *Sheridan*, January 1; Eleventh Regiment Cavalry, January 15; movement continue as directed till completed; Thirty-sixth Infantry is in the field; can not leave at present. Authority requested retain regular officers, volunteer service, whose regular organization here; also volunteer officers, now assigned to special duty, who so desire, with view muster out June 30. Important question policy involved as departure volunteers almost renders it impossible furnish officers for special duty, necessities for which increasing. Transport *Sherman* leaves December 15, about 500 volunteer convalescents; transport *Warren*, December 22, same number; any remaining on transport *Sheridan* January 1.

MACARTHUR.

ADJUTANT-GENERAL'S OFFICE,
Washington, December 13, 1900.

MacArthur, *Manila:*

With reference to your telegram of 2d, Secretary of State cabled consul-general, Hongkong, place himself under direction John S. Mallory (captain Second Infantry). Failing, recall will be considered. Volunteer officers not responsible for public property, and returning to the United States with a view to discharge, must bring with them affidavit and certificates required by section 2, General Orders, War Department, Adjutant-General's Office, series of 1899, No. 13.

CORBIN.

Manila. (Received December 14, 1900—9.11 a. m.)

Adjutant-General, *Washington:*

Killed—Luzon, December 8, Boot Peninsula, M, First Cavalry, Ernest Shrey; November 24, Cobo, C, Forty-seventh Infantry, Frank Herman. Wounded—Thomas G. G. Brydges, chest, mortal; December 8, Boot Peninsula, B, Twenty-first Infantry, Carl E. Schultz, slightly; D, Twenty-first Infantry, Michael C. O'Donnell, severely; November 30, Sorsogon, K, Forty-seventh Infantry, Artificer Aaron A Knee, arm, slight; Corpl. William B. Webb, hand, slight; Louis S. Nesbitt, head, serious; James A. Marsh, thigh, serious; H, Forty-seventh Infantry, George McBride, arm, serious

MACARTHUR.

Manila. (Received December 15, 1900—7.41 a. m.)

Adjutant-General, *Washington:*

Sick in hospital, 3,446; sick in quarters, 1,520; 7.85 per cent.

MACARTHUR.

ADJUTANT-GENERAL'S OFFICE,
Washington, December 17, 1900.

MACARTHUR, *Manila:*

With reference to your telegram of 13th, authority granted for retention of regular and volunteer officers Philippine Islands.

By direction of the Secretary of War:

CORBIN.

MANILA. (Received December 17, 1900—11.46 p. m.)

ADJUTANT-GENERAL, *Washington:*

With reference to your telegram of 13th, ice plant machinery inspected. No objection second payment.

MACARTHUR.

MANILA. (Received December 18, 1900—6.57 a. m.)

ADJUTANT-GENERAL, *Washington:*

Following deaths have occurred since last report: Dysentery—December 12, H, Thirty-second Infantry, Benonie Banning; M, Thirty-second Infantry, Colter Shaw; December 10, B, Seventeenth Infantry, George A. Newland; December 11, G, Twenty-fourth Infantry, Sergt. Pleasant H. Hammond; December 14, M, Eighth Infantry, John G. Hammer; November 24, F, Fortieth Infantry, Artificer James F. Barrett. Malarial fever—December 8, D, Fifth Infantry, Charles D. Phipps; December 9, F, Third Cavalry, Alfred J. Maud; November 5, F, Second Infantry, Richard B. Reddick. Typhoid fever—December 3, M, Twenty-fourth Infantry, Senos Daniels; December 4, E, Second Infantry, Corpl. Leonard B. Neal; December 11, L, Forty-first Infantry, Frank Dechert. Died from wounds received in action—December 9, D, Twenty-first Infantry, Michael O'Donnell; November 25, C, Forty-seventh Infantry, Thomas G. G. Brydges. Killed, kicked by horse—December 9, M, Seventh Artillery, Thomas J. Labreck. Murdered by Moro, neck severed by kris—November 25, A, Thirty-first Infantry, Oliver L. Harter. Peritonitis—December 6, B, Third Cavalry, Charles Conlin; November 28, A, Ninth Cavalry, John H. Anderson; Asthma—December 12, B, Forty-ninth Infantry, Edward Jones. Pneumonia—November 15, K, Forty-third Infantry, Robert F. Lane. Variola—December 10, G, Forty-eighth Infantry, Samuel Duncan. Tuberculosis—December 9, C, Twelfth Infantry, Lee V. Haynes. Diphtheria—December 12, F, Thirty-fifth Infantry, Charles W. Hake. Nephritis—December 10, Hospital Corps, Benjamin F. Jones. Drowned—December 4, C, Twenty-fifth Infantry, William T. Jackson.

MACARTHUR.

MANILA. (Received December 19, 1900—12.05 a. m.)

ADJUTANT-GENERAL, *Washington:*

Died, hospital, Manila, 11.45 night December 17, dysentery, abscess liver, Montgomery D. Parker, captain, Eighth Infantry.

MACARTHUR.

ADJUTANT-GENERAL'S OFFICE,
Washington, December 19, 1900.

MACARTHUR, *Manila:*

Acting Secretary of War directs absolutely essential for proper conduct and accomplishment muster-out work that regimental adjutants and regimental quartermasters, regular or volunteer, return to United States with their volunteer organization. Authority cabled December 17 modified accordingly. Frederick detail satisfactory.

CORBIN.

ADJUTANT-GENERAL'S OFFICE,
Washington, December 20, 1900.

MACARTHUR, *Manila:*
With reference to my telegram of 12th ultimo, trial Winchester rifles, awaiting reply.

WARD.

MANILA. (Received December 21, 1900—3.30 a. m.)
ADJUTANT-GENERAL, *Washington:*
If sufficient inducement is offered in nature of bounty, equal something less than cost placing recruit Manila, say $250, possibly many volunteers would reenlist under new army bill; accepting only worthy men standing most rigid physical examination, we would get trained soldiers, familiar with Philippine service, at less than cost recruit, thus insuring economy and professional efficiency.

MACARTHUR.

MANILA. (Received December 22, 1900—10.56 a. m.)
ADJUTANT-GENERAL, *Washington:*
Killed—November 24, Frocista, Luzon, M, Forty-seventh Infantry, Corpl. Arthur Burrows; November 25, D, Eleventh Cavalry, Sergt. Bernard Baker; between November 24 and December 7, Calbayon Matuguinao, Samar, H, Twenty-ninth Infantry, Welburn Watts. Wounded—M, Twenty-ninth Infantry, Hylas E. Smiley, severely; B, Twenty-ninth Infantry, Charles E. Mackey, moderately; December 15, Duero, Bohol, H, Signal Corps, U. S. Army, Corpl. Charles A. Wilson, mortally; December 8, Antique, Panay, G, Thirty-eighth Infantry, Martin L. Weatherman, neck, serious; December 18, San Ignacio, Luzon, G, Forty-ninth Infantry, Musician Hays Withers, leg above knee, moderate; October 30, Bugason, Panay, F, Forty-fourth Infantry, Lee Piatt, arm, slight; November 10, Subig, Luzon, L, Twenty-fifth Infantry, William Smith, shoulder, slight.

MACARTHUR.

MANILA. (Received December 25, 1900—1.47 p. m.)
ADJUTANT-GENERAL, *Washington:*
Expectations, based on result of election, have not been realized. Progress of pacification apparent to me, but still very slow. Condition very flexible and likely to become chronic. I have therefore initiated a more rigid policy by issue of proclamation, enjoining precise observance of laws of war, with special reference to sending supplies and information to enemy in field, from towns occupied by our troops, and also warning leaders that intimidation of natives, by kidnaping or assassination, must sooner or later lead to their trial for felonious crimes, unless they become fugitive criminals beyond the jurisdiction of the United States, which latter course would mean lifelong expatriation. Proclamation well received, but country expectant and awaiting practical application thereof. Am considering expediency of closing ports of both Camarines, Albay, Samar, and Leyte. Would like to emphasize new policy by deporting to Guam at early date a few prominent leaders now in my hands. Request authority accordingly. Pro-American natives Manila, with chief justice at the head, have organized party, which apparently has some elements of cohesion and usefulness. Field movements outlined in my message of October 26 will probably be somewhat interrupted by early return of volunteers. It is difficult to convince people, especially natives, that any of the volunteers will be replaced.

Early information of purpose of Department in regard to army legislation and the prospect of the passage of an army bill would greatly strengthen my administration here.

MACARTHUR.

MANILA. (Received December 26, 1900—6.25 a. m.)
ADJUTANT-GENERAL, *Washington:*

Following deaths have occurred since last report: Dysentery—December 11, E, Thirty-eighth Infantry, Edward A. Henry; December 18, D, Fifteenth Infantry, Corpl. George B. Hozak; December 14, A, Thirteenth Infantry, John Pettry; December 13, G, Eleventh Cavalry, William L. Stone, jr.; December 16, B, Forty-first Infantry, Edward L. Van Buren; December 19, K, Third Infantry, David J, Parcell; December 20, A, Thirty-ninth Infantry, George J. Rehm; H, Forty-fifth Infantry, Stephen Z. Delk. Diarrhea—December 7, F, Forty-seventh Infantry, Edward Fletcher. Variola—December 14, E, Forty-eighth Infantry, Thomas Love; G, Forty-eighth Infantry, Edward Clark. Malarial fever—December 13, C, Thirty-sixth Infantry, Alfred H. Bolton; December 15, C, Thirty-third Infantry, William J. Wright. Drowned—December 18, A, Sixth Artillery, Frank Lowe; December 15, I, Fifteenth Infantry, Howard L. Garron; November 28, E, Fortieth Infantry, Stephen F. Holmes. Killed by accident, target practice—December 18, K, Third Infantry, John Begley. Surgical shock—August 26, F, Forty-third Infantry, William E. Dennis. Died from wounds received in action—December 10, G, Thirty-eighth Infantry, Martin L. Weatherman; December 17, H, Signal Corps, Corpl. Charles A. Wilson. Peritonitis—December 15, F, Twenty-fourth Infantry, Pomp Dunkerson. Abscess liver—December 12, H, Forty-fourth Infantry, William E. Bell. Pulmonary œdema—December 15, A, Eleventh Cavalry, Sergt. Charles C. Crane. Pleurisy—E, Forty-ninth Infantry, Isaiah Braxton. Hepatitis—December 20, B, Third Cavalry, Henry A. Hall. Apoplexy—December 19, Forty-eighth Infantry, Sergt. Maj. Wooten R. Abernathy. Cerebral anæmia—November 25, B, Twenty-first Infantry, Michael F. Duffy.

MACARTHUR.

ADJUTANT-GENERAL'S OFFICE,
Washington, December 26, 1900.

MACARTHUR, *Manila:*

Secretary of War authorizes you to deport insurgent leaders to Guam. Send them under orders to deliver to custody of naval officer in command, who will be instructed by Secretary of the Navy to receive and keep. Secretary of War does not approve closing ports in Camarines, Albay, Samar, and Leyte. Army bill authorizing about 100,000 men will undoubtedly pass early in January.

CORBIN.

ADJUTANT-GENERAL'S OFFICE,
Washington, December 26, 1900.

MACARTHUR, *Manila:*

Reported Jacob. H. Smith (brigadier-general, volunteers) at Dagupan, at the instance of Archbishop Chappelle, required priest named Garces leave his parish, where another priest was substituted. Is it a fact? Information desired as to the condition of Lieutenant Lynch, Forty-fourth Regiment U. S. Volunteer Infantry, reported wounded.

CORBIN.

Manila. (Received December 27, 1900—12.38 a. m.)

Adjutant-General, *Washington:*

Died, dysentery, First Lieut. Walter T. Slack, Forty-seventh Infantry, 10.45 evening, December 25.

MacArthur.

Manila. (Received December 27, 1900—6.38 a. m.)

Adjutant-General, *Washington:*

Eleventh Regiment U. S. Volunteer Cavalry engaged important active operations Camarines, precluding shipment till February 1. Shall retain accordingly unless Department wishes otherwise; no other regiment available for shipment January 15.

MacArthur.

Adjutant-General's Office,
Washington, December 27, 1900.

MacArthur, *Manila:*

With reference to your telegram of 27th, Secretary of War approves delay starting Eleventh Regiment U. S. Volunteer Cavalry, for reasons stated, but wishes, if possible, you get another regiment under way. We must push this movement, otherwise will be trouble getting volunteers home. If no other, send convalescents.

Corbin.

Manila. (Received December 28, 1900—6.05 a. m.)

Adjutant-General, *Washington:*

With reference to your telegram of 22d, George W. Upperman, F, Forty-fifth Infantry, died in hospital Nueva Caceras, Luzon, November 4, acute dysentery.

MacArthur.

Manila. (Received December 28, 1900—9.30 a. m.)

Adjutant-General, *Washington:*

Many papers [belonging to] Trias, secured recent capture, one of which contains Filipino account conference between Trias and Japanese consul in remote part of Cavite Province October 11, this year. Paper carefully prepared, authenticated by Filipino secretary, measurably confirmed by other captured papers, most probably true. I accept it as such without any hesitation. Consul advised that Trias visit Japan to negotiate voluntary contributions of arms, and, concerning future of archipelago, Filipinos represented that concessions which they might be forced to make to Washington would be more agreeable if made to Japan, which, as a nation of kindred blood, would not be likely to assert —— superiority. Consul said Japan desired coaling stations, freedom to trade and build railways. That individual Japanese have assisted insurgents has been more than suspected, but if official intervention and encouragement has transpired, a new and strong light is thrown on situation—sufficient, perhaps, to account for defiant attitude of many leaders, especially the wavering policy of Trias, who on several occasions has apparently been on verge of surrender, and also explain unyielding character of resistance in southern Luzon. In view of delicate international questions involved, shall act only under advice of Department. Papers by mail.

MacArthur.

Manila. (Received December 29, 1900—12.35 a. m.)

Adjutant-General, *Washington:*

With reference to your telegram of 26th, Jacob H. Smith, [brigadier-general, volunteers], explains that native priest Garces removed because not loyal. Removal requested by majority communicants parish. Action necessary preserve peace. Garces not confined, as been necessary many cases native priests.

With reference to your telegram of 27th, will not be possible to send another regiment in place of Eleventh Regiment U. S. Volunteer Cavalry. All troops actively engaged field operations. Will send convalescents as directed. Retention Eleventh Regiment U. S. Volunteer Cavalry only deviation original programme that I will recommend.

MacArthur.

ADJUTANT-GENERAL'S OFFICE,
Washington, December 29, 1900.

MacArthur, *Manila:*

Name and post of Japanese consul referred to in your dispatch December 28 desired.

Corbin.

Manila. (Received December 30, 1900—6 a. m.)

Adjutant-General, *Washington:*

With reference to your letter of 1st ultimo, following officers, Regular Army, holding commissions Thirty-seventh Infantry, belong regular regiments, Division of the Philippines: Charles T. Boyd [second lieutenant, Fourth Cavalry], David E. W. Lyle [first lieutenant, Eighteenth Infantry], Francis A. Winter [captain, assistant surgeon], Ernest D. Scott [second lieutenant, Sixth Artillery].

With reference to my telegram of 13th, recommend that regular officers [be] discharged to date muster out of regiment, and that volunteers remaining here [on] special duty be discharged to date June 30; latter provision very important.

MacArthur.

Manila. (Received December 30, 1900—9.42 a. m.)

Adjutant-General, *Washington:*

Killed—November 28, Cabangan, Luzon, E, Sixteenth Infantry, Joseph Rockbud; December 14, Calinog, Panay, B, Thirty-eighth Infantry, William H. Mansker. Wounded: Passi, Panay, B, Twenty-sixth Infantry, Sergt. Roy Emigh, moderately; December 16, Duero, Bohol, Acting Asst. Surg. Edward Rockhill, slightly; December 19, Limbones Cove, Luzon, B, Fourth Cavalry, Andrew S. Steen, ear, slight; November 23, Palanan, Luzon, Ernest Hagedorn [second lieutenant, Sixteenth Infantry], leg above knee, slight; November 8, Angadanan, Luzon, L, Sixteenth Infantry, Edward L. Kershner, chest, serious; December 1, Jiminez, Mindanao, G, Fortieth Infantry, Sergt. Walter Huff, thigh, serious; November 5, Barugo, Leyte, I, Forty-third Infantry, Julius A. Percival, arm, moderate; H, Forty-third Infantry, Corpl. Robert C. Mason, thigh, serious; November 24, Cobo, Luzon, C, Forty-seventh Infantry, William F. Howard, arm, serious, John B. Goold, arm, serious; December 12, Teson, Panay, K, Eighteenth Infantry, Sergt. William J. Ayers, elbow, severe; November 22, Hilongos, Leyte, A, Forty-fourth Infantry, Evans F. Benner, thigh, serious, George B. Rezner, foot, moderate; November 24, Camilig, Luzon, E, Ninth Cavalry, Corpl. Martin Bacon, foot, slight, William R. Rushingbo, leg, above knee, serious.

MacArthur.

Manila. (Received December 30, 1900—9.30 a. m.)

Adjutant-General, *Washington:*

Replying to your telegram of December 29, Taiyo Hojo, chancellor of the imperial Japanese consulate of this city, and in full charge of said consulate in the absence of K. Mimashi, regular consul, from April 16, 1900, until arrival of Goro Narita, vice-consul, on 28th of November, 1900.

MacArthur.

ADJUTANT-GENERAL'S OFFICE,
Washington, December 31, 1900.

MacArthur, *Manila:*

Unless urgently required there send Transport *Relief* to Nagasaki, to remain until further orders as floating hospital for sick arriving Nagasaki en route to the United States or Philippine Islands.

Order May 4, reduction William F. Hancock [Captain, Sixth Artillery], received December. Cable dismissals, reductions officers.

With reference to your telegram of 30th, Secretary of War authorizes volunteers retained by you special duty discharged to date June 30.

CORBIN.

MANILA. (Received January 1, 1901—3.52 a. m.)

Adjutant-General, *Washington:*

Sick in hospital, 3,414; sick in quarters, 1,355; per cent, 7.39.

MACARTHUR.

MANILA. (Received January 2, 1901—11.36 a. m.)

Adjutant-General, *Washington:*

Following deaths have occurred since last report: Dysentery—December 20, M, Thirty-eighth Infantry, Simon P. Bechdolt; December 27, D, Forty-ninth Infantry, Oliver Smith; December 22, D, Eleventh Cavalry, Printis Sulteen; December 21, E, Eleventh Cavalry, Sergt. William P. Mynatt; December 23, C, Seventeenth Infantry, George Morgan; December 25, M, Eleventh Cavalry, Chester A. Markham; December 1, M, Sixteenth Infantry, Hughie Flynn. Enterocolitis—December 15, G, Forty-seventh Infantry, Charles H Williams; December 24, L, Third Cavalry, Corpl. Ross R. Bond. Peritonitis—December 27, I, Thirty-sixth Infantry, Samuel L. Sprouse. Drowned—December 1, E, Sixteenth Infantry, Samuel E. Swearingen. Variola—December 27, F, Seventeenth Infantry, James R. Lyon; December 22, B, Thirty-third Infantry, George Brown. Anæmia—December 25, I, Thirty-third Infantry, Sergt. Michael J. O'Brien Suicide—December 24, D, Third Infantry, Thomas J. McGuire; December 25, F, Twelfth Infantry, Emil Bettin. Killed by comrade—December 23, I, Fourth Infantry, Corpl. William O. Stephenson. Accidental shot, killed himself—December 24, M, Thirty-fourth Infantry, Knute Mason. With reference to my telegram of September 17, death Sloan should be September 5. Typhoid fever—December 10, H, Nineteenth Infantry, Thomas Welch.

MACARTHUR.

ADJUTANT-GENERAL'S OFFICE,
Washington, January 2, 1901.

MacArthur, *Manila:*

Secretary of War directs you cause inquiry made all volunteer regiments before leaving Manila and discharge all officers and men desiring remain Philippine Islands.

CORBIN.

MANILA. (Received January 4, 1901—9.45 a. m.)

Adjutant-General, *Washington:*

Troops throughout entire archipelago more active than at any time since November, '99. Result satisfactory and encouraging. Expect to be able to continue activity in every direction, and also provide for return of volunteers, excepting in Young's district, which gives me much concern. Can you send me six battalions of regulars without waiting for army bill, first three to reach here not later than April, one other as soon as possible. With this additional force I hope to carry out all wishes of Department, and at the same time insure most rigorous prosecution of campaign. Military necessity may demand temporary closing ports south Luzon, Samar, Leyte. Speculative effect upon hemp would be unimportant compared with military advantages expected to accrue. Remey, Bates, both agree with me as to the wisdom of such policy. If future operations demand such action, discretionary authority requested.

MacArthur.

MANILA. (Received January 5, 1901—12.15 a. m.)
ADJUTANT-GENERAL, *Washington:*
With reference to my telegram of 30th ultimo, answer requested regarding recommendation that regular officers be discharged date muster out volunteer service. With reference to your letter of 12th September, recommend volunteer medical officers who desire contract be discharged to date muster-out their regiment.

MacArthur.

MANILA. (Received January 5, 1901—2.40 a. m.)
ADJUTANT-GENERAL, *Washington:*
With reference to your telegram of 18th September, 1899, recommend in consideration of their services, transports with returning volunteers be authorized to stop Nagasaki, Yokohama, and Timansi. General Orders, War Department, Adjutant-General's Office, series of 1900, No. 92, that going ashore of men be left discretion commanding officers.

MacArthur.

MANILA. (Received January 5, 1901—6.52 a. m.)
ADJUTANT-GENERAL, *Washington:*
With reference to your telegram of 31st ultimo, recent efforts purchase hospital ship unsuccessful. Interests sick here require retention transport *Relief*.

MacArthur.

ADJUTANT-GENERAL'S OFFICE,
Washington, January 7, 1901.
MacArthur, *Manila:*
Secretary of War is not willing to authorize the proposed interference with the ordinary course of commerce from Philippine ports unless satisfied of the existence of a military necessity, and directs full reports as to the military advantages expected to accrue from closing hemp ports, and the reasons for your expectation.

Corbin.

ADJUTANT-GENERAL'S OFFICE,
Washington, January 7, 1901.
MacArthur, *Manila:*
Will arrange as far as possible send you six battalions at least to arrive in April. Secretary of War gratified to learn of increased activity troops, which should continue with all vigor until order established throughout. Complete your plans for returning volunteers so last of them will arrive San Francisco by July 1. Department will arrange to keep your command to 60,000.

Corbin.

MANILA. (Received January 7, 1901—11.22 a. m.)

ADJUTANT-GENERAL, *Washington:*

Killed—December 31, Ilagan, Luzon, I, Forty-ninth infantry, Corpl. James W. Bunn; December 30, Santo Tomas, Luzon, B, First Cavalry, Harvey L. Bradley; December 31, Longos, Luzon, Fifteenth Infantry, unassigned recruit, Andrew Brannon; December 30, Quiom, Luzon, A, Battalion Engineers, George H. Rea; July 19, murdered by natives, Cabatuan, Panay, body recovered December 20, George O. Hill, H, Eighteenth Infantry. Wounded—December 31, Longos, Luzon, L, Fifteenth Infantry, Anthony Kearney, neck, moderate; Sergt. Patrick Philbin, shoulder, moderate; December 17, Dingle Panay, K, Thirty-eighth Infantry, Charles R. Johnson, arm, serious; December 8, Antique, Panay, G, Thirty-eighth Infantry, Henry S. Sweeney, face, slight; December 23, Mount Bagombong, Panay, I, Eighteenth Infantry, Musician James Vankirk, back, serious; K, Eighteenth Infantry, Corpl. Harrison Noble, chest, serious; December 25, Cabiao, Luzon, M, Twenty-second Infantry, Musician William Quinn, head, slight; December 27, Matnog, Luzon, D, Forty-seventh Infantry, Sergt. Clarence F. Dunkle, head, slight; December 31, San Nicolas, Luzon, I, Thirty-second Infantry, Hiram W. Purtee, thigh, slight.

MACARTHUR.

ADJUTANT-GENERAL'S OFFICE,
Washington, January 8, 1901.

MACARTHUR, *Manila:*

Secretary of War authorizes discharge date of muster out volunteer regiments in cases regular officers and medical officers accepting contracts.

With reference to your telegram of 13th [December], cause second installment on refrigerator machinery paid to contractor by cable through depot quartermaster, New York, who will obtain receipt.

CORBIN.

MANILA. (Received January 8, 1901—6.53 a. m.)

ADJUTANT-GENERAL, *Washington:*

Louis P. Smith [first lieutenant, assistant surgeon] died hospital 6.50 this morning, septicæmia. Transport *Port Albert* sailed January 4.

MACARTHUR.

MANILA. (Received January 8, 1901—9.47 a. m.)

ADJUTANT-GENERAL, *Washington:*

Following deaths have occurred since last report: Dysentery—December 1, B, Thirty-fourth Infantry, Frank B. Huff; December 15, I, Eighteenth Infantry, Fred. J. Wilson; December 25, F, Twenty-fifth Infantry, Samuel A. Nelson; December 19, I, Eighteenth Infantry, George W. Elder; January 3, D, Forty-sixth Infantry, Hans Cofford; December 29, M, Third Cavalry, George T. Butler. Malarial fever—January 1, K, Thirty-seventh Infantry, Patrick W. Fitzgerald; December 28, I, Thirty-sixth Infantry, Allen Westfall; December 26, D, Twenty-fifth Infantry, Lawrence T. Gray. Drowned—November 27, Twenty-fourth Infantry, unassigned recruit, Charles G. Yeizer. Typhoid fever—December 21, C, Thirty-first Infantry, Daniel F. Griffin. Pulmonary hemorrhage—January 3, F, Twenty-first Infantry, Thomas Fenton. Tuberculosis—December 30, Twelfth Infantry, unassigned recruit, George W. Whalen. Necrosis—December 29, C, Twelfth Infantry, Rutledge Harden. Internal injuries, jumping out window while delirious, malarial fever—December 30, D, Thirty-fourth Infantry, Dell W. Barnard. Abscess liver—December 28, H,

Thirty-seventh Infantry, First Sergt. Robert Anderson. Gastritis—December 24, L, Thirty-sixth Infantry, Jos. Sommers. Mitral obstructions—December 29, F, Fourth Infantry, Louis E. Silver. Alcoholic marasmus—December 7, B, Thirty-first Infantry, Christian F. Kayser. Suicide, shot, head—January 3, H, Thirteenth Infantry, Sergt. John Coffey.

MACARTHUR.

MANILA. (Received January 9, 1901—2.43 a. m.)

ADJUTANT-GENERAL, *Washington:*

With reference to your telegram of 7th, Thirty-seventh Infantry sails January 10; Eleventh Cavalry February 1; thereafter a volunteer regiment every two weeks until May 1, making nearly 10,000. From May 1, troops can leave safely only as regiments arrive; three of six battalions should be here not later than April 1; sooner, if possible. Until new troops arrive, shall take only Thirty-sixth Infantry from General Young, retaining Thirty-third Infantry, Thirty-fourth Infantry, until something sent in order to relieve them

MACARTHUR.

MANILA. (Received January 9, 1901—6.28 a. m.)

ADJUTANT-GENERAL, *Washington:*

Hemp in Southern Luzon in same relation to present struggle as cotton during rebellion; fields nearly all in possession of insurgents; large sums collected from contraband trade, which can only be controlled by closing ports, the military advantage of which would arise from self-interested action of hemp dealers to induce pacification, and also action of natives to same end, in order to get rice in; if hemp could not get out or rice get in, two powerful interests would operate for tranquilization. Army now stronger than it will ever be again. Every effort being made to utilize this advantage for purpose of obtaining decisive results; temporary closure of ports powerful factor, which shall abandon with reluctance; final results can not be predicted, but we are now nearer pacification than at any time since outbreak.

MACARTHUR.

MANILA. (Received January 11, 1901—7.40 a. m.)

ADJUTANT-GENERAL, *Washington:*

Sheridan sailed January 10, 27 officers, 654 men, Thirty-seventh Infantry. Transports *Logan, Lennox,* arrived yesterday.

MACARTHUR.

ADJUTANT-GENERAL'S OFFICE,
Washington, January 11, 1901.

MACARTHUR, *Manila:*

With reference to your telegram of the 4th, after careful consideration Secretary of War constrained withhold approval for authority close certain ports southern Luzon.

CORBIN.

ADJUTANT-GENERAL'S OFFICE,
Washington, January 11, 1901.

MACARTHUR, *Manila:*

Secretary of War desires early return *Buford, Kilpatrick, Meade, Garonne,* and transport *Pennsylvania,* loaded their full capacity, giving preference to sick and convalescent volunteers. Will have to dock *Sherman* and *Warren.* This will make need of ships to sail from San Francisco.

AFFAIRS IN THE PHILIPPINE ISLANDS. 1245

Two squadrons Fifth Regiment U. S. Cavalry and two battalions Eleventh Regiment U. S. Infantry will be sent you in March. Infantry companies 150 strong.

With reference to your telegram of 5th, returning volunteers will be authorized to stop Nagasaki, and shore leave given men, discretion commanding officer. Secretary of War regrets necessity speedy transportation will not admit of stops Yokohama, Timansi. Except for sufficient guard duties en route, all arms and equipments should be turned into supply depot before the departure volunteers. Volunteer officers arriving United States before muster out can not be paid unless provided with certificate last payment, Philippine Islands.

CORBIN.

MANILA. (Received January 12, 1901—8.17 a. m.)
ADJUTANT-GENERAL, *Washington:*
With reference to your telegram of 8th, hospital equipment shipped Nagasaki, January 10. John McE. Hyde [major, quartermaster's department] reports no instructions received; nothing is known by him about establishment hospital there.

MACARTHUR.

MANILA. (Received January 15, 1901—11.27 a. m.)
ADJUTANT-GENERAL, *Washington:*
Following deaths have occurred since last report: Dysentery—January 5, D, Twenty-second Infantry, Leroy B. Wilson; September 8, M, Forty-fifth Infantry, Andrew Thompson; January 3, C, Forty-ninth Infantry, Robert James; January 6, K, Thirty-fifth Infantry, Corpl. Guy A. Price; October 21, M, Twenty-ninth Infantry, William L. Romans; January 11, M, Thirty-ninth Infantry, Samuel Tweed. Typhoid fever—January 5, H, Third Infantry, Leonard Wenzel; January 7, C, Forty-second Infantry, Herman Boehler. Tuberculosis—D, Thirty-sixth Infantry, Dan Winters. Enterocolitis—January 8, K, Fourth Cavalry, Solomon H. Neiffer. Syphilis—January 9, L, Fortieth Infantry, Arthur E. Gleason. Pyæmia—January 1, Hospital Corps, John H. Walmach. Malarial fever—December 15, H, Twenty-second Infantry, Richard Walker. Killed by accident—December 31, K, Twenty-fifth Infantry, Jesse B. Smith.

MACARTHUR.

MANILA. (Received January 12, 1901—8 a. m.)
ADJUTANT-GENERAL, *Washington:*
Delgado, commander in chief Iloilo Province, Panay, surrendered January 11 to Robert P. Hughes [brigadier-general volunteers] with 4 officers, 21 men, 14 rifles; his command much scattered; other surrenders expected during the next few days; important; signifies end organized armed resistance, Iloilo Province, Panay.

MACARTHUR.

MANILA. (Received January 16, 1901—7.40 a. m.)
ADJUTANT-GENERAL, *Washington:*
Referring your message January 10, wishes of Department will be executed substantially as expressed. I purpose returning troops on schedule calculated to prevent unfavorable reaction on military situation; to this end also am forcing organization of scouts and police, hiring watchmen to replace soldiers guarding property, by which means get a regiment from Manila and possibly another from vicinity for service in remote part of island, and, thereby, in connection with prompt arrival Eleventh Infantry, Fifth Cavalry, be enhanced to hold all territory now occupied, and also

continue some active operations until arrival of ample force. Margin of safety small during period of exchange of volunteers for regulars, and, as consequence, every detail requires most thoughtful consideration; possibly some volunteers may not reach home by July 1, although all will be afloat by that time. Specific views of Department requested upon my message January 9. Favorable conditions which now obtain will be maintained unless something very unexpected occurs.

MACARTHUR.

ADJUTANT-GENERAL'S OFFICE,
Washington, January 16, 1901.

MACARTHUR, *Manila:*
Telegraph the condition of army, Manila and elsewhere Philippine Islands, with reference to drunkenness and use intoxicating liquors. Are houses prostitution licensed, protected, or in any way encouraged by military authorities?

CORBIN.

ADJUTANT-GENERAL'S OFFICE,
Washington, January 16, 1901.

MACARTHUR, *Manila:*
With reference to your telegram of 16th, my message January 11 answers yours January 9.

CORBIN.

MANILA. (Received January 17, 1901—6.15 a. m.)
ADJUTANT-GENERAL, *Washington:*
Sick in hospital, 3,438; sick in quarters, 1,225; 7.49 per cent.

MACARTHUR.

MANILA. (Received January 17, 1901—9 a. m.)
ADJUTANT-GENERAL, *Washington:*
Total strength present and absent, December 31, ascertained as near as possible: First Cavalry, officers 35, enlisted men 833; Third Cavalry, 40, 1,324; Fourth Cavalry, 47, 1,352; Sixth Cavalry, 25, 413; Ninth Cavalry, 34, 835; Eleventh Cavalry, 50, 963; Philippine Cavalry, 13, 453. Battery E, First Artillery, 4, 151; Third Artillery, 13, 411; Battery E, Fourth Artillery, 3, 148; Sixth Artillery, 42, 1,373. First Infantry, 34, 1,075; Second Infantry, 35, 1,063; Third Infantry, 46, 1,396; Fourth Infantry, 46, 1,405; Fifth Infantry, 34, 1,033; Sixth Infantry, 45, 1,340; Eighth Infantry, 24, 1,013; Twelfth Infantry, 46, 1,071; Thirteenth Infantry, 47, 1,401; Fourteenth Infantry, 40, 1,114; Fifteenth Infantry, 40, 1,103; Sixteenth Infantry, 46, 1,445; Seventeenth Infantry, 46, 1,437; Eighteenth Infantry, 37, 1,110; Nineteenth Infantry, 46, 1,440; Thirtieth Infantry, 46, 1,546; Twenty-first Infantry, 46, 1,355; Twenty-second Infantry, 45, 1,400; Twenty-third Infantry, 34, 1,393; Twenty-fourth Infantry 39, 1,407; Twenty-fifth Infantry, 46, 1,534; Twenty-sixth Infantry, 50, 1,161; Twenty-seventh Infantry, 50, 1,137; Twenty-eight Infantry, 50, 1,209; Twenty-ninth Infantry, 49, 1,213; Thirtieth Infantry, 48, 1,129; Thirty-first Infantry, 50, 1,189; Thirty-second Infantry, 50, 1,099; Thirty-third Infantry, 50, 1,180; Thirty-fourth Infantry, 50, 1,183; Thirty-fifth Infantry, 50, 1,199; Thirty-sixth Infantry, 50, 915; Thirty-seventh Infantry, 50, 861; Thirty-eighth Infantry, 48, 1,012; Thirty-ninth Infantry, 50, 1,016; Fortieth Infantry, 49, 1,188; Forty-first Infantry, 50, 1,240; Forty-second Infantry, 50, 1,085; Forty-third Infantry, 49, 1,187; Forty-fourth Infantry, 49, 1,220; Forty-fifth Infantry, 50, 1,193; Forty-sixth Infantry, 50, 1,102; Forty-

seventh Infantry, 49, 1,223; Forty-eighth Infantry, 50, 1,264; Forty-ninth Infantry, 49, 1,200. Engineers, 9, 379. Hospital Corps, 166, 2,894. Signal Corps, 28, 495. Total, 2,513, 64,966. Acting assistant surgeons, 325.

MACARTHUR.

MANILA. (Received January 17, 1901—9.15 a. m.)
ADJUTANT-GENERAL, *Washington:*
Killed—December 15, Duero, Bohol, C, Forty-fourth Infantry, Jay R. Young, Troy P. Sliger, Corpl. William P. Ellett. Wounded (extent not reported)—Wayne Eskridge, David N. Stark, Solomon Dotterer; January 12, Gapan, Luzon, C, Twenty-second Infantry, Edward D. Mason, hand, side, slight; December 7, Donsol, Luzon, D, Forty-seventh Infantry, Philip A. Hollenbeck, thumb, severe.

MACARTHUR.

MANILA. (Received January 17, 1901—9.15 a. m.)
ADJUTANT-GENERAL, *Washington:*
Rosecrans sailed January 16, Guam, 32 deported insurgents. *Aztec* sailed to-day.

MACARTHUR.

MANILA. (Received January 17, 1901—12.15 p. m.)
ADJUTANT-GENERAL, *Washington:*
With reference to your telegram of 16th, drunkenness this army, no more noticeable here than in garrisons United States. Considering whole force as unit, probably very much less. In Manila drunken men very noticeable; effect one drunkard in public place creates impression among citizens of extensive disorders throughout whole force, which is not case. Army in splendid discipline, high state efficiency, doing hardest kind service, most faithful inspiring manner. Houses prostitution not licensed, protected, encouraged.

MACARTHUR.

MANILA. (Received January 19, 1901—8.23 a. m.)
ADJUTANT-GENERAL, *Washington:*

*   *   *   *   *   *   *

Killed, 3.55 afternoon, January 18, 3 miles west Gapan, John Morrison, jr. [fiirst lieutenant Fourth Cavalry.]

MACARTHUR.

MANILA. (Received January 21, 1901—5.10 a. m.)
ADJUTANT-GENERAL, *Washington:*
With reference to your telegram of 11th December, schedule arranged sending 10,000 volunteers by transports, referred to in your telegram January 10, by March 15. Is it satisfactory? After departure of above it is considered unsafe to relieve others, excepting as replaced by troops from United States of America.

MACARTHUR.

MANILA. (Received January 21, 1901—2.14 p. m.)
ADJUTANT-GENERAL, *Washington:*
Following deaths have occurred since last report: Dysentery—January 2, I, Eighteenth Infantry, Corpl. Charles Toll; January 17, M, Thirtieth Infantry, Corpl.

William C. Mueller; January 3, B, Thirty-first Infantry, Corpl. Frank A. McCowen; January 13, H, Thirty-fifth Infantry, Corpl. Herbert Hawes; I, Eighteenth Infantry, Gustav Ecklund. Psilosis—D, Thirty-ninth Infantry, Corpl. Charles B. Smith. Enteritis—G, Sixteenth Infantry, John Sheehy. Diarrhea—January 15, M, Forty-first Infantry, Allyn Dunlap. Meningitis—December 26, I, Forty-third Infantry, George E. Ricker. Died from wounds received in action—December 16, C, Forty-fourth Infantry, Solomon Dotterer. Killed by fall from window—January 18, O, Third Artillery, Ferdinand Fraenznick. Murdered by prisoner—December 25, D, Eleventh Cavalry, Columbus L. Black. Drowned—December 16, I, Fifteenth Infantry, Alexander E. Wirth. Pneumonia—December 9, G, Thirty-eighth Infantry, John T. Bell. Tuberculosis—January 19, A, Third Cavalry, Jesse Swanek.

MacArthur.

ADJUTANT-GENERAL'S OFFICE,
Washington, January 22, 1901.

MacArthur, Manila:

* * * * * * *

Whereabouts and condition Lieutenant Brewer, Twenty-seventh Infantry, desired. * * *

Corbin.

Manila. (Received January 24, 1901—9.38 a. m.)
Adjutant-General, Washington:

With reference to your telegram of 22d, see mine September 11; nothing is known further. Brewer, Gallagher, undoubtedly murdered; bodies concealed; thorough search has been made by troops, and Acting Asst. Surg. Brewer, brother deceased.

MacArthur.

ADJUTANT-GENERAL'S OFFICE,
Washington, January 25, 1901.

MacArthur, Manila:

With reference to your telegram of 21st, taken in connection with one from Colonel Miller to Quartermaster-General of the Army, is satisfactory. Secretary of War desires, however, every arrangement possible made for return of volunteers within limitation their enlistment.

Telegraph for information Senate whether Mabini been deported Guam as political prisoner and offense.

* * * * * * *

Corbin.

Manila. (Received January 26, 1901—2.55 a. m.)
Adjutant-General, Washington:

Mabini deported; a most active agitator, persistently and defiantly refusing amnesty, and maintaining correspondence with insurgents in the field while living in Manila, Luzon, under protection of the United States; also for offensive statement in regard to recent proclamation enforcing laws of war; his deportation absolutely essential.

MacArthur.

ADJUTANT-GENERAL'S OFFICE,
Washington, January 29, 1901.

MacArthur, Manila:
Reported here ports of Tabaco, Suriago, have been closed. What are facts?

CORBIN.

ADJUTANT-GENERAL'S OFFICE,
Washington, January 29, 1901.

MacArthur, Manila:
In sending two squadrons cavalry, do you desire horses accompany, or have you horses Eleventh Cavalry for them?

* * * * * * *

CORBIN.

ADJUTANT-GENERAL'S OFFICE,
Washington, January 29, 1901.

Wood, Habana:
Secretary of War is desirous to know if you can give your consent to the immediate withdrawal of the Tenth Infantry from Cuba. The long delay in passage of the army bill makes it imperative that we have immediate use of every available company that we can lay our hands on for service in the Philippines. Secretary War very much desires if possible that you can see your way clear to recommend the withdrawal of this regiment at once.

CORBIN.

MANILA. (Received January 29, 1901—11.11 a. m.)
Adjutant-General, Washington:

* * * * * * *

Pennsylvania sailed January 28, 15 officers, 487 enlisted men, Thirty-sixth Regiment U. S. Volunteer Infantry.

MacArthur.

MANILA. (Received January 29, 1901—12.40 p. m.)
Adjutant-General, Washington:
Following deaths have occurred since last report: Dysentery—January 24, E, Third Cavalry, Corpl. Emory J. McBride, C, Seventeenth Infantry, Bernard Schultz; January 20, D, Twenty-second Infantry, Henry Steffen. Nephritis—January 22, G, Thirty-sixth Infantry, Don C. Hedrick. Appendicitis—H, Third Infantry, Henry Scharff. Tuberculosis—H, Thirty-fourth Infantry, Henry W. Wright. Malarial fever—January 18, M, Seventeenth Infantry, William G. Dodsworth. Heart disease—January 21, M, Twenty-second Infantry, John E. Shea. Suicide—January 20, F, Forty-eighth Infantry, Henry Moore. Accidental explosion shell—January 23, F, Fourth Infantry, Council C. Ashley. Drowned—December 4, C, Twenty-second Infantry, Forest Mitchel. Overdose morphine—December 30, Acting Hospital Steward Clare D. Trumbull. Died from wounds received in action—January 2, F, Forty-seventh Infantry, George O'Donnell. Died from effects of gore from carabao—January 13, K, Thirty-eighth Infantry, Cirg Willmore.

MacArthur.

MANILA. (Received January 29, 1901—1.49 p. m.)
ADJUTANT-GENERAL, *Washington:*
Killed—January 17, Boac, Marinduque, A, First Infantry, Corpl. William S. Shey, George C. Breshears; January 5, near Pompone, Luzon, D, Forty-fifth Infantry, Alphonse Vanacker; December 14, Sabang, Leyte, L, Forty-third Infantry, Granville P. Sims, Arthur Carr, Henry L. Higgins, Edwin E. Hamilton. Wounded—Lorenzo D. Taylor, breast, moderate; K, Forty-third Infantry, Second Lieut. Louis H. Leaf, wounded in leg above knee, serious; Frank H. Lucier, hand, serious; January 1, Anislac, Albay, F, Forty-seventh Infantry, George O'Donnel, thigh, serious; December 17, Guinobatan, Albay, F, Ninth Cavalry, Sergt. Richard Miller, thigh, serious; December 27, H, Ninth Cavalry, William Withers, hand, serious; January 1, Banquiruham, Albay, I, Forty-seventh Infantry, William Taylor, thigh, serious, both; First Sergt. Clarence Lininger, groin, severe; John Beatty, groin, severe; January 8, Mauban, Luzon, H, Thirtieth Infantry, Corpl. Henry C. Nevins, face, slight; M, Thirtieth Infantry, Roberts C. Settle, leg above knee, moderate; October 15, Ormoc, Leyte, D, Forty-fourth Infantry, Don. E. Connely, thigh, slight; January 17, Boac, Marinduque, A, First Infantry, Alphonse J. Vanlaeys, leg above knee, slight; Gus P. Haln, leg above knee, slight; December 12, Pasagoagan, Bohol, L, Nineteenth Infantry, James N. Roder, back, serious; Corpl. Ernest Switzer, head, serious; B, Forty-fourth Infantry, Robert E. Mitchell, leg above knee, serious.

MACARTHUR.

MANILA. (Received January 31, 1901—2.41 a. m.)
ADJUTANT-GENERAL, *Washington:*
With reference to your telegram of 29th, desire horses accompany squadron. When will squadrons start?

Several volunteer officers belong home battalions, regular establishment; authority requested retain; assign them portion regiment here.

* * * * * * *

MACARTHUR.

MANILA. (Received February 2, 1901—5.33 a. m.)
ADJUTANT-GENERAL, *Washington:*
With reference to your telegram of 29th ultimo, no action has been taken division, department headquarters, closing ports Tabaco and Surigao. Whatever action been by local authorities; cable cut when opened; will ascertain the facts and report.

MACARTHUR.

MANILA. (Received February 2, 1901—6.45 a. m.)
ADJUTANT-GENERAL, *Washington:*
Meade sailed February 1; 24 officers, 562 enlisted men, Eleventh Regiment, U. S. Volunteer Cavalry.

* * * * * * *

MACAUTHUR.

MANILA. (Received February 2, 1901—8.20 a. m.)
ADJUTANT-GENERAL, *Washington:*
Sick in hospital, 3,327; sick in quarters, 1,184; 7 per cent.

* * * * * * *

MACARTHUR.

ADJUTANT-GENERAL'S OFFICE,
Washington, February 2, 1901.

MACARTHUR, *Manila:*

With reference to your telegram of 2d, Secretary of War directs instruct local authorities having control ports Tabaco and Surigao if have been closed to open forthwith; if have not closed to keep open.

Returning transports should bring troops equal to comfortable carrying capacity.

Army bill passed and approved substantially bill of Department, and you have doubtless seen in service papers.

* * * * * * *

CORBIN.

MANILA. (Received February 3, 1901—3.10 a. m.)

ADJUTANT-GENERAL, *Washington:*

Hughes reports surrender 300 men, 150 rifles, Delagado's command. Surrenders throughout Luzon continue considerable numbers; Cavite Province with indications favorable to entire collapse insurrection that province at early date. Kobbé's reports Mindanao very encouraging; military situation throughout archipelago very favorable; passage army bill insuring adequate force will undoubtedly result in complete pacification early date.

MACARTHUR.

MANILA. (Received February 4, 1901—11.19 a. m.)

ADJUTANT-GENERAL, *Washington:*

Killed—January 9, Terragona, Leyte, M, Forty-third Volunteer Infantry, Edward McGuyre. February 2, near Tayum, Luzon, Acting Asst. Surg. Charles B. Ross; Company D, Fifth Infantry, Corpl. Fred Moncrief, Corpl. John D. Campbell, Charles B. Fleming; Company A, Fifth Infantry, Elwood B. Warner. Wounded—Company D, Fifth Infantry, Corpl. Thomas Feeney, leg, below knee, serious; Martin H. Bergen, leg, above knee, slight; William W. Heaps, abdomen, serious; C, Fifth Infantry, Sim Eubanks, hip, severe. December 17, Igcabucao, Panay, M, Twenty-sixth Volunteer Infantry, Corpl. John Conway, back, slight; Walter Bruffee, face, severe. January 25, San Antonio, Luzon, M, Fifteenth Infantry, Patrick Horan, arm, serious; Corpl. Michael J. McAdams, arm, moderate; near Maragondon, Forty-sixth Volunteer Infantry, Capt. Robert J. Reaney, hand, slight; San Pablo, Luzon, G, Forty-ninth Volunteer Infantry, Benny Williamson, head, slight; B, Forty-ninth Volunteer Infantry, William Edmondson, leg, above knee, moderate.

MACARTHUR.

MANILA. (Received February 3, 1901—4.40 a. m.)

ADJUTANT-GENERAL, *Washington:*

In attack on enemy in Cebu, January 29, Second Lieut. E. J. Hincken and five men, Company M, Forty-fourth Regiment U. S. Volunteer Infantry, were killed; 4 wounded and 2 missing; result treachery native officials. Names later.

MACARTHUR.

ADJUTANT-GENERAL'S OFFICE,
Washington, February 5, 1901.

MACARTHUR, *Manila:*

"Sale of or dealing in beer, wine, or any intoxicating liquors by any person in any post exchange or canteen or any transport or upon any premises used for military purposes by the United States is hereby prohibited. The Secretary of War is hereby directed to carry the provisions of this section into full force and effect." Act of Congress approved February 2. Orders mailed.

CORBIN.

ADJUTANT-GENERAL'S OFFICE,
Washington, February 7, 1901.

MACARTHUR, Manila:

* * * * * *

Have last pay rolls returning regiments precede regiments at least two weeks. When it becomes necessary pay one month only.

Secretary of War desires to know for the information of Senate whether an editor named Rice been deported. By what authority? What was offense?

CORBIN.

MANILA. (Received February 8, 1901—12.23 p. m.)

ADJUTANT-GENERAL, Washington:

Editor Rice deported San Francisco, January 28. Offense, malicious publication of false charges affecting integrity of administration of office captain of the port, in which formerly employed. This with full knowledge of their falsity. Matter received exhaustive investigation, which Rice was heard in his own defense. He was informed he must give a bond not to republish or must leave islands, as his actions were creating strife and were menace military situation. He maintained attitude of defiance, and was necessarily sent home. Full report was forwarded, with all papers, February 1.

MACARTHUR.

ADJUTANT-GENERAL'S OFFICE,
Washington, February 9, 1901.

MACARTHUR, Manila:

Strong representation made to the Department that persons interested in a speculative corner in hemp have been stirring up insurrection in the hemp provinces for the purpose of preventing the flow of hemp to the open ports and giving information, colored to suit their purposes, to military commanders, and interested suggestions, for the purpose of interfering with the ordinary supply of hemp to consumers. Important banks and capitalists in Manila said to be deeply interested in keeping up the price. Department desires to avoid being used by speculators or dealers on either side, and considers the only safe course is to interfere as little as possible with the ordinary course of business. At the same time it does not wish in any manner to interfere with any action on your part which you consider required by military necessity. Thorough investigation desired.

CORBIN.

MANILA. (Received February 11, 1901—6.57 a. m.)

ADJUTANT-GENERAL, Washington:

Buford sailed February 10; 28 officers, 853 enlisted men Twenty-seventh Regiment U. S. Volunteer Infantry. Transport Thyra arrived to-day.

MACARTHUR.

MANILA. (Received February 11, 1901—10.28 a. m.)

ADJUTANT-GENERAL, Washington:

Following deaths have occurred since last report: Dysentery—January 27, Company K, Twenty-sixth Volunteer Infantry, Ned Vandewark; Company M, Thirty-eighth Volunteer Infantry, Peter G. Garrett; January 31, Company F, Thirty-fifth Volunteer Infantry, Robert Jackson; Band, Eighth Infantry, Pio G. Otermin. Typhoid fever—January 25, B, Thirty-eighth Volunteer Infantry, Charles Freeman; December 13, G, Eighteenth Infantry, Ernest C. Grout. Malarial fever—December 18, F, Second Infantry, John Pierce; January 28, D, Sixteenth Infantry, James A. McCarthy. Variola—January 30, M, Thirty-third Volunteer Infantry, Frederick J. Fisher. Pneumonia—January 6, F, Second Infantry, Harry A. Grinstead. Alcoholism—January 17, G, Sixth Infantry, John O'Leary. Tuberculosis—January 31, E, Forty-fourth Volunteer Infantry, Samuel Whiteside. Drowned—December 23, F, Second Infantry, Charles D. Weidnerre. Insolation—December 24, D, Twenty-eighth Volunteer Infantry, Edward E. Mountz.

MACARTHUR.

ADJUTANT-GENERAL'S OFFICE,
Washington, February 11, 1901.

MACARTHUR, *Manila:*

* * * * * * *

With reference to your telegram of 31st ultimo, officers home battalions must join. Direct volunteer regiments transfer band instruments depot quartermaster on arrival San Francisco.

CORBIN.

MANILA. (Received February 12, 1901—12.30 a. m.)
ADJUTANT-GENERAL, *Washington:*

January 10, Rio Suribao, Samar, E, First Infantry, John Merillat, wounded in shoulder, slight; Sergt. Willard A. Castle, shoulder, moderate; January 27, Naban, Luzon, L, Forty-fifth Volunteer Infantry, Corpl. John F. Grantham, arm, shoulder, moderate; January 29, Caytacoes, Luzon, D, Fifteenth Infantry, Corpl. Samuel Achuff, arm, slight.

MACARTHUR.

MANILA. (Received February 12, 1901—8.36 a. m.)
ADJUTANT-GENERAL, *Washington:*

Col. Simon Tecson, 7 officers, 71 soldiers, 59 guns, 2,000 rounds ammunition, surrendered unconditionally, February 11, San Miguel de Mayumo, Luzon. This breaks up group insurrectos heretofore operating mountains east Bulacan; removes from northern Luzon last formidable organized force, excepting in first district. Rigid enforcement proclamation December 20, spontaneous action people through Federal party, behalf peace, self-protection, are producing most satisfactory results; encourage hope entire suspension hostilities early date.

MACARTHUR.

MANILA. (Received February 14, 1901—8.22 a. m.)
ADJUTANT-GENERAL, *Washington:*

Consul Nagasaki informs Capt. Irving W. Rand, assistant surgeon, provisional governor states military hospital will not be permitted. Await instructions.

MACARTHUR.

1254 CORRESPONDENCE.

ADJUTANT-GENERAL'S OFFICE,
Washington, February 14, 1901.

MACARTHUR, Manila:
Transport Sheridan will leave San Francisco on February 16 with first battalions Twenty-sixth and Twenty-seventh United States Infantry.

* * * * * * *

CORBIN.

MANILA. (Received February 15, 1901—5.22 a. m.)
ADJUTANT-GENERAL, Washington:
One hundred and twelve rifles, 1,500 rounds ammunition surrendered Laganoy, February 13, mostly from supply secreted contiguous swamps; incident important, indicating great reaction, favorable American interests, region Bulacan, heretofore one of worst in Luzon. Result accomplished exclusively by long-continued, intelligent, persistent efforts officers Third U. S. Infantry.

MACARTHUR.

MANILA. (Received February 16, 1901—5.52 a. m.)
ADJUTANT-GENERAL, Washington:
Sick in hospital, 4,424; sick in quarters, 1,103; 7.57 per cent.

MACARTHUR.

MANILA. (Received February 18, 1901—4 a. m.)
ADJUTANT-GENERAL, Washington:
Hancock, Kilpatrick sailed February 17; Hancock, 26 officers, 751 enlisted men Thirtieth Regiment U. S. Volunteer Infantry. Kilpatrick, 400 sick.

MACARTHUR.

MANILA. (Received February 18, 1901—9.40 a. m.)
ADJUTANT-GENERAL, Washington:
Killed—January 19, Santa Ana, Mindanao, F, Twenty-eighth Volunteer Infantry, Oliver Himmelberger; January 28, Jiminez, Mindanao, Hospital Corps, John L. Corley; February 8, Bangued, Luzon, D, Fifth Infantry, Edward C. Lusk; January 1, Quiom, Luzon, K, Fifth Infantry, Eugene R. Lyons. Wounded—February 9, Bittin, Luzon, Hospital Corps, William Countee, knee, slight; E, Forty-ninth Volunteer Infantry, Charles Nesbitt, leg below knee, slight; James T. Wood, leg below knee, slight; Miller Scott, hip, slight; December 1, Jiminez, Mindanao, G, Fortieth Volunteer Infantry, Sergt. Walter Huff, thigh, serious; January 21, Herman E. Braden, thigh, serious, both; John Jacksap, abdomen, serious; E, Fortieth Volunteer Infantry, Corpl. Sydney O. Watson, face, neck, shoulder, serious; February 11, Amaroa, Luzon, Thirty-third Volunteer Infantry, Battalion Sergt. Maj. James L. Scott, ear, slight; February 14, Naic, Luzon, K, Forty-sixth Volunteer Infantry, Benjamin Johnson, mortally.

MACARTHUR.

MANILA. (Received February 20, 1901—12.05 p. m.)
ADJUTANT-GENERAL, Washington:
Following deaths have occurred since last report: Dysentery—January 31, M, Third Cavalry, Farrier Edward Canavan; February 12, H, Signal Corps, Elmer E. Reelhorn; February 10, A, Twenty-first Infantry, Corpl. Michael McCue; February 5, A, Twenty-seventh Volunteer Infantry, Corpl. R. Slonaker; January 23, D, Forty-

ninth Volunteer Infantry, William Parnell. Died from wounds received in action—February 3, D, Fifth Infantry, William W. Heaps; January 23, G, Fortieth Volunteer Infantry, John Jaksap; February 15, K, Forty-sixth Volunteer Infantry, Benjamin Johnson. Typhoid fever—February 13, H, Eighth Infantry, Daniel McLeer; February 14, I, Fourth Cavalry, William Boden; February 11, M, Fortieth Volunteer Infantry, William M. Ford. Heart disease—February 9, K, Fortieth Volunteer Infantry, Frank Ott; February 18, Hospital Corps, Frederick Schilling. Tuberculosis—February 9, F, Nineteenth Infantry, Gus Anderson; February 11, G, Twenty-fourth Infantry, Homer Patton; February 3, B, Thirty-fourth Volunteer Infantry, Corpl. Floyd Dakin. Malarial fever—February 12, K, Sixth Infantry, Charles C. Polkey; January 26, D, Sixteenth Infantry, James A. McCarthy. Nephritis—February 13, B, Fifth Infantry, Walter Cooley; February 9, G, Forty-seventh Volunteer Infantry, Samuel B. Hutslar. Carcinoma liver—February 12, L, Second Infantry, Corpl. James H. Wilson. Abscess liver—December 27, H, Twenty-second Infantry, David T. Crozier. Pneumonia—February 6, C, Thirty-fourth Volunteer Infantry, John Williams. Pyæmic abscess lung—February 3, Hospital Corps, Charles M. Adams. Suicide—February 14, E, Thirteenth Infantry, David Lober. Erysipelas—February 8, F, Thirty-fifth Volunteer Infantry, William Wells. Enteritis—January 31, E, Third Cavalry, Samuel Robertson. Pernicious anæmia—December 3, F, First Infantry, Stephen J. Jones. Variola—February 15, F, Ninth Cavalry, James T. Timms. Drowned, body recovered—February 9, A, Thirty-third Volunteer Infantry, William Weithorn.

MACARTHUR.

MANILA. (Received February 23, 1901—6.52 a. m.)
ADJUTANT-GENERAL, *Washington:*
Killed—January 27, Dumaguete, Negros, G, Sixth Infantry, Charles L. Leonard; January 26, San Juan del Seite, Mindanao, C, Fortieth Volunteer Infantry, Corpl. William J. Kelly; February 10, Taal, Batangas, K, Thirty-ninth Volunteer Infantry, John T. Kidney; February 13, Maravilla, Cebu, I, Nineteenth Infantry, Erwin F. Delitsch. Wounded—John L. Griffin, leg above knee, slight; Harry J. Schneider, knee, slight; February 15, Dingras, Luzon, K, Third Cavalry, John J. Alford, finger, ear, slight; Martin Schrader, arm, slight; Jacob T. Pierson, foot, serious.

MACARTHUR.

ADJUTANT-GENERAL'S OFFICE,
Washington, February 25, 1901.
MACARTHUR, *Manila:*
Send Thirty-fifth Regiment U. S. Volunteer Infantry Portland, Oreg., on *Garonne*, and Thirty-sixth Regiment U. S. Volunteer Infantry on *Thomas*.

CORBIN.

MANILA. (Received February 26, 1901—5.52 a. m.)
ADJUTANT-GENERAL, *Washington:*
With reference to your telegram of 25th, compliance therewith means confusion, delay, as carefully considered scheme has been adopted and partially executed, whereby transport *Thomas*, now en route Mindanao, takes Twenty-eighth Regiment U. S. Volunteer Infantry, Thirty-fifth Regiment U. S. Volunteer Infantry, and transport *Garonne* Twenty-sixth Regiment U. S. Volunteer Infantry. Details connected return volunteers exceedingly complex. Can manage only under conditions existing here day by day. Think can get all volunteers San Francisco on time if given full discretion; otherwise can not tell what the result will be.

MACARTHUR.

ADJUTANT-GENERAL'S OFFICE,
Washington, February 26, 1901.

MacArthur, Manila:

With reference to your telegram of 26th, movement of volunteers, disregard my telegram February 25. Your plan accepted.

CORBIN.

MANILA. (Received February 28, 1901—8.40 a. m.)

Adjutant-General, Washington:

With reference to your telegram of 27th, Frederick Funston engaged on important surrender, possibility capturing Aguinaldo; will retain him six weeks provided we hear nothing to the contrary.

MACARTHUR.

SAN FRANCISCO, CAL., March 1, 1901.
(Received 8.22 p. m.)

Adjutant-General, Washington, D. C.:

The *Meade* is now coming in. [Eleventh Cavalry, 556 enlisted men.]

SHAFTER, Major-General.

MANILA. (Received March 1, 1901—7.22 a. m.)

Adjutant-General, Washington:

Killed—February 21, San Francisco de Malabon, Luzon, Company F, Fourth Infantry, Thomas Knebel; January 29, Santa Lucia, Cebu, Company M, Forty-fourth Volunteer Infantry, Artificer Frank Thomas, Sergt. William H. Painter, Edward M. Crutchfield, Robert M. Keller, Charles E. McBride. Wounded (serious), missing—Corpl. George H. Nestell, Frank B. Cassady. Wounded—Corpl. Frederick J. Butz, arm, slight; Carrell S. Huston, legs, severe; Leslie Page, arm, serious; John O. Whatley, shoulder, serious; February 16, Guinobatan, Luzon, Troop F, Ninth Cavalry, Jake Cox, buttock, slight; February 17, Esperanza, Luzon, Company D, Fifteenth Infantry, Dennis Sullivan, side, serious; Battery C, Seventh Artillery, William C. Morse, knee, serious; January 27, Colivo, Panay, Company C, Sixth Infantry, Sergt. Samuel G. Shelato, shoulder, slight; February 14, Naic, Luzon, Company K, Forty-sixth Volunteer Infantry, Corpl. William G. Quirk, shoulder, slight; January 29, Mariano, Company D, Fifteenth Infantry, Corpl. Samuel Schuff, arm, slight; January 31, Guinobatan, Luzon, Troop H, Ninth Cavalry, Corpl. Philip Oliver, arm, slight.

MACARTHUR.

MANILA. (Received March 1, 1901—10.55 a. m.)

Adjutant-General, Washington:

Following deaths have occurred since last report: Dysentery—February 27, Company I, Twenty-first Infantry, Bertie C. Thompson; Company A, Twenty-fourth Infantry, Walter L. Smith; February 24, Company I, Eighth Infantry, Frederick Ernst. Anæmia—February 19, Company F, Forty-third Volunteer Infantry, Clarence L. Anderson. Malarial fever—February 7, Company I, Sixteenth Infantry, Sergt. Locke Castlebury. Drowned, body recovered—February 17, Battery A, Sixth Artillery, Sergt. Jesse C. Coplinger. Variola—January 26, Company B, Forty-third Volunteer Infantry, William H. Hartman. Killed by accident—February 19, Company K, Seventeenth Infantry, John Kellick. Eruptive fever—February 20, Acting Asst. Surg. James A. Rabbett. Fracture, skull—Company L, Sixteenth Infantry, George S. Smedley. Nephritis—Company I, Twenty-first Infantry, Joseph W. Spencer. Enteritis—February 19, Company E, Battalion of Engineers, U. S. Army, Harry W. Starbird.

MACARTHUR.

MANILA. (Received March 3, 1901—6.25 a. m.)

ADJUTANT-GENERAL, *Washington:*

Logan sailed March 1 via Nagasaki, Samuel B. M. Young, Luther R. Hare, 26 officers, 769 enlisted men, Thirty-third Regiment U. S. Volunteer Infantry; 21 officers, 785 enlisted men, Thirty-fourth Regiment U. S. Volunteer Infantry; 250 bodies deceased soldiers. Notify William R. Shafter.

* * * * * * *

Sick in hospital, 2,961; sick in quarters, 1,059—6.79 per cent.

Transport *Lawton* arrived March 1.

With reference to your telegram of December 17, many volunteer officers have been retained on very important duty who desire appointment Regular Army who can not be sent home without paralyzing civil administration. Authority requested to examine them here.

MACARTHUR.

MANILA. (Received March 3, 1901—8.26 a. m.)

ADJUTANT-GENERAL, *Washington:*

March 25 thirteen volunteer regiments will have been returned. In order to continue movement with safety and intelligence, request definite information regarding numbers, date of departure other troops to be sent from the United States.

MACARTHUR.

MANILA. (Received March 8, 1901—7.47 a. m.)

ADJUTANT-GENERAL, *Washington:*

Killed—September 20, San Miguel de Mayumo, Luzon, Company A, Thirty-fifth Regiment, U. S. Volunteer Infantry, Charles A. Baker; March 3, near Silang, Luzon, Company D, Forty-sixth Regiment U. S. Volunteer Infantry, Sergt. Walter A. Gilmore. Wounded—January 4, Mount Isarog, Luzon, Company E, Forty-seventh Regiment, U. S. Volunteer Infantry, Corpl. Thomas L. Casey, arm, serious; February 24, San Vicente, Luzon, Troop F, Third Regiment U. S. Cavalry, Charles W. Larzelere, thigh, moderate.

MACARTHUR.

MANILA. (Received March 9, 1901—11 a. m.)

ADJUTANT-GENERAL, *Washington:*

* * * * * * *

Transport *Garonne*, 41 officers, 849 enlisted men, Twenty-sixth Regiment, U. S. Volunteer Infantry, sail to-day via Nagasaki: inform William R. Shafter; Company F, Twenty-sixth Regiment U. S. Volunteer Infantry, 3 officers, 82 enlisted men follow on transport *Grant*.

MACARTHUR.

MANILA. (Received March 10, 1901—9.39 a. m.)

ADJUTANT-GENERAL, *Washington:*

Following deaths have occurred since last report: Dysentery—February 26, Company H, Thirty-eighth Volunteer Infantry, Cook John G. Freeman; March 4, F, Twenty-fourth Infantry, Edward Price; March 6, Troop F, Third Cavalry, Felix H. McCue. Abscess liver—February 28, Company K, Fortieth Volunteer Infantry, Cornelius O'Donovan. Gangrenous appendicitis—February 14, M, Eighteenth Infantry, William B. Saler. Sprue—March 1, D, Twenty-third Infantry, Corpl. Wallace E. Johnson. Icterus—March 6, Company G, Twelfth Infantry, Harry W.

Kugle. Nephritis—March 4, Acting Asst. Surg. Sherman A. Yule. Tuberculosis—Company C, Twenty-fourth Infantry, Lee Brown. Variola—February 10, Company L, Nineteenth Infantry, First Sergt. Albert R. Sisler. Fractured skull—February 6, Battery G, Sixth Artillery, George E. Wills. Drowned, body recovered—February 27, Company F, Twenty-fifth Infantry, Corpl. William Johnson.

* * * * * * *

MACARTHUR.

MANILA. (Received March 11, 1901—3.25 a. m.)
ADJUTANT-GENERAL, *Washington:*

With reference to your telegram of 9th, will examine here all commissioned candidates volunteers now on special duty. Will take no additional details candidates; this essential civil administration.

Gen. Mariano de Dios, 4 officers, 57 men, uniformed, armed, surrendered Naic. Regarded very important, indicating collapse insurrection territory heretofore obstinately defended. Conditions throughout entire archipelago very encouraging; captures, surrenders arms continue; 3,168 arms surrendered, captured since January 1.

With reference to my telegram of 12th ultimo, information requested great practical importance in arranging further departure volunteers, even if dates only approximate.

MACARTHUR.

ADJUTANT-GENERAL'S OFFICE,
Washington, March 11, 1901.

MACARTHUR, *Manila:*

Troops sail as follows: First Battalion Twenty-eighth Infantry, Company D, Tenth Regiment U. S. Infantry, *Indiana*, March 15; headquarters, band, First, Third Squadrons, Fifth Regiment U. S. Cavalry, Troops A, B, Fifteenth Cavalry, *Meade*, March 16; 7 companies Tenth Regiment U. S. Infantry, transport *Pennsylvania*, March 18; horses Fifth Regiment U. S. Cavalry, by animal transport. Further assignments will be telegraphed.

* * * * * * *

CORBIN.

MANILA. (Received March 12, 1901—9.31 a. m.)
ADJUTANT-GENERAL, *Washington:*

No direct interference export of hemp from open ports during my command; field mostly under insurgent control; trade from field to open port necessarily contraband to large circle; assistance insurrection contributed mostly large firms Manila; since proclamation December 20 fear consequence, reduced activity, but not entirely suspended, such contrabrand trade; rigid enforcement proclamation steadily, surely, suppressing insurrection, which so effectually controlled now; hemp minor military consideration; will not be interfered with excepting punish contrabandists when detected; names complainants will assist investigation here.

MACARTHUR.

SAN FRANCISCO., CAL., *March 12, 1901.*
(Received 3.35 p. m.)

ADJUTANT-GENERAL, *Washington:*

The *Hancock* arrived this morning. [Thirtieth Regiment U. S. Volunteer Infantry, 788 enlisted men.]

SHAFTER, *Major-General.*

AFFAIRS IN THE PHILIPPINE ISLANDS. 1259

SAN FRANCISCO, CAL., *March 15, 1901.*
(Received 10.25 p. m.)

ADJUTANT-GENERAL, *Washington:*

Transport *Buford* has just arrived. [Twenty-seventh Regiment U. S. Volunteer Infantry, 855 enlisted men.]

SHAFTER, *Major-General.*

MANILA. (Received March 16, 1901—5.57 a. m.)

ADJUTANT-GENERAL, *Washington:*

Referring to your cablegram March 15, repeatedly published here from Washington sources Gen. Adna R. Chaffee or Gen. James F. Wade will relieve me. If such is purpose would like to be consulted as to time, as relief before appointment civil governor might be construing censure my administration.

MACARTHUR.

MANILA. (Received March 16, 1901—5.50 a. m.)

ADJUTANT-GENERAL, *Washington:*

Mariano Trias, only lieutenant-general insurgent army, surrendered March 15, San Francisco de Malabon, with 9 officers, 199 well-armed men. Trias immediately took oath of allegiance presence several thousand natives; most auspicious event; indicates final stage armed insurrection. Prestige Trias Southern Luzon equal that Aguinaldo. Gen. John C. Bates, Lieut. Col. Frank D. Baldwin, entitled great credit for persistent intelligent work bringing this about.

MACARTHUR.

MANILA, P. I. (Received March 16, 1901—12 noon.)

ADJUTANT-GENERAL, *Washington:*

Killed—March 3, near Silang, Cavite, E, Signal Corps, George W. Patton; February 16, Baldhill, Leyte, M, Forty-third Volunteer Infantry, John Cremmins. Wounded—March 4, Signal Corps, First Lieut. William E. Davies, slightly; February 22, Gasan, Marinduque, G, Second Infantry, James Burke, hip, severe; K, Second Infantry, Corpl. Harry Dasher, chest, slight; February 18, Mount Masalopot, Marinduque, B, First Infantry, Thomas Millard, shoulder, serious; I, Second Infantry, Charles A. Lambert, thigh, moderate; January 26, Jiminez, Mindanao, C, Fortieth Volunteer Infantry, William L. Birch, think slight; Walter Lawrence, arm, slight; Ernest S. George, arm, slight; Corpl. Lemuel Woodyard, arm, slight.

Sick in hospital 3,074; sick in quarters, 1,064; 7 per cent.

* * * * * * *

Transport *Thomas, Rosecrans*, 66 officers, 1,846 enlisted men, Twenty-eighth Regiment U. S. Volunteer Infantry, Thirty-fifth Regiment U. S. Volunteer Infantry, *Lawton*, 27 officers, 668 enlisted men, Thirty-ninth Regiment U. S. Volunteer Infantry; Brig. Gen. James M. Bell; sail to-day via Nagasaki. Notify William R. Shafter.

MACARTHUR.

ADJUTANT-GENERAL'S OFFICE,
Washington, March 16, 1901.

MACARTHUR, *Manila:*

Secwar has no intention to relieve you before the termination of the military government and transfer of executive authority to civil government. As part of that new arrangement, you will be relieved and Chaffee assigned to military command of division without civil authority. Taft cabled March 10 that he had had satisfactory conference with you as to transfer and date. What date was agreed upon? Letter mailed February 27.

CORBIN.

MANILA. (Received March 17, 1901—4.10 a. m.)
ADJUTANT-GENERAL, *Washington:*
Referring your telegram March 16, proposed arrangement very satisfactory to me. Taft and I agreed earliest date transfer executive authority June 30.

MACARTHUR.

MANILA. (Received March 19, 1901—5.25 a. m.)
ADJUTANT-GENERAL, *Washington:*
Gen. Robert P. Hughes reports Diocno, most troublesome insurgent general Panay, captured March 18, wounded three times; thinks this will end war Capiz Province, Panay. In my opinion will terminate hostilities Panay.

Transport *Sheridan* arrived to-day.

* * * * * * *

MACARTHUR.

ADJUTANT-GENERAL'S OFFICE,
Washington, March 19, 1901.

MACARTHUR, *Manila:*
Associated Press complains censor Manila held Trias cable and allowed Sun Press Association send report. Secretary of War desires statement by cable. Understood here there is no censor. What are the facts?

Published here Major Smith, commanding in Marinduque, has ordered all natives to live in five principal towns and natives continuing live in country will be considered insurgents. Is there any foundation for statement? Answer as soon as possible.

CORBIN.

MANILA. (Received March 21, 1901—12.20 p. m.)
ADJUTANT-GENERAL, *Washington:*
Following deaths have occurred since last report: Dysentery—March 4, Company D, Forty-fourth Volunteer Infantry, Sergt. William C. Perkins; February 27, Company A, Twenty-second Infantry, Patrick Mellon; March 13, Company M, Forty-eighth Volunteer Infantry, Henry J. Holly; February 22, Company E, Twenty-eighth Volunteer Infantry, David B. Curry. Diarrhea—March 9, Company K, Forty-fifth Volunteer Infantry, Loyd F. Dempsey. Died from wounds received in action—March 6, Battery C, Seventh Artillery (Fourteenth Battery Field Artillery), William C. Morse. Drowned, body recovered—March 9, Company L, Forty-first Infantry, Fred M. Altmose; February 26, Company E, First Infantry, John J. Jennings. Drowned, bodies not recovered—March 2, Company L, Twenty-eighth Volunteer Infantry, William Stewart, Henry L. Hawley, Corpl. William Boyle, John Blumm; February 10, Company E, Forty-seventh Volunteer Infantry, Garfield Henderson. Suicide—March 1, Company E, Twenty-ninth Volunteer Infantry, Corpl. Horace D. Smith. Gastritis—March 7, Company D, Twenty-third Infantry, Frank Chaplewski. Pulmonary œdema—March 14, Company F, Fourteenth Infantry, Oscar Carlson. Pneumonia—March 11, Company E, Thirty-ninth Volunteer Infantry, Pearley W. Moyer. Endocarditis—March 6, Company C, Nineteenth

Infantry, Lewis Feil. Uræmia—March 7, Company D, Twelfth Infantry, Corpl. Patrick Jackson. Killed by accident—March 2, Troop D, Ninth Cavalry, First Sergt. Charles H. Roper; February 3, Company I, Twenty-second Infantry, Thomas Murphy; Company B, Twenty-second Infantry, February 17, Michael J. Hurley. Killed by comrade—March 10, Company C, Thirteenth Infantry, Steven Budziak. Fracture skull—March 13, Company I, Fifth Infantry, Corpl. Herman Ehrich.

MACARTHUR.

MANILA. (Received March 22, 1901—12.15 a. m.)
ADJUTANT-GENERAL, *Washington:*
Hughes reports surrender Fullon and command, Antique Province, Panay, 180 rifles; this ends insurrection Panay.

MACARTHUR.

MANILA. (Received March 22, 1901—2.12 p. m.)
ADJUTANT-GENERAL, *Washington:*
With reference to your telegram of 21st, have maintained during my command careful personal supervision details medical administration, suppression insurrection has involved wide distribution troops, creating necessity a large number medical officers to attend scattered detachments. Movement volunteers home, simultaneously final vigorous methods end insurrection, taxing every resource command, to exclusion all other considerations. Notwithstanding reduction force, same number posts maintained, requiring same number medical officers. At present not single unnecessary assignment medical officers Division of the Philippines. Hope report cessation hostilities before June 30, when such disposition can be made as will admit reduction medical officers. See letter forwarded my indorsement March 12, and letter mailed to-day.

No objection wives noncommissioned staff coming, provided husbands' applications approved these headquarters.

With reference to your telegram of 19th, personally ordered cable company hold press reports Trias surrender till official information forwarded. Sun report got off ahead my order.

Report regarding Major Smith, Marinduque, substantially correct. His action effective suppressing insurrection there which past three months has presented obstinate resistance; exclusively a military measure carried out without objectionable or offensive features and effected end in view. Full report Major Smith next record events.

* * * * * * *

MACARTHUR.

MANILA. (Received March 24, 1901—5.40 a. m.)
ADJUTANT-GENERAL, *Washington:*
Killed—February 18, Mount Masalowat, Marinduque, Company I, Second Infantry, Bert Mason; March 9, San Luis, Isabela, Company D, Sixteenth Infantry, Corpl. Alonzo C. Hocker; March 3, Buena Vista, Marinduque, Company K, Second Infantry, Alfred W. James. Wounded—Corpl. William G. Aldred, leg above knee, serious; James C. Brinkerhoff, buttock, moderate; Thomas Sparrow, arm, serious; February 25, Nena Swar, Company D, First Infantry, Jesse L. Gray, leg below knee, slight; March 15, Calauan, Luzon, Company L, Eighth Infantry, First Sergt. James Delaney, leg above knee, serious.

Transport *Grant* sailed yesterday via Nagasaki, 2 officers, 76 enlisted men Company F, Twenty-sixth Volunteer Infantry, 56 officers, 1,534 enlisted men Twenty-ninth Volunteer Infantry, Thirty-second Volunteer Infantry; 126 sick. Notify Department of California.

MACARTHUR.

MANILA. (Received March 25, 1901—3.25 a. m.)

ADJUTANT-GENERAL, *Washington:*

With reference to your telegram of 16th, signed Edwards, insular funds appropriated for clerks, division, department headquarters, must continue or corresponding annual amount, $90,000, furnished or work can not be done, and 63 thoroughly competent clerks discharged. No competent enlisted clerks available; number civil-service clerks entirely inadequate.

Payment 30 pesos for surrendered rifles most important future policy, should continue, necessary to present future control islands. Request necessary funds for this purpose, if insular funds not available.

* * * * * * *

First Lieut. William H. Mullay died Manila Hospital, typhoid fever, 9.54 evening March 23.

* * * * * * *

MACARTHUR.

WAR DEPARTMENT, *March 26, 1901.*

MACARTHUR, *Manila:*

With reference to your telegram of 25th, Secretary of War desires to know what funds do you require for surrendered rifles. Possibly can be furnished from emergency appropriation, War Department. Is it necessary to cable funds if it should be granted?

EDWARDS.

MANILA. (Received March 27, 1901—11.50 p. m.)

ADJUTANT-GENERAL, *Washington:*

General Funston has just returned from expedition to Palanan, province of Isabela, where he captured Aguinaldo, who is now in my possession at Malacanan. Particulars later.

MACARTHUR.

MANILA. (Received March 28, 1901—4.38 p. m.)

ADJUTANT-GENERAL, *Washington:*

Important messages fell into General Funston's hands February 28, from which Aguinaldo was located at Palanan, Isabela Province. Expedition organized, consisting Aguinaldo's captured messenger, 4 ex-insurgent officers, and 78 Macabebes, who spoke Tagalo; armed Mausers, Remingtons; dressed to represent insurgents. Funston commanded, accompanied by Capt. Russell T. Hazzard, Eleventh Cavalry; Capt. Harry W. Newton, Thirty-fourth Volunteer Infantry; Lieut. Oliver P. M. Hazzard, Eleventh Volunteer Cavalry; Lieut. Burton J. Mitchell, Fortieth Volunteer Infantry. Officers dressed as American privates, and represented prisoners. Expedition sailed Manila March 6, *Vicksburg.* Landed March 14 last, coast Luzon, 20 miles south Casiguran. Reached Palanan, marching three afternoons, March 23. Natives completely misled; supposed detachment insurgent reenforcements, for which supplies furnished Aguinaldo; also sent supplies, and had his escort, 40 men, paraded to extend proper honor. Short distance Aguinaldo's quarters disguise discarded. Combat followed, resulting 2 insurgents killed, 18 rifles, 1 000 rounds ammunition captured, together with Aguinaldo and two principal staff officers. No casualties our side. Splendid cooperation navy through Commander Barry. Officers, men *Vicksburg* indispensable to success. Funston loudly praises navy; entire army joins in thanks to sea service. The transaction was brilliant in conception and faultless in execution. All credit must go Funston, who, under supervision General Wheaton, organized and conducted expedition from start to finish. His reward should be signal and immediate. Concur with General Wheaton, who recommends Funston's retention volunteers until he can be appointed brigadier-general regulars. I hope speedy cessation hostilities throughout archipelago as consequence this stroke. As result of conference now in progress, probable Aguinaldo will issue address advising general surrender, delivery arms, acceptance American supremacy.

MacARTHUR.

ADJUTANT-GENERAL'S OFFICE,
Washington, March 29, 1901.

MACARTHUR, *Manila:*

President instructs me express his high appreciation of gallant conduct General Funston and officers and men of Army and Navy engaged with him Palanan expedition. Secwar personally joins in this expression. You will observe following instructions Secwar: Fact that Aguinaldo has made unfounded claims to have received promises from American officers should lead to especial care in communicating with him. All possibility misconstruction or misrepresentation should be avoided, and you should expressly state to him in such manner that it will be capable unquestionable proof that no officer of Government in Philippine Islands is authorized to make to him any promise not contained in your notice of amnesty June 21, 1900, with your explanatory statement July 2, 1900, or in public acts Philippine Commission heretofore enacted. He should be treated like other prisoners war, without severity, but with every precaution against escape, and he must determine course which he will pursue in view such assurances and guarantees as are contained in papers above enumerated and in view President's instructions to Philippine Commissioners and President's other public utterances. In case he should offer allegiance United States and undertake secure general acceptance American sovereignty by his former followers, you will nevertheless retain him in custody until practical results his efforts leave no doubt his good faith and no possibility retraction on his part. Should he take other course of refusing allegiance, he should be detained in custody in such manner that neither by act nor communication can he interfere with pacification of country; and your general order 4, January 7, 1901, special order 6 same date, and letter instructions to Major Orwig by General Barry January 14, 1901, all relating to deportation insurgent prisoners Guam, are approved both as to form and substance. If it should appear that he has violated laws war, he should be tried.

CORBIN.

MANILA. (Received March 29, 1901—9.12 a. m.)

ADJUTANT-GENERAL, *Washington:*

Killed—March 23, near Candelaria, Luzon, Company I, Twenty-first Infantry, Peter A. Peterson; near San Antonio, Laguna, Company A, Twenty-first Infantry, Mathew Migusik. Wounded—Martin E. Keavey, thighs, severe; March 22, San Antonio, Luzon, Company B, Forty-ninth Volunteer Infantry, Laddie Blackstock, hand, slight; March 19, near Olongapo, Company G, Forty-first Volunteer Infantry,

Hiram M. Yarbrough, face, slight; February 28, Capaz, Panay, Company D, Thirty-eighth Volunteer Infantry, Sergt. John E. Pierce, leg above knee, slight.

Shall candidates reported qualified by board be held Manila pending appointment second lieutenant Regular Army?

Brig. Gen. William A. Kobbé reports surrender Sumilao, Mindanao, 9 officers, 160 men, 187 rifles, 80 shotguns, Capistrano's command. This ends trouble Mindanao as far as Filipinos concerned. Brig. Gen. Robert P. Hughes reports Alipali and Ruiz, 34 guns, surrendered to Capt. David C. Shanks, at Mambuiao. Two hundred and six guns Fullon's command surrendered to Lieut. Col. William S. Scott, Forty-fourth Volunteer Infantry.

MACARTHUR.

SAN FRANCISCO, CAL., *March 29, 1901.*
(Received 2.31 p. m.)

ADJUTANT-GENERAL, *Washington:*

Transport *Logan* arrived this morning. [Thirty-fourth Infantry Volunteers, 790 enlisted men; Thirty-third Infantry Volunteers, 760 enlisted men.]

SHAFTER, *Major-General.*

MANILA. (Received March 30, 1901—1.23 p. m.)

ADJUTANT-GENERAL, *Washington:*

Following deaths have occurred since last report: Died from wounds received in action—March 3, Company I, Sixth Infantry, Corpl. Robert Hensley. Suicide—March 17, Company D, Fourth Infantry, Cook Hugh Nelson. Killed by accident—Company E, Forty-fifth Volunteer Infantry, James G. Smith. Killed by comrade—March 21, Company B, Twenty-fourth Infantry, James Wilson. Gored by carabao—March 6, Company L, Eighteenth Infantry, Thomas Lavey. Explosion gasoline stove—March 18, Company L, Thirteenth Infantry, Josepha Meyer. Variola—March 21, Company I, Sixteenth Infantry, Walter H. Townsend. Dysentery—March 2, Company I, Twenty-ninth Volunteer Infantry, John C. Tyson; Company K, Thirty-first Volunteer Infantry, Hugh Neiswonger; March 15, Company I, Eighteenth Infantry, Irwin L. Brown. Philosis—March 24, Company E, Fourth Infantry, August Schultz; March 21, Battery F, Fourth Artillery, Wallie Griffin. Typhoid fever—February 5, Company A, Fifteenth Infantry, Otis W. Puffer. Malarial fever—March 24, Company L, Forty-sixth Volunteer Infantry, Henry Howe; January 2, Company E, Eighteenth Infantry, Artificer Angel Calcari. Heart disease—March 26, Company D, Forty-second Infantry, Christopher A. Moring. Cirrhosis liver—March 17, Company M, Fourth Infantry, Axel Fredin. Pneumonia—March 8, Company B, Twenty-seventh Volunteer Infantry, Charles A. Miller; March 18, B, Twenty-sixth Volunteer Infantry, Harry C. Anderson. Alcoholism—March 18, Hospital Corps, William H. Bennett. Jaundice—March 21, Company C, Third Infantry, Andrew Pflaum.

With reference to your telegram of 19th ultimo, Frank O. Whitlock desires transfer Corps of Engineers, U. S. Army.

General Geronimo, commanding eastern Bulacan, Morong provinces, surrendered yesterday, with 12 officers, 29 men, 30 guns; took oath and returned mountains in order to secure more guns. Contreras, commanding northeast Panay and Sulzan, surrendered, Panay, with 30 guns.

MACARTHUR.

ADJUTANT-GENERAL'S OFFICE, *Washington, April 1, 1901.*

MACARTHUR, *Manila.*

With reference to your telegram of 27th, use *Indiana*, *Sumner*, handle China troops. Not including *Sheridan*, you will have 10 transports for volunteers without *Indiana*. *Buford* sails April 1, depot battalion Fifth Regiment U. S. Infantry, two troops Fifteenth Cavalry; *Kilpatrick,* April 5, headquarters, band, and battalion Eleventh Regiment. U. S. Infantry, two companies First Regiment U. S. Infantry; *Logan,* April 15, squadron Ninth Regiment U. S. Cavalry, squadron Tenth Regiment U. S. Cavalry, battalion Eleventh Regiment U. S. Infantry, two companies First Regiment U. S. Infantry; *Ohio,* April 8; *Warren, Thomas, Lawton* not later than April 20. Last four transports without troops. Will coal to reach you May 15 if possible. *Hancock* sailed March 25, four companies Seventh Infantry, second squadron Sixth Cavalry. Sensational press reports, grave frauds, commissary department, Manila. What are the facts?

CORBIN.

MANILA. (Received April 1, 1901—9.15 a. m.)
ADJUTANT-GENERAL, *Washington:*
Transport *Wyefield* arrived March 28. *Pingsuey,* March 29.
Sick in hospital, 2,833; sick in quarters, 908; per cent, 6.89.

* * * * * * *

MACARTHUR.

MANILA. (Received April 1, 1901—7.40 a. m.)
ADJUTANT-GENERAL, *Washington:*
With reference to your telegram of 25th September, rate of exchange is two Mexican dollars for one dollar United States currency present quarter.

MACARTHUR.

MANILA. (Received April 1, 1901—8 a. m.)
ADJUTANT-GENERAL, *Washington:*
Since arrival Manila Aguinaldo been [Malacanan] investigating conditions archipelago, has relied almost entirely upon [instructive] advice Chief Justice Arellano; as result to-day [subscribed, swore] declaration, page 11, my annual report. Proposes to address armed insurgents, advising surrender, delivery arms, acceptance American sovereignty. Has reached conclusion voluntarily, without semblance coercion or promises. United States absolutely uncommitted. He is satisfied people demand peace: believes interest of country need it, and has apparently sacrificed his own view for the benefit of the archipelago. In present attitude he appears to great advantage. Aguinaldo's action potential for pacification. To same end request authority renew amnesty notice June 21, to terminate June 1, after which all in arms considered outlaws, criminals, treated accordingly. Do not doubt Aguinaldo's present sincerity, but presence in island for some time to come very undesirable. As best solution situation, also calculated strengthen efforts to pacify, recommend Aguinaldo and two selected by himself, and Chief Justice Arellano, if he can be persuaded to go, and two distinguished pro-Americans, make party visit to United States for purpose of observation and study American institutions. If authorized will send *Sheridan.* Can furnish all funds necessary from money appropriated act June 9, 1898. Funston or J. Franklin Bell charge party, both speak Spanish. Have considered proposition carefully. Would like to submit further remarks if Department doubtful. Contents your message March 30 exactly complied with. So far as known Aguinaldo not violated laws of war.

MACARTHUR.

MANILA. (Received April 2, 1901—5.40 a. m.)
ADJUTANT-GENERAL, *Washington:*
William R. Hall [Major Medical Department] died Manila 12.45 morning April 2, acute osteomyelitis.

MACARTHUR.

ADJUTANT-GENERAL'S OFFICE,
Washington, April 3, 1901.

MACARTHUR, *Manila:*

With reference to your dispatch of April 1, it is considered important that Aguinaldo remain in custody or under military surveillance for considerable time while the good faith of his allegiance is established by his assistance in the pacification of the country; that this can better be accomplished in the Philippines than here; that if his declaration of allegiance is sincere he can be of more service in Manila than here, and that such visit as you propose would necessarily result in an exciting public spectacle not favorable to the study of institutions. The proposal that Aguinaldo should come to this country at this time is therefore disapproved. Cable for consideration draft of such notice as you propose for extension of amnesty.

CORBIN.

MANILA. (Received April 3, 1901—10.11 a. m.)

ADJUTANT-GENERAL, *Washington:*

[Brigadier-General] Robert P. Hughes reports surrender at Banga, northwest Panay, March 31, 30 officers, 185 men, 105 rifles. [Brigadier-General] William A. Kobbé reports 21 men, 21 guns, surrendered March 31, northern Mindanao.

With reference to your telegram of 1st, if transports troops enumerated arrive according to schedule, all volunteers will arrive San Francisco June 30 at latest.

Commissary frauds being investigated; not sufficient gravity cause concern; apparently due irregularity sales savings. Press reports inexact, misleading, as all have been since removal censorship.

MACARTHUR.

MANILA. (Received April 6, 1901—8 a. m.)

ADJUTANT-GENERAL, *Washington:*

Propose following notice for extension amnesty:

"The amnesty announced in orders from this office under date of June 21, 1900, and which expired on September 21, 1900, is, by direction of the President of the United States, renewed, and will remain in full force and effect until June 1, 1901. On and after that date all persons found in arms against the United States will be treated as outlaws and not entitled, upon capture, to the privileges of prisoners of war; and all persons directly or indirectly participating in the insurrection shall stand disqualified to exercise the elective franchise or hold any office of profit or trust under the insular government, and the property of all such persons shall be confiscated under such confiscation proceedings as may hereafter be established by law. For convenient reference the amnesty notice referred to above is republished herewith."

MACARTHUR.

MANILA. (Received April 6, 1901—12.50 a. m.)

ADJUTANT-GENERAL, *Washington:*

Nineteen officers, 173 men, 133 rifles, 9 revolvers, Pablo Tecson's command, surrendered at San Fernando yesterday, and took oath.

MACARTHUR.

ADJUTANT-GENERAL'S OFFICE,
Washington, April 9, 1901.

MACARTHUR, *Manila:*

Cable Department in full President's consideration any proclamation or communication which Aguinaldo proposes make to people before permitting it announced or published.

CORBIN.

AFFAIRS IN THE PHILIPPINE ISLANDS.

ADJUTANT-GENERAL'S OFFICE,
Washington, April 9, 1901.

MACARTHUR, *Manila:*

Following instructions Secretary War replying yours April 6, not deemed advisable to issue any further notice or proclamation relating to amnesty at his time.

CORBIN.

MANILA. (Received April 10, 1901—12.45 p. m.)

ADJUTANT-GENERAL, *Washington:*

Following deaths have occurred since last report: Dysentery—March 18, Company K, Eighteenth Infantry, Louis F. Beneke; March 28, Company I, Fifteenth Infantry, William K. Brown; March 25, Company F, Eighteenth Infantry, Aaron C. Hurst; March 30, Company A, Nineteenth Infantry, John J. Ragan; March 20, Hospital Corps, Walter R. Ogden. Typhoid fever—March 11, Troop B, Ninth Cavalry, Sergt. William Rutledge; April 3, Hospital Corps, Harvey M. Herrick. Died from wounds received in action—March 29, Copmany A, Twenty-first Infantry, Martin E. Keavey; April 4, Company L, Forty-first Volunteer Infantry, Corpl. James W. Colwell. Variola—April 2, Company H, Twenty-fifth Infantry, Richard D. Lewis; Company E, Twentieth Infantry, Otto Holm. Enteritis—Company B, Forty-eighth Volunteer Infantry, William McGee. Phthisis pulmonalis—Company A, Fifth Infantry, James O'Brien. Meningitis—March 28, Company A, Forty-eighth Volunteer Infantry, James Buckhalter. Malarial fever—March 14, Company B, First Infantry, August Kreger. Appendicitis—March 27, Troop D, Ninth Cavalry, William H. Green. Broncho-pneumonia—April 4, Company K, Forty-first Volunteer Infantry, Joseph C. Haught. Exhaustion, liver abscesses—April 1, Band, Twenty-sixth Volunteer Infantry, Chauncey S. Lewis. Cirrhosis liver—March 17, Company M, Eighth Infantry, William F. Briggeman. Opium poisoning—March 14, Company E, Twelfth Infantry, William C. Long, Shock operation abscess liver—March 26, Company B, Twenty-third Infantry, Frank Gately. Accidental discharge revolver—April 1, Company A, Fifth Infantry, Harry L. Mace. Suicide—April 5, Company A, Twenty-fourth Infantry, William H. Dorsey; March 29, Company G, Forty-second Volunteer Infantry, Wilfried Beaulien.

If early discharge J. C. Read, captain and commissary of subsistence, contemplated, suspend action, as trial probable.

MACARTHUR.

ADJUTANT-GENERAL'S OFFICE,
Washington, April 10, 1901.

MACARTHUR, *Manila:*

Secretary of War directs recall all army officers at Guam. Secretary of the Navy has given instructions guard for prisoners.

* * * * * * *

CORBIN.

MANILA. (Received April 10, 1901—7.30 p. m.)

ADJUTANT-GENERAL, *Washington:*

Referring messages requesting full text Aguinaldo's proposed address and announcing decision Secretary of War against further amnesty notice, respectfully submit following, which was prepared by Aguinaldo, assisted only by the two staff officers captured with him; original in Spanish and ready for printing and distribution whenever considered expedient by Department. So far as military situation concerned, its immediate publication simultaneously with amnesty proposed by me—April 6—would, in my opinion, almost instantly terminate hostilities throughout archipelago, insure delivery of several thousand guns still held by insurgents, and establish peace under conditions most favorable to immediate organization and permanent maintenance of stable civil government.

"*To the Philippine people:*

"I believe that I am not in error in presuming that the unhappy fate to which my adverse fortune has led me is not a surprise to those who have been familiar, day by day, with the progress of the war. The lessons thus taught, the full meaning of which has but recently come to my knowledge, suggest to me with irresistible force that the complete termination of hostilities and a long-lasting peace are not only desirable but absolutely essential to the welfare of the Philippines. The Filipinos have never been dismayed by their weakness, nor have they faltered in following the path pointed out by their fortitude and courage; the time has come, however, in which they find their advance along this path impeded by an irresistible force, a force which, while it restrains them, yet enlightens the mind and opens another course by presenting to them the cause of peace. This cause has been joyfully embraced by a majority of our fellow-countrymen, who are already united around the glorious and sovereign banner of the United States. In this banner they repose their trust, in the belief that under its protection our people will attain all the promised liberties which they are even now beginning to enjoy.

"The country has declared unmistakably for peace. So be it. Enough of blood, enough of tears and desolation. This wish can not be ignored by the men still in arms, if they are animated by no other desire than to serve this noble people which has thus clearly manifested its will. So also do I respect this will, now that it is known to me, and after mature deliberation resolutely proclaim to the world that I can not refuse to heed the voice of a people longing for peace, nor the lamentations of thousands of families yearning to see their dear ones in the enjoyment of the liberty promised by the generosity of the great American Union. By acknowledging and accepting the sovereignty of the United States throughout the entire archipelago, as I now do without any reservation whatsoever, I believe that I am serving thee, my beloved country. May hapiness be thine.

"EMILIO AGUINALDO."
MACARTHUR.

ADJUTANT-GENERAL'S OFFICE,
Washington, April 11, 1901.

MACARTHUR, *Manila:*

Referring to your dispatch received April 10, it is considered that the paper prepared by Aguinaldo should be published unless the Commission from their standpoint see some objection. Consult them; and if they see no reason to the contrary, publish it. It is considered that this paper should stand by itself, and that any further notice regarding amnesty which we may determine upon should be subsequent and separate.
CORBIN.

MANILA. (Received April 11, 1901—10.10 a. m.]
ADJUTANT-GENERAL, *Washington:*

* * * Colonel Arce surrendered Castillejos yesterday; 235 soldiers, 12 officers, 103 rifles. This and surrender Colonel Alva, Olongapo, April 8, with 13 officers, 394 men, 92 rifles, frees both Bataan, Zambales provinces.
MACARTHUR.

MANILA. (Received April 14, 1901—5.53 a. m.)

ADJUTANT-GENERAL, *Washington.*

* * * * * * *

[Major] William Monaghan died of heart disease, 6 a. m. Saturday, April 13.

* * * * * * *

MACARTHUR.

MANILA. (Received April 16, 1901—6.05 a. m.)

ADJUTANT-GENERAL, *Washington:*

Transport *Indiana* arrived yesterday. Sick in hospital, 2,987; sick in quarters, 946; per cent, 7.39.

MACARTHUR.

MANILA. (Received April 16, 1901—8.26 a. m.)

ADJUTANT-GENERAL, *Washington:*

* * * * * * *

With reference to your telegram of 10th, request you send necessary orders recalling officers at Guam by transport from San Francisco. There take them on. There are several enlisted men, employees, and property pertaining army supply department, Guam; instructions should be sent regarding accountability therefor if officers removed. Intended recommencing withdrawal entire party, return prisoners Manila before June 30, sending transports from here that purpose.

* * * * * * *

MACARTHUR.

ADJUTANT-GENERAL'S OFFICE,
Washington, April 16, 1901.

MACARTHUR, *Manila:*

Secretary of War directs you report immediately by telegraph on Associated Press report from Manila yesterday, implicating certain officers Subsistence Department of the Army fraudulent practices and again to enjoin upon you necessity taking immediate and drastic measures toward guilty.

* * * * * * *

CORBIN.

MANILA. (Received April 17, 1901—7.10 a. m.)

ADJUTANT-GENERAL, *Washington:*

A large number discharged regulars can not be returned United States account shipment volunteers. Can fill transport. Request that I be granted authority to charter *Tartar*, now Hongkong, three months or less, $800 gold per day; necessity urgent.

* * * * * * *

Colonel Abad, insurgent leader, Marinduque, 9 officers, 70 soldiers, 248 small arms, surrendered, [Maj.] Frederick A. Smith, April 15; oathed with impressive ceremony; released. This ends insurrection there.

With reference to my telegram of 29th ultimo, Shall qualified candidates commissioned and enlisted volunteers be retained here, mustered out when regiment is, or be sent home?

MACARTHUR.

CORRESPONDENCE.

MANILA. (Received April 18, 1901—5 a. m.)

ADJUTANT-GENERAL, *Washington:*
Recommend assignment [Brig. Gen.] James F. Wade, Department of Southern Luzon, vice [Brig. Gen.] John C. Bates; [Brig. Gen.] William Ludlow, Department of Visayas, vice [Brig. Gen.] Robert P. Hughes.

Transport *Pennsylvania* arrived April 16; transports *Meade, Pakling*, April 17.

MACARTHUR.

MANILA. (Received April 18, 1901—3.17 p. m.)

ADJUTANT-GENERAL, *Washington:*

* * * * * * *

With reference to your telegram of 16th, Associated Press report grossly exaggerated, misleading matters therein touched upon regarding officers subsistence department fully investigated proceedings transport *Sheridan* regarding theft commissary stores amount which grossly exaggerated by press reports; immediate most drastic measures already applied; 3 officers, number enlisted men, being tried court-martial; number citizens military commission.

* * * * * * *

MACARTHUR.

ADJUTANT-GENERAL'S OFFICE,
Washington, April 19, 1901.

MACARTHUR, *Manila:*
With reference to your telegram of 17th, charter *Tartar*. Telegraph terms and where *Tartar* can be discharged. *Meade* to return discharged regulars.

* * * * * * *

CORBIN.

MANILA. (Received April 19, 1901—7.07 a. m.)

ADJUTANT-GENERAL, *Washington:*
* * * Transports *Hancock, Petrarch* arrived to-day.

MACARTHUR.

MANILA. (Received April 19, 1901—11 a. m.)

ADJUTANT-GENERAL, *Washington:*
Extensive repairs are necessary transport *Meade*, taking thirty days. Propose charter *Tartar* immediately replace her. Seems indispensable to movement volunteers. Request that I be granted authority to charter another vessel to return discharged soldiers referred to in our telegram of April 17.

Will assign [Maj.] Clinton B. Sears, chief engineer, retain him here. [Capt.] John Biddle familiar Guam Harbor, [Maj.] Clinton B. Sears unfamiliar. Recommend relief [Capt.] John Biddle duty Division of the Philippines, reassignment Guam board, to proceed to San Francisco with board now here.

Several men Forty-eighth Regiment U. S. Volunteer Infantry, Forty-ninth Regiment U. S. Volunteer Infantry, desire reenlist here.

Can Twenty-fourth Regiment U. S. Infantry, Twenty-fifth Regiment U. S. Infantry, be increased 150 per company?

Strong presumptive evidence fraud disbursement public funds by Second Lieutenant Polk, Thirty-ninth Regiment U. S. Volunteer Infantry. Papers mailed. Polk sailed March 16.

* * * * * * *

MACARTHUR.

AFFAIRS IN THE PHILIPPINE ISLANDS. 1271

ADJUTANT-GENERAL'S OFFICE,
Washington, April 19, 1901.

MACARTHUR, *Manila:*
Is Aguinaldo's proclamation published same heretofore cabled?

CORBIN.

MANILA. (Received April 20, 1901—4.55 a. m.)
ADJUTANT-GENERAL, *Washington:*
With reference to your telegram of 19th, Aguinaldo's address published here this morning precisely as cabled to War Department, word for word.

MACARTHUR.

MANILA. (Received April 20, 1901—10.23 a. m.)
ADJUTANT-GENERAL, *Washington:*
Following deaths have occurred since last report: Dysentery—April 8, Company A, Battalion of Engineers, United States Army, Sergt. Patrick F. Duggan; April 9, Company B, Forty-first Volunteer Infantry, John A. Soby; March 19, Company M, Forty-fifth Volunteer Infantry, Corpl. William Lochead; March 15, Company I, Thirty-first Volunteer Infantry, John E. Hayes. Typhoid fever—April 14, Company E, Forty-sixth Volunteer Infantry, Sergt. Arthur B. Hersey; April 1, Hospital Corps, Joe Chapman. Pneumonia—March 20, Company M, Forty-seventh Volunteer Infantry, Corpl. Fred O. Brown. Abscess liver—April 3, Company A, Nineteenth Infantry, Nathaniel F. Power. Variola—March 31, Company I, Eighteenth Infantry, John Tolley. Pyæmia—April 14, Company G, Forty-second Volunteer Infantry, George L. Norton. Tuberculosis—April 13, Company H, Fourth Infantry, Cesario Torres. Meningitis—March 22, at sea, B, Twenty-eighth Infantry, Ira L. Walker. Pericarditis—April 8, Company A, Sixteenth Infantry, Alfred Fow. Drowned, body not recovered—March 30, Company K, Second Infantry, Alfred G. Fost. Died from the effects of fall—April 1, Company K, Fifteenth Infantry, Frank M. Danitz; March 27, Company C, Sixteenth Infantry, Patrick Burns; March 12, Company I, Seventeenth Infantry, Charles V. Molder.

Reported postal authorities holding mail Twenty-fifth Regiment U. S. Infantry by mistake. Please have forwarded.

MACARTHUR.

MANILA. (Received April 21, 1901—5.51 a. m.)
SECRETARY OF WAR, *Washington:*
With reference to your telegram of 12th, Commission recommends extending period of amnesty offered June 21, 1900, to June 15, 1901.

TAFT.

MANILA. (Received April 21, 1901—6.33 a. m.)
ADJUTANT-GENERAL, *Washington:*
Wounded—March 14, Laguna, Samar, Eighth Battery Field Artillery, Corpl. Robert L. McLauchlin, side, severe; March 19, Mayana, Bohol, Company G, Forty-fourth Volunteer Infantry, Willard W. May, wounded in leg above knee, slight; March 23, Candelaria, Luzon, Company I, Twenty-first Infantry, John McQueney, ankle, wounded in foot, slight; April 14, Norzagaray, Luzon, Hospital Corps, Henry V. Garland, wounded in chest, serious; March 16, Donsol, Luzon, Company A, Forty-seventh Volunteer Infantry, Richard Mason, wounded in thigh, serious; Antonio Laporta, elbow, severe; Hiram Blizzard, wounded in thigh, slight; Com-

pany D, Forty-seventh Volunteer Infantry, Frank Remars, wounded in thigh, slight; March 18, Peñaranda, Luzon, Troop A, Fourth Cavalry, Dwight F. Lawson, wounded in shoulder, slight; Troop G, Fourth Cavalry, Alan R. Blackburn, wounded in leg above knee, serious; Acting Asst. Surg. U. S. Grant Deaton, heel, slight; February 26, Narvacan, Luzon, Company G, Thirty-third Volunteer Infantry, James F. Treadaway, wounded in foot, moderate; March 29, Talisay, Luzon, Troop C, Sixth Cavalry, Ewing Wright, finger, slight; James Creed, wounded in thigh, moderate.

MACARTHUR.

MANILA. (Received April 21, 1901—10 a. m.)

ADJUTANT-GENERAL, *Washington:*
* * * No truth Associated Press report April 15, concerning *Lawton.*

MACARTHUR.

MANILA. (Received April 23, 1901.)

ADJUTANT-GENERAL, *Washington:*
Transport *Sheridan* sailed April 22 via Nagasaki; [Gen.] John C. Bates, [Gen.] Frederick D. Grant, 66 officers, 1,822 enlisted men, Forty-fifth Regiment U. S. Volunteer Infantry, Forty-sixth Regiment U. S. Volunteer Infantry. Notify Department of California.

Transport *Kintuck* arrived yesterday.

MACARTHUR.

MANILA. (Received April 25, 1901—1.15 a. m.)

ADJUTANT-GENERAL, *Washington:*
Stop shipments all animals Philippines. Cavalry en route whose mounts not already shipped can be furnished here. Have abundant animals supply every demand under improved conditions.

* * * * * * *

MACARTHUR.

ADJUTANT-GENERAL'S OFFICE,
Washington, April 26, 1901.

MACARTHUR, *Manila:*
Mail exact copy final treaty Biacnabato, with signatures. Copy received merely states was signed.

* * * * * *

CORBIN.

ADJUTANT-GENERAL'S OFFICE,
Washington, April 27, 1901.

MACARTHUR, *Manila:*
* * * Reenlist not exceeding 150 men Forty-eighth Regiment U. S. Volunteer Infantry, Forty-ninth Regiment U. S. Volunteer Infantry, giving Twenty-fourth Regiment U. S. Infantry and Twenty-fifth Regiment U. S. Infantry 75 each.

CORBIN.

AFFAIRS IN THE PHILIPPINE ISLANDS. 1273

MANILA. (Received April 27, 1901—10.18 a. m.)

ADJUTANT-GENERAL, *Washington:*

* * * Owing repair transport *Meade* detention transport *Kilpatrick*, Honolulu, transport *Grant* should be returned at once direct in order to provide against any contingency returning volunteers.

MACARTHUR.

ADJUTANT-GENERAL'S OFFICE,
Washington, April 29, 1901.

MACARTHUR, *Manila:*

* * * First Battalion, Thirtieth Regiment, U. S. Infantry, sailed *Ohio* April 16.

With reference to your telegram of 16th, *Solace* left San Francisco April 18, orders to transfer detachment Guam to Manila.

With reference to my telegram of 1st, Troop G, Fifteenth Regiment U. S. Cavalry, Company A, Tenth U. S. Infantry, sailed *Kilpatrick* April 5, replacing Company K, Eleventh Regiment U. S. Infantry, and Company L, Eleventh Regiment U. S. Infantry, which will sail on *Lawton* May 7.

CORBIN.

MANILA. (Received April 30, 1901—2.59 a. m.)

ADJUTANT-GENERAL, *Washington:*

Juan and Blas Villamor, leaders Abra, surrendered Bangued April 27; now engaged assembling scattered commands, delivering arms. Aglipay, ex-priest, leader Ilocos Norte Province [Luzon], surrendered Lacng, April 28; promises bring about surrender his followers and arms. Tinio still out; will be destroyed unless surrenders soon, which very probable. These events signify total collapse rebellion First District, terminate insurrection Department of Northern Luzon. In south Luzon, groups under Cailles, Malvar, still out; both pursued great energy; their surrender [or] destruction accomplished soon. Lucban, Samar, still out with rather formidable band. Unless he surrenders soon may be necessary concentrate considerable force against him, which may prolong operations several weeks. Excepting above, insurrection practically suppressed throughout archipelago.

MACARTHUR.

MANILA. (Received April 30, 1901—6.55 a. m.)

ADJUTANT-GENERAL, *Washington:*

Col. Cipriano Callao and Gregorio Katibac; Malvar's best officers, surrendered [Col.] Jacob Kline, Lipa, April 28. 23 officers, 108 men, 86 rifles.

MACARTHUR.

ADJUTANT-GENERAL'S OFFICE,
Washington, April 30, 1901.

MACARTHUR, *Manila:*

*   *   *   *   *   *   *

To avoid expense sending unnecessary force to Philippine Islands, Secretary of War desires your opinion, in view of existing conditions, number each arm service required.

*   *   *   *   *   *   *

CORBIN

MANILA. (Received April 30, 1901.)
ADJUTANT-GENERAL, *Washington:*
Following deaths have occurred since last report: Drowned—bodies recovered, April 11, A, Twenty-seventh Regulars, Oscar E. Weeding; April 17, A, Twenty-eighth Regulars, John Tesmar; April 26, Company A, Twenty-first Infantry, Corpl. James D. McGill, Robert L. Tipps. Tuberculosis—April 22, Company H, Twenty-fifth Infantry, Corpl. Elwood A. Forman; April 21, Company D, Sixth Infantry, John H. Halter. Typhoid fever—April 20, Company G, Third Infantry, Noah E. Gardner; April 24, Company D, Third Infantry, Robert C. Wood. Purpura hæmorrhagica—April 22, Troop H, Third Cavalry, Powell V. Dials. Sclerosis—April 19, Troop G, Ninth Cavalry, Samuel Boggs. Nephritis—April 17, Company H, Twenty-fifth Infantry, Green Badgett; April 27, Company A, Twenty-fourth Infantry, Sergt. Henry Thomas. Dysentery—April 26, Company A, Third Infantry, Joseph F. Hefferan. Psilosia—April 23, Company M, Fourth Infantry, Clarence Hill. Suicide—Company A, Battalion of Engineers, U. S. Army, Charles Norwood. Variola—April 20, Company I, Fifth Infantry, Elven Pace. Diarrhea—April 13, Troop D, Ninth Cavalry, Fred A. Robinson. Cerebral embolism—March 14, Company A, Fortieth Volunteer Infantry, Eugene E. Sigsbee. Gastro-enteritis—April 20, Company B, Twenty-first Infantry, Alonzo Smith. Abscess liver—April 19, Company L, Fifteenth Infantry, Corpl. Frank E. Waldron.

* * * * * * *

Quentin Sales surrendered Iloilo April 25. All organized opposition that island ended.

MACARTHUR.

MANILA. (Received April 30, 1901—8.25 a. m.)
ADJUTANT-GENERAL, *Washington:*
General Tinio surrendered to-day at Sinait. He will deliver all men and guns his command as soon as can be gathered together. This completely pacifies First District, Department of Northern Luzon, for many months worst in Luzon.

MACARTHUR.

MANILA. (Received May 1, 1901—5.12 a. m.)
ADJUTANT-GENERAL, *Washington:*
* * * Sick in hospital, 2,586; sick in quarters, 613; 5.86 per cent.

MACARTHUR.

ADJUTANT-GENERAL'S OFFICE,
Washington, May 1, 1901.
MACARTHUR, *Manila:*
Order captains and commissary of subsistencies, U. S. Volunteers, Fenton, Ryan, Street, Ingalls, San Francisco. Funds and property to be transferred to line officers you detail in their place. Close money and property accountability and forward final accounts and returns.

Retiring board dissolved, convened according to your telegram April 27. You are authorized to detail recorder board.

* * * * * * *

CORBIN.

ADJUTANT-GENERAL'S OFFICE,
Washington, May 2, 1901.

MACARTHUR, *Manila:*
* * * Order San Francisco all signal officers volunteers Philippine Islands not appointed Regular Army, to enable them to be discharged and ordered home by July 1.

CORBIN.

ADJUTANT-GENERAL'S OFFICE,
Washington, May 3, 1901.

MACARTHUR, *Manila:*
In reference to your telegram of 2d. You were authorized March 9 to examine only volunteer officers candidates for commission Regular Army belonging to regiments which had sailed before that date. Qualified candidates will be considered by President, but should be informed no assurance of commission. All other candidates are to return with regiments for examination United States unless names are cabled you.

* * * * * * *

CORBIN.

MANILA. (Received May 3, 1901—11.15 a. m.)
ADJUTANT-GENERAL, *Washington:*
With reference to your telegram of 30th ultimo. Forty thousand American troops sufficient Philippine Islands, with possibility considerable reduction during next year. Proportion each arm can be fixed as will be convenient War Department.

Following suggested: Thirty thousand infantry, 9,000 cavalry, 8 companies coast artillery, 2 field batteries, 3 mountain batteries. Large proportion cavalry based on strength that arm and not military necessity. If desirable, cavalry can be reduced to 5,000 and infantry increased accordingly.

All artillery equipments now here should remain, use emergency, personnel batteries only returning United States. In addition enlisted strength Engineers, Ordnance, Signal Corps of the Army remain as at present, suitable number Hospital Corps.

MACARTHUR.

MANILA. (Received May 3, 1901—10 a. m.)
ADJUTANT-GENERAL, *Washington:*
* * * Wounded—April 5, Eighth Battery Field Artillery, Calbayog, Samar, George H. Glover, wounded in thigh, slight; Corpl. Warren Faust, feet, slight; Salsona, Luzon, Company M, Twentieth Infantry, Franklin H. Gross, wounded in shoulder, slight; Louis Gregory, wounded in leg above knee, slight; April 17, Tacloban, Leyte, Company H, First Infantry, William Schlager, arms, slight; Clyde B. Ely, wounded in arm, slight; April 27, Cabugao, Luzon, Troop I, Third Cavalry, Corpl. Alfred Ballin, wounded in abdomen, slight; [Capt.] John B. McDonald lung, severe; April 24, Tacloban, Leyte, Company H, First Infantry, Q. M. Sergt. William Blake, wounded in abdomen, moderate.

Killed—April 10, Lagonoy, Luzon, Company M, Forty-seventh Volunteer Infantry, Harry A. Varner.

Transports *Buford, Wright* arrived yesterday.

* * * * * * *

MACARTHUR.

ADJUTANT-GENERAL'S OFFICE,
Washington, May 6, 1901.

MACARTHUR, *Manila:*
* * * All general staff vacancies filled. Useless forward recommendations except by mail.

CORBIN.

MANILA. (Received May 7, 1901—1.30 a. m.)

ADJUTANT-GENERAL, *Washington:*
With reference to your telegram of 3d. See mine December 13, yours December 17; especially mine March 3, March 10. Volunteer officers reported qualified in our telegram May 2 were part those referred to in our telegramMarch 10. Many others of the same class are being examined. All been informed no assurance appointment according to your telegram February 26.

MACARTHUR.

MANILA. (Received May 8, 1901—7.12 a. m.)

ADJUTANT-GENERAL, *Washington:*
Philippine Commission asks detail many volunteer officers applicant appointment Regular Army, services indispensable civil administration islands. Request that I be granted authority to retain and examine here.

Transport *Aztec* arrived to-day.

MACARTHUR.

MANILA. (Received May 10, 1901—8.58 a. m.)

ADJUTANT-GENERAL, *Washington:*
Have attached Samar temporarily Department Visayas. Ordered [Gen.] Robert P. Hughes there to expedite pacification. Recommend Samar be permanently so attached.

MACARTHUR.

MANILA. (Received May 10, 1901—12.21 p. m.)

ADJUTANT-GENERAL, *Washington:*
Following deaths have occurred since last report: Drowned, bodies recovered—April 19, Company H, Twenty-first Infantry, Robert L. Keeton; April 21, A, Twenty-seventh Regulars, Walter Ashworth; May 1, Band, Fifth Cavalry, Benjamin Evans. Dysentery—March 29, Company L, Eighteenth Infantry, Musician Charles R. Spurgeon; May 1, Company F, Eighteenth Infantry, Corpl. William D. Schultze; May 5, Company G, Twenty-second Infantry, Albert O. McIlvaine; April 25, Company F, Eighteenth Infantry, Roderick Littlefield; April 27, Company K, Fourteenth Infantry, Adam Eichelsdefer. Typhoid fever—April 30, Company B, Third Infantry, William R. Metzsker; May 3, Company F, Seventeenth Infantry, Columbus C. Sparks; May 4, Troop G, Sixth Cavalry, Lawrence Murphy. Tuberculosis—May 3, Company M, Seventeenth Infantry, Edward E. Dickey; Company K, Forty-ninth Volunteer Infantry, Isaiah Brooks. Pneumonia—April 20, at sea, Company E, Fifth Infantry, Frank X. Carter; May 6, Company H, Fifth Infantry, William Burns. Diabetes mellitus—May 2, Company H, Forty-second Volunteer Infantry, Harry J. McCloy. Variola—April 28, Company I, Forty-eighth Volunteer Infantry, Charles Johnson. Insolation—Troop I, Third Cavalry, Ralph Mollyneaux. Abscess liver—May 2, Company D, Fortieth Volunteer Infantry, Howard L. Martin. Sclerosis—Company L, Nineteenth Infantry, Corpl. Frank H. Edwards. Suicide—April 27, Company G, Second Infantry, Frank Mattice.

Transport *Ohio* arrived to-day.

* * * * * * *

MACARTHUR.

ADJUTANT-GENERAL'S OFFICE,
Washington, May 11, 1901.

MacArthur, Manila:
 * * * Secretary of War approves attaching Samar permanently Department of Visayas.

* * * * * * *

Corbin.

ADJUTANT-GENERAL'S OFFICE,
Washington, May 11, 1901.

MacArthur, Manila:
After the departure volunteers mail casualty reports instead of cabling. Economy use cable again enjoined by Secretary of War.

* * * * * * *

Corbin.

Manila. (Received May 12, 1901—8.55 a. m.).

Adjutant-General, Washington.
What captains, lieutenants, Thirtieth Infantry are now Philippine Islands? This with view their assignment battalion that regiment now here, which is without officers belonging thereto.

With reference to your telegram of 29th March, signed Edwards. Please expedite transfer $50,000 war emergency fund asked for by chief quartermaster May 8; will probably require $50,000 additional; will it be available on demand?

* * * * * * *

MacArthur.

ADJUTANT-GENERAL'S OFFICE,
Washington, May 13,.1901.

MacArthur, Manila.
Forward records examination appointment Regular Army first mail after the examination.

* * * * * * *

Corbin.

ADJUTANT-GENERAL'S OFFICE,
Washington, May 14, 1901.

MacArthur, Manila:
With reference to your telegram of 3d, Secretary of War directs following the volunteers you send Fourth Regiment U. S. Cavalry, Twenty-ninth, Thirtieth, Thirty-second, Thirty-third companies Coast Artillery, First, Eighth, Tenth, Twelfth, Thirteenth batteries Field Artillery, Fourteenth Regiment U. S. Infantry, Eighteenth Regiment U. S. Infantry, Twenty-third Regiment U. S. Infantry, San Francisco. Order mailed.

* * * * * * *

Order to San Francisco all quartermasters and assistant quartermasters volunteers not in Regular Army to enable them to be discharged and ordered home before June 30. Direct them close accounts before departure.

Corbin.

MANILA. (Received May 15, 1901—3.43 p. m.)

ADJUTANT-GENERAL, *Washington*:

Have ordered Ninth Regiment, U. S. Cavalry, Tenth Regiment, U. S. Cavalry, squadrons just arrived, to [Gen.] Robert P. Hughes for Malabare, Samar. If necessary, will send entire Ninth Regiment, U. S. Infantry there on arrival from China; if not sufficient, will continue concentrating troops Samar until Lucban, who is very obstinate, is forced submit. As paramount military necessity will close temporarily all ports Samar under authority contained yours March 9. An outlawry and amnesty proclamation, to end June 20—such insinuate mine April 1, April 6—will greatly assist military operations Samar—will probably result in immediate complete pacification entire archipelago.

MACARTHUR.

MANILA. (Received May 15, 1901—7.30 p. m.)

Recent commissary trials have resulted in sentence to periods of imprisonment of number of soldiers and civilians, all of which have been executed. Captain Read, commissary volunteers, and Lieutenant Boyer, Thirty-ninth Volunteer Infantry, similarly convicted and sentenced to dismissal and imprisonment, and a third conviction, Captain Barrows, seems probable soon. Highly important, under existing condition, to secure immediate example and uniformity of treatment to officers and men. Can not Articles of War be so construed as to give authority for final review in latter case by division commander, as commanding general of an army in the field?

MACARTHUR.

ADJUTANT-GENERAL'S OFFICE,
Washington, May 15, 1901.

MACARTHUR, *Manila:*

* * * Secretary of War directs no more enlisted men ordered for examination second lieutenant the current year.

CORBIN.

MANILA. (Received May 15, 1901—1.12 a. m.)

ADJUTANT-GENERAL, *Washington:*

* * * Transport *Logan* arrived yesterday; *Kilpatrick* May 12.

MACARTHUR.

WAR DEPARTMENT,
Washington, May 16, 1901.

Memorandum for the Adjutant-General to send the following dispatch to General MacArthur: You can not review sentence as commanding general of an army in the field, but it is not time of peace, and article 106 does not apply. Under article 104 the sentence of dismissal may be carried into execution after it shall have been approved by the officer ordering the court.

ELIHU ROOT, *Secretary of War.*

ADJUTANT-GENERAL'S OFFICE,
Washington, May 16, 1901.

MACARTHUR, *Manila:*

You can not review sentence as commanding general of an army in the field, but it is not time of peace, and article 106 does not apply. Under article 104 sentence dismissal may be carried into execution after approval by the officer ordering the court.

CORBIN.

MANILA. (Received May 16, 1901—8.23 a. m.)
ADJUTANT-GENERAL, *Washington:*
* * * Sick in hospital, 2,744; sick in quarters, 801; 6.47 per cent.

MACARTHUR.

MANILA. (Received May 17, 1901—7.39 a. m.)
ADJUTANT-GENERAL, *Washington:*
Boyer, Barrows tried court convened by department commander; Read, court convened provost-marshal-general as commander separate brigade. In each case sentence dismissed and imprisonment.

With reference to your telegram of 16th. Have returned cases Boyer, Barrows to department commander for final review; execution sentence very important. Read case be similarly returned provost-marshal if permissible. See article 107. Request decision.

MACARTHUR.

ADJUTANT-GENERAL'S OFFICE,
Washington, May 17, 1901.
MACARTHUR, *Manila:*
Sentence dismissal by court-martial convened by provost-marshal-general as commander separate brigade may be carried into execution by you. By direction of the Secretary of War.

Secretary of War approves your energetic measures suppression troubles Samar.

* * * * * * *

CORBIN.

MANILA. (Received May 17, 1901—2.10 a. m.)
ADJUTANT-GENERAL, *Washington:*
General Mascardo, 21 officers, 331 men and rifles, surrendered [Capt.] Joseph P. O'Neil, San Narciso, Zambales Province, May 16.

MACARTHUR.

ADJUTANT-GENERAL'S OFFICE.
Washington, May 18, 1901.
MACARTHUR, *Manila:*
Company A, Twenty-seventh Regiment U. S. Infantry, Company B, Twenty-seventh Regiment U. S. Infantry, Company C, Twenty-seventh Regiment U. S. Infantry, Company D, Twenty-seventh Regiment U. S. Infantry, charged to Company I, Twenty-sixth Regiment U. S. Infantry, Company K, Twenty-sixth Regiment U. S. Infantry, Company L, Twenty-sixth Regiment U. S. Infantry, Company M, Twenty-sixth Regiment U. S. Infantry. Organize Second Battalion, Twenty-sixth Regiment U. S. Infantry, by transfer from First and Third Battalion. Company A, Twenty-eighth Regiment U. S. Infantry, Company B, Twenty-eighth Regiment U. S. Infantry, Company C, Twenty-eighth Regiment U. S. Infantry, Company D, Twenty-eighth Regiment U. S. Infantry, changed to Company E, Thirtieth Regiment U. S. Infantry, Company F, Thirtieth Regiment U. S. Infantry Company G, Thirtieth Regiment U. S. Infantry, Company H, Thirtieth Regiment U. S. Infantry. Organize Third Battalion, Thirtieth Regiment U. S. Infantry, by transfer from First and Second battalions. Each company transferred will retain books, records, and property and change of designation entered on records. Battalion noncommissioned staff

are included in transfer; officers are not included. Total enlisted strength of each company, 104. Headquarters and bands Twenty-sixth Regiment U. S. Infantry, Thirtieth Regiment U. S. Infantry, and necessary recruits, will be sent Philippine Islands.

* * * * * * *

CORBIN.

VANCOUVER BARRACKS, WASH., *May 18, 1901.*
ADJUTANT-GENERAL, U. S. ARMY, *Washington, D. C.:*
Transport *Copack* will sail from Portland, Oreg., en route to Manila 3 p. m. to-day, with cargo consisting of hay and grain.

RICHARDS,
Acting Adjutant-General, in absence of Department Commander.

MANILA. (Received May 19, 1901—9.25 a. m.)
ADJUTANT-GENERAL, *Washington:*
Lacuna surrendered [Gen.] Frederick Funston to-day San Isidro, 31 officers, 200 men, 245 rifles, 40,000 ammunition.

[Gen.] Loyd Wheaton reports absolute termination armed resistance Department of Northern Luzon.

MACARTHUR.

MANILA. (Received May 19, 1901—12.55 a. m.)
ADJUTANT-GENERAL, *Washington:*
* * * Transport *Thyra* arrived yesterday.

MACARTHUR.

MANILA. (Received May 19, 1901—3.12 a. m.)
ADJUTANT-GENERAL, *Washington:*
Transport *Hancock*, 31 officers, 1,042 enlisted men Thirty-first Regiment U. S. Volunteer Infantry; transport *Aztec*, 2 officers, 62 enlisted men Company H, Forty-second Regiment U. S. Volunteer Infantry; transport *Buford*, 21 officers, 910 enlisted men Forty-first Regiment U. S. Volunteer Infantry—225 remains—sailed May 18 via Nagasaki. Notify Department of California.

MACARTHUR.

MANILA. (Received May 21, 1901—9.03 a. m.)
ADJUTANT-GENERAL, *Washington:*
Following deaths have occurred since last report: Dysentery—April 23, Company A, First Infantry, George Wilkensen; April 27, Company H, Sixth Infantry, John J. Whalen; May 1, Company H, Eighth Infantry, Robert H. McCaskey; May 15, Company I, Eighth Infantry, John Naughton. Typhoid fever—May 3, Company H, Signal Corps, U. S. Army, Sergt. James H. O'Donnell. Drowned, bodies not recovered—May 13, Troop F, Tenth Cavalry, Sergt. Walter W. Board, Shelley Moran. Abscess liver—April 26, Company D, Twenty-seventh Infantry, Corpl. William E. Hall; May 4, Company H, Eighteenth Infantry, George Heeb. Paralysis—March 22, Company F, Forty-third Volunteer Infantry, Charles E. Minard. Malarial fever—May 8, Company L, Third Infantry, Edward W. Hockley. Septicæmia—May 12, Troop I, Fourth Cavalry, Corpl. Henry P. Sullivan. Killed by comrade—April 26,

AFFAIRS IN THE PHILIPPINE ISLANDS. 1281

Company C, Twenty-seventh Infantry, Sergt. Willian G. Moreland; May 8, Company A, Twenty-eighth Infantry, Edward Roxbury. Appendicitis—April 30, Troop K, Fifth Cavalry, Jacob N. Buechel. Transport *Thomas* arrived yesterday.

MACARTHUR.

MANILA. (Received May 22, 1901—8.48 a. m.)
ADJUTANT-GENERAL, *Washington:*
With reference to my telegram of 12th. Has $50,000 war emergency fund been placed credit chief quartermaster? Indispensable it be made available immediately.

* * * * * * *

MACARTHUR.

ADJUTANT-GENERAL'S OFFICE,
Washington, May 22, 1901.
MCARTHUR, *Manila:*
* * * In cabling percentages use four figures instead of two code words.

* * * * * * *

CORBIN.

MANILA. (Received May 23, 1901—2.45 a. m.)
ADJUTANT-GENERAL, *Washington.*
Transport *Pennsylvania* sailed May 22, 32 officers, 910 enlisted men Fortieth Regiment U. S. Volunteer Infantry, direct San Francisco. Notify Department of California. Transport *Grant* arrived to-day.

MACARTHUR.

MANILA. (Received May 24, 1901—9 a. m.)
ADJUTANT-GENERAL, *Washington:*
Killed, April 28, Jiminez, Mindanao, G, Fortieth, John McElhone, May 17; near Pasacao, Luzon, Company I, Eighth Infantry, James C. Harvey; B, Twenty-sixth Infantry, Lawrence O'Hara, Samuel R. Cox.
Wounded, May 13, Lupi, Luzon, Troop B, Ninth Cavalry, First Sergt. Jesse Thrower, wounded in leg above knee, serious.

MACARTHUR.

ADJUTANT-GENERAL'S OFFICE,
Washington, May 27, 1901.
MACARTHUR, *Manila:*
German war ship *Hansa* visits Manila June 10 to June 14. Extend usual courtesies.
Account early expiration service volunteers Secretary of War desires to know probable dates of sailing remaining volunteer regiments.

* * * * * * *

CORBIN.

MANILA. (Received May 27, 1901—8.35 a. m.)
ADJUTANT-GENERAL, *Washington:*
Kintuck sailed May 26, Portland, 2 officers, 54 enlisted men Company B, Forty-second Regiment U. S. Volunteer Infantry. Arrange transportation company to San Francisco. Notify Department of California.

MACARTHUR.

1282 CORRESPONDENCE.

MANILA. (Received May 28, 1901—10.38 a. m.)

ADJUTANT-GENERAL, *Washington:*

Transport *Thomas* sailed May 27, via Nagasaki, Forty-seventh Regiment U. S. Volunteer Infantry, 33 officers, 972 enlisted men; battalion Forty-ninth Regiment U. S. Volunteer Infantry, 24 officers, 358 enlisted men; Band, three companies Thirty-eighth Regiment U. S. Volunteer Infantry, 10 officers, 285 enlisted men. *Ohio* sails to-morrow direct, headquarters, ten companies Forty-second Regiment U. S. Volunteer Infantry, 29 officers, 749 enlisted men. Notify Department of California. Transport *Grant* with Forty-eighth Regiment, U. S. Volunteer Infantry, two battalions Forty-ninth Regiment, U. S. Volunteer Infantry; transport *Kilpatrick* with Forty-third Regiment U. S. Volunteer Infantry; transport *Logan*, with two battalions Thirth-eighth Regiment U. S. Volunteer Infantry and the Forty-fourth Regiment U. S. Volunteer Infantry, sail June 1

MACARTHUR.

ADJUTANT-GENERAL'S OFFICE,
Washington, May 28, 1901.

MACARTHUR, *Manila:*

* * * With reference to your telegram of 28, is of the utmost importance commanding officers be instructed have muster-out work more thoroughly done. If possible send Frederick on *Logan*. Press reports arrest First Lieutenant Welch, Forty-third Regiment U. S. Volunteer Infantry. What are the facts?

CORBIN.

MANILA. (Received May 29, 1901—11.41 a. m.)

ADJUTANT-GENERAL, *Washington:*

* * * Several volunteer staff officers ordered United States desire discharge here June 30. Can it be done?

With reference to your telegram of 14th, will retain equipments light batteries, sending personnel only United States. Is this approved?

*　　　*　　　*　　　*　　　*　　　*　　　*

MACARTHUR.

MANILA. (Received May 30, 1901—7.05 a. m.)

ADJUTANT-GENERAL, *Washington:*

With reference to your telegram of 28th, Captain Spellman, Lieutenant Jones, Assistant Surgeon Welch, Forty-third Regiment, U. S. Volunteer Infantry, charged trading in permits to take hemp from closed ports Malitboc Bay, have been retained with view to court-martial.

Acting Asst. Surg. Charles St. John killed near Paricale, Luzon, May 22. * * *

MACARTHUR.

ADJUTANT-GENERAL'S OFFICE,
Washington, May 31, 1901.

MACARTHUR, *Manila:*

* * * All volunteer staff officers desiring can be discharged Philippine Islands June 30.

*　　　*　　　*　　　*　　　*　　　*　　　*

Retain equipment light batteries, sending personnel only United States.

*　　　*　　　*　　　*　　　*　　　*　　　*

CORBIN.

AFFAIRS IN THE PHILIPPINE ISLANDS. 1283

MANILA. (Received June 1, 1901—7.10 a. m.)
ADJUTANT-GENERAL, *Washington:*
* * * * * * *

Transport *Logan* sailed May 31 via Nagasaki; 2 battalions Thirty-eighth Volunteer Infantry, 21 officers, 577 enlisted men; Forty-fourth Volunteer Infantry, 36 officers, 1,061 enlisted men. Notify Department of California.

MACARTHUR.

MANILA. (Received June 2, 1901—12.45 a. m.)
ADJUTANT-GENERAL, *Washington:*
Thyra sailed June 1; 3 officers, 78 enlisted men, Company B, Thirty-eighth Volunteer Infantry, via Nagaski. Notify Department of California.
Sick in hospital, 2,729; sick in quarters, 661; 6.71 per cent.

MACARTHUR.

HEADQUARTERS DIVISION OF THE PHILIPPINES,
Manila, P. I., June 3, 1901.
The ADJUTANT-GENERAL, U. S. ARMY,
Washington, D. C.

SIR: With reference to your cablegram of May 11, 1901, I have the honor to inclose the following list of deaths in this command since last report or have not yet been reported: Abscess of liver—Private John A. Caniff, H, Sixth Infantry, Bacolod, Negros, May 15, 1901. Killed by comrade—Private William Cook, M, Second Infantry, Masbate, Masbate, May 4, 1901; Private George F. Sensabough, G, First Infantry, Hibutan, Samar, May 14, 1901. Peritonitis—Private George Goetz, F, Forty-seventh Infantry, Legaspi, Luzon, April 20, 1901. Insolation—Private Edward Grady, C, Seventh Artillery, Legaspi, Luzon, April 21, 1901. Variola—Private Luther E. Grider, F, Third Cavalry, Vigan, Luzon, May 23, 1901; Private George W. Smith, F, Third Cavalry, Vigan, Luzon, May 20, 1901. Suicide—Private Lewis Matson, A, Twenty-eighth Infantry, Panguil, Luzon, May 12, 1901. Dysentery—Sergt. William T. Morris, Band, Sixteenth Infantry, Aparri, Luzon, May 14, 1901; Saddler George Lutz, B, First Cavalry, Calamba, Luzon, May 17, 1901; Corpl. Henry Koch, First Battery Field Artillery, Hospital No. 3, Manila, May 19, 1901; Private John B. Tracy, F, Signal Corps, Hospital No. 3, Manila, May 21, 1901. Result of gunshot wounds in action—Corpl. John Haefner, I, Eighth Infantry, Santa Cruz, Luzon, May 16, 1901. Heat exhaustion—Musician William F. Iltis, Thirty-second Company Coast Artillery, First Reserve Hospital, Manila, May 22, 1901. Drowned, body recovered—Private Frederick W. Martin, C, Twentieth Infantry, Vigan, Luzon, May 8, 1901. Smallpox—Private Edward Brewer, E, Third Cavalry, Vigan, Luzon, May 25, 1901. Malarial fever—Private Bert Lewis, I, Forty-eighth Infantry, San Fernando, Luzon, May 26, 1901. With reference to our telegram of May 21, bodies of Sergt. Walter W. Beard and Private Shelley Moran, Troop F, Tenth U. S. Cavalry, have been recovered.

Very respectfully,
ARTHUR MACARTHUR,
Major-General, U. S. Army, Commanding.

MANILA. (Received June 6, 1901—12.50 a. m.)
ADJUTANT-GENERAL, *Washington:*
* * * * * * *

Transport *Kilpatrick* sailed to-day direct, 33 officers, 1,013 enlisted men Forty-third Regiment U. S. Volunteer Infantry. Department of California. Transport *Sumner* arrived to-day with Adna R. Chaffee.

MACARTHUR.

MANILA. (Received June 7, 1901—7.05 a. m.)
ADJUTANT-GENERAL, *Washington:*
Transport *Grant* sailed from Aparri via Nagasaki June 2, 38 officers, 1,086 enlisted men Forty-eighth Regiment U. S. Volunteer Infantry, two battalions Forty-ninth Regiment U. S. Volunteer Infantry. All volunteers now en route United States. Notify Department California. *Pakling* sailed June 6, 3 officers, 136 enlisted men Battery F, Fifth Artillery.

* * * * * * *

MACARTHUR.

MANILA. (Received June 7, 1901—3.33 a. m.)
ADJUTANT-GENERAL, *Washington:*
In providing for return of volunteers, 5,414 native scouts, including Philippine Cavalry employed now in service, in my judgment for time being they should be retained, but will be practically without officers after June 30. Recommend that provisional appointment be given such volunteer officers as necessary to maintain present organization as outlined section 36, act approved February 2, 1901. All scouts now paid from public civil funds; if continued, as herein recommended, how shall they be paid after June 30? Under present conditions regular regiments impossible spare regular officers for this duty. Services of scouts indispensable. Desired to have one first one second lieutenant dismounted each company, not to exceed 50 of each.

MACARTHUR.

ADJUTANT-GENERAL'S OFFICE,
Washington, June 8, 1901.
MACARTHUR, *Manila:*

* * * * * * *

Discontinue cabling sick report.

* * * * * * *

CORBIN.

MANILA. (Received June 10, 1901—8.44 a. m.)
ADJUTANT-GENERAL, *Washington:*
Under civil government scheme, to be established June 30, may capital sentences adjudged by military commissions and approved prior thereto be carried into execution? After that date may trial by military commission pending on June 30 be completed and sentences executed?

MACARTHUR.

ADJUTANT-GENERAL'S OFFICE,
Washington, June 10, 1901.
MACARTHUR, *Manila:*
Retain Philippine scouts and their deserving officers. Make provisional appointment not exceeding 50 first lieutenants, 50 second lieutenants. Cable their names and recommendations for rates pay native officers and men. Decision regarding funds for payment will be telegraphed soon.

* * * * * * *

CORBIN.

MANILA. (Received June 11, 1901—4 a. m.)

ADJUTANT-GENERAL, *Washington:*

A large number men regular regiments ordered United States wish to remain here. Authority requested transfer those desirable regiments remaining. Shall volunteer officers appointed regular army be mustered out volunteer service upon acceptance?

Morning June 10, William H. Wilhelm encountered a large force near Lipa. Walter H. Lee, Engineers, Anton Springer, jr., killed; William H. Wilhelm, [first lieutenant] Charles R. Ramsay seriously wounded; four enlisted men wounded; insurgents dispersed.

MACARTHUR.

ADJUTANT-GENERAL'S OFFICE,
Washington, June 12, 1901.

MACARTHUR, *Manila*:

*　　*　　*　　*　　*　　*　　*

With reference to your telegram of 11th, all volunteer officers should be mustered out on acceptance appointment Regular Army.

CORBIN.

MANILA. (Received June 12, 1901—13.33 a. m.)

ADJUTANT-GENERAL, *Washington:*

[Capt.] William H. Wilhelm died from wounds received in action 2 p. m. Wednesday, June 12, Lipa, Luzon.

MACARTHUR.

ADJUTANT-GENERAL'S OFFICE,
Washington, June 14, 1901.

MACARTHUR, *Manila:*

Is there any objection to sending United States, to be confined Fort Leavenworth, Kans., Read and other volunteer officers convicted fraud?

With reference to your telegram of 11th, make transfer to organizations remaining.

With reference to your telegram of 10th, regarding capital sentences and trials pending June 30, yes.

CORBIN.

ADJUTANT-GENERAL'S OFFICE,
Washington, June 16, 1901.

MACARTHUR, *Manila:*

Secretary of War directs present organization Philippine cavalry and scouts continued temporarily until otherwise ordered, officers to be paid from army appropriation, men as now from civil funds. This arrangement is subject to change. Cable your recommendations for first and second lieutenants, not exceeding 50 each. Decided necessary President make these appointments.

CORBIN.

MANILA. (Received June 16, 1901—6.30 a. m.)

ADJUTANT-GENERAL, *Washington:*

Sending Read, other convicted officers United States objectionable, as first step to defeat sentence would be considered here partial triumph condemned officers, and neutralize to that extent good effect of conviction. Should be confined here at least one year.

Will inauguration of civil government be deferred? To what date?

*　　*　　*　　*　　*　　*　　*

MACARTHUR.

ADJUTANT-GENERAL'S OFFICE,
Washington, June 17, 1901.

MacArthur, *Manila:*

* * * * * * *

Read and other convicts will not be sent United States until recommended by you.

* * * * * * *

CORBIN.

ADJUTANT-GENERAL'S OFFICE,
Washington, June 19, 1901.

MacArthur, *Manila:*

Secretary of War directs that you be advised William H. Taft will be appointed civil governor, to take office July 4, with Malacanan as his official residence. See proposed order in Secretary's dispatch to Taft June 14. Suitable official residence to be provided for Adna R. Chaffee as commanding general division and military governor. Transfer command to him at the same time. Adjutant-General of the Army leaves for Manila on *Hancock* June 25.

Cable names enlisted men killed, wounded, June 10, and organization.

* * * * * * *

CORBIN.

ADJUTANT-GENERAL'S OFFICE,
Washington, June 21, 1901.

Chaffee, *Manila:*

Orders to-day assign you to duty as commanding general Division Philippines and military governor, to take effect July 4. William H. Taft and Arthur MacArthur will show you their instructions bearing on your duties.

WARD.

EXECUTIVE MANSION,
Washington, June 21, 1901.

On and after the fourth day of July, 1901, until it shall be otherwise ordered, the president of the Philippine Commission will exercise the executive authority in all civil affairs in the government of the Philippine Islands heretofore exercised in such affairs by the military governor of the Philippines, and to this end the Hon. William H. Taft, president of the said Commission, is hereby appointed civil governor of the Philippine Islands. Such executive authority will be exetcised under and in conformity to the instructions to the Philippine Commission, dated April 7, 1900, and subject to the approval and control of the Secretary of war of the United States. The municipal and provincial civil governments which have been or shall hereafter be established in said islands, and all persons performing duties appertaining to the offices of civil government in said islands will, in respect of such duties, report to the said civil governor.

The power to appoint civil officers heretofore vested in the Philippine Commission or in the military governor will be exercised by the civil governor with the advice and consent of the Commission. The military governor of the Philippines is hereby relieved from the performance, on and after the said fourth day of July, of the civil duties hereinbefore described, but his authority will continue to be exercised as heretofore in those districts in which insurrection against the authority of the United States continues to exist or in which public order is not sufficiently restored to enable provincial civil government to be established under the instructions to the Commission, dated April 7, 1900.

WILLIAM McKINLEY.

MANILA. (Received June 21, 1901—7.35 a. m.)

ADJUTANT-GENERAL, *Washington:*

With reference to your telegram of 19th. Wounded—June 10, Lipa, Luzon, Company D, Twenty-first Regiment U. S. Infantry, First Sergt. Frank B. Stearns, wounded in leg above knee, moderate; Sergt. Delbert Gregory, wounded in leg above knee, serious; Rudolph Cork, wounded in leg above knee, slight. Died from wounds received in action—John J. Rogers.

MACARTHUR.

GENERAL ORDERS,} HEADQUARTERS OF THE ARMY,
No. 87. ADJUTANT-GENERAL'S OFFICE,
Washington, June 22, 1901.

By direction of the Secretary of War, the following order from the War Department is published to the Army for the information and guidance of all concerned:

"WAR DEPARTMENT, *Washington, June 21, 1901.*

"On and after the 4th day of July, 1901, until it shall be otherwise ordered, the president of the Philippine Commission will exercise the executive authority in all civil affairs in the government of the Philippine Islands heretofore exercised in such affairs by the military governor of the Philippines, and to that end the Hon. William H. Taft, president of the said Commission, is hereby appointed civil governor of the Philippine Islands. Such executive authority will be exercised under and in conformity to the instructions to the Philippine Commissioners dated April 7, 1900, and subject to the approval and control of the Secretary of War of the United States. The municipal and provincial civil governments which have been or shall hereafter be established in said islands, and all persons performing duties appertaining to the offices of civil government in said islands, will in respect of such duties report to the said civil governor.

"The power to appoint civil officers, heretofore vested in the Philippine Commission or in the military governor, will be exercised by the civil governor, with the advice and consent of the Commission.

"The military governor of the Philippines is hereby relieved from the performance, on and after the said 4th of July, of the civil duties hereinbefore described, but his authority will continue to be exercised as heretofore in those districts in which insurrection against the authority of the United States continues to exist, or in which public order is not sufficiently restored to enable provincial civil governments to be established under the instructions to the Commission dated April 7, 1900.

"By the President:

"ELIHU ROOT, *Secretary of War*"

By command of Lieutenant-General Miles:

THOMAS WARD,
Acting Adjutant-General.

ADJUTANT-GENERAL'S OFFICE,
Washington, June 22, 1901.

MACARTHUR, *Manila:*

Place ayuntamiento building at the disposal of civil governor and Commission July 4.

*   *   *   *   *   *   *

WARD.

MANILA. (Received June 22, 1901—7.12 a. m.)

ADJUTANT-GENERAL, *Washington:*

*   *   *   *   *   *   *

Transport *Indiana* sailed June 20, Twenty-ninth, Thirtieth, Thirty-second, Thirty-third Company Coast Artillery, First Battery Field Artillery, 145 general prisoners. Notify Department of California.

* * * * * * *

MacArthur.

MANILA. (Received June 24, 1901—9.22 a. m.)

Adjutant-General, *Washington:*

General Cailles surrendered to-day Santa Cruz, Luzon, 386 rifles, 4,000 rounds ammunition, about 600 officers, men; has taken oath of allegiance; very important, as it is most probable pacification all southern Luzon will follow quickly.

Transport *Lawton* arrived yesterday.

MacArthur.

MANILA. (Received June 26, 1901.)

Adjutant-General, *Washington:*

Urge prompt forwarding by transport school supplies now at San Francisco.

MacArthur.

MANILA. (Received June 27, 1901—5.10 a. m.)

Adjutant-General, *Washington:*

* * * * * * *

Transport *Samoa* arrived yesterday. Transport *Lennox* sails to-day.

MacArthur.

MANILA. (Received June 29, 1901—5.55 a. m.)

Adjutant-General, *Washington:*

With reference to your telegram of 27th. My recommendations did not contemplate battalion organization for scouts. Scarcity officers regular establishment Division of the Philippines will not permit appointment captains majors. Purpose was to continue in force present organization as temporary expedient under provisional officers recommended. Organization native troops such importance should be left decision Adna R. Chaffee when he has determined his policy this regard. My views decidedly against such organization, at least till number officers duty here Regular Army considerably more than at present.

* * * * * * *

Edward E. Downes killed southern Samar; particulars later. Transport *Sheridan* arrived yesterday.

MacArthur.

MANILA. (Received June 30, 1901—11.52 p. m.)

Adjutant-General, *Washington:*

With reference to your telegram of 25th September. Rate of exchange two Mexican dollars for one dollar United States currency present quarter.

MacArthur.

MANILA. (Received July 5, 1901—7.27 a. m.)

ADJUTANT-GENERAL, *Washington:*

Transport *Meade* sailed to-day, 3 officers, 140 enlisted men, Eighth Battery Field Artillery. Arthur MacArthur, who remains two weeks Japan awaiting transport *Sheridan*, going thence United States.

* * * * * * *

CHAFFEE.

MANILA. (Received July 6, 1901—1.38 a. m.)

ADJUTANT-GENERAL, *Washington:*

* * * * * * *

With reference to your telegram of 3d. Cavite commissary solely for Navy; should be discontinued. Manila depots accessible.

CHAFFEE.

MANILA. (Received July 11, 1901.)

ADJUTANT-GENERAL, *Washington:*

With reference to letter June 19 from William H. Taft, copy first seen to-day, strongly recommend commissary quartermaster privileges will not be extended. Very important Army Regulations orders strictly adhered to this respect. Economy enjoined by War Department on all commanders; hoped War Department will assist this respect. None so able forego said privileges as commission and attaches. Army appropriation should not bear extraordinary tax burden necessary supply civil service islands.

* * * * * * *

CHAFFEE.

MANILA. (Received July 13, 1901.)

ADJUTANT-GENERAL, *Washington:*

* * * * * * *

About 2,000 shotguns, many revolvers, in hand municipal police throughout islands; army officers responsible. This not desirable. Proposed sell these arms civil government in order to assist in equipping its civil force. Is this approved?

* * * * * * *

CHAFFEE.

MANILA. (Received July 16, 1901—11.35 a. m.)

ADJUTANT-GENERAL, *Washington:*

Transport *Sumner* sailed July 15; 164 sick, 9 insane. Notify Department of California.

* * * * * * *

CHAFFEE.

MANILA. (Received July 17, 1901—7.25 a. m.)

ADJUTANT-GENERAL, *Washington:*

Adna R. Chaffee desires organize separate brigades within several departments. This will improve administration and efficiency generally. Is it opinion Department that such separate brigade commanders could legally convene general court-martial, etc.? Favorable action recommended. Reply as soon as possible.

CORBIN.

ADJUTANT-GENERAL'S OFFICE,
Washington, July 18, 1901.

CHAFFEE, *Manila:*
Cable number of men, cavalry, infantry, in excess of authorized strength, from latest information.

* * * * * * *

WARD.

ADJUTANT-GENERAL'S OFFICE,
Washington, July 19, 1901.

CHAFFEE, *Manila:*
With reference to my telegram of 18th May, expedite departure officers ordered to the United States, particularly Twenty-eighth Infantry.

WARD.

ADJUTANT-GENERAL'S OFFICE,
Washington, July 19, 1901.

CHAFFEE, *Manila:*
Important *Sheridan* return at once. No other transport available to leave San Francisco September 1.

WARD.

ADJUTANT-GENERAL'S OFFICE,
Washington, July 19, 1901.

CHAFFEE, *Manila:*
Regular line transports must sail first and middle month. Arrangement here depends upon this.

WARD.

MANILA. (Received July 20, 1901—9.35 a. m.)
ADJUTANT-GENERAL, *Washington:*
With reference to your telegram of 18th, number of men in excess of authorized strength, cavalry, 1,375; infantry, 5,600.

* * * * * * *

CHAFFEE.

MANILA. (Received July 20, 1901—9.35 a. m.)
ADJUTANT-GENERAL, *Washington:*
Transport *Sheridan* sails to-day, Fourteenth Regiment U. S. Infantry, Company A, Battalion of Engineers, U. S. Army, 48 general prisoners.

* * * * * * *

CHAFFEE.

ADJUTANT-GENERAL'S OFFICE,
Washington, July 23, 1901.

CHAFFEE, *Manila:*
With reference to Corbin's telegram 17th, Secretary of War authorizes organization separate brigades. Commanders assigned will have full authority in general court-martial, etc.

WARD.

AFFAIRS IN THE PHILIPPINE ISLANDS.

MANILA. (Received August 1, 1901—5.55 a. m.)

ADJUTANT-GENERAL, *Washington:*

Suggest information desired by chiefs bureaus affecting administration Division of the Philippines be addressed to me, not chiefs departments.

* * * * * * *

CHAFFEE.

MANILA. (Received August 9, 1901—12.27 a. m.)

ADJUTANT-GENERAL, *Washington:*

Transport *Hancock* sailed 5th; 20 officers, 814 enlisted men, Fourth Regiment U. S. Cavalry. *Samoa* sailed yesterday, 326 deceased soldiers.

* * * * * * *

CHAFFEE.

ADJUTANT-GENERAL'S OFFICE,
Washington, August 10, 1901.

CHAFFEE, *Manila:*

Quarantine regulations Malta and Gibraltar require clean bill of health from Manila, Singapore, Colombo. Mail not to be received at and ships will hold no communication with Aden, Suez, Port Said. If coal required either three last points, must be taken on in quarantine, securing certificates to this effect. *Buford* due Manila August 15. Sail her for New York about September 1, with instructions coal at Colombo for Malta, purchasing open market. Instructions mailed chief quartermaster June 17 regarding coaling Manila to New York modified as to coaling Colombo. Troops to return on *Buford* will be named hereafter.

WARD.

MANILA. (Received August 13, 1901—7.45 a. m.)

ADJUTANT-GENERAL, *Washington:*

Transport *Grant* arrived yesterday. All are well.

CHAFFEE.

ADJUTANT-GENERAL'S OFFICE,
Washington, August 12, 1901.

CHAFFEE, *Manila:*

Cable Department of California whenever a large number sick is sent to San Francisco, in order to prepare. This was not done sailing *Meade.*

WARD.

ADJUTANT-GENERAL'S OFFICE,
Washington, August 16, 1901.

CHAFFEE, *Manila:*

Authorize chief commissary Manila invoice subsistence supplies as requested to marine officer acting commissary of subsistence, Cavite.

WARD.

MANILA. (Received August 27, 1901—2.22 a. m.)

ADJUTANT-GENERAL, *Washington:*

Transport *Grant* sailed August 25, Troop B, Fourth Cavalry, 2 officers, 81 enlisted men; Twelfth Battery Field Artillery, Thirteenth Battery Field Artillery, 5 officers, 288 enlisted men.

CHAFFEE.

ADJUTANT-GENERAL'S OFFICE,
Washington, August 30, 1901.

CHAFFEE, *Manila:*

If you can spare send on *Buford* nine companies Coast Artillery longest in Philippine Islands. Report action.

WARD.

MANILA. (Received August 30, 1901—4.30 a. m.)

ADJUTANT-GENERAL, *Washington:*

* * * * * * *

Buford can not leave before September 5, account repairs.

CHAFFEE.

MANILA. (Received September 1, 1901.)

ADJUTANT-GENERAL, *Washington:*

Twenty-five Hospital Corps men arrived *Buford;* no more needed Division of the Philippines.

With reference to your telegram of 30th, intend to send Twenty-third Regiment U. S. Infantry transport *Buford* New York, Eighteenth Regiment U. S. Infantry transport *Kilpatrick* San Francisco, afterwards 9 companies Coast Artillery transport *Kilpatrick* New York. Is this approved?

* * * * * * *

CHAFFEE.

MANILA. (Received September 5, 1901—9.04 a. m.)

ADJUTANT-GENERAL, *Washington:*

With reference to my telegram of 1st, is my request approved? Seventeenth Regiment U. S. Infantry ready relieve Twenty-third Regiment U. S. Infantry.

* * * * * * *

CHAFFEE.

ADJUTANT-GENERAL'S OFFICE,
Washington, September 5, 1901.

CHAFFEE, *Manila:*

Movements Eighteenth Regiment U. S. Infantry, Twenty-third Regiment U. S. Infantry, nine companies of Coast Artillery, proposed in your telegram September 1, approved.

GREENE.

ADJUTANT-GENERAL'S OFFICE,
Washington, September 11, 1901.

CHAFFEE, *Manila:*

With reference to your telegram of 7th, send Samuel M. Mills, Abner H. Merrill, Henry C. Danes, with nine companies of Coast Artillery, and to San Francisco instead of New York. Cable designations companies.

WARD.

AFFAIRS IN THE PHILIPPINE ISLANDS. 1293

MANILA. (Received September 13, 1901—2.02 p. m.)
ADJUTANT-GENERAL, *Washington:*

* * * * * *

With reference to your telegram of 11th, Sixtieth, Sixty-first, Sixty-second, Sixty-third, Sixty-fourth, Sixty-fifth, Sixty-eighth, Seventieth, and Seventy-first companies Coast Artillery.

CHAFFEE.

MANILA. (Received September 12, 1901—8.32 a. m.)
ADJUTANT-GENERAL, *Washington:*

* * * * * *

Will send Engineers to New York on *McClellan* if satisfactory about September 30.

CHAFFEE.

ADJUTANT-GENERAL'S OFFICE,
Washington, September 12, 1901.

CHAFFEE, *Manila:*

Proposed sending Engineers New York by *McClellan* approved.

WARD.

MANILA. (Received September 11, 1901—2.01 p. m.)
ADJUTANT-GENERAL, *Washington:*

* * * * * *

Teachers want purchase horse equipments; have plenty to spare.

CHAFFEE.

MANILA. (Received September 16, 1901—9.36 a. m.)
ADJUTANT-GENERAL'S OFFICE, *Washington:*

* * * * * *

Kilpatrick sails from Iloilo to San Francisco September 16, 27 officers, 896 enlisted men, Eighteenth Regiment U. S. Infantry.

CHAFFEE.

MANILA, *September 16, 1901—9.36 a. m.*
ADJUTANT-GENERAL, *Washington:*

Request that I be granted authority to transfer enlisted men of good character who desire remain islands after discharge from organization going United States to those remaining.

* * * * * * *

CHAFFEE.

ADJUTANT-GENERAL'S OFFICE,
Washington, September 16, 1901.

CHAFFEE, *Manila:*

Secretary of War grants authority transfer enlisted men good character who desire remain islands after discharge from organizations going United States to those remaining.

WARD.

MANILA. (Received September 18, 1901—8.28 a. m.)
ADJUTANT-GENERAL, *Washington:*
Transport *Meade* arrived yesterday.

* * * * * *

CHAFFEE.

MANILA. (Received September 21, 1901—9.41 a. m.)
ADJUTANT-GENERAL, *Washington:*
Buford grounded sand bar mouth Rio Grande River, Mindanao; no damage reported yet; vessels to lighter her en route; *Lawton* should be alongside her now.

CHAFFEE.

MANILA. (Received September 24, 1901—8.04 a. m.)
ADJUTANT-GENERAL, *Washington:*
Buford floated uninjured; now loading Twenty-third Regiment U. S. Infantry.

* * * * * *

CHAFFEE.

MANILA. (Received September 25, 1901—7.27 a. m.)
ADJUTANT-GENERAL, *Washington:*
With reference to your letter of 8th July, Regular Army, 1,111 officers, 42,123 enlisted men; volunteer surgeons, 172; native scouts, 73 officers and 4,973 enlisted men.

* * * * * *

CHAFFEE.

MANILA. (Received September 26, 1901—8.46 a. m.)
ADJUTANT-GENERAL, *Washington:*
Transport *Sheridan* arrived to-day.

* * * * * *

CHAFFEE.

ADJUTANT-GENERAL'S OFFICE,
Washington, September 28, 1901.

CHAFFEE, *Manila:*

Acting Secretary of War directs Philippine scouts in service United States heretofore paid from insular funds be enlisted and mustered from October 1 and paid from Regular Army appropriations. Your recommendation requested as to proper allowance pay, rations, and clothing.

He also directs sale of such horse equipments as may be acted on by inspector to teachers at prices you deem proper

CORBIN.

MANILA. (Received September 29, 1901—9.50 a. m.)
ADJUTANT-GENERAL, *Washington:*
Hughes reports following received from Basey, southern Samar: 24 men, Company C, Ninth Regiment U. S. Infantry, 11 wounded, has just arrived from Balangiga; remainder company killed; insurgents secured all company supplies and all rifles except three. Company was attacked during breakfast, morning September 28; company 72 strong; officers, Thomas W. Connell, captain; Edward A. Bumpus, first lieutenant; Dr. R. S. Griswold, major-surgeon. Investigation will be made.

CHAFFEE.

ADJUTANT-GENERAL'S OFFICE,
Washington, September 30, 1901.

CHAFFEE, *Manila:*

With reference to your telegram of 29th, report by telegraph names killed, wounded, missing, as soon as possible. What was the result of the investigation?

CORBIN.

MANILA. (Received October 1, 1901—12.23 p. m.)

ADJUTANT-GENERAL, *Washington:*

Buford sailed September 29.

With reference to your telegram of 28th ultimo, recommend pay native scouts as in our General Order 11, 1901, except sergeants, $12; corporals, $10; privates, $8; subsistence, regular ration; clothing allowance, $3 month, all ranks.

With reference to your telegram of 30th ultimo, will cable names missing enlisted men as soon as ascertained. Company was rushed about 6 o'clock morning; large party bolomen; about 400. General Hughes thinks surprise due confidence commanding officer assertions friendship from natives. Result investigation cabled as soon as obtained.

CHAFFEE.

MANILA. (Received October 2, 1901.)

ADJUTANT-GENERAL, *Washington:*

Transport *Meade* sailed October 1; 9 companies coast artillery.

* * * * * * *

CHAFFEE.

MANILA. (Received October 2, 1901—10.06 p. m.)

ADJUTANT-GENERAL, *Washington:*

* * * * * * *

On August 25, pursuant to writ of habeas corpus case Calloway ordered deported, I declined produce prisoner, court first instance making return that prisoner was held by authority United States; that court had no jurisdiction in such a case; court decided no jurisdiction; man was deported yesterday. Supreme court served writ for Brooks, civil-service messenger, who violated his contract, deserted, went Iloilo for employment private firm. Was arrested and ordered deported as disciplinary measure; offered make return as before; prisoner not produced in court; court refused to hear, and demanded presence prisoner. I have declined to produce him until peace these islands. Authority commanding general division, military governor, must not be subjected to review by courts, which I hold to be analogous to State courts; have acted accordingly, being careful to show respect by giving heedful attention to its demands; the influence of army, on which life of civil government depends in these islands, no matter whose opinion to contrary, will be seriously impaired if action of commanding general division is reviewable by civil courts. A respectful return will always be made. The only course that should be permitted is appeal from his decision to Secretary of War for final decision as to right or wrong of his action.

CHAFFEE.

MANILA. (Received October 4, 1901—10.05 p. m.)

ADJUTANT-GENERAL, *Washington:*

From those who escaped following September 29: While at breakfast 6.45 morning, company was attacked at signal ringing convent bells by about 450 bolomen, 200 from rear of quarters, 200 front simultaneously attack officers' quarters. Company completely surprised. Force attacking front gained possession arms. Fight ensued for them, in which most men met death mess room in rear. Enemy beaten off temporarily by about 25 men who gained their arms. Sergeant Betron assumed command; endeavored collect men, leave in boats, reattacked by enemy. Strength command, 3 officers, 72 men. Killed, 3 officers, 40 enlisted men; missing, 6; wounded, 13; present, 13. Party attacking officers in convent entered through church; large numbers led by presidente; probably 101 rifles with company, 26 saved; 15 of rifles lost, bolts drawn; 25,000 ammunition lost. Ninety-five prisoners outside cuartel joined in attack at signal. Boat of enlisted men capsized. Captain Bookmiller may pick up men. (Signed) Lieut. James P. Drouillard, Ninth Infantry. September 30: Have just returned Balangiga; Drouillard explains conditions correctly. Landed yesterday. Inhabitants deserted town, firing one shot. Buried 3 officers, 29 men; number bodies burned. Quarters, buildings fired as we entered; secured or destroyed most of rations; all ordnance gone. Insurgents secured 57 serviceable rifles, 28,000 cartridges. Forty-eight men Company C, Ninth Infantry, 1 Hospital-Corps man killed or missing; 28 men accounted for. Found 2 men in boat en route here. Buried dead, burned town, returned Basey. (Signed) Bookmiller. De Russey has sent strong company to chastise savages if found. (Signed) Hughes. No other details. Names of killed to be determined by elimination of survivors as soon as possible; June muster roll probably latest evidence to be had. Battalion seventh, Twenty-sixth Regiment, U. S. Infantry, Samar. Loss of arms serious matter, because of effect generally. Island inhabitants southern Samar generally savages.—Hughes. No information regarding prisoners reported; they are seldom caught. He thinks part of scheme of attack feel apprehension stations east coast; Hughes will strengthen. Lieut. Harry W. Bathiany, second lieutenant, Third Infantry, just from Sulat, says whole east coast hostile; will not intercourse with troops; destroyed all towns before our arrival there.

CHAFFEE.

MANILA. (Received October 4, 1901—4.31 p. m.)
ADJUTANT-GENERAL, *Washington:*

Taft dispatch Secretary of War received. Principle involved is more far-reaching and of more deadly importance to stability United States Army authority these islands until better sentiment masses obtains than put by Taft. Request complied with, following results: Habeas corpus for any deserter who may employ lawyer, any person now held for trial violation rules of war, inquiry into cases adjudged by military commission. Finnick case now before court; he was tried for commissary fraud. Informed writ preparing to take Howard, captured in Mindoro, out of my custody. The principle is so far-reaching that efforts of Army, its influence will be jeopardized, and beg to say in a state of insurrection military authority over prisoners should not be questioned by civil court. It will not do to believe court will not interfere except where it ought. It can not help itself; it must grant writs when asked, and service on me will be as frequent as there are prisoners. The case is vital for the influence of the military in these islands; lessen it, we arm the enemies of the United States Army; inspire them with hope. They are more numerous in sentiment, in my opinion, than reports indicate. There will never be any conflict between civil authorities and me if court refrains from interference with proper authority of commanding general of division, in a country known to all to be hostile, and in insurrection to United States Army in sentiment, and in considerable territory open and active. I have always given courtesy and support to the court. This conflict is not my seeking. Principle involved is that when court is informed that prisoners held by military authority of United States Army for crime, court shall not discharge prisoners, nor shall he be taken into court, nor is trial by authority of military law reviewable on habeas corpus by court.

CHAFFEE.

ADJUTANT-GENERAL'S OFFICE,
Washington, October 5, 1901.

CHAFFEE, *Manila:*

With reference to your telegram of 2d, Acting Secretary of War inquires was Brooks sentenced deportation by court-martial or by exercise your discretion as commanding officer? Was Brooks in military service United States or attached thereto as camp follower?

CORBIN.

MANILA. (Received October 6, 1901—8.19 a. m.)

ADJUTANT-GENERAL, *Washington:*

With reference to your telegram of 5th, Brooks ordered San Francisco, through exercise my discretion commanding general division; he was discharged military service to accept position messenger, and signed contract to serve as such two years, hence camp follower; deserted this service shortly after discharge to accept employment private firm. In my dispatch October 3, for court first instance read supreme court.

* * * * * * *

CHAFFEE.

EXECUTIVE MANSION,
Washington, October 8, 1901.

CHAFFEE, *Manila:*

I am deeply chagrined, to use the mildest possible term, over the trouble between yourself and Taft. I wish you to see him personally and spare no effort to secure prompt and friendly agreement in regard to the differences between you. Have cabled him also. It is most unfortunate to have any action taken which produces friction and which may have serious effect both in the Philippines and here at home. I trust implicitly that you and Taft will come to agreement.

THEODORE ROOSEVELT.

MANILA. (Received October 8, 1901—3.32 p. m.)

ADJUTANT-GENERAL, *Washington:*

Casualties engagement at Balangiga, Samar, September 28. Wounded will be reported as soon as received. Company C, Ninth U. S. Infantry: Killed—Sergt. John F. Martin, Sergt. James N. Randles, Corpl. Henry J. Scharer; Privates Joseph I. Godon, James Martin, John W. Aydelotte, Byron Dent, Eli Fitzgerald, Charles E. Sterling, Robert Sproull, John H. Miller, Richard Long, Joseph Turner, Gustav F. Schnitzler; Corpl. Frank McCormack; Privates Proal Peters, Leonard P. Schley; Artificer Joseph R. Marr; Privates James F. McDermott, Charles E. Davis, Harry M. Wood, John Wannebo, Joseph O. Kleinhample, Robert L. Booth, Guy C. Dennis, John D. Armani, Litto Armani, George Bony, John D. Burrer, James L. Cain, Frank Vobayda, Charles Powers. Died from wounds received in action—Corpl. Thomas E. Baird; Privates Chris F. Recard, Floyd J. Shoemaker. Missing bodies probably burned when insurgents deserted town—Musician John L. Covington; Privates Patrick J. Dobbins, Jerry J. Driscoll, Evans South, August F. Porczeng, Christian S. Williams, Claud C. Wingo, also Harry Wright, Hospital Corps.

CHAFFEE.

MANILA. (Received October 11, 1901—11.27 a. m.)

ADJUTANT-GENERAL, *Washington:*

Transport *Ingalls* arrived yesterday.

CHAFFEE.

CORRESPONDENCE.

MANILA. (Received October 12, 1901—11.17 a. m.)
ADJUTANT-GENERAL, *Washington:*

Engagement Balangiga, Samar, September 28:

Wounded—Company C, Ninth Infantry, Corpl. James Pickett, wounded in abdomen, serious; Henry Claas, wounded in back, serious; Ernest U. Ralston, severe; Henry W. Manire, wounded in arm, serious; John Uhtop, wounded in chest, serious; George E. Meyers, wounded in back, slight; Sergt. John D. Closson, scalp, ear, severe; Albert B. Keller, hip, severe; Charles F. Marak, wounded in arm, moderate; William J. Gibbs, moderate; Melvin M. Walls, wounded in chest, slight; Corpl. Arnold Irish, wounded in shoulder, moderate; Elbert B. DeGraffenreid, ear, severe; Clifford M. Mumby, elbow, slight; Sergt. Frank Betron, wounded in thigh, slight; Adolph Gamlin, wounded in head, serious; Richard Considine, elbow, slight; Corpl. Sylvester Burke, eye, slight; George Allen, finger, slight; all will recover. Died from wounds received in action—October 2, Private Cornelius F. Donahue.

CHAFFEE.

MANILA. (Received October 14, 1901.)
ADJUTANT-GENERAL, *Washington:*

* * * * * * *

Transport *Sumner* arrived to-day.

CHAFFEE.

MANILA. (Received October 15, 1901.)
ADJUTANT-GENERAL, *Washington:*

* * * * * * *

All reports indicate commands will be decreased about 50 per cent by March 31; these men ought to be replaced as they leave.

CHAFFEE.

MANILA. (Received October 17, 1901.)
ADJUTANT-GENERAL, *Washington:*

* * * * * * *

Sheridan sailed October 16; 271 sick, 19 insane, 748 short-term enlisted men.

CHAFFEE.

MANILA. (Received October 18, 1901.)
ADJUTANT-GENERAL, *Washington:*

* * * * * * *

Forty-six men Company E, Ninth Regiment United States Infantry, under First Lieut. George W. Wallace, in field Lower Gandara, Samar, were attacked by 400 bolomen October 16. Our loss 10 killed, six wounded, names not received; 81 enemy left dead on field; enemy beaten off.

CHAFFEE.

MANILA. (Received October 19, 1901.)
ADJUTANT-GENERAL, *Washington:*

* * * * * * *

With reference to my telegram of 18th, following casualties Gandara River, October 16, Company E, Ninth Infantry: Killed—George W. Teachout, William H. Ritchie, Edward F. Burns, Carl M. Johnson, William Loftin, Jack Pleoplis, Charlie Wilson, Orville J. Dromgoole. Died from wounds received in action—First Sergt.

William F. Gormly, John P. Kelly. Wounded—Martin G. Lyons, lung, back, serious; Robert L. Hampton, lung, skull, serious; Jack M. Russell, thigh serious; Henry Stierle, cheek, serious; Eugene Dewitt, wounded in thigh, serious; Frank McAndrew, back, head, slight; Musician Charles W. Buck, wounded in shoulder, slight.

CHAFFEE.

MANILA. (Received October 19, 1901.)

ADJUTANT-GENERAL, *Washington:*
* * * * * * *
Sailed for United States October 18, *McClellan.*

CHAFFEE.

MANILA. (Received October 22, 1901.)

ADJUTANT-GENERAL, *Washington:*
Col. Tully McCrea reports *Sheridan* disabled Nagasaki, three weeks repair. *Warren* sails 25th; takes sick from *Sheridan.* McCrea says can take care of other troops.

CHAFFEE.

ADJUTANT-GENERAL'S OFFICE,
Washington, October 23, 1901.
CHAFFEE, *Manila:*
What is the situation and what steps have been taken suppress disturbance Samar?

CORBIN.

MANILA. (Received October 23, 1901.)

ADJUTANT-GENERAL, *Washington:*
* * * * * * *
Department need not feel further apprehension serious loss Samar. As soon as additional troops sent there distributed to strengthen small garrisons bolomen will be cautious. Many rumors further disturbance other quarters, but do not regard same as being serious nature. Battalion Twelfth Infantry, 300 marines additional force named cable October 4 to Samar.

CHAFFEE.

MANILA. (Received October 27, 1901.)

ADJUTANT-GENERAL, *Washington:*
Sumner badly in want of repairs, $20,000. Can it be done San Francisco? If not, must send her Hongkong.

CHAFFEE.

ADJUTAN-GENERAL'S OFFICE,
Washington, October 28, 1901.
CHAFFEE, *Manila:*
With reference to your telegram of 27th, send transport *Sumner* Hongkong repairs. Report cost.

CORBIN.

MANILA. (Received October 29, 1901.)

ADJUTANT-GENERAL, *Washington:*

* * * * * * *

Transport *Warren* sailed October 26; takes sick from *Sheridan*, Nagasaki.

CHAFFEE.

MANILA. (Received October 29, 1901.)

ADJUTANT-GENERAL, *Washington:*

* * * * * * *

Transport *Hancock* arrived October 25.

CHAFFEE.

MANILA. (Received October 31, 1901.)

ADJUTANT-GENERAL, *Washington:*

Following from Brigadier-General Hughes: "Insurrecto forces Cebu Island have come in, laid down arms in good faith in obedience demand of people for peace; 150 rifles, 8 brass pieces, 60 officers, 470 men. Affairs not yet satisfactory Bohol Island; may move additional troops there force settlement." This settles for present at least disturbance hitherto existing Cebu. Further disorder that island will be matter deliberate action by inhabitants, as peace may be easily preserved if people disposed do so. Shall advise Hughes waste no time, but move on Bohol immediately.

CHAFFEE.

MANILA. (Received November 2, 1901.)

ADJUTANT-GENERAL, *Washington:*

* * * * * * *

With reference to your telegram of 25th September, request time for payment native scouts from army appropriation date from November 30 where impractical to enlist previous that time; paymaster says can not pay prior date enlistment. Nearly all insist on being sent home and discharged before enlistment; hence slow progress reorganization.

CHAFFEE.

ADJUTANT-GENERAL'S OFFICE,
Washington, November 4, 1901.

CHAFFEE, *Manila:*

Order transfer from Manila ordnance depots to Admiral Rodgers, Cavite, 400 each of magazine rifles, caliber .30, bayonet scabbards, and double-loop cartridge belts and 200,000, caliber .30, ball cartridges. Report action for payment here.

CORBIN.

MANILA. (Received November 6, 1901.)

ADJUTANT-GENERAL, *Washington:*

* * * * * * *

Transport *Warren* damaged inland sea now at Kobe. Can not proceed until repaired; must be docked. Transport *Hancock* sails to-morrow take passengers transport *Warren* San Francisco. Transport *Warren* to be repaired and return as soon as possible Manila.

CHAFFEE.

MANILA. (Received November 6, 1901.)

ADJUTANT-GENERAL, *Washington:*

* * * * * * *

Recommend First Battalion, Second Infantry, be sent here in order to relieve Third Battalion; former to be composed of men with at least one year to serve if practicable.

CHAFFEE.

ADJUTANT-GENERAL'S OFFICE,
Washington, November 5, 1901.

CHAFFEE, *Manila:*

How many Hospital Corps men will you require? One thousand enlistments expire next four months in Philippine Islands.

CORBIN.

ADJUTANT-GENERAL'S OFFICE,
Washington, November 5, 1901.

CHAFFEE, *Manila:*

With reference to your telegram of 2d, Secretary of War authorizes payment native scouts from Philippine funds to include November 30, where earlier enlistment impracticable. Civil governor informer.

CARTER.

MANILA. (Received November 7, 1901.)

ADJUTANT-GENERAL, *Washington:*

Forwarded by mail October 10 recommendation creating two departments Division Philippines, instead four. Mail delayed by accidents to transports Suggested Department of North Philippines, headquarters Manila, and Department South Philippines, headquarters Cebu, dividing line as follows: Passing southeastwardly through the west pass of Apo or Mindoro Strait to the twelfth parallel of north latitude; thence east along the 124th° 10′ east of Greenwich, but including the entire island of Masbate; thence north to San Bernardino Straits. North Philippines embraces 4 brigades, south Philippines 2 brigades, as heretofore organized by me. Request executive action by cable on this dispatch, to take effect November 30, if sufficiently broad and clear to be understood and suggestion meets approval. The insurrection in Batangas, Laguna, and Tayabas provinces must be put down, which I have in view by giving Wheaton Department of North Philippines, Wade to command South Philippines. Wheaton is excellent leader to conduct active campaign, and time is now ripe for it in provinces named. Public begin to fear that vigorous action in Samar may indicate future in store for other sections still in insurrection, which is fact, and I want to make the impression a reality if necessary. Prominent Filipino insurrecto sympathizers begin to feel their interests and persons are in danger, and I want to force them into active efforts for peace.

CHAFFEE.

ADJUTANT-GENERAL'S OFFICE,
Washington, November 9, 1901.

CHAFFEE, *Manila:*

Orders November 9 organizes two departments November 30, instead four; Wheaton, Wade assigned, as recommended in your telegram 7th.

WARD.

ADJUTANT-GENERAL, *Washington:*
MANILA. (Received November 10, 1901.)

Cable general orders, War Department, Adjutant-General's Office, current series, No. —, November 9, organizing two departments, full text.

CHAFFEE.

ADJUTANT-GENERAL, *Washington:*
MANILA. (Received November 10, 1901.)

* * * * * * *

Transport *Hancock* sailed November 7, 730 short-term enlisted men. Will transfer them to transport *Sheridan*, then will take all of the passengers from transport *Warren.*

CHAFFEE.

ADJUTANT-GENERAL, *Washington:*
MANILA. (Received November 12, 1901.)

* * * * * * *

Two companies Ilocano scouts in Samar will not reenlist there; will serve under present engagement until the end of the year. Commission will authorize pay for December, if Secretary of War authorizes. See your telegram November 5.

CHAFFEE.

ADJUTANT-GENERAL, *Washington:*
MANILA. (Received November 13, 1901.)

With reference to my telegram of 19th ultimo, relative pay scouts; awaiting reply.

* * * * * * *

CHAFFEE.

ADJUTANT-GENERAL'S OFFICE, *Washington, November 14, 1901.*
CHAFFEE, *Manila:*

GENERAL ORDERS, } HDQRS. OF THE ARMY, ADJUTANT-GENERAL'S OFFICE,
No. 148. } *Washington, November 9, 1901.*

The following order from the War Department is published to the Army for the information and guidance of all concerned:

"WAR DEPARTMENT, *Washington, November 9, 1901.*

"By direction of the President the Departments of Northern and Southern Luzon, of the Visayas, and of Mindanao and Jolo will be discontinued on November 30, 1901, and on and after that date the Division of the Philippines will be composed of the following departments:

"Department of North Philippines to include all that portion of the Philippine Archipelago lying north of a line passing southeastwardly through the West Pass of Apo or Mindoro Strait to the twelfth parallel of north latitude, thence east along said parallel 124° 10′ east of Greenwich, but including the entire island of Masbate, thence north to San Bernardino Straits.

"Maj. Gen. Loyd Wheaton, U. S. Army, is assigned to the command of this department, with headquarters at Manila, island of Luzon.

"Department of South Philippines to include all that portion of the Philippine Archipelago lying south of the dividing line as above described.

"Brig. Gen. James F. Wade, U. S. Army, is assigned to the command of this department, with headquarters at Cebu, island of Cebu.

"ELIHU ROOT, *Secretary of War.*"

The records of the discontinued departments will be disposed of as the division commander may direct.

By command of Lieutenant-General Miles:

THOMAS WARD, *Acting Adjutant-General.*

MANILA. (Received November 16, 1901.)

ADJUTANT-GENERAL, *Washington:*

* * * * * * *

Transport *Sheridan* will not sail before November 18 or 19. Transport *Thomas* will be ready to sail November 20.

CHAFFEE.

MANILA. (Received November 1901.)

ADJUTANT-GENERAL, *Washington:*

* * * * * * *

Information received to-day transport *Hancock* aground 8 yesterday morning entrance inland sea; reported not damaged; expected float high tide to-night. No more her class will be sent that route.

CHAFFEE.

ADJUTANT-GENERAL'S OFFICE,
Washington, November 18, 1901.

CHAFFEE, *Manila:*

Second Battalion Twenty-eighth Regiment U. S. Infantry, 70 men Eighth Regiment U. S. Infantry, sailed transport *Rosecrans* November 17.

WARD.

ADJUTANT-GENERAL'S OFFICE,
Washington, November 20, 1901.

CHAFFEE, *Manila:*
When did *Sheridan* sail?

CORBIN.

MANILA. (Received November 20, 1901.)

ADJUTANT-GENERAL, *Washington:*
Transport *Thomas* sailed to-day, 49 furloughed and discharged soldiers, 102 prisoners, 127 sick, 949 short-term men.

* * * * * * *

CHAFFEE.

MANILA. (Received November 29, 1901.)

ADJUTANT-GENERAL, *Washington:*
Transport *Wright* struck on uncharted rock near south end Daram Island and north entrance San Juanico Straits; badly injured.

CHAFFEE.

MANILA. (Received December 2, 1901.)

ADJUTANT-GENERAL, *Washington:*

* * * * * * *

Seventeenth Regiment U. S. Infantry can not be sent until Twenty-seventh Regiment U. S. Infantry arrives. Important that it arrives complete. When will Twenty-seventh Regiment U. S. Infantry sail? If not en route may send Company G, Twentieth Regiment U. S. Infantry before Seventeenth Regiment U. S. Infantry.

CHAFFEE.

CORRESPONDENCE.

MANILA. (Received December 2, 1901.)
ADJUTANT-GENERAL, *Washington:*

* * * * * * *

Transport *Kilpatrick* arrived Manila on December 2.

CHAFFEE.

ADJUTANT-GENERAL'S OFFICE,
Washington, December 4, 1901.
CHAFFEE, *Manila:*

Second and third battalion, Twenty-seventh Regiment U. S. Infantry, will sail from New York January 16 and December 5; headquarters and first battalion San Francisco, December 16. Not expected Seventeenth Regiment U. S. Infantry can be withdrawn before arrival Twenty-seventh Regiment U. S. Infantry.

* * * * * * *

CORBIN.

ADJUTANT-GENERAL'S OFFICE,
Washington, December 4, 1901.
CHAFFEE, *Manila:*

* * * * * * *

Enlistment papers native scouts received treated as reenlistment. Prior service was civil contract. Has no connection with enlistment. Provincial designation and nearest relative must be shown. Issue orders.

CORBIN.

ADJUTANT-GENERAL'S OFFICE,
Washington, December 6, 1901.
CHAFFEE, *Manila:*

Send *Kilpatrick* San Francisco, and hereafter all transports on regular line on regular dates. Sail independent transports sent you at your convenience. *Kilpatrick* for the present will be kept on the San Francisco line.

* * * * * * *

CORBIN.

ADJUTANT-GENERAL'S OFFICE,
Washington, December 10, 1901.
CHAFFEE, *Manila:*

Assign suitable staterooms to patients seriously ill requiring better accommodations than transport hospitals afford. Limit assignment other passengers accordingly.

CORBIN.

MANILA. (Received December 12, 1901.)
ADJUTANT-GENERAL, *Washington:*

Transport *Kilpatrick* sailed yesterday; 950 discharged and short-term men.

CHAFFEE.

MANILA. (Received December 12, 1901.)
ADJUTANT-GENERAL:

Transport *Grant* arrived yesterday.

* * * * * * *

CHAFFEE.

ADJUTANT-GENERAL'S OFFICE,
Washington, December 13. 1901.

CHAFFEE, *Manila:*
Transport *Crook* sailed from New York for Manila 5th with Second Squadron Eleventh Regiment U. S. Cavalry, Third Battalion Twenty-seventh Regiment U. S. Infantry, 51 Hospital Corps men.

CORBIN.

MANILA. (Received December 16, 1901.)

ADJUTANT-GENERAL, *Washington:*

* * * * * * *

Warren sailed December 15; 756 short-term enlisted men, Robert P. Hughes, Frederick Funston.

CHAFFEE.

ADJUTANT-GENERAL'S OFFICE,
Washington, December 17, 1901.

CHAFFEE, *Manila:*
Reported *Thomas* sailed from Nagasaki for San Francisco via Kobe and Yokohama. If ship so ordered, why?

CORBIN.

ADJUTANT-GENERAL'S OFFICE,
Washington, December 17, 1901.

CHAFFEE, *Manila:*
Headquarters seven troops Fifteenth Regiment U. S. Cavalry, 345 unassigned recruits, sailed transport *Hancock* December 16.

* * * * * * *

CORBIN.

ADJUTANT-GENERAL'S OFFICE,
Washington, December 19, 1901.

CHAFFEE, *Manila:*
Eleven hundred short-term men who arrived on *Sheridan* were discharged on ship. Secretary of War directs such men to be held in service and turned over to the commanding general, Department of California, who will order their discharge rapidly as they can be paid.

CORBIN.

MANILA. (Received December 20, 1901.)

ADJUTANT-GENERAL, *Washington:*
With reference to your telegram of 17th, transport *Thomas* was not authorized to sail by Kobe, Yokohama, from Nagasaki to San Francisco.

* * * * * * *

CHAFFEE.

MANILA. (Received December 24, 1901.)

ADJUTANT-GENERAL, *Washington:*
Meade arrived December 19, delayed, severe typhoon. *Egbert*, December 22.

* * * * * * *

CHAFFEE.

MANILA. (Received December 24, 1901.)

ADJUTANT-GENERAL, *Washington:*

* * * * * * *

Grant sails to-day, Fourth Infantry, William H. Taft, 114 sick, 5 insane, 35 general prisoners, 541 discharged short-term enlisted men.

CHAFFEE.

MANILA. (Received December 24, 1901.)

ADJUTANT-GENERAL, *Washington:*

* * * * * * *

Authority requested to sell civil government of the Philippine Islands such medical supplies not needed by army for one year at invoice prices or price made board appraisers.

CHAFFEE.

MANILA. (Received December 24, 1901.)

ADJUTANT-GENERAL, *Washington:*

* * * * * * *

Reference our General Orders Nos. 52 and 64, 1900, letter Division Insular Affairs, October 24, 1901; auditor calls for deposit without deductions of all fines collected provost courts. Fines collected by municipal courts go to municipalities for expenses. What is military to do for funds to run municipalities under its jurisdiction if fines turned in? Think it strained construction of term "revenues" to hold fines to be such. There is no objection accounting to auditor for such moneys, but we need them pay expenses municipal governments, to be disbursed by commanding officers.

CHAFFEE.

MANILA. (Received December 24, 1901.)

ADJUTANT-GENERAL, *Washington:*

* * * * * * *

Samson, leader insurgents Mutasaron, surrendered, with all officers, men, 28 cannon, 45 rifles.

CHAFFEE.

MANILA. (Received December 25, 1901.)

ADJUTANT-GENERAL, *Washington:*

Company F, Twenty-first Infantry, desperate hand-to-hand encounter in gorge 6 miles south San José, Batangas, December 23; 22 enemy killed. Patrick A. Connolly, ugly bolo wound left cheek; Private Carney, six bolo cuts, neck and shoulders. Hot time in Batangas.

* * * * * * *

CHAFFEE.

MANILA. (Received December 26, 1901.)

ADJUTANT-GENERAL, *Washington:*

J. Franklin Bell, Jacob H. Smith doing their utmost. Are greatly in want of stenographers.

* * * * * * *

CHAFFEE.

ADJUTANT-GENERAL'S OFFICE,
Washington, December 26, 1901.

CHAFFEE, Manila:
With reference to your telegram of 24th, Secretary of War authorizes sale medical supplies under restrictions mentioned.

CORBIN.

ADJUTANT-GENERAL'S OFFICE,
Washington, December 26, 1901.

CHAFFEE, Manila:
In sending you new cavalry regiment should it bring horses, or have you enough for all mounted purposes?

CORBIN.

MANILA. (Received December 27, 1901.)

ADJUTANT-GENERAL, Washington:
* * * * * *
Rosecrans arrived 22d.

CHAFFEE.

MANILA. (Received December 27, 1901.)

ADJUTANT-GENERAL, Washington:
With reference to your telegram of 26th, no horses required at present; probably have enough to mount, but these troops will have to do foot service for the present.
* * * * * * *

CHAFFEE.

MANILA. (Received December 27, 1901.)

ADJUTANT-GENERAL, Washington:
Request $10,000 made available as soon as possible for small-arms practice target division of the Philippines.
* * * * * * *

CHAFFEE.

MANILA. (Received December 27, 1901.)

ADJUTANT-GENERAL, Washington:
* * * * * * *

Jacob H. Smith reports following: During scout near Dapdap, Samar, December 24, [Capt.] Francis H. Schoeffel, with detachment 18 men Company E, Ninth Infantry, were attacked large force bolomen springing from thickets. Severe hand-to-hand fight ensued. Following casualties occurred:

Killed—Sergt. John P. Swisher, Corpl. James Gaughan, John Maren, Frank McAndrew, Joseph A. Weippert, George Bedford. Wounded—[Capt.] Francis H. Schoeffel, slightly; Corpl. John H. Russell, Daniel L. McPherson, George Claxton, severely; Arthur Bonnicastle, slightly. One other killed, one wounded, names later. No property lost. Enemy driven from field; lost severely. Lang's detachment Philippine Scouts arrived soon after, assisted caring for wounded and removing.

CHAFFEE.

ADJUTANT-GENERAL'S OFFICE,
Washington, December 28, 1901.

CHAFFEE, *Manila:*

Order officers returning to the United States account sickness to general hospital, Presidio, instead of granting sick leaves.

CORBIN.

MANILA. (Received January 1, 1902.)

ADJUTANT-GENERAL, *Washington:*

Proceeding now occupy Grande Island, Subig Bay, as prison confinement persons arrested Laguna, Batangas Province, Luzon; occupancy temporary, probably three, four months. By executive order this island now under control Navy. Is there any objection to my proceeding? Admiral Rodgers has just called attention exclusive control Navy. See no reason why it can not be temporarily occupied purpose stated. Reply asked for at earliest moment practicable. Am just landing troops prisoners there.

*   *   *   *   *   *   *

CHAFFEE.

MANILA. (Received January 2, 1902.)

ADJUTANT-GENERAL, *Washington:*

Must have sanitary dump carts purchased by Quartermaster's Department to turn over to Manila to replace same number used by Army, but purchased with public civil funds especially for Manila; unless this purchase made must gather in carts from many places where now used. Clearly Army now entitled these carts; city needs them. Advise by cable.

CHAFFEE.

MANILA. (Received January 2, 1902.)

ADJUTANT-GENERAL, *Washington:*

With reference to my telegram of 1st, Grande Island time mentioned not sufficient. Unless can occupy for a year or two, hardly worth while incur expense involved. Excellent place military prison. Unless Navy seriously object think Sscretary of War, Secretary of the Navy could effect satisfactory arrangement its use prison grounds.

CHAFFEE.

ADJUTANT-GENERAL'S OFFICE,
Washington, January 2, 1902.

CHAFFEE, *Manila:*

First squadron Eleventh Regiment U. S. Cavalry, Regimental Headquarters, and first battalion Twenty-seventh Regiment U. S. Infantry, 711 unassigned recruits sailed *Sheridan* January 1.

CORBIN.

ADJUTANT-GENERAL'S OFFICE,
Washington, January 3, 1902.

CHAFFEE, *Manila:*

With reference to your telegram of 2d, sanitary carts will be be bought. How many do you want for army use?

CORBIN.

AFFAIRS IN THE PHILIPPINE ISLANDS. 1309

MANILA. (Received January 5, 1902.)

ADJUTANT-GENERAL, *Washington:*
With reference to your telegram of 3d, want 35 sanitary carts to turn over Manila, replacing same number used Army belonging city; no others required.

CHAFFEE.

ADJUTANT-GENERAL'S OFFICE,
Washington, January 6, 1902.

CHAFFEE, *Manila:*
With reference to my telegram of 19th ultimo, are short-term men on *Grant* already discharged or to be held in service as directed?

CORBIN.

MANILA. (Received January 8, 1902.)

ADJUTANT-GENERAL, *Washington:*
* * * * * * *
With reference to your telegram of 19th ultimo, instructions given that short-term men transport *Grant* should not be discharged en route.

CHAFFEE.

ADJUTANT-GENERAL'S OFFICE,
Washington, January 8, 1902.

CHAFFEE, *Manila:*
Report whether Sergeant Markley, Company C, Ninth Regiment U. S. Infantry, or others engaged Balangiga, entitled special recognition, and what form.

CORBIN.

ADJUTANT-GENERAL'S OFFICE,
Washington, January 8, 1902.

CHAFFEE, *Manila:*
What rates pay been determined for all enlisted grades Philippine scouts?

CORBIN.

ADJUTANT-GENERAL'S OFFICE,
Washington, January 8, 1902.

CHAFFEE, *Manila:*
Send statements prisoners from all prison posts. See letter September 5.

CORBIN.

MANILA. (Received January 9, 1902.)

ADJUTANT-GENERAL, *Washington:*
With reference to your telegram of 8th, pay each grade Philippine scouts one-half, including 20 per cent increase for foreign service, provided law for pay enlisted men; army clothing allowance 9 cents day, or $2.70 month, all grades.

CHAFFEE.

ADJUTANT-GENERAL'S OFFICE,
Washington, January 10, 1902.

CHAFFEE, *Manila:*

Ask Rodgers for Secretary Long's cable to him regarding prison site.

CORBIN.

MANILA. (Received January 10, 1902.)

ADJUTANT-GENERAL, *Washington:*

With reference to my telegram of 27th ultimo, $10,000 target material. Request reply by telegram.

CHAFFEE.

MANILA. (Received January 13, 1902.)

ADJUTANT-GENERAL, *Washington:*

* * * * * * *

Hancock arrived January 11.

CHAFFEE.

ADJUTANT-GENERAL'S OFFICE,
Washington, January 13, 1902.

CHAFFEE, *Manila:*

With reference to your telegram of 7th, military authorities will conform to rates of exchange fixed by the proclamation civil governor.

CORBIN.

MANILA. (Received January 14, 1902.)

ADJUTANT-GENERAL, *Washington:*

Important surrender occurred January 13, Taal, Batangas; 1 colonel, 3 lieutenant-colonels, 1 major, 5 captains, 12 lieutenants, 245 men, 223 rifles. Marasigan, the colonel, hitherto leader much importance under Malvar for west third of province. That section now practically cleared of hostile force. Surrender unconditional every way and wholly due hard splendid service troops, officers, men. American native believe this surrender will influence hostile forces other sections province to surrender. Prisoners not charged with serious crimes released.

CHAFFEE.

MANILA. (Received January 15, 1902.)

ADJUTANT-GENERAL, *Washington:*

* * * * * * *

With reference to my telegram of 2d; with reference to my telegram of 5th, sanitary carts, take no action. Will purchase 20 from city Manila for army use and sell Manila wooden dump carts needed, which we can spare. In this way settle dispute about ownership 60 sanitary carts.

CHAFFEE.

ADJUTANT-GENERAL'S OFFICE,
Washington, January 15, 1902.

CHAFFEE, *Manila:*

You are authorized to proceed with barracks on the basis of $500,000 that will be sent in the course of the next few days.

CORBIN.

ADJUTANT-GENERAL'S OFFICE,
Washington, January 16, 1902.

CHAFFEE, Manila:
You are authorized to occupy Grande Island for military prisoners as long as public interests require.
CORBIN.

MANILA. (Received January 18, 1902.)
ADJUTANT-GENERAL, Washington:
* * * * * * *
Meade sailed January 16, 108 sick, 13 insane, 827 short-term enlisted men.
CHAFFEE.

MANILA. (Received January 18, 1902.)
ADJUTANT-GENERAL, Washington:
* * * * * * *
[Brig. Gen.] James F. Wade, Cebu, reports January 15, 365 insurgents surrendered January 14; January 15 took oath Tagbilaran, Bohol.
CHAFFEE.

MANILA. (Received January 18, 1902.)
ADJUTANT-GENERAL, Washington:
With reference to your telegram of 16th, we think $500,000 will clear the ground, which is practically wild land; make the roads, without which nothing can be done toward construction; prepare foundation with rock to be obtained in the vicinity, and cover labor for construction of the post. The material to be purchased and supplied from the United States, lumber, nails, iron roofing, large pump, water pipe, plumbing material, etc., probably cost $300,000; but it is large post, and as yet we have not worked out the bill of lumber; water and drainage pipe required can not be determined until ground cleared, carefully surveyed, and post plotted. We can not do more than to clear, survey, and plot ground this season. Have only four months to work before rains begin. Must have quartermaster with skill for this work and energy to supervise it. Send [Capt.] Joseph C. Byron and Thomas Humphreys; quartermasters out here are all engaged in other ways. My idea is to prepare this season for construction next. If post is to be constructed, authority to begin clearing requested. Think $200,000 sufficient for this calendar year.
* * * * * * *
CHAFFEE.

MANILA. (Received January 18, 1902.)
ADJUTANT-GENERAL, Washington:
* * * * * * *
Authority to occupy Grande Island came too late. Arrangements completed and am occupying small island Laguna de Bay for prison. Absent from Manila ten days to Samar.
CHAFFEE.

ADJUTANT-GENERAL'S OFFICE,
Washington, January 20, 1902.

CHAFFEE, Manila:
Kilpatrick sailed 16th; unassigned recruits, 460 infantry, 173 cavalry.
WARD.

1312 CORRESPONDENCE.

MANILA. (Received January 23, 1902.)
ADJUTANT-GENERAL, *Washington:*
* * * * * * *
With reference to your telegram of 27th ultimo, with reference to your telegram of 10th, regarding appropriation target practice, request reply by telegram. Unable utilize present favorable weather.

CHAFFEE.

MANILA. (Received January 23, 1902.)
ADJUTANT-GENERAL, *Washington:*
With reference to your telegram of the 8th, not thought Sergeant Markley, Company C, Ninth Infantry, or others engaged Balangiga affair deserve special recognition.
* * * * * * *

CHAFFEE.

MANILA. (Received January 24, 1902.)
ADJUTANT-GENERAL, *Washington:*
* * * * * * *
With reference to my telegram of 23d about Sergeant Markley, Company C, Ninth Regiment U. S. Infantry, hold until [Gen.] Adna R. Chaffee returns from Samar.

CHAFFEE.

ADJUTANT-GENERAL'S OFFICE,
Washington, January 24, 1902.
CHAFFEE, *Manila:*
Republish, distribute military governor's General Orders, No. 49, 1901, correcting to agree with General Orders, No. 87, this office.

CORBIN.

ADJUTANT-GENERAL'S OFFICE,
Washington, January 24, 1902.
CHAFFEE, *Manila:*
Require compliance Army Regulations 162 before the departure short-term men from stations, noting on descriptive list all information required for discharge certificates.

CORBIN.

ADJUTANT-GENERAL'S OFFICE,
Washington, January 24, 1902.
CHAFFEE, *Manila:*
Transport *Buford* sailed from New York for Manila, 21st, Third Squadron, Eleventh Regiment U. S. Cavalry; Second Battalion, Twenty-seventh Regiment U. S. Infantry; 50 men, Hospital Corps.

CORBIN.

MANILA. (Received January 25, 1902.)
ADJUTANT-GENERAL, *Washington:*
Rosecrans sailed 24th, 8 officers, 475 enlisted men Third Battalion, Twenty-second Regiment U. S. Infantry.

CHAFFEE.

AFFAIRS IN THE PHILIPPINE ISLANDS. 1313

MANILA. (Received January 27, 1902.)
ADJUTANT-GENERAL, *Washington:*

* * * * * * *

With reference to your telegram of 24th, Order 49 has been republished as directed.

CHAFFEE.

MANILA. (Received January 27, 1902.)
ADJUTANT-GENERAL, *Washington:*

* * * * * * *

Date of sailing Twenty-second Regiment U. S. Infantry, February 1; Twentieth Regiment U. S. Infantry, February 16; headquarters, First Battalion, Second Battalion, Seventeenth U. S. Infantry, February 28; Third Battalion Seventeenth Regiment U. S. Infantry after arrival Second Battalion Twenty-seventh Regiment U. S. Infantry.

CHAFFEE.

MANILA. (Received January 28, 1902.)
ADJUTANT-GENERAL, *Washington:*

* * * * * * *

Sheridan arrived January 26.

CHAFFEE.

MANILA. (Received January 28, 1902.)
ADJUTANT-GENERAL, *Washington:*

* * * * * * *

On January 27, 25 cases measles *Sheridan*. Necessary disinfect at quarantine. Will take probably two weeks before troops can be sent destination.

CHAFFEE.

MANILA. (Received January 28, 1902.)
ADJUTANT-GENERAL, *Washington:*

Do not need more cavalry; if sent must be for dismounted service. Most expensive, least useful arm these islands are mounted men.

* * * * * * *

CHAFFEE.

MANILA. (Received January 28, 1902.)
ADJUTANT-GENERAL, *Washington:*

Major Waller, 4 officers and 50 men of the Marine Corps, 36 native bearers, four days' rations, started last week of December from Lanang, on the east coast of Samar, to cross the island to Basey, about 35 miles on map. Trail at one time existed, but found in places only. Lieutenant Lyles, Twelfth U. S. Infantry, accompanied the command. Incessant rains from the start, swollen streams, and other natural obstacles made progress extremely slow. When rations consumed men exhausted rapidly, dropping on the way. Major Waller separated from Captain Porter, Lieutenant Williams, and major part of the men, proceeding toward Basey, where he arrived January 9 with 2 officers, 13 men; also Lieutenant Lyles. He returned to the mountains next day with relief, but returned to Basey about ten days later unsuccessful. Porter was to build rafts, but timber would not float. Second day after separating from Waller Porter moved toward Lanang, arriving January 11 with 2 men, all exhausted physically and mentally. Lieutenant Williams and over 30 men left in mountains in similar condition with native bearers. Relief expedition under Lieutenant Williams, First Infantry, delayed starting two days by storm raging and torrent river. Started 13th; reached Marines 18th, saving Lieutenant Williams and all except 10 men not found, who are no doubt dead from starvation, namely: Privates Fangule, E. Foster, G. M. Britt, T. Wards, Brown, F. F. Murry, T. Buffett, Baley, Baroni, Connell, R. Kettle died hospital, Tacloban, January 23. Captain Porter, Lieutenant Williams, and 18 men hospital, Tacloban, not very clear in mind regarding much of the time covered by period of suffering. All will probably recover. Major Waller at present disordered in his recollections. Suffering of this command twenty days can not be described. Efforts of Lieutenant Williams, First Infantry, and his relief party unequaled for courage and labor.

CHAFFEE.

MANILA. (Received January 28, 1902.)

ADJUTANT-GENERAL, *Washington:*

* * * * * * *

What further destination *Crook*, New York or San Francisco? If former, can she carry troops?

CHAFFEE.

ADJUTANT-GENERAL'S OFFICE,
Washington, February 1, 1902.

CHAFFEE, *Manila:*

With reference to your telegram of 28th ultimo, transport *Crook* assigned regular line San Francisco and Manila.

CORBIN.

ADJUTANT-GENERAL'S OFFICE,
Washington, February 3, 1902.

CHAFFEE, *Manila:*

Unassigned recruits, infantry, 1,115; cavalry, 307; sailed transport *Thomas* February 1.

* * * * * * *

With reference to your telegram of 23d ultimo, funds target practice included urgency deficiency bill. Will telegraph as soon as appropriated.

CORBIN.

MANILA. (Received February 3, 1902.)

ADJUTANT-GENERAL, *Washington:*

* * * * * * *

Hancock sailed February 1, Brig. Gen. Joseph C. Breckenridge, headquarters, First, Second Battalions, Twenty-second Regiment U. S. Infantry, 92 sick, 10 insane, 497 short term discharged enlisted men, 47 general prisoners.

CHAFFEE.

MANILA. (Received February 3, 1902.)

ADJUTANT-GENERAL, *Washington:*

* * * * * * *

Crook arrived February 3.

CHAFFEE.

AFFAIRS IN THE PHILIPPINE ISLANDS. 1315

MANILA. (Received February 7, 1902.)
ADJUTANT-GENERAL, *Washington:*
With reference to your telegram of 8th ultimo, have been unable to find any survivors Balangiga affair can be rewarded by promotion. List of three will be forwarded for mention in General Orders.

* * * * * * *

CHAFFEE.

ADJUTANT-GENERAL'S OFFICE,
Washington, February 5, 1902.
CHAFFEE, *Manila:*
To refute statements misconduct troops toward natives Secretary of War directs all petitions for retention commands various garrisons mailed immediately and cable stations of troops vacated since December 1 owing to general improved conditions.

CORBIN.

MANILA. (Received February 8, 1902.)
ADJUTANT-GENERAL, *Washington:*

* * * * * * *

With reference to your telegram of 5th, 134 stations abandoned, 39 newly occupied.

CHAFFEE.

ADJUTANT-GENERAL'S OFFICE,
Washington, February 7, 1902.
CHAFFEE, *Manila:*
Secretary of War desires to know approximate cost to the United States secure complete title reservation for Manila post if it can be secured.

CORBIN.

ADJUTANT-GENERAL'S OFFICE,
Washington, February 8, 1902.
CHAFFEE, *Manila:*
Secretary of War rules that offices in civil government of the Philippine Islands, for which elections are held under acts passed by Philippine Commission, are not civil offices within' meaning section 1222 Revised Statutes, and an officer chosen thereto by popular election may be ordered to perform duties of the office as agent of the military power which constituted the Commission itself. No acceptance by the officer or new oath of office will be required, but an order from you and obedience to the order of the officer.

WARD.

MANILA. (Received February 9, 1902.)
ADJUTANT-GENERAL, *Washington:*

* * * * * * *

Reference site post near Manila. For tract land 20,000 acres owners ask $1,000,000 gold; same returned for taxation last September at valuation $300,000 Mexican; for the ground located thereon staked off by myself am asked $158,000 gold, $101 acre, or rental $15,000 gold for a year. Consider price exorbitant. Col. Joseph T. Sanger working for reduction. Can not report approximate cost for few days.

CHAFFEE.

MANILA. (Received February 11, 1902.)
ADJUTANT-GENERAL, *Washington:*

* * * * * * *

With reference to my indorsement of 3d December letter Brig. Gen. George W. Davis, November 14, do not want home battalion Tenth Regiment U. S. Infantry.

CHAFFEE.

MANILA. (Received February 11, 1902.)
ADJUTANT-GENERAL, *Washington:*

* * * * * * *

Transport *Wright* afloat; owe Navy thanks; Lieutenant Andrews superintending work.

CHAFFEE.

ADJUTANT-GENERAL'S OFFICE,
Washington, February 12, 1902.
CHAFFEE, *Manila:*

Transport *Grant* sailed from San Francisco for Manila 8th, 20 Hospital Corps men, 196 infantry, 87 cavalry, unassigned recruits.

CORBIN.

ADJUTANT-GENERAL'S OFFICE,
Washington, Febuary 16, 1902.
CHAFFEE, *Manila:*

With reference to my telegram of 26th November, order discharge at sea short-term noncommissioned officers, cooks, and other special men whose enlistments expire en route. This to prevent exceeding legal limit when replaced by company commanders.

CORBIN.

ADJUTANT-GENERAL'S OFFICE,
Washington, February 17, 1902.
CHAFFEE, *Manila:*

Transport *Warren* sailed from San Francisco for Manila 16th, Second Battalion Fifteenth Regiment U. S. Infantry, 353 unassigned infantry recruits.

CORBIN.

MANILA. (Received February 17, 1902.)
ADJUTANT-GENERAL, *Washington:*

* * * * * * *

Sheridan sailed February 16, 97 sick, 6 insane, 1,189 short-term discharged enlisted men, headquarters, First and Third battalions Twentieth. Regiment U. S. Infantry; total enlisted strength rolls 588 present, absent 142 transferred remaining regiments.

CHAFFEE.

MANILA. (Received February 17, 1902.)
ADJUTANT-GENERAL, *Washington:*

* * * * * * *

Transport *Kilpatrick* arrived to-day.

CHAFFEE.

MANILA. (Received February 19, 1902.)
ADJUTANT-GENERAL, *Washington:*
Egbert sailed February 18, Second Battalion Twentieth Regiment U. S. Infantry; total enlisted strength rolls 213 present; absent 133 transferred remaining regiments: 312 short-term discharged enlisted men.

* * * * * * *

CHAFFEE.

ADJUTANT-GENERAL'S OFFICE,
Washington, February 19, 1902.

CHAFFEE, *Manila:*
Secretary of War desires you send by next mail original telegram to Aguinaldo, asking what rewards will be given troops entering Manila with Aguinaldo's promise to give titles nobility. Send copy of lists, members congress, showing which elected, which appointed, also complete copy Aguinaldo's diary, and letters sent book, secretary foreign affairs. John R. M. Taylor states these papers on file bureau military information, Manila. Send all such records for which you have no further need.

CORBIN.

ADJUTANT-GENERAL'S OFFICE,
Washington, February 17, 1902.

CHAFFEE, *Manila:*
Letter First Sergt. White, Company L, Ninth Regiment U. S. Infantry, Atlanta Constitution, 1900, reports Macabebes applying water torture natives in order to secure information about hidden arms. Telegraph as soon as possible if White wrote letter and his explanation. Matter before Senate. Early comprehensive reply desired.

CORBIN.

ADJUTANT-GENERAL'S OFFICE,
Washington, February 19, 1902.

MAJ. GEN. ADNA R. CHAFFEE,
Commanding Division of the Philippines,
Manila, P. I.

GENERAL: At the instance of the Secretary of War, I inclose herewith a copy of a report of Maj. Cornelius Gardener, Thirteenth U. S. Infantry, as provincial governor of the province of Tayabas, the same having been made by him to the civil governor of the Philippine Islands.

There is so much contained in this report, reflecting not only upon officers of the Army but the general conduct of affairs and the military branch of the Government, that the Secretary of War desires you to cause a careful inquiry to be made concerning these statements, and if they be found true that the necessary administrative and disciplinary measures be applied to correct these evils.

Your particular attention is invited to the portions of the report which are underscored.

You are requested to make a full report of the investigation herein directed as soon as possible.

Very respectfully,

H. C. CORBIN,
Adjutant-General, Major-General, U. S. Army.

MANILA. (Received February 22, 1902.)

ADJUTANT-GENERAL, *Washington:*

Associated Press reports battalions Tenth and Eleventh Infantry ordered here, battalion Fifteenth en route. Do not want Twenty-ninth to relieve Ninth, as mentioned in my letter January 30; under this new condition, unless organizations are ordered home, will have to extend occupation rather than contract, as I am now doing by calling in detachments. I will take away Third and Twelfth Infantry soon, which will enable me to cover their ground by fewer troops. Conditions favor this in section occupied by these regiments. Count on reduction by July to 35,000, including native troops.

CHAFFEE.

ADJUTANT-GENERAL'S OFFICE,
Washington, February 24, 1902.

CHAFFEE, *Manila:*

Secretary War desires you to continue process of contracting occupation, following policy described in your dispatch received February 22, as rapidly as civil governor is willing to take responsibility of maintaining order by use of constabulary and police. Return Ninth, Third, Twelfth, Twenty-first, and Thirteenth Infantry in order named. Use *Kilpatrick* and *Buford* on San Francisco route. The Twenty-ninth Infantry will be held in this country for the present. Home battalion system abandoned; those in United States will be sent to join regiments, not to increase your force, but enable you to relieve regiments longest on duty in islands.

CORBIN.

MANILA, *February 24, 1902.*

ADJUTANT-GENERAL, *Washington:*

With reference to your telegram of 17th, report following: First Sergeant White, Company L, Ninth Infantry, states he wrote personal private letter May, 1900, to brother at Atlanta. First letter written since arrival Philippine Islands, September, 1899; states said letter altered, part omitted, matter inserted to suit home correspondent's imagination; that after it was published copy reached him hardly recognized; same being nearly two years ago. Does not remember all contents. States positively he not author, knew nothing regarding paragraph relating hydraulic treatment. His full letter mail. White's character excellent every way. Irvine commanding. White's letter will be forwarded immediately when received.

CHAFFEE.

MANILA. (Received February 25, 1902.)

ADJUTANT-GENERAL, *Washington:*

Site selected for post at confluence Pasig-Tugig rivers, about 7 miles above Manila; good road front on Pasig about 1¼ miles; extends south about 2¼ miles, partly along Tugig, approximately 2,100 acres, exact area later. Site high, rolling, easily drained, considered sanitary; water from Tugig sterilized; good stone quarries; title to be determined courts; purchase price approximately $75,000. If we can arrange executory price, I may do so, and proceed with survey, clearing, plotting ground. This much cheapest site found. Think price very reasonable compared other demands.

*   *   *   *   *   *   *

CHAFFEE.

MANILA. (Received February 26, 1902.)
ADJUTANT-GENERAL, *Washington:*
Ninth too deeply involved Samar to get out just now without interference with work there. Will relieve after battalions Tenth, Eleventh, and Fifteenth arrive. Shall make use of transport sailing March 15 to send Third Infantry, unless you say no.
CHAFFEE.

MANILA. (Received March 2, 1902.)
ADJUTANT-GENERAL, *Washington:*
* * * * * * *
Kilpatrick sailed March 1; 86 sick, 4 insane; remains Lieut. Col. Benjamin F. Pope and family; headquarters, Second Battalion Seventeenth Regiment U. S. Infantry. Total enlisted strength rolls 195, transferred remaining regiments 129; 597 short-term enlisted men.
CHAFFEE.

MANILA. (Received March 2, 1902.)
ADJUTANT-GENERAL, *Washington:*
* * * * * * *
With reference to your telegram of 19th ultimo, telegrams from Aguinaldo, et cetera, mailed yesterday.
CHAFFEE.

ADJUTANT-GENERAL'S OFFICE,
Washington, March 3, 1902.
CHAFFEE, *Manila:*
Six hundred and sixty-two unassigned infantry recruits sailed transport *Meade* March 1.
WARD.

WAR DEPARTMENT,
Washington, March 4, 1902.
CHAFFEE, *Manila:*
Referring to reports which indicate frequent arrests by subordinate military officers in provinces under civil government, your General Order 179 and your confidential circular of January 10 on this subject accord with the rule laid down in President's instructions of April 7, 1900, and indicate the proper course to be followed, and are approved. Disciplinary measures, however, seem necessary to produce obedience. Military officers have no right to make any arrests in provinces under civil government unless under circumstances of immediate exigency or when called upon by civil authority, and in every such case the prisoner is to be immediately turned over to the civil authorities for trial. You will communicate the tenor hereof to Gen. J. H. Smith and relieve Maj. E. F. Glenn and Capt. James A. Ryan, Fifteenth Cavalry, from their present duties and order them to Manila to await investigation into their conduct, in accordance with instructions to follow by mail from this Department. Furnish copy to civil governor.
ROOT, *Secretary of War.*

MANILA. (Received March 5, 1902.)
ADJUTANT-GENERAL, *Washington:*
Thomas arrived March 3.
* * * * * * *
CHAFFEE.

ADJUTANT-GENERAL, *Washington:*

MANILA. (Received March 6, 1902.)

* * * * * * *

Will be absent to Aparri about six days.

CHAFFEE.

WAR DEPARTMENT,
Washington, March 6, 1902.

CHAFFEE, *Manila:*

Sensational Associated Press report here reports practical renewal warlike conditions in Morong; intense excitement and many inhabitants fleeing for their lives. Report immediately actual conditions by cable.

ROOT, *Secretary of War.*

MANILA. (Received March 7, 1902.)

ADJUTANT-GENERAL, *Washington:*

* * * * * * *

Crook sailed March 6; 489 short-term discharged enlisted men; Third Battalion, Seventeenth Regiment U. S. Infantry; 175 total enlisted strength rolls; 113 transferred remaining regiments.

CHAFFEE.

ADJUTANT-GENERAL'S OFFICE,
Washington, March 8, 1902.

CHAFFEE, *Manila:*

Transport *Meade* returned San Francisco account smallpox; sails again 17th.

WARD.

MANILA. (Received March 8, 1902.)

ADJUTANT-GENERAL, *Washington:*

With reference to your telegram of 6th, Secretary of War, facts from Morong are: About week ago Presidente Cainta was kidnaped. Perpetrators this act were new organization gathered Morong Province, about 60 strong; vigorously searched for; driven to hiding; probably captured in a day or two; have inflicted no material damage. No special significance need or should attach this event.

* * * * * * *

CHAFFEE.

MANILA. (Received March 12, 1902.)

ADJUTANT-GENERAL, *Washington:*

* * * * * * *

Grant arrived 10th.

CHAFFEE.

MANILA. (Received March 13, 1902.)

ADJUTANT-GENERAL, *Washington:*

With reference to my telegram of 14th December, contingent fund, awaiting reply. Need $10,000 emergency fund War Department pay for surrendered arms. Have to my credit $50,000, called contingency fund; can turn over $10,000 for the purpose mentioned if you authorize.

* * * * * * *

CHAFFEE.

ADJUTANT-GENERAL'S OFFICE,
Washington, March 13, 1902.

CHAFFEE, *Manila:*

Humphrey recommends $92,000 gold repair transport *Liscum.* Do you recommend expenditure?

WARD.

MANILA. (Received March 14, 1902.)

ADJUTANT-GENERAL, *Washington:*

With reference to your telegram of 13th, *Liscum* must be repaired, otherwise no use. When repaired most useful ship we own here because facility carrying animals. Good hull; boilers must have been poor when ship purchased; our service less than year. Recommend repair immediately.

CHAFFEE.

ADJUTANT-GENERAL'S OFFICE,
Washington, March 17, 1902.

CHAFFEE, *Manila:*

Headquarters, band, Second Battalion Tenth Regiment U. S. Infantry, 130 assigned recruits, 236 unassigned infantry recruits, sailed *Hancock* March 15.

CORBIN.

MANILA. (Received March 20, 1902.)

ADJUTANT-GENERAL, *Washington:*

* * * * * * *

Thomas should arrive on the 18th; 685 enlisted men Third Regiment U. S. Infantry, long-term men, accompanying; 63 transferred in accordance with their request remaining regiments; 780 short-term men; 10 general prisoners; 53 sick.

CHAFFEE.

ADJUTANT-GENERAL'S OFFICE,
Washington, March 21, 1902.

CHAFFEE, *Manila:*

Reduce issue hay to quarter ration and telegraph supply on hand, including that en route and period for which it will last.

CORBIN.

MANILA. (Received March 21, 1902.)

ADJUTANT-GENERAL, *Washington:*

* * * * * * *

Buford arrived March 21.

CHAFFEE.

ADJUTANT-GENERAL'S OFFICE,
Washington, March 21, 1902.

CHAFFEE, *Manila:*

Transport *Meade* sailed from San Francisco for Manila 19th; recruits unassigned infantry, 628; assigned colored cavalry, 59; Hospital Corps, 33; Signal Corps of the Army, 20.

CORBIN.

ADJUTANT-GENERAL'S OFFICE,
Washington, March 21, 1902.

CHAFFEE, *Manila:*

Secretary of War desires to know if you can substitute chartered vessels for all interisland transports, how soon same can be done, and whether *Relief, Lawton, and Wright,* American vessels, and *Sumner, Burnside, Liscum,* and *Ingalls,* foreign vessels, can be sold to advantage in Orient? How soon could you contract for lighterage service various ports Philippine Islands? Would it be cheaper than present system and what would you recommend done with owned harbor steam vessels and lighters?

CORBIN.

MANILA. (Received March 22, 1902.)

ADJUTANT-GENERAL, *Washington:*

Twenty cases cholera Manila last two days; number of cases fatal.

CHAFFEE.

ADJUTANT-GENERAL'S OFFICE,
Washington, March 22, 1902.

CHAFFEE, *Manila:*

Attention specially called to necessity to disinfect all cholera discharges, sterilize all drinking water, and confer with civil authorities regarding similar action for civilian population.

CORBIN.

MANILA. (Received March 23, 1902.)

ADJUTANT-GENERAL, *Washington:*

March 12, soldier Twenty-seventh Regiment U. S. Infantry, hunting near Parang, shot head, killed instantly. Col. Frank D. Baldwin believes Moros fired shot. On 15th detachment 17 men, Troop A, Fifteenth Regiment U. S. Cavalry, commanded by Lieutenant Forsyth, exploring toward Lake Lanao, aided by friendly Moros, were surrounded; attacked by 200 Moros dense jungle about 25 miles northeast Parang. Private Keller killed. Forsyth had to abandon 18 horses, 2 pack mules, etc., everything except men and arms. While returning next day detachment again attacked, fell back to Bulden, station of supplies, 18 miles Paran. Moros about lake have been generally friendly, except one dato, and opening trails, roads formed by them, Moros doing work. Probably unfriendly dato responsible for attacks on our troops. Shall require guilty parties delivered up, property returned.

*   *   *   *   *   *   *

CHAFFEE.

MANILA. (Received March 26, 1902.)

ADJUTANT-GENERAL, *Washington:*

Authority requested, under paragraph 581 Army Regulations, for publication four newspapers asking bids in order to supply long forage.

*   *   *   *   *   *   *

CHAFFEE.

AFFAIRS IN THE PHILIPPINE ISLANDS.

MANILA. (Received March 27, 1902.)

ADJUTANT-GENERAL, *Washington:*

Executory contract has been made for ground military post; by terms have immediate possession. May we proceed with roads, clearing land, water system, etc.? If yes, place Col. Charles F. Humphrey credit $100,000 of $500,000 appropriated for post. Title land will be perfect; cost $55,000; area 1,801 acres. Contract by next mail.

CHAFFEE.

MANILA. (Received March 28, 1902.)

ADJUTANT-GENERAL, *Washington:*

With reference to your telegram of 19th, we get short-term men home as soon as transportation permits; at sailing each transport have several hundred men left here; over 1,000 now which should be en route. *Grant* loaded Twelfth Regiment U. S. Infantry and men for discharge. *Buford* en route Mindanao, delivering Twenty-seventh Regiment U. S. Infantry. Arrival *Warren* uncertain. *Meade* and *Hancock* about April 20, sailing about May 1; therefore *Buford* only probable departure during April with Ninth and Twenty-first regiments U. S. Infantry, squadron Third Regiment U. S. Cavalry; over 2,000 short-term men in view for departure.

* * * * * * *

CHAFFEE.

ADJUTANT-GENERAL'S OFFICE,
Washington, March 29, 1902.

CHAFFEE, *Manila:*

You should sail transports *Warren* and *Hancock* for San Francisco, due in Manila 6th and 12th. Men for discharge should have preference over organizations; not less than one company with each transport for guard. Will send *Sheridan* April 1, *Kilpatrick* April 10, *Sherman* April 16, *Crook* April 20, and *Logan* May 1. Will these meet requirements?

* * * * * * *

CORBIN.

MANILA. (Received March 31, 1902.)

ADJUTANT-GENERAL, *Washington:*

* * * * * *

We should no longer delay construction storehouses, thereby reducing monthly expense about $7,000. Commerce greatly interfered with by our present location. Will have get away soon because public demand better custom-house facilities. Rainy season by July, hence haste work very important. Civil government consents to building on ground occupied. Land transportation undisputed for three years. Let us have funds storehouse immediately.

CHAFFEE.

MANILA. (Received April 1, 1902.)

ADJUTANT-GENERAL, *Washington:*

Grant sailed March 31, direct Honolulu. Has been held here five days quarantine. Twenty-eight officers, 648 enlisted men, Twelfth Regiment U. S. Infantry; 835 short-term men, 59 sick, 3 insane.

With reference to your telegram of 29th ultimo, transports mentioned sufficient for requirements to June 15.

* * * * * * *

CHAFFEE.

ADJUTANT-GENERAL'S OFFICE,
Washington, April 2, 1902.

CHAFFEE, *Manila:*

Secretary of War desires that investigation directed by letter of the Adjutant-General of the Army February 19th, into truth of the charges made by Cornelius Gardener, be prosecuted and report made thereon with all speed which is consistent with thorough, searching investigation. Full facilities should be afforded Cornelius Gardener to establish truth of the specifications, which, of course, he will be called upon to furnish.

CORBIN.

MANILA. (Received April 2, 1902.)

ADJUTANT-GENERAL, *Washington:*

* * * * * * *

It is insisted, and I think with justice, that service rendered in one quarter should be paid for at the rate of exchange established by the civil governor for that quarter, though paid at subsequent date; native labor accounts for last quarter should be paid at the 2.10 rate, not at the 2.27 rate fixed for the present quarter; payment was due on conclusion of service rendered, but it is rare that accounts can be paid immediately. It is not right for the government to do an injustice; therefore payment should be made at the rate ruling at the time of service rendered.

CHAFFEE.

ADJUTANT-GENERAL'S OFFICE,
Washington, April 2, 1902.

CHAFFEE, *Manila:*

Transport *Sheridan* sailed from San Francisco for Manila 1st; Twenty-ninth Regiment U. S. Infantry, 64 Hospital Corps, 158 Ninth Regiment U. S. Infantry, 25 miscellaneous recruits.

CORBIN.

ADJUTANT-GENERAL'S OFFICE,
Washington, April 2, 1902.

CHAFFEE, *Manila:*

Story Manila Times maltreatment Private Richter by Lieutenant Sinclair, Twenty-eighth Infantry, resulting in soldier's death, republished in papers here; have thorough investigation made and cable facts. If true as printed, Secwar directs that you apply drastic disciplinary measures.

CORBIN.

MANILA. (Received April 3, 1902.)

ADJUTANT-GENERAL, *Washington:*

* * * * * * *

Transport *Warren* arrived April 2.

CHAFFEE.

MANILA. (Received April 3, 1902.)

ADJUTANT-GENERAL, *Washington:*

* * * * * * *

From what funds are expenses of witnesses before military commissions paid?

CHAFFEE.

ADJUTANT-GENERAL'S OFFICE,
Washington, April 3, 1902.

CHAFFEE, *Manila:*

With reference to your telegram 31st ultimo, Secretary of War authorizes $75,000 sixteen storehouse. Understood material required from the United States additional. Have chief quartermaster telegraph as soon as possible material required. With reference to Col. Charles F. Humphrey cablegram March 31, it is understood that all funds for barracks and quarters required in addition to above to June 30 are $75,000 rents, $25,000 construction repair. Are we correct?

CORBIN.

MANILA. (Received April 4, 1902.)

ADJUTANT-GENERAL, *Washington:*

*   *   *   *   *   *   *

With reference to your telegram of 3d, construction, Col. Charles F. Humphrey, March 31, you are correct.

CHAFFEE.

MANILA. (Received April 4, 1902.)

ADJUTANT-GENERAL, *Washington:*

*   *   *   *   *   *   *

In case of Lieutenant Sinclair, was investigated at the time, officer tried, acquitted by the court. Papers were sent by last mail March 28. Facts, Richter drunk, very abusive, gagged by Sinclair, died soon after.

CHAFFEE.

ADJUTANT-GENERAL'S OFFICE,
Washington, April 4, 1902.

CHAFFEE, *Manila:*

Telegraph number enlisted men, cavalry, artillery, infantry, now actually in service division.

CORBIN.

MANILA. (Received April 7, 1902.)

ADJUTANT-GENERAL, *Washington:*

*   *   *   *   *   *   *

Request that I be granted authority to discharge without honor, for cause, Philippine scouts.

CHAFFEE.

ADJUTANT-GENERAL'S OFFICE,
Washington, April 7, 1902.

CHAFFEE, *Manila:*

Cable Sinclair and Richter not satisfactory to the Secretary of War. How far was Sinclair to blame if, as you report, "gagged by Sinclair and died?" On what grounds did court hold him guiltless? Great interest by the press and people; more extensive report desired by cable.

CORBIN.

MANILA. (Received April 7, 1902.)

ADJUTANT-GENERAL, *Washington:*

Sumner and *Relief* at Shanghai undergoing repair per authority of cable from Quartermaster-General March 2. *Relief* expected to return about three weeks; *Lawton* in constant use; probably two months before can obtain ships now in Europe desirable to charter. Prices are too high here and ships too large for what we want, viz, ships that can enter Pasig River. Col. Charles F. Humphrey can give no encouragement in offering our ships for sale in this vicinity. We shall be badly crippled to lose *Lawton* before middle June. *Relief* may depart as soon as returned. If *Burnside* is recalled new cable ship will have to be supplied or else submit to long delays and heavy charges to obtain repair ship from Singapore when needed. Two repairs to cable leading out from Zamboanga last month damaged by currents, wear of cable on rock. Communication with Zamboanga interrupted for week past. *Burnside* will effect repair in about five days. Renew recommendation that *Liscum* be repaired immediately; that she be not sold. Much hampered for ship to transport animals. Papers mailed. Col. Charles F. Humphrey and James B. Aleshire believe it is impracticable to contract for handling our freight Manila Bay at present. I believe to do so will largely increase expense. Dispose of our facilities we will be taken by the throat sure.

Leave to-day on *Princeton* for Zamboanga, consult Brig. Gen. George W. Davis, on Moro situation; absent about ten days.

* * * * * * *

CHAFFEE.

MANILA. (Received April 9, 1902.)

ADJUTANT-GENERAL, *Washington:*

* * * * * *

With reference to your telegram of 4th, cavalry 6,687, artillery 736, infantry 22,277.

CHAFFEE.

MANILA. (Received April 10, 1902.)

ADJUTANT-GENERAL, *Washington:*

With reference to your telegram of 7th, Richter prisoner guardhouse Dasmariñas awaiting trial general court-martial; very drunk, noisy, defiant; when ordered by Sinclair, officer of the day, keep quiet, became violently profane, abusive; forcibly taken from guardhouse to open air, hands tied, water thrown on face to quiet without effect. He called on other prisoners for help; then ordered gagged by Sinclair to force him to keep quiet. Gagged about ten, twelve minutes; became quiet; gag removed; returned to guardhouse; half hour later noticed very quiet. Surgeon summoned, pronounced soldier dead. Evidence before court indicates man died collapse lungs, due entrance foreign matter. From examination record trial presumably court acquitted Sinclair because his extreme action seemed necessary maintain prison discipline; trial Third Brigade approved by Bell. Record forwarded by next mail; inspectors report this case on *Grant*.

* * * * * * *

CHAFFEE.

WAR DEPARTMENT, ADJUTANT-GENERAL'S OFFICE,
Washington, April 10, 1902.

The COMMANDING GENERAL,
Division of the Philippines, Manila, P. I.

SIR: I am directed by the Secretary of War to inclose for your information copy of report of William P. Rohde [Rhode] to the attorney-general of the Philippines, dated February 7, 1902,[a] with special reference to the manner in which evidence was obtained by Capt. James A. Ryan, Fifteenth Cavalry, from prisoners at Jiminez, Mindanao, with instructions to ascertain whether the facts stated can be substantiated and if so to place Captain Ryan on trial.

Very respectfully,

GEO. ANDREWS,
Assistant Adjutant General.

---

[a] Printed on page 2198 of Proceedings of Senate Committee on the Philippines.

MANILA. (Received April 15, 1902.)

ADJUTANT-GENERAL, *Washington:*

With reference to my telegram of 23d ultimo, reporting attack by Moros reconnoissance under Forsyth March 15, soldier Twenty-seventh Regiment U. S. Infantry murdered by Moros vicinity Paran-Paran. March 3 two soldiers Twenty-seventh Regiment U. S. Infantry, having one gun, were approached with semblance friendship by six Moros, near Malabang; rifle seized, one soldier killed, other severely wounded, but escaped. Murder without provocation or justification in any way. Murderers known; demand has been made for their surrender. Thus far dattos refused deliver them. Have been Malabang; tried confer with them; waited three days. Dattos failed come or acknowledge receipt of my request conference. Expedition 1,200 men, under Col. Frank D. Baldwin, cavalry, artillery, being formed, leaving for Lake Lanao about April 27; purpose arrest murderers, punish dattos. Every care to be taken not bring general war with Moros about lake. Absolutely important our authority respected by these people, that sovereignty United States fully acknowledged. Have addressed letter to this effect to dattos, at the same time informing them of friendly disposition of Government; that purpose was punish only those given offense; that Government claims right explore country between Illana, Ilimar bays; that my purpose do so now and at any other time. Accomplishment this object necessary retain battalion Seventeenth two months longer. My belief present time large majority dattos will not support those implicated murders.

*　　*　　*　　*　　*　　*　　*

CHAFFEE.

MANILA. (Received April 16, 1902.)

ADJUTANT-GENERAL, *Washington:*

Unconditional surrender Malvar to-day to Brig. Gen. J. Franklin Bell. Organized armed resistance to United States terminated Department North Philippines.

*　　*　　*　　*　　*　　*　　*

CHAFFEE.

ADJUTANT-GENERAL'S OFFICE,
Washington, April 17, 1902.

CHAFFEE, *Manila:*

Acting Secretary of War directs me inform you President wishes through you to express his gratification and gratification American people at results campaign of J. Franklin Bell and officers and men his command in Batangas and Laguna Provinces which culminated in surrender insurgent forces under Malvar, and which will further extend the territory in which civil government is exercised.

CORBIN.

ADJUTANT-GENERAL'S OFFICE,
Washington, April 16, 1902.

CHAFFEE, *Manila:*

February 19 letter was sent you inclosing for investigation copy of charges made by Governor Gardener of Tayabas Province (Luzon), which contained general allegations of cruelties practiced by troops on natives, and generally of an insolent and brutal attitude of the army toward natives. On April 2 cablegram was sent you urging action with all speed consistent with thorough and searching investigation. March

4 cablegram was sent you directing disciplinary measures to produce obedience to President's instructions subordinating military officers to civil government in pacified provinces and instructing you to relieve Maj. Edwin F. Glenn and Capt. James A. Ryan from duty and order them to Manila to await investigation into their conduct, in accordance with instructions to follow by mail. March 24 instructions were mailed you containing statement of charges against those officers and Gen. Jacob H. Smith as the basis of the investigation ordered by the cable of March 4. Further instructions in both matters are required by the following facts: Press dispatches state that upon the trial of Major Waller, of the Marine Corps, testimony was given by Waller, corroborated by other witnesses, that Gen. Jacob H. Smith instructed him to kill and burn; that the more he killed and burned the better pleased General Smith would be; that it was no time to take prisoners; and that when Major Waller asked General Smith to define the age limit for killing he replied, "Everything over 10." If such testimony was given, and the facts can be established, you will place General Smith on trial by court-martial. Yesterday, before Senate Committee on Philippines, Sergt. Charles S. Riley and Private William Lewis Smith, of the Twenty-sixth Volunteer Infantry, testified that the form of torture known as the "water cure" was administered to the presidente of the town of Igbarras, Iloilo Province, Panay, by a detachment of the Eighteenth Regiment U. S. Infantry, under command Lieut. Arthur L. Conger, under orders of Maj. Edwin F. Glenn, then captain, Twenty-fifth Regiment U. S. Infantry, and that Capt. and Asst. Surg. Palmer Lyon, at that time a contract surgeon, was present to assist them. The officers named, or such of them as are found to be responsible for the act, will be tried therefor by court-martial. Conger and Lyon are in the United States. Twenty-sixth Volunteer Infantry and Eighteenth Regiment U. S. Infantry having returned to United States, and most of the witnesses being presumptively here, Secretary of War directs Maj. Edwin F. Glenn be directed proceed to San Francisco and report to commanding general, Department of California, with a view to his trial by court-martial under charges alleging the cruelties practiced by him upon a native of the Philippine Islands at Igbarras June 27, 1900. If you can discover any witnesses still in the service in the Philippine Islands who can testify in support of the charges, or if Major Glenn desires attendance of any persons now serving in the islands as witnesses for defense, direct them proceed to San Francisco for that purpose. As the two years allowed for the prosecution by statutes of limitation is nearly at an end, no time is to be lost. Take such course in advancing or postponing investigations previously ordered into conduct General Smith and Major Glenn as shall be required to enable you to execute these instructions. It is believed the violations of law and humanity, of which these cases, if true, are examples, will prove to be few and occasional and not to characterize the conduct of the army generally in the Philippine Islands, but the fact that any such acts of cruelty and barbarity appear to have been done indicates necessity of most thorough and searching and exhaustive investigation under the general charges preferred by Governor Gardener, and you will spare no effort in the investigation already ordered under these charges to uncover every such case which may have occurred and bring the offenders to justice. The President desires to know in the fullest and most circumstantial manner all the facts, nothing being concealed and no man being for any reason favored or shielded. For the very reason that the President intends back up the army in the heartiest fashion in every lawful and legitimate method of doing its work, he also intends to see that the most rigorous care is exercised to detect and prevent any cruelty or brutality, and that men guilty thereof are punished. Great as the provocation has been in dealing with foes who habitually resort to treachery, murder, and torture against our men, nothing can justify or will be held to justify the use of torture or inhuman conduct of any kind on the part of the American Army.

By direction of the Secretary of War:

CORBIN.

AFFAIRS IN THE PHILIPPINE ISLANDS. 1329

MANILA. (Received April 19, 1902.)

ADJUTANT-GENERAL, *Washington:*

* * * * * * *

Reference your cable 17th, inquiry into Waller case disclosed inference that presidente of Basey and two native prisoners had been shot through influence, direction, or knowledge Major Glenn and Lieutenant Cook, Philippine Scouts; that padre of Basey had been improperly treated by direction or knowledge of Major Glenn. Major Watts instructed ascertain fact. His report recently received (and) examined by me yesterday shows necessity trial Lieutenant Cook for murder [and] Lieutenant Gaujot for water cure of three padres. Probability both cases may involve Glenn to extent that officers acted according his instructions. Glenn should not therefore be ordered San Francisco. He can be charged with directing application water cure to president Igbarras as stated in your cable. Conger [and] Lyon, the presidente, Mr. Riley, and Smith to be cited as witnesses and sent out here. Two latter may not be required Glenn's case, but if Conger [and] Lyon be tried they doubtless will be needed witnesses. Inquiry will be sent [set] on foot obtain evidence at Igbarras. Waller testified incidence substance as cabled by you regarding conversation had with General Smith. Captain Porter, Marines, testified having conversation two other officers. Say Waller told them regarding it very soon after occurrence. Smith now on *Buford*, quarantined, sailing 20th, but as you direct will retain him bring trial. Of course he intended remarks to refer persons hostile to troops, not those friendly; any other inference will do him injustice. Sorely impossible convey in words correct idea difficulties been met with by officers in prosecution this war, nor can President fully comprehend that very much necessary success would have failed of accomplishment had not serious measures been used force disclosure information. Some officers have doubtless failed in exercise due discretion, blood grown hot in their dealings with deceit and lying, hence severity. some few occassions. This regretted. Record Waller trial not yet in. Sent probably May 1. Waller acquitted by court.

* * * * * * *

CHAFFEE.

ADJUTANT-GENERAL'S OFFICE,
Washington, April 20, 1902.

CHAFFEE, *Manila:*

Expedition ordered under Baldwin will not leave coast until you hear from here. This will not, however, interfere with complete preparation.

CORBIN.

ADJUTANT-GENERAL'S OFFICE,
Washington, April 21, 1902.

CHAFFEE, *Manila:*

SPECIAL ORDERS, } WAR DEPARTMENT,
No. 1. } ADJUTANT-GENERAL'S OFFICE,
Washington, April 21, 1902.

The following order is published for the information and guidance of all concerned:

WAR DEPARTMENT, *Washington, April 21, 1902.*

By direction of the President, a general court-martial is hereby appointed to meet at Manila, Philippine Islands, at 10 o'clock ante meridian, on Tuesday the 24th day of April, 1902, or as soon thereafter as practicable, for the trial of Brig. Gen. Jacob H. Smith, U. S. Army, and such other persons as may be brought before it. Detail for the court: Maj. Gen. Loyd Wheaton, U. S. Army; Brig. Gen. Samuel S. Sumner, U. S. Army; Brig. Gen. J. Franklin Bell, U. S. Army; Brig. Gen. William H. Bisbee, U. S. Army; Col. Chambers McKibbin, Twenty-fourth Regiment U. S. Infantry; Col. William A. Rafferty, Fifth Regiment U. S. Cavalry; Col. William E. Dougherty, Eighth Regiment U. S. Infantry; Col. Alfred C. Markley, Thirteenth Regiment U. S. Infantry; Col. Jesse M. Lee, Thirtieth Regiment U. S. Infantry; Maj. Harvey C. Carbaugh, judge-advocate, U. S. Army, judge-advocate of the court.

WM. CARY SANGER,
Acting Secretary of War.

By order of the Acting Secretary of War:

H. C. CORBIN, *Adjutant-General.*

MANILA. (Received April 21, 1902.)

ADJUTANT-GENERAL, *Washington:*

On behalf Brig. Gen. J. Franklin Bell, his officers and men, I beg to thank the President for expression of his personal gratification and for information that American people are also gratified each because surrender Malvar and forces hitherto supporting the cause of the insurrection under his leadership in province Batangas, Laguna, Tayabas, and island Mindoro.

CHAFFEE.

MANILA. (Received April 21, 1902.)

ADJUTANT-GENERAL, *Washington:*

* * * * * * *

Transports *Meade* and *McClellan* arrived April 21.

CHAFFEE.

ADJUTANT-GENERAL'S OFFICE,
Washington, April 22, 1902.

CHAFFEE, *Manila:*

Crook sailed April 21 with Second Battalion Eleventh Regiment U. S. Infantry and 36 Hospital Corps men.

CORBIN.

ADJUTANT-GENERAL'S OFFICE,
Washington, April 20, 1902.

CHAFFEE, *Manila:*

Expedition ordered under Baldwin will not leave coast until you hear from here. This will not, however, interfere with complete preparation.

* * * * * * *

CORBIN.

MANILA. (Received April 22, 1902.)

ADJUTANT-GENERAL, *Washington:*

With reference to my telegram of 15th, yours 21st, when at Malabang authorized Baldwin continue clearing trail toward lake if not opposed, but he was not to move in force until expedition was fully prepared, which I expected to accomplish by 25th. On 18th he pushed his advance from camp 8 miles out, with orders to clear blockaded trail, halt when it reached sufficient water, which was not found until second crossing Maliling River where it issues from Lake Tapao. Advance consisted one battalion Twenty-seventh Regiment U. S. Infantry, under Major Scott. He reached Tapao without opposition, but found trail badly obstructed fallen timber. Baldwin arrived same place noon 20th with Moore's battalion and mountain battery. In order to find defensive camp and grazing to north of him he sent forward Moore's battalion, one gun. Moore was fired on from hills in front and to his left. He returned fire, but did not advance. Baldwin brought forward rest of battery, three infantry companies, and drove off assailants; firing distance 1,100 down to 300 yards. Excellent firing by battery. Enemy driven 2 miles and scattered. No casualties our troops. Seven Moro bodies found. Opposing Moros from Pinellas village, whose fort is in sight, flying red flag. Yesterday morning delegation arrived at Baldwin's camp from Ganasi, making absolute submission United States authority under terms my proclamation. Yesterday morning there was an affair of few minutes with Sultan of Pualao's men, who attempted reoccupy ground cleared day before, and they were forcibly dispersed. Baldwin says will be necessary reduce fort at Pulas, if it continues hostile, before passing it. Altitude camp, 2,650 feet. Davis says he has ordered Baldwin not to assault any fort or occupy hostile places until the two weeks' time which I granted the Moros to surrender murderers has expired. Yours yesterday was sent at once to Davis; received by him 10.50 p. m. He has ordered Baldwin to abstain absolutely from any aggressive movement, but to favor in every way possible friendly conference. To withdraw all our forces will ruin our prestige; to withdraw part of force will be dangerous. Have ordered trail cleared to rear quickly. Eight miles was well opened when I was there. Shall maintain our position, but not advance further until you are heard from. Febiger's battalion of 200 is in reserve. Baldwin's advance to so great distance was premature, but occasioned by opportunity to seize advantage in situation and position for camping troops. Pershing at Iligan says everything quiet. He is confident Moros on north side have no idea of rising.

CHAFFEE.

ADJUTANT-GENERAL'S OFFICE,
Washington, April 22, 1902.

CHAFFEE, *Manila:*

The President is anxious that no expedition be made against Moros until all efforts by negotiation have been exhausted. To this end he desires that you confer freely with the acting civil governor. In the event the force has to be sent, he directs that it go under the immediate command of General Davis. The President will give you all support, but desires exercise of great care and prudence. If possible avoid by all honorable means general war.

CORBIN.

ADJUTANT-GENERAL'S OFFICE,
Washington, April 22, 1902.

CHAFFEE, *Manila:*

* * * * * * *

With reference to previous cables on subject it has been suggested to President that possibly surrender of the Moro murderers might be effected by instrumentality friendly dattos. President desires this considered in conference with Wright, and to have assurance every honorable peaceful remedy has been exhausted.

CORBIN.

ADJUTANT-GENERAL'S OFFICE,
Washington, April 23, 1902.

CHAFFEE, *Manila:*

Your cable of yesterday has been submitted by the Acting Secretary of War to the President, who directs that you keep in mind the President's orders, but of course do nothing that will impair our prestige or in any other way imperil the army. If, after the expiration of the time named in your proclamation, and after all possible diplomatic and friendly methods have been exhausted, your demand for the Moro murderers has not been met, you will act upon the lines that in your judgment will best serve to bring about peace and order in the island of Mindanao.

CORBIN.

MANILA. (Received April 23, 1902.)

ADJUTANT-GENERAL, *Washington:*

* * * * * * *

Buford sailed 22d; headquarters; 52 enlisted men; Troop E, Third Cavalry, 61 enlisted men; Troop F, Third Cavalry, 668 short-term enlisted men.

CHAFFEE.

MANILA. (Received April 23, 1902.)

ADJUTANT-GENERAL, *Washington:*

With reference to your telegram of 17th, instructions mailed March 24 not received, and have no charges against Brig. Gen. Jacob H. Smith other than arising from testimony adduced before Waller court.

* * * * * * *

CHAFFEE.

MANILA. (Received April 24, 1902.)

ADJUTANT-GENERAL, *Washington:*

* * * * * * *

With reference to your telegram of 22d, and two April 23, we will endeavor not become involved in war with Moros. All my actions and instructions have had in view avoiding any conflict at all. We must not fail duty which demands application Mosaic law, "An eye for an eye," when dealing with savages who know no other way obtaining redress for wrong, and count all as cowards who fail to make the demand and execute it. Every murder of a soldier by Moro must be satisfied by punishment of offender in our courts. If this be not done better to leave country so favorable for the crime. Certain it is that for each offense we condone 10 crimes will follow, and that great island will remain terra incognita. Better for Moros that army press into their settlements in friendly spirit than stand barred out at their gates and lose their respect. We can never become friends in such situation. Before Baldwin could be communicated with he had taken fort at Pulas after slight resistance; no casualties. Very soon after neighboring town of Ganasi opened its doors, hoisted white flag, and delivered red flag. Datto Lampok and others with strong following asked permission to call and make peace. Datto Amani Pack, of Ganasi, who sent threatening message in reply my letter, is one of those who have submitted. Camp is 2 miles from Ganasi, whose Sultan has asked Baldwin come there. Have directed him not to move. He is 10 miles from Datto. It is my purpose to have interview with General Davis; will go on *Hancock*, which left here to-day for Malabang with battalion Tenth Infantry. It is our purpose to show considerable force troops to lake Moros, converse with dattos, then retire troops by different trails to Malabang and Paran; thereafter to send expeditions occasionally to lake. We supposed Ganasi 35 miles from Malabang, actually short 21. No fighting; not necessary overcome opposition to advance to present location troops. Seven hundred and seventy-five men with Baldwin; 2 troops cavalry dismounted 12 miles in rear. Reserve Malabang telegraph line 3 miles from Baldwin. Every effort will be made prevent general war. Davis says situation this time very favorable.

CHAFFEE.

AFFAIRS IN THE PHILIPPINE ISLANDS. 1333

ADJUTANT-GENERAL'S OFFICE,
Washington, April 25, 1902.

CHAFFEE, *Manila.*

Your cable yesterday reference situation Mindanao has been submitted to President, who remarks that the portion down to the words "Before Baldwin" should have been sent by mail. Remainder message approved by President. Acting Secretary of War confirms previous instructions that no movement or action be made that will in any way impair prestige of army and settlement questions at issue.

CORBIN.

ADJUTANT-GENERAL'S OFFICE,
Washington, April 28, 1902.

CHAFFEE, *Manila:*

With reference to your telegram of 26th, Acting Secretary of War directs on completion trial Jacob H. Smith that court will adjourn. Cable names officers for trial of Glenn and others. President will order court at Catbalogan, you preparing charges in each case.

CORBIN.

MANILA. (Received May 1, 1902.)

ADJUTANT-GENERAL, *Washington, D. C.:*

Transport *Sheridan* arrived to-day.

CHAFFEE.

ADJUTANT-GENERAL'S OFFICE,
Washington, May 1, 1902.

CHAFFEE, *Manila:*

Has Cornelius Gardener filed specifications under investigation ordered February 19? State condition of investigation. Cable fully.

CORBIN.

ADJUTANT-GENERAL'S OFFICE,
Washington, May 1, 1902.

CHAFFEE, *Manila:*

Agents Warner, Barnes & Co. and Smith Bell & Co. charge discrimination. Secretary of War desires to know what action has been taken.

CORBIN.

ADJUTANT-GENERAL'S OFFICE,
Washington, May 2, 1902.

CHAFFEE, *Manila:*

On what information was trial Waller instituted, date of information, and order for court? Reply as soon as possible.

CORBIN.

ADJUTANT-GENERAL'S OFFICE,
Washington, May 2, 1902.

CHAFFEE, *Manila:*

Reply as soon as possible to cable yesterday concerning Gardener investigation.

CORBIN.

MANILA. (Received May 2, 1902.)

ADJUTANT-GENERAL, *Washington, D. C.:*

With reference to telegram of 1st, agents firms referred to expelled from Samar by Maj. Gen. Robert P. Hughes because while engaged in trade Samar paid leaders insurrection tax levied by them on hemp and supplied them rice. Recently British consul called behalf these firms wanting resume trade; application refused until ports opened. Alleged discrimination because other party on brigade commander's and my request had delivered rice, some other supplies, some ports in order prevent suffering among people. This military matter. When ports opened, probably May 10, firms may resume business.

CHAFFEE.

MANILA. (Received May 2, 1902.)

ADJUTANT-GENERAL, *Washington, D. C.:*

With reference to your telegram of 1st, Maj. Cornelius Gardener has filed few specifications; very general in character; practically paragraphing his report. One instance gives name an officer. Board, Col. Theodore J. Wint, Lieut. Col. Jos. W. Duncan, Capt. William T. Johnston; sitting Lucena, under instruction afford Major Gardener full opportunity substantiate every allegation. Maj. Cornelius Gardener has telegraphed Luke E. Wright that investigation has developed into attack on him. Asked counsel; Lieutenant Trent authorized aid him. Wint directed afford Gardener every opportunity. Following his reply, Capt. Harry H. Bandholtz, governor, has since yesterday acted counsel for Gardener, who up to the present declined furnish names any witnesses to board. He has brought several witnesses, but so far his procedure indicates he does not desire attack Gardener, but is pursuing rigid investigation his allegations, irrespective what he wishes, and will not permit him shape or dictate course investigation. Think any objection Maj. Cornelius Gardener lays in fact that board desires test accuracy his information and condition Tayabas when he was governor. Some time must necessarily elapse before report completed; probably many witnesses to be examined.

CHAFFEE.

WAR DEPARTMENT,
Washington, May 2, 1902.

CHAFFEE, *Manilla:*

Cable in full Major Gardener's specifications. Your directions to board to afford Gardener every opportunity are approved. Board should be especially enjoined not to permit the proceeding to assume a character giving the least color to a claim that there is an attack on him or allow it to be in any way diverted from a full and fair investigation of the truth of his charges.

ROOT.

ADJUTANT-GENERAL'S OFFICE,
Washington, May 3, 1902.

CHAFFEE, *Manila:*

Investigate *Sumner* collision Shanghai, ascertain responsibility, and submit report.

CORBIN.

ADJUTANT-GENERAL'S OFFICE,
Washington, May 3, 1902.

CHAFFEE, *Manila:*

Referring to letter of February 28, Secretary of War directs send telegrams, records, correspondence, captured Cabucabuan; also all similar insurgent papers not previously sent. Such papers invaluable here.

CORBIN.

ADJUTANT-GENERAL'S OFFICE,
Washington, May 3, 1902.

CHAFFEE, *Manila:*

When will natives collected near and in towns under General Bell's order December 8, 1901, be able to return their homes under last clause that order?

CORBIN.

ADJUTANT-GENERAL'S OFFICE,
Washington, May 3, 1902.

CHAFFEE, *Manila:*

Cable in full such statement and explanation as General Smith may have given court-martial proceedings regarding conversation with Waller mentioned by dispatch 15th April.

MANILA. (Received May 3, 1902.)

ADJUTANT-GENERAL, *Washington, D. C.:*

With reference to telegram of 2d, while I was at Tacloban, January 23, Lieutenant Day, Marines, talked presence Capt. George O. Squier regarding his shooting natives Basey two or three days before. Squier informed Capt. Frank DeW. Ramsey, who informed me. Ordered investigation immediately, resulting charges murder against Waller and Day. Conference was held with Remey. We agreed Waller, Day should be tried court-martial under army jurisdiction. Order for court Special Order No. 54, paragraph 10, amended by Special Order No. 58, paragraph 1; 60, paragraph 4, Division of the Philippines. Court met March 17; proceedings received April 25. Order has not been published. Review now in my hands.

MANILA. (Received May 3, 1902.)

ADJUTANT-GENERAL, *Washington, D. C.:*

After much talk with Datto Bayan, Brig. Gen. George W. Davis demanded May 1 that murderers and horses be given up or Datto send peace delegation talk with him by noon May 2. Message delivered noon May 1; messenger not returned 11 o'clock May 2. During night our troops fired upon. Did not reply. Moros again fired upon troops morning May 2; squads went out drove off approaching Moros. Eleven o'clock troops attacked took fort without loss; 1,300 yards beyond, another fort strongest work; attacked it. Dispatch from Davis says our troops surrounded fort 3 o'clock. Firing in progress 5 o'clock. About 20 men wounded; also First Lieut. Henry S. Wagner, General Davis's aid, and Lieutenant Jossman, Twenty-seventh Infantry; former seriously.

CHAFFEE.

WHITE HOUSE,
Washington, May 4, 1902.

CHAFFEE, *Manila:*

Accept for the army under your command, and express to General Davis and Colonel Baldwin especially, my congratulations and thanks for the splendid courage and fidelity which have again carried our flag to victory. Your fellow-countrymen at home will ever honor the memory of the fallen, and be faithful to the brave survivors who have themselves been faithful unto death for their country's sake.

THEODORE ROOSEVELT.

MANILA. (Received May 4, 1902.)

ADJUTANT-GENERAL, *Washington, D. C.:*

Report full substance [Brig. Gen.] George W. Davis's message May 3 from Bayan:
"Eighty-four survivors Bayan surrendered unconditionally this morning at 7. Sultan Bayan, Raja Muda Bayan, Sultan Pandapatan, and all leading dattos dead and many their followers. Assault principal fort which surrendered last night one most gallant performances American arms. Col. Frank D. Baldwin and his regiment deserve all praise, hand-to-hand struggle in four lines of ditches under walls of fort. These trenches are lined with Moro dead from rifle fire. Have never seen heard any performance excelling this gallantry grit. Painful duty report overthrow Moro power not accomplished without severe loss. One officer, 7 enlisted killed, 4 officers, 37 enlisted wounded. Telegraph list later. After 84 survivors marched out this morning as prisoners and was understood they were all, 8 others, who had concealed themselves in rubbish inside fort, made break for liberty; tried cut way out; none succeeded. Some Moro wounded tried stab soldiers trying help them. Impossible to state number Moros killed; many lying in tall grass. Surrender saves us from siege and starving out or escalade. Impossible to have carried works without scaling ladders, which were ready. Intend retain prisoners until two or three small adjacent forts occupied; then, with your consent, to retain hostages, 8 or 10 principals, release others; force in line for advance; 4 mountain guns, 470 rifles; this fully sufficient. Could not use more men advantageously. Had we sent strong column would only have swelled casualty list. One neighboring datto already presented himself as friend, and expect general coming in shortly, when weight blow known. Dead sent Malabang for burial. In light present knowledge could have besieged principal forts and in time forced surrender, but that would probably resulted in sortie for freedom and escape for many. By attacking them have been completely crushed. The only kind of lesson these wild Moros seem to be able to profit by. Shall invite Sultan Sarac pay me friendly visit, if he does not do so his own initiative; has fort further in plain sight and of same strength as was Bayan on beautiful tableland, thousand acres fine upland rice, and urging people to return its cultivation."

Result to follow this action very important, namely, it secures respect United States of America authority center Moro savagery.

CHAFFEE.

MANILA. (Received May 5, 1902.)

ADJUTANT-GENERAL, *Washington, D. C.:*

With reference to your telegram 3d, natives Laguna Province collected under orders Brig. Gen. J. Franklin Bell allowed return home more than month ago. Batangas Province, Luzon, last of natives relieved of all army surveillance April 16.

CHAFFEE.

MANILA. (Received May 5, 1902.)

ADJUTANT-GENERAL, *Washington, D. C.:*

Brig. Gen. Jacob H. Smith did not testify as witness. He plead not guilty; admitted in writing to court "that he did give certain instructions relating to hostiles under arms in field, and instructed him not to burden himself with prisoners, of which he, General Smith, already had so many that efficiency his command was impaired; that he did tell him he wanted kill and burn in interior and hostile country; further instructed him that the interior of Samar must be made a howling wilderness, and further instructed him that he wanted all persons killed who were capable of bearing arms and were engaged in hostilities against United States, and that he designated age limit 10 years, as boys that age were actively engaged hostilities against United States authorities, and were equally dangerous as an enemy as those more mature age."

CHAFFEE.

MANILA. (Received May 5, 1902.)
ADJUTANT-GENERAL, *Washington, D. C.:*
With reference to your telegram March 21, Buencamino sailed *Buford* April 22.
CHAFFEE.

MANILA. (Received May 6, 1902.)
ADJUTANT-GENERAL, *Washington, D. C.:*
Brig. Gen. George W. Davis reports, 1 p. m., Saturday, May 3, Moro prisoners that had been disarmed, sitting on open hilltop surrounded by strong guard, at concerted signal, sprang feet, rushed down hill. Several endeavored to seize rifles guards; one succeeded while soldier drinking from canteen; direction flight such as bring them rear company, so firing upon Moros would endanger our men. Guard and one company opened fire without orders, killing 35; recaptured 9; others escaped. Regret this accident; desire release prisoners except few leaders, encouraging others return peaceful labors.
CHAFFEE.

MANILA. (Received May 6, 1902.)
ADJUTANT-GENERAL, *Washington, D. C.:*
With reference to your telegram 3d, relative record Cabucabuan, papers voluminous. Several hundred being gotten out as soon as possible. Other captured insurgent records here amount several thousand. Needed here constantly for reference. Will be sent. Still some in Tagalog, Visayan. If translation will answer will send fast as prepared.
CHAFFEE.

MANILA. (Received May 6, 1902.)
ADJUTANT-GENERAL, *Washington, D. C.:*
Leave for Lake Lanao to-morrow evening; absent about twelve days; purpose, to view situation.
CHAFFEE.

ADJUTANT-GENERAL'S OFFICE,
Washington, May 7, 1902.
CHAFFEE, *Manila:*
Published letter Walker, Company I, Fifteenth Infantry, states a large number of native prisoners shot at Irocin, near Sorsogon, orders First Lieut. Frank S. Burr. Is there any foundation for story, and what?
CORBIN.

ADJUTANT-GENERAL'S OFFICE,
Washington, May 8, 1902.
CHAFFEE, *Manila:*
Retain Brig. Gen. Jacob H. Smith until further orders.
CORBIN.

ADJUTANT-GENERAL'S OFFICE,
Washington, May 8, 1902.
CHAFFEE, *Manila:*
Forward number posts and number American troops remaining in each province.
CORBIN.

ADJUTANT-GENERAL, *Washington, D. C.:*
MANILA. (Received May 8, 1902.)
Sailed from Batangas May 6, 28 officers, 854 enlisted men, Twenty-first Infantry.

CHAFFEE.

ADJUTANT-GENERAL, *Washington, D. C.:*
MANILA. (Received May 8, 1902.)
Following from Brig. Gen. George W. Davis, May 6: Situation to-day every way satisfactory. No hostile shot been fired since escape prisoners from guard. Would be exceedingly easy for Moros climb bluff, cut our telegraph traversing shore lake 4 miles; not molested. Two o'clock to-day Rinini Tampanga, of Tuburan, and delegation presented themselves. Sultan Ganasi says Datto (1901) Paygoag was killed Bayan Fort and his people dead or dispersed. Will investigate, but doubt whole report. Number prisoners escaped probably not exceeding 25; 10 recaptured unhurt. For miles about country much same its natural aspect as Camp Meade, Pennsylvania; enormous agricultural facilities. All wounded doing well. Lieutenant Jossman seriously hurt; bullet penetrated lung, ranged downward, lodged body; no amputation yet. Chief surgeon says one or two will likely be necessary; hopes recovery without. May 7 leave in morning for Malabang meet General Chaffee, expected morning 10th. No change situation. Wounded doing well. Datto from lower Bayan Fort presented himself, saying his people want peace, promising bring cattle, other supplies.

CHAFFEE.

ADJUTANT-GENERAL'S OFFICE,
Washington, May 10, 1902.
CHAFFEE, *Manila:*
Translation captured insurgent records Tagalog, Visayan, will answer.

CORBIN.

ADJUTANT-GENERAL, *Washington, D. C.:*
MANILA. (Received May 10, 1902.)
With reference to your telegram of 8th, number stations occupied, 253; province of Albay, 2 stations, 3 troops; Bataan, 1 station, 1 company; Batangas, 18, 9 troops, 5 companies; Bulacan, 3, 2 companies; Cagayan, 4, 6 companies; Camarines, 9, 2 troops, 6 companies; Cavite, 11, 2 troops, 6 companies; Ilocos Norte province, Luzon, Ilocos Sur province, Luzon, 7, 12 troops; Laguna, 25, 12 troops, 9 companies; Isabela, 8, 6 companies; Marinduque, 3, 3 companies; Masbate, 1, 2 companies; Mindoro, 6, 6 companies; Nueva Ecija, 5, 4 companies; Pampanga, 3, 3 troops; Pangasinan, 14, 1 troop, 11 companies; Principe, 1, 1. company; Rizal, 18, 6 artillery, 2 engineers, 2 signal, 10 troops, 20 companies; Romblon, 1, 1 company; Sorsogon, 5, 4 companies; Tarlac, 4, 4 companies; Tayabas, 15, 7 troops, 10 companies; Zambales, 3, 4 companies; Bohol, 1, 1 company; Busuanga, 1, 1 company; Capul, 1 detachment; Cebu, 4, 1 engineer, 1 signal, 5 companies; Jolo, 1, 1 troop, 2 companies; Leyte, 7, 5 companies; Mindanao, 21, 1 artillery, 1 engineer, 8 troops, 22 companies; Negros, 3, 2 companies; Panay, 6, 4 troops, 4 companies; Paragua, 2, 1 company; Samar, 37, 4 troops, 31 companies; Siassi, 1, 1 company; Tawi-tawi, 1, 1 company. Sixth, Ninth, Nineteenth Infantry not included; assembling Manila for shipment United States of America.

CHAFFEE.

MANILA. (Received May 13, 1902.)
ADJUTANT-GENERAL, *Washington, D. C.:*
Lanao, May 12: Been here past three days studying situation with Brig. Gen. George W. Davis. Think two battalions should remain if can be supplied. Ganasi trail very difficult, but another trail promises much better. Think withdrawal from Lake would seriously jeopardize safety weaker dattos; would have given friendly assistance, but believe if we remain the more powerful dattos will come in when it is apparent that our mission is friendly. From present indications further hostilities will not be necessary unless provoked by Moros. Bayan caused much astonishment; was extremely necessary wholesome lesson, which don't think will have to be repeated. Some dattos very suspicious and on defensive. Lake country beautiful; more suitable for the occupancy of Americans than any part of the archipelago; elevation, soil, and climate perfect, comparing favorably with any valley of the Alleghenies.

CHAFFEE.

MANILA. (Received May 14, 1902.)
ADJUTANT-GENERAL, *Washington:*
Warren sailed to-day Company I, Ninth Infantry, 650 casuals, 300 marines.

CHAFFEE.

MANILA. (Received May 17, 1902.)
ADJUTANT-GENERAL, *Washington, D. C.:*
Have missing orders and circulars specified my letter March 24 to adjutant-general of Department North Philippines been sent, and when?

CHAFFEE.

MANILA. (Received May 18, 1902.)
ADJUTANT-GENERAL, *Washington, D. C.:*
Col. Theodore J. Wint reports evidence contained 300 pages. Record fails this far prove statements or justify Major Cornelius Gardener's report December 16 as to general maltreatment and abuses. Some special cases. Maj. Cornelius Gardener still some witnesses to introduce, declines furnish names, number. Board already delayed five days, his request.

CHAFFEE.

ADJUTANT-GENERAL'S OFFICE,
Washington, May 19, 1902.
CHAFFEE, *Manila:*
Examine original Dewey's cablegram to Secretary of the Navy February 5, and Elwell S. Otis's cablegram February 5, 1899, and report hour and minute, Manila, time, they were filed in the cable office Manila. Answer quick.

CORBIN.

MANILA. (Received May 20, 1902.)
ADJUTANT-GENERAL, *Washington:*
With reference to your telegram 19th, records cable company show Dewey's message 41 words filed 6.02 evening February 5, message 20 words filed 11 morning February 6. Original messages sent London. Otis message, dated February 5, filed 8.32 morning February 6.

CHAFFEE.

MANILA. (Received May 21, 1902.)
ADJUTANT-GENERAL, *Washington:*
What transports sail from San Francisco June 16, July 1?

CHAFFEE.

ADJUTANT-GENERAL'S OFFICE,
Washington, May 22, 1902.
CHAFFEE, *Manila:*
Prohibit shipment on transports animals, snakes, to the United States and Hawaii.

CORBIN.

ADJUTANT-GENERAL'S OFFICE,
Washington, May 22, 1902.
CHAFFEE, *Manila:*
Telegraphic Circular No. 1, Third Separate Brigade, series 1901, not received. When was it mailed? Unless very long, cable in full immediately.

CORBIN.

ADJUTANT-GENERAL'S OFFICE,
Washington, May 22, 1902.
CHAFFEE, *Manila:*
With reference to your telegram of 21st, *Meade* sails June 16, none July 1, unless transport other than *Hancock* sails immediately for United States. *Hancock* ordered sold on arrival.

CORBIN.

ADJUTANT-GENERAL'S OFFICE,
Washington, May 22, 1902.
CHAFFEE, *Manila:*
Secretary of War desires to know is there any necessity, in your judgment, to modify any orders regarding intercourse with Philippine Islands during prevalence cholera?

CORBIN.

MANILA. (Received May 22, 1902.)
ADJUTANT-GENERAL, *Washington, D. C.:*
Crook arrived May 20.

CHAFFEE.

MANILA. (Received May 22, 1902.)
ADJUTANT-GENERAL, *Washington, D. C.:*
Kilpatrick sailed May 21, 658 casuals, 150 marines, 53 enlisted men Troop G, Third Cavalry, and 58 enlisted men Troop H, Third Cavalry.

CHAF

MANILA. (Received May 22, 1902.)
ADJUTANT-GENERAL, *Washington, D. C.:*
With reference to your telegram 17th, Department of Northern Luzon orders mailed May 5; Third District, First and Second Brigades, May 22; Third and Fourth Brigades, not mailed.

CHAFFEE.

AFFAIRS IN THE PHILIPPINE ISLANDS. 1341

MANILA. (Received May 24, 1902.)
ADJUTANT-GENERAL, *Washington, D. C.:*
Grant should have arrived San Francisco by April 30. Why not sail July 1? Will need for Eighth Infantry, sailing August 15.

CHAFFEE.

MANILA. (Received May 24, 1902.)
ADJUTANT-GENERAL, *Washington, D. C.:*
Warren left Nagasaki May 22; *Hancock*, *Sherman* quarantined here, depart four days; *Sheridan* under repairs; *Crook*, *McClellan* gathering troops for home; *Lawton* transferring last squadron Fifteenth Cavalry, Seventh Brigade; *Burnside* use court Catbalogan; *Sumner*, *Relief* under repairs Shanghai; *Ingalls* exchanging Third Cavalry, Eleventh Cavalry.

CHAFFEE.

MANILA. (Received May 24, 1902.)
ADJUTANT-GENERAL, *Washington, D. C.:*
Unnecessary modify orders regarding intercourse with Philippine Islands during prevalence cholera; due observance sanitary rules; danger slight.

CHAFFEE.

MANILA. (Received May 24, 1902.)
ADJUTANT-GENERAL, *Washington, D. C.:*
Bell's telegraph circular "No. 1" never mailed from here. Advises station commanders he will send them instructions circular form by wire, copies mail. Directs them keep separate file; transferred successors, receipts to be taken. Directs entered on this file any general authority sent an individual commander to pursue particular policy at his station or district. Bell will visit every station as soon as possible and will inspect this file of instructions; brigade inspector will examine it; station commanders to improvise file for filing instructions, and will also enter in station or company books. Any answer to telegram sent by Bell personally may be addressed to him direct.

CHAFFEE.

MANILA. (Received May 24, 1902.)
ADJUTANT-GENERAL, *Washington, D. C.:*
Following from New York Sun, dated Washington, March 31, with reference to bill governing Philippine Islands: "The bill conveys to present government of islands the public property transferred under treaty with Spain to the United States." As long as army remains Philippine Islands much said property occupied by military in Manila, some at other points, will be required its use, and should be retained as property United States. Think it too early for Government to dispossess itself of property which is occupied, and necessarily so.

CHAFFEE.

ADJUTANT-GENERAL'S OFFICE,
Washington, May 26, 1902.
CHAFFEE, *Manila:*
Referring to telegram from your office 26th instant, at the request of the Secretary of the Treasury you are advised Treasury quarantine regulations are applicable to army transports under Executive orders January 3, 1900. Cancel my telegram of May 24 on the same subject.

CORBIN.

ADJUTANT-GENERAL'S OFFICE,
Washington, May 26, 1902.

CHAFFEE, *Manila:*

The Secretary of War desires, if practicable, 50 men belonging to Ninth Infantry having two years' or more service, left by returning companies, to be transferred Company B, Ninth Infantry, and sent to Pekin, China, first opportunity. Report desired.

CORBIN.

ADJUTANT-GENERAL'S OFFICE,
Washington, D. C., May 26, 1902.

CHAFFEE, *Manila:*

Your dispatches May 24. *Grant* out of commission, undergoing repairs; *Buford* will sail on June 2; *Meade*, June 16; *Kilpatrick*, July 1; *Sherman*, July 16. Expedite.

CORBIN.

MANILA. (Received May 26, 1902.)

ADJUTANT-GENERAL, *Washington, D. C.:*

Referring to telegram from your office of 23d instant, was not understood refer quarantine regulations. I am of opinion it is not necessary quarantine transports. Five days thought to be sufficient; slight probability of cholera spreading board ship. Distilling apparatus food prepared as now; quarantine has cost hundred thousand dollars. Referring to telegram from your office 24th instant, unintelligible, but observed to refer quarantine.

CHAFFEE.

MANILA. (Received May 26, 1902.)

ADJUTANT-GENERAL, *Washington, D. C.:*

Referring to your telegram of March 16, 1901, signed Edwards, and instructions auditor for Philippine Islands, January, 1901, advise me from what funds payment accounts due March 31, 1901, but not presented until later will be paid; many such, principally rents, due shelter troops. Should they not be paid from Philippine Islands funds, as would have been done had accounts been presented March 31, 1901, when actually due? Civil government holds it can not appropriate for these accounts. I am of opinion such construction erroneous. Believe Secretary of War intended pay all rent (and) unliquidated damages to include March 31, from Philippine Islands funds.

CHAFFEE.

MANILA. (Received May 27, 1902.)

ADJUTANT-GENERAL, *Washington, D. C.:*

Referring to telegram from your office of 26th instant, men Ninth Infantry transferred. To dispatch will transfer 50 men Thirteenth Infantry, Company B, Ninth Infantry, until otherwise ordered.

CHAFFEE.

MANILA. (Received May 27, 1902.)

ADJUTANT-GENERAL, *Washington, D. C.:*

Transport *Logan* arrived May 26.

CHAFFEE.

ADJUTANT-GENERAL'S OFFICE,
Washington, *May 28, 1902.*

CHAFFEE, *Manila:*
Referring to telegram from your office of 26th instant, the Secretary of War instructed matter held up until condition of Philippine finances can be ascertained. Upon arrival at Manila William H. Taft and Commission afforded an opportunity to consider matters discussed by the Secretary of War with William H. Taft.

CORBIN.

MANILA. (Received May 28, 1902.)
ADJUTANT-GENERAL, *Washington, D. C.:*
Referring to your letter March 24, can secure about 50 suitable men from Thirteenth Infantry and other regiments if I am authorized to transfer. Will need 175 additional engineer recruits.

CHAFFEE.

MANILA. (Received May 29, 1902.)
ADJUTANT-GENERAL, *Washington, D. C.:*
Transport *Hancock* sailed May 27, headquarters, 10 companies, noncommissioned staff, Ninth Infantry—443 enlisted men, 50 prisoners, 314 casuals.

CHAFFEE.

MANILA. (Received May 29, 1902.)
ADJUTANT-GENERAL, *Washington, D. C.:*
Transport *Sherman* sailed May 28, 580 enlisted men Sixth Infantry, 568 enlisted men Nineteenth Infantry, Maj. Gen. Loyd Wheaton, Brig. Gen. Simon Snyder, 151 sick, 11 insane soldiers, 42 discharged soldiers.

CHAFFEE.

WASHINGTON, *June 4, 1902.*
CHAFFEE, *Manila:*
Transport *Buford* sailed June 2.

CORBIN.

MANILA. (Received June 10, 1902.)
ADJUTANT-GENERAL, *Washington:*
Is there any objection pay department receiving deposits enlisted men Philippine scouts?

CHAFFEE.

MANILA. (Received June 10, 1902.)
ADJUTANT-GENERAL, *Washington:*
Transport *Thomas* arrived June 9.

CHAFFEE.

MANILA. (Received June 10, 1902.)
ADJUTANT-GENERAL, *Washington:*
Trials Edwin F. Glenn, Julian E. Gaujot, Norman E. Cook, completed. The court adjourned. Investigation James A. Ryan not completed in time to try before this court. Several members ordered to the United States. Reassembled only much delay, expense, therefore recommend new court to meet Manila June 16—trial

James A. Ryan and others ordered before it. Suggest following several members: Brig. Gen. William H. Bisbee, Col. Theodore J. Wint, Col. William E. Dougherty, Col. Jesse M. Lee, Lieut. Col. John F. Stretch, Lieut. Col. Charles A. P. Hatfield, Lieut. Col. George S. Anderson, Maj. William L. Pitcher, Maj. William W. Wotherspoon, Maj. William C. Buttler, Capt. Hoel S. Bishop, Capt. William C. Brown, Capt. John P. Ryan, Maj. Millard F. Waltz, judge-advocate.

CHAFFEE.

MANILA. (Received June 13, 1902.)

ADJUTANT-GENERAL, *Washington:*

* * * * * * *

More troops Third and Sixth Brigades than desirable to keep there. Can spare Fifteenth Regiment U. S. Infantry, Eighth Regiment U. S. Infantry. Recommend departure in the order named. Eighth Infantry in the midst of cholera; Fifteenth Infantry, not. Am unable to concentrate into larger garrisons as no cover available without constructing.

CHAFFEE.

WASHINGTON, *June 14, 1902.*

CHAFFEE, *Manila:*

When were proceedings Waller case mailed?

* * * * * * *

CORBIN.

WASHINGTON, *June 14, 1902.*

CHAFFEE, *Manila:*

* * * * * * *

No objection Pay Department receiving deposits enlisted men Philippine Scouts.

CORBIN.

WASHINGTON, *June 14, 1902.*

CHAFFEE, *Manila:*

Special Orders, No. 2, War Department, Adjutant-General's Office, Washington, June 14, 1902, appointing a general court-martial to meet at Manila, P. I., Monday, June 16, 1902, for trial of Capt. James A. Ryan, Fifteenth Infantry, and such other persons as may be brought before it. Detail of court.

CORBIN.

WASHINGTON, *June 14, 1902.*

CHAFFEE, *Manila:*

With reference to your letter of May 5, your dispatch of the same day, the Secretary of War directs you convene at once a board consisting of yourself and three senior medical officers on duty at Manila, to determine and report upon Jacob H. Smith's fitness for further duty. He should then be ordered to proceed to San Francisco to report on arrival to the Adjutant-General of the Army for further orders. Early action and reply by telegraph desired.

CORBIN.

MANILA. (Received June 14, 1902.)

ADJUTANT-GENERAL, *Washington:*

* * * * * * *

Cornelius Gardener board completed work Lucena. Arrived at Manila, where few witnesses will be examined. One member ill. Cornelius Gardener declines to proceed unless full board present. Asks a few days returning and engage assistance. Not possible to send him *Sheridan* with his regiment next transport.

CHAFFEE.

AFFAIRS IN THE PHILIPPINE ISLANDS.

MANILA. (Received June 15, 1902.)
ADJUTANT-GENERAL, *Washington:*

Request permission to use authority Secretary of War for discharge enlisted men Philippine Scouts who have proved themselves worthless material. Propose to give them honorable discharge, withholding recommendation for reenlistment.

* * * * * * *

CHAFFEE.

MANILA. (Received June 15, 1902.)
ADJUTANT-GENERAL, *Washington:*

* * * * * * *

Referring to telegram from your office of 7th ultimo, Lieut. Frank S. Burr reports May 8 no foundation for published letter that large number prisoners shot Irocin, Sorsogon Province, by his order. [Maj.] Frank F. Eastman, inspector-general, Fourth Brigade, reports June 9 upon investigation alleged shooting prisoners Irocin [First Lieut.] Frank S. Burr, that Walker testified under oath he did not make statement alleged. Six noncommissioned officers and 12 privates, including Walker, at or near Irocin, during part of October and November, 1901, testify no prisoners shot at that or any other time. Records show that from October 7 to November 11, 1901, 4 companies Fifteenth Infantry, 3 detachments constabulary, and many people, commanded by Capt. Edmund Wittenmyer, joined in campaign over country south of Sorsogon Bay; object to rid country of ladrones and Anting Anting fanatics; that during which period 26 were killed, about 350 prisoners captured. Of the killed, Lieutenant Burr's command effected 14 of the number, 7 in one ambush, 4 in another. Night of October 27, Frank S. Burr, 2 soldiers, one native police, guided by natives, marched from Irocin to barrio near San Roque, 12 miles; 3.30 in the morning were surprised, killed Balalog, leader of gang, and 2 others; wounded 4. Commanding officer, Sorgoson, only 18 miles from Irocin, has not heard circumstances referred to your dispatch of May 8, and in my opinion the report is absolutely untrue.

CHAFFEE.

WASHINGTON, *June 16, 1902.*
CHAFFEE, *Manila:*

* * * * * * *

Eighth Regiment U. S. Infantry and Fifteenth Regiment U. S. Infantry will be returned by you as indicated your cable June 13. This will not modify orders already given for return of regiments.

CORBIN.

MANILA. (Received June 16, 1902.)
ADJUTANT-GENERAL, *Washington:*

* * * * * * *

Transport *Logan* sailed June 12 from Aparri, 377 enlisted men Seventh Regiment U. S. Infantry, 787 enlisted men Sixteenth Regiment U. S. Infantry, 27 general prisoners, 8 insane, 77 sick.

CHAFFEE.

MANILA. (Received June 16, 1902.)
ADJUTANT-GENERAL, *Washington:*

* * * * * * *

Five of 7 enlisted men Troop M, Fifth Cavalry, captured May 30, near Morong, murdered June 1; bodies recovered yesterday; buried Tanay. Information obtained from one of captured murderers. Two soldiers effected escape.

CHAFFEE.

MANILA. (Received June 16, 1902.)

ADJUTANT-GENERAL, *Washington:*

* * * * * *

Request authority to discontinue First Separate Brigade, consolidating with Second, with headquarters at San Fernando, Pampanga; also to discontinue Fourth Separate Brigade, consolidating Third, with headquarters at Batangas. Will result two brigades instead of four, Department North Philippines. Number of troops north of Pasig River has been considerably reduced; also in Camarines.

CHAFFEE.

MANILA. (Received June 16, 1902.)

ADJUTANT-GENERAL, *Washington:*

* * * * * *

Request authority to ship United States hospital medical supplies in excess of requirements 20,000 men two years; amount very considerable. Breaking up hospitals in interior calls for storage facilities Manila beyond capacity division depot.

CHAFFEE.

MANILA. (Received June 16, 1902.)

ADJUTANT-GENERAL, *Washington:*

* * * * * * *

See map of Laguna de Bay, Malagi Island, south end Talim. Request President proclaim Maligi Island military reservation to be used as military prison. Figuring to a great extent is uninhabited. Think it is public domain.

CHAFFEE.

WASHINGTON, *June 17, 1902.*

CHAFFEE, *Manila:*

Referring to telegram from your office of 14th instant, the Secretary of War directs you give Cornelius Gardener full time and opportunity to submit all evidence he has to offer in support of allegations under inquiry.

CORBIN.

WASHINGTON, *June 17, 1902.*

CHAFFEE, *Manila:*

Referring to telegram from your office of 15th instant, the Secretary of War approves your request to discharge Philippine Scouts as indicated.

CORBIN.

WASHINGTON, *June 18, 1902.*

CHAFFEE, *Manila:*

The Secretary of War approves your request to discontinue First and Fourth Separate Brigades.

CORBIN.

WASHINGTON, *June 18, 1902.*

CHAFFEE, *Manila:*

Referring to telegram from your office of 16th instant, cable the names men Troop M, Fifth Cavalry, murdered.

CORBIN.

AFFAIRS IN THE PHILIPPINE ISLANDS. 1347

WASHINGTON, *June 18, 1902.*

CHAFFEE, *Manila:*
Transport *Meade* sailed June 16.

CORBIN.

WASHINGTON, *June 18, 1902.*

CHAFFEE, *Manila:*
Referring to telegram from your office of 16th instant, medical supplies mentioned will be shipped to medical supply depot San Francisco. Care should be taken that articles worn-out and unfit for reissue be disposed of as authorized by Army Regulations.

CORBIN.

MANILA. (Received June 18, 1902.)

ADJUTANT-GENERAL, *Washington:*
Sheridan has been delayed until June 22, case cholera.

CHAFFEE.

MANILA. (Received June 18, 1902.)

ADJUTANT-GENERAL, *Washington:*
* * * * * * *
Consul Goodnow authorized by me to arbitrate amount of damage to Belgian ship *Ragnar* if *Sumner* responsible. Finds amount £1,752 2s. 6d., holds *Sumner* responsible. Shall I order payment?

CHAFFEE.

MANILA. (Received June 18, 1902.)

ADJUTANT-GENERAL, *Washington:*
Mongolian employees steward department *Sumner* and *Lawton* will perforce of circumstances serve on those ships to San Francisco, from there to be returned here at the expense of the Government. Forty-two on *Sumner*, 23 *Lawton*.
* * * * * * *

CHAFFEE.

MANILA. (Received June 18, 1902.)

ADJUTANT-GENERAL, *Washington:*
Do not advise board Brig. Gen. Jacob H. Smith. Certain to find him fit for duty. First Lieut. George H. Shields, jr., thinks excitement influenced his own judgment. Capt. Waldo E. Ayer gone. Dr. Stafford, Brig. Gen. Jacob H. Smith's host, warm friend, believes board must decide variable, erratic, egotistical statements, which are strongest points Jacob H. Smith, not unfit him for duty. Neither George H. Shields, jr., Stafford willing to testify. Board not familiar sufficient circumstances to develop evidence adequate test case. In good physical condition.
* * * * * * *

CHAFFEE.

MANILA. (Received June 18, 1902.)

ADJUTANT-GENERAL, *Washington:*
* * * * * * *
Referring to telegram from your office of 14th instant, Waller proceedings forwarded by mail May 19.

CHAFFEE.

WASHINGTON, *June 19, 1902.*
CHAFFEE, *Manila:*
Referring to telegram from your office of 18th instant, Secretary of War withdraws instructions for board of yourself and three medical officers. Jacob H. Smith will proceed to San Francisco and report by telegraph to Adjutant-General.
CORBIN.

WASHINGTON, *June 20, 1902.*
CHAFFFE, *Manila:*
With reference to reported surplus of medical supplies, are there not stores of other departments in excess of requirements that might be well returned?
CORBIN.

WASHINGTON, *June 21, 1902.*
CHAFFEE, *Manila:*
Claim for damages *Ragnar* can only be adjusted by Congress. Courts and Executive Departments are without authority to award or pay damages. No award of arbitrator is binding on United States, but Secretary has assumed the £1,752 2s. 6d. to be correctly ascertained and requested Congress to appropriate, and will doubtless be done early date.
CORBIN.

MANILA. (Received June 21, 1902.)
ADJUTANT-GENERAL, *Washington:*
*   *   *   *   *   *
Referring to telegram from your office of 20th instant, will probably have superfluous stores all departments in excess of wants 20,000 men one year. We are investigating matter to determine how much; slow, difficult. Because of large amount property scattered throughout the archipelago in excess of wants and gradual reduction troops being made, propose to sell here considerable excess, some articles, commissary stores, jams, ginger ale, etc., deteriorating. Ginger ale will about give away. Can malted milk be used United States? Considerable winter clothing, will be useful home, not here. Can make load *McClellan*, New York or San Francisco, combining all departments for shipment.
CHAFFEE.

MANILA. (Received June 21, 1902.)
ADJUTANT-GENERAL, *Washington:*
*   *   *   *   *   *   *
Referring to telegram from this office of 16th instant, awaiting reply regarding Malagi Island, about quarter mile wide, half mile long, much desirable stone, making roads, new post.
CHAFFEE.

MANILA. (Received June 22, 1902.)
ADJUTANT-GENERAL, *Washington:*
Insane native scouts are sent to Hospicio de San José, Manila. Can their pay be withdrawn to maintain them in this institution?
*   *   *   *   *   *   *
CHAFFEE.

MANILA. (Received June 23, 1902.)

ADJUTANT-GENERAL, *Washington:*

Transport *Sheridan* sailed June 22, 612 enlisted men Thirteenth Infantry; 154 enlisted men Third Cavalry; 534 casuals, Col. Stephen W. Groesbeck, 76 sick soldiers.

* * * * * * *

CHAFFEE.

MANILA. (Received June 23, 1902.)

ADJUTANT-GENERAL, *Washington:*

* * * * * * *

Report following showing temper two strong parties Lake Lanao who will probably have to be attacked soon in order to prevent war. Influence is extending and becoming chronic. Gen. George W. Davis and Col. Frank D. Baldwin of this opinion; but they are doing all they can to prevent resumption of hostilities. I regard our retirement from lake great mistake from any point of view; but to remain we must insist on respect for the lives of our soldiers, who are snipped and boloed very frequently. Datto Bacolod and Masui are at present the chief offenders and instigators of hostile spirit. Believe them now sparring for time to gather rice crop. Gen. George W. Davis and Col. Frank D. Baldwin think they will become actively hostile in two months or less. Quote following reply to-day, June 17, from Datto Tunan Dundan and Sultan of Bacolod: "We ask you to return to Malabang because we do not want you live (at) Lanao, but want you to return to Malabang. You must follow our religion and customs, and in not doing so you will be to blame, for all dattos of the Laguna will make war against you, because we profess only one religion, which is that of Stambul. This letter, burned in six places, shows to you that it means war." End.

CHAFFEE.

MANILA. (Received June 24, 1902.)

ADJUTANT-GENERAL, *Washington:*

* * * * * * *

Can definite time be fixed when appropriation payment land new post Manila will be available? Owner desires to leave for Spain, to be absent considerable length of time. Desires to know when payment may be expected.

CHAFFEE.

MANILA. (Received June 24, 1902.)

ADJUTANT-GENERAL, *Washington:*

* * * * * * *

Five men One hundred and first Company, Coast Artillery, attacked by 10 Moros with bolos on Makadar trail, 10 miles from Malabang, June 22. One man cut in the head, seriously; one wounded in arm, serious. Moros secured one rifle. This result our efforts to treat with Moros friendly, trusting to their honor, of which apparently they have not the least. Nearly every day our wires are cut and our men attacked, but thus far we have not inflicted wounds in return. Shall I permit this business to continue? General Davis asks that general policy of the United States toward Lake Moros be at once decided [upon] and announced. I concur in request. Until this is done have directed Davis to warn all friendly dattos not allow their people use Makadar trail when armed. This being understood by them soldiers will be instructed to use effective measures, and if necessary to kill every armed Moro found on that trail; also not allow an armed Moro to come nearer than

10 paces. Makadar trail must be made safe, or we must abandon Lake station. Practically impossible to have intercourse with any dattos who will not voluntarily come to us. Since we can not make progress toward peaceful relations, Bacolod, Masiu, and Buting dattos should be coerced, and sooner it shall be done the better for all concerned.

CHAFFEE.

Washington, June 25, 1902.

CHAFFEE, *Manila:*
The Secretary of War authorizes immediate establishment military prison Malagi Island, avoiding the occupation of private lands. Letter mailed.

CORBIN.

Washington, June 27, 1902.

CHAFFEE, *Manila:*
Referring to telegram from your office of 22d instant pay insane native scouts can not be drawn except by guardian appointed by competent court.

CORBIN.

Washington, June 27, 1902.

CHAFFEE, *Manila:*
The Secretary of War authorizes you to discharge by order of the Secretary of War enlisted men Twenty-fourth Regiment U. S. Infantry, and other colored regiments, married Filipinos.

CORBIN.

MANILA. (Received June 28, 1902.)

ADJUTANT-GENERAL, *Washington:*

* * * * * * *

Transport *Sumner* sailed June 25, 226 enlisted men Twenty-fourth Infantry, 203 enlisted men Seventeenth Infantry, 77 casuals.

CHAFFEE.

WASHINGTON, *July 1, 1902.*

CHAFFEE, *Manila:*
How many medical officers, regular and volunteer, will be required in your division for force of 20,000?

CORBIN.

ADJUTANT-GENERAL'S OFFICE,
Washington, July 2, 1902.

CHAFFEE, *Manila:*
I am directed by Secretary of War to send you the following for your information and guidance:

"WAR DEPARTMENT, *Washington, July 4, 1902.*

"The insurrection against the sovereign authority of the United States in the Philippine Archipelago having ended, and provincial civil governments having been established throughout the entire territory of the archipelago not inhabited by Moro tribes, under instructions of the President to the Philippine Commission dated April 7, 1900, now ratified and confirmed by the Act of Congress, approved July 1, 1902, entitled "An act temporarily to provide for the administration of affairs of civil government in the Philippine Islands and for other purposes,' the general commanding division of the Philippines is hereby relieved from the further performance of the duties of military governor and the office of the military governor in said archipelago is terminated. The general commanding division of the Philippines and all military officers in authority therein will continue to observe direction contained in the aforesaid instructions of the President, that the military forces in the division of the Philippines shall be at all times subject, under the orders of the military commander, to the call of the civil authorities for maintenance of law and the enforcement of their authority.

"By the President:

"ELIHU ROOT, *Secretary of War.*"

CORBIN.

WASHINGTON, *July 2, 1902.*

CHAFFEE, *Manila:*

Referring to telegram from this office of 1st instant, also report Hospital Corps men required.

CORBIN.

MANILA, P. I., *July 2, 1902.*

ADJUTANT-GENERAL, *Washington:*

Authority requested to transfer long-term men outgoing infantry regiments artillery corps.

CHAFFEE.

WASHINGTON, *July 2, 1902.*

CHAFFEE, *Manila:*

Referring to telegram from your office of 2d instant, long-term men outgoing infantry regiments may be transferred to the artillery under orders April 3, when willing.

CORBIN.

WASHINGTON, *July 3, 1902.*

CHAFFEE, *Manila:*

Transport *Kilpatrick* sailed July 1, second squadron Fifth Cavalry, 54 Hospital Corps men

CORBIN.

WASHINGTON, *July 3, 1902.*

CHAFFEE, *Manila:*

Direct all disbursing officers avail themselves Philippines treasury as the United States Government depository as far as practicable convenient.

CORBIN.

WASHINGTON, *July 3, 1902.*

CHAFFEE, *Manila:*

With reference to your telegram of 24th ultimo, $55,000 appropriation military post Manila now available payment land. Attorney-General of the United States concurs opinion of the attorney-general Philippine Islands that general warranty deed due form if accompanied by quitclaim deeds tenants occupants will suffice to invest valid title United States. Do you desire above amount placed to credit of [Col.] Charles F. Humphrey? If you desire, where?

CORBIN.

General Orders,	Headquarters of the Army,
No. 66.	Adjutant-General's Office,
	Washington, July 4, 1902.

The following has been received from the War Department:

"War Department, *Washington, July 4, 1902.*

" *To the Army of the United States:*

"The President upon this anniversary of national independence wishes to express to the officers and enlisted men of the United States Army his deep appreciation of the service they have rendered to the country in the great and difficult undertakings which they have brought to a successful conclusion during the past year.

"He thanks the officers and the enlisted men who have been maintaining order and carrying on the military government in Cuba, because they have faithfully given effect to the humane purposes of the American people. They have with sincere kindness helped the Cuban people to take all the successive steps necessary to the establishment of their own constitutional government. During the time required for that process they have governed Cuba wisely, regarding justice and respecting individual liberty; have honestly collected and expended for the best interests of the Cuban people the revenues, amounting to over sixty millions of dollars; have carried out practical and thorough sanitary measures, greatly improving the health and lowering the death rate of the island. By patient, scientific research they have ascertained the causes of yellow fever, and by good administration have put an end to that most dreadful disease which has long destroyed the lives and hindered the commercial prosperity of the Cubans. They have expedited justice and secured protection for the rights of the innocent, while they have cleansed the prisons and established sound discipline and healthful conditions for the punishment of the guilty. They have reestablished and renovated and put upon a substantial basis adequate hospitals and asylums for the care of the unfortunate. They have established a general system of free common schools throughout the island, in which over two hundred thousand children are in actual attendance. They have constructed great and necessary public works. They have gradually trained the Cubans themselves in all branches of administration, so that the new government upon assuming power has begun its work with an experienced force of Cuban civil-service employees competent to execute its orders. They have borne themselves with dignity and self-control, so that nearly four years of military occupation have passed unmarred by injury or insult to man or woman. They have transferred the Government of Cuba to the Cuban people amid universal expressions of friendship and good will, and have left a record of ordered justice and liberty, of rapid improvement in material and moral conditions, and progress in the art of government which reflects great credit upon the people of the United States.

"The President thanks the officers and enlisted men of the Army in the Philippines, both regulars and volunteers, for the courage and fortitude, the indomitable spirit and loyal devotion with which they have put down and ended the great insurrection which has raged throughout the archipelago against the lawful sovereignty and just authority of the United States. The task was peculiarly difficult and trying. They were required at first to overcome organized resistance of superior numbers, well equipped with modern arms of precision, intrenched in an unknown country of mountain defiles, jungles, and swamps, apparently capable of interminable defense. When this resistance had been overcome they were required to crush out a general system of guerrilla warfare conducted among a people speaking unknown tongues, from whom it was almost impossible to obtain the information necessary for successful pursuit or to guard against surprise and ambush.

"The enemies by whom they were surrounded were regardless of all obligations of good faith and of all the limitations which humanity has imposed upon civilized warfare. Bound themselves by the laws of war, our soldiers were called upon to meet every device of unscrupulous treachery and to contemplate without reprisal the infliction of barbarous cruelties upon their comrades and friendly natives. They were instructed, while punishing armed resistance, to conciliate the friendship of the peaceful, yet had to do with a population among whom it was impossible to distinguish friend from foe, and who in countless instances used a false appearance of friendship for ambush and assassination. They were obliged to deal with problems of communication and transportation in a country without roads and frequently made impassable by torrential rains. They were weakened by tropical heat and tropical disease. Widely scattered over a great archipelago, extending a thousand miles from north to south, the gravest responsibilities, involving the life or death of their commands, frequently devolved upon young and inexperienced officers beyond the reach of specific orders or advice.

"Under all these adverse circumstances the Army of the Philippines has accomplished its task rapidly and completely. In more than two thousand combats, great and small, within three years, it has exhibited unvarying courage and resolution. Utilizing the lessons of the Indian wars, it has relentlessly followed the guerrilla bands to their fastnesses in mountain and jungle and crushed them. It has put an end to the vast system of intimidation and secret assassination by which the peaceful natives were prevented from taking a genuine part in government under American authority. It has captured or forced to surrender substantially all the leaders of the insurrection. It has submitted to no discouragement and halted at no obstacle. Its officers have shown high qualities of command, and its men have shown devotion and discipline. Its splendid virile energy has been accompanied by self-control, patience, and magnanimity. With surprisingly few individual exceptions its course has been characterized by humanity and kindness to the prisoner and the noncombatant. With admirable good temper, sympathy, and loyalty to American ideals its commanding generals have joined with the civilian agents of the Government in healing the wounds of war and assuring to the people of the Philippines the blessings of peace and prosperity. Individual liberty, protection of personal rights, civil order, public instruction, and religious freedom have followed its footsteps. It has added honor to the flag which it defended, and has justified increased confidence in the future of the American people, whose soldiers do not shrink from labor or death, yet love liberty and peace.

"The President feels that he expresses the sentiments of all the loyal people of the United States in doing honor to the whole Army which has joined in the performance and shares in the credit of these honorable services.

"This general order will be read aloud at parade in every military post on the 4th day of July, 1902, or on the first day after it shall have been received.

"ELIHU ROOT, *Secretary of War.*"

By command of Lieutenant-General Miles:

H. C. CORBIN,
Adjutant-General, Major-General, U. S. Army.

WASHINGTON, *July 5, 1902.*

CHAFFEE, *Manila:*

Referring to telegram from your office of 21st ultimo, load *McClellan* for New York surplus serviceable clothing, equipage, commissary chests, hospital medical supplies. Condemn, advertise, sell superfluous subsistence stores, subsistence property, unserviceable medical supplies, unserviceable irregular quartermaster supplies. Malted milk can not be used here.

CORBIN.

MANILA, P. I., *July 7, 1902.*

ADJUTANT-GENERAL, *Washington:*

* * * * * * *

Transport *Buford* arrived July 4.

CHAFFEE.

WASHINGTON, *July 8, 1902.*

CHAFFEE, *Manila:*

Send all the insurgent records by first transport. They have become a matter of great importance. Should any these papers be required, either by military or civil government, certified copies will be furnished from here.

CORBIN.

WASHINGTON, *July 8, 1902.*

CHAFFEE, *Manila:*

Appropriation for the support of the Army fiscal year ending June 30, 1903, provides $1,500,000 for proper shelter and protection officers and enlisted men in the Philippines, including the acquisition of title to building sites where necessary. Rents for barracks and quarters will be paid from this fund also. This is in addition to $500,000 for post near Manila. All rents should be terminated as rapidly as the exigencies of the service will admit.

CORBIN.

MANILA, P. I., *July 8, 1902.*

ADJUTANT-GENERAL, *Washington:*

In consequence of the President's proclamation of amnesty and declaration of peace, are brigade commanders deprived of authority to convene general courts-martial?

CHAFFEE.

WASHINGTON, *July 8, 1902.*

CHAFFEE, *Manila:*

As a result of the President's proclamation of July 4, 1902, all powers in connection with the administration of military justice, which depend for their exercise upon the existence of a state of war, cease to be operative from the date of the receipt of such proclamation. Separate brigades may continue to exist as tactical organizations, but their commanders no longer have power to convene general courts-martial.

CORBIN.

WASHINGTON, *July 9, 1902.*

CHAFFEE, *Manila:*

Forward immediately all battle reports past year as per Troops in Campaign and Army Regulations.

CORBIN.

MANILA, P. I., *July 9, 1902.*

ADJUTANT-GENERAL, *Washington:*

Transport *Thomas* sailed July 6 (Brig. Gen.) Jacob H. Smith, 671 enlisted men Twenty-fourth Infantry, 389 enlisted men Twenty-fifth Infantry, 292 enlisted men Tenth Cavalry, 59 short-term enlisted men, 78 sick, 4 insane, 28 marines.

* * * * * * *

CHAFFEE.

MANILA, P. I., *July 11, 1902.*

ADJUTANT-GENERAL, *Washington:*

Will the War Department take steps looking to the release Filipino held custody Guam?

CHAFFEE.

WASHINGTON, *July 13, 1902.*

CHAFFEE, *Manila:*

Issues of extra rations convalescents limited by appropriation act current year to troops in camp United States. My telegram of August 15, 1900, revoked. This does not interfere with 40-cent allowance to enlisted patients in hospital.

CORBIN.

MANILA, P. I., *July 14, 1902.*

ADJUTANT-GENERAL, *Washington:*

Referring to telegram from your office of 2d instant referring to telegram from your office of 3d instant, chief surgeon estimates 304 surgeons as necessary. You may cut to 290 on my authority. Chief surgeon's estimate is for 61 hospital stewards, 253 acting hospital stewards, 1,297 privates, to which add 20 per cent on account of sickness, absence, delays in transportation, or a total of 1,996 men. My opinion 1,900 men is sufficient, but careful attention necessary to see this number available.

CHAFFEE.

MANILA, P. I., *July 14, 1902.*

ADJUTANT-GENERAL, *Washington:*

Transport *Lawton* sailed July 11 from Aparri; 277 enlisted men, Sixteenth Infantry; 155 enlisted men, Third Infantry; 57 casuals.

*   *   *   *   *   *   *

CHAFFEE.

WASHINGTON, *July 15, 1902.*

CHAFFEE, *Manila:*

Have not requirements your letter June 9 been met by the appropriation of $1,500,000 cabled you?

CORBIN.

MANILA, P. I., *July 16, 1902.*

ADJUTANT-GENERAL, *Washington:*

Transport *Meade* arrived July 16.

*   *   *   *   *   *   *

CHAFFEE.

MANILA, P. I., *July 16, 1902.*

ADJUTANT-GENERAL, *Washington:*

*   *   *   *   *   *   *

Want 109 recruits each, First Cavalry, Fifth Cavalry.

CHAFFEE.

MANILA, P. I., *July 16, 1902.*

ADJUTANT-GENERAL, *Washington:*

*   *   *   *   *   *   *

Referring to telegram from your office of 15th instant; yes.

CHAFFEE.

WASHINGTON, *July 17, 1902.*

CHAFFEE, *Manila:*

Transport *Sherman* sailed July 16.

CORBIN.

WASHINGTON, *July 18, 1902.*

CHAFFEE, *Manila:*

Referring to telegram from your office of 16th instant, requesting 109 recruits each, First Cavalry and Fifth Cavalry, you are authorized to transfer to those regiments long-term men, returning infantry regiments, when fit and willing. Will this enable you to bring troops to 75 each, strength established by General Orders, Headquarters of the Army, A. G. O. (c. s.), No. 48?

CORBIN.

WASHINGTON, *July 18, 1902.*

CHAFFEE, *Manila:*

Prisoners of war at Guam are no longer to be kept in confinement, but will be at liberty to go wherever they please, except that Secretary of War thinks the Philippine government should prohibit their return to the archipelago except on condition of taking the oath of allegiance prescribed in the amnesty proclamation. If any considerable number of the prisoners wish to take the oath of allegiance and return to Manila, a transport will be directed to stop at Guam for them. Furnish copy of this to Philippine Commission.

CORBIN.

MANILA, P. I., *July 19, 1902.*

ADJUTANT-GENERAL, *Washington:*

* * * * * * *

Referring to telegram from your office of 18th instant, probably can secure from infantry regiments Division of the Philippines having excess sufficient long-term men for First Cavalry, Fifth Cavalry. Take no action request recruits until further advised.

CHAFFEE.

MANILA, P. I., *July 21, 1902.*

ADJUTANT-GENERAL, *Washington:*

* * * * * * *

Transport *Crook* sailed July 17; 565 enlisted men, Twenty-fifth Infantry, 10 prisoners.

CHAFFEE.

MANILA, P. I., *July 22, 1902.*

ADJUTANT-GENERAL, *Washington:*

Transport *Relief* sailed July 21, Col. William P. Hall.

* * * * * * *

CHAFFEE.

MANILA, P. I., *July 23, 1902.*

ADJUTANT-GENERAL, *Washington:*

No further cases to refer general court-martial convened by President. June 14 the court adjourned sine die. Shall members join proper station—four in the United States?

* * * * * * *

CHAFFEE.

WASHINGTON, *July 24, 1902.*

CHAFFEE, *Manila:*

Referring to telegram from your office of 23d instant, members general court-martial will proceed to join their proper stations.

CHAFFEE.

WASHINGTON, *July 26, 1902.*

CHAFFEE, *Manila:*

The Secretary of War desires to know amount of unpaid accounts subject of correspondence your cable May 26 and letter May 29.

CARTER.

WASHINGTON, *July 26, 1902.*

CHAFFEE, *Manila:*

Executive order November 9, 1901, declaring naval reservation provinces Zambeles, Bataan, revoked by Executive order May 9, 1902.

CARTER.

WASHINGTON, *July 28, 1902.*

CHAFFEE, *Manila:*

President confirmed sentences Glenn and Gaujot, disapproved acquittal Cook July 24 without remark. The Secretary of War directs release.

CARTER.

MANILA, P. I., *July 29, 1902.*

ADJUTANT-GENERAL, *Washington:*

Transport *Buford* sailed July 29, 462 enlisted men, Eighth United States Infantry; 143, Fifteenth United States Infantry; 104, Twenty-fifth United States Infantry; 91 sick, 5 insane, 61 discharged soldiers.

CHAFFEE.

MANILA, P. I., *July 30, 1902.*

ADJUTANT-GENERAL, *Washington:*

Transport *Kilpatrick* arrived July 29.

*   *   *   *   *   *   *

CHAFFEE.

INDEX TO CORRESPONDENCE RELATING TO THE WAR WITH SPAIN, ETC.

1898-1902.

Aaron, Sibert P., pvt., Co. C, 34th Inf., U. S. V., wounded, 1192.
Abad, insurgent colonel, surrender, 1269.
Abbott, Charles W., jr., col., 1st R. I. Vol. Inf., mentioned, 521.
Abbott, Nathan J., pvt., Co. B, 7th U. S. Inf., mentioned, 206.
Abel, Jacob, pvt., Co. K, 22d U. S. Inf., death, 1109.
Abernathy, Wooten R., sergt. maj., 48th Inf., U. S. V., death, 1238.
Abernethy, Robert S., maj., 36th Inf., U. S. V., wounded, 807, 1050, 1051.
Ables, Arthur, pvt., Co. F, 9th U. S. Inf., wounded, 444.
Achuff, Samuel, corpl., Co. D, 15th U. S. Inf., wounded, 1253.
Ackley, John V., pvt., Co. K, 16th U. S. Inf., death, 1229.
Adair, Victor, pvt., Troop M, 4th U. S. Cav., death, 1172.
Adams, Allen P., pvt., Co. E, 3d U. S. Inf., death, 1221.
Adams, Bird L., pvt., ——, 1st Idaho Vol. Inf., death, 803.
Adams, Charles F., pvt., Co. D, 20th U. S. Inf., death, 1132.
Adams, Charles J., corpl., Co. M, 12th U. S. Inf., wounded, 1015.
Adams, Charles M., pvt., Hosp. Corps, U. S. A., death, 1255.
Adams, Claude A., corpl., Co. I, 40th Inf., U. S. V., wounded, 1162.
Adams, Emmet C., pvt., Co. M, 29th Inf., U. S. V., death, 1142.
Adams, Francis J., maj., surg., 1st Mont. Vol. Inf., wounded, 948.
Adams, Frank E., pvt., Co. L, 2d Oreg. Vol. Inf., wounded, 952.
Adams, Frank H., 1st lieut., 1st S. Dak. Vol. Inf., killed, 948, 949.
Adams, Henry H., letter of, 353.
Adams, Herman P., pvt., Co. B, 2d Oreg. Vol. Inf., killed, 945.
Adams, John C., artif., Co. A, 1st Mont. Vol. Inf., death, 803.
Adams, John E., pvt., Troop C, 3d U. S. Cav., drowned, 1167.
Adams, John F., pvt., Co. M, 1st Wash. Vol. Inf., killed, 914.
Adams, Jonas B., pvt., band, 18th U. S. Inf., death, 829.
Adams, Otto, pvt., Co. E, 30th Inf., U. S. V., wounded, 1199.
Adams Ralph W., pvt., Co. E, 14th U. S. Inf., wounded, 454.
Adams, Robert, jr., telegram of, 335, 338.
Adams, Vernon A., pvt., Co. E, 38th Inf., U. S. V., wounded, 1193.
Adams, William, pvt., Co. F, 20th U. S. Inf., mentioned, 216.
Adamson, Henry J., pvt., Co. D, 39th Inf., U. S. V., death, 1165.
Addison, Seymour, pvt., Co. I, 1st Mont. Vol. Inf., wounded, 950.
Addy, William S., pvt., Co. F, 18th U. S. Inf., killed, 1107.

Adee, Alvey A., Asst. Secy. State, letter of, 366, 367.
Adkins, William H., pvt., Co. E, 1st Wash. Vol. Inf., mentioned, 1015.
Affeldt, Elmer F., pvt., Co. B 6th U. S. Inf., wounded, 1087.
Agee, Edward M., pvt., Co. D, 44th Inf., U. S. V., killed, 1209.
Agidius, Adolph, pvt., Co. F, 1st Idaho Vol. Inf., death, 917.
Aglipay, Gregorio, ex-priest, surrender, 1273.
Aguinaldo, Don Emilio, insurgent general in chief:
  Aid or encouragement received by, from people in U. S., 1187, 1142.
  American naval commander refuses to recognize, 821.
  Amnesty, no further promise of, 1263.
  Bodyguard—
    Combat with, 1263.
    Destroyed by U. S. troops, 1121.
  Capture, 1260, 1262, 1263.
    Child and money belonging to mother, 1108.
    Plans for, 1256.
  Conduct toward members insurgent government, 840.
  Correspondence with American military commanders, 1134.
  Demands on General Merritt, reply to, 788.
  Desire for amicable relations with U. S. authorities, 845.
  Expedition for capture, organization, 1262.
    Commendation by President of members, 1263.
  Family protected by U. S. troops from Filipinos, 1110.
  Filipinos called to resist foreign invasion, 898.
  Influence—
    In southern islands, 836.
    Waning, 851.
  Instructions as to intercourse with, 1263.
  Memorandum of demands submitted to General Merritt, 816.
  Mentioned, 720, 778, 781, 786-788, 790, 804, 806, 807-812, 815, 817, 819, 821, 822, 827, 831, 836, 840, 843-845, 847, 849, 866-868, 872, 877, 879, 886, 898, 899, 901, 902, 908, 909, 911, 912, 944, 947, 918, 988, 1011, 1013, 1060, 1070, 1074, 1078, 1088, 1096, 1097, 1098, 1100, 1106-1109, 1116, 1121-1123, 1184, 1187, 1138, 1142, 1159, 1162, 1163, 1194, 1206 1256, 1262, 1263, 1265-1267, 1271, 1317, 1319.
  Movements in endeavoring to escape, 1107-1109, 1116
  Request for protection of American squadron, 821.
  Requests recognition of insurgent cooperation, 911.
  Self-proclaimed dictator and president, 781.
  Sentiment toward Americans, 806.
  To be held responsible for—
    Failure of insurgents to withdraw from Manila, 826.
    Injury to prisoners held by insurgents, 1098.
  Treatment, 1263.
  Views re conditions of withdrawal, 823.
  War declared by, 898.
Ahlers, Charles L., pvt., Co. G, 13th Minn. Vol. Inf., mentioned, 762.

INDEX.

Aiken, Blaine, 1st lieut., 10th Pa. Vol. Inf., wounded, 981.
Aikin, James, pvt., Co. F, 14th U. S. Inf., wounded, 454.
Akins, Lyle W., pvt., Co. I, 35th Inf., U. S. V., wounded and captured, 1186.
Alameda, U. S. transport, mentioned, 605, 723.
Alamo, U. S. transport, mentioned, 123, 150, 190, 208, 310, 326, 357, 372, 173, 396, 413, 623.
Albert, C. S., representative N. Y. World, letter to, 28.
Albert, Mickelson, pvt., Co. A, 1st Ill. Vol. Inf., mentioned, 216.
Albright, William S., capt., 20th Kans. Vol. Inf., wounded, 983.
Alden, Charles H., col., med. dept., U. S. A., letter, 153.
Alden, Frank E., qm. sergt., Co. L, 71st N. Y. Vol. Inf., mentioned, 224.
Alder, Alvin E., corpl., Co. G, 3d U. S. Inf., death, 1052.
Alderman, Thadeus G., pvt., Co. F, 20th Kans. Vol. Inf., wounded, 952.
Aldred, William G., corpl., Co. K, 2d U. S. Inf., wounded, 1261.
Aldrich, Archie A., artif., Co. E, 1st Colo. Vol. Inf., death, 972; wounded, 943.
Alejandrino, José, insurgent general, mentioned, 1110.
Aleshire, James B., maj., qm. dept., U. S. A., mentioned, 480, 482, 497, 1326.
To go to Manila, 494.
Alexander, Henry, pvt., Co. F, 24th U. S. Inf., death, 1149.
Alexander, James, 1st sergt., Troop A, 4th U. S. Cav., wounded, 1234.
Alexander, Jesse S., pvt., Co. B, 37th Inf., U. S. V., death, 1196.
Alexander, Jules D. St., pvt., Co. I, 33d Inf., U. S. V., death, 1219.
Alexander, Samuel H., pvt., Co. C. 22d U. S. Inf., death, 1082.
Alexieff, Russian Admiral, ranking admiral at Tientsin, 429.
Alford, Alfred C., 1st lieut., 20th Kans. Vol. Inf., killed, 898.
Alford, John J., pvt., Troop K, 3d U. S. Cav., wounded, 1255.
Alger, Frederick M., capt., A. A. G., U. S. V., commended, 128.
Mentioned, 76, 80, 89, 150, 283, 341.
Alger, Russell A., secy. war, correspondence, 8, 16, 19, 22-51, 55, 58-60, 62, 66-71, 73-79, 81-83, 89, 90, 92, 94, 99-101, 104, 105, 108, 110, 113 114, 116, 117, 123-128, 132, 134-138, 141, 142, 144, 146, 147, 150, 152-157, 159, 161, 163-165, 168, 170, 172-176, 179, 181, 183, 184, 186-188, 191, 192, 195, 196, 199, 204, 206-209, 212, 215, 216, 219, 224-226, 237, 241, 242, 245, 246, 261-273, 276, 277, 279-290, 292-294, 296, 297, 299-301, 304-316, 320, 324, 326, 329-337, 340-344, 346-354, 356-359, 361-375, 377-381, 384-386, 388, 390, 392, 393, 395, 396, 398-401, 404.
Alicante, hospital ship, mentioned, 212, 215, 991, 1133.
Alipali, insurgent, surrender, 1264.
Alison, Albert W., pvt., Co. B, 13th Minn. Vol. Inf., death, 894.
Allbriten, James P., pvt., Co. L, 44th Inf., U. S. V., death, 1220.
Allegheny, U. S. transport, mentioned, 184, 190, 233, 255, 330.
Allen, Charles H., Asst. Secy. Navy, mentioned, 23, 28, 29, 37, 39, 40, 41, 66, 240, 349.
Allen, David, pvt., Co. M., 28th U. S. Inf., killed, 1212.
Allen, Enick L., pvt., Co. K, 44th Inf., U. S. V., death, 1191.
Allen, Floyd, pvt., Co. K, 21st U. S. Inf., death, 1038.
Allen, George, pvt., Co. C, 9th U. S. Inf., wounded, 1298.
Allen, Henry T., maj., 43d Inf., U. S. V., mentioned, 77, 78, 442, 1168.
Allen, Ira, pvt., Co. F, 36th Inf., U. S. V., wounded, 1141.
Allen, James, lieut. col., sig. officer, U. S. V., mentioned, 57, 70, 75, 78, 80, 88, 92, 98, 100, 110, 120.
Allen, James, pvt., Batty. G, 3d U. S. Art., death, 1027.

Allen, James R., pvt., Co. K, 1st Nebr. Vol. Inf., wounded, 974.
Allen, John, pvt., Co. H, 16th U. S. Inf., wounded, 1182.
Allen, Robert H., 1st lieut., 14th U. S. Inf., mentioned, 442.
Allen, Samuel E., 1st lieut., 5th U. S. Art., mentioned, 75, 326.
Allen, Walter, pvt., Co. E, 9th U. S. Inf., death, 489.
Allen, William T., pvt., Co. L, 2d Oreg. Vol. Inf., wounded, 946.
Alley, John S., pvt., Co. D, 1st Nebr. Vol. Inf., death, 917.
Wounded, 914.
Alley, Lofer J., pvt., Co. K, 14th U. S. Inf., wounded and death, 454, 464.
Allison, Elvie, corpl., Co. K, 20th Kans. Vol. Inf., wounded, 983.
Allison, Henry L., pvt., Co. M, 6th U. S. Inf., death, 1226.
Allison, Walter, pvt., Co. B, 48th Inf., U. S. V., death, 1178.
Almen, Alfred C., pvt., Co. I, 1st N. Dak. Vol. Inf., killed, 967.
Alpbanalp, John, pvt., Batty. B, Utah Vol. Art., wounded, 974.
Alport, Joseph W., corpl., Co. H, 43d Inf., U. S. V., death, 1153.
Alpren, Samuel, pvt., Co. F, 3d U. S. Inf., wounded, 995.
Alstaetter, Frederick W., 1st lieut., Engr. Corps, U. S. A., capture by insurgents, 1196.
Release, 1230.
Alston, Douglas, pvt., Co. C, 49th Inf., U. S. V., drowned, 1223.
Altmann, Benno, act. hosp. stewd., U. S. A., wounded, 963.
Altmose, Fred M., pvt., Co. L, 41st Inf., U. S. V., death, 1260.
Alva, insurgent colonel, surrender, 1268.
Alvarado, gunboat, mentioned, 157.
Alvey, William G., pvt., Co. L, 23d U. S. Inf., wounded, 956.
Ames, Adelbert, brig. gen., U. S. V., mentioned, 181, 225, 525, 543, 545.
Opinion, re. health of army in Cuba, 202.
Ames, Butler, 1st lieut., 6th Mass. Vol. Inf., mentioned, 376.
Recommended for appointment as lieut. col., 375.
Ames, Marion, corpl., Co. H, 2d Mass. Vol. Inf., mentioned, 229.
Ammerman, Jake H., pvt., Co. B, 9th U. S. Inf., death, 497.
Ammons, Williams, pvt., Co. K, 49th Inf., U. S. V., death, 1231.
Amos, William R., pvt., Co. I, 1st S. Dak. Vol. Inf., wounded, 949.
Amphitrite, mentioned, 352.
Amsler, John J., corpl., Co. F, 47th Inf., U. S. V., wounded, 1185.
Ancona, German war ship, mentioned, 833.
Anderson, Andrew, pvt., Co. H, 35th Inf., U. S. V., death, 1146.
Anderson, Anton, pvt., Co. E, 3d U. S. Inf., mentioned, 241.
Anderson, August, pvt., Co. F, 20th U. S. Inf., mentioned, 253.
Anderson, Charles G., pvt., Co. L, 1st Wash. Vol. Inf., wounded, 1015.
Anderson, Charles H., maj., 1st Colo. Vol. Inf., wounded, 937.
Anderson, Charles H., pvt., Co. E, 23d U. S. Inf., wounded, 956.
Anderson, Chris H., pvt., Co. K, 30th Inf., U. S. V., wounded, 1147.
Anderson, Clarence, pvt., Co. E, 23d U. S. Inf., death, 1078.
Anderson, Clarence L., pvt., Co. F, 43d Inf., U. S. V., death, 1256.
Anderson, David S., pvt., Co. K, 6th U. S. Inf., killed, 1037, 1052.
Anderson, Edward E., cook, Co. M, 6th U. S. Inf., death, 1208.
Anderson, Eugene S., pvt., Co. E, 16th U. S. Inf., killed, 1152.
Anderson, Fred, pvt., Co. C, 3d U. S. Inf., death, 1060.

INDEX. 1361

Anderson, George S., col., 6th U. S. Cav., mentioned, 422, 424, 1132, 1214, 1344.
Anderson, Gus, pvt., Co. F, 19th U. S. Inf., death, 1255.
Anderson, Harry C., pvt., Co. B, 25th U. S. Inf., death, 1264.
Anderson, Harry C., pvt., Co. C, 13th Minn. Vol. Inf., wounded, 963.
Anderson, John, pvt., Co. F, 1st Idaho Vol. Inf., wounded, 917.
Anderson, John, pvt., Co. F, 32d Inf., U. S. V., death, 1205.
Anderson, John H., pvt., Troop A, 9th U. S. Cav., death, 1236.
Anderson, Julius, pvt., Co. A, 39th Inf., U. S. V., death, 1189.
Anderson, Larz, mentioned, 355.
Anderson, Milton E., pvt., Co. M, 34th Inf., U.S.V., drowned, 1210.
Anderson, Nels, pvt., Co. G. 12th U. S. Inf., drowned, 997.
Anderson, Peter, pvt., Batty. B, Utah Art., wounded, 896.
Anderson, Philip M., pvt., Co. K, 14th U. S. Inf., death, 469.
Wounded, 454.
Anderson, Raynard N., pvt., Co. A, 35th Inf., U. S. V., death, 1125.
Anderson, Robert, 1st sergt., Co. H, 37th Inf., U. S. V., death, 1244.
Anderson, Robert, corpl., Troop B, 10th U. S. Cav., mentioned, 229.
Anderson, Roy P., pvt., Co. K, 1st S. Dak. Vol. Inf., death, 833.
Anderson, Stanley, pvt., Co. C, 3d U. S. Inf., wounded, 999.
Anderson, Thomas, sergt., Co. B, 1st Mont. Vol. Inf., killed, 976.
Anderson, Thomas M., brig. gen., U. S. V., mentioned, 556-560, 635, 660-662, 664, 667-670, 672, 709, 711, 716, 758, 777, 815, 816, 820, 1134, 1216.
Andrews, Albium M., pvt., Co. A, 33d Inf., U.S.V., wounded, 1228.
Andrews, George M., pvt., Co. A, 1st Nebr. Vol. Inf., wounded, 906.
Andrews, Griffin, pvt., Co. F, 22d U. S. Inf., wounded, 1092.
Andrews, John N., brig. gen., U. S. V., mentioned, 512, 514-517, 541.
Andrews, Magruder, pvt., Co. C, 6th U. S. Inf., wounded, 1153.
Andrews, Philip, lieut., U. S. N., mentioned, 1316.
Andrews, Thomas W., pvt., Co. G, 14th U. S. Inf., death, 1016.
Andrews, William Augustus, pvt., U. S. Marine Corps, death, 486.
Andrews, William R., pvt., Co. F, 29th U. S. Inf., killed, 1219.
Andrewson, Peter, pvt., Batt. B, Utah Art., wounded, 896.
Angel Island, Cal., detention camp, establishment, 1021, 1022.
Anibal, Albert S., pvt., Co. G, 20th Kans. Vol. Inf., killed, 945.
Ankrim, Carl, pvt., Co. F, 31st Inf., U. S. V., death, 1208.
Annapolis, U. S. gunboat, mentioned, 22, 300, 301.
Annis, Frank E., pvt., Co. I, 35th Inf., U. S. V., death, 1196.
Antone, Jurich, jr., qm. sergt., Co. C, 1st S. Dak. Vol. Inf., wounded, 975.
Antrim, Ray L., pvt., Co. K, 2d Oreg. Vol. Inf., wounded, 946.
Apperti, Stefano, pvt., Co. H, 43d Inf., U. S. V., killed, 1168.
Apson, Frank, pvt., Co. C, 41st Inf., U. S. V., death, 1153.
Arab, U. S. transport, mentioned, 1223.
Arade, Frank A., pvt., Co. K, 18th U. S. Inf., wounded, 1216.
Aransas, U. S. transport, mentioned, 190, 304, 307, 347, 355, 401.
Arcadia, U. S. transport, mentioned, 83, 84, 213, 224, 232, 275, 278, 282, 309, 310.
Arce, insurgent colonel, surrender 1268.
Archbold, Harry, pvt., Co. M, 1st Mont. Vol. Inf., death, 875.
Arellano, chief justice of P. I., advises surrender of insurgents, 1265.

Arguellez, insurgent colonel, statement re suspension of hostilities, 1163, 1164.
Arguelles, Manuel, appointed on conference commission, 909.
Argyll, U. S. transport, mentioned, 484, 1217.
Arizona, U. S. transport, mentioned, 741, 742, 744, 748, 749, 751-753, 755, 756, 758, 759, 764, 784, 792, 794, 795, 797, 799, 832, 838-840, 922, 928, 929.
Arkell, B., mentioned, 301.
Arlington, James E., pvt., Co. H, 26th Inf., U. S. V., death, 1120.
Armani, John D., pvt., Co. C, 9th U. S. Inf., killed, 1297.
Armani, Litto, pvt., Co. C, 9th U. S. Inf., killed, 1297.
Armburst, Bert F., pvt., Co. I, 10th Pa. Vol. Inf., killed, 954.
Armfield, Joseph F., col., 1st N. C. Vol. Inf., mentioned, 553.
Armitage, William J., pvt., Co. B, 2d Oreg. Vol. Inf., wounded, 946.
Armour, William J., pvt., Co. K, 27th U. S. Inf., wounded, 1234.
Armstrong, Frank C., surg., 32d Inf., U.S.V., death, 1113.
Armstrong, Frank E., pvt., Co. H, 23d U. S. Inf., death, 1074.
Armstrong, Frank G., corpl., Co. C, 23d U. S. Inf., wounded, 956.
Armstrong, James, pvt., Co. L, 9th U. S. Inf., death, 1027.
Armstrong, Robert H., pvt., Co. D, 8th Ohio Vol. Inf., mentioned, 24.
Armstrong, Samuel T., maj., surg., U. S. V., mentioned, 189.
Army:
  Arrangements for payment, 16.
  Casualties in, 54, 55, 61, 74, 83, 121-124, 127, 171, 174, 175, 182, 183, 185, 187, 192, 193, 196, 197, 202, 204-206, 209, 211-214, 216, 218, 219, 223, 224, 226, 229, 235, 238, 240, 241, 244, 246, 248, 253, 317, 365, 372, 380, 390, 417, 426, 428-430, 435, 440, 443, 445, 449, 451, 453, 454, 459, 460, 461, 463-466, 469, 477, 478, 480, 482, 485-489, 491, 493-495, 497, 498, 500, 501, 504, 505, 748, 758, 760-762, 797, 798, 802-804, 828-831, 833, 837, 840-842, 850, 856, 861, 866, 875, 886, 892-903, 905, 907, 914-917, 921-926, 931, 934, 936, 937, 939-941, 943, 945-952, 954-957, 959-961, 963, 966-968, 972, 974-977, 979, 981-984, 986-988, 992-995, 997, 999, 1001, 1003, 1005, 1008, 1010, 1015-1021, 1026, 1027, 1029, 1031, 1082, 1037, 1038, 1042, 1044-1046, 1048, 1050-1052, 1055, 1057, 1060, 1062-1064, 1066, 1067, 1069, 1070, 1072-1075, 1078, 1079, 1081, 1082, 1084-1088, 1090, 1091, 1095, 1096, 1099, 1101, 1102, 1104, 1107, 1109, 1110-1115, 1117, 1119, 1120, 1123-1133, 1136, 1137, 1139, 1140-1153, 1155, 1156, 1160-1162, 1164-1168, 1170, 1172, 1174-1176, 1178, 1180-1187, 1189-1197, 1199-1203, 1205, 1206, 1208-1223, 1225, 1226, 1227, 1228, 1229, 1231-1238, 1240, 1241, 1243-1245, 1247-1251, 1253-1265, 1267, 1271, 1272, 1274, 1275, 1280, 1281, 1283, 1287, 1297-1299, 1306, 1322.
  Companies in Philippine Islands, increase in strength, 1013.
  Concentration of troops, 7, 11.
  Condition as to efficiency, 680, 704.
  Congratulations to, in Cuba, 105, 114.
  Corps, organization, etc.—
    Distribution, 257, 258.
    Nomination of staff officers, 706.
    Eighth—
      Command, authority for transfer, 708.
      Constituted from troops of Philippine expedition, 707, 708.
      Major-General Merritt assigned to command, 708.
      Organization, 556-579.
      Proposed award of medals to members, 1025.
    Fifth—
      Command, 82.
      Discontinuance, 257.
      General officers accompanying General Shafter, 47.
      Gunboat and steamer surrenders to Shafter, 157.
      Lieutenant Hobson, exchange of, 101.
      Organization, 13, 14, 539-547.

Army—Continued.
  Corps, organization, etc.—Continued.
    Fifth—Continued.
      Reduction of Santiago, health conditions, 87.
      Re, officers with rank of major-general, remaining with, 170.
      Strength, composition, etc., 15, 21, 22.
    First—
      Organization, 509–519.
      Reorganization and distribution, 257.
    Fourth—
      Departure from Tampa, 69.
      Organization, 534–539.
      Reorganization and distribution, 257, 258.
      Organization of Philippine expedition as, 701.
      Advantages of, 705.
    Second—
      First brigade, 3d division, organization, etc., 42.
      Organization, 519–529.
      Reorganization and distribution, 257.
      Two brigades to form part of Santiago expedition, 44.
    Seventh—
      Assignment of adjutants-general, 27.
      Organization, 13, 547–555.
    Sixth—
      Discontinuance, 257.
    Third—
      Discontinuance, 257.
      Organization, 530–534.
      Relief of General Wade, 340.
  Criticism of, in Cuba, 106, 113, 114.
  Danger to, of exposure in Philippine Islands, 691.
  Decision of Supreme Court U. S. re captures by Navy and, 164.
  Enlisted strength of certain regiments, 842.
  Equipment, conditions at Santiago, 242.
  Field returns, etc., 681, 682, 716.
  Hardships in Cuba, 213.
  Instruction, 776, 777, 1013.
  Interment of soldiers, 145.
  Mismanagement, 256.
  Officers, promotions, recommendations for, 85, 99, 104, 109, 110, 113, 116, 129, 179, 209, 225–227.
  Preparation for invasion of Cuba, 8.
  President's message of thanks, published to, 152, 153.
  Sick, return from Philippine Islands, 1023.
  Steamers available for use, 34.
  Stores for, shipment, 82.
  Strength in Philippine Islands, 1079, 1093.
  Troops—
    Arming with Krag-Jörgensen, 114.
    Commissary stores for, at Newport News, 336.
    Concentration, 266.
    Condition on transports, 293.
    Delay at—
      Chickamauga, 294.
      Newport News, 326.
    Disembarkation at—
      Cabañas and Guantanamo, Cuba, 273.
      Doraco, Porto Rico, 320.
      Ponce, Porto Rico, 318, 319.
    Equipment, 269, 273, 319.
    From Arizona to Cuba, Porto Rico, and Philippines, 345.
    Health conditions, 60, 74, 109, 123, 124, 173–175, 177, 182, 183, 184–187, 189–198, 200–202, 204–206, 209, 211–216, 218, 219, 223–227, 229, 230, 235, 238, 240, 241, 243, 244, 246, 248, 252–254, 265, 330, 367, 381, 385, 388, 392, 400, 921, 955, 970, 1014, 1019, 1034, 1037, 1100, 1108, 1111, 1193, 1194, 1201, 1203, 1209, 1214, 1219, 1224, 1228, 1235, 1241, 1246, 1250, 1254, 1257, 1259.
    Organization, 269.
    Payment, 131, 133, 137, 159, 164, 172, 173, 222, 233, 385, 396, 694.
    Porto Rico Expedition—
      Equipment, 171, 270, 303.
      Landing, protection of Navy, 297, 299.
      Movements in, 369.
      Needed in, 364.
      To, 261, 268, 272, 276, 281, 283–288, 289, 291, 292, 294, 295, 310, 311, 312, 315–317, 319, 320, 323, 324, 327, 328, 331, 340, 347, 352, 368, 377, 390.
      Transportation in, 357, 359.
    Postal relations, establishment, 696.

Army—Continued.
  Troops—Continued.
    Santiago de Cuba—
      At, for Porto Rican expedition, 274.
      For, 261.
      From, to Port Tampa, 304.
      Sailing for, 278, 279, 309.
      To Montauk Point from, 360.
      Transportation and accommodations on sea, 267.
      Inadequate, 307.
    Yellow-fever conditions, 272, 276, 283.
  Organizations—
    Artillery—
      Coast companies, return to U. S., 1277, 1287, 1292, 1293.
      Consolidation of batteries, 1191.
      Field batteries, return to U. S., 1277, 1289, 1291.
      Light and mountain batteries for P. I., 932, 933, 936.
      First, mentioned, 7, 33, 389, 394, 441, 540, 541, 543, 544, 546, 564–566, 568, 569, 572, 573, 575, 576, 578, 933, 967, 970, 1015, 1018, 1026, 1039, 1047, 1053, 1079, 1093, 1095, 1114, 1128, 1142, 1151, 1159, 1169, 1175, 1188, 1198, 1207, 1217, 1227, 1233, 1246.
      Second, mentioned, 7, 33, 369, 372, 389, 391, 394, 540, 541, 543, 544, 546, 554, 555.
      Third, mentioned, 7, 70, 304, 441, 446, 448, 469, 477, 486, 488, 491, 541, 556–566, 568, 569, 571–573, 575–579, 666, 681, 683–685, 721, 748, 1009, 1016, 1018–1020, 1025–1027, 1047, 1052, 1079, 1093, 1114, 1128, 1142, 1151, 1159, 1169, 1175, 1188, 1191, 1198, 1207, 1217, 1225–1227, 1233, 1246.
      Fourth, mentioned, 7, 33, 70, 156, 195, 202, 212, 278, 279, 329, 441, 540, 541, 543, 544, 546, 564, 565, 568–574, 576, 578, 933, 967, 970, 998, 1025, 1026, 1047, 1079, 1093, 1114, 1128, 1142, 1151, 1159, 1169, 1175, 1188, 1198, 1207, 1227, 1233, 1246.
      Fifth, mentioned, 7, 27, 70, 178, 304, 329, 347, 355, 369, 372, 389–391, 431, 441, 449, 454, 460, 461, 469, 484, 541, 544, 546, 564, 565, 566, 568–570, 572–574, 576, 578, 933, 970, 1026, 1047, 1079, 1093, 1114, 1128, 1142, 1151, 1159, 1169, 1175, 1188, 1198, 1207, 1217, 1227.
      Sixth, mentioned, 27, 329, 369, 372, 389, 391, 556–579, 721, 736, 862, 926, 929–931, 935, 936, 953, 954, 962, 971, 1015, 1018, 1019, 1025, 1026, 1039, 1047, 1056, 1075, 1079, 1091, 1093, 1099, 1114, 1123, 1128, 1142, 1151, 1159, 1169, 1175, 1178, 1188, 1198, 1207, 1217, 1227, 1233, 1246.
      Seventh, mentioned, 59, 276, 306, 309, 310, 318, 329, 369, 372, 389, 391, 434, 446, 484, 647, 681, 841, 1039, 1205–1207, 1217, 1219.
    Astor Battery—
      Arrival at San Francisco, 878.
      Tendered to Government, 687.
      To be returned from Manila, 851.
      Mentioned, 556–558, 687, 699, 717, 855, 878, 1039, 1131.
    Cavalry—
      First, mentioned, 7, 15, 33, 54, 55, 60, 61, 123, 174, 209, 212–214, 229, 275, 422, 441, 448, 449, 539–542, 544, 546, 1009, 1198, 1203, 1207, 1217, 1226, 1233, 1246, 1355, 1356.
      Second, mentioned, 7, 11, 33, 56, 183, 195, 197, 226, 244, 253, 306, 309, 310, 329, 539, 540, 542, 546.
      Third, mentioned, 7, 15, 33, 123, 206, 211, 227–229, 304, 422, 443, 446, 448, 456, 457, 539–542, 546, 570, 572, 574, 575, 578, 1036, 1048, 1053, 1054, 1057, 1059, 1062, 1079, 1093, 1100, 1114, 1120, 1128, 1142, 1151, 1159, 1169, 1175, 1188, 1195, 1198, 1203, 1207, 1211, 1212, 1217, 1221, 1226, 1233, 1246, 1323, 1332, 1340, 1341, 1349.
      Fourth, mentioned, 556–563, 565–578, 647, 667, 681–685, 688, 689, 721, 736, 931, 944, 972, 973, 976, 978, 979, 1052, 1054, 1057, 1060, 1062, 1063, 1151, 1159, 1169, 1175, 1188, 1198, 1207, 1217, 1226, 1233, 1246, 1277, 1291.
      Fifth, mentioned, 80, 56, 231, 273, 276, 311, 815–317, 326, 329, 334, 343, 350, 351, 361, 362, 364, 366, 539, 1003, 1008, 1010, 1012, 1018, 1019, 1021, 1023–1026, 1029, 1030, 1032, 1039, 1042, 1047, 1053, 1079, 1086, 1087, 1093, 1095–1097, 1100, 1112, 1114, 1120, 1128, 1131, 1138, 1142, 1245, 1258, 1345, 1346, 1351, 1355, 1356.

INDEX. 1363

Army—Continued.
  Organizations—Continued.
   Cavalry—Continued.
    Sixth, mentioned, 7, 15, 33, 123, 195, 211, 227, 292, 295, 302, 328, 333, 412, 416, 421–423, 427, 430–432, 434, 447, 460, 466, 469, 473, 476, 478, 485, 488, 489, 495, 497, 501, 505, 539–542, 546, 1009, 1227, 1233, 1246, 1265.
    Squadron of, to constitute legation guard, 480.
    Seventh, mentioned, 124, 517, 548, 552, 554, 555.
    Eighth, mentioned, 124, 380, 390, 539, 548, 552, 688, 689, 1224.
    Ninth, mentioned, 7, 15, 33, 124, 195, 204, 206, 216, 224, 232, 238, 422, 441, 457, 461, 495, 539–542, 546, 1009, 1207, 1213, 1216, 1217, 1227, 1233, 1246, 1265, 1278.
    Tenth, mentioned, 7, 15, 33, 54, 61, 124, 204, 216, 218, 224, 229, 246, 539–542, 544, 546, 1265, 1278, 1354.
    Eleventh, mentioned, 1151, 1159, 1169, 1175, 1188, 1198, 1207, 1217, 1227, 1233, 1235, 1239, 1240, 1244, 1246, 1249, 1250, 1256, 1305, 1312, 1322, 1341.
    Fifteenth, mentioned, 1258, 1265, 1273, 1305, 1322, 1344.
   Engineers, mentioned, 33, 267, 443, 446, 448, 540, 541, 543, 544, 556, 557, 559, 562–564, 566, 567, 569–571, 573, 574, 576, 577, 579, 1026, 1030, 1047, 1080, 1085, 1094, 1095, 1114, 1128, 1142, 1148, 1151, 1159, 1169, 1176, 1188, 1195, 1199, 1203, 1207, 1227, 1234, 1247, 1290, 1293.
   Hospital Corps, mentioned, 93, 105, 304, 309, 421, 426, 482, 571, 574, 576, 577, 579, 998, 1018, 1019, 1022, 1025, 1029, 1030, 1039, 1041, 1046, 1059, 1063, 1064, 1066, 1069, 1073, 1085–1087, 1142, 1151, 1159, 1169, 1176, 1188, 1199, 1207, 1218, 1227, 1234, 1247, 1292, 1321, 1324, 1330, 1351.
   Infantry—
    First, mentioned, 7, 15, 33, 128, 183, 187, 195, 202, 204, 224, 226, 239, 255, 535, 538, 540–543, 545, 1204, 1216, 1217, 1221, 1222, 1227, 1233, 1246, 1265.
    Second, mentioned, 7, 11, 15, 33, 105, 124, 127, 175, 193, 197, 212, 219, 229, 246, 361, 422, 459, 465, 520, 528, 529, 535, 538–541, 543, 545, 1204, 1208, 1217, 1227, 1233, 1246 1301.
    Third, mentioned, 7, 33, 202, 213, 219, 224, 235, 241, 535, 540, 542, 544, 545, 561–563, 565, 566, 568, 569, 571–573, 575, 576, 578, 838, 852, 854, 856, 855, 866, 870, 874, 881, 882, 884, 885, 887, 889, 890, 893, 982, 995, 998, 1001, 1015, 1016, 1019, 1025, 1026, 1032, 1041, 1047, 1052, 1053, 1055, 1060, 1062, 1063, 1079, 1093, 1114, 1128, 1135, 1142, 1159, 1169, 1175, 1188, 1198, 1207, 1217, 1227, 1233, 1246, 1254, 1318, 1319, 1321, 1355.
    Fourth, mentioned, 7, 15, 33, 124, 216, 224, 539–543, 545, 547, 562, 563, 565–567, 569, 570, 572–574, 576, 578, 666, 681, 838, 841–843, 852, 854, 856, 857, 859–861, 863, 865, 866, 869, 870, 873, 874, 878, 879, 1001, 1003, 1016–1018, 1020, 1021, 1025, 1026, 1029, 1032, 1039, 1041, 1047, 1052–1054, 1056, 1077, 1079, 1093, 1101, 1114, 1128, 1129, 1142, 1159, 1169, 1175, 1188, 1198, 1207, 1217, 1227, 1233, 1246, 1306.
    Fifth, mentioned, 7, 231, 234, 235, 237, 238, 245, 276, 292, 307, 309, 311, 315, 317, 329, 370, 422, 459, 465, 534–536, 539, 1208, 1211, 1217, 1227, 1233, 1246, 1264.
    Sixth, mentioned, 7, 15, 33, 124, 212, 214, 218, 225, 227, 539–541, 543–545, 565, 567, 568, 570, 571, 573, 574, 577, 579, 838, 926, 929, 953, 962, 980, 998, 1005, 1016, 1018, 1019, 1025, 1026, 1030, 1037, 1039, 1047, 1052, 1060, 1075, 1079, 1094, 1106, 1114, 1121, 1128, 1142, 1159, 1169, 1175, 1188, 1198, 1207, 1217, 1227, 1233, 1246, 1338, 1343.
    Seventh, mentioned, 7, 11, 15, 33, 124, 174, 193, 197, 202, 204, 206, 209, 212, 216, 226, 243, 245, 539–542, 544–546, 1126, 1265, 1345.
    Eighth, mentioned, 7, 11, 15, 33, 124, 204, 206, 213, 214, 218, 219, 224, 292, 302, 328, 333, 422, 459, 465, 535, 537–543, 545, 1208, 1211, 1217, 1221, 1225, 1227, 1233, 1246, 1341, 1344, 1345, 1357.
    Ninth, mentioned, 7, 15, 33, 124, 183, 193, 197, 219, 227, 246, 412, 415, 417–418, 419, 422–426,

Army—Continued.
  Organizations—Continued.
   Infantry—Continued.
    Ninth—Continued.
     428, 430–435, 438, 440, 441, 443–445, 449, 454, 460, 463, 464, 469, 477, 478, 481, 482, 489, 494, 495, 497, 500, 503–505, 535, 539, 540, 542–545, 563–566, 568, 571–573, 575, 576, 578, 926, 929, 936, 937, 943, 951, 967, 1008, 1009, 1015, 1016, 1018–1021, 1025–1027, 1030, 1032, 1038, 1041, 1047, 1050, 1052, 1055, 1076, 1080, 1094, 1114, 1128, 1142, 1151, 1159, 1175, 1188, 1198, 1207, 1217, 1227, 1278, 1294, 1309, 1318, 1323, 1324, 1338, 1339, 1342, 1343.
     To constitute legation guard, 480.
    Tenth, mentioned, 7, 15, 33, 124, 216, 219, 227, 229, 248, 535, 537, 538, 540, 541, 543, 545, 1008, 1053, 1249, 1258, 1273, 1316, 1318, 1319, 1321, 1382.
    Eleventh, mentioned, 7, 30, 273, 275, 306, 307, 309, 310, 329, 358, 359, 380, 382, 390, 534–537, 539, 1265, 1273, 1318, 1319, 1330.
    Twelfth, mentioned, 7, 11, 15, 33, 124, 171, 175, 195, 204, 214, 219, 224, 232, 235, 539–542, 544, 545, 563–565, 566, 568, 569, 571–573, 575, 576, 578, 838, 852, 854–857, 859, 860, 863, 865, 866, 869, 870, 874, 876, 882, 885, 889, 903, 904, 906, 1003, 1008, 1015, 1017, 1018, 1020, 1025–1027, 1029, 1032, 1041, 1047, 1050–1052, 1053, 1055–1057, 1060, 1062, 1080, 1094, 1114, 1128, 1142, 1151, 1159, 1169, 1175, 1188, 1198, 1207, 1217, 1227, 1233, 1246, 1299, 1318, 1323.
    Thirteenth, mentioned, 7, 15, 33, 124, 206, 212, 225–227, 229, 539, 540, 542, 543, 545, 564–573, 575, 577, 578, 953, 962, 976, 977, 978, 997, 1008, 1010, 1018–1020, 1026, 1027, 1030, 1032, 1039, 1047, 1056, 1060, 1080, 1082, 1094, 1114, 1128, 1142, 1151, 1159, 1169, 1175, 1188, 1198, 1207, 1217, 1227, 1233, 1246, 1318, 1342, 1343, 1849.
    Fourteenth, casualties in band, 480, 486.
     Mentioned, 54, 422, 426, 430, 431, 434, 449, 453, 454, 458, 460, 463–465, 469, 477, 481, 482, 484, 486–488, 491, 556–567, 569–574, 576, 577, 579, 640–642, 644, 647, 648, 660, 663, 664, 668, 669, 671, 721, 736, 769, 770, 772, 779, 917, 978, 979, 998, 1001, 1008, 1012, 1015–1019, 1021, 1023, 1025–1027, 1029, 1032, 1039, 1047, 1060, 1062, 1074, 1077, 1079, 1082, 1094, 1114, 1128, 1142, 1147, 1151, 1155, 1156, 1159, 1163, 1169, 1175, 1188, 1198, 1207, 1217, 1227, 1233, 1246, 1277, 1290.
    Fifteenth, mentioned, 7, 422, 428, 431, 443, 446, 448, 456, 466, 474, 481, 488, 493, 494, 535, 538, 647, 666, 682–684, 687, 1195, 1208, 1211, 1217, 1227, 1233, 1246, 1316, 1318, 1319, 1344, 1345, 1357.
    Sixteenth, mentioned, 7, 11, 15, 33, 124, 183, 192, 229, 253, 317, 535, 537–541, 543, 545, 565, 568, 569, 571, 572, 574, 575, 577, 578, 926, 929, 953, 962, 980, 998, 1018, 1025, 1026, 1032, 1039, 1047, 1080, 1094, 1114, 1124, 1128, 1142, 1151, 1159, 1169, 1175, 1188, 1198, 1207, 1217, 1227, 1233, 1246, 1345, 1355.
    Seventeenth, mentioned, 7, 15, 33, 124, 171, 185, 205, 223, 224, 539–542, 544, 545, 562, 563, 565, 566, 568, 569, 571–573, 575, 577, 578, 838, 852, 854, 856, 857, 859–861, 863, 865, 866, 869–871, 873, 874, 876, 878–882, 884, 885, 887, 889–893, 904, 905, 1008, 1017, 1019, 1021, 1025–1027, 1030, 1039, 1041, 1047, 1050–1052, 1055, 1060, 1062, 1063, 1080, 1094, 1095, 1098, 1114, 1128, 1142, 1151, 1159, 1169, 1175, 1188, 1198, 1207, 1217, 1227, 1233, 1246, 1292, 1303, 1304, 1313, 1319, 1320, 1350.
    Eighteenth, mentioned, 7, 556–565, 567, 568, 570, 571, 573–575, 577, 579, 662, 689, 701, 704, 721, 748, 839, 862, 978, 998, 1019, 1025, 1026, 1030, 1032, 1039, 1047, 1080, 1094, 1106, 1107, 1111, 1114, 1128, 1142, 1147, 1148, 1151, 1159, 1169, 1171, 1179, 1188, 1193, 1198, 1207, 1217, 1227, 1233, 1246, 1277, 1292, 1293, 1303, 1328.
    Nineteenth, mentioned, 7, 30, 273, 275, 294, 306, 307, 309, 310, 316, 329, 358, 359, 382, 534–537, 539, 568–571, 573–575, 577, 579, 980, 996, 1004, 1012, 1014, 1013, 1033, 1037, 1039, 1041, 1042, 1047, 1058, 1060, 1062, 1063, 1066, 1075, 1076, 1080, 1089, 1094, 1106, 1114, 1122, 1128, 1142, 1151, 1159, 1169, 1188, 1198, 1207, 1217, 1227, 1233, 1246, 1338, 1343.

Army—Continued.
　Organizations—Continued.
　　Infantry—Continued.
　　　Twentieth, mentioned, 7, 18, 33, 124, 183, 209, 216, 224, 226, 229, 253, 422, 535, 540, 542, 544, 545, 561–564, 566–568, 571, 573, 574, 576, 577, 579, 666, 681, 838, 841, 842, 852–857, 860, 862, 863, 865, 866, 868–871, 876, 886, 887, 889, 908, 917, 931, 1016, 1018, 1019, 1025, 1026, 1039, 1041, 1047, 1060, 1080, 1094, 1114, 1128, 1142, 1151, 1159, 1169, 1175, 1188, 1198, 1207, 1217, 1227, 1233, 1246, 1275, 1303, 1313, 1316, 1317.
　　　　Preparation for service in Philippine Islands, 842.
　　　　Strength and condition, 842, 860.
　　　Twenty-first, mentioned, 7, 15, 33, 124, 127, 206, 212, 220, 253, 539, 540, 543, 545, 564, 565, 567, 569, 572–574, 576, 578, 926, 929, 953, 959, 960, 962, 967, 969, 1008, 1009, 1015, 1018–1021, 1025–1027, 1038, 1041, 1042, 1047, 1054, 1060, 1062, 1063, 1080, 1114, 1126, 1128, 1142, 1151, 1159, 1169, 1175, 1188, 1198, 1217, 1227, 1233, 1246, 1306, 1318, 1323, 1338.
　　　Twenty-second, condition, 841.
　　　　Mentioned, 7, 15, 33, 124, 197, 206, 214, 219, 302, 540–543, 545, 561–563, 565, 566, 568, 569, 571–573, 575, 576, 578, 838, 841, 842, 852, 855, 856, 859, 865, 866, 870, 882, 883, 887–889, 892, 931, 938, 1001, 1008, 1019, 1025, 1026, 1039, 1041, 1047, 1050, 1053, 1062, 1077, 1080, 1087, 1094, 1100, 1109, 1114, 1128, 1142, 1151, 1159, 1169, 1175, 1188, 1198, 1217, 1227, 1233, 1246, 1312–1314.
　　　　Strength, present and absent, 843.
　　　Twenty-third, mentioned, 7, 556–565, 567, 568, 570–577, 579, 662, 689, 702, 704, 716, 721, 748, 758, 802, 841, 917, 918, 950, 997, 998, 1015, 1019, 1025, 1026, 1039, 1047, 1052, 1057, 1075, 1080, 1094, 1106, 1110, 1114, 1128, 1142, 1147, 1148, 1151, 1159, 1169, 1171, 1175, 1188, 1193, 1198, 1207, 1217, 1227, 1233, 1246, 1277, 1292, 1294.
　　　Twenty-fourth, mentioned, 7, 15, 33, 124, 183, 192, 193, 197, 202, 204, 209, 213, 214, 218, 223, 229, 241, 244, 248, 255, 540, 542, 543, 545, 567, 569, 570, 572, 573, 575, 576, 578, 838, 854, 856, 858, 918, 1009, 1012, 1013, 1017, 1018, 1020–1024, 1030, 1039, 1047, 1052, 1055, 1057, 1060, 1080, 1094, 1106, 1114, 1115, 1116, 1120, 1121, 1124, 1128, 1142, 1151, 1159, 1169, 1175, 1188, 1198, 1207, 1215–1217, 1227, 1233, 1246, 1270, 1272, 1350, 1354.
　　　Twenty-fifth, mentioned, 15, 33, 124, 171, 212, 224, 541–543, 545, 566, 567, 569, 571–573, 575, 577, 578, 1009, 1012–1014, 1018, 1020–1023, 1025, 1030, 1039, 1047, 1054, 1080, 1094, 1104, 1114, 1116, 1128, 1130, 1132, 1142, 1151, 1159, 1169, 1175, 1188, 1198, 1207, 1215–1217, 1227, 1233, 1246, 1270–1272, 1254, 1256, 1257.
　　Macabebe Scouts, mentioned, 1076, 1093, 1100, 1106, 1113.
　Signal Corps—
　　Interruption of Aguinaldo's communication by, 812.
　　Mentioned, 142, 143, 184, 209, 295, 304, 328, 419, 478, 541, 543, 544, 566, 567, 569–571, 573, 574, 576, 577, 579, 998, 1012, 1018, 1019, 1023, 1026, 1030, 1080, 1086, 1094, 1095, 1114, 1128, 1142, 1148, 1151, 1159, 1169, 1176, 1188, 1199, 1207, 1218, 1227, 1234, 1247, 1321.
　　Transportation, arranging for, 139, 142, 143.
　Volunteers. *See* Volunteers.
Arndt, Fred W., pvt., Co. E, 22d U. S. Inf., wounded, 946.
Arneson, Arnold, pvt., Co. A, 13th Minn. Vol. Inf., wounded, 947.
Arnold, Abraham K., brig. gen., U. S. V., mentioned, 535, 539, 547–551, 554, 555.
Arnold, John W., pvt., Co. F, 23d U. S. Inf., death, 1208.
Arnold, Louis, pvt., Batty. F, 5th U. S. Art., wounded, 1085.
Arnovitch, Morris, pvt., Hosp. Corps, U. S. A., wounded, 1176.
Arrick, Harry E., pvt., Co. E, 11th U. S. Inf., wounded, 390.
Arthur, George W., pvt., Co. C, 6th U. S. Inf., wounded, 1084.

Arvidson, Nels, pvt., Co. D, 22d U. S. Inf., wounded, 941.
Ashbery, Joe H., pvt., Co. M, 38th U. S. Inf., death, 1215.
Ashby, High R., mus., Co. C, 23d U. S. Inf., wounded, 956.
Ashcraft, Charles W., sergt., Co. C, 10th Pa. Vol. Inf., wounded, 954.
Ashcroft, Elmer H., pvt., Co. E, 20th Kans. Vol. Inf., wounded, 995.
Ashline, Michael, pvt., Co. I, 21st U. S. Inf., mentioned, 1042.
Ashley, Council C., pvt., Co. F, 4th U. S. Inf., death, 1249.
Ashmore, Joseph E., pvt., Co. D, 12th U. S. Inf., mentioned, 224.
Ashworth, Walter, pvt., Co. A, 27th U. S. Inf., death, 1276.
Asks, lieut. col., Japanese forces, member temporary government council, 438.
Asselstine, Charles, pvt, Troop G, 11th U. S. Cav., wounded, 1203.
Associated Press, reports of, 1036, 1135, 1136.
Astor, John Jacob, lieut. col., I. G., U. S. V., mentioned, 70, 164, 190, 196.
　On staff of General Shafter, 70.
Atchison, Fred, pvt., Co. G, 20th Kans. Vol. Inf., wounded, 954.
Athenian, U. S. transport, mentioned, 441, 448, 463, 465, 475, 1059, 1061, 1078, 1084, 1213, 1219.
Athey, Harry R., pvt., Co. A, 1st Mont. Vol. Inf., wounded, 950, 956.
Atkins, Harvey, pvt., Co. I, 2d Mass. Vol. Inf., mentioned, 183.
Atkinson, Edward, pamphlets sent out by, destruction, 973.
Atkinson, G. W., governor, West Virginia, mentioned, 324.
Atlanta, Ga., recruits to be equipped and drilled at, 47.
Attik, Dato, mentioned, 1118.
Attorney-General, United States, mentioned, 101, 103.
Atwater, Ernestine, missionary in China, murder, 471, 476.
Atwater, Mary, missionary in China, murder, 471, 476.
Atwater, ——, missionary in China, murder of, and family, 471, 476.
Augur, Jacob A., maj., 4th U. S. Cav., mentioned, 1031.
Augustin, Joseph N., 2d lieut., 24th U. S. Inf., killed, 124.
Augustine, Charles C., corpl., Co. M, 1st Wash. Vol. Inf., wounded, 898.
　Mentioned, 83.
Augustine, M. Isidore, Swedish and Norwegian consul, mentioned, 90.
Auspach, Francis G., pvt., Co. A, 1st Mont. Vol. Inf., wounded, 917.
Aust, Frank, pvt., Co. G, 1st Cal. Vol. Inf., wounded, 898.
Austin, John, pvt., Co. K, 24th U. S. Inf., death, 1152.
Austin, O. H., mentioned, 331.
Australia, U. S. transport, mentioned, 556, 605, 612, 624, 660, 661, 663, 664, 670, 671, 749, 758, 767, 776, 780.
Australia and China Telegraph Company (Eastern extension) requests U. S. recognition of Spanish concessions, 965.
Avery, Howard S., 2d lieut., 14th U. S. Inf., wounded, 1015.
Axline, Henry A., col., 10th Ohio Vol. Inf., mentioned, 526.
Axt, Albert E., pvt., Co. H, 22d U. S. Inf., wounded, 946.
Axtell, Hays, pvt., Co. G, 1st Mont. Vol. Inf., wounded, 945.
Axtell, William A., pvt., Co. K, 35d Inf., U. S. V., death of, 1125.
Aydelotte, John W., pvt., Co. C, 9th U. S. Inf., killed, 1297.
Ayer, Waldo E., capt., 12th U. S. Inf., mentioned, 1347.
Ayers, William J., sergt., Co. K, 18th U. S. Inf., wounded, 1240.
Aztec, U. S. transport, mentioned, 448, 457, 463, 465, 475, 1071, 1089, 1094, 1095, 1111, 1212, 1247, 1276, 1280.

INDEX. 1365

Babb, Alonzo J., pvt., Co. M, 14th U.S. Inf., wounded, 454.
Babcock, A. J., 1st lieut., 33d Mich. Vol. Inf., mentioned, 183.
Babcock, Campbell S., 2d lieut., 1st U. S. Cav., mentioned, 646.
Babcock, Delos D., pvt., Co. G, 1st Mont. Vol. Inf., wounded, 900.
Babcock, John B., lieut. col., a. g. dept.; brig. gen., U. S. V., 646, 652, 653, 667, 689, 766, 767, 782, 783, 815, 1134.
Back, Henry, pvt., Co. E, 19th U. S. Inf., death, 1070.
Bacolod, Dato, mentioned, 1349.
Bacon, Martin, corpl., Troop E, 9th U. S. Cav., wounded, 1240.
Bacon, John M., brig. gen., U. S. V., 841.
Badger, U. S. auxiliary cruiser, mentioned, 228, 230, 231, 234, 240, 599.
Badger, Lewis R., pvt., Co. F, 20th Kans. Vol. Inf., death, 879.
Badgett, Green, pvt., Co. H, 25th U. S. Inf., death, 1274.
Baehr, William L., sergt., Co. L, 1st Nebr. Vol. Inf., wounded, 967.
Baer, Richard G., pvt., Co. E, 10th Pa. Vol. Inf., wounded, 954.
Baggage, over-sea allowance, officers, 865.
Bailey, Alvin H., pvt., Hosp. Corps, U. S. A., wounded, 1085.
Bailey, Clarence M., lieut. col., 13th U. S. Inf., mentioned, 829.
Bailey, George, 1st sergt., Co. D, 9th U. S. Inf., wounded, 444, 460.
Bailey, John A., pvt., Co. L, 2d Oreg. Vol. Inf., wounded, 946.
Bailey, Sidney, pvt., Co. G, 1st Idaho Vol. Inf., wounded, 897.
Bailey, William T., pvt., Co. K, 6th U. S. Inf., death, 1181.
Baine, Horace G., pvt., Co. B, 30th Inf., U. S. V., wounded, 1147.
Baird, Jesse P., pvt., Co. C, 1st Nebr. Vol. Inf., wounded, 967.
Baird, Thomas E., corpl., Co. C, 9th U. S. Inf., death, 1297.
Baker, Albert T., pvt., Co. K, 13th U. S. Inf., death, 1164.
Baker, Alvin G., pvt., Co. B, 22d U. S. Inf., death, 1164.
Baker, Bernard, sergt., Troop D, 11th U. S. Cav., killed, 1237.
Baker, Charles A., pvt., Co. A, 35th Inf., U. S. V., killed, 1257.
Baker, Clinton S., sergt., Co. G, 26th U. S. Inf., death, 1217.
Baker, Edward, pvt., Co. A, 19th U S. Inf., killed, 1202.
Baker, Edward M., pvt., Co. D, 45th Inf., U. S. V., death, 1168.
Baker, Fred A., pvt., Co. F, 3d U. S. Inf., wounded, 995.
Baker, George W., pvt., Co. G, 13th Minn. Vol. Inf., wounded, 916.
Baker, Harvey, mus., Co. E, 14th U. S. Inf., wounded, 460.
Baker, Hiram C., capt., 39th Inf., U. S. V., wounded, 1131, 1146.
Baker, Homer A., pvt., Co. D, 1st S. Dak. Vol. Inf., wounded, 954.
Baker, James W., pvt., Co. K, 3d U. S. Inf., wounded, 995.
Baker, John, pvt., Co. D, 26th U. S. Inf., death, 1194.
Baker, Robert L., pvt., Co. A, 49th Inf., U. S. V., death, 1223.
Baker, William B., pvt., Astor Battery, U. S. A., wounded, 761.
Baker, William H., pvt., Co. I, 18th U. S. Inf., death, 1196.
Bakewell, Allen C., jun. vice-comdr. Lafayette Post, G. A. R., mentioned, 387, 399.
Balch, Lewis, maj., surg., U. S. V., mentioned, 1178.
Baldwin, Dorman, jr., 2d lieut., 1st N. Dak. Vol. Inf., wounded, 957.

Baldwin, Frank D., brig. gen., U. S. A., congratulated by President, 1335, 1336.
Expeditions against Moros, 1327, 1329–1331, 1333.
Mentioned, 1349.
Shooting of soldiers by Moros, 1322.
Baldwin, John A., capt., 9th U. S. Inf., mentioned, 371.
Baldwin, Theodore A., lieut. col., 10th U. S. Cav., mentioned, 546.
Baldwin, William H., lieut. col., sub. dept., U. S. A., mentioned, 887.
Baldwin, W. H., jr., mentioned, 206.
Bale, Frederick, pvt., Co. A, 36th Inf., U. S. V., death, 1109.
Baley, ——, pvt., U. S. Marine Corps, death, 1314.
Ball, Collin H., 2d lieut., 20th Kans. Vol. Inf., wounded, 976.
Ball, Sidney H., pvt., Co. F, 30th U. S. Inf., death, 1215.
Ballan, Fred L., pvt., Co. H, 1st Wash. Vol. Inf., wounded, 1044.
Ballance, John G., capt., 22d U. S. Inf., mentioned, 1103, 1109.
Ballanger, Charles, pvt., Co. L, 1st Nebr. Vol. Inf., killed, 897.
Ballard, Henry W., pvt., Co. F, 23d U. S. Inf., wounded, 760.
Ballard, Thorn H., pvt., Co. I, 14th U. S. Inf., wounded, 1015.
Ballenger, Charles O., pvt., Co. D, 1st Nebr. Vol. Inf., killed, 956.
Ballenger, Henry, pvt., Co. D, 48th Inf., U. S. V., death, 1189.
Ballin, Alfred, corpl., Troop I, 3d U. S. Cav., wounded, 1275.
Ballou, John E., pvt., Co. I, 20th Kans. Vol. Inf., wounded, 952.
Baltimore, U. S. cruiser, mentioned, 215, 832.
Bancroft, U. S. gunboat, mentioned, 22, 39.
Bancroft, William A., brig. gen., U. S. V., mentioned, 549.
Bandain, Felix George, pvt., Troop F, 11th Cav., U. S. V., death, 1149.
Bander, Charles L., pvt., Co. H, 51st Iowa Vol. Inf., wounded, 983.
Bandholtz, Harry H., capt., 2d U. S. Inf., mentioned, 1334.
Bank, Andrew, pvt., Co. I, 10th Pa. Vol. Inf., mentioned, 952.
Banker, William L., pvt., Co. L, 15th U. S. Inf., killed, 1211.
Banks, George T., corpl., Co. E, 1st Mont. Vol. Inf., wounded, 945.
Banks, Robert, pvt., Co. F, 49th Inf., U. S. V., drowned, 1221.
Banks, William, pvt., Co. B, 49th Inf., U. S. V., death, 1149.
Banning, Benonie, pvt., Co. H, 32d Inf., U. S. V., death, 1236.
Barber, Francis V., brig. gen., U. S. V., 732.
Barber, Fred, pvt., Co. I, 1st S. Dak. Vol. Inf., wounded, 948.
Barber, Herbert P., pvt., Co. A, 1st Nebr. Vol. Inf., wounded, 955.
Barber, Lewis F., pvt., Co. C, 1st S. Dak. Vol. Inf., wounded, 954.
Barber, Merritt C., col., a. a. g., U. S. A., sick in hospital at Manila, 1181.
Barber, Sim, pvt., Co. L, 20th Kans. Vol. Inf., death, 923.
Barber, Thomas H., col., 1st N. Y. Vol. Inf., brig. gen., U. S. A.; mentioned, 706, 707, 715, 720, 721, 725–727, 729, 758, 762, 783, 784, 851.
Barber, William C., pvt., Co. E, 20th Kans. Vol. Inf., wounded, 901.
Barclay, Morrison, pvt., Co. I, 10th Pa. Vol. Inf., wounded, 950.
Barclay, William, pvt., Co. I, 45th Inf., U. S. V., death, 1200.
Bardelson, Samuel, sergt., Co. I, 34th Inf., U. S. V., wounded, 1188.
Bare, Alonzo, pvt., Co. D, 32d Inf., U. S. V., death, 1156.
Barieau, Louis H., pvt., Co. G, 1st Cal. Vol. Inf., wounded, 924.
Barjaron, Ernest B., civilian scout, wounded, 1130.

Barker, Everet, pvt., Co. G, 31st Inf., U. S. V., death, 1136.
Barker, Everet, pvt., Co. G, 33d Inf., U. S. V., death, 1156.
Barker, George L., 1st sergt., Co. A, 1st S. Dak. Vol. Inf., wounded, 996.
Barker, John L., pvt., Co. M, 23d U. S. Inf., wounded, 916.
Barker, Joseph, pvt., Co. C, 3d U. S. Inf., death, 1221.
Barker, Simeon T., pvt., Co. B, 18th U. S. Inf., wounded, 1113.
Barker, Verne A., pvt., Co. I, 13th Minn. Vol. Inf., death, 923.
Barkla, Clarence S., corpl., Co. M, 27th Inf., U. S. V., death, 1136.
Barkley, Howard, corpl., Co. E, 1st Idaho Vol. Inf., wounded, 901.
Barkley, James H., brig. gen., U. S. V., mentioned, 551, 552.
Barkley, William, sergt., Co. M, 20th U. S. Inf., wounded, 936.
Barlow, Jesse E., pvt., Co. F, 36th Inf., U. S. V., death, 1189.
Barnard, Dell W., pvt., Co. D, 34th Inf., U. S. V., death, 1243.
Barnell, David O., pvt., Co. L, 1st Nebr. Vol. Inf., wounded, 946.
Barnes, Elmer E., mus., Co. C, 10th Pa. Vol. Inf., wounded, 946.
Barnes, ——, corpl., Co. E, 16th Pa. Vol. Inf., wounded in action, 378.
Barnes, Wiley, pvt., Co. L, 23d U. S. Inf., wounded, 956.
Barnes, William, corpl., Co. F, 12th U. S. Inf., wounded, 1055.
Barnes, William, pvt., Troop E, 3d U. S. Cav., killed, 1185.
Barnes, William T., pvt., Co. A, 41st Inf., U. S. V., death, 1200.
Barnett, James E., lieut. col., 10th Pa. Vol. Inf., request to join regiment in P. I., 734, 739, 752, 753.
Mentioned, 735, 742, 753.
Barnett, John T., col., 159th Ind. Vol. Inf., mentioned, 521.
Barnhart, Harry, pvt., Co. C, 41st Inf., U. S. V., death, 1201.
Barnum, Malvern H., 2d lieut., 10th U. S. Cav., wounded, 124.
Baron, Gilbert L., corpl., Co. C, 33d Inf., U. S. V., death, 1123.
Baroni, ——, pvt., U. S. Marine Corps, death, 1314.
Barrett, Gregory, capt., 10th U. S. Inf., mentioned, 216.
Barrett, James, pvt., Co. H, 13th Minn. Vol. Inf., wounded, 984.
Barrett, James, pvt., Batty. L, 3d U. S. Art., wounded, 947.
Barrett, James F., artif., Co. F, 40th Inf., U. S. V., death, 1236.
Barrett, Thomas J., pvt., Co. E, 17th U. S. Inf., 205.
Barrowman, Henry E., pvt., Co. E, 13th Minn. Vol. Inf., mentioned, 762.
Wounded, 761.
Barrows, Frederick J., 1st lieut., 30th Inf., U. S. V., probable dismissal, 1278, 1279.
Barry, John J., pvt., Co. A, 28th Inf., U. S. V., wounded, 1130.
Barry, John J., pvt., Co. L, 19th U. S. Inf., death, 1233.
Barry, Michael, pvt., Troop C, 3d U. S. Cav., killed, 1147.
Barry, Michael, pvt., Co. H, 21st U. S. Inf., death, 1090.
Barry, Thomas H., lieut. col., a. a. g., U. S. A.
General MacArthur requests, be made chief of staff, 1177, 1181.
Instructions to Major Orwig, 1263.
Mentioned, 453, 457, 458, 460, 469, 470, 700, 706, 1142.
Barth, Albert E., pvt., Co. M, 14th U. S. Inf., wounded, 895.
Barth, Edward, pvt., Co. G, 21st U. S. Inf., death, 1152.
Bartholomew, William, pvt., Troop D, 2d U. S. Cav., mentioned, 197.
Bartlett, Edward R., pvt., Co. D, 1st Wash. Vol. Inf., wounded, 941.
Bartlett, Franklin, col., 22d N. Y. Vol. Inf., mentioned, 293.

Bartlett, Robert M., pvt., Co. H, 42d Inf., U. S. V., death, 1149.
Bartlett, William J., corpl., Co. E, 35th Inf., U. S. V., wounded, 1176.
Barton, Clara, Miss, mentioned, 92, 165, 210, 214, 228, 231-233, 237, 239, 246.
Barton, Ross, 1st sergt., Co. G, 47th Inf., U. S. V., wounded, 1147.
Barton, Samuel F., pvt., Co. B, 20th Kans. Vol. Inf., wounded, 948.
Barton, Stephen L., chairman Central Cuban Relief Com., mentioned, 165, 167, 210.
Bartz, Gustav, corpl., Co. F, 9th U. S. Inf., wounded, 444.
Basford, Theodore B., pvt., Co. I, 8th U. S. Inf., death, 1215.
Bash, William H., pvt., Co. F, 20th Kans. Vol. Inf., death, 875.
Bassford, Joseph H., sergt., Co. E, 36th Inf., U. S. V., death, 1088.
Bastian, Edward, cook, Co. D, 41st Inf., U. S. V., death, 1170.
Batchelor, Joseph B., jr., capt., 24th U. S. Inf., mentioned, 1031, 1115, 1116, 1121, 1124.
Batdorf, Edwin, col. 1st Mo. Vol. Inf., mentioned, 531, 532, 533.
Bates, Arthur, pvt., Troop H, 4th U. S. Cav., captured by insurgents, 1196.
Bates, Charles E., corpl., Co. I, 18th U. S. Inf., wounded, 943.
Bates, Earl R., pvt., Co. L, 37th Inf., U. S. V., death, 1151.
Bates, John C., maj. gen., U. S. V.:
Mentioned, 47, 70, 101, 116, 181, 202, 216, 226, 255, 256, 516-518, 534, 542, 544, 545, 556, 559, 572, 574, 841, 995, 1027, 1052, 1058, 1060, 1074, 1075, 1099, 1117, 1118, 1121, 1129, 1131, 1135, 1138, 1144, 1148, 1154, 1155, 1158, 1159, 1192, 1242, 1270, 1272.
Opinion re health of Army in Cuba, 202.
Recommended for promotion, 104.
Bates, Milton T., pvt., Co. I, 25th U. S. Inf., death, 1200.
Bates, Robert F., maj., 22d U. S. Inf., mentioned, 1031.
Bates, Thomas O., pvt., Co. F, 43d Inf., U. S. V., death, 1168.
Batey, Frederick S., pvt., Co. B, 12th U. S. Inf., death, 1052.
Bath, ——, a. a. surg., U. S. A., captured by insurgents, released, 1222.
Bathe, Otto F. H., pvt., Co. L, 15th U. S. Inf., wounded, 1211.
Bathiany, Harry W., 2d lieut., 3d U. S. Inf., conditions in vicinity, Sulat, P. I., 1296.
Bathing facilities, transports, 773.
Batson, Matthew A., 1st lieut., 4th U. S. Cav., mentioned, 1076, 1093, 1100, 1197.
Wounded, 1113.
Battersly, George M., pvt., Co. M, 20th Kans. Vol. Inf., wounded, 897.
Bandreau, Edward, pvt., Co. G, 17th U. S. Inf., wounded, 1017.
Bauer, Frank, pvt., Co. E, 42d Inf., U. S. V., death, 1167.
Bauman, Edward, pvt., Co. E, 3d U. S. Inf., death, 1151.
Baumler, Henry, pvt., Co. E, 23d U. S. Inf., death, 1074.
Bayan, Sultan of:
Consultation with General Davis, 1335.
Death, 1336.
Baylis, Richard E., pvt., Batty. L, 6th U. S. Art., death, 1078.
Bay State, hospital ship, mentioned, 245, 246, 252, 254.
Bayern, steamer, 400 boxes rifles shipped from Bremerhaven to Hongkong, 1134.
Baytel, Edward M., pvt., Co. E, 37th Inf., U. S. V., wounded, 1193.
Beach, Charles H., pvt., Co. A, 39th Inf., U. S. V., death, 1215.
Beach, Fred S., qm. sergt., Co. K, 12th U. S. Inf., wounded, 1057.
Beach, Jack L., pvt., Co. M, 1st Nebr. Vol. Inf., wounded, 955.
Beach, Lewis B., pvt., Co. F, 1st Idaho Vol. Inf., wounded, 897.
Beall, Clarence W., pvt., Co. K, 4th U. S. Inf., death, 1109.
Beall, Fielder M. M., capt., 3d U. S. Inf., mentioned, 943.

INDEX. 1367

Beals, Frank L., pvt., Co. E, Sig. Corps, U. S. V., wounded, 1081.
Bear, P. E., judge, mentioned, 316.
Bearse, Richard, sergt., Co. B, 2d Mass. Vol. Inf., mentioned, 202.
Beattie, Archie, pvt., Co. C, 1st Ill. Vol. Inf., mentioned, 209.
Beattie, Edward W., pvt., Co. A, Batt. Engrs., death, 1152.
Beatty, Harry W., qm. sergt., Co. F, 35th Inf., U. S. V., wounded, 1124.
Beatty, John, pvt., Co. I, 47th Inf., U. S. V., wounded, 1250.
Beaty, Maurice P., pvt., Co. C, 13th Minn. Vol. Inf., killed, 963.
Beauchene, William, pvt., Co. F, 1st Idaho Vol. Inf., death, 1045.
Beaudette, Napoleon L., pvt., Co. H, 46th Inf., U. S. V., death, 1167.
Beaulien, Wilfried, pvt., Co. G, 42d Inf., U. S. V., death, 1267.
Beavers, Joseph F., pvt., Co. K, 9th U. S. Inf., wounded, 1008.
Bechdolt, Simon P., pvt., Co. M, 38th Inf., U. S. V., death, 1241.
Beck, Frederick W., mus., Co. C, 1st Idaho Vol. Inf., wounded, 897.
Beck, Porter, pvt., Co. K, 31st Inf., U. S. V., death, 1164.
Beck, James, lieut. col., 23d Kans. Vol. Inf., mentioned, 241.
Becker, Dr., geologist, mentioned, 721.
Becker, Ernest L., corpl., Co. G, 9th U. S. Inf., death, 1186.
Beckman, Joseph, pvt., Co. F, 1st Mont. Vol. Inf., killed, 945.
Beckwith, George, pvt., Co. B, 18th U. S. Inf., wounded, 1113.
Bedell, Edward L., pvt., Co. A, 21st U. S. Inf., death, 1048.
Bedford, Clifford R., pvt., Co. E, 14th U. S. Inf., death, 491.
Bedford, George, pvt., Co. E, 9th U. S. Inf., killed, 1307.
Beecher, Henry C., pvt., Co. A, 1st Mont. Vol. Inf., killed, 937.
Beehler, William H., commander, U. S. N., mentioned, 1126.
Beehmann, Fred C., pvt., Co. K, 1st Wash. Vol. Inf., death, 1063.
Beer, James, pvt., Co. B, 37th Inf., U. S. V., wounded, 1182.
Begley, John, pvt., Co. K, 3d U. S. Inf., killed by accident, 1238.
Behm, Alfred, pvt., Co. C, 22d U. S. Inf., wounded, 936.
Behm, John, pvt., Co. M, 51st Iowa Vol. Inf., wounded, 975.
Beiser, Charles, sergt., Co. K, 4th U. S. Cav., death, 875.
Belden, William O., pvt., Co. L, 1st Nebr. Vol. Inf., killed, 983.
Belding, William E., pvt., band, 46th Inf., U. S. V., death, 1202.
Belgian King, transport, mentioned, 459, 1069, 1071, 1085.
Belgic, U. S. transport, mentioned, 695.
Belk, Erasmus, corpl., Co. I, 21st U. S. Inf., death, 1194.
Belknap, Bruce F., pvt., Co. K, 1st Mont. Vol. Inf., wounded, 983.
Bell, Frederick J., sergt., Co. B, 33d Inf., U. S. V., killed, 1137.
Bell, Frank T., pvt., Co. L, 37th Inf., U. S. V., wounded, 1211.
Bell, George S., pvt., Co. I, 9th U. S. Inf., death, 495.
Bell, James M., brig. gen., U. S. V., mentioned, 578, 972, 1158, 1159, 1259.
Wounded, 54, 55, 123.
Bell, J. Franklin, brig. gen., U. S. A.
Memorandum by General Merritt for guidance in treating with Filipinos, 818.
Mentioned, 575, 577, 578, 808, 819, 1030, 1042, 1066, 1073, 1083, 1087, 1091, 1093, 1097, 1109–1111, 1126, 1196, 1265, 1330, 1327, 1330, 1335, 1336.
Operations, 1110, 1158.
Wounded, 926.
Bell, John, pvt., Co. E, 25th U. S. Inf., death, 1233.
Bell, John T., pvt., Co. G, 38th Inf., U. S. V., death, 1248.

Bell, Thomas, pvt., Co. A, 24th U. S. Inf., death, 1109.
Bell, William E., pvt., Co. H, 44th Inf., U. S. V., death, 1238.
Bell, Wilman H., pvt., Co. C, 1st Cal. Vol. Inf., death, 879.
Bell, Willard R., pvt., Co. K, 19th U. S. Inf., wounded, 1141.
Bellinger, John B., capt., qm. dept., U. S. A., mentioned, 56, 63, 64, 139, 141–143, 148, 282, 292, 370.
Bellis, Wilson, pvt., Co. G, 45th Inf., U. S. V., killed, 1150.
Bellman, Herman, pvt., Co. B, 1st S. Dak. Vol. Inf., wounded, 920.
Bement, Robert B. C., maj., eng. officer, U. S. V., mentioned, 667, 688, 819.
Benchley, Edward N., 2d lieut., 6th U. S. Inf., killed, 121.
Bender, Frederick W., pvt., Co. I, 18th U. S. Inf., wounded, 1216.
Benedict, C. A., pvt., Co. H, 1st Idaho Vol. Inf., wounded, 943.
Benedict, John H., pvt., Co. C, 1st S. Dak. Vol. Inf., wounded, 954.
Beneke, Louis F., pvt., Co. K, 18th U. S. Inf., death, 1267.
Benham, Daniel W., col., 7th U. S. Inf., mentioned, 124.
Benham, Henry W., 1st lieut., 2d U. S. Inf., mentioned, 124.
Benicia Arsenal, Cal., arms in, for U. S. troops, 639, 641, 642, 992.
Benjamin, Edward, pvt., Co. D, 33d Mich. Vol. Inf., mentioned, 192.
Benjamin, James, pvt., Co. C, 24th U. S. Inf., killed, 1220.
Benmohr, U. S. transport, mentioned, 1099, 1103, 1128.
Benner, Evans F., pvt., Co. A, 44th Inf., U. S. V., wounded, 1240.
Bennett, Charles, pvt., Co. M, 20th Kans. Vol. Inf., wounded, 903.
Bennett, Fred, col., 3d Ill. Vol. Inf., mentioned, 510.
Bennett, James A., pvt., Co. E, 33d Inf., U. S. V., killed, 1137.
Bennett, Marion O., pvt., Co. K, 17th U. S. Inf., death, 1221.
Bennett, Thomas E., pvt., Co. C, 40th Inf., U. S. V., killed, 1182.
Bennett, Thomas H., pvt., Troop G, 4th U. S. Cav., death, 1142.
Bennett, Thomas R., pvt., Co. H, 34th Mich. Vol. Inf., mentioned, 202.
Bennett, William H., pvt., Hosp. Corps, U. S. A., death, 1264.
Bennington, Manford, corpl., Co. D, 14th U. S. Inf., wounded, 898.
Bensel, Herman, pvt., Co. I, 1st Nebr. Vol. Inf., wounded, 950.
Benson, Abram, pvt., Co. E, 24th U. S. Inf., mentioned, 224.
Benson, Charles, pvt., Troop C, 3d U. S. Cav., killed 1147.
Benson, George D., pvt., Co. C, 1st S. Dak. Vol. Inf., wounded, 948.
Bentley, George H., capt., 47th Inf., U. S. V., death, 1204.
Wounded, 1187.
Bentley, James, pvt., Co. H, 24th U. S. Inf., wounded, 1149.
Berdine, Walter, pvt., Co. E, 23d U. S. Inf., mentioned, 761.
Death, 803.
Berg, Otto J., pvt., Co. F, 1st S. Dak. Vol. Inf., death, 889.
Bergen, Martin H., pvt., Co. D, 5th U. S. Inf., wounded, 1251.
Bergen, Roy, pvt., Co. M, 14th U. S. Inf., killed, 453.
Bergh, Joseph M., pvt., Troop F, 6th U. S. Cav., mentioned, 195.
Bergunde, Albert, pvt., Co. G, 13th U. S. Inf., mentioned, 183.
Berhanan, Smith, pvt., Co. M, 25th U. S. Inf., death, 1219.
Berkshire, U. S. transport, mentioned, 190, 192, 198, 255.
Berlin, Jack, pvt., Troop K, 1st U. S. Cav., killed, 61.

Berlin, steamship, mentioned, 179, 191, 192, 245, 248, 249, 255, 256, 594, 606.
Bernard, Alfred E., pvt., Hosp. Corps, U. S. A., death, 1086.
Bernard, Albert O., pvt., Co. B, 43d Inf., U. S. V., death, 1221.
Bernard, John J., 2d lieut., 4th U. S. Inf., killed, 124, 167.
Bernier, Joseph P., pvt., Co. M, 1st Wash. Vol. Inf., wounded, 897.
Berry, Alfred, corpl., Co. B, 19th U. S. Inf., wounded, 1141.
Berry, Augustin, pvt., Co. F, 14th U. S. Inf., wounded, 895.
Berry, Frank, pvt., Co. C, 18th U. S. Inf., death, 803.
Berry, James F., sergt., Co. B, 27th Inf., U. S. V., killed, 1173.
Berry, J. H., mentioned, 348.
Berry, Joseph L., pvt., Co. M, 2d Oreg. Vol. Inf., killed, 963.
Berry, Leslie D., pvt., Co. A, 37th Inf., U. S. V., killed, 1086.
Bert, August, pvt., Batty. F, 5th U. S. Art., wounded, 1113.
Bess, Charles, pvt., Co. E, 13th U. S. Inf., wounded, 1008.
Bessie, lighter, mentioned, 56, 58, 66, 192.
Bethea, William B., pvt., Co. G, 33d Inf., U. S. V., wounded, 1124.
Bethel, Elijah, pvt., Co. I, 24th U. S. Inf., killed, 1196.
Betron, Frank, sergt., Co. C, 9th U. S. Inf., mentioned, 1296.
Wounded, 1298.
Bettin, Emil, pvt., Co. F, 12th U. S. Inf., suicide, 1241.
Betwee, Eugene F., corpl., Co. E, 30th Inf., U. S. V., wounded, 1199.
Betzold, William, pvt., Co. D, 6th U. S. Art., wounded, 984.
Bevan, Oscar, pvt., Co. F, 3d U. S. Inf., wounded, 981.
Bevan, Samuel H., sergt., Co. C, 41st Inf., U. S. V., death, 1191.
Bevans, Charles E., pvt., Co. E, 14th U. S. Inf., wounded, 1081.
Beyrow, Albert, corpl., Co. H, 12th U. S. Inf., wounded, 1051.
Bibber, Marshall D., pvt., Co. B, 13th U. S. Inf., wounded, 1084.
Bickham, Abraham S., capt., asst. qm., U. S. V., mentioned, 352, 951.
Bickhart, Wesley, 1st sergt., Co. H, 9th U. S. Inf., wounded, 444.
Biddle, John, capt., Engr. Corps, U. S. A., lieut. col., U. S. V., assigned to duty Guam Harbor, 1270.
Mentioned, 372, 404, 1218, 1224.
Biddle, William P., maj., U. S. Marine Corps, mentioned, 442, 459.
Biddle, William S., jr., capt., 14th U. S. Inf., mentioned, 1156.
Bie, Otto, capt., snag boat Suwanee, mentioned, 129, 271, 272.
Biegler, George W., capt., 28th Inf., U. S. V., wounded, 1222.
Biehl, Louis, pvt., Co. B, 18th U. S. Inf., killed, 943.
Bigelow, John, capt., 10th U. S. Cav., mentioned, 83.
Wounded, 124.
Biggs, William E., pvt., Co. C, 40th Inf., U. S. V., wounded, 1150.
Bigley, Thomas, pvt., Co. C, 21st U. S. Inf., mentioned, 253.
Bigos, Frank L., pvt., Co. H, 26th Inf., U. S. V., death, 1167.
Billman, Warren, sergt., Co. F, Sig. Corps, U. S. V., killed, 1192.
Bills, Charles S., col., 2d Nebr. Vol. Inf., mentioned, 530-533.
Bimson, Harvey, pvt., Co. F, 18th U. S. Inf., death, 1232.
Bindnagel, Philip, pvt., Co. H, 13th U. S. Inf., death, 1189.
Bingham, Henry H., Hon., mentioned, 328, 338.
Binier, Henry G., pvt., Co. C, 20th U. S. Inf., death, 1104.

Binns, George, sergt. maj., 13th U. S. Inf., death, 1190.
Biork, Emil, pvt., Troop K, 1st U. S. Cav., killed, 61.
Birch, William L., pvt., Co. C, 40th Inf., U. S. V., wounded, 1259.
Bird, Charles, maj., qm. dept., U. S. A., mentioned, 118, 119, 312.
Bird, Miss, missionary, mentioned, 471.
Birds, ——, a. a. surg., U. S. A., mentioned, 197.
Birkhimer, William E., col., 28th inf., U. S. V., mentioned, 716, 1129.
Birlew, Orlin L., pvt., band, 20th Kans. Vol. Inf., killed, 954.
Bisbee, William H., col. 13th U. S. Inf., brig. gen., U. S. A., mentioned, 209, 569, 1031, 1330, 1344.
Bishop, Albert O., pvt., Batty. H, 3d U. S. Art., rescued, 1129.
Bishop, Hoel S., capt., 5th U. S. Cav., mentioned, 1344.
Bishop, William H., capt., 20th Kans. Vol. Inf., wounded, 977.
Bishop, William H., maj., 36th Inf., U. S. V., mentioned, 1138.
Bittler, William C., capt., 3d U S. Inf., mentioned, 1066.
Bixman, William, pvt., Co. C, 18th U. S. Inf., wounded, 943.
Bjork, Gustav A., pvt., Co. A, 12th U. S. Inf., mentioned, 214.
Black, Archie, pvt., Troop L, 3d U. S. Cav., wounded, 1163.
Black, Camp, N. Y., inspection, 135.
Troops to remain at, 149.
Black, Columbus L., pvt., Troop D, 11th Cav., U. S. V., death, 1248.
Black, James, pvt., Co. G, 1st S. Dak. Vol. Inf., wounded, 996.
Black, John, pvt., Co. B, 1st Nebr. Vol. Inf., death, 803.
Black, John D., maj., chief commissary, U. S. V., funds placed to credit, 376.
Black, William M., lieut. col., chief engineer, U. S. V., mentioned, 56, 126, 127. 129, 133, 139, 146, 148, 271, 272, 285, 305, 371, 392, 393.
Blackburn, Alan R., pvt., Troop G, 4th U. S. Cav., wounded, 1272.
Blackmon, Thomas D., corpl., Co. C, 29th Inf., U. S. V., wounded, 1212.
Blaesing, Henry G., pvt., Co. B, 30th Inf., U. S. V. death, 1189.
Blair, Alexander C., sergt., Co. F, Sig. Corps, U. S. V., killed, 1165.
Blair, Eteyl P., pvt., Co. A, 20th Kans. Vol. Inf., death, 879.
Blair, J., qm. sergt., 12th U. S. Inf., mentioned, 175.
Blaisdell, Jay, pvt., Co. H, 39th Inf., U. S. V., wounded, 1147.
Blake, Charles H., pvt., Co. G, 2d U. S. Inf., mentioned, 229.
Blake, Harold K., pvt., Co. D, 1st Nebr. Vol. Inf., wounded, 976.
Blake, John J., pvt., Co. H, 6th U. S. Inf., death, 1060.
Blake, William, qm. sergt., Co. H, 1st U. S. Inf., wounded, 1275.
Blakeley, Gaylord S., pvt., Co. L, 1st Nebr. Vol. Inf., wounded, 956.
Blakly, Bennett, pvt., Co. B, 40th Inf., U. S. V., killed, 1153.
Blakeman, Robert, 2d lieut., 49th Inf., U. S. V., mentioned, 1218.
Blanchard, N. C., mentioned, 356, 364.
Blanchard, William H., pvt., Troop A, 11th Cav., U. S. V., killed, 1148.
Blackstock, Laddie, pvt., Co. B, 49th Inf., U. S. V., wounded, 1263.
Blanco, Ramon, Spanish captain-general of Cuba, mentioned, 100, 126, 147, 151, 222.
Message to, reporting loss of squadron by Cervera, 100.
Bland, Ellis, pvt., Co. A, 8th Ohio Vol. Inf., mentioned, 224.
Blazek, John, pvt., Co. I, 22d U. S. Inf., wounded, 934.
Bleeker, Herman, pvt., Co. G, 4th U. S. Inf., wounded, 946.

INDEX.   1369

Blesh, Tolando, mus., Co. L, 20th Kans. Vol. Inf., wounded, 915.
Bliel, George F., pvt., Co. B, 13th U. S. Inf., wounded, 1084.
Bliler, Edward H., pvt., Co. H, 22d U. S. Inf., death, 1120.
Blizzard, Hiram, pvt., Co. A, 47th Inf., U. S. V., wounded, 1271.
Blocksom, Augustus P., capt., 6th U. S. Cav., wounded, 124.
Blood, Louis, corpl., Co. E, 21st U. S. Inf., wounded, 1052.
Blosser, John H., pvt., Co. M, 2d Oreg. Vol. Inf., wounded, 946.
Bloushier, Warren, pvt., Co. I, 21st U. S. Inf., death, 1125.
Blowers, Eugene E., corpl., Co. D, 26th Inf., U. S. V., wounded, 1112.
Blume, Rufus B, pvt., Batty. K, 3d U. S. Art., wounded, 901.
Blumm, John, pvt., Co. L, 28th Inf., death, 1260.
Blystone, Robert J., mus., Co. G, 47th Inf., U. S. V., wounded, 1187.
Boakler, Samuel E., sergt., I, 14th U. S. Inf., wounded, 895.
Board of officers, to select sites at Honolulu for military stations and defensive works 727.
Board, Walter W., sergt., Troop F, 10th U. S. Cav., body recovered, 1283; death, 1280.
Boardman, George W., corpl. and sergt., Co. A, 1st Mont. Vol. Inf., wounded, 901, 1017.
Boast, William J., pvt., Co. G, 1st Mont. Vol. Inf., wounded, 959.
Boatwright, Edwin S., mus., Co. C 12th U. S. Inf., killed, 1057.
Bobleter, Joseph, col., 12th Minn. Vol. Inf., mentioned, 511.
Boden, William, pvt., Troop I, 4th U. S. Cav., death, 1255.
Boeckling, A. A., pvt., Batty. K, 3d U. S. Art., wounded, 950.
Boehler, Herman, pvt., Co. C, 42d Inf., U. S. V., death, 1245.
Boehnke, Otto H., pvt., Troop G, 4th U. S. Cav., death, 1063.
Boese, William, pvt., Co. H, 46th Inf., U. S. V., death, 1150.
Wounded, 1137.
Boetther, Robert, pvt., Co. I, 1st Ill. Vol. Inf., mentioned, 219.
Boggs, Samuel, pvt., Troop G, 9th U. S. Cav., death, 1274.
Bogt, John, cook, Co. C, 28th U. S. Inf., wounded, 1229.
Bohner, Frank, pvt., Co. M, 23d U S. Inf., death, 1045.
Boland, James, pvt., Co. I, 45th Inf., U. S. V., death, 1208.
Bolin, Wallace A., qm. sergt., 51st Iowa Vol. Inf., death, 956.
Boling, William, pvt., Co. E, 38th Inf., U. S. V., death, 1226.
Bolkey, J. O., pvt., Co. B, 1st Mont. Vol. Inf., wounded, 950.
Bolles, Frank C., 2d lieut., 18th U. S. Inf., wounded, 905, 1149.
Bollinger, Samuel T., corpl., Co. D 17th U. S. Inf., killed, 1052.
Bolt, Julius E., pvt., Co. A, 43d Inf., U. S. V., wounded, 1167.
Bolton, Alfred H., pvt., Co. C, 36th Inf., U. S. V., death, 1238.
Boman, John J., pvt., Co. G, 1st Cal. Vol. Inf., death, 1045, 1059.
Bombacher, Fred, sergt., Co. K, 37th Inf., U. S. V., wounded, 1192.
Bonaparte, Clem, pvt., Co. K, 24th U. S. Inf., death, 1113.
Bond, Ross R., corpl., 3d U. S. Cav., death, 1241.
Bonesteel, Charles H., capt., 21st U. S. Inf. General MacArthur requests that he remain with command in P. I., 1167.
Bonham, William A., pvt., Co. I, 1st Mont. Vol. Inf., wounded, 916.
Bonner, Alphonso, pvt., Co. M, 14th U. S. Inf., killed, 895.
Bonnicastle, Arthur, pvt., Co. E, 9th U. S. Inf., wounded, 1307.

Bony, Anton M., pvt., Co. I, 39th Inf., U. S. V., death, 1130.
Bony, George, pvt., Co. C, 9th U. S. Inf., killed, 1297.
Booker, Charles A., 1st lieut., 1st Wash. Vol. Inf., wounded, 977.
Booker, Harry, pvt., Co. C, 23d U. S. Inf., wounded, 761.
Booker, James, pvt., Co. K, 24th U. S. Inf., death, 1125.
Bookmiller, Edwin V., capt., 9th U. S. Inf., mentioned, 1296.
Wounded, 428–430, 435, 443.
Boomer, George R., pvt., Co. C, 1st Nebr. Vol. Inf., wounded, 955.
Boone, Hilliard, pvt., Co. L, 25th U. S. Inf., killed, 1141.
Boone, Willie F., pvt., Co. H, 3d Inf., U. S. V., killed, 1101.
Booream, Henry S., 1st sergt., Co. I, 22d U. S. Inf., death, 1205.
Boostel, Harry, pvt., Co. A, 8th U. S. Inf., mentioned, 204.
Booth, Henry G., pvt., Co. B, 17th U. S. Inf., death, 1082.
Booth, Robert L., pvt., Co. C, 9th U. S. Inf., killed, 1297.
Booth, Walter C., pvt., Co. A, 44th Inf., U. S. V., killed, 1192.
Booze, Richard, pvt., Co. I, 24th U. S. Inf., death, 1200.
Borchart, Robert, pvt., Co. C, 16th U. S. Inf., wounded, 1152.
Borden, George L., pvt., Co. L, 18th U. S. Inf., wounded, 1202.
Borden, George P., maj., 5th U. S. Inf., mentioned, 459, 1211.
Borderwine, Alfred J., pvt., Co. H, 51st Iowa Vol. Inf., missing, 961.
Borkowski, William, pvt., Co. F, 1st Mont. Vol. Inf., wounded, 954.
Born, William L., sergt., Co. A, 4th U. S. Inf., wounded, 1085.
Borthwick, William J., pvt., Co G, 1st Mont. Vol. Inf., wounded, 900.
Borup, Henry D., capt., ord. dept., U. S. A., mentioned, 95, 156, 158.
Bosold, Christian, pvt., Co. M, 17th U. S. Inf., death, 1045.
Bostick, Benjamin F., pvt., Co. L, 6th Mass. Vol. Inf., wounded, 330.
Bostwick, William H., pvt., Co. K, 33d U. S. Inf., death, 1189.
Wounded, 1139.
Bothwell, Samuel C., 1st lieut., 1st Wash. Vol. Inf., mentioned, 994.
Bothwell, William H., pvt., Co. K, 48th Inf., U. S. V., death, 1197.
Bottino, Celestine, pvt., Co. D, 17th U. S. Inf., wounded, 1051.
Bottorff, John C., pvt., Co. D, 23d U. S. Inf., death, 1136.
Bouchard, Frank, pvt., Troop C, 4th U. S. Cav., wounded, 1031.
Bourns, Dr., citizen of Georgia, mentioned, 667.
Boutelle, Charles A., member of Congress, mentioned, 357.
Boutelle, Henry M., 2d lieut., 3d U. S. Art., killed, 1093.
Bouzey, William, corpl., Co. F, 38th Inf., U. S. V., death, 1215.
Bowan, Willie, pvt., Co. K, 49th Inf., U. S. V., death, 1167.
Bowen, Edward B., pvt., Co. F, 1st Mont. Vol. Inf., wounded, 953.
Bowen, H. C., maj., 2d Mass. Vol. Inf., mentioned, 245–247, 251, 253.
Bowen, Mortimer C., wag., Co. —, 1st S. Dak. Vol. Inf., killed, 975.
Bower, William A., pvt., Co. M, 38th Inf., U. S. V., death, 1213.
Bower, lieut. col., British forces, member temporary government council, 438.
Bowers, Horace M., pvt., Co. C, 1st Cal. Vol. Inf., death, 803.
Bowers, John B., pvt., Co. M, 41st Inf., U. S. V., death, 1226.

Bowers, Ralph R., pvt., Sig. Corps, U. S. A., death, 803.
Bowker, Ernest R., pvt., Co. F, 1st Wyo. Vol. Inf., death, 803.
Bowler, Michael, pvt., Troop K, 6th U. S. Cav., death, 505.
Bowling, Francis B., pvt., Co. K, 6th U. S. Inf., death, 1219.
Bowling, John M., pvt., Co. M, 18th U. S. Inf., death, 1208.
Bowling, John W., pvt., Co. M, 19th U. S. Inf., wounded, 1189.
Bowman, Daniel C., pvt., Co. D, 2d Oreg. Vol. Inf., wounded, 948.
Bowman, Daniel T., 1st lieut., 37th Inf., U. S. V., death, 1131.
Bowman, William, pvt., Co. D, 39th Inf., U. S. V., death, 1161.
Bowman, Charles G., commander, U. S. N., mentioned, 451.
Bowne, Fred W., corpl., Co. M, 2d Oreg. Vol. Inf., wounded, 941.
Bowser, Clifford H., 1st sergt., Co. K, 1st Colo. Vol. Inf., death, 1008. Wounded, 981.
Box, James M., pvt., Co. D, 1st Mont. Vol. Inf., wounded, 901.
Boy, Frank J., sergt., Co. L, 12th U. S. Inf.
Boyce, Charles B., pvt., Co. L, 1st Colo. Vol. Inf., wounded, 895.
Boyd, Charles T., maj., 37th Inf., U. S. V., mentioned, 1130, 1131, 1240.
Boyd, Frank, pvt., Co. D, 2d Oreg. Vol. Inf., mentioned, 1028.
Boyd, Grant, pvt., Co. K, 1st Nebr. Vol. Inf., wounded, 899.
Boyd, Jacob, sergt., Co. K, 4th U. S. Inf., drowned, 972.
Boyd, John J., pvt., Co. H, 33d Inf., U. S. V., missing, 1222.
Boyer, Frank, pvt., Co. A, 20th U. S. Inf., mentioned, 229.
Boyer, Frederick, 1st lieut., 39th Inf., U. S. V., conviction and dismissal, 1278, 1279.
Boyle, Benjamin N., pvt., Co. L, 14th U. S. Inf., wounded, 454.
Boyle, Gus A., lieut., 30th Inf., U. S. V., wounded, 1150.
Boyle, John J., pvt., Co. D, 1st Nebr. Vol. Inf., killed, 952.
Boyle, William, corpl., Co. L, 28th Inf., death, 1260.
Boynton, Henry V., brig. gen., U. S. V., mentioned, 71, 286.
Boyton, James, pvt., Co. E, 33d Inf., U. S. V., wounded, 1102.
Brackett, Charles F., pvt., Co. B, 13th Minn. Vol. Inf., wounded, 963.
Brackette, June M., corpl., Co. C, 12th U. S. Inf., death, 968.
Brackman, John, pvt., Co. L, 1st Ill. Vol. Inf., mentioned, 219.
Braddish, Stephen, pvt., Co. E, 12th U. S. Inf., wounded, 1057.
Braden, Herman E., pvt., Co. G, 40th Inf., U. S. V., wounded, 1254.
Braden, John Q. A., maj., 36th Inf., U. S. V., wounded, 1050, 1051.
Braden, William M., pvt., Co. H, 10th Pa. Vol. Inf., death, 803.
Bradenberg, Charles, pvt., Co. K, 44th Inf., U. S. V., killed, 1222.
Bradford, Oscar O., pvt., Troop L, 3d U. S. Cav., wounded, 1222.
Bradford, Royal B., capt., U. S. N., mentioned, 699.
Bradford, William S., 2d lieut., 17th U. S. Inf., mentioned, 1041.
Bradley, Harvey L., pvt., Troop B, 1st U. S. Cav., killed, 1243.
Bradley, John J., capt., asst. qm., U. S. V., mentioned, 1139.
Bradley, W. O., governor of Kentucky, mentioned, 329, 370.
Bradley, William S., pvt., Co. L, 37th Inf., U. S. V., wounded, 1211.
Brady, Edward F., pvt., Co. K, 1st Colo. Vol. Inf., wounded, 761.
Brady, Edward M., pvt., Co. C, 20th U. S. Inf., wounded, 937.

Brady, Frederick L., 1st U. S. Vol. Cav., mentioned, 219.
Brady, John, pvt., Co. D, 14th U. S. Inf., wounded, 898.
Brady, John, jr., pvt., Co. I, 10th Pa. Vol. Inf., death, 803.
Brady, Jasper E., capt., Sig. Corps, U. S. V., mentioned, 42, 43, 44.
Brady, Thomas F., pvt., Co. B, 33d Inf., U. S. V., killed, 1152.
Brady, William, pvt., Co. H, 9th U. S. Inf., death, 1136.
Braedler, William F., pvt., Co. B, 31st Inf., U. S. V., death, 1208.
Braham, Edward, pvt., Co. E, 1st Cal. Vol. Inf., death, 803.
Brain, Frank, pvt., Co. C, 10th Pa. Vol. Inf., death, 886.
Brainard, David L., lieut. col., chief commissary, U. S. V., mentioned, 646, 647, 1059.
Braman, Edward, pvt., Co. H, 43d Inf., U. S. V., killed, 1168.
Braman, John, pvt., Batty. B, Utah Vol. Art., wounded, 975.
Brambrila, Robert M., 2d lieut., 23d U. S. Inf., mentioned, 917.
Branagan, Charles, pvt., Troop E, 3d U. S. Cav., death, 1119.
Brandon, Arthur A., pvt., Co. D, 30th Inf., U.S.V., death, 1160.
Brandon, William N., pvt., Co. E, 33d Inf., U.S.V., killed, 1137.
Brandt, Charles, pvt., Co. D, 30th Inf., U. S. V., killed, 1176.
Brandt, Jacob, pvt., Co. K, 30th Inf., U. S. V., death, 1152.
Branigan, Patrick, pvt., Troop C, 4th U. S. Cav., wounded, 1003, 1008.
Brann, Leonard T., corpl., Co. G, 32d Inf., U.S.V., killed, 1143.
Brannen, John, pvt., Co. A, 14th U. S. Inf., death, 1015.
Brannon, Andrew, unassigned recruit, 15th U. S. Inf., killed, 1243.
Brant, Allen, pvt., Co. C, 1st Cal. Vol. Inf., wounded, 904.
Bratchey, John T., pvt., Co. K, 21st U. S. Inf., wounded, 1084.
Brathor, Thomas, sergt., Co. B, 9th U. S. Inf., death, 1045.
Bratton, steamer, mentioned, 181.
Braunwart, Frank, sergt., Co. M, 6th U. S. Inf., death, 1226.
Brawley, Judge, mentioned, 95, 117.
Braxton, Isaiah, pvt., Co. E, 49th Inf., U. S. V., death, 1238.
Bray, Howard W., American citizen, mentioned, 927.
Bray, William, pvt., Co. C, 9th U. S. Inf., death, 464.
Brayton, William, pvt., Co. C, 9th U. S. Inf., death, 463.
Brazee, A. J., 1st lieut., 2d Oreg. Vol. Inf., wounded, 946.
Breakwater, U. S. transport, mentioned, 189, 190, 224.
Breckinridge, Ethelbert L. D., 2d lieut., 7th U. S. Inf., wounded, 1124, 1126.
Breckinridge, Joseph C., Insp. Gen., U. S. A., mentioned, 27, 46, 47, 63, 89, 128, 242, 257, 340, 354, 359, 363, 509, 510, 513–515, 530, 1314.
Breed, Harvey M., corpl., Co. B, 1st S. Dak. Vol. Inf., killed, 975.
Breeding, Thomas H., pvt., Co. H, 13th U. S. Inf., death, 1208.
Brefka, Anthony, pvt., Co. A, 3d U. S. Inf., wounded, 995.
Breiner, Halfdam Rye, hosp. stewd., 9th Mass. Vol. Inf., mentioned, 219.
Bremer, William H., sergt., Troop H, 4th U. S. Cav., killed, 1227.
Bremerhaven, shipment from, of arms for insurgents, 1134.
Brendel, Frederick, pvt., Co. K, 40th Inf., U.S.V., killed, 1162.
Brendel, Senro J., pvt., Co. A, 14th U. S. Inf., wounded, 1015.
Brenholts, Harry P., pvt., Co. M, 51st Iowa Vol. Inf., wounded, 1052.

Brennan, Carmac, pvt., Co. I, 21st U. S. Inf., death, 1213.
Brennan, John A., pvt., Co. G, 22d U. S. Inf., killed, 1052.
Brennan, Martin, pvt., Co. K, 21st U. S. Inf., rescued, 1129.
Brent, William, mus., Co. H, 24th U. S. Inf., mentioned, 192.
Brereton, John J., capt., 24th U. S. Inf., mentioned, 83.
Wounded, 124.
Breshears, George C., pvt., Co. A, 1st U. S. Inf., killed, 1250.
Breslin, Daniel J., pvt., Co. I, 21st U. S. Inf., death, 1196.
Bretch, Brayton, pvt., Co. C., 9th U. S. Inf., wounded, 1015.
Bretherton, William M., pvt., Troop A, 11th Cav., U. S. V., death, 1132.
Brett, James E., capt., 24th U. S. Inf., mentioned, 83, 124.
Brett, William L., pvt., Troop K, 4th U. S. Cav., wounded, 1096.
Brevets, recommendations for, 766.
Not entertained except for services in battle, 766.
Brewer, Edward, pvt., Co. E, 3d U. S. Cav., death, 1283.
Brewer, George W., pvt., Co. L, 38th Inf., U. S. V., death, 1217.
Brewer, Isaac W., actg. asst. surg., U. S. A., mentioned, 1248.
Brewer, John H., pvt., Co. E, 35th Inf., U. S. V., killed, 1225.
Brewer, Richard H., 1st lieut., asst. surg., 27th Inf., U. S. V., disappearance, 1208, 1248.
Brewer, Thomas L., 2d lieut., 21st U. S. Inf., mentioned, 1019.
Brewer, Walter, pvt., Co. H, 4th U. S. Cav., wounded, 1196.
Brewster, André W., capt., 9th U. S. Inf.:
Mentioned, 1066.
Selected for legation guard, 503.
Wounded, 428, 429.
Brewster, Charles S., corpl., Co. C, 1st Nebr., Vol. Inf., wounded, 975.
Brice, Pressley K., 2d lieut., 14th U. S. Inf., mentioned, 442.
Brickdale, Richard E., pvt., Co. F, 2d Oreg. Vol. Inf., wounded, 948.
Brickey, Wiley J., sergt., Co. H, 47th Inf., U. S.V., death, 1165.
Bridges, Douglas F., pvt., Co. F, 1st Nebr., Vol. Inf., wounded, 897, 899.
Bridgman, Victor H., capt. 6th U. S. Art., mentioned, 1107.
Brierer, E., maj., 10th Pa. Vol. Inf., wounded, 895.
Briggeman, William F., pvt., Co. M, 8th U. S. Inf., death, 1267.
Briggs, Clarence, pvt., Co. H, 1st Mont. Vol. Inf., wounded, 900.
Briggs, Clarence G., pvt., band, 1st Mont. Vol. Inf., death, 907.
Briggs, George, pvt., Co. G, 1st Wyo. Vol. Inf., death, 967.
Briggs, William F., pvt., Co. A, 18th U. S. Inf., killed, 924.
Brill, Charles, pvt., Co. M, 1st Colo. Vol. Inf., wounded, 947.
Briney, William, pvt., Co. L, 14th U. S. Inf., wounded, 1085.
Brink, John P., pvt., Co. L., 15th U.S. Inf., killed, 1211.
Brinkerhoff, Henry R., maj., 3d U. S. Inf., mentioned, 1000.
Brinkerhoff, James C., pvt., Co. K, 2d U. S. Inf., wounded, 1261.
Brinton, Charles, pvt., Co. B, 1st Mont. Vol. Inf., wounded, 903.
Bristow, Joseph L., 4th asst. P. M. General, mentioned, 292.
Britenstine, Charles, hosp. stewd., 32d Inf., U. S. V., death, 1109.
British deserters from Malta, disposition, 940, 967, 968.
Secreted on American transport, 939, 940.
Britt, C. A., civilian teamster, qm. dept., death, 504.
Britt, G. M., pvt., U. S. Marine Corps, death, 1314.

Brittain, Cyrus E., pvt., Co. A, 35th Inf., U. S. V., death, 1146.
Brittles, John, pvt., Troop D, 11th Cav., U.S. V., wounded, 1225.
Britton, William, sergeant, Troop 3, 1st U. S. Cav., mentioned, 174.
Brock, Henry R., pvt., Co. B, 12th U. S. Inf., death, 1208.
Brocker, Charles, pvt., Co. C, 45th Inf., U. S. V., wounded, 1209.
Broderick, John F., pvt., Co. H, 20th Inf., U.S. V., wounded, 1174.
Brodie, ——, maj., 1st U. S. Vol. Cav., wounded, 55.
Brogden, Walter, pvt., Co. F., 14th U. S. Inf., wounded, 1008.
Bromm, Andrew, pvt., Batty. F, 5th U. S. Art., wounded, 454.
Bronson, John L., pvt., Co. B, 1st Nebr. Vol. Inf., wounded, 897.
Bronston, Tevis, pvt., Co. K, 25th U. S. Inf., killed, 1141.
Brook, Preston B., pvt., Co. H, 33th Inf., U. S. V., death, 1144.
Brooke, James M., corpl., Co. L, 2d Mass. Vol. Inf., mentioned, 202.
Brooke, John R., maj.-gen., U. S. A., assigned to command at Chickamauga Park, 7, 8.
Commissioner to arrange for evacuation of Porto Rico, 397.
Correspondence, 58, 182, 286, 292, 294, 295, 298, 299, 301, 302, 306, 308, 312, 317, 318, 319, 321, 322, 323, 324, 325, 326, 327, 328.
Mentioned, 8, 11, 44–46, 52, 53, 57, 71, 76, 80, 82, 83, 86, 90–92, 96, 97, 102, 111, 112, 122, 126, 130, 131, 189, 267–269, 290, 296, 301, 304, 308, 312, 315, 320, 321, 324, 329, 333, 346, 360, 365, 369, 377, 378, 390, 398, 399, 403, 509, 510, 513, 539.
Number troops Porto Rico, 302.
Requests to have his whole corps, 323.
Brooke, Thomas M., pvt., Co. H, 56th Inf., U.S.V., death, 1150.
Brooke, William, 1st lieut., 4th U. S. Inf., mentioned, 99, 227.
Brookling, Robert E., pvt., Co. B, 18th U. S. Inf., wounded, 1117.
Brooklyn, U. S. cruiser, mentioned, 418, 420, 484, 1080.
Brooks, Charles A., pvt., Co. F 9th U. S. Inf., killed, 1055.
Brooks, Charles F., sergt., Co. L, 22d U. S. Inf., killed, 948.
Brooks, Charles L., corpl., Co. D, 40th Inf., U.S.V., wounded, 1160.
Brooks, Clarence G., pvt., Co. M, 30th Inf., U. S. V., death, 1156.
Brooks, Isaiah, pvt., Co. K, 49th Inf., U. S. V. death, 1276.
Brooks, John P., pvt., Co. C, 12th U. S. Inf., killed, 1057.
Brooks, Robert H., pvt., Co. I, 24th U. S. Inf., captured by insurgents, 1196.
Brooks, Tomas, consul, Guantanamo, Cuba, mentioned, 188.
Brooks, ——, civilian, connection with commissary frauds in P. I., 1297.
Brookover, Harry, pvt., Co. K, 1st Nebr. Vol. Inf., wounded, 974.
Brooley, ——, pvt., Co. G, 1st U. S. Inf., mentioned, 183.
Brophy, Thomas, corpl., U. S. Marine Corps, death, 454.
Brothers, Thomas P., pvt., Co. D, 21st U. S. Inf., killed, 1081.
Brouillet, George H., pvt., Co. H, 4th U. S. Inf., wounded, 1081.
Brown, Albert L., pvt., Co. E, 34th Inf., U. S. V., death, 1190.
Brown, Alonzo, pvt., Co. B, 9th U. S. Inf., killed, 1131.
Brown, Charles, pvt., Co. M, 26th Inf., U. S. V., death, 1162.
Brown, David, civilian, rescue, 1129.
Brown, Edward F., pvt., Co. C, 51st Iowa Vol. Inf., wounded, 1026.
Brown, Fred O., corpl., Co. M, 47th Inf., U. S. V., death, 1271.
Brown, George, pvt., Co. B, 33d Inf., U. S. V., death, 1241.
Brown, Harry, pvt., Co. F, 1st Nebr. Vol. Inf., wounded, 897.

Brown, Harry D., corpl., Co. E, 33d Inf., U. S. V., wounded, 1124.
Brown, Herbert H., pvt., Co. B, 26th Inf., U.S.V., killed, 1225.
Brown, Irwin L., pvt., Co. I, 18th U. S. Inf., death, 1264.
Brown, Jacob, corpl., Co. I, 14th U. S. Inf., death, 1109.
Brown, James, pvt., Co. E, 9th U. S. Inf., wounded, 1055.
Brown, James F., pvt., Co. G, 1st Cal. Vol. Inf., mentioned, 1043.
Brown, John H., pvt., Co. C, 44th Inf., U. S. V., wounded, 1212.
Brown, Judson, pvt., Co. H, 48th Inf., U. S. V., death, 1172.
Brown, Justus M., lieut. col., med. dept., U. S. A., mentioned, 169, 170.
Brown, Laurel, pvt., Co. A, 31st Inf., U. S. V., death, 1210.
Brown, Lee, pvt., Co. C, 24th U. S. Inf., death, 1258.
Brown, Mathew W., pvt., Co. G, 38th Inf., U.S.V., death, 1213.
Brown, Robert, pvt., Co. G, 1st Mont. Vol. Inf., death, 956.
Wounded, 945.
Brown, Thomas, pvt., Co. C, 24th U. S. Inf., wounded, 1188.
Brown, Thomas, pvt., Co. C, 38th Inf., U. S. V., wounded, 1141.
Brown, Thomas, corpl., Co. C, 38th Inf., U. S. V., death, 1149.
Brown, Walter E., pvt., Co. G, 1st S. Dak. Vol. Inf., wounded, 946.
Brown, Walter E., corpl., Co. D, 10th Pa. Vol. Inf., death, 803.
Brown, William, pvt., Co. M, 30th Inf., U. S. V., death, 1197.
Brown, William, pvt., Co. D, 32d Inf., U. S. V., death, 1130.
Brown, William, capt., 45th Inf., U. S. V., killed, 1203.
Brown, William C., capt., 1st U. S. Cav., mentioned, 1344.
Brown, William K., pvt., Co. I, 15th U. S. Inf., death, 1267.
Brown, William M., pvt., Co. E, 25th U. S. Inf., death, 1152.
Brown, William S., pvt., Co. I, 41st Inf., U. S. V., death, 1233.
Brown, ——, pvt., U. S. Marine Corps, death, 1314.
Brownell, Cornelius M., capt., 26th Inf., U. S. V., mentioned, 1126.
Brubaker, Abraham H., mus., Co. B, 41st Inf., U. S. V., death, 1196.
Bruce, Alexander S., pvt., Co. B, 29th Inf., U.S.V., death, 1153.
Bruce, Edward S., pvt., Co. I, 12th U. S. Inf., death, 1090.
Bruce, William, 1st Nev. Vol. Cav., rescued, 1129.
Bruffee, Walter, pvt., Co. M, 26th Inf., U. S. V., wounded, 1251.
Brum, Paul, pvt., Co. F, 30th Inf., U. S. V., death, 1213.
Bruner, John, pvt., Co. H, 4th U. S. Inf., death, 1162.
Brunger, Fred C., pvt., Co. L, 1st S. Dak. Vol. Inf., wounded, 949.
Bruning, John, corpl., Light Batty. D, 5th U. S. Art., wounded, 390.
Bruschke, William, pvt., Co. B, 18th U. S. Inf., wounded, 943.
Brunson, Everett, pvt., Co. E, 51st Iowa Vol. Inf., wounded, 983.
Brunston, Charles, sergt., Co. G, 13th Minn. Vol. Inf., mentioned, 761, 762.
Bryan, Edgar J., 2d lieut., 2d Oreg. Vol. Inf., mentioned, 780, 810.
Bryan, John E., pvt., Co. I, 47th Inf., U. S. V., death, 1210.
Bryan, Tom, pvt., Co. H, 1st Cal. Vol. Inf., killed, 895.
Bryant, James H., corpl., Co. E, 20th Kans. Vol. Inf., wounded, 946.
Bryant, Richard M., pvt., Co. K, 1st Colo. Vol. Inf., death, 923.
Bryant, William C., corpl., Co. G, 12th U. S. Inf., death, 1130.
Brydges, Thomas G. G., pvt., Co. C, 47th Inf., U. S. V., wounded, 1235, 1236.

Bryon, John C., corpl., Co. I, 1st N. Dak. Vol. Inf., death, 997.
Buchan, Fred E., 2d lieut., 6th U. S. Cav., mentioned, 421.
Buchanan, Henry, pvt., Co. C, 38th Inf., U. S. V., wounded, 1141.
Buchanan, John, pvt., Co. E, 34th Inf., U. S. V., death, 1217.
Buchholz, William F., corpl., Co. G, 39th Inf., U. S. V., wounded, 1147.
Buck, Alfred E., U. S. minister to Japan, mentioned, 427, 440, 450, 455, 1063.
Buck, Charles W., mus., Co. E, 9th U. S. Inf., wounded, 1299.
Buck, Dimitri C., pvt., Co. A, 22d U. S. Inf., death, 1125.
Buck, Hammond H., corpl., Co. B, 1st S. Dak. Vol. Inf., wounded, 977.
Buck, Howard G., corpl., Co. B, 39th Inf., U.S. V., death, 1185.
Buckendorf, Fred W., pvt., Co. L, 13th Minn. Vol. Inf., killed, 984.
Buckhalter, James, pvt., Co. A, 48th Inf., U.S. V., death, 1267.
Buckingham, David E., pvt., Co. I, 21st U. S. Inf., death, 1123.
Buckley, George H., pvt., Co. A, 9th U. S. Inf., killed, 443, 445.
Buckley, John, pvt., Co. C, 1st Nebr. Vol. Inf., death, 803.
Bucklin, Robert E., corpl., Co. K, 1st Wash. Vol. Inf., wounded, 941.
Buencamino, Felipe, insurgent secretary of state, mentioned, 814; capture, 1108.
Budziak, Steven, pvt., Co. C, 13th U. S. Inf., death, 1261.
Buechel, Jacob N., pvt., Troop K, 5th U. S. Cav., death, 1281.
Buenos Ayres, Spanish vessel, mentioned, 836, 991.
Buffett, T., pvt., U. S. Marine Corps, death, 1314.
Buford, U. S. transport, mentioned, 1224, 1227, 1244, 1252, 1259, 1264, 1275, 1280, 1291, 1292, 1294, 1295, 1312, 1321, 1323, 1329, 1332, 1337, 1342, 1343, 1353, 1357.
Buhl, Arthur, pvt., Co. L, 1st Cal. Vol. Inf., wounded, 914.
Buhlert, Julius C., pvt., Batty. H, 3d U. S. Art., wounded, 946.
Bullan, John C., pvt., Co. A, 1st Mont. Vol. Inf., wounded, 900.
Bullard, Noah W., pvt., Co. F, 39th Inf., U. S. V., wounded, 1152.
Bullard, Percy G., pvt., Co. C, 1st Mont. Vol. Inf., wounded, 901.
Bullard, Robert L., col., 37th Inf., U. S. V., mentioned, 422, 424, 1131.
Bullington, James C., corpl., Co. F, 1st Tenn. Vol. Inf., killed, 1081.
Bullis, John L., maj., pay dept., U. S. A., mentioned, 646.
Bullis, William, pvt., Co. A, 37th Inf., U. S. V., wounded, 1146.
Bullman, Conoway O., pvt., Co. I, 47th Inf., U. S. V., death, 1228.
Bullock, Edmund, artif., Co. B, 40th Inf., U. S. V., killed, 1153.
Bulson, Henry O., pvt., Co. H, 9th U. S. Inf., death, 1066.
Bumiller, Frederick A., pvt., Batty. B, Utah Art., death, 979.
Wounded, 975.
Bumpus, Edward A., 1st lieut., 9th U. S. Inf., attacked by insurgents 1294.
Bunce, George J., pvt., Co. L, 3d Wis. Vol. Inf., wounded, 388.
Bunker, Russell S., lieut., 13th Minn. Vol. Inf., mentioned, 829, 943.
Bunn, James W., corpl., Co. I, 49th Inf., U. S. V. killed, 1243.
Bunton, William E., pvt., Co. E, 10th Pa. Vol. Inf., death, 803.
Burbank, Frank B., pvt., Co. E, Sig. Corps, U. S. A., death, 1190.
Burbee, Raymond D., pvt., Co. D, 6th U. S. Inf., wounded, 1126.
Burchard, Easton, 1st lieut., asst. surg., 40th Inf., U. S. V., death, 1205.
Burchill, Thomas J., pvt., Co. G, 22d U. S. Inf., death, 1130.
Burd, Albert H., pvt., Co. H, 1st Nebr Vol. Inf. death, 804.

INDEX. 1373

Burdell, Stephen, pvt., Co. M, 1st Cal. Vol. Inf., death, 993.
Burdett, Charles L., col., 1st Conn. Vol. Inf., mentioned, 524.
Burdick, George E., pvt., Co. K, 36th Inf., U. S. V., wounded, 1096.
Burdt, Herman F., pvt., Co. H, 3d U. S. Inf., wounded, 1191.
Burg, George, pvt., Co. I, 12th U. S. Inf., death, 1125.
Burger, George E., lance corpl., Co. M, 23d U. S. Inf., killed, 1067.
Burgess, Louis R., 1st lieut., 5th U. S. Art., wounded, 1079, 1081.
Burgess, William, pvt., Co. E, 1st Idaho Vol. Inf., death, 979.
Burgey, James T., pvt., Co. C, 26th Inf., U. S. V., killed, 1205.
Burgoyne, Napoleon D., corpl., Co. I, 39th Inf., U. S. V., wounded, 1146.
Burgstaller, Vincent, sergt., Co. I, 33d Inf., U. S. V., killed, 1223, 1225.
Burke, Claus A., pvt., Co. H, 42d Inf., U. S. V., death, 1156.
Burke, Daniel W., lieut. col., 11th U. S. Inf., mentioned, 393.
Burke, Frank, corpl., Co. B, 41st Inf., U. S. V., death, 1213.
Burke, James, pvt., Co. G, 2d U. S. Inf., wounded, 1259.
Burke, James H., pvt., Co. E, 9th U. S. Inf., death, 505.
Burke, Patrick, pvt., Troop I, 11th Cav., U. S. V., wounded, 1124.
Burke, Patrick, sergt., Troop L, 11th Cav., U. S. V., death, 1215.
Wounded, 1182.
Burke, Sylvester, corpl., Co. C, 9th U. S. Inf., wounded, 1298.
Burke, Thomas, 1st sergt., Co. D, 19th U. S. Inf., death, 1192.
Burke, Thomas P., pvt., Co. C, 1st Idaho Vol. Inf., wounded, 897.
Burke, William, pvt., Co. B, 35th Inf., U. S. V., death, 1190.
Burket, John, pvt., Co. K, 39th Inf., U. S. V., wounded, 1214.
Burleigh, E. C., mentioned, 357.
Burles, William, pvt., Co. L, 25th U. S. Inf., killed, 1233.
Burlingame, Walter H., pvt., Co. F, 39th Inf., U. S. V., death, 1150.
Burlingham, George M., corpl., Co. H, 1st Wash. Vol. Inf., wounded, 971.
Burlingham, William B., sergt., Co. K, 13th Minn. Vol. Inf., wounded, 981.
Burnett, Brady F., corpl., Co. M, 2d Oreg. Vol. Inf., wounded, 946.
Burnham, Arthur, pvt., Co. K, 2d Mass. Vol. Inf., mentioned, 241.
Burns, Alexander F., pvt., Co. M, 13th Mont. Vol. Inf., wounded, 899.
Burns, David, pvt., Co. M, 1st Mont. Vol. Inf., wounded, 901.
Burns, Edward F., pvt., Co. E, 9th U. S. Inf., killed, 1298.
Burns, Frank W., sergt., Co. H, 47th Inf., U. S. V., killed, 1191.
Burns, James F., pvt., Co. C, 43d Inf., U. S. V., death, 1155.
Wounded, 1155.
Burns, John J., pvt., Co. M, 33d Inf., U. S. V., death, 1213.
Burns, Mark, pvt., Troop D, 3d U. S. Cav., killed, 1148.
Burns, Patrick, pvt., Co. C, 16th U. S. Inf., death, 1271.
Burns, Richard M., pvt., Co. G, 34th Inf., U. S. V., death, 1226, 1233.
Burns, William, pvt., Co. H, 5th U. S. Inf., death, 1276.
Burns, William B., corpl., Co. F, 44th Inf., U. S. V., mentioned, 1231.
Burns, William G., pvt., Co. L, 9th U. S. Inf., death, 1151.
Burns, Robert, maj. surg., U. S. V., mentioned, 863, 865, 1127.
Burnsen, Charles, sergt., Co. G., 13th Minn. Vol. Inf., death, 803.
Burnside, William A., 1st lieut., 17th U. S. Inf., mentioned, 769, 772.
Burnside, U. S. transport, mentioned, 1322, 1326, 1341.
Burr, Edward, capt., Corps of Engineers, U. S. A., mentioned, 543, 544.
Burr, Frank S., 1st lieut., 15th U. S. Inf., mentioned, 1337, 1345.
Burr, Theodore, pvt., Co. B, 18th U. S. Inf., wounded, 943.
Burrer, John D., pvt., Co. C, 9th U. S. Inf., killed, 1297.
Burrows, Arthur, corpl., Co. M, 47th Inf., U. S. V., killed, 1237.
Burt, Andrew S., col. 25th U. S. Inf., brig. gen., U. S. V., mentioned, 548–551, 1025.
Burtchell, George, pvt., Co. B, Batt. Engrs., U. S. A., death, 1130.
Burton, Frank, pvt., Co. L, 33d Mich. Vol. Inf., mentioned, 229.
Burto, Frederick G., pvt., Co. M, 40th Inf., U. S. V., death, 1191.
Burton, James R., corpl., Co. C, 9th U. S. Inf., wounded, 443.
Burton, John, civilian clerk, Manila, P. I., mentioned, 979.
Bury, Fred, 2d lieut., 11th Cav., U. S. V., wounded, 1185.
Bush, James A., corpl., Co. C, 16th U. S. Inf., death, 1217.
Bush, William, pvt., Co. A, 14th U. S. Inf., wounded, 899, 916.
Bush, William H., pvt., Co. I, 1st Colo. Vol. Inf., death, 947.
Bushfield, Lewellyn N., 2d lieut., 17th U.S. Inf., wounded, 1124.
Bushnell, Asa, Hon., governor of Ohio, mentioned, 404, 405.
Busic, Pearley M., pvt., Co. M, 1st Nebr. Vol. Inf., wounded, 950.
Bussman, Charles F., pvt., Co. B, 1st Cal. Vol. Inf., wounded, 919.
Buster, William, pvt., Co. E, 18th U. S. Inf., wounded, 943.
Butcher, Charles A., corpl., Co. A, 10th U. S. Inf., mentioned, 248.
Butler, Charles, pvt., Co. C, 1st S. Dak. Vol. Inf., mentioned, 732.
Butler, Charles L., sergt., Co. B, 1st Nebr. Vol. Inf., wounded, 975, 977.
Butler, George T., pvt., Troop M, 3d U. S. Cav., death, 1243.
Butler, Matthew C., maj. gen., U. S. V., commissioner to arrange for evacuation of Porto Rico, 397.
Mentioned, 521, 522.
Butler, Smedley D., capt., U. S. Marine Corps, wounded, 429, 459, 460.
Butner, Edwin R., capt., asst. qm., U. S. V., mentioned, 930.
Butterfield, Daniel, Gen., commander Lafayette Post, G. A. R., mentioned, 365, 368, 369, 386, 387, 398, 399, 403, 404.
Buttermore, Albert J., 1st lieut., 10th Pa. Vol. Inf., wounded, 895.
Buttler, William C., maj., 25th U. S. Inf., mentioned, 1344.
Buttner, Frederick H., pvt., Co C, Batt. Engrs., U. S. A., wounded, 983.
Button, Henry, pvt., Co. A, 49th Inf., U. S. V., death, 1205.
Butts, Frank M., pvt., Co. L, 2d Oreg. Vol. Inf., wounded, 992.
Butts, Rutherford B., pvt., Co. I, 23d Inf., U. S. V., wounded, 1167.
Butz, Frederick J., corpl., Co. M, 44th Inf., U. S. V., wounded, 1256.
Byers, Samuel, pvt., Troop H, 3d U. S. Cav., death, 1233.
Byers, William H., pvt., Co. G, 17th U. S. Inf., mentioned, 185.
Byram, George L., 1st lieut., 1st U. S. Cav., mentioned, 54, 55.
Wounded, 123.
Byrd, Clarence, pvt., Co. K, 24th U. S. Inf., death, 1197.
Byrne, Bernard A., lieut. col., 40th Inf., U. S. V., mentioned, 1035, 1037, 1062, 1373, 1088, 1116.
Byrne, John G., a. a. surg., U. S. V., wounded, 1198.
Byrne, Patrick J., 1st sergt., Co. B, 22d U. S. Inf., wounded, 948.

INDEX.

Byrne, William J., pvt., Troop G, 11th Cav., U. S. V., wounded, 1182.
Byrnes, Patrick, pvt., Co. L, 20th U. S. Inf., death, 1001.
Byron, John C., corpl., Co. D, 1st N. Dak. Vol. Inf., wounded, 957.
Byron, Joseph C., capt. qm. dept., U. S. A., mentioned, 441, 456, 468, 474, 480, 482, 494, 504, 505, 1311.
  Wounded, 380, 390.
Byunes, Joseph O., pvt., Co. C, 30th Inf., U. S. V., killed, 1147.
Cabell, De Rosey C., capt., 6th U. S. Cav., mentioned, 492.
Cadiz, Spain, Spanish fleet at, 28.
Cadiz, Spanish steamship, transporting Spanish prisoners to Spain, 991.
Cadwell, Charles I., pvt., Co. F, 1st Nebr. Vol. Inf., wounded, 975.
Cailles, Juan, insurgent general, mentioned, 1211, surrender, 1288.
Cain, James L., pvt., Co. C, 9th U. S. Inf., killed, 1297.
Cain, Maurice, pvt., Co. A, 22d U. S. Inf., death, 1144.
Cain, Spurgeon, mus., Co. K, 22d U. S. Inf., wounded, 948.
Cainta, Rizal, P. I., presidente, reported kidnaped, 1320.
Calanary, John, pvt., Co. E, 1st Mont. Vol. Inf., wounded, 945.
Calbi, Dato, mentioned, 1118.
Calcari, Angel, artif., Co. E, 18th U. S. Inf., death, 1264.
Caldwell, Edward, pvt., Co. D, 10th Pa. Vol. Inf., wounded, 895.
Caldwell, Harry, pvt., Co. M, 30th U. S. Inf., death, 1194.
Calhoun, James S., pvt., Co. C, 40th Inf., U. S. V., killed, 1182.
Califf, Albert J., pvt., Co. M, 2d Oreg. Vol. Inf., wounded, 946.
California, Department of:
  Hawaiian Islands attached to, 725, 726.
  Instructions for sailing of transports, 463.
  Nagasaki as distributing point for China, instructions re, 427, 439.
  Staff officers and clerks for, necessity, 673.
  Troops remaining from Philippine expedition to report to commanding general, 725.
California, State of, volunteers:
  Alleged deplorable health condition at San Francisco, 784.
  Alleged discrimation against, 755.
  Urged for service at front, 744, 746, 789.
California, U. S. transport, mentiond, 431.
Calkins, Charles, pvt., Co. E, 3d U. S. Inf., death, 1015.
Call, William E., pvt., Co. D, 44th Inf., U. S. V., wounded, 1167.
Callaghan, Riley G., pvt., Co. H, 18th U. S. Inf., wounded, 943.
Callahan, James A., pvt., Co. K., 1st Mont. Vol. Inf., killed, 976.
Callahan, Joseph, pvt., Co. M, 1st Mont. Vol. Inf., wounded, 903.
Callahan, William A., 1st lieut., 20th Kans. Vol. Inf., wounded, 915.
Callao, Cipriano, insurgent colonel, surrender, 1273.
Callao, Spanish gunboat, mentioned, 745.
Callaway, Christopher C., corpl., Co. D, 33d Inf., U. S. V., wounded, 1152.
Callender, Thomas S., Mr., mentioned, 240, 246-248, 250, 253.
Callender, Thomas S., jr., pvt., Co. G, 71st N. Y. Vol. Inf., mentioned, 240, 241, 246-248, 250, 253, 254.
Callis, Joseph M., pvt., Co. H, 6th U. S. Inf., death, 1082.
Calloway, Mason, pvt., Batty. L, 3d U. S. Art., wounded, 948.
Calvert, Robert B., 2d lieut., 18th U. S. Inf., wounded, 1117.
Calwerel, Frank R., corpl., Co. B, 1st Idaho Vol. Inf., killed, 895.
Camara, Admiral, Spanish navy, mentioned, 712, 714.

Cambon, Jules, French ambassador to U. S., mentioned, 126, 220, 322, 346, 383.
Camel, Charles A., pvt., band, 24th U. S. Inf., death, 1190.
Cameron, James R., pvt., Co. E, 3d U. S. Inf., death, 1088.
Cameron, Joseph O., pvt., Co. D, 39th Inf., U. S. V., death, 1152.
Camgobell, Daniel, pvt., Co. M, 1st Wash. Vol. Inf., wounded, 897.
Camp Merritt, San Francisco, Cal., abandonment directed, 735.
Camp, T. J., pvt.. ——, 71st N. Y. Vol. Inf., mentioned, 254.
Camp, Wilber E., sergt., Co. G, 1st Nebr. Vol. Inf., wounded, 906.
Camps, location, at Honolulu, 758, 839.
  Care and protection, 7.
  Difficulty in locating suitable, 13.
  Muster out at San Francisco, 1041, 1042.
  Selection of, 35-39.
Campbell, Daniel, pvt., Co. M, 1st Nebr. Vol. Inf., wounded, 899.
Campbell, David, pvt., Co. M, 1st Wash. Vol. Inf., death, 956.
Campbell, David L., pvt., Co. E, 20th Kans. Vol. Inf., death, 886.
Campbell, Edward A., pvt., Co. F, 14th U. S. Inf., death, 1001.
Campbell, Edward A., col., 1st N. J. Vol. Inf., mentioned, 520, 521.
Campbell, Franklin, pvt., Co. G, 7th U. S. Inf., mentioned, 216.
Campbell, George H., pvt., Co. L, 30th U. S. Inf., death, 1200.
Campbell, Harry, pvt., Co. B, 6th U. S. Inf., wounded, 1087.
Campbell, H. S., clerk, General Brooke's headquarters, mentioned, 302.
Campbell, James, pvt., Co. L, 6th U. S. Inf., death, 1200.
Campbell, James, col., 9th Ill. Vol. Inf., mentioned, 555.
Campbell, James A., capt., asst. qm., U. S. V., mentioned, 302.
Campbell, James R., pvt., Co. B, 43d Inf., U. S. V., death, 1210; wounded, 1202.
Campbell, John D., corpl., Co. D, 5th U. S. Inf., killed, 1251.
Campbell, John J., pvt., Co. M, 1st Mont. Vol. Inf., wounded, 900, 907.
Campbell, Joseph F., pvt., Co. L, 9th U. S. Inf., killed, 1081.
Campbell, Roy G., pvt., Co. C, 1st Nebr. Vol. Inf., wounded, 955.
Canaly, James J., pvt., Co. G, 21st U. S. Inf., wounded, 1052.
Canavan, Edward, farrier, Troop M, 3d U. S. Cav., death, 1254.
Caney, Francis W., pvt., Co. H, 9th Mass. Vol. Inf., mentioned, 209.
Caniff, John A., pvt., Co. H, 6th U. S. Inf., death, 1283.
Cannon, Horace, corpl., Co. K, 48th Inf., U. S. V., wounded, 1176.
Cannon, John F., pvt., Co. C, 16th U. S. Inf., wounded, 1152.
Cannon, Spanish, captured by American troops, 1163.
  Request by Spain for return, 1188.
  Refused by U. S., 1188.
Canon, insurgent general, mentioned, 1112.
Canton, William J., maj., 1st Wash. Vol. Inf., mentioned, 992.
Capistrano, insurgent commander, surrender, 1264.
Caplick, Albert, corpl., Co. K, 13th U. S. Inf., wounded, 1113.
Capron, Allyn K., capt., 1st U. S. Vol. Cav., killed, 61, 124; mentioned, 54, 369.
Caralaski, Jacob, pvt., Co. F, 21st U.S. Inf., death, 1095.
Carbaugh, Henry C., lieut. col., judge-advocate, U. S. V., mentioned, 1330.
Carden, Alfred O., pvt., Co. D, 2d Oreg. Vol. Inf., wounded, 934.
Cardenas, Daniel W. de, batt. sergt. maj., 27th Inf., U. S. V., wounded, 1231.
Cardoza, James F., pvt., Co. A, Batt. Engrs., U. S. A., death, 803.

Cardwell, ——, civilian clerk, Manila P. I., mentioned, 979.
Carey, John, pvt., Co. G, 14th U. S. Inf., wounded, 898.
Carey, John B., pvt., Troop K, 4th U. S. Cav., wounded, 974
Carl, John G., sergt., Co. L, 18th U. S. Inf., death, 1156; wounded, 1155.
Carleton, Mervin M., sergt., Co. E, 13th Minn. Vol. Inf., death, 861; mentioned, 762; wounded, 760.
Carlile, John J., pvt., Co. M, 1st Wash. Vol. Inf., wounded, 898.
Carlson, Carl A., pvt., Co. H, 22d U. S. Inf., death, 1008; wounded, 992.
Carlson, Carl F., pvt., Co. D, 43d Inf., U. S. V., killed, 1209.
Carlson, Charles, pvt., Co. L, 1st Colo. Vol. Inf., death, 895.
Carlson, Oscar, pvt., Co. F, 14th U. S. Inf., death, 1260.
Carlyle, Allen E., pvt., Co. I, 1st Wash. Vol. Inf., death, 886.
Carmen, Sr., Filipino, appointed by Aguinaldo to meet commissioners, 909.
Carnahan, Henry, pvt., Co. M, 47th Inf., U. S. V., death, 1234.
Carnes, Joseph F., pvt., Co. F, 34th Inf., U. S. V., death, 1146.
Carney, Edward, pvt., Co. F, 21st U. S. Inf., wounded, 1306.
Carney, Frank, pvt., Co. G, 47th Inf., U. S. V., wounded, 1187.

Caroline and Ladrone islands:
Harbors, anchorages, defenses, 746
Means of communication with Manila, 746.
Memorandum on, 744, 745.
Spanish colony at Ponape Island, condition, number, and defenses, 745.
Spanish Government requests to send native soldiers, prisoners of U. S., as garrison for, 961.
Weather conditions, 746.

Carpenter, Gilbert S., brig. gen., U. S. V.
Mentioned, 55, 538, 539, 545, 1031, 1107.
Recommended for promotion, 225, 1122.
Wounded, 124.
Carpenter, Herbert, pvt., Co. B, 34th Inf., U. S. V., wounded, 1212.
Carpenter, John D., pvt., Co. L, 46th Inf., U. S. V., death, 1230.
Carpenter, Louis H., brig. gen., U. S. V., mentioned, 530, 535, 536, 537, 552.
Carpenter, Raymond, pvt., Batty. L, 3d U. S. Art. death, 1125.
Carr, Elmer E., pvt., Co. F, 39th Inf., U. S. V., wounded, 1152.
Carr, Frank, pvt., Co. F, 26th Inf., U. S. V., killed, 1137.
Carr, Fred, pvt., Co. G, 34th Inf., U. S. V., wounded, 1147.
Carr, James, pvt., Co. L, 17th U. S. Inf., wounded, 1222.
Carregie, Frank, pvt., Co. F, 7th U. S. Inf., mentioned, 197.
Carrick, James I., pvt., Co. K, 25th U. S. Inf., wounded, 1216.
Carrington, Frank de L., lieut. col., 8th Cal. Vol. Inf., mentioned, 722.
Carroll, Charles A., pvt., Co. A, 6th U. S. Inf., death, 1226.
Carroll, Daniel, pvt., Co. A, 2d Oreg. Vol. Inf., mentioned, 1028.
Carroll, Daniel W., pvt., Co. A, 22d U. S. Inf., wounded, 934.
Carroll, Henry, brig. gen., U. S. V.
Promotion, 116.
Recommended for, 113.
Wounded, 123.
Carroll, James A., pvt., Co. I, 1st Nebr. Vol. Inf., wounded, 952.
Carroll, Richard, pvt., Co. B, 3d U. S. Inf., death, 979.
Carroll, William, pvt., Co. D, 20th Kans. Vol. Inf., killed, 949.
Carroll, William O., pvt., Co. E, 17th U. S. Inf., wounded, 1021.
Carruthers, Elmer R., pvt., Co. L, 16th U. S. Inf., death, 1164,

Carson, jr., John M., maj., qm., U. S. V., mentioned, 302.
Carter, Albert, pvt., Co. C, 15th U. S. Inf., death, 493.
Carter, Albert, pvt., Co. H, 48th Inf., U. S. V., death, 1190.
Carter, Albin E., pvt., Co. G, 44th Inf., U. S. V., killed, 1218.
Carter, Charles F., pvt., Co. G, 1st N. Y. Vol. Inf., death, 838.
Carter, Charles H., pvt., Co. D, 27th U. S. Inf., wounded, 1206.
Carter, Cornelius E., pvt., Co. E, 24th U. S. Inf., death, 1153.
Carter, Edward, pvt., Troop C, 11th U. S. Cav., death, 1205.
Carter, Frank, pvt., Co. E, 5th U. S. Inf., death, 1276.
Carter, Fred, pvt., Co. E, 20th Kans. Vol. Inf., wounded, 954.
Carter, Harry, pvt., Co. D, 35th Inf., U. S. V., wounded, 1182.
Carter, John Q. A., pvt., Co. L, 12th U. S. Inf., killed, 1128.
Carter, Robert, pvt., Co. F, 3d U. S. Inf., death, 979.
Carter, Thomas A., U. S. Senator, letter of, 330.
Carter, Thomas H., Hon., mentioned, 333, 367.
Carter, ——, surg., U. S. Marine Hosp. Serv., appointed sanitary inspector at Santiago, 218.
Carter, William, pvt., Co. F, 24th U. S. Inf., death, 1057, 1060.
Carter, William H., lieut. col., A. A. G., U. S. A., correspondence, 62, 102, 141, 145, 178, 254, 307, 319, 336, 349, 376.
Carter, William T., pvt., Co. H, 23d U. S. Inf., wounded, 1147.
Carter, Willard V., pvt., Co. L, 1st Nebr. Vol. Inf., wounded, 975.
Cartner, Alexander L., corpl., Co. A, 19th U. S. Inf., death, 1213.
Carty, Charles S., pvt., Co. E, 1st Colo. Vol. Inf., wounded, 955.
Case, James Francis, capt., 2d Oreg. Vol. Inf., mentioned, 780.
Casebeer, James A., pvt., Co. D, 1st Mont. Vol. Inf., wounded, 1015.
Casey, Joseph, pvt., Co. B, 18th U. S. Inf., wounded, 1108.
Casey, Thomas L., corpl., Co. E, 47th Inf., U. S. V., wounded, 1257.
Casey, William H., pvt., Co. G, 4th U. S. Inf., death, 1074.
Cashemire, Spanish ship.
Transporting Spanish prisoners from P. I., to Spain, 991, 1069.
Cashmore, Alfred, pvt., band, 1st Mont. Vol. Inf., wounded, 922.
Cason, Oliver B., pvt., Co. E, 23d U. S. Inf., wounded, 956.
Cassady, Frank B., pvt., Co. M, 44th Inf., U. S. V., wounded, missing, 1256.
Cassels, Arthur F., 2d lieut., 7th U. S. Art., mentioned, 1039, 1178.
Cassidy, James P., pvt., Co. K, 1st Cal. Vol. Inf., killed, 914.
Cassidy, Robert V., pvt., Co. K, 22d U. S. Inf., wounded, 994.
Casteel, Delphey T. E., col., 2d W. Va. Vol. Inf., mentioned, 525, 526.
Casteel, Lovell E., sergt., Co. H, 33d Inf., U. S. V., killed, 1101.
Castillo, Demetrio, brig. gen., Cuban Army, mentioned, 21, 54.
Castillo, Lazaro, pvt., Co. E, 33d Inf., U. S. V., wounded, 1102.
Castillo, Pedro Lopez de, pvt., Spanish Army, letter to "Soldiers of American Army," 249, 250.
Castine, U. S. dispatch boat, mentioned, 22, 50, 415.
Castle, Charles W., 2d lieut., 16th U. S. Inf., mentioned, 301.
Castle, Willard A., sergt., Co. E, 1st U. S. Inf., wounded, 1253.
Castlebury, Locke, sergt., Co. I, 16th U. S. Inf., death, 1256.
Castner, Alonzo B., pvt., Co. F, 14th U. S. Inf., wounded, 999.

Casualties:
American, at Manila, 754.
Call for, by Secretary of War, 759.
In assault on, and other causes, 760, 761.
At—
Caloocan, 900, 903.
Sea, 763.
En route to U. S., 829.
List of—
Desired, 800.
Sent to people of Minnesota, 762.
Philippine Islands, 921, 949, 956, 957, 960, 966.
Jan. 1 to Apr. 1, 1900, 1156.
List to be furnished A. G. O. weekly, 801.
Number and causes of, to Feb. 1, 1899, 893.
Number and causes, report desired by U. S. Senate, 890.
Total resulting from engagements, Feb. 4–8, 899.
See also Army and Volunteers.
Cataluña, Spanish ship:
Transporting Spanish prisoners to Spain, 991, 1069.
Catania, transport, mentioned, 69, 72, 73, 88, 123, 192, 198, 224, 234, 237.
Catchings, T. C., Hon., mentioned, 362, 364.
Cathelin, George, pvt., Batty. D, Cal. H. Art., wounded, 995.
Catron, Frank B., pvt., Batty. K, 3d U. S. Art., wounded, 950.
Cauble, Thomas O., pvt., Co. D, 3d U. S. Inf., death, 972.
Cavanaugh, Harry G., capt., 13th U. S. Inf., mentioned, 83; wounded, 124.
Cavanaugh, John, pvt., Co. E, 1st Mont. Vol. Inf., wounded, 954.
Cavenaugh, William A., 2d lieut., 20th U. S. Inf., mentioned, 994.
Cawetzka, Charles, pvt., Co. F, 30th Inf., U. S. V., wounded, 1130.
Ceasor, William, pvt., Co. B, 37th Inf., U. S. V., death, 1202.
Ceballos, J. M. & Co., Re. contract for transportation of Spanish prisoners, 222, 223, 964, 965, 976, 987.
Release of ships belonging to, 967.
Cecil, John, pvt., Co. G, 24th U. S. Inf., wounded, 1052.
Censor of news at Manila:
Charges of favoritism and neglect against, 1135, 1136.
Complaints of discrimination by, 1023.
Unfounded, 1025.
Complaints regarding, 973, 1260.
Reasons for, 1221.
Removal, 1036, 1065, 1066, 1221, 1225, 1229.
Centennial, steamship, mentioned, 661, 1028, 1091.
Cerveny, John, pvt., Co. D, 18th U. S. Inf., death, 1196.
Cervera, Pascual, Spanish admiral:
Fleet of—
Report of destruction, 78, 81.
Effect on Army, 81.
Mentioned, 16, 22, 23, 25, 73, 78, 81, 100, 157, 171, 234, 261.
Ordered to shell Santiago, 74.
Telegram to Captain-General Blanco, reporting destruction of his fleet, 100.
Chaffee, Adna R., maj. gen., U. S. A.
Assigned to command China Relief Expedition, 419, 420, 431, 433.
Detail as military governor, P. I., 1259.
Mentioned, 47, 116, 181, 418, 420, 421, 424, 427, 431–436, 438–441, 443–458, 460–466, 468–506, 535, 538, 541, 542, 544, 545, 667, 841, 1283, 1286, 1288, 1289, 1338.
Nominated for major-generalcy, 498.
President U. S. regrets friction between Taft and, 1297.
Recommended for promotion, 104.
Chaffee, Mark J., pvt., Co. C, 45th Inf., U. S. V., wounded, 1203.
Chaffee, William K., col., 2d Mo. Vol. Inf., mentioned, 518, 519.
Chaffin, George H., lieut. col., 6th Mass. Vol. Inf., resignation, 374, 376.
Chalker, ——, chief engineer, U. S. Navy, mentioned, 769, 770, 772.
Chamberlain, Edgar J., corpl., Co. K, 2d Oreg. Vol. Inf., wounded, 983.

Chamberlain, Clarence C., pvt., Co. I, 34th Mich Vol. Inf., mentioned, 219.
Chamberlain John L., maj., chief ordnance officer, U. S. V., mentioned, 397.
Chamberlain, W. P., civilian employee on tug Oceania, wounded, 1090.
Chambers, Arthur N., pvt., Co. L, 9th U. S. Inf., killed, 1081.
Chambers, John L., pvt., Co. H, 16th U. S. Inf., death, 1226.
Chambers, Merritt, pvt., Co. A, 4th U. S. Inf., mentioned, 216.
Chamblin, Ross, pvt., Co. L, 14th U. S. Inf., wounded, 454.
Chance, William W., capt., sig. officer, U. S. V., mentioned, 1000.
Recommended for commission in Army, 785.
Chandler, Bert B., pvt., Co. C, 2d Oreg. Vol. Inf., death, 972; wounded, 946.
Chandler, Elias, col., 1st Ark. Vol. Inf., mentioned, 530, 531.
Chapin, Edward H., pvt., Co. D, 38th Inf., U. S. V., wounded, 1141.
Chaplains, U. S. Army—
Appointment, 698.
Priests recommended for, 693.
To accompany General Merritt to P. I., 711.
Chaplewski, Frank, pvt., Co. D, 23d U. S. Inf., death, 1260.
Chapline, Alexander R., pvt., Co. M, 14th U. S. Inf., death, 931.
Chapman, Albert J., pvt., Co. A, 34th Mich. Vol. Inf., mentioned, 202.
Chapman, Arden R., corpl., Co. M, 1st Nebr. Vol. Inf., wounded, 974.
Chapman, Charles A., corpl., Co. H, 47th Inf., U. S. V., wounded, 1166.
Chapman, Frank, pvt., Co. D, 37th Inf., U. S. V., wounded, 1146.
Chapman, Joe, pvt., Hosp. Corps, U. S. A., death, 1271.
Chappell, Clarence E., pvt., Batty. L, 3d U. S. Art., wounded, 950.
Chappelle, Catholic Archbishop, P. I., mentioned, 1145, 1238.
Charette, Adolph T., pvt., Co. A, 1st Mont. Vol. Inf., wounded, 903.
Charles, Nelson, mentioned, 748, 1078, 1079, 1094, 1097.
Charleston, S. C.:
Equipment for troops, 80.
Funds requested by Gen. Wilson for supply depts. at, 91, 132, 135, 141.
Movement of troops, 77, 85, 91, 92, 97, 98, 101, 102, 105–109, 111, 120, 133.
Rita, Spanish steamer, appraisement by admiralty court, 95, 117, 118, 119.
Transfer to War Department, 103.
Transportation facilities, 83, 87, 88, 93, 96, 97, 98, 101–103, 105, 106, 108, 112, 115, 121, 122, 127, 132, 133, 138, 144.
Charleston, U. S. cruiser, mentioned, 637, 664, 670, 775.
Charlton, Thomas E., pvt., Co. D, 4th U. S. Inf., wounded, 1017.
Chase, George F., capt., 3d U. S. Cav., mentioned, 1059.
Chase, Herbert H., corpl., Co. D, 29th U. S. Inf., killed, 1229.
Chase, James T., maj., 1st N. Y. Vol. Inf., mentioned, 748.
Chase, Lewis, pvt., Co. E, 1st S. Dak. Vol. Inf., killed, 949.
Chatman, William, pvt., Co. L, 37th Inf., U. S. V., death, 1223.
Chaxel, Fred, pvt., Co. F, 1st Mont. Vol. Inf., wounded, 915.
Cheastey, William J., pvt., Co. M, 1st Mont. Vol. Inf., wounded, 920.
Cheatham, B. Frank, maj., 37th Inf., U. S. V., mentioned, 1086, 1131, 1132.
Cheatham, William, pvt., Co. H, 3d U. S. Inf., killed, 1187.
Checks, issue to officers and soldiers recommended, to send money to families, 693, 694.
Cheek, William D., sergt., Co. L, 20th U. S. Inf., wounded, 937.
Cheevers, William, pvt., Co. I, 71st N. Y. Vol. Inf., mentioned, 202.

INDEX. 1377

Cheney, Ward, 1st lieut., 4th U. S. Inf., killed, 1129, 1130.
Chenoweth, Claude M., pvt., Co. G, 1st Nebr. Vol. Inf., mentioned, 955.
Cheribon, steamer, mentioned, 222, 223.
Cherokee, U. S. transport, 80, 95, 98, 99, 112, 113, 121, 157, 275, 278, 282, 309, 310, 333.
Cherry, Matthias H., pvt., Co. E, 1st Wash. Vol. Inf., killed, 895.
Chestnut, Willie, pvt., Co. A, 22d U. S. Inf., death, 1151.
Chevalier, Elmer H., pvt., Co. E, 21st U. S. Inf., death, 986.
Chidester, Walter C., a. a. surgeon, U. S. A., wounded, 1150.
Childers, Robert E., pvt., Co. B, 1st Nebr. Vol. Inf., wounded, 899.
Childs, Leroy L., pvt., Co. I, 1st Wash. Vol. Inf., wounded, 906.

Chickamauga Park, Ga.:
Brooke, General, to command troops at, 8.
Concentration of troops, 7.
Condition of camp at, 36, 43.
Equipment and movement of troops, 48, 49, 52, 53, 71–82, 91, 92.
Organization of division, 44, 45, 46, 47.
Wade, General, to command troops at, 57.

China Relief Expedition, correspondence relating to, 409–506.
Allied forces advance on Pekin, 454.
Territory assigned to each, 501.
American interests, protection of, 410, 411, 412, 413, 414, 420, 462.
Astronomical instruments, removal from observatory, 493, 494.
Austrian forces in Pekin, 416.
Number, 439.
Barracks for legation guard, 498, 501, 504.
Boxers at Tientsin, 413.
In vicinity of Pekin, 474.
Canton, conditions, 420.
Catholic Christians, annoying villagers at Ho-si-wu and Matow, 495.
Chefoo, conditions, 414.
Troops at, 420.
Cheng-ting-fu, Belgian engineers in danger, 485.
Held by Germany, 488.
China, allied troops for, 423.
Conditions, 426.
Forts, dismantling, 504.
Military occupation, 504.
Postal officials, telegrams held by, 414.
Postal service, 487, 488, 490, 491, 494, 495, 496.
Relief expedition, command of, 431.
Retention troops in, 482, 484.
Troops for, 415, 416, 417, 424.
Wintering in, 470, 479.
Withdrawal of, 476.
Troops from, to be used in P. I., 1224.
Chinese fleet, leaving Yangtse River, 448.
Ching-wang-tao, pier at, 491.
Postal service, 491.
To be taken by allied forces, 430.
Port of, when open, 457.
Christians, killed and burned near Sanho, 495.
Conference, commanders, allied forces, 410.
Naval commanders, policy in Pekin, 465.
England, forces of, advance on Pekin, 411, 444, 447.
Capture Peitsang, 448.
In Pekin, 416.
Landing Cheefoo and Pekin, 415.
Landing Taku, 409.
Number, 439.
Occupation of Shanghai, 450, 451.
Temporary loan to Tientsin provincial government, 483.
Fenchow-fu, foreigners shot by Chinese escort, 474, 476.
French forces, advance on Pekin, 447.
Engagement near Tssotshon, 495.
In Pekin, 416.
Landing Taku, 409.
Number 439, 473.
Funds, discovery in Forbidden City, policy, 502.
Payment troops, extortionate charges exchange by Hongkong bank, 488, 489.
Placed to credit of General Chaffee, 458.

China Relief Expedition—Continued.
German forces, blown up at Petang, 477.
Burial Christians at Meaofingshen and Tingling, 496.
In Pekin, 416.
Landing Cheefoo, 415.
Number, 439 473.
Transfer of railroad, 483, 488.
German minister, murder of, 422.
Germany, influence in China, 493.
Guns, U. S. light artillery, complimentary remarks by General Linivitch, 490.
Inferiority in action, criticism, 490.
Hongkong Bank, extortionate charges, exchange money, 491.
Horses, authority to purchase, 500, 501.
Ho-si-wu, villagers annoyed by Catholic Christians, 495.
Hospitals, in Japan for U. S. troops, 454–456.
Hostilities, cessation, 452.
Italian forces, in Pekin, 416.
Strength of, 439.
Japan, hospital for U. S. troops, 454–456.
Postal service in China, 487–491, 494–496.
Temporary loan to Tientsin provisional government, 483.
Japanese forces, advance on Pekin, 444, 447.
Capture of Peitsang, 448.
Casualties, 443.
Engagement, Taku, 495.
In Pekin, 416.
Strength of, 425, 439, 473.
Legation, American guard for, 435, 478, 480.
Reduction, 499, 501.
Legations, blockaded by Chinese, 457.
Burned, 422.
Guard, reductions, 499.
Relieved, 461.
Li Hung Chang, cessation of hostilities, 452, 462.
Conference naval commanders, policy in Pekin, 465.
Settlement of differences, 479, 480.
Mafang, murder of native Christians, 497.
Marines, fuel and forage to, 445.
Matow, villagers annoyed by Catholic Christians, 495.
Meaofingshen, Christians murdered, 496.
Messages, delay of, 428, 430, 432, 467, 468, 471–473.
Ming-Tombs, expedition to, 490.
Missionaries, murder of, at Tayuan, 476.
Protection of, 478.
Relief of, 471, 472.
Rescue American and British, 414.
Nagasaki, distributing point, landing troops, 427, 431, 439, 440.
Newchwang, advance on, by Boxers, 449.
Bombardment, seizure by Russians, 449.
General conditions, 449.
Robbers, activity of, 490.
Pao-ting-fu, Americans murdered, 487, 488.
Execution of accomplices in murders, 488.
Expedition to, 475, 485.
Troops at, 483, 488.
Pechili, held by Germany, 488.
Pei-tang Ho, bridge destroyed, 486, 491.
Pekin, advance on, 435, 444, 453.
Capture of, casualties, etc., 458–460, 465.
Cessation of hostilities against legations, 442.
Communication interrupted, 410.
Conditions, 413, 422, 426, 433, 435, 437, 438, 450, 454, 469, 470, 472, 474, 476, 477, 481, 485, 490.
Escort for ministers, etc., 451, 452.
Troops to winter at, 479.
Continued occupation, 499.
Delay of march on, 443.
Engagement near, casualties, 488, 421.
Forces in, 414.
General Chaffee to command forces, 418–420, 431, 433.
German troops burn Tsung-li-Yamen, 426.
Ministers, arrangements for delivery, etc., 455.
Occupation of ground, 498.
Proposition to relieve, 452.
Removal of instruments from observatory, 493, 494.
Restoration railroad to Shan-hai-kuan, 483.
Retention of troops in, 469, 470.
Treasure in Forbidden City, 502.
Troops to, 409–411, 415, 422.

China Relief Expedition—Continued.
  Pietsang, engagement, 446-448.
    Capture by Japanese, 448.
  Petang, attack on, 477.
  Philippines, troops for China, 412, 415-419, 422, 424, 426, 472.
  Phinwang, British to build bridge, 466.
  Postal service, 487, 488, 490, 491, 494-496.
  Proclamation, issue of, 416.
  Railroad, near Pekin, repair, 461, 462.
    Repair by Russians, 453, 470, 474, 481.
    Shan-hai-kuan to Pekin, restoration, 483.
    Transfer from Russian to German forces, repair of, etc., 483, 488.
  Rice, relief distress, 483.
  Robbers, engagement with, near Pekin, 492.
  Russian forces, advance on Pekin, 447.
    Blown up at Petang, 477.
    Bombardment of Newchwang—seizure of, 449.
    Engagement near Tientsin, 417.
    In Pekin, 416.
    Landing Chefoo and Pekin, 415.
    At Taku, 409, 414.
    Strength of, 439, 473.
    To Pekin, 411.
    Temporary loan to Tientsin provisional government, 483.
    Transfer of railroad, 483, 488.
  Sanho, Christians killed and burned, 495.
    German troops to, 495.
  Shanghai, objections to landing of soldiers, 449-451.
  Shan-hai-kuan, British to build pier, 491.
    Occupation by Russian forces, 481.
    Restoration railroad to Pekin, 483.
    Surrender of, 481.
  Shan-Tung, exempt from military operations, 484.
  Sian Fu, allied forces proposed march on, 498, 499.
  Supplies, authority to sell, 500.
    And equipment for Relief Expedition, 441, 446, 453.
  Taku, engagement Japanese and Chinese near, 495.
    Firing on ships, 415, 422.
    Forts, capture of, 415, 422.
    Marines to, 418.
    Occupation of ground, 498.
    Surrender of, 412, 413.
    Troops, difficulty in landing, 409, 443, 444.
    At, 412, 422, 432.
  Taiyuan, murder of missionaries, 476.
    Expedition to, 488.
  Temple agricultural grounds, concession to U. S., 493, 498, 501.
  Tientsin, Boxers at, 413.
    Boxers, dispersion of, 460.
    Capture, 437, 438, 440.
    Casualties, 417, 426, 429, 440, 443, 445, 466, 469.
    Colonel Liscum killed at, 426.
    Communication interrupted, 410.
    Conditions, 410, 418, 422, 425, 442.
    Troops to winter at, 479.
    Engagements at and near, 417, 422, 466.
    Firing on, 415,
    Hospital, deaths in, 464.
    Loan by England to provisional government of, 483.
    Looting, 434, 436, 438, 440, 442.
    Occupation of ground, 498.
    Preservation of, 428.
    Rice, for relief of distress, 483.
    Siege guns, disposition of, 479.
    Silver, requests return of, 483.
    Supplies for, 437.
    Troops to, 409, 410, 432.
  Tingling, Christians murdered, 496.
  Tsangchow, China, British mission looted, 414.
  Tssotshon, engagement near, between French and Chinese, 495.
  Tsung-li-Yamen, burning of, 426.
  Tu-liu, expedition to, 474.
  United States, concession Temple agricultural grounds, 493, 498, 501.
    Capture Peitsang, 448.
    Forces, advance on Pekin, 444, 447.
    Policy in China, 462.
    Strength of, 439.
    Von Waldersee, field marshal German army, to command allied forces, 450, 451.

China Relief Expedition—Continued.
  Yangtsun, casualties, 453.
    Occupation, casualties, etc., 449, 451.
  Yangtze, military camp, 437.
China:
  Detail of officers to gather military information in, 1169, 1171.
  Troops from Philippine Islands for service in, 1180.
China, U. S. transport, mentioned, 556, 585, 620, 660, 661, 665, 667, 683, 685, 691, 699, 700, 701, 704, 730, 738, 792.
China Sea, Spanish reserve fleet sail for, 705.
Chinese consular representative, correction of name at Manila, 789, 790.
Chinese Government, standing in re rule of Chinese exclusion in P. I., 1073.
Chinese minister, Washington, D. C., requests admission of 700 Chinese to P. I. as exception to expulsion rule, 1073.
Chinese, request for landing in P. I., 1073.
Chinese, safety in P. I., 901.
Ching, Prince, mentioned, 473-475, 502.
Chinn, Ben D., pvt., Co. C, 38th Inf., U. S. V., wounded, 1141.
Chinn, Grant, pvt., Co. K, 1st Nebr. Vol. Inf., wounded, 983.
Chittenden, Hiram M., lieut. col., chief engineer, U. S. V., mentioned, 336, 379, 386, 393, 646.
Chitty, William D., 2d lieut., 3d U. S. Cav., mentioned, 1062.
Chrisler, Charles, pvt., Co. G, 14th U. S. Inf., death, 487.
Christenberry, Silas A., corpl., Co. D, 9th U. S. Inf., wounded, 444.
Christensen, Boyle, sergt., Co. D, 13th U. S. Inf., wounded, 1008.
Christie, Peter, pvt., Co. D, 21st U. S. Inf., mentioned, 1042; wounded, 1044.
Christman, Claude B., corpl., Co. K, 27th Inf., U. S. V., death, 1125.
Christy, Charles M., capt., 20th Kans. Vol. Inf., wounded, 903.
Church, George, pvt., Co. A, 13th Minn. Vol. Inf., mentioned, 920.
Church, Rodney S., pvt., Co. C, 1st Wash. Vol. Inf., wounded, 936.
Churches, religious worship, and educational establishments to be safe-guarded by American Army, 757.
Cilley, Jonathan, 1st lieut., 43d U. S. V., Inf., death, 1179.
Cincinnati, U. S. gunboat, mentioned, 297, 299-301.
Citizens of United States, unity of action in case of attack on sovereignty, etc., 826.
City of Chester, U. S. transport, mentioned, 233, 336, 360, 366, 372, 373, 392, 395, 590, 598, 621, 624, 627.
City of Macon, U. S. transport, mentioned, 60, 63, 65, 67, 69, 72, 88, 95, 122, 211, 224, 373.
City of Para, U. S. transport, mentioned, 599, 1014, 1018, 1024, 1026, 1030, 1051, 1061, 1063, 1075, 1082, 1094, 1095, 1101.
City of Pekin, U. S. transport:
  Amidship sleeping quarters untenable, 768.
  Bathing accommodations, 768.
  Chartering of, 637, 638.
  Cooking facilities, 776.
  Mentioned, 556, 584, 637, 638, 649, 658, 660, 663-665, 667, 669-671, 673, 767, 774, 775, 792, 1090, 1091, 1105, 1110, 1120, 1128.
  Sanitary condition, report, 774, 767.
City of Puebla, U. S. transport, mentioned, 604, 618, 695, 720, 721, 724, 729, 733, 758, 791, 832, 850, 928, 943, 953, 971, 985, 1000, 1082, 1091, 1092, 1106, 1123.
City of Sydney, U. S. transport:
  Arrangements for messing, 769.
  Bathing facilities, 769.
  Cleanliness of quarters, responsibility for, 770.
  Commissary department, 769, 771, 773, 776.
    Inadequacy, 769.
  Cooking facilities, 771, 773.
    Inadequacy, 768, 769.
  Discipline and health of troops, 770.
  Enlisted men, recommendations for schools for, 771, 773.
  Improvement, recommendations, 773, 774.
  Inspection, 770.
  Mentioned, 556, 612, 660, 661, 663, 664, 667, 670-672, 736, 749, 758, 768, 770-772, 777, 780, 1049, 1071, 1074, 1078, 1089, 1102, 1128.
  Quarters, assignment, 770, 772, 775.

INDEX. 1379

City of Sidney, U. S. transport—Continued.
Sanitary conditions, 770–772, 774–775.
Precautions, 770.
Sleeping accommodations, 772, 775 777.
Supplies and equipment, 777.
Inadequacy, 769.
Troops, health, and discipline, 770, 771, 774, 777.
Instruction, 773, 774.
Ventilation, imperfect, 772.
City of Washington, U. S. transport, mentioned, 120, 123, 157, 317, 324, 328, 333.
To be used as hospital ship, 120.
Claas, Henry, pvt., Co. C, 9th U. S. Inf., wounded, 1298.
Clampffer, George, pvt., Co. B, 9th U. S. Inf., wounded, 1015.
Clampitt, Eli E., pvt., Batty. G, 3d U. S. Art., death, 917.
Clampitt, Neimeyer E., pvt., Batty. E, 3d U. S. Art., wounded, 897.
Clancy, James H., pvt., Co. H, 43d Inf., U. S. V., wounded, 1160, 1168.
Clancy, Oliver, qm. sergt., 1st Wash. Vol. Inf., wounded, 896.
Clanton, Charles A., pvt., Co. I, 14th U. S. Inf., wounded, 898.
Clanz, William H., pvt., Co. A, 10th U. S. Inf., mentioned, 229.
Clapin, Frank, pvt., Co. C, 9th U. S. Inf., death, 495.
Clapp, Chris W., jr., pvt., Co. I, 20th Kans. Vol. Inf., wounded, 983.
Clapp, Hugh E., sergt., Co. D, 1st Nebr. Vol. Inf., wounded, 955.
Clapp, Mr. and Mrs., missionaries in China, murder, 471, 476.
Clark, Birt I., pvt., Co. A, 2d Oreg. Vol. Inf., killed, 952.
Clark, Charles, pvt., Co. G, 36th Inf., U. S. V., wounded, 1233.
Clark, Charles N., 1st lieut., 13th Minn. Vol. Inf., wounded, 963.
Clark, Edward, pvt., Co. G, 48th Inf., U. S. V., death, 1238.
Clark, Frank, pvt., Co. H, 29th Inf., U. S. V., wounded, 1124.
Clark, Frank J., pvt., Troop C, 11th Cav., U. S. V., wounded, 1124.
Clark, Fred, pvt., Batty. K, 3d U. S Art., wounded, 946.
Clark, Henry, 1st sergt., Co. L, 12th U. S. Inf., wounded, 1008.
Clark, James E., pvt., Co. K, 43d Inf., U. S. V., death, 1217.
Clark, James M., pvt., Co. K, 1st S. Dak. Vol. Inf., death, 840.
Clark, John B., pvt., Co. A, 33d Inf., U. S. V., wounded, 1228.
Clark, Osmond D., col., 1st Vt. Vol. Inf., mentioned, 530, 531.
Clark, Ralph L., pvt., Co. I, 23d U. S Inf., death, 1213; wounded, 1176.
Clark, Raymond, qm. sergt., Co. I, 37th Inf., U. S. V., death, 1210.
Clark, Raymond, pvt., Co. D, 20th Kans. Vol. Inf., wounded, 898.
Clark, Robert E., pvt., Co. L, 35th Inf., U. S. V., death, 1186.
Clark, Robert S., pvt., Co. F, 35th Inf., U. S. V., wounded, 1124.
Clark, Rodney, pvt., Co. B, 51st Iowa Vol. Inf., death, 1052.
Clark, Rufus B., qm. sergt., 1st Wash. Vol. Inf., wounded, 896.
Clark, William D., pvt., Co. E, 18th U. S. Inf., death, 979.
Clark, William J., pvt., Co. F, 1st Cal. Vol. Inf., mentioned, 1043.
Clarke, Adna G., capt., 20th Kans. Vol. Inf., wounded, 946.
Clarke, William A., pvt., Troop I, 3d U. S. Cav., drowned, 1215.
Clase, Ransom, pvt., Co. M, 14th U. S Inf., killed, 898.
Clauer, James, pvt., Co. C, 21st U. S. Inf., death, 1104.
Claus, John W., col., judge-advocate, U. S. A., mentioned, 400, 646.

Claxton, George, pvt., Co. E, 9th U. S. Inf., wounded, 1307.
Clay, Adolph M., pvt., Co. F, 1st Mont. Vol. Inf., wounded, 976.
Clay, Charles D., capt., 17th U. S. Inf., mentioned, 994; wounded, 946.
Clay, George P., corpl., Co. M, 43d Inf., U. S. V., death, 1178.
Clay, Willie, pvt., Troop C, 9th U. S. Cav., drowned, 1226.
Claypool, Jerry, pvt., Co. C, 12th U. S. Inf., death, 1194.
Clayton, George, pvt., Co. C, 19th U. S. Inf., death, 1086.
Clayton, William C., pvt., Batty. E, 1st U. S. Art., wounded, 1015.
Clayton, William H., sergt., Co. K, 29th U. S. Inf., death, 1168.
Cleary, Patrick, pvt., Co. G, 35th Inf., U. S. V., death, 1095.
Clease, John H., pvt., Co. E, 2d U. S. Inf., mentioned, 193.
Cleer, Edward F., sergt., Batty. G, 6th U. S. Art., killed, 1227.
Cleland, Leslie E., pvt., Co. L, 9th U. S. Inf., wounded, 1087.
Clem, Abraham, pvt., Co. D, 1st Mont. Vol. Inf., wounded, 1008.
Clements, Hugh, pvt., Co. C, 28th U. S. Inf., wounded, 1189.
Clemmens, Charles, pvt., Co. H, 34th Inf., U. S. V., mentioned, 183.
Clerical force, inadequacy of, at San Francisco, 673.
Cleveland, U. S. transport, mentioned, 985, 986.
Cleveland, Jeremy R., pvt., Batty. H, 3d U. S. Art., wounded, 901.
Cleveland, William J., pvt., Co. M, 16th U. S. Inf., death, 1164.
Cliff, Fred, pvt., Co. H, 30th Inf., U. S. V., wounded, 1150.
Cline, Jacob O., pvt., Co. H, 10th Pa. Vol. Inf., killed, 949.
Cline, Thomas A., pvt., Co. F, 34th Inf., U. S. V., wounded, 1227.
Clintman, William D., corpl., Co. D, 27th U. S. Inf., killed, 1206.
Clinton, mentioned, 190, 228, 231, 233, 234, 237, 239, 246, 370, 394.
Clinton, James W., 1st lieut., 22d U. S. Inf., mentioned, 951.
Closson, John D., sergt., Co. C, 9th U. S. Inf., wounded, 443, 1298.
Clother, George L., pvt., Co. B, 1st Nebr. Vol. Inf., wounded, 899.
Clother, George L., Batty. B, Utah Vol. Art., wounded, 897.
Clough, Bert E., pvt., Co. G, 22d U. S. Inf., wounded, 946.
Coad, Alfred, pvt., Co. L, 40th Inf., U. S. V., wounded, 1162.
Coak, William, pvt., Co. B, 4th U. S. Inf., death, 1017.
Coakley, John H., pvt., Co. K, 34th Inf., U. S. V., death, 1144.
Coal supply for transports at Honolulu, 730.
Coan, William J., pvt., Co. C, 44th Inf., U. S. V., wounded, 1212.
Coates, John F., pvt., Co. E, 33d Inf., U. S. V., wounded, 1101.
Coates, Ralph C., pvt., Co. K, 1st Cal. Vol. Inf.:
Death, 1048.
Mentioned, 1043.
Missing, 991.
Coats, Christopher C., pvt., Co. C, 18th U. S. Inf., wounded, 1113.
Coats, John D., pvt., Co. C, 16th U. S. Inf., wounded, 1152.
Coba, E. G., civilian teamster, mentioned, 183.
Cobb, Samuel R., pvt., Co. I, 11th U. S. Inf., wounded, 390.
Coburn, Edward C., pvt., Co. L, 15th U. S. Inf., killed, 1211.
Cochran, Melville A., col., 6th U. S. Inf., mentioned, 540.
Cochrane, Helen D., contract nurse, death, 1202.
Cockayne, Albert H., sergt., Co. E, Sig. Corps, U. S. A., killed, 1191.
Cockrane, Charles E., pvt., Co. G, 2d Oreg. Vol. Inf., mentioned, 948.

Coe, Charles H., pvt., Troop I, 4th U. S. Cav., wounded, 987.
Coe, John N., maj., 21st U. S. Inf., mentioned, 124.
Coffee, Nathan, pvt., Co. A, 24th U. S. Inf., death, 1141.
Coffel, Marvin A., late pvt., Co. G, 17th U. S. Inf., death, 1104.
Coffey, John, sergt., Co. H, 13th U. S. Inf., death, 1244.
Coffield, Maurice, pvt., Troop I, 4th U. S. Cav., wounded, 1003.
Coffin, John W., 1st lieut., asst. surg., 10th Pa. Vol. Inf., mentioned, 994.
Cofford, Hans, pvt., Co. D, 46th Inf., U. S. V., death, 1243.
Cogan, John H., pvt., Co. F, 3d U. S. Inf., death, 1141.
Cohen, Jay W., pvt., Co. M, 46th Inf., U. S. V., death, 1167.
Cohen, Morris J., sergt., Co. B, 20th Kans. Vol. Inf., killed, 948.
Colbe, Gustave, pvt., Troop K, 1st U. S. Cav., killed, 61.
Colby, Leonard W., brig. gen., U. S. Vols., mentioned, 294, 531-533, 538, 539.
Coldwell, C. E. Payson, pvt., Co. A, 13th Minn. Vol. Inf., death, 803.
Cole, Adelbert F., pvt., Co. C, 26th U. S. Inf., killed, 1192.
Cole, Andrew O., pvt., Co. D, 14th U. S. Inf., death, 917.
Cole, Edwin T., 1st lieut., 6th U. S. Inf., mentioned, 1056.
Cole, Jesse J., pvt., Co. L, 13th Minn. Vol. Inf., killed, 963.
Cole, Nelson, brig. gen., U. S. V., mentioned, 522-528.
Cole, Otis D., pvt., Co. L, 34th Inf., U. S. V., death, 1196.
Cole, William A., pvt., Co. I, 31st Inf., U. S. V., death, 1187.
Cole, James A., 1st lieut., 6th U. S. Cav., mentioned, 124.
Coleman, Frank E., pvt., Co. L, 36th Inf., U.S. V., death, 1202.
Coleman, George W., pvt., Co. M, 8th Ohio Vol. Inf., mentioned, 209.
Coleman, Thomas H., pvt., Co. E, 1st S. Dak. Vol. Inf., wounded, 975.
Coleman, Walter F., pvt., Co. G, 9th U. S. Inf., wounded, 444.
Coleran, Daniel E., pvt., Co. G, 1st S. Dak. Vol. Inf., killed, 996.
Coles, Robert R., pvt., Co. H, 40th Inf., U. S. V., killed, 1188.
Colgan, Edward R., qm. sergt., Co. K, 2d Oreg. Vol. Inf., mentioned, 952.
Collins, Charles L., capt., 23d U. S. Inf., death, 1066; mentioned, 1041.
Collins, Dennis A., corpl., Co. I, 21st U. S. Inf., wounded, 1015.
Collins, Daniel H., pvt., Co. F, 17th U. S. Inf., death, 1150.
Collins, Fred P., batt. sergt. maj., 14th U. S. Inf., death, 1142.
Collins, Harve, pvt., Co. A, 38th U. S. Inf., death, 1201.
Collins, Harry G., pvt., Co. L, 1st Cal. Vol. Inf., mentioned, 1043.
Collins, John W., pvt., Co. H, 46th Inf., U. S. V., death, 1200.
Collins, Joseph, pvt., Co. B, 39th Inf., U. S. V., death, 1196.
Collins, Walling, pvt., Co. B, 22d U. S. Inf., killed, 1052.
Collins, Walter E., pvt., Co. H, 43d Inf., U. S. V., killed, 1168.
Collins, William D., pvt., Co. C, 10th Pa. Vol. Inf., mentioned, 1026; wounded, 948.
Collins, ——, representative Associated Press, complaint against press censor, 1023, 1025.
Collison, Thomas H., pvt., Co. I, 16th U. S. Inf., death, 1164.
Colombo, Ceylon, U. S. soldiers buried in general cemetery, 968.
Colon, steamer. mentioned, 100, 556, 620, 660, 661, 665, 667, 683, 685, 691, 699, 700, 701, 704, 730, 731.
Cotton, Charles S., capt., U. S. N., mentioned, 78.

Columbia, U. S. steamship, mentioned, 77, 88, 93, 97, 101-103, 105, 106, 108, 112, 115, 131, 273, 280, 297, 299, 300, 301, 660, 1066, 1067, 1084, 1085, 1112, 1128.
Columbia, Department of:
  Gen. S. S. Sumner recommended for command, 841.
  Headquarters established at San Francisco, 647.
  Officers relieved from, and assigned to, duty in, 636.
Colvin, Livious S., pvt., Co. F, 29th U. S. Inf., wounded, 1219.
Colwell, James W., corpl., Co. L, 41st Inf., U. S. V., death, 1267.
Comal, U. S. transport, mentioned, 184, 190, 330.
Comanche, U. S. transport, mentioned, 60, 63, 65, 67, 69, 72, 73, 86, 88, 95, 122, 224, 273, 373.
Comba, Richard, brig. gen., U. S. V., mentioned, 538, 539.
Combs, Walter R., corpl., Co. M, 51st Iowa Vol. Inf., wounded, 999.
Comegys, Edward T., maj., med. dept., U. S. A., mentioned, 479.
Comerford, James, corpl., Co. M, 22d U. S. Inf., wounded, 941.
Comfort, Charles D., capt., 32d Inf., U. S. V., mentioned, 1126.
Commer, Garfield, pvt., Co. C, 12th U. S. Inf., death, 1140.
Commission to Philippine Islands:
  Constitution, 883.
  Departure of members, 883.
Commons, John, pvt., Co. E, 48th Inf., U. S. V., death, 1231.
Commutation of quarters to staff of Philippine expedition at San Francisco, 708.
Compton, Charles E., brig. gen., U. S. V., mentioned, 516, 530-533.
Concas, Spanish naval officer, mentioned, 100.
Concepción, Filipino general, surrender, 1121.
Conchman, Benjamin, pvt., band, 20th Kans. Vol. Inf., wounded, 983.
Concho, U. S. steamship, mentioned, 190, 191, 197, 208, 305-307, 310, 326, 357, 399, 602.
Conde del Venadito, Sp. cruiser, mentioned, 22.
Condlin, John B., pvt., Batty. G, 3d U. S. Art., death, 1232.
Condon, Clarence M., 2d lieut., Philippine Cav., wounded, 1231.
Condon, Dennis, pvt., Co. I, 18th U. S. Inf., death, 1194.
Condon, Patrick, sergt., Co. B, 12th U. S. Inf., death, 1156.
Conemaugh, U. S. transport, mentioned, 421, 431, 445, 447, 448, 660, 921, 930, 931, 958, 970, 979, 981, 1055.
Congar, Alfred B., pvt., Co. D, 6th U. S. Inf., death, 1190.
Conger, Arthur L., 1st lieut., 18th U. S. Inf., mentioned, 1328, 1329.
Conger, Edwin H., U. S. minister to China, mentioned, 409, 412-415, 433, 434, 438, 442, 443, 449-452, 454, 462, 463, 466, 478, 482, 483, 486, 490, 493, 497, 499.
Conger, Hiram C., pvt., Co. H, 10th Pa. Vol. Inf., wounded, 895, 920.
Conklin, Chester A. A., pvt., Co. H, 43d Inf., U. S. V., killed, 1168.
Conklin, Frank B., pvt., Co. F, 4th U. S. Inf., wounded, 1086.
Conklin, Frederick B., pvt., Co. G, 12th U. S. Inf., wounded, 1195.
Conley, Charles C., pvt., Co. D, 13th Minn. Vol. Inf., wounded, 966.
Conley, George, sergt., Co. G, 30th U. S. Inf., death, 1197.
Conley, James, pvt., Troop C, 1st U. S. Cav., mentioned, 214.
Conley, John L., pvt., Hosp. Corps, U. S. A., killed, 1254.
Conlin, Charles, pvt., Troop B, 3d U. S. Cav., death, 1236.
Connell, Thomas W., capt., 9th U. S. Inf., mentioned, 1294.
Connell, ——, pvt., U. S. Marine Corps, death, 1314.
Connelly, Charles, sergt., Co. C, 14th U. S. Inf., death, 833.

Connelly, James, sergt., Co. E, 21st U. S. Inf., wounded, 1064.
Connelly, John, jr., corpl., Co. K, 13th Minn. Vol. Inf., wounded, 947.
Connelly, Don E., pvt., Co. D, 44th Inf., U. S. V., wounded, 1250.
Conner, H. Cleide, pvt., Co. I, 36th Inf., U. S. V., death, 1141.
Conner, William H., Co. G, 14th U. S. Inf., death, 477; mentioned, 481.
Conners, Thomas, pvt., Co. M, 12th U. S. Inf., death, 1027.
Connolly, Patrick A., pvt., Co. F, 21st U. S. Inf., wounded, 1306.
Connolly, Patrick A., 1st lieut., 21st U. S. Inf., wounded, 1015.
Connor, Lawrence P., pvt., Co. E 1st Nebr. Vol. Inf., wounded, 760.
Connors, Henry, sergt., Co. G, 33d Mich. Vol. Inf., mentioned, 248.
Connors, Humphrey E., corpl., Co. A, 43d Inf., U. S. V., wounded, 1166.
Connox [William N. Connor], pvt., Co. G, 14th U. S. Inf., mentioned, 481.
Conroy, Michael, corpl., Co. B, 9th U. S. Inf., wounded, 443.
Considine, Richard, pvt., Co. C, 9th U. S. Inf., wounded, 1298.
Converse, Llewellyn H., corpl., Co. E, 6th U. S. Inf., death, 1162.
Conway, Daniel, pvt., Co. F, 20th Kans. Vol. Inf., wounded, 897.
Conway, James, pvt., Co. A, 6th U. S. Inf., wounded, 1084.
Conway, James, cableman, transport Hooker, death, 1125.
Conway, John, corpl., Co. M, 25th U. S. Inf., wounded, 1251.
Conway, John A., corpl., Co. C, 9th U. S. Inf., death, 478.
Conway, Martin J., pvt., Co. D, 26th U. S. Inf., death, 1189.
Conway, Thomas, pvt., Co. M, 12th U. S. Inf., wounded, 1048.
Cook, Allen, pvt., Co. L, 26th U. S. Inf., death, 1156.
Cook, Casper, pvt., Co. F, 21st U. S. Inf., wounded, 1008.
Cook, Charles C., pvt., Co. B, 9th U. S. Inf., killed, 1131.
Cook, Charles H., pvt., Co. G, 21st U. S. Inf., death, 1178.
Cook, Ermine, pvt., Co. E, 24th U. S. Inf., death, 1219.
Cook, Frank N., pvt., Co. I, 21st U. S. Inf., death, 1086.
Cook, Jack, corpl., Co. I, 40th Inf., U. S. V., wounded, 1171.
Cook, Joseph P., pvt., Co. B, 9th U. S. Inf., death, 1133; wounded, 1131.
Cook, Morton H., qm. sergt., Co. I, 45th Inf., U. S. V., death, 1194.
Cook, Norman E., 1st lieut., Philippine Scouts, mentioned, 1329, 1343.
Cook, Virgil Y., col., 2d Ark. Vol. Inf., mentioned, 348, 357.
Cook, William, pvt., Co. M, 2d U. S. Inf., killed, 1283.
Cook, William, pvt., Co. F, 1st Cal. Vol. Inf., death, 833.
Cook, William D., pvt., Co. E, 50th U. S. Inf., wounded, 1188.
Cook, Warren H., sergt., Co. F, 1st Nebr. Vol. Inf., death, 917; wounded, 906.
Cook, William M., pvt., Co. D, 2d Oreg. Vol. Inf., killed, 946.
Cooke, George F., capt., 15th U. S. Inf., mentioned, 1211.
Cooledge, Leon D., pvt., Co. M, 37th Inf., U. S. V., death, 1196.
Cooley, Walter, pvt., Co. B, 5th U. S. Inf., death, 1255.
Coolidge, Charles A., lieut. col., 9th U. S. Inf., mentioned, 428, 429, 434-438, 440, 442, 1025.
Coombs, Marshal E., pvt., Co. C, 22d U. S. Inf., wounded, 936.
Coombs, ——, capt., 5th U. S. Cav., mentioned, 316.
Coonce, Sidney L., pvt., Co. L, 32d Inf., U. S. V., death, 1205.
Cooney, George F., pvt., Co. F, 12th U. S. Inf., death, 1095.
Cooney, Michael J., pvt., Troop D, 3d U. S. Cav., wounded, 1152.
Cooney, Patrick, pvt., Batty. K., 3d U. S. Art., wounded, 946.
Coons, Charles A., sergt., Co. H, 1st U. S. Inf., mentioned, 195.
Cooper, Alex., pvt., Co. C, 33th Inf., U. S. V., killed, 1160.
Cooper, Charley, pvt., Troop K, 6th U. S. Cav., death, 495.
Cooper, George A., 2d lieut., 15th U. S. Inf., killed, 1211; mentioned, 1213, 1214.
Cooper, Henry M., mentioned, 348.
Cooper, Isaac, pvt., Co. B, 20th Kans. Vol. Inf., death, 894.
Cooper, Thomas E., pvt., Co. M, 21st U. S. Inf., death, 1200.
Cooper, William, pvt., Co. A, 14th U. S. Inf., wounded, 1015.
Cooper, Woll, pvt., Co. D, 35th Inf., U. S. V., wounded, 1081.
Cootey, George H., pvt., Co. M, 13th Minn. Vol. Inf., death, 803.
Copack, transport, mentioned, 1280.
Copes, Saul, pvt., Co. C, 24th U. S. Inf., death, 1078.
Copley, Ulysses G., pvt., Batty F, 6th U. S. Art., death, 1078.
Coplinger, Jesse C., sergt., Batty. A, 6th U. S. Art., death, 1256.
Coppinger, John J., maj. gen., U. S. V.:
Assigned to command at Mobile, Ala., 7, 8.
Correspondence, 59, 62, 63, 64, 65, 66, 71, 72, 73, 84, 94, 98, 111, 112, 121, 133, 138, 139, 143, 146, 166, 182, 189, 193, 198, 199, 208, 270, 277, 278, 279, 282, 288, 289, 292, 305, 306, 307, 308, 309, 310, 311, 313, 315, 316, 317, 318, 319, 325, 328, 329, 330, 332, 335, 341, 343, 360, 361, 362, 366, 368, 370.
Mentioned, 8, 12, 17, 18, 24, 47, 49, 51, 53, 55-57, 67, 69, 85, 268, 288, 319, 320, 325, 328-330, 332, 335, 341-343, 367, 377, 379, 509, 534, 535, 537.
Corbet, Albert J., pvt., Batty G, 3d U. S. Art., wounded, 897.
Corbett, John, pvt., Co. G, 22d U. S. Inf., death, 993.
Corbett, Louis E., pvt., Co. D, 9th U. S. Inf., death, 1074.
Corbett, Richard P., pvt., Co. C, 26th U. S. Inf., death, 1113; wounded, 1108.
Corbin, Henry C., Adjt. Gen., U. S. A., correspondence, 1-506, 635-1357.
Corbit, John, pvt., Co. C, 28th Inf., U. S. V., wounded, 1130.
Corbusier, William H., maj., med. dept., U. S. A., mentioned, 657, 766.
Corby, Joseph A., col., 4th Mo. Vol. Inf., mentioned, 524.
Corcoran, Michael P., pvt., Co. B, Batt. Engrs., U. S. A., death, 1215.
Corder, John W., pvt., Batty. H, 3d U. S. Art., wounded, 917.
Cordner, John O., pvt., Co. C, 4th Ohio Vol. Inf., wounded, 356.
Cork, Israel, pvt., Co. I, 18th U. S. Inf., death, 1167.
Corley, Michael E., pvt., Co. A, 43d Inf., U. S. V., killed, 1153.
Corliss, Augustus W., maj., 7th U. S. Inf., mentioned, 546; wounded, 124.
Cornell, Sidney J., sergt., Co. C, 1st S. Dak. Vol. Inf., wounded, 949.
Cornett, Bert, pvt., Co. E, 20th Kans. Vol. Inf., death, 875.
Cornin, William, pvt., Co. C, 22d U. S. Inf., mentioned, 206.
Corning, James G., pvt., Co. L, 18th U. S. Inf., wounded, 1160.
Cornish, William A., pvt., Co. H, 1st Cal. Vol. Inf., wounded, 905.

Corren, Jose, mus., Co. B, 29th U. S. Inf., killed, 1197.
Corrigan, Fred, trump., Troop A, 6th U. S. Cav., wounded, 466.
Corrigan, Michael, pvt., Co. K, 1st Mont. Vol. Inf., death, 1038.
Cosgrave, James P., 1st lieut., 1st Nebr. Vol. Inf., wounded, 956.
Cosgrove, Peter, sergt., Co. H, 22d U. S. Inf., wounded, 992.
Cosper, Emmet D., pvt., Co. M, 2d Oreg. Vol. Inf., wounded, 946.
Costa, August, pvt., Co. B, 41st Inf., U. S. V., killed, 1143.
Costello, Edward, pvt., Co. H, 37th Inf., U. S. V., death, 1190.
Costello, Jow, pvt., Troop K, 4th U. S. Cav., wounded, 994.
Cotay, Charles N., pvt., Co. A, 6th U. S. Inf., killed, 1087.
Cotchett, Walter V., 1st lieut., 11th Cav., U. S. V., wounded, 1124, 1126.
Cotter, John, pvt., Troop K, 4th U. S. Cav., wounded, 947.
Cotton, Earl R., pvt., Co. H, 9th U. S. Inf., death, 1020.
Cottril, Burton C., pvt., Co. E, 30th Inf., U. S. V., death, 1165.
Coughlan, John, pvt., Troop H, 4th U. S. Cav., captured by insurgents, 1196.
Coulter, Alex., pvt., Co. A, 10th Pa. Vol. Inf., mentioned, 953.
Countee, Thomas W., sergt., Co. F, 24th U. S. Inf., death 1057, 1060.
Countee, William, pvt., Hosp. Corps, U. S. A., wounded, 1254.
Courcey, William S., clerk to Adjutant-General, U. S. A., mentioned, 247.
Coursen, Henry A., col., 13th Pa. Vol. Inf., mentioned, 521.
Coursey, Oscar W., sergt., Co. G, 1st S. Dak. Vol. Inf., wounded, 981.
Courtney, William C., pvt., Co. B, 1st Wash. Vol. Inf., death, 956; wounded, 947.
Covety, F. G., pvt., Co. M, 34th Mich. Vol. Inf., mentioned, 216.
Covey, James, sergt., Co. K, 19th U. S. Inf., wounded, 1084.
Covington, John L., mus., Co. C, 9th U. S. Inf., missing, 1297.
Covington, William D., qm. sergt., Co. B, 1st Wash. Vol. Inf., wounded, 947.
Cowan, Charles A., pvt., Co. M, 38th Inf., U. S. V., death, 1202.
Cox, G. K., mentioned, 247, 251, 253.
Cox, Ira W., pvt., Co. D, 22d U. S. Inf., killed, 1052.
Cox, Jake, pvt., Troop F, 9th U. S. Cav., wounded, 1256.
Cox, James S., pvt., Co. L, 25th U. S. Inf., wounded, 1228.
Cox, John W., pvt., Co. K, 38th Inf., U. S. V., death, 1200.
Cox, Joseph B., pvt., Co. E, 22d U. S. Inf., wounded, 934.
Cox, Patrick, pvt., Co. B, 9th U. S. Inf., wounded, 443.
Cox, Samuel R., pvt., Co. B, 26th U. S. Inf., killed, 1281.
Cox, Shelby G., actg. hosp. stewd., U. S. A., mentioned, 662.
Coxe, Francis M., col., pay dept., U. S. A., mentioned, 646.
Coyle, John J., pvt., Co. L, 6th U. S. Inf., death, 1189.
Crabb, Albert B., pvt., Co. A, 20th U. S. Inf., death, 1213.
Crable, William H., pvt., Co. C. 10th Pa. Vol. Inf., death, 803.
Crabtree, Edmond, mus., Co. K, 6th U. S. Inf., death, 1130.
Cradock, Prestwood B., pvt., Troop F, 4th U. S. Cav., death, 1133.
Crafer, Joseph, pvt., Co. F, 1st Mont. Vol. Inf., wounded, 900.
Craig, Benjamin, sergt., Troop C, 4th U. S. Cav., death, 1003.
Craig, Charles, pvt., Co. F, 1st Nebr. Vol. Inf., mentioned, 732.

Craig, Charles, sergt., Co. E, 47th Inf., U. S. V., wounded, 1187.
Craig, Curran C., pvt., Co. E, 20th Kans. Vol. Inf., killed, 945.
Craigie, David J., maj., 25th U. S. Inf., mentioned, 860.
Crandall, Carl E., pvt., Co. A, 9th U. S. Inf., death, 1104.
Crane, Charles C., sergt., Troop A, 11th Cav., U. S. V., death, 1238.
Crane, Edward, pvt., Co. D, 20th Kans. Vol. Inf., wounded, 954.
Crane, Felix G., pvt., Co. H, 41st Inf., U. S. V., death, 1191.
Crane, Joseph A., pvt., Co. F, 17th U. S. Inf., death, 1132.
Crann, Patrick W., pvt., Co. C, 28th U. S. Inf., wounded, 1229.
Cravens, George H., pvt., Co. E, 20th Kans. Vol. Inf., wounded, 946.
Crawford, Duncan G., pvt., Co. M, 16th U. S. Inf., death, 1187.
Crawford, Elmo, pvt., Co. G, 33d Inf., U. S. V., wounded, 1124.
Crawford, Elwin, pvt., Co. C, 2d Oreg. Vol. Inf., wounded, 946.
Crawford, Robert, pvt., Co. B, 9th U. S. Inf., wounded, 443.
Crawford, Ward C., pvt., Co. L, 1st Nebr. Vol. Inf., wounded, 946.
Crawford, William, corpl., Co. K, 25th U. S. Inf., death, 1146.
Cravens, George H., corpl., Troop A, 11th Cav., U. S. V., wounded, 1199.
Creed, James, pvt., Troop C, 6th U. S. Cav., wounded, 1272.
Creekbaum, Lawrence, pvt., Troop M, 3d U. S. Cav., wounded, 1176.
Creelman, William, pvt., Co. B, 1st Tenn. Vol. Inf., death, 1066.
Cremmins, John, pvt., Co. M, 43d Inf., U. S. V., killed, 1259.
Crenshaw, Henry T., pvt., Co. A, Batt. Engrs., U. S. A., captured by insurgents, 1196.
Cress, Chester A., pvt., Co. D, 33d Inf., U. S. V., killed, 1152.
Cress, George O., capt., 4th U. S. Cav., mentioned, 1042.
Crimmens, Dennis, sergt., Astor Batty., U. S. A., death, 802.
Crispen, William, pvt., Co. K, 18th U. S. Inf., wounded, 1174.
Crispi, Joseph, mus., Co. A, 17th U. S. Inf., death, 1136.
Criss, Ernest, pvt., Co. H, 20th Kans. Vol. Inf., wounded, 954.
Cristobal Colon, Spanish cruiser, mentioned, 81.
Critchfield, Thomas B., corpl., Co. D, 10th Pa. Vol. Inf., wounded, 953.
Crites, Clarence W., pvt., Troop D, 3d U. S. Cav., death, 1130.
Crittenden, John J., capt., 22d U. S. Inf., reported killed, 124.
Crogan, Joseph, pvt., Co. I, 21st U. S. Inf., death, 1021.
Cromer, Edward J., pvt., Troop H, 4th U. S. Cav., captured by insurgents, 1196.
Crook, U. S. transport, mentioned, 1305, 1314, 1320, 1323, 1330, 1340, 1341, 1356.
Crook, Fort, Nebr., condition of troops at, 841.
Crook, John, pvt., Co. E, 4th U. S. Inf., death, 1197.
Crosby, Frank H., pvt., Co. D, 26th U. S. Inf., death, 1230.
Crosby, Paul M., pvt., Co. E, 13th Minn. Vol. Inf., death, 801, 803.
Crosby, William, pvt., Co. B, 17th U. S. Inf., wounded, 1087.
Crosiar, Warren E., pvt., Co. I, 1st S. Dak. Vol. Inf., wounded, 949.
Cross, Abraham, corpl., Co. K, 16th U. S. Inf., death, 1168.
Cross, George L., pvt., Batty. H, 3d U. S. Art., death, 1189.
Crosswhite, Worley T., pvt., Co. L, 37th Inf., U. S. V., wounded, 1211.
Crowder, Enoch H., maj., judge-advocate, U. S. A., mentioned, 667, 700, 706, 909.
Recommended for censor in P. I., 973.

Crowe, Edward A., pvt., Co. B, 37th Inf., U. S. V., death, 1205.
Crowell, Charles C., 2d lieut., 10th Pa. Vol. Inf., mentioned, 739.
Crowell, George W., sergt., band, 1st Mont. Vol. Inf., wounded, 959.
Crowell, William W., pvt., Co. H, 13th U. S. Inf., death, 1170.
Crowninshield, Arent S., rear-admiral, U. S. Navy, mentioned, 42, 49, 131, 411.
Crowl, Frank M., pvt., Co. G, 13th Minn. Vol. Inf., mentioned, 762; wounded, 760.
Crowley, Charles, pvt., Co. B., 13th U. S. Inf., death, 803.
Crowley, Michael J., pvt., Batty. K, 3d U. S. Art., wounded, 917.
Crowley, Michael P., pvt., Co. D, 2d Oreg. Vol. Inf., death, 903.
Crozier, David T., pvt., Co. H, 22d U. S. Inf., death, 1255.
Crozier, William, capt., ord. dept., U. S. A., mentioned, 424, 426, 428, 430.
Crumpacker, E. D., member of Congress, mentioned, 377.
Crumpholz, Carl, pvt., Co. E, 22d U. S. Inf., mentioned, 941.
Crumrine, Harry R., pvt., Co. F, 1st Wyo. Vol. Inf., wounded, 917, 899.
Crutchfield, Edward M., pvt., Co. M, 44th Inf., U. S. V., killed, 1256.
Crystal, Robert A., pvt., Co. F, 1st Wash. Vol. Inf., death, 1063.
Cuba, Dept. of, establishment, 205, 217, 381.
Cuba, Island of, West Indies.
  Aguadores, establishment of telegraph communication, 57.
  Appointment of commissaries and quartermasters for forces in, 804.
  Arming troop for, with Krag-Jörgensen, 114.
  Attitude of European governments toward Spain, relative to, 28.
  Captured—
    Property, troops required to protect, 235.
    Ships, merchant, disposition of, 182, 184.
    Taken possession by Navy, 170, 175, 180, 181.
    Use of, 170.
  Central Cuban Relief Committee, requests assistance in distributing supplies, 210.
  Cipher messages, 76, 80, 93.
  Clothing—
    Gratuitous issue, 217.
    Sterilizing, 216.
  Cobre road, General Garcia charged with blocking, 87.
  Coffins, request for supply, 216.
  Concert of movement between army and navy, 19, 20.
  Congratulations of President to troops in, 105, 114.
  Contingent fund, for use of expedition, 27.
  Convalescents, transportation, 198, 199.
  Convoy for invading army, 16.
  Criticisms as to operations and treatment of troops, 106, 113, 114.
  Cruisers, carrying capacity, 49.
  Cubans, treatment, 185.
  Customs service—
    Organization and instructions for, 157-159, 163, 180-183, 186, 195, 199, 215, 238, 255.
    Recommends appointment of officer, 158.
    Tonnage tax on cargoes abolished, 159, 163.
  Daiquiri—
    Arrival of transports, 80.
    Building of crib wharves at, 121.
    Casualties in skirmish at, 61.
    Facilities at, for disembarkation, 121.
    Landing of troops at, 50, 53, 54, 62, 121-123.
    Lighters and tug wanted at, 54, 56.
    Spanish troops entrenched at, 25.
  Daily reports required for, 74.
  Danger of landing army during rainy season, 8, 9.
  Dead, marking of graves, 58, 60.
  Dead and wounded, inquiries about, 93.
  Information concerning Santiago garrison and reinforcements, 62.
  Destruction of Spanish fleet, 100.
  Dos Caminos, evacuated by Spanish, 125.
  Dry Tortugas, Fla., shipment of troops to, 11, 12.
    Transports and convoys at, 22, 48.

Cuba, Island of, West Indies—Continued.
  El Caney—
    Capture of, 70.
    Noncombatants to occupy, 79.
    Wounded Spanish officers and men returned to their command, 99.
  English cable, use by Spanish general in connection with surrender of Santiago, 109, 113.
  Closing of, 386.
  Exchange of prisoners, 101.
  Expedition—
    Composition and organization, 30, 31, 45, 46, 57, 58.
    Convoy for, 34, 37-40.
    Departure, necessity for early, 28, 30.
    Directed, 80.
    To announce departure, 33, 34.
    Delay, cause, etc., 25, 26.
    Increase in, 32, 35.
    Lack of transportation for 33.
    Landing at Daiquiri, 50, 53, 54.
    Sailing of, 23, 28, 30, 31, 34, 35, 39, 42-44.
    Sailing orders countermanded, 31.
    Volunteers to accompany first, 24.
  Expedition No. 2, organization and equipment, 34, 45, 46.
  French Cable Company—
    Censorship of, 67, 68, 70.
    To protect neutral operators of, 50.
  General orders, A. G. O.—
    No. 50, Fifth Army Corps, disbandment, 257.
    No. 111, organizing 1, 2, 3, 4, 5, and 6 brigades, 345.
    No. 163, Army corps, discontinuance and reorganization of, 257.
  Government property, troops required to protect, 235.
  Guantanamo—
    Building of docks at, 118.
    Harbor, excellent for Navy, 114.
    Marines in camp at, 150.
    Not desirable as landing place, 114.
    Recovery of mines in channel, 50.
    Sailing of *Resolute* from, 115.
    Telegraphic communication established, 50.
    Transports held in bay by naval authorities, 92, 93.
    Troops not to land at, 146.
    To rendezvous at, 154.
  Guantanamo Bay, excellent landing place, 100.
  Gunboats, turning over to Navy, 157, 164.
  Habana, blockade, provisions for, 16.
    Evacuation commission to meet at, 751.
  Holguin—
    Number of Spanish soldiers at, 52.
    Spanish forces, evacuation terms, 116, 117, 119.
    Instructions for military governor, 159-163.
  Isle of Pines, scheme for occupancy, 71.
  Juragua, occupation by U. S. troops, 53, 54.
    Cuban army to join U. S. troops at, 54.
  Juraguacito, Spanish troops intrenched at, 25.
  Landing place for invading army, 11.
  Lighters and tugs for, 54, 56, 58, 66, 107, 115, 120, 124.
    Handling of transports hampered for want of, 104.
  Loss at sea, 113.
  Manzanillo, number Spanish troops at 21, 52.
  Mariel, General Shafter to seize and hold, 11.
  Medical attendance, complaint, re, 197.
  Medical supplies—
    Arrival of, 107.
    Lack of, 102, 195, 197.
  Moron de Cuba, Spanish troops intrenched at, 25.
  Morro Castle, light at, injured by cannonading, 168.
  Nicolas Channel, Spanish fleet seen in, 31, 32.
  Nuevitas, point for interior campaign, 51.
    Operations, confidential daily reports requested by General Greely, 61.
    Gen. Miles' scheme of, 261.
  Ordnance—
    Captured—
      Cannon for Omaha Exposition, 191, 197.
      Mausers and Remingtons sent to arsenal, 248.
      Rifles, arming of volunteers with, 170.
      Shipment of guns, 251.

1384 INDEX.

Cuba, Island of, West Indies—Continued.
Ordnance—Continued.
Mauser and Remington rifles, General Shafter recommends shipment to arsenal, 248.
Ordnance stores, shipment of, 104.
Palma Soriano—
French consul and French citizens at, 75.
Troops sent to receive Spanish surrender, 171.
Peace, declaration of, 220.
Playa del Este, establishment of telegraphic communication, 57.
Port of Banes, landing of expedition at, 21.
Puerto Principe, proposed base for interior campaign, 51.
Postal service, establishment and instructions concerning, 169.
Press boats, seizure directed, 23.
Press censorship, 223, 224.
Red Cross Society, discharge of steamer and unloading supplies at Santiago, 165, 167.
Recruits—
Equipment and assignment, 49.
Joining regiments, 13.
To be held at Atlanta, Ga., equipped, etc., 47.
Reenforcements for, 87, 105, 106.
Regular troops to form advance in invasion, 14, 15.
Relics, cannon, flags, etc., to be divided between Army and Navy, 212.
Relief stores, distribution, 237.
Relinquishment of Spanish sovereignty over, 751.
Rendezvous for invading army, 11.
Route to be taken by transports going to, 39.
San Juan River—
Held by Spanish forces, 81, 82.
U. S. troops in vicinity, 74.
San Luis—
Spanish decline to surrender, 170, 171.
Troops sent to, to receive Spanish surrender, 171.
Santiago de Cuba—
American counsel needed, 157.
Archbishop asks permission to come inside U. S. lines, 134.
Arms and ammunition—
For use of troops, 110, 111.
Surrendered, 158, 164, 176.
Assault on, in re., 68, 70, 97, 137, 138.
General Garcia to take part in, 68.
Postponement, 134, 135.
Preparation, 88, 89, 90, 91, 92, 115.
At mercy of U. S. guns, 125.
Bombardment by Army and Navy, 29, 30, 40, 87, 105, 122, 123, 125.
Delayed, 79, 81.
Effect of, 132.
Cable communication, 67, 70.
Campaign—
Criticism of, 172, 190, 197.
Mismanagement of, 256.
Casualties, American, 176-178, 185, 204-206, 211-213, 223, 224, 226, 240, 241, 248.
Civil government, customs, etc., re, 156, 206, 214, 215, 226, 230, 231, 235, 255.
Condition of affairs at, 109, 140.
Entered by General Pando, 87.
Evacuation by Spanish, terms, etc., 116, 117, 119, 122, 133, 134.
Facilities for reaching, 402, 404.
Food supplies at, 128, 131, 180.
Foreign consuls, retirement from, 73, 74.
Franking privilege, recommendations re, 13.
Freight, importance of early discharge of, 167, 169, 171, 173, 174.
Ships with, to touch, 158.
Gunboat and seamen surrender to General Shafter, 157.
Harbor—
Closing, 125.
Scheme for destroying submerged mines in, 94.
Spanish ships in, 22, 23.
Re possession of ships and boats in, 155, 156.
Hospital—
Attendants, immune doctors and nurses wanted, 164.
Establishment and equipment, 140, 215.
Hospital ship and medical officers needed, 72, 74.

Cuba, Island of, West Indies—Continued.
Santiago de Cuba—Continued.
Instructions for movement against, 16, 18, 19.
Means of landing troops near, 19.
Immune regiments needed, 166, 167, 172.
Ordered to, 138, 144.
Killed, wounded, etc., list of, 149.
Land transportation, inadequacy, 121, 122, 138.
Light-House Service, establishment, 158, 168.
Lines of U. S., surrounding—
Condition, 120.
Impregnability, 122, 123.
Picket line, advance of, 67, 68.
Strengthening of, 81, 130.
Mails, disinfection, 153.
Mauser rifles and ammunition to be sent to Springfield Arsenal, 168.
Merchants, permission granted to import supplies, request arrangements as to duties, 159.
Military government, instructions for, 159-163.
Miles, Nelson A., major-general, departure of, for, 110.
Arrival of, at, 131.
Navy—
Disinclined to force entrance to harbor, 105.
To cooperate with Army in assault on, 136, 141.
To force entrance to harbor, 88, 89.
No attempt by, to enter harbor, 132.
Newspaper correspondent, return to U. S., 147.
North American Trust Company to locate at, as U. S. agents, 168.
Nurses—
Volunteer, sent to, 208.
Wanted at, 164.
Old bronze cannon and Mausers sent to Fort Monroe, 191, 197.
Operations, plan of, 125.
Opening of fire, by Spanish, 125.
Peace, Spanish Government asks for, 182.
Ports, reopening, for commerce, 157.
Postal service, establishment and instructions concerning, 169.
President's proclamation, 178.
Prisoners, exchange of, 95.
Railroad held by General Garcia, 74, 75.
Refugees and destitute people—
Relief and supplies for, 68, 73, 92, 132, 237.
Suffering among, 130, 133.
Shafter's command of troops not to be interfered with, 110.
Gunboat and seamen surrender to, 157.
Health, 945.
To use own judgment in taking, 84.
Situation at, stated by foreign consuls, 90, 91.
Spanish fleet—
Bottling in harbor, 16, 25, 77, 78.
Destruction, 78, 81, 100.
Spanish troops at, 21, 52.
Captain-general asks for list of Spanish officers, prisoners in hands of Americans, 126.
Re number of, to be returned to Spain, 136, 137, 142, 143, 155, 157, 158, 164, 166, 167, 169, 176, 215.
Spanish surrenders from interior, 170.
Supreme Court, U. S., decision re captures by Army and Navy, 164.
Surrender of, 143-145, 147, 150.
Capitulation, conditions, terms, 151, 152, 154.
Approved by Secretary of War, 155.
Commissioners to arrange details, 146, 147.
Appointment, 140.
Re signing of articles by Sampson, 163.
Cause of delay, 149.
Congratulations by President and Secretary of War, 150, 152.
Considering proposition, 130.
Correspondence relating to, 150, 151.
Cubans hurt at not being permitted to take part in conference, 175.
Demand for, 78, 79, 105, 130.
Spanish reply, 79.
General Toral asks for additional time, 136, 137.
Authorized to capitulate, 153, 154.
Hoisting of American flag, 155-157.
Possibility of General Toral gaining time to get reenforcements, 147, 148.

INDEX. 1385

Cuba, Island of, West Indies—Continued.
 Santiago de Cuba—Continued.
  Surrender of—Continued.
   Re Spanish carrying away their arms, 147-150.
   Spanish generals fear consequences, 148, 149.
   Terms of acceptance, 136.
   Territory embraced in, 142, 143.
   Unconditional only, to be accepted by U. S., 116, 119.
    Demand refused, 122, 123.
    Spanish to be returned to Spain, 125, 130.
    Instructions re, 140.
   Telegraph cables, instructions re, 163, 165-168, 171, 172, 174, 175, 177, 178, 222-224.
   Transportation, lack of wagon, etc., 94, 95.
  Transports—
   Carrying wounded, ordered to Tampa, 98.
   Sailing of, countermanded, reasons, 31.
   Use of, to force entrance in harbor, 91, 94, 105.
  Troops—
   Approximate number in vicinity, 40.
   Immune, for Porto Rico, 380.
   Movements to and from, 67, 94, 139, 143, 144, 274, 278, 279, 309, 381.
   Payment, 159, 164, 172, 173.
   Placing in camps, 158.
   Removal of, 360, 363, 366.
   Yellow fever conditions, 272.
  Water supply cut, 147.
  Wharf construction, 127, 131, 132, 137.
  Yellow fever situation, 134, 137, 140, 143, 157, 166, 171, 173-175, 178, 179, 182, 184, 186, 187, 189, 192-194, 196, 197, 200-202, 204, 206, 209, 213, 214, 216, 218, 219, 235, 243, 253.
   Precautions to prevent spread, 135, 139, 141.
 Sardinero, U. S. troops to take position near, 74.
 Scheme for operations, by General Miles, 51, 52, 261.
 Sevilla—
  Occupied by U. S. troops, 60, 74.
   Character of defenses, 74.
  Skirmish near, 54, 55.
   Casualties in, 54.
 Siboney—
  Arrival of troops at, 60, 122, 123, 125, 128.
  Condition of affairs, 99.
  Engagement at, 70.
  Not adapted to disembarking troops, 121.
  Occupied by U. S. troops, 74.
  Wounded in hospital at, care, 101.
  Wounded, Spanish soldiers, return of, to their command, 99.
  Yellow fever at, 117, 284.
 Siege batteries, armament, 389, 390, 392, 394-397.
 Siege guns for, 59, 66, 67.
 Siege train, equipment, 379, 382.
 Spanish—
  Arms, disposition, 190.
  Army, reported strength, 52.
  Bank notes, commanding general takes possession of, 204.
  Fleet—
   Bottling, in Santiago Harbor, 16, 25, 77, 78.
   Destruction, 78, 81, 100.
    Effect on troops, 81.
    Object of expedition, 20.
   Identification, 22.
   Location, 12, 16, 31, 32, 77, 78, 261.
   Orders for destruction, 19.
   Reported at Cadiz, Spain, 28.
   Reported distribution, 131.
  Officers, captain general asks for list of, prisoners in hands of Americans, 126.
  Prisoners—
   Disposition, 188.
   Protection, 176.
   Rations for, 184, 303.
   Release, 194.
   Sick in hospital, 193, 196, 204.
   Transportation for, 204, 207.
   Treatment by Cubans, 99, 101.
  Troops, 52.
   Arms turned in by, 176.
   Condition, 187.
   Departure for Spain, express good wishes for Americans, 249.
   Distribution of rations to, 200.
   Removal, 203.
   Surrender, 176, 187.

Cuba, Island of, West Indies—Continued.
 Spanish—Continued.
  Troops—Continued.
   Wounded officers and men, return to command, 99.
  Staff officers needed, 804.
  Subsistence stores—
   Authority to sell to civilians, 185, 186.
   Beef for troops, 192, 198.
   Distribution, 200.
   Relative to supply, 195.
   Secretary of Navy asks what disposition shall be made of, 188.
  Supplies needed, 64.
  Torpedoes, removal of, 188.
  Transportation of sick and wounded, 83.
  War correspondent's pass, 300.
  Withdrawal of troops for service in P. I., 1249.
  Yellow fever—
   Cases, 140.
   Conditions, 272, 284.
   Handling, 144.
   Precautions to prevent spread, 135, 139, 141.
   Preparations for handling, 156.
   Preventive measures, 124.
Cuban forces:
 Arms and equipment for, 21.
 Subsistence supplies for destitute persons and, 68.
 Unreliability for fighting, 122.
Cudney, Dell, pvt., Co. C, 17th U. S. Inf., wounded, 1101.
Cuite, Gilbert, pvt., Co. C, 10th Pa. Vol. Inf., wounded, 919.
Culberson, C. A., governor of Texas, mentioned, 342.
Culberson, Tom, pvt., Batty. L, 3d U. S. Art., wounded, 950.
Cull, Henry E., ccrpl., Co. L, 35th Inf., U. S. V., death, 1164.
Cullams, Grant, pvt., Co. C, 10th Pa. Vol. Inf., mentioned, 922.
Cullen, James, pvt., Co. D, 22d U. S. Inf., death, 1205.
Cullen, James E., pvt., Co. L, 30th U. S. Inf., death, 1160.
Cullinane, John, pvt., Co. G, 26th U. S. Inf., killed, 1191.
Cullman, George, pvt., Co. L, 34th Mich. Vol. Inf., mentioned, 216.
Cullom, Shelby M., U. S. Senator, mentioned, 331, 335-337.
Culross, Alexander M., pvt., Co. K, 4th U. S. Inf., death, 1090.
Culver, Harry S., pvt., Co. D, 14th U. S. Inf., death, 803.
Culver, James S., col., 5th Ill. Vol. Inf., mentioned, 380, 390, 514.
Culyon, U. S. naval vessel, not wanted by Army, 1074.
Cumberland, U. S. steam lighter, mentioned, 192.
Cummings, Joseph, pvt., Co. M, 23d U. S. Inf., killed, 1067.
Cummings, Patrick, pvt., Co. D, 10th Pa. Vol. Inf., wounded, 953.
Cummings, Richard C., pvt., Co. L, 16th U. S. Inf., killed, 1212.
Cummings, Martan, corpl., Co. M, 3d U. S. Inf., killed, 945.
Cummins, Albert S., capt., 4th U. S. Art., mentioned, 544, 546, 1073.
Cunningham, Henry, pvt., Co. F, 24th U. S. Inf., death, 1125.
Cunningham, James J., pvt., Co. G, 31st Inf., U. S. V., death, 1196.
Cunningham, John, corpl., Co. F, 12th U. S. Inf., death, 1082.
Cunningham, John, pvt., Co. L, 9th U. S. Inf., death, 1142.
Cunningham, Robert, pvt., Co. L, 28th Inf., U. S. V., wounded, 1132.
Cunningham, Walter O., pvt., Co. C, 22d U. S. Inf., death, 1217.
Curley, Charles, pvt., Co. H, 21st U. S. Inf., death, 1095.
Curley, Edward M., pvt., Co. E, 1st Wash. Vol. Inf., wounded, 977.
Curley, Lawrence, pvt., Co. L, 35th Inf., U. S. V., death, 1210.
Curram, Patrick, pvt., Co E, 14th U. S. Inf., wounded, 454.

Curran, James, pvt., Co. I, 21st U. S. Inf., wounded, 1021.
Curran, James J., pvt., Co. K, 4th U. S. Inf., death, 1162.
Curran, James P., pvt., Co. B, 16th U. S. Inf., mentioned, 1129.
Curran, John, pvt., Co. H, 20th U. S. Inf., wounded, 926.
Curren, Thomas H., corpl., Co. G, 9th U. S. Inf., wounded, 444.
Currie, Daniel, pvt., Co. F, 30th U. S. Inf., death, 1219.
Currier, Harry L., pvt., Co. A, 13th Minn. Vol. Inf., death, 803.
Currier, William J., pvt., Co. E, 1st Idaho Vol. Inf., wounded, 1008.
Curry, David B., pvt., Co. E, 28th U. S. Inf., death, 1260.
Curry, John J., pvt., Troop C, 11th Cav., U. S. V., death, 1219.
Curry, William, pvt., Co. D, 14th U. S. Inf., wounded, 1015.
Curry, William M., pvt., Co. H, 6th U. S. Inf., death, 1104.
Curtis, G., pvt., Batty. D, 5th U. S. Art., wounded, 390.
Curtis, George W., pvt., Co. G, 18th U. S. Inf., death, 1133.
Curtis, James E., pvt., Co. A, 39th Inf., U. S. V., death, 1201.
Curtis, Orin F., 1st sergt., Co. C, 1st Nebr. Vol. Inf., wounded, 897.
Cushing, Frank P., pvt., Co. I, 35th Inf., U. S. V., death, 1178.
Cushing, John H., corpl., Co. C, 51st Iowa Vol. Inf., wounded, 983.
Cusker, Mira, pvt., Co. I, 1st Wash. Vol. Inf., wounded, 897.
Cutting, David A., pvt., Co. I, 1st Cal. Vol. Inf., wounded, 897.
Cyan, Robert, pvt., Co. L, 14th U. S. Inf., wounded, 1017.
Dabney, James M., pvt., Co. G, 1st Cal. Vol., death, 1048; mentioned, 1043.
Dabney Vostock, U. S. transport, mentioned, 1111, 1128.
Dade, Alexander L., 1st lieut., 3d U. S. Cav., mentioned, 123.
Daft, Thomas L., pvt., Troop D, 4th U. S. Cav., death, 1215.
Daggett, Aaron S., col., 14th U. S. Inf., mentioned, 225, 424, 434, 435, 441, 442, 570, 1018.
Dague, David E., corpl., Co. A, 14th U. S. Inf., death, 1015.
Dahl, George J., pvt., Co. D, 14th U. S. Inf., death, 1062.
Daily, George B., pvt., Co. K, 20th Kans. Vol. Inf., wounded, 954.
Daily, Joseph O., pvt., —— 13th Minn. Vol. Inf., death, 803.
Daily, Melvin, P., pvt., Troop G, 4th U. S. Cav., death, 1008.
Daily, Nelson E., pvt., Troop G, 4th U. S. Cav., wounded, 1003.
Daily, Robert L., pvt., Co. L, 51st Iowa Vol. Inf., wounded, 974.
Dakin, Floyd, corpl., Co. B, 34th Inf., U. S. V., death, 1255.
Dalts, George, artif., Co. D, 4th U. S. Inf., death, 1020.
Daly, Joseph, pvt., Co. B, 18th U. S. Inf., wounded, 943.
Daly, William L., pvt., Co. A, 26th U. S. Inf., death, 1196.
Daly, ——, surg., mentioned, 381.
Dame, William E., capt., 34th Inf., U. S. V., mentioned, 1126.
Dance, Willie, pvt., Co. K, 24th U. S. Inf., death, 1130.
Danes, Henry C., capt., 3d U. S. Art., mentioned, 1292.
Danforth, ——, contract surg., U. S. A., mentioned, 83.
Daniel, Charles O., artif., Co. K, 34th Inf., U. S. V., death, 1213.
Daniel, Fred, pvt., Co. B, 16th U. S. Inf., killed, 1150.
Daniel, John W., U. S. Senator, mentioned, 358.
Daniels, Senos, pvt., Co. M, 24th U. S. Inf., death, 1236.

Danitz, Frank M., pvt., Co. K, 15th U. S. Inf., death, 1271.
Danner, James D., 2d lieut., 28th U. S. Inf., death, 1213.
Danner, Norman E., pvt., Batty. E, 1st U. S. Art., wounded, 1015.
Dapray, John A., capt., 23d U. S. Inf., mentioned, 1011.
Darcey, Samuel, sergt., Co. M, 23d U. S. Inf., killed, 1067.
Dare, Edmund I., pvt., Co. L, 28th U. S. Inf., death, 1226.
Darras, Orian L., pvt., Co. G, 1st Idaho Vol. Inf., killed, 898.
Dasher, Harry, corpl., Co. K, 2d U. S. Inf., wounded, 1259.
Daum, Sam M., pvt., Co. G, 40th Inf., U. S. V., death, 1196.
Davidson, Alexander H., 1st sergt., Troop E, 4th U. S. Cav., wounded, 947.
Davidson, George F., qm. employee, death, 1119.
Davidson, Ira F., qm. employee, death, 498.
Davidson, Ralph M., mus., Co. I, 23d U. S. Inf., wounded, 1183.
Davidson, Robert, pvt., Co. G, 14th U. S. Inf., death, 840.
Davidson, Thomas J., pvt., Co. H, 20th Kans. Vol. Inf., wounded, 983.
Davies, Henry, pvt., Co. M, 14th U. S. Inf., wounded, 460.
Davies, William E., 1st lieut., Sig. Corps, U. S. A., wounded, 1259.
Davis, Albert R., pvt., Co. D, 17th U. S. Inf., wounded, 1021.
Davis, Andrew, pvt., Co. B, 1st Mont. Vol. Inf., wounded, 981.
Davis, Charles A., pvt., Co. H, 20th U. S. Inf., death, 939; wounded, 934.
Davis, Charles E., pvt., Co. C, 9th U. S. Inf., killed, 1297.
Davis, Charles N., corpl., Co. —, 1st Cal. Vol. Inf., wounded, 974.
Davis, Clyde M., pvt., Co. M, 38th Inf., U. S. V., killed, 1188.
Davis, Cushman K., U. S. Senator, mentioned, 356.
Davis, David, pvt., Co. E, 35th Inf., U. S. V., death, 1174.
Davis, David J., pvt., Batty. A, Utah Vol. Art., wounded, 974.
Davis, Edward, capt., 3d U. S. Art., maj., a. a. g., U. S. V., mentioned, 36, 42.
Davis, Edward E., pvt., Co. E, 4th U. S. Inf., drowned, 1228.
Davis, Enoch, pvt., Co. H, 1st Nebr. Vol. Inf., wounded, 915.
Davis, Frederick A., pvt., Co. L, 4th U. S. Inf., wounded, 1017.
Davis, George W., maj. gen., U. S. A., mentioned, 521, 522, 524, 525, 667, 1316, 1326, 1331, 1335–1339, 1349.
Davis, Guy P., pvt., Co. C, 1st S. Dak. Vol. Inf., wounded, 961.
Davis, H. S., pvt., Co. E, 2d Mass. Vol. Inf., mentioned, 219.
Davis, James E., pvt., Co. L, 19th U. S. Inf., death, 1160.
Davis, James H., pvt., Co. L, 1st S. Dak. Vol. Inf., wounded, 975.
Davis, John E., pvt., Co. E, 2d Oreg. Vol. Inf., wounded, 946.
Davis, John G., maj., surg., U. S. V., death, 1225.
Davis, Noah, pvt., Batty. K, 3d U. S. Art., death, 866.
Davis, Oliver W., pvt., Co. D, 1st S. Dak. Vol. Inf., death, 979.
Davis, Richard Harding, newspaper correspondent, mentioned, 106, 172.
Davis, Samuel, pvt., Troop L, 3d U. S. Cav., killed, 1225; missing, 1222.
Davis, Samuel G., pvt., Troop C, 3d U. S. Cav., killed, 1152.
Davis, Samuel L., pvt., Co. G, 28th Inf., U. S. V., death, 1109.
Davis, Thomas, pvt., Troop D, 9th U. S. Cav., death, 1220.
Davis, Thomas B., pvt., Co. I, 33d Inf., U. S. V., wounded, 1223, 1225.
Davis, Webster, Assist. Secy. Interior, mentioned, 356.

INDEX. 1387

Davis, William B., maj., med. dept., U. S. A., mentioned, 755.
Davis, William G., col. 49th Iowa Vol. Inf., mentioned, 555.
Davis, William R., pvt., Co. A, 34th Inf., U. S. V., death, 1197.
Davis, Charles H., commander, U. S. Gunboat *Dixie*, mentioned, 330.
Davis, Julian L., 2d lieut., 36th Inf., U. S. V., killed, 1100.
Davis, Austin R., capt., U. S. Marine Corps, killed, 429.
Davis, ——, American missionary in China, mentioned, 471.
Daw, Herbert, pvt., Co. F, 33d Mich. Vol. Inf., mentioned, 214.
Dawson, Eli, pvt., ——, 3d U. S. Art. death, 802.
Dawson, John F., pvt., Troop F, 8d U. S. Cav., death, 1172.
Dawson, Tilden W., pvt., Troop L, 1st U. S.V. Cav., killed, 61.
Day, Claude B., pvt., Hosp. Corps, U. S. A., wounded, 1092.
Day, David, pvt., Co. L, 37th Inf., U. S. V., wounded, 1211.
Day, Edward, pvt., Co. A, 1st Nebr. Vol. Inf., death, 917.
Day, Edward D., pvt., Co. A, 1st Nebr. Vol. Inf., wounded, 906.
Day, George W., corpl., Co. E, 18th U. S. Inf., death, 1152.
Day, John H A., 1st lieut., U. S. Marine Corps, mentioned, 1335.
Day, Thomas G., corpl., Co. M, 45th Inf., U.S. V., killed, 1182.
Day, Selden A., maj., 5th U. S. Art. mentioned, 139.
Day, William R., Secretary of State mentioned, 159, 165, 209, 210, 220, 264, 265, 346, 359, 383.
Day, Matthias W., lieut. col. 1st Ohio Vol. Cav., mentioned, 283, 292.
Daywalt, ——, a. a. surg., U. S. A., mentioned, 794, 796.
D'Azavedo, in charge steamer *Bratton*, mentioned, 181.
Dean, Charles H., pvt., Co. E, 35th Inf., U.S.V., wounded, 1176.
Dean, David C., pvt., Co. L, 1st S. Dak. Vol. Inf., death, 979; wounded, 975.
Dean, James T., 1st lieut., 14th U.S. Inf., mentioned, 301.
Dean, John, pvt., Co. F, 24th U. S. Inf., death, 1057, 1060.
Dean, John D., qm. employee, death 1090.
Dean, Arthur L., corpl., Batty. G, 3d Art., killed, 897.
Deaner, George, sergt., Co. K, 3d Inf. killed, 1197.
Dearmond, Samuel, pvt., Co. B, 32d Inf., U.S.V., death, 1189.
Deasy, John E., pvt., Co. D, 21st U. S. Inf., death, 1152.
Deaton, Jerry, pvt., Co. H, 4th U. S. Inf., death, 1190.
Deaton, U. S. Grant, a. a. surg., U. S. A., mentioned, 1272.
Debaugh, Charles R., pvt., Co. L, 15th U. S. Inf., death, 1213; wounded, 1211.
Debolt, Carl W., pvt., Co. C, 10th Pa. Vol. Inf., wounded, 895.
Dechert, Frank, pvt., Co. L, 41st Inf., U. S. V., death, 1236.
Deck, Frederick, pvt., Co. B, 6th U. S. Inf., death, 1226.
Declaiment, Lorenzo A., corpl., Troop B, 4th U. S. Cav., wounded, 1127.
De Dout, Andrew P., 1st sergt., Co. M, 35th Inf., U. S. V., wounded, 1162.
Defenses, Pacific coast, number of troops needed for, 673-675.
Deforest, George L., pvt., Co. B, 9th U. S. Inf., wounded, 1015.
Degnan, William J., pvt., Co. K, 30th Inf., U. S. V., wounded, 1163.
Dehart, Charles C., pvt., Co. M, 8d U. S. Inf., wounded, 956.
De Hart, Evremonde, sergt., Co. L, 15th U. S. Inf., killed, 1211.
Dehaven, Ota L., pvt., Co. H, 18th U. S. Inf., death, 1175.
Deitrich, Charles, pvt., Co. A, 3d U. S. Inf., wounded, 995.

De Jean, Harlowe, pvt., Co. L, 1st S. Dak. Vol. Inf., killed, 975.
Delaney, James, 1st sergt., Co. L, 8th U. S. Inf., wounded, 1261.
Delaney, John, sergt., Troop E, 11th Cav., U. S. V., death, 1123.
Delgado, insurgent commander, surrender, 1251.
Delitsch, Erwin F., pvt., Co. I, 19th U. S. Inf., killed, 1255.
Delk, Stephen Z., pvt., Co. H, 45th Inf., U. S. V., death, 1238.
Dellinger, Eldo, pvt., Co. F, 30th Inf., U. S. V., death, 1205.
Deloga, Charles F., corpl., Co. A 1st Wash. Vol. Inf., wounded, 896.
Deming, Peter S., capt., asst. com. sub., U. S. V., mentioned, 107.
Dempsey, Loyd F., pvt., Co. K, 45th Inf., U. S. V., death, 1260.
Denby, Charles, member Philippine Commission, mentioned, 883, 998.
Dene, Moneton, hosp. stewd., U. S. A., mentioned, 732.
Denham, Frank, pvt., Co. C, 71st N. Y. Vol. Inf., mentioned, 247, 250-253.
Dennehy, Albert M., corpl., Co. L, 26th Inf., U. S. V., killed, 1182.
Dennis, Albert E., pvt., Co. H, 13th Minn. Vol. Inf., death, 803.
Dennis, Guy C., pvt., Co. C, 9th U. S. Inf., killed, 1297.
Dennis, James N. C., pvt., Co. D 1st Mont. Vol. Inf., wounded, 1017.
Dennis, John, pvt., Co. D, 1st Colo. Vol. Inf., wounded, 956.
Dennis, William E., pvt., Co. F 43d Inf., U. S. V., death, 1238; wounded, 1214.
Denniston, Minott C., pvt., Co. L, 4th U. S. Inf., wounded, 1017.
Denno, Otis L., corpl., Co. K, 1st Wash. Vol. Inf., wounded, 1057.
Denny, John H., pvt., Co. K, 18th U. S. Inf., killed, 1143.
Dent, Byron, pvt., Co. C, 9th U. S. Inf., killed, 1297.
Derby, George McC., lieut. col., chief engr., U. S. V., mentioned, 100, 118.
Derr, Louis, pvt., Co. G, 19th U. S. Inf., death, 1191.
Derry, Edward J., pvt., Batty. E 6th U. S. Art., death, 1130.
De Russy, Isaac D., brig. gen., U. S. V., mentioned, 55, 535.
Descriptive lists, soldiers returning to United States to be furnished, 926, 938.
Desmond, M. W., pvt., Co. L, 9th Mass. Vol. Inf., mentioned, 212.
Detention camp, establishment at Angel Island, Cal., 1021, 1022.
Detroit, U. S. cruiser, mentioned, 39, 50.
Devlin, George, pvt., Co. M, 3d U. S. Inf., death, 952.
Devoe, Peter H., pvt., Co. E, 7th U. S. Inf., mentioned, 219.
Dewald, Joseph, sergt., Co. K, 20th Kans. Vol. Inf., wounded, 952, 981.
Dewar, J. J., pvt., Co. K, 1st Cal. Vol. Inf., killed, 895.
De Wayary, ——, col., Russian forces, mentioned, 438.
Dewey, George, rear-admiral, U. S N,, mentioned, 234, 640, 645, 648, 649, 654, 655, 668, 669, 674-676, 682, 688, 693, 694, 697, 699, 704, 708. 710-714, 718, 720, 721, 724, 752, 778, 780, 782, 788, 799, 805, 819, 821, 826, 827, 833, 850, 851, 858, 864, 872, 876 883, 884, 893, 896, 897, 900, 911, 912, 919, 927, 982, 989 991, 1080, 1339.
Dewitt, Eugene, pvt., Co. E, 9th U. S. Inf., wounded, 1299.
De Wolf, Egbert V., pvt., Co. H, 23d U. S. Inf., killed, 1147.
D. H. Miller, U. S. transport, mentioned, 80, 98, 219, 221, 239, 275, 292, 294, 309, 310, 382, 921.
Dials, Powell V., pvt., Troop H, 3d U. S. Cav., death, 1274.
Dibble, John S., pvt., Co. M, 19th U. S. Inf., killed, 1162.
Dibble, Zeth H., pvt., Co. D, 1st Mont. Vol. Inf., wounded, 900.
Dibler, Frank, pvt., Co. F, 8th Ohio Vol. Inf., mentioned, 213.
Dickelman, Francis, pvt., Hosp. Corps, U. S. A., death, 803.

Dickerman, George P., pvt., Co. C, 1st Colo. Vol. Inf., wounded, 959.
Dickey, Edward E., pvt., Co. M, 17th U. S. Inf., death, 1276.
Dickens, Randolph, maj., U. S. Marine Corps, landing of command, 459.
Dickinson, Ralph M., pvt., Co. I, 23d U. S. Inf., wounded, 1176.
Dickinson, Sidney O., pvt., Co. H, 1st Wash. Vol. Inf., wounded, 926, 977.
Dickinson, Walter M., capt., 17th U. S. Inf., killed, 124.
Dickman, Joseph T., lieut. col., 26th Inf., U. S. V., mentioned, 89, 284; 433, 1106, 1107.
Dickson, Henry, pvt., Co. L, 13th Minn. Vol. Inf., death, 803; mentioned, 761, 762, 828.
Diedel, Charles L., pvt., Co. C, 22d U. S. Inf., wounded, 999.
Diehl, Adam, pvt., Co. I, 17th U. S. Inf., death, 1132.
Dietz, Louis V., pvt., Co. D, 14th U. S. Inf., killed, 895.
Diggles, Arthur M., maj., 13th Minn. Vol. Inf., death, 997; wounded, 987.
Diggs, Charles, pvt., Co. D, 24th U. S. Inf., mentioned, 213.
Dillenback, John W., maj., 2d U. S. Art., mentioned, 543.
Dillinger, John, pvt., Troop A, 3d U. S. Cav., wounded, 1124.
Dillon, Samuel H., pvt., Co. B, 19th U. S. Inf., death, 1194.
Dillon, Thomas S., capt., 1st Mont. Vol. Inf., wounded, 983.
Dilts, George, artif., Co. D, 4th U. S. Inf., wounded, 1017.
Dimler, Frederick M., pvt., Co. E, 18th U. S. Inf., death, 1160.
Dimmick, William, pvt., Co. I, 30th Inf., U. S. V., death, 1200.
Dimond, John J., pvt., Co. A, 9th U. S. Inf., wounded, 443.
Dimond, John P., pvt., Co. F, 9th U. S. Inf., wounded, 444.
Dindinger, Philip F., pvt., Co. M, 19th U. S. Inf., death, 1226.
Dingey, William H., pvt., Co. A, 12th U. S. Inf., wounded, 1026.
Dingler, Herman C., cook, band, 6th U. S. Inf., death, 1200.
Dinneen, Lawrence, sergt., Co. B, 13th U. S. Inf., death, 1109.
Dinsmore, Luther H., pvt., Co. B, 1st Cal. Vol. Inf., death, 1059.
Diocno, insurgent general, mentioned, 1260.
Dios, Mariano de, insurgent general, mentioned, 1258.
Dirks, Harrison, pvt., Co. K, 48th Inf., U. S. V., drowned, 1170.
Disbrow, William H., mus., Co. H, 1st Nebr. Vol. Inf., wounded, 907.
Discharge:
At San Francisco, of soldiers from P. I., 1094.
Enlisted men from regiments destined for P. I., 854, 860.
Enlisted men, volunteers, to enter business, 1220.
Married enlisted men recommended, 842.
Officers for sickness, etc., 1171.
Soldiers from service in P. I., 1093.
Travel allowances on, for men reenlisting in P. I., 1004.
Discharged soldiers, payment on final statements, 1004, 1061.
Dismukes, Martin, 1st lieut., 1st Tenn. Vol. Inf., mentioned, 839.
Ditman, Willard L., corpl., Co. C, 6th U. S. Inf., killed, 1206.
Diwell, William, pvt., Co. L, 35th Inf., U. S. V., death, 1152.
Dix, Alva L., pvt., Co. G, 20th Kans. Vol. Inf., killed, 954.
Dix, Peter H., pvt., Troop K, 1st U. S. Cav., killed, 61.
Dixie, U. S. cruiser, mentioned, 301, 330, 590, 619, 626.
Dixon, Frank, pvt., Co. D, 17th U. S. Inf., death, 1201.
Dixon, James, pvt., Troop M, 4th U. S. Cav., drowned, 1210.

Dixon, Mr., and wife, mentioned, 476.
Dobbins, Patrick J., pvt., Co. C, 9th U. S. Inf., missing, 1297.
Dobel, Gustave D., pvt., Co. G, 39th Inf., U. S. V., death, 1190.
Doble, George D., pvt., Co. C, 19th U. S. Inf., wounded, 1113.
Dobman, Joseph, pvt., Co. G, 1st Wash. Vol. Inf., wounded, 1008.
Dockery, Oliver H., 2d lieut., 3d U. S. Inf., mentioned, 1019.
Dodd, George A., capt., 3d U. S. Cav., mentioned, 1138; wounded, 123.
Dodds, Edwin E., artif., Co. I, 40th Inf., U. S. V., wounded, 1171.
Dodds, Frank L., capt., 9th U. S. Inf., mentioned, 1018.
Dodge, Charles, capt., 24th U. S. Inf., mentioned, 193.
Dodge, Francis S., maj., pay dept., U. S. A., mentioned, 189, 233, 243, 251, 396.
Dodson, F. D. B., pvt., Co. D, 2d Oreg. Vol. Inf., wounded, 934.
Dodson, Jesse C., corpl., Co. K, 35th Inf., U. S. V., death, 1231.
Dodsworth, William G., pvt., Co. M, 17th U. S. Inf., death, 1249.
Doering, John J., pvt., Co. A, 36th Inf., U. S. V., killed, 1064.
Dolan, John, pvt., Co. K, 37th Inf., U. S. V., death, 1216; mentioned, 1234.
Dolan, John A., corpl., Co. C, 27th Inf., U. S. V., mentioned, 1234.
Dolan, John J., pvt., Co. H, 26th Inf., U. S. V., death, 1219.
Dolan, William J., pvt., Co. D, 34th Mich. Vol. Inf., mentioned, 193.
Dold, William, pvt., Co. L, 22d U. S. Inf., wounded, 1234.
Dollard, William, pvt., Co. C, 33d Mich. Vol. Inf., mentioned, 183.
Dollen, Oscar E., pvt., Co. G, 34th Inf., U. S. V., death, 1125; wounded, 1124.
Dolloff, Charles, pvt., Co. I, 43d Inf., U. S. V., death, 1168; wounded, 1162.
Domce, Albert L., pvt., Co. E, 37th Inf., U. S. V., wounded, 1148.
Donahue, Cornelius F., pvt., Co. C, 9th U. S. Inf., death, 1298.
Donahue, James, pvt., Co. I, 31st Inf., U. S. V., death, 1178.
Donaldson, George, pvt., Co. G, 40th Inf., U. S. V., killed, 1148.
Donaldson, William A., collector, custom-house, Santiago, Cuba, mentioned, 232, 255.
Donall, Thomas G., pvt., Co. D, 44th Inf., U. S. V., wounded, 1209.
Donalm, Timothy, pvt., Co. H, 12th U. S. Inf., mentioned, 921.
Donegan, Jack, qm. employee, mentioned, 174.
Don Juan de Austria, Spanish cruiser, mentioned, 650.
Donnally, William F., pvt., Co. D, 4th U. S. Inf., wounded, 1017.
Donnelly, Frederick, chief clerk, Division of the Philippines, mentioned, 979.
Donnelly, John, pvt., Co. M, 1st S. Dak. Vol. Inf., wounded, 954.
Donohue, Timothy, pvt., Co. H, 12th U. S. Inf., death, 968.
Donohue, William, pvt., Co. F, 1st Colo. Vol. Inf., death, 923.
Donovan, Daniel, pvt., Co. D, 4th U. S. Inf., death, 1017.
Donovan, Harry W., pvt., Co. H, 1st N. Dak., Vol. Inf., wounded, 948, 955.
Donovan, Joseph L., 1st lieut., 21st U. S. Inf., wounded, 1015.
Dooley, Albert, corpl., Co. L, 20th Kans. Vol. Inf., wounded, 995.
Doolittle, Elmer L, pvt., Co. C, 2d Oreg. Vol. Inf., wounded, 1003.
Doolittle, Walter S., 2d lieut., 1st S. Dak. Vol. Inf., wounded, 981.
Doran, Elmer F., pvt., Co. I, 1st Colo. Vol. Inf., death, 895.
Doran, George L., pvt., Co. F, 18th U. S. Inf., death, 923.
Doran, Walter, pvt., Co. E, 2d Oreg. Vol. Inf., wounded, 936.

INDEX. 1389

Dorey, William H., mus., Co. A, 19th U. S. Inf., death, 1232.
Dorman, Erskin H., corpl., Co. M, 40th Inf., U. S. V., death, 1170.
Dorn, Siegfried A. G., 1st lieut., 1st Mont. Vol. Inf., mentioned, 1000.
Dorsey, William H., pvt., Co. A, 24th U. S. Inf., death, 1267.
Dorst, Joseph H., capt., 2d U. S. Cav.; lieut. col., a. a. g., U. S. V., mentioned, 21, 27, 79, 90.
Dorton, Bert M., pvt., Batty. K, 3d U. S. Art., wounded, 901.
Dorward, A. B., gen., British forces, mentioned, 438, 440.
Dory, Joseph A., sergt., Co. C, 9th U. S. Inf., wounded, 443.
Dotterer, Solomon, pvt., Co. C, 44th Inf., U. S. V., death, 1248; wounded, 1247.
Doty, Dr. Alva H., health officer, Staten Island, N. Y., mentioned, 324, 325.
Doty, Pearl, pvt., Co. B, 2d Oreg. Vol. Inf., death, 894.
Doty, William H., pvt., Co. F, 40th Inf., U. S. V., death, 1140.
Dougherty, Andrew J., 2d lieut., 17th U. S. Inf., mentioned, 1019.
Dougherty, Charles B., col., 9th Pa. Vol. Inf., mentioned, 511.
Dougherty, John J., pvt., Co. B, 34th Inf., U. S. V., death, 1156.
Dougherty, Joseph E., pvt., Co. A, 1st Wash. Vol. Inf., wounded, 896.
Dougherty, William E., col., 8th U S. Inf., mentioned, 1330, 1344.
Douglas, Charles W., pvt., Co. M, 14th U. S. Inf., death, 895.
Douglas, George C., pvt., Hosp. Corps, U. S. A., wounded, 1096.
Douglas, Henry T., brig. gen., U. S. V., mentioned, 550, 551, 552, 554.
Dousley, William, pvt., Co. C, 1st Cal. Vol. Inf., death, 1001.
Dove, Wilber E., 1st lieut., 12th U S. Inf., mentioned, 998; wounded, 124.
Dow, Thomas H., pvt., Batty. K, 3d U. S. Art., wounded, 1092.
Dowdall, Patrick, sergt., Batty. E, 6th U. S. Art., death, 1152.
Dowdy, James T., corpl., Co. D, 39th Inf., U. S. V., death, 1208.
Dowel, William, pvt., Co. L, 35th Inf., U. S. V., death, 1190.
Dowis, Jonathan, pvt., Co. G, 1st Nebr. Vol. Inf., wounded, 955.
Downer, Alfred, pvt., Troop L, 3d U. S. Cav., wounded, 1222.
Downes, Edward E., 2d lieut., 1st U. S. Inf., killed, 1288.
Downing, Edward S., pvt., Co. H, 1st Nebr. Vol. Inf., wounded, 955.
Downing, Walter, pvt., Co. —, 1st Colo. Vol. Inf., death, 840.
Downs, Ralph W. E., pvt., Co. C, 10th Pa. Vol. Inf., wounded, 953.
Doyle, Myles, corpl., Co. L, 12th U S. Inf., death, 1020.
Doyle, Shan, pvt., Co. B, 45th Inf., U. S. V., death, 1234.
Doyle, Thomas H., pvt., Co. A, 13th U. S. Inf., death, 1231.
Doxsee, Harry L., pvt., Co. C, 1st Colo. Vol. Inf., killed, 994.
Draney, John, mus., Co. E, 16th U S. Inf., death, 1104.
Drehr, John J., pvt., Co. F, 9th U. S. Inf., killed, 443, 445.
Drennan, James W., maj., 1st Mont. Vol. Inf., death, 1017.
Drew, Alfred W., 1st lieut., 12th U. S. Inf., killed, 1056, 1057.
Drew, Jarvis, pvt., Troop H, U. S V., 11th Cav., death, 1181.
Drew, Otis W., pvt., Co. B, 2d Oreg. Vol. Inf., death, 850.
Drew, ——, chief, customs and imperial posts, Tientsin, China, mentioned, 491.
Driscoll, Isadore, corpl., Co. I, 1st N. Dak. Vol. Inf., killed, 967.
Driscoll, Jerry J., pvt., Co. C, 9th U. S. Inf., missing, 1297.

Driver, Gerry W., a. a. surgeon, U. S. A., mentioned, 1059.
Driver, James O., pvt., Co. B, 20th U. S. Inf., death, 1194.
Dromgoole, Orville J., pvt., Co. E, 9th U. S. Inf., killed, 1298.
Dronin, Joseph A., sergt., Co. F, Sig. Corps, U. S. A., death, 1202.
Drouillard, James P., 1st lieut., 9th U. S. Inf., mentioned, 1296.
Drum, John, capt., 10th U. S. Inf., killed, 124.
Drummond, James, pvt., Co. K, 6th Mass. Vol. Inf., wounded, 330.
Dubois, Edmund, capt., 42d Inf., U. S. V., wounded, 1146.
Ducat, Arthur C., capt., 24th U. S. Inf., mentioned, 83; wounded, 124.
Duckland, Fred, mus., Co. —, 13th Minn. Vol. Inf., death, 803.
Duddy, James, corpl., Co. D, 28th Inf., U. S. V., death, 1152.
Dudley, George N., pvt., Co. F, 14th U. S. Inf., death, 1130.
Dudley, John, sergt., Co. B, 19th U. S. Inf., death, 1234.
Duff, Hugh M., pvt., Co. I, 34th Inf., U. S. V., wounded, 1182.
Duffield, Henry M., brig. gen., U. S. V., mentioned, 42, 58–30, 76, 78, 87, 128, 192, 193, 196, 199, 265, 326, 522–524.
Duffy, Michael F., pvt., Co. B, 21st U. S. Inf., death, 1238.
Duffy, Patrick, corpl., Co. H, 21st U. S. Inf., death, 1052.
Duffy, Patrick, pvt., Co. I, 43d Inf., U. S. V., wounded, 1148.
Dugan, William, pvt., Co. F, 26th U. S. Inf., U. S. V.: Killed, 1150.
Mentioned, 1144.
Missing, 1145.
Dugard, Walter, pvt., Co. G, 1st Idaho Vol. Inf., death, 894.
Duggan, Fred, pvt., Co. L, 15th U. S. Inf., reported killed, 1211; wounded, 1212.
Duggan, Patrick F., sergt., Co. A, Batt. Engrs., U. S. A., death, 1271.
Duggan, William J., maj., 51st Iowa Vol. Inf., wounded, 975.
Duggan, Walter T., capt., 10th U. S. Inf., wounded, 124.
Duke of Fife, U. S. transport, mentioned, 1105, 1128.
Dumas, Henry, pvt., Co. H, 43d Inf., U. S. V., killed, 1168.
Dunaway, William, pvt., Co. C, 3d U. S. Inf., death, 1082.
Duncan, George M., pvt., Co. B, 4th U. S. Inf., wounded, 1112.
Duncan, George M., pvt., Co. G, 1st Wash. Vol. Inf., wounded, 896.
Duncan, Hugh B., pvt., Co. A, 33d Inf., U. S. V., death, 1190.
Duncan, James W., maj., 13th, U. S. Inf., mentioned, 1324.
Duncan, John F., pvt., Co. E, 1st Nebr. Vol. Inf., wounded, 760.
Duncan, Samuel, pvt., Co. G, 48th Inf., U. S. V., death, 1236.
Dunken, Roy, pvt., Co. H, 1st Nebr. Vol. Inf., wounded, 955.
Dunkerson, Pomp, pvt., Co. F, 24th U. S. Inf., death, 1238.
Dunkle, Clarence F., sergt., Co. D, 47th Inf., U. S. V., wounded, 1243.
Dunlap, Allyn, pvt., Co. M, 41st Inf., U. S. V., death, 1248.
Dunlap, Ralph C., pvt., band, 40th Inf., U. S. V., death, 1221.
Dunlap, William J., pvt., Co. L, 22d U. S. Inf., wounded, 948.
Dunmore, John V., pvt., 1st Cal. Vol. Inf., death, 803.
Dunn, Charles, pvt., Astor Battery, U. S. A., death, 802; mentioned, 761.
Dunn, Chester Q., pvt., Co. E, 34th Inf., U. S. V., death, 1153.
Dunn, Frank S., sergt., Co. M, 4th U. S. Inf., killed, 1213.
Dunn, Irving, pvt., Troop A, 6th U. S. Cav., death, 478.

1390　INDEX.

Dunn, James W., pvt., Co. I, 25th U. S. Inf., killed, 1140.
Dunn, John, corpl., Co. B, 8th U. S. Inf., mentioned, 218.
Dunn, John F., pvt., Co. C, 1st Mont. Vol. Inf., wounded, 916.
Dunn, John H., pvt., Co. D, 4th U. S. Inf., death, 1056.
Dunn, Owen V., pvt., Co. E, 4th U. S. Inf., death, 1066.
Dunn, Robert A., sergt., Co. E, 47th Inf., U. S. V., wounded, 1187.
Dunn, Thomas D., pvt., Co. L, 1st Mont. Vol. Inf., wounded, 916.
Dunne, William F., sergt., Co. C, 1st Cal. Vol. Inf., wounded, 409.
Dunning, Benjamin F., pvt., Co. E, 1st Nebr. Vol. Inf., wounded, 983.
Dunphy, Martin, pvt., Co. A, 9th U. S. Inf., wounded, 443.
Dunseth, B. F., pvt., Co. L, 2d Oreg. Vol. Inf., wounded, 946.
Dunstore, John G., pvt., ——, 1st Cal. Vol. Inf., mentioned, 761.
Duplisser, W. L., pvt., Batty. G, 3d U. S. Art., wounded, 946.
Dupree, John E., pvt., Co. E, 12th U. S. Inf., killed, 1214.
Durand, Albert, pvt., Co. I, 9th U. S. Inf., wounded, 1087.
Durbin, Carey E., pvt., Co. I, 14th U. S. Inf., wounded, 460.
Durbin, Winfield F., col., 161st Ind. Vol. Inf., mentioned, 349, 552.
Durhem, Charles F., pvt., Co. C, 1st Nebr. Vol. Inf., wounded, 955.
Durkin, Edward S., pvt., Co. C, 4th U. S. Inf., wounded, 1110.
Duschen, Albert, pvt., Co. E, 1st Ill. Vol. Inf., mentioned, 197.
Dusling, Albert, pvt., Hosp. Corps, U. S. A., death, 1125.
Dutran, Peter, pvt., Co. C, 26th Inf., U. S. V., death, 1189; wounded, 1183.
Dutton, Harry L., corpl., Co. C, 18th U. S. Inf., wounded, 1113.
Duvall, Frank, pvt., Co. E, 1st Colo. Vol. Inf., death 1032; wounded, 1008.
Dwent, Frank, sergt., Co. A, 1st Idaho Vol. Inf., death, 833.
Dwyer, Edward L., wagoner, Co. C, 1st Wash., Vol. Inf., wounded, 906.
Dwyer, John, corpl., Co. G, 14th U. S. Inf., wounded, 1084.
Dwyer, John J., pvt., Co. E, 9th U. S. Inf., death, 1181.
Dwyer, Patrick, pvt., Co. A, 39th Inf., U. S. V., death, 1178.
Dwyer, Patrick H., pvt., Co. D, 51st Iowa Vol. Inf., wounded, 975.
Dye, Charles B., pvt., Co. D, 37th Inf. U. S. V., death, 1215.
Dyer, Alexander B., capt., 6th U. S. Art., mentioned, 560–563, 1046.
Dyer, Elisha, jr., Hon., gov. R. I., mentioned, 236.
Dyer, George L., capt., U. S. cruiser *Baltimore*, mentioned, 928.
Dyer, George W., pvt., Co. B, 25th U. S. Inf., death, 1153.
Eagan, Charles P., Commissary-General, U. S. A., mentioned, 171.
Eagar, John, pvt., Co. B, 18th U. S. Inf., wounded, 1117.
Eager, Frank D., maj., 1st Nebr. Vol. Inf., wounded, 975.
Eagle, U. S. gunboat, mentioned, 31; 39.
Ealy, William A., pvt., Co. F, 20th U. S. Inf., wounded, 937.
Earle, William H., corpl., Co. I, 1st Colo. Vol. Inf., wounded, 895.
Earle, William W., pvt., Co. E, 14th U. S. Inf., wounded, 460.
Earley, Frank J., pvt., Co. K, 21st U. S. Inf., killed, 124.
Easley, Charles F., pvt., band, 34th Inf. U. S. V., death, 1132.
Easly, Charles I., corpl., Co. B, 22d U. S. Inf., wounded, 934.
East, Department of, General Merritt relieved from command, 637.

Easter, Harry A., pvt., Co. C, 32d Inf., U. S. V., killed, 1161.
Easterly, James E., pvt., Co. L, 38th Inf., U. S. V., killed, 1192.
Eastman, Francis B., corpl., Co. D, 17th U. S. Inf., wounded, 1060.
Eastman, Frank F., maj., I. G. dept., U. S. A., relative shooting of prisoners, 1345.
Eastman, John, pvt., Co. K, 35th Inf., U. S. V., suicide, 1215.
Eastman, Joseph W., pvt., Co. C, 40th Inf., U. S. V., wounded, 1193.
Easton, Ira A., pvt., Troop A, 11th U. S. V. Cav., wounded, 1203.
Eastwick, Philip G., jr., maj., 2d Oreg. Vol. Inf., mentioned, 770, 772, 777.
Eastwood, Lewis L., pvt., Co. C, 37th Inf., U. S. V., death, 1123.
Eaton, Edward, pvt., Co. I, 39th Inf., U. S. V., death, 1185.
Ebbert, William, 1st sergt., Co. A, 43d Inf., U. S. V., wounded, 1187.
Eberhardt, Tony, pvt., Co. E, 33d Inf., U. S. V., wounded, 1101.
Ebert, William A., pvt., Co. F, 20th Kans. Vol. Inf., wounded, 952.
Ebig, Edward A., mus., Co. B, 43d Inf., U. S. V., killed, 1162.
Echols, Charles P., 1st lieut., Engr. Corps, U. S. A., mentioned, 667, 716.
Eckert, Peter J., pvt., Co. L, 16th U. S. Inf., death, 1160.
Eckhardt, Louis, pvt., Co. M, 20th U. S. Inf., death, 1191.
Ecklund, Gustav, pvt., Co. I, 18th U. S. Inf., death, 1248.
Edder, Angus, corpl., Co. A, 28th Inf., U. S. V., wounded, 1132.
Edelsten, Ernest, 1st sergt. Co. H, 35th Inf., U. S. V., death, 1194.
Edgell, George E,, pvt., Batt. H, 3d U. S. Art., death, 802.
Edgerton, Arthur J., pvt., Co. L, 32d Inf., U.S. V., death, 1130.
Edie, Guy L., maj., med. dept., U. S. A., mentioned, 971.
Edling, Leonard J., pvt., Co. E, 21st U. S. Inf., death, 1020; wounded, 994.
Edlund, Gustave E., artif., Co. B, 1st Nebr. Vol. Inf., killed, 899.
Edmonds, Charles W., pvt., Batty. E, 1st U. S. Art., death, 1015.
Edmondson, William, pvt., Co. B, 49th Inf., U. S. V., wounded, 1251.
Edmonston, Raphael A., 1st lieut., asst. surg., 34th Inf., U. S. V., death, 1175.
Edwards, Clarence R., maj., a. a. g., U. S. V., clerks in P. I., 66, 67, 69, 1262.
Edwards, Daniel R., pvt., Co. E, 18th U. S. Inf., death, 1066.
Edwards, Earl, pvt., Co. K, 22d U.S. Inf., wounded, 941.
Edwards, Frank E., corpl., Co. M, 2d Oreg. Vol. Inf., wounded, 948.
Edwards, Frank H., corpl., Co. L, 19th U. S. Inf., death, 1276.
Edwards, George F., corpl., Co. C, 40th Inf., U. S. V., killed, 1182.
Edwards, Herbert H., corpl., Co. H, 43d Inf., U. S. V., killed, 1168.
Edwards, Thomas R., pvt., Co. K, 16th U. S. Inf., death, 1160.
Edwards, Vernie J., sergt., Troop F, 11th U. S. V. Cav., death, 1233.
Edwards, Eaton A., capt., 25th U. S. Inf., wounded, 124.
Egan, Condrad, pvt., Co. K, 1st Nebr. Vol. Inf., wounded, 897.
Egan, George M., pvt., Co. L, 40th Inf., U. S. V., wounded, 1162.
Egbert, Harry C., col., 6th U. S. Inf.:
　Killed, 945.
　Mentioned, 83, 956.
　Wounded, 124.
Egbert, U. S. transport, mentioned, 503, 505, 1305, 1317.
Egger, Albert, pvt., Co. C, 1st Cal. Vol. Inf., wounded, 904.
Ehrheart, Thomas A., pvt., Co. K, 42d Inf., U. S. V., death 1156.

Ehrich, Herman, corpl., Co. I, 5th U. S. Inf., death, 1261.
Eichelsdefer, Adam, pvt., Co. K, 14th U. S. Inf., death, 1276.
Eichhammer, George, pvt., Co. G, 2d Oreg. Vol. Inf., wounded, 946.
Eichholtz, Levi B., corpl., Troop B, 4th U. S. Cav., killed, 1212.
Eicknorth, William, pvt., Co. M, 20th U. S. Inf., wounded, 1017.
Eide, Albert A., pvt., Co. G, 2d Oreg. Vol. Inf., wounded, 925.
Eide, Martin, pvt., Co. M, 1st S. Dak. Vol. Inf., wounded, 915.
Eidsness, Asked O., pvt., Co. D, 1st S. Dak. Vol. Inf., death, 833.
Eighth Army Corps, organization, 556–579.
Eisenach, Richard, pvt., Co. K, 45th Inf., U. S. V., killed, 1161.
Ekman, Fred, pvt., Co. I, 13th Minn. Vol. Inf., wounded, 947.
Ekola, Matt, pvt., Co. C, 34th Inf., U. S. V., death, 1189.
Elder, George W., pvt., Co. I, 18th U. S. Inf., death, 1243.
Eldridge, Bogardus, capt., 14th U. S. Inf., killed, 1079.
Elfgang, Gottfried, pvt., Co. C, 4th U. S. Inf., death, 1099.
Elifritz, Walter A., pvt., Co. H, 1st Nebr. Vol. Inf., wounded, 955, 974.
Elkins, Heber, pvt., Troop F, 11th U. S. V. Cav., wounded, 1148.
Ellery, John, pvt., Co. C, 46th Inf., U. S. V., death, 1196.
Ellett, Luther M., pvt., Co. A, 24th U. S. Inf., death, 1078.
Ellett, William P., corpl., Co. C, 44th Inf., U. S. V., killed, 1247.
Elliot, William L., 1st lieut., 12th U. S. Inf., mentioned, 219, 251.
Elliott, Archie, pvt., Co. I, 37th Inf., U. S. V., death, 1208.
Elliott, David S., capt., 20th Kans. Vol. Inf., killed, 920.
Elliott, Jesse, corpl., Co. B, 21st U. S. Inf., wounded, 1090.
Elliott, John B., pvt., Co. B, 12th U. S. Inf., death, 993.
Elliott, Milton A., jr., 2d lieut., 13th U. S. Inf., mentioned, 1019.
Elliott, Russell T., pvt., Co. K, 14th U. S. Inf., killed, 460.
Elliott, Walter B., capt., 40th Inf., U. S. V., mentioned, 1171, 1183.
Ellis, Arthur H., pvt., Co. H, 1st Wash. Vol. Inf., wounded, 977.
Ellis, Arthur J., pvt., Co. H, 44th Inf., U. S. V., death, 1141.
Ellis, Carson E., pvt., Co. L, 1st Wash. Vol. Inf., wounded, 914.
Ellis, Charles F., pvt., Co. D, 6th U. S. Inf., death, 1202.
Ellis, Harry K., mus., Co. C, 9th U. S. Inf., wounded, 443.
Ellis, Herbert E., pvt., Co. A, 22d U. S. Inf., death, 1189.
Ellis, James T., 1st sergt. Co. A, 29th U. S Inf., wounded, 1197.
Ellis, Matthew H., maj., surg., 2d Oreg. Vol. Inf., wounded, 1003.
Ellis, Philip H., maj., 13th U. S. Inf., mentioned, 83; wounded, 124.
Ellis, William, pvt., Co. E, 22d U. S. Inf., wounded, 941.
Elmes, David, mus., Co. M, 1st S. Dak. Vol. Inf., wounded, 949.
Eltinge, Le Roy, 2d lieut., 4th U. S. Cav., wounded, 962, 976.
Elwood, Willard, pvt., Co. M, 34th Inf., U. S. V., death, 1220.
Ely, Clyde B., pvt., Co. H, 1st U. S. Inf., wounded, 1275.
Emery, Harry C., pvt., Co. C, 14th U. S. Inf., wounded, 1017.
Emery, ——, Associated Press representative, to relieve Martin at Manila, 1225.
Emigh, Roy, sergt., Co. B, 26th U. S. Inf., wounded, 1240.
Emma Luyken, German steamer, shipment of arms and ammunition from Bremerhaven by, 1126.
Emmert, Harry N., sergt., Co. I, 40th Inf., U. S. V., wounded, 1195.
Emmett, William J., 1st sergt., Co. L, 14th U. S. Inf., wounded, 454.
Engberg, Joseph J., pvt., Batty. H, 3d U. S. Art., wounded, 905.
Engelhardt, John, pvt., Co. B, 28th U. S. Inf., death, 1223.
England, Berton, pvt., Co. F, 30th U. S. Inf., death, 1215.
England, Edward C., sergt., Batty. G, 6th U. S. Art., wounded, 1112.
England, Lloyd, 2d lieut., 3d U. S. Art., wounded, 959.
England, John J., pvt., Co. I, 37th Inf., U. S. V., death, 1223.
Engleheart, William M., pvt., Co. C, 10th Pa. Vol. Inf., injured, 555.
Englehorn, George, pvt., Co. K, 1st Nebr. Vol. Inf., wounded 760.
Englesby, Charles H., capt., 1st S. Dak. Vol. Inf., wounded, 981.
English, William B., pvt., Co. E, 30th U. S. Inf., killed, 1199.
Engstron, Richard, pvt., Co. L, 13th U. S. Inf., death, 1185.
Ennis, Edward R., pvt., Co. L, 1st Wash. Vol. Inf., wounded, 977.
Ennis, William, capt., 4th U. S. Art., mentioned, 543.
Eno, Joseph, pvt., Co. H, 1st Wash. Vol. Inf., killed, 977.
Enright, James, pvt., Co. E, 1st Mont. Vol. Inf., wounded, 945.
Enright, Patrick J., corpl., Co. G, 16th U. S. Inf., killed, 1150.
Enright, Timothy, pvt., Co. B, 13th Minn. Vol. Inf., death, 939.
Enslow, Raymond S., 1st lieut., 11th Cav. U. S. V., wounded, 1127.
Eoff, Calvin H., corpl., Troop A, 3d U. S. Cav., drowned, 1190.
Epp, Henry, corpl., Co. C, 1st Nebr. Vol. Inf., wounded, 897.
Ericcson, mentioned, 39.
Erickson, Albert, pvt., Co. H, 13th Minn. Vol. Inf., wounded, 991.
Erickson, Ole S., corpl., Co. H, 4th U. S. Inf., wounded, 1081.
Ericson, Henry W., pvt., Co. A, 19th U. S. Inf., killed, 1202.
Erikson, August M., pvt., Co. C, 4th U. S. Inf., killed, 1130.
Erisman, Alfred J., pvt., Co. G, 1st Nebr. Vol. Inf., death, 831.
Ernsberger, Frank A., sergt., Batty. L, 3d U. S. Art., wounded, 947.
Ernst, Frederick, pvt., Co. I, 8th U. S. Inf., death, 1256.
Ernst, Oswald H., brig. gen., U. S. V.; lieut. col., Engr. Corps, U. S. A., mentioned, 71, 76, 82, 92, 98, 106, 109, 115, 119, 126, 133, 145, 274, 277, 278, 280, 283, 287, 289, 291, 330, 369, 372, 511, 513–515.
Ervine, William J., pvt., Troop F, 1st U. S. V. Cav., killed, 61.
Erwin, Walter, pvt., Co. B, 2d Oreg. Vol. Inf., wounded, 934.
Erwin, William H., pvt., Troop A, 4th U. S. Cav., death, 1144.
Escario, Don Federico, brig. gen., Spanish army, mentioned, 151, 152.
Eschels, Charles, pvt., Co. B, 1st S. Dak. Vol. Inf., death, 967.
Esig, Jesse, pvt., Co. H, 40th Inf., U. S. V., wounded, 1183.
Eskridge, Richard T., maj., 10th U. S. Inf., mentioned, 83; wounded, 124.
Eskridge, Wayne, pvt., Co. C, 44th Inf., U. S. V., wounded, 1247.
Esmerelda, Spanish steamer, mentioned, 1073.
Espenson, Hans E., pvt., Co. E, 37th Inf., U. S. V., death, 1178.
Esshom, Merton W., pvt., Co. E, 1st Colo. Vol. Inf., wounded, 947.
Estes, William R., pvt., Co. C, 17th U. S. Inf., death, 1205.
Estry, Julius J., mentioned, 342.

Etheridge, Perry G., pvt., Co. A, 22d U. S. Inf., killed, 1174.
Eubanks, Sim, pvt., Co. C, 5th U. S. Inf., wounded, 1251.
Eulate, Spanish officer, mentioned, 100.
European governments, attitude toward Spain, in re Cuba, 28.
Eustis, W. H., mentioned, 347.
Euston, Arthur, pvt., Co. E, 26th Inf., U. S. V., death, 1132.
Evacuation commissions, to meet at Habana, Cuba, and San Juan, P. R., 751.
Evans, Alfred, pvt., Co. E, 14th U. S. Inf., wounded, 465.
Evans, Andrew W., pvt., Co. E, 20th Kans. Vol. Inf., wounded, 946.
Evans, Benjamin, pvt., band, 5th U. S. Cav., death, 1276.
Evans, Daniel J., pvt., Co. H, 1st Cal. Vol. Inf., mentioned, 761.
Evans, Houston V., 1st lieut., 6th U. S. Inf., mentioned, 1037, 1090.
Evans, John, pvt., Co. K, 19th U. S. Inf., death, 1109.
Evans, John, pvt., Co. C, 49th Inf., U. S. V., death, 1197.
Evans, John W., pvt., Co. F, 21st U. S. Inf., death, 1060.
Evans, Samuel H., pvt., Troop E, 4th U. S. Cav., wounded, 947.
Everett, Dickson A., pvt., Co. A, 14th U. S. Inf., mentioned, 924; wounded, 895.
Everett, William E., pvt., Co. A, 1st Wash. Vol. Inf., wounded, 897.
Everington, Joseph W., pvt., Co. C, 18th U. S. Inf., killed, 924.
Everson, John M., pvt., Co. K, 1st Nebr. Vol. Inf., wounded, 956.
Ewers, Ezra P., brig. gen., U. S. V.:
Assigned to Department of Santiago, 219, 381.
Mentioned, 194.
Request for service in Cuba, 209.
Wounded, 124.
Ewing, John A., pvt., Co. G, 1st N. Dak. Vol. Inf., death, 923.
Faber, Charles H., pvt., Co. A, 17th U. S. Inf., death, 1197.
Fahrenwald, William, pvt., Co. C, 1st S. Dak. Vol. Inf., death, 993.
Fairbanks, Charles W., U. S. Senator, mentioned, 320, 332, 342.
Fairchild, Benjamin R., pvt., Co. L, 26th Inf., U. S. V., death, 1109.
Fairchild, Tray E., pvt., Co. D, 20th Kans. Vol. Inf., killed, 948.
Fairfax, Albert D., pvt., Batty. G, 3d U. S. Art., death, 802.
Fait, William R., pvt., Co. A, 1st Wash. Vol. Inf., wounded, 897.
Falkenburg, Harry C., prin. mus., 1st Colo. Vol. Inf., death, 886.
Fallen, Oscar, pvt., Co. M, 1st S. Dak. Vol. Inf., killed, 954.
Fallis, Enoch M., pvt., Co. C, 16th U. S. Inf., wounded, 1152.
Fallon, John E., pvt., Co. H, 1st Ill. Vol. Inf., mentioned, 226.
Fallon, Michael, pvt., Co. L, 26th U. S. Inf., death 1202.
Fallon, Patrick, pvt., Co. H, 12th U. S. inf., death, 1130.
Fallon, Peter M., pvt., Co. D, 6th U. S. Inf., death, 1153.
Falls, John J., pvt., Troop K, 3d U. S. Cav., wounded, 1113.
Fanita, ship, mentioned, 32, 182, 275, 278, 282, 325.
Fanning, J., sergt., U. S. Marine Corps, killed, 459.
Fargo, George B., pvt., Co. F, 1st Wash. Vol. Inf., death, 960.
Farmer, Garrett, pvt., Co. B, 39th Inf., U. S. V., wounded, 1209.
Farnham, Eugene S., pvt., Co. A, 37th Inf., U. S. V., death, 1176.
Farnoff, Charles, pvt., Co. L, 20th U. S. Inf., mentioned, 937.
Faron, Michael J., pvt., Co. H, 43d Inf., U. S. V., wounded, 1168.
Farral, George P., pvt., Co. A, U. S. Marine Corps, wounded, 460.

Farrar, Arthur V., pvt., Co. L, 17th U. S. Inf., wounded, 1222.
Farrell, Edward, pvt., Co. A, 19th U. S. Inf., death, 1226.
Farrell, George P., pvt., U. S. Marine Corps, death, 482.
Farrell, James F., pvt., Co. H, 9th Mass. Vol. Inf., mentioned, 185.
Farrell, John E., pvt., Co. C, 26th Inf., U. S. V., death, 1189.
Farrell, Joseph, 1st sergt., Co. A, 16th U. S. Inf., death, 1215.
Farrell, Michael J., pvt., Co. F, 21st U. S. Inf., death, 1167.
Farrow, Frank E., pvt., Co. I, 40th Inf., U. S. V., wounded, 1162.
Farrow, George, farrier, Troop M, 4th U. S. Cav., death, 1190.
Farthing, Abner, pvt., Co. B, 39th Inf., U. S. V., death, 1161.
Fauber, William E., pvt., Co. K, 6th U. S. Inf., death, 1090.
Faul, George A., pvt., Co. M, 13th U. S. Inf., death, 1161.
Faulkner, Harry, pvt., Co. A, 4th U. S. Inf., wounded, 1086.
Faust, Samuel, pvt., Co. G, 34th Inf., U. S. V., wounded, 1124.
Faust, Warren, corpl., 8th Batty. Field Art., U. S. A., wounded, 1275.
Favier, ——, comsy. sergt., U. S. A., mentioned, 970.
Fawke, Harry W., pvt., Co. C, 1st Cal. Vol. Inf., wounded, 905.
Fay, Clarence A., pvt., Co. L, 1st Nebr. Vol. Inf., wounded, 946.
Fay, Hiram, pvt., Co. I, 1st S. Dak. Vol. Inf., wounded, 895.
Febiger, George L., 1st lieut., 33d Inf., U. S. V., killed, 1222; mentioned, 1221.
Febiger, Lea, maj., 17th U. S. Inf., expedition against Moros, 1331.
February, Samuel J., pvt., Co. I, 18th U. S. Inf., death, 972.
Federica, mentioned, 461, 484, 1206, 1217, 1227, 1228, 1247, 1259, 1303, 1307, 1312.
Feeney, Thomas, corpl., Co. D, 5th U. S. Inf., wounded, 1251.
Fehl, Samuel M., rct., 14th U. S. Inf., death, 1060.
Fehr, Egidius J., pvt., Co. M, 13th Minn. Vol. Inf., wounded, 916.
Feil, Lewis, pvt., Co. C, 19th U. S. Inf., death, 1261.
Feist, Edd F., corpl., Co. E, 32d Inf., U. S. V., wounded, 1191.
Feley, Charles J., pvt., Co. C, 18th U. S. Inf., killed, 1026.
Felker, Oscar, pvt., Co. C, 1st S. Dak. Vol. Inf., killed, 915.
Felland, Olavus T., pvt., Co. M, 1st S. Dak. Vol. Inf., death, 894.
Fellowes, Kendall, corpl., Co. A, 1st Wash. Vol. Inf., wounded, 896.
Felts, John W., pvt., Co. K, 19th U. S. Inf., wounded, 1146.
Fenneberg, Frederick, pvt., Co. D, 11th U. S. Inf., killed, 390.
Wounded, 380.
Fenniger, Oscar A., pvt., Batty. A, Utah Vol. Art., death, 1008.
Fent, Ottis V., pvt., Co. K, 1st Nebr. Vol. Inf., wounded, 946.
Fenton, Charles W., 1st lieut., 5th U. S. Cav., wounded, 1084.
Fenton, Eben B., capt., asst. comy. subs., U. S. V., mentioned, 1274.
Fenton, John H., pvt., Co. B, 2d Oreg. Vol. Inf., death, 837.
Fenton, Thomas, pvt., Co. F, 21st U. S. Inf., death, 1243.
Ferguson, Arthur M., 1st lieut., 36th Inf., U. S. V., wounded, 1091.
Ferguson, David A., pvt., Troop I, 4th U. S. Cav., death, 1150.
Ferguson, Harley B., 1st lieut., Corps of Engrs., U. S. A., mentioned, 419.
Ferguson, Lewis W., pvt., Co. B, 20th Kans. Vol. Inf., death, 866.
Ferguson, Virgil J., pvt., Co. C, 12th U. S. Inf., death, 1141.

Fern, U. S. gunboat, mentioned, 115.
Fernald, Roy L., 2d lieut., 26th U. S. Inf., drowned, 1204.
Fernandina, Fla.—
Concentration of troops, 266, 273, 289, 361.
Harbor facilities for embarkation of troops, 144.
Healthful camp, 43.
Recommended camp be located at, 37.
Fessenden, Walter W., pvt., Co. K., 17th U. S. Inf., death, 1219.
Fessler, Jacob, pvt., Hosp. Corps, U. S. A., death, 1104.
Fidel, insurgent colonel, killed, 1211.
Fidler, Louie, pvt., Co. H, 40th Inf., U. S. V., killed, 1183.
Field, Ashley, pvt., Co. M, 1st Ill. Vol. Inf., mentioned, 241.
Field, Burt, pvt., Co. E, 43d Inf., U. S. V., killed, 1218.
Field, Robert, 2d lieut., 14th U. S. Inf., mentioned, 1156.
Field, William J., pvt., Co. I, 9th U. S. Inf., wounded, 454.
Fields, Allie D., pvt., Co. L, 21st U. S. Inf., wounded, 1084.
Fields, Eddie, pvt., Co. I, 24th U. S. Inf., killed, 1196.
Fields, William, pvt., Hosp. Corps, U. S. A., death, 803.
Fife, William J., lieut. col., 1st Wash. Vol. Inf., mentioned, 827, 992.
Fifth Army Corps, organization, 13, 14, 539-547.
Fike, Alonzo M., pvt., Co. F, 1st Nebr. Vol. Inf., wounded, 914.
Files, Herbert L., pvt., Co. I, 1st N. Dak. Vol. Inf., wounded, 967.
Filley, Thomas, pvt., Co. F, 20th U. S. Inf., wounded, 937.
Filipinos, Spanish regiment of, distribution, 655.
Finger, John, pvt., Batty. F, 5th U. S. Art., wounded, 1112.
Finke, William J., pvt., Co. I, 1st Nebr. Vol. Inf., wounded, 948.
Finncan, John, pvt., Co. M, 35th Inf., U. S. V., death, 1191.
Finney, Rufus N., pvt., Co. M, 30th U. S. V. Inf., death, 1201.
Finnick, [?] ——, comsy. sergt., U. S. A., trial for commissary fraud, 1296.
Firn, Philip, mus., Co. G, 18th U. S. Inf., mentioned, 761.
First Army Corps, organization, 509-519.
First Brigade, U. S. Expeditionary Forces, report of voyage, 767.
Fischer, Ernest H. A., pvt., Co. I, 1st Wash. Vol. Inf., wounded, 897.
Fisette, Arthur, pvt., Co. C, 33d Mich. Vol. Inf., mentioned, 197.
Fish, Charles L., pvt., Co. I, 26th Inf., U. S. V., wounded, 1202.
Fish, Edward B., 1st lieut., 2d Mass. Vol. Inf., mentioned, 254.
Fish, Hamilton, sergt., Troop L, 1st U. S. V., Cav., killed, 61; mentioned, 59.
Fished, H., pvt., U. S. Marine Corps, killed, 459.
Fisher, Charles, pvt., Co. M, 23d U. S. Inf., wounded, 1072.
Fisher, Earl, sergt., Batty. K, 3d U. S. Art., wounded, 946.
Fisher, Ernest H. A., pvt., Co. I, 1st Wash. Vol. Inf., wounded, 897.
Fisher, Ford, sergt., Batty. A, Utah Vol. Art., killed, 991.
Fisher, Frederick J., pvt., Co. M, 33d Inf., U.S.V., death, 1253.
Fisher, Jacob, corpl., Co. G, 3d U. S. Inf., wounded, 981.
Fisher, Peter H. S., pvt., Co. M, 1st Cal. Vol. Inf., death, 803.
Fisk, C. Harry, pvt., Co. D, 1st Nebr. Vol. Inf., mentioned, 828.
Fisk, Philip B., mus., Co. A, 18th U. S. Inf., death, 803.
Fiske, Edward S., pvt., Hosp. Corps, U. S. A., death, 829, 830.
Fitch, Graham D., capt., Corps of Engrs., U. S. A., mentioned, 541.
Fitch, William C., pvt., Co. D, 13th Minn. Vol. Inf., wounded, 902.

Fitchie, Harry E., pvt., Co. D, 1st Nebr. Vol. Inf., wounded, 948.
Fitzgerald, Edward, corpl., Co. A, 28th U. S. Inf., death, 1228.
Fitzgerald, Edward, corpl., Troop B, 4th U. S. Cav., mentioned, 1078.
Fitzgerald, Eli, pvt., Co. C, 9th U. S. Inf., killed, 1297.
Fitzgerald, Henry, pvt., Co. F, 9th U. S. Inf., death, 1150.
Fitzgerald, Maurice, pvt., Co. G, 9th U. S. Inf., death, 1181.
Fitzgerald, Patrick W., pvt., Co. K, 37th Inf., U. S. V., death, 1243.
Fitzgerald, Thomas, pvt., Co. C, 71st N. Y. Vol. Inf., mentioned, 247, 250-253.
Fitzgerald, Thomas F., mus., band, 23d U. S. Inf., death, 830.
Fitzgerald, William, pvt., Co. K, 4th Inf., U.S.V., death, 1191.
Fitzgerald, William, 1st sergt., Co. L, 15th U. S. Inf., killed, 1211.
Fitzgerald, William E., pvt., Co. M, 3d U. S. Inf., wounded, 946.
Fitzgerald, John J., member of Congress, mentioned, 217.
Fitzloff, Henry, pvt., Co. C, 13th Minn. Vol. Inf., mentioned, 762; wounded, 761.
Fitzpatrick, Albert W., pvt., Co. D, 9th U. S. Inf., wounded, 454.
Fitzpatrick, Timothy, corpl., Batty. H, 3d U. S. Art., wounded, 946.
Fitzpatrick, William E., pvt., Co. F, 47th Inf., U. S. V., wounded, 1198.
Fitzsimmons, John F., pvt., Co. B, 21st U. S. Inf., death, 1095.
Flags, captured during Santiago campaign wanted at Omaha exposition, 191, 197.
Flanagan, Francis P., pvt., Co. L, 15th U. S. Inf., wounded, 1211.
Flanders, Bert G., pvt., Co. K, 4th U. S. Inf., death, 1109.
Fleming, Adrian S., 1st lieut., 6th U. S. Art., mentioned, 1046.
Fleming, Charles B., pvt., Co. D, 5th U. S. Inf., killed, 1251.
Fleming, Courtland, pvt., band, 20th Kans. Vol. Inf., wounded, 954, 961.
Fleming, John, pvt., Co. L, 20th U. S. Inf., wounded, 1199.
Flemming, Clarence T., pvt., Co. F, 49th Inf., U. S. V., death, 1221.
Flemming, William, sergt., Co. H, 23d U. S. Inf., death, 1208.
Fletcher, Edward, pvt., Co. F, 47th Inf., U. S. V., death, 1238.
Fletcher, Loren, member of Congress, mentioned, 353.
Fletcher, Mert, pvt., Co. F, 18th U. S. Inf., killed, 1113.
Fletcher, Royal E., pvt., Co. B, 1st Wash. Vol. Inf., death, 894.
Flewelling, Joseph, pvt., Co. E, 37th Inf., U.S.V., wounded, 1193.
Flinn, Pinkney, pvt., Co. E, 37th Inf., U. S. V., death, 1150.
Flint, Grover, 1st lieut., 35th Inf., U. S. V., wounded, 1182.
Flint, John W., pvt., Co. C, 13th Minn. Vol. Inf., death, 994.
Flint, Eddy & Co., Messrs., mentioned, 181, 182.
Flintshire, U. S. transport, mentioned, 424, 426, 427, 430, 437, 439, 442, 445.
Flood, Edward N., corpl., Co. F, 46th Inf., U.S.V., death, 1170.
Flood, Henry J., sergt., Co. A, 28th U. S. V., wounded, 1130.
Flood, John P., pvt., Co. F, 14th U. S. Inf., wounded, 1084.
Florentine, Edward, pvt., Batty. K, 3d U. S. Art., death, 1020.
Flores, Eufrasio, appointed by Aguinaldo as member of commission to confer with Gen. Otis, 909.
Florida, steamer, mentioned, 33, 51, 52, 240, 245, 245, 252, 255, 275, 278, 282, 309, 310, 350, 398, 595, 619, 625.
Flosser, William A., pvt., Co. A, 18th U. S. Inf., death, 803.

Floyd, George, artif., Co. B, 37th Inf., U. S. V., death, 1187.
Floyd, Robert W., pvt., Co. E, 29th Inf., U. S. V., death, 1170.
Flynn, Hughie, pvt., Co. M, 16th U. S. Inf., death, 1241.
Flynn, Timothy J., pvt., Co. F, 18th U. S. Inf., wounded, 1113.
Flynn, William J., pvt., Batty. F, 5th U. S. Art., death, 1086.
Fogarty, William, sergt., Batty. H, 3d U. S. Art., killed, 945.
Foin, Harry F., pvt., Co. L, 39th Inf., U. S. V., death, 1210.
Folds, Henry S., pvt., Co. E, 38th Inf., U. S. V., death, 1215.
Folger, Lester M., pvt., Co. G, 20th U. S. Inf., wounded, 934.
Folkner, Horace L., pvt., Co. F, 1st Nebr. Vol. Inf., death, 803.
Fontan, Ventura, lieut. col., Spanish army, mentioned, 151, 152.
Foote, Frank M., maj., 1st Wyo. Vol. Inf., mentioned, 717.
Foote, Stephen M., 1st lieut., 4th U. S. Art., commended, 129.
Foraker, J. B., U. S. Senator, mentioned, 329, 339.
Forbis, John L., pvt., Co. G, 20th U. S. Inf., suicide, 1221.
Forby, Lee, capt., 1st Nebr. Vol. Inf., death, 956; wounded, 946.
Forche, Elisha, pvt., Co. C, 24th U. S. Inf., drowned, 1167.
Ford, Charles, pvt., Co. G, 17th U. S. Inf., wounded, 1017.
Ford, Clyde S., 1st lieut., med. dept. U. S. A., mentioned, 1018.
Ford, Joseph H., 1st lieut., med. dept., U. S. A., mentioned, 1018.
Ford, Joseph W., pvt., Troop A, 11th U. S. V. Cav., wounded, 1212.
Ford, William M., pvt., Co. M, 40th Inf., U. S. V., death, 1255.
Forden, James V., sergt., band, 14th U. S. Inf., death, 480.
Fordyce, S. W., mentioned, 351.
Forgerel, Louis A., pvt., Co. E, 14th U. S. Inf., wounded, 454.
Forman, Elwood A., corpl., Co. H, 25th U. S. Inf., death, 1274.
Fornance, James, capt., 13th U. S. Inf., killed, 124; mentioned, 83.
Forsberg, Nels G., pvt., Co. H, 1st Nebr. Vol. Inf., wounded, 967.
Forse, Albert G., maj., 1st U. S. Cav., killed, 123.
Forsyth, William D., 1st lieut., 15th U. S. Cav., attacked by Moros, 1322.
Forsyth, William W., capt., 6th U. S. Cav., mentioned 476, 495.
Fort, Charles O., 1st sergt., Co. A, 44th Inf., U. S. V., wounded, 1216.
Fortson, George H., capt., 1st Wash. Vol. Inf., death, 956; wounded, 947.
Foss, Henry, pvt., Co. B, 13th Minn. Vol. Inf., wounded, 963.
Foster, Alexander, corpl., Co. C, 21st U. S. Inf., wounded, 1052.
Foster, Charles E., pvt., Co. M, 14th U. S. Inf., wounded, 454.
Foster, D. Jack, col., 6th Ill. Vol. Inf., mentioned, 520.
Foster, Ernest M., pvt., Co. C, 14th U. S. Inf., death, 804; mentioned, 829.
Foster, Fangule E., pvt., U. S. Marine Corps, death, 1314.
Foster, Fay, pvt., Co. D, 9th U. S. Inf., death, 1113.
Foster, Frank W., pvt., Co. E, 30th Inf., U. S. V., suicide, 1161.
Foster, Herbert S., capt., 20th U. S. Inf., mentioned, 561.
Foster, Perrent, corpl., Co. L, 25th U. S. Inf., drowned, 1213.
Foster, Pierce C., 2d lieut., 3d U. S. Inf., death, 994.
Foster, William, pvt., Co. A, 3d U. S. Inf., death, 1156; wounded, 1055.
Fouke, Frank J., pvt., Co. K, 1st Nebr. Vol. Inf., wounded, 974.

Foulkes, Jesse A., pvt., Co. K, 14th U. S. Inf., wounded, 460.
Foulks, Nicholas N., pvt., Co. C, 14th U. S. Inf., wounded, 898.
Foultz, Stewart C., pvt., Co. C, 16th U. S. Inf., wounded, 1152.
Fourth Army Corps, organization, 534–539.
Fountaine, Alfred, pvt., Co. I, 43d Inf., U. S. V., death, 1178.
Fow, Alfred, pvt., Co. A, 16th U. S. Inf., death, 1271.
Fowler, A. S., mentioned, 348.
Fowler, Godfrey R., capt., 33d Inf., U. S. V., mentioned, 1109.
Fowler, John, American consul, Chefoo, China, mentioned, 414, 433, 434, 438–441, 443, 445–452, 455–458, 460, 467, 473, 475.
Fowlis, Kirk, pvt., Co. G, 24th U. S. Inf., wounded, 1160.
Fox, George O., sergt., Co. E, 14th U. S. Inf., wounded, 460.
Fox, Joseph, corpl., Co. H, 22d U. S. Inf., killed by comrade, 1208.
Fox, Paul, pvt., Co. K, 22d U. S. Inf., drowned, 1189.
Fox, Robert L., pvt., Co. C, 10th Pa. Vol. Inf., death, 803.
Fox, Walter P., pvt., Co. E, 1st Wash. Vol. Inf., wounded, 896.
Fox, John C., 1st lieut., 1st S. Dak. Vol. Inf., mentioned, 1000.
Fraenznick, Ferdinand, pvt., Batty. O, 3d U. S. Art., killed, 1248.
Frager, Frank, pvt., Co. G, 14th U. S. Inf., wounded, 1085.
Frame, Robert, pvt., Co. C, 28th U. S. Inf., death, 1185.
Francis, John J., pvt., Co. C, 43d Inf., U. S. V., wounded, 1187.
Frank, C. C., pvt., Co. C, 16th Pa. Vol. Inf., wounded, 378.
Frank, Edward P., pvt., Co. C, 34th Inf., U. S. V., wounded, 1192.
Frank, Richard T., pvt., Co. C, 3d U. S. Inf., wounded, 995.
Frank, Royal T., brig. gen., U. S. V., mentioned, 509, 513, 520, 528, 529, 530, 532, 533, 535, 538, 539.
Franking privilege, recommendation relative to, 13.
Franklin, Samuel, pvt., Co. D, 28th Inf., U. S. V., wounded, 1189.
Franks, Benjamin, pvt., Co. E, 25th U. S. Inf., death, 1205.
Frantzen, Joseph, pvt., Co. F, 1st Mont. Vol. Inf., wounded, 995.
Franz, Arthur, pvt., Co. L, 14th U. S. Inf., wounded, 1015.
Franz, Felix, corpl., band, 13th U. S. Inf., death, 1228.
Franz, Friedrik W., pvt., Co. M, 4th U. S. Inf., drowned, 1170.
Frappier, Abraham, pvt., Co. A, 26th Inf., U. S. V., wounded, 1112.
Frazee, Charles W., pvt., Troop A, 3d U. S. Cav., killed, 1126.
Frazer, Clements L., pvt., Co. M, 43d Inf., U. S. V., wounded, 1176.
Frazer, S. J., surg., U. S. V., mentioned, 985.
Frazier, James, pvt., Co. C, 1st Idaho Vol. Inf., killed, 895.
Frazier, Joseph, 1st lieut., 9th U. S. Inf., mentioned, 256, 978.
Fredendall, Ira L., capt., asst. qm., U. S. V., ordered to Taku, China, 463, 482.
Fredericks, Charles W., pvt., Co. E, 22d U. S. Inf., killed, 941.
Fredin, Axel, pvt., Co. M, 4th U. S. Inf., death, 1264.
Free, John J., pvt., Co. K, 6th U. S. Inf., death, 1125.
Freeman, Charles, pvt., Co. B, 38th Inf., U. S. V., death, 1253.
Freeman, Henry B., col., 24th U. S. Inf.; lieut. col., 5th U. S. Inf., mentioned, 238, 255, 1199.
Freeman, James, pvt., Troop C, 11th Cav. U. S. V., killed, 1148.
Freeman, John G., cook, Co. H, 38th Inf., U. S. V., death, 1257.
Freestrom, Tage Fred, pvt., Co. B, 1st Cal. Vol. Inf., death, 830.

French, Charles, capt., 36th Inf., U. S. V., death, 1091.
French, Eugene S., 2d lieut., 1st Mont. Vol. Inf., killed, 915.
French, Francis H., capt., 19th U. S. Inf., mentioned, 1041.
French, William B., pvt., Batty. L, 3d U. S. Art., wounded, 959.
Frey, George W., pvt., Co. H, 16th U. S. Inf., death, 1191.
Frey, Leonard, pvt., Co. L, 18th U. S. Inf., death, 1228.
Friedeck, Charles, pvt., Co. M, 9th U. S. Inf., death, 464.
Friedrick, John H., lieut. col., 13th Minn. Vol. Inf., mentioned, 998.
Friel, James A., late pvt., Co. F, 9th U. S. Inf., mentioned, 486.
Frink, Charles S., 1st sergt., Co. K 1st Ill. Vol. Inf., mentioned, 230.
Frisby, Albert W., pvt., Co. E, 17th U. S. Inf., death, 1223.
Frisch, Herman H., pvt., Co. F, 39th Inf., U. S. V., death, 1160; wounded, 1152.
Frish, Lewis L., pvt., Co. H, 9th U. S. Inf., wounded, 444.
Fritch, Hermon, pvt., Co. K, 23d U. S. Inf., killed, 1140.
Fritsch, Joseph L., pvt., Co. M, 9th U. S. Inf., death, 464; wounded, 454.
Fritscher, Robert E., pvt., Co. L, 1st Nebr. Vol. Inf., wounded, 946.
Fritz, Ernest, pvt., Co. I, 20th Kans. Vol. Inf., wounded, 898.
Fritz, John G., pvt., Co. L, 13th U. S. Inf., wounded, 1113.
Fritzon, Fred C., pvt., Co. E, 13th Minn. Vol. Inf., death, 1027.
Froggatt, Arthur, pvt., Co. H, 9th U. S. Inf., death, 1027.
Fromberg, Gustave, corpl., Co. B, 30th Inf., death, 1196.
Fromherz, Charles, pvt., Co. L, 14th U. S. Inf., death, 488.
Frost, Alfred S., col., 1st S. Dak. Vol. Inf., mentioned, 948.
Fry, Norman M., sergt., Co. L, 33d Inf., U. S. V., killed, 1137.
Fry, Samuel G., pvt., Batty. D, 5th U. S. Art., wounded, 390.
Fryberger, Albert, pvt., Co. C, 34th Inf., U. S. V., killed, 1192.
Frye, Maurice, pvt., Co. E, 30th Inf., U. S. V., wounded, 1199.
Frykman, Oscar, pvt., Co. M, 13th Minn. Vol. Inf., wounded, 916.
Fuesguss, Jacob, pvt., Co. H, 42d Inf., U. S. V., death, 1156.
Fugate, John W., pvt., Hosp. Corps, U. S. A., death, 1062.
Fuller, Dwight M., pvt., Co. L, 14th U. S. Inf., wounded, 454.
Fuller, Frank, pvt., Co. M, 33d Mich. Vol. Inf., mentioned, 218.
Fuller, John, pvt., Co. A, 48th Inf., U. S. V., drowned, 1205.
Fuller, Lawson M., 1st lieut., ord. dept., U. S. A., mentioned, 646, 1041.
Fullon, insurgent general, surrender, 1264.
Fulmer, William H., pvt., Co. C, 27th U. S. Inf., death, 1202.
Fulton, Willis C., pvt., Co. C, 17th U. S. Inf., death, 1149.
Funistas, auxiliary gunboat, mentioned, 321.
Funston, Frederick, brig. gen., U. S. V.:
 Mentioned, 564-566, 575, 576, 578, 898, 977, 1005, 1006, 1256, 1262, 1263, 1265, 1305.
 Praised on account capture of Aguinaldo, 1263.
 Recommended for promotion, 1263; wounded, 983.
Furguson, Frank E., pvt., Co. D, 1st S. Dak. Vol. Inf., wounded, 954.
Furman, John, pvt., Co. C, 48th Inf., U. S. V., death, 1167.
Furman, Quince E., pvt., Co. C, 4th U. S. Inf., wounded, 1109.
Furor, Spanish torpedo destroyer, mentioned, 81.
Furr, Guy A., sergt., Troop B, 11th U. S. V., Cav., killed, 1191.

Gaddy, Charles, pvt., Co. H, 3d U. S. Inf., killed, 1187.
Gaffary, T. St. John, mentioned, 823, 324.
Gage, Henry, pvt., Co. H, 25th U. S. Inf., death, 1233.
Gage, Lyman J., Secretary of Treasury, correspondence, 183, 331; mentioned, 395.
Gage, Roy, pvt., Co. K, 35th Inf., U. S. V., wounded, 1220.
Gaines, Paul, pvt., Co. L, 29th Inf. U. S. V., death, 1125.
Gains, Moseley, pvt., Troop B, 10th U. S. Cav., mentioned, 246.
Galbreath, Hugh, pvt., Co. G, 7th U. S. Inf., mentioned, 204.
Gale, Lewis E., prin. mus., 35th Inf., U. S. V., suicide, 1233.
Galicia, ship, mentioned, 22.
Gallagher, Francis, pvt., Co. I, 27th Inf., U. S. V., disappearance, 1208; reported murdered, 1248.
Gallagher, Hugh J., capt., 3d U. S. Cav.; maj., comsy., U. S. V., mentioned, 468, 472.
Gallagher, Philip, sergt., Co. B, 21st U. S. Inf., death, 1161.
Gallagher, William, pvt., Co. L, 14th U. S. Inf., death, 1095.
Gallaher, James C., pvt., Co. E, 19th U. S. Inf., wounded, 1152.
Gallant, John, corpl., Co. B, 9th U. S. Inf., wounded, 443.
Galleher, John B., 1st lieut., 40th inf., U. S. V., death, 1148, 1150.
Gallivan, Matthew pvt., Co. F, 47th Inf., U. S. V., wounded, 1147.
Galveston, Tex., immune regiments at, for Santiago, 166.
Galvin, Thomas A., corpl., Batty. L, 3d U. S. Art., wounded, 947.
Galvin, Thomas F, pvt., Co. C, 13th Minn. Vol. Inf., wounded, 915.
Galvin, William J, pvt., Co. A, 8th U. S. Inf., mentioned, 214.
Gamble, Charles J., pvt., Co. C 3d U. S. Inf., death, 1015; wounded, 999.
Gamble, Henry, pvt., Co. D, 35th Inf., U. S. V., wounded, 1182.
Gamble, John M., pvt., Batty. K, 3d U. S. Art., death, 1045.
Gamlin, Adolph, pvt., Co. C, 9th U. S. Inf., wounded, 1298.
Ganong, James, pvt., Co. D, 1st Idaho Vol. Inf., death, 917.
Gantenbein, Rudolph, corpl., Co. I, 2d Oreg. Vol. Inf., wounded, 946.
Garber, M. C., editor Courier, mentioned, 316.
Garces, priest in Philippines, mentioned, 1238, 1239.
Garcia, Calixto, brig. gen., Cuban army, mentioned, 40, 51, 54, 64, 68, 74, 78, 87, 125, 175, 185, 235, 261-263.
Garcia, Pantaleon, insurgent general, mentioned, 1076.
Gardener, Cornelius, col., 31st Mich. Vol. Inf.:
 Colonel Wint reports evidence in case of, 1339.
 Completion board on case, 1344
 Mentioned, 71, 511, 512, 515.
 Re to charges against, 1324, 1333, 1334.
 Report as governor of Tayabas, 1317.
 Secretary War directs time be given him to submit evidence, 1346.
Gardenhire, William, 2d lieut., 1st Mont. Vol. Inf., wounded, 901, 906.
Gardinell, Charles, pvt., Co. F, 1st Cal. Vol. Inf., death, 1044.
Gardner, Algernon A., pvt., Co. G, 4th U. S. Inf., death, 967.
Gardner, Benjamin, pvt., Troop D, 4th U. S. Cav., death, 1132.
Gardner, Carl M., pvt., Co. L, 51st Iowa Vol. Inf., wounded, 974.
Gardner, George D., pvt., Co. K, 14th U. S. Inf., wounded, 454.
Gardner, Henry, sergt., Co. F, 47th Inf., U. S. V., wounded, 1185.
Gardner, Homer, pvt., Co. H, 47th Inf., U. S. V., wounded, 1187.
Gardner, James P., pvt., Co. G, 40th Inf., U.S.V., death, 1210.
Gardner, John W., corpl., Co. M, 21st U. S. Inf., death, 1205.

Gardner, Noah E., pvt., Co. G, 3d U. S. Inf., death, 1274.
Gardner, Oliver F., pvt., Co. F, 30th Inf., U. S. V., wounded, 1198.
Gardner, Philip S., sergt., Co. B, 28th Inf., U. S. V., wounded, 1189.
Gardner, Thomas E., pvt., Co. L, 17th U. S. Inf., killed, 1107.
Gardner, William J., pvt., Co. K, 18th U. S. Inf., death, 1217.
Garland, Henry V., pvt., Hosp. Corps, U. S. A., wounded, 1271.
Garretson, George A., brig. gen., U. S. V., mentioned, 44, 61, 77, 80, 81, 85, 93, 97, 101-103, 105, 106, 108, 109, 112, 117-121, 188, 277, 283, 284, 294, 297, 350, 369, 375, 521-523, 667, 674, 678.
Garrett, Andrew S., pvt., Co. B, 37th Inf., U. S. V., wounded, 1087.
Garrett, Edgar H., pvt., Co. C, 40th Inf., U. S. V., wounded, 1150.
Garrett, Peter G., pvt., Co. M, 38th Inf., U. S. V., death, 1253.
Garrett, Sidney T., pvt., Co. F, 13th Minn. Vol. Inf., death, 833.
Garrison, Frank L., pvt., Co. I, 17th U. S. Inf., death, 1008.
Garritty, Michael H., pvt., Co. L, 20th Kans. Vol, Inf., wounded, 954.
Garron, Howard L., pvt., Co. I, 15th U. S. Inf., drowned, 1238.
Garonne, U. S. transport, mentioned, 441, 448, 449, 464, 471, 477, 1057, 1078, 1082, 1084, 1102, 1198, 1207, 1227, 1228, 1244, 1255, 1257.
Garsuch, Leonard, pvt., Sig. Corps, U. S. A., death, 803.
Gartz, William, pvt., Batty. E, 1st U. S. Art., wounded, 1055.
Garvey, James A., pvt., Co. A, 1st Tenn. Vol. Inf., death, 903.
Garvey, John, pvt., Co. L, 9th U. S. Inf., death, 1048.
Garvin, Theodore F., pvt., Co. G, 45th Inf., U. S. V., death, 1208.
Gaskins, John, pvt., Co. L, 49th Inf., U. S. V., drowned, 1185.
Gate City, U. S. transport, mentioned, 60, 63, 65, 67, 69, 72, 88, 95, 122, 192, 198, 210, 211, 227, 588.
Gately, Frank, pvt., Co. B, 23d U. S. Inf., death, 1267.
Gatewood, George, pvt., Co. K, 25th U. S. Inf., death, 1136.
Gatto, Harry S., pvt., Co. B, 27th Inf., U. S. V., wounded, 1231.
Gaughan, James, corpl., Co. E, 9th U. S. Inf., killed, 1307.
Gaujot, Julien E, 1st lieut., 10th U. S. Cav.
Cruel treatment of natives, 1329.
Sentence confirmed by President, 1357.
Trial, 1343.
Gaut, Frank, pvt., Co. I, 1st Mont. Vol. Inf., missing, 902.
Gautier, Conrad, pvt., Co. M, 6th U. S. Inf., death, 1231.
Gavan, Michael B., pvt., Co. H, 30th Inf., U. S. V., death, 1095.
Gavett, Edwin L., pvt., Co. I, 6th U. S. Inf., death, 1016.
Gavigan, Thomas, pvt., Co. C, 26th Inf., U. S. V., death, 1189; wounded, 1182.
Gayer, Henry H., pvt., Co. M, 14th U. S. Inf., death, 1082.
Gaylord, Harry L., Co. E, 18th U. S. Inf., wounded, 1152.
Gearhart, Foy F., pvt., Co. C, 43d Inf., U. S. V., death, 1210.
Gearin, Nicholas, pvt., Co. M, 22d U. S. Inf., wounded, 946.
Gearny, P. D., pvt., Co. G, 16th U. S. Inf., mentioned, 192.
Geary, Dennis, capt., Cal. Heavy Art., mentioned, 769, 770, 772.
Geary, Woodbridge, capt., 13th U. S. Inf., death, 1085.
Geere, Frank, corpl., Co. G, 1st Wyo. Vol. Inf., mentioned, 1045.
Gehleff, Max, pvt., Co. E, 14th U. S. Inf., wounded, 1081.
Gehring, Theodore, pvt., Co. C, 4th U.S. Inf., death, 1130.

Geib, Robert L. C., pvt., Co. G, 13th Minn. Vol. Inf., wounded, 948.
Geiger, Charles G., unassigned recruit, 24th U. S. Inf., death, 1233.
Geiger, Richard, corpl., Co. C, 33d Inf., U. S. V., wounded, 1234.
Geiger, William C., 1st lieut., 14th U. S. Inf., death, 1186; wounded, 1137.
Geisman, Arnold, pvt., Co. K, 71st N. Y. Vol. Inf., mentioned, 229.
Gemas, George B., pvt., Co. D, 10th Pa. Vol. Inf., wounded, 959.
General officers, list of, accompanying Gen. Shafter, 47.
Gentry, Cornelius, pvt., Co. L, 37th Inf., U. S. V., mentioned, 1211.
George, Charles, pvt., Co. D, 44th Inf., U. S. V., wounded, 1167.
George, Dustin L., sergt., Co. H, 43d Inf., U.S. V., killed, 1168.
George, Ernest S., pvt., Co. C, 40th Inf., U. S. V., wounded, 1259.
George W. Elder, U. S. transport, mentioned, 1073, 1087.
Gerhard, Adolf, clerk, General Brooke's headquarters, mentioned, 302.
Gerity, William J., pvt., Troop H, 4th U. S. Cav., captured by insurgents, 1196.
Geronimo, insurgent general, surrender, 1264.
Gerrick, Henry, pvt., Co. E, 11th U. S. Inf., wounded, 390.
Gerstner, John B., corpl., Co. F, 21st U. S. Inf., death, 1021.
Gertz, John, pvt., Co. A, 39th Inf., U. S. V., death, 1205.
Geyer, William, pvt., Co. A, 22d U. S. Inf., wounded, 948.
Ghant, Joseph, pvt., Troop I, 11th U. S. V. Cav., death, 1202.
Gibb, James, pvt., Co. B, 1st S. Dak. Vol. Inf., wounded, 975.
Gibbons, James, Catholic cardinal, mentioned, 831.
Gibbons, John A., pvt., Hosp. Corps, U. S. A., killed, 900.
Gibbons, Webster F., sergt., Co. H, 23d U. S. Inf., killed, 1147.
Gibbs, Frederick, pvt., Co. K, 1st Nebr. Vol. Inf., wounded, 974.
Gibbs, William J., pvt., Co. C, 9th U. S. Inf., wounded, 1298.
Gibman, Walter, pvt., Co. F, 20th U. S. Inf., mentioned, 229.
Gibson, Edward J., capt., 6th Mass. Vol. Inf., wounded, 330.
Gibson, Ernest H., pvt., Co. F, 14th U. S. Inf., wounded, 454.
Gibson, Frank A., pvt., Co. H, 1st Mont. Vol. Inf., wounded, 950.
Gibson, Frederick, pvt., Troop G, 11th U. S. V. Cav., death, 1210.
Gibson, George E., capt., 34th Inf., U. S. V., wounded, 1192.
Gibson, Oral F., pvt., Co. E, 1st Wash. Vol. Inf., missing, 898; wounded, 899.
Gibson, John, lieut. commander, U. S. N., mentioned, 643, 647, 664, 665.
Gibson, William, Co. G, 7th U. S. Inf., mentioned, 206.
Giffin, Ira, A., pvt. Co. E, 1st Nebr. Vol. Inf., death, 830.
Gifford, Willard C., pvt., ——, 30th Inf., U. S. V., death, 1233.
Gihon, Edward J., capt., 6th Mass. Vol. Inf., mentioned, 374.
Gilbert, Bertram C., 2d lieut., Art. Corps, U. S. A., mentioned, 1041.
Gilbert, Nelson, jr., pvt., Co. —, 21st U. S. Inf., wounded, 127.
Gilbert, William, pvt., Co. E, 9th U. S. Inf., wounded, 444.
Gilbert, William L., pvt., Co. K, 1st Nebr. Vol. Inf., wounded, 967, 982.
Gildersleve, Emmet W., pvt., Co. C, 14th U. S. Inf., death, 803.
Giles, Henry, qm. sergt., Co. C, 24th U. S. Inf., death, 1202.
Gillenwater, William H., capt., 31st Inf., U. S. V., mentioned, 1178.

INDEX. 1397

Gillespie, Daniel, pvt., Co. K, 23d U. S. Inf., death, 1161.
Gillespie, George L., col., Engr. Corps, U. S. A.; brig. gen., U. S. V., mentioned, 33, 84, 135, 149, 178, 189, 313.
Gillespie, Thomas, pvt., Co. G, 18th U. S. Inf., death, 1162.
Gillespie, William D., qm. sergt., 1st Idaho Vol. Inf., death, 829.
Gilliardy, William J., pvt., Co. L, 14th U. S. Inf., wounded, 1017.
Gillilan, John, pvt., Co. B, 20th Kans. Vol. Inf., wounded, 898.
Gillilan, John D., pvt., Batty. K, 3d U. S. Art., wounded, 950.
Gillispie, David E., pvt., Co. E, 1st Nebr. Vol. Inf., wounded, 975.
Gillman, John E., corpl., Co. L, 21st U. S. Inf., wounded, 1081.
Gillmore, James C., lieut. commander, U. S. N., prisoner in hands of insurgents, 980, 1124, 1129.
Gilman, Benjamin H., capt., 13th U. S. Inf., mentioned, 124.
Gilmore, John C., brig. gen., U. S. V., correspondence, 58, 62, 63, 75, 291, 344.
  Mentioned, 9, 52, 213, 233, 236, 270, 275, 276, 357, 361, 368, 373, 375, 378, 382, 384, 385, 392, 396, 398, 399-403, 683.
Gilmore, Walter A., sergt., Co. D, 46th Inf., U. S. V., killed, 1257.
Gilpin, Charles W., corpl., Co. B, 34th Inf., U. S. V., death, 1189.
Gilpin, Hiram, pvt., Co. K, 45th Inf., U. S. V., death, 1231.
Gindici, Charles J., sergt. maj., 36th Inf., U. S. V., death, 1082.
Gingras, Aleade, pvt., Co. B, 43d Inf., U. S. V., killed, 1225.
Girard, Alfred C., maj., med. dept., U. S. A., mentioned, 208.
Girton, Charles S., pvt., Co. K, 14th U. S. Inf., wounded, 1017.
Gislason, Bjorn B., pvt., Co. C, 13th Minn. Vol. Inf., wounded, 963.
Givens, George, sergt., Co. M, 49th Inf., U. S. V., killed by comrade, 1234.
Givens, Jacob, pvt., Co. D, 17th U. S. Inf., death, 1180.
Glancey, Francis, pvt., Co. C, 21st U. S. Inf., wounded, 1038.
Glassford, William A., maj., sig. officer, U. S. V., mentioned, 302.
Glazier, Harry M., pvt., Co. L, 13th Minn. Vol. Inf., wounded, 947.
Gleason, Arthur E., pvt., Co. L, 40th Inf., U. S. V., death, 1245.
Gleason, Fred C., corpl., Co. F, 40th Inf., U. S. V., death, 1194.
Gleason, Frederick I., pvt., Co. K, 39th Inf., U. S. V., death, 1164.
Gleason, Harry E., pvt., Co. F, 12th U. S. Inf., death, 1120.
Gleason, James, pvt., Batty. L, 3d U. S. Art., wounded, 895.
Gleerupp, Charles, pvt., Co. L, 4th U. S. Inf., killed, 1042.
Glenn, Edwin F., maj., 5th U. S. Inf.
  Conduct in P. I., 1319.
  Investigation of "water-cure" case, 1328, 1329.
  Mentioned, 1329, 1333, 1343, 1357.
Glenn, William J., col., 14th Pa. Vol. Inf., mentioned, 526.
Glenogle, U. S. transport, mentioned, 1078, 1079, 1091, 1097.
Gloucester, U. S. gunboat, mentioned, 300, 301, 321, 322.
Glover, Frank S., pvt., Co. A, 1st Nebr. Vol. Inf., death, 853.
Glover, George H., pvt., 8th Batty., Field Art., wounded, 1275.
Glover, John A., sergt., Co. A, 1st Nebr. Vol. Inf., death, 829, 830.
Glover, John H., pvt., Co. G, 18th U. S. Inf., killed, 1182.
Glumm, Frank E., pvt., Co. B, 34th Inf., U. S. V., death, 1223.
Glynn, Martin, pvt., Co. G, 18th U. S. Inf., death, 1200.
Gobin, John P. S., brig. gen., U. S. V., mentioned, 521-527.

Godahl, Edwin J., pvt., Co. L, 37th Inf., U. S. V., killed, 1211.
Godfrey, George J., capt., 22d U. S. Inf., killed, 1174; wounded, 124.
Godley, Forest, pvt., Co. G, 7th U. S. Inf., mentioned, 219.
Godon, Joseph I., pvt., Co. C, 9th U. S. Inf., killed, 1297.
Godwin, Edward A., col., 7th and 40th Inf., U. S. V., mentioned, 515, 1148, 1171.
Goebel, Frank H., pvt., Co. B, 1st S. Dak. Vol. Inf., wounded, 975.
Goeke, Albert, corpl., Co. G, 3d U. S. Inf., killed, 1187.
Goethals, George W., lieut. col., chief engr., U. S. V., mentioned, 301, 646.
Goetz, George, pvt., Co. F, 47th Inf., U. S. V., death, 1283.
Goetz, Herman W., pvt., Co. F, 1st Ill. Vol. Inf., mentioned, 218.
Goezenback, Fred, pvt., Co. G, 14th U. S. Inf., wounded, 898.
Goff, Charles J., capt., asst. qm., U. S. V., mentioned, 103.
Golambeski, John, corpl., Troop K, 4th U. S. Cav., killed, 982.
Golden, Ralph, pvt., Batty. K, 3d U. S. Art., wounded, 966.
Golden, Robert B., pvt., Co. B, 9th U. S. Inf., killed, 443, 445.
Goldman, Benin F., corpl., Co. I, 1st Wash. Vol. Inf., wounded, 1015.
Goldman, David, pvt., Co. I, 30th Inf., U. S. V., killed, 1150.
Goldsberry, Frank J., pvt., Co. I, 36th Inf., U. S. V., wounded, 1096.
Goldsmith, David S., pvt., Co. G, 12th U. S. Inf., death, 1003.
Goldsworthy, steamer, mentioned, 66.
Goldthwaite, William B., recruit, 23d U. S. Inf., death, 1070.
Gombert, Charles, pvt., Co. K, 71st N. Y. Vol. Inf., mentioned, 241.
Gómez, Máximo, gen., Cuban army, mentioned, 51, 175, 285, 261, 263.
Gompertz, Paul, pvt., Hosp. Corps, U. S. A., killed, 975.
Gompman, Joseph, pvt., Co. G, 18th U. S. Inf., death, 972.
Gongo, George, pvt., Co. B, 27th Inf., U. S. V., death, 1153.
Gonyea, Barney, pvt., Co. C, 9th U. S. Inf., killed, 443, 445; wounded, 1008.
Gonzales, insgt. maj., mentioned, 719.
Good, Fred, pvt., Batty. K, 3d U. S. Art., killed, 902.
Good, Michael, trumpeter, Troop E, 4th U. S. Cav., drowned, 1185; wounded, 936.
Goodale, Greenleaf A., maj., 23d U. S. Inf., mentioned, 567, 568.
Goodell, Ulysses A., capt., 6 Mass. Vol. Inf., resignation, 374, 376.
Goodling, John W., pvt., Co. H, 13th U. S. Inf., death, 1136.
Goodman, John, pvt., Co. M, 25th U. S. Inf., killed, 1140.
Goodman, W. A., pvt., Batty. D, 6th U. S. Art., killed, 895.
Goodman, Wilhelm I., pvt., Batty. A, Utah Vol. Art., killed, 896.
Goodnow, John, U. S. consul-general, Shanghai, China, mentioned, 449, 450, 474, 484, 1347.
Goodon, Frank A., pvt., Co. A, 14th U. S. Inf., wounded, 898.
Goodreau, Eli, pvt., Co. D, 14th U. S. Inf., death, 1016.
Goodrich, William, sergt., Co. C, 1st N. Y. Vol. Inf., death, 838.
Goodrich, Caspar F., capt., U. S. Navy, mentioned, 125.
Goodrich, Dewane, artif., Co. D, 9th U. S. Inf., death, 1113.
Goodrich, James A., pvt., Co. L, 28th Inf., U. S. V., wounded, 1132.
Googins, Laurence M., pvt., Co. G, 14th U. S. Inf., killed, 453.
Goold, John B., pvt., Co. C, 47th Inf., U. S. V., wounded, 1240.
Goorskey, Pete, corpl., Co. B, 4th U. S. Inf., death, 1017.

Gordon, Archie H., pvt., Co. K, 3d U. S. Inf., rescued, 1129.
Gordon, Charles H., capt., 47th Inf., U. S. V., mentioned, 1061.
Gordon, Fred, pvt., Co. L, 16th U. S. Inf., death, 1201.
Gordon, Lem, pvt., Co. C, 31st Inf., U. S. V., death, 1172.
Gordon, Morris, pvt., Co. L, 13th U. S. Inf., death, 1190.
Gordon, William W., brig. gen., U. S. V., member commission to Cuba, to arrange evacuation, 397.
Mentioned, 55, 403, 517, 547, 549.
Gorgas, William C., maj., med. dept., U. S. A., mentioned, 140.
Gorman, Edward, sergt. and pvt., Co. D, 9th U. S. Inf., wounded, 444, 1064.
Gormly, William F, 1st sergt., Co. E, 9th U. S. Inf., death, 1299.
Gotti, Frank, pvt., Co. I, 1st Mont. Vol. Inf., wounded, 901.
Gottreux, Abraham, pvt., Co. H, 12th U. S. Inf., death, 1060.
Gould, Francis, cook, Co. L, 6th U. S. Inf., death, 1217.
Gould, Frank, corpl., Co. M, 39th Inf., U. S. V., death, 1181.
Gould, Miss Helen M., mentioned, 487.
Gould, Howard, mentioned, 358.
Gould, Thomas J., pvt., Co. I, 47th Inf., U. S. V., wounded, 1155.
Govryck, Charles, pvt., Co. K, 1st Nebr. Vol. Inf., wounded, 914.
Gowing, Louis W., pvt., Co. G, 39th Inf., U. S. V., death, 1174.
Grabow, Frederic, pvt., Co. F, 14th U. S. Inf., death, 1001.
Grabowsky, Joseph, pvt., Troop C, 4th U. S. Cav., death, 972; wounded, 963.
Grace, Benjamin V., pvt., Co. K, 6th U. S. Inf., death, 1132.
Grace, Bertram H., pvt., Co. H, 51st Iowa Vol. Inf., wounded, 981.
Grace, Charles W., pvt., Troop K, 3d U. S. Cav., wounded 1137.
Grace, Leo D., pvt., Co. A, 2d Oreg. Vol. Inf., wounded, 948.
Grady, Edward, pvt., Batty. C, 7th U. S. Art., death, 1288.
Grady, Michael J., pvt., Co. C, 4th U. S. Inf., wounded, 1140.
Grady, Patrick J., maj., 9th Mass. Vol. Inf., mentioned, 193.
Grady, Richard J., pvt., Co. K, 40th Inf., U. S. V., killed, 1166.
Graem, Gus, pvt., Co. L, 71st N. Y. Vol. Inf., mentioned, 193.
Graff, Joseph V., member of Congress, mentioned, 331, 334.
Graffenreid, Elbert B., pvt., Co. C, 9th U. S. Inf., wounded, 1298.
Graft, George W., cook. Troop C, 4th U. S. Cav., death, 1202.
Gragert, John, pvt., Co. K, 3d U. S. Inf., death, 1220.
Graham, Clint W., pvt., Co. I, 14th U. S. Inf., death, 463, 464; wounded, 454.
Graham, Frank A., pvt., Co. E, 1st Nebr. Vol. Inf., wounded, 967.
Graham, James M., 1st lieut., 19th U. S. Inf., mentioned, 1178.
Graham, William M., brig. gen., U. S. A., maj. gen., U. S. V., mentioned, 42, 75, 77, 80, 81, 85, 86, 93, 105, 111, 208, 257, 267, 308, 509, 519, 520, 1178.
Graham, William T., pvt., Co. B, 39th Inf., U. S. V., death, 1213.
Grand Duchess, U. S. transport, mentioned, 75, 77, 96, 133, 138, 139, 192, 198, 273, 275, 277, 280, 291, 293, 341.
Grandy, Luther B., maj., surg., 35th Inf., U. S. V., mentioned, 998.
Grane, Mikal D., pvt., Co. L, 34th Inf., U. S. V., death, 1149.
Grant, Frank A., capt., Utah Vol. Art., mentioned, 938.

Grant, Frederick D., brig. gen., U. S. V., mentioned, 295, 315, 317, 321, 328, 333, 336, 337, 340, 347–349, 352, 354, 357, 360, 362–364, 367, 368, 380, 390, 513, 530, 532, 533, 566, 567, 569, 571–573, 575, 576, 578, 995, 1082, 1115, 1116, 1272.
Grant, Tony, pvt., Co. H, 25th U. S. Inf., wounded, 1160.
Grant, Zeb, pvt., Co. C, 29th Inf., U. S. V., wounded, 1212.
Grant, U. S. transport, mentioned, 416, 418–422, 427, 430–433, 439, 441, 444, 453, 456, 457, 460, 492, 588, 609, 624, 875, 879, 892, 893, 897, 928, 930, 933, 934, 940, 944, 952, 958, 962, 980, 983, 998, 1021, 1027, 1030, 1040, 1044, 1045, 1047, 1061, 1075, 1089, 1096, 1124, 1138, 1142, 1178, 1195, 1205, 1225, 1257, 1262, 1273, 1281, 1282, 1284, 1291, 1304, 1306, 1309, 1316, 1320, 1323, 1326, 1341, 1342.
Grantham, John F., corpl., Co. L, 45th Inf., U. S. V., wounded, 1253.
Grateg, James J., pvt., Batty. K, 3d U. S. Art., wounded, 899.
Gravely, Frank, pvt., Co. H, 27th Inf., U. S. V., death, 1090.
Graves, Daniels, pvt., Co. G, 11th U. S. Inf., wounded, 390.
Gray, Alex., clerk to Paymaster Thrift, mentioned, 254.
Gray, James, pvt., Co. H, 3d U. S. Inf., death, 1197.
Gray, Jesse L., pvt., Co. D, 1st U. S. Inf., wounded, 1261.
Gray, John A., pvt., Batty. K, 3d U. S. Art., wounded, 897.
Gray, John W., pvt., Co. H, 33d Inf., U. S. V., wounded, 1222.
Gray, Lawrence T., pvt., Co. D, 25th U. S. Inf., death, 1243.
Gray, Lincoln G., pvt., Co. L, 16th U. S. Inf., death, 1164.
Gray, Samuel, pvt., Co. M, 45th Inf., U. S. V., death, 1185; wounded, 1182.
Gray, Thomas M., pvt., Co. M, 18th U. S. Inf., death, 1189.
Gray, Ulysses H., pvt., Co. B, 13th U. S. Inf., wounded, 1113.
Gray, William B., pvt., Co. H, 20th U. S. Inf., death, 1016.
Greathouse, John A., pvt., Co. H, 23d U. S. Inf., wounded, 1147.
Greely, Adolphus W., Chief Signal Officer, U. S. A., mentioned, 50, 57, 61, 67, 73, 78, 100, 163, 165, 166, 177, 178, 334.
Green, Charles P., corpl., Co. G, 1st S. Dak. Vol. Inf., wounded, 981.
Green, Frank E., capt., 1st Mont. Vol. Inf., wounded, 981.
Green, Frank W., pvt., Co. C, U. S. Marine Corps, wounded, 460.
Green, Fred E., pvt., Co. I, 1st S. Dak. Vol. Inf., death, 895.
Green, Henry O., pvt., Co. G, 18th U. S. Inf., death, 1150.
Green, James H., pvt., Co. L, 49th Inf., U. S. V., mentioned, 1205.
Green, John F., capt., 33d Inf., U. S. V., wounded, 1101.
Green, Oliver E., pvt., Co. L, 13th U. S. Inf., suicide, 1190.
Green, Robert, pvt., Co. D, 37th Inf., U. S. V., death, 1181.
Green, Walter D., artif., Co. M, 30th Inf., U. S. V., death, 1228.
Green, Warren, pvt., Co. H, 24th U. S. Inf., mentioned, 209.
Green, William, pvt., Co. H, 2d Mass. Vol. Inf., mentioned, 216.
Green, William H., pvt., Troop D, 9th U. S. Cav., death, 1267.
Green, ——, pvt., U. S. Marine Corps, wounded, 459.
Greenan, Philip, 2d lieut., 1st Mont. Vol. Inf., wounded, 915.
Greene, Francis V., maj. gen., U. S. V., mentioned, 548, 552, 553, 556, 667, 674, 678, 686, 701, 711, 716, 758, 765, 781, 834.
Greene, Frank, capt., Sig. Cps., U. S. A., lieut, col., sig. officer, U. S. V., mentioned, 61, 163, 208, 541, 543, 544, 546, 547.
Greene, Henry A., maj., a. a. g., U. S. A., mentioned, 463.
Greene, Marshall, sergt., Co. E, Sig. Corps, U. S. A., death, 1202.

Greenleaf, Charles R., col., med. dept., U. S. A., mentioned, 36–38, 43, 140, 266, 303, 375, 378, 381, 385, 396, 1192, 1198.
Greenlee, Ed, pvt., Co. G, 48th Inf., U. S. V., death, 1168.
Greenough, George G., maj., 7th U. S. Art., mentioned, 1206.
Greens, James A., pvt., Troop B, 4th U. S. Cav., death, 1197.
Greenslit, Fred, C., pvt., D, 1st S. Dak. Vol. Inf., death, 804.
Greenwell, George W., pvt., Hosp. Corps, U. S. A., wounded, 1057.
Gregg, Edwin F., pvt., Co. I, 1st Nebr. Vol. Inf., wounded, 974.
Gregg, John C., 1st lieut., 4th U. S. Inf., killed, 954, 956.
Gregg, John E., pvt., Co. I, 1st Ill. Vol. Inf., mentioned, 229.
Gregg, La Vergne, sergt., Co. M, 22d U. S. Inf., wounded, 946.
Gregory, Delbert, sergt., Co. D, 21st U. S. Inf., wounded, 1287.
Gregory, Louis, pvt., Co. M, 20th U. S. Inf., wounded, 1275.
Gregory, William, pvt., Troop H, 11th U. S. V. Cav., wounded, 1140.
Gregory, repr. Chesapeake and Ohio R. R., mentioned, 296.
Greik, James F., pvt., Co. A, 1st Wash. Vol. Inf., wounded, 896.
Greiner, Joseph, pvt , Co. D, 34th Mich. Vol. Inf., mentioned, 205.
Greller, George, pvt., Co. A, 12th U. S. Inf., death, 1045.
Grennan, James H., pvt., Co. D, 20th U. S. Inf., death, 1095.
Grennan, Lawrence E., corpl., Batty. L, 6th U. S. Art., wounded, 1112.
Gresham, John C., capt., 7th U. S. Cav., mentioned, 344, 345.
Gretzer, John, jr., pvt., Co. D, 1st Nebr. Vol. Inf., wounded, 950.
Grider, Luther E., pvt., Troop F, 3d U. S. Cav., death, 1283.
Griewatz, Peter P., pvt., Troop D, 4th U. S. Cav., death, 1119.
Griffin, Daniel F., pvt., Co. C, 31st Inf., U. S. V., death, 1243.
Griffin, Eugene, col., 1st U. S. V. Engrs., mentioned, 319, 336, 337, 340, 366.
Griffin, E. J., pvt., Co. H, 8th U. S. Inf., mentioned, 219.
Griffin, John L., pvt., Co. I, 19th U. S. Inf., wounded, 1255.
Griffin, Joseph H., corpl., Co. E, 44th Inf., U. S. V., killed, 1173.
Griffin, Thomas, pvt., Co. L, 34th Inf., U. S. V., killed, 1143.
Griffin, Wallie, pvt., Batty. F, 4th U. S Art., death, 1264.
Griffin, William P., pvt., Batty. G, 6th U. S. Art., death, 802.
Griffith, Jesse J., sergt., Co. C, 1st Ill. Vol. Inf., mentioned, 209.
Griffiths, Harold F., pvt., Co. G, 27th Inf., U. S. V., death, 1119.
Griffiths, John J., pvt., Co. L, 20th U. S. Inf., wounded, 937.
Griggs, Austin, pvt., Co. C, 24th U. S. Inf., death, 1132.
Grigsby, Melvin, col., 3d U. S. V. Cav. mentioned, 304, 330, 363, 367, 512.
Grigsby, Robert L., corpl., Co. A, 18th U. S. Inf., killed, 914.
Grils, Alrich J., pvt., Co. H, 34th Mich Vol. Inf., mentioned, 212.
Grimes, Avery, pvt., Co. L, 13th Minn. Vol. Inf., wounded, 947.
Grimes, George M., 1st lieut., 20th U. S. Inf., mentioned, 1019.
Grimes, Samuel, pvt., Co. G, 18th U. S Inf., death, 1153.
Grimm, Charles, unassigned recruit, 18th U. S. Inf., death, 1189.
Grinnell, Merton G., pvt., Co. D, 13th Minn. Vol. Inf., wounded, 915.
Grinsel, Alexander W., pvt., Co. G, 26th Inf., U. S. V., wounded, 1166.

Grinstead, Harry A., pvt., Co. F, 2d U. S. Inf., death, 1253.
Grisard, John S., 1st lieut., 7th U. S. Inf., wounded, 124.
Griscom, Redgway H., pvt., Troop —, 11th Cav., U. S. V., wounded, 1130.
Griswold, Richard S., maj., surg., U. S. V., killed, 1294.
Groesbeck, Stephen W., col., judge advocate, U. S. A., mentioned, 1349.
Groff, ——, member National Relief Commission, distribution of supplies in P. E., 392.
Groh, Joseph, pvt., Co. M, 12th U. S Inf., drowned, 1187.
Groll, Raymond, pvt., Co. I, 36th Inf., U. S. V., death, 1120.
Groome, John C., capt., Philadelphia Troop Cav., mentioned, 316.
Gross, Franklin H., pvt., Co. M, 20th U. S. Inf., wounded, 1275.
Gross, William, pvt., Co. C, 17th U. S. Inf., death, 1223.
Gross, Louis H., 2d lieut., 6th U. S. Inf., mentioned, 83, 124.
Grossman, Damian, pvt., Co. C, 1st Wash. Vol. Inf., death, 907.
Grossman, Emory W., pvt., Co. H, 1st Nebr. Vol. Inf., wounded, 952.
Groth, Heinrich, sergt., Co. A, 17th U. S. Inf., death, 1205.
Grottendick, Charles, pvt., Co. F, 21st U. S. Inf., wounded, 1044.
Grout, Ernest C., pvt., Co. G, 18th U. S. Inf., death, 1258.
Grove, William R., lieut. col., 36th Inf., U. S. V., wounded, 1096.
Grovens, Jeronemé S., mentioned 483.
Grubbs, Haydon Y., 1st lieut., 6th U. S. Inf., killed, 1079.
Gruber, Daniel, pvt., Co. C, 8th U. S. Inf., mentioned, 213.
Gruettert, August, pvt., Co. M, 19th U. S. Inf., death, 1130.
Grundhand, Leroy, pvt., Troop E 4th U. S. Cav., wounded, 947.
Grundy, William, pvt., Co. E, 1st S. Dak.Vol. Inf., wounded, 956.
Guenther, Charles A., pvt., Co. B, 34th Inf., U. S. V., death, 1104.
Guenther, Francis L., brig. gen., U. S. V., mentioned, 519, 520, 522, 523, 524, 526.
Guess, George, corpl., Co. I, 9th U. S. Inf., death, 1063.
Guilbert, Holden P., corpl., Co. I, 13th Minn.Vol. Inf., wounded, 963.
Guinan, Thomas P., pvt., Co. K, 12th U. S. Inf., death, 1066.
Guiney, Patrick W., 2d lieut., 6th U. S. Cav., mentioned, 423.
Guiteras, James, Dr., yellow-fever expert, mentioned, 8.
Guiteras, John, maj., surg., U. S. V., mentioned, 135.
Gumbinger, Jacob, capt., Wilson Batty., Florida State Troops, mentioned, 363.
Gump, Daniel, sergt., Co. B, 27th Inf., U. S. V., wounded, 1231.
Gunderson, Ole, corpl., Co. E, Sig Corps, U.S.A., death, 1082; wounded, 1081.
Gunder, George W., col., 160th Ind. Vol. Inf., mentioned, 518.
Gurney, John A., 2d lieut., 24th U. S. Inf., killed, 124.
Gurule, Petronilo, pvt., Co. L, 34th Inf., U. S. V. death, 1149.
Guss, Ellis L., corpl., Co. C, 47th Inf., U. S. V., death, 1191.
Gussie, U. S. transport, mentioned, 80, 92, 98, 192, 198, 275, 278, 279, 282.
Gustafson, Oscar, pvt., Batty. L, 3d U. S. Art., wounded, 946.
Guthrie, John B., capt., 13th U. S. Inf., wounded, 124.
Guy, Robert C., pvt., Troop D, 2d U. S. Cav., mentioned, 244.
Guyer, Charles E., pvt., Co. K, 40th Inf., U. S. V., killed, 1162.
Guynn, Elzy J., corpl., Co. L, 33d Inf., U. S. V., wounded, 1152.

Guyton, Earl E., pvt., Co. A, 17th U. S. Inf., drowned, 1194.
Gwinn, Arthur, 1st sergt., Co. D, 32d Inf., U. S. V., death, 1162.
Gyger, George R., capt., sig. officer, U. S. V., mentioned, 554, 555.
Gypsum King, U. S. transport, mentioned, 378.
Haag, Braney, pvt., Batty. G, 3d U. S. Art., killed, 899.
Haan, Peter D., pvt., Co. D, 34th Mich. Vol. Inf., mentioned, 205.
Haan, William G., 1st lieut., 3d U. S. Art., mentioned, 558, 559, 561.
Habana, evacuation commission to meet at, 751.
Hackett, Adrian L., jr., pvt., Co. M, 51st Iowa Vol. Inf., wounded, 974.
Hackett, Frank W., Asst. Secy. Navy, mentioned, 410, 411, 413, 414, 422, 423, 436, 444, 468.
Hackett, Powhatan T., pvt., Co. F, 20th Kans. Vol. Inf., death, 879.
Hackworth, Charles A., pvt., Co. D, 30th Inf. U. S. V., wounded, 1150.
Haeffele, Robert, pvt., Co. H, 22d U. S. Inf., death, 1088.
Haefner, Charles L., pvt., Co. L, 32d Inf., U. S. V., death, 1142.
Haefner, John, corpl., Co. I, 8th U. S. Inf., death, 1283.
Hagadorn, Ernst, 2d lieut., 16th U S. Inf., mentioned, 1041, 1240.
Hagberg, Ole G., sergt., Co. D, 1st Idaho Vol. Inf., death, 861.
Hagebaum, William, artif., Co. F, 22d U. S. Inf., wounded, 948.
Hagen, Faitz O., pvt., Hosp. Corps, U. S. A., death, 1213.
Haggerty, Michael, pvt., Co. H, 36th Inf., U. S. V., wounded, 1096.
Hahr, W. H., clerk, Railway Mail Service, mentioned, 298.
Haight, George A., pvt., Co. L, 37th Inf., U. S. V., killed, 1211.
Hagland, Andrew, pvt., Co. M, 37th Inf., U. S. V., wounded, 1148.
Hague, Harry, pvt., Co. H, 8th Ohio Vol. Inf., mentioned, 195.
Haines, Harry S., pvt., Co. C, 4th Ohio Vol. Inf., wounded, 378.
Hains, John P., mentioned, 388.
Hains, Peter C., brig. gen., U. S. V., mentioned, 71, 76, 82, 95, 96, 98, 117, 133, 137, 138, 145, 274, 277, 286, 288–290, 292, 294–296, 305, 306, 312, 313, 317, 321, 328, 333, 365, 378, 511, 513–515.
Hairston, Peter, pvt., Co. H, 48th Inf., U. S. V., death, 1168.
Hake, Charles W., pvt., Co. F, 35th Inf., U. S. V., death, 1236.
Hakel, George E., pvt., Astor Batty., U. S. A., wounded, 761.
Hale, Earl, pvt., Co. H, 34th Inf., U. S. V., wounded, 1225.
Hale, Edward, pvt., Co. A, 21st U. S. Inf., death, 1161.
Hale, Ezekiel E., pvt., Co. B, 9th U. S. Inf., death, 464.
Hale, Irving, brig. gen., U. S. V., mentioned, 557, 565, 835; wounded, 981.
Hale, Irwing W., pvt., Co. D, 42d U. S. V., death, 1202.
Hale, Jesse A., pvt., Co. A, 14th U. S. Inf., killed, 895.
Hale, Harry C., maj., 44th Inf., U. S. V., mentioned, 686, 982.
Haler, William, pvt., Co. L, 17th U. S. Inf., wounded, 1222, 1225.
Haley, Charles E., pvt., Co. G, 22d U. S. Inf., wounded, 941.
Haley, Frank, pvt., Co. H, 48th Inf., U. S. V., death, 1178.
Haley, Robert H., pvt., Co. K, 22d U. S. Inf., wounded, 966.
Halfry, Frank J., pvt., Co. E, 12th U. S. Inf., death, 1052.
Hall, Curt E., pvt., Co. L, 42d Inf., U. S. V., death, 1128.
Hall, Fred, pvt., Co. I, 1st Mont. Vol. Inf., killed, 900.
Hall, George W., pvt., Co. G, 1st Idaho Vol. Inf., death, 895.

Hall, Henry A., pvt., Troop B, 3d U. S. Cav., death, 1238.
Hall, Henry N., sergt., Co. L, 21st U. S. Inf., death, 1189.
Hall, Homer A., pvt., Co. A, 17th U. S. Inf., wounded, 999.
Hall, James O., pvt., Co. E, 9th U. S. Inf., killed, 460.
Hall, John S., pvt., Co. K, 39th Inf., U. S. V., death, 1180.
Hall, Martin G., pvt., Co. F, 1st Mont. Vol. Inf., wounded, 981.
Hall, Parker J., pvt., Batty. B, Utah Vol. Art., wounded, 947.
Hall, Robert H., brig. gen., U. S. V., mentioned, 55, 535–538, 541, 556, 562–567, 569, 570, 573, 574, 576, 578, 585, 683, 982, 1001, 1042, 1044.
Hall, Sam A., corpl., Co. C, 30th Inf., U. S. V., death, 1208.
Hall, William, pvt., Troop E, 11th U. S. V. Cav., death, 1228.
Hall, William E., corpl., Co. D, 27th Inf., U. S. V., death, 1280.
Hall, William J., sergt., Co. H, 43d Inf., U. S. V., death, 1168, 1174.
Hall, William P., lieut. col., a. a. g., U. S. A., mentioned, 1356.
Hall, William R., maj., med. dep., death, 1265; mentioned, 145.
Hallaner, Conrad, corpl., Co. D, 14th U. S. Inf., wounded, 1008.
Hallecka, Joseph, pvt., Co. D, 18th U. S. Inf., death, 1109.
Haller, Joseph B., pvt., Co. C, 12th U. S. Inf., death, 1219.
Hallinan, James J., pvt., Co. G, 27th Inf., U. S. V., death, 1161.
Hallor, Howard, pvt., Co. C, 1st Idaho Vol. Inf., wounded, 897.
Haln, Gus P., pvt., Co. A, 1st U. S. Inf., wounded, 1250.
Halter, John H., pvt., Co. D, 6th U. S. Inf., death 1274.
Haly, Thomas C., pvt., Co. L, 1st Cal. Vol. Inf., wounded, 914.
Hamberg, Henry E., pvt., Co. L, 35th Inf., U. S. V., death, 1168.
Hamberger, Jacob, pvt., Co. H, 18th U. S. Inf., death, 960.
Hamby, James P., sergt., Co. C, 29th Inf., U. S. V., wounded, 1212.
Hamer, Thomas R., capt., 1st Idaho Vol. Inf., mentioned, 920; wounded, 901.
Hamill, W. D., pvt., Troop A, 2d U. S. Cav., mentioned, 183.
Hamilton, Alston, 1st lieut., 1st U. S. Art., mentioned, 1095.
Hamilton, Edwin E., pvt., Co. L, 43d Inf., U. S. V., killed, 1250.
Hamilton, Ernest L., 1st sergt., Co. E, 30th Inf., U. S. V., wounded, 1188.
Hamilton, Jack, pvt., Co. E, 13th Minn. Vol. Inf., wounded, 948.
Hamilton, Jack, pvt., Co. E, 3d U. S. Inf., wounded, 961.
Hamilton, James, sergt., Co. B, 21st U. S. Inf., death, 1099.
Hamilton, James W., pvt., Troop B, 3d U. S. Cav., mentioned, 229.
Hamilton, John F. J., corpl., Co. H, 43d Inf., U. S. V., killed, 1168.
Hamilton, John M., lieut. col., 9th U. S. Cav., killed, 124.
Hamilton, Thomas V., pvt., Co. E, 30th Inf., U. S. V., death, 1215.
Hammel, John, pvt., Co. G, 17th U. S. Inf., wounded, 1051.
Hammer, John G., pvt., Co. M, 8th U. S. Inf., death, 1236.
Hammerberg, James C., corpl, Co. G, 20th Kans. Vol. Inf., wounded, 954.
Hammermanson, Henry, pvt., Co. A, 47th Inf., U. S. V., wounded, 1176.
Hammerson, Alfred T., pvt., B, 1st Cal. Vol. Inf., wounded, 761.
Hammond, Charles A., pvt., Co. F, 20th Kans. Vol. Inf., wounded, 897.
Hammond, Harold, 1st lieut., 9th U. S. Inf., wounded, 428, 429.

INDEX. 1401

Hammond, Pleasant H., sergt., Co. G, 24th U. S. Inf., death, 1236.
Hammons, David H., pvt., Co. F, 9th U. S. Inf., wounded, 444.
Hampson, Percy, sergt., Co. A, 44th Inf., U. S. V., killed, 1192.
Hampton, Ed. W., pvt., Co. H, 2d Oreg. Vol. Inf., killed, 914.
Hampton, Robert L., pvt., Co. E, 9th U. S. Inf., wounded, 1299.
Hanche, Fred, pvt., Co. B, 1st S. Dak. Vol. Inf., wounded, 975.
Hancock, William F., capt., 6th U. S. Art., reduction, 1241.
Hancock, U. S. transport, mentioned, 432, 441, 446, 448, 456, 463, 603, 620, 936, 959, 960 962, 967, 969, 986, 1005, 1016, 1026, 1041, 1044, 1106, 1123, 1139, 1174, 1179, 1199, 1215, 1216, 1223, 1254, 1258, 1265, 1270, 1280, 1286, 1291, 1300,-1302, 1303, 1305, 1310, 1314, 1321, 1323, 1332, 1340, 1341, 1343.
Hand, John L., pvt., Troop M, 4th U. S. Cav., death, 1090.
Hand, Norman E., pvt., Co. L, 20th Kans. Vol. Inf., death, 886.
Hane, Charles H., pvt., Co. L, 12th U. S. Inf., wounded, 1057.
Haniacker, Noble W., pvt., Co. C, 4th Ohio Vol. Inf., wounded, 378.
Hankins, Charles E., pvt., Co. F, 45th Inf., U. S. V., death, 1215.
Hankley, Frank, pvt., Co. F, 40th Inf., U. S. V., death, 1192.
Hanley, William M., pvt., Co. A, 6th U. S. Inf., killed, 1075.
Hanks, Cornelius, pvt., Hosp. Corps, U. S. A., mentioned, 241.
Hann, Matthew E., pvt., Co. C, 36th Inf., U. S. V., wounded, 1051.
Hanna, Philip C., U. S. consul, San Juan, P. R., mentioned, 264, 265, 306, 344, 366, 367.
Hanna, Marcus A., U. S. Senator, mentioned, 336, 339, 679.
Hannigs, Carl, pvt., Co. D, 12th U. S. Inf., wounded, 1059, 1227.
Hanrahan, John M., pvt., Co. M, 25th Inf., U. S. V., death, 1200.
Hansa, German war ship, to visit Manila, P. I., 1281.
Hanscom, Eugene, 1st sergt., Co. A, 13th Minn. Vol. Inf., wounded, 963.
Hansen, Albert S., pvt., Co. F, 13th Minn. Vol. Inf., mentioned, 762; wounded, 761.
Hansen, Andrew, seaman, transport Relief, drowned, 477.
Hansen, Christ E., pvt., Co. K, 3d Inf., killed, 1197.
Hansen, Francis E., corpl., Co. L, 1st Nebr. Vol.
Hansen, George, pvt., Co. A, 1st Nebr. Vol. Inf., death, 829; wounded, 760.
Hansen, Henry E., pvt., Co. K, 16th U. S. Inf., death, 1164.
Hansen, Herman, pvt., Batty. G, 3d U. S. Art., wounded, 899.
Hansen, Isadore, pvt., Co. I, 27th Inf., U. S. V., killed, 1212.
Hansen, James, pvt., Co. H, 1st Idaho Vol. Inf., wounded, 897.
Hansen, Nels, pvt., Hosp. Corps, U. S. A., death, 1217.
Hansen, Nicholas, pvt., Co. A, 13th Minn. Vol. Inf., wounded, 971.
Hansen, Samuel E., pvt., Co. B, 18th U. S. Inf., death, 1164.
Hanson, Charles, pvt., Co. C, 40th Inf., U. S. V., killed, 1182.
Inf., death, 979; wounded, 899, 975.
Hanson, Otto O., corpl., Co. A, 6th U. S. Inf., wounded, 1202.
Hanson, Walter N., pvt., Co. L, 1st Wash. Vol. Inf., killed, 895.
Hapner, Charles E., pvt., Co. I, 17th U. S. Inf., wounded, 1107.
Harbach, Abram A., lieut. col., 3d U. S. Inf., mentioned, 544, 545.
Harber, Richard B., pvt., Co. D, 32d Inf., U. S. V., death, 1162.
Harbeson, James P., 1st lieut., 12th U. S. Inf., wounded, 1015.
Harbour, Benjamin A., pvt., Co. I, 14th U. S. Inf., wounded, 895.

Hard, Curtis V., col. 8th Ohio Vol. Inf., mentioned, 203, 338.
Harden, Edward W., reappointment as secretary Philippine Commission, 884.
Harden, Frank M., pvt., Co. K, 1st Nebr. Vol. Inf., death, 840.
Harden, Richard, 1st lieut., 1st Dist. Columbia Vol. Inf., mentioned, 216.
Harden, Rutledge, pvt., Co. C, 12th U. S. Inf., death, 1243.
Harden, William K., pvt., Co. G, 48th Inf., U. S. V., death, 1234.
Hardenberg, Raymond W., 2d lieut., 4th U. S. Inf., mentioned, 1041.
Hardin, Edward T., col., 29th Inf., U. S. V., mentioned, 1081.
Harding, Sherman, pvt., Co. I, 1st Wash. Vol. Inf., killed, 895.
Hardwick, Arthur, pvt., Co. D, 16th U. S. Inf., killed, 1152.
Hardy, Alexander W., corpl., Co. G, 1st S. Dak. Vol. Inf., wounded, 949.
Hardy, Andrew, pvt., Co. K, 49th Inf., U. S. V., killed, 1229.
Hardy, Samuel, pvt., Co. I, 49th Inf., U. S. V., death, 1190.
Hardy, Samuel, pvt., Co. H, 48th Inf., U. S. V., death, 1234.
Hardy, Thomas, pvt., Co. C, 17th U. S. Inf., honorable discharge, 900.
Hardy, William, pvt., Co. D, 16th U. S. Inf., killed, 1075.
Hare, Luther R., brig. gen., U. S. V.:
Mentioned, 1116, 1122, 1124, 1128, 1129, 1216, 1257.
Pursuit of insurgents, 1122.
Lt. Gillmore and party, 1124.
Rescue of American prisoners, 1128, 1218.
Hare, Thomas D., hosp. stewd., U. S. A., killed, 1152; mentioned, 662.
Hargrave, James W., pvt., Co. L, 22d U. S. Inf., death, 1208.
Harkins, Daniel O., pvt., Co. L, 3d U. S. Inf., wounded, 1232.
Harlow, Alfred, pvt., Batty. K, 3d U. S. Art., wounded, 946.
Harlton, John J., 1st sergt., Co. H, 1st Wash. Vol. Inf., wounded 967.
Harman, Willett M., pvt., Co. D, 22d U. S. Inf., wounded, 934.
Harms, William J., pvt., Co. L 4th U. S. Inf., death, 947.
Harned, Pomroy, pvt., Co. A, 14th U. S. Inf., wounded, 1015.
Harney, Thomas W. P., pvt., Co. E, 14th U. S. Inf., death, 831.
Harney, William E., corpl., Co. C, 31st Inf., U. S. V., death, 1196.
Harper, William D., pvt., Hosp. Corps, U. S. A., killed, 1220.
Harpster, Edward L., pvt., Co. E, 47th Inf., U. S. V., wounded, 1187.
Harpold, Herbert B., sergt., Co. G, 33d Inf., U. S. V., wounded, 1101.
Harriff, Peter J., pvt., Co. C, 51st Iowa Vol. Inf., wounded, 1051.
Harrington, James, qm. sergt., Co. A, 14th U. S. Inf., death, 1070.
Harrington, James, pvt., Co. G, 2d Oreg. Vol. Inf., killed, 991.
Harrington, Patrick H., pvt., Co. D, 43d Inf., U. S. V., death, 1191.
Harris, Albert, pvt., Co. M, 25th U. S. Inf., death, 1228.
Harris, Charles A., pvt., Troop A, 3d U. S. Cav., killed, 1163.
Harris, Edward, corpl., Co. F, 21st U. S. Inf., death, 1090.
Harris, Edward K., pvt., Co. K, 20th Kans. Vol. Inf., wounded, 976.
Harris, Eldridge, pvt., Co. B, 34th Inf., U. S. V., killed, 1206.
Harris, Harry S., pvt., Co. B, 20th Kans. Vol. Inf., wounded, 901.
Harris, Henry S. T., maj., chief surg., U. S. V., opinion as to health of army in Cuba, 201.
Harris, Joseph, pvt., Troop A, 3d U. S. Cav., death, 1174.
Harris, Lawrence V., pvt., Co. I, 21st U. S. Inf., death, 1086.

Harris, Matthias L., corpl., Co. I, 14th U. S. Inf., death, 1086.
Harris, Robert L., pvt., Co. B, 33d Inf., U. S. V., wounded, 1216.
Harris, Samuel P., pvt., Co. H, 33d Inf., U. S. V., missing, 1222.
Harris, Walter W., pvt., Co. E, 40th Inf., U. S. V., death, 1136.
Harris, William C., pvt., Co. C, 44th Inf., U.S. V., wounded, 1212.
Harrison, Charles, pvt., Co. H, 26th Inf., U. S. V., death, 1130.
Harrison, Charles F., pvt., Co. F, 22d U. S. Inf., mentioned 197.
Harrison, Oatis, pvt., Co. K, 34th Inf., U .S. V., killed, 1189.
Harrison, Webber, corpl., Co. G, 12th U. S. Inf., drowned, 997.
Harrison, William, pvt., Co. K, 13th U. S. Inf., death, 1056.
Harrison, William H., pvt., Co. I, 1st S. Dak. Vol. Inf., wounded, 981.
Harrison, William R., 2d lieut., 47th Inf., U. S. V., wounded, 1187.
Harsch, August, pvt., Co. C, 4th U. S. Inf., killed, 1130.
Hart, Henry F., corpl., Co. F, 42d Inf., U. S. V., killed, 1176.
Hart, James, oiler on *Yorktown*, death, 1090.
Hart, James M., pvt., Co. A, 9th U. S. Inf., death, 1113.
Hart, Robert, Sir, Chief, Chinese Customs service, mentioned, 469.
Hart, William, pvt., Troop G, 4th U. S. Cav., death, 1213.
Hart, William H., pvt., Co. K, 27th Inf., U. S. V., killed, 1231.
Harter, Charles E., pvt., Co. H, 18th U. S. Inf., death, 1132.
Harter, Oliver L., pvt., Co. A, 31st Inf., U. S. V., murdered by Moros, 1236.
Hartfield, John, pvt., Co. D, 13th Minn. Vol. Inf., wounded, 919.
Harting, Edwin A., 1st lieut., 1st S. Dak. Vol. Inf., drowned, 904.
Harting, William, corpl., Co. L, 13th U. S. Inf., death, 1060.
Hartley, Alfred, pvt., Troop F, 3d U. S. Cav., suicide, 1234.
Hartley, James, pvt., Co. D, 13th Minn. Vol. Inf., wounded, 902.
Hartman, Theodore, pvt., Co. H, 8th U. S. Inf., mentioned, 214.
Hartman, William H., pvt., Co. B, 43d Inf.,U. S. V., death, 1256.
Hartmann, Edward T., 1st lieut., 19th U. S. Inf., mentioned, 1041.
Hartrigsen, Albert W., pvt., Troop E, 4th U. S. Cav., accidentally shot, 931, 959.
Hartsfield, Samuel E., pvt., Troop A, 6th U. S. Cav., wounded, 466.
Hartwell, J. A., Catholic priest, mentioned, 402.
Hartwick, Herbert L., sergt., Co. K, 9th U. S. Inf., wounded, 1038.
Harvard, auxiliary cruiser, mentioned, 49, 55, 78, 80, 87, 91, 93, 96, 97, 102, 103, 108, 223, 245, 313, 598, 599, 602.
Harvey, Eugene A., pvt., Co. B, 13th Minn. Vol. Inf., wounded, 963.
Harvey, Edward B., pvt., Co. I, 1st Mont. Vol. Inf., wounded, 976.
Harvey, James C., pvt., Co. I, 8th U. S. Inf., killed, 1281.
Harvey, John, pvt., Co. K, 25th U. S. Inf.,wounded, 1132.
Harvey, Joseph J., sergt., Co. A, 47th Inf., U.S. V., wounded, 1176.
Harwood, Justice W., civilian, mentioned, 246.
Hasbrouck, Henry C., brig. gen., U. S. V., mentioned, 63, 65, 547, 549–555.
Haskell, A., pvt., Co. I, 1st S. Dak. Vol. Inf., wounded, 895.
Haskell, Charles W., corpl., Co. L, 1st Colo. Vol. Inf., wounded, 937.
Haskell, Joseph T., lieut. col., 17th U. S. Inf., mentioned, 83; wounded, 124.
Haskell, Harry L., capt., 12th U. S. Inf., wounded, 124.
Hassard, Morley L., pvt., Co. A, 1st Wyo. Vol. Inf., death, 836.

Hassaurek, Frank, 2d lieut., Co. K, 17th U. S. Inf., death, 993.
Hassett, George, pvt., Co. B, 33d Mich Vol. Inf., detailed with Miss Clara Barton, 214.
Hasson, John P., 2d lieut., 35th Inf., U. S. V., wounded, 1162.
Hast, William, corpl., Co. H, 4th U. S. Inf., death, 993.
Hastings, Byron F., pvt., Co. I, 1st S. Dak. Vol. Inf., wounded, 948.
Hatfield, Adrian, pvt., Co. K, 20th Kans. Vol. Inf., death, 952; wounded, 952.
Hatfield, Charles A. P., lieut. col., 5th U. S. Cav., mentioned, 1344.
Hatfield, John W., sergt., Troop F, 11th U. S. V. Cav., murdered, 1148; wounded, 1166.
Haught, Joseph C., pvt., Co. K, 41st Inf., U. S. V., death, 1267.
Haughwont, Charles, 1st lieut., 1st Colo. Vol. Inf., wounded, 895.
Haugse, Arne, artif., Co. K, 1st S. Dak. Vol. Inf., wounded, 948.
Hauk, Melvin M., pvt., Troop B, 11th Cav., U.S.V., death, 1229.
Hause, Adam, pvt., Co. F, 14th U. S. Inf., wounded, 454.
Hauser, John, sergt., Co. G, 14th U. S. Inf., wounded, 460.
Havana, steamship, mentioned, 592, 624, 625.
Havard, Valery, maj., med. dept., U. S. A., mentioned, 175, 184, 192, 217.
Opinion as to health of army in Cuba, 201.
Haven, George, corpl., Co. D, 1st Ill. Vol. Inf., mentioned, 209.
Havens, Richard F., pvt., Co. H, 21st U. S. Inf., death, 1020.
Haverman, Aaron P., pvt., Co. K, 32d Inf., U. S. V., death, 1217.
Haviland, Albert, pvt., Co. F, 1st Colo. Vol. Inf., death, 917.
Hawaiian Islands:
Attached to Department of California, 726
Garrison for, 726, 728, 733.
Military station in, site for, 733.
Organization of volunteer battalion, 743.
Provision for officers and men left at, 739.
Transports to carry mail to, 702.
Hawes, Herbert, corpl., Co. H, 35th Inf., U. S. V., death, 1248.
Hawkins, Alexander L., col., 10th Pa. Vol. Inf., mentioned, 658, 659, 1062; wounded, 981.
Hawkins, Amasa J., pvt., Co. I, 13th Minn. Vol. Inf., death, 852.
Hawkins, Frank B., 1st. lieut., 10th Pa. Vol. Inf., mentioned, 1001.
Hawkins, Hamilton S., brig. gen., U. S. V.:
Mentioned, 47, 74, 83, 100, 116, 181, 145, 541, 548.
Recommended for promotion, 104.
Wounded, 124.
Hawkins, Holmer E., pvt., Batty. K, 3d U. S. Art., wounded, 897.
Hawkins, Robert W., pvt., Co. B, 1st S. Dak. Vol. Inf., wounded, 975.
Hawley, Henry L., pvt., Co. L, 28th Inf., death, 1260.
Haworth, Benjamin, pvt., Co. C, 3d U. S. Inf., death, 1132.
Hawthorne, Wister, pvt., Co. C, 2d Oreg. Vol. Inf., death, 886.
Haxton, Ralph C., corpl., Co. C, 4th U. S. Inf., wounded, 1086.
Hay, John, Secy. of State, correspondence, 306, 344, 346, 358, 387, 414, 424, 427, 428, 430, 432, 433, 436, 437, 440, 449–451, 454, 455, 457, 467, 475, 484, 1119.
Hayden, Frank C., pvt., Co. D, 14th U. S. Inf., death, 861.
Hayden, Thomas, pvt., Astor Batty., U. S. A., wounded, 760.
Hayes, B. C., pvt., Co. B, 20th U. S. Inf., mentioned, 209.
Hayes, Denis L., pvt., Co. F, 26th Inf., U. S. V., killed, 1150; mentioned, 1144, 1145.
Hayes, Denny, pvt., Co. E, 22d U. S. Inf., death, 997.
Hayes, Edward M., lieut. col., 4th U. S. Cav., mentioned, 1100, 1103, 1138, 1139.
Hayes, John E., pvt., Co. I, 31st Inf., U. S. V., death, 1271.

Hayes, John F., corpl., Co. A, 46th Inf., U. S. V., death, 1213.
Hayes, John W., pvt., Co. B, 9th U. S. Inf., death, 1070.
Hayes, Patrick, pvt., Co. M, 21st U. S. Inf., death, 1185.
Hayes, Tilden H., pvt., Co. C, 33d Inf., U. S. V., death, 1197.
Hayes, William J., pvt., Co. G, 1st Wash. Vol. Inf., wounded, 897.
Hayes, ——, corpl., Co. H, 1st Mcnt. Vol. Inf., missing, 895.
Hayes, Webb C., maj., 1st Ohio Vol. Cav., mentioned, 284, 287, 350, 351, 361, 366, 369.
Hayne, Arthur P., 1st lieut., Batty. A, Cal. Vol. Art., to collect information for Secretary of Agriculture, 803, 804.
Haynes, Joseph, pvt., Troop E, 9th U. S. Cav., mentioned, 206.
Haynes, Lee V., pvt., Co. C, 12th U. S. Inf., death, 1236.
Haynes, Samuel K., pvt., Co. D, 4th U. S. Inf., wounded, 1017.
Hays, William J., pvt., Co. G, 1st Wash. Vol. Inf., wounded, 897.
Hayson, Thomas R., capt., 32d Inf., U. S. V., mentioned, 1126.
Haywood, John H., pvt., Co. H, 40th Inf., U. S. V., killed, 1183.
Hazard, Howard D., pvt., Co. E, 1st Wash. Vol. Inf., wounded, 914.
Hazzard, Oliver P. M., 1st lieut., 11th Cav., U. S. V., mentioned, 1262.
Hazzard, Russell T., capt., 11th Cav., U. S. V., mentioned, 992, 1262.
Haze, Henry, pvt., Co. A, 1st Cal. Vol. Inf., death, 1151.
Heaberling, William H., corpl., Co. G, 3d U. S. Inf., death, 957; wounded, 946.
Head, Claud F., mus., Co. A, 1st Nebr. Vol. Inf., wounded, 760.
Headlee, D. J. C., pvt., Co. A, 2d Oreg. Vol. Inf., wounded, 946.
Heafnoe, Harry, pvt., Troop G, 1st U. S. V. Cav., killed, 61.
Heald, Edwin W., pvt., Co. G, 1st S. Dak. Vol. Inf., wounded, 996.
Healy, James, pvt., Co. I, 18th U. S. Inf., death, 856.
Healy, John, pvt., Batty. K, 3d U. S. Art., death, 1066.
Healy, John M., pvt., Co. K, 17th U. S. Inf., death, 1132.
Healy, Patrick J., pvt., Co. F, 34th Mich. Vol. Inf., mentioned, 206.
Healy, Thomas, pvt., Co. M, 13th U. S. Inf., wounded, 1010.
Healy, Thomas F., pvt., Co. M, 10th U. S. Inf., death, 1008.
Heaps, William W., pvt., Co. D, 6th U. S. Inf., death, 1255; wounded, 1251.
Heard, Floyd H., pvt., Co. H, 33d Inf., U. S. V., wounded, 1222.
Heartery, Richard, messenger, General Brooke's headquarters, mentioned, 302.
Heath, Herbert L., capt., 2d Oreg. Vol. Inf., wounded, 984.
Heath, Louis C., pvt., Co. G, 71st N. Y. Vol. Inf., mentioned, 216.
Heath, Ulysses G., pvt., Co. K, 48th Inf., U. S. V., death, 1197; wounded, 1176.
Heatwole, Joel P., member of Congress, mentioned, 347.
Heck, Walter, pvt., Co. K, 37th Inf., U. S. V., wounded, 1198.
Heckathorn, Jerry A., pvt., Co. K, 14th U. S. Inf., wounded, 898.
Hecker, Frank J., col., ch. qm., U. S. V., mentioned, 102, 132, 137, 222, 291, 292, 305, 312, 336, 349.
Heckerman, Gerhart, corpl., Co. H, 9th U. S. Inf., wounded, 444.
Heckman, Henry M., pvt., Co. G, 1st Nebr. Vol. Inf., wounded, 955.
Hedekin, Charles A., 1st lieut., 3d U. S. Cav., mentioned, 457.
Hedges, Herbert, pvt., Co. B, 1st Nebr. Vol. Inf., wounded, 926, 955.
Hedges, William T., pvt., Co. M, 37th Inf., U. S. V., death, 1196.

Hedrick, Don C., pvt., Co. G, 36th Inf., U. S. V., death, 1249.
Heeb, George, pvt., Co. H, 18th U. S. Inf., death, 1280.
Heely, Frank H., pvt., Hosp. Corps, U. S. A., death, 831.
Heer, William, pvt., Troop I, 4th U. S. Cav., wounded, 981.
Hefferan, Joseph F., pvt., Co. A, 3d U. S. Inf., death, 1274.
Heflin, Joseph H., pvt., Co. E, 20th Kans. Vol. Inf., wounded, 946.
Hegel, Edward H., pvt., Co. E, 30th Inf., U. S. V., death, 1208.
Hegner, Harry H., pvt., Co. E, 1st Idaho Vol. Inf., wounded, 1008.
Hegwein, Frederick, pvt., Co. H, 27th Inf., U. S. V., death, 1146.
Hehl, John B., pvt., Co. M, 14th U. S. Inf., wounded, 454.
Heibeck, Louis, blacksmith, Batty. D, 6th U. S. Art., wounded, 925.
Heiberg, Elvin R., 1st Lieut., 6th U. S. Cav., mentioned, 421.
Heichener, John, pvt., Co. K, 23d U. S. Inf., killed, 1052.
Heide, Thomas A., pvt., Co. D, 6th U. S. Inf., death, 1119.
Heidt, Grayson V., 2d lieut., 3d U. S. Cav., mentioned, 1221.
Heilig, William, pvt., Troop G, 11th U. S. V. Cav., death, 1185.
Heimroth, Oscar H., pvt., Co. H, 1st Cal. Vol. Inf., wounded, 897.
Heinz, Jacob, pvt., Co. A, 13th U. S. Inf., death, 1197.
Heisig, Harry J., pvt., Co. M., 1st Colo. Vol. Inf., death, 1032.
Heisler, Leo, pvt., Batty. H, 3d U. S. Art., wounded, 901.
Heistand, Henry O. S., lieut. col., a. a. g., U. S. A., mentioned, 36, 59, 93, 111, 142, 236, 239, 241, 321, 382, 393, 397, 503.
Helder, James K., pvt., Co. C, 47th Inf., U. S. V., death, 1167.
Helena, U. S. gunboat, mentioned, 22, 409, 410, 1135.
Hellen, Edward G., pvt., Co. D, 21st U. S. Inf., wounded, 1092.
Hellriegel, Jacob, sergt., Co. K, 3d U. S. Inf., wounded, 999.
Hellriegle, J. Lewis, pvt., Co. F, 14th U. S. Inf., death, 1082.
Helmcke, Max G. C., pvt., Co. G, 3d U. S. Inf., wounded, 1212.
Helsen, Palmer, pvt., Co. H, 3d U. S. Inf., death, 1062.
Helvie, Peter W., pvt., Co. D, 45th Inf., U. S. V., death, 1142.
Hely, Harold T., pvt., Co. A, 21st U. S. Inf., wounded, 1081.
Hembd, Otto, pvt., Co. K, 1st Nebr. Vol. Inf., wounded, 974.
Hemphill, Albert G., corpl., Co. E, 40th Inf., U. S. V., death, 1191.
Hemphill, George, corpl., Co. C, 6th U. S. Inf., wounded, 1153.
Hempstead, Frank L., act. hosp. stewd., U. S. A., wounded, 897.
Henchy, John, pvt., Co. F, 21st U. S. Inf., wounded, 1015.
Henderly, John A., corpl., Co. M, 31st Inf., U. S. V., death, 1196.
Henderson, Charles, corpl., Co. K, 13th U. S. Inf., killed, 1046.
Henderson, Dallas, corpl., Co. I, 1st Nebr. Vol. Inf., wounded, 974.
Henderson, Garfield, pvt., Co. E, 47th Inf., U. S. V., death, 1260.
Henderson, Guy W., pvt., Co. F, 45th Inf., U. S. V., death, 1194.
Henderson, Thomas, pvt., Co. E, 47th Inf., U. S. V., death, 1205.
Henderson, Samuel J., corpl., Co. C, 27th Inf., U. S. V., drowned, 1089.
Hendrickson, John, pvt., Co. E, 27th Inf., U. S. V., death, 1149.
Heneger, Burt, pvt., Troop K, 4th U. S. Cav., death, 1119.

Heneghan, Timothy, pvt., Co. H, 47th Inf., U. S. V., killed, 1147.
Henessy, Wesley J., pvt., Co. D, 22d U. S. Inf., killed, 934.
Heney, Arthur H., sergt., 33d Mich. Vol. Inf., mentioned, 218.
Henig, Albert, pvt., Co. K, 9th U. S. Inf., death, 482.
Henley, Alonzo, pvt., Co. D, 18th U. S. Inf., death, 1168.
Henna, J. J., mentioned, 313, 314.
Hennessey, John A., pvt., Co. C, 10th Pa. Vol. Inf., wounded, 919.
Hennessey, Michael J., pvt., Co. L, 15th U. S. Inf., wounded, 1211.
Hennessy, Arthur, civilian employee, drowned, 1193.
Hennessy, Murtha, sergt., Co. B, 13th U. S. Inf., death, 1086.
Henry, Charles, corpl., Co. I, 24th U. S. Inf., death, 1228.
Henry, Edward A., pvt., Co. E, 38th Inf., U. S. V., death, 1238.
Henry, Francis J., pvt., Co. B, 1st Idaho Vol. Inf., wounded, 1008.
Henry, Guy V., brig. gen., U. S. V., mentioned, 24, 36, 37, 77, 94, 111, 114, 123, 125, 130, 132, 283, 284, 330, 341, 369, 382, 547, 548.
  Ordered to Santiago, Cuba, 94.
Henry, M. M., pvt., Co. E, 13th U. S. Inf., wounded, 1008.
Henry, Ralph, pvt., Co. A, 37th Inf., U. S. V., wounded, 1152.
Henry, William F., pvt., Co. I, 16th U. S. Inf., drowned, 1156.
Henry, William G., pvt., Co. D, 4th U. S. Inf., death, 1070; wounded, 1017.
Hensel, Bernhart C., pvt., Co. F, 14th U. S. Inf., wounded, 902.
Hensil, August W., pvt., Co. K, 1st N. Dak. Vol. Inf., wounded, 981.
Hensley, Robert, corpl., Co. I, 6th U. S. Inf., death, 1264.
Herman, Frank, pvt., Co. C, 47th Inf., U. S. V., killed, 1235.
Hernandez, col., Cuban army, mentioned, 40.
Hermandez, Milton D., mus., Co. D, 6th U. S. Inf., death, 1172.
Herndon, John E., pvt., Troop G, 4th U. S. Cav., death, 1219.
Herpolsheimer, Martin, capt., 1st Nebr. Vol. Inf., wounded, 957.
Herrfeldt, Edward, pvt., Co. E, 33d Inf., U. S. V., killed, 1152.
Herrick, Charles F., pvt., Batty. G, 6th U. S. Art., death, 1150.
Herrick, Harvey M., pvt., Hosp. Corps, U. S. A., death, 1267.
Herrington, Charles R., qm. sergt., Co. F, 2d Oreg. Vol. Inf., wounded, 1017.
Herrmann, Ernest, corpl., Co. G, 12th U. S. Inf., drowned, 997.
Herron, Izariah, pvt., Co. K, 38th Inf., U. S. V., death, 1146.
Hersey, Arthur B., sergt., Co. E, 46th Inf., U. S. V., death, 1271.
Hersey, Henry B., maj., 1st U. S. V. Cav., mentioned, 128, 182, 325.
Herter, Fritz, pvt., Co. H, 22d U. S. Inf., wounded, 957.
Hertwick, Joseph C., corpl., Troop A, 11th U. S. V. Cav., wounded, 1203.
Heskett, James T., pvt., Co. C, 37th Inf., U. S. V., death, 1170.
Hess, Burton E., cook, Co. H, 43d Inf., U. S. V., killed, 1168.
Hess, Frank W., maj., 3d U. S. Art., mentioned, 685.
Hested, James E., artif., Co. D, 20th Kans. Vol. Inf., wounded, 948.
Hestilow, Charles, pvt., Co. I, 31st Inf., U. S. V., death, 1196.
Hewitt, Dan, pvt., Co. B, 20th Kans. Vol. Inf., wounded, 898.
Hezlep, James R., pvt., Co. M, 19th U. S. Inf., wounded, 1189.
Hiatt, Charles, sergt., Troop E, 4th U. S. Cav., death, 1029; wounded, 947.
Hibbard, Harry G., corpl., Co. K, 2d Oreg. Vol. Inf., death, 853.

Hibbs, Frank M., pvt., Co. A, 2d Oreg. Vol. Inf., death, 853.
Hickade, Frank, pvt., Co. K, 4th U. S. Inf., wounded, 1085.
Hickey, James L., corpl., Co. E, 17th U. S. Inf., death, 1221.
Hickman, Charles P., pvt., Co. A, 1st Colo. Vol. Inf., wounded, 1003.
Hicks, Albert S., pvt., Co. C, 1st Mont. Vol. Inf., mentioned, 926; wounded, 917.
Hicks, Charles, pvt., Co. F, 24th U. S. Inf., mentioned, 224.
Hicks, Philip S., pvt., Co. M, 14th U. S. Inf., death, 803.
Hicks, William, pvt., Co. A, 19th U. S. Inf., wounded, 1126.
Hicks, Wyatt G., pvt., Co. I, 14th U. S. Inf., killed, 453.
Hicks, ——, a. a. surg., U. S. A., mentioned, 197.
Hieronymus, Reuben C., pvt., Co. L, 38th Inf., U. S. V., wounded, 1145.
Hiett, Benjamin H., sergt., Batty. H, 3d U. S. Art., wounded, 950.
Higgin, Thomas M., pvt., Co. G, 14th U. S. Inf., wounded, 460.
Higgins, Henry L., pvt., Co. L, 43d Inf., U. S. V., killed, 1250.
Higgins, James F., pvt., Co. D, 36th Inf., U. S. V., wounded, 1051.
Higgins, James J., corpl., Co. H, 13th U. S. Inf., death, 1032.
Higgins, James J., pvt., Co. C, 21st U. S. Inf., death, 1070.
Higgins, Peter, pvt., Co. H, 3d U. S. Inf., wounded, 995.
Higgins, William L., corpl., Co. B, 9th U. S. Inf., drowned, 984.
Higginson, Francis J., capt., U. S. N., mentioned, 322, 330.
Higley, Brainard S., 1st lieut., med. dept., U. S. A., death, 1144.
Hildebrant, Martin, pvt., Co. E, 2d Oreg. Vol. Inf., wounded, 919.
Hill, Charles B., pvt., Batty. B, Utah Vol. Art., wounded, 902.
Hill, Clarence, pvt., Co. M, 4th U. S. V., death, 1274.
Hill, Claude, pvt., Co. A, 1st Idaho Vol. Inf., wounded, 948.
Hill, Edward J., pvt., Co. K, 43d Inf., U. S. V., wounded, 1162, 1225.
Hill, Frederick A., lieut. col., judge-advocate, U. S. V., mentioned, 331.
Hill, George O., pvt., Co. H, 18th U. S. Inf., murdered by natives, 1243.
Hill, Henry F., pvt., Co. G, 33d Inf., U. S. V., killed, 1124.
Hill, Herbert, pvt., Troop K, 10th U. S. Cav., mentioned, 229.
Hill, James H. F., pvt., Co. C, 19th U. S. Inf., death, 1104.
Hill, James T., pvt., Co. M, 45th Inf., U. S. V., killed, 1155.
Hill, John P., pvt., Co. C, 29th Inf., U. S. V., death, 1146.
Hill, Owen B., pvt., Co. G, 14th U. S. Inf., wounded, 1085.
Hill, Thomas, pvt., Co. H, 48th Inf., U. S. V., death, 1165.
Hill, William I., pvt., Co. A, 14th U. S. Inf., death, 803.
Hill, William H., pvt., Hosp. Corps, U. S. A., death, 1029.
Hill, William L., capt., 1st Mont. Vol. Inf., mentioned, 994; wounded, 900.
Hilliker, Frank, pvt., Co. K, 36th Inf., U. S. V., wounded, 1233.
Hillis, Mark A., corpl., Co. E, 36th Inf., U. S. V., death, 1123.
Hillman, Henry C., pvt., Co. G, 13th U. S. Inf., death, 1210.
Hillman, Herman H., pvt., Co. D, 13th Minn. Vol. Inf., wounded, 916.
Himmelberger, Oliver, pvt., Co. F, 28th Inf., U. S. V., killed, 1254.
Hinchcliffe, William, pvt., Co. K, 1st Wash. Vol. Inf., wounded, 947.
Hincken, Elias J., 2d lieut., 44th Inf., U. S. V., killed, 1251.

Hinckley, W. D., clerk, General Brooke's headquarters, mentioned, 302.
Hinds, Loring, pvt., Troop L, 4th U. S. Cav., wounded, 1042.
Hines, Joseph, pvt., Co. D, 19th U. S. Inf., death, 1078.
Hines, John, pvt., Co. B, 6th U. S. Inf., death, 1196.
Hinman, William W., corpl., Troop F, 11th U.S.V. Cav., wounded, 1108.
Hippart, John, pvt., Co. K, 36th Inf., U. S. V., wounded, 1096.
Hippler, Charles L., pvt., Co. G, 3d U. S. Inf., killed, 1187.
Hires, Frederick, pvt., Co. B, 17th U. S. Inf., death, 1178.
Hiscock, Harry, sergt., Co. H, 26th Inf., U. S. V., death, 1113; wounded, 1112.
Hisey, Albert S., pvt., Co. E, 1st Nebr. Vol. Inf., wounded, 956.
Hite, Ernest, pvt., Co. E, 35th Inf., U. S. V., wounded, 1176.
Hizon, insurgent general, capture, 1170, 1179; mentioned, 1133.
Hoadley, Charles, pvt., Co. L, 1st Ill. Vol. Inf., mentioned, 214.
Hoar, George F., U. S. Senator, mentioned, 254.
Hoar, George F., corpl., Co. H, 9th U. S. Inf., wounded, 444.
Hoar, Thomas, sergt., Troop D, 11th U. S. V. Cav., death, 1156.
Hobbs, Horace P., 2d lieut., 17th U. S. Inf., mentioned, 1019.
Hobbs William, pvt., Co. B, Batt. U. S. V. Engrs., death, 1217.
Hobby, Leander, pvt., Co. M, 36th Inf., U. S. V., death, 1144.
Hobson, Charles, pvt., Co. K, 34th Inf., U. S. V., death, 1226.
Hobson, Richmond P., naval constructor, U. S. N., mentioned, 25, 81, 95 101.
Hochberg, Alexander, pvt., Co. H, 21st U. S. Inf., wounded, 1075.
Hocker, Alonzo C., corpl., Co. D, 16th U. S. Inf., killed, 1261.
Hockley, Edward W., pvt., Co. L, 3d U. S. Inf., death, 1280.
Hodge, William, pvt., Co. C, 14th U. S. Inf., death, 1032.
Hodge, Dr. and Mrs., missionaries in China, murder, 487.
Hodgens, Ralph M., pvt., Co. H, 10th Pa. Vol. Inf., wounded, 948.
Hodges, Nathan A., pvt., Co. D, 51st Iowa Vol. Inf., wounded, 975.
Hoeft, Ernest L., pvt., Co. D, 32d Inf., U. S. V., wounded, 1218.
Hofman, John D., pvt., Co. M, 16th U. S. Inf., wounded, 1231.
Hoff, J. Van R., lieut. col., med. dept., U. S. A., mentioned, 646.
Hoffman, Charles P., pvt., Co. D, 32d Inf., U.S.V., killed, 1218.
Hoffman, Edward, pvt., Co. M, 2d Oreg. Vol. Inf., killed, 963.
Hoffman, John E., corpl., Co. F, 20th U. S. Inf., wounded, 934.
Hoffman, Joseph, pvt., Co. E, 22d U. S. Inf., wounded, 934.
Hoffman, Theodore F., col., 8th Pa. Vol. Inf., mentioned, 526, 528, 529.
Hoffman, William B., cook, Co. M, 4th U. S. Inf., wounded, 460.
Hoffmaster, Nathan, pvt., Co. H, 14th U. S. Inf., death, 487.
Hogan, Charles J., 1st lieut., 1st Cal. Vol. Inf., wounded, 897.
Hogan, James, pvt., Co. F, 21st U. S. Inf., death, 1066.
Hogan, John, pvt., Co. D, 34th Mich. Vol. Inf., mentioned, 216.
Hogan, Joseph, sergt., Co. M, 4th U. S. Inf., death, 1006.
Hogan, William A., qm. sergt., Troop G, 11th Cav., U. S. V., death, 1216.
Hogebom, John A., pvt., Co. I, 22d U. S. Inf., wounded, 950.

Hogolen Island [Turk Island], Carolines, harbor and defenses, 745.
Hogue, Walter, pvt., Co. G., 1st Nebr. Vol. Inf., death, 803; mentioned, 828.
Hogue, William, pvt., Co. F, 1st Cal. Vol. Inf., wounded, 897.
Hohlfeld, Julius, corpl., Co. M, 4th U. S. Inf., death, 967.
Hohne, Max, corpl., Co. L, 18th U. S. Inf., killed, 1155.
Hojo, Taiyo, chancellor, Japanese consulate, Manila, P. I., 1240.
Holbrook, Isa, pvt., Co. I, 1st Nebr. Vol. Inf., wounded, 950.
Holbrook, Rufus K., pvt., Co. C, 2d Oreg. Vol. Inf., death, 802; mentioned, 761.
Holbrow, Joseph H., pvt., Co. A, 41st Inf., U.S.V., death, 1172.
Holden, David, sergt., Co. F, 24th U. S. Inf., wounded, 1085.
Holdermess, George, prin. mus. 34th Mich. Vol. Inf., mentioned, 192.
Holland, Elijah, pvt., Co. H, 48th Inf., U. S. V., death, 1187.
Holland, Howard H., pvt., Co. D, 1st Wash. Vol. Inf., wounded, 905.
Holland, Leon G., pvt., Co. M, 2d Oreg. Vol. Inf., wounded, 946.
Hollars, George, pvt., Co. H, 40th Inf., U. S. V., wounded, 1188.
Hollenback, Arthur, pvt., Co. E, 35th Inf., U.S.V., death, 1123.
Hollenbaugh, Newton, pvt., Batty. L, 6th U. S. Art., death, 1140.
Hollenbeck, Philip A., pvt., Co. D, 47th Inf., U.S.V., wounded, 1247.
Holliday, Thomas, pvt., Co. A, 24th U. S. Inf., death, 1074.
Hollingshead, Arthur, pvt., Co. E, 20th Kans. Vol. Inf., wounded, 995.
Hollingsworth, Albert H., capt., 1st Nebr. Vol. Inf., wounded, 906.
Hollingsworth, Thomas W., pvt., Co. L, 47th Inf., U. S. V., killed, 1231.
Hollingsworth, William O., pvt., Co. C, 44th Inf., U. S. V., killed, 1219.
Hollis, Leonidas O., sergt., Co. G, 29th Inf., U. S. V., wounded, 1214.
Hollis, Magnus O., capt., 4th U. S. Inf., death, 1101.
Hollister, John F., pvt., Co. D, 21st U. S. Inf., mentioned, 1042.
Holloway, Fred, pvt., Co. H, 40th Inf., U. S. V., killed, 1183.
Holly, Henry J., pvt., Co. M, 45th Inf., U. S. V., death, 1260.
Holm, Otto, pvt., Co. E, 20th U. S. Inf., death, 1267.
Holmes, Marcus, 1st sergt., Astor Batty., U. S. A., death, 802.
Holmes, Stephen F., pvt., Co. E, 40th Inf., U.S.V., drowned, 1238.
Holoman, John, pvt., Co. H, 17th U. S. Inf., death, 1027.
Holt, Edward M., pvt., Co. L, 37th Inf., U. S. V., wounded, 1146.
Holt, William A., pvt., Co. F, 33d Inf., U. S. V., death, 1140.
Holter, Albert E., pvt., Troop I, 4th U. S. Cav., death, 1130.
Homfeld, John, pvt., Co. M, 4th U. S. Inf., wounded, 1110.
Hongkong, launch, mentioned, 435.
Hongkong, China:
  American agent for insurgents at, 1023.
  American consul at, information re Spanish troops in P. I., 665.
  Cable connection with Manila, 702.
  Deaths from disease, 1075.
  Hospital for U. S. troops, 756.
  Insurgent arms, shipment under German flag, 836.
  Junta, insurgent—
    Investigation by officer from P. I., 1170, 1171.
    Cooperation of American consul-general, 1235.
    Recall of officer investigating, 1202.
Honnyman, Elmer, First Troop, Nev. Vol. Cav., rescued, 1129.

Honolulu, H. I.:
American minister at, memo. on Caroline and Ladrone islands, 745.
Arrival of Philippine expeditions, 730, 740.
Treatment by Hawaiians, 730, 740.
Convalescents, transportation to homes, 731.
Deaths at, 731, 732, 1020.
Departure of troops for Manila, 832, 1092, 1099.
Detachment Philippine expedition to await orders at, 756.
Detention at, of transportation for P. I., 798, 799.
Garrison for, 721, 722, 724, 725-729, 732, 733, 748, 755, 763, 766, 802, 837, 930, 936, 953, 954.
Health conditions at, 838.
Natives endangered by diseases brought by troops, 731.
Officers and men left at, provision for, 731.
Provisions for care of officers and men left at, 731, 732.
Request for 8th California to go to, 728.
Retention of military camp, 839.
Sick soldiers left at, 838, 1058, 1089.
Sites for military station, selection, 727, 729, 731, 758.
Stragglers from second Philippine expedition, 738.
Supplies at, for transports, 699.
Transportation of troops to, 723, 728, 729.
Troops remaining at, 832.
Use by army transports of navy coal at, 701, 730.
Hood, Charles C., col., 16th U. S. Inf., mentioned, 574, 575, 577, 578, 1159.
Hood, Duncan N., col., 2d U. S. Vol. Inf., mentioned, 138, 192, 203, 230, 235.
Hoofer, Robert N., pvt., Co. K, 16th U. S. Inf., death, 1168.
Hook, Edward R., pvt., Co. H, 20th Kans. Vol. Inf., wounded, 946.
Hooker, U. S. transport, mentioned, 1055, 1078, 1125.
Responsibility for grounding, 1055.
Hoor, Herbert G., pvt., Co. K, 22d U. S. Inf., death, 1120.
Hoover, Edward, pvt., Co. B, 34th Inf., U. S. V., death, 1232.
Hoover, William D., pvt., Co. I, 38th Inf., U. S. V., wounded, 1153.
Hope, Charles, pvt., Co. K, 4th U. S Inf., death, 1017.
Hopkins, Ford, pvt., Co. M, 34th Inf., U. S. V., death, 1178.
Hopkins, George H., maj., a. a. g., U. S. V., mentioned, 44.
Hopkins, Henry, 1st sergt., Co. H, 14th U. S. Inf., wounded, 460.
Hopkins, Herbert A., pvt., Co. F, 1st Cal. Vol. Inf., death, 979.
Hopkins, Oscar C., corpl., Co. I, 41st Inf., U. S. V., death, 1208.
Hoppe, Otto H., pvt., Co. A, 1st Wash. Vol. Inf., wounded, 897.
Hoppe, Reno D., sergt., Co. I, 1st Wash. Vol. Inf., wounded, 906.
Hopper, George L., corpl., Co. H, 8th Ohio Vol. Inf., mentioned, 213.
Hoppin, Curtis B., capt., 2d U. S. Cav., mentioned, 301, 306, 309.
Hopwood, William C., pvt., Co. D, 1st Wash. Vol. Inf., killed, 903; wounded, 896.
Horan, James, pvt., Co. A, 9th U. S. Inf., death, 1099.
Horan, Patrick, pvt., Co. M, 15th U. S. Inf., wounded, 1251.
Horan, Robert, pvt., Co. M, 14th U. S. Inf., death, 464.
Horan, William, pvt., Co. D, 9th U. S. Inf., wounded, 1081.
Hordemon, Joseph L., sergt., Troop D, 11th U. S. V., Cav., wounded, 1128.
Horgan, Patrick, pvt., Co. G, 14th U. S. Inf., wounded, 898.
Horkman, David M., pvt., Co. H, 20th Kans. Vol. Inf., wounded, 901.
Horn, Charles A., pvt., Co. C, 2d Oreg. Vol. Inf., death, 804.
Horn, Christian O., pvt., Co. E, 1st Wash. Vol. Inf., wounded, 914.
Horn, Samuel M., sergt., Co. C, 17th U. S. Inf., death, 1226.

Horn, George W., pvt., Co. G, 1st Colo. Vol. Inf. mentioned, 1033.
Horne, Max, pvt., Co. L, 18th U. S. Inf., wounded, 943.
Horner, Reginald H., pvt., Co. M, 36th Inf., U. S. V., death, 1104.
Hornet, U. S. gunboat, mentioned, 22.
Hornsby, David J., pvt., Co. C, 29th Inf., U. S. V., wounded, 1212.
Horton, George R., pvt., Co. L, 15th U. S. Inf., killed, 1211.
Horton, Ira W., pvt., Troop K, 3d U. S. Cav., wounded, 1113.
Horton, Lewis, pvt., Co. I, 49th Inf., U. S. V., death, 1228.
Horton, Ray, pvt., Batty. —, 6th U. S. Art., death, 802.
Hosier, Harry E., corpl., Co. B, 37th Inf., U. S. V., killed, 1146.
Hoskins, Isaac M., pvt., Co. H, 48th Inf., U. S. V., death, 1170.
Hoskinson, Walter H., pvt., Co. E, 39th Inf., U. S. V., killed, 1147.
Hospital ship and surgeons for Santiago, 72, 74.
Hosty, Thomas, pvt., Co. L, 19th U. S. Inf., wounded, 1152.
Hotter, Henry, secretary Memphis Cotton Exchange, mentioned, 361.
Hotchkiss, Adam, pvt., Co. L, 13th Minn. Vol. Inf., wounded, 963.
Hotchkiss Mountain Gun Battery, organization, 638, 639, 688, 689.
Houck, William S., pvt., Co. K, 22d U. S. Inf., death, 1062.
Hough, Elmer D., pvt., Co. D, 14th U. S. Inf., wounded, 898.
Houle, George E., 1st lieut., 3d U. S. Inf., mentioned, 1135.
Houlihan, Patrick, corpl., Co. I, 21st U. S. Inf., wounded, 1015.
House, Frank E., pvt., Co. F, 4th U. S. Inf., death, 1136.
House, William E., pvt., band, 23d U. S. Inf., death, 961; wounded, 956.
Householder, Edward E., pvt., Co. D, 12th U. S. Inf., killed, 1157.
Householder, S. S., corpl., Co. F, 20th U. S. Inf., mentioned, 937.
Hover, Roy W., sergt. maj., 1st S. Dak. Vol. Inf., death, 831.
Hovey, George W., corpl., Co. H, 1st Wash. Vol. Inf., death, 979; wounded, 977.
Hovey, Robert, pvt., Co. H, 1st Wash. Vol. Inf., wounded, 977.
Howard, Arthur, insurgent lieut. col., deserter from U. S. Army, mentioned, 1296.
Howard, George W., pvt., Co. E, 21st U. S. Inf., wounded, 1052.
Howard, Guy., capt., qm. dept., U. S. A., lieut. col., U. S. V., mentioned, 86, 102, 116, 1018, 1088.
Howard, Harry M., 1st sergt. Co. K, 13th Minn. Vol. Inf., wounded, 991.
Howard, Herbert, pvt., Co. H, 1st Colo. Vol. Inf., mentioned, 782.
Howard, Ivers J., pvt., Co. B, 20th Kans. Vol. Inf., death, 903.
Wounded, 901.
Howard, John C., pvt., Co. C, 19th U. S. Inf., death, 1165.
Howard, Neil, pvt., Hosp. Corps, U. S. A., death, 803.
Howard, Perry H., pvt., Co. B, 1st U. S. Inf., mentioned, 224.
Howard, William, pvt., Co. K, 14th U. S. Inf., wounded, 898.
Howard, William, pvt., Co. E, 22d U. S. Inf., wounded, 946.
Howard, William E., pvt., Co. H, 1st Wash. Vol. Inf., wounded, 977.
Howard, William F., pvt., Co. C, 47th Inf., U. S. V., wounded, 1240.
Howe, Arthur C., pvt., Co. C, 20th Kans. Vol. Inf., wounded, 931.
Howe, George W., pvt., Troop C, 11th Cav., U. S. V., death, 1165.
Howe, Harry, pvt., Troop E, 4th U. S. Cav., wounded, 947.
Howe, Henry, pvt., Co. L, 46th Inf., U. S. V., death, 1264.

INDEX. 1407

Howe, Thomas P. A., 1st sergt., Co. L, 37th Inf., U. S. V., killed, 1211.
Howe, William J., teamster, mentioned, 174.
Howe, Willis, corpl., Co. G, 24th U. S. Inf., wounded, 1052.
Howell, Duke H., pvt., Co. M, 33d Inf., U. S. V., wounded, 1102.
Howell, Samuel F., pvt., Co. D, 14th U. S. Inf., killed, 760, 803.
Howland, Harry S., 2d lieut., 23d U. S. Inf., wounded, 1072.
Howley, Bartholomew W., pvt., Co. G, 19th U. S. Inf., death, 1185.
Howze, Robert L., lieut. col., 34th Inf., U. S. V., Mentioned, 1069, 1116, 1120, 1124, 1128, 1129.
  Pursuit of prisoners, 1124.
  Rescue of American prisoners, 1128.
Hoyt, Edward, pvt., Co. A, 43d Inf., U. S. V., killed, 1176.
Hoyt, Henry T., maj., chief surg., U. S. V., wounded, 955.
Hozack, George B., corpl., Co. D, 15th U. S. Inf., death, 1238.
Hubbard, Benjamin, pvt., Co. G, 14th U. S. Inf., death, 947.
Hubbard, Chester W., pvt., Co. K, 2d Oreg. Vol. Inf., death, 894; mentioned, 904.
Hubbard, Lorenzo D., pvt., Co. F, 35th Inf., U. S. V., wounded, 1124.
Hubbard, Lucius F., brig. gen., U. S. V., mentioned, 547, 550, 551, 552.
Hubbard, Walter A., pvt., Co. K, 20th Kans. Vol. Inf., wounded, 975.
Hubart, Charles, pvt., Co. L, 2d Oreg. Vol. Inf., killed, 945.
Hubberd, John, sergt., Co. C, 19th U. S. Inf., death, 1221.
Huber, Harry F., pvt., Hosp. Corps, U. S. A., mentioned, 958; rescued, 1129.
Hubert, Edgar, capt., 8th U. S. Inf., mentioned, 139.
Huchison, Archie, pvt., Co. F, 22d U. S. Inf., wounded, 1085.
Hudson, George H., pvt., Utah Vol. Art., death, 803.
Hudson, U. S. transport, mentioned, 60, 63, 65, 67, 69, 72, 88, 95, 122, 157, 236, 243, 304, 349, 354, 378, 594.
Hudson, Joseph K., brig. gen., U. S. V., mentioned, 292, 329, 335, 536, 537.
Hudson, Simon, pvt., Co. E, 39th Inf., U. S. V., death, 1152; wounded, 1149.
Huennekens, John A. C., act. hosp. stewd., U. S. A., death, 1217.
Huesman, William W., pvt., Co. M, 30th Inf., U. S. V., death, 1215.
Huey, Charles V., sergt., Co. C, 40th Inf., U. S. V., killed, 1153.
Huff, Claude W., pvt., Co. E, 1st Cal. Vol. Inf., mentioned, 1043.
Huff, Frank B., pvt., Co. B, 34th Inf., U. S. V., mentioned, 1243.
Huff, Walter, sergt., Co. G, 40th Inf., U. S. V., wounded, 1240, 1254.
Hug, Adolph, cook, Co. A, 9th U. S. Inf., death, 1189.
Huggard, William, pvt., Co. D, 6th U. S. Inf., wounded, 1126.
Hughes, Frank, pvt., Co. E, 47th Inf., U. S. V., killed, 1184.
Hughes, John, corpl., Batty. D, 3d U. S. Art., death, 477.
Hughes, John H., 2d lieut., 4th U. S. Inf., mentioned, 83; reported killed, 124.
Hughes, Marvin P., sergt., Co. G, 35th Inf, U. S. V., wounded, 1124.
Hughes, Richard, pvt., Co. M, 14th U. S. Inf., wounded, 895.
Hughes, Robert P., brig. gen., U. S. A., mentioned, 557-563, 565, 567, 568, 570, 571, 573, 574, 575, 577, 579, 646, 689, 718, 766, 909, 1006, 1011, 1059, 1062, 1073, 1077, 1088, 1091, 1096, 1098, 1105, 1106, 1107, 1111, 1116, 1122, 1125, 1126, 1133, 1134, 1154, 1155, 1159, 1223, 1245, 1251, 1260, 1261, 1264, 1266, 1270, 1276, 1278, 1295, 1300, 1305.
  Reports outbreak in Bohol, P. I., 1204.
Huhn, Paulinus, pvt., Co. M, 13th Minn. Vol. Inf., wounded, 947.
Huidekoper, Rush S., lieut. col., chief surg., U. S. V., mentioned, 301.

Hulbe, Henry, pvt., Co. A, 14th U. S. Inf., wounded, 1015.
Hulbert, Elwyn C., pvt., Batty. L, 3d U. S. Art., wounded, 1124.
Hulf, Claude W., pvt., Co. E, 1st Cal. Vol. Inf., wounded, 1038.
Hulgan, James C., pvt., Co. K, 33d Inf., U. S. V., death, 1090, 1095.
Huling, Frank A., pvt., Co. K, 20th Kans. Vol. Inf., wounded, 906.
Hulings, Willis J., col., 16th Pa. Vol. Inf., mentioned, 71, 294, 372, 511, 512.
Hull, Harry L., corpl., Co. A, 1st Nebr. Vol. Inf., wounded, 897.
Hull, Jacob, jr., pvt., Co. E, 10th Pa. Vol. Inf., death, 803.
Hulme, Charley, pvt., Co. D, 28th inf., U. S. A., death, 1231.
Hulseberg, Frederick W., act. asst. surg., U. S. A., killed by insurgents, 1195.
Hultberg, Charles, Co. M, 1st S. Dak. Vol. Inf. mentioned, 974.
Hummer, Lloyd, sergt., Co. G, 37th Inf., U. S. V., wounded, 1155.
Hummer, Robert, pvt., Co. A, 36th Inf., U. S. V., death, 1088.
Humphrey, Charles F., col., qm. dept., U. S. A., constructions in P. I., 1325, 1326.
  Mentioned, 10, 73, 80, 92, 94, 100, 110, 120, 122, 123, 139, 141, 174, 197, 198, 208, 210, 290, 296, 297, 299, 303, 304, 310, 311, 318, 351, 470, 482, 485, 486, 488, 491, 494, 495, 497, 502, 503, 1321, 1323, 1351.
Humphrey, Chauncey B., 2d lieut., 3d U. S. Inf., wounded, 957.
Humphrey, Orson E., pvt., Co. M, 1st Nebr. Vol. Inf., wounded, 974.
Humphreys, Daniel W., pvt., Co. K, 18th U. S. Inf., killed, 1111.
Humphreys, Thomas, capt. and qm., Chaffee requests services of, 1311.
Humphris, William, sergt., Co. D, 14th U. S. Inf., death, 1086.
Hunker, John J., comdr., U. S. Navy, mentioned, 42.
Hunricker, Merton, pvt., Co. L, 22d U. S. Inf., wounded, 946.
Hunt, Arthur, pvt., Co. A, 49th Inf., U. S. V., death, 1219.
Hunt, Arthur S., pvt., Co. K, 3d U. S. Inf., death, 988.
Hunt, Charles B., col., 1st Ohio Vol. Inf., mentioned, 510.
Hunt, John C., pvt., Co. C, 43d Inf., U. S. V., death, 1168.
Hunter, Alfred M., 1st lieut., 4th U. S. Art., mentioned, 397.
Hunter, Ed., pvt., Co. A, 45th Inf., U. S. V., death, 1228.
Hunter, Edward, lieut. col., j. a. dept., U. S. A., mentioned, 302.
Hunter, Frank, pvt., Co. G, 48th Inf., U. S. V., death, 1229.
Hunter, Fred M., pvt., Co. G, 28th Inf., U. S. V., wounded, 1222.
Hunter, George K., capt., 3d U. S. Cav., wounded, 123.
Hunter, George W., pvt., Co. I, 47th Inf., U. S. V., wounded, 1166.
Hunter, Leo W., pvt., Co. K, 1st Nebr. Vol. Inf., wounded, 982.
Hunter, Louis L., corpl., Co. E, 51st Iowa Vol. Inf., wounded, 974.
Hunter, Swift D., pvt., Co. M, 1st Mont. Vol. Inf., wounded, 987.
Hunter, William, pvt., Co. C, 34th Inf., U. S. V., killed, 1192.
Hunter, William E., pvt., Troop L, 3d U. S. Cav., wounded, 1222.
Hunter, William E., corpl., Co. G, 27th Inf., U. S. V., death, 1089.
Hunting, Walter J., corpl., Co. F, 1st Nebr. Vol. Inf., wounded, 925.
Huntington, C. P., mentioned, 358, 364.
Huntley, Charles D., pvt., Co. F, 18th U. S. Inf., death, 1200.
Hurbough, Edgar J., pvt., Co. F, 33d Inf., U. S. V., death, 1151.
Hurd, Benjamin F., pvt., Co. E, 1st Cal. Vol. Inf., mentioned, 1043.
Hurd, Glen W., pvt., Co. C, 1st Mont. Vol. Inf., wounded, 916.

Hurley, Jeremiah H., corpl., Co. G, 46th Inf., U. S. V., death, 1185.
Hurley, Marion, pvt., Co. A, 18th U. S. Inf., death, 803.
Hurley, Michael J., pvt., Co. B, 22d U. S. Inf., death, 1261.
Hursh, Ray L., pvt., Co. C, 1st Cal. Vol. Inf., wounded, 904.
Hurst, Aaron C., pvt., Co. F, 18th U. S. Inf., death, 1267.
Hurst, Henry H., pvt., Co. M, 14th U. S. Inf., wounded, 454.
Hurst, James H., corpl., Co. F, 14th U. S. Inf., wounded, 454.
Hurst, John H., pvt., Co. H, 14th U. S. Inf., death, 464.
Hurth, Edward A., pvt., Co. H, 33d Inf., U. S. V., wounded, 1102.
Husby, Olof, pvt., Co. L, 34th Mich. Vol. Inf., mentioned, 226.
Husketh, James L., pvt., Co. H, 29th Inf., U. S. V., wounded, 1160.
Huss, Charles H., pvt., Co. D, 40th Inf., U. S. V., wounded, 1160.
Huss, Frank, pvt., Co. B, 4th U. S. Inf., wounded, 1017, 1085.
Hussey, William H., pvt., Co. C, 17th U. S. Inf., death, 1027.
Hustead, Phineas F., pvt., Co. L, 40th Inf., U. S. V., wounded, 1162.
Huston, Carrell S., pvt., Co. M, 44th Inf., U. S. V., wounded, 1256.
Huston, Harry C., pvt., Co. E, 14th U. S. Inf., wounded, 454.
Hutberg, Charles, mus., Co. M, 1st S. Dak. Vol. Inf., wounded, 915.
Hutcheson, Grote F., capt., 6th U. S. Cav., mentioned, 487, 488.
Hutchinson, Charles L., pvt., Co. C, 1st Colo. Vol. Inf., wounded, 956.
Hutchinson, De Forest V., pvt., Co. B, 9th U. S. Inf., death, 1020; wounded, 1010.
Hutchinson, Elias, pvt., Co. M, 2d Oreg. Vol. Inf., death, 771, 803; mentioned, 774.
Hutchinson, Horace, pvt., Co. C, 6th U. S. Inf., wounded, 1087, 1153.
Hutchinson, Hugh, pvt., Co. L, 1st Idaho Vol. Inf., mentioned, 1008.
Hutchison, Earl R., pvt., Co. C, 40th Inf., U. S. V., wounded, 1150.
Hutchison, Walter E., pvt., Co. A, 51st Iowa Vol. Inf., death, 1052.
Hutfils, Frederick, qm. sergt., Co. H, 21st U. S. Inf., death, 1062.
Huth, Jacob, pvt., Co. K, 14th U. S. Inf., death, 917.
Hutslar, Samuel B., pvt., Co. G, 47th Inf., U. S. V., death, 1255.
Hutton, James A., 2d lieut., 1st Cal. Vol. Inf., mentioned, 1000.
Huttuna, Adolph, pvt., Co. C, 6th U. S. Inf., death, 1200.
Hyland, Edward T., pvt., Co. M, 45th Inf., U. S. V., death, 1220; wounded, 1218.
Hyde, John McE., maj., qm. dept., U. S. A., mentioned, 427, 445, 451, 452, 455, 456, 459, 461, 463, 464, 489, 494, 495, 506.
  Reestablishing hospital at Nagasaki, 1245.
Hyer, Benjamin B., 1st lieut., 6th U. S. Cav., mentioned, 473.
Hylin, Edward, corpl., Batty. D, 6th U. S. Art., death, 997.
Hylton, Asa C., corpl., Co. C, 36th Inf., U. S. V., death, 1228.
Hyman, Martin, pvt., Co. B, 1st Mont. Vol. Inf., wounded, 915.
Hyner, Frederick, pvt., Hosp. Corps, U. S. A., death, 1208.
Hyners, Pompy, pvt., Co. G, 49th Inf., U. S. V., death, 1160.
Iberia, Spanish regiment of, distribution, 655.
Ill, James B., pvt., Co. A, 24th U. S. Inf., mentioned, 244.
Illeroa, Spanish commander, killed, 372.
Iltis, William F., mus., 32d Co., Coast Art., death, 1283.
Inderbitzen, Edward J., corpl., Troop H, 11th U. S. V. Cav., drowned, 1221.
Indian reservations, need for troops near, 689.

Indiana, U. S. battleship, mentioned, 16, 22, 31, 39, 40, 299.
Indiana, U. S. transport, 424, 426, 427, 430, 436, 437, 439, 441, 442, 444-446, 453, 456-459, 463, 464, 471, 477, 481, 484, 488, 503-506, 593, 609, 695, 704, 715, 740, 792, 802, 841, 853, 922, 1016, 1074, 1076, 1081, 1082, 1098, 1108, 1128, 1227, 1228, 1258, 1264, 1269, 1287.
Infanta Maria Theresa, Spanish cruiser, mentioned, 81.
Infantry and cavalry schools, officers on duty at ordered to join their commands, 8.
Ingalls, Ralph, pvt., Co. F, 5th Mo. Vol. Inf., mentioned, 343.
Ingalls, Ralph, capt., commissary, U. S. V., ordered to San Francisco, 1274.
Ingalls, U. S. transport, mentioned, 1297, 1322, 1341.
Ingersoll, Guy M., pvt., Co. C, 40th Inf., U. S. V., wounded, 1150.
Ingeterson, Louis J., corpl., Co. D, 36th Inf., U. S. V., wounded, 1081.
Ingle, Conley A., pvt., Co. G, 16th U. S. Inf., death, 1070.
Ingle, Reuben, pvt., Co. A, 20th U. S. Inf., mentioned, 226.
Innis, James A., pvt., Troop K, 4th U. S. Cav., death, 1232.
Intoxicating liquors, prohibition of sale, 1251.
Irene, German war ship, mentioned, 833.
Irish, Arnold, corpl., Co. C, 9th U. S. Inf., wounded, 1298.
Irons, James A., maj., I. G., U. S. V., mentioned, 256.
Iroquois, U. S. transport, mentioned, 80, 95, 99, 121, 155, 190, 275, 332.
Irvine, Albert, pvt., Co. M, 12th U. S. Inf., death, 1060; wounded, 1057.
Irwin, Edward K., 1st lieut., 1st Wash. Vol. Inf., wounded, 896.
Isenbarger, Dock R., pvt., Co. B, 35th Inf., U. S. V., death, 1162.
Isla de Luzon, steamship transporting Spanish prisoners to Spain, 991, 1069.
Issinghausen, Frank H., pvt., Co. M, 14th U. S. Inf., killed, 895.
Iverson, Gerhard W., pvt., Co. F, 1st Cal. Vol. Inf., mentioned, 1403.
Ives, Frank J., maj., chief surg., U. S. V., opinion re health conditions in Cuba, 201, 244, 256, 505.
Jabelman, Charles, pvt., Troop B, 4th U. S. Cav., wounded, 1052.
Jackman, Samuel C., pvt., Co. L, 47th Inf., U. S. V., death, 1189.
Jacksap, John, pvt., Co. G, 40th Inf., U. S. V., mentioned, 1255; wounded, 1254.
Jackson, Arlington D., pvt., Co. M, 22d U. S. Inf., killed, 1182.
Jackson, Charles H., pvt., Co. L, 1st S. Dak. Vol. Inf., wounded, 949.
Jackson, Douglas V., col., 50th Iowa Vol. Inf., mentioned, 548.
Jackson, Frank R., pvt., Co. L, 14th U. S. Inf., wounded, 454.
Jackson, Frederick J., a. a. surg., U. S. A., wounded, 1234.
Jackson, George W., pvt., Co. I, 24th U. S. Inf., captured by insurgents, 1196; wounded, 1222.
Jackson, Glan H., corpl., Co. G, 46th Inf., U. S. V., death, 1220.
Jackson, Harold L., 1st lieut., 22d U. S. Inf., mentioned, 994; wounded, 946.
Jackson, Harry J., pvt., Co. B, 39th Inf., U. S. V., death, 1178.
Jackson, James, pvt., Co. D, 40th Inf., U. S. V., death, 1165.
Jackson, Jesse G., pvt., Co. F, 44th Inf., U. S. V., death, 1197.
Jackson, John B., chargé d'affaires, Berlin, Germany, mentioned, 450, 451.
Jackson, John F., pvt., Troop K, 4th U. S. Cav., wounded, 1096.
Jackson, John W., corpl., Co. C, 47th Inf., U. S. V., wounded, 1231.
Jackson, Logan B., pvt., Co. G, 30th U. S. Inf., death, 1223.
Jackson, Max, pvt., Co. C, 3d U. S. Inf., death, 1075.

INDEX. 1409

Jackson, Milo, pvt., Co. I, 47th Inf., U. S. V., death, 1215.
Jackson, Patrick, corpl., Co. D, 12th U. S. Inf., death, 1261.
Jackson, Robert, pvt., band, 8th U. S. Inf., death, 1253.
Jackson, Robert D., pvt., Co. F, 29th U. S. Inf., wounded, 1219.
Jackson, Romeo, pvt., Co. K, 24th U. S. Inf., death, 1152.
Jackson, Rufus A., pvt., Troop K, 3d U. S. Cav., wounded, 1113.
Jackson, Sherman E., corpl., Co. D, 9th U. S. Inf., wounded, 444.
Jackson, William, pvt., Co. F, 48th Inf., U. S. V., death, 1229.
Jackson, William B., pvt., Troop L, 4th U. S. Cav., killed, 974.
Jackson, William T., pvt., Co. C, 25th U. S. Inf., death, 1236.
Jacksonville, Fla.—
  Concentration of troops, 26
  Dangerous as camp, 38.
  General Lawton, to command troops at, 13.
  Laborers to be sent to Cuba from, 118, 120, 121, 126.
  Movement of troops from, 38, 45, 48.
  Volunteer regiments temporarily stopped at, 13, 14.
Jacobs, Frank, pvt., Co. E, 9th U. S. Inf., death, 1191.
Jacobs, Frederick G., pvt., Hosp. Corps, U. S. A., death, 798, 803.
Jacobs, Harry, pvt., Co. A, 20th U. S. Inf., death, 1194.
Jacobs, Joshua W., maj., qm. dept., U. S. A., mentioned, 27, 123.
Jacobs, William, pvt., Co. M, 45th Inf., U. S. V., death, 1226.
James, Alfred W., pvt., Co. K, 2d U. S. Inf., killed, 1261.
James, Arthur W., pvt., Co. B, 39th U. S. Inf., death, 1174.
James, Robert, pvt., Co. C, 49th Inf., U. S. V., death, 1245.
James, William H. W., maj., 23d U. S. Inf., mentioned, 1025.
Jamison, Clyde J., pvt., Co. G, 9th U. S. Inf., killed, 443, 445.
Janch, Charles, pvt., Co. A, 2d U. S. Inf., wounded, 127.
Janes, William, pvt., Troop A, 11th U. S. V. Cav., death, 1202.
Jansen, Louis, corpl., band, 34th Inf., U. S. V., death, 1095.
Janzen, John, pvt., Co. K, 2d Oreg. Vol. Inf., wounded, 946.
Jaques, Edward, pvt., Co. M, 2d Oreg. Vol. Inf., injured, 952.
Jarvis, Jose A., pvt., Hosp. Corps, U. S. A., death, 1189.
Jarvis, Walter C., corpl., Co. A, 9th U. S. Inf., mentioned, 246.
Jaudenes, Don Fermin, Spanish capt. gen., P. I., mentioned, 757, 799, 828, 913.
Jeans, Earl A., pvt., Co. I, 1st Wash. Vol. Inf., death, 889.
Jeddington, William, pvt., Co. A, 4th Ohio Vol. Inf., wounded, 378.
Jefferson, Richard, pvt., Co. E, 25th U. S. Inf., death, 1088.
Jeffrey, John B., capt., asst. qm., U. S. V., mentioned, 1031.
Jeffries, James E., pvt., Co. H, 40th Inf., U. S. V., wounded, 1183.
Jenkins, Daniel P., pvt., Co. M, 22d U. S. Inf., death, 1146.
Jenkins, Fred W., pvt., Co. A, 32d Inf., U. S. V., killed, 1182.
Jenkins, Paul, pvt., Co. A, 33d Inf., U. S. V., killed, 1216.
Jenks, ——, corpl., mentioned, 383.
Jenks, Albert C., pvt., Co. K, 6th U. S. Inf., wounded, 1037, 1064.
Jenks, Newell E, pvt., Co. L, 1st S. Dak. Vol. Inf., death, 803.
Jennewine, Frederick M., pvt., Co. C, 10th Pa. Vol. Inf., killed, 954.

Jennings, Edward J., civilian teamster, death, 491.
Jennings, Frank W., capt., Utah Vol. Art., mentioned, 1046.
Jennings, Henry J., corpl., Co. K, 9th Mass. Vol. Inf., mentioned, 226.
Jennings, John J., pvt., Co. E, 1st U. S. Inf., death, 1260.
Jennings, Robert, sergt., Co. A, 18th U. S. Inf., wounded, 914.
Jens, Charles W., capt., 1st Nebr. Vol. Inf., wounded, 950.
Jensen, Andrew, capt. 1st Mont. Vol. Inf., wounded, 977.
Jensen, Hans, pvt., Co. B, 14th U. S. Inf., wounded, 898.
Jensen, Lauritz, corpl., Co. L, 15th U. S. Inf., killed, 1211.
Jensen, Mourits C., corpl., Batty. B, Utah Vol. Art., death, 979; wounded, 975.
Jensen, Robert P., capt., asst surg., 1st Nebr. Vol. Inf., mentioned, 994.
Jenson, Christian, corpl., Co. C, 17th U. S. Inf., wounded, 1031.
Jentzen, Richard, pvt., Co. H, 1st Cal. Vol. Inf., wounded, 897.
Jessien, Emil, pvt., Batty. K, 3d U. S. Art., death, 1052.
Jette, Joseph E., pvt., Co. H, 1st Mont. Vol. Inf., wounded, 975.
Jewel, W. M., pvt., Co. H, 2d U. S. Inf., mentioned, 197.
Jifkins, Edward, post-office clerk, mentioned, 298.
Jilbert, Thomas W., pvt., Co. D, 34th Mich. Vol. Inf., mentioned, 209.
Joakanain, Dato, Moro chief, mentioned, 1118.
Jobbling, Arthur, pvt., Co. H, 18th U. S. Inf., death, 803; mentioned, 761.
Johannsen, Julius, pvt., Co. A, 45th Inf., U. S. V., death, 1190.
John, Fred J. A., pvt., Batty. L, 3d U. S. Art., wounded, 959.
Johns, Asa T., pvt., Co. E, 48th Inf., U. S. V., death, 1197.
Johnson, Alonzo L., sergt., Co. K, 12th U. S. Inf., killed, 1160.
Johnson, Alonzo R., pvt., Co. K, 14th U. S. Inf., wounded, 967.
Johnson, Andrew, pvt., Batty. K, 3d U. S. Art., wounded, 897.
Johnson, Andrew, pvt., Troop F, 2d U. S. Cav., mentioned, 183.
Johnson, Andrew T., pvt., Troop L, 3d U. S. Cav., killed, 1222.
Johnson, Anson B., U. S. consul, Amoy, China, mentioned, 1074.
Johnson, Asa L., pvt., Co. E, 43d Inf., U. S. V., killed, 1176.
Johnson, August L., pvt., Co. E, 34th Mich. Vol. Inf., mentioned, 246.
Johnson, Benjamin, capt., asst. qm., U. S. V., mentioned, 133.
Johnson, Benjamin, pvt., Co. K, 46th Inf., U. S. V., death, 1255; wounded, 1254.
Johnson, Carl M., pvt., Co. E, 9th U. S. Inf., killed, 1298.
Johnson, Carter P., 1st lieut., 10th U. S. Cav., mentioned, 51, 52.
Johnson, Charles, pvt., Co. E, 4th U. S. Inf., wounded, 454.
Johnson, Charles, pvt., Batty G, 3d U. S. Art., killed, 951.
Johnson, Charles, pvt., Co. I, 48th Inf., U. S. V., death, 1276.
Johnson, Charles R., pvt., Co. K, 38th Inf., U. S V., wounded, 1243.
Johnson, Christian, pvt., Co. A, 1st U. S. Inf., death, 202, 204.
Johnson, David R., pvt., Co. I, 13th U. S. Inf., death, 997, 1020.
Johnson, Edgar J., pvt., Co. D, 2d Oreg. Vol. Inf., mentioned, 761.
Johnson, Edgar J., pvt., Co. D, 2d Oreg. Vol. Inf., death, 803.
Johnson, Edward, pvt., Troop F, 11th U. S. V. Cav., wounded, 1108.
Johnson, Edward C., pvt., Co. C 34th Inf., U. S. V., killed, 1212.

Johnson, E. John L., pvt., Co. D, 11th U. S. Inf., wounded, 390.
Johnson, Ernest, pvt., Troop F, 10th U. S. Cav., mentioned, 229.
Johnson, Frank A., corpl., Co. C, 1st Wash. Vol. Inf., wounded, 925.
Johnson, Frank B., pvt., Co. A, 22d U. S. Inf., killed, 1082.
Johnson, Frank W., pvt., Co. M, 34th Inf., U. S. V., drowned, 1210.
Johnson, Handy B., pvt., Co. K, 22d U. S. Inf., wounded, 1092.
Johnson, Henry L., pvt., Co. C, 20th Kans. Vol. Inf., wounded, 954.
Johnson, Henry S., pvt., Co. H, 33d Inf., U. S. V., mentioned, 1229; wounded, 1222, 1228.
Johnson, Henry W., pvt., Co. K, 22d U. S. Inf., killed, 941.
Johnson, Isaac, pvt., Co. D, 1st S. Dak. Vol. Inf., wounded, 949.
Johnson, James G., pvt., Co. T, 24th U. S. Inf., death, 1057, 1060.
Johnson, John J., corpl., Co. H, 24th U. S. Inf., death, 1123.
Johnson, Joshua W., pvt., Co. G, 9th U. S. Inf., death, 1066.
Johnson, Martin, pvt., Co. D, 3d U. S. Inf., death, 1074.
Johnson, Norwin, corpl., Co. B, 45th Inf., U. S. V., killed, 1182.
Johnson, Ole, corpl., Co. C, 20th U. S. Inf., killed, 937.
Johnson, Oscar E., corpl., Co. H, 1st S. Dak. Vol. Inf., killed, 975; wounded, 954.
Johnson, Oscar F., pvt., Co. G, 34th Inf., U. S. V., killed, 1161.
Johnson, Otto T., pvt., Co. F, 14th U. S. Inf., death, 1070.
Johnson, Rasmus M., pvt., Batty. O, 3d U. S. Art., death, 486.
Johnson, S. O., pvt., Co. F, 7th U. S. Inf., mentioned, 193, 202.
Johnson, Thomas, pvt., Co. L, 37th Inf., U. S. V., killed, 1203.
Johnson, Toliver G., pvt., Co. F, 29th U. S. Inf., wounded, 1219.
Johnson, Wallace E., corpl., Co. D, 23d U. S. Inf., death, 1257.
Johnson, William, corpl., Co. F, 25th U. S. Inf., death, 1258.
Johnson, William I., pvt., Co. K, 1st Nebr. Vol. Inf., wounded, 983.
Johnson, Willie, pvt., Co. G, 49th Inf., U. S. V., death, 1226.
Johnson, Willis J., pvt., Co. H, 25th U. S. Inf., wounded, 1160.
Johnson, Winnie, pvt., Co. B, 39th Inf., U. S. V., death, 1208.
Johnson, W. H., chairman, Georgia Republican State committee, mentioned, 348.
Johnson, W. O., pvt., Batty. F, 4th U. S. Art., mentioned, 202.
Johnson, W. S., pvt., Co. D, 1st Colo. Vol. Inf., mentioned, 829.
Johnston, Fred S., pvt., Co. I, 33d Inf., U. S. V., death, 1149.
Johnston, John A., maj., a. a. g., U. S. A., mentioned, 328.
Johnston, Taylor, pvt., Co. F, 22d U. S. Inf., death, 1149.
Johnston, William H., maj., 46th Inf., U. S. V., mentioned, 1025, 1136.
Johnston, William T., capt., 15th U. S. Cav., mentioned, 1062, 1334.
Joiner, Miles, pvt., Co. L, 30th Inf., U. S. V., death, 1196.
Jolley, Errol V., pvt., Co. F, 16th Pa. Vol. Inf., wounded, 378.
Jolly, Wade L., 2d lieut., U. S. Marine Corps, sick, 435.
Jolo, Spanish regiment of, distribution, 655. Sultan of, mentioned, 1118.
Jones, Benjamin F., pvt., Hosp. Corps, U. S. A., death, 1236.
Jones, Burgher R., pvt., Co. F, 23d U. S. Inf., death, 894.
Jones, Daniel W., governor of Arkansas, mentioned, 357.
Jones, Delbert R., 1st lieut., 43d Inf., U. S. V., mentioned, 1282.

Jones, Die E., pvt., Co. L, 21st U. S. Inf., death, 986.
Jones, Edward, pvt., Co. B, 49th Inf., U. S. V., death, 1236.
Jones, Edward, pvt., Co. F, 24th U. S. Inf., death, 1057, 1060.
Jones, Emmet L., pvt., Co. K, 2d Oreg. Vol. Inf., wounded, 946.
Jones, Francis B., maj., qm. dept., U. S. A., mentioned, 906.
Jones, Frank B., capt., 22d U. S. Inf., wounded, 124, 941.
Jones, Guy, pvt., Co. H, 1st S. Dak. Vol. Inf., killed, 975.
Jones, Harry A., pvt., Troop F, 3d U. S. Cav., drowned, 1187.
Jones, Ira, pvt., Co. E, 24th U. S. Inf., death, 1088.
Jones, James, sergt., Co. F, 18th U. S. Inf., death, 1191.
Jones, James D., pvt., Co. C, 1st Idaho Vol. Inf., death, 833.
Jones, James L., pvt., Co. E, 30th Inf., U. S. V., wounded and death, 1150.
Jones, John A., corpl., Co. L, 23d U. S. Inf., wounded, 959.
Jones, John M., pvt., Co. E, 25th U. S. Inf., death, 1232.
Jones, John W., lieut. col., 1st Idaho Vol. Inf., mentioned, 717.
Jones, Larry, pvt., Co. D, 20th Kans. Vol. Inf., wounded, 917.
Jones, Leroy C., pvt., Co. H, 48th Inf., U. S. V., death, 1187.
Jones, Lewis E., pvt., Co. L, 13th U. S. Inf., death, 1086.
Jones, Lewis W., pvt., Co. C, 35th Inf., U. S. V., wounded, 1182.
Jones, Miles D., pvt., Co. D, 6th U. S. Inf., death, 1156.
Jones, Morradey E., pvt., Co. I, 14th U. S. Inf., death, 1082.
Jones, Oliver H., pvt., Co. K, 36th Inf., U. S. V., wounded, 1096.
Jones, Richard B., pvt., Co. B, 1st Idaho Vol. Inf., wounded, 898.
Jones, Robert, pvt., Co. B, 1st Idaho Vol. Inf., wounded, 897.
Jones, Samuel, saddler, Troop E, 4th U. S. Cav., killed, 936.
Jones, Samuel F., pvt., ——, 4th Ohio Vol. Inf., wounded, 378.
Jones, Sam R., maj. qm. dept., U. S. A., mentioned, 807, 808.
Jones, Stephen J., pvt., Co. F, 1st U. S. Inf., death, 1255.
Jones, William A., pvt., Co. G, 13th Minn. Vol. Inf., mentioned, 762; wounded, 761.
Jones, William H., pvt., Co. I, 24th U. S. Inf., killed, 1222.
Jones, William H., corpl., Co. C, 1st Idaho Vol. Inf., death, 830.
Jordan, Albert J., pvt., Co. G, 2d Oreg. Vol. Inf., wounded, 946.
Jordan, John, pvt., Co. K, 3d U. S. Inf., death, 1196.
Jordens, Herman J. A., farrier, Troop B, 3d U. S. Cav., death, 1233.
Jorgensen, Christian A., pvt., Co. C, 19th U. S. Inf., wounded, 1140.
Jorgenson, Charles J., pvt., Co. F, 18th U. S. Inf., death, 831.
Jossman, Albert L., 2d lieut., 27th U. S. Inf., wounded by Moros, 1335, 1338.
Judy, Joseph M., pvt., Co. D, 32d Inf., U. S. V., death, 1190.
Juhl, Albert, corpl., Co. H, 9th U. S. Inf., wounded, 444.
Jumper, Ulysses S., pvt., Co. C, 9th U. S. Inf., wounded, 443.
Junker, Frank, pvt., Co. C, 30th Inf., U. S. V., wounded, 1147.
Jusseaume, Ulric, pvt., Co. F, 36th Inf., U. S. V., mentioned, 1234; wounded, 1233.
Justh Maurice, 1st sergt., Co. A, 1st Cal. Vol. Inf., death, 803.
Kaester, Henry, pvt., Co. L, 34th Mich. Vol. Inf., mentioned, 205.
Kahl, George, pvt., Co. L, 13th Minn. Vol. Inf., mentioned, 762; wounded, 761.

INDEX. 1411

Kaiser, Charles A., pvt., Co. K, 1st Mont. Vol. Inf., death, 967.
Kaiserin Augusta, German steamship, mentioned, 752.
Kalkins, Henry M., pvt., Co. K, 1st Cal. Vol. Inf., wounded, 898.
Kamp, J. H., railway mail clerk mentioned, 298.
Kanawha, water boat, mentioned, 192, 198.
Kane, James, pvt., Co. K, 14th U. S. Inf., wounded, 898.
Kane, John, pvt., Co. K, 17th U. S. Inf., death, 1062.
Kane, Michael E., pvt., Co. C, 28th Inf., U. S. V., killed, 1130.
Kane, Thomas, pvt., Co. A, 26th U. S. Inf., death, 1226.
Kang, Chen, Chinese consular agent at Manila, correction of name, 789.
Kankiwicz, Peter, pvt., Co. G, 13th U. S. Inf., wounded, 1085.
Kanters, Lex M., mus., Co. K. 40th Inf., U. S. V., wounded, 1183.
Kappner, Lawrence P., pvt., Co A, 42d Inf., U. S. V., killed, 1231.
Karger, Charles, pvt., Co. M, 3d U. S. Inf., death, 1001.
Karns, Thomas F., pvt., Co. H, 18th U. S. Inf., wounded, 1166.
Katibac, Gregorio, insurgent officer, surrender, 1273.
Kauffman, James F., pvt., Co. D 11th U. S. V. Cav., death, 1208.
Kauffman, Joseph C., corpl., Co. G, 47th Inf., U. S. V., wounded, 1187.
Kaufman, Emanuel, pvt., Co. L, 15th U. S. Inf., killed, 1211; wounded, 1212.
Kaufmann, George C., pvt., Co. E, 14th U. S. Inf., death, 465; wounded, 460.
Kayser, Christian F., pvt., Co. B, 51st Inf., U. S. V., death, 1244.
Kayser, Frank J., pvt., Troop K, 3d U. S. Cav., wounded, 1137.
Kean, Peter H., sergt., Troop H, 4th U. S. Cav., death, 1130.
Kearnes, Joseph P., pvt., Co. M, 1st Colo. Vol. Inf., wounded, 1010.
Kearney, Anthony, pvt., Co. L, 15th U. S. Inf., wounded, 1211, 1243.
Keath, George W., pvt., Co. D, 33d Inf., U. S. V., death, 1205.
Keavey, Martin E., pvt., Co. A, 21st U. S. Inf., death, 1267; wounded, 1263.
Keckley, Charles, pvt., Co. A, 1st Nebr. Vol. Inf., wounded, 899.
Keeble, John R., pvt., Co. H, 47th Inf. U. S. V., wounded, 1202.
Keefe, William, pvt., Co. I, 31st Inf., U. S. V., death, 1178.
Keen, Frank B., pvt., Co. H, 25th U. S. Inf., death, 1152.
Keen, Henry, jr., pvt., Co. I, 21st U. S. Inf., death, 1060.
Keenan, James T., pvt., Co. I, 1st Nebr. Vol. Inf., wounded, 974.
Keenan, Richard E., pvt., Co. C, 9th U. S. Inf., wounded, 1055.
Keene, William, pvt., Co. I, 20th Kans. Vol. Inf., killed, 949.
Keeney, John D., pvt., Co. F, 1st Nebr. Vol. Inf., wounded, 982.
Keeney, Reed M., pvt., Co. M, 6th U. S. Inf., wounded, 1126.
Keeton, Robert L., pvt., Co. H, 21st U. S. Inf., death, 1070.
Kehoe, J. J., pvt., Co. G, 2d Oreg. Vol. Inf., death, 1008.
Keifer, J. Warren, maj. gen., U. S. V., mentioned, 285, 548-554.
Keith, Walter S., pvt., Co. M, 36th Inf., U. S. V., death, 1201.
Keithley, Ira, sergt., Co. D, 20th Kans. Vol. Inf., wounded, 904.
Kelch, William D, pvt., Co. C, 8d U. S. Inf., drowned, 1213.
Keleher, Timothy D., maj., addl. p. m., U. S. V., duties, 792.
Kelleher, Matthew, corpl., Co. L, 17th U. S. Inf., death, 1070.

Keller, Albert B., pvt., Co. C. 9th U. S. Inf., wounded, 1298.
Keller, Herbert L., pvt., Co. C, 13th Minn. Vol. Inf., death, 993.
Keller, James A., pvt., Co. D, 39th Inf., U. S. V., death, 1189.
Keller, Robert M., pvt., Co. M, 44th Inf., U. S. V., killed, 1256.
Keller, William J., pvt., Co. F, 3d U. S. Inf., death, 1181.
Keller, William M , pvt., Co. B, 1st Idaho Vol. Inf., wounded, 897.
Keller, Charles, pvt., Troop A, 15th U. S. Cav., killed by Moros, 1322.
Kellett, Bert, pvt , Co. G, 1st S. Dak. Vol. Inf., wounded, 996.
Kelley, Myles, 2d lieut., 1st Mont. Vol. Inf., wounded, 954.
Kellick, John, pvt., Co. K, 17th U. S. Inf., death, 1256.
Kelliher, Robert J., corpl., Co. E 13th Minn. Vol. Inf., wounded, 966.
Kellock, C. J., sergt., U. S. Marine Corps, killed, 445.
Kellock, W., pvt., Co. G, 22d U. S. Inf., mentioned, 214.
Kellogg, Edgar R., col., 6th U. S. Inf., mentioned, 1016.
Kellogg, Hurley B., pvt., Troop D, 4th U. S. Cav., death, 1153.
Kellogg, Sanford C., maj., 4th U. S. Cav., mentioned, 666, 667, 685.
Kells, Ralph W., pvt., Co. L, 1st Nebr. Vol. Inf., killed, 917.
Kelly, Alonzo B., pvt., Co. F, 24th U. S. Inf., wounded, 1148.
Kelly, Frederick J., pvt., Batty. D, 6th U. S. Art., drowned, 866; wounded, 948.
Kelly, Ira L., pvt., Troop K, 4th U. S. Cav., drowned, 866.
Kelly, James, pvt., Batty. G, 3d U. S. Art., death, 1130.
Kelly, James, pvt., Co. G, 2d Oreg. Vol. Inf., death, 988.
Kelly, James F., pvt., Co. C, 22d U. S. Inf., death 1189.
Kelly, John, pvt., Co. K, 9th U. S. Inf., wounded, 1087.
Kelly, John, pvt., Troop K, 11th U. S. V. Cav., death, 1175.
Kelly, John H., pvt., Co. B, 22d U. S. Inf., killed, 1140.
Kelly, John P., pvt., Co. E, 9th U. S. Inf., death, 1299.
Kelly, Joseph, pvt., Co. A, 36th Inf., U. S. V., killed, 1201.
Kelly, Michael, pvt., Co. L, 15th U. S. Inf., wounded, 1211.
Kelly, Mike, pvt., Co. C, 20th U. S. Inf., wounded, 937.
Kelly, Peter, sergt. Co. K, 21st U. S. Inf., wounded, 1084.
Kelly, Richard H , pvt., Co. L, 13th Minn. Vol. Inf., wounded 963.
Kelly, Thomas, corpl., U. S. Marine Corps, killed, 445.
Kelly, Thomas P., pvt., Co. L, 15th U. S. Inf., killed, 1211.
Kelly, Vernon, pvt., Co. K, 10th Pa. Vol. Inf., wounded, 945.
Kelly, William, pvt., Co. G, 9th U. S. Inf., suicide, 477.
Kelly, William J., Corpl., Co. C, 40th Inf., U.S.V., killed, 1255.
Kelsay, Lyman, pvt., Co. D, 2d Oreg. Vol. Inf., death, 1001.
Kelson, Charles A., artif., Co. B, 20th Kans. Vol. Inf., wounded 898.
Kemano, Edward H., pvt., Troop L, 4th U. S. Cav., death, 1066.
Kemp, Walter, pvt., Co. F, 20th Kans. Vol. Inf., wounded, 952.
Kemper, Oran A., mus., Co. M, 14th U. S. Inf., wounded, 454.
Kempff, Louis, rear-admiral, U. S. N., mentioned, 409-423, 426, 436.
Kenan, Owen T., capt., 29th Inf., U. S. V., wounded, 1126.

Kendall, Hampton, pvt., Co. F, 24th U. S. Inf., death, 1057, 1060.
Kendall, Lucius, col., 1st Me. Vol. Inf., mentioned, 530, 531.
Kenly, William L., 1st lieut., 1st Art., mentioned, 1131.
Kennan, Cortland L., col., 5th Ohio Vol. Inf., mentioned, 55.
Kennedy, David J., pvt., Co. D, 9th U. S. Inf., wounded, 444.
Kennedy, David V., pvt., Co. L, 37th Inf., U. S. V., wounded, 1150.
Kennedy, George, pvt., Co. M, 47th Inf., U. S. V., death, 1215; wounded, 1214.
Kennedy, Horace F., sergt., Co. M, 1st Nebr. Vol. Inf., wounded, 974.
Kennedy, J., pvt., U. S. Marine Corps, killed, 459.
Kennedy, James, pvt., Co. K, 1st Mont. Vol. Inf., drowned, 979.
Kennedy, James A., pvt., Co. E, 12th U. S. Inf., wounded, 1214.
Kennedy, James W., pvt., Co. G, 1st Mont. Vol. Inf., wounded, 900, 906.
Kennedy, John T., corpl., Batty. A, Utah Vol. Art., death, 939.
Kennedy, Michael, pvt., Co. F, 14th U. S. Inf., wounded, 895.
Kennedy, Thomas A., corpl., Co. H, 43d Inf., U. S. V., wounded, 1214.
Kennedy, William, pvt., Co. G, 1st Mont. Vol. Inf., wounded, 901, 906.
Kennedy, William G., pvt., Co. C, 20th U. S. Inf., death, 1109.
Kennedy, William H., pvt., Co. G, 9th U. S. Inf., death, 1066.
Kennedy, William S., pvt., Co. I, 14th U. S. Inf., wounded, 898.
Kenney, Frank, pvt., Co. A, 2d Oreg. Vol. Inf., mentioned, 1028.
Kennon, Lyman W. V., col., 34th Inf., U. S. V., mentioned, 570.
Kenny, Edgar A., pvt., Co. E, 19th U. S. Inf., death, 1090.
Kenny, John N., pvt., Co. A, 30th Inf., U. S. V., death, 1216.
Kenoyer, Hugh, pvt., Co. M, 1st Nebr. Vol. Inf., wounded, 897.
Kent, George, pvt., Co. A, 34th Mich. Vol. Inf., mentioned, 253.
Kent, J. Ford, brig. gen., U. S. A., health of army in Cuba, 202.
Mentioned, 47, 54, 101, 109, 113, 116, 181, 202, 216, 219, 226, 228, 540, 541, 543.
Kent, William A., 2d lieut., 23d U. S. Inf., mentioned, 1041.
Kent, William S., pvt., Co. K, 3d U. S. Inf., death, 1202.
Keogel, Christopher C., pvt., Co. B, 13th U. S. Inf., death, 1232.
Keogh, Harry R., pvt., Co. E, 1st S. Dak. Vol. Inf., killed, 949.
Kerbey, Everette, pvt., Co. C, 39th Inf., U. S. V., death, 1189.
Kerens, R. C., Hon., mentioned, 344, 345.
Kerins, Joseph J., pvt., Co. H., 43d Inf., U. S. V., killed, 1168.
Kernan, Francis J., capt., 2d U. S. Inf., mentioned, 646, 668.
Kernen, John, pvt., Co. B, 51st Iowa Vol. Inf., wounded, 975.
Kerr, Benjamin M., pvt., Co. M, 38th Inf., U. S. V., death, 1189.
Kerr, Harry B., pvt., Co. H, 1st Colo. Vol. Inf., wounded, 950.
Kerr, Howard L., pvt., Co. M, 1st Nebr. Vol. Inf., wounded, 897.
Kerr, John B., capt., 6th U. S. Cav., wounded, 123.
Kerr, Robert C., pvt., Co. I, 14th U. S. Inf., killed, 453.
Kerr, Robert D., 2d lieut., Engr. Corps, U. S. A., death, 803.
Kerrigan, Anthony, corpl., Co. B, 43d Inf., U. S. V., death, 1125.
Kerrigan, Herbert W., pvt., Co. H, 2d Oreg. Vol. Inf., mentioned, 1028.
Kershner, Edward L., pvt., Co. L, 16th U. S. Inf., wounded, 1240.
Kershner, James W., corpl., Co. A, 20th Kans. Vol. Inf., wounded, 903, 976.

Kerth, Monroe C., 2d lieut., 21st U. S. Inf., wounded, 1015.
Kessinger, Joseph C., pvt., Troop D, 11th U. S. V. Cav., death, 1125; wounded, 1124.
Kessler, Frank, corpl., Co. K, 18th U. S. Inf., death, 1174.
Kessler, Henry C., col., 1st Mont. Vol. Inf., mentioned, 567.
Kessler, James, pvt., Co. D, 10th Pa. Vol. Inf., wounded, 897.
Kettle, R., pvt., U. S. Marine Corps, death, 1314.
Key, Albert L., lieut., U. S. N., mentioned, 456.
Key West, Fla.:
Convoys at, 29, 62, 66, 88.
To be met during daylight, 42.
Lighters and tugs sent to Cuba from, 120.
Medical officer, request detail of, 86.
Rendezvous for Army of Invasion, 11.
Seizure of press boats at, directed, 23.
Surgeon at, to report list of wounded, 98.
Transports, movement to and from, 86, 95.
Repairs on, 88.
To proceed without convoy, 129.
With sick and wounded sail for, 80.
Water supply at, inadequacy, 12.
Wounded, to be taken to hospital at, 112.
Keyes, Maxwell, 2d lieut., 3d U. S. Inf., killed, 1109.
Kidd, George A., pvt., Co. L, 17th U. S. Inf., death, 1008.
Kiddoo, Frank R., pvt., Co. E, 14th U. S. Inf., wounded, 454.
Kidney, John T., pvt., Co. K, 39th Inf., U. S. V., killed, 1255.
Kilbourne, Charles E., maj., pay dept., U. S. A., mentioned, 635, 766, 791.
Kilbourne, Henry S., maj., med. dept., U. S. A., opinion as to health condition of army in Cuba, 201.
Kilkenny, Lawrence E., pvt., Co. E, 18th U. S. Inf., wounded, 1227.
Kille, ——, missionary in China, mentioned, 497.
Killian, John H., pvt., Co. H, 13th U. S. Inf., death, 1008.
Killion, Mathew W., pvt., Troop D, 4th U. S. Cav., wounded, 1087.
Killough, Rollie B., pvt., Co. L, 40th Inf., U. S. V., killed, 1162.
Killough, Thomas A., pvt., Co. E, 40th Inf., U. S. V., wounded, 1148.
Killpatrick, Chester L., pvt., Co., G, 33d Inf., U. S. V., wounded, 1124.
Kilpatrick, U. S. transport, mentioned, 595, 619, 1224, 1227, 1244, 1254, 1265, 1273, 1278, 1282, 1283, 1292, 1293, 1304, 1311, 1316, 1319, 1323, 1340, 1342, 1350, 1357.
Kilpatrick, William, pvt., Co. C, 32d Inf., U. S. V., killed by comrade, 1220.
Kimball, Amos S., lieut. col., qm. dept., U. S. A., mentioned, 12, 39, 173, 179, 246, 247, 291, 308, 315, 874, 879, 881, 882, 884, 885.
Kimball, Amos W., capt., qm. dept., U. S. A., mentioned, 985.
Kimble, Doughton H., pvt., Co. K, 44th Inf., U. S. V., wounded, 1227.
Kincaid, Ernest R., corpl., Co. K, 20th Kans. Vol. Inf., wounded, 977.
Kind, Henry, pvt., Co. M, 27th Inf., U. S. V., death, 1230.
Kinder, Mr., representative of railroad in China, mentioned, 483.
Kindred, Ellis, pvt., Co. F, 30th Inf., U. S. V., killed, 1195.
King, Charles, brig. gen., U. S. V., mentioned, 559, 678, 757, 758, 759, 795, 797, 832, 838, 970, 1000.
King, C. B., pvt., U. S. Marine Corps, killed, 459.
King, Edward L., 2d lieut., 7th U. S. Cav., mentioned, 227.
King, Ernest, pvt., Co. G, 24th U. S. Inf., drowned, 1208.
King, Frank E., pvt., Co. G, 9th U. S. Inf., death, 1020.
King, George, pvt., Co. H, 14th U. S. Inf., wounded 460.
King, George W., pvt., Co. E, 17th U. S. Inf., wounded, 1031.
King, John B., corpl., Troop C, 3d U. S. Cav., killed, 1152.
King, Loda B., pvt., Co. G, 9th U. S. Inf., wounded, 444.

King, Richard, pvt., Batty. H, 3d U. S. Art., wounded, 959.
King, Stewart, pvt., Co. B, 27th Inf., U. S. V., death, 1174.
King, Thomas, pvt., Co. L, 14th U. S. Inf., wounded, 460.
Kingery, William H., pvt., Co. L, 17th U. S. Inf., death, 1205.
Kingsbury, Henry P., maj., 3d U. S. Cav., mentioned, 1211.
Kingsland, L. D., prest. Manufacturers' Ass'n, St. Louis, Mo., mentioned, 343.
Kingsmore, S. W., post-office clerk, mentioned, 298.
Kinniey, Oscar C., pvt., Co. C, 20th U. S. Inf., wounded, 937.
Kinnison, Henry L, 1st lieut., 25th U. S. Inf., wounded, 124.
Kinsell, William F., pvt., Co. D, 37th Inf., U. S. V., death, 1149.
Kintuck, U. S. transport, mentioned, 448, 471, 503, 1272, 1281.
Kiphart, Edgar, artif., Co. K, 4th U. S. inf., wounded, 1017.
Kirby-Smith, Reynold M., asst. surg., 1st Tenn. Vol. Inf., mentioned, 839.
Kirkland, Henry B., pvt., Co. B, 9th U. S. Inf., death, 486.
Kirley, John, pvt., Co. K, 1st Mont. Vol. Inf., wounded, 977.
Kirtz, Ezra A., pvt., Co. H, 2d Oreg. Vol. Inf., wounded, 1008.
Kistler, Robert C., pvt., Co. D, 3d U. S. Inf., wounded, 956.
Kitchen, George, pvt., Co. K, 24th U. S. Inf., death, 1132.
Kitchen, Zade E., pvt., Co. M, 17th U. S. Inf., death, 1144.
Kitchen, Chauncey A., sergt., Co. F, 44th Inf., U. S. V., status of, 1230.
Klein, Jacob, pvt., Co. L, 9th U. S. Inf., death, 1185.
Kleinhample, Joseph O., pvt., Co. C, 9th U.S. Inf., killed, 1297.
Klick, Paul H., pvt., Co. H, 13th U. S. Inf., death, 1125.
Kline, Elza, pvt., Co. F, 30th Inf., U. S. V., death, 1194.
Kline, Jacob, brig. gen., U. S. V., mentioned, 55, 526–528, 534, 536, 537, 565, 578, 1088, 1273.
Kline, James W., pvt., Co. L, 20th Kans. Vol. Inf., wounded, 934.
Kline, John C., pvt., Co. A, 1st Wash. Vol. Inf., wounded 896.
Kline, Louis, pvt., Co. E, 48th Inf., U. S. V., death, 1229.
Kling, George, pvt., Co. D, 21st U. S. Inf., death, 1213.
Klinke, Frederick, pvt., Co. B, 39th Inf., U. S. V., death, 1172.
Klockenkemper, Henry J., cook, Co. L, 6th U. S. Inf., death, 1210.
Knapp, Charles, pvt., Co. D, 1st Nebr. Vol. Inf., wounded, 952.
Knapp, Ernest C., pvt., Co. G, 9th U. S. Inf., death, 1082.
Knapp, George G., pvt., Co. G, 36th Inf., U. S. V., killed, 1143.
Knapp, Russell, pvt., Co. B, 3d U. S. Inf., death, 1196.
Knaub, George, pvt., Troop H, 4th U. S. Cav., captured by insurgents, 1196.
Knebel, Thomas, pvt., Co. F. 4th U. S. Inf., killed, 1256.
Knee, Aaron A., artif., Co. K, 47th Inf., U. S. V., wounded, 1235.
Knepa, Charles H., pvt., Co. C, 9th U. S. Inf., wounded, 994.
Knickerbocker, U. S. transport, mentioned, 190, 245, 249, 255, 332.
Kniffen, Addison E., pvt., Co. B, 42d Inf., U.S.V., death, 1205.
Knight, Daniel, pvt., Co. K, 49th Inf., U. S. V., death, 1153.
Knight, James Harvey, pvt., Co. M, 14th U. S. Inf., killed, 895.
Knight Vallie, pvt., Co. L, 33d Inf., U. S. V., death, 1190.

Knighton, Charles E., pvt., Co. B, 12th U. S. Inf., wounded, 1057.
Knitter, John J., pvt., Co. D, 9th U. S. Inf., death, 477.
Knittle, Albert, pvt., Batty. O, 6th U. S. Art., death, 1150.
Knoffke, Frank J., pvt., Co. L, 23d U. S. Inf., wounded, 1195.
Knoll, Frank, sergt., Co. E, 14th U. S. Inf., wounded, 454.
Knouse, Frank M., pvt., Co. C, 1st Nebr. Vol. Inf., death, 861.
Knox, Joseph, pvt., Co. K, 9th U. S. Inf., death, 494.
Knox, Lyle L., pvt., Co. I, 20th Kans. Vol. Inf., wounded, 976.
Knox, Roy J. D., pvt., Co. E, 10th Pa. Vol. Inf., wounded, 955.
Knox, Thomas T., capt., 1st U. S. Cav., wounded, 54, 55, 123.
Knowles, Ernest, pvt., Co. D, 21st U. S. Inf., wounded, 1090.
Knuckles, William, pvt., Co. E, 42d Inf., U. S. V., death, 1153.
Kobbé, William A., brig. gen., U. S. V., mentioned, 572, 575, 577, 579, 1133, 1135, 1139, 1141, 1144, 1154, 1155, 1159, 1223, 1251, 1264, 1266.
See *Expedition*, under *Philippine Islands*.
Kocarnik, Louis, pvt., Batty. F, 4th U. S. Art., mentioned, 195.
Koch, Albert E., corpl., Co. A, 2d U. S. Inf., mentioned, 212.
Koch, Alfred H., pvt., Co. F 21st U. S. Inf., death, 1027.
Koch, Henry, corpl., 1st Batty., Field Art., death, 1283.
Koehler, Adolph G., pvt., Co. M, 20th U. S. Inf., wounded, 934.
Koehler, Edgar F., 1st lieut., 9th U. S. Inf., killed, 1148.
Koehler, George B., corpl., Co. I, 23d U. S. Inf., killed, 1166.
Koenig, Ernest, sergt., Batty. A, Cal. Vol. Art., death, 1058.
Koontz, Howard M., 1st lieut., 44th Inf., U. S. V., killed, 1229.
Koontz, Spencer S., pvt., Co. F, 36th Inf., U.S.V., death, 1140.
Koopman, William J., pvt., Co. L, 1st Nebr. Vol. Inf., wounded, 946.
Koops, Carl, 1st lieut., 10th U. S. Inf., wounded, 124.
Koplen, Adolph, pvt., Co. A, 1st N. Dak. Vol. Inf., drowned, 956.
Kopp, John, pvt., Co. I, 43d Inf., U. S. V., wounded, 1176.
Koskela, M. W., pvt., Co. F, 1st Idaho Vol. Inf., wounded, 902.
Kosling, J., pvt., Co. H, 33d Inf., U. S. V., mentioned, 195.
Koth, Enoch, pvt., Co. F, 1st Idaho Vol. Inf., wounded, 897.
Krafft, Hugo C., pvt., Co. G, 14th U. S. Inf., death, 486.
Kramer, Herman W., pvt., Co. L 30th Inf., U.S.V., death, 1210.
Kramer, Jerry, pvt., Batty. E, 3d U. S. Art., wounded, 901.
Kramer, William, pvt., Co. D, 1st Mont. Vol. Inf., wounded, 1008.
Kramer, William F., pvt., Co. D, 1st Mont. Vol. Inf., wounded, 915.
Kranz, Henry J., pvt., Co. C, 45th Inf., U. S. V., death, 1200.
Krayenbuhl, Maurice G., capt., 2d U. S. Art., mentioned, 948, 956; mortally wounded, 945.
Kreanert, Joseph, sergt., Co. K, 16th U. S. Inf., death, 1164.
Kreeger, Charles F., pvt., Co. K, 4th U. S. Inf., wounded, 1017.
Kreger, August, pvt., Co. B, 1st U. S. Inf., death, 1267.
Kreidler, John P., pvt., Co. H, 38th Inf., U. S. V., missing, 1216.
Kreitzer, Adolph M., pvt., Batty. F, 6th U. S. Art., death, 1056.
Kretz, John G., pvt., Co. H, 33th Inf., U. S. V., wounded, 1233.

INDEX.

Krider, David, pvt., Batty. M, 3d U. S. Art., wounded, 897.
Kriger, Charles J., pvt., Co. F, 30th Inf., U. S. V., killed, 1195.
Krohn, Emil, pvt., Co. A, 3d U. S. Inf., wounded, 956.
Kroupa, Edward C., pvt., Co. F, 71st N. Y. Vol. Inf., mentioned, 219.
Krueger, Albert R., sergt., Co. I, 39th Inf., U. S. V., death, 1233.
Krueger, Fred, pvt., Co. K, 3d U. S. Inf., death, 1001.
Krueger, Gustav A., pvt., Co. A, 39th Inf., U. S. V., death, 1170.
Krueger, William, pvt., Co. D, 30th Inf., U. S. V., death, 1228.
Kruger, Herman F., pvt., Co. K, 1st S. Dak. Vol. Inf., wounded, 956.
Kruger, Otto, pvt., Co. L, 3d U. S. Inf., wounded, 1232.
Krupp, Otto, pvt., Troop B, 1st U. S. Cav., killed, 61.
Kruse, Max R., pvt., Co. L, 1st Cal. Vol. Inf., wounded, 914.
Kuck, Edward, pvt., Co. E, 44th Inf., U. S. V., wounded, 1174.
Kuert, Julius A., col., 2d Ohio Vol. Inf., mentioned, 515.
Kuester, Jules, pvt., Batty. K, 3d U. S. Art., wounded, 946.
Kugle, Harry W., pvt., Co. G, 12th U. S. Inf., death, 1257.
Kugler, Lewis, pvt., Co. A, 41st Inf., U. S. V., death, 1200.
Kuhn, Fred, pvt., Co. C, 1st Nebr. Vol. Inf., wounded, 899.
Kuhn, Frederick, pvt., Co. L, 17th U. S. Inf., drowned at sea, 952.
Kuhn, John E., pvt., Co. H, 43d Inf., U. S. V., killed, 1168.
Kuhns, Harris E., pvt., Co. L, 20th Kans. Vol. Inf., wounded, 954.
Kunkel, Henry, corpl., Co. C, 28th Inf., U. S. V., wounded, 1229.
Kunzig, William, pvt., Co. B, 6th U. S. Inf., death, 1052.
Kustenborder, William Otto, pvt., Co. H, 1t Nebr. Vol. Inf., death, 979; wounded, 955.
Kutschinsky, Frank, pvt., Co. H, 47th Inf., U. S. V., killed, 1162.
Kuver, Ernest A., corpl., Co. H, 3d U. S. Inf., wounded, 956.
Kyger, Daniel T., pvt., Co. I, 1st Wash. Vol. Inf., death, 903.
Kyger, Miles E., corpl., Co. I, 1st Wash. Vol. Inf., death, 894.
Kyle, James H., U. S. Senator, mentioned, 304.
Kynan, Michael, pvt., Co. F, 18th U. S. Inf., death, 1156.
Kysela, Henry J., pvt., Co. G, 14th U. S. Inf., wounded, 460.
Kysh, William B., corpl., Co. H, 33d Inf., U. S. V., wounded, 1152.
Kyte, John, corpl., Co. L, 8th Mass. Vol. Inf., mentioned, 214.
Labodie, Julius, 1st sergt., Co. L, 6th U. S. Inf., death, 1082.
Labreck, Thomas J., pvt., Batty. M, 7th U. S. Art., killed, 1236.
Lacharite, Fred, pvt., Troop L, 3d U. S. Cav., death, 1210.
Ladd, Ira B., a. a. surg., U. S. A., mentioned, 1007.
Ladrones group, island of to be ceded to U. S., 751.
La Duke, ——, 2d Wis. Vol. Inf., mentioned, 391.
Lafeyth, William A., pvt., Co. L, 20th U. S. Inf., wounded, 937.
Laffler, William, jr., pvt., Co. B, 40th Inf., U. S. V., wounded, 1160.
Lafflin, Gilbert B., pvt., Co. B, 34th Inf., U. S. V., death, 1213.
La Garde, Louis A., maj., med. dept., U. S. A., mentioned, 141, 197-199, 205.
Lageman, Charles B., pvt., Co. H, 17th U. S. Inf., death, 1228.
La Grande Duchesse, U. S. transport, mentioned, 93, 102-104, 108, 109, 116-119, 125, 127, 294, 295.
Lahey, Michael T., pvt., Co. K, 16th U. S. Inf., death, 1164.

Laidler, Holland I., pvt., Hosp. Corps, U. S. A., killed, 975.
Laigle, Albert C., pvt., Co. K, 18th U. S. Inf., death, 1210.
Laird, Ridgley M., pvt., Co. G, 43d Inf., U. S. V., wounded, 1163.
Laird, Robert Ed., pvt., Co. E, 26th Inf., U. S. V., death, 1168.
Laine, J., pvt., Co. G, 9th U. S. Inf., mentioned, 183.
Lake, Oscar, pvt., Co. C, 34th Inf., U. S. V., wounded, 1192.
Lakes, Dept. of, General Bates to command, 841.
Lakken, Ole T., pvt., Co. K, 1st N. Dak. Vol. Inf., death, 840.
Lamb, Charles S., pvt., Co. F, 1st Idaho Vol. Inf., mentioned, 934. Wounded, 917.
Lamb, Charles W., pvt., Co. K, 34th Inf., U. S. V., death, 1109.
Lamb, Samuel H., corpl., Co. H, 17th U. S. Inf., wounded, 1055.
Lamb, William G., pvt., Co. I, 1st N. Dak. Vol. Inf., killed, 967.
Lambert, Charles A., pvt., Co. I, 2d U. S. Inf., wounded, 1259.
Lambert, Clinton, pvt., Co. C, 14th U. S. Inf., wounded, 760.
Lamkin, George A. G., pvt., Co. H, 37th Inf., U. S. V., killed, 1128.
Lammers, Edward H., pvt., Co. M, 22d U. S. Inf., wounded, 946.
Lamon, Isaac J., pvt., Co. G, 3d U. S. Inf., wounded, 1212.
Lamoree, Nelson T., pvt., Co. I, 14th U. S. Inf., death, 1015.
Lampasas, U. S. transport, mentioned, 94, 112, 126, 127, 133, 134, 143, 146, 148, 293, 341.
Lampman, Frank, pvt., Co. I, 4th U. S. Inf., killed, 1052.
Lampok, Datto, Moro, mentioned, 1332.
Lancaster, James M., maj., 4th U. S. Art., mentioned, 388.
Land, Noah B., pvt., Co. E, 1st Nebr. Vol. Inf., death, 976.
Land, [Sands] John R., hosp. stewd., U.S.A., mentioned, 662.
Landenschlager, William, pvt., Co. C, 20th Kans. Vol. Inf., wounded, 988.
Landerman, Frank M., pvt., Co. G, 1st Mont. Vol. Inf., wounded, 959.
Landfeohr, Henry W., pvt., Co. E, 35th Inf., U. S. V., killed, 1112.
Landis, Claude B., member of Congress, mentioned, 844, 845.
Landis, Jacob, corpl., Co. C, 10th Pa. Vol. Inf., killed, 897.
Landolt, Harry B., pvt., Co. I, 28th Inf., U. S. V., wounded, 1132.
Landreth, Alvin, pvt., Co. M, 40th Inf., U. S. V., killed, 1183.
Landrum, Benton W., pvt., Co. I, 3d U. S. Inf., wounded, 987.
Lane, Bert R., pvt., Co. K, 18th U. S. Inf., killed, 1143.
Lane, Edward G., pvt., Co. F, 19th U. S. Inf., death, 1189.
Lane, Godwin J., corpl., Co. I, 21st U. S. Inf., wounded, 1044.
Lane, James A., pvt., Co. H, 33d Inf., U. S. V., wounded, 1124.
Lane, Joseph, pvt., Co. I, 9th Mass. Vol. Inf., mentioned, 216.
Lane, Josh, pvt., Co. A, 49th Inf., U. S. V., death, 1190.
Lane, Milton, pvt., Co. H, 42d Inf., U. S. V., wounded, 1146.
Lane, Robert F., pvt., Co. K, 43d Inf., U. S. V., death, 1236.
Lane, Sidney, mus., Co. D, 47th Inf., U. S. V., wounded, 1176.
Lane, William E., pvt., Co. D, 38th Inf., U. S. V., wounded, 1192.
Lang, Frank R., 1st lieut., 9th U. S. Inf., mentioned, 1041. Wounded, 429, 430, 443, 449, 454.
Lang, John L., sergt., Co. H, 3d U. S. Art., killed, 966.
Lang, Louis M., capt., 42d Inf., U. S. V., mentioned, 1307.

INDEX. 1415

Lang, William T., corpl., Co. L, 4th U. S. Inf., wounded. 1017.
Lange, Frank, sergt., Co. E, 42d Inf. U.S.V., death, 1196.
Langevin, David, sergt., band, 46th Inf., U. S. V., killed, 1176.
Langfitt, William C., maj., U. S. Vol. Engrs., mentioned, 802.
Langford, G. W., civilian, mentioned, 1129.
Langford, Henry, corpl., Co. L, 22d U. S. Inf., killed, 992.
Langhlin, James H., sergt., Co. C, 17th U. S. Inf., wounded, 1017.
Lanker, Thomas A., pvt., Co. L, 14th U. S. Inf., wounded, 460.
Langworthy, Samuel R., capt., 35th Inf., U. S. V., death, 1146.
Lanman, George B., lieut. col. 1st Ill. Vol. Inf., mentioned, 256.
Lanter, John, pvt., Co. C, 38th Inf., U. S. V., killed, 1225.
Lanterman, Stewart E., pvt., Co. M 1st Nebr. Vol., Inf., mentioned, 1026.
Lanza, Conrad H., 2d lieut., 3d U.S. Art., wounded, 966.
Laporta, Antonio, pvt., Co. A. 47th Inf., U. S. V., wounded, 1271.
Laporte, Peter, pvt., Hosp. Corps, U. S. A., death, 988.
Lapp, Oliver C., sergt., Co. I, 1st S. Dak. Vol. Inf., wounded, 975.
Lapp, William, pvt., Co. L, 12th U. S. Inf., wounded, 1015, 1027.
La River, Philip E., corpl., Co. I, 25th Inf., U. S. V., killed, 1166.
Larkin, John S., pvt., Co. C, 34th Inf., U. S. V., wounded, 1132.
Larkin, John T., pvt., Co. G, 42d Inf., U. S. V., killed, 1146.
Larnenn, J., sergt., Troop C, 3d U S. Cav., mentioned, 178.
La Rose, Charles A., pvt., Troop B, 4th U. S. Cav., death, 1086.
La Rowe, John, pvt., Co. H, 4th U. S. Inf., death, 1104.
Larrimore, Aly C., pvt., Co. A, 38th Inf., U. S. V., death, 1130.
Larsen, Charles E., pvt., Co. E, 30th Inf., U. S. V., death, 1196.
Larsen, Christian, sergt., Co. F, 12th U. S. Inf., mentioned, 204.
Larsen, Hans, pvt., Co. H, 3d Inf., U. S. V., mentioned, 213.
Larsen, Peter, corpl., Co. G, 3d U. S. Inf., death, 1075.
Larson, George O., corpl., Batty. A, Utah Vol. Art., death, 856.
Larson, Herman A., pvt., Co. K, 46th Inf., U. S. V., death, 1142.
Larson, Scott L., pvt., Co. G, 39th Inf., U. S. V., death, 1170.
Larson, Theodore, pvt., Co. K, 1st Nebr. Vol. Inf., death, 803.
Larson, Walter C., pvt., Co. L, 51st Iowa Vol. Inf., wounded, 974.
Larue, Edward H., corpl., Co. C, 40th Inf., U. S. V., killed, 1182.
La Rue, William H., pvt., Co. K, 1st Nebr. Vol. Inf., wounded, 974.
Larzelere, Charles W., pvt., Troop F, 3d U. S. Cav., wounded, 1257.
Lash, William M., corpl., Co. F, 30th Inf., U. S. V., death, 1208. Wounded, 1203.
La Shell, George M., sergt., Co. B, 1st Idaho Vol. Inf., wounded, 1008.
Lashley, Mark E., corpl., Co. G, 39th Inf., U. S. V., wounded, 1192.
Lasseigne, Armand, capt., 14th U. S. Inf., mentioned, 1156.
Lassiter, William, capt., 16th U. S. Inf., wounded, 124.
Latimer, Grant, pvt., Co. E, 48th Inf., U. S. V., death, 1234.
Latimer, Julian L., lieut., U. S. N., mentioned, 457, 459.
Lattimore, John W., corpl., Co. C, 9th U. S. Inf., wounded, 1086.
Lauer, Clemens, pvt., Co. F, 23d U. S. Inf., killed, 760, 803.

Laura, steam tug, mentioned, 54, 58, 104, 192.
Laurence, Hardy L., pvt., Co. H, 36th Inf., U.S.V., death, 1123; wounded, 1092.
Lautzanheiser, Irvine, pvt., Co. —, 8th Ohio Vol. Inf., mentioned, 226.
La Verne Co., ice plant erected by, 1235.
Lavey, Thomas, pvt., Co. L, 18th U. S. Inf., killed, 1264.
Lavier, Charles J., jr., pvt., Co. H, 9th U. S. Inf., killed, 1052.
Law, George A., sergt., Co. I, 23d U. S. Inf., killed, 1166.
Lawrence, Capt., Englishman, commanding Aguinaldo's artillery, mentioned, 1108.
Lawrence, J. E., pvt., Co. M, 2d Oreg. Vol. Inf., mentioned, 1028.
Lawrence, Walter, pvt., Co. C, 40th U. S. Inf., wounded, 1193, 1259.
Lawrence, Willse, pvt., Co. K, 14th U. S. Inf., wounded, 454.
Laws, Albert, 1st lieut., 24th U. S. Inf., wounded, 124.
Laws, Thomas J., sergt., Co. L, 14th U. S. Inf., death, 1015.
Lawson, Charles H., corpl., Co. B, 37th Inf., U. S. V., wounded, 1075.
Lawson, Dwight F., pvt., Troop A, 4th U. S. Cav., wounded, 1272.
Lawson, Laurin L., pvt., Co. B, 1st Wash. Vol. Inf., wounded, 897.
Lawton, Henry W., maj. gen., U. S. V.:
 Assigned to command Dept. Santiago, 217, 381.
 Customs business transferred to, 255.
 Desires to remain in Cuba, 203, 204, 209.
 Killed at San Mateo, Luzon, 1123.
 Mentioned, 9, 13, 47, 70, 76, 87, 100, 101, 116, 129, 146–148, 151, 152, 181, 216, 224, 226, 227, 230, 231, 233, 235, 237, 239, 242–244, 246–249, 252, 535, 542, 543, 556, 561–563, 565–567, 569, 570, 572, 585, 866, 869, 879, 881, 931, 944, 960–963, 968, 971, 975, 977, 980–984, 988, 990, 993, 995, 1005–1008, 1010, 1042, 1062, 1067–1069, 1076, 1082, 1085, 1087–1089, 1091, 1093, 1095–1098, 1100–1104, 1106–1109, 1111, 1115, 1116, 1121, 1123, 1126, 1272.
 Opinion re. health of Army in Cuba, 202.
 Recommended for promotion, 104.
 (See *Expedition* under *Philippine Islands*.)
Lawton, Louis B., 1st lieut., 9th U. S. Inf., wounded, 428–430, 435, 443.
Lawton, R. M., pvt., Co. E, 1st Nebr. Vol. Inf., killed, 956.
Lawton, U. S. transport, mentioned, 1257, 1259, 1265, 1273, 1288, 1294, 1322, 1325, 1326, 1341, 1347, 1355.
Lawyer, Rufus, pvt., Co. G, 14th U. S. Inf., wounded, 460.
Layman, Charles A., pvt., Co. K, 4th U. S. Inf., wounded, 1017.
Lazelle, Jacob H. G., 1st lieut. 18th U. S. Inf., death, 803.
Lea, William E., pvt., Co. C, 39th Inf., U. S. V., death, 1185.
Leach, Brice, pvt., Co. C, 18th U. S. Inf., wounded, 1113.
Leach, James M., pvt., Co. A 17th U. S. Inf., death, 1070.
Leadberter, Percy, corpl., band, 13th U. S. Inf., death, 1144.
Leadly, Lewis J., pvt., Co. M, 37th Inf., U. S. V., death, 1156.
Leaf, Louis H., 2d lieut., 43d Inf., U. S. V., wounded, 1250.
Leahy, Cornelius J., pvt., Co. A, 36th Inf., U. S. V., killed, 1233.
Leahy, James T., pvt., Co. L, 3d U. S. Art., wounded, 899.
Learnard, Henry G., 1st lieut., 14th U. S. Inf., wounded, 1017.
Learneshock, Garatt, pvt., Co. E, 2d U. S. Inf., mentioned, 175.
Lears, William P., pvt., Co. E, 1st Nebr. Vol. Inf., wounded, 760.
Leary, James, pvt., Co. I, 34th Inf., U. S. V., death, 1132.
Leary, James, pvt., Co. K, 43d Inf., U. S. V., wounded, 1167.
Leasor, Elmer E., pvt., Co. C, 38th Inf., U. S. V., wounded, 1141.

1416　INDEX.

Leclaire, John, pvt., Co. I, 13th U. S. Inf., death, 1074.
Ledgerwood, Benjamin E., pvt., Co. H, 3d U. S. Inf., wounded, 995.
Ledyard, Augustus C., 1st lieut., 6th U. S. Inf., killed, 1115.
Lee, Benjamin A., col., 3d N. J. Vol. Inf., mentioned, 528.
Lee, B., pvt., Co. —, 23d U. S. Inf., death, 831.
Lee, Charles, pvt., Co. E, 26th Inf., U. S. V., death, 1150.
Lee, Fitzhugh, maj. gen., U. S. V., mentioned, 37, 43–45, 266, 268, 395, 509, 547, 548, 552.
Lee, Harry C., pvt., Co. H, 43d Inf., U. S. V., wounded, 1168.
Lee, Harry O., pvt., Co. B, 9th U. S. Inf., killed, 1112.
Lee, James G. C., col., qm. dept., U. S. A., mentioned, 646.
Lee, Jesse M., col., 30th Inf., U. S. V., wounded, 428, 429; mentioned, 1031, 1330, 1344.
Lee, John S., corpl., Co. G, 8th Ohio Vol. Inf., mentioned, 235.
Lee, Orison P., capt., 45th Inf., U. S. V., death, 1181.
Lee, Robert M., pvt., Co. F, 20th Kans. Vol. Inf., death, 1075.
Lee, Thomas, pvt., Co. C, 26th Inf., U. S. V., killed, 1189.
Lee, Walter H., 2d lieut., Engr. Corps, U. S. A., killed, 1285.
Lee, William, pvt., Co. K, 49th Inf., U. S. V., death, 1187.
Leek, A. H., pvt., Co. E, 22d U. S. Inf., mentioned, 219.
Leelanaw, U. S. transport, mentioned, 421, 431, 445, 957, 958, 979, 981, 1010, 1230.
Leeman, Harvey L., pvt., Co. F, 18th U. S. Inf., death, 1149.
Leers, Frank, pvt., Co. B, 37th Inf., U. S. V., wounded, 1148.
Legaspi, Spanish regt., distribution, 655.
Legg, Martin O., pvt., Co. L, 1st Nebr. Vol. Inf., death, 979.; wounded, 975.
Leggett, E., pvt., Troop A, 1st U. S. Vol. Cav., killed, 61.
Lehman, Frank W., pvt., Co. B, Engr. Corps, U. S. A., death, 1168.
Lehfeld, George, pvt., Co. C, 22d U. S. Inf., death, 1130.
Lehmay, Henry, pvt., Co. M, 3d U. S. Inf., death, 1044.
Leghton, James E., pvt., Batty. F, 4th U. S. Art., death, 1228.
Leimbacher, Henry, pvt., Co. G, 1st Wash. Vol. Inf., death, 947.
Leland, Lewis L., chapl., 1st Tenn. Vol. Inf., death, 920.
Lemay, William P., mus., Co. F, 3d U. S. Inf., wounded, 995.
Lemeter, Ball, pvt., Co. L, 1st Ill. Vol. Inf., mentioned, 197.
Leininger, John A., capt., 8th Ohio Vol. Inf., death, 214.
Mentioned, 240.
Shipment of remains, 236, 240.
Lemly, Henry R., capt., 7th U. S. Art., mentioned, 59, 306, 309.
Lemly, William B., capt., U. S. Marine Corps, wounded, 429.
Lemon, Charles B., sergt., Co. B, 1st Cal. Vol. Inf., death, 837.
Lemon, Thomas F., pvt., Co. A, 1st N. Y. Vol. Inf., death, 838.
Lenehan, John, pvt., Co. H, 46th Inf., U. S. V., wounded, 1137.
Lennox, Charles, pvt., Co. K, 27th Inf., U. S. V., death, 1223.
Lennox, U. S. transport, mentioned, 423, 431, 445, 447, 448, 503, 506, 1244, 1288.
Lenoir, Joseph E., pvt., Co. I, 14th U. S. Inf., wounded, 454.
Lenoir, Noah, pvt., Co. D, 48th Inf., U. S. V., death, 1189.
Lenox, James P., pvt., Co. E, 1st Mont. Vol. Inf., wounded, 954.
Lentki, Charles, pvt., Co. B, 2d U. S. Inf., wounded, 127.
Lentz, Emil, pvt., Co. B, 30th Inf., U. S. V., death, 1185.
Leon XIII, Spanish ship, mentioned, 991, 1069.

Leona, U. S. transport, mentioned, 190, 208, 232, 305–307, 310, 326, 364.
Leonard, Charles L., pvt., Co. G, 6th U. S. Inf., killed, 1255.
Leonard, Frank M., corpl., Co. F, 9th U. S. Inf., wounded, 444.
Leonard, Henry, 1st lieut., U. S. Marine Corps, mentioned, 442; wounded, 429.
Leonard, Ivers W., 1st lieut., 22d U. S. Inf., mentioned, 971.
Leonard, James, pvt., Co. K, 3d U. S. Art., wounded, 901.
Leonard, Stephen H., drum-major, 46th Inf., U. S. V., killed, 1176.
Leonard, William H., mus., Co. H, 3d U. S. Inf., mentioned, 224.
Leonhaeuser, Harry A., capt., 25th U. S. Inf., mentioned, 1104, 1130.
Le Page, Romeo, pvt., Co. A, 26th Inf., U. S. V., death, 1202.
Leppman, John H., pvt., Troop K, 4th U. S. Cav., death, 833.
Leroy, Victor, corpl., Co. M, 22d U. S. Inf., death, 1205.
Lesher, Isaiah, pvt., Co. H, 26th Inf., U. S. V., wounded, 1166.
Leslie, Claude D., pvt., Co. I, 14th U. S. Inf., death, 1193.
Lesser, ——, surg. of Red Cross, mentioned, 197.
Lester, Isaac A., pvt., Co. E, 24th U. S. Inf., mentioned, 197.
Levack, Theodore, 1st lieut., 44th Inf., U. S. V., mentioned, 1204, 1206.
Lewis, Bert, pvt., Co. I, 48th Inf., U. S. V., death, 1283.
Lewis, Charles A., pvt., Co. I, 1st Nebr. Vol. Inf., wounded, 925.
Lewis, Chauncey S., pvt., band, 26th Inf., U. S. V., death, 1267.
Lewis, Frank C., pvt., Co. F, 13th Minn. Vol. Inf., killed, 981, 987.
Lewis, Frederick W., 2d lieut., 22d U. S. Inf., mentioned, 124.
Lewis, James H., member of Congress, mentioned, 299.
Lewis, Jasper A., sergt., Batty. G, 3d U. S. Art., wounded, 915.
Lewis, John A., pvt., Co. B, 25th U. S. Inf., mentioned, 212.
Lewis, Louis H., 2d lieut., 9th U. S. Inf., killed, 124.
Lewis, Richard D., pvt., Co. H, 25th U. S. Inf., death, 1267.
Lewis, William D., pvt., Co. C, 10th Pa. Vol. Inf., wounded, 954.
Lewis, William F., capt., med. dept., U. S. A., mentioned, 17, 487.
Lewis, William P., pvt., Co. —, 1st Nebr. Vol. Inf., death, 803.
Lewis, William Z., pvt., Co. I, 1st S. Dak. Vol. Inf., death, 895.
Ley, Peter, pvt., Co. L, 22d U. S. Inf., death, 1178.
Leyden, U. S. transport, mentioned, 88, 95, 300, 301, 352.
Lichamer, George, pvt., Co. G, 2d Oreg. Vol. Inf., death, 979.
Lichtman, Harry, pvt., Co. F, 33d Inf., U. S. V., wounded, 1176.
Lick, Frank M., pvt., Troop H, 4th U. S. Cav., death, 1221.
Lien, Jonas H., 1st lieut., 1st S. Dak. Vol. Inf., killed, 948, 949.
Liever, Louis, pvt., Batty. F, 5th U. S. Art., wounded, 1085.
Lightell, Charles, pvt., Co. C, 19th U. S. Inf., death, 1162.
Lightfoot, James R., sergt., Co. K, 25th U. S. Inf., killed, 1191.
Li Hung Chang, viceroy of Chili, China, appointment to negotiate cessation hostilities, 452.
Mentioned, 418, 431, 443, 444, 462, 465, 469, 474–477, 479, 480, 485, 486, 501.
Lillard, Ben F., pvt., Co. G, 38th Inf., U. S. V., wounded, 1193.
Lille, Louis, corpl., Co. G, 41st Inf., U. S. V., death, 1150.
Lilley, Robert J., pvt., Troop F, 4th U. S. Cav., death, 1226.
Lillie, Charles, pvt., Co. I, 1st Colo. Vol. Inf., death, 903.

INDEX. 1417

Lillie, William H., pvt., Co. D, 1st Idaho Vol. Inf., wounded, 919.
Lincoln, James R., brig. gen., U. S. V., mentioned, 525-528, 536, 537.
Lincoln, Sumner H., maj., 10th U. S. Inf., mentioned, 83; wounded, 124.
Lindberg, J. P., pvt., Co. F, 1st Ill. Vol. Inf., mentioned, 219.
Linde, Milton F., pvt., Co. A, 1st Nebr. Vol. Inf., killed, 954.
Lindenberg, Charles A., pvt., Co. H, 33d Inf., U. S. V., killed, 1222.
Linderbeck, Charles P., pvt., Co. C, 46th Inf., U. S. V., death, 1202.
Linderman, Victor J., corpl., Batty. A, 3d U. S. Art., death, 491.
Lindsay, J. P., mentioned, 347.
Lindsay, William F., pvt., Troop G, 4th U. S. Cav., death, 1132.
Lindsey, Maurice F., pvt., Co. G, 29th Inf., U. S. V., wounded, 1149.
Linehan, William, pvt., Co. F, 37th Inf., U. S. V., death, 1153.
Ling, Charles J., pvt., Co. B, 13th U. S. Inf., wounded, 1113.
Linguist, John W., pvt., Co. C, 3d U. S. Inf., mentioned, 235.
Lininger, Clarence, 1st sergt., Co. I, 47th Inf., U. S. V., wounded, 1250.
Linivitch, General, Russian Army, mentioned, 481, 490.
Link, James E., pvt., Co. —, 1st S. Dak. Vol. Inf., death, 850.
Linn, John W., pvt., Co. L, 33d Inf., U. S. V., killed, 1152.
Linscott, F. M., capt., 1st Nev. Vol. Cav., mentioned, 697.
Linsener, Carl, pvt., Co. F, 12th U. S. Inf., mentioned, 235.
Linsley, Joel R., sergt., Co. L, 30th Inf., U. S. V., death, 1196.
Linstad, Hardus, qm. sergt., 34th Inf., U. S. V., killed, 1161.
Lintner, A. W., pvt., Batty. G, 3d U. S. Art., wounded, 946.
Linton, James, pvt., Co. D, 9th U. S. Inf., wounded, 1055.
Linton, John, pvt., Troop F, 3d U. S. Cav., death, 1219.
Lippincott, Henry, lieut. col., med. dept., U. S. A., mentioned, 657, 766, 994, 1013.
Lippitt, Thomas M., asst. surg., U. S. N., wounded, 459.
Lipscomb, Spencer K., corpl., Co. G, 14th U. S. Inf., wounded, 898.
Liscum, Emerson H., brig. gen., U. S. V.:
  Killed, 426, 428, 429, 436, 443.
  Mentioned, 83, 412, 415, 416, 419, 423-426, 433-435, 438, 440, 489, 575, 576, 578, 995, 1050, 1180.
  Wounded, 124.
Liscum, Mrs. Emerson H., mentioned, 1195.
Liscum, U. S. transport, mentioned, 1321, 1322, 1326.
Lisk, Raymond, pvt., Co. G, 27th Inf., U. S. V., death, 1231.
Lissak, Ormond, maj., ord. dept., U. S. A., mentioned, 321.
Litchford, John J., pvt., Co. C, 40th Inf., U. S. V., killed, 1182.
Little, Andrew, pvt., Co. G, 2d Mass. Vol. Inf., mentioned, 253.
Little, Charles, pvt., Co. F, 13th Minn. Vol. Inf., mentioned, 760, 762.
Littlefield, Charles A., pvt., Co. C, 27th Inf., U. S. V., wounded, 1124.
Littlefield, Roderick, pvt., Co. F, 18th U. S. Inf., death, 1276.
Littleton, James E., pvt., Troop I, 4th U. S. Cav., death, 1162.
Littrell, Samuel M., pvt., Co. E, 16th U. S. Inf., death, 1099.
Litzinger, William, pvt., band, 16th U. S. Inf., death, 1187.
Livingston, H. G., pvt., Co. M, 1st Nebr. Vol. Inf., killed, 899.
Lizer, James A., pvt., Co. K, 1st S. Dak. Vol. Inf., killed, 975.
Llennoc, Alexander, corpl., Troop, 1st U. S. Cav., killed, 61.

Llewellyn, William G., pvt., Co. H, 6th U. S. Inf., death, 1133.
Lober, David, pvt., Co. E, 13th U. S. Inf., death, 1255.
Lochead, William, corpl., Co. M, 45th Inf., U. S. V., death, 1271.
Lock, William H., sergt., Co. G 1st S. Dak. Vol. Inf., wounded, 901.
Lockett, James, col., 11th Cav, U. S. V., mentioned, 1032, 1042, 1053, 1127.
Lockhart, Edward E., pvt., Co. C, 18th U. S. Inf., wounded, 1117.
Lockhart, Percy R., pvt., Co. G, 1st Mont. Vol. Inf., killed, 945.
Lodge, Henry C., U. S. Senator mentioned, 308, 311.
Loewenstein, Prince, killed while conveying refreshments to troops on firing line, 949.
Loftin, William, pvt., Co. E, 9th U. S. Inf., killed, 1298.
Logan, Edward, pvt., Co. L, 43 Inf., U. S. V., killed, 1143.
Logan, Glen H., maj., addl. p. m., U. S. V., killed, 1101.
Logan, Tilden A., pvt., Co. B, 29th Inf., U. S. V., death, 1149.
Logan, U. S. transport, mentioned, 412, 423, 427, 431, 436, 592, 603, 626, 1104, 1112, 1114, 1117, 1128, 1204, 1214, 1215, 1244, 1257, 1264, 1265, 1278, 1282, 1283, 1323, 1342.
Logsdon, William, pvt., Co. C, 1st Nebr. Vol. Inf., wounded, 955.
Lohman, William, pvt., Co. C, 18th U. S. Inf., wounded, 943.
Lomia, Luigi, capt., 5th U. S. Art., mentioned, 156, 278, 279, 304.
Londrigan, William, pvt., Co. A, 21st U. S. Inf., death, 1167.
Long, Avery E., sergt., Batty. E, 1st Art., wounded, 1015.
Long, Edward, pvt., Co. A, Batt. Engr. U. S. A., wounded, 1196.
Long, Frank S., capt., 39th Inf., U. S. V., mentioned, 1131.
Long, John D., Secretary of Navy, 16, 19, 23, 28, 40, 42, 50, 52, 69, 75, 81, 88, 115, 136, 141, 173, 187, 200, 269, 270, 281, 284, 293, 297, 298, 352, 409, 423, 425, 427, 429, 432, 436, 442, 451, 467, 468, 477, 480, 481, 490, 492.
Long, John H., pvt., Co. L, 12th U. S. Inf., wounded, 1017.
Long, Oscar, lieut. col., ch. qm., U. S. V., mentioned, 643, 865, 979, 1067.
Long, Richard, pvt., Co. C, 9th U. S. Inf., killed, 1297.
Long, Samuel D., pvt., Co. C, 22d U. S. Inf., death, 1142.
Long, William C., pvt., Co. E 12th U. S. Inf., death, 1267.
Looker, Henry B., capt., 1st D. C. Vol. Inf., mentioned, 73.
Loos, John G., pvt., Co. F, 32d Inf., U. S. V., wounded, 1231.
Loose, Otto B., pvt., Co. H, 43d Inf., U. S. V., killed, 1168.
Lopez, ——, capt., Spanish army, killed, 372.
Lopez, Ignacio, insurgent general, mentioned, 1073.
Lord, Allie W., pvt., Co. E, 12th U. S. Inf., death, 1056.
Lorenz, Joseph, pvt., Co. F, 1st Mont. Vol. Inf., wounded, 950.
Lorenzen, Fred C., pvt., Co. L, 1st S. Dak. Vol. Inf., wounded, 948.
Louis, Bert, pvt., band, 7th U. S. Inf., mentioned, 174.
Louis, Norman, pvt., Co. K, 14th U. S. Inf., death, 1104.
Louisiana, U. S. transport, mentioned, 80, 188-190, 194.
Loundy, S. D., pvt., Co. F, 20th U. S. Inf., mentioned, 224.
Louth, Raymond D., pvt., Batty. M, 6th U. S. Art., death, 1066.
Lov Christof, pvt., Co. G, 20th U. S. Inf., death, 993.
Love, James M., 2d lieut., 21st U. S. Inf., wounded, 1046.
Love, Thomas, pvt., Co. E, 48th Inf., U. S. V., death, 1238.

1418 INDEX.

Lovejoy, Frank A., pvt., Co. C, 1st Wash. Vol. Inf., killed, 925.
Lovell, Joseph, pvt., Co. K, 39th Inf., U. S. V., death, 1180.
Lovell, Seth, sergt., Troop C, 4th U. S. Cav., death, 1003.
Lovering, Hon. William C., mentioned, 303.
Low, John W., pvt., Co. G, 33d Inf., U. S. V., death, 1232.
Lowe, Bertie A., pvt., Co. E, 14th U. S. Inf., wounded, 975.
Lowe, Frank, pvt., Batty. A, 6th U. S. Art., death, 1238.
Lowe, Harvey J., pvt., Co. A, 14th U. S. Inf., killed, 1027; wounded, 1015.
Lowe, Howard W., sergt., Batty. G, 6th U. S. Art., killed, 1107.
Lowe, Irwin S., pvt., Co. C, 22d U. S. Inf., death, 1202.
Lowenberg, Jesse G., 1st lieut., 37th Inf., U. S. V., wounded, 897, 1218.
Lowman, George E., sergt., Co. D, 1st Mont. Vol. Inf., wounded, 903.
Loyd, Preston A., pvt., Co. G, 26th Inf., U. S. V., wounded, 1141.
Loyeaa, Fred W., pvt., Co. E, 33d Inf., U. S. V., wounded, 1137.
Lucas, Charles E., pvt., Co. D, 51st Iowa Vol. Inf., wounded, 1017.
Lucas, Jacob, pvt., Co. D, 30th Inf., U. S. V., wounded, 1150.
Lucban, insurgent general, mentioned, 1141.
Lucban, insurgent officer, mentioned, 1273.
Luchsinger, Charles J., pvt., Troop H, 4th U. S. Cav., mentioned, 1196.
Lucier, Frank H., pvt., Co. K, 43d Inf., U. S. V., wounded, 1250.
Ludington, Marshall I., Q. M. General, U. S. A., mentioned, 66, 100, 118, 120, 142, 210, 267, 318, 351, 357, 402, 404.
Ludlow, William, brig. gen., U. S. V.:
  Mentioned, 47, 63, 130, 181, 224, 516, 517, 542, 543, 545.
  Opinion regarding health of Army in Cuba, 202.
  Recommended for promotion, 225.
  To remain in Cuba, 209.
Lukes, Frank, pvt., Co. B, 4th U. S. Inf., wounded, 1017.
Lumbert, John, pvt., Co. H, 12th U. S. Inf., killed, 1229.
Luna, Maximiliano, 2d lieut., 34th Inf., U. S. V., death, 1103, 1109.
Luna, ——, lieut. gen., insurgent forces, mentioned, 1009, 1011.
Lundberg, John C., pvt., Co. I, 30th Inf., U. S. V., death, 1160.
Lundin, Frederick, pvt., Co. D, 1st Cal. Vol. Inf., death, 979.
Lundlom, Victor W., corpl., Co. C, 16th U. S. Inf., wounded, 1152.
Lundstrom, Edward, pvt., Batty. L, 3d U. S. Art., wounded, 895.
Lundy, William, pvt., Troop A, 11th Cav., U. S. V., death, 1201.
Lungan, W. G., 2d lieut., 1st Nebr. Vol. Inf., wounded, 975.
Lunskeenan, A. K., pvt., Co. I, 1st Mont. Vol. Inf., wounded, 950.
Lurienne, M., manager, French cable, Cuba, mentioned, 177, 178.
Lusk, Edward C., pvt., Co. D, 5th U. S. Inf., killed, 1254.
Lutjens, John N., pvt., Co. D, 1st Idaho Vol. Inf., wounded, 898.
Lutz, George, saddler, Troop B, 1st U. S. Cav., death, 1283.
Lutz, William J., 1st lieut., 2d U. S. Inf., wounded, 127.
Lyle, David E. W., 1st lieut., 18th U. S. Inf., mentioned, 1240.
Lyles, De Witt C., 2d lieut., 12th U. S. Inf., mentioned, 1313.
Lymons, John, mus., Co. E, 34th Inf., U. S. V., mentioned, 248.
Lynch, Daniel, pvt., Co. C, 22d U. S. Inf., death, 1189.
Lynch, Frank E., 1st. lieut., 44th Inf., U. S. V., mentioned, 1238.
Lynch, James G., pvt., Co. A, 30th Inf., U. S. V., death, 1174.
Lynch, James S., pvt., Co. C, 9th U. S. Inf., death, 984.
Lynch, John, pvt., Co. H, 14th U. S. Inf., wounded, 460.
Lynch, John F., pvt., Co. E, 37th Inf., U. S. V., death, 1153.
Lynch, Robert R., mus., Co. I, 47th Inf., U. S. V., wounded, 1190.
Lynch, Thomas, pvt., Co. F, 16th U. S. Inf., wounded, 1087.
Lynch, Thomas F., pvt., Batty. G, 3d U. S. Art., wounded, 946.
Lynn, Edward J., pvt., Co. I, 1st Mont. Vol. Inf., wounded, 945.
Lynn, William, pvt., Co. D, 28th Inf., U. S. V., wounded, 1189.
Lyon, Edward E. trumpeter, Troop C, 6th U. S. Cav., wounded, 466.
Lyon, Henry G., 1st lieut., 24th U. S. Inf., wounded, 83, 124.
Lyon, James R., pvt., Co. F, 17th U. S. Inf., death, 1241.
Lyon, Palmer, capt., med. dept., U. S. A., mentioned, 1328, 1329.
Lyons, Daniel, pvt., Co. H, 24th U. S. A., death, 1152.
Lyons, Eugene, pvt., Co. K, 5th U. S. Inf., killed, 1254.
Lyons, Fred R., pvt., Troop A, 11th Cav., U. S. V., death, 1217.
Lyons, George, pvt., Co. G, 26th Inf., U. S. V., death, 1215.
Lyons, James J., pvt., Troop K, 3d U. S. Cav., missing, 1209.
Lyons, Joseph, pvt., band, 14th U. S. Inf., death, 486.
Lyons, Martin G., pvt., Co. E, 9th U. S. Inf., wounded, 1299.
Lyons, Thomas J., pvt., Troop D, 3d U. S. Cav., death, 1130.
Lysle, William, pvt., Co. F, 24th U. S. Inf., death, 1208.
Lytle, Wesley, pvt., Co. —, 1st Wyo. Vol. Inf., death, 1045.
Mabini, Apolinario, insurgent agent, mentioned, 1248.
Mabry, William H., col., 1st Tex. Vol. Inf., mentioned, 535, 551, 552.
Macabulos, ——, insurgent general, mentioned, 1180.
MacAndrew, William J., pvt., Co. I, 4th U. S. Inf., death, 1185.
MacArthur, Arthur, maj. gen., U. S. A. and U. S. V.
  Assignment to command Division of the Philippines, 1157, 1164.
  Relief from, 1259.
  Correspondence, 411, 412, 415-419, 422-430, 432-437, 439, 441, 443-450, 452, 455, 456, 461, 463-465, 469, 471, 472, 475, 478-480, 484, 485, 487, 492, 494, 502-504.
  Mentioned, 556-569, 571-573, 575, 576, 578, 683, 684, 715, 716, 758, 900, 915, 944, 945, 947, 948, 950-953, 962, 971, 972, 975, 977, 982, 984, 985, 988, 990, 991, 994, 995, 1013, 1049-1051, 1053, 1062, 1071, 1076, 1086, 1092, 1093, 1095-1098, 1100, 1102-1104, 1108-1110, 1116, 1121, 1135, 1138, 1139, 1154, 1157, 1164, 1183, 1184, 1186, 1220, 1286, 1289.
  See *Expedition* under *Philippine Islands.*
Maccoe, Malcolm H., pvt., Co. M, 1st Colo. Vol. Inf., wounded, 947.
MacDonald, Donald, pvt., Co. C, 32d Inf., U. S. V., killed, 1161.
MacDonald, M. A., member post-office committee, mentioned, 405.
Mace, Harry L., pvt., Co. A, 5th U. S. Inf., death, 1267.
Machias, U. S. gunboat, mentioned, 88, 95.
Macias, ——, Spanish capt. gen., mentioned, 359, 396.
Mackay, Charles E., pvt., Co. B, 29th Inf., U. S. V., wounded, 1237.
Mackay, Mr. J. W., mentioned, 104.
Mackay, Miss, mentioned, 488.
Macklem, Harry, pvt., Co. E, 1st Idaho Vol. Inf., wounded, 1008.
Macnab, Alexander J., jr., 2d lieut., Co. I, 23d U. S. Inf., wounded, 1057.
Macomb, Montgomery M., capt., 7th U. S. Art., mentioned, 59, 273, 276, 306, 309.
Macon, steamship, mentioned, 588.

Macy, Bruce E., pvt., Co. C, 1st Nebr. Vol. Inf., death, 972; wounded, 952.
Madden, Ernest, 1st sergt., Co. D, 1st S. Dak. Vol. Inf., wounded, 949.
Madden, Joseph J., pvt., Batty. L, 3d U. S. Art., death, 1016.
Madden, Martin A., sergt., Co. G, 17th U. S. Inf., death, 1217.
Madden, Peter, pvt., Troop B, 4th U. S. Cav., death, 1136.
Maddex, Elmer B., pvt., Co. B, 13th U. S. Inf. death, 803.
Madill, Benjamin W., pvt., Co. C, 45th Inf., U. S. V., wounded, 1209.
Madison, Max, pvt., Batty. B, Utah Art., U. S. V., killed, 975.
Madox, William, pvt., Co. I, 1st Nebr. Vol. Inf., wounded, 897.
Magallanes, Spanish regiment of, distribution, 655.
Magee, Francis J., pvt., Co. F, 9th U. S. Inf., wounded, 444.
Magnus, Raphael, pvt., Co. K, 21st U. S. Inf., death, 1228.
Magnusen, John, pvt., band, 34th Inf., U. S. V., death, 1146.
Maguic, Michael, pvt., Co. G, 26th Inf., U. S. V., wounded, 1166.
Mahaffy, Robert, sergt., Co. L, 37th Inf., U. S. V., wounded, 1211.
Mahan, Virgil H., pvt., Co. L, 20th U. S. Inf., wounded, 937.
Maher, James, pvt., Co. C, 4th U. S. Inf., wounded, 1110.
Maher, Joseph, pvt., Co. M, 1st Cal. Vol. Inf., killed, 895.
Maher, Joseph F., pvt., Co. A, 37th Inf., U. S. V., killed, 1086.
Maher, Roy C., pvt., Co. —, 1st Nebr. Vol. Inf., death, 803.
Maher, Thomas, sergt., Co. H, 21st U. S. Inf., mentioned, 253.
Mahoney, Alfred A., pvt., Co. I, 9th U. S. Inf., death, 1021.
Mahoney, John J., pvt., Co. K, 1st S. Dak. Vol. Inf., death, 850.
Mahoney, Oscar C., pvt., Co. G, 46th Inf., U. S. V., death, 1178.
Mahoney, P. H., pvt., Co. D, 20th U. S. Inf., mentioned, 183.
Maicel, Arno H., pvt., Co. H, 1st Wash. Vol. Inf., killed, 895.
Maine, U. S. hospital ship, casualties on, 486. Mentioned, 455, 480, 481.
Majayjay, Matthew, pvt., Co. D, 35th Inf., U.S.V., wounded, 1225.
Major, Charles J., pvt., Co. G, 18th U. S. Inf., death, 1162.
Major, Edward G., pvt., Co. L, 17th U. S. Inf., death, 1132.
Major, S. J., pvt., Co. C, 2d Mass. Vol. Inf., mentioned, 209.
Majors, Harvey W., pvt., Co. L, 1st Nebr. Vol. Inf., wounded, 975.
Malakie, John W., pvt., Troop M, 4th U. S. Cav., death, 1196.
Malaney, Daniel J., pvt., Co. G, 33d Mich. Vol. Inf., mentioned, 226.
Malchus, Henry, pvt., Co. C, 12th U. S. Inf., wounded, 1057.
Maleham, Arthur, pvt., Co. L, 33d Mich. Vol. Inf., mentioned, 238.
Mallicoat, Oscar, pvt., Co. K, 20th Kans. Vol. Inf., wounded, 915.
Mallonee, Joseph, artif., Co. H, 32d Inf., U. S. V., wounded, 1191.
Mallory, John S., lieut. col., 41st Inf., U. S. V., mentioned, 1171, 1232, 1235.
Mallory, Harris W., pvt., Co. B, 9th U. S. Inf., death, 984.
Mallory, Thomas J., pvt., Co. C, 33d Inf., U. S. V., wounded, 1198.
Malloy, Thomas, pvt., Co. K, 1st Mont. Vol. Inf., mentioned, 900, 902.
Malone, Patrick, sergt., Co. E, 22d U. S. Inf., death, 1168.
Malone, William I., pvt., Co. L, 1st Nebr. Vol. Inf., mentioned, 782.
Maloney, John, mus., Co. H, 13th U. S. Inf., death, 1226.

Maloney, Patrick, corpl., Co. G, 43d Inf., U. S. V., death, 1226.
Maloney, Thomas, pvt., Co. E, 17th U. S. Inf., death, 1052.
Maloney, Thomas L., pvt., Co. D, 9th U. S. Inf., wounded, 444.
Maloney, William F., 1st sergt., Co. F, 14th U. S. Inf., wounded, 454.
Malvar, insurgent officer, mentioned, 1330.
Manahan, Resiel, pvt., Co. A, 20th Kans. Vol. Inf., killed, 976.
Manauense, U. S. transport, mentioned, 1089, 1091, 1105, 1110.
Manches, Edward, pvt., Co. M, 1st S. Dak. Vol. Inf., death, 831.
Manchester, Otis, pvt., Co. H, 26th Inf. U. S. V., wounded, 1232.
Manchester, Theodore E., pvt., Co. G, 1st Mont. Vol. Inf., wounded, 916.
Manderville, George, pvt., Troop E, 4th U. S. Cav., death, 1210.
Mandig, John, pvt., Co. K, 16th U. S. Inf., mentioned, 229.
Manduka, John, pvt., Co. E, 12th U. S. Inf., wounded, 1214.
Mangold, Joseph F., pvt., Troop K, 3d U. S. Cav., wounded, 1113.
Mangum, George A., pvt., Co. L 23d U. S. Inf., wounded, 1167.
Manila, Spanish regiment of, distribution, 655.
Manire, Henry W., pvt., Co. C 9th U. S. Inf., wounded, 1298.
Manitoba, U. S. transport, mentioned, 349, 354, 360, 362, 378, 606, 607, 616, 619, 623.
Manley, Emmet W., pvt., Co. D 23d U. S. Inf., death, 866.
Mann, George T., pvt., Co. K, 38th Inf., U. S. V., death, 1141.
Manning, Edgar J., pvt., Co. A, 9th U. S. Inf., death, 1150.
Manning, George B., pvt., Co. C, 1st Idaho Vol. Inf., wounded, 975.
Manning, Henry G., corpl., Co, I, 32d Inf., U. S. V., wounded, 1190.
Manning, James, pvt., Co. B, 37th Inf., U. S. V., death, 1205.
Manning, Patrick, pvt., Co. L, 17th U. S. Inf., death, 979.
Manning, U. S. transport, mentioned, 22, 39.
Mansfield, Arthur S., pvt., Co. L, 15th U. S. Inf., killed, 1211.
Mansfield, Claude M., pvt., Troop K, 4th U. S. Cav., wounded, 1113.
Mansker, William H., pvt., Co. B, 38th Inf., U. S. V., killed, 1240.
Manson, George, cook, Co. E, 46th Inf., U. S. V., death, 1190.
Manteo, lighter, mentioned, 192, 198
Mantle. Lee, mentioned, 304.
Manz, Peter, pvt., Co. F, 3d U. S. Inf., death, 1045.
Marak, Charles F., pvt., Co. C, 9th U. S. Inf., wounded, 1298.
Marasigan, insurgent officer, mentioned, 1310.
Marble, Frank, lieut., U. S. N., mentioned, 157.
March, Peyton C., maj., 33d Inf., U. S. V., mentioned, 717, 971, 1101, 1111, 1120, 1121.
Marcy, C. A., corpl., Co. G, 2d Oreg. Vol. Inf., wounded, 946.
Marek, Joe, pvt., Co. M, 33d Inf. U. S. V., death, 1205.
Maren, John, pvt., Co. E, 9th U. S. Inf., killed, 1307.
Marietta, U. S. gunboat, mentioned, 418.
Marine Corps, 1st Regt., U. S., casualties in, 429, 435, 445, 451, 453, 454, 460, 463, 477, 482, 486.
Marine Hospital Service, jurisdiction as to sanitary matters, 218.
Marine, James A., pvt., Co. H, 33d Mich. Vol. Inf., mentioned, 183.
Mariner, George E., corpl., Co. E, 1st Nebr. Vol. Inf., wounded, 974.
Mariposa, U. S. transport, mentioned, 723, 748.
Markham, Chester A., pvt., Troop M, 11th Cav., U. S. V., death, 1241.
Markle, John G., corpl., Co. F, 19th U. S. Inf., death, 1185.
Markley, Alfred C., col., 13th U. S. Inf., mentioned, 1330.
Markley, George F., sergt., Co. C, 9th U. S. Inf., mentioned, 1312.

Markley, James J., pvt., Co. M, 51st Iowa Vol. Inf., wounded, 999.
Marks, George J., pvt., Co. F, 22d U. S. Inf., death, 1123.
Markwood, William, pvt., Co. K, 18th U. S. Inf., wounded, 943.
Marlan, Wilford B., pvt., Co. A, 44th Inf., U. S. V., death, 1161.
Marlinson, William O., pvt., Co. —, 13th Minn. Vol. Inf., death, 803.
Marlow, T. A., pvt., Co. L, 1st Cal. Vol. Inf., wounded, 943.
Marr, Joseph R., artif., Co. C, 9th U. S. Inf., killed, 1297.
Marrion, John C., pvt., Co. K, 3d U. S. Art., death, 903.
Marrs, Ward, pvt., Co. E, 33d Mich. Vol. Inf., mentioned, 182.
Marsfelder, Henry W., pvt., Co. M, 13th U. S. Inf., wounded, 1010.
Marsh, B. F., mentioned, 357.
Marsh, Elmer G., pvt., Co. B, 28th Inf., U. S. V., wounded, 1189.
Marsh, Elwin R., pvt., Co. M, 46th Inf., U. S. V., death, 1174.
Marsh, James A., pvt., Co. K, 47th Inf., U. S. V., wounded, 1235.
Marshall, Alpha E., pvt., Co. C, 44th Inf., U. S. V., killed, 1212.
Marshall, Ben H., pvt., Co. B, 40th Inf., U. S. V., wounded, 1160.
Marshall, Charles, sergt., Co. I, 40th Inf., U. S. V., death, 1164; wounded, 1162.
Marshall, Edward, newspaper correspondent, mentioned, 68.
Marshall, Francis C., 1st lieut., 6th U. S. Cav., mentioned, 423.
Marshall, George, corpl., Co. M, 12th U. S. Inf., death, 1015.
Marshall group, supply of coal at Jaluit, 746.
Marshall, John C., pvt., Co. H, 1st Nebr. Vol. Inf., wounded, 955.
Marshall, Robert, pvt., Co. D, 13th U. S. Inf., death, 1078.
Marshall, Warner, pvt., Co. M, 1st Wash. Vol. Inf., wounded, 931.
Marshall, William G., pvt., Co. D, 1st Mont. Vol. Inf., death, 961; wounded, 953.
Marshall, William J., pvt., Co. D, 1st Wash. Vol. Inf., wounded, 977.
Marshall, Winfield, pvt., Co. C, 24th U. S. Inf., death, 1132.
Mart, Joseph, pvt., Co. C, 1st Mont. Vol. Inf., death, 923.
Martens, Theodore J., pvt., Co. M, 20th U. S. Inf., death, 1060.
Martenson, Andrew, pvt., Co. A, 13th Minn. Vol. Inf., wounded, 947.
Martin, Charles W., pvt., Troop L, 3d U. S. Cav., wounded, 1222.
Martin, Clarence C., pvt., Co. D, 4th U. S. Inf., wounded, 1017.
Martin, Frank M., pvt., Co. I, 23d U. S. Inf., death, 956.
Martin, Frederick W., pvt., Co. C, 20th U. S. Inf., death, 1283.
Martin, George, pvt., Co. L, 34th Mich. Vol. Inf., mentioned, 205.
Martin, Howard L., pvt., Co. D, 40th Inf., U. S. V., death, 1276.
Martin, James, pvt., Co. C, 9th U. S. Inf., killed, 1297.
Martin, John A., pvt., Co. H, 36th Inf., U. S. V., death, 1056.
Martin, John F., sergt., Co. C, 9th U. S. Inf., killed, 1297.
Martin, John P., corpl., Troop G, 4th U. S. Cav., wounded, 1084.
Martin, Joseph F., pvt., Hosp. Corps, U. S. A., death, 1149.
Martin, Joseph W., pvt., Co. L, 30th Inf., U. S. V., death, 1194.
Martin, Ned, pvt., Co. M, 25th U. S. Inf., death, 1156.
Martin, Oliver H., pvt., Co. G, 32d Inf., U. S. V., killed, 1143.
Martin, Patrick J., pvt., Co. M, 21st U. S. Inf., death, 1223.

Martin, William F., pvt., Co. L, 37th Inf., U. S. V., wounded, 1203.
Martin, William H., pvt., Co. H, 40th Inf., U. S. V., killed, 1148.
Martin, newspaper correspondent, Associated Press, mentioned, 1221, 1225.
Martindale, David, corpl., Co. C, 1st S. Dak. Vol. Inf., wounded, 996.
Martonchik, Mike, pvt., Co. C, 44th Inf., U. S. V., wounded, 1212.
Marvine, Walter, chaplain, U. S. A., mentioned, 505.
Maryland, State of, history 1st and 5th regts., Vol. Inf., 596.
Mascardo, insurgent general, mentioned, 1133, 1279.
Mason, Arnold A., pvt., Co. L, 4th U. S. Inf., wounded, 1017.
Mason, Bert, pvt., Co. I, 2d U. S. Inf., killed, 1261.
Mason, Charles F., maj., med. dept., U. S. A., mentioned, 302.
Mason, Clarence W., pvt., band, 51st Iowa Vol. Inf., death, 1048.
Mason, Edward D., pvt., Co. C, 22d U. S. Inf., wounded, 1247.
Mason, Knute, pvt., Co. M, 34th Inf., U. S. V., killed, 1241.
Mason, Patrick, pvt., Co. I, 24th U. S. Inf., death, 1132.
Mason, Richard, pvt., Co. A., 47th Inf., U. S. V., wounded, 1271.
Mason, Robert, British proconsul, Santiago, Cuba, mentioned, 90, 151, 152.
Mason, Robert C., corpl., Co. H, 43d Inf., U. S. V., wounded, 1240.
Mason, Willard B., pvt., Co. L, 1st Nebr. Vol. Inf., wounded, 983.
Mason, William E., U. S. Senator, mentioned, 333, 337.
Massa, Anthony, pvt., Co. A, 7th U. S. Inf., mentioned, 212.
Massachusetts, U. S. transport, mentioned, 292, 300, 301, 312, 317, 324, 328, 333, 356, 362, 366, 400, 608, 616, 875.
Masten, John M., member post-office committee, mentioned, 405.
Mathias, Fred W., sergt., Co. F, 27th Inf., U. S. V., death, 1140.
Mathieson, Hans C., pvt., Troop K, 4th U. S. Cav., wounded, 994.
Matson, Lewis, pvt., Co. A, 28th Inf., U. S. V., death, 1283.
Matteawan, U. S. transport, mentioned, 184, 186, 188, 190, 192, 194, 198, 212, 330, 332.
Matter, Edward M., chief mus., 3d U. S. Inf., death, 952.
Matthews, Edward, pvt., Co. E, 1st Nebr. Vol. Inf., wounded, 967.
Matthews, Wesley D., pvt., Co. G, 20th Kans. Vol. Inf., wounded, 961.
Mattice, Frank, pvt., Co. G, 2d U. S. Inf., death, 1276.
Mattock, Everette, pvt., Co. L, 15th U. S. Inf., wounded, 1211.
Mattock, George A., artif., Co. A, 33d Inf., U. S. V., wounded, 1102.
Mattocks, Charles P., brig. gen., U. S. V., mentioned, 357, 532-534.
Mattson, Alex, pvt., Co. L, 45th Inf., U. S. V., death, 1127.
Matuchewica, Thomas, trumpeter, Troop E, 4th U. S. Cav., wounded, 1231.
Maud, Alfred J., pvt., Troop F, 3d U. S. Cav., death, 1236.
Mauk, Abram L., pvt., Troop L, 4th U. S. Cav., mentioned, 1152.
Mautte, George C., pvt., Co. L, 6th U. S. Inf., death, 1205.
Maus, Marion P., lieut. col., I. G., U. S. V., mentioned, 94.
Maupin, Socrates, pvt., Co. G, 1st D. C. Vol. Inf., mentioned, 229.
Maverick, tug, mentioned, 56, 192, 335.
Maxfield, Fred L., pvt., Co. B, 20th Kans. Vol. Inf., death, 1016.
Maxfield, Joseph E., lieut. col., sig. officer, U. S. V., mentioned, 543, 551-553.
Maxwell, Fred, pvt., Co. K, 20th Kans. Vol. Inf., death, 894.

Maxwell, John W., pvt., Troop E, 11th Cav., U. S. V., wounded, 1148.
May, Will, pvt., Co. I, 1st S. Dak. Vol. Inf., death, 957; wounded, 949.
May, Willard W., pvt., Co. G, 44th Inf., U. S. V., wounded, 1271.
Mayer, Charles, pvt., Co. A, 19th U. S. Inf., death, 1217.
Mayse, Arlington, pvt., Co. H, 22d U. S. Inf., death, 1146.
McAdams, Frank, pvt., Co. M, 22d U. S. Inf., death, 1210.
McAdams, Michael J., corpl., Co. M, 15th U. S. Inf., wounded, 1251.
McAdoo, David A., pvt., Co. B, 18th U. S. Inf., death, 1109.
McAllister, Loss I., pvt., Troop —, 6th U. S. Cav., wounded, 466.
McAllister, ——, surg., 10th Pa. Vol. Inf., mentioned, 732.
McAlvey, George, sergt., Co. F, 19th U. S. Inf., death, 1202.
McAndrew, Frank, pvt., Co. E, 9th U. S. Inf., killed, 1307; wounded, 1299.
McArthur, John C., 1st lieut., 3d U. S. Inf., wounded, 995.
McAvoy, John, pvt., Co. L, 20th U. S. Inf., killed, 937.
McBride, Charles E., pvt., Co. M, 44th Inf., U.S.V., killed, 1256.
McBride, Clarence J., pvt., Co. B, 9th U. S. Inf., wounded, 443.
McBride, Emory J., corpl., Troop E, 3d U. S., Cav., death, 1249.
McBride, George, pvt., Co. H, 47th Inf., U. S. V., wounded, 1235.
McBride, John, pvt., Co. F, 28th Inf., U. S. V., killed, 1222.
McBride, Patrick, 1st sergt., Co. K, 1st Mont. Vol. Inf., wounded, 987.
McCafferty, David, pvt., Co. E, 2d U. S. Inf., mentioned, 193.
McCaffrey, Owen, pvt., Co. H, 23d U. S. Inf., wounded, 1188.
McCain, Henry P., capt., 14th U. S. Inf., mentioned, 423, 442, 780, 829.
McCall, Frank A., pvt., Co. B, 1st Idaho Vol. Inf., wounded, 897.
McCall, Howard M., pvt., Co. C, 37th Inf., U.S.V., death, 1170.
McCall, Hugh, pvt., Co. A, 18th U. S. Inf., death, 1153.
McCall, John M., pvt., Co. B, 22d U. S. Inf., death, 1066.
McCalla, Bowman H., capt., U. S. N., mentioned, 409, 410, 1121; wounded, 421.
McCandless, Edward R., pvt., Co. K, 32d, Inf., U. S. V., death, 1091.
McCandless, John, pvt., Batty. H 3d U. S. Art., wounded, 950.
McCann, John D., pvt., Co. K, 19th U. S. Inf., death, 1164.
McCann, Robert, pvt., Co. C, 14th U. S. Inf., killed, 760; mentioned, 803.
McCann, Robert E, pvt., Co. C, 23d U. S. Inf., wounded, 760.
McCart, Harry O., pvt., Co. I, 1st Nebr. Vol. Inf., killed, 975.
McCarter, George A., sergt., Troop M, 11th Cav., U. S. V., wounded, 1148.
McCarthy, Daniel, pvt., Co. E, Sig. Corps, U. S. A., death, 1086.
McCarthy, Edward J., pvt., Co. L 19th U. S. Inf., death, 1228.
McCarthy, James A., pvt., Co. D, 16th U. S. Inf., death, 1253, 1255.
McCarthy, John, pvt., Co. D, 29th Inf., U. S. V., death, 1217.
McCarthy, Michael, pvt., Co. M, 26th Inf., U. S. V., wounded, 1052.
McCarthy, Thomas F., pvt., Co. I, 9th U. S. Inf., wounded, 1081.
McCarthy, Webster, pvt., Co. A, 1st N. Y. Vol, Inf., death, 838.
McCarron, James, corpl., Co. B, 21st U.S. Inf., death, 1169.
McCarty, James, pvt., Co. A, 4th U. S. Inf., wounded, 1003.

McCarty, William G., pvt., Co. H, 36th Inf., U. S. V., wounded, 1092.
McCarty, William H., pvt., Co. G, 1st Mont. Vol. Inf., wounded, 945.
McCaskey, Robert H., pvt., Co. H, 8th U. S. Inf., death, 1280.
McCaskey, Walter B., 2d lieut., 21st U. S. Inf., mentioned, 1019.
McCaskey, William S., lieut. col., 20th U. S. Inf., mentioned, 865.
McCaul, Albert J., pvt., Troop K, 4th U. S. Cav., death, 802.
McCauley, John P., pvt., Co. A, 1st Nebr. Vol. Inf., wounded, 760.
McClain, A. Brent, pvt., Co. G, 1st Tenn. Vol. Inf., death, 879.
McClellan, Hugh P., pvt., Co. I, 14th U. S. Inf., death, 947; wounded, 895.
McClellan, Joseph, corpl., Co. K, 43d Inf., U. S. V., killed, 1176.
McClellan, Randall, pvt., Co. I, 47th Inf,, U.S.V., wounded, 1202.
McClellan, U. S. transport, mentioned, 1293, 1299, 1330, 1341, 1348, 1353.
McClelland, Paul D., 1st lieut., S. Dak, Vol. Inf., wounded, 948, 949.
McClernand, Edward J., lieut. col., a. a. g., U. S. V., mentioned, 90, 102, 252, 257.
McClintock, Guy E., farrier, Troop L, 3d U. S. Cav., killed, 1222.
McClintock, James H., capt., 1st U. S. Vol. Cav., wounded, 55.
McCloud, Ulysses G., pvt., Co. G, 40th Inf., U. S. V., death, 1205.
McCloy, Harry J., pvt., Co. H, 42d Inf., U. S. V., death, 1276.
McClure, A. K., mentioned, 316.
McClure, Charles, maj., pay dept., U. S. A., mentioned, 693, 1235.
McClure, Charles, capt., 18th U. S. Inf., mentioned, 960.
McClure, George D., pvt., Co. F, 44th Inf., U. S. V., killed, 1182.
McClure, Harry, pvt., Co. H, 1st Idaho Vol. Inf., killed, 901.
McCollister, Charles, pvt., Co. H, 12th U. S. Inf., wounded, 1229.
McConkey, J. E., pvt., U. S. Marine Corps, killed, 445.
McConnell, Carl W., pvt., Co. G, 1st S. Dak. Vol. Inf., wounded, 996.
McConnell, John A., pvt., Co. C, 1st Wyo. Vol. Inf., wounded, 931.
McConnell, Robert B., sergt., Co. H, 1st Nebr. Vol. Inf., wounded, 955.
McConville, Edward, maj., 1st Idaho Vol. Inf. killed, 895; mentioned, 922.
McCordie, Horace G., pvt., Co. F, 1st S. Dak. Vol. Inf., death, 947.
McCorkle, John T., corpl., Co. G, 1st Colo. Vol. Inf., wounded, 956.
McCorkle, Henry L., 2d lieut., 25th U. S. Inf., killed, 124.
McCormack, Frank, corpl., Co. C, 9th U. S. Inf., killed, 1297.
McCormick, Hale Y., pvt., Troop A, 6th U. S. Cav., wounded, 466.
McCormick, James, pvt., Co. B, 4th U. S. Inf., death, 1001.
McCormick, James, pvt., Co. L, 25th U. S. Inf., killed, 1228.
McCouch, Alexander, sergt., Co. C, 10th Pa. Vol. Inf., wounded, 940.
McCowen, Frank A., corpl., Co. B, 31st Inf., U. S. V., death, 1248.
McCoy, Burt, corpl., Co. H, 25th U. S. Inf., wounded, 1127.
McCoy, Frank R., 2d lieut., 8th U. S. Cav., wounded, 124.
McCoy, Henry B., col., 1st Colo. Vol. Inf., mentioned, 835.
McCoy, R. G., pvt., Co. M, 2d Oreg. Vol. Inf., mentioned, 1028.
McCoy, Walter A., pvt., Co. I, 39th Inf., U. S. V., death, 1156.
McCrancken, Horace J., pvt., Co. H, 1st S. Dak. Vol. Inf., death, 895.

McCray, Lawrence, corpl., Co. G, 22d U. S. Inf., death, 1001.
McCray, William V., pvt., Troop G, 11th Cav., U. S. V., death, 1161.
McCrea, Tully, col., Art. Corps, U. S. A., mentioned, 1299.
McCreary, James, pvt., Co. E, 1st Mont. Vol. Inf., wounded, 945.
McCreary, Joseph R., pvt., Co. C., 18th U. S. Inf., wounded, 943.
McCue, Felix H., pvt., Troop F, 3d U. S. Cav., death, 1257.
McCue, James, pvt., Co. F, 21st U. S. Inf., wounded, 1015.
McCue, Michael, corpl., Co. A, 21st U. S. Inf., death, 1254.
McCulloch, Oscar, pvt., Co. K, 16th U. S. Inf., wounded, 1110.
McCulloch, T. A., a. a. surg., U. S. A., mentioned, 992, 1042.
McCullough, John, pvt., Co. M, 3d U. S. Inf., wounded, 961.
McCully, Edward, pvt., Co. C, 16th U. S. Inf., wounded, 1152.
McCurry, James B., pvt., Co. E, 32d Inf., U. S. V., death, 1185.
McCutcheon, Marbel. pvt., Co. I, 27th Inf., U. S. V., wounded, 1212.
McDaniel, David, pvt., Co. B, 9th U. S. Inf., death, 504.
McDaniel, Ernest W., corpl., Co. D, 32d Inf., U. S. V., wounded, 1218.
McDaniel, John C., cook, Co. K, 31st Inf., U. S. V., death, 1196.
McDermott, James F., pvt., Co. C, 9th U. S. Inf., killed, 1297.
McDill, John R., maj. and surg., U. S. V , mentioned, 552.
McDonal, Andrew, corpl., Co. C, 44th Inf., U. S. V., wounded, 1212.
McDonald, Frank, sergt., Co. L, 21st U. S. Inf., mentioned, 1129.
McDonald, Frederick, pvt., Co. H, 19th U. S. Inf., death, 1060.
McDonald, John A., pvt., Co. D, 34th Mich. Vol. Inf., mentioned, 195.
McDonald, John B., capt., 3d U. S. Cav., wounded, 1275.
McDonald, Robert, pvt., Co. K, 1st Colo. Vol. Inf., wounded, 761.
McDonald, T. M., mus., Co. D, 17th U. S. Inf., mentioned, 223.
McDonnell, Patrick, pvt., Co. A, 28th Inf., U. S. V., wounded, 1132.
McDonwell, Harry A., pvt., Co. M, 1st Colo. Vol. Inf., death, 852.
McDougall, Miles M., corpl., Co. I, 1st Wash. Vol. Inf., wounded, 896.
McDougall, William, pvt., Co. F, 20th Kans. Vol. Inf., wounded, 983.
McDuffy. pvt., Co. H, 23d U. S. Inf., killed, 1042.
McEachran, John, corpl., Co. B, 37th Inf., U. S. V., death, 1149.
McElwain, William, pvt., Co. H, 2d Oreg. Vol. Inf., death, 1003.
McEntee, Joseph, sergt., Co. C, 17th U. S. Inf., killed, 1210.
McElhour, John, pvt., Co. G, 40th Inf., U. S. V., killed, 1281.
McElliot, Daniel, pvt., Co. A, 1st Mont. Vol. Inf., death, 830.
McFadden, Henry S., 1st sergt., 23d U. S. Inf., wounded, 924.
McFadden, Joseph W , pvt., Troop G, 1st U. S. Cav., mentioned, 229.
McFarland, Andrew, pvt., Co. F, 21st U. S. Inf., wounded, 1008.
McFarland, George, pvt., Co. L, 20th U. S. Inf., wounded, 937.
McFarland, William, pvt., Co. K, 37th Inf., U. S. V., death, 1123.
McFarland, William C., capt. 10th U. S. Inf., wounded, 124.
McFarland, Willis L., pvt., Troop K, 4th U. S. Cav., death, 1190.
McGee, James C., pvt , Co. K, 13th Minn. Vol. Inf., wounded, 947.
McGee, John J., corpl., Co. G, 14th U. S. Inf., death, 1130.

McGee, Thomas, pvt., Co. D, 26th Inf., U. S. V., wounded, 1227.
McGee, William, pvt., Co. B, 48th Inf., U. S. V., death, 1267.
McGibb, Charles J., corpl., Co, D, 35th Inf., U. S. V., wounded, 1182.
McGill, James D., corpl., Co. A, 21st U. S. Inf., death, 1274.
McGillicuddy, Willam J., pvt., Co. L, 12th U. S. Inf., wounded, 1015.
McGillioray, James B., pvt., Co. D, 17th U.S. Inf., wounded, 1060.
McGinnis, James S., pvt., Co. D, 39th Inf., U. S. V., wounded, 1222.
McGlachlin, Edward F., jr., 1st lieut., 5th U. S. Art., mentioned, 27, 397.
McGlinche, James, pvt., Co. E, 4th U. S. Inf., wounded, 1085.
McGoldrics, Michael, pvt., 1st U. S. Inf., mentioned, 187.
McGonagle, John, mus., Co. C, 28th Inf., U. S. V., death, 1142.
McGovern, Michael F., corpl., Co. F, 43d Inf., U. S. V., killed, 1212.
McGowan, George W., corpl., Co. A, 1st Wash. Vol. Inf., killed, 895.
McGrath, Frank J., pvt., Troop M, 4th U. S. Cav., wounded, 1081.
McGrath, Hugh J., capt., 4th U. S. Cav., death, 1096; wounded, 1082.
McGrath, Michael, pvt., Co. M, 12th U. S. Inf., death, 1066.
McGraw, John F., pvt., Co. L, 9th U. S. Inf., wounded, 1086.
McGraw, William A., pvt., Co. I, 20th Kans. Vol. Inf., wounded, 898.
McGreevy, James F., pvt., Troop K, 4th U. S. Cav., wounded, 982.
McGregor, John, pvt., Troop C, 4th U. S. Cav., wounded, 1046.
McGuire, Ellison, mayor, Madison, Wis., mentioned, 316.
McGuire, Harvey, pvt., Co. E, 6th U. S. Inf., mentioned, 218.
McGuire, James, qm. sergt., Co. B, 16th U. S. Inf., death, 1045.
McGuire, Philip F., pvt., Co. F, 12th U. S. Inf., death, 955, 968.
McGuire, Thomas J., pvt., Co. D, 3d U. S. Inf., death, 1241.
McGurrin, William T., col., 32d Mich. Vol. Inf., mentioned, 548.
McGuyer, Porter, pvt., Co. D, 44th Inf., U. S. V., death, 1146.
McGuyre, Edward, pvt., Co. M, 43d Inf., U. S. V., killed, 1251.
McHaffy, Robert, sergt., Co. L, 37th Inf., U. S. V., wounded, 1193.
McHale, P., Rev., Catholic priest, mentioned, 402.
McHenry, John W., pvt., Co. L, 12th U. S. Inf., wounded, 1015.
McHenry, Marvin R., pvt., Co. H, 14th U. S. Inf., death, 1048.
McHugh, James, pvt., Co. M, 12th U. S. Inf., death, 1048.
McHugh, John, pvt., Co. L, 4th U. S. Inf., wounded, 1017.
McHuner, John C., pvt., Co. E, 17th U. S. Inf., killed, 1026.
McIlrath, John A., pvt., Batty. H, 3d U. S. Art., death, 802; mentioned, 761.
McIlvaine, Albert O., pvt., Co. G, 22d U. S. Inf., death, 1276.
McInness, Edward, sergt., Co. I, 13th Minn. Vol. Inf., wounded, 947.
McIntosh, James E., pvt., Co. F, 33d Inf., U. S. V., death, 1190.
McIntosh, Wallace, pvt., Co. M, 39th Inf., U. S. V., death, 1194.
McIntyre, Hugh, pvt., Co. L, 40th Inf., U. S. V., death, 1151.
McIntyre, Thomas H. R., 2d lieut., 6th U. S. Art., mentioned, 1178.
McIntyre, William H., pvt., Co. K, 45th Inf., U. S. V., death, 1228.
McIntyre, John A., pvt., Co. G and I, 35th Inf., U. S. V., mentioned, 1186.
McKay, Oren A., pvt., Batty. K, 3d U. S. Art., wounded, 950.

INDEX. 1423

McKee, William J., brig. gen., U. S. V., mentioned, 71, 512–518, 520, 528.
McKellar, Nelson B., pvt., Co. F, 1st S. Dak. Vol Inf., death, 956.
McKelvey, David C., corpl., Batty. K, 3d U. S. Art., wounded, 901.
McKenna, E. A., capt., sig. officer, U. S. V., mentioned, 717.
McKenna, Frank B., 1st lieut., 15th U. S. Inf., mentioned, 301.
McKenna, James, pvt., Co. K, 16th U. S. Inf., death, 1160.
McKenzie, Herbert A., pvt., Batty. L, 3d U. S. Art., wounded, 947.
McKibbin, Chambers, brig. gen., U. S. V.:
Mentioned, 104, 116, 157, 181, 524, 525, 527–529, 543, 545, 1330.
Opinion re health of army in Cuba, 202.
Wounded, 124.
McKinley, William, President United States:
Mentioned, 19, 25, 26, 28–30, 34, 44, 71, 74, 76, 79, 82, 89, 90, 99, 101, 105–107, 109, 114, 116, 119, 143, 144, 147–149, 152, 156, 159, 161–164, 168–170, 175, 178, 182, 187, 191, 217, 229, 231–233, 238, 242, 256, 263, 264, 283, 285, 287, 296–299, 322, 323, 326, 329, 341, 344, 351, 356, 357, 379, 381, 386, 387, 389, 403, 415, 419, 428, 429, 431–433, 437, 461, 462, 470, 482, 494, 502, 1117–1119, 1203; message to Army, 153; proclamations by, 220, 383; reported illness, 498.
McKinney, James P., pvt., Co. L, 1st Nebr. Vol. Inf., wounded, 897.
McKinnish, Robert G., pvt., Co. M, 35th Inf., U. S. V., killed, 1161.
McKinnon, Charles, pvt., Co. F, 2d Oreg. Vol. Inf., death, 840.
McKinnon, William D., chaplain, U. S. A., mentioned, 923.
McKinzie, Job, pvt., Troop G, 9th U. S. Cav., mentioned, 1229; wounded, 1228.
McKnight, Joshua L., pvt., Co. E, 24th U. S. Inf., death, 1132.
McLain, Frank G., pvt., Co. G, 1st S. Dak. Vol. Inf., wounded, 895.
McLauchlin, Robert L., corpl., 8th Batty. Field Art., wounded, 1271.
McLaughlin, Eugene A., pvt., Co. A, 9th Mass. Vol. Inf., mentioned, 238.
McLaughlin, George P., pvt., Co. B, 9th Mass. Vol. Inf., mentioned, 212.
McLaughlin, Harold, corpl., Co. M, 29th Inf., U. S. V., death, 1210.
McLaughlin, James F., pvt., Co. C, 13th U. S. Inf., death, 1217.
McLaughlin, John, corpl., Co. M, 9th U. S. Inf., death, 1156.
McLaughlin, John T., pvt., Co. G, 1st Mont. Vol. Inf., wounded, 961.
McLean, Courtland, pvt., Co. L, 30th Inf., U. S. V., death, 1217.
McLean, George H. H., pvt., Co. F, 22d U. S. Inf., death, 1125.
McLean, Richard H., pvt., Co. A, 1st Wash. Vol. Inf., death, 923; wounded, 896.
McLean, Thomas C., commander, U. S. N., mentioned, 418, 420.
McLean, Walter J., pvt., Co. L, 1st Mont. Vol. Inf., death, 831, 833.
McLeer, Daniel, pvt., Co. H, 8th U. S. Inf., death, 1255.
McLenathan, G. T., pvt., Troop A, 2d U. S. Cav., mentioned, 183.
McLeod, James, sergt., Co. E, 19th U. S. Inf., death, 1088.
McMahan, William J., pvt., Troop E, 3d U. S. Cav., wounded, 1222.
McMahon, John M., pvt., Co. I, 23d U. S. Inf., wounded, 1167.
McMahon, Joseph, pvt., Co. E, 9th U. S. Inf., wounded, 444.
McMaken, William, col., 6th Ohio Vol. Inf., mentioned, 329, 515.
McMartin, Willis C., corpl., Co. G, 45th Inf., U. S. V., death, 1146.
McMillan, Albert C., 1st lieut., 30th Inf., U. S. V., mentioned, 1178.
McMillan, Emmett, pvt., Co. F, 24th U. S. Inf., death, 1057, 1060.
McMillan, Norman, pvt., Co. M, 71st N. Y. Vol. Inf., mentioned, 246.

McMillan, Robert F., 2d lieut., 14th U. S. Inf. mentioned, 1019.
McMillan, James H., capt., asst. qm., U. S. V., mentioned, 310, 311.
McMillen, Victor, pvt., Co. C, 30th Inf., U. S. V., wounded, 1147.
McMurray, William S., pvt., Co. C, 1st Colo. Vol. Inf., death, 883.
McNally, Frank S., sergt., Co. G, 1st Cal. Vol. Inf., wounded, 924.
McNally, Henry J., pvt., Co. K, 20th U. S. Inf., death, 1070.
McNamara, J. M., pvt., Co. K, 9th Mass. Vol. Inf., mentioned, 229.
McNamara, William H., pvt., Co. H, 35th Inf., U. S. V., death, 1194.
McNarney, Frank T., 2d lieut., 36th Inf., U. S. V., wounded, 1150.
McNeil, Clarence H., 2d lieut., 5th U. S. Art., mentioned, 397.
McNeil, George, pvt., Co. G, 1st Wash. Vol. Inf., wounded, 897.
McNerney, James, pvt., Co. B, 22d U. S. Inf., death, 1181.
McNerney, James H., pvt., Co. D, 9th U. S. Inf., death, 1190.
McNulty, Matthew, pvt., Co. B, 22d U. S. Inf., death, 1140.
McNulty, William O., pvt., Co. M, 18th U. S. Inf., wounded, 1152.
McPartland, John, pvt., Co. B, 9th U. S. Inf., killed, 443, 445.
McPherson, Daniel L., pvt., Co. E, 9th U. S. Inf., wounded, 1307.
McPherson, Floyd W., pvt., Co. H, 33d Inf., U. S. V., wounded, 1222.
McPherson, Fort, Ga., recruits at, assignment, 49; wounded to be sent to, 112.
McPherson, Louis, pvt., Co. A, 35th Inf., U. S. V., death, 1142.
McQuade, William, sergt., Batty. E 3d U. S. Art., death, 1136; wounded, 897.
McQuary, John H., mus., Co. E, 1st Mont. Vol. Inf., wounded, 954.
McQueney, John, pvt., Co. I, 21st U. S. Inf., wounded, 1271.
McQuinston, Charles, capt., 4th U. S. Cav., death, 1209.
McQuirk, Michael J., pvt., Co. M, 40th Inf. U. S. V., killed, 1183.
McRae, James H., capt., 3d U. S. Inf., mentioned, 1135, 1139.
McReynolds, Richard H., wagoner, Troop G, 4th U. S. Cav., death, 988.
McRobert, Hugh, pvt., Troop G, 4th U. S. Cav., death, 1191.
McShearer, James, pvt., Co. A, 19th U. S. Inf., death, 1219.
McSweeney, John P., pvt., Co. H, 9th U. S. Inf., wounded, 444.
McTaggart, William A., 2d lieut., 20th Kans. Vol. Inf., killed, 983.
McVay, Clyde A., pvt., Co. A, S. Dak. Vol. Inf., wounded, 915.
McVay, Clyde E., pvt., Co. A, 1st Colo. Vol. Inf., wounded, 899.
McVay, Harlan E., capt., med. dept., U. S. A., death, 875, mentioned, 657, 766, 769, 772.
McVay, John A., pvt., Co. E, 10th Pa. Vol. Inf., wounded, 940.
McWhood, Fred J., 1st sergt., Co. L, 28th Inf., U. S. V., wounded, 1132.
McWilliams, Hugh, asst. engr. *Pechili*, death, 477.
McWrarer, Edward, pvt., Co. E, 1st Mont. Vol. Inf., wounded, 945.
Mead, George E., pvt., Co. F, 47th Inf., U. S. V., killed, 1161.
Mead, Joseph T., pvt., Troop D, 11th Cav., U. S. V., killed, 1215.
Meade, Francis K., 1st lieut., 21st U. S. Inf., death, 1213; mentioned, 1126.
Meade, Robert L., col., U. S. Marine Corps, mentioned, 425, 436–440.
Meade, U. S. transport, mentioned, 432, 443, 446, 448, 456, 459, 461, 463, 464, 597, 627, 1102, 1103, 1110, 1112, 1119, 1128, 1165, 1173, 1195, 1208, 1244, 1250, 1256, 1258, 1270, 1278, 1289, 1291, 1294, 1295, 1305, 1311, 1319–1321, 1323, 1330, 1340, 1341, 1347, 1355.

1424 INDEX.

Meadows, Frank, pvt., Co. D, 16th U. S. Inf., mentioned, 229.
Mealey, Joseph F., pvt., Troop H, 4th U. S. Cav., mentioned, 1196.
Mear, Clinton E., pvt., Co. H, 43d Inf., U. S. V., wounded, 1160.
Medal of honor, special, for members Eighth Army Corps, 1025.
Medlock, Andrew B., pvt., Hosp. Corps, U. S. A., mentioned, 1216.
Meggison, Charlie J., pvt., Co. B, 13th Minn. Vol. Inf., wounded, 963.
Mehailik, Frank E., pvt., Co. G, 28th Inf., U.S.V., wounded, 1222.
Meidle, Andrew J., pvt., Co. H, 13th Minn. Vol. Inf., wounded, 918.
Meiklejohn, George D., Assistant Secretary of War, mentioned, 298, 347, 348, 353, 354, 373, 379.
Meksa, Stanislaw, pvt., Co. B, 6th U. S. Inf., wounded, 1067.
Melchor, Anton, pvt., Co. D, 23d U. S. Inf., death, 1200.
Mellick, Charles, sergt., Co. H, 1st Nebr. Vol. Inf., killed, 974.
Mellin, Ranger, pvt., Co. I, 9th Mass. Vol. Inf., mentioned, 213.
Mellingerm, Levi P., corpl., Co. F, 13th U. S. Inf., death, 1048.
Mellon, Patrick, pvt., Co. A, 22d U. S. Inf., death, 1260.
Melonson, Ambrose J., Co. M, 9th U. S. Inf., death, 482.
Melse, Milton S., pvt., Co. D, 1st Wash. Vol. Inf., death, 947.
Melville, Paul E., qm. sergt., Co. D, 31st Inf., U. S. V., death, 1185.
Mengel, Jacob, corpl., Co. H, 9th U. S. Inf., wounded, 444.
Mercer, Albert C., pvt., Co. D, 21st U. S. Inf., death, 1194.
Mercer, William S., pvt., Co. M, 34th Inf., U.S.V., killed, 1214.
Mercier, Oscar H., actg. hosp. stewd., U. S. A., killed, 1101.
Merillat, John, pvt., Co. E, 1st U. S. Inf., wounded, 1253.
Merriam, Alfred W., sergt., Co. H, 3d U. S. Inf., killed, 1187.
Merriam, Henry C., brig. gen., U. S. A., mentioned, 643, 683–685, 688, 732, 758, 764, 841, 1012, 1020.
Merriam, Henry C., pvt., Co. G, 21st U. S. Inf., death, 1125.
Merriam, Henry M., 2d lieut., 3d U. S. Art., mentioned, 1046.
Merrill, Abner H., capt., 1st U. S. Art., mentioned, 112, 1292.
Merrill, William J., pvt., Co. M, 3d U. S. Inf., killed, 945.
Merrimac, U. S. collier, mentioned, 25.
Merritt, Thomas E., 2d lieut., 1st U. S. Art., mentioned, 998.
Merritt, Wesley, pvt., Co. K, 48th Inf., U. S. V., death, 1164.
Merritt, Wesley, maj. gen., U. S. A.:
  Arrival at Manila, 781, correspondence, 220, 383.
  Intentions toward Aguinaldo, 821.
  Memorandum for guidance of Major Bell in treating with Filipinos, 818.
  Mentioned, 28, 509, 556, 638, 639, 643, 648, 654, 657, 666, 669, 674–676, 679, 682–685, 689, 695, 696, 698, 699, 704, 705, 707–709, 714, 716, 719, 720, 726, 730, 738, 739, 741, 750, 757, 762, 765, 781, 783, 786, 806, 808–810, 814, 818, 821–823, 846, 849, 913, 1134, 1181.
  Recommends steamer Newport for permanent transport, 737.
  Requests suspension of orders, 638.
  To command Philippine expedition, 639.
  Transfer command to General Otis, 765.
Merryweather & Sons, London, England, mentioned, 727.
Mertner, David, pvt., Troop E, 3d U. S. Cav., mentioned, 206.
Merwin, Eugene, corpl., Co. M, 1st Cal. Vol. Inf., death, 879.
Mesick, Charles E., pvt., Co. G, 43d Inf., U. S. V., wounded, 1195.
Messenheimer, William I., pvt., Co. H, 12th U. S. Inf., wounded, 1057.

Messer, Alfred M., pvt., Co. L, 14th U. S. Inf., wounded, 454.
Messler, Clarence L., pvt., Co. H, 18th U. S. Inf., wounded, 1160.
Metcalf, Everett, pvt., Co. B, 1st Mont. Vol. Inf., wounded, 900.
Metcalf, Wilder S., maj., 20th Kans. Vol. Inf., wounded, 952.
Metzler, W. E., pvt., Co. L, 14th U. S. Inf., killed, 453.
Metzsker, William R., pvt., Co. B, 3d U. S. Inf., death, 1276.
Mexico, U. S. transport, mentioned, 181, 182, 249, 255, 256.
Meyer, Ferdinand W., pvt., Co. I, 43d Inf., U. S. V., killed, 1155.
Meyer, George, pvt., Co. K, 20th Kans. Vol. Inf., wounded, 961.
Meyer, Joseph P., pvt., Co. G, 1st Mont. Vol. Inf., wounded, 945.
Meyer, Josepha, pvt., Co. L, 13th U. S. Inf., killed, 1264.
Meyer, Oren B., 1st lieut., 3d U. S. Cav., wounded, 123.
Meyer, Ralph E., 2d lieut., 12th U. S. Inf., death, 966, 968.
Meyer, William A., pvt., Batty. L, 3d U. S. Art., wounded, 1124.
Meyers, George E., pvt., Co. C, 9th U. S. Inf., wounded, 1298.
Meyersick, William R, pvt., Co. I, 1st Mont. Vol. Inf., wounded, 895.
Miami, Fla.—
  Accommodations at, 38, 39.
  Camp at—
    Advantages, 43, 45.
    Location recommended, 37.
  Concentration point for troops, 33, 266.
  Not suitable for camp site, 44.
Miami, U. S. transport, mentioned, 184, 186, 188, 190, 192, 194, 198, 212, 228, 330, 332.
Michie, Dennis M., 2d lieut., 17th U. S. Inf., killed, 124.
Michigan, State of, history of volunteer regiments, 598, 599.
Michigan, U. S. transport, mentioned, 192, 317, 326, 341, 351, 589, 596, 597, 619.
Michler, Francis, lieut. col., a. a. g., U. S. V., mentioned, 37, 39, 46, 47.
Mickelson, Andrew, pvt., Troop A, Nev. Vol. Cav., death, 939.
Mickey, J. C., pvt., Co. I, 10th Pa. Vol. Inf., wounded, 950.
Mickler, Walter J., pvt., Co. B, 29th Inf., U. S. V. killed, 1197.
Middleton, George, pvt., Co. F, 17th U. S., Inf., death, 1201.
Middleton, Howard, pvt., Co. G, 14th U. S. Inf., wounded, 898.
Middleton, Johnson V. D., col., med. dept., U. S. A., mentioned, 764.
Meitschke, William, pvt., Co. M, 1st Mont. Vol. Inf., killed, 945.
Mifflin, Herbert, pvt., Co. B, 4th U. S. Inf., death, 1020; wounded, 1017.
Migusik, Mathew, pvt., Co. A, 21st U. S. Inf., killed, 1263.
Mikkula, Mathieu, pvt., Co. G, 45th Inf., U.S.V., death, 1167.
Mikulhki, Michael J., corpl., Co. I, 21st U. S. Inf., wounded, 1015.
Mileage, payment in advance, 706.
Mileon, Edward, pvt., Batty. L, 3d U. S. Art., wounded, 1124.
Miles, Arthur W., mus., Co. F, 47th Inf., U. S. V., death, 1210; wounded, 1187.
Miles, Charles A., pvt., Co. D, 35th Inf., U. S. V., death, 1231.
Miles, Earl B., pvt., Troop G, 3d U. S. Cav., wounded, 1003.
Miles, Evan, col., 1st U. S. Inf., mentioned, 542.
Miles, Nelson A., maj. gen., U. S. A.:
  Arrival at Santiago, Cuba, 131.
  Correspondence, 24–39, 41–49, 51, 67, 69–71, 78, 80, 92, 94, 100, 110, 114, 128, 131, 132, 134–136, 142, 144–146, 148, 150, 153, 154, 156, 157, 205, 219, 220, 261–290, 293, 296, 301, 303–305, 313, 314, 320, 322, 326, 327, 330, 333–335, 337, 341, 344, 350–353, 355, 356, 357, 359–362, 364–366, 368, 372–379, 381–388, 390–393, 395–402.

INDEX. 1425

Miles, Nelson A.—Continued.
　Mentioned, 40, 42, 52, 63, 110, 115, 117–120, 128, 131, 139, 144, 145, 147, 184, 188, 192, 198, 210, 211, 218, 228, 233, 269, 270, 277, 280, 281, 284, 286–293, 297, 298, 302, 304, 308, 310–314, 318, 319, 321, 324–327, 334, 335, 337, 344, 346, 350, 351, 355, 357–363, 365, 367, 368, 370–375, 377–379, 384, 386, 393–395, 398, 683, 750.
　Occupancy of Isle of Pines, 71.
　Operations in Cuba, scheme, 51, 52, 261, 263.
　Ordered to Washington, D. C., 48.
　Porto Rico—
　　Fixing money values, 350, 353.
　　Movement against, 261, 271, 277, 280, 282, 283.
　Submarine mines, destruction, 94.
Miley, John D., lieut. col., I. G. U. S. V., mentioned, 87, 89, 90, 91, 109, 209, 225.
Milkowski, Charles, corpl., Co. F, 22d U. S. Inf., death, 997.
Millar, Thomas, capt., 40th Inf., U. S. V., mentioned, 1188.
Millard, Everett, pvt., Co. M, 2d Oreg. Vol. Inf., wounded, 963.
Millard, Guy, pvt., Co. L, 2d Oreg. Vol. Inf., killed, 945.
Millard, Stanley, pvt., Co. C, 4th U. S. Inf., wounded, 1130.
Millard, Thomas, pvt., Co. B, 1st U. S. Inf., wounded, 1259.
Miller, Charles, pvt., Co. B, 22d U. S. Inf., death, 1190.
Miller, Charles A., pvt., Co. B, 27th Inf., U. S. V., death, 1264.
Miller, Clarence E., 1st sergt. Co. B, 45th Inf., U. S. V., killed, 1182.
Miller, Claude H., 2d lieut., 24th U. S. Inf., mentioned, 124.
Miller, Crosby P., maj., qm. dept., U. S. A., mentioned, 502, 1049, 1071.
Miller, Edward B., pvt., Co. E, 22d U. S. Inf., wounded, 946.
Miller, Edward P., pvt., Co. K, 42d Inf., U. S. V., death, 1228.
Miller, Francis C., pvt., Co. I, 21st U. S. Inf., death, 1056.
Miller, Frederick, pvt., Co. M, 3d U. S. Inf., wounded, 981.
Miller, Frederick, ord. sergt., U. S. A., death, 1192.
Miller, Henry J., pvt., Co. A, 39th Inf., U. S. V., death, 1172.
Miller, Howard E., pvt., Co. K, 16th U. S. Inf., death, 1160.
Miller, Jacob, pvt., Co. G, 26th Inf., U. S. V., wounded, 1166.
Miller, James, pvt., Co. M, 14th U. S. Inf., wounded, 898.
Miller, John, pvt., Co. I, 22d U. S. Inf., death, 956; wounded, 948
Miller, John, pvt., Co. K, 19th U. S. Inf., death, 1109.
Miller, John E., pvt., Co. A, 17th U. S. Inf., wounded, 1107.
Miller, John G., corpl., Co. F, 2d Oreg. Vol. Inf., wounded, 987.
Miller, John H., pvt., Co. C, 9th U. S. Inf., killed, 1297.
Miller, John J., pvt., Co. C, 38th Inf., U. S. V., wounded, 1163.
Miller, John R., maj., 1st Mont. Vol. Inf., wounded, 977.
Miller, Joseph N., rear-admiral, U. S. N., mentioned, 729.
Miller, Joseph W., sergt., Co. H, 3d U. S. Inf., wounded, 995.
Miller, Lewis E., pvt., Co. A, 2d Oreg. Vol. Inf., death, 836.
Miller, Lincoln, pvt., Co. A, 37th Inf., U. S. V., killed, 1146.
Miller, Marcus P., brig. gen., U. S. V., mentioned, 559–562, 674, 678, 683, 758, 762, 794, 795, 801, 834, 862, 865, 866, 867, 872, 873, 876, 877, 927, 928, 994, 1248.
Miller, Myron C., pvt., Co. 5th U. S. Inf., missing, 444.
Miller, Ollie, pvt., Batty. L, 3d U. S. Art., wounded, 946.
Miller, Paul, pvt., Co. D, 23d U. S. Inf., U. S. V., mentioned, 732.

Miller, Richard, sergt., Troop F, 9th U. S. Cav., wounded, 1250.
Miller, Ross G., pvt., Troop A, 4th U. S. Cav., wounded, 1145.
Miller, Thomas, pvt., Co. K, 20th U. S. Inf., wounded, 934.
Miller, Thomas, capt., 40th Inf., U. S. V., wounded, 1183.
Miller, William, pvt., Co. I, 14th U. S. Inf., wounded, 454.
Miller, William, pvt., Co. K, 4th U. S. Inf., death, 1029.
Miller, William J., pvt., Co. F, 41st Inf., U. S. V., death, 1223.
Miller, William L., pvt., Co. D, 38th Inf., U. S. V., death, 1133.
Miller, William M., corpl., Co. A, 33d Inf., U. S. V., wounded, 1228.
Miller, William P., pvt., Co. F, 22d U. S. Inf., death, 1229.
Milligan, Manley F., pvt., Co. C, 30th Inf., U. S. V., death, 1200.
Mills, Albert L., 1st lieut., 1st U. S. Cav., wounded, 123.
Mills, C. W., pvt., Co. M, 2d Oreg. Vol. Inf., mentioned, 1028.
Mills, Ivan L., pvt., Co. C, 26th Inf., U. S. V., death, 1191.
Mills, James S., pvt., Co. E, 20th Kans. Vol. Inf., wounded, 901.
Mills, John T., pvt., Co. D, 44th Inf., U. S. V., wounded, 1209
Mills, Orville H., corpl., Co. B, 33d Inf., U. S. V., wounded, 1219
Mills, Robert, corpl., Troop E, 11th Cav., U. S. V., death, 1136.
Mills, Samuel M., maj., 6th U. S. Art., mentioned, 487, 541, 980, 1292.
Milner, James, pvt., Co. G, 14th U. S. Inf., 1084.
Milzkie, Paul I., pvt., Co. E, 11th U. S. Inf., wounded, 390.
Mimashi, K., Japanese consul at Manila, mentioned, 1240.
Minnich, Leroy S., pvt., Co. —, 1st Wyo. Vol. Inf., death, 803.
Minard, Charles E., pvt., Co. F, 43d Inf., U. S. V., death, 1280.
Mindanao, Spanish regiment, mentioned, 655.
Miner, Cassius A., pvt., Co. B, 39th Inf., U. S. V., death, 1185.
Miner, Charles, pvt., Co. —, 2d Oreg. Vol. Inf., death, 803.
Miner, Charles W., lieut. col., 6th U. S. Inf., mentioned, 545.
Mingee, Leander, pvt., Co. E, 22d U. S. Inf., wounded, 941.
Minneapolis, U. S. transport, mentioned, 16.
Minnesota, U. S. transport, mentioned, 592, 594, 595.
Minnewaska, U. S. transport, mentioned, 253, 336, 337, 340, 615, 624.
Minnich, Leroy S., pvt., Co. C, 1st Wyo. Vol. Inf., mentioned, 761.
Minnis, John F., pvt., Co. H, 2d U. S. Inf., mentioned, 193.
Minor, Guy E., pvt., Co. H, 1st Nebr. Vol. Inf., wounded, 974.
Misner, Theodore A., pvt., Co. A, 22d U. S. Inf., wounded, 934.
Missal, Adolphe, pvt., Co. F, 3d U. S. Inf., mentioned, 224.
Mississippi, U. S. transport, mentioned, 83, 84, 128, 138, 143, 155, 171, 192, 275, 351, 356, 597, 608, 616.
Missouri, Dept. of, Gen. Chaffee to command, 841.
Missouri, U. S. hospital ship, mentioned, 241, 245, 249, 1110, 1128.
Mitchel, Forest, pvt., Co. C, 22d U. S. Inf., death, 1249.
Mitchell, Alexander M., pvt., Co. B, 20th Kans. Vol. Inf., wounded, 902.
Mitchell, Burton J., 1st lieut., 40th Inf., U. S. V., mentioned, 1262.
Mitchell, David D., capt., 15th U. S. Inf., killed, 1211; mentioned, 1213, 1214.
Mitchell, Edward B., pvt., Co. L, 14th U. S. Inf., death, 460.
Mitchell, Edward B., 2d lieut., 24th U. S. Inf., wounded, 1188.
Mitchell, George, pvt., Co. I, 21st U. S. Inf., killed, 1090.

Mitchell, George J., pvt., Troop E, 3d U. S. Cav., killed, 1143.
Mitchell, J., seaman, U. S. N., wounded, 459.
Mitchell, James, 1st lieut., 14th U. S. Inf., death, 895; mentioned, 442.
Mitchell, John F., corpl., Co. A, 1st Wash. Vol. Inf., wounded, 896.
Mitchell, John M., member of Congress, mentioned, 348.
Mitchell, Leonard A., 1st lieut., 51st Ia. Vol. Inf., 943.
Mitchell, Louis, pvt., Co. K, 48th Inf., U. S. V., death, 1190.
Mitchell, Robert E., pvt., Co. B, 44th Inf., U.S. V., wounded, 1250.
Mitchell, Roscoe L., pvt., Batty. E, 3d U. S. Art., wounded, 897.
Mitchell, Smack, pvt., Co. L, 33d Inf., U. S. V., killed, 1101.
Mixon, Thomas, pvt., Co. K, 43d Inf., U. S. V., death, 1197; wounded, 1176.
Moale, Edward, col., 15th U. S. Inf., mentioned. 469.

Mobile, Ala. :
Camp at, condition, accommodations, 35, 36.
Concentration of troops, 7, 266.
General Coppinger to command troops at, 8.
Immunes at, 45.
Lighters ordered to General Shafter from, 58.
Troops at—
  Available for embarkation, 18.
  Ordered to Tampa, 35, 36.
  To be ordered to other corps, 47.
Withdrawal of troops from, 24, 43, 45, 49.

Mobile, U. S. transport, mentioned, 205, 213, 240–242, 244, 326, 334, 335, 361–363, 366, 592, 596, 615, 619, 621, 871, 873, 875.
Moffett, Richard K., corpl., Co. A, 19th U. S. Inf., wounded, 1227.
Moffett, Mr., correspondent, mentioned, 300, 301.
Mohawk, U. S. transport, mentioned, 83, 84, 128, 138, 148, 205, 221, 232, 236, 275, 278, 282, 309, 310, 326, 334, 335, 350, 361, 362, 366, 384, 869, 875, 880.
Mohlin, Ludwig P., pvt., Co. B, 12th U. S. Inf., death, 1032.
Mohun, Louis W., corpl., Co. I, 9th U. S. Inf., death, 1113.
Molcan, Gottlieb, pvt., Co. C, 1st Mont. Vol. Inf., wounded, 981.
Molder, Charles V., pvt., Co. I, 17th U. S. Inf., death, 1271.
Moles, Robert, pvt., Batty. L, 3d U. S. Art., wounded, 966.
Mole St. Nicolas, Hayti, naval vessels to coal at, 16.
Moller, Henry, pvt., Co. B, 18th U. S. Inf., death, 1086.
Moller, Joseph B., pvt., Co. H, 14th U. S. Inf., death, 1190.
Mollyneaux, Ralph, pvt., Troop I, 3d U. S. Cav., death, 1276.
Moloney, James, pvt., Co. H, 26th Inf., U. S. V., death, 1144.
Moloney, William, corpl., Co. L, 19th U. S. Inf., death, 1130.
Momeny, George, corpl., Co. I, 47th Inf., U.S. V., wounded, 1155.
Monadnock, U. S. gunboat, mentioned, 415, 744.
Monaghan, William, maj., pay dept., U. S. V., death, 1267.
Monahan, Cornelius, pvt., Hosp. Corps, U. S. A., wounded, 925.
Moncrief, Fred, corpl., Co. D, 5th U. S. Inf., killed, 1251.
Monocacy, U. S. gunboat, mentioned, 411, 415, 422, 484.

Monroe, Fort, Va. :
Movement of troops, 58, 59.
Sick and wounded to be sent to, 93, 99.
Thence to New York, 142.

Monroe, James G., pvt., Co. H, 10th Pa. Vol. Inf., 833.
Monroe, George H., pvt., Co. F, 20th Kans. Vol. Inf., wounded, 915.
Monsen, Christ, sergt., Troop I, 4th U. S. Cav., death, 1161.
Monserrat, Spanish ship, mentioned, 991.
Montag, George, pvt., Co. C, 35th Inf., U. S. V., death, 1119.

Montauk Point, N. Y., troops from Cuba sent to, 360.
Monterey, U. S. monitor, mentioned, 740, 782.
Montero, Spanish general, death, 997.
Montgomery, Benjamin F., capt., Sig. Corps, U. S. A., mentioned, 42, 43, 44, 48, 73.
Montgomery, Humphrey, pvt., Co. A, 24th U. S. Inf., mentioned, 241.
Montgomery, James R., mus., Co. B, 33d Inf., U. S. V., wounded, 1137.
Montgomery, John, sergt., Batty. K, 3d U. S. Art., death, 972; wounded, 959.
Montgomery, John, mus., Co. F, 22d U. S. Inf., wounded, 1192.
Montgomery, William A., col., 2d Miss. Vol. Inf., mentioned, 551.
Montojo, admiral, Spanish navy, mentioned, 799.
Moody, George, pvt., Co. F, 24th U. S. Inf., death, 1057, 1060.
Moody, Jesse G., corpl., Co. M [L?], 40th Inf., U. S. V., killed, 1183; mentioned, 1206.
Moon, Henry C., capt., 20th U. S. Inf., mentioned, 842; wounded, 124.
Mooney, Terrence J., pvt., Batty. F, 5th U. S. Art., wounded, 1130.
Mooney, William, member post-office committee, mentioned, 405.
Moore, Arthur K., pvt., Co. H, 20th Kans. Vol. Inf., wounded, 984.
Moore, Charles, pvt., Co. E, 22d U. S. Inf., death, 1142.
Moore, Edson B., pvt., Co. C, 26th Inf., U. S. V., death, 1210.
Moore, Edward S., pvt., Co. G, 1st Mont. Vol. Inf.. death, 923; wounded, 918.
Moore, Ellridge W., 2d lieut., 2d Oreg. Vol. Inf., 829.
Moore, E. B., pvt., Co. H, 8th U. S. Inf., mentioned, 224.
Moore, George A., pvt., Co. C, 1st S. Dak. Vol. Inf., wounded, 949.
Moore, George D., 1st lieut., 23d U. S. Inf., mentioned, 1039.
Moore, Henry, pvt., Co. F, 48th Inf., U. S. V., death, 1249.
Moore, James T. capt., 27th U. S. Inf., mentioned, 1331.
Moore, John, pvt., Troop K, 11th Cav., U. S. V., death, 1174.
Moore, John, pvt., Co. H, 12th U. S. Inf., death, 1095.
Moore, John A., sergt., Co. K, 4th U. S. Inf., death, 984.
Moore, John H., corpl., Co. L, 14th U. S. Inf., death, 1015.
Moore, John L., 1st lieut., 51st Iowa Vol. Inf., death, 1038.
Moore, John M., Co. C, 32d Inf., U. S. V., death, 1152.
Moore, Milton, col., 5th Mo. Vol. Inf., mentioned, 530–533.
Moore, Robert H., pvt., Co. K, 23d U. S. Inf., killed, 1052.
Moore, William K., 1st lieut., 1st Nebr. Vol. Inf., wounded, 974.
Moore, William S., pvt., Co. L, 13th Minn. Vol. Inf., mentioned, 762; wounded. 761.
Moore, ——, secretary, mentioned, 264, 367.
Moran, James W., pvt., Co. A, 26th Inf., U. S. V., death, 1170.
Moran, John, pvt., Batty. E, 1st U. S. Art., death, 1078.
Moran, John E., capt., 37th Inf., U.S. V., wounded, 1211.
Moran, Paul E., sergt., Co. E, 6th U.S. Inf., death, 1095.
Moran, Shelley, pvt., Troop F, 10th U. S. Cav., death, 1280; mentioned, 1283.
Mordin, John, pvt., Co. G, 46th Inf., U. S. V., death, 1151.
Moreau, Henry, pvt., Batty. F, 5th U. S. Art., death, 1078.
Morehouse, Charles, pvt., Co. M, 46th Inf., U. S. V., death, 1172.
Moreland, William G., sergt., Co. C, 27th Inf., U. S. V., killed, 1281.
Morelock, A. Lee, sergt., Co. D, 2d Oreg. Vol. Inf., wounded, 946.

Morfoed, Fred, pvt., Co. K, 34th Inf., U. S. V., death, 1125.
Morgan, Charles, corpl., Co. H, 14th U. S. Inf., wounded, 460.
Morgan, Charles A., pvt., Co. C, 23d U. S. Inf., wounded, 760.
Morgan, Elijah, pvt., Co. D, 1st N. Dak. Vol. Inf., wounded, 957.
Morgan, Eugene R., pvt., Co. D, 10th Pa. Vol. Inf., wounded, 945.
Morgan, George, pvt., Co. C, 17th U. S. Inf., death, 1241.
Morgan, Jesse M., civilian, wounded, 897.
Morgan, John, pvt., Co. H, 1st N. Dak. Vol. Inf., death, 831.
Morgan, Joseph C., pvt., Co. A, 29th Inf., U. S. V., death, 1233.
Morgan, J. Pierpont, mentioned, 321.
Morgan, Louis, corpl., Co. A, 24th U. S. Inf., death, 1231.
Morgan, Walter, pvt., Co. A, 39th Inf., U. S. V., death, 1217.
Morgan City, U. S. transport, mentioned, 80, 92, 98, 275, 278, 282, 316, 317, 399, 588, 704, 715, 740, 791, 868, 869, 871, 886, 889, 919, 922, 929, 930, 936, 962, 996, 1023, 1038, 1049, 1063, 1064, 1069, 1071, 1072, 1074.
  Mail lost in wreck, 1072.
  Stranded in Inland Sea, Japan, 1063.
Morgans, Thomas, pvt., Co. L, 16th U. S. Inf., death, 1160.
Moriarty, Dennis, corpl., Co. G, 9th U. S. Inf., wounded, 444.
Moriarty, J. D., pvt., Co. E, 9th Mass. Vol. Inf., mentioned, 241.
Morin, E., pvt., Co. C, 1st Wash. Vol. Inf., wounded, 948.
Moring, Christopher A., pvt., Co. D, 42d Inf., U. S. V., death, 1264.
Morisette, Joseph T., pvt., Co. A, 37th Inf., U. S. V., killed, 1086.
Morley, Frank A., lieut., 13th Minn. Vol. Inf., death, 784, 803.
Morning Star, American missionary vessel, mentioned, 746.
Morray, Henry, corpl., Co. I, 9th U. S. Inf. wounded, 1081.
Morrell, Miss, mentioned, 487.
Morrill, Asa P., pvt., Co. D, 1st Idaho Vol. Inf., wounded, 1008.
Morris, Courtney, pvt., Co. L, 36th Inf., U. S. V., wounded, 1233.
Morris, David H., pvt., Co. H, 9th U. S. Inf., wounded, 444.
Morris, Edward R., capt., med. dept., U. S. A., mentioned, 657, 658.
Morris, Frederick, pvt., Co. M, 28th Inf., U. S. V., death, 1200.
Morris, George W., pvt., Co. A, 19th U. S. Inf., killed, 1148.
Morris, Louis T., lieut. col., 4th U. S. Cav., mentioned, 685.
Morris, Philip, pvt., Co. L, 4th U. S. Inf., death, 1070.
Morris, Thomas P., pvt., Co. M, 3d U. S. Inf., killed, 961.
Morris, Warren J., pvt., Co. C, 1st Mont. Vol. Inf., wounded, 1017.
Morris, William T., sergt., band, 15th U. S. Inf., death, 1283.
Morrisey, Michael, pvt., Co. L, 26th Inf., U. S. V., wounded, 1190.
Morrison, Charles S., pvt., Co. B, 1st Colo. Vol. Inf., wounded, 895.
Morrison, Henry H., pvt., Co. M, 20th Kans. Vol. Inf., death, 979; wounded, 977.
Morrison, John, jr., 1st lieut., 4th U. S. Cav., killed, 1247; mentioned, 1057.
Morrison, John P., pvt., Co. A, 47th Inf., U. S. V. killed, 1150.
Morrison, Sidney, pvt., Co. M, 20th Kans. Vol. Inf., wounded, 901.
Morrison, Sidney E., 2d lieut., 1st S. Dak. Vol. Inf., killed, 948, 949.
Morrison, Temple B., pvt., Co. C, 39th Inf., U. S. V., death, 1172.
Morrison, Theophilus W., capt., 16th U. S. Inf., killed, 124.

Morrissey, Edward, pvt., Co. B, 1st Mont. Vol. Inf., wounded, 948.
Morros, James J., pvt., Co. M, 1st Tenn. Vol. Inf., death, 917.
Morrow, Frank J., 1st lieut., 17th U. S. Inf., wounded, 1160.
Morse, Arthur, pvt., Co. D, 18th U. S. Inf., death, 1048.
Morse, J. B., 2d lieut., Cal. Vol. Heavy Art., mentioned, 763.
Morse, John O., sergt., Co. K, 20th Kans. Vol. Inf., wounded, 901.
Morse, Joseph B., 2d lieut., 9th U. S. Inf., death, 1056.
Morse, Lee K., sergt., Co. L, 2d Oreg. Vol. Inf., death, 875.
Morse, William C., pvt., Batty. C, 7th U. S. Art. (14th Batty. Field Art.), death, 1260; wounded, 1256.
Mortenson, Martin C., pvt., Co. E, 1st S. Dak. Vol. Inf., death, 803.
Morton, Ben A., corpl., Co. M, 6th U. S. Inf., wounded, 1067.
Morton, I. W., president Commercial Club, St. Louis, Mo., mentioned, 343.
Morton, Hon. Levi P., mentioned, 235.
Mosby, William, pvt., Co. F, 22d U. S. Inf., wounded, 1192.
Moseback, William H., pvt., Co. E, 28th Inf., U. S. V., death 1226.
Moseley, William J., pvt., Co. H, 24th U. S. Inf., mentioned, 218.
Moseley, ——, consul, mentioned, 1099.
Moses, Cassius M., lieut. col., 1st Colo. Vol. Inf., wounded, 1008.
Mosher, Theodore capt., 22d U. S. Inf., mentioned, 83; wounded, 124.
Moss, James A., 1st lieut., 24th U. S. Inf., mentioned, 1018.
Motley, George, pvt., Co. H, 24th U. S. Inf., death, 1125.
Motsinger, Roy B., pvt., Co. D, 36th Inf., U. S. V., wounded, 1096.
Mott, T. Bently, 1st lieut., 7th U. S. Art., mentioned, 686.
Motz, Joseph J., pvt., Batty. K, 3d U. S. Art., death, 961; wounded, 946.
Mount, Earl, pvt., Co. C, 2d Oreg. Vol. Inf., wounded, 946.
Mount, James A., governor of Indiana, mentioned, 349, 357.
Mount Vernon, Ala., concentration of troops, 49, 266.
Mountz, Edward E., pvt., Co. D, 28th Inf., U. S. V., death 1253.
Mowrey, Joseph L., pvt., Co. G, 38th Inf., U. S. V., death, 1233.
Moyer, Pearley W., pvt., Co. E, 39th Inf., U. S. V., death, 1260.
Moyers, John A., pvt., Co. H, 1st Tenn. Vol. Inf., death, 889.
Muck, Frank J., pvt., Co. D, 34th Mich. Vol. Inf., mentioned, 218.
Muda, Rajah, Moro chief, mentioned, 1118.
Mueller, Alfred J., pvt., Co. L, 37th Inf., U. S. V., killed, 1211; mentioned, 1214.
Mueller, William C., corpl., Co. M, 30th Inf., U. S. V., death, 1248.
Muggy, Hubert, pvt., Troop D, 3d U. S. Cav., wounded, 1137.
Muhlson, G., pvt., Co. I, 1st Mont. Vol. Inf., wounded, 981.
Muhr, John C., pvt., Co. E, 20th Kans. Vol. Inf., wounded, 948.
Muir, Charles H., maj., 38th Inf., U. S. V., mentioned, 433, 1136; wounded, 1147.
Mulhey, William A., pvt., Co. B, 4th U. S. Inf., wounded, 1021.
Mulholland, David, pvt., Co. I, 22d U. S. Inf., wounded, 934.
Mullaney, John, corpl., Co. F, 21st U. S. Inf., death, 1048.
Mullay, William H., 1st lieut., 21st U. S. Inf., death, 1262.
Mullen, Barney, corpl., Co. H, 14th U. S. Inf., killed, 1081.
Mullen, Henry, pvt., Co. C, 1st Wash. Vol. Inf., wounded, 906.
Mullen, Patrick, pvt., Co. G, 3d U. S. Inf., killed, 1187.

Muller, Andrew, pvt., Co. G, 27th U. S. Inf., U. S. V., death, 1196.
Muller, Martin, pvt., Batty. E, 1st U. S. Art., death 1070.
Mulligan, John, pvt., Co. M, 14th U. S. Inf., wounded, 454.
Mullin, Thomas, pvt., Co. C, 21st U. S. Inf., wounded, 1010.
Mulray, Thomas, pvt., Co. L, 15th U. S. Inf., killed, 1211.
Mulvahill, John, pvt., Co. D, 22d U. S. Inf., wounded, 934.
Mulvahill, Patrick, J., pvt., Co. L, 12th U. S. Inf., wounded, 1015.
Mumby, Clifford M., pvt., Co. C, 9th U. S. Inf., wounded, 1298.
Munch, Joseph, jr., pvt., Co. D, 9th U. S. Inf., wounded, 444.
Mundi, Dato, Moro chief, mentioned, 1060.
Munro, Horace N., pvt., Troop C, 4th U. S. Cav., wounded, 1145.
Munro, James N., 2d lieut., 4th U. S. Cav., mentioned, 1112.
Munroe, Thomas L., pvt., Co. K, 1st Wash. Vol. Inf., wounded, 961.
Munson, William N., pvt., Co. K, 9th U. S. Inf., killed, 1055.
Munson, Wynne P., pvt., Co. K, 22d U. S. Inf., killed, 934.
Murdock, James E., pvt., Co. F, 43d Inf., U. S. V., wounded, 1176.
Murnan, ——, pvt., Co. C, 3d U. S. Inf., death, 1060.
Murphy, Charles S., pvt., Co. M, 1st Mont. Vol. Inf., killed, 977.
Murphy, David A., pvt., Co. F, 9th U. S. Inf., wounded, 444.
Murphy, Dennis, pvt., Co. I, 35th Inf., U. S. V., death, 1217.
Murphy, Dennis, pvt., Co. I, 13th U. S. Inf., death, 1223.
Murphy, Edward, qm. sergt., Co. I, 21st U. S. Inf., death, 1201.
Murphy, George F., pvt., Co. A, 9th U. S. Inf., wounded, 443.
Murphy, Henry, corpl., Co. B, 28th Inf., U. S. V., death, 1185.
Murphy, James E., pvt., Co. C, 34th Inf., U. S. V., death, 1155; wounded, 1155.
Murphy, James T., pvt., Batty. G, 6th U. S. Art., wounded, 1112.
Murphy, Jeremiah, pvt., Co. E, 9th U. S. Inf., death, 1187.
Murphy, John, capt., 14th U. S. Inf., mentioned, 769, 770, 772.
Murphy, John, corpl., Co. A, 1st Cal. Vol. Inf., wounded, 897.
Murphy, John, pvt., Co. D, 1st S. Dak. Vol. Inf., wounded, 975.
Murphy, John W., capt., 1st Idaho Vol. Inf., 829.
Murphy, Joseph P., pvt., Troop L, 3d U. S. Cav., death, 1226.
Murphy, Lawrence, pvt., Troop G, 6th U. S. Cav., death, 1276.
Murphy, Lee S., pvt., Co. G, 32d Inf., U. S. V., killed, 1148.
Murphy, Patrick, jr., pvt., Co. E, 9th U. S. Inf., wounded, 460.
Murphy, Patrick J., pvt., Co. G, 34th Inf., U. S. V., wounded, 1147.
Murphy, Robert, pvt., Co. K, 1st Mont. Vol. Inf., wounded, 981.
Murphy, Stephen, pvt., Co. M, 2d Oreg. Vol. Inf., mentioned, 1028.
Murphy, Thomas, pvt., Co. I, 22d U. S. Inf., death, 1261.
Murphy, William, pvt., Co. E, 8th U. S. Inf., mentioned, 206.
Murphy, William, pvt., Co. D, 9th U. S. Inf., wounded, 444.
Murphy, William, pvt., Co. C, 13th U. S. Inf., killed, 1046.
Murphy, William, pvt., Co. I, 23d U. S. Inf., death, 1190; wounded, 1189.
Murphy, William L., capt., 24th U. S. Inf., killed, 1230.
Murphy, William L., pvt., Co. A, 27th Inf., U. S. V., death, 1104.
Murphy, John W., capt., 1st Idaho Vol. Inf., mentioned, 829.
Murray, Arthur, col., 43d Inf., U. S. V., call for troops, 1159; mentioned, 1112, 1114, 1122, 1125.
Murray, Charles H., pvt., Co. M, 39th Inf., U. S. V., death, 1194.
Murray, Elmore E., pvt., Co. F, 29th Inf., U.S.V., killed, 1219.
Murray, Frank J., pvt., Co. A, 1st Cal. Vol. Inf., death, 1044.
Murray, Joseph W., sergt., Co. L, 20th Kans. Vol. Inf., wounded, 954.
Murray, Thomas J., sergt., Co. A, 23d U. S. Inf., death, 1120.
Murray, William H., pvt., Co. K, 21st U. S. Inf., death, 1048.
Murray, William L., pvt., Co. C, 21st U. S. Inf., death, 1038.
Murray, ——, capt., 8th Cal. Vol. Inf., mentioned, 726.
Murry, F. F., pvt., U. S. Marine Corps, death, 1314.
Murvin, Harry B., pvt., Co. L, 4th U. S. Inf., death, 1215.
Mussler, Ernest A., pvt., Troop K, 3d U. S. Cav., wounded, 1209.
Myer, Fort, Va., movement of artillery from, 59.
Myer, Gustave, pvt., Co. E, 1st Nebr. Vol. Inf., wounded, 952.
Myers, Allison, pvt., Co. L, 1st S. Dak. Vol. Inf., wounded, 948, 949.
Myers, Bert, pvt., Co. G, 29th Inf., U. S. V., death, 1136.
Myers, Charles F., pvt., Co. H, 1st Mont. Vol. Inf., wounded, 954.
Myers, Fred, pvt., Co. F, 43d Inf., U. S. V., wounded, 1183, 1214.
Myers, Henry C., pvt., Troop C, 3d U. S. Cav., wounded, 1152.
Myers, Howard G., pvt., Troop E, 3d U. S. Cav., wounded, 1184.
Myers, John T., capt., U. S. Marine Corps, mentioned, 459.
Myers, William, pvt., Co. F, 22d U. S. Inf., wounded, 946.
Myersick, William B., pvt., Co. I, 1st Mont. Vol. Inf., wounded, 907.
Myhre, Christ L., corpl., Co. E, 1st S. Dak. Vol. Inf., wounded, 975.
Mynatt, William P., sergt., Troop E, 11th Cav., U. S. V., death, 1241.
Mynott, Mark D., pvt., Batty. D, 6th U. S. Art., death, 1015; wounded, 1015.
Mynott, Edward, pvt., Co. L, 34th Mich. Vol. Inf., mentioned, 226.
Nadean, John, pvt., Co. H, 26th Inf., U. S. V., wounded, 1126.
Naftzger, Fern R., pvt., Co. D, 8th Ohio Vol. Inf., mentioned, 246.
Nagasaki, launch, mentioned, 435.
Nagele, Herman, pvt., Co. L, 18th U. S. Inf., death, 1210.
Nagle, Thomas, pvt., Co. E, 17th U. S. Inf., death, 1095.
Nall, Amon, pvt., Troop G, 4th U. S. Cav., wounded, 1051.
Nance, Mack C., pvt., Co. F, 24th U. S. Inf., wounded, 1148.
Nanney, Willie P., pvt., Batty. F, 5th U. S. Art., wounded, 460.
Napier, Robert, pvt., Troop I, 11th Cav., U. S. V., killed, 1131.
Narita, Goro, Japanese vice-consul at Manila, mentioned, 1240.
Narver, Elmer F., pvt., Co. D, 51st Iowa Vol. Inf., wounded, 975.
Nash, Frank, pvt., Co. D, 20th U. S. Inf., wounded, 934.
Nash, Harry E., pvt., Co. D, 19th U. S. Inf., death, 1162.
Nashville, U. S. gunboat, mentioned, 410, 415, 420, 425, 1135, 1139.
Naughton, John, pvt., Co. I, 8th U. S. Inf., death, 1280.
Navarro, Angel, secretary to governor, Santiago de Cuba, mentioned, 90.
Navy:
  Bombardment of Santiago to be made by, 105.
    by Army and, 122, 123.
  Censorship of cable, in re., 67, 70.
  Cooperation with Army, 16, 18, 19, 88, 89, 97, 98, 136, 141.

Navy—Continued.
Decision of Supreme Court in re. captures by, 164.
Destruction of Spanish fleet by, 81.
Entrance to Santiago Harbor by, 38, 89, 91.
Disinclined to force entrance to harbor of Santiago, 105, 132.
Firing by, near Aguadores, 125.
Supply of water for, 9, 10.
To assist in caring for wounded, 72.
Naylor, William K., 1st lieut., 9th U. S. Inf., mentioned, 505; wounded, 428, 429.
Nazor, Robert M., pvt., Co. E, 9th U. S. Inf., death, 1062.
Neal, Amos O., pvt., Co. F, 39th Inf., U. S. V., death, 1146.
Neal, Edward M., pvt., Co. L, 15th U. S. Inf., death, 1211.
Neal, Leonard B., corpl., Co. E, 2d U. S. Inf., death, 1236.
Neary, James, corpl., Co. M, 14th U. S. Inf., wounded, 895.
Neary, William C., 1st lieut., 4th U. S. Inf., wounded, 124.
Neatherly, Henry M., pvt., Co. F, 37th Inf., U. S. V., death, 1119.
Nebergall, Guy, pvt., Co. I, 20th Kans. Vol. Inf., death, 984.
Nebinger, Rankins, farrier, Troop I, 4th U. S. Cav., wounded, 947.
Neeves, Eden C., pvt., Co. D, 39th Inf., U. S. V., death, 1178.
Neiffer, Solomon H., pvt., Co. K, 4th U. S. Cav., death, 1245.
Neill, Howard, pvt., Hosp. Corps, U. S. A., mentioned, 761.
Neipp, Charles J., pvt., Co. D, 23d U. S. Inf., death, 1213.
Neiswonger, Hugh, pvt., Co. K, 31st Inf., U. S. V., death, 1264.
Nelson, Andrew J., pvt., Co. D, 30th U. S. Inf., death, 1233.
Nelson, Algert T., pvt., Co. G, 46th Inf., U. S. V., wounded, 1137.
Nelson, Arthur, pvt., Co. B, 8th Ohio Vol. Inf., mentioned, 197.
Nelson, Augustus, pvt., Co. L, 47th Inf., U. S. V., wounded, 1231.
Nelson, James W., pvt., Co. D, 1st S. Dak. Vol. Inf., killed, 949.
Nelson, John E., pvt., Co. K, 2d U. S. Inf., wounded, 995.
Nelson, John Ingham, pvt., Co. G, 3d U. S. Inf., killed, 961.
Nelson, Herbert R., pvt., Co. F, 46th Inf., U. S. V., death, 1178.
Nelson, Hugh, cook, Co. D, 4th U. S. Inf., suicide, 1264.
Nelson, Louis O., pvt., Co. G, 12th U. S. Inf., death, 1144.
Nelson, N. P., sergt., Co. I, U. S. Marine Corps, death, 477.
Nelson, Oscar C., corpl., Co. C, 1st. Cal. Vol. Inf., wounded, 905.
Nelson, Otto, pvt,, Co. A, 1st Mont. Vol. Inf., wounded, 916.
Nelson, Peter, pvt., Co. A, 2d U. S. Inf., killed, 127.
Nelson, Samuel A., pvt., Co. F, 25th U. S. Inf., death, 1243.
Nelson, William, pvt., Co. F, 20th Kans. Vol. Inf., wounded, 897.
Nesbitt, Charles, pvt., Co. E, 49th Inf., U. S. V., wounded, 1254.
Nesbitt, Louis S., pvt., Co. K, 47th Inf., U. S. V., wounded, 1235.
Nesbitt, Oscar, pvt., Co. K, 20th Kans. Vol. Inf., wounded, 981.
Ness, Henry O., pvt., Co. D, 1st Wash. Vol. Inf., wounded, 941.
Nessel, Carl L., pvt., Troop C, 4th U. S. Cav., death, 1146.
Nestell, George H., corpl., Co. M, 44th Inf., U.S.V., wounded, missing, 1256.
Netherton, Charles M., pvt., Co. D, 39th Inf., U. S. V., death, 1174.
Nettingham, Martin C., corpl., Co. C, 33d Mich., Vol Inf., mentioned, 209.

Neugass, Max, pvt., Co. E, 4th U. S. Inf., death, 1020.
Neumann, Richard C., pvt., Co. E, 14th U. S. Inf., wounded, 1081.
Neuvians, Charles, corpl., Co. L, 21st U. S. Inf., wounded, 1015.
Nevins, Henry C., corpl., Co. H, 30th U. S. Inf., wounded, 1250.
Nevins, Michael, pvt., Co. I, 9th U. S. Inf., death, 497.
Newark, U. S. cruiser, mentioned, 299, 409, 410, 436, 1121.
Newby, Otis C., corpl., Co. C, 45th Inf., U. S. V., killed, 1209.
Newell, Alex, pvt., Co. E, 10th Pa. Vol. Inf., killed, 945.
Newell, Fred E., pvt., Co. D, 9th U. S. Inf., wounded, 444.
Newell, Isaac, 1st lieut., 22d U. S. Inf., mentioned, 994.
Newfeldt, Erich, pvt., Co. D, 1st Nebr. Vol. Inf., wounded, 955.
Newhoff, George, pvt., Co. A, 1st Nebr. Vol. Inf., wounded, 950.
Newland, George A., pvt., Co. B, 17th U. S. Inf., death, 1236.
Newman, Andrew, pvt., Co. G, 19th U. S. Inf., death, 1202.
Newman, Charles M., pvt., Troop H, 4th U. S. Cav., wounded, 1196.
Newman, Edward, pvt., Co. C, 22d U. S. Inf., wounded, 1060.
Newman, Fenton F., pvt., Co. C, 23d U. S. Inf., wounded, 760.
Newmann, Louis F., pvt., Co. G, 2d Oreg. Vol. Inf., mentioned, 1028.
New Orleans, La.:
Concentration of troops, 7.
General Shafter to command troops at, 8.
Immune regiments at for Santiago, 166.
Troops at, ordered to Tampa, 35.
New Orleans, U. S. cruiser, mentioned, 50, 297, 299, 415, 484, 488, 490, 492.
Newport News, Va.:
As shipping point, 144.
Transports and troops, movement, 77, 102, 116, 117, 133.
Wounded returned to, 55.
Newport, U. S. transport, mentioned, 556, 593, 612, 624, 710, 713, 715, 717, 737, 740, 741, 781, 792, 796, 803, 832–834, 851, 922, 928, 936, 959, 960, 962, 994, 1005, 1007, 1010, 1030, 1034, 1041, 1042, 1058, 1061, 1064, 1083, 1089, 1091, 1105, 1107.
Purchase, 737.
Ventilation facilities, 737.
Newton, Harry W., capt., 34th Inf., U. S. V., in capture of Aguinaldo, 1262.
Newton, Henry, pvt., Co. M, 14th U. S. Inf., killed, 898.
New York, N. Y.:
Movement of troops to and from, 133, 869, 870, 881, 882, 887, 889–891, 904.
Transports, movement to and from, 82, 84, 85, 87, 98, 106, 109, 111, 117.
New York, U. S. cruiser, mentioned, 16.
New York Herald, criticism by, as to operations and treatment of troops in Cuba, 106, 113, 114.
New York Journal, treatment of Spanish prisoners by Cubans, reports published in, 99, 101.
New York World, location of Spanish fleet, 28.
Niagara, U. S. transport, mentioned, 115.
Nichols, Daniel J., pvt., 1st Cal. Vol. Inf., death, 803.
Nichols, Edward, pvt., Hosp. Corps, U. S. A., death, 1210.
Nichols, Ferd, pvt., Co. G, 44th Inf., U. S. V., death, 1168.
Nichols, George C., pvt., Co. D, 20th Kans. Vol. Inf., wounded, 946.
Nichols, Ray S., pvt., Co. K, 1st S. Dak. Vol. Inf., wounded, 949.
Nichols, Reuben, pvt Co. H, 39th Inf., U. S. V., wounded, 1147.
Nichols, William H., pvt., Co. E, 4th U. S. Inf., death, 1045.
Nickel, William, pvt., Co. A, 3Sd Inf., U. S. V., wounded, 1228.

Niemis, Louis, pvt., Troop F, 3d U. S. Cav., drowned, 1187.
Nihart, Ray W., pvt., Co. F, 38th Inf., U. S. V., death, 1233.
Niles, John, pvt., Co. K, 39th Inf., U. S. V., killed, 1214.
Nilson, Anton B., pvt., Co. C, 1st Cal. Vol. Inf., killed, 902.
Nilsson, Abel, pvt., Co. H, 1st Wash. Vol. Inf., wounded, 977.
Niske [Fish?], C. H., pvt., ——, 1st Nebr. Vol. Inf., death, 803.
Noble, Don L., recruit, 18th U. S. Inf., death, 967.
Noble, Harrison, corpl., Co. K, 18th U. S. Inf., wounded, 1243.
Noble, Henry L., pvt., Co. G, 51st Iowa Vol. Inf., death, 1066.
Noble, Hugh B., pvt., Co. G, 17th U. S. Inf., death, 1063.
Noble, James L., corpl., Co. C, 43d Inf., U. S. V., killed, 1225; wounded, 1167.
Noble, John W., mentioned, 342.
Noeil, Joseph, pvt., Co. H, 43d Inf., U. S. V., killed, 1168.
Noel, Ernest L., pvt., Co. C, 44th Inf., U. S. V., wounded, 1212.
Noel, Jack, pvt., Co. G, 39th Inf., U. S. V., wounded, 1147.
Noid, James, pvt., Co. E, 24th U. S. Inf., killed, 1052.
Nolan, John, pvt., Co. H, 19th U. S. Inf., death, 1074.
Nolan, Nicholas J., pvt., Co. D, 17th U. S. Inf., wounded, 1051.
Nolan, Philip H., pvt., Co. B, 26th U. S. Inf., killed, 1153.
Nolan, William, pvt., Troop C, 4th U. S. Cav., killed, 1026.
Nolan, William J., pvt., Co. K, 16th U. S. Inf., death, 1160.
Noland, John, pvt., Co. E, 4th U. S. Inf., wounded, 1021.
Nolte, August, pvt., Co. A, 4th U. S. Inf., death, 1032.
Nooman, John M., pvt., Co. G, 1st Cal. Vol. Inf., mentioned, 1043.
Noonan, Thomas, pvt., Co. L, 18th U. S. Inf., wounded, 1227.
Noriel,? insurgent general, mentioned, 1129.
Norris, Henry, pvt., Co. C, 35th Inf., U. S. V., wounded, 1182.
North American Trust Company, agent to U. S. Government, 168.
North, Edwin N., pvt., Co. H, 47th Inf., U. S. V., wounded, 1187.
North, Ludlow F., sergt., Sig. Corps, U. S. A., killed, 1206.
North, Thomas C., pvt., Co. G, 1st Nebr. Vol. Inf., death, 866.
Northcross, William P., sergt., Co. H, 40th Inf., U. S. V., missing, 1183.
Northrop, Arthur A., sergt., Co. E, 1st S. Dak. Vol. Inf., wounded, 949.
Norton, Fred J., pvt., Co. F, 2d Oreg. Vol. Inf., death, 853.
Norton, George L., pvt., Co. G, 42d Inf., U. S. V., death, 1271.
Norton, Harry A., pvt., Co. F, 9th U. S. Inf., wounded, 444.
Norton, John, corpl., Co. C, 26th U. S. Inf., wounded, 1183.
Norton, John H., pvt., Co. A, 6th U. S. Inf., wounded, 1084.
Norton, Norman, pvt., Co. F, 13th U. S. Inf., wounded, 1085.
Norton, William F., pvt., Co. M, 9th U. S. Inf., wounded, 460.
Norval, Edward E., pvt., Co. E, 12th U. S. Inf., wounded, 1131.
Norwood, Charles, pvt., Co. A, Batt. Engrs., U.S. A., death, 1274.
Noss, Jesse, pvt., ——, 10th Pa. Vol. Inf., death, 803.
Novrcki, James, pvt., Co. D, 10th Pa. Vol. Inf., wounded, 954.
Nowland, James E., sergt, Co. E, 27th Inf., U.S.V., killed, 1140.
Noyes, Charles R., capt., 9th U. S. Inf., wounded, 428–430, 435, 443.

Noyes, Henry E., maj., 2d U. S. Cav., mentioned, 534.
Noyes, Samuel W., 2d lieut., 23d U. S. Inf., mentioned, 1041.
Nueces, steamship, mentioned, 94, 112, 122, 126, 127, 134, 138, 139, 143, 156, 233, 278, 279, 293.
Nuneville, Joseph, pvt., Co. G, 12th U. S. Inf., drowned, 997.
Nuñez, Emilio, brig. gen., Cuban army, mentioned, 51.
Oates, William C., brig. gen., U. S. V., mentioned, 524–526.
Obdam, U. S. transport, mentioned, 126, 341, 362–364, 367, 368, 378, 380, 382, 390, 396, 402, 596, 597, 602, 603, 615, 623.
Oberhansen, Edward, pvt., Troop C, 4th U. S. Cav., wounded, 1046.
Oberle, William J., pvt., Co. B, 13th Minn. Vol. Inf., wounded, 963.
O'Brian, Maurice, 1st sergt., Troop G, 4th U. S. Cav., killed, 1182.
O'Brien, Frank, pvt., Co. I, 30th Inf., U. S. V., death, 1189.
O'Brien, James, pvt., Co. A, 5th U. S. Inf., death, 1267.
O'Brien, John D., capt., 1st Wyo. Vol. Inf., wounded, 926.
O'Brien, J. W., civilian, rescue, 1129.
O'Brien, Lyster M., maj., 17th U. S. Inf., mentioned, 1095.
O'Brien, Michael, sergt., Co. F, 9th U. S. Inf., wounded, 454.
O'Brien, Michael J., sergt., Co. I, 33d Inf., U.S. V., death, 1241.
O'Brien, Patrick, pvt., Batty. K, 3d U. S. Art., wounded, 948.
O'Brien, Peter J., pvt., Co. B, 47th Inf., U. S. V., wounded, 1234.
O'Brien, William S., pvt., Co. D, 22d U. S. Inf., wounded, 984.
Occurren, Mr., missionary in China, murder of, and wife, 476.
Oceania, tug, mentioned, 1090.
Ocker, Frank O., pvt., Co. B, 6th U. S. Inf., death, 1150.
O'Connell, James, pvt., Co. C, 18th U. S. Inf., wounded, 1113.
O'Connell, James H., pvt., Co. D, 22d U. S. Inf., wounded, 1057.
O Connell, John J., 1st lieut., 21st U. S. Inf., mentioned, 1186.
O'Connell, Patrick J., pvt., Co. L, 35th Inf., U. S. V., death, 1226.
O'Connor, Daniel, corpl., Co. E, 9th U. S. Inf., wounded, 454.
O'Connor, Daniel J., pvt., Co. D, 14th U. S. Inf., death, 760.
O'Connor, John, pvt., Co. K, 71st N. Y. Vol. Inf., mentioned, 229.
O'Connor, John C., 1st sergt., Batty. G, 3d U. S. Art., wounded, 951.
O'Connor, John M., sergt., Co. L, 9th U S. Inf., death, 494.
O'Connor, Michael J., maj., 9th Mass. Vol. Inf., mentioned, 212.
O'Connor, Patrick, pvt., Troop K, 4th U S. Cav., wounded, 974.
O'Day, Patrick, pvt., Co. L, 12th U. S. Inf., death, 1233.
Odell, Ralph A., pvt., Co. A, 2d Oreg. Vol. Inf., death, 1008.
Odin, Arthur S., pvt., Co. I, 9th U. S. Inf., wounded, 1015.
O'Donnell, Charles F., mus., Co. F, 1st Idaho Vol. Inf., death, 850.
O'Donnell, George, pvt., Co. F, 47th Inf., U. S V., death, 1249; wounded, 1250.
O'Donnell, James H., sergt., Co. H, Sig. Corps, U S. A., death, 1280.
O'Donnell, Michael C., pvt. Co. D, 21st U. S. Inf., mentioned, 1236; wounded, 1235.
O'Donnell, Terrence E, pvt., Co. B, 6th U. S. Inf., wounded, 1067.
O'Donovan, Cornelius, pvt., Co. K, 40th Inf., U. S. V., death 1257.
O'Donovan, Frank, pvt., Co. A, 35th Inf., U.S.V., death, 1174.
O'Dowd, James T., pvt., Co. M, 14th U. S. Inf., wounded, 454.

INDEX. 1431

O'Dea, Stephen, corpl., Co. G, 9th U. S. Inf., wounded, 444.
Oesch, Edward D., pvt., Co. E, 2d Oreg. Vol. Inf., wounded, 936.
O'Flaherty, Henry O., pvt., Co. L, 2d Oreg. Vol. Inf., death, 931.
Officers, commissioned:
Certificates necessary for payment, 1245.
Commendation of, 128, 129, 172, 209, 225, 226, 227, 1016.
Discharge and muster-out in P. I., 1240, 1242.
Discharge of, holding volunteer commissions, 1242.
Need of regular, among volunteers, 46.
Promotions, recommendations for, 85, 99, 104, 109, 110, 113, 116, 129, 179, 209, 225-227.
Relative rank, 36, 37.
Retention in P. I., 1006, 1256, 1257.
Assignment to special duty, 1235.
Selection of, for regiments raised in P. I., 1004.
Staff:
Lack of experienced, 36.
Reappointment of, 43.
Ogden, Walter R., pvt., Hosp. Corps, U. S. A., death, 1267.
Ogden, William A., pvt., Co. M, 32d Inf., U. S. V., death, 1144.
Ogilvie, Herbert W., pvt., Batty. L, 3d U. S. Art., wounded, 946.
Oglesby, George, pvt., Co. B, 32d Inf., U. S. V., death, 1200.
O'Hara, James, capt., 3d U. S. Art. mentioned, 716.
O'Hara, John, pvt., Co. H, 28th U. S. Inf., killed, 1222.
O'Hara, Lawrence, pvt., Co. B, 26th U. S. Inf., killed, 1281.
O'Hare, Timothy, pvt., Co. I, 26th U. S. Inf., death, 1151.
O'Hern, Richard, pvt., Co. I, 26th U. S. Inf., killed, 1209.
Ohio, U. S. transport, mentioned, 604, 612, 622, 623, 660, 695, 704, 715, 740, 792, 801, 802, 840, 873, 880, 881-883, 887, 889, 892, 923, 933, 940, 962, 976-978, 997, 1005, 1007, 1010, 1030, 1034, 1041, 1042, 1058, 1061, 1069, 1071, 1077, 1094, 1108, 1128, 1265, 1273, 1276, 1282.
Ohtan, Ben, pvt., Co. L, 13th Minn. Vol. Inf., wounded, 901.
O'Keefe, Frank, alias Frank G. Armstrong, corpl., Co. C, 23d U. S. Inf., death, 960.
Olbright, Frank C., pvt., Co. F, 14th U. S. Inf., wounded, 454.
Olds, Howard A., pvt., Co. F, 20th Kans. Vol. Inf., death, 923; wounded, 918.
O'Leary, James, corpl., Co. M, 1st Mont. Vol. Inf., wounded, 981.
O'Leary, John, pvt., Co. G, 6th U. S. Inf., death, 1253.
O'Leary, William C., pvt., Co. I, 1st Mont. Vol. Inf. death, 803.
Olesen, Peter O., pvt., Co. C, 23d U. S. Inf., wounded, 956.
Olimb, Lewis, sergt., Troop C, 11th Cav., U. S. V., death, 1142.
Oliver, Alra K., pvt., Co. D, 21st U. S. Inf., wounded, 1084.
Oliver, Benjamin F., pvt., Co. H, 20th Kans. Vol. Inf., wounded, 983.
Oliver, Charles P., pvt., Co. H, 2d Oreg. Vol. Inf., death, 833.
Oliver, George, pvt., Co. E, 40th Inf., U. S. V., death, 1191.
Oliver, John, sergt., Co. E, 34th Mich. Vol. Inf., mentioned, 197.
Oliver, Philip, corpl., Troop H, 9th U. S. Cav., wounded, 1256.
Olivette, U. S. transport, mentioned, 45, 68, 142, 157, 169, 170, 172, 177-179, 192, 195, 198, 200, 207, 229, 237, 249, 308, 315, 325, 351, 589, 617.
O'Loghlen, Julius J., civilian clerk, rating, 979.
Olsen, Peter O., pvt., Co. C, 23d U. S. Inf., death, 1078.
Olson, Charles, pvt., Co. E, 2d Oreg. Vol. Inf., wounded, 934.
Olson, John, pvt., Co. A, 45th U. S. Inf., death, 1205.
Olson, Oscar, pvt., Co. F, 9th U. S. Inf., killed, 443, 445.

Olstad, Charles, pvt., Co. G, 1st N. Dak. Vol. Inf., wounded, 987.
Olympia, U. S. cruiser, mentioned, 719, 1116.
Omaha exposition, captured flags and cannon desired for, 191, 197.
O'Malley, Martin, pvt., Co. E, 3d U. S. Inf., wounded, 946.
O'Malley, Michael, pvt., Co. K, 9th Mass. Vol. Inf. mentioned, 248.
O'Mally, John, sergt., Co. F, 34th Inf., U. S. V., death, 1164.
O'Neil, Edward J., pvt., Co. E, 1st Cal. Vol. Inf., wounded, 903.
O'Neil, James, pvt., Co. G, 4th U. S. Inf., wounded, 946.
O'Neil, James, sergt., Co. H, 13th U. S. Inf., wounded, 1101.
O'Neil, James A., pvt., Batty. H, 3d U. S. Art., killed, 945.
O'Neil, James J., pvt., Co. C, 9th U. S. Inf., death, 444; wounded, 443.
O'Neil, Joseph P., capt., 25th U. S. Inf., mentioned, 1132, 1279.
O'Neill, Barney, pvt., Co. M, 1st Mont. Vol. Inf., wounded, 996.
O'Neill, James, corpl., Co. I, 40th Inf., U. S. V., killed, 1171.
Ouellette, Joseph, pvt., Co. M, 14th U. S, Inf., death, 464.
Openheimer, Louis M., col., 2d Tex. Vol. Inf., mentioned, 550.
Oquendo, Spanish cruiser, mentioned, 81, 100.
Ord, Jules G., 1st lieut., 6th U.S. Inf., killed, 124.
Ordd, Charles E., pvt., Co. M, 6th U. S. Inf., death, 1189.
Ordway, Elliot W., pvt., Co. H, 2d Oreg. Vol. Inf., death, 829.
Oregon, governor of, requests recruits for 2d Oregon be either mustered out or sent to regiment, 787.
Oregon, U. S. battleship, mentioned, 410, 413, 415, 423, 425, 1110, 1111.
Oregon Railway and Navigation Company, mentioned, 723.
O'Reilly, James A., pvt., Co. F, 6th U. S. Inf., wounded, 1087.
O'Reilly, Robert M., lieut. col. med. dept., mentioned, 234, 238, 315, 318, 360.
Organ, Charlie, pvt., Co. M, 14th U.S. Inf., death, 464.
Orizaba, transport, mentioned, 21, 192, 198, 228, 233, 243, 252-255.
O'Rourke, Joseph P., pvt., Co. I, 4th U. S Inf., death, 1078.
O Rourke, Thomas, pvt., Co. E, 27th Inf., U. S. V., death, 1142; wounded, 1140.
Orr, William S., pvt., Co. A, 1st Nebr. Vol. Inf., killed, 954.
Orth, John, artif., Co. B, 35th Inf., U. S. V., killed, 1161.
Ortman, John W., pvt., Co. L, 1st S. Dak. Vol. Inf., wounded, 954.
Orwig, Henry B., maj., 37th Inf., U. S. V., General Barry's instructions to, 1263.
Osberger, Jos. W., mus., Co. M, 14th U. S. Inf., wounded, 895.
Osborn, Herbert E., pvt., Co. E, 1st Wash. Vol. Inf., wounded, 897.
Osborn, Roy L., corpl., Co. A, 46th Inf., U S. V., death, 1202.
Osborn, Thomas, pvt., Co. C, 12th U. S. Inf., death, 1165.
Osborn, Wilson M., corpl., Co. F, 1st S. Dak. Vol. Inf., death, 907.
Osborne, David R., pvt., Co. I, 21st U. S. Inf., death, 1095.
Osborne, Herbert L., pvt., Co. C, 1st Wash. Vol. Inf., wounded, 920.
Osceola, U. S. transport, mentioned, 22, 39.
Osgood, Carl H., corpl., Co. F, 1st S. Dak. Vol. Inf., wounded, 895.
Osgood, Charles K., sergt., Co. C, 26th U. S. Inf., wounded, 1183.
Osgood, Henry B., maj., sub. dept., U. S. A., mentioned, 234.
O'Shea, James P., pvt., Co. G, 6th U. S. Inf., death, 1162.
Osleurn, Arthur L., pvt., Co. M, 14th U. S. Inf., wounded, 895.

Osorio, Don Antonio, citizen of Cavite, mentioned, 810.
Ossowski, Paul, pvt., Co. C, 1st Nebr. Vol. Inf., wounded, 982.
Osterhout, Earl W., pvt., Co. E, 1st Nebr. Vol Inf., death, 831.
Oswald, Campbell, sergt., Co. E, 18th U. S. Inf., death, 1133.
Oswald, Charles, corpl., Co. L, 15th U. S. Inf., wounded, 1211.
Oswald, Harry, pvt., Troop M, 11th Cav., U. S. V., drowned, 1187.
Otermin, Pio G., pvt., band, 8th U. S. Inf., death, 1253.
Otis, Albert H., capt., 1st Wash. Vol. Inf., wounded, 896, 992.
Otis, Elwell S., maj. gen., U. S. V.:
 Command in Philippines, transfer to, 765.
 Mentioned, 556–563, 565–567, 569–571, 573–575, 577, 638–640, 661, 667, 669, 701, 708, 720, 722, 733, 758, 765, 766, 769, 770, 772, 793, 795, 798, 799, 827, 850, 853, 859, 870, 879, 883, 900, 911–913, 919, 924, 942, 943, 957, 958, 964–966, 988, 989, 1011, 1025, 1061, 1096, 1098, 1154, 1163–1165, 1168, 1173, 1193, 1220, 1339.
 Relief from duty in P. I., 1156, 1157, 1164, 1165.
 Reply to demands of Aguinaldo, 823.
 To command P. I. expeditionary troops at San Francisco, 661, 664.
 To take up duties of Anderson until arrival of General Merritt, 661.
Otis, Harrison G., brig. gen., U. S. V., mentioned, 556–562, 678, 720, 755.
O'Toole, Thomas A., corpl., Co. L, 37th Inf., U. S. V., killed, 1203.
Ott, Fayette, pvt., Co. G, 38th Inf., U. S. V., death, 1208.
Ott, Frank, pvt., Co. K, 40th Inf., U. S. V., death, 1255.
Otto, George H., pvt., Co. C, 43d Inf., U. S. V., wounded, 1163.
Ought, Claude H., capt., Co. B, 1st Nebr. Vol. Inf., mentioned, 994; wounded, 926.
Ovenshine, Samuel, brig. gen., mentioned, 557–563, 565, 716, 982, 1006, 1007, 1010.
Overstreet, Jesse, member of Congress, mentioned, 344.
Overbay, Henry, corpl., Co. H, 14th U. S. Inf., wounded, 1092.
Overton, Charles, pvt., Co. I, 21st U. S. Inf., wounded, 1021.
Overton, Clarence W., pvt., Co. G, 22d U. S. Inf., death, 923.
Overton, Samuel J., corpl., Co. I, 44th Inf., U. S. V., death, 1208.
Overton, Winfield S., 2d lieut., 3d U. S. Art., wounded, 946.
Overturf, George, pvt., Troop E, 11th Cav., U. S. V., death, 1172.
Oviatt, F. D., clerk, General Brooke's headquarters, mentioned, 302.
Oviatt, Joseph S., pvt., Co. A, 1st Nebr. Vol. Inf., wounded, 760.
Owen, Abert W., pvt., Co. A, 1st Wash. Vol. Inf., wounded, 897.
Owen, Basil, pvt., Co. B, 37th Inf., U. S. V., death, 1174.
Owen, Eugene J., pvt., Hosp. Corps, U. S. A., wounded, 946.
Owen, James, pvt., Batt. L, 3d U. S. Art., death, 894.
Owen, William O., capt., med. dept., U. S. A., mentioned, 657, 658.
Owens, Benjamin, pvt., Co. L, 15th U. S. Inf., wounded, 1211.
Owens, George S., pvt., Co. M, 3d U. S. Inf., wounded, 946.
Owens, John F., pvt., Co. H, 29th Inf., death, 1178.
Owens, Lee, corpl., Co. K, 14th U. S. Inf., mentioned, 454.
Owens, Temple H., 1st lieut., 45th Inf., U. S. V., accidentally shot himself, 1217.
Owens, William, civilian teamster, q. m. dept., death, 497.
Ozman, Roscoe C., pvt., Co. C, 1st Nebr. Vol. Inf., wounded, 946.
Pace, Elven, pvt. Co. I, 5th U. S. Inf., death, 1274.
Pacific coast, troops needed for defense of, 673, 674, 675.

Pacific coast, inadequacy of force of staff officers and clerks, 673.
Pacific, Dept. of:
 Discontinued, 1154; established, 649.
Pack, Dato Amani, Moro chief, sends threatening letter to Gen. Chaffee, 1332.
Packer, Guy V., pvt., Co. C, 1st Cal. Vol. Inf., killed, 902.
Paddock, Richard B., capt., 6th U. S. Cav., death, 501; mentioned, 505.
Paden, Leslie B., pvt., Co. E, 13th Minn. Vol. Inf., death, 803; mentioned, 761, 762.
Padesky, Albert, pvt., Co. I, 36th Inf. U. S. V., wounded, 1233.
Page, Henry, 1st lieut., med. dept., U. S. A., mentioned, 657, 658.
Page, Henry, maj., chief comsy., U. S. V., reports death of Lieut. Burchard, 1205.
Page, James, pvt., Co. D, 2d Oreg. Vol. Inf., killed, 941.
Page, John H., col., 3d U. S. Inf., mentioned, 194, 535, 890, 893.
 Recommended for promotion, 225.
Page, Larrance, qm. sergt., Co. H, 20th Kans. Vol. Inf., wounded, 961.
Page, Leslie, pvt., Co. M, 44th Inf., U. S. V., wounded, 1256.
Pagner, L., pvt., Co. G, 13th U. S. Inf., 206, death.
Paige, Robert, pvt., Hosp. Corps, U. S. A., death, 1086.
Painter, William H., sergt., Co. M, 44th Inf., U. S. V., killed, 1256.
Pakling, U. S. transport, mentioned, 441, 448, 449, 463, 471, 488, 503, 506, 672, 1198, 1207, 1284.
Pakshan, U. S. transport, mentioned, 672.
Pallat, Louis, pvt., Co. H, 1st Mont. Vol. Inf., wounded, 945.
Palmer, Ernest L., pvt., Co. E, 13th U. S. Inf., death, 1181.
Palmer, Irving H., pvt., Troop A, 3d U. S. Cav., killed, 1137.
Palmer, Lewis B., pvt., Co. C, 3d U. S. Cav., killed, 1152.
Pandapatan, Sultan, Moro chief, death, 1336.
Pando, Spanish general, mentioned, 68, 75, 82, 87, 123.
Pangborn, Lucius W., pvt., Co. I, 1st Nebr. Vol. Inf., wounded, 975.
Panke, William F., pvt., Co. E, 1st S. Dak. Vol. Inf., wounded, 949.
Parcell, David J., pvt., Co. K, 3d U. S. Inf., death, 1238; wounded, 995.
Pareja, Spanish general, mentioned, 188.
Parham, William G., pvt., Co. H, 34th Inf., U. S. V., death, 1220.
Parke, Glen V., pvt., Co. G, 28th U. S. Inf., death, 1181.
Parker, Clarence, pvt., Co. G, 17th U. S. Inf., wounded, 1225.
Parker, Clyde B., 1st lieut., 44th Inf., U. S. V., wounded, 1219.
Parker, Frederick F., pvt., Co. C, 19th U. S. Inf., killed, 1148.
Parker, George W., pvt., Co. G, 47th Inf., U. S. V., wounded, 1187.
Parker, James, lieut. col., 45th Inf., U. S. V., mentioned, 1114.
Parker, John H., 1st lieut., 13th U. S. Inf., mentioned, 232.
Parker, Montgomery D., capt., 8th U. S. Inf., death, 1236.
Parker, Orville E., pvt., Co. G, 20th Kans. Vol. Inf., wounded, 946.
Parker, Robert R., pvt., Co. C, 23d U. S. Inf., wounded, 760.
Parker, Robert S., 2d lieut., 20th Kans. Vol. Inf., wounded, 995.
Parker, Thomas, pvt., Co. K, 4th U. S. Inf., wounded, 1017.
Parker, William, pvt., Co. L, 17th U. S. Inf., killed, 1087.
Parker, William B., corpl., Co. D, 44th Inf., U. S. V., wounded, 1209.
Parker, Zeph, mus., Co. I, 48th Inf., U. S. V., 1153.
Parkhurst, Charles B., capt., 4th U. S. Art., mentioned, 83.
Parkhurst, Maurice, pvt., Co. B, 1st Colo. Vol. Inf., wounded, 895.
Parks, Charles E., pvt., Co. F, 1st Nebr. Vol. Inf., wounded, 906.

Parks, George B., pvt., Troop E, 4th U. S. Cav., wounded, 936.
Parks, Harold E., pvt., Co. K, 1st Cal. Vol. Inf., wounded, 920.
Parmer, Charles E., pvt., Co. E, 22d U. S. Inf., wounded, 941.
Parnell, Edward, mus., Co. E, 25th U. S. Inf., death, 1086.
Parnell, William, pvt., Co. D, 49th Inf., U. S. V., death, 1255.
Parnow, John W., pvt., Co. L, 1st Cal. Vol. Inf., wounded, 914.
Parrot, John W., pvt., Co. M, 3d U. S. Inf., wounded, 961.
Parsons, Bert W., pvt., Co. C, 13th Minn. Vol. Inf., wounded, 947.
Parsons, Charles, pvt., Co. A, 1st Wash. Vol. Inf., death, 972.
Parsons, Charles P., pvt., Co. C, 16th U. S. Inf., drowned, 1213.
Parsons, Williams, pvt., Co. C, 22d U. S. Inf., death, 1150.
Partlon, William L., pvt., Co. G, 9th U. S. Inf., wounded, 444.
Partridge, Miss, American missionary in China, mentioned, 471.
Partridge, I. W., pvt., U. S. Marine Corps, killed, 445.
Paryibel, H. Daniel, pvt., Astor Batty., U. S. A., death, 804.
Passmore, Louis D., pvt., Co. I, 1st Nebr. Vol. Inf., death, 829.
Pate, Edgar T., pvt., Co. H, 1st Colo. Vol. Inf., wounded, 1010.
Pathan, U. S. transport, mentioned, 1102, 1120.
Patten, George H., 1st lieut., 22d U. S. Inf., mentioned, 124.
Patten, James, pvt., Co. M, 16th U. S. Inf., death, 1191.
Patten, William, pvt., Batty. H, 3d U. S. Art., killed, 945; wounded, 946.
Paterno, Pedro, Filipino, requests permission to organize banquet and fiesta at Manila, P. I., 1194.
Patterson, Archie, mus., Co. I, 13th Minn. Vol. Inf., death, 803.
Patterson, Edward, pvt., Co. C, 3d U. S. Inf., death, 1001.
Patterson, Henry G., pvt., Hosp. Corps, U. S. A., death, 1219.
Patterson, John, pvt., Co. M, 33d Inf., U. S. V., wounded, 1137.
Patterson, John H., lieut. col., 22d U. S. Inf., recommended for promotion, 225; wounded, 124.
Patterson, Joseph C., pvt., Co. L, 3d U. S. Inf., death, 1178.
Patterson, Ralph B., pvt., Co. M, 33th Inf., U. S. V., death, 1161.
Patterson, Reginald S., pvt., Co. B, 1st Wash. Vol. Inf., 947.
Pattie, James, pvt., Co. G, 4th U. S. Inf., death, 1119.
Patton, Frank A., pvt., Co. K, 3d U. S. Inf., death, 1156.
Patton, George W., pvt., Co. E, Sig. Corps, U. S. A., killed, 1259.
Patton, Homer, pvt., Co. G, 24th U. S. Inf., death, 1255.
Patton, Richard M., pvt., Co. L, 17th U. S. Inf., death, 1178.
Patton, Wilburn, pvt., Co. L, 3d U. S. Inf., wounded, 1212.
Patton, William A., mus., Co. H, 1st Mont. Vol. Inf., wounded, 975.
Patton, William G., pvt., Co. I, 46th Inf., U. S. V., wounded, 1128.
Pauley, Joseph C., pvt., Co. K, 18th U. S. Inf., death, 1205.
Paup, Homer W., pvt., Co. A, 35th Inf., U. S. V., death, 1123.
Pausler, Max H., pvt., Co. C, 33d Mich. Vol. Inf., mentioned, 192.
Paygoag, Dato, Moro chief, killed 1338.
Payne, Henry, pvt., Co. M, 2d Oreg. Vol. Inf., killed, 963.
Payne, Ira M., pvt., Co. A, 20th Kans. Vol. Inf., wounded, 903.
Payne, James, pvt., Co. C, 1st Idaho Vol. Inf., wounded, 897.

Payne, John M., pvt., Co. H, 37th Inf., U. S. V., wounded, 1198.
Payne, Will C., pvt., Co. G, 1st Idaho Vol. Inf., wounded, 897.
Paxton, Clifton J., pvt., Co. D, 13th U. S. Inf., death, 1151.
Peacock, William, pvt., Co. E, 2d U. S. Inf., mentioned, 175.
Pearce, Fred A., 2d lieut., 6th U. S. Art., death, 1005.
Pearson, Arthur, pvt., Co. A, 1st Idaho Vol. Inf., wounded, 963.
Pearson, Charles, pvt., Co. A, 30th U. S. Inf., death, 1197.
Pearson, Claude L., pvt., Co. D, 22d Inf., U.S.V., wounded, 1145.
Pearson, Edward P., col., 10th U. S. Inf., mentioned, 540, 541, 543, 545.
Pearson, John S., pvt., Co. M, 45th Inf., killed, 1218.
Pease, Charles M., pvt., Co. B, 20th Kans. Vol., wounded, 954.
Pease, H. L., pvt., Co. H, 8th U. S. Inf., mentioned, 206.
Pechili, U. S. transport, mentioned, 477.
Peck, Earl H., sergt., Co. D, 26th U. S. Inf., death, 1174, 1190.
Pedigo, Rubert S., pvt., Co. I, 12th U. S. Inf., wounded, 1182.
Peel, Gordon A., pvt., Hosp. Corps, U. S. A., mentioned, 952; wounded, 946.
Pegan, Edward A., pvt., Co. L, 1st Nebr. Vol., wounded, 946.
Pegler, Lewis, pvt., Co. I, 1st Nebr. Vol., killed, 897.
Pelham, John P., pvt., Co. H, 40th Inf., U. S. V., killed, 1183.
Peltzer, Charles E., pvt., E, 1st Nebr. Vol., wounded, 760.
Pence, Ira N., pvt., Co. B, 29th U. S. Inf., killed, 1219.
Pender, John A., pvt., Batty. B, Utah Art. Vol., wounded, 961.
Pender, John G., pvt., Co. I, 12th U. S. Inf., wounded, 994.
Pendergrass, Oliver M., pvt., Co. E, 43d Inf., U. S. V., death, 1168; wounded, 1133.
Penn, Edward, pvt., Co. B, 24th U. S. Inf., mentioned, 209.
Penn, Julius A., maj., 34th Inf., U. S. V., mentioned, 1120.
Pennington, Alexander C. M., brig. gen., U. S. A., mentioned, 238, 343, 345, 358.
Pennsylvania, U. S. transport, mentioned, 437, 445, 471, 593, 602, 618, 622, 720–722, 729, 763, 792, 832, 851, 922, 985, 986, 1010, 1012–1014, 1017–1025, 1045, 1046, 1049, 1061, 1064, 1083, 1093, 1116, 1227, 1228, 1244, 1249, 1256, 1270, 1281.
Penrose, Bois, Hon., mentioned, 315, 335, 339, 418.
Peoria, U. S. gunboat, mentioned, 52.
Pepke, Emil J., pvt., Co. I, 1st N. Dak. Vol., wounded, 981.
Pepper, John, pvt., Co. E, 6th U. S. Inf., mentioned, 214.
Percival, Fred A., pvt., Co. F, 33d Mich. Vol. Inf., mentioned, 174, 221.
Percival, Herbert A., pvt., band, 46th Inf., U. S. V., killed, 1176.
Percival, Julius A., pvt., Co. I, 43d Inf., U. S. V., wounded, 1240.
Perg, Peter, pvt., Co. H, 23d U. S. Inf., wounded, 761.
Perkins, Clyde, pvt., Co. K, 2d Oreg. Vol. Inf., death, 840.
Perkins, Frederick, 1st lieut., 8th U. S. Inf., mentioned, 124.
Perkins, George H., pvt., Co. B, 1st Cal. Vol. Inf., death, 803; mentioned, 761.
Perkins, M. D., pvt., Co. G, 7th U. S. Inf., mentioned, 216.
Perkins, Ray C., pvt., band, 34th Inf., U. S. V., death, 1170.
Perkins, William C., sergt., Co. D, 44th Inf., U. S. V., death, 1260.
Perley, Harry O., maj., med. dept., U. S. A., mentioned, 478, 480, 486–488, 491.
Pernitski, Albert, pvt., Co. A 21st U. S. Inf., death, 1052.
Perrine, Gilbert C., pvt., Co. D 13th Minn. Vol. Inf., death, 875.

Perry, Albert L., pvt., Co. A, 32d Inf., U. S. V., death, 1146.
Perry, Alexander W., capt., qm. dept., U. S. A., mentioned, 1073.
Perry, Edward H., pvt., Co. I, 1st Wash. Vol. Inf., killed, 895.
Perry, Fred L., 2d lieut., 1st Col. Vol. Inf., wounded, 955.
Perry, Harry, pvt., Co. L, 15th U. S. Inf., wounded, 1211.
Perry, Richard E., pvt., Co. A, 2d Oreg. Vol. Inf., death. 803.
Perry, Roland L., pvt., Co. K, 14th U. S. Inf., killed, 453.
Perry, Romeo T., 1st sergt., Co. C, 9th U. S. Inf., wounded, 443, 1021.
Perry, Wilburn, pvt., Co. L, 36th Inf., U. S. V., wounded, 1096.
Pertinax, Donaldson, pvt., Co. K, 1st Nebr. Vol. Inf., wounded, 956.
Peru, U. S. transport, mentioned, 720, 721, 724, 729, 733, 758, 800.
Peruzzy, Arnold, corpl., Co. A, 9th U. S. Inf., wounded, 443.
Peterman, John P., col., 34th Inf., U. S. V., mentioned, 546.
Peters, Charles G., pvt., Co. B, 22d U. S. Inf., death, 1189.
Peters, John, corpl., Co. A, 27th U. S. Inf., wounded, 1124.
Peters, Otto J., pvt., Co. A, 19th U. S. Inf., death, 1215.
Peters, Proal, pvt., Co. C, 9th U. S. Inf., killed, 1297.
Peterson, Axel, pvt., Co. E, 1st Mont. Vol. Inf., wounded, 954.
Peterson, Andrew, corpl., Batty. B, Utah Vol. Art., mentioned, 922; wounded, 901.
Peterson, Carl H., pvt., Co. B, 38th Inf., U. S. V., death, 1174.
Peterson, Carl J., pvt., Co. G, 1st Mont. Vol. Inf., wounded, 900.
Peterson, Charles, pvt., Co. F, 36th Inf., U. S. V., death, 1201.
Peterson, Charles W., pvt., Co. H, 1st S. Dak. Vol. Inf., killed, 975.
Peterson, Christian, sergt., Co. B, 12th U. S. Inf., wounded, 1131.
Peterson, Edwin O., pvt., Co. D, 1st Nebr. Vol. Inf., wounded, 974.
Peterson, Frank A., pvt., Co. F, 1st Nebr. Vol. Inf., wounded, 950.
Peterson, Knut K., pvt., Co. L, 1st S. Dak. Vol. Inf., wounded, 954.
Peterson, Oscar, pvt., Co. H, 46th Inf., U. S. V., death, 1189.
Peterson, Peter A., pvt., Co. I, 21st U. S. Inf., killed, 1263.
Petite, Albert M., 1st lieut., 39th Inf., U. S. V., wounded, 1131, 1146.
Petrarch, U. S. transport, mentioned, 1270.
Petro, Alva W., pvt., Co. K, 45th Inf., U. S. V., death, 1213.
Petro, Thomas W., pvt., Co. M, 4th U. S. Inf., death, 1029.
Pettis, Nathaniel, pvt., Co. K, 48th Inf., U. S. V., wounded, 1176.
Pettit, James S., col., 31st Inf., U. S. V., mentioned, 281, 576, 577.
Pettry, John, pvt., Co. A, 13th U. S. Inf., death, 1238.
Pettus, Andrew, pvt., Co. E, 3d Inf., U. S. V., killed, 1101.
Pew, William A., col., 8th Mass. Vol. Inf., mentioned, 511.
Pflaum, Andrew, pvt., Co. C, 3d U. S. Inf., death, 1264.
Phelan, Patrick M., pvt., Troop I, 11th Cav., U. S. V., death, 1149.
Phelps, Benjamin, pvt., Co. I, 1st S. Dak. Vol. Inf., wounded, 895.
Phelps, T. S., lieut. comdr., U. S. N., mentioned, 772.
Phelps, William B., pvt., Co. H, 18th U. S. Inf., death, 1223.
Phenix, Charles, pvt., ——, 1st Col. Vol. Inf., death, 803.
Phenuer, Paul P., pvt., Troop F, 11th U. S. Cav., wounded, 1108.

Philadelphia, U. S. cruiser, mentioned, 186, 703, 704, 710, 712.
Philbin, Patrick, sergt., Co. L, 15th U. S. Inf., wounded, 1243.

Philippine Islands, affairs in:
Abricay, Luzon, casualties in action, 1231.
Absentees from 22d Inf. and other regular regiments, 841.
Accident, deaths among U. S. troops, 1020.
Accommodations, transports, insufficiency, 865, 881.
Ackle, Luzon, casualties in action, 1212.
Acquisition—
  By either United States or Great Britain desired, 718.
  By United States should follow victory, Manila, 719.
Adherence to United States—
  Of Dattos, 1075.
  When expected from better-class Filipinos, 908.
Administration (McKinley), insurgents expectant of overthrow, 1051.
Affairs, administration—
  Instructions of President, 858, 863, 1080.
  Protest by Aguinaldo against, 913.
Agreement—
  Between Gen. Bates and Sultan of Jolo, 1058.
  Conditional approval by President, 1118.
  Instructions regarding, 1117.
Agriculture, collection of information re, 803.
Agsarab, Panay, casualties in action, 1206.
Aguinaldo, to be responsible for injury to prisoners, 1098.
  Conduct of, effect on American affairs, 821.
  Influence in southern group, destruction, 927.
  Self-proclaimed dictator and president, 778.
Agusan, Mindanao—
  Engagement at, 1171.
  Casualties, 1171.
Agutag, Panay, casualties in action, 1206.
Alang-Alang, Leyte, casualties in action, 1214.
Alava, Luzon, casualties in action, 1176.
Albay, Luzon, casualties in action, 1148, 1187.
Alcula, Pangasinan, capture of insurgent Gen. Cavestany, 1179.
Aliaga, Luzon, action near, 1093.
Aliang, Luzon, casualties in action, 1185.
Alilem, Luzon, casualties in action, 1152.
Alimodian, Panay, casualties in action, 1126.
Alipali, surrender of, 1264.
Allegiance to United States—
  Administration of oath to insurrectos, 1232, 1259.
  Declaration by Spaniards under Paris treaty, 1161.
  Filipinos would take oath, 719.
Amaroa, Luzon, casualties in action, 1254.
American—
  Authorities—
    Aguinaldo advised to present case to, 818.
    Relations of Aguinaldo with, 913.
  Citizens, trouble caused by intermeddling, 927.
  Commanders—
    Decline to recognize insurgent cooperation, 911.
    Military to confer with Admiral Dewey, 668.
    Unanimity in measures for enforcement of U. S. demands, 827.
  Defeat—
    False rumors of, cause revolt in Negros, 1122.
    Demands for withdrawal of insurgents from Manila, Aguinaldo denies receipt, 845.
  Entry into Manila—
    Accomplished without Filipino aid, 822.
    Flag, raised by Dattos of archipelago, 1075.
  Forces—
    Filipino expectations in regard, 911.
    Limits of territory to be occupied by, 849.
    Transportation, Aguinaldo requested to obtain, 810.
  Naval commander—
    Attitude toward Aguinaldo, 821.
    Organizing forces near Cavite, 674.
    Refusal to recognize Aguinaldo, 821.
    Protection of Filipino boats, 819.
    Request for, 821.

INDEX. 1435

Philippine Islands, affairs in—Continued.
American—Continued.
Noninterference requested by insurgents, 805.
Prisoners of insurgents—
Condition, 980, 1144, 1186.
Escape from insurgents, 1216.
Insurgents request permission to send into American lines, 1071.
Measures for release, 1122.
Petitioned by business men of Iloilo, Panay, 853.
Release, 1078, 1100, 1109, 1122, 1124, 1128, 1129, 1130, 1139, 1140, 1147, 1218, 1230.
Protection, sought by insurgents, 957, 1019.
Rule, welcome to insurgents of southern islands, 827.
Soldiers, death and wounding, investigation, 820.
Sovereignty, contract for recognition, denial by Aguinaldo, 912.
Negros inhabitants enthusiastic for, 935.
Vessels, two, to convey Spanish prisoners to Manila, 1072.
Insurgents close Philippine ports to, 1050.
Victories, effect of, 824, 858.
Americans—
Aguinaldo asserts, must be driven from Philippines, 836.
Arrested by insurgents, 958.
Avoidance of conflict with Filipinos, 806.
Employment in conducting affairs of Manila, 818.
Insurgents and Spaniards intensify sentiment against, 886.
Precarious situation in Manila, 651.
Proclamation directing uprising against, 913.
Threats against, by Spaniards, 650.
Unopposed landing at Zamboanga and Jolo, 997.
Amigos—
Killing by insurgents, 1158.
Insurgents appear as, 1211.
Ammunition for insurgents, order placed at Kynoch's, England, 1114.
Amnesty—
Notice—
Amended by direction of President, 1179.
Banquet and fiesta in celebration of, 1194.
Conditions given former insurgents, 1183, 1184.
Issuance to insurgents, 1175, 1177, 1179, 1180, 1181.
With time limit, 1177; meager results, 1203.
No additional promises to be made, 1263.
Promised insurgents on surrender, 978.
Refusal by Mabini, 1248.
Supplementary action required, 1203.
Treatment of those availing of, 1177, 1178.
Amontoc, Luzon, casualties in action, 1173.
Amulug, Luzon, casualties in action, 1231.
Anabo, Luzon, casualties in action, 1108, 1109.
Angadanan, Luzon, casualties in action, 1240.
Angeles, Luzon—
Engagements at and near, 1053, 1056, 1085, 1086, 1093, 1126.
Casualties, 1054–1057, 1073, 1075, 1086, 1087, 1096, 1126.
Fired into by insurgents, 1062.
Insurgents driven from, 1053.
And from vicinity, 1095.
Occupation by U. S. troops, 1054.
Railway to, completion, 1062.
Animals—
Lost in typhoon, 1080, 1230.
Required for troops in, 1054, 1083, 1084, 1209.
Anislac, Albay, casualties in action at, 1198, 1250.
Anistac, Luzon, casualties at, 1198.
Annexation—
Effect on Filipinos of word, 903.
Men of property desire, 864.
Withdraw from Aguinaldo, 872.
Antipolo, Luzon—
Advance on, 1001.
Capture by U. S. troops, 1004.
Antique, Panay—
Casualties in action, 1140, 1145, 1237, 1243.
Surrender of insurgents, 1261.
Antique River, Panay—
Engagement at crossing, 1134.
Casualties, 1134.

Philippine Islands, affairs in—Continued.
Antwerp, Holland, insurgent arms and ammunition shipped via, 1126.
Aparri, Luzon, occupation by U.S. troops recommended, 851.
Appointments—
Chief justice, and restoration judicial system, 852.
Chaplains, U. S. Army, 693, 698.
Representative Filipinos to civil offices, 872.
Staff officers, 804.
Treasurer, army officer as, 985.
Appropriations, from insular revenues, 1199, 1206.
Aptitude for civil life, demonstration by Filipinos, 888.
Aquino, insurgent general, surrender, 1186.
Arayat, Luzon—
Engagements at and near, 1088, 1095.
Casualties, 1085–1088, 1101.
Insurgents driven from vicinity, 1086.
Occupied by U. S. troops, 1085.
Arayat Mountain, Luzon, dispersal of robber bands on, 1130.
Argogila, Negros, bandits driven from, 1062.
Aritao, Nueva Vizcaya, engagement at, 1126.
Armistice, general, requested by insurgent commissioners, 981, 993; denied, 994.
Arms and ammunition—
For insurgents, prevention of delivery, 840, 864, 1120.
In possession of guerrillas and ladrones, 1159.
Not landed without authority, 841.
Payment for surrender of, under amnesty, 1178.
Permits to carry, given by insurgent officials to citizens in violation of instructions of U. S. officials, 825.
Return of, to insurgents, 816.
Sale to insurgents by Spaniards, 1011.
Shipment for insurgents from China, efforts for prevention, 864, 1017.
German ports, 1116, 1134, 1148.
Japan, 867.
Supplied volunteers, 990.
Supply for insurgents in, 836
Army—
Commendation of men engaged in capture of Aguinaldo, 1263.
Condition as to drunkenness, etc., 1246, 1247.
Examination of candidates for commissions, 1258.
Relations with Navy, 1035.
See *Army* and *Volunteers.*
Arrests, by local presidentes, instructions violated, 825.
Arsenal, insurgent, destruction by U. S. troops, 1139.
Assassinations by insurgents, 1011, 1158.
Associated Press representatives—
Allege favoritism and neglect by censor at Manila, 1025, 1135, 1136, 1220–1225, 1260.
Complaint of prejudice unfounded in fact, 1025.
Hongkong, use position to send insurgent dispatches, 1025.
Associated Press of U. S. alleges discrimination by censor at Manila, 1025.
Antimonan, Luzon, casualties in action, 1163.
Atlao, Panay, casualties in action, 1188.
Australian horses for U. S. service, 938.
Authority—
Aguinaldo's, not recognized in southern islands, 836.
Aguinaldo with Filipinos, exercise, 840.
Avoidance of conflict, 806, 825.
Authority, United States—
Submission to, favored by majority of revolutionary government, 851.
To what end to be expected, 858.
Bacolor, Luzon, casualties in action, 1057.
Bacoor, Luzon, casualties in action, 1079, 1081, 1129, 1130, 1140.
Badoc, Luzon, casualties in action, 1152, 1192, 1195, 1214.
Bagbag, Batangas, casualties in action at, 1145.
Baggage, over-sea allowance, officers, 865.
Bagnotan, Luzon, casualties in action, 1151.
Bagombong, Mount, Panay, casualties in action, 1243.

Philippine Islands, affairs in—Continued.
Balanga, Luzon, casualties in action, 1182.
Balasan, Panay, casualties in action, 1227.
Balayan, Luzon, engagement near, 1136.
Balahill, Leyte, casualties in action, 1259.
Balinag, Luzon—
  And villages in vicinity captured, 980, 981.
  Casualties in action, 1117, 1227.
  Engagement near, 1054.
  Troops returning to, attacked by insurgents, 995.
Balincaguing, Luzon, casualties in action, 1141.
Bamban Luzon, captured by U. S. troops, 1100.
  Casualties in action, 1101.
Bamgo, Leyte, casualties in action, 1240.
Bandits—
  Engagement with, in Cebu Mountains, 1040.
  Casualties, 1040.
  Robbing and impressing people of Cebu, 1039.
  Stronghold at Argogila destroyed, 1062.
Bangao, Tawi-Tawi group, casualties in action, 1147.
Bangar, Luzon, casualties in action, 1147.
Bangued, Luzon—
  Captured by U. S. troops, 1116.
  Casualties in action, 1151, 1152, 1198, 1219, 1223, 1228, 1254.
Banna, Luzon, casualties in action, 1126.
Banquirubam, Albay, casualties in action, 1250.
Bataan, Luzon, casualties in action, 1227.
Bataan Province, Luzon—
  Capture of insurgent corral in, 1126.
  Engagement in mountains of, 1126.
  Casualties, 1126.
Batac, Luzon, casualties in action, 1161, 1163.
Batangas, Luzon, casualties in action, 1160, 1192.
Batangas Mountains, Luzon—
  Engagement in, 1135.
  Casualties, 1135.
Bantagas Province—
  Conditions in, 1132.
  In possession of American troops, 1133.
  Insurgents retreating from, 1135.
Barotac, Panay, casualties in action, 1183.
Barrack furniture, for troops, 948, 950.
Barracks, construction of, 1014, 1015.
Barrio Tenabang, Panay, casualties in action, 1107.
Basilan, garrisoned by U. S. troops, 1121.
Basilan Islands, placing of American troops, 1060.
Bayambang, Luzon, casualties in action, 1222, 1225.
Baybay, Leyte, casualties in action, 1218.
Bayombong, Luzon—
  Capital of insurgent government, 1091.
  Insurgents driven to, 1097, 1098, 1103, 1106.
  Surrender of insurgents at, 1111.
Beef supply, for troops, 1161.
Belligerency of Filipinos, U. S. recognition claimed by Aguinaldo, 913.
Belligerents, U. S. and Spain recognized as, 824.
Biacnabato, insurgent stronghold, capture by U. S. troops, 1121.
Bimmauya, Luzon, casualties in action, 1143.
Biñang, Luzon—
  Capture by U. S. troops, 1131.
  Casualties in action, 1137, 1150, 1212.
  Engagement at, 1129.
Bittin, Luzon, casualties in action, 1254.
Blockhouse No. 4, Manila, casualties near, 940.
Blockhouses, occupation by Filipinos, importance, 848.
Boac, Marinduque, casualties in action, 1197, 1250.
Bobon, Negros, casualties in action, 1052, 1064.
Bodies, embalming and shipment, 955.
Bohol, Bohol—
  Outbreak in, 1204; cause, 1206.
Bolijoon Mountains, Cebu, casualties in engagement at, 1183.
Bombardment of Manila, postponement, reasons, 824.
Bonanguran, Luzon, casualties in action, 1176.
Bongabon, Luzon, casualties in action, 1160.
Bongao, Tawi-Tawi, U. S. troops occupy, 1074.
Boot Peninsula, Luzon, casualties in action, 1235.

Philippine Islands, affairs in—Continued.
Booty—
  Not admitted by laws of war, 825.
  Share in, demanded by Aguinaldo, 825.
Botolan, Luzon, casualties in action, 1160.
Bremerhaven, shipment of arms for insurgents, 1134.
Bridge and railroads destroyed by insurgents, 947, 948.
Bridges, utility, 656.
Buena Vista, Marinduque, casualties in action at and near, 1085, 1261.
Bugason, Panay, casualties in action, 1229–1231, 1237.
Buhi, Camarines Sur, casualties in action, 1182.
Bulacan, Luzon—
  Casualties in action, 1140.
  Reaction favoring American interests, 1253, 1254.
Bulacan-Morong provinces, surrender of insurgents, 1264.
Bulacan Province, Luzon—
  Covered by U. S. troops, 990, 993.
  Insurgents concentrated in mountains, 1115.
  Insurgents driven from, 990, 1120, 1121.
Bulacan River, operations of American gunboats, 949.
Bulasan, Panay, casualties in action, 1231, 1234.
Bulong, Negros, casualties in action, 1038.
Business in Manila, impeded by cyclonic storms, 1033.
Bustos, Luzon, casualties in engagement, 1055.
Butaritari, Gilbert group, coal supply at, 746.
Cabanatuan, Luzon—
  Casualties in action, 1130, 1189, 1192, 1212, 1214.
  Insurgents driven from line of advance, 1091.
Cabang, Leyte, casualties in action, 1163.
Cabangan, Luzon, casualties in action, 1191, 1199, 1240.
Cabaruan, Luzon, casualties in action, 1124.
Cabatuan, Panay—
  Casualties in action, 1232.
  Insurgent capital, captured by U. S. troops, 1107.
  Murder by natives at, 1243.
Cabiao, Luzon, casualties in action, 1162, 1234, 1243.
Cabinet, revolutionary, dissensions in, and resignation, 908.
Cable communication, 983, 984.
  Extension from Capiz to Iloilo, 918.
  Interruption between Manila and Iloilo, 1169.
Cable concessions, Spanish, recognition by United States, 965, 966.
Cabugao, Luzon, casualties in action, 1152, 1209.
Cabug-Cabug, Panay, casualties in action, 1155, 1160.
Cabuyao, capture by U. S. troops, 1131.
Cagayan, Mindanao—
  Engagement at, 1162.
  Casualties in action, 1162, 1166.
Cagayan Province, surrenders to Navy, 1121.
Cagayan River, Mindanao—
  Casualties in action, 1183.
  Reconnaissance up, 1183.
  U. S. troops ambushed, 1183.
Cagayan Valley, Mindanao towns attacked by insurgents, 1159.
Caigan, casualties in action, 1140.
Cainta, Luzon, casualties in action, 937, 1015.
Calabanga, Luzon, casualties in action, 1150, 1183.
Calaca, Luzon, action at, 1136.
Calamba, Luzon—
  Attacked by insurgents, 1079, 1088.
  Capture by U. S. troops, 1042.
  Casualties in action, 1044, 1046, 1052, 1064, 1079, 1081, 1084, 1090, 1092, 1131, 1146, 1147, 1191, 1209, 1222.
  Engagements at and near, 1126, 1131.
Calauan, Luzon, casualties in action, 1261.
Calbayog, Samar—
  Casualties in action, 1162, 1163.
  Insurgents endeavor to burn, 1141.
  Occupation by U. S. troops, 1141.
Calbayog, Leyte, casualties in action, 1195.
Calbayon, Samar, casualties in action, 1237.
Calbiga, Samar, casualties in action, 1176.
Calinog, Panay, casualties in action, 1240.
Calivo, Panay, casualties in action, 1202.

Philippine Islands, affairs in—Continued.
Callios (Papaya), Luzon, casualties in action, 1182.
Caloocan, Luzon—
　Advance on, by U. S. troops, 944.
　Casualties in action, 898, 904, 917, 918, 920, 921, 931, 934, 937.
　Construction of barracks, 1015.
　Demonstration by insurgents near, 915.
　Engagements at, 898, 915, 921, 971.
　Insurgents driven from, 900.
Calulut, Luzon, action near, 1095.
Calumpit, Luzon—
　Insurgents destroy railroad near, 982.
　Occupied by U. S. troops, 975.
Camalaningan, Luzon, casualties in action, 1150, 1152.
Camarines Sur, Luzon—
　Activity of insurgents in, 1144.
　Operations in, 1144.
Camilig, Luzon, casualties in action, 1148, 1155, 1225, 1228, 1240.
Camiling, Luzon, casualties, 1160.
Campaign, active, in Panay and Cebu, prevented by withdrawal of volunteers and discharged regulars, 1060.
Campaigns, preparation for future, 1027.
Candaba, Luzon, casualties in action, 1182.
Candelaria, Luzon, casualties in action, 1199, 1263.
Cannon, Spanish—
　Captured by American troops, 1163.
　Request by Spain for return, refused by U. S., 1188.
Capas, Luzon—
　Capture by U. S. troops, 1100.
　Casualties in action, 1112, 1234.
Capaz, Panay, casualties in action, 1264.
Capitulation, articles of, 757.
　Obligations and rights of U. S. under, 824
　Territory transferred, 845.
Carig, Isabela, Luzon—
　Casualties in action, 1211, 1214.
　Engagement in vicinity, 1211.
Carmen, Bohol, casualties in action, 1204, 1206, 1219,
Carmen, Luzon, casualties in action, 1124, 1212.
Carmona, Luzon—
　Casualties in action, 1206.
　Engagement at, 1131.
Carranglan, Luzon, casualties in action, 1143.
Castellano, Negros, surrender of insurgents, 1073.
Castillejos, Luzon, casualties in action, 1216.
Casualties, American. See *Army* and *Volunteers.*
Casualties—
　To February 1, 1899, number and cause, 893.
　From January 1 to April 1, 1900, 1156.
　Total resulting from engagements, February 4-8, 1899, 899.
　Weekly list to be cabled Adjt. Gen, 801.
Catarman, Samar, casualties in action, 1183.
Catbalogan, Samar—
　Casualties in action, 1143, 1212, 1229.
　Insurgents endeavor to burn, 1141.
　Occupation by U. S. troops, 1142.
Catholic bishop and priests—
　Capture and maltreatment by insurgents, 790.
　Protection by U. S. forces, 793.
Catubig, Samar—
　Attack by insurgents, 1168.
　Casualties in action, 1165, 1176, 1214.
　Convent burned by insurgents, 1168.
Cavalry—
　Mounts and equipments, 1032.
　Mounting, need and difficulty, 1030.
　Volunteer regiment, organization, 1033.
Cavinti, Luzon, casualties in action, 1148, 1198, 1199.
Cavitan, Panay, casualties in action, 1152, 1153.
Cavite, Luzon—
　Americans to be encamped at, 818.
　Base for operations, 676, 805.
　Condition of American land and naval forces, 780.
　Defenses, 778.
　Garrison, 558, 559, 567, 568, 570, 571.
　Health of forces in, 738.
　In possession U. S. naval forces, 676.

Philippine Islands, affairs in—Continued.
Cavite, Luzon—Continued.
　Location and condition, 778.
　Monk prisoners of insurgents, danger, 743.
　Nature of buildings, 778.
　Naval forces organizing near, 674, 694.
　Number in hospital at, 766.
　Scarcity of supplies, 778.
　U. S. troops land at, 720.
　War material at, conceded property of Spain, 1066, 1076.
Cavite Province, Luzon—
　All occupied by U. S. troops, 1131.
　American troops welcomed by people, 1012.
　Collapse of insurrection, 1251.
　Conditions, 1131, 1132.
　Engagements, 1011.
　Insurgents driven from, 1011.
　Surrender promised, 1027.
Cavite Viejo, Luzon—
　Casualties in action, 1084.
　Engagement at, 1082.
Cayan, Lepanto Province—
　Action at, 1121.
　Casualties, 1121.
Caytacoes, Luzon, casualties in action, 1253.
Ceballos & Co., J. M., merchants, Manila, transportation to Spain of Spanish prisoners of war, 964.
Cebu, Cebu Island—
　American soldiers ambushed, killed, and mutilated, 1059.
　Casualties in action, 1067, 1075, 1084, 1087, 1140, 1141, 1227, 1251.
　Engagement at, 1075, 1251.
　Situation at, 935.
　Vice-consul at, recommendation for appointment, 798.
Cebu Island—
　American occupation, 867, 916, 918, 1027, 1106.
　Conditions in, 1060, 1077.
　Extension of cable to, 983, 984.
　Inhabitants request U. S. protection, 1011.
　Police of island, American, troops, 1122.
　Probable result of American occupation, 927.
　Robbers impressing and robbing, 1039.
Censorship at Manila—
　Complaints regarding, 973, 1023, 1036, 1135, 1136, 1220, 1260; reasons for, 1221.
　Discontinuance, 1036, 1065, 1065, 1221, 1225, 1229.
Cervantes, Luzon—
　Action with Aguinaldo's rear guard near, 1116.
　Casualties in, 1116.
Characteristics of Filipinos, 809.
Chinese and opium, U. S. laws applied to admission, 791.
Church—
　Administration, interference in, 1238.
　Number established by law, 1184.
Church property—
　Protection by American officers, 1070.
　Treatment by American troops, 1070, 1072.
Churches and convents, occupation by American troops 1072.
Civil administration—
　Retention of volunteer officers necessary for proper, 1227.
　Temporary inauguration in conquered country, 986.
Civil affairs, administration by American officials, result of interference, 825.
Civil authority, assumption by Aguinaldo, ignored by American commander, 809, 810.
Civil conference commission, tendered by Aguinaldo, declined by American authorities, 1078.
Civil government—
　Establishment essential, 852
　Inauguration in Negros Island, 1060, 1091.
　No insurgent, 1019.
　Policy of Philippine Commission, re., 1002.
　Reception by Filipinos, 719.
　Transfer of executive authority to, 1259.
Civil government, Manila, administration of San Jose College, 1141.
Civil government, Vigan, Luzon, tender allegiance to U. S., 1192.
Civil life, capacity of Filipinos for, 888.

Philippine Islands, affairs in—Continued.
Civil marriages—
Provision for, 1125.
Validity, 1125.
Civil war threatening in Sulu Archipelago, 916, 918.
Civil officials, Spanish, captured by insurgents, 921.
Civilized powers, rupture of relations with U. S., set forth by Aguinaldo to, 910.
Clerical force—
Necessity for, and appropriations, 1262.
Number and compensation, 979.
Coast and harbors, requirements for defenses, 851.
Cobo, Luzon, casualties in action, 1235, 1240.
Colasi, Panay, casualties in action, 1163.
Colivo, Panay, casualties in action, 1256.
Collectors of customs—
Appointment, 1003.
Regular Army officers, 935.
Comansi, Luzon—
Casualties in action, 1131, 1132.
Insurgents kill American prisoners, 1131.
Commendation—
By President, of troops composing Eighth Army Corps, 1025.
Of officers, 1016.
Commerce and navigation, in Sulu Islands, to be treated by U. S., 1099.
Commerce, interisland, seriously affected by complications, 827.
Commission, insurgent—
Appointed by Aguinaldo, 814, 909, 912.
Hostilities, propositions for termination, 1163.
Reception by Admiral Dewey, 912.
Sending to Manila, by Aguinaldo, 1088, 1090.
Commission, U. S. Philippine—
Constitution of, 873, 876, 883.
Departure of civilian members for, 883.
In hearty accord with Army and Navy, 1029.
Recommendation for secretary, 884.
Communication—
Lack of, between Manila and Iloilo, 862.
Line of, destroyed by storms, 1084.
Difficulty of, under Spanish law, 650.
Insurgent, interrupted by U. S. Signal Corps, 812.
Concepcion, Luzon, capture by U. S. troops, 1100.
Concessions—
Appeal to American commander, by insurgent leaders, 908.
By Aguinaldo, re. occupation of Manila, 815.
By Filipinos, accepted by Americans as indications of weakness, 912.
Demanded by Aguinaldo résumé by Gen. Otis, 825.
Refused by Gen. Otis, 826, 849.
Regulations for granting, 861.
Conditions and military situation, 830, 1164, 1237, 1241, 1245.
Difficulty of making Filipinos understand, 908.
Information regarding, 682.
Little improvement shown, 1204.
Similarity to those in Cuba, 650.
Conditions—
Aguinaldo's, precedent to withdrawal of Filipinos, 823.
For retirement of Filipinos, Aguinaldo's objection to, 821.
Conduct, Aguinaldo's, toward Filipinos, 849.
Conduct of insurgents such as to arouse indignation of friendly nations, 847.
Conferences—
Aguinaldo and Merritt, desired by latter, 818.
Desired by insurgent commission, 878, 908, 988, 1071.
Gen. Merritt and Aguinaldo's commission, 823.
Gen. Otis and Filipino leaders, 872.
Insurgent and American commission, 814, 879, 909, 978.
Japanese consul and Gen. Trias, 1239.
Spanish commander and insurgents, 997.
Leading members revolutionary government, 851.
Requested by Aguinaldo, 909, 1078.
With insurgent leaders re. amnesty, 1184.
Confidence, leading Filipinos as to pacification, 1165.

Philippine Islands, affairs in—Continued.
Conflict—
Avoidance of, by U. S. forces, 815, 866, 910.
Effect on Filipinos, if precipitated, 909.
Merchants of Iloilo request avoidance, 865.
Slight danger of, 928.
Congratulations of President to American forces, 897, 978, 1002, 1003.
Congress of U. S., insurgents encouraged by reports of attitude, 1148.
Congress, revolutionary, control by radicals, 908.
Conquest, effected by American victories over Spanish, 858.
Consolacion, Cebu, casualties in action, 1146.
Constabulary, native, organization, 1177.
Constitution, Philippine Republic, promulgation by Aguinaldo, 888.
Consular agent—
Chinese, recognition, 747, 784, 785.
Request for privileges, 747.
Contention among insurgent leaders, 1019.
Contingent fund, A. G. O., allotment for Philippine expedition, 681, 682, 697, 698, 700.
Control by Germany, 713.
Control, disposition, and government ceded to U. S. by treaty, 858.
Control of religious orders, exercise by U. S., 1145.
Convalescent camp, establishment for U. S. troops, 847.
Convalescents—
Disbursement of funds for, 1197.
Return to U. S., 1240.
Convents near Manila—
Occupation by insurgents, 815.
Ordered evacuated, 816.
Convoy for transports, 703, 704.
Cooperation of insurgents, Aguinaldo requests recognition of, 911.
Corona, Mount, Luzon, casualties in action, 1192.
Corregidor Island, construction of hospital, 1014.
Correspondence re. affairs in, 635–1357.
Correspondents—
Allege misrepresentation of conditions, 1036.
Gen. Otis's answer, 1036.
No discrimination against, 881.
Cosucos, Luzon, casualties in action, 1228.
Cotabato, Mindanao—
Garrison, 1121.
New government calls for U. S. troops, 1105.
Country occupied by U. S. troops, 1019.
Courts, operation under Filipinos, 1019.
Criminal procedure, preparation, 1157.
Cristina, Panay, casualties in action, 1202.
Criticism of military operations—
Alleged, by Gen. Lawton, 1068.
Denial by Lawton, 1067, 1069.
Cruelty of insurgents to religious orders, 804.
Cuartero, casualties in action, 1226.
Cuenca, Luzon, casualties in action, 1153.
Custom and taxes, receipts, 765, 843, 891, 969.
Customs authorities, refusal to allow landing of supplies from transport at San Francisco, 830.
Customs duties—
Collection at Iloilo, method, 883.
Exaction at insurgent ports, 791.
Monthly receipts, 791.
Customs regulations, establishment in Sulu Archipelago, 1075.
Customs tariff and regulations for, 738.
Cuyapo, Luzon, surrender of insurgents, 1172.
Dagami, Leyte, prisoner of war beheaded at, 1153.
Dagupan, Luzon, hdqrs. Dept. No. Luzon, established at, 1077.
Insurgents in mountains near, 1109.
Occupation by U. S. troops, 851, 1069, 1070.
Unsuitability for dept. hdqrs., 1165.
Damageo Bridge, Luzon, casualties in action, 1188.
Danao, Cebu, casualties in action, 1160.
Dasmariñas, Luzon, capture by U. S. troops, 1016.
Casualties in action, 1017.
Dasol, Luzon, casualties in action, 1143, 1150.
Datos, trouble between insurgents and, 1074.

INDEX. 1439

Philippine Islands, affairs in—Continued.
Davao, Mindanao, garrison for, 1121.
Dead soldiers, shipment to U. S., 935.
Declaration of war between U. S. and Spain:
 Influence of Filipinos, 911.
 Made by Aguinaldo, 898, 1163.
Decrees, etc., re. establishment of civil government, 1065.
Defenses, abandonment by insurgents in Panay, 1098.
 Of Manila, indefiniteness of line, 846.
 Effect of removal of Filipinos from, 848.
 Spanish, location, 846.
Demand, Gen. Otis's, for withdrawal of insurgents from Manila, 846.
 Opinion of insurgent officials as to justice of, 848.
 Of Aguinaldo, reply of Gen. Otis, 823.
Democratic triumph in U. S., insurgents put hope in, 1098.
Denunciation, of act of U. S. Government, 912.
Department commanders, for assignment, 841.
Department, military, organization, 1153, 1154.
Deportation and bribery, by Spanish Government, effect of, 650.
Deportations to Guam, 1263.
 To San Francisco of Editor Rice, 1252.
Deposito, Luzon, casualties in engagement, 1052.
Descriptive lists, soldiers to be furnished, 926, 935.
Dictator, American commander refuses to recognize Aguinaldo as, 810.
Difficulties attending campaigning, 968.
Dinalupijan, Luzon, casualties in action, 1143, 1145.
Dingle, Panay, casualties in action, 1216, 1243.
Dingras, Luzon, casualties in action, 1124, 1255.
Discharge and reenlistment in P. I. under G. O. 40, 1006, 1007.
 At San Francisco of soldiers from P. I., 1093, 1094.
 Enlisted men from regiments destined for P. I., 854, 860.
 Married enlisted men recommended, 842.
 Officers for sickness, etc., 1171.
 Payment on final statements, 1081.
 Travel allowances on, for men reenlisting in P. I., 1004.
 Volunteers to enter business in P. I., 1220.
Disappearance, officers and enlisted men, 1208.
Dissensions among insurgent cabinet and congress, 843.
Distinguished services of officers, 877.
Division and departments, military, establishment, 1076.
Division, organization, 1153, 1154.
Doninglay, Luzon, casualties in action, 1145.
Donsol, Luzon, casualties in action, 1150, 1247.
Drunkenness, condition of army as to, 1246, 1247.
Duero, Bohol, casualties in action, 1237, 1240, 1246.
Dumaguete, Negros, casualties in action, 1255.
Dumangas, Panay, casualties in action, 1182, 1189, 1190, 1192, 1209.
Duties, collected at Iloilo by insurgents, 879.
Eastern extension Australia C. Tel. Co. requests recognition of Spanish concession, 965.
Echagüe, Luzon, casualties in action, 1182.
Eighth Army Corps, commendation by President, of troops composing, 1025.
Elections, holding of, in various parts, 1073, 1077.
Electric-light lines, grants, etc., for construction, 861.
El Pardo, Cebu, casualties in engagement near, 1072.
Emergency ration—
 For use in, 1050, 1058, 1059.
 Not suitable to Tropics, 1051.
Enemy's property and money, disposition, 825.
Engagement, precipitation of, to be avoided, 812.
 At Manila Feb. 4, 1899, first of the insurrection, 748, 893, 894, 896.
English cemetery, funeral party from British war ship to, interference by insurgents, 847.
Enlisted men—
 Discharge from regiments destined for, 860.
 To enter business, 1220.

Philippine Islands, affairs in—Continued.
Enlisted men—Continued.
 Of married, recommended, 842.
 Volunteer, desiring to remain in, 1220, 1241.
 Or transfer from regiments ordered to, 854.
 Drowned while crossing San Mateo River, 1057.
 Home battalion for invalided and short-term, 1143, 1144, 1147, 1148.
 Missing, 980, 1054, 1197, 1208, 1216, 1256.
 Murdered by insurgents, 1248.
 Not to receive travel pay when discharged in, 932.
 Recommended for commission, 785.
 Transfer to Hosp. Corps, 658.
 Transportation of families, 861, 877.
Enlisted strength, reports, 867, 1035, 1046, 1064, 1079, 1093, 1114, 1128, 1142, 1151, 1159, 1169, 1175, 1188, 1198, 1207, 1217, 1226, 1233.
Enlistment, additional volunteer regiments, 1003.
Enlistments, dispatches discouraging, 972.
Enrique, Iloilo, reception of U. S. troops, 949.
Equipments—
 Disposition of volunteer, 991.
 For troops, 1048, 1050.
Escalante, Negros Island, cable party ambushed, 997, 998.
Esperanza, Luzon, casualties in action, 1256.
Estella, Luzon, engagements near, 1211.
Evacuation of conquered territory, avoidance, 1180,
Exclusion of Chinese from, request for landing, 1073, 1074.
Executive authority, transfer to civil government, 1259, 1260.
Expedition to—
 Composition, estimate, 639, 643–645, 649, 666, 669.
 Recommendation by Gen. Miles, 647.
 Contingent fund for, 681, 682, 697, 698, 700.
 Convoy for, 698, 700, 712–714.
 Enlisted personnel, condition and disposition, 718.
 Equipment, etc., 675, 680, 697.
 General Merritt assigned to command, 636, 637, 639, 676.
 General officers assigned to, 674.
 Instructions to commander, 669.
 Murat Halstead to accompany, 702, 703, 705.
 Railway mail service connected with, 696.
 Sanitary conditions and precautions, 767, 768.
 Staff officers, and clerical force, 635–637, 639, 641, 642, 646, 652, 653, 656–658, 660–662, 664–667.
 Troops of to be constituted an army corps, 703, 705, 706.
 Constituted Eighth Army Corps, 707, 708.
 To Iloilo, 862.
Expenditure of money and lives, by U. S. in war with Spain, 824.
Exports and duty on, from Iloilo, 1153.
Families, officers' and soldiers'—
 Advisability of having, at Manila, 1083.
 Going to Manila, 971.
 Not to accompany troops to Manila, 930.
 Perplexity caused by presence, 1084.
 Provision for officers', 971, 972.
 Transportation, 861, 865, 867–839, 877.
Female nurses, for service in, 887.
Field artillery, German, purchase for insurgents, 1059.
Field operations, nature and extent, 931.
Field return of troops, to be cabled monthly, 1035.
Filipino—
 Assistance to U. S. troops, 809.
 Further concessions requested denied, 848.
 Good will of American Government toward, 820.
 Refusal to furnish means of transportation to U. S. troops, 808.
 Suspicions of, how may be quieted, 849.
Filipino bank, endeavor to establish, 840.
Filipino flag, unfurling, as emblem of independence, 913.
Filipino leaders—
 Bribes given by Spanish Government, 650.
 Deportation, by Spanish Government, 650.
 Effect of bribery and deportation, 650.

1440 INDEX.

Philippine Islands, affairs in—Continued.
Filipino people, desire peace and American protection, 1019.
Filipino regiments, of Spanish forces—
  Insubordination and desertion, 651.
  Organizations, number and distribution, 654, 655.
Filipino Republic, Aguinaldo self-declared president and dictator, 806, 807.
Filipino soldiers, provision for destitute, taking advantage of amnesty, 1178.
Filipino withdrawal, extension requested of time for, 848.
Filipinos—
  Aguinaldo, medium of communication with, 809.
  Aim of military administration of U. S. troops, 859.
  Allowed to depart for U. S., 1044.
  Anxiety for peace in certain provinces, 991.
  Appointment of representative to civil offices, 872.
  Armed in vicinity of Manila, 765.
  Aspirations, 879.
  Assistance requested in furnishing supplies, etc., for U. S. troops, 807.
  Attitude as to peace, 968, 969.
    Toward American troops, 910, 1019.
    Toward religious orders, 1145.
    Toward U. S., 718, 719, 806, 820, 1159.
  Believe Aguinaldo unable to gather considerable force, 901.
  Capacity for self-government, 836.
  Characteristics, 765, 809.
  Claim of assistance rendered, 821.
  Claim that Americans take advantage of their friendly feeling, 911.
  Concessions to, latitude of American commanders in, 826.
  Condition in region held by U. S. troops, 984, 985.
  Conservative, decline to participate in deliberations of revolutionary congress, 908.
  Conservatives fear for personal safety, 886.
  Course of action recommended for, 826.
  Death of Gen. Luna viewed with satisfaction, 1011.
  Demand for restitution of original position, 786.
  Desire free entrance and exit in ports under American control, 817, 819, 825.
  Desire for change of flag, 719.
  Desire protection of American squadron for boats, 817, 821.
  Desire to be organized and led by U. S. officers, 719.
  Desire to live in harmony with Americans, 849.
  Desires as to form of government, 872.
  Difficulty in protecting those with American tendencies, 1070.
  Disinclination to assist U. S. forces in regard to supplies, etc., 807.
  Distribution of rifles found in Cavite Arsenal, 911.
  Effect of declination to comply with demands of U. S. Government, 826.
  Effect of words "protection" and "independence," 908.
  Encroachments on American outposts, 822.
  Evacuation of Manila suburbs, 817.
  Expectations in regard to American forces, 911.
  Fear of return of Spanish authority, 843.
  Form of government adopted, 888.
  Free entry to Manila, of products, 816, 819.
  Friendly, charge Spaniards with fomenting discord, 1011.
  Futile efforts to obtain rights from Spanish, 718.
  Futility of efforts to capture Manila, 822.
  Hail with joy, advent of Aguinaldo, 911.
  If needed for office, to be nominated by Aguinaldo, 815.
  Incentive in pursuing hostilities, 913.
  Influence of certain, gaining influence in revolutionary councils, 827.
  Intractability, 909.
  Investigation of death and wounding of American soldiers, 820.
  Leaders can not control army and masses, 872.

Philippine Islands, affairs in—Continued.
Filipinos—Continued.
  Leading, of Luzon desire to send families to Manila, 1005.
  Masses dominated by army and secret clubs, 872.
  Measures to encourage self-protection, 1173.
  Misconception of services rendered, 844.
  Necessity for caution in handling, 1029.
  Objects in proclaiming republic, 888.
  Occupation of suburbs of Manila, withdrawal, 816, 819.
  Opinion of leading, as to means of bringing about peace, 998.
  Organization of native troops from, 1000, 1197.
  Pamphlets, etc., circulated among, 1137.
  Policy of U. S. Government toward, 927.
  Positions in Manila, captured by, 821.
  Profess friendship to, and ask protection of 1005.
  Protection against insurgent abuses, 986.
  Quiet conduct of U. S. troops, viewed as weakness or fear, 909.
  Reasons to be given by Aguinaldo, in case demands are not acceeded to, 822.
  Recommendation for civil offices, 816, 818.
  Refusal to furnish supplies to U. S. troops, except by orders of Aguinaldo, 811.
  Results achieved against Spaniards, 822.
  Retirement beyond line of demarcation, 848.
    Objections by Aguinaldo, 820.
  Returning to homes, 994, 1132.
  Sacrifices made in cause of liberty, 823.
  Safety of lives and property, 824.
  Treatment by U. S. Government, 813.
  Unarmed, free ingress and egress from Manila, 816.
  Wanton killing of unarmed, by Spanish troops, 652.
  Withdrawal from Aguinaldo of, who desire annexation to U. S., 872.
Final statements, payment on, of men discharged in, 1061.
Fire apparatus for Manila, contract for, 727, 927.
Firearms for insurgents, American at Hongkong, as agent, 1023.
Fires, in Manila, 915.
Flag, Filipino, recognition, 872, 913.
Flag, U. S., German warships fail to salute, 833.
Florida Blanca, Luzon—
  Action near, 1091.
  Casualties in action, 1091, 1189.
  Insurgents driven from vicinity, 1093.
Force required to suppress insurrection, 1052, 1053.
  Needed in southern waters, 1055.
Foreign interests, protection in San Fernando de Dilao, guaranteed by Aguinaldo, 817.
Foreign invasion, all Filipinos called by Aguinaldo to resist, 898.
Foreign powers, Aguinaldo's independent status not recognized by, 810.
Fortifications, insurgent, near Cebu, captured by U. S. troops, 1075.
Franchises, regulation for granting, 861.
Free trade in Sulu Archipelago, question of, under protection, 1099, 1885, 1887.
Transit for foreign merchandise, 798.
Freedom of press, abuse of, 827.
Friars, rescue from insurgents, 1121.
Friction, decrease of, between insurgents and U. S. authorities, 843.
Frorista, Luzon, casualties in action, 1237.
Funds, disbursement for sick and convalescent, 1194, 1197, 1200, 1201.
Funds, appropriation for harbor improvements, 1218.
Funds, public, delivery to Spanish Government, demanded, 963.
Funeral party from British warship, interference with, by insurgents, 847.
Gapan, Luzon, casualties in action, 1209, 1247.
Gasan, Marinduque, casualties in action, 1259.
General prisoners, transfer to Dept. California, 1083.
German subjects, protection, 919.
German warships, failure to salute U. S. flag, 833.
Germany, control by, of, 713.

INDEX. 1441

Philippine Islands, affairs in—Continued.
Gerona, Luzon—
Casualties in action, 1160.
Occupied by U. S. troops, 1103.
Gibraltar—
U. S. transport Grant, quarantined at, 892.
U. S. troops at, 1110.
Ginigaran, Samar, casualties in attack on, 1126.
Goods and wares, admittance to ports, 859.
Government, civil—
Despotic, Aguinaldo's—
Attitude of American commander toward, 809.
Reasons for not formally protesting against, 809.
Establishment, 1159.
Filipino, form and organization, 807.
Form, 872.
Interference with ordinary course of business forbidden, 1252.
Military-civil, inauguration in Negros, 1091.
Orders, decrees, etc., providing for, 1065.
United States, assurances of policy to be given insurgents, 1186.
Working, in island of Negros, 1108.
Grants, etc., for construction public or quasi-public works, regulation, 861.
Graves at Manila, deceased members 10th Pa. Vols., decorated, 1062.
Greeting to President, from civil government of Negros, 1095.
Guadalupe, Cebu, casualties in action, 934, 936, 1057, 1231.
Guadalupe Hill, Cebu, casualties in action, 1021.
Guagua—
Casualties in engagement, 1081.
Country in vicinity, cleared of insurgents, 1083.
Guam Island, Ladrones—
Communication with, 1071.
Deportation to, 1237, 1238, 1247, 1248, 1263.
Harbor, anchorages, and defenses, 746.
Supervision, 982.
Guerrilla warfare—
Insurgents to prosecute, 968.
Directed by Hongkong junta, 1148.
Guerrillas and ladrones, operations, 1159.
Guiguinto, Luzon, casualties in action, 1087, 1212.
Guinobatan, Luzon, casualties in action, 1155, 1190, 1191, 1220, 1250, 1256.
Gunboats, Spanish—
Arms, etc., insurgents permitted to take from, 1011.
Purchase by U. S., 938, 1001.
Turning over to U. S. Navy, 1002.
Gunboats, U. S. Army—
Efficiency, 945, 985.
Operations, 949, 985–987, 990.
Seizure by insurgents, 980.
Hamburg, Germany, insurgent arms and ammunition shipped via, 1116, 1126, 1134, 1148.
Harbor defenses, necessity for, 850.
Harbor improvements, appropriation for, 1218.
Health conditions, 691, 795, 802, 842, 893, 970, 1019.
Improvement in, 1144.
Remedial action needed, 1192.
Hemp—
Exporting of, 1258.
Relation to continuance of insurrection, 1244.
Hemp and tobacco, shipments since opening of ports, 1147.
Hemp districts, opening of main, 1130, 1131.
Hemp ports—
American occupation, 1139.
Opening, 1133.
Hemp provinces, insurrection stirred up by interested persons, 1252.
Hemp trade, complaints of military interference with, 1258.
Herald of the Revolution, Filipino organ, proclamation of Aguinaldo published in, 912.
Hilongos, Leyte, casualties in action, 1155, 1188, 1192, 1216, 1240.
Home battalions—
Designation and composition, 1147, 1148, 1155, 1156.
For troops in, 1143, 1144, 1148.
Officers to join, 1253.
Return to U. S., 1172, 1190.

Philippine Islands, affairs in—Continued.
Hongkong, China—
American agent for insurgents at, 1023.
Cable communication with Manila, 702.
Cooperation of American consul-general, 1235.
Deaths from disease, 1075.
Hospital for U. S. troops, 756.
Insurgent arms, shipment under German flag, 836.
Investigation by U. S. officer, 1170, 1171.
Recall of officer investigating, 1232.
Horses, etc.—
For cavalry, 978.
For troops, 981, 1048.
Hospital—
Construction at Corregidor Island, 1014.
Establishment, 1253.
Hospitals—
Establishment, 1245.
For troops at Manila, 766, 1058, 1064.
Funds desired for, 766.
Need for Philippine troops, 756.
Hospital ship—
Needed for interisland service, 753, 759, 1221, 1242.
Relief to be sent to Manila for duty, 884.
Hostilities—
Attitude of Filipinos as to, 910.
Cessation requested by Aguinaldo, 993.
Insurgent statement, re. precipitation, 1163.
Measures for cessation, 1164.
Not to be inaugurated by Americans, 868.
Opening of, by Filipinos, assumed justification for, 912.
Suspension desired by insurgents, 978, 981.
Suspension directed by insurgent government, pending negotiations, 977.
Suspension of, 750.
Termination in Panay, 1260.
Hotels, licensed, number and character in Manila, 1150.
Iba, Luzon—
Casualties in action, 1127, 1143.
Engagement at, 1132.
Occupied by U. S. troops, 1121.
Ice plant, inspection and payment, 1233, 1236, 1243.
Igcabucao, Panay, casualties in action, 1251.
Ilagan, Luzon, casualties in action, 1152, 1243.
Iligan, Mindanao, occupation by U. S. troops, 852.
Ildefonso, Luzon—
Capture by U. S. forces, 988.
Casualties in action, 1109, 1124.
Illaya, Panay, casualties in action, 1117.
Ilocos Sur, Luzon, reaction among inhabitants, 1232.
Iloilo, Panay—
Active hostilities at, 851.
American protection petitioned for, 853.
Capture determined on, 896.
Casualties in engagements, 920, 1081, 1112, 1113, 1150, 1168.
Conditions, 867, 872, 879, 927, 935, 949.
Consequence of conflict, 821.
Customs duties at, method of collection, 883.
Danger of conflict at, slight, 928.
Departure of expedition for, 862, 866, 1060, 1089.
Engagement at, and capture of, 903.
Evacuation by Spanish troops, 862.
Exodus from, after American occupation, 928.
Expected result of capture, by U. S. troops, 872.
Exports and duty, 1153.
Gen. Miller instructed to occupy, 899.
Hdqrs., Dept. Visayas, to be established at, 1077.
Insurgent forces near, disintegration, 914.
Contemplate attack on, 787.
Driven into mountains from, 1107.
In possession of, 862, 865.
Native portion fired by insurgents, 903.
Occupation, probable result, 927.
Resumption of business, etc., 928.
Spanish forces, concentration at, 833.
Strength, etc., of insurgents, 928.
U. S. troops to protect life and property, 857.
Vice-consul at, appointment, 798.

Philippine Islands, affairs in—Continued.
Iloilo and Cebu—
  Cable communication, 966.
  Necessity for occupation, 851.
Iloilo Province, Panay—
  Insurgents cleared from, 1111.
  Termination of armed insurrection, 1245.
Imus, Luzon—
  Attack by insurgents, 1108.
  Casualties in actions, 1021, 1085, 1086, 1092, 1110, 1112, 1113, 1130.
  Engagement at, and near, 1016, 1129.
  Insurgents driven from, 1104.
    Retire to, from Zapote River country, 1010, 1011.
  Reconnaisance from, 1016.
Indang, Luzon, casualties in action, 1148, 1176.
Independence—
  Aguinaldo and advisers cry for, 836.
  Declared by Aguinaldo, 787, 872.
  Desired by Filipinos, 912.
  Influence on certain Filipinos, 840.
Insurgent government asserting unqualified, 850.
Reconquering of, reason for Aguinaldo's return, 912.
Indian reservations, need for troops near, 689.
Inefficiency of Spanish forces, 650.
Infantry companies, increased strength for service in, 1003.
Influence on soldiers, of newspaper and State advice against reenlistment, 970.
Information from Gen. Merritt, to be enciphered, 764.
Information regarding, 675, 689–691.
Inhabitants—
  Attitude toward U. S. troops, 1103, 1109.
  Protection by U. S. troops, 1148.
  Robbed and murdered by insurgent bands, 1115.
  Voluntary assistance rendered American troops, 1116.
Instruction of troops destined for, 776, 777, 1013, 1024.
Instructions, correspondence regarding, 678, 679.
Instructions, President's, to American commanders, 873.
Instructions to Gen. Bates re. treaty with Sultan of Sulu, 1138.
Insurgents—
  Activity among, 787, 833.
  Admiration for achievements of American Army, 977.
  Agents endeavor to cause outbreaks by rumors of American defeats, 1122.
  Aguinaldo orders withdrawal from Manila, 845.
  Aguinaldo requests permission to enter Manila, 814.
  All officials dominated by Gen. Luna, 872.
  American forces not to pass through lines, 815.
  Americans in hands of, 980.
  And overthrow of U. S. administration, 1050.
  Application to send commission to Manila, 1088, 1090.
  Arms and ammunition—
    Captured and surrendered, 896, 947, 995, 1011, 1056, 1062, 1075, 1079, 1082, 1083, 1087, 1088, 1091, 1093, 1095, 1097, 1100, 1103, 1104, 1106, 1107, 1109–1111, 1114, 1120, 1121, 1126, 1127, 1129, 1131, 1133, 1134–1136, 1138, 1139, 1141, 1148, 1157, 1165, 1171, 1245, 1251, 1253, 1254, 1258, 1263, 1264.
    Shipment from Hongkong, 1017.
    Supplied by Japanese Government, 805.
  Army, condition, 651, 968, 1100.
    Disintegration, 898, 957, 981, 982, 1008, 1019, 1093, 1100, 1103, 1106, 1107, 1109, 1110, 1120, 1131, 1139, 1140.
    Spaniards serving in, 1011.
    Strength and condition as to armament, etc., 896.
  Assurances by American Government to, accepting amnesty, 1184.
  Attacked and defeated at Zamboanga by Moros, 1060.
  Attitude reg. American demands for evacuation of Manila, 805.

Philippine Islands, affairs in—Continued.
Insurgents—Continued.
  Attitude toward U. S. forces, 743, 778, 781, 786, 791, 808, 927.
  Authority, acknowledgment in Luzon, 827.
  Avoidance of conflict with, desired by President, 866, 873.
  Barbarous treatment of priests and nuns by, 831.
  Belief in recognition, by Europe, 1050.
  Build hopes on withdrawal of volunteers, 968.
  Buildings in Manila and vicinity, desired by, 815.
  Capture all Spanish garrisons in Luzon, 788.
  Capture and maltreatment of bishop and priests, 790. 793.
  Captured, 902, 906, 915, 921, 934, 947, 968, 980, 995, 1007, 1011, 1062, 1066, 1076, 1083, 1087, 1088, 1091, 1095, 1097, 1100, 1103, 1104, 1106–1108, 1120, 1121, 1126, 1127, 1130, 1131, 1135, 1138, 1139, 1148, 1157, 1162, 1173, 1177, 1179, 1186, 1260, 1262, 1263.
  Cartridge factories, 1017.
  Casualties, 896, 900, 902, 906, 915, 931, 934, 938, 945, 961, 962, 977, 980, 982, 990, 995, 997, 1005, 1007, 1010, 1011, 1013, 1016, 1050, 1054, 1056, 1060, 1073, 1076, 1082, 1084, 1087, 1088, 1090, 1091, 1093, 1095, 1097, 1098, 1101, 1104, 1106–1108, 1110, 1114, 1120–1122, 1126, 1127, 1131–1135, 1136, 1138, 1139, 1141, 1148, 1157, 1162, 1168, 1171, 1204, 1205, 1211, 1222, 1260, 1263.
  Casualties and captures from, during April, 1900, 1165.
  Cause, collapse expected, 1020.
  Claim part of booty of war, 815.
  Collected near Manila, 900, 906.
  Commission—
    Appointed by Aguinaldo, to confer with Gen. Anderson, 814.
    Arrival at Manila for consultation, 993.
    Request for note from Gen. Otis, asking Aguinaldo to withdraw troops, 844.
    Statement by, 879.
  Comply with demand for withdrawal from Manila, 790.
  Concentration near Manila, 900, 906, 1107.
  Concentration from southern Luzon, 944.
  Concessions—
    By commissioners of Aguinaldo, 815.
    Demanded by, indefinitely stated, 825.
    Requested, denied by Gen. Otis, 844.
  Condition of, 719, 944.
  Conflict with, in Iloilo, to be avoided, 857.
  Congress—
    Adoption of constitution, 886.
    Peace measures supported by members, 991.
  Control confined to Luzon, 935.
  Cooperation with Americans, in military operations against Spanish desired, 805.
  Cruel treatment of religious orders, 804.
  Decline to deliver Spanish prisoners to American vessel, 1072.
  Decree closing ports to American vessels, 1050.
  Delegation sent to Hongkong, to purchase arms, 840.
  Demands, 650.
    For release of Spanish prisoners, 1043.
    For withdrawal of U. S. troops from Manila, 786.
    Joint occupation of city of Manila, 754.
    Memorandum by Aguinaldo, 816.
    On Spanish Government, 650.
  Demonstrations met, and blocked by U. S. forces, 982.
  Deportation, 1263.
    Of leaders to island of Guam, 1239, 1247.
  Desire of civil officers filled by, 815.
  Desire to appear well before civilized world, 791, 824.
  Desire to surrender Iloilo, 879.
  Disintegration, 994.
    And demoralization, 990, 1007, 1100.
    Manifestation of, 986.
    Of army, 1084.
  Disposition and condition, 853, 960.
  Dissatisfaction in ranks of, 864.
  Division of opinion among leaders, 805.
  Driven from—
    Line, to Dasmariñas to Imus, 1086.
    Lines near Manila, 894, 915.

INDEX. 1443

Philippine Islands, affairs in—Continued.
Insurgents—Continued.
  Driven from—Continued.
    Pasig River line, 928.
    Towns along Rio Grande, 993.
    Works near Cebu, Cebu, 1075.
  Establishment of provisional government by Americans, would precipitate conflict with, 781.
  Evacuation of Manila and its defenses, 804.
  Expectant of European recognition, 1050.
  Expedition against Spaniards, 785.
  Fear resumption of Spanish authority, 786.
  Force in vicinity of Iloilo, strength and condition, 928.
  Generals' council, accedes to demand of American commander, 847.
  Government—
    Announced, 743.
    Attack on Manila, not ordered by, 896.
    Beheading of members, 1105.
    Capture of officials, 1108.
    Dependence on U. S. Government, 878.
    Endeavor to present communication from, 1078.
    Inefficiency to restrain people, 378.
    Not recognized by Gen. Otis, 982.
    Officials in hands of U. S. troops, 1107.
    Disposition, 1107.
    People of Manila directed to rise en masse, 906.
    Perilous condition, 957.
    Secretary of interior, capture by U. S. troops, 1103.
    Weakening, 866.
    Withdrawal of conservatives from, 908.
  Grounds for proposal of joint occupation of Manila, 824.
  Hopes based on recognition by European powers and Democratic triumph in U. S. election, 1098, 1116.
  Hostilities, proposed suspension, 1164.
  In control of affairs outside of Cavite and Manila, 788.
  In Iloilo to be informed of purpose of U. S. Government, 866.
  In southern islands would welcome American rule, 827.
  Instructions as to treatment, 812.
  Irresponsible military organizations, inability to control, 805.
  Islands in possession of, 836.
  Junta, activity of, necessitates watching, 1148.
  Killing of Gen. Luna, result, 1009.
  Leaders—
    Effort to hold together until after U. S. election, 1203.
    Fears for individual safety, 872.
    Hope for U. S. aid, 1019.
    Ignored by American generals in stipulations for capitulation, 911.
    Powerlessness of, to control people, 876.
    Pretending submission and loyalty to U. S., by Aguinaldo's advice, 1206.
    Proclaim overthrow McKinley Administration and independence and recognition by U. S., 1019.
    Surrendering, 1165.
  Lines—
    Held by, at time of American entry into Manila, 822.
    Spaniards passing through, be considered as spies, 816.
  Make efforts to concentrate and attack Manila before arrival of reenforcements, 908.
  Manila invested by, 781.
  Measures for release of Spanish prisoners, 1045.
  Merchant vessels destroyed, 1050.
  Money captured, 1109, 1110, 1132, 1141.
  Monk prisoners, danger of, 743.
  Must recognize military occupation and authority of U. S., 754.
  Negotiations with Spanish Government for release of prisoners, 1050.
  No conditions except unqualified acceptance of amnesty to be allowed former, 1183, 1184.
  Not to acknowledge U. S. sovereignty longer than necessity demands, 815.
  Not to hold a line encircling city of Manila, 815.

Philippine Islands, affairs in—Continued.
Insurgents—Continued.
  Number and armament, 652, 758, 791, 805.
  Occupation of suburb of Manila, 786.
  Officers—
    Arrest and imprisonment for kidnaping, 84.
    Difficulty of Aguinaldo in controlling, 8448.
    Of rank, deserting, 994.
    Surrender, 1157.
  Of Iloilo recognize authority of Aguinaldo, 865.
  Organize congress at Malolos, 791.
  Part taken by, forcing surrender of Manila, 911.
  Payments for release of Spanish prisoners, 1043.
  Plan to capture and burn Manila, 65.
  Ports—
    Blocked, effect on revenues, 1015.
    In possession, danger in exacting duties at, 791.
  Position, from Caloocan to Malolos, 945.
  Preparation for offensive operations, 787.
  Prisoners in hands of, 806, 1166.
  Proclamation by leader, directing uprising against Americans, 913.
  Procurement of rapid-fire guns for, 1055, 1059.
  Progress made, to what due, 815.
  Pronounced, think can tire out U. S. by keeping people in unrest, 1148.
  Property captured from, 1100, 1102–1104, 1109, 1110, 1112, 1120, 1121, 1126, 1127, 1129–1131, 1133, 1135, 1136, 1138, 1139, 1141, 1148, 1157, 1165.
  Proposed issue of amnesty to, 1175, 1177, 1179, 1180.
    Issue of, 1181.
  Proposition regarding U. S. garrison for Zamboanga, 1074.
  Punishment of officers' murderers, 999.
  Records captured, 1101, 1104, 1120, 1129, 1131, 1239.
  Relations between U. S. troops and, 813.
  Relations between Americans and Iloilo, 928.
  Release of Spanish prisoners, through American intercession, 1040.
  Remnant compelling by violence contributions and secret support, 1184.
  Republic, organization, 650.
  Request for buildings denied, 816.
  Request return of arms taken by U. S. forces, 816.
  Representative at Washington telegraphs drive Americans from, before arrival of reenforcements, 902.
  Rifles needed for, 665.
  Ruse to obtain acknowledgment by U. S. authorities, 1078.
  Sale of arms by Spaniards to, 1011.
  Settlement of differences among leaders, 787.
  Spanish subjects, interests of confided to French consul, 920.
  Stores, etc., captured from, 983, 1062, 1079, 1083, 1090, 1091, 1093, 1097, 1100.
  Strained relations with, 831.
  Strength and location of only organized force, 1019.
  Supplies, etc., for, 651.
    Necessity of cutting off, 1069.
  Surrenders, 1073, 1100, 1108, 1109, 1111, 1112, 1121, 1157–1159, 1165, 1171, 1172, 1180, 1186, 1199, 1232, 1245, 1251, 1253, 1256, 1258, 1259, 1261, 1264.
  Treatment—
    Of captured Americans, 1195.
    Of inhabitants, 969.
  Trenches occupied by American forces, 813, 911.
  Troops driven from Tarlac and officials murdered, 866.
  Trouble—
    Threatened with U. S. forces, 813.
    With, not anticipated, 827.
  Understanding between Spaniards and, 989.
  Unfriendly attitude toward U. S. forces, 808.
  View of conduct of U. S. troops, 909.
  Vessels, arrests in Manila Bay, by American naval forces, 911.
  Weakness, 985.

1444 INDEX.

Philippine Islands, affairs in—Continued.
Insurgents—Continued.
  Withdrawal from Manila, 791.
    Action of Gen. Otis approved by War Department, 789.
    Demanded by American commander, 788.
    Its suburbs and defenses, 843, 844.
Insurrection—
  Assistance to, by merchants, Manila, 1258.
  Force required to suppress, 1051, 1052.
  Length, dependent upon celerity with which troops sent, 1053.
  Organized, given place to brigandage, 1159.
  Participation, no bar to employment in civil or military service 1184.
  Termination in Panay, 1261.
Interisland trade, effect of interdiction on revenues, 1015.
Commerce and customs receipts, 969.
Intoxicating liquors, use by Army, 1246.
Invalided volunteers, return to U. S., 1204.
Isarog, Mount, Luzon, casualties in action, 1153, 1257.
Island revenues, payments for road supplies to be made from, 1199.
Japanese Government—
  Arms and ammunition supplied insurgents, 805.
  Asserted has promised protection to Filipinos, 836.
  Attitude toward insurgents, 1239.
  Authorizes landing of animals at Kobe and Nagasaki, 1054.
  Permits landing at Nagasaki of troops from Morgan City, 1063.
Japanese consul, conference with insurgent Gen. Trias, 1239, 1240.
Jaro, Leyte, casualties in action, 1162, 1209.
Jaro, Panay—
  Action at and near, 905, 1106, 1126.
  Casualties, 905, 943, 1106, 1108, 1117, 1126.
  Insurgents driven from, 1107.
Jean, Luzon, casualties in action, 1220.
Jiminez, Mindanao, casualties in action at, 1240, 1254, 1259.
Joint note of American commanders to Spanish commander, Manila, demanding surrender of city, 754.
Joint occupation of Manila—
  Condemnation of, in equity, 824.
  Grounds for, proposed by Aguinaldo, 824.
  Impracticability, 824.
Jolo Archipelago—
  Danger to Chinese in, 901.
  Occupation by U. S. forces, 1058.
  Troops required for, 960.
  U. S. sovereignty of, acknowledged by Sultan and Datos, 1058.
Jolo, Jolo—
  Desire of Spaniards to evacuate, 980.
  Free port, used as a feint for other ports, 1099.
  Garrison, 567, 568, 570, 571.
  Improvement of conditions, 997, 1027.
  Occupation by U. S. troops, 1158.
  Spain responsible for conditions until confirmation of treaty, 919.
  Spanish forces at and near, 655.
  U. S. troops to relieve Spanish garrison, 991.
Judicial system, restoration, 852.
Jurisdiction of American commander, 826.
Justice of U. S. Government, Aguinaldo's appeal to, 821.
Kansas City Star, transportation for correspondent, 990.
Katipunan insurrectos—
  Administration of oath of allegiance, 1232.
  Surrender at Santa Maria, Luzon, 1232.
Khaki—
  Cause of unsatisfactoriness, 1028.
  Uniform, procurable in, superior to U. S., 1024.
Kidnaping and robbery in Manila by insurgents, 825, 846.
Killing of soldiers, by pretended pacificos, to be treated as murder, 1206.
Kobbé's expedition, operations, 1135, 1139, 1141, 1144.
Kobe, Japan, landing of American animals authorized, 1054.
Krag-Örgensen rifles, supply for troops, 992.

Philippine Islands, affairs in—Continued.
Kynochs, England, insurgent order for ammunition placed at, 1114.
Labo, Luzon, casualties in action, 1182, 1192.
Ladrone Islands, capture of, 778.
Ladrones—
  Insurgents operating in Luzon with, 1159.
  Troublesome in all islands, 1144.
Ladrones and Caroline Islands, memorandum on, 745.
La Granja, Samar, casualties in action, 1126.
Laguan, Samar, casualties in action, 1225.
Laguna de Bay, Luzon—
  Coast and surrounding country opened to traffic, 1138.
  In possession of U. S. gunboat, 938.
Laigo, Luzon, casualties in action, 1166.
Lambuanao, Panay, casualties in action, 1193, 1202.
Lampag, Leyte, casualties in action, 1166.
Lanang, Samar, casualties in action, 1155.
Land cultivation, resumption within American lines, 1019.
Langbasa, Luzon, casualties in action, 1225.
Laoag, Luzon, captured by joint army and navy force, 1120.
Lapaz, Leyte, casualties in action, 1153, 1166, 1189, 1195, 1229.
Lapo, Luzon, casualties in action, 1189, 1190.
Las Piñas, Luzon, casualties in action, 1016, 1017, 1075.
Laundry for troops, 1013, 1014.
Law of nations, in re course of action of insurgent leaders, 824.
Laws of war—
  Observance, 1237.
  Violators not to receive benefit of amnesty, 1175, 1177.
Lawton's expedition, 959-963, 968, 971, 972, 973, 975, 977, 980-982, 984, 988, 990, 993, 995, 1001, 1006-1008, 1010, 1011, 1062, 1069, 1076, 1081, 1085, 1087, 1089, 1091, 1095-1098, 1100-1104, 1106, 1108, 1109, 1111, 1116, 1121, 1123.
Layagon, Panay, casualties in action, 1174.
Legaspi, Luzon—
  Casualties in action, 1139, 1147, 1161, 1187, 1191, 2022, 1225.
  Engagement at, 1139.
Lemery, Luzon—
  Casualties in action, 1137, 1182.
  Engagement at, 1136.
Leon, Panay, casualties in action, 1112, 1202.
Leyte, Island—
  Attitude of inhabitants, 935.
  Conditions in, 1164.
  Occupation of hemp ports, 1139.
Libmanan, Luzon—
  Casualties in action, 1148, 1150, 1182.
  Engagement at, 1148.
Licenses, sale for lotteries and pastimes opposed by public morals, discontinued, 791.
Ligao, Luzon, casualties in action, 1190.
Lilio, Luzon, insurgents driven from, 1139.
Limbones Cove, Luzon, casualties in action, 1240.
Linao, Luzon, casualties in action, 1150-1152.
Lingayen Gulf, Luzon—
  Expedition to, 1095.
  Landing of expedition, 1096.
  Prevented by heavy storm, 1108.
Line of communication—
  Attack by insurgents on, 962, 1079.
  Imus-Bacoor, attacked by insurgents, 1082.
  American casualties, 1082.
  Insurgent, use by U. S. forces, 812.
  Insurgents attack MacArthur's railway, 962.
  Insurgents driven from, 963.
Lipa, Batangas, casualties in action, 1185.
Lipa, Luzon, casualties in action, 1140, 1145, 1150, 1193.
Llana Hermosa, Luzon, casualities in action, 1191.
Laculan, Mindanao, casualties in action, 1182, 1193.
Longos, Luzon, casualties in action, 1243.
Los Baños, Luzon—
  Capture of insurgents near, 1130.
  Casualties in action, 1081, 1152.
Lucamo, Leyte, casualties in action, 1166.
Lucena, Luzon, insurgents driven from, 1139.
Lumbaro Barrio, Luzon, casualties in action, 1131.

Philippine Islands, affairs in—Continued.
Luna, ——, lieut. gen., insurgent forces—
  Attitude and character, 1011.
  Murdered by insurgents, 1011.
Lupao, Luzon—
  Casualties in action, 1092.
  Insurgents driven from, 1100.
Luzon, Island of—
  Acknowledgment of insurgent authority, 827.
  Assistance to U. S. troops by inhabitants, 1162.
  Attitude of inhabitants, 1116.
  Blocking of roads in west coast, 1092.
  Casualties in actions in, 1121.
  Conditions, 650, 827, 969, 1029, 1158, 1162, 1165, 1253.
  Disposition of American troops in, 1124.
  Provincial government establishment, 852.
  Influence of Aguinaldo, destruction, 898.
  Insurgents driven from northern part, 1120.
  Location and number of insurgents, 864, 1019, 1211.
  Military operations, 1100–1116, 1120–1124, 1126–1133, 1135, 1136, 1138–1140, 1144, 1148, 1158, 1159, 1162, 1167, 1211, 1222.
  Natives of southeast combining to drive out insurgents, 1019.
  Number of Spanish prisoners held by insurgents, 1050.
  Occupation by U. S. troops, 851, 908, 1120, 1148.
  Operations of insurgents, 1159, 1211.
  Ports to be closed, 1050.
  Rainy season interrupts campaigning, 1019.
  Reenforcements for U. S. troops, 1158, 1159.
  Reported insurgent victories cause outbreak in Negros, 1115.
  Revolutionary government, progress, 836.
  Spanish forces in, 655.
  Spanish garrisons in, capture by insurgents, 788.
  Stations occupied by U. S. troops, 1100.
  Surrenders of insurgents, 1251.
  Troops in northwest, attacked by insurgents, 1162.
    Casualties, 1162.
Luzon, Northern—
  Action in, 1138.
  Casualties in action, 1129, 1139.
  Conditions, 1128.
  Inhabitants refuse to be subject to Aguinaldo's authority, 843.
Luzon Province, conditions, 960.
Maasin, Luzon,
  Casualties in action, 982, 1117, 1225.
  Engagement on river at, 982.
Mabalacat, Luzon,
  Action in vicinity, 1097, 1135.
  Casualties in action at, 1101, 1113, 1143, 1160.
  Seized by U. S. troops, 1096.
Mabini, Apolinario,
  Corresponding with insurgents while under protection U. S., 1248.
  Deportation to Guam, 1248.
  Founder of insurgent government, capture by U. S. troops, 1121.
  Refusal of amnesty, 1248.
Macabebe scouts, organization, 1076.
  Work done by, 1076.
  Desire to accept military service with Spain, as garrison for Caroline Islands, 961.
MacArthur's expedition, operations, 951, 953, 959, 962, 971–973, 975, 977, 982, 984, 988, 990, 993, 1049–1051, 1053, 1062, 1076, 1086, 1092, 1095, 1097, 1098, 1100, 1102–1104, 1106, 1108–1111, 1116, 1121, 1135, 1138, 1139.
Macato, Panay, casualties in action, 1149.
Machine guns—
  And ammunition, for troops, 1039, 1200.
  Need of, to strengthen garrisons, 1199.
Mandalog, Panay, casualties in action, 1147.
Madrid Government—
  Action of, regarding release of Spaniards held by insurgents, 1053.
  Instructions regarding release of Spanish prisoners held by insurgents, 1050.
Madrigal, Negros, action at, 1122.
Magalang, Luzon—
  Captured by U. S. forces, 1095.
  Casualties in action 1095, 1096, 1098.
  Concepcion road, action on, 1098.

Philippine Islands, affairs in—Continued.
Magat-Rio Grande Junction—
  Engagement at, 1121.
  Casualties, 1121.
Magat River, Luzon, expedition down, 1115.
Magdalena, Luzon, casualties in action, 1145, 1148, 1152, 1192.
Majayjay, Luzon—
  Casualties in action, 1195.
  Insurgents concentrated at, 1139.
Malabagun, Luzon, casualties in action, 1190.
Malabog, Luzon, casualties in action, 1166.
Malabog Hill, Luzon, casualties in action, 1185.
Malindy, Mount, Panay, casualties at, 1218.
Malinta, Luzon, Col. Egbert killed in action at, 945, 956.
Malitbog, Leyte, casualties in action, 1162.
Malolos, Luzon—
  Americans arrested by insurgents, 958.
  Captured by U. S. troops, 953.
  Casualties in action, 952, 953, 1187, 1212, 1232.
  Engagement at, 952.
  Fired by retreating insurgents, 953.
  Reconnaissance from, 955.
  U. S. troops at, 959.
Malta, island of—
  American soldiers and seamen left at, disposition and care, 932–934, 937–939, 942, 943.
  Arrival at, of U. S. troops, 1112.
Malunu, Luzon, casualties in action, 1182.
Mambusao, Panay, casualties in action, 1227.
  Surrender of insurgents, 1264.
Manadaan, Panay, Panay, casualties in action, 1191.
Mandurriao, Panay, casualties in action, 1108.
Mangataren, Luzon—
  Action in mountains near, 1110.
  Casualties in action, 1126, 1140.
  Insurgents driven from, 1109.
Maniclin, Luzon, casualties in action, 1212.
Manila, Luzon—
  Aguinaldo endeavoring to capture without American assistance, 806.
  Requests that insurgents enter, 814.
  Americans entry into, without Filipino assistance, 822.
  Precarious situation, 651.
  To conduct municipal affairs, 818.
  And suburbs—
    American demand for evacuation by Filipinos, 826.
    Instructions from U. S. Government, prohibit joint occupation, 826.
  Approaches, 782, 808.
  Arms, ammunition funds etc., 765.
  Arms to be returned upon evacuation, 757.
  Assault on, distribution of forces, 758.
  Attack by American forces, 754.
    Plans and preparations, 781.
  Attack on, not ordered by insurgent government, 896.
  Attempted concentration of insurgents to north, 848.
  Banquet and fiesta, in celebration of amnesty, 1194.
  Battle of, conditions on day of, 837.
  Billeting of insurgent troops in vicinity, 815.
  Bombardment by U. S. naval forces, and unconditional surrender, 752.
  Cable to Hongkong, establishment, 702.
  Capitulation, 754, 757, 824.
    Commission composition, 757.
    Fall occupancy granted to U. S., by articles of, 824.
    Persons included in, to remain at liberty, conditional upon good behavior, 757.
  Garrison, how forced, 911.
  Capture, plans for, 717.
  Casualties—
    Among troops at, 760, 761.
    In skirmishes in vicinity, 915, 919, 931.
  Cause of attack on, 902.
  Chinese consul—
    Correction of name, 789, 790.
    Recognition, 747, 784, 785.
    Request for privileges, 747.
  Climate, location, conditions, etc., 690, 743, 754, 760, 765, 788, 790, 834–836, 848, 851, 860, 864, 866, 868, 872, 876–879, 886, 888, 898, 906, 943, 945, 960, 991, 1019.

Philippine Islands, affairs in—Continued.
Manila, Luzon—Continued.
Coal supply for transports, 703, 709, 711, 912, 713.
Concentration of insurgents near, 902, 1107.
Condition of Spanish forces and noncombatants, 754.
Cooperation between Army and Navy, 669.
Customs and taxes, receipts, 891.
Deaths of American soldiers, investigation, 820.
Defenses, nature and extent, 652, 691, 778–781.
Defenses on R. R., constructed by insurgents, 787.
Delay in opening waterworks, cause, 819.
Demand—
  For removal of insurgents from defenses, effect, 831.
  Of Aguinaldo, that U. S. troops retire within the city, 821.
  Of American commander, for withdrawal of insurgents, 788.
Departure—
  Citizens, 876, 877.
  Gen. Merritt and officers, 783.
  Spanish transport with prisoners of war, 833.
Detail of collector customs at, 1002, 1003, 1212,
Details of capitulation, 757.
Determination of lines of defenses and municipal limits, 846.
Difficulty of communication with, 691.
Directions for insurgent attack on, 914.
Discharge of volunteers at, 785, 786.
Disposition conceded by insurgent commission, 815.
Disposition of—
  Ordnance stores, 763.
  Public property, 757.
District occupied by U. S. troops after capitulation, 754.
Engagements at and near, 748, 893–896, 899, 914, 931, 945, 1006, 1054.
Engagement between Spaniards and insurgents near, 650.
Establishment of—
  Convalescent camp for U. S. troops, 847.
  Department headquarters at, 1166.
Evacuation—
  By insurgents, 760, 786, 791, 804, 805, 816, 844, 911.
  Filipino, conditions, 817.
Expected attack on, 652.
Fitting up of hospital ship for, 752, 753.
Free entry and exit of unarmed Pilipinos, 816, 819.
Futile endeavors of Filipinos to capture, 822.
General engagement inaugurated by Filipinos Feb. 4, 1899, 893.
Gen. Merritt arrives at, 742.
Harbor defenses, recommendations regarding, 841.
Hdqrs., Dept. So. Luzon, establishment, 1077.
Health conditions, 691, 834, 835, 885.
Holding by U. S., conceded by insurgents, 824.
Hospital accomodations, 1058, 1064.
Hospital ship to be sent to, 884.
Inhabitants, etc., to be safe guarded by American Army, 757.
Insurgents—
  Cease interference in city affairs, 843.
  Expectation of uprising not realized, 898.
  Grounds for joint occupation, 824.
  In vicinity, 719, 765, 805, 973, 982, 1104, 1115.
  Intrench in outskirts of, 915.
  Not to hold a line encircling, 815.
  Plan to capture and burn, 651, 915.
  Threaten attack on, 985.
Invested by insurgents, 781.
Joint occupation—
  Condemned by equity, 813, 819, 824.
  Demanded by insurgents, 754.
  Not to be permitted, 814.
Jurisdiction municipal designation, 815, 845.
Lines, insurgent, at time of American entry, 822.
Location conditions, etc., 690.
Martial law declared by Aguinaldo, 781, 808.
Means of communication, 780.
Military and political conditions, 650.

Philippine Islands, affairs in—Continued.
Manila, Luzon—Continued.
Municipal limits, evacuation by U. S. forces, 815.
Necessity for water and sanitation, 818.
Not affected by closing of Luzon ports, 1050.
Number and character licensed saloons and hotels, 1150.
Obligations of U. S. Government, articles of capitulation, 824.
Organization of pro-American party, 1237.
People of, driven to eating horses, 779.
Political situation, 718.
Port and Rio Pasig, insurgents request free entrance, exit, 815.
Granted insurgent steamer *Patria*, 816.
Positions, restitution to Filipinos demanded in case of resumption of Spanish domination, 817, 826.
President of U. S. thanks troops for conduct in campaign against, 759.
Private property, under safeguard of American Army, 757.
Province, city, garrison and civil affairs in hands military governor, 1167.
Public funds, on hand, collected, expended, 843, 884.
Quarters for officers, 785.
Reasons for, postponement, of bombardment, 824.
Receipt of proclamation suspending hostilities, 756.
Reconnaissance of lines and approaches, assistance of Aguinaldo in making, requested, 807, 808.
Reconnaissances of, and surrounding country, 780, 898.
Removal from, of noncombatants, 754.
Repatriation of officers, soldiers, and families, 757.
Reported disorderly conduct of troops, 857.
Reports from American consul, 650, 651, 652.
Retention of transports, 756.
Retirement of—
  American troops to lines designated by Aguinaldo, 826.
  Filipinos, lines to which made, 821.
Rising of inhabitants against Americans, 906, 908, 913.
Second Philippine expedition arrives, 738.
Shipment of Spanish prisoners of war, 850.
Shipment of troops, suspension, 751.
Sick at, 766.
Situation for hospital at, 760, 891, 894, 898, 902, 909, 915, 916, 918, 945, 1005, 1065, 1066.
Spanish—
  Forces at, and in vicinity, 655, 675, 691, 778.
  In, closely besieged by insurgents, 780.
  Prisoners in, 765.
Supplies for troops in, 757, 761, 764.
Supply lines cut off by U. S. troops and Filipinos, 719.
Surrender demanded by American commanders, 754.
Surrender, forcing of, 719, 782.
Unhealthfulness, 847.
U. S. authority over, 824.
Uprising of Filipino organizations threatened, 868.
Wanton killing of defenseless Filipinos by Spanish forces, 652.
Water supply, 896.
Withdrawal of insurgents from, 790, 819, 843, 844.
Manila Bay—
  Battle, Spanish naval force annihilated, 718.
  Submarine mines not practicable for, 674, 694.
  U. S. in possession of, and tributaries, 825.
Manila-Hongkong cable concession, recognition requested of Spanish grant, 965.
Maniling, Luzon, casualties in action, 1188.
Maradudon, Monte, Luzon, casualties in action, 1184.
Maragondon, Luzon, casualties in action, 1251.
Maravilla, Cebu, casualties in action, 1255.
Marianao, casualties in action, 1256.
Marilao—
  Engagement at, and capture, 947.
  Engagement near, 948.

INDEX.   1447

Philippine Islands, affairs in—Continued.
Marilao Guiguinto, engagements on advance, 951.
Marinduque Island—
Casualties on, 1219.
Operations, 1216, 1218, 1222.
Suppression of insurrection, 1261.
Treatment of natives, 1260, 1261.
Troops ordered to, to suppress revolt, 1216.
Marines, landing at Vigan, 1110.
Mariquina, Luzon—
Attack and capture, by U. S. troops, 952.
Casualties in action, 937, 943, 1052, 1085, 1173.
Engagements near, 953.
Killed in engagement at, 956.
Mariquina Road, Luzon—
Skirmish on, 906.
Casualties, 906.
Martial law—
Declared by Aguinaldo, 808.
Proclamation by Aguinaldo, nonrecognition, 810.
Masalopot, Mount, Marinduque casualties in action, 1259.
Masalowat, Mount, Marinduque casualties in action, 1261.
Matnog, Luzon, casualties in action, 1243.
Matuguinao, Samar, casualties in action, 1153, 1155, 1160, 1176, 1183, 1237.
Mauban, Luzon, casualties in action, 1250.
Mavitac, Luzon—
Casualties in action, 1211, 1214.
Engagement at, 1211.
Medal of honor, special, recommended for officers and soldiers, 8th Army Corps, 1025.
Medical administration, necessities and methods, 1261.
Medical officers, additional, needed, 874, 884, 1024, 1026, 1192, 1193.
Medical supplies, etc., needed, 709, 711, 766, 884, 1198.
Memorandum—
For guidance of Maj. J. F. Bell in treating with Filipinos, 818.
Of insurgents' demands, 816.
Gen. Merritt's reply, 816.
Merchants, efforts to establish trade in Sulu Islands, trouble caused by, 1099.
Merchant vessels, seizure for violating regulations, 1099.
Messages, cable, from, authority for sending business, 890.
Messages, important, to be enciphered, 851.
Mexico, Luzon, casualties in engagement near, 1081.
Meycauyan, Luzon—
Casualties in action, 1075.
Lieut. Krayenbuhl, killed in action, 945, 956.
Mileage, payment in advance to disabled officers, 706.
Military authority—
Defied by press correspondents, 1036.
To remain supreme until otherwise provided, 859.
Military departments—
Assignment of troops, 1155.
Designation of headquarters, 1155.
Establishment and limits, 1004, 1033, 1034, 1070, 1076, 1077.
Modification, 1166, 1167, 1170.
Organization deferred, 1035.
Military governor—
Accused of prejudice against press representatives, 1023.
Protest of Aguinaldo against assumption of title, 912.
Relief of MacArthur and appointment of Chaffee, 1259.
Military government—
Duties toward Filipinos, 859.
Extension to whole archipelago, 858.
Insurgent, put in operation by Aguinaldo, 809.
Relations between religious orders, native church, Tagologs, and, 1145.
Relations with Philippine Commission, 1002.
Restoration in southern islands, 852.
Military grasp, relaxation of, would hinder favorable outcome, 1184.

Philippine Islands, affairs in—Continued.
Military information, detail of officer to gather in China, 1169, 1171.
Military operations—
Alleged criticism by Gen. Lawton, 1067.
Denial, 1068, 1069.
Difficulties attending, 1031, 1033, 1034, 1049-1051, 1090-1093, 1095, 1096, 1098, 1100.
Rainy season interferes with, 1049.
Military situation in, 645, 646, 1251.
Information needed of, 645, 646, 650-652.
Mindanao Island—
American occupation, 1158.
Conditions, 919.
Eastern, proffered surrender to U. S., 1076
Garrisons for, 1105, 1110, 1111, 1232.
Operations, 1222, 1223.
Spanish forces in, 655.
Termination of insurrection 1264.
Troops required for, 960.
Mindanao and Jolo, department of—
Brig. Gen. Kobbé, assigned to command, 1154, 1155.
Organization and limits, 1077, 1154, 1155.
Mindanao and Jolo district, garrison, 572, 574, 575, 577, 579.
Mission of U. S. in, 807.
Moalbual, Cebu, casualties in action at, 1222, 1227.
Money, insurgent, use as trust fund, 1184.
Monks, insurgent prisoners, danger, 743.
Montalban, Luzon—
Capture by American troops, 1126.
Casualties in action, 1126.
Capture of insurgent stronghold in mountains near, 1127.
Casualties in, 1127.
Casualties in action at, 1128, 1131.
Morong, Luzon—
Advance of U. S. troops on, 1001.
Casualties in action, 1015, 1038, 1140.
Garrisoned by U. S. troops, 1005.
Murders and robberies by insurgents, 1001.
Morong Province—
Insurgents driven into, 938.
Towns captured by U. S. troops, 1005.
Moros, disposition toward U. S., 1058.
Mounted infantry, advisability of using, 1029, 1030.
Mounts—
For cavalry in, 1032.
For troops, 1030.
Municipal government, installation, 1192.
Municipal law, continue in force until otherwise provided, 859.
Municipal limits of Manila, determination by chief engineer U. S. forces, 846.
Munitions of war, not to be landed without consent of American commander, 841.
Muñoz, Luzon, casualties in action, 1222.
Muntinlupa, Luzon—
Casualties in action, 1026, 1086, 1087.
Insurgents driven from, 1086.
Murders and robberies, insurgent, 1001, 1060, 1070, 1115, 1243, 1248.
Muster-in rolls, volunteers, 707.
Muster-out—
Arrangements for volunteer, 1041, 1236.
Volunteers desire, at San Francisco, 1015.
Naban, Luzon, casualties in action, 1253.
Naga, Cebu, casualties in action, 1189.
Nagasaki, Japan—
Deaths in hospital, 1045.
Establishment of floating hospital at, 1241.
Establishment of hospital, 885, 1245.
Forbidden by Japanese governor, 1253.
Japanese Government permits landing of troops, 1063.
Sick left at, 1071.
Transports to stop at, returning to U. S., 1245.
Naguilian, Luzon, casualties in action, 1148.
Niac, Luzon—
Captured by U. S. troops, 1131.
Casualties in action near, 1131, 1148, 1166, 1212, 1254, 1256, 1258.
Surrender of insurgents, 1258.
Naporo, Samar, casualties in action, 1176.

Philippine Islands, affairs in—Continued.
Narvacan, Luzon—
  Casualties in action, 1115, 1222, 1225.
  Engagement at and near, 1115, 1221.
Nasugbu, Luzon, casualties in action, 1222.
National or civil recognition by American commander, 910.
Native church, relations with military government, 1145.
Native constabulary—
  Arming, 1180, 1197.
  Organization, 969, 1173, 1179.
Native force, enlargement, 1195.
Native officials, treachery, 1251.
Native organizations, inadvisability of use, 1000, 1001.
Native Spanish regiments, eager to desert to U. S. flag, 719.
Native volunteer force—
  Enlargement not recommended, 1197.
  Number and distribution, 1197.
Native wine (vino), no licensed sale in Manila, 1151.
Natives—
  Disposition, condition, characteristics, 690.
  Intimidation, kidnaping, assassination by insurgents, penalty, 1237.
  Pro-American party organization, 1237.
Natives of southern, disposition, 852.
Naval forces—
  Landing at Vigan and reception, 1111.
  Organizing near Cavite, 694.
  Participation in operations in Luzon, 1007, 1082.
  Zamboanga, turned over to, by insurgent government, 1105.
Naval officers, transferred to Asiatic fleet at Manila, 724.
Navigation, freedom of, in Manila Bay and its tributaries, to vessels of all nations, 825.
  Of ports in P. I. in control of U. S. forces, protection to Filipino in, free, 817.
Navy—
  Bombardment of Manila, 752.
  Cooperation with Army, 1012, 1069, 1097, 1111, 1115, 1116, 1120, 1122, 1133, 1135, 1136, 1139, 1148, 1260, 1263.
  Force surrender of Manila, 719, 752.
  Increase of, at Manila, 1080.
  Relations with Army, 1035.
  Surrender of Cagayan Province to, 1121.
  To exercise supervision over island of Guam, 982.
  Turning over Spanish gunboats to, 1001.
  Necessity for presence of officers with command, 467.
Negotiations—
  Between Gen. Bates and Sultan of Jolo, 1052.
  Made in writing and ratified by generals in chief, 816.
Negotiations and conferences, result of, with insurgents, 1002.
Negotiations for peace, progress, 1027.
Negotiations with Aguinaldo, refusal of Americans to enter into, 1097.
Negros Island—
  American casualties in action, 1035, 1037.
  American protection requested, 914.
  Attack by insurgents on inhabitants of, 997.
  Conditions, 969, 1091, 1125.
  Development of internal government, 949.
  Eastern coast under American flag, 999.
  Engagements with robber bands, 1035, 1037, 1044, 1059, 1079, 1090, 1133.
    American casualties, 1079.
    Robber casualties, 1090.
  Fine imposed on towns engaged in revolt, 1123.
  Members of civil government, memorialize the President U. S., 1095.
  Occupation by U. S. troops, 918, 1027.
  Outbreak of natives, in southern district, 1115.
  Panay insurgents driven out of, 1088.
  People send salute to American commander in southern island, 924.
  Revolt in, cause, 1122, 1123.
  Situation, 935, 1077, 1108.
  Surrender of chief insurgent leader, 1108.
  Troops welcomed by people of, 924.

Philippine Islands, affairs in—Continued.
Neutral zone, establishment between insurgents and U. S. troops, 1163.
New Segovia, bishop, priests, and nuns being barbarously treated by insurgents, 831.
Newspaper articles, defamatory, cause much trouble, 1116.
Newspaper correspondents—
  Complaint of discrimination, settlement, 1041.
  Disagreement between military governor and, 1036.
  Dispatch alleging discord in administration, 1034, 1035.
  Treatment at Manila, 1065, 1066.
Noncommissioned staff officers, need for, 802.
Northern expedition, casualties, 1124.
Northern Luzon, department of—
  Assignments to command, 1154, 1157, 1164, 1165.
  Headquarters established in Manila, 1167.
  Modification, 1165, 1167, 1170.
  Organization and limits, 1077, 1154.
Northern Luzon—
  Operations, military, in, 1069.
  Reenforcements needed for, 1158.
  Spanish officials requested to send vessels to obtain Spanish prisoners, 1072.
Norzagaray, Luzon, casualties in action, 1017, 1176, 1182, 1231.
Notice of amnesty, 1177, 1180, 1181.
  Amended by direction of President, 1179.
Novaliches, Luzon—
  Advance on, 944.
  Casualties in action, 1117, 1212, 1216, 1234.
Novaleta, Luzon—
  Casualties in action, 1052.
  Naval demonstration on, 1082.
Nueva Caceres, Luzon—
  Casualties in action, 1161, 1209.
  Inhabitants flee to mountains, 1148.
  Offer of natives to drive insurgents from Bayombong, 1110.
  Surrender to U. S. troops, 1112.
Nurses—
  Need of, 744.
  Transportation for Red Cross, 744.
  Volunteer, for service in, 958, 959.
Obligations contracted in regard to conferences between Aguinaldo and U. S. military commander, 823.
Obligations of U. S. Government to inhabitants of Manila, under articles of capitulation, 824.
Obsolete cannon—
  Property of Spain, 989.
  Use in States and for monuments, 987.
Occupation—
  American, necessity, 635–640, 676.
  Joint, objection to by Aguinaldo, 820.
  Joint, prohibited by U. S. Government, 813, 814, 819, 826.
  Lines of, not to be extended, 907.
  Of ports, prosecution by U. S. forces, 864.
  Of various points, by U. S. forces, necessity for, 851, 852, 969, 1010, 1127, 1144.
O'Donnell, Luzon, casualties in action, 1104, 1227.
Office, appointment of Spaniards objected to, 1011.
Officers, commissioned—
  Allowance of baggage, increase for over-sea service, 865.
  Appointed treasurer, 985.
  Assignment as collectors of customs, 985.
  Assignment of brigade commanders, 689.
  Commendation by Gen. Merritt, 717.
  Designation for brig. gen. vol., 1176, 1177.
  Disabled, payment in advance of mileage, 706.
  Discharge or resignation, 1171, 1220, 1241.
  Discharge of regular holding volunteer commissions, 1243.
  Dismissals and reductions, 1241.
  Examination for appointment in Regular Army, 1257.
  Families not desired in, 930, 933, 1039, 1040, 1084, 1143, 1149.
  For Philippine expedition, 683, 688, 701, 765, 832, 834, 931.
  Home battalion, for invalided, 1143, 1144, 1147, 1148.

INDEX. 1449

Philippine Islands, affairs in—Continued.
Officers, commissioned—Continued.
  Horses, transportation not permitted, 925, 858, 859.
  Missing, 980, 997, 999, 1208.
  Investigation, 1140.
  Murdered by insurgents, 998, 1243.
  Punishment of murderers, 999.
  Promotion, 793.
  Recommended, 760, 785.
  Recruiting, detail and duties, 686, 687.
  Retention in, 1006, 1235, 1236, 1250.
  Staff—
    For Philippine expedition, 645, 653, 657, 667, 672, 686, 801, 804.
      Appointment, etc., 674.
    Recommendations for, 8th Army Corps, 706.
  To be sent to China and Asia points, 1171.
  Travel allowances for volunteers, 1004.
Olongapo, Luzon, casualties in action, 1263.
Operations—
  Against Spanish cooperation of insurgent, requested by American commanders, 805.
  Military difficulties attending, 963, 973, 975, 981, 1102, 1104, 1108, 1111, 1115, 1144, 1211, 1225, 1226, 1245, 1246.
  Military, preparation by American forces, 806, 953.
  Resumption of active military, 1053.
Orion, Luzon, casualties in action, 1161, 1162, 1182, 1218, 1225.
Ormoc, Leyte, casualties in action, 1250.
Oroquieta, Mindanao, casualties in action, 1195, 1209.
Osaka and Hiogo, Japan, shipment of arms to Aguinaldo, 867.
Otis, Gen. E. S., assumes command, 764, 783.
Outbreak, in Negros, caused by reported victories of insurgents, 1115.
Outlaws, insurgents who decline amnesty, to be declared, 1175.
Outlying districts, measures for protection, 1173.
Outposts, American encroachment upon by Filipinos, 822.
Pacific, Department of the—
  Discontinued, 1154.
  Established, 649.
  Gen. Merritt, assigned to command, 649, 652.
  Lieut. Col. Babcock, assigned as adjutant-general, 652.
Pacification, progress, 1237, 1244, 1251, 1253.
Paco, District of Manila—
  Difficulty experienced by Aguinaldo, in withdrawing from, 845.
  Illegal maintenance of insurgents at, 847.
Paete, Luzon, casualties in action, 1152, 1206.
Pagsajan, Luzon, casualties in action, 1146, 1203, 1212.
Palanan, Luzon—
  Capture of Aguinaldo at, 1262.
  Casualties in action, 1240.
Palanas, Masbate, casualties in action, 1219.
Palanig, Luzon, casualties in action, 1176.
Palistina, Luzon, casualties in action, 1197.
Pambujan, Samar, casualties in action, 1176.
Pamphlets—
  Anti-American, 973.
  Precautions against circulation of antigovernment, 976.
  Speeches, etc., defamatory of U. S., circulated among Filipinos and soldiers, 1137.
Pamplona, Luzon, casualties in action, 1182.
Panay Island—
  Conditions in, 1060, 1125.
  Dissensions between insurgent Tagalos and Visayans, 1077.
  Insurrection, terminated in, 1261.
  Northern, Tagalos driven from, 1122.
  Operations against insurgents, 1091, 1096, 1101, 1105-1108, 1111, 1116, 1120, 1122, 1125, 1133, 1134, 1139, 1222, 1223, 1232, 1245.
  Impeded by typhoons, 1098.
  Population flies to mountains, 1134.
  Surrender of insurgents, 1245, 1251, 1264.
  Termination of hostilities, 1260.
  Western coast, opened for trade, 1138.
Panda, Panay, casualties in action, 1219.
Pandacan, Luzon—
  Occupation by insurgents, reasons for, 849.
  Retention under jurisdiction of Filipinos requested, 848.

Philippine Islands, affairs in—Continued.
Panguil, Luzon, casualties in action, 1193, 1203.
Paniqui, casualties in action, 1128.
Panitan, Panay, casualties in action, 1143.
Pantijan, Luzon, casualties in action, 1231.
Paquil, Luzon, casualties in action, 1146.
Paragua Island, conditions, 919.
Paranas, Samar, casualties in action, 1176.
Paranaqui, U. S. troops to encamp in vicinity, 807.
Pardo, Cebu, casualties in action, 1052.
Paris treaty, Sulu Island not within line of cession, 1075.
Parole, given by insurgent soldiers, 1078.
Parole of Spanish officers, returning to Spain, 828.
Pasagoagan, Bohol, casualties in action, 1250.
Pasay, Luzon, construction of barracks, 1015.
Pasig, Luzon—
  Casualties in action, 937, 941.
  Engagement near, 938.
  Occupied by U. S. troops, 934.
Pasig River line, Luzon—
  Captured from insurgents, 981.
  Disturbances in country north and south, 1211.
  Effect of American occupation, 935.
  Engagements on, 934.
Passi, Panay, casualties in action, 1240.
Pasuquin, Luzon, casualties in action, 1227.
Pateros, Luzon—
  Casualties in action, 905, 936.
  Occupied by U. S. troops, 934.
  Skirmish at, 905.
Patnongon, Panay, casualties in action, 1148, 1173, 1174.
Pavia, Panay—
  Actions at, 1107, 1111.
  Casualties in action, 1107, 1111, 1117, 1195, 1215.
Payment, advance, of troops, 874, 876.
Payments to insurgents—
  For release of Spanish prisoners, 1044, 1046, 1072.
  Effect, 1046.
  Not to be permitted, 1049.
Payo, Isla Catanduanes, casualties in action, 1231.
Peace—
  Continuance desired by American commander, 877.
  Insurgents desire to arrange terms, 978, 988, 991.
  Philippine Commission's policy for establishing, 1002.
Peace, general, Filipinos will contribute to establishment, upon official recognition of their government, 888.
Peace Commission, Paris—
  Gen. Merritt, ordered to confer with, 765.
  Gen. Whittier, to report to, 828.
Peñaranda, Luzon, casualties in action, 1150, 1155.
Personal rights, guaranteed to insurgents, accepting amnesty, 1184.
Philippine Commission—
  Confidence of leading Filipinos gained by, 998.
  Differences in, and with military government, 1002.
  Instructions of President, 1158.
  Policy for terminating war, etc., 1002.
  Reception, 1158.
  Relations with military government, 998, 1002, 1158.
  Sails for Manila, 890, 892.
Philippine Republic—
  Aguinaldo proclaimed president, 886.
  Promulgation of political constitution by Aguinaldo, 888.
Picilla, Luzon, casualties in action, 1031.
Pili, Luzon, casualties in action, 1218.
Pilar, Luzon, casualties in action, 1233.
Point Baño, Luzon, casualties in action, 1229.
Polangui, Luzon, casualties in action, 1155.
Police, native, organization, 1245.
Policy, toward insurgents who accept amnesty, 1184.
Political situation, 649-652.
  Report by Consul Williams, 718.
Polo, Leyte—
  Casualties in action, 1187.
  Engagement near, 945.

Philippine Islands, affairs in—Continued.
Pompone, Luzon, casualties in action, 1250.
Ponape Island—
  Anchorages, condition of, 745.
  Armament, 745.
  Hostility of natives to Spaniards, 745.
  Spanish colony, number, condition, and defenses, 745.
Porac, Luzon—
  Abandoned by insurgents, 1050.
  Captured by U. S. troops, 1076.
  Casualties in action, 1076, 1081, 1087, 1096.
  Insurgent post near, capture, 1139.
Ports of entry—
  Closing, 1237, 1238, 1242, 1244, 1249-1251.
  Advantages accruing therefrom, 1242, 1244.
  Declared by Executive order, 985.
  Of Luzon, opened to Filipinos by American victories over Spanish forces, 824.
  Opened for trade, 1027, 1125, 1130, 1131.
  Under American control—
    Filipinos desire free entrance and departure, 817.
    Opened to commerce of all nations, 859.
  Under Spanish control, 833.
  Vessels other than American not permitted to enter, 1050.
Positions, ceded by insurgents, 814.
Positions, Spanish—
  Captured by Filipinos, 821.
  Claims to conquering, validity, 822.
Post exchanges, prohibition of sale of intoxicating liquors in, 1251.
Pototan, Panay, casualties in action, 1153.
Potable water, source, conceded by insurgents, 815.
Powers, limitations of U. S. commanders, 826.
President, Biscayan Republic, character and disposition, 928.
President of Filipino Republic, protest against U. S. intrusion, 913.
President of U. S.—
  Congratulations upon success in, 1002.
  Message in re treatment of Filipinos, 873.
  Policy compromised by speech of Gen. Merritt, 715.
  Proclamation—
    Effect in Iloilo of publication, 927.
    For suspension of hostilities, 750.
    Issuance to Filipinos, 868.
  Thanks to troops for conduct in Manila campaign, 759.
Press—
  Censor, no discrimination by, 881.
  Dispatches from Manila to be censored, 878.
  Messages, copies required by military governor, 1229.
  Reports held at Manila, 1261.
Priest, native, removal by American military authorities, 1238, 1239.
Priests and nuns, barbarous treatment by insurgents, 831.
  Release of, endeavors for, 831, 886.
Priests, Filipino, mixed up in revolt in Negros, 1123.
Prisoner of war beheaded by insurgents, 1153.
Prisoners of insurgents—
  American authorities to assist in release of Spanish, 1008.
  American course in relation to, 1098.
  Harm done to, insurgents to be responsible for, 1098.
  Measures for recovery, 1097.
  Number American, 921.
  Number Spanish, 806.
  Spanish and American—
    Location, 1111.
    Release from insurgents, 1110, 1112, 1115.
  Spanish, in hands of Tagals, release urged by Spanish Government, 885.
Private property—
  Disposition under amnesty, 1184.
  Protection by U. S. forces, 859.
  Transference to Aguinaldo, status, 810.
Privileges extended to prisoners at Manila, 1185.
Procedure of American generals in regard to Filipinos. effect on intercourse, 912.
Proclamation regarding occupation, 676-678.
  Administration of affairs, avoidance of conflict, 678.

Philippine Islands, affairs in—Continued.
Proclamation regarding churches, schoolhouses, etc., protection, 677.
Confiscation, state and private property, 677.
Contributions, levying, exercise of right, 677.
Enemy's territory, effect of occupation, 676.
  Inhabitants' rights, 676.
Expenses government, defrayment, 677.
Justice, administration under U. S. occupancy, 677.
Law and order, measures for preservation, 677.
Military occupant, powers, 676.
Municipal laws, continuance, 677.
Native officials, retention in office, 677.
Occupation by U. S., purpose, 676.
Peace with Spain, measures to further, 676.
People, freedom of, abridgment, 677.
Ports and places open to commerce of all neutral nations, 678.
Private rights, laws relating to, continuance of, 677.
Property, treatment of, 677, 678.
Revenue measures, formulation, 678.
Revenues, collection, 677.
Taxes and duties, payable to military occupant, 677.
Transportation, means of, retention, 677.
U. S. authority, acceptance of, necessary to holding of judicial offices, 677.
Proclamation—
  American reception by Spanish and Filipinos, 872.
  By Aguinaldo, 872, 910, 912.
  Dec. 20, effect, 1258.
  Gen. Luna, directs burning of all abandoned towns, 949.
  Insurgent leader, directing uprising against American forces, 913.
  Issuance to Filipinos, 872.
  Of amnesty, preparation and issue, 1175, 1177, 1179-1181.
  Commission, effect, 960.
  President, suspending hostilities, receipt at Manila, 750, 756.
  Providing for establishment of civil government, to be submitted to Sec. of War, 1065.
  Regarding observance laws of war, 1237.
Prohibition against landing arms, 841.
Property—
  Disposition, 966.
  In Manila, destruction by incendiary fire, 915.
  No confiscation by U. S. troops, 809.
  Occupation by U. S. troops objected to, 810.
  Ownership, 941, 942.
  Public and private, treatment, 859.
  Public movable, delivery requested by Spanish Government, 963.
  Spanish Government, disposition, 974.
  U. S. Government insures safety of lives and, of Filipinos, 824.
Prostitution, houses of, licensing, or protection, 1246, 1247.
Protection—
  Against insurgents requested, 982, 999, 1011.
  American, desired by mass of Filipinos, 1019.
  Of towns, measures for, 1077.
  Requested, causes wide dissemination of American forces, 1053.
Protest, Aguinaldo's, against proclamation of Gen. Otis, 912.
Protocol—
  Between Spain and U. S., prisoners, 750, 751.
  Hostilities, suspension, 751.
  Ladrones group, island in, to be ceded to U. S., 751.
  Manila, city, bay, and harbor, to be held by U. S., 751.
Protocols of 1877 and 1885, application of, to trade with Sulu Islands, 1099.
Provinces of northwestern Luzon, garrisons, 575, 578.
Provincial governments, establishment, cause conflict with insurgents, 807.
  Recommended, 802.
Provisional government, establishment by Americans, probable effect, 781.
Provost guard, composition, 557-561, 563-564, 568, 571, 573-575, 577, 579.

INDEX. 1451

Philippine Islands, affairs in—Continued.
Public funds—
Appropriation for sick soldiers at Manila, 835.
Received, expended, etc., at Manila, 884.
Spanish, disposition, 974.
U. S. officials connected with, necessity for retention, 791.
Public means of transportation, reserved to U. S. Government, 859.
Public misconception in U. S., created by allegations, Manila press correspondents, 1065, 1066.
Public or quasi-public works, grants or concessions for construction, regulations for, 861.
Public property, certificates for volunteer officers, 1235.
Public property and state revenues, pass to U. S., with cession, 859.
Public records, delivery requested by Spanish Government, 963.
Pulilan, Luzon, casualties in action, 1161, 1162.
Pumping station near Manila—
Attack on, 944.
Casualties in action, 926, 945.
Engagement at, 906.
Puruyan, Mount, Luzon, casualties in action, 1185.
Putol, barrio, Luzon, casualties in action, 1132.
Quadruple alliance, hopes of insurgents fixed on, between powers of Europe, 1098.
Quarters—
Extra, at posts, to be occupied by families of officers on foreign service, 842.
Officers, line, authorized, 787.
Scarcity, at Manila for officers' families, 1149.
Quiangan, Luzon, casualties in action, 1151.
Quingua, Luzon—
Casualties in action, 972
Engagement at, 972.
Reconnaissance to, 972.
Quingua River, Luzon, engagement along, 973.
Quiom, Luzon, casualties in action, 1243, 1254.
Railroad—
Condition from Bamban to Dagupan, 1104.
Destruction by insurgents, 994, 1097, 1100, 1103.
Insurgent director, captured, 1108.
Reconstruction by U. S. troops, 1101, 1103.
Railroads or tramways, grants of franchises for construction, 861.
Railway and telegraph lines, destruction, 950.
Railway mail service, equipment with Philippine expedition, 695, 696.
Rainy season—
Effect on troops, communication, 1034.
Precludes military operations and impedes business, 1031, 1033.
Rapid-fire guns, insurgent measures to procure in Europe, 1055.
Ration—
Emergency, not suitable to Tropics, 1051.
For troops serving in tropical climates, 984.
Issue of, exceptional for convalescents, 1200, 1201.
Issue to Spanish prisoners, 811.
Modification of soldier's, 797, 1000.
Reasons for acceptance by U. S., 873.
Recognition—
By U. S. military governor of national or civil powers, 910.
Insurgents expectant of European, 1050.
Recommendations—
For brevets, 766.
Harbor defenses of Manila, 841.
Medal of honor, for 8th Army Corps, 1025.
Gen. Funston, for brig. gen., U. S. A., 1263.
Officers, 760, 785.
Ration for troops, 1000.
Regarding expedition, 643, 645-648.
Reconnaissance in vicinity of Manila, Aguinaldo requested to facilitate, 810.
Records, captured insurgent, to be forwarded to Washington, 1134.
Recruiting—
Home battalion, scheme for, 1226.
In States, for volunteer regiments, 1014, 1029.
Recruiting parties—
Composition, 686.
Detail to raise maximum strength, 686.
Instructions for officers, 687.

Philippine Islands, affairs in—Continued.
Recruits—
Assignment of surplus, 1074, 1077.
Equipment, 717.
Number required to fill companies, 1026.
Organization for discipline, 996.
Red Cross Society, transportation of trained nurses, 744, 799.
Red Cross Society of Hawaii, soldiers cared for by, 731.
Red Cross supplies, landing at San Francisco, refused by custom authorities, 830.
Reenforcements—
Need for, in Luzon, 1158.
Needed for Jolo and Zamboanga, 1105.
Reenlistments, 1014.
Advice of newspaper and State against, effect on soldiers, 970.
Bounty for, 1237.
Dispatches, etc., tending to discourage, 973.
Of volunteers, 935, 1002-1004, 1054.
Under G. O., 67, s. 99, 1034.
Refrigerating plant, construction at Manila, 924-926.
Regiments—
Additional required, 1053.
Organization, 1004, 1005, 1020, 1028-1030, 1038, 1042, 1047.
Regular Army, appointments to, 1264.
Regular regiments, condition as to absentees, etc., 841.
Reenlistments in, 1000.
Relations, insurgent, with U. S. authorities, desire for continuance of friendly, 844.
Relations military government with Philippine Commission, 998.
Relations with U. S.—
Avoidance by Aguinaldo of rupture, 911.
Rupture of, explained by Aguinaldo, 910.
Religious liberty not to be interfered with, 1184.
Religious orders—
Cruel treatment by insurgents, 804.
Disposition of property, 1145.
No public funds to be used for support, 1184.
Reinstatement, 1145.
Relations with military government, 1145.
U. S. supervision over property, 1145.
Repatriation of Spanish prisoners, civil and military, 1040.
Replacement of troops, 924.
Reports, American consul's, difficulty in transmitting, 650, 651.
Report of operations, rendition 1083.
Representatives of Aguinaldo, Admiral Dewey refuses to receive, 821.
Republic of U. S., policy regarding legitimate holdings in, 826.
Requisitions for means of transportation, Aguinaldo to assist in supplying, 811.
Restraint of insurgent hostilities against Spaniards, 788.
Retention of officers, connected with public funds, necessity for, 791.
Retention of volunteers, 964.
Returns, monthly, of troops to be rendered from all stations, 867.
Revenues, 891
Decrease of, due to blockaded ports, 1015.
Insurgent source of, interdicted by U. S. possession, 1019.
Receipts, monthly diminution, 827.
Revolt in Negros Island—
Caused by Hongkong junta, 1123.
Character, 1116.
Revolution, declaration by Aguinaldo, 787.
Revolutionary councils, influence of certain Filipinos on, 827.
Revolutionary forces, assistance due U. S. troops from, through sense of justice, 824.
Revolutionary government—
Admit that destruction of Spanish fleet influenced the progress of their arms, 911.
Agitation due to removal of Filipinos from Manila defenses, 848.
American authorities refuse to recognize the so-called, 908.
Desire of members for conference with General Otis, 876.
Dissensions among members, 840.

Philippine Islands, affairs in—Continued.
Revolutionary government—Continued.
Division of cabinet, 836.
Loan for, 840.
Majority favor submission to U. S. authority, 851.
Territory ruled by, 911.
Why representatives not officially received, 910.
Revolutionary priest, justification for acting without observance of rules of intercourse, 912.
Revolutionary proclamation, reason for issuance, 876.
Revolutionary republic [?], Aguinaldo, self-proclaimed president, 720.
Revolutionary troops, attitude toward U. S. forces, 910.
Rifles, payment for surrendered, 1262.
Rio Cagayan Mindanao, casualties in action, 1206.
Rio Chico de Pampanga, Luzon—
American civilian killed by insurgents, 1090.
Casualties in action on, 1234.
Rio Grande, Luzon, casualties in action, 1206.
Engagement at, 977.
Passage by U. S. forces, 977.
Rio Suribao, Samar, casualties in action, 1253.
Road building—
Allotment of funds for, 1206.
Payments, how made, 1199.
Measures for, 1186, 1187.
Roads and bridges, necessity for, and cost, 1173.
Robber bands—
Actions with American troops, 1044, 1079, 1090.
Robber casualties, 1090.
Activity in islands, 1148.
Arms, stock, etc., captured from, 1035, 1037.
Dispersed in northern Luzon, 1130.
Increase in numbers, 999.
Scattering in Negros Island, 1035, 1037, 1059.
Robberies and murders committed by guerrillas and ladrones, 1159.
Romblon Island—
Casualties in action, 1126.
Garrisoned by U. S. troops, 1122.
Insurgents in, surrendering arms, 1126.
Rosario, Luzon—
Casualties in action, 1082, 1113, 1188.
Engagement at, 1082.
Rotation of service, 1144.
Sabang, Leyte, casualties in action, 1250.
Saloons, licensed, number and character, 1150.
Salvacion, Luzon, casualties in action, 1203.
Samar Island—
Attitude of inhabitants, 935.
Casualties in engagements on, 1165.
Conditions, 1164.
Insurgents driven into mountains, 1141.
Occupation of hemp ports, 1139, 1141.
Operations in, 1222, 1223, 1232.
Sampaloc, Luzon, casualties in action, 1149, 1150.
San Antonio, Luzon, casualties in action, 1251, 1263.
San Blas, Panay, casualties in action, 1209.
San Diego, Luzon—
Engagement at, 1138.
Casualties, 1138.
San Fabian, Luzon—
Action near, 1101.
Casualties, 1101.
Insurgents driven from, 1097.
San Felipe, Luzon, casualties, 931.
San Fernandino, casualties in action, 1017.
San Fernando de Dilao, Manila, occupation by Filipinos, 817.
San Fernando, Luzon—
Attack on U. S. forces, 982, 1013.
Casualties in action, 982, 1013, 1021, 1026, 1031, 1044, 1049, 1050–1052, 1055–1057, 1060–1064, 1081.
Engagement in vicinity, 995.
Fired by insurgents, 983.
Insurgents retreat from, to Tarlac, 991.
Members of picket post near, killed by insurgents, 1079.
Reconnoissance from, 1079.
American casualties, 1079.
San Francisco, Luzon, casualties in action, 1146, 1147, 1152.

Philippine Islands, affairs in—Continued.
San Francisco de Malabon, Luzon—
Casualties in action, 1085, 1256.
Insurgents driven from, 1084.
Surrender of insurgents, 1259.
San Gregorio, Luzon, casualties in action, 1234.
San Ignacio, Luzon, casualties in action, 1237.
San Ildefonso, Luzon, casualties in action, 1234.
San Isidro, Luzon—
Action on road to, 1087.
Casualties, 1087.
Aguinaldo and government in mountains near, 991.
Attitude of inhabitants in vicinity, 1087.
Casualties in action, 1052, 1092, 1190, 1222.
Insurgent capital captured by U. S. troops, 990.
Permanent station established near, 1089.
Sanitarium, U. S. Army, establishment within insurgent lines, 849.
San Jacinto—
Action at, and near, 1101, 1108.
Casualties, 1101.
San José, Luzon, casualties in action, 1160.
San José College, Manila, administration, 1141.
San José de Buenavista, Panay, casualties in action, 1160.
San José, Samar, casualties in action, 1162.
San José, insurgents driven from, 1100.
San Juan, Luzon, casualties in action, 1148.
San Juan del Siete, Mindanao, casualties in action, 1255.
San Luis, Luzon, casualties in action, 1038, 1052, 1057, 1147, 1148, 1261.
San Manuel, Luzon, casualties in action, 1166.
San Mateo, Luzon—
Capture by American troops, 1126.
Casualties in action, 1055, 1101, 1110, 1117, 1124, 1126, 1128, 1203, 1206.
San Mateo River, enlisted men drowned while crossing, 1057.
San Miguel de Mayumo, Luzon—
Casualties in action, 1161, 1166, 1173, 1174, 1196, 1220, 1257.
Engagement at and near, 1173, 1196.
Surrender of insurgents, 1253.
San Miguel Bay, Camarines, landing of Bates expedition, 1148.
San Miguel, Leyte, casualties in action, 1212, 1214.
San Miguel, Luzon, capture by U. S. forces, 988.
San Nicolas, Luzon—
Casualties in action at, 1082, 1085, 1087, 1113, 1137, 1243.
Engagement at, 1082.
San Nicolas-San Manuel road, skirmishes on, 1103.
San Pablo, Luzon, casualties in action, 1149, 1150, 1251.
San Pedro Macati—
Casualties in action, 915, 919, 920, 922, 924, 925, 931, 936, 943, 1057.
Skirmish near, 914.
San Pedro Magalang, Luzon, casualties in action, 1113.
San Quintin, Luzon—
Casualties in action, 1216, 1225.
Insurgents driven from, 1100.
San Rafael, insurgents driven from, 1066.
San Remedio, Panay, casualties in action, 1152.
San Roque, Luzon—
Casualties in action, 1234.
Occupied by U. S. troops, 899.
San Vicente, Luzon, casualties in action, 1233, 1257.
Santa Ana, Mindanao, casualties in action, 1085, 1254.
Santa Barbara, Panay, insurgents driven from, 1106, 1107.
Santa Cruz, Egaña, Panay, casualties in action, 1182.
Santa Cruz, Laguna, casualties in action, 1182.
Santa Cruz, Luzon, casualties in action, 1146, 1150, 1198, 1220, 1231.
Santa Cruz, Marinduque—
Disappearance of reconnoitering party from, 1214.
Measures for relief, 1214.
Santa Cruz—
Captured by U. S. troops, 961.

INDEX. 1453

Philippine Islands, affairs in—Continued.
Santa Cruz—Continued.
  Casualties in action, 961, 962, 1031.
  Dispersion of insurgents in vicinity, 963.
  Engagement with ladrones at, 1135.
  Evacuated by insurgents, 1138.
  Occupied by U. S. troops, 1139.
Santa Fe, Leyte, casualties in action, 1202.
Santa Lucia, Cebu, casualties in action, 1256.
Santa Lucia, Luzon—
  Casualties in action, 1176.
  Engagements near, 1138.
Santa Maria, Luzon, surrender of Katipunan insurrectos, 1232.
Santa Rio, casualties in action, 1064.
Santa Rita, Samar—
  Action near, 1087, 1088.
  Capture by U. S. troops, 1051.
  Casualties in action, 1055.
  Insurgent demonstration against, 1066.
  Reconnaissances in vicinity, 1051.
Santa Rosa—
  Casualties in action, 1090, 1128.
  Engagement near, 1090.
Santiago, Luzon—
  Casualties in action, 1146.
  Engagement at, 713.
Santo Tomas, Batangas, casualties in action, 1147.
Santo Tomas, Luzon, casualties in action, 1131, 1137, 1243.
Santo Tomas—
  Casualties in action, 983, 1132, 1135, 1146.
  Destroyed by fire by insurgents, 983.
  Engagement near, 1132.
  Pack train ambushed near, 1135.
Sariaya, Tayabas, casualties in action, 1145, 1148, 1195, 1198, 1203, 1225.
Savagery of insurgents, causes desperation among Filipinos, 1035.
Schedule of tariff, 804.
Schools, superintendent of, Manila, Chaplain McKinnon performing duties, 923.
Schwan's expedition, operations, 1082–1086, 1128, 1129, 1131–1133, 1135, 1136.
Scouts, native, organization, 1245.
Secret clubs in Manila, endeavors to foment discord, 872.
Secretary of War congratulates Army on victory, 897.
Self-government, capacity of Filipinos, 836.
Senate of U. S., report of casualties desired by, 890.
Service, length of tour, 854.
Service in, rotation in, 1144.
Settlement of Spanish civil affairs, 875.
Siassi, Tawi-Tawi group, American occupation, 1074.
Sibalon, Panay, casualties in action, 1227.
Sibul, Luzon—
  Advance on, 1127.
  Casualties in action, 1182.
Sick and convalescent, return to U. S., 1017, 1021, 1195, 1227, 1234, 1235, 1244.
Sick and wounded—
  Necessity for additional supplies, 1198.
  Return to U. S., 1204.
  Disposition on arrival, 926.
Sickness and casualties among troops in, 795, 827.
Sick report of troops, 1214, 1219, 1224, 1228, 1232, 1235, 1241, 1246, 1250, 1254, 1257, 1259.
Silang, Luzon—
  Captured by U. S. troops, 1129, 1131.
  Casualties in action, 1148, 1257, 1259.
Silang Line, Luzon, insurgents driven from position north, 1131.
Simms-Dudley dynamite guns, for troops in, 1038, 1039.
Sinait, Luzon, casualties in action, 1212, 1222.
Singalon road, Luzon, complaint of presence of insurgents on, 846.
Siniloan, Luzon, casualties in action, 1176, 1198.
Situation, improvement in, 675, 1157.
Situation, presentation of, to Aguinaldo, 826.
Skirmishes, Jan. 1–Mar. 31, 1900, number and casualties, 1156.
Slavery in Sulu Archipelago—
  Character of, 1118.

Philippine Islands, affairs in—Continued.
Slavery in Sulu Archipelago—Continued.
  Course of action looking to abolition, 1118.
  Existence and extent, 1117.
  Instructions to Gen. Bates regarding character, extent, etc., 1117.
  Neither authorized nor recognized, 1118.
Slaves, market price, 1118.
Soldiers—
  Ambushed, killed, and mutilated, 1059.
  Captured by insurgents, 1214.
  Discharge at San Francisco, 1093, 1094.
  Killing by pretended pacificos, treatment, 1206.
Sorsogon, Luzon, casualties in action, 1214, 1235.
Southern islands—
  Conditions, 836, 852, 908.
  Excitement sustained by stories of insurgent victories, 997.
  Garrisons, where should be located, 908.
  Measure to allay excitement, 994.
  Occupation of hemp ports, 852, 1139.
  Operations, 1110, 1141.
  Petition for U. S. occupancy, 927.
Southern Luzon, department—
  Headquarters, establishment, 1167.
  Maj. Gen. Bates assigned to command, 1154, 1155.
  Organization and limits, 1077, 1154.
  Modification, 1166, 1167, 1170.
Sovereignty, American, Aguinaldo's protest against, 913.
Release of insurgent generals, accepting, 1185.
Unity of U. S. citizens in case of attack on, 826.
"Sovereignty," effect on Filipinos, of word, 908.
Spain—
  No just claim for arms recaptured from insurgents, 1188.
  Proclamation for suspension of hostilities, 750.
  Return of Spanish troops, 830, 838, 839.
  Right arm broken at battle of Manila Bay, 719.
  Sympathizers of, agitate fears of Filipinos, 843.
Spaniards—
  Attitude toward U. S. Government, 1011.
  Declaration of allegiance to U. S., time for, 1161.
  Effect on Americans' position by premature evacuation of southern islands, 927.
  Expulsion, effect on conditions, 719.
  In Manila, endeavor to defeat ratification of treaty, 878.
  Insurgents protest against filling of offices by, 815.
  Natives of Ponope hostile to, 745.
  Passing through insurgent lines will be considered spies, 816.
  Restraint of insurgent hostilities against, 788.
  Sentiment against Americans intensified by insurgents and, 878, 886.
  Source of trouble experienced by U. S. authorities, 860.
Spanish—
  Barbarities, 718.
  Casualties, 997.
  Natives of Iloilo advised by, to resist foreign nations, 872.
  Opinions of American proclamation, 872.
Spanish authority, condition at Iloilo, Panay, 853.
Spanish authorities—
  Aguinaldo secretly negotiating with, 808.
  Connivance with insurgents, 980.
  Request delivery war material at Cavite, 1066.
Spanish authority in southern islands, precariousness of, 827.
Spanish captain-general summoned to Spain, 799, 800.
Spanish central government, movable public property remains to, 942.
Spanish civil affairs, settlement, 875.
Spanish civil prisoners, transportation to Spain, 1040.
Spanish colony at Ponope, number, condition, and defenses, 745.
Spanish commission, for release of Spanish prisoners, not treated with, by Aguinaldo, 1096.

Philippine Islands, affairs in—Continued.
Spanish domination, Filipinos demand suburbs of Manila in case of continuance, 817, 826.
Spanish fleet—
  Movements, uncertainty of, 712.
  Plans of American commanders in case of arrival at Manila, 780.
Spanish forces—
  Attack by insurgents at Zamboanga, cause, 1011.
  Composition, armament, and distribution, 645, 648.
  Concentrated at and surrounded in Iloilo, Panay, 836.
  Condition, 836.
  Cooperation of insurgents in operations against, 805.
  Effect upon, of American victories, 824.
  Estimated strength, 718, 719.
  Evacuation of certain stations, 862.
  Expulsion, claimed by insurgents, 911.
  Insubordination among native, 651.
  Military stations turned over to inhabitants, 864.
  Number, organization, distribution, 654, 655.
  Participation by insurgents in forcing surrender, 821, 911.
  Retirement from Manila forced by U. S. troops, 821.
Spanish funds and property in Manila, 765.
Spanish garrisons—
  Relief, by U. S. troops, 989, 991.
  To be held at southern points until arrival of U. S. troops, 980.
Spanish Government—
  Acknowledgment of cession of rights, 910.
  Agreement for suspension of hostilities, 750.
  Barbarities and cruelties practiced by, 652.
  Condition, 651.
  Evacuation of Mindoro and Jolo, 963.
  Duplicity in arranging for release of Spanish prisoners, 1050.
  Private claims against, 791.
  Relations with insurgents not countenanced by American Government, 1072.
  Requests delivery of funds, property, etc., 963, 964.
  Urges release of prisoners held by Tagalos, 885.
Spanish gunboats and transports, purchase for service in, 980, 1146.
Spanish insular bonds, disposition, 976.
Spanish intrigues with—
  Insurgents, trouble caused by, 1011.
  Sultan of Sulu, defeated by arrival American troops, 1011.
Spanish liquidation commission, delivery of all movable public property requested by, 963.
Spanish officers—
  Return to Spain on parole, 828.
  To retain side arms, horses, and private property, 757.
Spanish officials—
  Deposition from positions, 818.
  In hands of insurgents, escape of, 1022.
  Transportation to Spain, 1022, 1023.
Spanish prisoners in hands of insurgents—
  Care and condition, 1070, 1121.
  Direct official Spanish negotiation not countenanced by American Government, 1072.
  Instructions from Madrid regarding ransom, 1050.
  Intentions of insurgents with regard to, 1043, 1097.
  Release and measures for, 886, 941, 1011, 1040, 1042, 1043, 1045, 1049, 1053, 1072, 1088, 1090, 1096, 1097, 1100, 1109, 1111, 1116, 1120-1122, 1124, 1132, 1135, 1139, 1140, 1144, 1147-1149.
  Transportation to Spain, 1119, 1121, 1129.
Spanish prisoners of war—
  Confined temporarily within limits of walled city, 790.
  Danger of American troops contracting disease from, 830.
  Issue of rations to, 811.
  Number captured, repatriated, and remaining at Manila, 896.
  Desired by Secretary of War, 893.

Philippine Islands, affairs in—Continued.
Spanish prisoners of war—Continued.
  Repatriation, 799, 800, 830, 833, 850, 895, 904, 916, 920, 921, 976, 995, 1014, 1069, 1133, 1134, 1139, 1151, 1158.
  No vessels available for, 886.
  Transportation to Spain, 964, 965.
    Expense account, 987, 1013.
    Vessels for, use and disposition, 964, 967, 968.
Spanish position and strength, reconnoissance of, 808.
Spanish reserve fleet, movements and strength, 705.
Spanish residents, plotting to inaugurate hostilities between forces of U. S. and insurgents, 827.
Spanish responsibility in, duration, 919.
Spanish sovereignty, suspension effected by American victories, 858.
Spanish subjects, interests of, confided to French consul, 920.
Spanish tariff, no codification, 804.
Spanish troops—
  Armament and equipment, 654-656, 665, 675, 757.
  Besieged by insurgents, 988, 989.
  Casualties at Zamboanga, 988.
  Discipline and efficiency, 676.
  Evacuation of Iloilo, 862.
  Number, condition, disposition, 654, 655, 665, 675, 691, 778, 988, 989.
  Proportion, white and native, 654, 656, 676.
  Relations with insurgents, 980.
  Repatriation, 873, 976, 991, 995.
Spies, Spaniards passing through lines without permission considered as, 816.
Spoils of war, existence not recognized by U. S., 825.
Storms prevent landing troops and loading transports, 1031.
Strategic points—
  Occupation of, directed, 863, 1127.
  Surreptitiously turned over to Filipinos by Spaniards, 864.
Subig, Luzon, casualties in action, 1141, 1228, 1231, 1237.
Subig Bay, Luzon—
  Advantages in case of reverse by Spaniards, 780.
  Insurgents driven from country, 1120.
  Naval station occupied by marines, 1120.
Submarine mines not practicable in Manila Bay, 674, 694.
Subsistence supplies—
  Character and quantity, 952.
  For Army and Navy, 1005.
Substitute of ration, issue for convalescents, 1201.
Sulu, Sultan of—
  Agreement with Gen. Bates, 1027, 1058, 1117.
  Conditional approval, 1117.
  Anxious for Americans to replace Spaniards, 918.
  Intrigue with Spaniards defeated by arrival American troops, 1011.
Sulu Archipelago—
  American troops placed in, 1060.
  Dattos desire to raise American flag on, 1075.
  Evacuation by Spaniards, 916.
  Free trade in, 1094.
  Insurgent plotting and trade subject causing trouble in, 1099.
  Navigation and commerce of, treatment of by U. S., 1099.
  Situation, 916, 1074.
  Slavery—
    Existence and extent, 1118.
    Neither authorized nor recognized, 1118.
Sulug, engagement near, 1126.
Sumilao, Mindanao, surrender of insurgents, 1264.
Superintendent of schools, appointment, 923.
Supplies for troops, etc., 639-641, 680, 794, 949, 970, 1012, 1039, 1048, 1049, 1127, 1180, 1182.
  Not to be furnished except on Aguinaldo's order, 809.
  Requisitions on Filipinos, 811.
  Sufficiency and character, 676, 779, 929, 951.
Surigao, Mindanao, closing of port, 1249-1251.

Philippine Islands, affairs in—Continued.
Surrendered territory, duties of American commander re, 826.
Surrenders, eastern Mindanao, offered to U. S. 1076.
Taal, Luzon—
Casualties in action, 1136, 1141, 1189, 1255.
Engagement at, 1136.
Tabaco, Luzon—
Casualties in action, 1184, 1187.
Closing of port, 1249, 1250, 1251.
Tabuan, Negros Island, casualties in action, 1067, 1079, 1087.
Tacloban, Leyte—
American occupation, 1141.
Casualties in action, 1166, 1225.
Engagement at, 1141.
Tagalo insurrection, effect of surrender Cavite province, 1027.
Tagalog domination, necessity for supplanting, 1069.
Tagalog people, relations with U. S. military government, 1145.
Tagals—
Release of prisoners of, urged by Spanish Government, 885.
Severely punished in Negros Island, 1059.
Tagatay, Luzon, casualties in action, 1191.
Tagudin, Luzon, casualties in action, 1160.
Taguig, Luzon—
Attack on U. S. troops, 977.
Casualties near, 940, 941.
Insurgents cleared from, 1007.
Talavera, Luzon—
American soldiers ambushed near, 1196.
Casualties in action, 1196, 1222.
Tanauan, Batangas, casualties in action, 1192.
Tanauan, Leyte, casualties in action, 1140, 1163, 1201, 1214.
Tangadan Mountain, Luzon, casualties in action, 1124, 1137, 1147, 1148.
Tangalan, Panay, casualties in action, 1153.
Tariff and customs regulations, working, 738, 843.
Tariff revision, report of board, 1207.
Tariff schedule, 804.
Tarlac, Luzon—
Captured by U. S. troops, 1100.
Casualties in action, 1127.
Insurgent force at, diminished, 994.
People looking for advance of American troops, 1035.
Surrender of insurgents at, 1171, 1172, 1180.
Tarlac Province, Luzon, Aguinaldo's troops driven from, and officials murdered, 866.
Taxes and duties, payable to U. S. authorities, 859.
Tayabas, Luzon—
Casualties in action, 1150.
Insurgents driven from, 1139.
Tayabas Province, Luzon, casualties in action, 1176.
Taysan, Luzon, casualties in action, 1163.
Tayug, Luzon—
Insurgents driven from, 1100.
Surrender of insurgent command, 1199.
Tayum, Luzon—
Engagement near, 1251.
Casualties, 1251.
Telegraph or telephone lines, concessions or grants for construction, 861.
Telegraphic communication, establishment, 1107.
Terragona, Leyte, casualties in action, 1251.
Territory—
In rightful possession of U. S., 825, 849.
Occupied by American troops, misunderstanding as to limits, 845.
Occupied, holding by American forces, 1245.
Seizure by U. S., Filipino view, 912.
Teson, Panay, casualties in action, 1240.
Tiamo, Luzon, casualties in action, 1192.
Tibaguin, Luzon, casualties in action, 1187, 1191.
Tibuan, Negros Island—
Casualties in action, 1056.
Insurgents routed by American troops, 1056.
Tila Pass, Luzon, casualties in action, 1124.
Tinuba, Luzon, casualties in action, 1148.

Philippine Islands, affairs in—Continued.
Toboatin Bridge, Luzon, casualties in action, 1112.
Topographical features, 656.
Towns burned by insurgents, 950.
Trade conditions—
In Sulu Archipelago, trouble caused by, 1099.
Investigation, 828, 829, 1148.
Trade privileges, effect on Filipinos of interdiction, 1049.
Trade restrictions, relaxation extended without discrimination, 825.
Transfer, enlisted men from regiments ordered to, 861.
Transfers, to Hosp. Corps, 1193
Transportation—
Families of officers and men 863.
Light batteries, and mountain guns, 936, 937.
Means of, Aguinaldo's assistance in obtaining, requested, 810, 811.
Requirements, 778, 798–800, 807, 852–856, 860, 921, 957, 958, 1028, 1032, 1087, 1209, 1210, 1224, 1229, 1230.
Volunteers reenlisting, 1003.
Travel pay, men discharged not to receive, 932.
Treasury deposits, delivery requested by Spanish Government, 963.
Treaty of peace—
Acknowledgments contained in, 910.
Confirmation, Spanish responsibility continues until, 919.
Control, disposition, and government ceded to U. S., 858.
Declaration by Spaniards, of allegiance under, 1161.
Disposition of Manila suburbs under, 819.
Endeavors of Spaniards in Manila to defeat ratification, 878.
Filipinos' demands in case conclusion, 821.
Shipment of Spanish prisoners under, 920.
Spaniards endeavor to defeat ratification, 878.
Trenches, insurgent, occupation by U. S. troops, 812.
Trinidad, movement of insurgents toward, 1106.
Troops—
Calls for, from Southern ports, 862.
Casualties, number, and cause, report desired by U. S. Senate, 890.
Changes in ration, 794.
Condition as to efficiency, etc., 874.
Measures necessary to maintain, 1167.
Conduct commended by Filipinos, 860.
Conduct in engagement at Manila, 894.
Credit due for victory at Manila, 898.
Extensive distribution, necessitates concentration at central points 1173.
Health and comfort, provisions for, 759, 960.
Hospital ship for Manila, 766.
Hospitals, establishment, 756.
Instruction and discipline, 734, 776.
Monthly return, rendition from all stations, 867, 1035.
Necessary for suppression of insurrection, 836, 1051.
Occupation of southern islands, 980.
Required for holding, 839, 908, 969, 1003, 1020, 1173.
Required for permanent garrison, 840.
Supplies and equipment, 680, 734, 758, 761, 764, 779, 797, 871, 874, 887, 888, 924, 952.
Suspension of shipment under protocol, 751.
Work of, causes gratification, 944.
Tropical climates, rations for troops serving, 984.
Tropical service, insurgents, preparation of, for, 838.
Trust fund, for disabled soldiers, widows, and orphans, establishment, 1184.
Tubangan, Panay, casualties in action, 1225.
Typhoons, interfere with movement of troops, 1031, 1033, 1046.
Ubay, Bohol, garrison threatened by insurgents, 1206.
Umbao, Luzon, casualties in action, 1232.
Uniform—
Issue of defective, to troops, 1028.
Khaki procured in U. S., unfit for issue, 1024.
Supply for troops in, 901, 902, 1028, 1042.
United States—
Attitude of insurgents toward, 719, 786, 806.

Philippine Islands, affairs in—Continued.
United States—Continued.
Desires of Chief Executive, regarding conditions, 850.
Filipinos allowed to depart for, 1044.
Insurgents must recognize military occupation and authority, 754.
Natives of Iloilo, advised by Spaniards to resist authority, 872.
Obligations, purpose to discharge, 676.
Proclamation suspending hostilities, 750.
Purpose of occupation, 676.
Reconnoissance of approaches to Manila, 807.
Sanitary precautions, 806.
Sentiment of Aguinaldo toward, 807, 809.
Spaniards misrepresent intentions, 878.
United States authorities—
Alleged promise to Aguinaldo, 913.
Decrease of friction with insurgents, 843.
United States commander—
Aguinaldo's military leadership recognized, 809.
Attitude toward insurgents, 805.
Duties, 826.
Position not understood by Aguinaldo, 910.
Power and duties, 826, 910.
Rifles distributed to Filipinos by, 911.
United States Philippine Commission—
Constitution, 883.
Reported disagreement with Gen. Otis, 996.
United States control, effect of words on Filipinos, 908.
United States consuls, trouble caused by intermeddling, 909.
United States forces—
Attitude toward inhabitants, 858.
Commander ignores Aguinaldo's assumption of civil authority, 809.
Joint demand for withdrawal of insurgents, 788.
Not to pass insurgent lines without permission, 815.
Purpose as claimed by Aguinaldo, 913.
Requisition for means of transportation, etc., 806, 807, 809.
Territory in rightful possession, under terms of armistice, 825.
Unarmed, to be permitted to pass through insurgent lines, 816.
Weakness, 969.
Would be aided by all natives and almost all foreigners, 719.
United States Government—
Acts of, denounced by Aguinaldo as cause for hostilities, 912.
Aguinaldo's appeal to, 821.
Attitude toward insurgents, 805, 815, 818, 820, 872, 910, 1097.
Can not share nor delegate power of administering civil affairs of Manila, 825.
Capability constantly prejudiced by Spanish prisoners of war and citizens, 872.
Commander, merely agent of, 910.
Control, disposition, and government, ceded by treaty of peace to, 858.
Demand for withdrawal of insurgents from municipal area of Manila, 911.
Does not recognize existence of spoils of war, 825.
Duties and powers, 754, 910.
Effect of declination of Filipinos to comply with demands, 826.
Extension of military government, 858.
Friendship professed by Aguinaldo, 817.
Furtherance of Filipino interest desired by, 910.
Indignities suffered from insurgents, 847.
Instructions prohibiting joint occupation of Manila and its suburbs, 826.
Insults by insurgents, responsibility for, 847.
Intrusion protested against by Aguinaldo, 913.
Mission, 807, 858, 859.
Misunderstanding with insurgent representatives and, 910.
Obligations preclude granting of concessions demanded by Aguinaldo, 826.
Obligations under articles of capitulation, 824, 1119.
Policy toward Filipino, 840, 910, 927.

Philippine Islands, affairs in—Continued.
United States Government—Continued.
Preservation of peace and protection of persons and property, 826.
Protection demanded for Filipino vessels, intent not stated, 825.
Purposes of, 866, 876, 1177, 1179.
Reasons for war with Spanish Government, 824.
Right to hold and administer affairs of Manila conceded by insurgents, 824.
Unanimity of commanders in enforcing demands, 827.
United States lines not to be extended, 812.
United States naval commander, jurisdiction and scope of authority, 826.
United States officers—
Arrests by, to preserve domestic tranquillity, 825.
Unarmed, arrested, and turned back to Manila by insurgents, 846.
United States sovereignty—
Amnesty for insurgents who accept, 1175, 1177.
Not to be acknowledged by insurgents longer than necessity demands, 816.
United States troops—
Acquirement of booty, etc., forbidden, 825.
Demand for their retirement within the city, 821.
Disease, danger of contraction, from Spanish prisoners, 830.
Landed at Cavite, Luzon, 720.
Landing, prevention of foreign interference with, 713.
Means of transportation, Aguinaldo requested to furnish, 811.
Filipinos refuse to furnish, 808.
Needed for conquest and occupancy, 719.
Occupation of warehouse objected to by Aguinaldo, 810.
Opinion of officers regarding Filipinos, 818.
Placing of guns in insurgent trenches, 812.
Relations with insurgents, 813.
Retirement to lines designated by Aguinaldo, 826.
Uprising of Filipinos, proclamation directing, against Americans, 913.
Valderrama, Panay, casualties in action, 1160.
Veterinary surgeons and farriers, 1043.
Vice-consuls, U. S., recommendations for appointment, 798.
Vigan, Luzon—
American occupation, 851.
Casualties in action, 1114, 1124, 1137.
Engagement at, 1114.
Landing of naval forces, 1111.
Reception by inhabitants, 1111.
Rumored capture by insurgents, 787.
Villavieja, Luzon, casualties in action, 1203.
Vintar, Luzon, casualties in action, 1225.
Visayan cable lines, recognition requested of Spanish subsidy, 965.
Viscayan Islands—
Activity of insurgents, 1165.
American occupation effect, 912.
Conditions, 969, 1029.
Disposition toward U. S. troops, 1107.
Troops required for, 960.
Use of native organizations, 969.
Visayas, department of the—
Brig. Gen. Hughes assigned to command, 1154, 1155.
Organization and limits, 1077, 1154, 1155.
War contributions, Aguinaldo endeavoring to levy, 851.
War material at Cavite—
Deemed property of Spain, 1076.
Spanish authorities request delivery, 1066.
War with Spain, why undertaken by U. S., 824.
Water supply—
Distillation and supply to camps, etc., 692, 696.
Expenses for machine and waterworks, 696.
Waterworks, near Manila—
Captured from insurgents, 896.
Delay in opening, 819.
Object of Aguinaldo in permitting use by U. S. troops, 820.
To be opened by Filipinos, 816-819.
Wharves, available sites for construction, 1045.

INDEX. 1457

Philippine Islands, affairs in—Continued.
  Wheaton's expedition, operations, 962, 963, 1016, 1092, 1095–1097, 1100, 1101, 1104, 1106, 1108–1110, 1128, 1129, 1131, 1132, 1135, 1136.
  Withdrawal of insurgents—
    As a means of preventing friction, 849.
    From Manila not made as requested, 846.
  Works, public or quasi-public, grants, etc., for construction, 861.
  Yap Island, harbor, anchorages and defenses, 746.
  Yokohama, Japan, hospital for Philippine troops, 756.
  Young's expedition, operations, 1083, 1085–1087, 1089–1091, 1097, 1098, 1100, 1103, 1106, 1108–1111, 1113–1116, 1120, 1122, 1125, 1128, 1158, 1211, 1222, 1223.
  Zambales Province—
    Engagements in, 1126, 1138.
    Casualties, 1126, 1138.
    Insurgents in, operations of, 1104.
  Zamboanga, Mindanao—
    Arms, etc., surrendered by insurgents, 1110.
    Attack by insurgents, 1105.
    Attack by insurgents on Spanish troops at, 988.
    Cause of, 1011.
    Conditions at, 1106, 1110, 1111, 1121.
    Desire of Spaniards to evacuate, 980.
    Hdqrs., Dept. Mindanao and Jolo, establishment, 1077.
    Insurgents attacked and defeated by Moros, 1060.
    Insurgents desire U. S. garrison, conditional upon withdrawal, 1074.
    Marines to be used if needed, 1105.
    Natives serenade U. S. troops, 1111.
    Relief of Spanish troops, 989.
    Spanish garrison withdrawn from, after battle with insurgents, 997.
    Surrender of insurgents, 1109.
    Turned over to U. S. naval forces, 1105.
  Zapote Bridge, Luzon, casualties, 1015–1017, 1021.
  Zapote River, Luzon—
    Engagement at crossing, 1008.
    Casualties, 1010.
    Insurgents driven from intrenchments at crossing, 1010.
    Scout along, 1010.
  Zone to be occupied by U. S. troops, map requested by Aguinaldo, 814.
Philippines, Division of:
  Appointment of adjutant-general 1177, 1181.
  Assignment of chief of staff, 1183.
  Assignments to command, 1154, 1157, 1164.
  Creation, 1004.
  Determination of number and character of troops, 1157.
  Organization, 170, 1154.
  See *Philippine Islands.*
Philips, James M., pvt., Co. B, 45th Inf., U. S. V., killed, 1192.
Philips, Turley, pvt., Co. H, 40th Inf., U. S. V., wounded, 1183.
Phillippi, Leonard E., corpl., Co. G, 1st Colo. Vol. Inf., death, 960; wounded, 956.
Phillips, George S., pvt., Co. M, 13th U. S. Inf., death, 1215.
Phillips, Jacob P., pvt., Co. E, 24th U. S. Inf., mentioned, 229.
Phillips, Paul H., pvt., Troop E, 4th U. S. Cav., death, 1149.
Phillips, William H., pvt., Co. H, 21st U. S. Inf., wounded, 1042, 1044.
Philo, A. D., pvt., Batty G, 3d U. S. Art., wounded, 899.
Philpot, William, pvt., Co. F, 1st Nebr. Vol. Inf., killed, 899.
Phineas, Charles, pvt., Co. I, 1st Colo. Vol. Inf., mentioned, 761.
Phipps, Charles D., pvt., Co. D, 5th U. S. Inf., death, 1236.
Phœnix, U. S. transport, mentioned, 414.
Piatt, Lee, pvt., Co. F, 44th Inf., U. S, V., wounded, 1237.
Pickard, ——, capt., 1st N.Y. Vol. Inf., mentioned, 748.
Picken, William, pvt., Co. K, 13th U. S. Inf., death, 1194.

Pickett, James, corpl., Co. C, 9th U. S. Inf., wounded, 1298.
Pierce, Charles C., chaplain, U. S A., mentioned, 1062.
Pierce, Charles H., pvt., Co. I, 22d U. S. Inf., wounded, 1092.
Pierce, James, mus., Co. C, 1st Nebr. Vol. Inf., wounded, 897.
Pierce, John, pvt., Co. F, 47th Inf., U. S. V., killed, 1191.
Pierce, John E., sergt., Co. D, 38th Inf., U. S. V., wounded, 1264.
Pierce, John, pvt., Co. F, 2d U. S. Inf., death, 1253.
Pierce, Joseph, unassigned recruit, 23d U. S. Inf., death, 1099.
Pierce, William L., corpl., Co. K, 21st U. S. Inf., death, 1194.
Pierestoff, Lester, pvt., Co. C, 1st Mont. Vol. Inf., wounded, 899.
Pierson, Charles O., 2d lieut., Sig. Corps, U. S. V., mentioned, 143, 145, 239, 386.
Pierson, Edward, pvt., Co. E, 14th U. S. Inf., death, 1233.
Pierson, Jacob T., pvt., Troop K, 3d U. S. Cav., wounded, 1255.
Pigmy, British gunboat, mentioned, 481.
Pike, Albert C., pvt., Batty. L, 3d U. S. Art., wounded, 950.
Pilar, Gregorio del, insurgent general, killed, 1121.
Pilar, Pio del, insurgent general, capture, 1177. Mentioned, 1115, 1121.
Pilgrim, William H., pvt., Co. M 13th Minn. Vol. Inf., death, 1020.
Pillans, William, corpl., Co. M, 4th U. S. Inf., wounded, 1081.
Pillsbury, Ross L., corpl., Co. C, 40th Inf., U. S.V., wounded, 1193.
Pines, Isle of Cuba, cession to U. S., 351.
Pingree, Carrol L., pvt., Co. D 9th U. S. Inf., wounded, 444.
Pinny, Frank, pvt., Co. B, 1st Wash. Vol. Inf.
Piper, Richard J., pvt., Co. M, 20th U. S. Inf., wounded, 934.
Pipes, Ashel E., corpl., Co. M 3d U. S. Inf., killed, 995.
Pitcher, Thomas I, pvt., Co. L, 15th U. S. Inf., killed, 1211.
Pitcher, William L, capt. and maj., 8th U. S. Inf., mentioned, 1344.
Pitt, James, pvt., Co. C, 36th Inf., U. S. V., wounded, 1092.
Pitts, Clyde D., pvt., Batty. L, 3d U. S. Art., death, 850.
Pitts, Edwin E, pvt., Co. A, 1st Colo. Vol. Inf., wounded, 947.
Pitts, John W., pvt., Co. G, 14th U. S. Inf., killed, 963.
Plants, Leroy W., pvt., Troop M 4th U. S. Cav., drowned, 1219.
Platt, Thomas C., U. S. Senator, mentioned, 59, 294, 302, 323, 324, 334, 402, 403.
Pleasant, John, pvt., Co. F, 32d Inf., U. S. V., death, 1142.
Plemons, E., pvt., Co. I, 27th Inf., U. S. V., wounded, 1234.
Pleoplis, Jack, pvt., Co. E, 9th U. S. Inf., killed, 1298.
Ploeger, Christ B., pvt., Batty. K, 3d U. S. Art., wounded, 897; mentioned, 922.
Plottner, Alvin F., pvt., Co. A, 1st Mont. Vol. Inf., wounded, 920.
Plowman, Harry L., pvt., Co. H, 1st Idaho Vol. Inf., death, 923.
Plume, Joseph W., brig. gen., U. S. V., mentioned, 522, 523.
Plummer, George, pvt., Co. M 12th U. S. Inf., wounded, 1055.
Plummer, H. L., pvt., Co. E, 20th Kans. Vol. Inf., killed, 945.
Plummer, ——, pvt., Co. G, 4th U. S. Inf., wounded, 1042.
Pluton, Spanish torpedo destroyer, mentioned, 81.
Pogorzelski, Mike, pvt., Co. A, 43d Inf., U. S. V., mentioned, 1153.
Poland, Homer W., pvt., Co. G, 30th Inf., U.S. V., death, 1219.

Poland, John S., brig. gen., U. S. V., mentioned, 36, 71, 295, 511-513.
Polk, Frank M., 2d lieut., 39th Inf., U. S. V., mentioned, 1270.
Polk, Lucius E., capt., 43d Inf., U. S. V., wounded, 1187.
Polkey, Charles C., pvt., Co. K, 6th U. S. Inf., death, 1255.
Polley, William H., pvt., Co. L, 15th U. S. Inf., wounded, 1211.
Pollock, William S., pvt., Troop L, 3d U. S. Cav., death, 1133.
Polly, Nocholas C., pvt., Co. D, 1st Wash. Vol. Inf., wounded, 896.
Pomelow, Trefflie, pvt., Co. H, 43d Inf., U. S. V., killed, 1168.
Ponath, William W., corpl., Co. G, 2d Oreg. Vol. Inf., wounded, 917.
Pool, Victor A., pvt., Co. K, 33d Inf., U. S. V., death, 1205.
Poole, John E., pvt., Co. H, 24th U. S. Inf., mentioned, 1057, 1060.
Poole, Juan B., pvt., Co. F, 29th U. S. Inf., wounded, 1219.
Poor, Walter, sergt., Co. A, 1st Nebr. Vol. Inf., killed, 945.
Poore, Benjamin A., capt., 6th U. S. Inf., mentioned, 1079.
Poore, William Francis, pvt., Co. D, 1st D. C. Vol. Inf., mentioned, 183.
Pope, Benjamin F., lieut. col., med. dept., U. S. A., mentioned, 174, 1319.
Pope, Bert, pvt., Co. C, 22d U. S. Inf., death, 1082.
Pope, James W., col., chief qm., U. S. V.; maj. qm. dept., U. S. A., mentioned, 646, 948.
Pope, Percival C., col., U. S. Marine Corps, mentioned, 970.
Porczeng, August F., pvt., Co. C, 9th U. S. Inf., missing, 1297; wounded, 1010.
Porro, Richard S., citizen of Santiago, Cuba, mentioned, 22.
Port Albert, U. S. transport, mentioned, 412, 430, 437, 439, 445, 1083, 1243.
Port Stephens, U. S. transport, mentioned, 437, 439, 445, 446, 450, 465, 469, 471, 472, 475, 477.
Port Tampa, Fla.:
Immune doctors, commissary stores, etc., depart for Cuba, 155.
Movement of troops and transports, 65, 67, 69, 73, 75, 134, 270.
Transportation, etc., at 63, 94.
Port Victor, U. S. transport, mentioned, 184, 192, 198, 309, 351.
Porter, Clarence H., pvt., Co. H, 1st N. Y. Vol. Inf., death, 838.
Porter, David D., capt., U. S. Marine Corps, mentioned, 1313, 1329.
Porter, John, pvt., Co. B, 39th Inf., U. S. V., death, 1197.
Porter, John Addison, secretary to President, mentioned, 353.
Porter, John B., maj., 28th U. S. Inf., mentioned, 1089.
Porter, John H., pvt., Co. D, 9th U. S. Inf., killed, 443, 445.
Porter, John L., mus., Co. H, 24th U. S. Inf., death, 1132.
Porter, John W., pvt., Batty. C, 6th U. S. Art., death, 1095.
Porter, Lennard, pvt., Co. I, 13th Minn. Vol. Inf., wounded, 947.
Porter, Meritt, pvt., Co. E, 22d U. S. Inf., wounded, 941.
Portland, U. S. transport, mentioned, 961, 968, 992.
Porto Rico, campaign in, correspondence relating to.
Alabama, troops sent to, 285, 345.
Arizona, troops sent to, 345.
Arkansas, troops sent to, 345, 347, 348, 351, 354, 357.
Army and Navy Christian Commission to Porto Rico, 305.
Asomanta, engagement, casualties in, 388.
Banes, Bay of, rendezvous for U. S. troops, 262, 263.
Bonds, cancelling, notaries public, 384.
Cabañas, disembarkation of troops, 273.
Capron, Fort, naming of, 369.
Catholic Priest, salary of, 369.
Cession to U. S., 751.

Porto Rico, campaign in, correspondence relating to—Continued.
Charleston, S. C., sailing of troops from, 274, 275, 276, 277, 278, 294, 295.
Wagons left at, 378.
Chickamauga Park, Ga., troops at, 266, 294, 296.
Cienfuegos, Cuba, blockading of port, 263.
Coamo, capture of, casualties, 372, 378.
Connecticut, troops sent to, 345, 353, 365.
Crab Island, rendezvous, 150, 286.
Cuba, scheme for movement of troops from, 262, 268.
Culebra Island, landing place for expedition to, 150.
Customs duties, 381, 391
Delaware, troops sent to, 345.
Doraco, landing of troops, 320.
Enlisted men, discharge, 373, 376, 359.
Equipment, disposition, 389, 390, 392-397.
Equipment and transportation for troops, 303, 325, 379.
Evacuation by Spaniards, 395, 398, 399, 403.
Exodus, 306.
Expedition to—
Embarkation, 276, 279.
Organization, 140, 268.
Facilities for reaching, 402, 404.
Fajardo Point, P. R., rendezvous, troops landing at, 276, 280, 281, 285, 286, 289, 291, 297, 299, 310, 311, 318, 319, 337.
Laborers for, 281.
Flags for public schools, 365, 368, 386, 398.
Florida, troops for foreign service, 285, 335, 363.
French ambassador, place of neutrality for foreigners, San Juan, P. R., 346, 355.
Georgia, troops sent to, 285, 335, 348.
Gibara, port, Cuba, troops in, 262.
Guanica, port of, landing of troops, 321, 322, 338.
Guantanamo, Cuba, disembarkation of troops, rendezvous, 273, 274, 337.
Guayamo, capture of, casualties, 365, 378.
Health conditions, 381, 385.
Hormigueros, casualties at, 390.
Hospital at Ponce, 373, 378.
Hostilities, suspension, 383, 389, 393.
Immunity for natives, 377.
Indiana, troops sent to, 316, 320, 332, 342-344, 345, 349, 353, 377.
Protest against troops sailing on certain transports, 357.
Illinois, troops sent to, 329, 331, 333-335, 377, 339, 349, 352, 354, 357, 365; return of, 401, 402.
Iowa, troops sent to, 345.
Jacksonville, Fla., concentration of troops, 266.
Kentucky, troops sent to, 329, 363, 369, 370.
Key West, Fla., movement of transports from, 262.
Lighters and tugs, for expedition to, 305, 306.
Louisiana, troops sent to, 285, 356, 364.
Mail, for troops in, 370-373.
Maine, troops sent to, 345, 355, 357.
Manití, port of, troops in, 262.
Mariel, landing of troops at, 262.
Marines, for, 296.
Maryland, troops sent to 335, 345, 355.
Massachusetts, troops sent to, 308, 311, 373, 374, 375.
1st Art. asks to be sent to, 303.
Matanzas, Cuba, landing of troops at, 262.
Mayaguez, engagement at, casualties, 380, 381.
Miami, Fla., concentration of troops, 266.
Troops to Porto Rico, 285.
Minnesota, troops sent to, 347, 353, 356.
Mississippi, troops sent to, 285, 362, 364.
Missouri, troops sent to, 342-345, 356.
Mobile, Ala., concentration of troops, 266.
Money, standard value, 350, 353.
Montana, troops sent to, 304, 330, 363, 367.
Montauk Point, N. Y., troops from Santiago, Cuba, 360.
Mount Vernon, Ala., concentration of troops, 266.
Movement against, 67, 144-146, 150, 154, 155, 261-265, 267 2"2, 277, 279, 281, 301, 304, 306-309, 330, 335, 340, 364, 366-369.
National Relief Commission, supplies, 392.
Navy, interference of, at San Juan, 379, 380.
New Hampshire, troops sent to, 345.
New Jersey, troops sent to, 345.

Porto Rico, campaign in, correspondence relating to—Continued.
   Newport News, Va., sailing of troops, 274, 328. 333.
      Movement of troops to, 305, 306, 308, 312, 326.
   New York, equipment for troops, 319.
      Troops sent to, 320, 323, 334, 336, 337, 340, 345, 347, 348, 353, 358, 364.
      Return of troops and muster-out, 400, 402.
   Nipe, Bay of, Cuba, troops in, rendezvous, 262, 263.
      Landing troops, 283, 286.
   North Carolina, troops sent to, 345.
   Nuevitas, Cuba, landing troops, 286.
   Nuevitas, Cuba, troops in, 262.
   Officers, commissioned, death, 344.
   Ohio, troops sent to, 329, 336, 338, 339, 342, 343, 346, 350, 351, 354, 361, 366.
      Return of troops from, 404.
   Operations, suspension, 383, 389.
   Paymasters for, 285.
   Payment of troops, 396.
   Pennsylvania, equipment of troops for, 313.
      Troops sent to, 312, 315, 316 328, 331, 335–339, 362, 368, 370, 390.
      Return of troops, and muster-out 400, 402.
   Point Fajardo, rendezvous of transports for Porto Rico expedition, 155.
   Ponce, collector of port, 344, 356.
      General conditions, customs receipts, 341.
      Excluding vessels, 400.
      Hospital at, 373, 378.
      Disembarkation of troops, engagement at, 318, 319, 330, 341, 347.
      Rendezvous, 338.
      Transports to, 349, 350.
      Prisoners, political, relief, 377.
      Proclamation, by President U. S., 383, 384, 389.
   Postal service, 298, 405.
   Public schools, opening, flags for, 365, 368, 386, 398, 399, 403, 404.
   Puerto Padre, Cuba, troops in port 262.
   Puerto Principe, Cuba, occupation by troops, 262.
   Red Cross ambulances, 310.
   Rhode Island, troops sent to, 318, 345.
   Rio Grande Valley, skirmish, 393.
   Sabaña la Mar, port, troops in, 262.
   San Juan—
      Fortifications, 264.
      Landing of Navy at, 372, 379, 380.
      Place of neutrality for foreigners, 346, 355.
   San Juan, Cape de, P. R., landing of troops, 285, 286, 337.
      Rendezvous of transports for, 155.
      Transports to, 352.
   Santa Clara Province, Cuba, occupation by troops, 262.
   Ships, grounding, 362.
   Subsistence for inhabitants, 384.
   Supplies, etc., 291, 303, 350, 362.
   Surrender, refusal of, at San Juan, P. R., 359.
   St. Thomas, dispatches to, 327.
   Tampa, Fla., concentration of troops, 266.
      O'Reilly, lieut. col. to remain at, 360.
      Stores and equipment, disposition of, 367.
      Transports, movement of, 262, 275, 278, 306, 307, 335, 310, 318, 326, 330, 332.
      Troops, health conditions, 367–368, 388.
   Tennessee, troops to, 345, 358, 361.
   Texas, troops to, 285, 342, 345.
   Transportation, by sea, 266.
      And equipment for troops in, 325.
   Transports, aground, 362.
      Atlantic liners to be used as, 284.
      Inadequate supply, 292.
   Troops at Santiago for, 274.
      Payment, 385.
      Return, 400, 401.
      Surrender, 351.
      Transportation, 311.
   United States money for, 367.
   Proclamation of President, 383, 389.
   Vermont, troops sent to, 311, 345, 340, 342, 359.
   Vieques Island, ceded to U. S., 351.
      Rendezvous, 286.
   Virginia, troops sent to, 345, 355.
   Volunteer troops, muster-out from, 400.
   West Virginia, troops sent to, 324, 345.
   Wisconsin, return of troops, 401, 402.
   Yauco, occupation by troops, 330.

Portwich, Oscar, pvt., Batty. G, 3d U. S. Art., wounded, 901.
Post, Alfred G., pvt., Co. K, 2d U. S. Inf., drowned, 1271.
Postmaster-General, U. S., mentioned, 169, 371, 384, 496.
Posts, military, families of absent officers and soldiers, to retain quarters, 930.
Potter, Carroll H., maj., 14th U. S. Inf., mentioned, 709.
Potter, Charles L., lieut. col., chief engr. officer, U. S. V., mentioned, 667, 700, 845.
Potter, John A., pvt., Co. A, 9th U. S. Inf., killed, 443, 445.
Potter, Joseph M., cook, Co. M, 13th U. S. Inf., wounded, 1231.
Potter, William, Hon., mentioned, 361.
Potter, ——, col., National Relief Commission, mentioned, 392, 862.
Powell, Archibald W., pvt., Co. I, 10th Pa. Vol. Inf., wounded, 953.
Powell, William H., col., 9th U. S. Inf., mentioned, 139, 995.
Power, Alfred, pvt., Co. E, 14th U. S. Inf., death, 477.
Power, Charles, trumpeter, Troop K, 4th U. S. Cav., wounded, 974.
Power, Nathaniel F., pvt., Co. A, 19th U. S. Inf., death, 1271.
Powerful, British war ship, mentioned, 846.
Powers, Charles, pvt., Co. C, 9th U. S. Inf., killed, 1297.
Powers, H. M., pvt., ——, 1st Cal. Vol. Inf., mentioned, 828.
Powers, John, pvt., Co. K, 14th U. S. Inf., wounded, 898.
Powers, Samuel J., pvt., Troop F, 2d U. S. Cav., mentioned, 195.
Prager, Arthur E., pvt., Co. E, 9th U. S. Inf., wounded, 1008.
Prairie, U. S. ship, mentioned, 223, 230, 231, 245, 344.
Pratt, Charles E., pvt., Co. M, 20th Kans. Vol. Inf., killed, 898.
Pratt, Edward, pvt., Co. L, 13th Minn. Vol. Inf., death, 956.
Pratt, Hiram A., sergt., Co. I, 1st S. Dak. Vol. Inf., wounded, 948.
Pratt, Sidney, pvt., Co. A, 13th Minn. Vol. Inf., death, 803; mentioned, 761, 762.
Pratt, ——, U. S. consul, mentioned, 909.
Pray, Albert F., pvt., Co. B, 1st Wash. Vol. Inf., wounded, 897.
Preacher, Charles B., 1st sergt., Co. M, 1st S. Dak. Vol. Inf., death, 957; wounded, 949.
Prescott, Philip R., pvt., Co. E, 46th Inf., U. S. V., death, 1172.
Pressen, Clinton G., pvt., Co. H, 40th Inf., U. S. V., death, 1161.
Pressley, Algernon S., pvt., Co. G, 32d Inf., U. S. V., killed, 1143.
Preston, John M., pvt., Co. G, 12th U. S. Inf., death, 1078.
Preston, William, corpl., Co. A, 24th U. S. Inf., death, 1202.
Preston, Winfield S., pvt., Co. C, 19th U. S. Inf., wounded 1153.
Prettyman, ——, pvt., Co. M, 17th U. S. Inf., death, 892.
Price, Charles S., civilian, wounded, 1073.
Price, Edward, pvt., Co. F, 24th U. S. Inf., death, 1257.
Price, Elmer A., pvt., Co. L, 25th U. S. Inf., wounded, 1228.
Price, Eliphalet, pvt., Batty. E, 6th U. S. Art., death, 1099.
Price, Guy A., corpl., Co. K, 35th Inf., U. S. V., death, 1245.
Price, John, pvt., Co. D, 12th U. S. Inf., wounded, 1227.
Price, Lewis H., corpl., Co. E, 24th U. S. Inf., wounded, 1052.
Price, Walter B., pvt., Hosp. Corps, U. S. A., death, 1213.
Prickett, Nathaniel F., pvt., Co. G, 23d U. S. Inf., death, 967.
Prignitz, William, pvt., Co. L, 4th U. S. Inf., wounded, 1017.
Princeton, U. S. aux. cruiser, mentioned, 418, 420, 1326.

Prior, J. H., capt., 6th Mass. Vol. Inf., wounded, 330.
Pritchard, Moses P., pvt., Co. A, 14th U. S. Inf., wounded, 967.
Proclamation for suspension of hostilities, 750.
Proctor, Redfield, U. S. Senator, mentioned, 307, 311, 359.
Proffett, Shannon, pvt., Co. I, 25th U. S. Inf., killed, 1194.
Proske, Oscar, pvt., Co. G, 14th U. S. Inf., death, 1125.
Protocol, between American and Spanish governments, for establishment of peace, 750.
Protz, William, pvt., Batty. F, 5th U. S. Art., wounded, 1130.
Proudfoot, Rolla, pvt., Co. I, 1st Wash. Vol. Inf., wounded, 897.
Prouty, Charles K., pvt., Co. C, 1st S. Dak. Vol. Inf., death, 1015.
Pruitt, John, pvt., Co. L, 1st Wash. Vol. Inf., wounded, 897.
Pruitt, Norman A., pvt., Co. F, U. S. Marine Corps, wounded, 454.
Pryor, James J., pvt., Co. K, 24th U. S. Inf., death, 1149.
Przykalla, Fred., corpl., Co. H, 9th U. S. Inf., death, 1027.
Pstrom, Robert B., pvt., Batty. D, 3d U. S. Art., wounded, 899.
Puckett, Dale, pvt., Co. D, 33d Inf., U. S. V., killed, 1137.
Puehl, George, pvt., Co. E, 33d Inf., U. S. V., wounded, 1101.
Puffer, Otis W., pvt., Co. A, 15th U. S. Inf., death, 1264.
Puget Sound, defense of, 674.
Pugh, Paul B., pvt., Co. L, 51st Iowa Vol. Inf., death, 1027.
Pullen, Arthur, pvt., Co. M, 2d Oreg. Vol. Inf., wounded, 963.
Purdy, Clarence N., 2d lieut., 6th U. S. Inf., mentioned, 83; wounded, 124.
Puritan, U. S. monitor, mentioned, 352.
Purtee, Hiram W., pvt., Co. I, 32d Inf., U. S. V., wounded, 1243.
Putnam, Herbert A., pvt., Co. I, 1st S. Dak. Vol. Inf., wounded, 975.
Putzker, Bruno L., pvt., Batty. K, 3d U. S. Art., death, 907; wounded, 901.
Pyncheon, Edward R., pvt., Co. K, 1st Colo. Vol. Inf., death, 947; wounded, 937.
Pyncheon, William, pvt., Co. B, 1st Wash. Vol. Inf., mentioned, 959.
Quarles, James T., pvt., Co. L, 25th U. S. Inf., wounded, 1132.
Quartermaster-General, U. S. A., memorandum for, 108.
Mentioned, 128, 227, 237, 416, 489, 494, 659, 1010, 1014, 1054.
Quay, Matthew S., U. S. Senator, mentioned, 320, 330, 339, 368, 370.
Quick, Charlie, pvt., Co. D, 39th Inf., U. S. V., death, 1215.
Quigley, John J., pvt., Co. A, 16th U. S. Inf., wounded, 1117.
Quillion, Clarence, pvt., Co. E, 35th Inf., U. S. V., killed, 1176.
Quinlin, Dennis P., 2d lieut., 11th U. S. V. Cav., wounded, 1140.
Quinlin, John, sergt., band, 18th U. S. Inf., death, 1032.
Quinn, Edward, pvt., Troop K, 4th U. S. Cav., mentioned, 974.
Quinn, George E., corpl., Co. E, 39th Inf., U. S. V., wounded, 1149.
Quinn, John, pvt., Co. K, 26th U. S. Inf., death, 1194.
Quinn, John J., pvt., Co. A, 21st U. S. Inf., death, 1208.
Quinn, Thomas, pvt., Co. H, 13th U. S. Inf., killed, 1166.
Quinn, William, mus., Co. M, 22d U. S. Inf., wounded, 1243.
Quinne, Thomas, pvt., Troop E, 4th U. S. Cav., death, 1062.
Quint, Willis, pvt., Co. B, 43d Inf., U. S. V., wounded, 1163.
Quinton, Wiliam, maj., 14th U. S. Inf., mentioned, 1018.

Quirk, William G., corpl., Co. K, 46th Inf., U. S. V., wounded, 1256.
Quiros, Spanish gunboat, mentioned, 745.
Rabbett, James A., a. a. surg., U. S. A., death, 1256.
Rabi, Jesus, brig. gen., Cuban army, mentioned, 54.
Radcliffe, Charlie A., pvt., Troop A, 4th U. S. Cav., killed, 1081.
Radebaugh, Harry, pvt., Co. G, 27th Inf., U. S. V., death, 1142.
Rader, brig. gen., Cuban army, mentioned, 54.
Radzinski, Arthur D., sergt. maj., 33d Inf., U. S. V., death, 1125; wounded, 1101.
Rafferty, Ogden, maj., med. dept., U. S. A., mentioned, 123.
Rafferty, William A., lieut. col., 2d, and col., 5th U. S. Cav., mentioned, 542, 544, 1330.
Raft, Frank J., corpl., Co. C, 12th U. S. Inf., wounded, 1057.
Ragan, John J., pvt., Co. A, 19th U. S. Inf., death, 1267.
Ragsdale, James W., U. S. consul, Tientsin, China, mentioned, 495.
Ragnar, Belgian ship, mentioned, 1347.
Railway Mail Service, equipment of with exp., 696; placed in touch with Phil. exp., 695.
Rains, Paul, pvt., Co. L, 33d Inf., U. S. V., wounded, 1152.
Rains, newspaper correspondent, mentioned, 147.
Rainwater, Charles O., pvt., Co. C, 22d U. S. Inf., death, 1123.
Ralph, Richard H., pvt., Batty. B, Utah Vol. Art., U. S. V., death, 1045, 1048.
Ralph, Thomas S., pvt., Co. M, 22d U. S. Inf., death, 1063.
Ralston, Ernest U., pvt., Co. C, 9th U. S. Inf., wounded, 1298.
Ralston, Francis W., jr., 2d lieut., 30th Inf., U. S. V., mentioned, 1185.
Rambo, Isaac E., pvt., Co. E, 4th U. S. Inf., death, 1074.
Ramdles, John M., pvt., Co. A, 30th Inf., U. S. V., death, 1233.
Rampolla, M., Catholic cardinal, mentioned, 790, 793, 831.
Ramsay, Charles R., 2d lieut., 21st U. S. Inf., wounded, 1285.
Ramsay, Robert, pvt., Co. C, 24th U. S. Inf., mentioned, 209.
Ramsey, Charles E., pvt., Co. C, 33d Inf., U. S. V., death, 1149.
Ramsey, Frank De W., capt., 9th U. S. Inf., mentioned, 1335.
Rand, Irving W., brig. gen., U. S. V., mentioned, 240.
Randall, George M., brig. gen., U. S. V., mentioned, 526, 527, 529.
Randall, Wesley, pvt., Co. A, 48th Inf., U. S. V., death, 1144.
Randles, James N., sergt., Co. C, 9th U. S. Inf., killed, 1297.
Randolph, Wallace F., brig. gen., U. S. V., mentioned, 15, 65, 70, 73, 86–88, 95, 104, 120, 141, 275, 541, 544, 546, 1155.
Ranney, Archie J., pvt., Co. G, 14th U. S. Inf., death, 464.
Ranous, Don J., pvt., Co. K, 1st S. Dak. Vol. Inf., wounded, 975.
Ranous, Roy E., pvt., Co. K, 1st S. Dak. Vol. Inf., wounded, 981.
Ransey, Arthur, pvt., Co. F, 1st Colo. Vol. Inf., death, 917.
Ransom, William P. H., pvt., Co. F, 14th U. S. Inf., wounded, 902.
Ranson, Clayton L., pvt., Co. L, 2d Oreg. Vol. Inf., wounded, 1008.
Rasmunson, William O., corpl., Co. F, 12th U. S. Inf., death, 1048.
Rasmussen, Herbert, pvt., Co. B, 1st Nebr. Vol. Inf., wounded, 967.
Rass, Herbert, pvt., Batty. G, 3d U. S. Art., killed, 945.
Ratcliff, Henry, pvt., Co. F, 20th Kans. Vol. Inf., wounded, 952.
Rath, Henry J., mus., Batty. H, 3d U. S. Art., wounded, 950.
Rathmaner, Frank, pvt., Co. A, 36th Inf., U. S. V., wounded, 1064.
Rattler, U. S. gunboat, mentioned, 928.

INDEX. 1461

Raub, Harry T., mus., Co. A, 17th U. S. Inf., death, 1229.
Rauch, William, pvt., Co. C, 19th U. S. Inf., death, 1189.
Ray, Charles W., sergt., Co. I, 22d U. S. Inf., wounded, 1162.
Ray, John, pvt., Co. M, 36th Inf., U. S. V., wounded, 1052.
Ray, Johnson H., pvt., Co. B, 37th Inf., U. S. V., death, 1153.
Ray, P. Henry, col., 3d U. S. Vol. Inf. mentioned, 191, 208, 212, 223, 234.
Rayburn, John, pvt., Co. H, 33d Inf., U. S. V., wounded, 1203.
Raymond, Elmer, pvt., Co. E, 19th U. S. Inf., death, 1058, 1063.
Raymond, George B., pvt., Co. G, 1st Mont. Vol. Inf., wounded, 995.
Raymond, John W., pvt., Co. H, 17th U. S. Inf., wounded, 1051.
Rayne, Thomas M., corpl., Co. I, 21st U. S. Inf., wounded, 1015.
Rea, Edward, pvt., Co. K, 3d U. S. Inf., wounded, 987.
Rea, George H., pvt., Co. A, Batt. of Engrs., U. S. A., killed, 1248.
Rea, Guy A., pvt., Troop K, 4th U. S. Cav., death, 1228.
Read, Charles, pvt., Co. G, 14th U. S. Inf., wounded, 898.
Read, James C., capt., com. sub., U. S. V., mentioned, 1267, 1278, 1279, 1285, 1286; wounded, 950.
Read, William C., 1st lieut., 36th Inf., U. S. V., wounded, 1126.
Reade, Frederick G., sergt., Co. F, 17th U. S. Inf., death, 1167.
Reaman, William W., corpl., Co. F, 1st S. Dak. Vol. Inf., wounded, 975.
Reaney, Robert J., capt., 46th Inf., U. S. V., wounded, 1251.
Reason, Walker D., pvt., Co. L, 25th U. S. Inf., wounded, 1228.
Reasoner, Daniel, pvt. Co. K, 9th U. S. Inf., death, 482.
Reaver, Edward, pvt., Co. F, 23d U. S. Inf., killed, 916.
Rebecca Shoal, convoy to meet transports at, 39, 40.
Reber, Samuel, maj., sig. officer, U. S. V.; 1st lieut., Sig. Corps, U. S. A., mentioned, 275.
Reberger, Beaure, pvt., Co. F, 34th Inf., U. S. V., death, 1217.
Recard, Chris F., pvt., Co. C., 9th U. S Inf., death, 1297.
Recob, Fred A., corpl., Co. A., 20th Kans. Vol. Inf., wounded, 950.
Recommendation, establishment military camp or sanitarium, at Honolulu, H. I., 731.
Reddick, Richard B., pvt., Co. F, 2d U. S. Inf., death, 1236.
Redmond, Henry E., pvt., Co. G, 1st Colo. Vol. Inf., wounded, 956.
Reed, Amos, pvt., Co. A, 49th Inf., U. S. V., death, 1228.
Reed, Bayles T., pvt. Co. F, 3d U. S. Inf., death, 1151.
Reed, Bert J., corpl., Co. F, 18th U. S. Inf., wounded, 1113.
Reed, Cosley, pvt., Co. A, 24th U. S. Inf., death, 1051, 1056.
Reed, Henry A., capt., 5th U. S. Art., mentioned, 347, 355.
Reed, Lewis E., pvt., Co. G, 1st Nebr. Vol. Inf., wounded, 952.
Reed, Robert F., corpl., Co. E, 1st Idaho Vol. Inf., wounded, 1008.
Reed, William H., pvt., Co. M, 37th Inf., U. S. V., death, 1213.
Reelhorn, Elmer E., pvt., Co. H, Sig. Corps, U. S. A., death, 1254.
Reese, James A., pvt., Troop G, 4th U. S. Cav., wounded, 1044.
Reese, Newton W., pvt., Troop I, 4th U. S. Cav., death, 1130.
Reeve, Charles McC., brig. gen., U S. V., mentioned, 716, 793.
Reeve, Horace M., 1st lieut., 3d U. S. Inf., mentioned, 256.
Reeves, Edward, pvt., Troop C, 4th U. S. Cav., wounded, 1031.

Reeves, Ira L., 1st lieut., 4th U. S. Inf., wounded, 1031.
Reeves, Isaac, pvt., Co. B, 48th Inf., U. S. V., death, 1233.
Reeves, John T., pvt., Co. A, 2d Oreg. Vol. Inf., wounded, 983.
Reeves, Walter, pvt., Co. G, 24th U. S. Inf., mentioned, 214.
Reffitt, John F., pvt., Co. M, 33d Inf., U. S. V., wounded, 1102.
Regan, James, maj., 9th U. S. Inf., mentioned, 563, 564, 943; wounded, 428–430, 435, 443.
Regan, William J., pvt. Co. G, 17th U. S. Inf., death, 1189.
Regnier, Samuel E., corpl., Co. G, 46th Inf., U. S. V., death, 1189.
Rehl, George E., pvt., Co. E, 39th Inf., U. S. V., death, 1140.
Rehm, George J., pvt., Co. A, 39th Inf., U. S. V., death, 1238.
Reichart, George B., pvt., Co. E, 1st Wash. Vol. Inf., killed, 895.
Reichelt, Alfred B., corpl., Co. C, 1st Wash. Vol. Inf., wounded, 920.
Reid, Hugh J., —— Iowa Vol. Inf., mentioned, 358.
Reid, James J., pvt., Co. M, 2d Oreg. Vol. Inf., death, 803.
Reid, Whitelaw, Hon., mentioned, 959.
Reid, Mrs. Whitelaw, mentioned, 958.
Reid, ——, gen., British army, mentioned, 491.
Reilly, Hugh J., capt., 5th U. S. Art., killed, 460, 461; mentioned, 424, 426, 441, 505.
Reilly, Michael, sergt., Co. G, 17th U. S. Inf., death, 1160.
Reilly, Owen, pvt., Co. E, 33d Inf., U. S. V., death, 1234.
Reina Cristiana, trans-Atlantic steamship, mentioned, 886, 888, 904, 991.
Reina Mercedes, Spanish cruiser, mentioned, 22.
Relief, U. S. hospl. ship, mentioned, 196, 199, 241, 425, 442, 451, 452, 466, 471, 472, 477–480, 482, 486, 884, 932–934, 937, 938, 963, 1017, 1032, 1046, 1116, 1193, 1221, 1241, 1322, 1325, 1326, 1341, 1356.
Remaley, Augustus C., 1st sergt., Co. I, 10th Pa. Vol. Inf., wounded, 954.
Remars, Frank, pvt., Co. D, 47th Inf., U. S. V., wounded, 1272.
Remey, George C., rear-admiral, U. S. N., mentioned, 31, 37–40, 51, 52, 66, 86, 88, 410, 414–418, 420–422, 425, 426, 429, 432, 433, 435, 436, 438, 439, 443, 444, 447, 448, 451, 454, 456–460, 463, 465, 467, 468, 471–474, 476, 477, 480, 481, 484, 492, 1242.
Renned, William A., pvt., Co. H, 21st U. S. Inf., killed, 1046.
Renner, William M., pvt., Troop E, 3d U. S. Cav., death, 1233.
Reno, Harry, sergt., Troop K, 4th U. S. Cav., death, 1125.
Resolute, auxiliary cruiser, mentioned, 31, 44, 96, 102, 103, 108, 109, 115, 117, 119, 132, 133, 177, 208, 234, 240.
Reyer, Adolph T., pvt., Co. E, 13th U. S. Inf., death, 1202.
Reyer, Ira N., pvt., Co. K, 8th Ohio Vol. Inf., mentioned, 213.
Reynolds, Charles E., corpl., Co. F, 33d Inf., U. S. V., wounded, 1190.
Reynolds, Henry G., pvt., Co. D, 1st Mont. Vol. Inf., wounded, 900.
Reynolds, Maurice, pvt., Batty. F, 3d U. S. Art., wounded, 946.
Reynolds, Edward G., pvt., Co. D, 1st Mont. Vol. Inf., wounded, 895.
Rezner, George B., pvt., Co. A, 44th Inf., U. S. V., wounded, 1240.
Rhode, Paul J., pvt., Co. K, 13th Minn. Vol. Inf., death, 1027.
Rhode, William P., civilian, mentioned, 1326.
Rhodes, Albert V., pvt., Co. C, 26th U. S. Inf., wounded, 1209.
Rhodes, Charles D., capt., a. a. g., U. S. V., commended, 89, 128, 129; mentioned, 421.
Rhodes, Ernest W., pvt., Co. C, 17th U. S. Inf., death, 1109.
Rhodes, Joseph E., pvt., Co. M, 47th Inf., U. S. V., death, 1165.
Riblet, Oscar, pvt., Co. A, 37th Inf., U. S. V., death, 1201.
Ricarte, insurgent gen., mentioned 1186.

Rice, Archie, pvt., Co. F, 29th Inf., U. S. V., death, 1217.
Rice, Charles, pvt., Co. A, 27th Inf., U. S. V., death, 1200.
Rice, Clarence T., pvt., Co. E, 13th Minn. Vol. Inf., mentioned, 762; wounded, 761.
Rice, Cushman A., capt. 34th Inf., U. S. V., wounded, 1214.
Rice, Edmund, lieut. col., I. G., U. S. V.; appointed col., 6th Mass. Vol. Inf., 375, 376. Mentioned, 59, 60, 62–65, 67, 69, 72, 73, 134, 138, 275, 279, 376.
Rice, Ernest, pvt., Co. A, 48th Inf., U. S. V., death, 1202.
Rice, James, pvt., Co. K, 14th U. S. Inf., wounded, 454, 464.
Rice, James T., pvt., Co. D, 20th Kans. Vol. Inf., wounded, 954.
Rice, Robert, pvt., Co. E, 22d U. S. Inf., wounded, 941.
Rice, Walter, pvt., Co. M, 45th Inf., U. S. V., death, 1202.
Rice, ——, editor, mentioned, 1251; deported to San Francisco, 1252.
Rich, Harry, pvt., Co. K, 3d U. S. Inf., death, 1231.
Richar, Ralph L., pvt., Co. K, 34th Inf., U. S. V., death, 1144.
Richard, Frank, pvt., Co. G, 14th U. S. Inf., wounded, 1084.
Richard, James, pvt., Co. D, 1st Nebr. Vol. Inf., wounded, 974.
Richards, George C., pvt., Co. D, 22d U. S. Inf., wounded, 946.
Richards, John, pvt., Co. C, 24th U. S. Inf., mentioned, 248.
Richards, John J., pvt., Co. D, 4th U. S. Inf., death, 1187.
Richards, John T., adjt. gen., Maine, mentioned, 355, 356.
Richards, Ralph E., pvt., Co. H, 9th U. S. Inf., wounded, 444.
Richards, William C., pvt., Co. B, 1st Nebr. Vol. Inf., wounded, 974.
Richards, William V., lieut. col., a. a. g., U. S. V., mentioned, 301.
Richardson, C. W., pvt., Co. L, 1st Ill. Vol. Inf., mentioned, 248.
Richardson, Vinton, pvt., Co. L, 44th Inf., U. S. V., death, 1185.
Richardson, Winthrop, corpl., Troop H, 4th U. S. Cav., wounded, 1127.
Riché, Charles S., col., 1st U. S. Vol. Inf., mentioned, 188, 191.
Richmond, Ephraim T. C., col., 41st Inf., U. S. V., mentioned, 1112, 1114, 1117, 1122, 1127.
Richmond, L. S., corpl., Co. F, 1st S. Dak. Vol. Inf., wounded, 956.
Richter, Edward C., pvt., Co. I, 28th U. S. Inf., mentioned, 1324, 1325.
Richter, Fred, pvt., Co. M, 26th Inf., U. S. V., death, 1197.
Richter, Rembold, capt., 1st Cal. Vol. Inf., death, 803.
Richwine, Robert M., pvt., Co. E, 37th Inf., U. S. V., death, 1090.
Rickard, Thomas, pvt., Co. D, 1st Mont. Vol. Inf., wounded, 945.
Ricker, George E., pvt., Co. I, 43d Inf., U. S. V., death, 1248.
Rickets, Alonzo, pvt., Co. I, 20th Kans. Vol. Inf., killed, 900.
Rickle, Lewis, pvt., Troop I, 11th U. S. V. Cav., wounded, 1197.
Rickman, Emanuel, pvt., Co. D, 1st S. Dak. Vol. Inf., wounded, 954.
Riddet, Alexander, pvt., Co. L, 28th Inf., U. S. V., wounded, 1152.
Rider, Ernest L., pvt., Co. L, 13th Minn. Vol. Inf., mentioned, 762; wounded, 761.
Ridner, Rufus, pvt., Co. A, 37th Inf., U. S. V., wounded, 1140.
Rie, Charles, pvt., Troop E, 4th U.S. Cav., wounded, 947.
Rieffennacht, Fred E., pvt., Co. G, 9th U. S. Inf., killed, 443, 445.
Rietz, Fred L., pvt., Batty. F, 4th U. S. Art., killed, 1225.
Riffee, Clarence W., pvt., Co. A, 4th Ohio Vol. Inf., wounded, 365.
Riles, Augustus, pvt., Co. H, 48th Inf., U. S. V., death, 1205.
Riley, Charley P., pvt., Co. H, 9th U. S. Inf., wounded, 444.
Riley, Charles S., sergt., 26th U. S. Inf., mentioned, 1328, 1329.
Riley, Edwin R., pvt., Co. H, 13th U. S. Inf., death, 1178.
Riley, Fred E., pvt., Co. A, 42d Inf., U. S. V., wounded, 1231.
Riley, James E., pvt., Co. C, 20th Kans. Vol. Inf., wounded, 915.
Riley, R. E., pvt., Co. L, 1st Nebr. Vol. Inf., wounded, 950.
Riley, Thomas B., pvt., Co. L, 45th Inf., U. S. V., death, 1219.
Riley, Walter M., corpl., Co. F, 1st Nebr. Vol. Inf., death, 967.
Rinehart, Alton A., pvt., Co. K, 1st Wash. Vol. Inf., killed, 914.
Ring, John H., pvt., Hosp. Corps, U. S. A., death, 482.
Ringgold, Ga., movement of troops to, 92.
Rink, Paul, pvt., Batty. L, 6th U. S. Art., death, 1119; wounded, 1112.
Rio Janeiro, U. S. transport, mentioned, 618, 720–722, 729, 742, 763, 791, 794, 796, 797, 830, 1080, 1081, 1095.
Rio Grande, U. S. transport, mentioned, 190, 220, 224, 305, 306, 310.
Rio Negros, Spanish ship, mentioned, 916, 991.
Riordan, William F., pvt., Co. I, 13th U. S. Inf., wounded, 1010.
Rios, Spanish gen., mentioned, 862, 997.
Rique, Richard, pvt., Co. C, 9th U. S. Inf., mentioned, 246.
Risner, George I., pvt., Co. E, 42d Inf., U. S. V., death, 1196.
Rist, Charlie, pvt., Troop F, 3d U. S. Cav., death, 1123.
Rita, captured Spanish vessel, appraisement, 95, 103, 117–119; mentioned, 106, 108, 109, 117–120, 122, 127, 128, 142, 280, 341, 370.
Ritchey, John P., pvt., Co. C, 12th U. S. Inf., wounded, 1234.
Ritchie, William H., pvt., Co. E, 9th U. S. Inf., killed, 1298.
Ritchie, William B., 2d lieut., 10th Pa. Vol. Inf., mentioned, 731.
Ritter, Henry, corpl., Co. H, 1st Cal. Vol. Inf., wounded, 904.
Rivers, Frank, pvt., Co. A, 1st Wash. Vol. Inf., wounded, 897.
Rivers, William C., 1st lieut., 1st U. S. Cav., wounded, 123.
Rizal, insurgent gen., mentioned, 1129, 1131.
Roach, Thomas, pvt., Co. L, 21st U. S. Inf., death, 1104.
Robb, Charles N., pvt., Co. E, 1st Mont. Vol. Inf., wounded, 1017.
Robberson, William B., pvt., Hosp. Corps, U. S. A., death, 803.
Robbins, Charles B., 1st sergt., Co. B, 1st Nebr. Vol. Inf., wounded, 952.
Robbins, Weldon R., pvt., Co. A, 1st Nebr. Vol. Inf., wounded, 948.
Robe, Charles H., maj., 14th U. S. Inf., mentioned, 635.
Roberts, Archibald, pvt., Co. M, 39th Inf., U. S. V., death, 1191.
Roberts, A. L., corpl., Co. D, 2d Oreg. Vol. Inf., wounded, 946.
Roberts, Charles D., capt., 35th Inf., U. S. V., mentioned, 1186.
Roberts, Earl E., corpl., Co. A, 37th Inf., U. S. V., wounded, 1152.
Roberts, Elmer O., pvt., Co. C, 2d Oreg. Vol. Inf., wounded, 946.
Roberts, Los H., pvt., Co. B, 28th Inf., U. S. V., wounded, 1189.
Roberts, Ray S., pvt., Co. K, 14th U. S. Inf., wounded, 454.
Roberts, Samuel A., pvt., Co. H, 36th Inf., U. S. V., wounded, 1233.
Roberts, Thomas A., 2d lieut., 10th U. S. Cav., mentioned, 83; wounded, 123.
Roberts, Ward G., pvt., Co. G, 1st Nebr. Vol. Inf., wounded, 946.

INDEX.   1463

Robertson, James, sergt., Troop B, 4th U. S. Cav., killed, 1052.
Robertson, John, 2d lieut., 6th U. S. Inf., mentioned, 83; wounded, 124.
Robertson, Samuel, pvt., Troop E, 3d U. S. Cav., death, 1255.
Robeson, William B., pvt., Hosp. Corps, U. S. A., mentioned, 761.
Robine, Hiram G., pvt., Co. A, 39th Inf., U. S. V., death, 1178.
Robinson, Fred A., pvt., Troop D, 9th U. S. Cav., death, 1274.
Robinson, George W., pvt., Troop A, 3d U. S. Cav., drowned, 1190.
Robinson, H. M., chief clerk, Railway Mail Service, mentioned, 298.
Robinson, James, corpl., Co. L, 49th Inf., U. S. V., death, 1219.
Robinson, John A., corpl., Co. H, 33d Inf., U. S. V., killed, 1101.
Robinson, John E., pvt., Co. M, 1st Mont. Vol. Inf., wounded, 946, 954.
Robinson, Joseph A., sergt., Co. D, 20th Kans. Vol. Inf., wounded, 983.
Robinson, Leonard, pvt., Co. C, 34th Inf., U. S. V., wounded, 1220.
Robinson, Noyes C., capt., 13th Minn. Vol. Inf., wounded, 915.
Robinson, Peter T., pvt., Co. K, 34th Inf., U. S. V., death, 1132.
Robinson, William S., pvt., Co. D, 46th Inf., U. S. V., death, 1172.
Roche, Thomas J., pvt., Batty. K, 3d U. S. Art., death, 802.
Rock, Thomas, pvt., Co. F, 20th U. S. Inf., death, 1001.
Rockafellow, Nathan D., pvt., Co. D, 51st Iowa Vol. Inf., wounded, 1017.
Rockbud, Joseph, pvt., Co. E, 16th U. S. Inf., killed, 1240.
Rockefeller, Charles M., capt., 9th U. S. Inf., mentioned, 951, 980, 999, 1140.
Rockefeller, Christopher, corpl., Co. F, 23d U. S. Inf., death, 829.
Rockhill, Edward, a. a. surg., U. S. A., wounded, 1240.
Rockhill, William W., U. S. commissioner to China, mentioned, 434, 470, 476, 501 502.
Rockwell, Allen B., pvt., Co. C, 10th Pa. Vol. Inf. wounded, 897.
Rockwell, James J., capt., ord. dept., U. S. A., mentioned, 80.
Rocky Mountain News, allegations re. condition Colo. Vols., 834.
Rodden, Edward A., pvt., Co. L, 18th U. S. Inf., death, 1208.
Roddin, George, pvt., Co. C, 39th Inf., U. S. V., death, 1170.
Roddy, Edward G., pvt., Co. D, 13th U. S. Inf., death, 1153.
Roddy, Steve R., pvt., 23d U. S. Inf., death, 803.
Rode, Moss B., pvt., Co. C, 19th U. S. Inf., death, 1149.
Roden, Andrew, pvt., Co. H, 9th U. S. Inf., wounded, 444.
Rodenberger, Kenneth M., pvt., Co. A, 22d U. S. Inf., death, 1125.
Rodenberger, William R., pvt., Co. E 18th U. S. Inf., wounded, 943.
Roder, James N., pvt., Co. L, 19th U. S. Inf., wounded, 1250.
Rodes, Ernest W., pvt., Co. C, 17th U. S. Inf., wounded, 1101.
Rodgers, Charles A., pvt., Co. K, 14th U. S. Inf., wounded, 465.
Rodgers, Frederick, capt., U. S. N., mentioned, 288, 289, 352, 1300, 1308, 1310.
Rodgers, John E., pvt., Co. C, 18th U. S. Inf., wounded, 943.
Rodgers, John H., pvt., Troop H, 4th U. S. Cav., wounded, 1227.
Rodgers, John I., brig. gen., U. S. V., mentioned, 27, 59, 62, 69, 156, 273, 277–279, 289, 292, 294, 301, 305, 310, 311, 317, 318, 347, 355, 367, 368, 372, 379, 382, 388, 390, 392, 394–397, 399.
Rodman, John B., maj., 20th U. S. Inf., mentioned, 1018; wounded, 124.
Rodney, George B., maj., 4th U. S. Art., mentioned, 333.

Roe, Charles F., brig. gen., U. S. V, mentioned, 71, 513, 514.
Roeder, Alfred, sergt., Co. K, 6th U. S. Inf., mentioned, 1122.
Roeder, Milton M., mus., Co. D, 12th U. S. Inf., death, 1194; wounded, 1057.
Rofeno, Frank E., pvt., Co. G, 2d Oreg. Vol. Inf., death, 803.
Rogers, Clay M., pvt., Co. H, 36th Inf., U. S. V., wounded, 1096.
Rogers, Dewey, pvt., Co. G, 9th U. S. Inf., killed, 443, 445.
Rogers, George, sergt., Co. C, 1st Wyo. Vol. Inf., killed, 897.
Rogers, George W., pvt., Co. K, 22d U. S. Inf., death, 1120.
Rogers, John, pvt., Co. C, 16th U. S. Inf., wounded, 1117.
Rogers, John F., pvt., Co. L, 1st S. Dak. Vol. Inf., wounded, 961.
Rogers, John H., pvt., Troop L, 4th U. S. Cav., wounded, 1225.
Rogers, John J., pvt., Co. D, 21st U. S. Inf., death, 1287.
Rogers, John T., pvt., Troop C, 4th U. S. Cav., death, 1060.
Rogers, Jordon, pvt., Co. D, 12th U. S. Inf., wounded, 1057.
Rogers, Thomas H., pvt., Co. L, 20th U. S. Inf., wounded, 937.
Rogers, William A., pvt., Co. H, 1st Cal. Vol. Inf., wounded, 897.
Roller, John S., artif., Co. C, 1st Nebr. Vol. Inf., wounded, 975.
Rollins, George T., 1st sergt., Co. B, 21st U. S. Inf., wounded, 1052.
Romanonicz, Ignacy, sergt., Co. D, 3d U. S. Inf., death, 1104.
Romans, William L., pvt., Co. M, 29th Inf., U. S. V., death, 1245.
Roob, Daniel E., pvt., Co. A, 45th Inf., U. S. V., death, 1219.
Rooney, James E., pvt., Co. A, 26th Inf., U. S. V., death, 1113; wounded, 1108.
Rooney, Patrick B., pvt., Co. M, 17th U. S. Inf., death, 1229.
Roormon, Lahue H., pvt., Co. A, 13th U. S. Inf., death, 1132.
Roos, Albert, pvt., Co. D, 16th U. S. Inf., death, 1048.
Roosevelt, Theodore, col., 1st U. S. V. Cav., mentioned, 209, 544.
Opinion re health of army in Cuba, 202.
Roper, Andrew C., pvt., Co. E, 17th U. S. Inf., death, 1200.
Roper, Charles H., 1st sergt. Troop D, 9th U. S. Cav., death, 1261.
Roper, Fred, pvt., Co. H, 21st U. S. Inf., mentioned 206.
Ros, Modesto, Portuguese consul, mentioned, 90.
Rose, Edward, pvt., Co. I, 46th Inf., U. S. V., death, 1190.
Rose, Elmer E., pvt., Co. I, 23d U.S. Inf., wounded, 1167.
Rose, Frank L., pvt., Co. K, 1st Wash. Vol. Inf., wounded, 925.
Rosebrook, Arthur, pvt., Co. L, 11th U. S. Inf., wounded, 1015.
Rosecrans, U. S. transport, mentioned, 459, 461, 494.
Rosenecker, Charles, pvt., Co. D, 10th Pa. Vol. Inf., wounded, 961.
Rosenberg, Emil W., 1st Ill. Vol. Inf., mentioned, 235.
Ross, Alfred L., pvt., Co. I, 33d Inf., U. S. V., death, 1153.
Ross, Charles B., a. a. surg., U. S. A., killed, 1251.
Ross, George, pvt., Co. E, 19th U. S. Inf., wounded, 1152.
Ross, Harry, pvt., Troop L, 11th U. S. V. Cav., wounded, 1128.
Ross, James, pvt., Co. E, 35th Inf., U. S. V., death, 1136.
Ross, Ora, pvt., Co. F, 1st Nebr. Vol. Inf., wounded, 967.
Ross, Robert B., pvt., Co. L, 1st S. Dak. Vol. Inf., wounded, 920.
Rosselit, William C., corpl., Co. D, 17th U. S. Inf., wounded, 1087.

Rosser, Henry, corpl., Co. A, 17th U. S. Inf., wounded, 1087.
Rosser, Thomas L., brig. gen., U. S. V., mentioned, 358, 512, 513.
Rossiter, William, pvt., Co. G, 11th U. S. Inf., wounded, 390.
Roth, Edward C., pvt., Hosp. Corps, U. S. A., death, 1219.
Rothbone, Elmer R., pvt., Co. I, 21st U. S. Inf., death, 1060.
Rothe, Timothy, pvt., Co. G, 18th U. S. Inf., mentioned, 197.
Rothemeyer, Edward A., pvt., Co. A, 20th Kans. Vol. Inf., death, 879.
Rothwell, Sylvester F., sergt., Co. F, 37th Inf., U. S. V., death, 1153.
Roumania, U. S. transport, mentioned, 312, 317, 324, 328, 333, 362, 366, 400, 588–590, 592, 598, 602, 609, 617.
Rouse, Louis J., pvt., Co. B, 20th Kans. Vol. Inf., mentioned, 951.
Row, Charles T., pvt., Co. K, 30th Inf., U. S. V., death, 1160.
Rowe, Charles E., corpl., Co. M, 33d Inf., U. S. V., wounded, 1102.
Rowell, Charles W., capt., 2d U. S. Inf., killed, 127.
Rowland, George W., pvt., Co. H, 1st Mont. Vol. Inf., wounded, 898.
Rowlands, Owen H., corpl., Co. L, 1st Mont. Vol. Inf., killed, 959.
Rowley, William S., pvt., Co. B, 9th U. S. Inf., wounded, 443.
Roxbury, Edward, pvt., Co. A, 28th Inf., U. S. V., death, 1281.
Royden, Herbert N., 1st lieut., 23d U. S. Inf., mentioned, 1019.
Rubart, Charles R., pvt., Co. L, 2d Oreg. Vol. Inf., wounded, 952.
Rucker, Clarence, pvt., Co. E, 24th U. S. Inf., wounded, 1052.
Rucker, Louis H., maj., 4th U. S. Cav., mentioned, 685.
Rudd, Alson J., 1st lieut., sig. officer, U. S. V., mentioned, 994.
Ruedy, Charles W., pvt., Co. F, 2d Oreg. Vol. Inf., wounded, 946.
Ruefer, Frank, pvt., Co. G, 22d U.S. Inf., wounded, 941.
Ruffin, James, pvt., Co. G, 24th U. S. Inf., death, 1082.
Ruggles, Arthur W., pvt., Co. B, 9th U. S. Inf., wounded, 443.
Ruhl, Charles H., pvt., Co. H, 2d Oreg. Vol. Inf., death, 830.
Ruhlen, George, lieut. col., ch. qm., U. S. V., mentioned, 643, 752, 758, 799.
Ruiz, insurgent, mentioned, 1264.
Rumbley, William M., corpl., Co. I, 20th Kans. Vol. Inf., wounded, 931.
Rumery, Alton J., pvt., Troop L, 3d U. S. Cav., death, 1223.
Rummels, Charles, pvt., Co. H, 1st Mont. Vol. Inf., wounded, 895.
Rundy, William, pvt., Co. N, 26th Inf., U. S. V., death, 1130.
Rupel, William M., pvt., Co. E, 17th U. S. Inf., death, 1232; wounded, 1055.
Ruppert, Albert J., pvt., Co. H, 1st Wash. Vol. Inf., killed, 915.
Ruppert, Lennie L., corpl., Troop A, 4th U. S. Cav., wounded, 1209.
Rush, Curtis J., pvt., Batty. B, 6th U. S. Art., death, 1221.
Rush, Solomon F., pvt., Co. A, 10th Pa. Vol. Inf., 954.
Rushingbo, William R., pvt., Troop E, 9th U. S. Cav., wounded, 1240.
Rushworth, Lester, pvt., Co. H, 43d Inf., U. S. V., wounded, 1168.
Russel, Edgar, capt., sig. officer, U. S. V., mentioned, 419.
Russel, Isaac, discharged, Batty. A, Utah Vol. Art., U. S. V., wounded, 897.
Russell, Jack M., pvt., Co. E, 9th U. S. Inf., wounded, 1299.
Russell, John C., jr., corpl., Co. F, 42d Inf., U. S. V., death, 1156.
Russell, John H., corpl., Co. E, 9th U. S. Inf., wounded, 1307.

Russel, Marcus B., sergt., Troop G, 1st U. S. V. Cav., killed, 61.
Russell, Solomon, pvt., Co. H, 1st Wash. Vol. Inf., wounded, 925.
Russell, Thomas, pvt., Co. F, 24th U. S. Inf., death, 1057, 1060.
Russell, Thomas, pvt., Co. F, 26th Inf., U. S. V., wounded, 1126.
Russell, William, pvt., Co. H, 47th Inf., U. S. V., wounded, 1202.
Rutherford, Harry, pvt., Co. G, 1st Idaho Vol. Inf., wounded, 897.
Rutledge, Jesse, pvt., Hosp. Corps., U. S. A., wounded, 1092.
Rutledge, William, sergt., Troop B, 9th U. S. Cav., death, 1267.
Ryan, Ernest, pvt., Co. L, 20th Kans. Vol. Inf., death, 997; wounded, 995.
Ryan, James, pvt., Co. C, 1st Idaho Vol. Inf., wounded, 898.
Ryan, James A., capt., 15th U. S. Cav., mentioned, 1319, 1326, 1328, 1343, 1344; wounded, 124.
Ryan, James C., pvt., Co. B, 39th Inf., U. S. V., killed, 1145.
Ryan, James J., pvt, Co. M, 45th Inf., U. S. V., killed, 1218.
Ryan, John, corpl., Co. G, 44th Inf., U. S. V., killed, 1173.
Ryan, John P., capt., 6th U. S. Cav., mentioned, 302, 1344.
Ryan, Joseph, pvt., Co. D, 9th U. S. Inf., wounded, 444.
Ryan, Joseph M., pvt., Co. E, 34th Inf., U. S. V., death, 1205.
Ryan, Joseph P., corpl., Co. C, 11th U. S. Inf., wounded, 390.
Ryan, Matthew N., pvt., Co. D, 1st S. Dak. Vol. Inf., killed, 949.
Ryan Michael, sergt., Co. A, 14th U. S. Inf., death, 972.
Ryan, Orian, pvt., Batty. L, 3d U. S. Art., wounded, 895.
Ryan, Patrick, pvt., Co. C, 20th U. S. Inf., death, 1086.
Ryan, Peter, pvt., Co. E, 1st S. Dak. Vol. Inf., killed, 949.
Ryan, Thomas, sergt., Co. F, 4th U. S Inf., death, 1170.
Ryan, William, pvt., Co. C, 16th U. S. Inf., wounded, 1152.
Ryan, William J., capt., com. sub., U. S. V., mentioned, 1274.
Ryberg, Walfred A., corpl., Co. I, 13th Minn. Vol. Inf., wounded, 963.
Rydeberg, Andrew, pvt., Co. B, 3d U. S. Inf., mentioned, 202.
Rylott, Thomas, corpl., Co. E, 1st Idaho Vol. Inf., wounded, 1008.
Rymer, W. T., pvt., Co. B, 1st Nebr. Vol. Inf., wounded, 950.
Rysdyk, Sidney, pvt., Co. F, 13th U. S. Inf., death, 1078.
Saal, Emil, pvt., Co. L, 1st Nebr. Vol. Inf., wounded, 956.
Sackett, George T., pvt., Co. H, 3d U. S. Inf., rescued, 1129.
Saffold, Marion B., capt., 13th U. S. Inf., killed, 1082.
Safford, Frank, pvt., Co. M, 14th U. S. Inf., killed, 482; mentioned, 481, 482.
Sagasta, Spanish prime minister, mentioned, 234.
Sailsbury, Frank, pvt., Co. H, 40th Inf., U. S. V., killed, 1183.
Saiter, Arthur, pvt., Co. G, 12th U. S. Inf., wounded, 1195.
Saler, William B., pvt., Co. M, 18th U. S. Inf., death, 1257.
Sales, Quintin, insurgent officer, surrender, 1274.
Saling, Philip, pvt., Co. H, 43d Inf., U. S. V., killed, 1168.
Salisbury, Austin J., pvt., Co. H, 2d Oreg. Vol. Inf., wounded, 1003.
Salisbury, Burton, pvt., Co. B, 21st U. S. Inf., mentioned, 212.
Sallisbury, William, pvt., Co. H, 30th Inf., U.S.V., killed, 1147.
Salmon, Charles S., corpl., Co. F, 26th Inf., U. S. V., wounded, 1189.

INDEX. 1465

Saltgaver, Theodore P., pvt., Co. D, 51st Iowa Vol. Inf., wounded, 1060.
Saltzman, Charles McK., 2d lieut., 1st U. S. Cav., mentioned, 123.
Salvadora, Spanish steamer, mentioned, 1074.
Salwitshka, Joseph, pvt., Co. E, 3d U. S. Inf., wounded, 997.
Samar, U. S. gunboat, mentioned, 1111.
Samoa, U. S. transport, mentioned, 1288, 1291.
Sample, Frank I., pvt., Co. C. 20th Kans. Vol. Inf., wounded, 983.
Sampsel, George M., pvt., Co. L.. 30th Inf., U. S. V., death, 1210.
Sampson, William T., rear-admiral, U. S. N., designated a commissioner to arrange evacuation by Spanish of Porto Rico, 397.
Mentioned, 16, 19, 25, 28-30, 34, 40, 50, 67-69, 74, 78, 81, 87, 89, 90, 92, 93, 105, 115, 128, 136, 154, 155, 157, 163, 181, 187, 200, 262, 273, 276, 280-287, 293, 297-300, 379.
Samson, Edgar, pvt., Co. G, 2d Oreg. Vol. Inf., wounded, 946.
Samson, Pedro, comandante of police mentioned, 1206.
Samson, insurgent general, surrender, 1306.
San Antonio, steamship, mentioned, 592, 621.
Sanders, Carleton E., pvt., Co. L, 2d Oreg. Vol. Inf., wounded, 946.
Sanders, Guy N., pvt., Co. L, 2d Oreg. Vol. Inf., wounded, 946.
Sanders, William H., pvt., Co. A, 18th U. S. Inf., death, 803.
Sandico, insurgent chief, mentioned, 1187, 1138, 1203.
Work done, and positions held by, 1138.
Sandidge, John F., corpl., Co. A, 40th Inf., U. S. V., wounded, 1150.
Sandman, Henry A., pvt., Co. C, 22d U. S. Inf., death, 1153.
Sands, A., pvt., Co. D, 11th U. S. Inf., wounded, 390.
Sands, Herbert, corpl., Co. F, 20th Kans. Vol. Inf., wounded, 915.
Sands, Joseph, pvt., Co. I, 36th Inf., U. S. V., death, 1178.
Sands, James H., capt., U. S. N., mentioned, 362.
Sanford, George, pvt., Co. I, 21st U. S. Inf., death, 1120.
San Francisco, Cal.:
Alleged deplorable health conditions in 7th Cal. Vol. Inf., 783.
Arrangements for care of sick, 1021.
Camp at, insanitary condition alleged, 787.
Expeditionary troops at, 748.
Disposition, 749.
General Otis to command troops at, 661, 662, 665.
Landing of surplus stores from transport, refused by customs authorities, 880.
Movement of troops to and from, 83, 84, 689, 882, 883, 886, 887, 1012.
Number and strength of regiments at, 736.
Presidio reservation, camp to be established on, 735.
Sanger, Joseph P., brig. gen., U. S. V., mentioned, 295, 512-518, 1315.
San Juan, P. R., evacuation commission to meet at, 715.
San Marcon, transport, mentioned 184, 190, 198, 330.
San Miguel, insurgent gen., mentioned, 1110.
Sanson, Bert, pvt., Co. K, 20th Kans. Vol. Inf., wounded, 901.
Sanson, ——, pvt., Co. C, 4th U. S. Inf., mentioned, 1042.
Santiago de Cuba, W. I. See under *Cuba.*
Santiago, steamship, mentioned, 189, 190, 192, 199, 233, 243, 310, 370, 379, 386, 393.
Saratoga, U. S. transport, mentioned, 190, 245, 249, 255, 332, 591, 625.
Sarazin, Herbert J., pvt., Co. B, 1st Colo. Vol. Inf., death, 803.
Sargent, Herbert H., col., 5th U. S. Vol. Inf., mentioned, 191, 208, 212, 220, 230, 235, 422, 424.
Sargent, Thomas, pvt., Hosp. Corps, U. S. A., death, 803.
Sario, steamer, mentioned, 1134.
Sarratt, Edwin O., 1st lieut., 6th U. S. Art., mentioned, 1019.
Sater, William A., 1st lieut., 18th Inf., killed 124.

Satrustegui, Spanish ship, mentioned, 991, 1069.
Saturnus, Spanish merchant steamer, mentioned, 746.
Sauer, Clemens, pvt., Co. F, 23d U. S. Inf., mentioned, 828.
Saunders, Arthur, pvt., Co. C, 13th U. S. Inf., death, 875.
Saunders, David I., pvt., Co. I, 1st Colo. Vol. Inf., death, 861.
Saunders, Henry K., pvt., Co. F, 14th U. S. Inf., death, 917.
Saunders, James, pvt., Co. K, 48th Inf., U. S. V., drowned, 1205.
Saunders, James F., corpl., Co. K, 18th U. S. Inf., wounded, 914.
Saunders, Joseph R., pvt., Co. B, 27th Inf., U. S. V., death, 1201.
Saunders, William H., pvt., Troop B, 1st U. S. Cav., mentioned, 226.
Savage, Preston, pvt., Co. B, 15th U. S. Inf., wounded, 943.
Savannah, Ga.:
Harbor facilities for embarkation of troops, 114.
Movement of troops to, equipment, 73.
Saville, Matthew E., 1st lieut., 10th U. S. Inf., wounded, 124.
Savoia, steamship, Mauser rifles shipped by, 1126.
Sawyer, Charles, pvt., Co. I, 3d U. S. Inf., death, 1178.
Sawyer, J. Estcourt, maj., qm. dept., U. S. A., mentioned, 48, 73, 146.
Saxton, John A., pvt., Co. M, 1st Mont. Vol. Inf., death, 1008.
Sayer, Frank B., pvt., Co. E, 47th Inf., U. S. V., wounded, 1187.
Sayers, Roy, pvt., Co. I, 17th U. S. Inf., death, 1167.
Sayles, Maynard E., pvt., Co. L, 1st Nebr. Vol. Inf., death, 979; wounded, 950.
Sayre, Farrand, 1st lieut., 8th U. S. Cav., mentioned, 638, 688.
Scales, Wallace B., 2d lieut., 6th U. S. Cav., mentioned, 421.
Scallon, Thomas, pvt., Co. K, 1st Mont. Vol. Inf., killed, 983.
Scandia, U. S. transport, mentioned, 605, 741, 742, 744, 748, 752, 753, 755, 758, 759, 761-764, 766, 784, 798-800, 830, 852, 853, 855-857, 860, 862-865, 867, 868, 871, 886, 889, 915, 922, 929, 930.
Scanlan, Harry J., pvt., Co. A, 22d U. S. Inf., wounded, 948.
Schafer, Charles P., pvt., Co. E, 40th Inf., U. S. V., death, 1181.
Schaffer, Charles E., pvt., Co. I 1st Nebr. Vol. Inf., wounded, 982.
Schaffer, Marion F., pvt., Co. C, 37th Inf., U. S. V., wounded, 1146.
Schall, John W., col., 6th Pa. Vol. Inf., mentioned, 521-523.
Schall, William P., pvt., Co. B, 3d U. S. Inf., death, 1217.
Schander, Fred W., corpl., Co. A, 1st Wash. Vol. Inf., wounded, 896.
Scharer, Henry J., corpl., Co. C, 9th U. S. Inf., killed, 1297; wounded, 444.
Scharff, Henry, pvt., Co. H, 3d U. S. Inf., death, 1249.
Schenck, William T., 1st lieut., 25th U. S. Inf., killed, 1141.
Schenk, William G., pvt., Co. M, 3d U. S. Inf., wounded, 946.
Scherer, A. F., pvt., Co. G, 1st Cal. Vol. Inf., wounded, 897.
Scherrer, John, corpl., Co. G, 20th Kans. Vol. Inf., killed, 949.
Scheule, Theodore, pvt., Co. C, 1st Mont. Vol. Inf., wounded, 1008.
Schilling, Frederick, pvt., Hosp. Corps, U. S. A., death, 1255.
Schisler, John A., pvt., Co. I, 12th U. S. Inf., death, 1217.
Schlachter, Gustav F., 2d lieut., 44th Inf., U. S. V., wounded, 1174.
Schlager, William, pvt., Co. H, 1st U. S. Inf., wounded, 1275.
Schleicher, Charles, corpl., Co. M, 21st U. S. Inf., death, 1153.
Schlewing, Gottlieb D., sergt., Co. I, 23d U. S. Inf., wounded, 1195.
Schaley, Lanier, corpl., Co. G, 39th Inf., U. S. V., death, 1191; wounded, 1149,

Schley, Leonard P., pvt., Co. C, 9th U. S. Inf., killed, 1297.
Schley, Winfield S., rear-admiral, U. S. N., designated commissioner to arrange for evacuation of Porto Rico, 397.
Mentioned, 16, 19, 22, 262, 282, 403.
Schmidt, August, pvt., Co. K, 22d U. S. Inf., wounded, 941.
Schmidt, Emil R., messenger, Gen. Brooks's hdqrs., mentioned, 302.
Schmidt, Frank, qm. sergt., Co. L, 16th U. S. Inf., death, 1187.
Schmidt, Frank G., pvt., Co. D, 32d Inf., U. S. V., wounded, 1218, 1225.
Schmidt, John, pvt., Co. E, 22d U. S. Inf., killed, 940.
Schmidt, Richard F., corpl., Co. H, 4th U. S. Inf., wounded, 956.
Schneebele, William, pvt., Co. H, 14th U. S. Inf., death, 1125.
Schneider, Anthony L., pvt., Co. M, 37th Inf., U. S. V., wounded, 1146.
Schneider, Charles, pvt., Co. L, 1st Ill. Vol. Inf., mentioned, 219.
Schneider, George, pvt., Co. E, 22d U. S. Inf., injured, 941.
Schneider, Harry J., pvt., Co. I, 19th U. S. Inf., wounded, 1255.
Schoeffel, John B., 1st lieut., 9th U. S. Inf., wounded, 435.
Schoeffel, Francis H., capt., 9th U. S. Inf., mentioned, 1307.
Schoenknecht, August, mus., Co. L, 17th U. S. Inf., suicide, 1156.
Schofield, Victor E., pvt., Co. I, 1st S. Dak. Vol. Inf., killed, 903.
Schomers, Peter, pvt., Co. A, 33d Inf., U. S. V., wounded, 1228.
Schooler, Balious, mus., Co. M, 39th Inf., U. S. V., death, 1178.
Schork, Frank W., pvt., Co. L, 9th U. S. Inf., wounded, 1086.
Schott, Otto, pvt., Troop K, 3d U. S. Cav., missing, 1209.
Schrader, Clyde J., pvt., Troop E, 11th U. S. V. Cav., wounded, 1192.
Schrader, Martin, pvt., Troop K, 3d U. S. Cav., wounded, 1255.
Schreiber, William G., capt., 35th Inf., U. S. V., wounded, 1212.
Schreiner, Edward R., 1st lieut., med. dept., U. S. A., mentioned, 1018.
Schroeder, J., pvt., U. S. Marine Corps, wounded, 459.
Schroeder, Henry F., sergt., Co. L, 16th U. S. Inf., wounded, 1214.
Schroeder, William, sergt., Co. E, 17th U. S. Inf., wounded, 1060.
Schryver, Percy, pvt., Co. G, 46th Inf., U. S. V., death, 1197.
Schuelr, Matt, pvt., Co. M, 1st S. Dak. Vol. Inf., wounded, 949.
Schueller, George J., mus., Co. I, 1st N. Dak. Vol. Inf., killed, 967.
Schuetz, August, artif., Co. A, 12th U. S. Inf., killed, 1160.
Schuff, Samuel, corpl., Co. D, 15th U. S. Inf., wounded, 1256.
Schuitzler, Gustav F., pvt., Co. C, 9th U. S. Inf., killed, 1297.
Schulemrie, George S., pvt., Batty. M, 3d U. S. Art., wounded, 897.
Schultz, August, pvt., Co. E, 4th U. S. Inf., death 1264.
Schultz, Bernard, pvt., Co. C, 17th U. S. Inf., death, 1249.
Schuller, Simon, pvt., Co. L, 22d U. S. Inf., wounded, 994.
Schultz, Carl E., pvt., Co. B, 21st U. S. Inf., wounded, 1235.
Schultz, George, pvt., Co. A, 23d U. S. Inf., death, 1015.
Schultz, Harry H., pvt., Co. H, 44th Inf., U. S. V., death, 1162.
Schultz, John T., pvt., Co. I, 1st Mont. Vol. Inf., wounded, 977.
Schultze, William D., corpl., Co. F, 18th U. S. Inf., death, 1276.
Schupp, Benjamin, pvt., Co. C, 39th Inf., U. S. V., death, 1215.

Schurman, Jacob G., prest., P. I. Com., mentioned, 883, 998, 1002.
Schuster, George J., pvt., Co. A, 30th Inf., U. S. V., death, 1196.
Schurchard, George A., pvt., Co. L, 6th U. S. Inf., killed, 1145.
Schuyler, Walter S., col., 203d N. Y. Vol. Inf., mentioned, 524, 527-529.
Schwan, Theodore, brig. gen., U. S. V., mentioned, 8, 16, 55, 267, 268, 276, 278, 289, 292, 294, 301, 305, 307, 309, 310, 316, 321, 329, 333, 369, 380, 381, 393, 536, 537, 547, 549, 576, 578, 902, 1014, 1030, 1082, 1083, 1085, 1086, 1128, 1129, 1131-1133, 1135, 1136, 1138, 1139, 1154.
Schwartz, Charles W., pvt., Co. H, 13th Minn. Vol. Inf., death, 803.
Schwartz, Christ, pvt., Co. A, 3d U. S. Inf., death, 1078.
Schwartz, John, sergt., Troop A, 4th U. S. Cav., wounded, 1234.
Schwartz, William F., pvt., Co. K, 2d Oreg. Vol. Inf., wounded, 946.
Schwarzhoff, Gen., lost in burning hdqrs. of Gen. Waldersee, 505.
Schwertfeger, Casper, pvt., Co. F, 9th U. S. Inf., killed, 443, 445.
Schwoebel, Jacob, pvt., Co. M, 14th U. S. Inf., wounded, 454.
Schwed, Fred, pvt., Troop L, 3d U. S. Cav., missing, 1222.
Scorpion U. S. gunboat, mentioned, 22.
Scott, Albert B., 1st lieut., 13th U. S. Inf., killed, 124; mentioned, 83.
Scott, Andrew, pvt., Co. G, 40th Inf., U. S. V., death, 1228.
Scott, Campbell, pvt., Co. D, 20th Kans. Vol. Inf., wounded, 917.
Scott, Edward J., pvt., Co. E, 17th U. S. Inf., death, 1156.
Scott, Ernest, qm. sergt., Co. B, 1st Idaho Vol. Inf., wounded, 897.
Scott, Ernest D., 2d lieut., 6th U. S. Art., mentioned, 1240.
Scott, George, corpl., Co. G, 1st Idaho Vol. Inf., killed, 994.
Scott, George W., pvt., Co. D, 6th U. S. Inf., death, 1208.
Scott, James L., batt. sergt. maj., 33d Inf., U. S. V., wounded, 1254.
Scott, Joe, pvt., Co. A, 1st Nebr. Vol. Inf., wounded, 950.
Scott, Joseph, pvt., Co. I, 20th Kans. Vol. Inf., wounded, 976.
Scott, Miller, pvt., Co. E, 49th Inf., U. S. V., wounded, 1254.
Scott, Walter, pvt., Co. G, 4th U. S. Inf., death, 1082.
Scott, Walter S., maj., 27th U. S. Inf., mentioned, 1330.
Scott, William S., capt., a. a. g., U. S. V., mentioned, 133, 219, 373, 379, 395, 1264.
Scovel, Sylvester, N. Y. World representative, mentioned, 175, 176, 179.
Scribner, Ellet, pvt., Co. D, 32d Inf., U. S. V., wounded, 1183.
Scriven, Dee M., pvt., Co. B, 1st Nebr. Vol. Inf., wounded, 950.
Scriven, George P., maj., sig. officer, U. S. V., mentioned, 766, 767, 783.
Scroggs, John A., pvt., Co. A, 1st Colo. Vol. Inf., death, 803.
Scudder, Marshall S., capt., 1st Wash. Vol. Inf., mentioned, 992.
Scully, Thomas E., pvt., Co. H, 17th U. S. Inf., wounded, 1087.
Seabrooke, Harry, pvt., Co. H, 1st Nebr. Vol. Inf., wounded, 899.
Seaholm, Otto, pvt., Co. L, 17th U. S. Inf., killed, 1222.
Seaman, George A., 2d lieut., Utah Vol. Art., wounded, 903, 922.
Searcy, William E., corpl., Co. D, 2d Oreg. Vol. Inf., wounded, 946.
Sears, Clinton B., maj., Engr. Corps, U. S. A., mentioned, 1030, 1270.
Sears, Elijah, pvt., Co. H, 48th Inf., U. S. V., death, 1168.
Sears, George L., pvt., Co. M, 1st Nebr. Vol. Inf., wounded, 950.
Sears, James W., pvt., Co. H, 40th Inf., U. S. V., death, 1208.

Sebilus, Nick, sergt., Troop F, 4th U. S. Cav., killed, 1052.
Seckler, Harry H., 1st lieut. 20th Kans. Vol. Inf., mentioned, 960.
Second Army Corps, organization, 519-529.
Secrist, Frank P., pvt., Co. B, 17th U. S. Inf., death, 1095.
Sedgwick, U. S. transport, mentioned, 626.
Seeberger, John, pvt., Co. G, 42d Inf., U. S. V., wounded, 1146.
Seeholts, Albert M., pvt., Co. M, 34th Inf., U. S. V., death, 1190.
Seeley, Ernest, pvt., Co. E, 30th Inf., U. S. V., death, 1180.
Seeman, Maurice L., pvt., Co. A, 14th U. S. Inf., killed, 895.
Segal, Charles, corpl., Co. L, 30th Inf., U. S. V., death, 1160.
Segurança, transport, mentioned, 184, 186, 190, 245-247, 249, 250, 253. 330, 382.
Sehon, John L., 1st lieut., 20th U. S. Inf., capt. retired, mentioned, 842.
Seifert, Ernest, pvt., Batty. L, 3d U. S. Art., killed, 966.
Seigenthaler, A. W., pvt., Co. C, 22d U. S. Inf., wounded, 931.
Seil, Frank, pvt., Co. B, 14th U. S. Inf., death, 1070.
Seitz, Charles A., pvt., Co. M, 14th U. S. Inf., killed, 895.
Seitz, Julius, pvt., Co. D, 19th U. S. Inf., death, 1217.
Sellers, Thomas, pvt., Co. K, 6th U. S. Inf., death, 1190.
Sellman, John F., corpl., Co. C, 27th Inf., U. S. V., death, 1144.
Selmer, Emil F., pvt., Batty. A, Utah Vol. Art., wounded, 976.
Sempson, William, pvt., Co. E, 20th U. S. Inf., wounded, 934.
Senator, transport, mentioned, 556, 585, 593, 603, 614, 628, 660, 699-701 704, 722, 730, 792, 799, 802, 839, 855, 873, 880-883, 887, 889, 892, 922, 929, 933, 936, 940, 962, 976-978 997, 1026, 1041, 1046, 1049, 1073, 1088, 1103, 1123 1128.
Seneca, hospital ship, mentioned, 123, 137, 139, 141, 157, 191, 197, 224, 312, 317, 319, 323-325, 328, 333, 402, 403.
Senechal, Victor J., pvt., Co. F, 4th U. S. Inf., death, 1165.
Senn, Nicholas, lieut. col., chief surg, U. S. V., mentioned, 378.
Typhoid fever situation, report, 385.
Sensabough, George F. pvt., Co. G, 1st U. S. Inf., death, 1283.
Sentman, John F., sergt., Co. G, 12th U. S. Inf., wounded, 1212.
Serenson, John, pvt., Co. L, 1st Mont. Vol. Inf., wounded, 895.
Sergeant, Thomas H., pvt., Hosp. Corps, U. S. A., mentioned, 761.
Settle, Robert C., pvt., Co. M, 30th Inf., U. S. V., wounded, 1250.
Setzer, Leslie G., pvt., Co. L, 20th Kans. Vol. Inf., wounded, 950.
Seumore, William, pvt., Astor Batty., U. S. A., wounded, 761.
Sevenson, Gotfried, pvt., Co. A, 9th U. S. Inf., killed, 445.
Seventh Army Corps, organization, 547-555.
Seventh Regiment Spanish Inf.; mentioned, 778.
Sewall, Harold M., U. S. minister to Hawaii, memo. on Caroline and Ladrones islands, 745.
Seward, William P., pvt., Co. G, 21st U. S. Inf., death, 1063.
Sexton, Edward F., pvt., Hosp. Corps, U. S. A., reported death, 1213.
Sexton, Semon H., pvt., Co. E, 42d Inf., U. S. V., death, 1165.
Seyburn, John R., 1st lieut., 5th U. S. Inf., mentioned, 83 wounded, 124.
Seymour, Edward, vice-admiral British navy, mentioned, 425, 429.
Seymour, Harry T., 1st sergt., Co. D, 37th Inf., U. S. V., wounded, 1146.
Seymour, John, pvt., Co. A, 9th U. S. Inf., wounded, 443.
Shaffer, Elmer E., pvt., Co. M, 40th Inf., U. S. V., wounded, 1162.

Shaffer, Theodore, pvt., Co. D, 32d Inf., U. S. V., death, 1150.
Shafter, James M., collector of customs, So. Pac. Ry. Co., mentioned, 158.
Shafter, William R., maj. gen., U. S. V.:
Assigned to command of troops at—
New Orleans, 7, 8.
Tampa, Fla., 9.
Condition of command, 360.
Congratulations on surrender, 150, 152.
Correspondence, 9, 10, 13, 14, 15, 16, 17, 18, 19, 20, 21, 22, 23, 24, 25, 26, 27, 29, 30, 31, 32, 33, 35, 36, 38, 40, 49, 50, 53, 54, 55, 57, 58. 59, 60, 61, 62, 64, 65-68, 70, 72, 85, 87, 88, 89, 91, 92, 93, 94, 95, 97, 99-101, 103, 104, 105, 106, 107, 109, 110, 111, 113, 114, 115, 116, 117, 119, 120, 121, 122, 123-125, 126, 127, 129, 130, 132-134, 135, 137, 138, 139, 140, 141, 142, 143, 144, 145, 147, 148, 149, 150, 151, 152, 153, 154, 155, 156, 157, 158, 159, 161-163, 163, 164, 165, 166, 167, 168, 169, 170, 171, 172, 173, 174, 175, 176, 177, 178, 179, 180, 181, 182, 183, 184, 185, 186, 187, 188, 189, 190, 191, 192, 193, 194, 195, 196, 197, 198-200, 201, 202, 203, 204, 205, 206, 207, 208, 209, 210, 211, 212, 213, 214, 215, 216, 217, 218, 219, 220, 221, 222, 223, 224, 225, 226, 228, 229, 230, 231, 232, 233, 234, 235, 236, 237, 238, 239, 240, 241, 242, 243, 244, 245, 246, 248, 249, 250, 251, 252, 253, 254, 255, 256, 257, 290, 299, 305, 306, 310, 318 325; with Gen. José Toral, Spanish commander, Santiago de Cuba, 79, 130, 133, 153, 154.
General officers accompanying, 47.
Health, 87, 94, 95, 100, 109, 120, 125.
Instructions to in cipher, 17.
Mentioned, 8, 11, 28, 34, 39, 40, 41, 44, 46, 47, 49, 50, 55-57, 66, 72, 73, 84, 86, 90-92, 110, 113, 116, 118, 120-122, 128, 129, 134, 136, 139, 143-145, 150, 151, 153, 163, 173, 183, 186, 188, 203, 208, 210, 219, 221, 227, 230, 235, 236, 240-242, 248, 250, 251, 255, 263, 265, 269, 272, 279, 291, 303, 310, 311, 313, 317, 330, 333, 338, 359-361, 363-367, 370, 377, 381, 383, 385, 392-395, 398, 400, 401, 416, 419, 421-423, 425, 428, 431, 441, 443, 449, 457, 459, 461, 464, 534, 539, 540, 750, 931, 990, 1013, 1257.
Reporting arrival at Montauk, 256.
Reports on transports Grant and Sherman, 980.
Re reduction of Santiago, situation, 87.
Shallenberger, Hon. W. S., Asst. P. M. Gen., mentioned, 695.
Shan Tung, Chinese governor, mentioned, 424.
Shaner, George R., mus., Co. C, 43d Inf., U. S. V., wounded, 1187.
Shank, Daniel F., pvt., Co. K, 9th U. S. Inf., death, 1140.
Shanks, David C., capt. 18th U. S. Inf., mentioned, 884, 1264.
Shannon, George, pvt., Co. C, 51st Iowa Vol. Inf., wounded, 984.
Shannon, William, pvt., Co. L, 25th U. S. Inf., killed, 1141.
Shapiro, Joseph S., pvt., Hosp. Corps, U. S. A., wounded, 1087.
Sharland, Frederick C., corpl., Co. B, 20th Kans. Vol. Inf., death, 1063.
Sharp, Bernard, sergt., Batty. L, 3d U. S. Art., wounded, 895.
Sharp, Charles, pvt., Co. C., 19th U. S. Inf., death, 1210.
Sharp, Chris, president Merchants' Exchange, St. Louis, Mo., mentioned, 343.
Sharp, Frank, sergt., Co. K, 10th Pa. Vol. Inf., wounded, 961.
Sharp, Frank E., pvt., Co. C, 33d Mich. Vol. Inf., mentioned, 243.
Sharp, George W., pvt., Co. G, 17th U. S. Inf., wounded, 1055.
Sharpe, Henry G., lieut. col., sub. dept., U. S. A., mentioned, 302.
Sharpless, Charles F., pvt., Co. H, 20th U. S. Inf., wounded, 934.
Shaughnessy, Albert, pvt., Co. E, 20th Kans. Vol. Inf., wounded, 954.
Shaw, Colter, pvt., Co. M, 32d Inf., U. S. V., death, 1236.
Shaw, Harry, corpl., Co. F, 24th U. S. Inf., mentioned, 202.
Shaw, John H., pvt., Co. F, 71st N. Y. Vol. Inf., mentioned, 219.

Shaw, John W., pvt., Co. I, 40th Inf., U. S. V., killed, 1171.
Shays, Arthur, pvt., Co. G, 11th U. S. Inf., wounded, 390.
Shea, Dennis, sergt., Batty. G, 3d U. S. Art., wounded, 922.
Shea, Dennis, pvt., Co. M, 9th U. S. Inf., death, 464.
Shea, Jeremiah, sergt., Batty. A, Cal. Vol. Art., death, 992.
Shea, John E., pvt., Co. M, 22d U. S. Inf., death, 1249.
Shea, Patrick, pvt., Co. M, 14th U. S. Inf., wounded, 454.
Shea, Timothy, corpl., Co. A, 19th U. S. Inf., wounded, 1160.
Sheafe, Mark W., brig. gen., U. S. V., mentioned, 521-523.
Sheahan, Joseph V., pvt., Hosp. Corps, U. S. A., death, 1174.
Shearer, Henry C., pvt., Co. K, 30th Inf., U. S. V., death, 1208.
Shearer, Merrill E., pvt., Co. E, 12th U. S. Inf., death, 1123.
Shearer, Ralph E., pvt., Co. E, 1st Wash. Vol. Inf., killed, 897.
Sheed, Rinaldo K., pvt., Co. H, 34th Mich. Vol. Inf., mentioned, 193.
Sheehan, Cornelius, qm. sergt., Co. K, 3d Inf., killed, 1197.
Sheehan, John, pvt., Co. L, 17th U. S. Inf., death, 979.
Sheehy, John, pvt., Co. G, 16th U. S. Inf., death, 1248.
Sheeley, William J., pvt., Hosp. Corps, U. S. A., wounded, 1126.
Sheets, Lon D., corpl., Co. K, 51st Iowa Vol. Inf., wounded, 1017.
Shelato, Samuel G., sergt., Co. C, 6th U. S. Inf., wounded, 1256.
Sheldon, Jay, sergt., Co. I, 20th Kans. Vol. Inf., killed, 903; wounded, 898.
Sheldon, Joseph, sergt., Co. H, 10th Pa. Vol. Inf., wounded, 895.
Sheldon, Raymond, 2d lieut., 17th U. S. Inf., mentioned, 884.
Shen, director-general at Shanghai, China, mentioned, 487.
Shepard, Sherman, pvt., Co. F, 25th U. S. Inf., killed, 1143.
Shepard, Sherman T., pvt., Co. H, 1st Wash. Vol. Inf., death, 1020; wounded, 977.
Shell, Fred, pvt., Co. G, 1st Idaho Vol. Inf., wounded, 897.
Shelledy, Allen M., pvt., Co. E, 14th U. S. Inf., wounded, 975.
Shelton, Ewing, pvt., Co. C, 9th U. S. Inf., death, 1181.
Shepherd, Lee, pvt., Co. A; 13th U. S. Inf., death, 1170.
Sheppard, George K., sergt., Co. C, 13th Minn. Vol. Inf., wounded, 915.
Sherbourne, Thomas L., 1st lieut., 33d Inf., U. S. V., wounded, 1234.
Sheridan, Michael, pvt., Co. K, 4th U. S. Inf., wounded, 1042.
Sheridan, U. S. transport, mentioned, 503, 600, 891, 893, 903-905, 907, 921, 923, 933, 937-940, 944, 960, 962, 966-968, 975, 980, 994-996, 1000-1002, 1010, 1012, 1014, 1017, 1018, 1023, 1038, 1040, 1046, 1047, 1049, 1051, 1054, 1064, 1077, 1079, 1090, 1095, 1100, 1235, 1244, 1254, 1260, 1264, 1265, 1270, 1272, 1289, 1290, 1294, 1298, 1299, 1300, 1302, 1303, 1305, 1308, 1313, 1323, 1324, 1333, 1341, 1344, 1347, 1349.
Sheridan, Michael V., brig. gen., U. S. V., mentioned, 286, 290, 301.
Sherman, U. S. transport, mentioned, 372, 464, 465, 584, 585, 618, 890, 893, 905, 907, 933, 940, 941, 944, 952, 957, 958, 980, 995, 1016, 1026, 1027, 1033, 1040, 1041, 1043, 1047, 1058, 1075, 1087, 1094, 1115, 1128, 1157, 1163, 1210, 1235, 1244, 1323, 1341-1343, 1355.
Sherratt, E. L., 1st sergt., Co. G, 1st N.Y.Vol. Inf., mentioned, 226.
Sherrell, William J., pvt., Co. K, 6th U. S. Inf., death, 1120.
Shew, John, pvt., Co. F, 29th Inf., U. S. V., wounded, 1219.

Shewman, William H., artif., Co. E., 34th Inf., U. S. V., death, 1161.
Shey, William S., corpl., Co. A, 1st U. S. Inf., killed, 1250.
Shiba, Japanese Lieut. Col., mil. attaché, legation of Pekin, mentioned, 442.
Shibley, Joseph H., pvt., Troop A, 4th U. S. Cav., death, 1191.
Shields, Devereux, capt., 29th Inf., U. S. V., captured by insurgents, 1214; wounded, 1218, 1219.
Shields, George H., jr., 1st lieut., 12th U. S. Inf., mentioned, 1347.
Shierloh, Henry P., pvt., Co. I, 9th U. S. Inf., wounded, 1055.
Shilling, Edward, pvt., Troop L, 3d U. S. Cav., death, 1191.
Shillock, Paul, capt., med. dept., U. S. A., mentioned, 1041, 1079.
Shimerhorn, William, corpl., Co. L, 1st Wash. Vol. Inf., wounded, 984.
Shine, Eugene, pvt., Co. L, 6th U. S. Inf., death, 1217.
Shinke, August E., pvt., Co. E, 36th Inf., U. S. V., wounded, 1096.
Shiperd, Moro C., pvt., Co. M, 1st Nebr. Vol. Inf., wounded, 899.
Shipp, William E., 1st lieut., 10th U. S. Cav., killed, 124.
Shirk, Frank E., corpl., Co. M, 12th U. S. Inf., wounded, 1015.
Shoecraft, Frederick E., pvt., Co. F, 9th U. S. Inf., wounded, 444.
Shoemaker, Floyd J., pvt., Co. C, 9th U. S. Inf., death, 1297.
Shores, Leslie, pvt., Co. F, 16th U. S. Inf., wounded, 1087.
Shorey, Fred C., pvt., Co. M, 1st Wash. Vol. Inf., mentioned, 925.
Short, Noah L., pvt., Co. H, 44th Inf., U. S. V., wounded, 1147.
Short, Walter C., 2d lieut., 6th U. S. Cav., wounded, 124.
Shrey, Ernest, pvt., Troop M, 1st U. S. Cav., killed, 1235.
Shroeder, Frank A., pvt., Co. E, 1st S. Dak. Vol. Inf., killed, 949.
Shueller, Simon, pvt., Co. L, 22d U. S. Inf., wounded, 992.
Shufelt, Herbert C., pvt., Co. F, 47th Inf., U.S. V., wounded, 1187.
Shultz, William, pvt., Co. G, 42d Inf., U. S. V., killed, 1146.
Shuler, C. A., corpl., ——, mentioned, 732.
Shuman, Harry A., pvt., Co. C, 1st Nebr. Vol. Inf., wounded, 946.
Shuman, Robert, sergt., Co. L, 28th Inf., U. S. V., killed, 1130.
Shunk, Francis R., capt., Engr. Corps, U. S. A., mentioned, 562-564.
Shupard, Harry B., pvt., Troop M, 6th U. S. Cav., death, 485.
Shuter, Henry D., pvt., Astor Batty., U. S. A., death, 829.
Sibert, Christer, pvt., Co. E, 10th Pa. Vol. Inf., wounded, 951.
Sibley, Richard B., pvt., Co. G, 33d Inf., U. S. V., wounded, 1124.
Sicard, Montgomery, rear-admiral, U. S. N., mentioned, 23.
Sick, Alois C. J., corpl., Co. B, 40th Inf., U. S. V., wounded, 1150.
Sidener, Otis H., pvt., Co. F, 39th Inf., U. S. V., wounded, 1149.
Siemens, George H., pvt., Co. K, 9th U. S. Inf., wounded, 460.
Sigler, Victor E., pvt., Troop G, 11th U. S. V. Cav., death, 1197.
Sigsbee, Eugene E., pvt., Co. A, 40th Inf., U. S. V., death, 1274.
Silence, William, mus., Co. M, 12th U. S. Inf., wounded, 1015.
Siler, Leno A., pvt., Co. H, 24th U. S. Inf., death, 1215.
Silk, Martin A., pvt., Co. F, 9th U. S. Inf., wounded, 460.
Sillman, Robert H., sergt., Astor Batty., U. S. A., wounded, 761.
Sills, James T., pvt., Co. C, 33d Inf., U. S. V., mentioned, 235.

INDEX. 1469

Silver, Charles, pvt., Co. D, 37th Inf., U. S. V., wounded, 1146.
Silver, David, pvt., Co. M, 1st Mont. Vol. Inf., death, 1020; wounded, 1017.
Silver, Louis E., pvt., Co. F, 4th U. S. Inf., death, 1244.
Silvers, William H., pvt., Co. E, 18th U. S. Inf., death, 1229.
Simcox, missionary in China, mentioned, 487.
Simila, Matthew, sergt., Troop K, 3d U. S. Cav., killed, 1209.
Simmons, J. Edward, mentioned, 352.
Simmons, Moses S., pvt., Batty. D, 6th U. S. Art., wounded, 976.
Simon, Charles, pvt., Co., B, 20th U. S. Inf., wounded, 934.
Simon, Frederick, sergt., band, 6th U. S. Inf., death, 1074.
Simonds, Ralph W., pvt., Co. A, 1st Wash. Vol. Inf., killed, 895.
Simons, William H., 1st lieut. 6th U. S. Inf., mentioned, 83, 1090; wounded, 124.
Simonson, Simon J., pvt., Co. K, 1st Nebr. Vol. Inf., wounded, 897.
Simpkins, Daniel W., pvt., Co. E, 14th U. S. Inf., killed, 460.
Simpson, A. H., pvt., Co. M, 8th Ohio Vol. Inf., mentioned, 197.
Simpson, George N., pvt., Co. E, 30th Inf., U.S.V., killed, 1199.
Simpson, Wendell L., capt., 6th U. S. Inf., mentioned, 1044.
Simpson, William A., maj., a. a. g., U. S. A., mentioned, 646, 667, 718, 767, 783, 796, 805.
Sims, Arthur C., corpl., Co. F, 1st Nebr. Vol. Inf., death, 831.
Sims, George R., corpl., Co. I, 33d Inf., U. S. V., wounded, 1102.
Sims, Granville P., pvt., Co. L, 43d Inf., U. S. V., killed, 1250.
Sinclair, David J., pvt., Co. E, 1st Cal. Vol. Inf., wounded, 898.
Sinclair, Joseph P., pvt., Co. B, 41st Inf., U.S.V., death, 1202.
Sinclair, William S., 2d lieut., 28th U. S. Inf., mentioned, 1324, 1325.
Singlemann, Charles W., pvt., Troop G, 11th U. S. V. Cav., death, 1136.
Sisk, William B., pvt., Co. F, 31st Inf., U. S. V., death, 1136.
Sisler, Albert R., 1st sergt., Co. L, 19th U. S. Inf., death, 1258.
Sisler, Charles W., pvt., Co. M, 19th U. S. Inf., wounded, 1141.
Sissenouth. D. C., sergt., Batty. L, 3d U. S. Art., wounded, 899.
Sisson, Eli I., pvt., Co. K, 1st Nebr. Vol. Inf., wounded, 974.
Sisson, Lester E., 2d lieut., 1st Nebr. Vol. Inf., killed, 972, 974.
Sites, William, pvt., Co. K, 45th Inf., U. S. V., death, 1228.
Sjoblom, Alex S., pvt., Co. L, 1st S. Dak. Vol. Inf., wounded, 975.
Skaggs, James S., pvt., Co. E, 38th Inf., U. S. V., killed, 1192.
Skillman, Lewis T., pvt., Co. M, 22d U. S. Inf., wounded, 946.
Skinner, Charles, pvt., Co. H, 4th U. S Inf., death, 1090.
Skinner, Edward, pvt., Co. I, 24th U. S. Inf., wounded, 1222.
Skinner, Guy E., pvt., Co. K, 1st S. Dak. Vol. Inf., wounded, 975.
Skinner, I., corpl., Co. I, 1st Mont. Vol. Inf., wounded, 895.
Skinner, William K., pvt., Troop I, 4th U.S. Cav., killed, 974.
Skinner, Wort, pvt., Co. H, 47th Inf., U. S. V., death, 1196.
Sklensky, John, mus., Co. F, 18th U. S. Inf., death, 1152.
Skogsberg, Axel, pvt., Co. F, 9th U. S. Inf., killed, 443, 445; wounded, 1086.
Slack, George A., pvt., Co. H, 43d Inf., U. S. V., killed, 1168.
Slack, Harry, pvt., Co. B, 1st Mont. Vol. Inf., wounded, 901.
Slack, Joseph M., pvt., Co. M, 3d U. S. Inf., wounded, 961.

Slack, Walter T., 1st lieut., 47th Inf., U. S. V., death, 1239.
Slade, John, pvt., Co. A, 1st Cal. Vol. Inf., wounded, 897.
Sladen, Fred W., capt., 14th U. S. Inf., mentioned, 442, 1173.
Slater, Charles H., pvt., Hosp. Corps, U. S. A., wounded, 975.
Slater, Charles H., pvt., Co. B, 21st U. S. Inf., death, 1090.
Slater, Richard B., corpl., Co. B, 9th U. S. Inf., killed, 443, 445.
Slatten, Amon M., pvt., Co. A, 51st Iowa Vol. Inf., wounded, 1060.
Slavens, Thomas H., 1st lieut., 4th U. S. Cav., mentioned, 1093, 1095, 1197.
Sliger, Troy P., pvt., Co. C, 44th Inf., U. S. V., killed, 1247.
Sliter, William E., pvt., Co. I, 33d Inf., U. S. V., death, 1160.
Sloan, John A., pvt., Co. M, 6th U. S. Inf., death, 1210; mentioned, 1241.
Sloat, William, pvt., Co. K, 14th U. S. Inf., wounded, 895.
Slocum, Charles L., artif., Co. K 37th Inf., U. S. V., death, 1149.
Slocum, Stephen L'H., 1st lieut., 8th U. S. Cav., correspondence, 131.
Slonaker, R., corpl., Co. A, 27th Inf., U. S. V., death, 1254.
Small, George E., mus., Co. G, 1st Wyo. Vol. Inf., wounded, 926.
Smart, Milton L., pvt., Co. D, 38th Inf., U. S. V., death, 1150.
Smedley, George S., pvt., Co. L, 16th U. S. Inf., death, 1256.
Smedley, Walker L., pvt., Co. E, 1st Nebr. Vol. Inf., wounded, 948.
Smiley, Hylas E., pvt., Co. M 29th Inf., U. S. V., wounded, 1237.
Smith, Alfred, pvt., Co. H, 1st Mont. Vol. Inf., wounded, 954.
Smith, Alfred T., col., 13th U. S. Inf., mentioned, 139, 540, 545, 564.
Smith, Alonzo, pvt., Co. B, 21st U. S. Inf., death, 1274.
Smith, Arthur J., ret. com. sergt., U. S. A., death, 907.
Smith, Arthur M., pvt., Co. F, 1st Cal. Vol. Inf., wounded, 920.
Smith, Arthur R. D., corpl., Co. I, 25th U. S. Inf., death, 1231; wounded, 1231.
Smith, Benjamin F., jr., pvt., Co. F, 2d Oreg. Vol. Inf., wounded, 952.
Smith, Bernard, pvt., Co. G, 4th U. S. Inf., death, 1215.
Smith, Bernard J., mus., band, 1st Colo. Vol. Inf., death, 947.
Smith, Charles B., corpl., Co. D, 39th Inf., U.S.V., death, 1248.
Smith, Charles E., pvt., Co. H, 13th U. S. Inf., wounded, 1085.
Smith, Charles E., P. M. General, mentioned, 372.
Smith, Charles H., sergt., Co. I, 24th U. S. Inf., killed, 1196.
Smith, Charles L., connected with Boston office, mentioned, 690.
Smith, Charles M., 2d lieut., 18th U. S. Inf., death, 1109.
Smith, Charles Stewart, of N. Y., mentioned, 358.
Smith, Charles T., pvt., Co. I, 46th Inf., U. S. V., wounded, 1231.
Smith, Claude, pvt., Co. G, 14th U. S. Inf., killed, 465.
Smith, Courtney, pvt,, Co. F, 44th Inf., U. S. V., death, 1165.
Smith, Demarest H., pvt., Co. E, 17th U. S. Inf., death, 1082.
Smith, Edmund D., capt., 19th U.S. Inf., wounded, 1142, 1143.
Smith, Edward, capt., 1st Idaho Vol. Inf., wounded, 931.
Smith, Edward D., corpl., Co. C 1st Wash. Vol. Inf., wounded, 906.
Smith, Ernest, pvt., Co. F, 10th U. S. Inf., mentioned, 229.
Smith, Ewen W., pvt., Co. M, 36th Inf., U. S. V., death, 1119.

Smith, Frank, pvt., Co. F, 13th Minn. Vol. Inf., mentioned, 987.
Smith, Frank, pvt., Co. A, 28th Inf., U. S. V., death, 1185; wounded, 1182.
Smith, Frank, pvt., Co. E, 1st Wash. Vol. Inf., killed, 895.
Smith, Frank, pvt., Co. F, 1st Colo. Vol. Inf., wounded, 761.
Smith, Frank A., pvt., Co. A, 26th Inf., U. S. V., death, 1192.
Smith, Frank C., corpl., Co. G, 47th Inf., U. S. V., death, 1205.
Smith, Frank G., lieut. col., 6th U. S. Art., mentioned, 390.
Smith, Frank J., pvt., Co. A, 19th U. S. Inf., death, 1232.
Smith, Fred, pvt., Co. A, 18th U. S. Inf., wounded, 905, 1163.
Smith, Frederick, pvt., Troop I, 11th U. S. V. Cav., death, 1200.
Smith, Frederick A, maj., 1st U. S. Inf., mentioned, 1269.
Smith, Fred W., pvt., Co. C, 1st Mont. Vol. Inf., wounded, 983.
Smith, George, pvt., Co. D, 21st U. S. Inf., wounded, 1090.
Smith, George J., pvt., Co. H, 1st Nebr. Vol. Inf., death, 939.
Smith, George R., maj., pay dept., mentioned, 646.
Smith, George W., pvt., Troop F, 3d U. S. Cav., death, 1283.
Smith, Gilbert, pvt., Co. E, 24th U. S. Inf., death, 1052.
Smith, Guy H. B., 1st lieut., 4th U. S. Inf., mentioned, 254.
Smith, Harry B., col., 158th Ind. Vol. Inf., mentioned, 511, 514.
Smith, Harvey R., pvt., Co. F., 1st Wash. Vol. Inf., wounded, 977.
Smith, Henry J., sergt., Co. G, 33d Inf., U. S. V., wounded, 1124.
Smith, Horace D., corpl., Co. E, 29th Inf., U.S.V., death, 1205.
Smith, Horace H., pvt., Troop E, 4th U. S. Cav., wounded, 936.
Smith, Hugh, pvt., Co. K, 32d Inf., U. S. V., death, 1217.
Smith, Ira B., pvt., Co. C, 13th Minn. Vol. Inf., wounded, 919.
Smith, Jacob H., brig. gen., U. S. V., mentioned, 563, 564, 949, 998, 1005, 1006 1019, 1025, 1053, 1095, 1097, 1122, 1123, 1238, 1239, 1260, 1261, 1306, 1307, 1319, 1328, 1329, 1332, 1333, 1335–1337, 1344, 1347, 1348, 1354.
Smith, Jacob N., pvt., Co. E, 2d Oreg. Vol. Inf., wounded, 946.
Smith, James, pvt., Co. F, 24th U. S. Inf., wounded, 1085.
Smith, James, pvt., Co. G, 34th Inf., U. S. V., wounded, 1147.
Smith, James F., col., 1st Cal. Vol. Inf., mentioned, 558, 564, 768, 909, 970.
Smith, James G., pvt., Co. E, 45th Inf., U. S. V., death, 1264.
Smith, James S., pvt., Co. B, 2d U. S. Inf., mentioned, 246.
Smith, Jay A., pvt., Co. G, 1st S. Dak. Vol. Inf., death, 839.
Smith, Jesse B., pvt., Co. K, 25th U.S. Inf., killed, 1245.
Smith, Joe, 2d lieut., 1st Wash. Vol. Inf., wounded, 896.
Smith, John, pvt., Co. K, 1st Wash. Vol. Inf., death, 1056.
Smith, John, pvt., Co. C, 6th U. S. Inf., death, 1125.
Smith, John P., pvt., Co. L, 14th U. S. Inf., death, 984.
Smith, John P., pvt., Co. G, 9th U. S. Inf., killed, 443, 445.
Smith, John W., pvt., Co. B, 4th U.S. Inf., wounded, 1085.
Smith, John W., pvt., Co. H, 40th Inf., U. S. V., wounded, 1183.
Smith, Joseph, pvt., Co. K, 40th Inf., U. S. V., death, 1190.
Smith, Joseph, pvt., Co. H, 23d U. S. Inf., wounded, 760.
Smith, Leland S., pvt., Sig. Corps, U. S. A., mentioned, 1129.

Smith, Louis P., 1st lieut. med. dep., U. S. A., death, 1243.
Smith, Mack D., pvt., Co. K, 40th Inf., U. S. V., wounded, 1171.
Smith, Nathan A. C., post-office clerk, mentioned, 298.
Smith, Odis, pvt., Co. A, 45th Inf., U. S. V., wounded, 1155.
Smith, Oliver, pvt., Co. D, 49th Inf., U. S. V., death, 1241.
Smith, Paschal Y., pvt., Co. M, 14th U. S. Inf., wounded, 454; death, 464.
Smith, Perrin L., 1st lieut., 39th Inf., U. S. V., killed, 1146.
Smith, Reuben, 2d lieut., 9th U. S. Inf., mentioned, 1019.
Smith, Robert H., pvt., Co. E, 12th U. S. Inf., death, 1090.
Smith, Robert L., pvt., Co. K, 1st Nebr. Vol. Inf., wounded, 974.
Smith, Royal H., corpl., Co. E, 1st S. Dak. Vol. Inf., death, 831.
Smith, Sandy, pvt., Co. H, 24th U. S. Inf., mentioned, 248.
Smith, Scott L., pvt., Co. L, 15th U. S. Inf., killed, 1211.
Smith, Soren H., corpl., Co. H, 1st Mont. Vol. Inf., wounded, 952.
Smith, Thomas, pvt., Co. K, 22d U. S. Inf., wounded, 1113.
Smith, Thomas, pvt., Co. K, 18th U. S. Inf., death, 1123.
Smith, Thomas, corpl., Co. G, 12th U. S. Inf., wounded, 1195.
Smith, Thomas M. K., lieut. col., 10th U. S. Inf., mentioned, 537.
Smith, Walter L., pvt., Co. A, 24th U. S. Inf., death, 1256.
Smith, William, pvt., Co. I, 48th Inf., U. S. V., death, 1205.
Smith, William, pvt., Co. I, 25th U. S. Inf., mentioned, 1161.
Smith, William, pvt., Co. L, 25th U. S. Inf., wounded, 1237.
Smith, William B., sergt., Co. M, 1st S. Dak. Vol. Inf., death, 915.
Smith, William C., col., 1st Tenn. Vol. Inf., mentioned, 707, 831, 895, 924, 935.
Smith, William E., pvt., Co. K, 2d Oreg. Vol. Inf., wounded, 1003.
Smith, William H., 1st lieut., 10th U. S. Cav., killed, 124.
Smith, William L., pvt., Co. —, 26th U. S. Inf., mentioned, 1328, 1329.
Smith, William T., sergt., Co. E, 18th U. S. Inf., death, 1229.
Smith, Wilson B., pvt., Co. B, 20th Kans. Vol. Inf., wounded, 954
Snapp, George D., pvt., Co. E, 14th U. S. Inf., wounded, 1084.
Snell, Robert E., pvt., Co. K, 14th U. S. Inf., wounded, 454.
Sniffin, Culver C., maj., pay dept., U. S. A., mentioned, 198, 222.
Snodgrass, Charles, pvt., Co. B, 20th Kans. Vol. Inf., death, 894.
Snodgrass, James E., pvt., Co. C, 2d Oreg. Vol. Inf., wounded, 946.
Snow, Arthur C., sergt., Co. K, 20th Kans. Vol. Inf., wounded, 975.
Snow, Lucius, pvt., Co. D, 14th U. S. Inf., wounded, 760.
Snow, Shubbell A., pvt., Co. G, 21st U. S. Inf., death, 1074.
Snowden, Albert S., pvt., Troop L, 4th U.S. Cav., death, 837.
Snowden, A. Lowden, col., ———, mentioned, 315.
Snyder, Geo. C., pvt., Co. E, 2d Oreg. Vol. Inf., wounded, 946.
Snyder, Lee, pvt., Co. E, 10th Pa. Vol. Inf., death, 803; mentioned, 761.
Snyder, Simon, brig. gen., U. S. V., mentioned, 12, 36, 55, 57, 71, 76, 292, 319, 320, 329, 368, 382, 511, 516, 517, 534–537, 1033, 1039, 1076, 1343.
Snyder, William, pvt., Co. E, 21st U. S. Inf., death, 1130.

INDEX. 1471

Soby, John A., pvt., Co. B., 41st Inf., U. S. V., death, 1271.
Soden, Guy B., corpl., Co. E, 14th U. S. Inf., death, 895.
Sodergren, Peter, pvt., Co. D, 45th Inf., U. S. V., death, 1219.
Solace, U. S. hosp. ship, mentioned, 410–412, 414, 425, 429, 435, 442, 445, 1218, 1273.
Solomon, Charles L., qm. employee death, 495.
Sorley, Lewis S., 1st lieut., 16th U. S. Inf., wounded, 124.
Somers, William S., pvt., Co. D, 14th U. S. Inf., death, 1016; wounded, 963.
Sommers, Frank, pvt., Co. D, 32 Inf., U. S. V., wounded, 1218.
Sommers, Joseph, pvt., Co. L, 36th Inf., U. S. V., death, 1244.
Soper, George I., pvt., Co. E, 22d U. S. Inf., death, 1200.
Soper, Jesse R., corpl., Co, E, 4th U. S. Inf., wounded, 1110.
Soper, Ward, pvt., Co. A, 30th Inf., U. S. V., death, 1213.
Sorensen, Emil S., pvt., Co. F, 30th Inf., U. S. V., death, 1191.
Sorensen, John, pvt., Co. L, 1st Mont. Vol. Inf., death, 917.
Sorrensen, Peter M., pvt., Co. B, 20th Kans. Vol. Inf., wounded, 995.
Soto, colonel, Spanish forces, mentioned, 393.
South, Evans, pvt., Co. C, 9th U. S. Inf., death, 1297.
South, John, pvt., Co. L, 43d Inf., U. S. V., wounded, 1225.
South, William M., pvt., Co. B, 20th U. S. Inf., death, 1161.
Southard, James H., member of Congress, mentioned, 329, 339.
Southern, Edward E., 1st lieut. 1st Wash. Vol. Inf., wounded, 967.
Southers, Henry L., corpl., Batty. B, Utah Vol. Art., wounded, 947.
Southwood, Frank, pvt., Co. B, 31st Inf., U. S. V., death, 1161.
Southworth, Frank W., pvt., Co. B, 6th U. S. Inf., wounded, 443.
Sowards, Oscar, pvt., Co. A, 1st Wash. Vol. Inf., wounded, 896.
Spaeth, Joseph M., pvt., Co. C, 1st Wyo. Vol. Inf., death, 931; wounded, 926.
Spain—
Protocol between U. S. and, provisions, 751.
Relinquishment of sovereignty over Cuba, 751.
Termination of war with, 323.
Spanish minister for foreign affairs, mentioned, 322.
Spanish to evacuate islands in West Indies, 751.
Sparks, Columbus C., pvt., Co. F, 17th U. S. Inf., death, 1276.
Sparks, Hugh, corpl., Co. A, 18th U. S. Inf., wounded, 905, 1163.
Sparrow, Thomas, pvt., Co. K, 2d U. S. Inf., wounded, 1261.
Spaulding, Oliver L., Asst. Secy. of Treasury, mentioned, 186.
Speaker, Lee, mus., Co. E, 35th Inf., U. S. V., wounded, 1176.
Spears, Frank E., pvt., Co. A, 30th Inf., U. S. V., death, 1174.
Specialist, U. S. transport, mentioned, 60, 63, 65, 67, 69, 72, 73, 86, 88, 95, 122, 253, 541.
Spellman, Michael J., capt., 43d Inf. U. S. V., mentioned, 1282.
Spence, Monroe W., pvt., Co. M, 1st Nebr. Vol. Inf., wounded, 952.
Spence, Robert E. L., maj., 32d Inf. U. S. V., mentioned, 83, 1126; wounded, 124.
Spencer, Herbert V., pvt., Co. I, 26th Inf., U. S. V., wounded, 1202.
Spencer, John W., pvt., Co. F, 33d Inf., U. S. V., killed, 1189.
Spencer, Joseph W., pvt., Co. I, 21st U. S. Inf., death, 1256.
Spencer, Lawrence L., qm. sergt. Co. B, 33d Inf., U. S. V., killed, 1137.
Sperlock, Claude, corpl., Co. B, 20th Kans. Vol. Inf., wounded, 954.
Sperry, Hon. N. D., member of Congress, mentioned, 354, 365.

Spicer, George, pvt., Co. G, 2d Oreg. Vol. Inf., wounded, 946.
Spierings, John, pvt., Co. H, 2d Oreg. Vol. Inf., death, 939.
Spilman, Baldwin D., col. 1st W. Va. Vol. Inf., mentioned, 518.
Spivy, James H., pvt, Co. G, 1st Nebr. Vol. Inf., killed, 983.
Spottenstein, Lloyd, pvt., Co. H, 1st Nebr. Vol. Inf., wounded, 955.
Spressor, Christian R. corpl., Co. K, 18th U. S. Inf., death, 1048.
Springer, Anton, jr., 1st lieut., 21st U. S. Inf., killed, 1285.
Springfield Armory, sample of Mauser rifle and ammunition sent to, 168.
Springfield Volunteer Aid Association, mentioned, 209.
Springstead, F. E., pvt., Co. —, 1st Colo. Vol. Inf., death, 803.
Sproull, Robert, pvt., Co. C, 9th U. S. Inf., killed, 1297.
Sprouse, Samuel L., pvt., Co. I, 36th Inf., U. S. V., death, 1241.
Spurgeon, Charles R., mus., Co. L, 18th U. S. Inf., death, 1276.
Squier, George O., capt., Sig. Corps, U. S. A., mentioned, 1335.
Squire, Guy P., pvt., Co. F, 1st S. Dak. Vol. Inf., wounded, 949.
Squires, Benjamin W., pvt., Co. L, 20th Kans. Vol. Inf., death, 886.
Squires, Grant, censor at New York, mentioned, 116, 143, 145, 174, 177, 208, 327, 385, 386, 389.
Stacey, Coleman S., corpl., Co. K, 25th U. S. Inf., death, 1201.
Stackpole, Horatio P., col., 1st N. Y. Vol. Inf., mentioned, 762.
Stadleman, John, pvt., Batty. K, 3d U. S. Art., wounded, 899.
Stader, Charles, pvt., Co. A, 36th Inf., U. S. V., death, 1109.
Staffeldt, William A., pvt., Co. E, 35th Inf., U. S. V., wounded, 1225.
Stafford, Frank, corpl., Co. M, 14th U. S. Inf., killed, 453.
Stafford, H. Eugene, a. a. surg., U. S. A., mentioned, 1347; wounded, 1087.
Stafford, Leonard, sergt., Co. E, 1st Nebr. Vol. Inf., mentioned, 732.
Stafford, William, pvt., Co. H, 21st U. S. Inf., death, 1052.
Stallcup, Edward, pvt., Co. L, 37th Inf., U. S. V., killed, 1211.
Stallings, James S., pvt., Co. B, 12th U. S. Inf., mentioned, 195.
Stalmaker, Morton, pvt., Co. B, 9th U. S. Inf., death, 504.
Stamford, Henry W., 2d lieut., Sig. Corps, U. S. A., mentioned, 419.
Stampff, Rudolph F., pvt., Co. G, 16th U. S. Inf., death, 1185.
Stanley, David S., 1st lieut. 22d U. S. Inf., mentioned, 887, 888, 1173.
Stanley, Fred, sergt., Troop M, 11th U. S. V. Cav., wounded, 1128.
Stanley, Ira N., sergt., Co. I, 40th Inf., U. S. V., killed, 1195.
Stanley, William F., pvt., Co. F, 1st Mont. Vol. Inf., death, 917.
Stanley, Windsor R., pvt., Co. G, 36th Inf., U. S. V., killed, 1092.
Stanon, Herbert, pvt., Co. —, 1st Colo. Vol. Inf., mentioned, 732.
Stanton, Harold L., pvt., Co. G, 2d Oreg. Vol. Inf., wounded, 925.
Stanton, William, capt., 6th U. S. Cav., wounded, 124.
Starbird, Harry W., pvt., Co. E, Batt. Engrs., death, 1256.
Stark, David N., pvt., Co. C, 44th Inf., U. S. V., wounded, 1247.
Stark, Jesse K., pvt., Troop K, 1st U. S. Cav., killed, 61.
Starkey, Anthony H., pvt., Co. B, 31st Inf., U. S. V., death, 1213.
Stassen, Jacob, pvt., Co. H, 23d U. S. Inf., death, 907.
State of California, steamship, mentioned, 660.

State of Texas, steamer, mentioned, 165, 167, 172.
Stauffer, William H., pvt., Co. I, 10th Pa. Vol. Inf., wounded 948.
Stauke, John, pvt., Co. E, 1st S. Dak. Vol. Inf., wounded, 949.
St. Clair, George, pvt., Co. E, 46th Inf., U. S. V., death, 1174.
Steadman, William A., pvt., Co. L, 1st Mont. Vol. Inf., mentioned, 926; wounded, 915.
Stedman, Clarence A., capt., 9th U. S. Cav., killed, 124.
Stearns, Charles T., pvt., Co. F, 39th Inf., U. S. V., death, 1223.
Stearns, Frank B., 1st sergt., Co. D, 21st U. S. Inf., wounded, 1287.
Stearns, Myron O., sergt., Co. B, 1st Nebr. Vol. Inf., death, 984.
Steel, James, pvt., Co. K, 6th U. S. Inf., death, 1119.
Steele, James B., 1st lieut., Sig. Corps, U. S. A., mentioned, 205, 209.
Steele, Sam, pvt., Co. I, 17th U. S. Inf., wounded, 1073.
Steelman, Monticue, pvt., Co. C, 32d Inf., U. S. V., death, 1202.
Steen, Andrew S., pvt., Troop B, 4th U. S. Cav., wounded, 1240.
Steen, Charles W., corpl., Co. E, 41st Inf., U. S. V., death, 1160.
Steere, Louis, sergt., Co. E, 16th U. S. Inf., wounded, 1060.
Steever, Edgar Z., maj., 3d U. S. Cav., mentioned, 1036, 1138.
Steffen, Henry, pvt., Co. D, 22d U. S. Inf., death, 1249.
Steiger, Fred P., pvt., Co. C, 12th U. S. Inf., wounded, 1057.
Steiger, George, pvt., Co. G, 22d U. S. Inf., death, 1070.
Steiner, William F., corpl., Co. L, 17th U. S. Inf., killed, 1222.
Steinhagen, Herman, pvt., Co. I, 14th U. S. Inf., wounded, 895.
Steinhart, Frank, clerk, Gen. Brooke's staff, mentioned, 302.
Steinhauser, Albert, capt., 45th Inf., U. S. V., mentioned, 1212.
Stephan, Charles, pvt., Co. L, 12th U. S. Inf., wounded, 1015.
Stephens, Fred, pvt., Co. D, 39th Inf., U. S. V., death, 1194.
Stephens, Jerry W., pvt., Co. B, 38th Inf., U. S. V., wounded, 1147.
Stephenson, Harry W., pvt., Co. C, 23d U. S. Inf., wounded, 956.
Stephenson, William O., corpl., Co. I, 4th U. S. Inf., killed, 1241.
Sterling, Charles E., pvt., Co. C, 9th U. S. Inf., killed, 1297.
Sterling, William W., pvt., Co. K, 1st Colo. Vol. Inf., wounded, 760.
Sternberg, George M., surg. gen., U. S. A., mentioned, 108, 140, 142, 186, 187, 196, 197, 227, 229, 234, 254, 303, 315, 357, 1021, 1024, 1028.
Stevens, Daniel W., pvt., Co. I, 10th Pa. Vol. Inf., killed, 954.
Stevens, Elmer, pvt., Co. G, 12th U. S. Inf., death, 1029.
Stevens, Eugene E., corpl., Co. K, 1st S. Dak. Vol. Inf., wounded, 895.
Stevens, Fatlick, pvt., Troop F, 1st U. S. Cav., mentioned, 213.
Stevens, Frank B., sergt., Co. C, 1st S. Dak. Vol. Inf., wounded, 955.
Stevens, Frank O., pvt., Co. E, 4th U. S. Inf., wounded, 1086.
Stevens, George, sergt., Co. A, 6th U. S. Inf., wounded, 1087.
Stevens, George W., general manager C. & O. R. R., mentioned, 296.
Stevens, Ira A., pvt., Co. K, 42d Inf., U. S. V., death, 1187.
Stevens, Joseph S., corpl., Troop K, 1st U. S. V. Cav., mentioned, 235, 236.
Stevens, Steve, pvt., Co. G, 1st Mont. Vol. Inf., killed, 945.
Stevens, William F., pvt., Co. F, Sig. Corps, U. S. A., death, 1213.

Stevenson, Clifford P., pvt., Co. H, 51st Iowa Vol. Inf., wounded, 999.
Stevenson, Erwin A., pvt., Co. L, 17th U. S. Inf., death, 1095.
Steward, Frank, pvt., Co. A, 20th Kans. Vol. Inf., wounded, 946.
Stewart, Cecil, 1st lieut., 4th U. S. Cav., mentioned, 943.
Stewart, Edward J., pvt., Co. L, 18th U. S. Inf., wounded, 1202.
Stewart Fred E., sergt., Maine Vol. Sig. Corps, mentioned, 224.
Stewart, George E., pvt., Co. B, 22d U. S. Inf., killed, 934.
Stewart, John S., capt., 1st Colo. Vol. Inf., killed, 945.
Stewart, Robert D., pvt., Co. C, 40th Inf., U. S. V., wounded, 1150.
Stewart, Walter E., jr., 2d lieut., 3d U. S. Inf., mentioned, 1019.
Stewart, William, pvt., Co. L, 28th Inf., U. S. V., death, 1260.
Stewart, William D., pvt., Co. G, 1st Cal. Vol. Inf., mentioned, 1043.
Stickel, Frank, pvt., Co. D, 17th U. S. Inf., wounded, 1060.
Stickle, Horton W., 1st lieut., Engr. Corps, U. S. A., mentioned, 943.
Stickles, Robert, pvt., Co. C, 49th Inf., U. S. V., death, 1168.
Stierle, Henry, pvt., Co. E, 9th U. S. Inf., wounded, 1299.
Stiles, Charles V., pvt., Co. H, 44th Inf., U. S. V., death, 1162.
Still, Charles, pvt., Co. C, 13th Minn. Vol. Inf., wounded, 966.
Stillings, Henry E., pvt., Co. B, 9th U. S. Inf., wounded, 443, 445.
Stillwagon, William H., pvt., Co. E, 10th Pa. Vol. Inf., death, 803.
Stillwater, U. S. transport, mentioned, 80, 92, 98, 120, 157, 190, 192, 275.
Stinnett, Charles H., pvt., Co. C, 17th U. S. Inf., death, 1234.
Stirewalt, Jefferson M., pvt., Co. E, 18th U. S. Inf., death, 1130.
St. John, Charles, a. a. surg., U. S. A., killed, 1282.
St. Louis, auxiliary cruiser, mentioned, 77, 102, 103, 205, 212, 215, 219, 227, 312, 313, 319, 323, 324, 327, 328, 333, 370-373, 589.
Stokes, John W., pvt., Co. M, 33d Inf., U. S. V., wounded, 1102.
Stockham, William E., capt., 1st Nebr. Vol. Inf., mentioned, 1000.
Stockley, Paul D., 2d lieut., 21st U. S. Inf., missing, 1137, 1139, 1140, 1143.
Stockmyer, Jacob H., pvt., Co. I, 1st S. Dak. Vol. Inf., wounded, 949.
Stockton, E. A., pvt., Batty. L, 3d U. S. Art., wounded, 946.
Stockton, Walter P., pvt., Co. F, 1st Nebr. Vol. Inf., wounded, 956.
Stockstill, Verni, pvt., Co. C, 44th Inf., U. S. V., death, 1223.
Stoddard, Charles H., capt., 71st N. Y. Vol. Inf., mentioned, 135.
Stolkman, ——, pvt., Troop E, 4th U. S. Cav., mentioned, 959.
Stoltsz, John K., pvt., Co. B, 16th U. S. Inf., death, 1132.
Stone, Daniel A., pvt., Co. D, 1st Ill. Vol. Inf., mentioned, 175.
Stone, David L., 2d lieut., 22d U. S. Inf., mentioned, 124.
Stone, Edward C., pvt., Co. G, 26th Inf., U. S. V., wounded, 1193.
Stone, Frank, pvt., Sig. Corps, U. S. A., mentioned, 1129.
Stone, Frank J., pvt., Co. L, 26th Inf., U. S. V., death, 1161.
Stone, Herman H., pvt., Co. K, 22d U. S. Inf., killed, 1128.
Stone, John, pvt., Co. L, 39th Inf., U. S. V., death, 1210.
Stone, L., pvt., Co. A, 3d U. S. Inf., wounded, 1117.
Stone, Roy, brig. gen., U. S. V., mentioned, 117-122, 126, 128, 131, 275, 280, 285, 306, 336, 352, 357.
Stone, William H., pvt., Co. H, 45th Inf., U. S. V., killed, 1163.

INDEX. 1473

Stone, William L., jr., pvt., Troop G, 11th U. S. V. Cav., death, 1238.
Stoner, Lee H., pvt., Co. D, 1st Nebr. Vol. Inf., wounded, 974.
Storch, James F., qm. sergt., Co. B 1st Nebr. Vol. Inf., killed, 974.
Storch, Joseph A., 1st lieut., 1st Nebr. Vol. Inf., wounded, 948.
Storer, Bellamy, U. S. minister to Spain, mentioned, 1049, 1050.
Storment, Peter M., pvt., Co. I, 14th U. S. Inf., killed, 895 917.
Stormer, George W, pvt., Co. B, 2d Oreg. Vol. Inf., death, 803.
Stroup, Ed., pvt., Co. K, 38th Inf., U. S. V., death, 1149.
Storrs, Roy, pvt., Co. L, 3d U. S. Inf., death, 1113.
Story, Frank A., corpl., Co. L, 37th Inf., U. S. V., wounded, 1211.
Stotsenburg, John M., col., 1st Nebr. Vol. Inf., killed, 972, 974; mentioned, 906.
Stovall, James O., pvt., Batty. D, 6th U. S. Art., death, 956.
Stovall, William, pvt., Co. A, 6th U. S. Inf., wounded, 1087.
Stowe, Charles T., qm. sergt., Co. H, 14th U. S. Inf., death, 1189.
St. Paul, auxiliary cruiser, mentioned, 77, 80–82, 87, 94, 97, 98, 103, 106, 107, 123, 126, 205, 215, 219, 228, 312, 313, 317, 319, 324, 328, 333, 344, 350, 611, 618, 660, 721, 722, 729, 735, 784, 791, 839, 922, 986, 1007, 1049, 1059, 1061, 1079, 1106, 1128.
Strain, Edward W., corpl., Co. F, 1st Wash. Vol. Inf., killed, 977.
Stranahan, Harry B., pvt., Troop K, 3d U. S. Cav., death, 1152.
Strand, Harry R. S., corpl., Co. L, 1st Wash. Vol. Inf., death, 917.
Strathgyle, U. S. transport, mentioned, 461, 463, 465, 475, 1210, 1216.
Stratman, Joseph, pvt., Co. M, 16th U. S. Inf., killed, 1182.
Stratton, William, pvt., Co. K, 34th Inf., U. S. V., wounded, 1192.
Straub, Albert R., pvt., Co. D, 1st Wash. Vol. Inf., wounded, 971.
Strauch, George H. B., pvt., Co. G, 9th U. S. Inf., wounded, 1055.
Strawderman, Liew, pvt., Co. L, 2d Oreg. Vol. Inf., killed, 948.
Streater, Herbert, pvt., Co. C, 13th U.S. Inf., death, 1027.
Street, Harlow L., capt., com. sub., U. S. V., mentioned, 1274.
Street, William H., pvt., Co. G, 36th Inf., U. S. V., death, 1144.
Streeter, Fred H., pvt., Co. C, 1st Idaho Vol. Inf., wounded, 897.
Stretch, Harley M., pvt., Co. I, 51st Iowa Vol. Inf., wounded, 999.
Stretch, John F., col., 27th U. S. Inf., mentioned, 1344.
Strickland, Isaac A. J., pvt., Batty. G, 3d U. S. Art., death, 802.
Strickland, Joseph, pvt., Co. H, 48th Inf., U. S. V., death, 1153.
Strobel, Benjamin, pvt., Co. F, 1st S. Dak. Vol. Inf., wounded, 949.
Strohm, Carl, pvt., Co. B, 18th U. S. Inf., wounded, 1113.
Strong, Fred E., civilian employee, wounded, 981.
Strong, Putnam Bradlee, maj., a. a. g., U. S. V., mentioned, 653; wounded, 955.
Strong, William L. ex-mayor, N. Y. City, mentioned, 104, 108, 126, 358.
Strother, Lewis H., maj., engr. officer, U. S. V., mentioned, 686.
Stroup, Louis R., pvt., Co. M, 12th U. S. Inf., wounded, 1057.
Stroutman, Fred, corpl., Co. M, 32d Inf., U. S. V., death, 1109.
Strumper, Gerard, pvt., Co. D, 14th U. S. Inf., death, 1021.
Stuart, James E., member post-office committee, 405.
Stuart, James T., mus., Co. —, 51st Iowa Vol. Inf., wounded, 1060.
Stuart, Moore, qm. employee, mentioned, 183.
Stuart, Stanley M., asst. surg., 11th Cav., U. S. V., death, 1226.

Stube, Henry A., pvt., Co. F, 1st Cal. Vol. Inf., death, 829, 830.
Stucker, Edgar M., pvt., Co. M, 31st Inf., U. S. V., death, 1142.
Stulz, Charles, pvt., Co. H, 1st S. Dak. Vol. Inf., killed, 975.
Sturgis, Samuel D., maj., a. a. g., U. S. V., mentioned, 667, 782.
Sturman, Lionel, pvt., Batty. D, Cal. Vol. Art., wounded, 961.
Stvan, Stanislaus, pvt., Co. D, 4th U. S. Inf., death, 1078.
Suether, Harry A., pvt., Batty. G, 6th U. S. Art., death, 802.
Suffoan, Melville B., pvt., Co. C, 9th U. S. Inf., mentioned, 197.
Sugg, William M., pvt., Co. D, 23d Inf., U. S. V., killed, 1225.
Sullivan, David J., pvt., Batty K, 3d U. S. Art., wounded, 946.
Sullivan, Dennis, pvt., Co. D, 15th U. S. Inf., wounded, 1256.
Sullivan, Fred P., pvt., Troop K, 4th U. S. Cav., death, 1223.
Sullivan, Henry P., corpl., Troop I, 4th U. S. Cav., death, 1280.
Sullivan, James H., pvt., Co. C, 19th U. S. Inf., death, 1144.
Sullivan, James P., pvt., Co. K, 13th U. S. Inf., death, 1219.
Sullivan, Jerry, pvt., Co. C, 17th U. S. Inf., death, 1088.
Sullivan, John B., pvt., Co. M, 21st U. S. Inf., death, 1233.
Sullivan, Michael, pvt., Co. M, 9th U. S. Inf., death, 1032.
Sullivan, Michael, pvt., Troop A, 4th U. S. Cav., death, 1119.
Sullivan, Michael J., pvt., Co. B, 21st U. S. Inf., death, 1226.
Sullivan, Neil C., sergt., Co. H, 1st Colo. Vol. Inf., death, 808.
Sullivan, Patrick, pvt., Co. C 18th U. S. Inf., wounded, 1117.
Sullivan, Patrick, pvt., Co. E, 7th U. S. Inf., mentioned, 174.
Sullivan, Thomas, pvt., Co. I, 17th U. S. Inf., death, 1167.
Sullivan, Walter S., pvt., Co. F, 14th U. S. Inf., death, 833.
Sullivan, William, pvt., Co. L 13th Minn. Vol. Inf., death, 803.
Sullivan, William, pvt., Co. A, 20th Kans. Vol. Inf., killed, 995.
Sullivan, William, pvt., Co. I, 33d Inf., U. S. V., death, 1160.
Sullivan, William R., corpl., Co. E, 30th Inf., U. S. V., wounded, 1199.
Sulteen, Printis, pvt., Troop D, 11th U. S. V. Cav., death, 1241.
Sulu, Sultan of.
   See under *Philippine Islands*.
Sulzer, Hon. M. R., rep. State com., mentioned, 316.
Sumers, Matt, pvt., Co. M, 1st Nebr. Vol. Inf., death, 956; wounded, 948.
Summerfield, Frank W., mus. Co. F, 36th Inf., U. S. V., killed, 1140.
Summerhayes, John W., capt., qm. dept., U. S. A., mentioned, 257.
Summers, Edwin L., pvt., Co. B, 37th Inf., U. S. V., death, 1219.
Summers, Henry W., corpl., Co. I, 19th U. S. Inf., wounded, 1141.
Summers, Jeff, pvt., Co. L, 30th Inf., U. S. V., death, 1201.
Summers, Owen, col., 2d Oreg. Vol. Inf., mentioned, 982.
Sumner, Edwin V., col. 7th U. S. Cav., mentioned, 667, 841.
Sumner, U S. transport, mentioned, 428, 431, 436, 437, 439, 444–446, 453, 456, 459, 464, 471, 488, 503–506, 1156, 1171, 1174, 1216, 1227, 1228, 1264, 1283, 1289, 1298, 1299, 1322, 1325, 1334, 1342, 1347, 1350.
Sumner, Samuel S., brig. gen., U. S. A., mentioned, 47, 179, 181, 202, 224, 225, 227, 528, 529, 541, 542, 544, 546, 841, 1330.
Sundwall, Olof, pvt., Co. F, Sig. Corps, U. S. A., death, 1216.
Suplee, Edwin M., 1st lieut., 3d U. S. Cav., mentioned, 1057.

Suppinal, Fred, qm. sergt., Co. I, 21st U. S. Inf., killed, 1044.
Supreme Court of U. S., decision re. captures by Army and Navy, 164.
Suter, Frederick S., pvt., Co. A, 43d Inf., U. S. V., death, 1190.
Sutherland, Garland B., pvt., Co. M, 6th U. S. Inf., death, 1162.
Sutherland, Joseph H., chaplain, U. S. A., mentioned, 1039, 1062.
Sutton, Charles W., pvt., Co. F, 42d Inf., U. S. V., death, 1153.
Sutton, Edward, pvt., Troop G, 9th U. S. Cav., mentioned, 195.
Sutton, Edward J., pvt., Co. I, 13th Minn. Vol. Inf., death, 931.
Suwanee, U. S. gunboat, mentioned, 50, 129, 148, 271, 371, 378, 392–394.
Svenson, Gotfried, pvt., Co. B, 9th U. S. Inf., killed, 443.
Swanek, Jesse, pvt., Troop A, 3d U. S. Cav., death, 1248.
Swank, John F., corpl., Co. C, 36th Inf., U. S. V., wounded, 1092.
Swann, Thomas E., pvt., Co. C, 49th Inf., U. S.V., death, 1189.
Swanson, Charlie, pvt., Co. F, 30th Inf., U. S. V., death, 1181.
Swanson, Edward N., pvt., Co. M, 21st U. S. Inf., death, 1125.
Swartz, Charles M., pvt., Co. D, 1st Nebr. Vol. Inf., death, 979; wounded, 974.
Swearingen, Samuel E., pvt., Co. E, 16th U. S. Inf., drowned, 1241.
Sweeney, Chase, corpl., Batty. E, 6th U. S. Art., death, 1170.
Sweeney, Henry S., pvt., Co. G, 38th Inf., U.S.V., wounded, 1243.
Sweeney, Joseph T., 1st lieut., 43d Inf., U. S. V., wounded, 1160.
Sweeney, Raymond, pvt., Co. F, 28th Inf., U.S.V., wounded, 1222.
Sweeney, Thomas M., pvt., Co. A, 17th U. S. Inf., killed, 1222.
Sweeney, Walter C., 1st lieut., 24th U. S. Inf., mentioned, 1168.
Sweenie, Walter T., pvt., Co. E, 1st Cal. Vol. Inf., killed, 1038.
Sweet, Edmund, pvt., Co. D, 26th Inf., U. S. V., wounded, 1112.
Sweet, Grover C., pvt., Co. H, 47th Inf., U. S. V., wounded, 1202.
Sweet, Joseph D., pvt., Co. M, 3d U. S. Inf., wounded, 961.
Sweet, Owen J., maj., 23d U. S. Inf., mentioned 1041.
Sweger, Harry, pvt., Troop A, 3d U. S. Cav., killed, 1126.
Swenson, Arthur W., sergt., Co. B, 1st S. Dak. Vol. Inf., wounded, 975.
Swick, Arthur J., pvt., Co. K, 13th U. S. Inf., death, 1202.
Swigert, Samuel M., maj., 3d U. S. Cav., mentioned, 1036, 1103.
Swink, Fred, pvt., Troop B, 11th Cav., U. S. V. wounded, 1185.
Swisher, John P., sergt., Co. E, 9th U. S. Inf., killed, 1307.
Switzens, John, pvt., Co. B 1st Idaho Vol. Inf., wounded, 897.
Switzer, Charles W., pvt., Co. B, 38th Inf., U.S.V., wounded, 1147.
Switzer, Ernest, corpl., Co. L, 19th U. S. Inf., wounded, 1250.
Taber, Claude, pvt., Co. A., 26th Inf., U. S. V., death, 1194.
Tacoma, U. S. transport, mentioned, 722, 799, 800, 802, 832, 833, 901, 902, 919, 970, 973, 979, 981, 1042, 1073, 1086, 1094.
Taft, Millard, pvt., Co. H, 3d U. S. Inf., mentioned, 241.
Taft, William H., civil governor, P. I., mentioned, 1174, 1175, 1286, 1287, 1289, 1297, 1306, 1343.
Taggart, Elmore F., capt., 6th U. S. Inf., mentioned, 256.
Taggert, Vernon E., pvt., Co. F, 13th Minn. Vol. Inf., death, 997.
Tague, Frank J., pvt., Co. D, 26th Inf., U. S. V., killed, 1188.

Tahl, John G., pvt., Co. K, 36th Inf., U. S. V., wounded, 1057.
Talley, James, pvt., Co. D, 32d Inf., U. S. V., death, 1202.
Talmadge, Louis, pvt., Co. A, 30th Inf., U. S. V., death, 1228.

Tampa, Fla.:
Change of base from, 43, 44, 45.
Concentration of troops, 7, 11, 12, 28, 29, 30, 32, 59, 111, 112, 523.
Convoy for transports, 22, 24, 29, 39, 40, 51, 52, 60.
Embarkation, difficulty, 32, 33.
Health and condition of troops, 36.
Press boats, seizure directed, 23.
Re movement from, 12, 34, 35, 39–44, 63, 69, 72, 73, 85, 87, 139.
Selection of camping ground at, 8, 35, 36.
Shafter, General, assigned to command, 9.
Sick and wounded sent to, 98, 114.
Siege train, composition, 27, 62.
Strength of organizaitons at, 33, 36, 55, 56, 65, 66.
Supply and equipment of troops, 14, 24, 27, 29, 45, 49, 53, 65, 66, 97, 110, 111.
Table of distances to cities of Cuba, 26.
Transportation facilities, inadequacy, 32.
Wade, General, assigned to command, 8.
Water supply, 13.

Tampanga, Rinini, Moro chief, mentioned, 1338.
Tangney, Thomas J., pvt., Co. A, 19th U. S. Inf., wounded, 1163.
Tanner, Francis C., pvt., Co. E, 33d Inf., U. S. V., wounded, 1102.
Tanner, Howard L, pvt., Co. K, 1st Mont. Vol. Inf., wounded, 920.
Tanner, John R., governor, Illinois, mentioned, 207, 331, 332, 337, 365.
Tanzy, James E., corpl., Co. G, 34th Inf., U. S. V., death, 1221.
Tappe, William, pvt., Co. M, 12th U. S. Inf., death, 1151.
Tarpon, tow steamer, mentioned, 129, 271.
Tartar, U. S. transport, mentioned, 594, 1089, 1047, 1057, 1061, 1063, 1067, 1068, 1071, 1085, 1089, 1091, 1105, 1107, 1269, 1270.
Tarvera, Dr. Pardo de, insurgent, mentioned, 848.
Tate, Francis L., pvt., Co. D, 30th Inf., U. S. V., death, 1196.
Tate, Frank E., pvt., Co. F, 1st Mont. Vol. Inf., wounded, 976.
Taussig, Edward D., comdr., U. S. N., mentioned, 412–414, 427, 436, 446.
Taussig, Joseph K., ensign, U. S. N., wounded, 421.
Taylor, Albert C., mus., Co. I, 1st Nebr. Vol. Inf., wounded, 950.
Taylor, Alfred H., pvt., Co. H, 21st U. S. Inf., mentioned, 206.
Taylor, Andrew J., pvt., Co. H, 39th Inf., U. S. V., death, 1226.
Taylor, Charles W., capt., 9th U. S. Cav., wounded, 124.
Taylor, Clarence V., pvt., Co. L, 40 Inf., U. S. V., wounded, 1162.
Taylor, Edward R., 1st lieut., 12th U. S. Inf., death, 1127.
Taylor, Elton A., pvt., Co. L, 45th Inf., U. S. V., wounded, 1182.
Taylor, Frank, corpl., Co. G, 48th Inf., U. S. V., death, 1231.
Taylor, Fred, pvt., Co. L, 1st Nebr. Vol. Inf., death, 861.
Taylor, George A., pvt., Co. H, 10th Pa. Vol. Inf., death, 957; wounded, 954.
Taylor, George H., maj., 6th Mass. Vol. Inf., mentioned, 374, 376.
Taylor, Hayes B., pvt., Co. L, 2d Oreg. Vol. Inf., killed, 948.
Taylor, Ismal S., pvt., Co. E, 14th U. S. Inf., wounded, 454.
Taylor, James, pvt., Co. F, 1st Mont. Vol. Inf., death, 803.
Taylor, James B., pvt., Co. F. 9th U. S. Inf., killed, 443, 445.
Taylor, Jay, pvt., Co. B, 3d Oreg. Vol. Inf., death, 972.
Taylor, John, pvt., Co. G, 24th U. S. Inf., death, 1208.
Taylor, John H., pvt., Co. F, Sig. Corps, U. S. A., death, 1223.
Taylor, John R. M., 1st lieut., 23d U. S. Inf., mentioned, 1317.

Taylor, Joseph C., corpl., Co. F, 1st Mont. Vol. Inf., wounded, 995.
Taylor, Leroy, pvt., Co. K, 32d Inf., U S. V., death, 1234.
Taylor, Lorenzo D., pvt. Co. L, 43d Inf. U. S. V., wounded, 1250.
Taylor, Richard, pvt., Co. L, 15th U. S. Inf., killed, 1211.
Taylor, Robert F., pvt., Troop H, 4th U. S. Cav., mentioned, 1196.
Taylor, Samuel, sergt., Co. K, 48th Inf., U. S. V., death, 1191.
Taylor, Shelby H., pvt. Co. C, 22d U. S. Inf., death, 1141.
Taylor, Sherman, pvt., Co. D, 37th Inf., U. S. V., death, 1185.
Taylor, Sidney W., capt., 4th U. S. Art., mentioned, 422, 424, 572.
Taylor, Thomas A., corpl, Co. D, 40th Inf., U.S.V., death, 1152.
Taylor, Wallace C., capt., 1st Nebr. Vol. Inf., wounded, 946.
Taylor, William, pvt., Co. I, 47th Inf., U. S. V., wounded, 1250.
Teachout, George W., pvt., Co. E, 9th U. S. Inf., killed, 1298.
Tecson, Pablo, insurgent commander, surrender, 1266.
Tecson, Simon, insurgent col., surrender, 1253.
Teibell, Louis H., pvt., Co. E, 42d Inf., U. S. V., wounded, 1152.
Teller, William, sergt., Co. D, 1st Idaho Vol. Inf., wounded, 898.
Temple, Frank, pvt., Co. I, 1st Cal. Vol. Inf., death, 850.
Templin, Howard, pvt., Co. I, 47th Inf., U. S. V., death, 1170.
Ten Eyck, William G. pvt., Co. E, 43d Inf., U. S. V., wounded, 1176.
Ten Eyck, Benjamin L., capt., med. dept., U.S.A., mentioned, 86.
Tennay, Dallas, pvt., Co. K, 34th Mich. Vol. Inf., mentioned, 212.
Tenton, Charles, pvt., Co. M, 3d U. S. Inf., wounded, 946.
Terry, Albert H., pvt., Co. L, 20th Kans. Vol. Inf., death, 979; wounded, 977.
Tesh, Chauncey, pvt., Batty. H, 3d U. S. Art., wounded, 946.
Tesmar, John, pvt., Co. A, 28th Inf., U. S. V., death, 1274.
Tew, Martin E., pvt., Co. F, 13th Minn. Vol. Inf., wounded, 992.
Texas, U. S. battleship, mentioned, 50.
Thackhara, Joseph B., pvt., Co. H, 17th U. S. Inf., wounded, 1087
Thayer, Arthur, 1st lieut., 3d U. S. Cav., missing, 1103; wounded, 123.
Theaker, Hugh A., co.., 16th U. S. Inf., mentioned, 543.
Theiss, Charles D. A., pvt., Co. M, 1st S. Dak. Vol. Inf., mentioned, 955.
Thelen, Peter J., pvt., Co. B, 20th U. S. Inf., wounded, 934.
Therrien, George, corpl., Co. L, 19th U. S. Inf., wounded, 1152.
Thiede, Otto, pvt., Co. L, 27th Inf., U. S. V., wounded, 1216.
Thiel, Frank S., pvt., Co. E, 13th U. S. Inf., death, 1140.
Third Army Corps, organization, 530-534.
Thollen, Augustus, pvt., Co. F, 2d U. S. Inf., death, 803.
Thoman, Charles, pvt., Co. A, 8th Ohio Vol. Inf., mentioned, 206.
Thomas, Bert, pvt., Co. M., 51st Iowa Vol. Inf., wounded, 974.
Thomas, Charles M., capt., U. S. N., mentioned, 436, 438.
Thomas, Clarence H., corpl., Co. F, Sig. Corps, U. S. A., death, 1158.
Thomas, Edward, pvt. Co. K, 37th Inf., U. S. V., death, 1172.
Thomas, Frank, artif., Co. M, 44th Inf., U. S. V., killed, 1256.
Thomas, Fretzsh., pvt., Co. H, 11th U. S. V. Cav., death, 1226.
Thomas, George, pvt., Co. I, 32d Inf. U. S. V., death, 1160.
Thomas, George F., pvt., Co. M, 47th Inf., U. S. V., death, 1229.
Thomas, Harry, pvt., Co. G, 17th U. S. Inf., death, 1132.
Thomas, Harry W., pvt., Co. B, 45th Inf., U. S. V., death, 1190.
Thomas, Henry, sergt., Co. A, 24th U. S. Inf., death, 1274.
Thomas, Isaac, pvt., Co. B, 34th Inf., U. S. V., death, 1234.
Thomas, James H., pvt., Co. G, 24th U. S. Inf., wounded, 1160.
Thomas, James M., pvt., Co. M, 25th U. S. Inf., death, 1213.
Thomas, Monroe M., corpl., Co. E, 48th Inf., U. S. V., death, 1213.
Thomas, Moses, pvt., Co. E, 48th Inf., U. S. V., death, 1197.
Thomas, R. E., pvt., U. S. Marine Corps, killed, 459.
Thomas, William H., pvt., Co. L, 32d Inf., U.S.V., death, 1172.
Thomas, U. S. transport, mentioned, 439, 446, 455, 489, 591, 598, 625, 626, 1094, 1121, 1124, 1155, 1159, 1165, 1181, 1195, 1211, 1282, 1303, 1305, 1314, 1319, 1321, 1343, 1354.
Thompson, Ambrose W., pvt., Co. F, 43d Inf., U. S. V., wounded, 1176.
Thompson, Andrew, pvt., Co. M, 45th Inf., U. S. V., death, 1245.
Thompson, Bertie C., pvt., Co. I, 21st U. S. Inf., death, 1256.
Thompson, Charles, pvt., Co. B, 1st Mont. Vol. Inf., wounded, 981.
Thompson, Charles H., pvt., Co. H, 1st N. Y. Vol. Inf., death, 838.
Thompson, Charles H., pvt., Co. K, 16th U. S. Inf., death, 1160.
Thompson, Christ, corpl., Co. K, 20th U. S. Inf., wounded, 934.
Thompson, Edward O., capt., 4th Ohio Vol. Inf., wounded, 878.
Thompson, Frank D., pvt., Troop M, 6th U. S. Cav., death, 497.
Thompson, Frank H., pvt., Co. H, 2d Oreg. Vol. Inf., wounded, 946.
Thompson, Garfield, pvt., Co. G, 24th U. S. Inf., death, 1082.
Thompson, George A., pvt., Co. I, 23d U. S. Inf., wounded, 1167.
Thompson, George S., sergt., band, 25th U. S. Inf., wounded, 1176.
Thompson, Henry F., corpl., Co. M, 14th U. S. Inf., killed, 895.
Thompson, H. Hugh, pvt., Troop I, 4th U. S. Cav., death, 1170.
Thompson, James, pvt., Co. D, 48th Inf., U. S. V., death, 1150.
Thompson, James E., sergt., Troop C, 4th U. S. Cav., death, 1119.
Thompson, John G., 2d lieut., 10th Pa. Vol. Inf., wounded, 940.
Thompson, John H., sergt., Co. H, 10th Pa. Vol. Inf., mentioned, 981.
Thompson, John R., chaplain, 1st Wash. Vol. Inf., death, 907; mentioned, 917.
Thompson, John T., col., chief ordnance officer, U. S. V., mentioned, 389, 395-397.
Thompson, J. Milton, maj., 24th U. S. Inf., mentioned, 1018.
Thompson, Lewis E., pvt., Co. L, 19th U. S. Inf., death, 1202.
Thompson, Maryland, pvt., Troop G, 10th U. S. Cav., mentioned, 218.
Thompson, Pete, pvt., Co. E, 35th Inf., U. S. V., wounded, 1176.
Thompson, Peter, pvt., Co. H, 29th Inf., U. S. V., wounded, 1128.
Thompson, Richard E., maj., Sig. Corps, U. S. A., mentioned, 646, 686, 899, 973.
Thompson, Thomas, pvt., Batty. K, 3d U. S. Art., killed, 945.
Thompson, William R., pvt., Co. A, 31st Inf., U. S. V., death, 1213.
Thorn, Andrew, pvt., Co. G, 9th U. S. Inf., mentioned, 193.
Thorne, Oscar G., pvt., Co. F, 20th Kans. Vol. Inf., killed, 931.
Thornton, E. C., pvt., Co. G, 2d Oreg. Vol. Inf., wounded, 952.

Thornton, Edward S., sergt. maj., 3d U. S. Cav., mentioned, 1179.
Thornton, George F., pvt., Co. G., 38th Inf., U. S. V., death 1223.
Thornton, Owen, Co. B, 34th Inf., U. S. V., mentioned, 206.
Thorsen, James, pvt., Troop E, 4th U. S. Cav., mentioned, 922; wounded, 902.
Thorssell, Guinnar, artif., Co. H, 13th Minn. Vol. Inf., wounded 761, 762.
Thrift, William H., maj., pay dept., U. S. A., mentioned, 252, 254.
Throckmorton, Charles T., pvt., Co. L, 33d Inf., U. S. V., wounded, 1102.
Thrower, Jesse, 1st sergt., Troop B, 9th U. S. Cav., wounded, 1281.
Thygeson, Carl M., pvt., Co. D, 1st Wash. Vol. Inf., death, 1008.
Thyra, U. S. transport, mentioned, 1252, 1280, 1283.
Tierney, James, pvt., Co. B, 1st Mont. Vol. Inf., wounded, 977.
Tierney, John, pvt., Co. I, 1st Mont. Vol. Inf., wounded, 950.
Tierney, Peter J., pvt., Co. F, 1st S. Dak. Vol. Inf., wounded, 949.
Tiernon, George, sergt., Co. M, 12th U. S. Inf., wounded, 1015.
Tiernon, John L., maj., 1st U. S. Art., mentioned, 564, 933, 970.
Tingley, Walter G., mus., Co. F, 1st Nebr. Vol. Inf., wounded, 974.
Tinio, insurgent gen., mentioned, 1120, 1121, 1138.
Tilden, Arthur W., pvt., Co. K, 14th U. S. Inf., death, 886.
Tilden, Samuel J., pvt., Co. M, 51st Iowa Vol. Inf., wounded, 981.
Tilley, Henry, qm. sergt., Co. G, 9th U. S. Inf., death, 1149.
Tilly, George H., capt., Sig. Corps, U. S. A., mentioned, 999; missing, 997, 998.
Timewell, James A., corpl., Co. A, 1st Wash. Vol. Inf., wounded, 896.
Timke, Anthony M., employee, sub. dept., U. S. A., mentioned, 839.
Timmerman, George, corpl., Co. M, 6th U. S. Inf., wounded, 1067.
Timmons, William C., pvt., Co. G, 12th U. S. Inf., death, 1082.
Timms, James T., pvt., Troop F, 9th U. S. Cav., death, 1255.
Tinch, William W., pvt., Co. K, 16th U. S. Inf., wounded, 1117.
Tinkler, James C., corpl., Co. C, 20th U. S. Inf., wounded, 937.
Tippie, Robert L., pvt., Co. M, 14th U. S. Inf., wounded, 454.
Tipps, Robert L., pvt., Co. A, 21st U. S. Inf., death, 1274.
Tischler, Richard, pvt., Troop H, 4th U. S. Cav., killed, 1196.
Titania, U. S. transport, mentioned, 720-722.
Titus, Calvin P., mus., Co. E, 14th U. S. Inf., wounded, 460.
Tjarnel, Henry V., pvt., Batty. L, 3d U. S. Art., wounded, 966.
Tobin, Fred, pvt., Co. B, 1st S. Dak. Vol. Inf., wounded, 915.
Tobin, Richard W., pvt., Co. F, 21st U. S. Inf., death, 1066.
Tochel, James J., pvt., Co. H, 47th Inf., U.S.V., death, 1229.
Todd, Charles, sergt., Co. E, 19th U. S. Inf., death, 1063.
Todd, Charles C., 2d lieut., 3d U. S. Inf., wounded, 981.
Todd, Eugene, pvt., Co. A, 33d Inf., U. S. V., wounded, 1216.
Todd, Robin J., sergt., Co. F, Sig. Corps, U. S. A., killed, 1231.
Todd, Henry D., jr., 1st lieut., 7th U. S. Art., mentioned, 397.
Tohorty, George, corpl., Troop A, 1st U.S.V. Cav., killed, 61.
Toiza, John, pvt., Batty. G, 3d U. S. Art., death, 924.
Tolbert, Thomas, pvt., Co. K, 48th Inf., U. S. V., death, 1191.
Tolbert, William H., corpl., Co. A, Mont. Vol. Inf., wounded, 952.
Tolck, Alfred, pvt., Co. D, 21st U. S. Inf., death, 1167.

Toll, Charles, corpl., Co. I, 18th U. S. Inf., death, 1247.
Tollefson, Benjamin A., pvt., Co. B, 3d U. S. Inf., death, 1074.
Tolley, John, pvt., Co. I, 18th U. S. Inf., death, 1271.
Tomelenson, Emmett L., mus., Co. C, 40th Inf., U. S. V., wounded, 1160.
Tomei, Joseph J., pvt., Co. D, 1st Cal. Vol. Inf., death, 803.
Tompkins, J. Peter W., wagoner, Co. I, 1st N. Dak. Vol. Inf., killed, 967.
Tomsett, Jesse M., 2d lieut., 1st Nebr. Vol. Inf., mentioned, 1007.
Toncray, James P., 1st lieut., 36th Inf., U. S. V., death, 1143.
Toomey, Jeremiah J., corpl., Co. K, 14th U. S. Inf., wounded, 454.
Toral, José, Spanish commander, Santiago de Cuba, correspondence, 79, 91, 95, 105, 113, 117, 123, 130, 133, 134, 136, 137, 140, 142, 147-154, 157, 164, 170, 171, 174, 176, 177, 205.
Torney, George H., maj., med. dept., U. S. A., mentioned, 378, 381.
Tornquest, Nels A., pvt., Batty. D, 6th U. S. Art., wounded, 975.
Torres, Cesario, pvt., Co. H, 4th U. S. Inf., death, 1271.
Torres, insurgent gen., mentioned, 1163.
Torrey, Jay L., col., 2d U. S. V. Cav., mentioned, 551.
Torrey, Zenas W., capt., 6th U. S. Inf., mentioned, 83; wounded, 124.
Totten, Thomas, pvt., Troop L, 4th U. S. Cav., death, 1048; wounded, 1042.
Towle, Ira S., pvt., Co. F, 13th Minn. Vol. Inf., wounded, 975.
Townsend, Thomas C., pvt., Co. K, 2d Oreg. Vol. Inf., wounded, 953.
Townsend, Walter H., pvt., Co. I, 16th U. S. Inf., death, 1264.
Townsley, Clarence P., 1st lieut., 4th U. S. Art., mentioned, 369, 372, 397.
Tozier, Charles W., sergt., Co. L, 20th Kans. Vol. Inf., wounded, 995.
Tracey, William J., pvt., Co. C, 1st Idaho Vol. Inf., death, 947.
Trackler, Frank M., pvt., Troop B, 11th U. S. V. Cav., wounded, 1220.
Tracy, Herbert, pvt., Co. K, 4th U. S. Inf., wounded, 1042.
Tracy, Herbert S., pvt., Co. K, 21st U. S. Inf., death, 1048.
Tracy, John B., pvt., Co. F, Sig. Corps, U. S. A., death, 1283.
Tracy, Leslie N., pvt., Co. K, 30th Inf., U. S. V., wounded, 1147.
Tracy, Michael, pvt., Co. F, 26th Inf., U. S. V., killed, 1150; mentioned, 1144, 1145.
Trahern, Walter, corpl., Co. E, 33d Inf., U. S. V., wounded, 1182.
Transports, U. S.:
Accommodations for troops, etc., 637, 638, 643, 660, 663, 664, 685, 768, 864, 865.
Arrangements for coaling, 699, 701, 703, 709-713, 730, 1049, 1052, 1053.
Casualties on, 771, 774, 798, 829, 830, 892, 923, 925, 929, 952, 968, 986, 992, 994, 997, 1016, 1051, 1058, 1089-1091, 1095, 1125, 1128, 1178, 1193, 1205.
Character of, 683, 721, 722, 1010, 1014.
Condition, 672, 686, 767-770, 884, 921.
Convoy, question of, 664, 665, 670, 693, 695, 697, 698, 700, 703, 704, 710, 712-714.
Cooking and storage facilities, 695, 767, 768, 803.
Danger of infectious diseases on, 1022.
Defects discovered in *Sheridan*, 1000.
Equipment, etc., 9, 12, 36, 125, 198.
Gate City reported stripped of all conveniences, 210, 211.
In quarantine, 193.
Inspection, 643, 880, 881, 886, 1012.
Investigation of conditions on, 191.
Mail lost by wreck of *Morgan City*, 1072.
Permanent purchase, 741, 742.
Prohibition of sale of intoxicating liquors, etc., on, 1251.
Recommendations regarding, 668, 767, 772.
Renaming, 875.
Reported overloading of *Tartar*, 1067.

Transports, U. S.—Continued.
Retention at Manila, 705, 738, 756, 759, 790, 791, 1228.
Route and where touching, 710, 714, 1070, 1242.
Sick and convalescent, return of, 207.
Subsistence and equipment, 653, 654.
To carry mail to Hawaiian Islands, 702.
To utilize for hospital purposes, 72.
Use for Spanish prisoners of war, 976.
Who carried on, 798, 799.
Treadaway, James F., pvt., Co. G, 33d Inf., U. S. V., wounded, 1272.
Treaty of peace, commissioners to negotiate, appointment and place of meeting, 751.
Trenham, Milton A., pvt., Co. D, 13th Minn. Vol. Inf., mentioned, 762; wounded, 761.
Trent, Grant T., 1st lieut., 39th Inf., U. S. V., mentioned, 1334.
Trepto, Ernest F., pvt., Co. D, 30th Inf., U. S. V., wounded, 1150.
Treuman, W. C., col., 1st N. Dak. Vol. Inf., mentioned, 717.
Trias, Mariano, insgt. lieut. gen. character and influence, 1259; surrender, 1259.
Trimble, John, pvt., Co. I, 1st Nebr. Vol. Inf., wounded, 925.
Triton, tug, mentioned, 210, 211.
Tross, Adolph, 1st sergt., Batty. C, 6th U. S. Art., death, 1174.
Trotter, Charles F., Post-Office Committee, mentioned, 405.
Troutman, August P., pvt., Co. G. 14th U. S. Inf., wounded, 460.
True, William M., 2d lieut., 33d Inf., U. S. V., wounded, 1203.
Truitt, Fred M., pvt., Co. E, 30th Inf., U. S. V., death, 1178.
Trulock, William A., pvt., Co. C, 1st N. Dak. Vol. Inf., wounded, 991.
Truman, Ralph E., pvt., Co. F, 20th U. S. Inf., wounded, 937.
Trumbull, Clare D., actg. hosp. stewd., U. S. A., death, 1249.
Tsung-li-Yamen, Peking, China, mentioned, 433, 434, 437, 448.
Tucker, Arlendon, pvt., Co. E, 48th Inf., U. S. V., death, 1144.
Tucker, Frank W., pvt., Co. C, 23d U. S. Inf., death, 829, 830.
Tucker, J. W., pvt., U. S. Marine Corps, killed, 459.
Tucker, Thomas C., pvt., Co. I, 33d Inf., U. S. V., wounded, 1223, 1225.
Tucker, Warren F., pvt., band, 12th U. S. Inf., death, 1132.
Tucker, W. B., corpl., Co. H, 1st Wash. Vol. Inf., wounded, 914.
Tudor, Wiley M., pvt., Co. A. 22d U. S. Inf., death, 1161.
Tufts, William E., pvt., Troop E, 4th U. S. Cav., death, 961; wounded, 947.
Tull, William, pvt., Co. I, 20th Kans. Vol. Inf., wounded, 946.
Turk, Richard L., pvt., Co. C, 23d U. S. Inf., wounded, 760.
Turman, Reuben S., 2d lieut., 6th U. S. Inf., mentioned, 83; wounded, 124.
Turner, A., pvt., killed, 459.
Turner, Henry L., col., 1st Ill. Vol. Inf., mentioned, 256, 544, 545.
Turner, James, pvt., Co. I, 24th U. S. Inf., wounded, 1101.
Turner, John, pvt., Co. H, 51st Iowa Vol. Inf., death, 967.
Turner, Joseph, pvt., Co. C, 9th U. S. Inf., killed, 1297.
Turner, Thomas H., pvt., Troop K, 4th U. S. Cav., wounded, 994.
Turner, William E., pvt., Co. I, 46th Inf., U. S. V., wounded, 1231.
Turpie, David, ex-U. S. Senator, mentioned, 343, 353.
Turpin, John G., pvt., Co. F, 39th Inf., U. S. V., death, 1185.
Turton, Frank N., sergt., Co. K, 1st Cal. Vol. Inf., wounded, 914.
Tweed, Elisha, pvt., Co. I, 47th Inf., U. S. V., wounded, 1166.
Tweed, Samuel, pvt., Co. M, 39th Inf., U. S. V., death, 1245.

Twenty, George T., pvt., Co. E, 13th Minn. Vol. Inf., mentioned, 762; wounded, 761.
Twever, Orton, pvt., Co. B, 1st Colo. Vol. Inf., wounded, 895.
Tyler, Charles R., capt., 19th U. S. Inf., mentioned, 1178.
Tyler, Ora F., pvt., Co. H, 14th U. S. Inf., wounded, 460.
Tyon, Eugene L., pvt., Co. I, 9th U. S. Inf., death, 500.
Tyson, James R., corpl., Co. B, 35th Inf., U. S. V., death, 1165.
Tyson, John C., pvt., Co. I, 29th Inf., U. S. V., death, 1264.
Ubold, L., pvt., Co. —, 16th Pa. Vol. Inf., wounded, 378.
Uhtop, John, pvt., Co. C, 9th U. S. Inf., wounded, 1298.
Ulary, Charles, pvt., Co. E, 32d Inf., U. S. V., wounded, 1102.
Uline, Michael, pvt., Co. L, 12th U. S. Inf., wounded, 1015.
Uline, Willis, 1st lieut., 12th U. S. Inf., wounded, 1056, 1057.
Ulmer, Louis, pvt., Co. L, 13th Minn. Vol. Inf., mentioned, 762; wounded, 761.
Umstetter, agent Great American Exposition, mentioned, 970.
Undergrave, Silas, pvt., Co. H, 2d Mass. Vol. Inf., mentioned, 197.
Underhill, Christy, corpl., Co. E, 32d Inf., U. S. V., death, 1144.
Underwood, Edward C., pvt., Co. I, 40th Inf., U. S. V., wounded, 1209.
Underwood, James A., pvt., Co. H, 40th Inf., U. S. V., killed, 1148.
Unger, Otto, pvt., Co. M, 4th U. S. Inf., death, 1123.
Ungerman, William B., pvt., Co. A, 2d Oreg. Vol. Inf., wounded, 946.
Unie, Elmer E., pvt., Co. B, 20th Kans. Vol. Inf., wounded, 901.
Unionist, U. S. transport, mentioned, 60, 63, 65, 67, 69, 72, 73, 86, 88, 95, 233, 255.
United States:
President of—
Congratulations to Army, 150, 152.
Mentioned, 509.
Message of thanks published to Army, 152, 153.
Proclamation, 178.
Regrets friction between Taft and Chaffee, 1297.
Protocol between Spain and, provisions, 751.
Spanish islands in W. I., to be ceded to, 751.
Unsinn, Adam, pvt., Co. H, 43d Inf., U. S. V., killed, 1162.
Upham, Frank, pvt., Co. C, 1st N. Dak. Vol. Inf., death, 923.
Uppendah, Henry, pvt., Co. E, 1st S. Dak. Vol. Inf., death, 1066.
Upperman, George W., pvt., Co. F, 45th Inf., U. S. V., death, 1239.
Upshaw, Jefferson A., corpl., Co. A, 29th U. S. Inf., wounded, 1197.
Uruguay, U. S. transport, transporting Spanish prisoners, 886, 888, 904, 991.
Utz, Otto M., pvt., Co. K, 26th U. S. Inf., wounded, 1195.
Vaille, F. W., asst. supt., railway mail service in P. I., 696.
Valdez, Frank J., corpl., Co. K, 18th U. S. Inf., death, 1162.
Vale, George E., pvt., Co. F, 14th U. S. Inf., wounded, 454.
Valencia, U. S. transport, mentioned, 584, 589, 603, 609, 622, 704, 715, 740, 792, 801, 802, 827, 839, 878, 958, 968, 1010, 1012-1014, 1017, 1018-1023, 1044, 1046, 1049, 1057, 1059, 1075, 1082, 1095, 1101.
Valentine, Watts C., 2d lieut., 19th U. S. Inf., mentioned, 316, 1178.
Vanacker, Alphonse, pvt., Co. D, 45th Inf. U. S. V., killed, 1250.
Van Berger, Clarence, corpl. Co. B, 37th Inf., U. S. V., death, 1146.
Van Beuren, George, pvt., Co. M, 1st N. Y. Vol. Inf., death, 838.
Vanburen, Alex. B., sergt., Co. F, 18th U. S. Inf., death, 1185.
Van Buren, Edward L., pvt., Co. B, 41st Inf., U. S. V., death, 1238.

Van Buskirk, Ralph E., pvt., Co. E, 1st Wash. Vol. Inf., killed, 934.
Vancel, William P., pvt., Co. I, 20th Kans. Vol. Inf., death, 853.
Vanderboem, Peter L., pvt., Co. L, 34th Mich. Vol. Inf., mentioned, 206.
Van Deusen, George W., capt., 7th U. S. Art., mentioned, 1127, 1131.
Vandewark, Ned, pvt., Co. K, 26th Inf., U. S. V., death, 1252.
Van Duzee, Charles A., col., 14th Minn. Vol. Inf., mentioned, 511, 514.
Vandyke, Allie D., pvt., Co. A., 33d Mich. Vol. Inf., mentioned, 241.
Van Eman, Robert L., pvt., Co. I, 13th Minn. Vol. Inf., death, 917.
Van Hook, Robert, mus., Co. K, 1st S. Dak. Vol. Inf., wounded, 983.
Van Horn, Hallard, corpl., Astor Batty., U. S. A., wounded, 761.
Van Horn, James J., col., 8th U. S. Inf., mentioned, 124, 541.
Van Horn, Robert O., 1st lieut., 17th U. S. Inf., mentioned, 1135.
Vankirk, James, mus., Co. I., 18th U. S. Inf., wounded, 1243.
Vanlaeys, Alphonse J., pvt., Co. A, 1st U. S. Inf., wounded, 1250.
Van Leer, Harry, pvt., Co. B, 9th U. S. Inf., wounded, 443.
Van Leer, Sam, capt., 37th Inf., U. S. V., wounded, 1148.
Van Ness, John I., pvt., Co. A, Batt. Engrs., U. S. A., wounded, 1085.
Vannice, William J., 1st lieut., 1st Colo. Vol. Inf., mentioned, 1000.
Van Orden, Ezra L., pvt., Co. H, 47th Inf., U. S. V., wounded, 1202.
Van Ornum, Arthur P., pvt., Co. C, 31st Inf., U. S. V., death, 1160.
Van Pelts, Charles E., pvt., Astor Batty. U. S. A., wounded, 761.
Van Rensselaer, National Relief Commission, mentioned, 392.
Vans, William J., sergt., Co. —, 1st Nebr. Vol. Inf., death, 803.
Van Schaick, Louis J., 2d lieut., 4th U. S. Inf., mentioned, 1041.
Van Sickle, John S., pvt., Troop A, 6th U. S. Cav., wounded, 466.
Van Uxem, National Relief Commission, mentioned, 392.
Van Valzah, David D., col., 18th U. S. Inf., mentioned, 557–559, 563, 716.
Van Veghton, Clinton, pvt., Co. D, 13th U. S. Inf., drowned, 1187.
Van Vliet, Robert C., capt., 10th U. S. Inf., wounded, 124.
Van Way, Charles, capt., 33d Inf., U. S. V., wounded, 1228.
Vanza, William A., pvt., Co. C, 17th U. S. Inf., death, 1060.
Vanzandt, John, pvt., Co. G, 22d U. S. Inf., death, 1232.
Varley, Thomas, pvt., Co. G, 20th U. S. Inf., wounded, 937.
Varner, Harry A., pvt., Co. M, 47th Inf., U. S. V., killed, 1275.
Vaughan, Elmer E., pvt., B, 23d U. S. Inf., death, 803.
Vaughn, Edward, pvt., Co. C, 51st Iowa Vol. Inf., death, 984.
Very, Samuel W., capt., U. S. N., mentioned, 1105.
Vesper, Paul L., pvt., Co. B, 2d Mass. Vol. Inf., mentioned, 218.
Vestal, Ora, sergt., Co. M, 43d Inf., U. S. V., death, 1174.
Vesuvius, dynamite gunboat, mentioned, 22, 39.
Veyon, Harry, pvt., Co. K, 43d Inf., U. S. V., killed, 1225.
Vice-consuls in Philippines, appointment, 798.
Vickers, Arthur H., 1st sergt., Co. F, 1st Nebr. Vol. Inf., death, 961; wounded, 954.
Vicksburg, U. S. gunboat, mentioned, 1262, 1263.
Viele, Charles D., lieut. col., 1st U. S. Cav., recommended for promotion, 225.
Vigan, P. I., marines landing at, 1110.
Vigilancia, U. S. transport, mentioned, 190, 192, 198, 212, 227, 245, 249, 594, 607, 609.
Villalobos, U. S. gunboat, mentioned, 1214.

Villamil, Spanish officer, mentioned, 100.
Villamor, Blas, insurgent officer, surrender, 1273.
Villamor, Juan, insurgent officer, surrender, 1273.
Vine, Frank A., pvt., Troop E, 9th U. S. Cav., mentioned, 238.
Virgin, John, pvt., Batty. L, 3d U. S. Art., wounded, 1044.
Visayan Military District, garrison at, 561–565, 567, 568, 570, 571, 573–575, 577, 579.
Visayas, Spanish regiment of, distribution, 655.
Viscaya, Spanish cruiser, mentioned, 81, 100.
Vitale, lieut., military attaché, Italian embassy, mentioned, 943.
Vivian, Francis J., pvt., Co. D, 34th Mich. Vol. Inf., mentioned, 195.
Vixen, U. S. gunboat, mentioned, 938.
Vobayda, Frank, pvt., Co. C., 9th U. S. Inf., killed, 1297.
Voget, Henry G. E., pvt., Co. K, 3d U. S. Inf., death, 1201.
Volkey, Theodore, pvt., Co. C, 1st Mont. Vol. Inf., wounded, 954.
Volunteers:
Arming with captured rifles, 170.
Casualties, 55, 61, 74, 83, 174, 175, 182, 183, 185, 192, 193, 195, 197, 202, 204–206, 209, 211–214, 216, 218, 219, 223, 224, 226, 229, 235, 238, 240, 241, 244, 246, 248, 253, 256, 330, 365, 378, 731, 748, 758, 760–763, 771, 774, 797, 801–804, 828–831, 833, 836–842, 850, 852, 853, 856, 861, 866, 875, 879, 886, 889, 893–907, 914–920, 922–926, 931, 934, 937, 939–941, 943, 945–957, 959–961, 966, 967, 971, 972, 974–977, 979, 981–984, 987, 988, 992–996, 999, 1001, 1003, 1008, 1010, 1011, 1015–1017, 1020, 1026, 1027, 1032, 1033, 1038, 1044–1046, 1048, 1050–1052, 1055, 1057–1060, 1063, 1064, 1066, 1075, 1081, 1086–1091, 1095, 1096, 1100–1104, 1109, 1112, 1113, 1115, 1119, 1120, 1123–1128, 1130, 1133, 1135–1137, 1139–1153, 1155, 1156, 1160–1162, 1164–1176, 1178, 1180–1197, 1199–1203, 1205, 1206, 1208–1223, 1225–1241, 1243–1245, 1247–1251, 1259, 1260, 1262–1264, 1267, 1269, 1271, 1272, 1274, 1275, 1280, 1281, 1283.
Condition of preparedness, 643, 704, 707, 748, 831.
Dead, to be brought to U. S. with each regiment, 1002.
Desire to return to U. S., 1001, 1005, 1014.
To enter business in P. I., 1220.
Designation of organized in P. I., 1029.
Discharge of, 785.
Disposition of field equipage, 1006.
Enlistment of, 1040.
And transfer to Vol. Sig. Corps, 686.
Additional regiments, 1003.
In P. I. authorized, 924.
Equipment, instruction, disposition, etc., 726, 729, 758, 837, 990, 991.
General field, return of, 681, 1032.
Homeward movement deferred, 1222.
Honolulu, designated for station, 722, 724, 763.
Return from, 851.
Selection of, for service at, 727, 728, 732, 733.
Equipment, etc., 727.
Selection of organization to garrison, 728.
Inspection of, 802.
Muster-in rolls, 707.
Muster-out, 964, 1015.
Need for in P. I., 908, 992.
Need of regular officers among, 46.
Number available for regiments in P. I., 1001.
Officers, commissioned—
Certificates necessary for payment, 1245.
Discharge and muster-out in P. I., 1240, 1241.
Discharge of regulars holding commissions in, 1242.
For regiments raised in P. I., selection, 1004.
Nomination of, 1028.
Retention in P. I., 1006, 1256, 1257.
Assignment to special duty, 1235.
Organization of—
Cavalry regiment in P. I., 1032.
Hawaiian military force as, 743.
Regiments in P. I., 970, 1003, 1011, 1014, 1020, 1028, 1029, 1038, 1042, 1047.
Strength, 1068.
Regiments, and instruction, in U. S., 1047.

INDEX. 1479

Volunteers—Continued.
  Place of muster-out, determined by regiments, 100.
  Recommended for service in P. I., 728, 732, 735, 736, 743, 747.
  Reenlistment in P. I., 935, 968, 1000, 1004.
  Bounty for, 1237.
  Recruitment of, 686, 687.
  Replaced by regular troops, 1019.
  Retention in P. I., 935, 936.
  Return to U. S., 906, 922, 939, 962, 978, 986, 997, 1001, 1007, 1016, 1019, 1026, 1027, 1031, 1033, 1039, 1040, 1041, 1043–1046, 1049, 1054, 1055, 1058, 1059, 1061–1065, 1069, 1072–1074, 1076, 1077, 1080, 1081, 1083–1085, 1088, 1094, 1098, 1194, 1204, 1222, 1223, 1227, 1228, 1234, 1235, 1239–1242, 1244–1248, 1250, 1252, 1255–1259, 1262, 1264.
  Delayed by typhoons, 1072.
  Insurgents build hopes on, 968.
  Interruption of field operations by, 1237.
  Of dead, sick, etc., desired, 1005.
  Strength, date of sailing to be reported, 1002.
  San Francisco—
    Desire muster-out at, 1015.
    Number and strength of regiments at, 736.
  State—
    Alabama—
      Infantry—
        1st, 35, 345, 534, 535, 547, 549, 550.
        2d, 547, 549, 550.
        3d, 520, 528, 529, 535, 538, 539.
        History of regiments, 583.
    Arkansas—
      Infantry—
        1st, 345, 348, 351, 354, 357, 531, 532, 533.
        2d, 348, 354, 520, 528, 532, 533, 535, 538, 539.
        History of regiments, 583, 584.
    Arizona—
      Troops, to Cuba, P. R., and P. I., 345.
    California—
      Alleged discrimination against, 755.
      Artillery, heavy, 556, 669, 671, 728, 732, 736, 748, 763, 769, 770, 792, 793, 827, 1026, 1027.
      For service in Honolulu, 837.
      History of regiments, 584, 585.
      Infantry—
        1st, 556, 640–642, 644, 663, 664, 368, 669, 671, 748, 775, 780, 905, 909, 1001, 1005, 1016, 1026, 1027, 1030, 1038, 1040–1042, 1058.
        6th, 789.
        7th—671, 734–736, 740, 741, 748, 755, 783, 789.
          Condition at San Francisco, 783.
          Report upon, 785.
        8th—722, 724, 728, 736, 743, 744, 746, 748, 789, 837.
          Character of enlisted personnel, 728.
          Desires service at front, 744.
          Men of, left in P. I., 1043.
          Selection for service in P. I. urged, 789.
          Sending to Manila, 755, 762, 763.
        Signal Corps, 1030.
    Colorado—
      Anxiety as to health condition of, at Manila, 834.
      Hardships suffered at Manila, and causes therefor, 835.
      History, 585, 586.
      1st Infantry, 556, 664, 671, 701, 704, 742, 658, 834, 835, 999, 1003, 1008, 1009, 1016, 1026, 1030, 1032, 1033, 1041, 1055, 1068.
        First to enter Spanish works at Manila, 835.
        Food and health conditions, 835.
    Connecticut—
      History, 586.
      Infantry—
        1st, 345, 524.
        3d, 520, 524–528.
        Yale Battery, 353, 354, 365.
    Delaware—
      1st Infantry, 345, 520, 523–525.
      History, 586.
    District of Columbia—
      1st Infantry, 69, 72, 73, 123, 183, 216, 229, 243, 253, 292, 530, 534–537, 540, 544, 545.
      History, 587.
    Florida—
      1st Infantry, 69, 309, 316, 329, 335, 534–539, 547, 548.
      History, 587.

Volunteers—Continued.
  State—Continued.
    Georgia—
      Artillery—Batteries A & B, 588.
      Infantry—
        1st, 348, 512–514.
        2d, 15, 308, 309, 316, 329, 335, 534, 536, 537, 539, 547, 548.
        3d, 520.
      History, 587, 588.
    Idaho—
      1st Infantry, 716, 999, 1008, 1026, 1027, 1030, 1040, 1044, 1045, 1061.
      History, 588.
      Members left in P. I., 1045.
    Illinois—
      Artillery, 590.
      Cavalry, 1st, 590.
      Infantry—
        1st, 62, 63, 65, 67, 69, 70, 72, 125, 132, 155, 175, 197, 206, 209, 214, 216, 218, 219, 226, 229, 238, 241, 248, 255, 256, 275, 337, 511, 512, 534, 536, 537, 540, 544, 545.
        2d, 15, 539, 547–555.
        3d, 306, 333, 337, 365, 510, 511, 513–515.
        4th, 547–549, 551–555.
        5th, 329, 331–336, 349, 352, 354, 357, 362, 380, 510, 511, 513, 514.
        6th, 105, 107, 108, 117, 120, 122, 142, 183, 194, 304, 308, 337, 385, 401, 402, 520–523, 540.
        7th, 521–523.
        8th, 207, 215, 246, 365.
        9th, 548, 550–555.
      History, 588–590.
    Indiana—
      Artillery, 592.
      Infantry—
        157th, 511, 534, 536.
        158th, 71, 342–344, 353, 511–514.
        159th, 316, 521–523.
        160th, 71, 357, 362, 510–518.
        161st, 349, 548, 551–555.
        To Porto Rico, 316, 320.
      History, 591, 592.
    Iowa—
      Artillery, 593.
      Infantry—
        1st, 556.
        5th, 15, 539.
        49th, 547, 549, 550–555.
        50th, 547–550.
        51st, 736, 739, 748, 749, 832, 862, 972, 999, 1015, 1017, 1026, 1027, 1038, 1047, 1051, 1052, 1055, 1060, 1062, 1069, 1073, 1088.
        52d, 345, 531–535.
      History, 592, 593.
      Number left at Manila, 1073.
      Recommended for service in P. I., 739.
    Kansas—
      Arrival in P. I., 841.
      Infantry—
        20th, 671, 736, 748, 834, 995, 999, 1005, 1016, 1017, 1026, 1047, 1062, 1063, 1085.
          Recommended for service in P. I., 739.
        21st, 511–514.
        22d, 521–523.
        23d, 239, 245.
      History, 593, 594.
    Kentucky—
      Cavalry, 512, 595.
      Infantry—
        1st, 328, 329, 354, 364, 511, 513, 515.
        2d, 531–533.
        3d, 370, 510, 512–518.
        4th, 515, 535, 538, 539.
      History, 594, 595.
    Louisiana—
      Artillery, 596.
      Infantry—
        1st, 35, 356, 364, 547, 549–551.
        2d, 35, 547–554.
      History, 595, 596.
    Maine—
      Artillery, 553–555.
      Infantry, 1st, 345, 355, 356, 531–534.
      Signal Corps, 224.
      History, 596.
    Maryland—
      Infantry—
        1st, 345, 355, 519, 524–528.
        5th, 292, 309, 316, 329, 335, 355, 530, 534–537.
      History, 596.

Volunteers—Continued.
State—Continued.
Massachusetts—
Artillery, 1st, 303, 308, 598.
Infantry—
2d, 12, 15, 33, 183, 197, 202, 209, 216, 218, 219, 221, 224, 229, 241, 252, 253, 385, 539, 540–545.
5th, 520, 524–529.
6th, 105, 111, 283, 304, 308, 373–376, 385, 520–523, 540, 630.
8th, 214, 308, 510–518.
9th, 42, 185, 193, 209, 212, 213, 216, 217, 219, 226, 229, 238, 241, 244, 248, 255, 519, 522–524, 540, 544, 546.
History, 597, 598.
Michigan—
Infantry—
31st, 71, 510–518.
32d, 15, 35, 289, 536, 537, 539, 547, 584.
Without arms, 24.
33d, 42, 182, 174, 182, 183, 192, 195, 197, 209, 214, 218, 226, 229, 235, 238, 241, 245, 246, 248, 253, 303, 519, 522–524, 540, 544, 546.
34th, 42, 183, 192, 193, 195, 197, 202, 205, 206, 209, 212, 213, 216, 219, 226, 232, 234, 243, 248, 253, 519, 522–524, 540, 543, 544, 546.
35th, 216, 519, 524–529.
History, 598, 599.
Minnesota—
Casualties, list, 762.
Inquiry as to, 759, 786, 795.
Infantry—
12th, 511–514.
13th, 556, 639, 671, 716, 742, 982, 999, 1000, 1020, 1026, 1027, 1040, 1045–1047, 1049, 1054, 1065.
Number left at Manila, 1054.
14th, 347, 353, 511–514.
15th, 524–529.
History, 599, 600.
Mississippi—
Infantry—
1st, 362, 364, 531–534.
2d, 547, 550, 551.
3d, 510, 516–519, 528.
History, 600, 601.
Missouri—
Artillery, 602.
Infantry—
1st, 343, 344, 530–533.
2d, 510–512, 514–519, 528.
3d, 521–523.
4th, 286, 345, 520–528.
5th, 342, 343, 356, 514, 531, 532, 533.
6th, 548, 551–555.
History, 601, 602.
Montana—
Infantry—
1st, 734, 785, 995, 999, 1001, 1003, 1008, 1015, 1017, 1020, 1026, 1038, 1039, 1048, 1049, 1057–1059, 1074, 1075.
Discharge, 785, 786.
History, 602.
Nebraska—
Infantry—
1st, 556, 671, 701, 704, 716, 758, 906, 972, 987, 999, 1016, 1019, 1026, 1041, 1044.
2d, 530–533.
3d, 547, 548, 550–555.
History, 603.
Nevada—
Cavalry, 832, 1026, 1030, 1069, 1077, 1094.
1st Infantry, 604.
History, 604.
Tender of services, 744.
New Hampshire—
Infantry—
1st, 345, 511–515.
History, 604.
New Jersey—
Infantry—
1st, 345, 520–523.
2d, 547, 549, 550.
3d, 521, 526–528.
4th, 520, 525–529.
History, 604, 605.
New York—
Artillery, 608.
Cavalry, 305, 333, 361, 400, 402, 403, 405.
Equipment, 3.9.

Volunteers—Continued.
State—Continued.
New York—Continued.
Infantry—
83, 706, 716, 720, 721, 725–727, 729, 748, 755, 762, 763, 766, 801, 802, 837, 838, 851.
1st—
Arrival from Honolulu, 851.
Disposition, 726, 801, 802, 851.
2d, 292, 530, 534–536.
3d, 347, 521–523.
8th, 348, 531–533.
9th, 531–533.
12th, 510–517, 747.
14th, 353, 364, 530–533.
21st, 540, 541.
22d, 345, 520.
65th, 520–523.
69th, 323, 334, 531–539.
71st, 12, 14, 15, 33, 126, 135, 149, 193, 202, 216, 219, 221, 224, 226, 227, 229, 241, 246, 539–541, 543, 545.
Target practice for, 14.
201st, 520, 524–529.
202d, 520, 524–528.
203d, 520, 524–529.
History, 606–608.
Request service in P. I., 747.
To go to Honolulu, 748, 762, 763, 766.
North Carolina—
Infantry—
1st, 15, 339, 345, 547–555.
3d, 510, 515–518.
History, 609.
North Dakota—
Infantry—
1st, 556, 717, 999, 1008, 1026, 1027, 1030, 1040, 1044, 1045, 1061.
History, 609.
Members left in P. I., 1045.
Ohio—
Artillery, 612.
Cavalry, 1st, 111, 112, 148, 275, 276, 283, 284, 342, 343, 350, 351, 361, 364, 366, 512.
Infantry—
1st, 287, 510, 534, 536, 550.
2d, 346, 352, 354, 510–518, 548.
3d, 15, 534, 536, 537, 539, 547, 548.
4th, 306, 333, 365, 378, 404, 405, 510, 511, 513–515.
5th, 15, 534, 536, 537, 539, 547, 548.
6th, 329, 336, 510–518.
7th, 520–523.
8th, 81, 82, 87, 93, 94, 188, 195–197, 209, 213, 214, 224, 226, 232, 235, 241, 246, 303, 520–523, 544, 545.
9th, 520, 521, 525–527.
10th, 519, 524–529.
History, 610–612.
Oregon—
Artillery, 612.
Infantry—
1st, 660, 664, 668, 999.
556, 669, 671, 769, 770, 772, 774, 778–780, 787, 832, 982, 997, 999, 1001–1003, 1005, 1007, 1008, 1010, 1014, 1017, 1028, 1030, 1032, 1033.
2d—
Deplorable condition at San Francisco, 787.
General field return, 1033.
History, 612.
Members left in P. I., 1028.
To be sent to Portland, 1002.
To be sent to San Francisco, 1007.
Pennsylvania—
Artillery, 312, 313, 317, 328, 335, 353, 362.
Cavalry, 305, 316, 333, 361, 362, 400, 402, 405.
Infantry—
1st, 511–514.
3d, 316, 511, 534, 536, 537.
4th, 306, 333, 401, 402, 510, 511, 513–515.
5th, 511–514.
6th, 521–523.
8th, 521–523.
9th, 511, 512, 514, 515.
556, 649, 658, 671, 701, 704, 735, 739, 748, 1001, 1016, 1019, 1026, 1041, 1046, 1062.
10th—
Graves of deceased decorated, 1062.
12th, 521–523.

INDEX.   1481

Volunteers—Continued.
State—Continued.
Pennsylvania—Continued.
13th, 521–529.
14th, 520, 524–528.
15th, 520, 525–527, 663, 999.
16th, 71, 92, 294, 295, 372, 378, 385, 511–515, 523.
18th, 523.
History, 613–616.
Rhode Island—
Artillery, 617.
Infantry—
1st, 318, 345, 520–528.
History, 617.
South Carolina—
Artillery, 617.
Infantry—
1st, 512, 548, 551.
2d, 348, 552–554.
History, 617.
South Dakota—
Infantry—
1st, 513, 547, 550, 736, 742, 763, 948, 987, 990, 999, 1000, 1015, 1026, 1039, 1046, 1048, 1049, 1065, 1068.
History, 618.
Tennessee—
Debark from transport to participate in action against insurgents near Cebu, 1031, 1076.
Infantry—
1st, 736, 748, 802, 831, 840, 899, 941, 1000, 1011, 1026, 1047, 1062, 1066, 1069, 1071, 1075, 1076, 1080, 1081, 1083, 1098.
Inspection of, 802.
Sail for Manila, 831.
Whereabouts and condition, 94.
2d, 358, 361, 520–528.
3d, 345, 531–533, 535, 538, 539.
4th, 510, 515–518.
History, 618, 619.
Texas—
Cavalry, 620.
Infantry—
1st, 35, 534, 535, 547–553.
2d, 35, 345, 534, 535, 547, 549, 550.
History, 619, 620.
Utah—
Artillery, 556, 704, 746, 748, 831, 832, 972, 982, 1000, 1008, 1016, 1019, 1026, 1041, 1044.
Cavalry, 620.
Disposition, 746.
History, 620.
Vermont—
1st Infantry, 307, 345, 359, 531–533.
History, 621.
Troops for Porto Rico, 340.
Virginia—
Infantry—
2d, 547, 549, 550.
3d, 345, 524.
4th, 547–555.
6th, 510, 515–518.
History, 621.
Washington—
Infantry—
1st, 736, 752, 753, 827, 992, 997, 1008, 1015, 1020, 1026, 1042, 1044, 1048, 1056, 1057, 1062–1064, 1083.
Departure for P. I., 827.
Friction in, 992.
History, 622.
Number left at Manila, 1064.
Service in P. I. urged, 753.
West Virginia—
Infantry—
1st, 324, 345, 510–518.
2d, 520, 523–529.
History, 622.
Troops to P. R., 324.
Wisconsin—
Artillery, 623.
Infantry—
1st, 547–550.
2d, 15, 92, 294, 295, 385, 401, 402, 511–515, 539.
3d, 92, 294, 295, 385, 510, 511, 513–515.
4th, 520, 528, 535, 538, 539.
History, 622, 623.

Volunteers—Continued.
State—Continued.
Wyoming—
Artillery, 624, 832, 834, 1000, 1026, 1040, 1044, 1061.
Infantry—
1st, 556, 717, 999, 1000, 1026, 1029, 1040, 1044, 1061.
History, 623.
Members left in P. I., 1045.
Strength of organizations, Philippine expedition, 716, 717.
Supplies, etc., for, 639–642, 644, 659, 660, 663, 671, 680, 707, 717.
Tender of services for P. I., 663, 684, 696, 699, 706, 711, 712, 741, 744, 746.
Travel pay and transportation, on muster-out, 999, 1000.
Reenlistment in P. I., 1004.
United States—
Cavalry—
1st, 33, 54, 55, 60, 61, 74, 128, 212, 226–228, 377, 540, 542, 544, 546.
History, 625.
2d, 547, 550.
History, 625.
3d, 512.
History, 625.
11th, 1043, 1063, 1068, 1079, 1093, 1114, 1126–1128, 1131, 1142, 1151, 1159, 1169, 1175, 1188, 1198, 1207, 1217, 1227, 1233, 1235, 1239, 1240, 1244, 1246, 1249, 1250, 1256, 1302, 1305, 1308, 1309.
Engineers—
1st, 233, 366, 392, 395, 401.
History, 624.
2d, 748.
History, 624.
3d, 510, 516–518, 528, 546, 547, 553–555.
History, 625.
Engineer Batt., 736.
Infantry—
1st Territorial, 510, 516–519.
1st, 138.
History, 626.
2d, 138, 231.
History, 626.
3d, 225, 231.
History, 626.
4th, 281, 550, 551.
History, 626.
5th, history, 626.
6th, 532, 533.
History, 626.
7th, 510, 515, 516, 518, 528.
History, 627.
8th, 213.
History, 627.
9th, 245, 248.
History, 627.
10th, 510, 515, 516, 518, 528.
History, 627.
26th, 1029, 1056, 1076, 1089, 1094, 1106, 1114, 1128, 1142, 1151, 1159, 1169, 1175, 1188, 1198, 1207, 1217, 1227, 1233, 1246, 1254, 1255, 1257, 1262, 1279, 1296.
27th, 1055, 1073, 1089, 1094, 1114, 1127, 1128, 1142, 1151, 1159, 1169, 1175, 1188, 1198, 1207, 1217, 1227, 1233, 1246, 1252, 1254, 1259, 1279, 1303–1305, 1308, 1312, 1313.
28th, 1089, 1091, 1105, 1107, 1114, 1128, 1129, 1131, 1142, 1151, 1159, 1169, 1175, 1188, 1198, 1207, 1222, 1227, 1232, 1233, 1246, 1255, 1258, 1259, 1279, 1290, 1303.
29th, 1081, 1082, 1091, 1114, 1128, 1142, 1151, 1159, 1169, 1175, 1188, 1198, 1207, 1214, 1218, 1222, 1227, 1233, 1246, 1262, 1277, 1318, 1324.
30th, 1075, 1087, 1094, 1114, 1128, 1131, 1135, 1138, 1139, 1142, 1151, 1159, 1169, 1175, 1188, 1198, 1207, 1217, 1227, 1233, 1246, 1254, 1258, 1273, 1277, 1279.
31st, 1056, 1088, 1090, 1091, 1105, 1110, 1111, 1114, 1128, 1142, 1151, 1159, 1169, 1175, 1188, 1198, 1207, 1217, 1227, 1233, 1246, 1280.
32d, 1078, 1080, 1091, 1094, 1113, 1114, 1126, 1128, 1142, 1151, 1159, 1169, 1175, 1188, 1198, 1207, 1217, 1227, 1233, 1246, 1262, 1277.

Volunteers—Continued.
United States—Continued.
Infantry—Continued.
33d, 1077, 1079, 1090, 1094, 1101, 1109–1111, 1113–1115, 1120, 1121, 1128, 1142, 1151, 1159, 1169, 1175, 1188, 1198, 1207, 1217, 1221, 1227, 1233, 1244, 1246, 1257, 1264, 1277.
34th, 570, 1056, 1066, 1067, 1069, 1071, 1085, 1094, 1103, 1114, 1115, 1126, 1128, 1133, 1142, 1151, 1159, 1169, 1175, 1188, 1198, 1207, 1217, 1227, 1233, 1244, 1246, 1257, 1264.
35th, 1029, 1080, 1081, 1095, 1114, 1128, 1142, 1151, 1159, 1169, 1175, 1188, 1198, 1207, 1218, 1227, 1234, 1246, 1255, 1259.
36th, 1029, 1047, 1051, 1056, 1057, 1063, 1064, 1068, 1076, 1080, 1087, 1088, 1091, 1093, 1094, 1097, 1109, 1110, 1114, 1126, 1128, 1138, 1142, 1151, 1159, 1169, 1175, 1188, 1198, 1207, 1218, 1222, 1227, 1234, 1235, 1244, 1246, 1249, 1255.
37th, 1029, 1047, 1063, 1068, 1080, 1086, 1094, 1114, 1128, 1130–1132, 1138, 1142, 1151, 1159, 1169, 1175, 1188, 1198, 1207, 1211, 1218, 1227, 1234, 1235, 1240, 1244, 1246.
38th, 1105, 1106, 1126, 1128, 1136, 1142, 1151, 1159, 1169, 1175, 1188, 1198, 1207, 1214, 1218, 1222, 1227, 1234, 1246, 1282, 1283.
39th, 1093, 1116, 1128, 1131, 1139, 1142, 1151, 1159, 1169, 1175, 1188, 1198, 1207, 1218, 1227, 1234, 1246, 1259.
40th, 1108, 1126, 1128, 1142, 1148, 1151, 1159, 1162, 1169, 1171, 1175, 1188, 1198, 1207, 1218, 1227, 1234, 1246, 1281.
41st, 1112, 1114, 1117, 1122, 1127, 1142, 1151, 1159, 1169, 1175, 1188, 1198, 1207, 1218, 1227, 1234, 1246, 1280.
42d, 1112, 1128, 1142, 1151, 1159, 1168, 1169, 1175, 1188, 1198, 1207, 1218, 1227, 1234, 1246, 1280–1282.
43d, 1102, 1103, 1106, 1110, 1112, 1114, 1119, 1122, 1125, 1128, 1135, 1142, 1151, 1159, 1169, 1176, 1188, 1199, 1207, 1218, 1227, 1234, 1246, 1282, 1283.
44th, 1106, 1122, 1125, 1128, 1142, 1151, 1159, 1169, 1176, 1188, 1199, 1207, 1218, 1227, 1234, 1246, 1282, 1283.
45th, 1098, 1103, 1115, 1123, 1127, 1128, 1131, 1135, 1142, 1148, 1151, 1159, 1169, 1176, 1188, 1199, 1207, 1218, 1227, 1234, 1246, 1272.
46th, 1102, 1121, 1127, 1128, 1131, 1136, 1142, 1151, 1159, 1176, 1188, 1199, 1207, 1218, 1227, 1234, 1246, 1272.
47th, 1094, 1102, 1124, 1128, 1135, 1142, 1151, 1159, 1169, 1176, 1188, 1199, 1207, 1218, 1227, 1234, 1247, 1282.
48th, 1138, 1142, 1151, 1159, 1169, 1176, 1188, 1199, 1207, 1218, 1227, 1234, 1247, 1270, 1272, 1284.
49th, 1112, 1115, 1124, 1142, 1151, 1159, 1169, 1176, 1188, 1199, 1207, 1218, 1227, 1234, 1247, 1270, 1272, 1282, 1284.
Signal Corps. 205, 295, 309, 516–518, 546, 547, 717, 899, 1010, 1084.
Transfers to, and enlistments for, 686.
Vondle, Frank D., pvt., Co. G, 21st U. S. Inf., wounded, 1052.
von Ketteler, Baroness, mentioned, 473.
von Shlick, Robert H., pvt., Co. C, 9th U. S. Inf., wounded, 444.
Voorhies, Porter H., pvt., Co. I, 18th U. S. Inf., death, 1217.
Vorfeld, Robert H., pvt., Batty. K, 3d U. S. Art., wounded, 948.
Vosburg, Clyde, sergt., Co. I, 1st Nebr. Vol. Inf., wounded, 974.
Vost, William P., maj., 6th U. S. Art., mentioned, 564.
Votrie, Albert, pvt., Co. K, 39th Inf., U. S. V., killed, 1145.
Vought, Fred J., pvt., Co. L, 3d Wis. Vol. Inf., mentioned, 388.
Vroom, Peter D., lieut. col., I. G. dept., U. S. A., mentioned, 301.
Wabster, Samuel, pvt., Co. E, 24th U. S. Inf., wounded, 1052.
Wachs, Adam R., corpl., Troop L, 3d U. S. Cav., wounded, 1222.

Wachs, Alfred P., corpl., Co. D, 33d Inf., U. S. V., killed, 1137.
Waddington, Amos H., pvt., Co. E, 1st Wash. Vol. Inf., wounded, 914.
Wade, Charles, pvt., Co. H, 3d U. S. Inf., wounded, 1191.
Wade, Gish, pvt., Co. E, 25th U. S. Inf., wounded, 1127.
Wade, James F., brig. gen., U. S. A.:
Assigned to command troops at Tampa, Fla., 7, 8.
Member evacuation committee, 397.
Mentioned, 8, 11, 12, 53, 57, 268, 290, 312, 313, 315, 317, 320, 340, 342–346, 348, 349, 355–357, 359, 363, 365, 509, 513, 530, 531, 539, 1259, 1270, 1301, 1302, 1311.
Wadlington, David H., pvt., Co. G, 4th U. S. Inf., wounded, 1021.
Wadsworth, James W., mentioned, 326.
Wadsworth, William A., maj., qm. dept., U. S. A., mentioned, 783, 785, 829.
Wageck, George A., pvt., Co. L, 1st Nebr. Vol. Inf., wounded, 975.
Wagner, Arthur L., lieut. col., a. a. g., U. S. A., mentioned, 32, 62, 114, 373.
Wagner, Burton R., mus., Co. H, 43d Inf., U. S. V., killed, 1168.
Wagner, Charles P., pvt., Co. I, 1st S. Dak. Vol. Inf., wounded, 975.
Wagner, Fred R., pvt., Co. D, 1st Nebr. Vol. Inf., wounded, 948.
Wagner, Henry M., pvt., Co. B, 22d Oreg. Vol. Inf., wounded, 1003.
Wagner, Henry S., 1st lieut., 14th U. S. Inf., wounded, 1335.
Wagner, John, pvt., Co. M, 14th U. S. Inf., wounded, 454.
Wagner, Louis L., corpl., Co. M, 36th Inf., U. S. V., killed, 1051.
Wagner, Max, 2d lieut., 26th Inf., U. S. V., killed, 1215.
Wagner, Paul, pvt., Co. B, 4th U. S. Inf., wounded, 1017.
Wagner, Walter, pvt., Co. A, 51st Iowa Vol. Inf., death, 1015.
Wagoner, Todd L., pvt., Co. F, 20th Kans. Vol. Inf., wounded, 955.
Wahl, Joseph A., pvt., Co. H, 20th Vol. Inf., death, 957; wounded, 950.
Wainwright, Richard, comdr., U. S. N., mentioned, 322.
Wainwright, Robert P. P., capt., 1st U. S. Cav., mentioned, 55; wounded, 54.
Waite, Augustus F., pvt., Co. G, 34th Inf., U. S. V., death, 1229.
Waite, Harry M., corpl., Co. C, 30th Inf., U. S. V., wounded, 1147.
Waldersee, Count von, field marshal, German army, mentioned, 447, 450, 451, 466, 480, 481, 483, 486, 488, 493, 494, 497, 499, 501, 505.
Waldo, Rhinelander, 2d lieut., 17th U. S. Inf., mentioned, 1019.
Waldron, Frank E., corpl., Co. L, 15th U. S. Inf., death, 1274.
Waldron, William H., 2d lieut., 9th U. S. Inf., mentioned, 998; wounded, 428, 429, 469.
Waldron, ——, pvt., Co. A, 1st Ill. Vol. Inf., mentioned, 256.
Waldschmidt, Henry, pvt., Co. I, 2d U. S. Inf., death, 1234.
Walfe, Henry N., interpreter, mentioned, 839.
Walker, Adelbert, sergt., Co. C, 9th U. S. Inf., wounded, 443.
Walker, Charles O., pvt., Co. C, 10th Pa. Vol. Inf., wounded, 945.
Walker, George B., capt., 6th U. S. Inf., mentioned, 83; wounded, 124.
Walker, Guy C., pvt., Co. G, 1st Nebr. Vol. Inf., killed, 926.
Walker, Ira L., pvt., Co. B, 28th Inf., U. S. V., death, 1271.
Walker, John F., corpl., Co. G, 51st Iowa Vol. Inf., death, 1045.
Walker, John W., pvt., Co. H, 29th Inf., U. S. V., killed, 1160.
Walker, Joseph, pvt., Troop M, 4th U. S. Cav., death, 1052.
Walker, Joseph L., pvt., Co. B, 1st Tenn. Vol. Inf., death, 947.

Walker, Philip E. M., 1st lieut., 3d U. S. Inf., mentioned, 998.
Walker, Pres, pvt., Co. C, 19th U. S. Inf., death, 1109.
Walker, Richard, pvt., Co. H, 22d U. S. Inf., death, 1245.
Walker, Samuel, pvt., Troop D, 9th U. S. Cav., killed, 1232.
Walker, William, pvt., Co. L, 9th U. S. Inf., death, 1149.
Walker, William O., pvt., Co. A, 2d Oreg. Vol. Inf., wounded, 971.
Walker, ——, Co. I, 15th U. S. Inf., mentioned, 1337, 1345.
Walkup, Harry B., pvt., Troop A, 4th U. S. Cav., wounded, 1209.
Wall, Edwin W., sergt., Co. K, 3d U. S. Art., killed, 959.
Wall, George, 1st sergt., Co. A, 14th U. S. Inf., wounded, 975.
Wall, Thomas B., pvt., Co. E, 27th Inf., U. S. V., wounded, 1113.
Wall, William L., sergt., Co. M, 1st Cal. Vol. Inf., wounded, 897.
Wallace, Al, pvt., Co. K, 48th Inf., U. S. V., death, 1191.
Wallace, Archer B., pvt., Co. K, 71st N. Y. Vol. Inf., mentioned, 236.
Wallace, Archer B., pvt., Co. K, N. Y. Vol. Inf., mentioned, 232, 236, 242-244, 247, 252.
Wallace, Charles T., sergt., Co. K, 10th Pa. Vol. Inf., wounded, 948.
Wallace, George A., pvt., Co. G, 39th Inf., U. S. V., death, 1215.
Wallace, George W., 1st lieut., 9th U. S. Inf., mentioned, 243, 1298.
Wallace, Joseph, pvt., Co. M, 9th U S. Inf., mentioned, 244.
Wallace, Lewis H., pvt., Co. H, 13th Minn. Vol. Inf., mentioned, 762; wounded, 761.
Wallace, Robert B., col., 37th Inf., U. S. V., mentioned, 902, 1030, 1042; wounded, 900.
Wallace, William, pvt., Co. L, 1st Tenn. Vol. Inf., death, 947.
Wallace, William J., pvt., Co. F, 18th U. S. Inf., death, 1109.
Waller, Littleton W. T., maj., U. S. Marine Corps:
  Charges against, 1335.
  Expedition in search of, 1313, 1314.
  Mentioned, 417, 426, 439.
  Orders of Gen. Smith to, 1328, 1329.
  Proceedings of trial, 1333, 1347.
Wallgreen, Enoch, pvt., Co. L, 14th U. S. Inf., wounded, 1017.
Walling, David, pvt., Co. C, 51st Iowa Vol. Inf., wounded, 1017.
Wallington, Charles, pvt., Co. B, 21st U. S. Inf., wounded, 1052.
Walls, John, pvt., Co. M, 38th Inf., U. S. V., death, 1208.
Walls, Melvin M., pvt., Co. C, 9th U. S. Inf., wounded, 1298.
Walmach, John H., pvt., Hosp. Corps, U. S. A., death, 1245.
Walsh, Henry J., pvt., Co. A, Batt. Engrs., U. S. A., mentioned, 1196.
Walsh, James J., pvt., Troop F, 3d U. S. Cav., death, 1215.
Walsh, Joseph, pvt., Co. L, 13th Minn. Vol. Inf., mentioned, 1054.
Walsh, Michael, pvt., Co. H, 6th U. S. Inf., death, 1048.
Walsh, Michael, pvt., Co. H, 21st U. S. Inf., death, 1099.
Walsh, Robert E., pvt., Co. C, 9th U. S. Inf., killed, 460.
Walsh, William C., pvt., Co. C, 1st Cal. Vol. Inf., wounded, 409.
Walter, John W., corpl., Co. H, 47th Inf., U. S. V., death, 1208, wounded, 1187.
Walter, Rudolph, corpl., Co. D, 31st Inf., U. S. V., death, 1208.
Walters, George H., pvt., Co. I, 38th Inf., U. S. V., death, 1144.
Walters, H. William, pvt., Co. M, 13th U. S. Inf., death, 1202.
Walthus, William, civilian, mentioned, 253.
Walton, Piley, pvt., Co. C, 1st Idaho Vol. Inf., wounded, 897.

Walton, Wesley, pvt., Co. M, 1st Wash. Vol. Inf., wounded, 897.
Waltz, Millard F., maj., 1st U. S. Inf., mentioned, 1344.
Walve, Ole, 1st sergt., Co. F, 22d U. S. Inf., wounded, 948.
Wampler, George C., pvt., Batty. L, 3d U. S. Art., wounded, 966.
Wanderer, U. S. transport, mentioned, 275.
Wangle, Charles E., pvt., Co. E 24th U. S. Inf., mentioned, 183.
Wansboro, Thomas A., 2d lieut., 7th U. S. Inf., killed, 124.
Wannebo, John, pvt., Co. C, 9th U. S. Inf., killed, 1297.
War, Secretary of, mentioned, 416, 422-424, 427, 428, 430, 432, 433, 436, 437, 443, 444, 447, 454, 457, 461, 467, 468, 490, 492, 1051, 1113, 1133, 1134-1137, 1143, 1145.
Warburton, Barclay H., capt., Light Batty. A, Pa. Vol. Art., mentioned, 313, 325.
Ward, Clarence E., pvt., Co. G, 40th Inf., U.S.V., death, 1194.
Ward, Earl C., corpl., Co. A, 30th Inf., U. S. V., death, 1150.
Ward, Elmer R., pvt., Co. A, 38th Inf., U. S. V., death, 1201.
Ward, Henry C., maj., 16th U. S. Inf., wounded, 1152.
Ward, James, corpl., Co. F, 25th U. S. Inf., killed, 1191.
Ward, John J., pvt., Co. F, 21st U.S. Inf., wounded, 1015.
Ward, Matthew T. E., 2d lieut., 27th Inf., U. S. V., wounded, 1216.
Ward, Oliver D., pvt., Co. B, 1st Wash. Vol. Inf., wounded, 947.
Ward, Thomas, col., a. a. g., U. S. A., mentioned, 49, 359, 394, 458, 489.
Ward, Miss, nurse, mentioned, 246, 247, 253.
Wardlaw, George B., corpl., Batty. B, Utah Vol. Art., wounded, 896.
Wards, T., pvt., U. S. Marine Corps, death, 1314.
Wardsworth, Andrew S., 2d lieut., 1st Nebr. Vol. Inf., wounded, 974.
Ware, Ansel T., pvt., Co. D, 12th U. S. Inf., wounded, 1057.
Ware, Loudon, pvt., Co. E, 24th U. S. Inf., wounded, 1055.
Wareham, James, pvt., Co. B, 28th Inf., U. S. V., wounded, 1132.
Warfield, Henry, pvt., Co. L, 25th U. S. Inf., wounded, 1228.
Warner, Barnes & Co., mentioned, 1333.
Warner, Cassius E., sergt. maj., 20th Kans. Vol. Inf., wounded, 983.
Warner, Converse P., pvt., Co. G, 4th U. S. Inf., death, 1003.
Warner, Elwood B., pvt., Co. A, 5th U. S. Inf., killed, 1251.
Warner, Herman E., pvt., Batty. L, 3d U. S. Art., wounded, 946.
Warner, Worthy, pvt., Co. B, 41st Inf., U. S. V., death, 1202.
Warrell, ——, pvt., U. S. Marine Corps, wounded, 459.
Warren, U. S. transport, mentioned, 457, 464, 465, 477, 488, 585, 936, 962, 971, 991, 1026, 1027, 1030, 1033, 1041, 1055, 1063, 1084, 1085, 1112, 1128, 1207, 1210, 1227, 1228, 1235, 1244, 1265, 1299, 1300, 1302, 1305, 1316, 1323, 1324, 1339, 1341.
Warren, Walter, pvt., Co. I, 49th Inf., U. S. V., death, 1226.
Warren, William K., pvt., Co. A, 14th Inf., U. S. V., mentioned, 974.
Warrick, Oliver B., capt., 18th U. S. Inf., killed, 1111.
Warrick, W. F., lieut, 10th Pa Vol. Inf., mentioned, 732.
Warrington, George W., pvt., Co. I, 1st Colo. Vol. Inf., death, 1032.
Washburn, Ray L., pvt., Co. D, 1st S. Dak. Vol. Inf., wounded, 949.
Washburn, Russell, pvt., Co. F, 47th Inf., U. S. V., death, 1185.
Washington, James H., pvt., Co. A, 24th U. S. Inf., death, 1149.
Washington, Lewis, corpl., Co. E, 48th Inf., U. S. V., killed, 1173.

Washington, Morgan G., corpl., Co. B, 25th U. S. Inf., killed, 1131.
Washington, Walter L., sergt., Co. C, 24th U. S. Inf., killed, 1212.
Washington, U. S. transport, mentioned, 400.
Wasp, U. S. gunboat, mentioned, 39, 50, 300, 301.
Wassell, William H., 1st lieut., 22d U. S. Inf., wounded, 124.
Waterman, Leslie R., qm., 1st N. Dak. Vol. Inf., death, 1119.
Waters, Charles A., pvt., Co. A, 20th Kans. Vol. Inf., wounded, 954.
Waters, Charles A., ccrpl., Co. D, 36th Inf. U. S. V., wounded, 1081.
Waters, Hugh, pvt., Co. D, 1st Wash. Vol. Inf., wounded, 941.
Waters, William J., pvt., Co. B, 8th U. S. Inf., mentioned, 218.
Waties, James R., brig. gen., U. S. V., mentioned, 342, 512–515, 527, 528.
Watkins, John P., pvt., Batty. F, 4th U. S. Art., death, 1229.
Watson, C. H., bandmaster, 13th Minn. Vol. Inf., death, 803.
Watson, Edward, farrier, Troop D, 3d U. S. Cav., death, 1170.
Watson, Harry G., pvt., Co. C, 13th Minn. Vol. Inf., death, 803; mentioned, 786.
Watson, Isaac, pvt., Co. F, 25th U. S. Inf., death, 1125.
Watson, James T., pvt., Co. H, 24th U. S. Inf., death, 1210.
Watson, John C., rear-admiral, U. S. N., mentioned, 9, 10, 281, 287, 1115, 1129.
Watson, Joseph, pvt., Co. D, 26th Inf., U. S. V., wounded, 1227.
Watson, Sidney O., corpl., Co. E, 40th Inf., U. S. V., wounded, 1254.
Watson, William J., capt., 20th Kans. Vol. Inf., wounded, 954.
Watson, William J., capt., 40th Inf., U. S. V., wounded, 1162.
Watts, Bert W., pvt., Co. C, 1st Nebr. Vol. Inf., wounded, 955.
Watts, Charles H., maj., 5th U. S. Cav., mentioned, 1329.
Watts, Clarence V., pvt., Batty. K, 3d U. S. Art., killed, 945.
Watts, Welburn, pvt., Co. H, 29th Inf., U. S. V., killed, 1237.
Waugh, Joseph D., wagoner, Co. C, 1st S. Dak. Vol. Inf., wounded, 956.
Way, Henry N., 2d lieut., 4th U. S. Inf., killed, 1203.
Weakley, William A., pvt., Co. I, 25th U. S. Inf., death, 1205.
Weatherby, J. B., cook, Co. M, 1st Wash. Vol. Inf., wounded, 897.
Weatherman, Martin L., pvt., Co. G, 38th Inf., U. S. V., death, 1238; wounded, 1237.
Weathers, Reuben, pvt., Co. L, 25th U. S. Inf., death, 1130.
Weaver, Edward, pvt., Co. C, 38th Inf., U. S. V., wounded, 1141.
Weaver, Edward M., pvt., Co. I, 1st Mont. Vol. Inf., wounded, 954.
Weaver, Henry H., pvt., Co. K, 10th Pa. Vol. Inf., death, 831.
Webb, Elijah, pvt., Co. H, 44th Inf., U. S. V., death, 1190.
Webb, Walter G., pvt., Co. E, 17th U. S. Inf., death, 1152.
Webb, Will, pvt., Co. C, 24th U. S. Inf., killed, 1188.
Webb, William B., corpl., Co. K, 47th Inf., U. S. V., wounded, 1235.
Webb, Richard W., corpl., Co. C, 9th U. S. Inf., wounded, 443.
Webb, William, pvt., Co. M, 9th U. S. Inf., death, 454.
Webb, Merrell E., maj., 33d Mich. Vol. Inf., mentioned, 174.
Webber, John M., pvt., Co. I, 20th Kans. Vol. Inf., wounded, 915.
Webber, Wilbon L. pvt., Co. K, 27th Inf., U. S. V., death, 1132.
Weber, Charles, corpl., Co. F, 18th U. S. Inf., wounded, 1113.
Weber, Edwin H., pvt., Co. E, 3d U. S. Inf., death, 1063.

Weber, Julius, pvt., Co. L, 12th U. S. Inf., wounded, 1057.
Weber, Louis P., 2d lieut., 42d Inf., U. S. V., death, 1150.
Webster, Alfred, pvt., Co. A, 12th U. S. Inf., mentioned, 171.
Webster, Daniel E., pvt., Co. L, 9th U. S. Inf., death, 1095.
Webster, Edward B., pvt., Co. K, 9th U. S. Inf., killed, 1038.
Webster, Elbridge H., pvt., Co. H, 43d Inf., U. S. V., killed, 1155.
Webster, George K., pvt., Co. D, 9th U. S. Inf., death, 1164; wounded, 1087.
Webster, Robert J., corpl., Co. I, 37th Inf., U. S. V., wounded, 1203.
Weden, Charles H., pvt., Co. L, 43d Inf., U. S. V., wounded, 1218.
Weed, Clayton S., pvt., Co. F, 42d Inf., U. S. V, death, 1165.
Weeden, Dickson W., pvt., Co. C, 1st Mont. Vol. Inf., death, 1060.
Weeding, Oscar E., pvt., Co. A, 27th Inf., U. S. V., death, 1274.
Weeks, Marion Merle, 2d lieut., 21st U. S. Inf., wounded, 1052.
Weeks, Thurston, pvt., Co. M, 29th Inf., U. S. V., death, 1200.
Weibner, Henry, cook, Co. G, 42d Inf., U. S. V., death, 1162.
Weidberg, Excelsion H., pvt., Co. A, 4th U. S. Inf., wounded, 999.
Weidnerre, Charles D., pvt., Co. F, 2d U. S. Inf., death, 1253.
Weidoff, Ernest, pvt., Co. I, 3d U. S. Inf., death, 1032.
Weidriech, William L., pvt., Co. K, 6th U. S. Inf., death, 1185.
Weigand, Frank, pvt., Co. F, 29th Inf., U. S. V., killed, 1219.
Weigle, ——, lieut., 1st Wash. Vol. Inf., mentioned, 1046.
Weiker, Leonard L., artif., Co. H, 8th Ohio Vol. Inf., mentioned, 197.
Weimer, Schuyler, corpl., Co. F, 39th Inf., U. S. V., death, 1221.
Weippert, Joseph A., pvt., Co. E, 9th U. S. Inf., killed, 1307.
Weis, Ambrose, ——, 7th U. S. Inf., mentioned, 209.
Weisenberger, maj., 1st Wash. Vol. Inf., mentioned, 992.
Weiss, Paul, pvt., Co. G, 1st S. Dak. Vol. Inf., wounded, 975.
Weithorn, William, pvt., Co. A, 33d Inf., U. S. V., death, 1255.
Welbon, Calvin, corpl., Co. D, 1st Wash. Vol. Inf., wounded, 966.
Welch, Benjamin F., pvt., Co. L, 40th Inf., U. S. V., death, 1162.
Welch, Charles, pvt., Batty. F, 4th U.S. Art., death, 1231.
Welch, Dudley W., 1st lieut., asst. surg., 43d Inf., U. S. V., mentioned, 1282.
Welch, Frank A., pvt., Co. I, 45th Inf., U. S. V., death, 1187; wounded, 1183.
Welch, Lyman, 2d lieut., 24th U. S. Inf., mentioned, 124.
Welch, Michael, pvt., Co. K, 8th U. S. Inf., death, 1234.
Welch, Thomas, pvt., Co. H, 19th U. S. Inf., death, 1241.
Welch, Thomas J., pvt., Co. E, 26th Inf., U. S. V, death, 1165.
Weld, John H., pvt., Co. E, 43d Inf., U. S. V., death, 1231.
Weldon, Edward, pvt., Co. K, 14th U. S. Inf., death, 1029.
Weldon, James E., pvt., Co. K, 1st Nebr. Vol. Inf., wounded, 924.
Welles, George S., corpl., Co. D, 9th U. S. Inf., killed, 1052.
Wellette, Joseph, pvt., Co. M, 14th U. S. Inf., wounded, 454.
Wells, Briant H., 2d lieut., 2d U. S. Inf., wounded, 124.
Wells, D. H., 2d lieut., 16th U. S. Inf., mentioned, 83.
Wells, Frank, pvt., Co. A, 34th Inf., U. S. V., death, 1123.

Wells, Frank M., chaplain, 1st Tenn. Vol. Inf., mentioned, 951.
Wells, George W., pvt., Co. K, 40th Inf., U. S. V., wounded, 1183.
Wells, H. L., capt., 2d Oreg. Vol. Inf., wounded, 952.
Wells, Joseph N., pvt., Co. L, 37th Inf., U. S. V., killed, 1214.
Wells, Samuel C., pvt., Co. B, 34th Inf., U. S. V., wounded, 1163.
Wells, William, pvt., Co. F, 35th Inf., U. S. V., death, 1255.
Welsh, George, pvt., Co. G, 32d Inf., U. S. V., killed, 1143.
Welsh, Lewis S., mentioned, 353.
Welsh, Robert E., pvt., Co. A, 23d U. S. Inf., death, 1119.
Welsh, Thomas H., pvt., Co. L, 9th Mass. Vol. Inf., mentioned, 229.
Wenks, ——, pvt., Co. —, 1st S. Dak. Vol. Inf., mentioned, 763.
Wentink, Martin, pvt., Co. A, 28th Inf., U. S. V., wounded, 1132.
Wentworth, Samuel S., pvt., Batty. E, 1st U. S. Art., wounded, 1015.
Wenzel, Leonard, pvt., Co. H, 3d U. S. Inf., death, 1245.
Wenzelburger, William, pvt., Co. L, 19th U. S. Inf., wounded, 1152.
Wessells, Henry W. jr., maj., 3d U. S. Cav., mentioned, 1059, 1100, 1101, 1136; wounded, 123.
West, Benjamin F., pvt., Co. L, 16th U. S. Inf., death, 1164.
West, James, 1st sergt., Co. D, 2d Oreg. Vol. Inf., wounded, 946.
West, James C., pvt., Co. L, 37th Inf., U. S. V., killed, 1211.
West, Peter F., pvt., Hosp. Corps. U. S. A., wounded, 946.
West, William H., pvt., Co. E, 10th Pa. Vol. Inf., wounded, 953.
Wester, ——, capt., Swedish army mentioned, 347, 348.
Westerhoff, John H., pvt., Co. D, 21st U. S. Inf., wounded, 1081.
Westervelt, Jesse I., pvt., Co. H, 9th U. S. Inf., wounded, 444.
Westever, John, pvt., Co. D, 1st Nebr. Vol. Inf., wounded, 956.
Westfall, Allen, pvt., Co. I, 36th Inf., U. S. V., death, 1243.
West Indies, islands of, to be evacuated by Spanish, 751.
Westminster, U. S. transport, mentioned, 437, 439.
Weston, John F., col., sub. dept., U. S. A., mentioned, 171, 240, 290, 299, 303.
Weston, Orin C., pvt., Co. F, 9th U. S. Inf., wounded, 444.
Westphal, Louis E., jr., pvt., Co. D, 1st Cal. Vol. Inf., death, 931.
Westran, Axel W., pvt., Co. A, 23d U. S. Inf., wounded, 1183.
Westrate, Anthony, pvt., Co. F, 30th Inf., U.S. V., wounded, 1150.
Wetherby, John C., pvt., Co. L, 4th U. S. Inf., death, 1113; wounded, 1110.
Wetherill, Alexander M., capt., 6th U. S. Inf., killed, 124.
Wetmore, Hon. G. P., mentioned, 318.
Wetter, Fred, pvt., Co. G, 31st Inf., U. S. V., death, 1213.
Wetzel, George, pvt., Hosp. Corps, U. S. A., death, 1196.
Whalen, George W., unassigned recruit, 12th U. S. Inf., death, 1248.
Whalen, James A., pvt., Co. A, 33d Inf., U. S. V., killed, 1148.
Whalen, John C., corpl., Co. L, 21st U. S. Inf., wounded, 1015.
Whalen, John J., pvt., Co. H, 6th U. S. Inf., death, 1280.
Whalery, Lewis, pvt., Co. A, 49th Inf., U. S. V., death, 1144.
Whatley, John O., pvt., Co. M, 44th Inf., U. S. V., wounded, 1256.
Wheadon, Bert D., 2d lieut., 1st Nebr. Vol. Inf., wounded, 906, 907.
Wheaton, Fred H., pvt., Co. H, 1st Mont. Vol. Inf., death, 957; wounded, 952.

Wheaton, Loyd, maj. gen., U. S. A., assigned to command, Dept. N. Luzon, 1164, 1165.
  Mentioned, 55, 547–553, 560–563, 566, 568, 572, 578, 889, 931, 944, 962, 963, 982, 1006, 1007, 1010, 1016, 1050, 1076, 1092, 1095–1097, 1101, 1103, 1104, 1106–1110, 1128, 1129, 1131–1133, 1135, 1136, 1171, 1263, 1301, 1302, 1329, 1343.
  See *Expedition* under *Philippine Islands*.
Wheaton, Roxie, pvt., Co. H, 40th Inf., U. S. V., wounded, 1183.
Wheeler, Charles W., sergt., Batty. H, 3d U. S. Art., wounded, 915.
Wheeler, Frank E., corpl., Co. E, 1st S. Dak. Vol. Inf., wounded, 949.
Wheeler, Fred, capt., 4th U. S. Cav., wounded, 936.
Wheeler, James W., pvt., Co. C, 2d Mass. Vol. Inf., mentioned, 202.
Wheeler, Joseph, maj. gen., U. S. V.
  Assigned to command, 4th Army Corps, 258.
  Mentioned, 14, 24, 27, 47, 54, 74, 82, 90, 100, 101, 136, 146–148, 151, 152, 181, 188, 189, 191, 216, 228, 240, 534, 535, 538, 541, 542, 544, 546, 568, 569, 571–573, 1034.
  Opinion, re health of army in Cuba, 202.
Wheeler, Harry M., pvt., Co. —, 2d Oreg. Vol. Inf., death, 803.
Wheeler, Oscar R., corpl., Co. E, 1st N. Y. Vol. Inf., death, 838.
Wheeler, Wilban H., pvt., Co. L, 1st Cal. Vol. Inf., wounded, 924.
Wheeler, William S., sergt., Co. —, 11th U. S. Inf., wounded, 390.
Whelan, John T., pvt., Co. K, 13th Minn. Vol. Inf., wounded, 947.
Wherry, William, lieut. col., 2d U. S. Inf., mentioned, 225.
Whims, Jasper L., pvt., Co. G, 12th U. S. Inf., death, 997.
Whipple, Charles H., maj., pay dept., U. S. A., mentioned, 635, 718, 766, 791, 830.
Whipple, Charles W., capt., ord. dept., U. S. A. mentioned, 700, 706.
Whipple, George E., corpl., Co. M, 2d Mass. Vol. Inf., mentioned, 224.
Whipps, Samuel F., corpl., Co. C, 9th U. S. Inf., wounded, 443.
Whitaker, Alfred H., sergt., Co. A, 1st N. Dak. Vol. Inf., death, 967.
Whitcomb, William L., pvt., Co. D, 1st Nebr. Vol. Inf., wounded, 956.
White, Cass, pvt., Co. D, 1st Colo. Vol. Inf., death, 900.
White, C. D., pvt., Co. D, 1st Colo. Vol. Inf., missing, 895.
White, Charles E., pvt., Co. K, 13th U. S. Inf., death, 1125; wounded, 1115.
White, Claude R., pvt., Co. A, 23d U. S. Inf., death, 997.
White, Daniel E., pvt., Co. C, 18th U. S. Inf., death, 907.
White, George W., pvt., Co. G, 3d U. S. Inf., death, 1213.
White, Grant A., 1st lieut., 33d Inf., U. S. V., death, 1161.
White, Herbert A., 1st lieut., 11th Cav., U. S. V., mentioned, 505.
White, John W., pvt., Co. F, 1st Nebr. Vol. Inf., wounded, 974.
White, Napoleon, pvt., Co. K, 4th U. S. Inf., wounded, 1042.
White, Peter F., corpl., Co. F, 43d Inf., U. S. V.
White, Ralph T., pvt., Co. E, 22d U. S. Inf., wounded, 941.
White, Robert H., maj., med. dept., U. S. A., mentioned, 657, 673.
White, William L., corpl., Troop E, capt., 10th U. S. Cav., killed, 61.
White, ——, 1st sergt., Co. L, 9th U. S. Inf., mentioned, 1317, 1318.
Whitecotton, William E., pvt., Co. I, 4th U. S. Inf., death, 1095.
Whitehead, Frank L., 1st sergt., Co. K, 14th U. S. Inf., wounded, 460.
Whitehead, John E., corpl., Co. F, 43d Inf., U. S. V., death, 1202.
Whiteker, Lossen B., pvt., Co. A, 20th Kans. Vol. Inf., wounded, 977.
Whitely, William, qm. employee, death, 478.

INDEX.

Whitemore, James H., pvt., Co. L, 1st Nebr. Vol. Inf., killed, 954.
Whiteside, Christopher E., pvt., Co. F, 9th U. S. Inf., wounded.
Whiteside, Samuel, pvt., Co. E, 44th Inf., U. S. V., death, 1253.
Whiteside, Thomas F., pvt., Co. M, 1st Colo. Vol. Inf., death, 956.
Whitesides, Alexander, cook, Co. A, 49th Inf., U. S. V., death, 1213.
Whitford, Clarence, pvt., band, 34th Inf., U. S. V., death, 1132.
Whiting, Charles, pvt., Co. G, 3d U. S. Inf., mentioned, 219.
Whiting, David C., pvt., Co. C, 35th Inf., U. S. V., death, 1220.
Whiting, E. W., pvt., Co. A, 1st Ill. Vol. Inf., mentioned, 214.
Whitlock, Frank O., 2d lieut., 14th Cav., U. S. V., mentioned, 1264.
Whitlock, George, pvt., Co. C, 16th Pa. Vol. Inf., wounded, 378.
Whitlock, Guy L., pvt., Co. M, 3d U. S. Inf., killed, 995.
Whitmore, Joseph, pvt., Co. —, 1st S. Dak. Vol. Inf., death, 803.
Whitney, Folliot A., maj., 6th U. S. Inf., death, 1200.
Whitney, I. J., sergt., Batty. G, 3d U. S. Art., killed, 951.
Whitney, Jack, corpl., Co. E, 6th U. S. Inf., death, 1130.
Whitney, Jophanus H., col., 5th Mass. Vol. Inf., mentioned, 529.
Whitney, Millet L., pvt., Co. H, 16th U. S. Inf., wounded, 1182.
Whitney, U. S. transport, mentioned, 80, 92, 98, 275, 278, 282, 309, 310, 350, 400, 589, 621.
Whitside, Samuel M., lieut. col., 5th U. S. Cav., mentioned 317, 326, 340.
Whitson, Robert C., pvt., Co. B, 38th Inf., U. S. V., wounded, 1192.
Whittaker, Edward, sergt., Co. K, 3d U. S. Art., killed, 897.
Whittier, George R., pvt., Co. L, 45th Inf., U. S. V. wounded, 1233.
Whittier, Charles A., brig. gen., U. S. V., mentioned, 828, 829.
Whitting, Harold, pvt., Hosp. Corps, U. S. A., death, 1208.
Wholly, John H., 1st lieut., 24th U. S. Inf.; col., 1st Wash. Vol. Inf., mentioned, 992.
Whorton, Henry C., pvt., Co. E, 17th U. S. Inf., death, 1132.
Whritenor, Harry N., pvt., Co. I, 21st U. S. Inf., death, 1086.
Wiber, James C., pvt., Co. M, 14th U. S. Inf., killed, 460.
Wiberg, cor. with Sec'y War, 342.
Wick, Lewis F., Co. G, 33d Mich. Vol. Inf., mentioned, 229.
Wickham, Frank D., 1st lieut., 18th U. S. Inf., mentioned, 998.
Wickham, Henry J., mus., Co. A, 1st Nebr. Vol. Inf., wounded, 760.
Wicks, Harry D., alias Briggs, George, pvt., Co. G, 1st Wyo. Vol. Inf., death, 967.
Widick, Albert A., corpl., Co. A, 40th Inf., U. S. V., wounded, 1150.
Wiedeer, Ray, pvt., Co. C, 1st Wyo. Vol. Inf., wounded, 897.
Wiegant, Thaddeus J. A., pvt., Co. C, 20th Vol. Inf., wounded, 946.
Wienecke, George C. O., pvt., Co. K, 9th U. S. Inf., death, 1165.
Wightman, William, sergt., Co. I, 3d U. S. Inf., death, 1158.
Wigley, Charles V., pvt., Co. C, 46th Inf., U. S. V.
Wikoff, Charles, col., 22d U. S. Inf., killed, 124. Mentioned, 252, 542.
Wilburn, Thomas G., mus., Co. K, 25th U. S. Inf., death, 1190.
Wilcox, Ernest, pvt., Troop E, 4th U. S. Cav., wounded, 936.
Wilcox, Merton A., pvt., Co. H, 20th Kans. Vol. Inf., killed, 983.
Wild, Charles W., pvt., Co. G, 46th Inf., U. S. V., death, 1191.
Wilder, Wilber E., col., 14th N. Y. Vol. Inf., mentioned, 353,

Wilder, ——, pvt., Co. G, 1st Colo. Vol. Inf., 1033.
Wildman, Rounsevelle, consul-general, U. S., at Hongkong, China, mentioned, 738.
Wiley, Everett S., pvt., Co. M, 39th Inf., U. S. V., death, 1228.
Wiley, John A., brig. gen., U. S. V., mentioned, 315, 331, 335, 512-518.
Wilford, Ward, pvt., Co. B, 8th Ohio Vol. Inf., mentioned, 235.
Wilhelm, Fred, pvt., Batty. G, 6th U. S. Art., death, 1168.
Wilhelm, William H., capt., 14th U. S. Inf., death, 1285.
Wilkander, John, comsy. sergt., U. S. A., mentioned, 943.
Wilkensen, George, pvt., Co. A, 1st U. S. Inf., death, 1280.
Wilkerson, James W., pvt., Co. M, 41st Inf., U.S.V., death, 1172.
Wilkes, Lewis, pvt., Co. A, 16th U. S. Inf., wounded, 1117.
Wilkie, Ames, corpl., Co. E, 11th U. S. Inf., wounded, 390.
Wilkins, David H., pvt., Co. I, 1st Nebr. Vol. Inf., wounded, 974.
Wilkinson, John C., president, Business Men's League, St. Louis, Mo., mentioned, 343.
Will, Gustave, 1st sergt., Troop D, 4th U. S. Cav., wounded, 1087.
Willard, James R., pvt., Co. D, 1st Idaho Vol. Inf., wounded, 901.
Willett, Irving J., mus., Co. F, 1st S. Dak. Vol. Inf., death, 850.
Williams, Allan T., pvt., Co. G, 13th Minn. Vol. Inf., wounded, 987.
Williams, Charles H., pvt., Co. G, 47th Inf., U.S.V., death, 1241.
Williams, Christian S., pvt., Co. C, 9th U. S. Inf., missing, 1297.
Williams, Clarence C., 1st lieut., ord. dept., U. S. A., mentioned, 830.
Williams, Constant, lieut. col., 15th U. S. Inf. mentioned, 443, 471, 1195.
Williams, David L., pvt., Co. F, 1st Mont. Vol. Inf., death, 1001.
Williams, David M., corpl., Co. B, 41st Inf., U.S.V., death, 1185.
Williams, Edwin E., pvt., Co. M, 40th Inf., U. S. V., wounded, 1183.
Williams, Ennis N., pvt., Co. H, 28th Inf., U. S. V., death, 1133; wounded, 1132.
Williams, Ezra W., sergt., Co. I, 42d Inf., U.S.V., death, 1228.
Williams, Fletcher, corpl., Co. K, 48th Inf., U.S.V., death, 1191.
Williams, Fred A., maj., 1st Nebr. Vol. Inf., mentioned, 922.
Williams, Gomer, pvt., Co. G, 1st Mont. Vol. Inf., wounded, 945.
Williams, Hardy, pvt., Co. M, 34th Inf., U. S. V., death, 1181.
Williams, Henry E., corpl., Co. E, 13th Minn. Vol. Inf., mentioned, 762; wounded, 760.
Williams, James, pvt., Co. C, 13th U. S. Inf., death, 1104.
Williams, James L., pvt., Co. E, 40th Inf., U. S. V., death, 1191.
Williams, John, 1st sergt., Co. F, 25th U. S. Inf., death, 1172.
Williams, John, pvt., Co. C, 34th Inf., U. S. V., death, 1255.
Williams, John, pvt., Co. G, 1st Nebr. Vol. Inf., wounded, 906.
Williams, John W., pvt., Batty. F, 6th U. S. Art., death, 1113.
Williams, Joseph F., pvt., Co. K, 14th U. S. Inf., death, 1119.
Williams, Kenneth P., 2d lieut., 1st U. S. Inf., mentioned, 1313, 1314.
Williams, Lamont A., 2d lieut., 51st Iowa Vol. Inf., wounded, 1050, 1055.
Williams, Levie, pvt., Co. K, 24th U. S. Inf., death, 1194.
Williams, Oliver, pvt., Co. M, 48th Inf., U. S. V., death, 1213.
Williams, Price, pvt., Co. H, 34th Inf., death, 1132.
Williams, Rowell, qm. employee, mentioned, 235.
Williams, Sam, pvt., Co. M, 36th Inf., U. S. V., wounded, 1087.

INDEX.

Williams, Thomas, pvt., Co. F, 31st Inf., U. S. V., death, 1213.
Williams, Thomas, pvt., Co. H, 48th Inf., U. S. V., death, 1229.
Williams, Thomas J., sergt., Co. G, 31st Inf., U. S. V., death, 1132.
Williams, William, pvt., Co. D, 22d U. S. Inf., death, 1181.
Williams, William H., 1st lieut., 12th U. S. Inf., wounded, 1051.
Williams, William H., pvt., Co. E, 14th U. S. Inf., death, 1186.
Williamson, Benny, pvt., Co. G, 49th Inf., U. S. V., wounded, 1251.
Williamson, Fred L., pvt., Co. B, 34th Inf., U. S. V., killed, 1190.
Williamson, George McK., capt., asst. qm., U. S. V., 1st lieut., 8th U. S. Cav., mentioned, 302.
Williamson, ——, veterinary, mentioned, 1042.
Williard, Harry O., 2d lieut., 10th U. S. Cav., wounded, 124.
Willing, David G., pvt., band, 18th U. S. Inf., death, 837.
Willing, Edward D., corpl., Co. B, 20th Kans. Vol. Inf., mentioned, 926; wounded, 901.
Williston, Edward B., brig. gen., U. S. V., mentioned, 240, 552-555, 564, 566-568, 571, 573-575, 577, 579, 971.
Willits, George, mentioned, 358.
Willmore, Cirg, pvt., Co. K, 38th Inf., U. S. V., death, 1249.
Wills, George E., pvt., Batty. G, 3th U. S. Art., death, 1258.
Wilmer, ——, adjt. gen., mentioned, 355.
Wilmington, U S. transport, mentioned, 88, 95.
Wilmot, Allyn B., pvt., Co. A, 12th U. S. Inf., death, 1078.
Wilseck, Charles, pvt., Co. G, 1st Wyo. Vol. Inf., death, 1029.
Wilson, Benton, pvt., Co. L, 36th Inf., U. S. V., wounded, 1081.
Wilson, Charles, pvt., Co. H, 24th U. S. Inf., wounded, 1149.
Wilson, Charles, pvt., Batty. F, 4th U. S. Art., wounded, 1085.
Wilson, Charles, pvt., Co. C, 29th Inf., U. S. V., death, 1228.
Wilson, Charles A., corpl., Sig. Corps, U. S. A., mentioned, 1238; wounded, 1237.
Wilson, Charles A., pvt., Co. I, 37th Inf., U. S. V., killed, 1206.
Wilson, Charles F., pvt., Troop C 4th U. S. Cav., death, 1070.
Wilson, Charles S., pvt., Co. I, 9th U. S. Inf., wounded, 1087.
Wilson, Charlie, pvt., Co. E, 9th U. S. Inf., killed, 1298.
Wilson, Clarence, corpl., Co. M, 17th U. S. Inf., death, 1095.
Wilson, Dudley, corpl., Co. G, 8th Ohio Vol. Inf., mentioned, 213.
Wilson, Edward F., pvt., Co. M. 22d U. S. Inf., wounded, 941.
Wilson, Fred J., pvt., Co. I, 18th U. S. Inf., death, 1243.
Wilson, George J., pvt., Co. E, 16th U. S. Inf., death, 1032.
Wilson, James, pvt., Co. B, 24th U. S. Inf., killed, 1264.
Wilson, James H., maj. gen., U. S. V.
 Arrival at Taku, Japan, 473.
 Mentioned, 37, 39, 44, 45, 53, 57, 58, 71, 76, 80, 82, 86, 91, 92, 95-98, 101, 103, 106, 108, 109, 115, 117, 122, 125-128, 130, 131-133, 135, 137-142, 144-146, 268, 269, 272, 274, 275, 277, 278, 280, 286, 287-291, 293-295, 297, 298, 321, 330, 331, 339, 372, 373, 404, 405, 470, 476-478, 486-489, 509-511, 513-518.
 Ordered to duty with Gen. Chaffee, 435.
Wilson, James H., corpl., Co. L, 2d U. S. Inf., death, 1255.
Wilson, James H., pvt., Co. M, 24th U. S. Inf., death, 1230.
Wilson, John, pvt., Troop I, 10th U. S. Cav., mentioned, 216.
Wilson, Joe D., pvt., Co. L, 23d U S. Inf., death, 861.
Wilson, Joseph C., sergt., Co. F, 23d U. S. Inf., death, 1141.
Wilson, Leroy B., pvt., Co D, 22d U. S. Inf., death, 1245.

Wilson, M., pvt., Co. E, 12th U. S. Inf., death, 979.
Wilson, M. Andrew, corpl., Co. M, 36th Inf., U. S. V., killed, 1051.
Wilson, Robert E., sergt. maj., 33d Inf., U. S. V., wounded, 1145.
Wilson, Samuel C., pvt., Co. F, 22d U. S. Inf., death, 1191.
Wilson, Samuel M., pvt., Co. M, 20th Kans. Vol. Inf., killed, 954.
Wilson, Thomas, pvt., Co. C, 36th Inf., U. S. V., death, 1185.
Wilson, William F., pvt., Co. H 33d Inf., U. S. V., killed, 1222.
Wilson, William G., pvt., Co. K, 9th U. S. Inf., death, 1200.
Wilson, W. W., sergt., Co. L, 2d Oreg. Vol. Inf., wounded, 952.
Winders, William M., pvt., Co. D, 1st Wash. Vol. Inf., mentioned, 974; wounded, 971.
Winfield, Charles, pvt., Batty. H, 3d U. S. Art., death, 802; mentioned, 761.
Wing, Eugene G., 2d lieut., 35th Inf., U. S. V., death, 1137, 1140.
Wingate, Fort, N. Mex., garrison at, 7.
Wingate, Noah P., pvt., Co. I, 38th Inf., U. S. V., wounded, 1153.
Wingo, Claud C., pvt., Co. C, 9th U. S. Inf., missing, 1297.
Winkler, Joseph H., pvt., Co. F, 3d U. S. Inf., killed, 1232.
Winkler, Walter C., 1st sergt., Co. C, 40th Inf., U. S. V., wounded, 1193.
Wint, Theodore J., col., 6th U. S. Cav., mentioned, 83, 466, 489, 495-498, 1324, 1339, 1344.
 Wounded, 124.
Winter, Francis A., capt., med. dept., U. S. A., mentioned, 1240.
Wintergill, ——, 2d Mass. Vol. Inf., mentioned, 254.
Winters, Alvin B., pvt., Co. H, 48th Inf., U. S. V., death, 1172.
Winters, Charles W., pvt., Co. K, 21st U. S. Inf., wounded, 1046.
Winters, Dan, pvt., Co. D, 36th Inf., U. S. V., death, 1245.
Winters, Willard, pvt., Co. H, 36th Inf., U. S. V., killed, 1087.
Wintler, Ralph, pvt., Troop K, 4th U. S. Cav., wounded, 905, 974.
Wipf, Alexander D., pvt., Troop B, 11th Cav., U. S. V., wounded, 1190.
Wiplinger, Frank, pvt., Co. D, 13th Minn. Vol. Inf., wounded, 987.
Wirth, Alexander E., pvt., Co I, 15th U. S. Inf., death, 1248.
Wischman, Walter, pvt., Troop F, 2d U. S. Cav., mentioned, 183.
Wise, Aaron C., pvt., Co. F, 12th U. S. Inf., wounded, 1026.
Wise, Eugene, corpl., Co. M, 16th U. S. Inf., death, 1088.
Wise, Frederick M., comdr., U. S. N., mentioned, 421, 422, 473, 477.
Wise, Isaac N., artif., Co. B, 39th Inf., U. S. V., death, 1170.
Wise, John K., pvt., Co. B, 39th Inf., U. S. V., death, 1181.
Wise, Walter W., pvt., Co. I, 1st Colo. Vol. Inf., death, 803.
Wisler, Jacob, pvt., Co. G, 4th U. S. Inf., death, 1233.
Witcher, J. S., paymaster, mentioned, 636.
Wither, Joseph A., pvt., Co. L, 1st Nebr. Vol. Inf., wounded, 952.
Witherby, John C., pvt., Co. —, 4th U. S. Inf., death, 1113.
Withers, Austin A., pvt., Troop M, 3d U. S. Cav., death, 1189.
Withers, Hays, mus., Co. G, 49th Inf., U. S. V., wounded, 1237.
Withers, William, pvt., Troop H, 9th U. S. Cav., wounded, 1235.
Witt, Buston, sergt., Co. H, 17th U. S. Inf., wounded, 1113.
Wittenmeyer, Edmund, capt., 15th U. S. Inf., mentioned, 1345.
Wiltshire, Leon W., pvt., Co. E, 9th U. S. Inf., death, 1150.
Wolcott, Roger, governor of Mass., mentioned, 373-376.

Wolcott, S. W., pvt., Co. —, 4th Ohio Vol. Inf., wounded, 365.
Wolf, Herman P., corpl., 1st N. Dak. Vol. Inf., wounded, 963.
Wolf, William, pvt., Co. L, 20th Kans. Vol. Inf., wounded, 915.
Wolfe, Orrin R., 1st lieut., 22d U. S. Inf., wounded, 1155.
Wolper, Henry, sergt., band, 9th U. S. Inf., death, 1123.
Womack, Payton M., pvt., Co. M, 6th U. S. Inf., wounded, 1126.
Womack, Samuel, pvt., Co. H, 9th U. S. Inf., death, 494.
Wampatuck, U. S. transport?, 22, 39.
Wonn, John W., corpl., Co. K, 3d U. S. Inf., death, 1187.
Wood, Charles P., pvt., Co. E, 13th Minn. Vol. Inf., mentioned, 762; wounded, 761.
Wood, Dennis H., pvt., Troop K, 3d U. S. Cav., wounded, 1113.
Wood, Elmer E., col., 2d La. Vol. Inf., mentioned, 554.
Wood, Harry M., pvt., Co. C, 9th U. S. Inf., killed, 1297.
Wood, James T., pvt., Co. E, 49th Inf., U. S. V., wounded, 1254.
Wood, John S., pvt., Co. —, 13th Minn. Vol. Inf., death, 803.
Wood, Leonard, brig. gen., U. S. V.:
  Appointed brig. gen., U. S. V., 116.
  Mentioned, 33, 54, 66, 181, 217.
  Opinion re. health of army in Cuba, 202.
  Ordered to duty at Santiago, Cuba, 217, 381.
  Recommended for promotion, 104.
  Recommended to remain in Cuba, 203, 209.
Wood, Marshall W., maj., med. dept., U. S. A. opinion re. health of army in Cuba, 201.
Wood, Palmer G., jr., 2d lieut., 12th U. S. Inf., death, 1229.
Wood, Robert C., pvt., Co. D, 3d U. S. Inf., death, 1274.
Wood, William C., pvt., Co. L, 44th Inf., U. S. V., death, 1221.
Wood, William J., pvt., Batty. L, 6th U. S. Art., death, 1150.
Wood, William M., 2d lieut., 12th U. S. Inf., mentioned, 224.
Wood, Winthrop S., capt., asst. qm., U. S. A., mentioned, 483, 486; wounded, 124.
Woodard, John H., artif., Co. L, 18th U. S. Inf., death, 1104.
Woodbury, Thomas C., capt., 16th U. S. Inf., mentioned, 83, 568; wounded, 124.
Woodbury, Urban C., cor. with Sec'y War, 340.
Woodford, Oliver G., pvt., Co. C, 40th Inf., U. S. V., killed, 1182.
Wooding, George S., pvt., Co. C, 13th Minn. Vol. Inf., wounded, 915.
Woodland, James M., pvt., Co. M, 17th U. S. Inf., death, 1149.
Woodley, Levi C., corpl., Co. B, 37th Inf., U. S. V., death, 1201.
Woodruff, Charles A., maj., sub. dept., U. S. A., mentioned, 256, 291.
Woodruff, Charles E., maj., med. dept., U. S. A., mentioned, 646, 667, 709.
Woodruff, Frank, pvt., Co. C, 2d Oreg. Vol. Inf., wounded, 952.
Woodruff, Lewis S., pvt., Co. D, 51st Iowa Vol. Inf., wounded, 1017.
Woodruff, Spawn, pvt., Co. C, 1st Wash. Vol. Inf., wounded, 1046.
Woods, Arthur A., pvt., U. S. Marine Corps, death, 463.
Woods, Charles, pvt., Co. D, 39th U. S. V., death, 1185.
Woods, Clyde Z., pvt., Co. H, 1st Wash. Vol. Inf., death, 979; wounded, 977.
Woods, Edward, pvt., Co. H, 17th U. S. Inf., wounded, 1051.
Woods, John J., pvt., Co. D, 17th U. S. Inf., wounded, 1051.
Woodson, Robert S., capt., med. dept., U. S. A., mentioned, 315.
Woodward, Charles F., col., 6th Mass. Vol. Inf., mentioned, 374, 375, 376.
Woodyard, Lemuel, corpl., Co. C, 40th Inf., U. S. V., wounded, 1259.

Woolworth, Charles A., sergt., Co. A, 20th Kans. Vol. Inf., wounded, 977.
Wooten, Guy F., pvt., Co. G, 28th Inf., U. S. V., death, 1229.
Wooters, Albert M., pvt., Co. B, 23d U. S. Inf., death, 988.
Worcester, ——, member Philippine Commission, mentioned, 863, 883, 998, 1127.
Work, Edson, pvt., Co. A, 9th U. S. Inf., death, 486.
Workosky, Andrew, pvt., Troop D, 11th Cav., U. S. V., wounded, 1190.
Worth, William S., lieut. col., 13th U. S. Inf., mentioned, 83, 116; wounded, 124.
Worthington, W. J., pvt., Co. H, 13th Minn. Vol Inf., mentioned, 1054.
Wotherspoon, William W., capt., 12th Inf., mentioned, 1003, 1344.
Woughtel, Clem., pvt., Co. B, 4th U. S. Inf., wounded, 1052.
Wren, Charles, pvt., Co. G, 8th U. S. Inf., mentioned, 213.
Wrenn, Willie L., pvt., Co. A, 41st Inf., U. S. V., death, 1132.
Wright, Arthur, pvt., Co. A, 33d Inf., U. S. V., killed, 1137.
Wright, Charles, pvt., Co. C, 34th Inf., U. S. V., wounded, 1192.
Wright, Edward, pvt., Co. F, 9th U. S. Inf., wounded, 444.
Wright, Ewing, pvt., Troop C, 6th U. S. Cav., wounded, 1272.
Wright, Harry, pvt., Hosp. Corps, U. S. A., missing, 1297.
Wright, Henry W., pvt., Co. H, 84th Inf., death, 1249.
Wright, H. E., pvt., Co. H, 1st Nebr. Vol. Inf., wounded, 950.
Wright, Ira, pvt., Co. —, 20th U. S. Inf., wounded, 948.
Wright, James G., pvt., Co. K, 16th U. S. Inf., wounded, 1101.
Wright, John B., pvt., Co. I, 27th Inf., U. S. V., death, 1196.
Wright, John C., qm. employee, mentioned, 246.
Wright, Joseph, pvt., Co. B, 1st Mont. Vol. Inf., wounded, 966.
Wright, Joseph L., pvt., Co. A, 26th Inf., U. S. V., death, 1200.
Wright Luke E., vice-governor, Philippine Islands, mentioned, 1331, 1334.
Wright, O. B., pvt., Co. I, 14th U. S. Inf., wounded, 895.
Wright, William J., pvt., Co. C, 33d Inf., U. S. V., death, 1238.
Wright, William T., pvt., Troop C, 11th Cav., U. S. V., wounded, 1148.
Wright, U. S. transport, mentioned, 1275, 1303, 1316, 1322.
Wubnig, Philip, pvt., Co. G, 9th U. S. Inf., wounded, 444.
Wu Ting Fang, Chinese minister to U. S., mentioned, 437.
Wyatt, James F., pvt., Co. M, 36th Inf., U. S. V., wounded, 1101.
Wyatt, Walter A., pvt., Co. L, 20th Kans. Vol. Inf., wounded, 952.
Wyefield, U. S. transport, mentioned, 424, 437, 439, 445, 447, 1128, 1230, 1265.
Wyeth, Guy A., 1st sergt., Co. I, 23d U. S. Inf., death, 1168; wounded, 1167.
Wyland, Louis E., corpl., Co. C, 51st Iowa Vol. Inf., wounded, 975.
Wyles, Lewis L., pvt., Co. G, 26th Inf., U. S. V., wounded, 1141.
Wyman, Walter, surg. gen., Marine Hosp. Service, mentioned, 140.
Wynn, Claud, pvt., Co. B, 41st Inf., U. S. V., death, 1196.
Wysor, Frank, sergt., Co. B, 19th U. S. Inf., death, 1160; wounded, 1160.
Yale, auxiliary cruiser, mentioned, 49, 55, 58, 62, 77, 80, 87, 88, 91, 93, 96–98, 101, 102, 103, 105, 106, 108, 111, 112, 115, 131, 135, 156, 157, 184, 206–208, 213, 215, 217, 233, 235, 240, 273, 280, 281, 283–285, 297, 299, 300, 301, 305, 313, 337, 341, 349, 362, 381, 404, 590, 599.
Yankee, U. S. cruiser, mentioned, 16.

INDEX.

Yarbrough, Hiram M., pvt., Co. G, 41st Inf., U. S. V., wounded, 1263.
Yarmouth, steamship, mentioned, 589, 617, 621.
Yates, Richard, governor of Illinois, mentioned, 329, 339.
Yax, Frank, pvt., Co. D, 21st U. S. Inf., wounded, 1081.
Ybor, Fla., arrival of troops and ordnance supplies, 69.
Yeagley, Edward A., pvt., Co. M, 16th U. S. Inf., death, 1200.
Yeatman, Richard T., capt., 14th U. S. Inf., mentioned, 1156.
Ycizer, Charles G., unassigned recruit, 24th U. S. Inf., death, 1243.
Yoder, Ephraim S., corpl., Co. K, 22d U. S. Inf., killed, 1092.
Yorktown, U. S. gunboat, mentioned, 413, 414, 420, 427, 980, 1090, 1214.
Yosemite, U. S. transport, mentioned, 321.
Yost, William H., pvt., Co. G, 1st Mont. Vol. Inf., wounded, 950.
Youell, Frank E., pvt., Co. H, 39th Inf., U. S. V., wounded, 1147.
Young, Alexander B., pvt., Co. H, 10th Pa. Vol. Inf., wounded, 953.
Young, Berry H., pvt., Co. D, 22d U. S. Inf., wounded, 941.
Young, Bert E., pvt., Co. B, 1st Idaho Vol. Inf., wounded, 1008.
Young, Boyd M., pvt., Co. B, 38th Inf., U. S. V., drowned, 1201.
Young, Charles E., pvt., Co. G, 1st Mont. Vol. Inf., wounded, 954.
Young, C. E., pvt., Co. G, 1st Nebr. Vol. Inf., wounded, 946.
Young, Edward C., pvt., Co. A, 2d Oreg. Vol. Inf., death, 803; mentioned, 761.
Young, Frank, pvt., Co. M, 20th U. S. Inf., wounded, 926.
Young, Harry A., sergt., Batt. A, Utah Art., killed, 896.
Young, Henry J., corpl., Co. L, 14th U. S. Inf., wounded, 454.
Young, Jay R., pvt., Co. C, 44th Inf., U. S. V., killed, 1247.
Young, John D., pvt., Co. A, 20th Kans. Vol. Inf., death, 886.
Young, John F., pvt., Co. A, 21st U. S. Inf., death, 1190.
Young, John G., corpl., Batty. A, Utah Art., killed, 896.
Young, John J., pvt., Co. C, 13th Minn. Vol. Inf., wounded, 963.
Young, Jonathan A., 2d lieut., 2d Oreg. Vol. Inf., wounded, 967.
Young, Roscoe, pvt., Co. B, 1st Nebr. Vol. Inf., killed, 926.
Young, Samuel B. M., brig. gen., U. S. A.:
Assigned to temporary command at Montauk Point, 211.
Calls for more troops, 1211.
Young, Samuel B. M., brig. gen., U. S. A.—Cont'd.
Mentioned, 74, 82, 100, 109, 113, 116, 123, 181, 227, 228, 240, 519, 520, 525–527, 541, 542, 546, 567, 569, 570, 572, 574, 575, 578, 1018, 1054, 1083, 1085–1087, 1089, 1090, 1091, 1098, 1103, 1106, 1108–1111, 1113–1116, 1120, 1122, 1124, 1135, 1138, 1158, 1159, 1162, 1192, 1223, 1232, 1241, 1244, 1257.
Reports numerous small engagements, 1211.
Young, Thomas, pvt., Co. A, 41st Inf., U. S. V., death, 1178.
Young, Walter C., corpl., Co. L, 38th Inf., U. S. V., killed, 1140.
Young, W. Harland, pvt., Co. I, 1st Ill. Vol. Inf., mentioned, 238.
Young, Willard, col., 2d U. S. V. Engrs., mentioned, 546, 547.
Young, William A. S., sergt., Co. E, 71st N. Y. Vol. Inf., mentioned, 193.
Young, William H., chief of scouts, died of wounds, 991.
Youngs, Charles H., pvt., Co. H, 1st Nebr. Vol. Inf., wounded, 952.
Yount, Frank, pvt., Co. D, 22d U. S. Inf., wounded, 941.
Yucatan, steamship, mentioned, 190, 198, 233, 243, 330.
Yule, Sherman A., a. a. surg., U. S. A., death, 1258.
Yungedu, Chinese prince, mentioned, 458.
Zafiro, U. S. gunboat, mentioned, 484.
Zaisser, Charles A., pvt., Co. D, 6th U. S. Inf., death, 1095.
Zamback, Paul, pvt., Co. K, 1st Ill. Vol. Inf., mentioned, 206.
Zealandia, transport, mentioned, 556, 603, 614, 618, 620, 661, 685, 691, 699, 700, 701, 704, 730, 792, 831, 840, 885, 888, 928, 951, 953, 985, 1001, 1012–1014, 1017, 1018, 1023, 1037, 1046, 1049, 1051, 1059, 1074, 1081, 1082, 1091, 1096, 1097.
Zeller, William J., pvt., Co. M, 37th Inf., U. S. V., death, 1187.
Zeloder, Augustus, pvt., Co. C, 1st Wash. Vol. Inf., wounded, 897.
Ziebel, Edward, pvt., Co. M, 20th Kans. Vol. Inf., wounded, 898.
Ziegenheim, Henry, mayor St. Louis, Mo., mentioned, 343.
Ziegler, Ernest B., pvt., Co. F, 34th Inf., U. S. V., wounded, 1124.
Ziegler, Robert M., pvt., Co. I, 16th U. S. Inf., mentioned, 253.
Ziemans, Charles, pvt., Hosp. Corps, U. S. A., killed, 1073.
Zinn, George A., capt., Engr. Corps, U. S. A., mentioned, 1224.
Ziun, Ralph H., pvt., Co. H, 43d Inf., U. S. V., killed, 1168.
Zlatnicki, Vincent, pvt., Troop D, 1st U. S. Cav., drowned, 1234.
Zollars, Charles O., 2d lieut., 1st Colo. Vol. Inf., mentioned, 994.
Züginfuss, Charles H., general manager Juragua Iron Co., mentioned, 22.
Zwiefel, Andrew P., pvt., Co. D, 12th U. S. Inf., death, 1132.

O

www.ingramcontent.com/pod-product-compliance
Lightning Source LLC
Chambersburg PA
CBHW081751300426
44116CB00014B/2091